Law School Publications

of

WEST PUBLISHING COMPANY

St. Paul, Minnesota 55102

ACCOUNTING

Fiflis and Kripke's Accounting for Business Lawyers, 687 pages, 1971.

ADMINISTRATIVE LAW

Davis' Basic Text, about 700 pages, 1971.
Davis' Cases, Text and Problems, 2nd Ed., 609 pages, 1965.

ADMIRALTY

Healy and Currie's Cases and Materials on Admiralty, 872 pages, 1965.

AGENCY

Seavey and Hall's Cases, 431 pages, 1956.
Seavey's Studies, 451 pages, 1949.
Seavey's Text, 329 pages, 1964.
See Agency-Partnership.

AGENCY PARTNERSHIP

Seavey, Reuschlein & Hall's Cases, 599 pages, 1962.
Steffen's Cases, 3rd Ed., 733 pages, 1969.

BANKRUPTCY

MacLachlan's Text, 500 pages, 1956.
See Creditors' Rights.

BILLS AND NOTES

Aigler and Steinheimer's Cases, 670 pages, 1962.
Britton's Text, 2nd Ed., 794 pages, 1961.
See Commercial Transactions.

COMMERCIAL TRANSACTIONS

Speidel, Summers and White's Teaching Materials, 1144 pages, 1969.

COMMON LAW PLEADING

Koffler and Reppy on Common Law Pleading, 663 pages, 1969.
McBaine's Cases, Introduction to Civil Procedure, 399 pages, 1950.
Shipman's Text, 3rd Ed., 644 pages, 1923.

COMMUNITY PROPERTY

Burby's Cases, 4th Ed., 342 pages, 1955.
Huie's Texas Cases on Marital Property Rights, 681 pages, 1966.
Verrall and Sammis' Cases on California Community Property, 2nd Ed., 398 pages, 1971.

CONFLICT OF LAWS

Cramton and Currie's Cases—Comments—Questions, 915 pages, 1968.
Ehrenzweig's Text, 824 pages, 1962.
Ehrenzweig's Conflicts in a Nutshell, 2nd Ed., 392 pages, 1970.
Ehrenzweig and Louisell's Jurisdiction in a Nutshell, 2nd Ed., 315 pages, 1968.
Goodrich's Text, 4th Ed., 483 pages, 1964.
Scoles and Weintraub's Cases, 956 pages, 1967.
Selected Readings, 1151 pages, 1956.
Stumberg's Cases, 499 pages, 1956.

CONSTITUTIONAL LAW

Lockhart, Kamisar and Choper's Cases — Comments — Questions, 3rd Ed., 1,487 pages, 1970.
Lockhart, Kamisar and Choper's Cases and Materials on The American Constitution, 3rd Ed., 1970.
Lockhart, Kamisar and Choper's Annual Supplement.
Selected Essays, 971 pages, 1963.
See Constitutional Rights and Liberties.

CONSTITUTIONAL RIGHTS & LIBERTIES

Lockhart, Kamisar and Choper's Cases and Materials on Constitutional Rights and Liberties, 3rd Ed., 1970.
Lockhart, Kamisar and Choper's 1970 Supplement.

CONSUMER CREDIT

Kripke's Cases, 454 pages, 1970.
Young's Cases on Consumer Credit. Pamphlet reprint from Dodyk, et al. Law and Poverty, 115 pages, 1969.

CONTRACTS

Calamari & Perillo's Text, 621 pages, 1970.

Corbin's Cases, 3rd Ed., 1381 pages, 1947. 1953 Supplement, 36 pages.

Corbin's Text, Student Edition, 1224 pages, 1952.

Fuller and Braucher's Cases, 907 pages, 1964.

Simpson's Cases, 592 pages, 1956.

Simpson's Text, 2nd Ed., 510 pages, 1965.

COPYRIGHT

Nimmer's Cases on Copyright and Other Aspects of Law Pertaining to Literary, Musical and Artistic Works, about 877 pages, 1971.

CORPORATIONS

Henn's Text, 2nd Ed., 956 pages, 1970.

Stevens and Henn's Statutes, Cases and Materials on Corporations and Other Business Enterprises, 1448 pages, 1965.

Stevens and Henn's Practice Projects Supplement, 81 pages, 1965.

CREDIT TRANSACTIONS

Maxwell & Riesenfeld's California Cases on Security Transactions, 371 pages, 1957.

Maxwell & Riesenfeld's Supplement, 68 pages, 1963.

CREDITORS' RIGHTS

Riesenfeld's Cases on Creditors' Remedies and Debtors' Protection, 669 pages, 1967.

Riesenfeld's Statutory Supplement, 1969.

Riesenfeld's Case Supplement, 1970.

CRIMINAL LAW

Hall & Glueck's Cases, 2d Ed., 699 pages, 1958.

Miller's Text, 649 pages, 1934.

Stumberg's Texas Cases, 505 pages, 1954.

Stumberg and Maloney's Texas Cases Supplement, 117 pages, 1965.

CRIMINAL PROCEDURE

Hall, Kamisar, LaFave and Israel's Materials on Modern Criminal Procedure, 3rd Ed., 1456 pages, 1969.

Hall, Kamisar, LaFave and Israel's Materials on Basic Criminal Procedure, 3rd Ed., 617 pages, 1969.

Hall, Kamisar, LaFave and Israel's Annual Criminal Procedure Supplement.

Israel and LaFave's Constitutional Criminal Procedure in a Nutshell, 423 pages, 1971.

DAMAGES

Crane's Cases, 3rd Ed., 337 pages, 1955.

McCormick's Text, 811 pages, 1935.

DICTIONARIES

Black's, one volume.

Bouvier's, two volumes.

DOMESTIC RELATIONS

Clark's Cases, 870 pages, 1965.

Clark's Text, 754 pages, 1968.

Paulsen's Cases on Family Law and Poverty Pamphlet, reprint from Dodyk, et al. Law and Poverty, 266 pages, 1969.

See Juvenile Courts.

DRUGS AND DRUGGISTS

Arthur's Text, 4th Ed., 399 pp., 1955.

ENGINEERING LAW

Simpson & Dillavou's Text, 4th Ed., 506 pages, 1958.

Sweet's Legal Aspects of Architecture, Engineering and the Construction Process, 953 pages, 1970.

EQUITY

Cook's Cases, 4th Ed., 1192 pp., 1948.

McClintock's Text, 2nd Ed., 643 pages, 1948.

Van Hecke's Cases on Equitable Remedies, 651 pages, 1959.

See Remedies.

EVIDENCE

Cleary and Strong's Cases, 967 pages, 1969.

McCormick's Cases, 3rd Ed., 663 pages, 1956.

McCormick, Elliott & Sutton's Cases, 4th Ed., about 1100 pages, 1971.

McCormick's Text, 774 pages, 1954.

Rothstein's Evidence in a Nutshell, 406 pages, 1970.

Selected Writings, 1232 pages, 1957.

FEDERAL ANTI-TRUST LAWS

Oppenheim's Cases on Robinson-Patman Act, Pamphlet, 295 pages, 1967.

Oppenheim and Weston's Cases, 3rd Ed., 952 pages, 1968.

Oppenheim and Weston's Supplement, 1970.

FEDERAL ESTATE AND GIFT TAXATION

See Taxation.

FEDERAL INCOME TAXATION

See Taxation.

FEDERAL JURISDICTION AND PROCE-DURE

Currie's Cases on Federal Courts, 823 pages, 1968.

Ehrenzweig and Louisell's Jurisdiction in a Nutshell, 2nd Ed., 315 pages, 1968.

Forrester, Currier and Moye's Cases, 2nd Ed., 933 pages, 1970.

Wright's Text, 2nd Ed., 745 pages, 1970.

FUTURE INTERESTS

Gulliver's Cases, 624 pages, 1959.

Powell's Cases, 3rd Ed., 1961.

Simes Text, 2nd Ed., 355 pages, 1966.

See Wills, Intestate Succession, Trusts, Gifts and Future Interests.

GRATUITOUS TRANSFERS

See Wills.

HOUSING AND URBAN DEVELOPMENT

Berger's Cases on Housing, Pamphlet reprint from Dodyk, et al. Law and Poverty, 277 pages, 1969.

Krasnowiecki's Cases, 697 pages, 1969.

Krasnowiecki's Statutory Supplement 1969.

See Land Use.

INSURANCE

Keeton's Cases on Basic Insurance Law, 655 pages, 1960.

Keeton's Basic Text, 712 pages, 1971.

Keeton's Case Supplement to Keeton's Basic Text, 398 pages, 1971.

Keeton & Keeton's Compensation Systems, Pamphlet Reprint from Keeton & Keeton's Cases on Torts, about 82 pages, 1971.

Vance's Text, 3rd Ed., 1290 pages, 1951.

INTERNATIONAL BUSINESS

Ebb's Cases, 885 pages, 1964.

Ebb's 1968 Supplement.

INTERNATIONAL LAW

Friedmann, Lissitzyn and Pugh's Cases, 1,205 pages, 1969.

INTRODUCTION TO LAW

Fryer and Orentlicher's Cases and Materials on Legal Method and Legal System, 1,043 pages, 1967.

Kimball's Historical Introduction to Legal System, 610 pages, 1966.

Kinyon's Introduction to Law Study and Law Examinations in a Nutshell, about 368 pages, 1971.

Smith's Cases on Development of Legal Institutions, 757 pages, 1965.

See Legal Method.

JURISPRUDENCE

Wu's Cases, 719 pages, 1958.

JUVENILE COURTS

Fox's The Law of Juvenile Courts in a Nutshell, 286 pages, 1971.

LABOR LAW

Sovern's Cases on Racial Discrimination in Employment, Pamphlet reprint from Dodyk et al. Law and Poverty, 188 pages, 1969.

LAND USE

Beuscher and Wright's Cases on Land Use, 788 pages, 1969.

Hagman's Text on Urban Planning and Land Development Control Law, about 542 pages, 1971.

LEGAL BIBLIOGRAPHY

Cohen's Legal Research in a Nutshell, 2nd Ed., about 220 pages, 1971.

How To Find The Law, with Special Chapters on Legal Writing, 6th Ed., 313 pages, 1965.

How To Find The Law Student Problem Book.

LEGAL ETHICS

Pirsig's Cases on Professional Responsibility, 2nd Ed., 447 pages, 1970.

Selected Readings Legal Profession, 565 pages, 1962.

LEGAL HISTORY

Kimball's Historical Introduction to Legal System, 610 pages, 1966.

Radin's Text, 612 pages, 1936.

Smith's Cases on Development of Legal Institutions, 757 pages, 1965.

LEGAL INTERVIEWING AND COUNSELING

Freeman's Cases, 253 pages, 1964.

LEGAL METHOD—LEGAL SYSTEM

Fryer and Orentlicher's Cases & Materials, 1043 pages, 1966.

See Introduction to Law.

LEGAL WRITING STYLE

Weihofen's Text, 323 pages, 1961.

See Legal Bibliography.

LEGISLATION

Nutting, Elliott and Dickerson's Cases 4th Ed., 631 pages, 1969.

LOCAL GOVERNMENT LAW

Michelman and Sandalow's Materials on Government in Urban Areas, 1216 pages, 1970.

Stason and Kauper's Cases, 3rd Ed., 692 pages, 1959.

See Land Use.

MASS COMMUNICATION LAW

Gillmor and Barron's Cases and Comment, 853 pages, 1969.

MORTGAGES

Osborne's Cases Secured Transactions, 559 pages, 1967.

Osborne's Text, 2nd Ed., 805 pages, 1970.

MUNICIPAL CORPORATIONS

Michelman and Sandalow's Materials on Government in Urban Areas, 1216 pages, 1970.

Stason and Kauper's Cases, 3rd Ed., 692 pages, 1959.

See Local Government Law.

See Land Use.

NATURAL RESOURCES

Trelease, Bloomenthal and Geraud's Cases and Materials on Natural Resources, 1131 pages, 1965.

OFFICE PRACTICE

A.B.A. Lawyer's Handbook, 557 pages, 1962.

See Legal Interviewing and Counseling.

OIL AND GAS

Hemingway's Text, 486 pages, 1971.

Huie, Walker and Woodward's Cases, 848 pages, 1960.

See Natural Resources.

PARTNERSHIP

Crane and Bromberg's Text, 695 pages, 1968.

See Agency-Partnership.

PERSONAL PROPERTY

Aigler, Smith and Tefft's Cases on Property, 2 Vols., 1339 pages, 1960.

Bigelow's Cases, 3rd Ed., 507 pages, 1942.

Fryer's Readings, 3rd Ed., 1184 pages, 1938.

PLEADING AND PROCEDURE

Brown, Karlen, Meisenholder, Stevens, and Vestal's Cases and Materials on Procedure Before Trial, 784 pages, 1968.

PLEADING AND PROCEDURE—Cont'd

Cleary's Cases on Pleading, 2d Ed., 434 pages, 1958.

Cound, Friedenthal and Miller's Cases on Civil Procedure, 1075 pages, 1968.

Cound, Friedenthal and Miller's Cases on Pleading, Discovery and Joinder, 643 pages, 1968.

Cound, Friedenthal and Miller's Civil Procedure Supplement, 1970.

Ehrenzweig and Louisell's Jurisdiction in a Nutshell, 2nd Ed., 315 pages, 1968.

Elliott & Karlen's Cases, 441 pages, 1961.

Hodges, Jones and Elliott's Cases on Texas Trial and Appellate Procedure, 623 pages, 1965.

Hodges, Jones, Elliott and Thode's Texas Judicial Process Prior to Trial, 935 pages, 1966.

Karlen's Cases on Trials and Appeals, 436 pages, 1961.

Karlen and Joiner's Cases and Materials on Trials and Appeals, 536 pages, 1971.

McBaine's Cases, Introduction to Civil Procedure, 399 pages, 1950.

POVERTY LAW

Dodyk, Sovern, Berger, Young and Paulsen's Cases on Law and Poverty, 1,234 pages, 1969.

Dodyk's Cases on Income Maintenance, Pamphlet reprint from Dodyk, et al. Law and Poverty, 379 pages, 1969.

REAL PROPERTY

Aigler, Smith & Tefft's Cases on Property, 2 Vols., 1339 pages, 1960.

Berger's Cases on Housing, Pamphlet reprint from Dodyk, et al. Law and Poverty, 277 pages, 1969.

Browder, Cunningham & Julin's Basic Property Law, 1209 pages, 1966.

Burby's Text, 3rd Ed., 490 Pages, 1965.

Jacobs' Cases Landlord and Tenant, 2nd Ed., 815 pages, 1941.

Moynihan's Introduction, 254 pages, 1962.

Phipps' Titles in a Nutshell—The Calculus of Interests, 277 pages, 1968.

Smith and Boyer's Survey of the Law of Property, 2nd Ed., 510 pages, 1971.

See Housing and Urban Development.

REMEDIES

Cribbet's Cases on Judicial Remedies, 762 pages, 1954.
Wright's Cases, 498 pages, 1955.
York and Bauman's Cases, 1271 pages, 1967.

REVIEW MATERIALS

Ballantine's Problems.
Burby's Law Refreshers.
Nutshell Series.
Smith Reviews.

SALES

Nordstrom's Text, 600 pages, 1970.
Nordstrom and Lattin's Problems and Materials on Sales and Secured Transactions, 809 pages, 1968.
See Commercial Transactions.

SECURED TRANSACTIONS

See Commercial Transactions.
See Sales.

SURETYSHIP AND GUARANTY

Osborne's Cases, 221 pages, 1966.
Simpson's Cases, 538 pages, 1942.

TAXATION

Chommie's Text on Federal Income Taxation, 742 pages, 1968.
Chommie's Supplement, 1970.
Hellerstein's Cases on State and Local Taxation, 3rd Ed., 741 pages, 1969.
Kragen & McNulty's Cases on Federal Income Taxation, 1,182 pages, 1970.
Lowndes & Kramer's Text on Federal Estate and Gift Taxes, 2nd Ed., 951 pages, 1962.
Rice's Problems and Materials in Federal Estate & Gift Taxation, 504 pages, 1966.
Rice's Problems and Materials in Federal Income Taxation, 2nd Ed., about 502 pages, 1971.

TORTS

Green, Pedrick, Rahl, Thode, Hawkins and Smith's Cases, 1311 pages, 1968.
Green, Pedrick, Rahl, Thode, Hawkins and Smith's Cases on Injuries to Relations, 466 pages, 1968.

TORTS—Cont'd

Keeton and Keeton's Cases, about 1176 pages, 1971.
Prosser's Text, 4th Ed., 1208 pages, 1971.
Seavey, Keeton and Keeton's Cases, 2nd Ed., 1055 pages, 1964.
Seavey, Keeton and Keeton's Supplement, 1970.

TRADE REGULATION

See Federal Anti-Trust Laws.
See Unfair Trade Practices.

TRUSTS

Bogert's Text, 4th Ed., 528 pages, 1963.
Powell's Cases, Trusts and Wills, 639 pages, 1960.
Smith's Survey, 167 pages, 1949.
See Wills, Intestate Succession, Trusts, Gifts and Future Interests.

UNFAIR TRADE PRACTICES

Oppenheim's Cases, 783 pages, 1965.
Oppenheim and Weston's Supplement.
Oppenheim's Robinson-Patman Act Pamphlet, 295 pages, 1967.

WATER LAW

Trelease's Cases, 364 pages, 1967.

WILLS

Atkinson's Text, 2nd Ed., 975 pages, 1953.
Turrentine's Cases, 2nd Ed., 483 pages, 1962.
See Wills, Intestate Succession, Trusts, Gifts and Future Interests.

WILLS, INTESTATE SUCCESSION, TRUSTS, GIFTS AND FUTURE INTERESTS

Gulliver, Clark, Lusky and Murphy's Cases and Materials on Gratuitous Transfers: Wills, Intestate Succession, Trusts, Gifts and Future Interests, 1017 pages, 1967.

WORKMEN'S COMPENSATION

Malone and Plant's Cases, 622 pages, 1963.

THE LAW

OF

CONTRACTS

By

JOHN D. CALAMARI
Professor of Law, Fordham University

and

JOSEPH M. PERILLO
Professor of Law, Fordham University

HORNBOOK SERIES

ST. PAUL, MINN.
WEST PUBLISHING CO.
1970

Calamari & Perillo Law of Contracts HB
2—1971

PREFACE

Contract law is rapidly changing. In particular, the enactment of the Uniform Commercial Code by forty-nine states has caused a major change of approach in some of the fundamental doctrines. It is believed that the time is ripe for a new introductory text which emphasizes new developments, without, however, neglecting traditional rules and doctrines. This volume is offered as such a text.

An attempt to introduce so vast a subject matter in a one volume text has obvious dangers. Over-simplifications are inevitable. Generalizations are always more dogmatic than the law in action. Nonetheless, the practitioner is aware and the student soon becomes aware of the uses and limitations of introductory texts. A text of this kind seeks to provide an introduction to the doctrines, concepts and fundamental rules of the subject. Its citations are designed to provide a guide to deeper knowledge of the subject.

We wish to express our indebtedness to the two giants in the field, Professors Arthur L. Corbin and Samuel Williston, whose treatises are cited liberally throughout the text, as well as to innumerable scholars and students who have contributed to the literature in legal periodicals and texts. We are indebted to Professors Paul S. Graziano and Joseph M. McLaughlin and Dean Malachy T. Mahon for their valued comments on portions of the manuscript. We particularly express our gratitude to George W. Bacon, Professor Emeritus, for making available to his successors the insights gained from his many years as a teacher and scholar.

We express our appreciation to Dean William Hughes Mulligan of the Fordham University School of Law who in many ways facilitated our task. We are grateful to Miss Anne McKim who ably prepared each draft of the manuscript and to Sandra Behrle, Manuel Bernardo, Andrew Bongiorno, Benjamin Goldman, Frederic Ingraham and James Maloney, each of whom gave us invaluable help in the checking of citations.

Last, but most important, we express our thanks to our wives for their patience and understanding.

JOHN D. CALAMARI
JOSEPH M. PERILLO

March, 1970

*

COPYRIGHT ACKNOWLEDGMENTS

The authors are indebted for the generous permission of various publishers to reprint published materials. A particular debt is owed to the American Law Institute for extensive quotes from the Restatements and to the American Law Institute and the National Conference of Commissioners on Uniform State Laws for permission to reproduce Official Comments on the Uniform Commercial Code. In addition various quotations from Duesenberg & King, Sales and Bulk Transfers and Williston on Contracts are reproduced with the permission of Matthew Bender & Co. and Baker Voorhis & Co., Inc., respectively. The consent of the Brooklyn Law Review for a quotation from Vol. 30, p. 185, is gratefully acknowledged as is the consent of the Fordham Law Review for adaptation of an article in Vol. 27, p. 332, and the Indiana Law Journal for adaptation of an article in Vol. 42, p. 333. Acknowledgment is also given to Yale University for its permission to reproduce quotations from Corbin on Contracts.

*

SUMMARY OF CONTENTS

Chapter		Page
1.	Introduction	1
2.	Offer and Acceptance	12
	A. Intent to Contract	13
	B. The Offer	17
	C. Other Matters Relating to Mutual Assent	27
	D. Acceptance	38
3.	Parol Evidence and Interpretation	74
	A. Introduction	74
	B. The Parol Evidence Rule	75
	C. Interpretation	89
4.	Consideration	103
5.	Informal Contracts Without Consideration or Detrimental Reliance	149
	A. Past Consideration and Moral Obligation as Consideration	150
	B. Consideration Not Required in Certain Commercial and Written Contracts	163
	C. Stipulations	170
6.	Promissory Estoppel: Detrimental Reliance as a Substitute for Consideration	171
	A. History of the Doctrine	171
	B. Modern Trends in Doctrine	180
7.	Contracts under Seal	188
8.	Capacity of Parties	197
	A. Infants	198
	B. The Mentally Infirm	216
9.	Conditions	223
	A. General Principles	224
	B. Express Conditions	237
	C. Constructive Conditions	243
	D. Excuse of Condition	264
10.	Breach of Contract—Repudiation	278
11.	Impossibility of Performance and Frustration of the Venture	296
12.	Damages	323
	A. Introduction	324
	B. Non-Compensatory Damages	326
	C. Compensatory Damages	327
	D. Foreseeability	329
	E. Certainty	334
	F. The Concept of Value	342
	G. Avoidable Consequences	345
	H. Damages in Particular Actions	350
	I. Agreed Damages	366

SUMMARY OF CONTENTS

Chapter				Page
13.	Restitution as a Remedy for Breach			371
14.	Third Party Beneficiaries			378
15.	Assignment and Delegation			401
16.	Statute of Frauds			437
	I.	When a Writing is Necessary		439
		A.	Suretyship Agreements	443
		B.	Agreements in Consideration of Marriage	460
		C.	Agreements for the Sale of Land or Interests in Land	461
		D.	Agreements for the Sale of Goods: The Uniform Commercial Code	466
		E.	Contracts Not to be Performed Within One Year	471
	II.	What is a Sufficient Writing or Memorandum and the Effect Thereof		480
	III.	Restitutionary Remedies		491
	IV.	Estoppel		498
17.	Joint and Several Contracts			501
18.	Discharge of Contracts			515
	A.	Rescission		517
	B.	Destruction or Surrender		519
	C.	Executory Bilateral Contract of Accord—Accord and Satisfaction—Substitute Agreement—Unilateral Accord		520
	D.	Three Party Situations		525
	E.	Account Stated		527
	F.	Release and Covenant Not to Sue		529
	G.	Gifts and Rejection of Tender		531
	H.	Merger		532
	I.	Union of Right and Duty in the Same Person		533
	J.	Alteration		534
	K.	Bankruptcy		535
	L.	Performance		535
19.	Illegal Bargains			537
	I.	Illegal Bargains		539
		A.	Bargains in Restraint of Trade	540
		B.	Bargains Harmful to Public or to Fiduciary Duties	544
		C.	Bargains to Commit a Tort or to Exonerate or Indemnify From Tortious Liability	549
		D.	Bargains Tending to Obstruct the Administration of Justice	553
		E.	Bargains Harmful to Marriage	555
		F.	Other Illegal Bargains	557
	II.	The Effect of Illegality		564
		A.	Illegal Executory Contracts	565
		B.	Illegal Contract Which is Performed in Whole or Part	567
Table of Cases				581
Index				607

TABLE OF CONTENTS

CHAPTER 1. INTRODUCTION

Sec.   Page

1. What is a Contract? --------------------------------------- 1
2. Contracts Distinguished from Executed Agreements ----------- 3
3. Freedom of Contract --------------------------------------- 4
4. Scope of the Law of Contracts ----------------------------- 6
5. Sources of Contract Law ----------------------------------- 6
6. Classification of Contracts ------------------------------- 9
7. Formal and Informal Contracts ----------------------------- 9
8. Unilateral and Bilateral Contracts ------------------------ 9
9. Enforceable, Void, Voidable and Unenforceable Contracts ------ 10
10. Express and Implied Contracts (Quasi Contracts) ------------- 10

CHAPTER 2. OFFER AND ACCEPTANCE

A. INTENT TO CONTRACT

11. Mutual Assent -- 13
12. Objective and Subjective Intention ----------------------- 14
13. Must the Parties be Serious? ----------------------------- 15
14. Must the Parties Intend Legal Consequences? -------------- 16

B. THE OFFER

15. What is an Offer? -- 17
16. Offer Distinguished from an Expression of Opinion --------- 17
17. Offers Distinguished from Statements of Intention and Preliminary Negotiations --------------------------------------- 19
18. Is the Ordinary Advertisement, Catalog or Circular Letter an Offer? -- 21
19. Offers at Auctions --------------------------------------- 23
20. Price Quotations Contrasted With Offers ------------------ 25

C. OTHER MATTERS RELATING TO MUTUAL ASSENT

21. Intention That the Agreement be Memorialized in a Formalized Writing -- 27
22. Questions of Law and Fact -------------------------------- 28
23. Indefiniteness --- 29
24. Unilateral, Bilateral and Reverse Unilateral Contracts and Some of Their Implications ------------------------------- 36

D. ACCEPTANCE

25. Must the Offeree Know of the Offer and if so at What Point of Time? --- 38
26. Must the Offeree Intend to Accept? ----------------------- 40

TABLE OF CONTENTS

Sec.   Page

27. Who May Accept the Offer? --------------------------------- 41
28. Must the Offeree Give Notice of Acceptance of an Offer to a
      Unilateral Contract? ------------------------------------- 43
29. Acceptance of an Offer Looking to a Series of Contracts ------ 43
30. The Necessity for Communicating Acceptance of an Offer to a
      Bilateral Contract -- 45
31. Promises Inferred from Conduct or Silence -------------------- 45
32. Acceptance Varying from Offer ------------------------------ 50
33. Termination of the Power of Acceptance Created by Revocable
      Offers --- 55
    (a) Lapse of Time -- 56
    (b) Death or Lack of Capacity of the Offeror --------------- 58
    (c) Revocation, Direct and Indirect ----------------------- 59
    (d) Rejection—Counter-Offer ------------------------------ 60
    (e) Death or Destruction --------------------------------- 61
    (f) Supervening Illegality ------------------------------- 61
34. Up to What Point of Time May an Offeror Revoke a Revocable
      Offer Looking to a Unilateral Contract? --------------------- 61
35. Up to What Point in Time May a Revocable Offer Looking to a
      Bilateral Contract be Revoked? ---------------------------- 63
    (a) Parties at a Distance --------------------------------- 63
    (b) Parties in the Presence of One Another ---------------- 66
36. Risk of Mistake in Transmission ---------------------------- 66
37. Termination of Irrevocable Offers (Option Contracts) --------- 67
    (a) What Makes an Offer Irrevocable? --------------------- 67
    (b) Termination of Irrevocable Offers --------------------- 69
38. Modern Trend Limiting the Importance of the Distinction Be-
      tween Unilateral and Bilateral Contracts --------------- 70
    (a) § 2–206 of the Uniform Commercial Code -------------- 70
    (b) Proposed Restatement -------------------------------- 72

CHAPTER 3. PAROL EVIDENCE AND INTERPRETATION

A. INTRODUCTION

39. The Difficulty of the Subject Matter --------------------------- 75

B. THE PAROL EVIDENCE RULE

40. The Area of Substantial Agreement --------------------------- 75
41. The Parol Evidence Rule: The Major Area of Conflict -------- 79
42. The Parol Evidence Rule Does Not Apply Until It is Decided
      That There is a Contract ---------------------------------- 86
43. The Parol Evidence Rule is a Rule of Substantive Law ---------- 86
44. The Parol Evidence Rule Does Not Apply to Subsequent Trans-
      actions -- 86
45. Some Miscellaneous Observations --------------------------- 87
46. Parol Evidence and The Uniform Commercial Code ----------- 87

TABLE OF CONTENTS

C. INTERPRETATION

Sec.   Page

47. Standards of Interpretation --- 89
48. Rules of Interpretation and Their Relationship to Standards of Interpretation --- 94
49. Are Questions of Interpretation Questions of Fact or Questions of Law? --- 96
50. The Relationship Between the Parol Evidence Rule and Rules and Standards of Interpretation --- 96
51. Some Practical Observations About Parol Evidence and Interpretation --- 98
52. Course of Dealing, Course of Performance and Usage --- 99

CHAPTER 4. CONSIDERATION

53. What is Consideration? --- 103
54. Motive and Past Consideration are Not Consideration: Necessity of an Exchange --- 106
55. Adequacy of the Detriment --- 107
56. Unconscionable Inadequacy of Consideration and Unconscionable Contracts --- 109
57. Conditions to Gifts Distinguished from Bargained for Detriment 114
58. Of Sham and Nominal Consideration and Cases Where the Promise is Only in Part Induced by the Detriment --- 116
59. Surrender of or Forbearance to Assert an Invalid Claim as Detriment --- 118
60. The Pre-existing Duty Rule: Duties Imposed by Law --- 120
61. The Pre-existing Duty Rule: The Two Party Cases --- 120
62. The Pre-existing Duty Rule: The Three Party Cases --- 123
63. Pre-existing Duty Rule—Agreements to Accept Part Payment as Satisfaction of a Debt: Pinnel's Case and Foakes v. Beer --- 124
64. The Rule of Foakes v. Beer: Minority Views --- 127
65. The Relationship of the Rule of Foakes v. Beer to the Doctrine of Accord and Satisfaction—Of Liquidated and Unliquidated Claims --- 127
66. Consideration in Bilateral Contracts --- 130
67. Mutuality of Obligation: Introduction --- 130
68. The Unilateral Contract: A So-called Exception to the Mutuality Requirement --- 131
69. Voidable and Unenforceable Promises as Consideration --- 132
70. Illusory and Optional Promises --- 133
71. A Conditional Promise May be Sufficient Consideration: Aleatory Promises --- 138
72. Requirement and Output Contracts --- 140
73. Consideration Supplied by Implied Promises --- 143
74. A Void Contract is Not Necessarily a Nullity --- 144
75. One Consideration Will Support Many Promises --- 146
76. All of the Consideration Need Not be Valid --- 147
77. Consideration and the Parol Evidence Rule --- 147

TABLE OF CONTENTS

CHAPTER 5. INFORMAL CONTRACTS WITHOUT CONSIDERATION OR DETRIMENTAL RELIANCE

A. PAST CONSIDERATION AND MORAL OBLIGATION AS CONSIDERATION

Sec.		Page
78.	Introduction	150
79.	The Relationship Between Past Consideration and Moral Obligation	151
80.	Promises to Pay Pre-existing Debts	151
81.	Promises to Pay for Acts Previously Performed at Request	152
82.	Promises to Pay for Benefits Previously Received Without Request	154
83.	Promises to Pay Debts Discharged by Operation of Law: Rationale	155
84.	Promises to Pay Debts Discharged in Bankruptcy	156
85.	Promises to Pay Debts—Effect on Statute of Limitations	157
86.	Promises to Perform Voidable Duties	160
87.	New Promise Based Upon a Previous Promise Within the Statute of Frauds	160
88.	Miscellaneous Promises Supported by Antecedent Events	162
89.	To Whom the Promise Must be Made	162

B. CONSIDERATION NOT REQUIRED IN CERTAIN COMMERCIAL AND WRITTEN CONTRACTS

90.	Scope of the Discussion	163
91.	The Model Written Obligation Act	163
92.	Modification of Contracts	164
93.	Modifications Under Compulsion	166
94.	Release and Accord and Satisfaction	167
	(a) Release	167
	(b) Accord and Satisfaction	168
95.	Firm Offers	169
96.	Past Consideration	169

C. STIPULATIONS

97.	Stipulations Defined	170
98.	Consideration and Formality in Stipulations	170

CHAPTER 6. PROMISSORY ESTOPPEL: DETRIMENTAL RELIANCE AS A SUBSTITUTE FOR CONSIDERATION

A. HISTORY OF THE DOCTRINE

99.	Introduction	172
100.	Promises in the Family	173

TABLE OF CONTENTS

Sec.   **Page**

101. Oral Gifts of Land ---- 173
102. Gratuitous Agencies and Bailments ---- 175
103. Charitable Subscriptions ---- 176
104. Other Roots of the Doctrine of Promissory Estoppel ---- 178
105. Traditional Approach to the Promissory Estoppel Doctrine ---- 179

B. MODERN TRENDS IN DOCTRINE

106. Modern Trends Generally ---- 180
107. Offers by Subcontractors ---- 180
108. Promises of Franchises: Is Promissory Estoppel a Non-contractual Cause of Action? ---- 182
109. Pensions and Other Fringe Benefits ---- 183
110. Flexibility of Remedy ---- 185
111. The Future of Promissory Estoppel ---- 186

CHAPTER 7. CONTRACTS UNDER SEAL

112. Introduction ---- 188
113. Sufficiency of the Writing ---- 189
114. What Constitutes a Seal ---- 189
115. The Adoption of a Seal Already On the Instrument ---- 190
116. Delivery of a Sealed Instrument ---- 191
117. Is Acceptance by the Obligee Necessary to Complete a Delivery? 191
118. Delivery in Escrow—Conditional Delivery ---- 192
119. Some Effects of the Seal ---- 193
120. Statutory Changes Affecting the Seal ---- 194

CHAPTER 8. CAPACITY OF PARTIES

121. Introduction ---- 197

A. INFANTS

122. Introduction ---- 199
123. Transactions Which the Infant Cannot Avoid ---- 201
124. Avoidance and Ratification ---- 202
    (a) Failure to Make a Timely Disaffirmance ---- 203
    (b) Express Ratification ---- 205
    (c) Ratification by Conduct ---- 206
125. Effect Upon Ratification of Ignorance of Law or Fact ---- 207
126. Obligations of Restitution upon Disaffirmance ---- 207
    (a) Infant as Defendant ---- 207
    (b) Infant as Plaintiff ---- 208
127. Torts Connected with Contracts ---- 209
    (a) Infant's Torts Stemming from His Contracts ---- 210
    (b) False Representations by the Infant ---- 210
    (c) Torts and Agency Relationships ---- 212
128. Liability of an Infant for Necessaries ---- 212
129. Infant's Liability for Benefits Received: The New Hampshire View ---- 215

TABLE OF CONTENTS

B. THE MENTALLY INFIRM

Sec.		Page
130.	Introduction	216
131.	Requirement of Restitution	218
132.	Avoidance and Ratification	219
133.	Liability for Necessaries	220
134.	Intoxicated Persons	220
135.	Exploitation of Alcoholics and Weak Minded Persons	221

CHAPTER 9. CONDITIONS

A. GENERAL PRINCIPLES

136.	Meaning of Condition in a Contract	225
137.	Classification of Conditions	226
138.	Conditions Precedent	226
139.	Concurrent Conditions	226
140.	Conditions Subsequent	227
141.	Express (True) and Constructive Conditions	229
142.	Illustrations and Effect of Express Conditions	230
143.	Distinction Between an Express Condition and a Promise	232
144.	Express Language of Condition May be Implied Language of Promise	233
145.	Express Language of Promise Giving Rise to Implied or Constructive Conditions	235
146.	The History of Constructive Conditions	235
147.	Constructive Conditions Distinguished from Implied in Fact Conditions	235
148.	Conditions as Related to Unilateral and Bilateral Contracts	236
149.	Importance of Distinguishing Between Express and Constructive Conditions: Substantial Performance and Material Breach	236

B. EXPRESS CONDITIONS

150.	Strict Compliance	237
151.	Conditions of Satisfaction	238
152.	Conditions of Satisfaction: Satisfaction of a Third Person	238
153.	Conditions of Satisfaction: Satisfaction of a Party to the Contract	240
154.	Demand as a Condition	242

C. CONSTRUCTIVE CONDITIONS

155.	Introduction	243
156.	Required Order of Performance in a Bilateral Contract	244
157.	Material Breach and Substantial Performance	245
	(a) Material Breach	245
	(b) Substantial Performance	248
158.	A Note on Terminology: "Failure of Consideration"	250

TABLE OF CONTENTS

Sec.   **Page**

159. Recovery for Less than Substantial Performance: Quasi Contractual and Statutory Relief 251
160. Recovery by a Party in Default: Divisibility 253
161. Divisibility: Other Uses of the Concept 256
162. Independent Promises 257
163. Present or Prospective Inability and Unwillingness to Perform as Constructive Conditions 259

D. EXCUSE OF CONDITION

164. Introduction 264
165. Hindrance or Failure to Cooperate as an Excuse of Condition: Duty to Cooperate 264
166. Estoppel and Waiver Compared 268
167. Waiver Contemporaneous with the Formation of the Contract .. 269
168. Waiver and Estoppel: Waiver before Failure of Condition but after Formation of the Contract 270
169. Waiver after Failure of Condition: Election 273
170. Giving Unjustifiable Reasons for Refusing to Perform as an Excuse of a Condition 274
171. Waiver of Condition is Not Waiver of Right to Damages for Breach 275
172. Excuse of Conditions Involving Forfeitures 276
173. Excuse of Condition by Impossibility 277

CHAPTER 10. BREACH OF CONTRACT—REPUDIATION

174. Introduction 278
175. Repudiation 278
176. What Constitutes a Repudiation 282
177. Positive Statement of Unwillingness or Inability to Perform as a Repudiation 282
178. Transferring or Contracting to Transfer Specific Property to a Third Person or Performing Any Voluntary Affirmative Act Which Renders Performance Substantially Impossible 283
179. Repudiation and Good Faith 284
180. What Constitutes Repudiation Under the Uniform Commercial Code 284
181. Insolvency and Bankruptcy as Equivalents of Repudiation 284
182. Retraction of a Repudiation 286
183. Courses Open to the Promisee 287
184. Does a Repudiation Always Justify an Immediate Action for Total Breach? 289
185. Successive Actions for Breach—Splitting an Indivisible Cause of Action 293

TABLE OF CONTENTS

CHAPTER 11. IMPOSSIBILITY OF PERFORMANCE AND FRUSTRATION OF THE VENTURE

Sec.   Page

186. Impossibility of Performance: Introduction 296
187. Destruction, Deterioration or Unavailability of the Subject Matter or Tangible Means of Performance 298
188. Failure of the Contemplated Mode of Delivery or Payment 303
189. Supervening Prohibition or Prevention by Law 304
190. Failure of the Intangible Means of Performance 306
191. Death or Illness 307
192. Reasonable Apprehension of Impossibility or Danger 308
193. Impracticability 309
194. Impossibility as an Excuse of Condition 310
195. Frustration of the Venture 312
196. Temporary Impossibility or Frustration 314
197. Personal versus Objective Impossibility or Frustration 315
198. Contributory Fault, Foreseeability, Assumption of the Risk 316
199. Assumption of the Risk—Technological Impossibility 318
200. Effect of Impossibility Upon a Prior Repudiation 319
201. Impossibility and Frustration Under the Uniform Commercial Code 320

CHAPTER 12. DAMAGES

A. INTRODUCTION

202. Damages Defined 324

B. NON–COMPENSATORY DAMAGES

203. Nominal Damages 326
204. Punitive Damages 327

C. COMPENSATORY DAMAGES

205. The General Standard 327

D. FORESEEABILITY

206. The Rule of Hadley v. Baxendale 329
207. Application of the Rule in Carrier and Telegraph Cases 332
208. Application of the Rule in Other Cases 334

E. CERTAINTY

209. Certainty as a Limitation Upon Recovery of Damages 334
210. Alternative Recovery: Reliance Interest Protected Where Expectation Interest is Uncertain or Nonexistent 338
211. Alternative Recovery: Value of a Chance or Opportunity 339
212. Alternative Recovery: Rental Value of Property that Might have Produced Profits 341

TABLE OF CONTENTS

F. THE CONCEPT OF VALUE

Sec.		Page
213.	Market Value as the Usual Standard	342
214.	Proof of Value	343
215.	Value a Variable Concept	344

G. AVOIDABLE CONSEQUENCES

216.	The "Duty" to Mitigate Damages	345
217.	Non-exclusive Contracts—An Apparent Exception to the Doctrine of Avoidable Consequences	348
218.	Recovery of Expenses Sustained in Avoiding Consequences of a Breach	349

H. DAMAGES IN PARTICULAR ACTIONS

219.	Wrongful Discharge of Employee	351
220.	Wrongful Termination by Employee	352
221.	Total Breach of Sales Contracts—Buyer's General Damages	353
222.	Buyer's General Damages for Seller's Breach of Warranty or Fraud	354
223.	Consequential and Incidental Damages for Seller's Breach	355
224.	Seller's General Damages for Non-acceptance or Repudiation	356
225.	Seller's General Damages Following Resale	358
226.	Seller's Consequential and Incidental Damages	358
227.	Seller's Action for the Price	359
228.	Seller's Damages for Contracts to Manufacture Special Goods Under the Code	360
229.	Construction Contracts: Measure of Recovery by Contractor	361
230.	Construction Contracts: Measure of Recovery by Owner	362
231.	Contracts to Sell Realty: Measure of Damages for Total Breach	364

I. AGREED DAMAGES

232.	Liquidated Damages Distinguished from Penalties	366
233.	Two Pitfalls of Draftsmanship: The Shotgun Clause and The Have Cake and Eat It Clause	368
234.	Availability of Specific Performance When Damages are Liquidated	369
235.	Liquidated Damages and Penalties Distinguished from Alternative Promises	369
236.	Liquidated Damages Under the Uniform Commercial Code	370

CHAPTER 13. RESTITUTION AS A REMEDY FOR BREACH

237.	Introduction	371
238.	What is Meant by Restitution? The Concept of Unjust Enrichment	371
239.	Restitution as an Alternative Remedy for Breach	372

Sec.   **Page**

240. Measure of Recovery in an Action for Restitution Based on Breach 374
241. Restitution Not Available if a Debt Has Been Created 375
242. May the Plaintiff Recover Both Damages and Restitution? 376

CHAPTER 14. THIRD PARTY BENEFICIARIES

243. Introduction 378
244. Categories of Beneficiaries 379
    (a) Creditor and Donee Beneficiaries 379
    (b) Intended and Incidental Beneficiaries 380
245. Relationship of Third Party Beneficiary Doctrine to the Statute of Wills 384
246. The Mortgage Assumption Cases and Vrooman v. Turner 384
247. Public Contracts 387
248. Intent to Benefit in the Creditor Beneficiary Context—Promises of Indemnity 390
249. The Surety Bond Cases 392
250. Promisor's Defenses 393
251. Vesting—Voluntary Discharge or Modification 395
252. Rights of the Beneficiary Against the Promisee 398
253. Rights of the Promisee Against the Promisor 399

CHAPTER 15. ASSIGNMENT AND DELEGATION

254. Terminology 401
255. History 402
256. Nature of an Assignment 403
257. Coverage of the Uniform Commercial Code and of this Chapter 404
258. Formalities 406
259. Gratuitous Assignments 407
260. Are There Rights Which Are Not Assignable? Problem in General 409
261. Where the Assignment Would Materially Change the Duty of the Other Party 409
262. Where the Assignment Would Vary Materially the Burden or Risk of the Obligor 410
263. Where the Assignment Would Impair Materially the Other Party's Chance of Obtaining Return Performance: Executory Bilateral Contracts 411
264. The Assignability of Option Contracts 413
265. Necessity of Precise Distinctions: Partnership as an Illustration 414
266. Assignments Contrary to Public Policy 415
267. Effect of Contractual Prohibition or Authorization of an Assignment 416
268. Voidable Assignments, Assignments of Conditional Rights and Conditional Assignment of Rights 418

Sec.   Page

269. Defenses of the Obligor Against the Assignee 419
270. Other Limitations Upon the Rights of the Assignee: Counter-
claims, Set-off, and Recoupment 422
271. Other Limitations Upon the Rights of the Assignee: Latent
Equities 423
272. Priorities Between Successive Assignees of the Same Claim 424
273. Rights of the Assignee Against an Attaching Creditor 426
274. Assignment of Future Rights: Equitable Assignments 427
275. Partial Assignments 429
276. Implied Warranties of the Assignor and Sub-Assignor 430
277. Delegation of Duties: Generally 430
278. Non-delegable Duties 431
279. Liability of the Delegate 434
280. Effect of Repudiation by Delegating Party 435
281. Effect of Delegation of a Non-delegable Duty 436

CHAPTER 16. STATUTE OF FRAUDS

I. WHEN A WRITING IS NECESSARY

282. Introduction 441

A. SURETYSHIP AGREEMENTS

283. Promise by Executor or Administrator 443
284. Promise to Answer for the Debt, Default or Miscarriage of Another 444
285. Cases Where There is No Prior Obligation Owing from TP to C
to Which D's Promise Relates 445
    (a) TP Must Come Under at Least a Voidable Obligation to
C 445
    (b) There Must be a Principal-Surety Relationship Between
TP and D 448
    (c) C Must Know or Have Reason to Know of the Principal-
Surety Relationship 449
    (d) The Promise Must Not be Joint 450
    (e) Summary 451
286. Cases Where There is a Prior Obligation Owing from TP to C
to Which D's Promise Relates 451
    (a) Novation 451
    (b) Where the Promise to Pay is Made to TP 452
    (c) Where the Promise is Made to C but is Co-extensive with
D's Obligation to C 452
287. The Main Purpose (or Leading Object) Rule 453
288. Some Illustrations 454
289. The Peculiar New York Rule 455
290. Promises of Indemnity 457
291. The Promise of the Del Credere Agent 459
292. The Promise of the Assignor to His Assignee Guaranteeing
Performance by the Obligor 459
293. A Promise to Buy a Claim 460

TABLE OF CONTENTS

B. AGREEMENTS IN CONSIDERATION OF MARRIAGE

Sec.   Page

294. When the Statute of Frauds Applies ------------------------- 460

**C. AGREEMENTS FOR THE SALE OF LAND OR
INTERESTS IN LAND**

295. Contracts for the Sale of Land ---------------------------- 461
   (a) Introduction --- 461
   (b) Is a Promise to Pay for an Interest in Real Property
       Within the Statute? ------------------------------- 461
   (c) Interests in Land ------------------------------------ 462
      1. In General ----------------------------------- 462
      2. Liens --------------------------------------- 462
      3. Fructus Industriales ------------------------- 463
      4. Standing Timber, Buildings Attached to the Land
         and Other Things Attached to the Earth Not In-
         cluded in the Concept Fructus Industriales ---- 463
      5. Miscellaneous Items Deemed Not to be Within this
         Section of the Statute of Frauds Relating to In-
         terests in Land ----------------------------- 464

296. Performance as Causing a Contract Within the Statute to be En-
     forceable --- 465

**D. AGREEMENTS FOR THE SALE OF GOODS: THE
UNIFORM COMMERCIAL CODE**

297. Contracts for the Sale of Goods --------------------------- 466
   (a) Introduction --- 466
   (b) Price or Value --------------------------------------- 467
   (c) Goods --- 468
   (d) Choses in Action ------------------------------------- 469
   (e) Part Performance ------------------------------------- 469
      1. Accept and Receive ---------------------------- 469
      2. Payment or Earnest --------------------------- 470
   (f) Admission in Court ----------------------------------- 471

E. CONTRACTS NOT TO BE PERFORMED WITHIN ONE YEAR

298. Computation of the One Year Period ------------------------ 471
299. Possibility of Performance Within One Year ---------------- 472
300. Promises Performable Within One Year but Conditional Upon
     an Uncertain Event --------------------------------- 473
301. A Promise of Extended Performance that Comes to an End
     Upon the Happening of a Condition that May Occur Within a
     Year --- 474
302. Contracts for Alternative Performances and Contracts with Op-
     tion to Terminate, Renew or Extend ----------------- 475
303. Is a Promise or a Contract Within the One Year Section of the
     Statute of Frauds? --------------------------------- 476

TABLE OF CONTENTS

Sec. | Page

304. Effect of Performance Under the One Year Section ---------- 476
305. Unilateral Contracts ------------------------------------ 477
306. Relationship of the One Year Provision to Other Subdivisions of the Statute -- 479

II. WHAT IS A SUFFICIENT WRITING OR MEMORANDUM AND THE EFFECT THEREOF

307. Introduction -- 480
308. Parol Evidence and the Memorandum --------------------- 480
309. The Contents of the Memorandum ----------------------- 482
310. The Form of the Contract and When It is to be Prepared—Necessity for Delivery -- 483
311. Signed by the Party to be Charged --------------------- 483
312. Problems Presented When the Memorandum is Contained in More Than One Writing ----------------------------------- 485
313. The Memorandum Under U.C.C. § 2–201—The Sale of Goods Section -- 485
314. Is the Oral Contract Which Does Not Comply with the Statute "Unenforceable" or "Void"? ----------------------------- 487
315. Effect of Part of a Contract being Unenforceable Because of the Statute -- 489
316. Oral Rescission or Variation of a Contract Within the Statute-- 489
317. To What Extent May an Oral Contract Which is Not Enforceable Because of the Statute of Frauds be Used as a Defense? 490
318. Some Miscellaneous Rules ------------------------------ 491

III. RESTITUTIONARY REMEDIES

319. Introduction -- 491
320. The Plaintiff Must Not be in Default ------------------ 492
321. Effect of Defendant's Restoration of the Status Quo ---------- 493
322. Restitution Denied Where Policy of the Statute Would be Thwarted -- 493
323. Measure of Recovery ---------------------------------- 494
324. The Contract Price as Evidence of Value: Contrast between Damages and Restitution ------------------------------- 495
325. Specific Restitution in Equity ------------------------ 497

IV. ESTOPPEL

326. Equitable Estoppel and the Statute of Frauds ---------------- 498
327. Promissory Estoppel ---------------------------------- 499

CHAPTER 17. JOINT AND SEVERAL CONTRACTS

328. Multiple Promisors ----------------------------------- 501
329. When Promisors are Bound Jointly, Severally, or Jointly and Severally -- 502

TABLE OF CONTENTS

Sec.   Page
330. Consequences of Joint Liability ----------------------------------- 503
      (a) Compulsory Joinder of Joint Promisors ----------------- 503
      (b) The Discharge of other Joint Promisors by a Judgment
          Against One -- 504
      (c) Only a Joint Judgment Can be Entered Against Joint
          Promisors -- 505
      (d) The Rule of Survivorship -------------------------------- 506
      (e) A Discharge of One Joint Obligor Releases the Others -- 506
331. Consequences of Joint and Several Liability -------------- 508
332. Consequences of Several Liability ---------------------------- 509
333. Relation of Co-Obligors to Each Other—Contribution --------- 510
334. Multiple Promisees -- 511
335. Compulsory Joinder of Joint Obligees ----------------------- 513
336. Discharge by One Joint Obligee ------------------------------ 513
337. Survivorship of Joint Rights -------------------------------- 514

CHAPTER 18. DISCHARGE OF CONTRACTS

338. Introduction --- 516

A. RESCISSION

339. Mutual Rescission -- 517

B. DESTRUCTION OR SURRENDER

340. Cancellation or Surrender, if the Contract is Formal ---------- 519

C. EXECUTORY BILATERAL CONTRACT OF ACCORD— ACCORD AND SATISFACTION—SUBSTITUTE AGREEMENT—UNILATERAL ACCORD

341. Background of the Problem ---------------------------------- 520
342. Consequences of Enforceability of an Executory Bilateral Con-
      tract of Accord -- 523
343. Distinguishing an Executory Bilateral Contract of Accord from
      a Substituted Agreement ----------------------------------- 524
344. An Offer of Accord Looking to a Unilateral Contract --------- 524

D. THREE PARTY SITUATIONS

345. Assignment, Novation or Contract for the Benefit of a Third
      Person -- 525

E. ACCOUNT STATED

346. Account Stated -- 527

F. RELEASE AND COVENANT NOT TO SUE

347. Release --- 529
348. Covenant Not to Sue --------------------------------------- 531

G. GIFTS AND REJECTION OF TENDER

349. Renunciation, Rejection of Tender, or Executed Gift --------- 531

TABLE OF CONTENTS

H. MERGER

Sec.   Page

350. Merger _____ 532

I. UNION OF RIGHT AND DUTY IN THE SAME PERSON

351. Acquisition by the Debtor of the Correlative Right _____ 533

J. ALTERATION

352. Discharge by Alteration _____ 534

K. BANKRUPTCY

353. Bankruptcy _____ 535

L. PERFORMANCE

354. Performance of the Duty—To Which Debt Should Payment be
      Applied _____ 535

CHAPTER 19. ILLEGAL BARGAINS

355. Introduction _____ 539

I. ILLEGAL BARGAINS

A. BARGAINS IN RESTRAINT OF TRADE

356. Agreement by a Seller of a Business Not to Compete with the
      Buyer _____ 540
357. Agreement by an Employee Not to Compete after the Termina-
      tion of His Employment _____ 541
358. Divisibility of a Contract in Restraint of Trade _____ 543
359. Monopolies and Restraint _____ 544

B. BARGAINS HARMFUL TO PUBLIC OR TO FIDUCIARY DUTIES

360. Lobbying Agreements to Influence Legislative Action _____ 544
361. Bargain to Procure Government Contracts _____ 545
362. Some Other Bargains Harmful to Public Service _____ 547
363. Bargain in Breach of a Fiduciary Obligation _____ 548
364. Agreement by a Citizen to Violate a Civic Duty _____ 549

C. BARGAINS TO COMMIT A TORT OR TO EXONERATE OR INDEMNIFY FROM TORTIOUS LIABILITY

365. Bargain to Commit a Tort or Injure Third Persons _____ 549
366. Bargains to Indemnify Against the Consequences of Illegal and
      Tortious Acts _____ 549
367. Agreement to Exempt a Person from Willful or Negligent Mis-
      conduct _____ 550

TABLE OF CONTENTS

D. BARGAINS TENDING TO OBSTRUCT THE ADMINISTRATION OF JUSTICE

Sec.   Page

368. Maintenance and Champerty ----- 553
369. Agreements Tending to Interfere with the Proper Functioning of the Judicial Machinery ----- 554

E. BARGAINS HARMFUL TO MARRIAGE

370. Contracts Tending to Prevent or Disrupt the Marriage Relationship ----- 555

F. OTHER ILLEGAL BARGAINS

371. Sunday Contracts: What Activities Included ----- 557
372. Effect of Violation of a Sunday Law Statute ----- 557
373. Wagering Contracts and Lotteries ----- 558
374. Usurious Bargains ----- 560
    (a) Was there a Loan of Money? ----- 561
    (b) Does the Loan Exceed the Legal Rate of Interest? ----- 562

II. THE EFFECT OF ILLEGALITY

375. Introduction ----- 565

A. ILLEGAL EXECUTORY CONTRACTS

376. General Rule ----- 565
377. Cases Where a Party May Successfully Sue Upon an Illegal Executory Bilateral Contract ----- 565
    (a) Ignorance of Facts and Law ----- 565
    (b) Bargain Illegal by Virtue of Wrongful Purpose ----- 566
    (c) Where a Particular Statute is Directed Against One of the Parties ----- 567

B. ILLEGAL CONTRACT WHICH IS PERFORMED IN WHOLE OR PART

378. Introduction ----- 567
379. Will the Courts Always Deny a Remedy in the Case of an Illegal Bargain Which Violates a Criminal Statute? ----- 568
380. Effect of Licensing Statutes ----- 570
381. Remoteness of the Illegality ----- 571
382. A Mere Depositary May Not Assert the Defense of Illegality -- 571
383. Quasi Contractual Recoveries Based Upon Performance ----- 573
384. Divisibility of Illegal Bargains ----- 573
385. The Doctrine of Pari Delicto ----- 574
386. Locus Poenitentiae ----- 577
387. Change of Law or Facts after the Bargain is Made ----- 579

Table of Cases ----- 581

Index ----- 607

†

HANDBOOK

OF THE

LAW OF CONTRACTS

CHAPTER 1

INTRODUCTION

Analysis

Sec.
1. What is a Contract?
2. Contracts Distinguished from Executed Agreements.
3. Freedom of Contract.
4. Scope of the Law of Contracts.
5. Sources of Contract Law.
6. Classification of Contracts.
7. Formal and Informal Contracts.
8. Unilateral and Bilateral Contracts.
9. Enforceable, Void, Voidable and Unenforceable Contracts.
10. Express and Implied Contracts (Quasi Contracts).

§ 1. What is a Contract?

No entirely satisfactory definition of the term "contract" has ever been devised. The difficulty of definition arises from the diversity of the expressions of assent which may properly be denominated "contracts" and from the various perspectives from which their formation and consequences may be viewed.

Every contract involves at least one promise that has legal consequences. The usual, but not the inevitable, legal consequence is that performance of the promise may be enforced in court by a decree for specific performance or a money judgment. The promissory element present in every contract is stressed in a widely quoted definition: "A contract is a promise, or set of promises, for breach of which the law gives a remedy, or the performance of which the law in some way recognizes as a duty." [1] This, like similar definitions, is somewhat

---

[1] 1 Williston, Contracts § 1 (3d ed. 1957) [hereinafter cited as Williston; except where reference is made to the earlier revised edition which will be

misleading. While it is true that a promise is a necessary element in almost every contract, frequently the promise is coupled with other elements such as physical acts, recitals of fact, and the immediate transfer of property interests. In ordinary usage the contract is not the promise alone, but the entire complex of these elements. The definition also fails to point out that a contract usually requires the assent of more than one person. An additional criticism is that there are "voidable" and "unenforceable" contracts containing promises which at times may be dishonored with impunity. While promises contained in such contracts may have legal consequences, to say that the law recognizes them as duties is to stretch the concept of duty beyond its usual limitations.[2]

Another common definition of a contract is that it is a legally enforceable agreement. While this definition has the advantage of emphasizing that "agreement"[3] is at the core of the law of contracts, the troublesome fact is that there are certain kinds of contracts which may be formed without an agreement.[4] Also, like other definitions of the term "contract," it is unenlightening, and of little help in determining whether a given complex of words and acts constitutes a contract. Knowledge of much of the law of contracts is a prerequisite to an understanding of what a contract is.

Apart from the difficulty, even when there is little or no substantive disagreement, of defining a legal term so as to achieve universal acceptance, it should be stressed that technical terms share an affliction in common with non-technical language. Words, carefully defined in one context, have the frequently disagreeable habit of appearing in different contexts with widely divergent meanings. To illustrate, Article I, Section 10, of the United States Constitution, pro-

---

cited as Williston (rev'd ed.)]; Restatement, Contracts § 1 (1932) [hereinafter cited as Restatement, Contracts]. The definition is carried over into the tentative draft of Restatement, Contracts (2d) § 1 (Tentative Draft 1964) [hereinafter cited as Restatement, Contracts (2d)]. Compare, 1 Corbin, Contracts § 3 (1963) [hereinafter cited as Corbin] (" . . . a contract is a promise enforceable at law directly or indirectly.")

2. "A duty is a legal relation that exists whenever certain action or forbearance is expected of an individual, and in default of it the representatives of organized society will act in some predetermined manner injurious

to the defaulting individual." 1A Corbin § 182. While the aggrieved party to an unenforceable or voidable contract sometimes has a remedy against the defaulting promisor, quite often there is none. Where there is no remedy for non-performance it seems inappropriate to speak of a "duty" of performance.

3. The term "agreement" may also be defined in various ways. The definition adopted by the Restatement, Contracts (2d) § 3 is: "An agreement is a manifestation of mutual assent on the part of two or more persons." Compare 1 Corbin § 9; 1 Williston § 2.

4. See ch. 5 infra.

vides that "No State shall . . . pass any . . . Law impairing the Obligation of Contracts." The United States Supreme Court has held that this clause prohibited the Legislature of New Hampshire from modifying a charter granted by King George III to Dartmouth College.[5] A study of the treatises on the law of contracts would indicate clearly that this charter is not a contract as that term is used in the law of contracts. Nonetheless, by considering the purpose of the constitutional clause, and the presumed intention of the framers of the Constitution, the court held that the charter was a contract within the meaning of the Constitution. The re-defining of a term based on the purpose for which the term was used in its particular context is one of the subtler and widely used techniques of the legal art.

Sometimes a legislative act will define terms used in the act in a manner different from standard definitions. The Uniform Commercial Code in essence defines a contract as the total legal obligation created by a bargain.[6] Thus by act of the legislature, the term "contract" for purposes of the Uniform Commercial Code, has a somewhat different meaning than it has in transactions not governed by the Code, since the term "bargain" as used in legal parlance includes transactions in which no promise is made, such as the immediate sale of property without warranty in exchange for cash.[7]

The term "contract" is also used by laymen and lawyers alike to refer to a document in which the terms of a contract is written. Use of the word in this sense is by no means improper so long as it is clearly understood that rules of law utilizing the concept "contract" rarely refer to the writing itself. Usually, the reference is to the agreement; the writing being merely a memorial of the agreement.

§ 2. Contracts Distinguished from Executed Agreements

The law gives effect to certain agreements other than contracts. These include barters, gifts, sales of goods, conveyances of interests in real property, and the creation of bailments.[8] The distinction is that a contract is executory in nature. It contains a promise or promises that must be executed, that is, performed. For example, an

---

5. Trustees of Dartmouth College v. Woodward, 17 U.S. (4 Wheat.) 518, 4 L.Ed. 629 (1819).

6. See U.C.C. § 1–201(11), read with § 1–201(3).

7. See Reporter's Note, Restatement, Contracts (2d) § 4. In addition, for purposes of Article 2 of the U.C.C., § 2–106(1) specifically includes sales of goods within the term "contracts."

8. See 1 Corbin § 4. A bailment is not necessarily formed by agreement. For example, a finder of personal property is a bailee. Brown, Personal Property § 73 (2d ed. 1955).

agreement to sell an automobile is a contract; the sale of an automobile is not.

The distinction, like many legal distinctions, is helpful for the purpose of analysis, but is not rigid and is often artificial. Looked at from a transactional perspective, probably most sales, conveyances and bailments are mixed transactions, involving both an executed transfer of property interests or possession and promises such as warranties or promises to surrender possession.

Even from a purely analytic point of view, the distinction between executed agreements and contracts is not firm. As noted in the preceding section, the Uniform Commercial Code includes sales of goods within its definition of contract. This was not an arbitrary legislative decision. One of the basic purposes of Article 2 of the Code is to bring the rules governing sales of goods closer to the rules governing contracts to sell goods than had been true under the Uniform Sales Act which the Code has replaced in most jurisdictions.[9]

§ 3.   Freedom of Contract

The law of contracts permeates every aspect of our society. Every day it reaches into the life of the individual, governing to some extent his employment, his purchase and sale of land and goods, the insuring of his possessions and the financing of these transactions. On a vaster scale it enters into practically every aspect of domestic and international trade.

It was not always thus. In medieval England contract law barely existed.[10] The protection of expectations engendered by promissory agreements was generally not regarded as important enough for the state to concern itself with. True, a remedy might sometimes be had in local courts, the proceedings of which we have few records. The ecclesiastical courts took jurisdiction over some contract cases and merchants and craftsmen often utilized their own courts and arbitrators. However, the central parts of the legal system—the courts of common law and the chancery—tended to regard the non-performance of promises as too trivial for consideration unless the promise was made pursuant to certain solemn forms.[11] The feudal society of

9. See U.C.C. § 2–106, Comment 1 (". . . the rights of the parties do not vary according to whether the transaction is a present sale or a contract to sell unless the Article expressly so provides.") Contrast, Uniform Sales Act § 1.

10. See Pollock, Contracts in Early English Law, 6 Harv.L.Rev. 389 (1893), Selected Readings on the Law of Contracts 10 (1931) [hereinafter cited as Selected Readings.]

11. See Hazeltine, The Formal Contract of Early English Law, 10 Colum.L.Rev. 608 (1910), Selected Readings 1.

the time assigned each man a niche, a status, which rather rigidly delineated the conduct expected of him and which he might expect from others. Enforcement of a voluntary assumption of duties of the kind we now call contractual tended to disrupt this status oriented society.

No attempt will be made here to trace the step by step evolution of the law of contracts. The crux is that as England changed from a relatively primitive backwater to a commercial center with a capitalistic ethic, the law changed with it. As freedom became a rallying cry for political reforms, freedom of contract was the ideological principle for development of the law of contract. In Maine's classic phrase, it was widely believed that "the movement of the progressive societies has hitherto been a movement *from Status to Contract*." [12] Williston adds: "Economic writers adopted the same line of thought. Adam Smith, Ricardo, Bentham, and John Stuart Mill successively insisted on freedom of bargaining as the fundamental and indispensable requisite of progress; and imposed their theories on the educated thought of their times with a thoroughness not common in economic speculation." [13]

In the twentieth century the tide has turned away from the nineteenth century tendency toward unrestricted freedom of contract. While the parties' power to contract as they please for lawful purposes remains a basic principle of our legal system, it is hemmed in by increasing legislative restrictions. Two areas of the law serve to illustrate this. Contracts of employment are controlled by a wide range of Federal and state laws concerning minimum wages, hours, working conditions and required social insurance programs. Contracts of insurance, perhaps to a greater extent than labor contracts, are controlled by law. Often terms of the policy are dictated by statute.

Apart from legislative restrictions on freedom of contract it seems likely that in the future there will be greater restrictions imposed by courts in the exercise of their function of developing the common law. There has been increasing recognition in legal literature that the bargaining process has become more limited in modern society. In purchasing a new automobile, for example, the individual may be able to dicker over price, model, color and certain other factors, but, if he wishes to consummate the contract to purchase, he usually must sign the standard form prepared by the manufacturer (although he is contracting with an independent dealer). He has no real choice. He must take that form or leave it. Such contracts,

---

12. Maine, Ancient Law 165 (3rd American ed. 1873).

13. Williston, Freedom of Contract, 6 Cornell L.Q. 365, 366 (1921), Selected Readings 100, 101–102.

called contracts of "adhesion," [14] have frequently been denied their intended effect by a process of strained interpretation.[15] In the landmark case of Henningsen v. Bloomfield Motors, Inc.,[16] the court dealt with the matter in more forthright fashion, denying any effect to a clause in an adhesion contract deemed by it to be unfair. How great an impact this decision will have is as yet unknown, but it has already given impetus to a trend.[17]

§ 4. Scope of the Law of Contracts

Contract law interlocks with and overlaps all other legal disciplines. In particular, labor, sales, commercial financing, agency, suretyship, quasi-contracts, damages, personal property—to name but a few—are contract permeated subjects about which specialized treatises have been written. A volume on the law of contracts can attempt only to discuss selected basic problems, principles, and concepts utilized in all of these disciplines.

The selection of the particular topics to be discussed in a volume of this kind is in part guided by traditional classifications and in part by the authors' perhaps arbitrary judgment of what topics best serve to orient the reader through the fundamentals of the laws governing consensual transactions.

§ 5. Sources of Contract Law

Except in a few American jurisdictions the basic law of contracts is not codified. Contract law is thus primarily common law, embodied in court decisions. Many legislative enactments do, however, bear on the subject. Generally, only a few statutes purport to modify a principle running throughout contract law. For the most part legislatures have concentrated on regulating particular types of contracts such as insurance policies and employment contracts. Of particular relevance in recent legislation is Article 2 of the Uniform Commercial Code. While this Article governs only sales and contracts to sell goods, there is reason to believe that in other contexts

---

14. See Kessler, Contracts of Adhesion —Some Thoughts About Freedom of Contract, 43 Colum.L.Rev. 629 (1943).

15. Compare Boll v. Sharp & Dohme, Inc., 281 App.Div. 568, 121 N.Y.S.2d 20 (1st Dep't 1953), aff'd 307 N.Y. 646, 120 N.E.2d 836 (1954) (blood donor's agreement to relieve drug company of liability rendered ineffective by narrow construction), with Tunkl v. Regents of Univ. of Cal., 60 Cal.2d 92, 32 Cal.Rptr. 33, 383 P.2d 441 (1963) (agreement by patient to relieve hospital of liability held void).

16. 32 N.J. 358, 161 A.2d 69, 75 A.L.R. 2d 1 (1960).

17. The trend has been reinforced by U.C.C. § 2–302, concerning "unconscionable" contracts or clauses. See § 56 infra.

courts will look to the Code rules for guidance in formulating decisions.[18]

For the guidance of the bench and bar, the American Law Institute in 1932 published a code-like document called the Restatement of Contracts. The Restatement, having been issued by a private organization, does not have the force of law. Nevertheless, it is highly persuasive authority. Leaders of the profession analyzed the often conflicting maze of judicial decisions, attempted to cull the sound from the less sound and to state the sounder views in systematic form.[19] The principal draftsman of the Restatement of Contracts was Samuel Williston.

After a passage of some thirty years, it was felt that there had been sufficient developments in the law for a new Restatement to be issued. In 1964 the first tentative draft of the initial portion of a second edition was circulated. The guiding spirit of the second edition is Arthur Linton Corbin.

The law of contracts is the subject of two of the best treatises in Anglo-American legal literature. The first edition of Professor Williston's treatise was published in 1920 and has had enormous impact on the law. Professor Corbin's, first published in 1950, promises to be equally influential. Research into any contract problem necessarily requires consultation of both of these authors' views as well as the cases and statutes. Both treatises are masterful analyses. To capsulate the basic difference in approach of the two authors, requires an introduction to two schools of jurisprudence: the so-called positivist and realist schools.

Stated in its extreme form the positivist idea is this:

> "Justice is an irrational idea . . . that only one of two orders is 'just' cannot be established by rational cognition. Such cognition can grasp only a positive order . . . This order is positive law . . . It presents the law as it is, without defending it by calling it just, or condemning it to call it unjust." [20]

The positivist usually believes that the legal system may be analyzed into component rules, principles and concepts and that any fact situation may be solved by the careful pigeonholing of the facts into the appropriate legal concepts, principles and rules. In other words,

---

18. See Note, The Uniform Commercial Code as a Premise for Judicial Reasoning, 65 Colum.L.Rev. 880 (1965).

19. For a fuller discussion, see Preface, Restatement of Contracts (1932).

20. Kelsen, General Theory of Law and State 13 (1961). Kelsen is the leading modern exponent of the positivist approach.

once the facts are determined, a carefully programmed computer would produce the correct decision. This approach has been criticized as "mechanical jurisprudence." [21]

The realist is skeptical whether decisions are in fact so arrived at and furthermore questions the propriety of such an approach. Again stated in extreme form, the realist believes:

> "[T]he law, with respect to any particular set of facts, is a decision of a court with respect to those facts so far as that decision affects that particular person. Until a court has passed on those facts no law on that subject is yet in existence." [22]

The realist is skeptical of the formulation of generalizations and definitions. He believes that courts in reaching a decision do in fact and should take into account the moral, ethical, economic and social situation in reaching a decision. This approach is subject to criticism in that it tends toward the creation of a legal system based on non-law and to defeat society's expectations of order and certainty in legal relationships.

Neither Professor Williston nor Professor Corbin adopt either of the extreme positions just discussed. However, the reader might find his comprehension of their treatises enhanced if he realizes at the outset that the former tends towards the positivist position and the latter towards the realist school.

The neophyte should also be apprised that although courts usually articulate their decisions in positivist terms, it is only the unsophisticated attorney who will phrase his argument purely in those terms without reference to social, economic and ethical considerations. While this volume is primarily an analysis of positive law, this is not because the authors are unaware of the increasing reliance by courts on other kinds of arguments. Nor are limitations of space the primary motive for concentration on analysis. This book is designed primarily for first year law students. During this concentrated year of study of fundamental courses, it is essential that they acquire firm command of the analytic method. Analytic ability alone will not make them great lawyers, but without this skill they cannot be capable lawyers.[23]

---

21. Pound, Mechanical Jurisprudence, 8 Colum.L.Rev. 605 (1908).

22. Frank, Law and the Modern Mind 46 (1930). See generally, Savarese, American Legal Realism, 3 Houston L.Rev. 180 (1965).

23. For a contrary view, attacking the use of the analytic method in the teaching of contract law, see the preface to Friedman, Contract Law in America (1965).

§ 6.   Classification of Contracts

Contracts have been classified and distinguished in various ways for different purposes. Some of these classifications will be discussed briefly in the following sections.

§ 7.   Formal and Informal Contracts

The distinction between formal and informal contracts is based on the method of the formation of the contract. Under the early common law a promise was not binding unless accompanied by certain formalities.[24] Three kinds of formal contracts are still important: (1) the contract under seal;[25] (2) the recognizance[26] and (3) negotiable instruments and letters of credit.[27]

All other kinds of contracts are considered to be informal[28] and are enforceable not because of the form of the transactions but because of their substance.

§ 8.   Unilateral and Bilateral Contracts

Every contract involves at least two contracting parties. In some contracts, however, only one party has made a promise and therefore only he is subject to a legal obligation. Such a contract is said to be unilateral. If both parties have made promises, the contract is bilateral.[29]

If A says to B, "If you walk across Brooklyn Bridge, I promise to pay you ten dollars," A has made a promise but he has not asked B for a return promise. He has requested B to perform an act, not a commitment to do the act. A has thus made an offer to a unilateral contract which arises when and if B performs the act called for. If A had said to B, "If you promise to walk across Brooklyn Bridge, I promise to pay you ten dollars," his offer requests B to make a commitment to walk the bridge. A bilateral contract arises when the requisite return promise is made by B.

24. See Hazeltine, The Formal Contract of Early English Law, 10 Colum.L.Rev. 608 (1910); Selected Readings 1 (1931).

25. The seal has lost all or some of its effect in many jurisdictions. See ch. 7 infra.

26. A recognizance is an acknowledgment in court by the recognizor that he is bound to make a certain payment unless a specified condition is performed. Restatement, Contracts § 9. Recognizances are discussed in works on suretyship.

27. Negotiable instruments and letters of credit are treated in specialized works.

28. These are also called simple or parol contracts.

29. Of course this assumes that there are only two parties to the contract. If there are more than two, the contract is deemed bilateral if one party is both a promisor and a promisee. Restatement, Contracts § 12.

A number of recent authorities, including the Second Restatement and the Uniform Commercial Code avoid the terms "bilateral" and "unilateral." Their abandonment of this terminology is part of an effort to soften the rigor of some of the rigid consequences thought to flow from the mechanical application of this dichotomy.[30]

§ 9. Enforceable, Void, Voidable and Unenforceable Contracts

When a promisee is entitled to either a money judgment [31] or specific performance because of a breach, the contract is said to be enforceable.

A contract is void, a contradiction in terms, when it produces no legal obligation upon the part of a promisor. For example, an exchange of promises which lacks consideration is frequently said to be a void contract. It would be more exact to say that no contract has been created.

A contract is voidable if one or more of the parties has the power to elect to avoid the legal relations created by the contract or by ratification to extinguish the power of avoidance. This power to avoid or ratify is sometimes given to an infant contracting party and to persons who have been induced to enter contracts by fraud, mistake or duress.

Unenforceable contracts are those which have some legal consequences but which may not be enforced in an action for damages or specific performance in the face of certain defenses such as the Statute of Frauds and the statute of limitations. While a voidable contract may be ratified an unenforceable contract may not. Certain contracts which are tainted by illegality but which are neither wholly void nor voidable may also be classified as unenforceable.[32]

§ 10. Express and Implied Contracts (Quasi Contracts)

When the parties manifest their agreement by words the contract is said to be express. When it is manifested by conduct it is said to be implied in fact. If A telephones a plumber to come to A's house to fix a broken pipe, it may be inferred that A has agreed to pay the plumber a reasonable fee for his services although nothing is said of this. The contract is partly express and partly implied in fact.

---

30. See Reporter's Note, Restatement, Contracts (2d) § 12. For a fuller discussion see § 38 infra.

31. A money judgment may be based on either the remedy of damages or of restitution, or both. See chs. 12, 13 infra.

32. Restatement, Contracts (2d) § 14, Comment b.

There are cases of contracts wholly implied in fact.[33]   The distinction between this kind of contract and a contract expressed in words is unimportant; both are true contracts formed by a mutual manifestation of assent.[34]

A contract implied in law is not a contract at all but an obligation imposed by law to do justice even though it is clear that no promise was ever made or intended.   To illustrate, if a physician gives a child necessary medical care in the face of parental neglect, the physician may recover from the parents, in quasi contract, the value of his services.[35]   There is nothing contractual about this at all.   The quasi contractual label arose from a procedural quirk.   Since in the earlier law there was no writ for an obligation of this kind, courts permitted the use of the contractual writ of assumpsit and allowed the plaintiff's attorney to plead a fictitious promise.   The crux is that a quasi contract is not a peculiar brand of contract.   It is a non-contractual obligation that used to be treated procedurally *as if it were* a contract.

33.   E. g., Day v. Caton, 119 Mass. 513
      (1876).

34.   See 1 Corbin § 18.

35.   Greenspan v. Slate, 12 N.J. 426, 97
      A.2d 390 (1953), 39 Cornell L.Q. 337
      (1953).

CHAPTER 2

OFFER AND ACCEPTANCE

Analysis

		Sections
A.	Intent to Contract	11–14
B.	The Offer	15–20
C.	Other Matters Relating to Mutual Assent	21–24
D.	Acceptance	25–38

Analysis

A. INTENT TO CONTRACT

Sec.
11. Mutual Assent.
12. Objective and Subjective Intention.
13. Must the Parties be Serious?
14. Must the Parties Intend Legal Consequences?

B. THE OFFER

15. What is an Offer?
16. Offer Distinguished from an Expression of Opinion.
17. Offers Distinguished from Statements of Intention and Preliminary Negotiations.
18. Is the Ordinary Advertisement, Catalog or Circular Letter an Offer?
19. Offers at Auctions.
20. Price Quotations Contrasted With Offers.

C. OTHER MATTERS RELATING TO MUTUAL ASSENT

21. Intention That the Agreement be Memorialized in a Formalized Writing.
22. Questions of Law and Fact.
23. Indefiniteness.
24. Unilateral, Bilateral and Reverse Unilateral Contracts and Some of Their Implications.

D. ACCEPTANCE

25. Must the Offeree Know of the Offer and if so at What Point of Time?
26. Must the Offeree Intend to Accept?
27. Who May Accept the Offer?
28. Must the Offeree Give Notice of Acceptance of an Offer to a Unilateral Contract?

Sec.
29. Acceptance of an Offer Looking to a Series of Contracts.
30. The Necessity for Communicating Acceptance of an Offer to a Bilateral Contract.
31. Promises Inferred from Conduct or Silence.
32. Acceptance Varying from Offer.
33. Termination of the Power of Acceptance Created by Revocable Offers.
    (a) Lapse of Time.
    (b) Death or Lack of Capacity of the Offeror.
    (c) Revocation, Direct and Indirect.
    (d) Rejection—Counter-Offer.
    (e) Death or Destruction.
    (f) Supervening Illegality.
34. Up to What Point of Time May an Offeror Revoke a Revocable Offer Looking to a Unilateral Contract?
35. Up to What Point in Time May a Revocable Offer Looking to a Bilateral Contract be Revoked?
    (a) Parties at a Distance.
    (b) Parties in the Presence of One Another.
36. Risk of Mistake in Transmission.
37. Termination of Irrevocable Offers (Option Contracts).
    (a) What Makes an Offer Irrevocable?
    (b) Termination of Irrevocable Offers.
38. Modern Trend Limiting the Importance of the Distinction Between Unilateral and Bilateral Contracts.
    (a) § 2–206 of the Uniform Commercial Code.
    (b) Proposed Restatement.

A. INTENT TO CONTRACT

Analysis

Sec.
11. Mutual Assent.
12. Objective and Subjective Intention.
13. Must the Parties be Serious?
14. Must the Parties Intend Legal Consequences?

§ 11. Mutual Assent

Usually, as an essential prerequisite to the formation of an informal contract there must be an agreement; a mutual manifestation of assent to the same terms.[1] The agreement ordinarily is reached by a process of offer and acceptance.[2]

1. It is ordinarily stated that the requisites of a contract are (1) a promise by a party having legal capacity to act, (2) two or more contracting parties, because the common law rule is that no man may contract with himself, (3) mutual assent, (4) consideration, (5) the agreement must not be void. 1 Williston § 18. As we shall see, in some instances requisites (3) and (4) are not necessary.

2. If A and B are together and C suggests the terms of a contract for them

§ 12. Objective and Subjective Intention

Words are notoriously slippery symbols and there may be a wide divergence between the meaning a person intended to convey with his expressions and the meaning reasonably or unreasonably understood by the person to whom he was communicating. For at least a century the objective theory of contracts has been dominant. Under this theory the subjective intention of the parties is ordinarily irrelevant. As stated by a great judge:

> "A contract has, strictly speaking, nothing to do with the personal, or individual, intent of the parties. A contract is an obligation attached by mere force of law to certain acts of the parties, usually words, which ordinarily accompany and represent a known intent. If, however, it were proved by twenty bishops that either party, when he used the words, intended something else than the usual meaning which the law imposes upon them, he would still be held, unless there were some mutual mistake, or something else of the sort." [3]

The objective theory lays stress on the outward manifestation of assent made to the other party in contrast to the older idea that a contract was a true "meeting of the minds." [4] Despite the ascendency of the objective theory, there are a number of instances when the subjective intention of the parties may be decisive. These will be discussed as they arise in the following chapters and especially in chapter 3. In the meantime, a tentative working objective test will be stated: A party's intention will be held to be what a reasonable man

and they both simultaneously agree to these terms there would be a contract without any process of offer and acceptance. However, if a writing is prepared by C and A signs it first and B signs later, it has been said that A is the offeror and B the offeree. See 1 Corbin § 12. In the first case posed in this note, if A and B were not together and expressed their assent separately to C, there would be no contract because although the parties expressed their assent to the same proposition they did not manifest the assent to each other unless C could be considered the agent of both. If a written contract is prepared in duplicate and one copy is signed by each party there would not necessarily be a contract, unless there were a prior understanding that the contract could be so formed, because presumably the manifestations of assent are not made with reference to each other. 1 Corbin § 12; Restatement, Contracts (2d) § 23; cf. Schwartz v. Greenburg, 304 N.Y. 250, 107 N.E.2d 65 (1952). See § 25 infra, particularly the discussion relating to identical cross offers.

3. Learned Hand, in Hotchkiss v. National City Bank of N.Y., 200 F. 287, 293 (S.D.N.Y.1911), aff'd 201 F. 664 (2d Cir.), aff'd 231 U.S. 50, 34 S.Ct. 20, 58 L.Ed. 115, and 231 U.S. 60, 34 S.Ct. 22, 58 L.Ed. 121 (1913).

4. See Williston, Freedom of Contract, 6 Cornell L.Q. 365 (1921), reprinted Am. Ass'n of Law Schools Selected Readings on the Law of Contracts 100 (1931) [hereinafter cited as Selected Readings].

in the position of the other party would conclude his manifestations to mean.[5] By testing the meaning to be given to a party's words from the point of view of the reasonable man in the second party's position, the subjective element of this party's particular knowledge is incorporated into the objective test. In other words, the test considers what the second party knows or should know about the intention of the first party.

§ 13. Must the Parties be Serious?

If A and B enter into what otherwise appears to be a contract and, at the trial, B asserts as a defense that he was "joking" would there be an enforceable contract? Under the tentative test proposed in the preceding section the issue would be whether a reasonable man in the position of A would conclude from the manifestations of the parties that B was serious. Under this test, if it is determined that B did not *appear* serious there is no contract. If he appeared to be serious there is a contract unless A knows or should know he is joking.[6] The same rules would apply if a party claims that he was not serious because he was angry or excited,[7] or because the entire matter was intended as a "frolic and banter."[8] Very often these issues are questions of fact rather than questions of law.[9]

---

5. The test is described as a tentative working test since other tests are sometimes employed. For example, the Restatement, Contracts § 227, Comment a, as a general rule attaches to unintegrated agreements "the meaning the person employing them should reasonably have apprehended that they would convey to the other party." In addition, other tests may be applied to integrated agreements. This matter is discussed in more detail in chapter 3 infra.

6. Lucy v. Zehmer, 196 Va. 493, 84 S. E.2d 516 (1954); 1 Williston § 21. If a purely objective theory were followed B should not be permitted to testify that he was not serious but could only point to words and conduct which showed that he was not serious. Since the test is partially subjective, B should be permitted to testify that he was not serious because, as stated, if A knew or should have known that he was joking there would be no contract. See also 1 Cor-

bin § 34. Analogous cases, permitting the annulment of marriages entered into in jest, are McClurg v. Terry, 21 N.J.Eq. 225 (1870); Davis v. Davis, 119 Conn. 194, 175 A. 574 (1934).

7. Higgins v. Lessig, 49 Ill.App. 459 (1893).

8. Keller v. Holderman, 11 Mich. 248 (1863); see also Graves v. Northern N.Y. Pub. Co., 260 App.Div. 900, 22 N. Y.S.2d 537 (4th Dep't 1940), appeal dism'd 285 N.Y. 547, 32 N.E.2d 832 (1941) (offer published in newspaper's "joke column" to pay $1,000 to anyone who would provide defendant with telephone number of Western Union).

9. Theiss v. Weiss, 166 Pa. 9, 31 A. 63 (1895); Chiles v. Good, 41 S.W.2d 738 (Tex.Civ.App.1931), rev'd on other grounds 57 S.W.2d 1100 (Tex.Comm. App.1933). On the distinction between questions of law and questions of fact, see § 22 infra.

Sometimes in a business setting, parties will enter into what appears to be a contract for such purposes as to give the impression to third persons that ownership of a business is in different hands than is actually the case, or to inflate the assets of one of the parties. In these cases it may be proved that both parties expressed to each other an intention to enter a merely sham arrangement.[10] Despite the appearance of a contract, these cases are consistent with the objective test. Although outsiders reasonably thought that there was a contract, the reasonable man in the position of the parties knew that there was no contract.

§ 14.   Must the Parties Intend Legal Consequences?

It has sometimes been stated that in order to have a contract the parties must act "in contemplation of legal consequences."[11] This is not literally true. As Corbin points out, if two ignorant persons agreed to exchange a horse for a cow, there would be an enforceable contract even if they were unaware that society offers a remedy for the enforcement of such an agreement.[12]

But it is also incorrect to say that intent to effect legal relations is always immaterial. Thus, if A invites B to dinner and B accepts the invitation and arrives at A's house at the appointed time and A is not there, B would not ordinarily have a cause of action because it is a reasonable factual presumption that the parties intended that only a social obligation shall result.[13] The same presumption exists when a husband and wife live together amicably and make an agreement with respect to the wife's support.[14]

10. Nice Ball Bearing Co. v. Bearing Jobbers, 205 F.2d 841 (7th Cir. 1953), cert. den. 346 U.S. 911, 74 S.Ct. 242, 98 L.Ed. 408 (1953); New York Trust Co. v. Island Oil & Transport Corp., 34 F. 2d 655 (2d Cir. 1929). Contra, 9 Wigmore, Evidence § 2406 (3d ed. 1940), and cases cited therein. If third parties rely on the sham agreement to their prejudice, the parties to the agreement may be estopped from denying its contractual effects. Mt. Vernon Trust Co. v. Bergoff, 272 N.Y. 192, 5 N.E.2d 196 (1936).

11. Balfour v. Balfour, [1919] 2 K.B. 571 (C.A.).

12. 1 Corbin § 34; Restatement, Contracts (2d) § 21B.

13. See McDowell, Contracts in the Family, 45 B.U.L.Rev. 43 (1965). Absence of contractual intention will also be assumed when a candidate for public office makes pre-election promises to the electorate. O'Reilly v. Mitchel, 85 Misc. 176, 148 N.Y.S. 88 (Sup.Ct.1914) (candidate for mayor promised not to change Civil Service Law). If contractual intention existed in such a case, however, the agreement so formed would doubtless be void on grounds of public policy.

14. Balfour v. Balfour, supra note 11. It should be noted that there are three important factual elements in this case. One, the parties are husband and wife; two, they are living in amity; three, the agreement relates to the wife's support. Separation agreements (where the parties are not living in amity) are ordinarily enforceable. Husband and wife, al-

Conversely, where the transaction is one which might be denominated a business transaction, the presumption is that the parties intend legal consequences; but, if they manifest an intention that only a moral obligation is undertaken, the agreement is not binding[15] unless the parties have in fact acted under the agreement in which event other doctrines may come into play.[16]

B. THE OFFER

Analysis

Sec.
15. What is an Offer?
16. Offer Distinguished from an Expression of Opinion.
17. Offers Distinguished from Statements of Intention and Preliminary Negotiations.
18. Is the Ordinary Advertisement, Catalog or Circular Letter an Offer?
19. Offers at Auctions.
20. Price Quotations Contrasted with Offers.

§ 15. What is an Offer?

Except in the unusual case of offers to enter into so-called "reverse unilateral" contracts,[17] an offer is a promise, a commitment to do or refrain from doing some specified thing in the future. The offer creates a power of acceptance permitting the offeree by accepting the offer to transform the offeror's promise into a contractual obligation.[18]

§ 16. Offer Distinguished from an Expression of Opinion

A father consulted with the doctor about a certain operation and asked "How long will the boy be in the hospital" and the doctor replied "Three or four days, not over four; then the boy can go home and it will be just a few days when he will go back to work with a good hand." The son's hand did not heal for a month after the operation. The Court held that the doctor was not liable because he

though living in amity, could certainly enter into a binding business arrangement.

15. Rose and Frank Co. v. J. R. Crompton, [1923] 2 K.B. 261 (C.A.); Smith v. MacDonald, 37 Cal.App. 503, 174 P. 80 (1918). Such a provision will be strictly construed. See Novack v. Bilnor Corp., 26 A.D.2d 572, 271 N.Y.S.2d 117 (2d Dep't 1966).

16. Restatement, Contracts (2d) § 21B, Comment b; 1 Corbin § 34.

17. See § 24 infra.

18. The Restatement, Contracts (2d) § 24 defines an offer as a "manifestation of willingness to enter into a bargain, so made as to justify another person in understanding that his assent to that bargain is invited and will conclude it."

had not made a promise (offer) [19] but merely a prediction.[20] In another case [21] the plaintiff questioned the defendant doctor about the electric shock therapy which the defendant proposed to use. The defendant told her that the treatments were perfectly safe. When she came out of the treatment she found she had a broken arm. The defendant explained that she had had a "convulsive seizure" which ensued as a result of the electric shock treatment. The Court indicated that whether the defendant's statement was a promise or an expression of opinion was a question of fact which, as is explained in § 22, means that the determination is to be made by the trier of fact.[22]

In another well known case [23] B, a tenant farmer, was behind in his rent. He told A, his landlord, about his problems, and A suggested that he should get more cattle. B replied "If I stock up too heavy in the pasture and there be a short spell I will be up against it and that is the reason I am waiting for you." A then told B "Never mind the water, John, I will see there will be plenty of water because it never failed in Minnesota yet." On the strength of A's statement B purchased 107 cattle and lost money when the water supply failed. The court held as matter of law that A's statement was not a promise; it was nothing more than an opinion or a weather prediction. If A had said "I will make good any loss you suffer due to a water shortage," the result could well have been different even though the rainfall was not within the control of the promisor.[24]

The important considerations are: (1) that in each of these cases the question is whether the defendant made an offer or merely ex-

---

19. The Restatement, Contracts (2d) § 2 defines a promise as "a manifestation of intention to act or refrain from acting in a specified way, so made as to justify a promisee in understanding that a commitment has been made."

20. Hawkins v. McGee, 84 N.H. 114, 146 A. 641 (1929). However, a statement by the doctor in the same case that "I will guarantee to make the hand a hundred percent perfect hand" was held to present a question of fact as to whether the doctor had made a promise. In Robins v. Finestone, 308 N.Y. 543, 127 N.E.2d 330 (1955) an allegation that a doctor promised to cure plaintiff in two or three days was held to state a cause of action that sounded in contract for purposes of the statute of limitations. This case is annotated in 7 Syracuse L.Rev. 165 (1955). Of course a medical doc-

tor's liability may be predicated upon grounds other than contract. The plaintiff may have a cause of action based upon malpractice (negligence) or assault. See, for example, Pearl v. Lesnick, 20 A.D.2d 761, 247 N.Y.S.2d 561 (1st Dep't 1964), aff'd 19 N.Y.2d 590, 278 N.Y.S.2d 237, 224 N.E.2d 739 (1967), where violation of a surgeon's promise not to perform an operation was held not to be a breach of contract, but an assault barred by the shorter tort statute of limitations.

21. Johnston v. Rodis, 102 U.S.App.D.C. 209, 251 F.2d 917 (1958).

22. See § 22 infra.

23. Anderson v. Backlund, 159 Minn. 423, 199 N.W. 90 (1924).

24. Restatement, Contracts (2d) § 2, Comment d.

pressed an opinion; (2) under the tentative standard adopted this is determined by inquiring whether a reasonable man in the position of the plaintiff would conclude that the defendant made a promise or merely stated his opinion; and (3) that sometimes this is a question of law and at other times this is a question of fact.[25]

§ 17. Offers Distinguished from Statements of Intention and Preliminary Negotiations

If A says to B "I am going to sell my car for $500.00," and B replies "All right, here is $500.00, I will take it," there is no contract because a reasonable man would conclude that A was stating his future intention and not making a promise.[26] So also an announcement that an auction will be held is deemed to be a statement of future intention.[27]

An inquiry or an invitation to make an offer must also be distinguished from an offer. For example, in one case the defendant, in reply to an inquiry as to whether he would sell the plaintiff his store property for $6,000, answered "it would not be possible for me to sell it unless I was to receive $16,000.00 cash." Plaintiff replied accepting the "offer." The court held that the defendant had not made an offer. The defendant had not said that he promised to sell for $16,-000.00; he was really saying "make me an offer." Consequently he did not confer upon the plaintiff the power to create a contract by accepting.[28]

Another interesting case is Mellen v. Johnson.[29] The defendant wrote the plaintiff that his price for certain property was $7,500 and that he was so writing to several other interested persons. The plaintiff wired stating that he accepted. The court held that a reasonable man should have concluded that the defendant was not making an offer especially since it would be unreasonable to assume that defendant was willing to subject himself to the possibility of being bound by more than one contract. This is not to say that a person may not be held to have made offers to sell the same property to more than

---

25. See § 22 infra.

26. Randall v. Morgan, 33 Eng.Rep. 26 (1805).

27. Benjamin v. First Citizens Bank and Trust Co., 248 App.Div. 610, 287 N.Y.S. 947 (1936) (plaintiff's assignor came from South Africa to attend an auction announced to be without reserve which was cancelled; no recovery; see § 19 infra); cf. Peters v. Bower, 63 So.2d 629 (Fla.1953) (affida-

vit of intent to grade streets in a subdivision held not enforceable). Statement of hopes and desires are also not considered to be promises or offers. 1 Corbin § 15.

28. Owen v. Tunison, 131 Me. 42, 158 A. 926 (1932). Accord, Blakeslee v. Nelson, 212 App.Div. 219, 207 N.Y.S. 676 (3d Dep't 1925), aff'd 240 N.Y. 697, 148 N.E. 763 (1925).

29. 322 Mass. 236, 76 N.E.2d 658 (1948).

one offeree. If he is so unwise, each of the offerees who has accepted will have a remedy against the offeror. When a person is interested in disposing of property, however, he is likely to negotiate with more than one potential buyer. If in some way he indicates that proposals to sell have been addressed to others, in the absence of a clear promise to sell at given terms, his proposal is not reasonably to be construed as an offer.

In Harvey v. Facey,[30] the plaintiff sent a telegram to the defendant saying "Will you sell us Bumper Hall Pen? Telegraph lowest cash price." The defendant answered "Lowest Price for Bumper Hall Pen £900." Plaintiff purported to accept this "offer." The court held that there was no contract: since the plaintiff's first question had not been answered, defendant's communication did not contain a promise to sell. The case has been criticized as overly technical.[31] It is arguable that the plaintiff, in the light of his previous inquiry, could reasonably conclude that the defendant made an offer to sell for 900 pounds. Nonetheless, courts are quite properly reluctant to construe a proposal as an offer unless it is quite clear a promise has been made. Once a contract is made, courts tend to interpret language freely and, if justice seems to require, without finicky regard for grammatical nicety. However, they will not lightly determine that a person has taken the significant step of creating a power of acceptance unless he quite clearly made a commitment.[32] Until he has done this, the person with whom he is dickering is not justified in relying upon the negotiations. This is particularly true when, as in Harvey v. Facey, the supposed offeree is aware that negotiations are in progress with other potential purchasers of the same subject matter.[33] The failure of the defendant to reply to the first question in the light of this circumstance is referable to an unwillingness to make a definite commitment.[34]

30. [1893] A.C. 552 (P.C.) (Jamaica); see also Courteen Seed Co. v. Abraham, 129 Or. 427, 275 P. 684 (1929).

31. 1 Corbin § 26 n. 20.

32. See United States v. Braunstein, 75 F.Supp. 137, 139 (S.D.N.Y.1947), appeal dism'd 168 F.2d 749 ("It is true that there is much room for interpretation once the parties are inside the framework of a contract, but it seems that there is less in the field of offer and acceptance. Greater precision of expression may be required, and less help from the court given, when the parties are merely at the threshold of a contract.") But cf. Restatement,

Contracts (2d) § 21A, esp. ill. 5. Compare Restatement, Contracts (2d) § 58. See § 47 infra.

33. In Harvey v. Facey, [1893] A.C. 552 (P.C.) (Jamaica), the plaintiffs, who were solicitors in Kingston, dispatched their initial telegram the day after the City Council had publicly debated negotiations with the defendant to sell the premises to the city. Although the opinion does not state that the plaintiffs were aware of the Council meeting, the inference is clear that they were.

34. The court's opinion in Harvey v. Facey does not come to grips with the

The essential point is that under the objective theory of contracts the test is whether a reasonable man in the position of the plaintiff would conclude that the defendant had made a commitment. Under such a test it is not surprising to find that there are often differences of opinion as to the correct result in a concrete case.[35]

§ 18. Is the Ordinary Advertisement, Catalog or Circular Letter an Offer?

If a clothing store advertised a well known brand of suits in the following terms, "nationally advertised at $220, today only at $150" and A came to the store in response to the advertisement, selected a suit and tendered $150, would there be a contract?[36] The answer is in the negative.[37] Since the store has not stated any quantity, the cases hold that an advertisement of this kind is only a statement of intention to sell or a preliminary proposal inviting offers. Would the reasonable man so conclude? While it would be onerous to hold that the advertiser has committed himself to have an unlimited supply of the article, it could be argued that he was impliedly promising to sell one to a customer or a reasonable number to a customer on a first come, first served basis so long as the supply lasts. The reasonable man test tends to be used by the courts to resolve cases of first im-

problem in these terms. As pointed out in the previous note the plaintiff knew that the defendant was negotiating with the Town of Kingston and defendant undoubtedly knew that the plaintiff knew. When the defendant received the telegram he should have known that the plaintiff was looking for an offer so that he might purchase before the Town of Kingston and it is certainly arguable that when the plaintiff received the reply as a reasonable man he could believe it was a statement of "selling price" (offer) rather than a price quotation or a statement of "asking price." Cf. Fairmount Glass Works v. Crunden-Martin Woodenware Co., 106 Ky. 659, 51 S.W. 196 (1899). However, the argument cuts both ways. Shouldn't the plaintiff as a reasonable man know that the defendant, while he was dickering with the Town of Kingston, might be unwilling to make a commitment and that the noncommital language used under the circumstances should lead a reasonable man to con-clude that an offer had not been made? Courteen Seed Co. v. Abraham, 129 Or. 427, 275 P. 684 (1929), criticized in 9 Ore.L.Rev. 72 (1929) presents a similar problem.

35. Grismore, Contracts § 14. (rev. ed. 1965) [hereinafter cited as Grismore].

36. Whether the advertiser may be held to some kind of liability if the advertising is fraudulent is beyond the scope of this book. See, for example, 69 Yale L.J. 830 (1960).

37. Georgian Co. v. Bloom, 27 Ga.App. 468, 108 S.E. 813 (1921); Craft v. Elder & Johnston Co., 38 N.E.2d 416 (Ohio App.1941); Restatement, Contracts (2d) § 25. In some cases it has been held that no offer has been made because the goods are insufficiently described. Lovett v. Frederick Loeser & Co., Inc., 124 Misc. 81, 207 N.Y.S. 753 (Mun.Ct.1924). This involves a question of indefiniteness. See § 23 infra.

pression which then serve as precedents in later cases. By this process certain hardened categories emerge. The newspaper advertisement cases relating to the sale of goods illustrate this process. Rightly or wrongly, at an early date it was decided and the law is now settled that there is no offer in cases such as the hypothetical illustration just discussed.

It does not follow that an advertisement for the sale of goods never makes an offer. In a recent case [38] the following advertisement appeared in the newspaper. "1 Black Lapin Stole, Beautiful, Worth $139.50 . . . . . $1.00 FIRST COME FIRST SERVED." The plaintiff was the first to present himself and tendered a dollar. The court held that there was an offer. The Restatement Second indicates that the basis of the decision is that the words "FIRST COME FIRST SERVED" are language of promise which is ordinarily lacking in advertisements for the sale of goods.[39] However, it would appear more likely that the critical factor was the statement of a quantity, to wit, one, which is ordinarily lacking in advertisements.[40] Perhaps it is the combination of the two which motivated the court in reaching its decision.

So also if an advertiser announces that "We will pay $10.00 for each share of the common stock of the XYZ Company mailed to us before July 1," an offer has been made.[41] Here again it should be observed that there is a quantity, "each share" (every share), and also language of promise ("We will pay"). If an advertiser promises to pay a fixed sum to anyone who contracts influenza after using his patent medicine, an offer has been made.[42] The problem here is quite different because there is language of promise and no problem with respect to quantity as in the case of the advertisement for the sale of goods.

---

38. Lefkowitz v. Great Minneapolis Surplus Store, 251 Minn. 188, 86 N.W. 2d 689 (1957).

39. Restatement, Contracts (2d) § 25, ill. 1.

40. "One" is not only a quantity but a quantity per person. Would there be an offer if the advertisement did not state the quantity allocated per person?

41. Crummer & Co. v. Nuveen, 147 F.2d 3, 157 A.L.R. 739 (7th Cir. 1945); Sey-

mour v. Armstrong, 62 Kan. 720, 64 P. 612 (1901).

42. Carlill v. Carbolic Smoke Ball Co., [1893] 1 Q.B. 256 (C.A.1892); accord, Minton v. F.G. Smith Piano Co., 36 App.D.C. 137 (1911); Whitehead v. Burgess, 61 N.J.L. 75, 38 A. 802 (1897); Johnson v. Capital City Ford Co., 85 So.2d 75 (La.App.1955). See also Crowe v. Hertz Corp., 382 F.2d 681 (5th Cir. 1967); Turner v. Central Hardware Co., 353 Mo. 1182, 186 S.W. 2d 603, 158 A.L.R. 1402 (1945) as to representations and warranties made in advertisements.

In the same category as advertisements for the sale of goods are catalogues,[43] circular letters[44] and price lists.[45]

§ 19. Offers at Auctions

If the auctioneer says, "What am I bid?", it seems clear that he is not making an offer to sell, but is inviting offers to purchase which he is free to accept or reject. The law so decided at an early date.[46] On the other hand if the auctioneer announces that he will sell to the highest bidder, a number of authorities have concluded that the auctioneer has made an offer.[47] The majority view, however, appears to be that such a statement does not constitute an offer,[48] presumably because a reasonable man would not believe that the auctioneer has manifested a willingness to risk a sale of the property at a price far below its value.

The rules governing auctions, at least as to the sale of goods, are now incorporated in § 2–328 of the Uniform Commercial Code.[49] In an auction "with reserve," the common law rule is retained. The bidder is the offeror and the contract is complete when the auctioneer so announces, usually by the fall of the hammer. The auctioneer may

---

43. Schenectady Stove Co. v. Holbrook, 101 N.Y. 45, 4 N.E. 4 (1885).

44. Moulton v. Kershaw, 59 Wis. 316, 18 N.W. 172 (1884); Montgomery Ward & Co. v. Johnson, 209 Mass. 89, 95 N.E. 290 (1911).

45. 1 Corbin § 28.

46. Payne v. Cave, 100 Eng.Rep. 502 (1789).

47. Restatement, Contracts (2d) § 27, ill. 3.

48. 1 Corbin § 108; Drew v. John Deere Co. of Syracuse, Inc., 19 App. Div.2d 308, 241 N.Y.S.2d 267 (4th Dep't 1963); Spencer v. Harding, L.R. 5 C.P. 561 (1870); Anderson v. Wisconsin Cent. Ry. Co., 107 Minn. 296, 120 N.W. 39 (1909).

49. The Uniform Commercial Code has nine separate articles covering various subject matters. The citation "2–328" indicates that the section is in Article 2 of the Code. Article 2 deals with sales of goods and contracts for the sale of goods. The Uniform Commercial Code does not concern itself primarily with contract law and almost all of the provisions which it contains with respect to contract law are contained in Article 2. This means that the contract provisions found in Article 2 relate only to cases involving the sale of goods. The term goods is defined in § 2–105 with a cross reference to § 2–107. This definition is discussed in detail in § 297 infra. The terms "contract for sale" and "sale" are defined in § 2–106. The contract provisions of Article 2 of the Code tend to change the traditional contract law with the result that very often there is a different rule for "contracts for sale" than there is for other contracts such as for work, labor and services and for the sale of land. The result of having two sets of contract rules has been criticized. Williston, The Law of Sales in the Proposed Uniform Commercial Code, 63 Harv.L.Rev. 561, 576 (1950); but cf. Corbin, The Uniform Commercial Code—Sales; Should it be Enacted? 59 Yale L.J. 821 (1950). However, the Code does not change all of the traditional rules; where it is silent, the traditional rules prevail even as to contracts for sale. U.C.C. § 1–103. Conversely, it is likely that the Code will frequently be employed, by analogy, to transactions outside its cover-

withdraw the goods until he announces his acceptance; the bidder may withdraw his bid before that time.[50]

An anomaly exists in the rules governing auctions announced to be "without reserve." The Code retains the common law rule that the auctioneer may not withdraw the article from sale after he calls for a bid on an article (provided that a bid is received within a reasonable time),[51] but it permits the bidder to withdraw until the article is knocked down to him.[52] This rule diverges substantially from standard contract principles. It is difficult to identify the offeror. If the auctioneer is deemed the offeror, then it must be said that the bid is a conditional acceptance, subject to no higher bid being made and subject to the bidder's right to withdraw. If the bidder is said to be the offeror, a unique situation exists since the offeree is not free to reject the offer. Since the rule is statutory, identification of the offeror is of purely intellectual interest.

Subdivision 4 of § 2–328 is quite puzzling. It reads:

"If the auctioneer knowingly receives a bid on the seller's behalf or the seller makes or procures such a bid, and notice has not been given that liberty for such bidding is reserved, the buyer may at his option avoid the sale or take the goods at the last good faith bid prior to completion of the sale. This subsection shall not apply to any bid at a forced sale."

This subdivision is designed to protect a buyer who has purchased at a price higher than he would have paid had he not been the victim of puffing by by-bidders on behalf of the seller. Consequently, if the auction is with reserve, this subdivision offers no remedy to a disappointed bidder if an agent for the seller is the high bidder.[53] The disappointed bidder is not a "buyer."

age. Cf. Freeman v. Poole, 37 R.I. 489, 93 A. 786 (1915), reh. denied 94 A. 152 (provisions of Uniform Sales Act applied to land auction).

50. A bid terminates all prior bids. See Note, 12 B.U.L.Rev. 240 (1932); U.C.C. § 2–328(3), final clause.

51. Zuhak v. Rose, 264 Wis. 286, 58 N. W.2d 693, 37 A.L.R.2d 1041 (1953); 1 Williston § 30. For the sale to be "without reserve" the goods must be put up without reserve "in explicit terms."

52. U.C.C. § 2–328(3).

53. Whenever the auction is with reserve, since the seller has the privilege of removing the goods from the auction block, he breaches no contrac-

tual obligation if he accomplishes the same result by the subterfuge of having his agent make the high bid. Drew v. John Deere Co. of Syracuse, Inc., supra n. 48; Calamari, The Impact of the Commercial Code on the New York Law of Offer and Acceptance and Consideration, 1 N.Y.C.L.E. No. 3, 83, 94 (1964), Freeman v. Poole, supra n. 49. If the auction is without reserve the highest legitimate bidder would have an action for breach of contract. This remedy does not arise, however, from § 2–328(4), but from the third sentence of § 2–328(3). The discussion relates solely to the existence of a contract and not to possible criminality or licensing difficulties. See, for example, McKinney's N.Y. General Business Law § 24.

The difficult phrase in the subdivision is "the last good faith bid prior to the completion of the sale." Suppose only B and A, a by-bidder, have bid and the goods are knocked down to B at $100. If the bidding was started by B at $40 and went in the sequence of $50, $60, $70, $80, $90, $100, at which price may B claim the goods? Since the Code provision was designed to protect him against puffing, it has been suggested that he should have the goods at $40, despite the fact that all of his bids were literally in good faith, including the last. But suppose that C, a legitimate bidder, had made the $90 bid? Although there has been puffing, a third person bid $90. It has also been suggested that, in order to protect C's interests, B if he elects to buy must pay $90.[54] It is difficult to see, however, what legally protected interest C has at this stage of the transaction. Nevertheless, the suggestion that B should pay $90 for the goods seems sound in that a third person in good faith valued the goods to be worth this sum and B himself valued them at a higher sum.

The common law principles governing auctions are generally applicable to invitations to submit bids, including, except as modified by statute, proposals by government agencies and public corporations to let contracts through competitive bidding.[55]

§ 20. Price Quotations Contrasted With Offers

A price quotation is usually a statement of intention to sell at a given price per unit. Since, as in the case of advertisements, circulars and catalogs, quotations usually do not indicate the quantity available and often omit other crucial terms such as quality, they are held not to constitute offers. This is true even when the communication is addressed to a particular customer.[56] However, the mere use of the word "quote" or "offer" is not crucial. It is the communication as a whole rather than the label the party puts upon it that must be interpreted. In a well known case the plaintiff asked for the defendant's price on 1000 gross of Mason green jars. The defendant answered stating a price and using the word "quote," but also stated that the price was "for immediate acceptance." The court decided that the defendant's communication, read as a whole and in the context of the plaintiff's inquiry, was not a quotation, but an offer.[57] Conversely, where the word "offer" is used but no quantity is stated

54. See 1 Hawkland, A Transactional Guide to the Uniform Commercial Code 40 (1964). [hereinafter cited Hawkland]

55. See 1 Corbin § 46; 1 Williston § 31.

56. Restatement, Contracts (2d) § 25, Comment c.

57. Fairmount Glass Works v. Crunden-Martin Woodenware Co., 106 Ky. 659, 51 S.W. 196 (1899).

or other facts show that no commitment has been made, the communication will be held to be a quotation rather than an offer.[58]

In the case discussed above there were three factors which led the court to the conclusion that the word "quote" in context meant "offer." First, it came in response to an inquiry that obviously sought an offer. Second, the defendant's communication was quite detailed as to terms and, of course, included by implication the quantity of 1000 gross inquired about by the plaintiff. Finally, there was the use of the words "for immediate acceptance."

Of these, obviously the most important was the existence of detailed terms including quantity. In another case [59] S wrote to B, "we quote you . . . Hungarian [flour] $5.40 [per barrel] car lots only and subject to sight draft with bill of lading. We would suggest your using wire to order as prices are rapidly advancing that they may be beyond reach before a letter would reach us." The court held that there was no offer because S's communication did not specify any quantity. Under these circumstances it would appear that there would be no offer even if the word "offer" had been used in place of the word "quote."

The question then arises what should be the result if S sends a letter to B saying "We quote you two cars Hungarian flour at $5.40 per barrel." Is this an offer? Williston indicates that it is when he says "Where the property to be sold is accurately defined and an amount stated as the price in the communication made, not by general advertisement, but to one person individually, no reasonable interpretation seems possible except that the writer offers to sell the property described for the price mentioned." [60] The Restatement Second appears to adopt this reasoning at least if S's communication contains "detailed terms" including quantity.[61] However, if the seller was dickering with others for the disposal of the same subject matter and the buyer knew this or should have known it, the problems discussed at length in footnote 34 supra would arise.

58. Moulton v. Kershaw, 59 Wis. 316, 18 N.W. 172 (1884).

59. Johnston Brothers v. Rogers Brothers, 30 Ont. 150 (1899).

60. 1 Williston § 27.

61. Restatement, Contracts (2d) § 25, ill. 3.

C. OTHER MATTERS RELATING TO MUTUAL ASSENT

Analysis

Sec.
21. Intention That the Agreement be Memoralized in a Formalized Writing.
22. Questions of Law and Fact.
23. Indefiniteness.
24. Unilateral, Bilateral and Reverse Unilateral Contracts and Some of Their Implications.

§ 21. Intention That the Agreement be Memorialized in a Formalized Writing

During the process of negotiation parties often manifest an intention that when an agreement is reached it should be formalized. In such a situation, does a contract arise when the parties reach an otherwise binding agreement or is there no contract unless the formal document is adopted by both parties?

The problem is analogous to the question of intending legal consequences.[62] If the parties make it clear that they do not intend that there should be legal consequences unless and until a formal writing is executed, there is no contract until that time.[63] Conversely, if they make it clear that the prospective writing is merely to be a convenient memorial of the agreement previously reached, the agreement is binding when reached even though the memorial is never adopted.[64] In this case a party's refusal to execute the memorial constitutes a breach of contract.[65]

The difficult case is where the parties have not expressly manifested their intent other than by the fact that they intended that there should be a writing. In this situation some of the cases have held that the parties are not bound until the writing is executed.[66] But the better view appears to be that in such a case the contract arises when the agreement is reached.[67]

---

62. See § 14 supra.

63. Warrior Constructors, Inc. v. International Union, 383 F.2d 700 (5th Cir. 1967); Smissaert v. Chiodo, 163 Cal. App.2d 827, 330 P.2d 98 (1958).

64. 1 Corbin § 30; 1 Williston §§ 28, 28A.

65. Restatement, Contracts (2d) § 26.

66. Wharton v. Stoutenburgh, 35 N.J. Eq. 266 (1882); Berman v. Rosenberg, 115 Me. 19, 97 A. 6 (1916).

67. H. B. Zachry Co. v. O'Brien, 378 F.2d 423 (10th Cir. 1967); Miles v. City of Wichita, 175 Kan. 723, 267 P. 2d 943 (1954); Dohrman v. Sullivan, 310 Ky. 463, 220 S.W.2d 973 (1949); Peoples Drug Stores, Inc. v. Fenton Realty Corp., 191 Md. 489, 62 A.2d 273 (1948); Sanders v. Pottlitzer Bros. Fruit Co., 144 N.Y. 209, 39 N.E. 75 (1894).

Of course, there may be cases where the parties have not expressly stated their intent but there is evidence of their intention from the surrounding circumstances as, for example, where the agreement is very complex and is customarily not considered binding until a formal contract is executed.[68]

In the previous discussion it has been assumed that the parties had manifested the same intent or had not manifested any intention. Obviously, in the majority of cases only one party claims that he did not intend to be bound until there was a formal writing. This issue is to be determined by the tentative test previously suggested. If a reasonable man in the position of the other party either knew or should know that the other party did not intend to be bound in the absence of a formal agreement there is no agreement until the formal agreement is executed.[69]

§ 22.   Questions of Law and Fact

The distinction between questions of law and fact is analyzed in detail in treatises on procedure. Here it is sufficient to note that at the trial level questions of fact are determined by the triers of fact, often a jury, and questions of law are determined by the trial judge. Appellate courts as a general rule, subject to some exceptions, review only questions of law.

To illustrate: Whether and to what extent subjective intention is relevant in making a particular determination is a question of law. Whether a person said "50" or "100" on a particular occasion is a question of fact. Whether a reasonable man in the position of the

---

68. Thus, in a case involving an alleged oral contract relating to a complex corporate underwriting, the court said, "In this record there is no rational basis for a finding that the parties departed from all that is customary or expected in corporate underwritings and made a definitive agreement by parol . . ." Biothermal Process Corp. v. Cohu & Co., 283 App.Div. 60, 65, 126 N.Y.S.2d 1, 6 (1st Dep't 1953), aff'd 308 N.Y. 689, 124 N. E.2d 323 (1954). Some of the surrounding circumstances to be considered are listed in Comment c of § 26 of the Restatement, Contracts (2d).

69. Restatement, Contracts (2d) § 26, Comment b. "In New York, as elsewhere it is quite plain that if either of the parties manifests an intention not to be bound until a written contract is executed then the parties are not bound until that event occurs." Lizza & Sons, Inc. v. D'Onfro, 186 F. Supp. 428, 432 (D.Mass.1959) aff'd (1st Cir.) 282 F.2d 175; Merritt-Chapman & Scott Corp. v. Public Utility Dist. # 2, 237 F.Supp. 985 (S.D.N.Y.1965). At times the rule is stated as if the parties are bound upon agreement "in the absence of a positive agreement that it should not be binding until so reduced to writing and formally executed," Disken v. Herter, 73 App.Div. 453, 455, 77 N.Y.S. 300, 302 (1st Dep't 1902), aff'd 175 N.Y. 480, 67 N.E. 1081 (1903); accord, 12 Am.Jur., Contracts §§ 23, 25 (1938). This statement is incorrect since it implies that the manifest intent of one of the parties may be ignored by the other.

plaintiff would conclude that the defendant had made a commitment is a question of fact unless the court rules that reasonable men could reach only one reasonable conclusion.   Even where reasonable men could reach different conclusions the question is often held to be one of law when it involves the interpretation of a writing.[70]   There is also a tendency to rule as a matter of law in certain recurring situations, as in the advertising situation,[71] where the law has hardened as to the proper decision.

The interpretation of a writing is a question of law in the sense that it is determined by the trial judge.   As Corbin points out "since two cases are never identical   .   .   .   the decision made in one of them can never be regarded as a conclusive precedent for the other." [72] It must also be remembered that the printed report never gives all of the facts and may well omit one of the decisive factors that led to the decision.

§ 23.   Indefiniteness

Although the parties may have had and manifested an intention to make a contract, if the content of their agreement is unduly uncertain and indefinite no contract is formed.[73]   The rule is that an "offer must be so definite as to its material terms [74] *or require such definite terms in the acceptance* that the promises and performances to be rendered by each party are reasonably [75] certain." [76]   The italicized words indicate that it is the *contract* which must be definite and not the offer.   For example, if A makes an offer to B to sell from 1 to 10 copies of a specified book at a certain price and adds "state the

---

70. This point is discussed in greater detail at § 49 infra.

71. See § 18 supra.

72. 1 Corbin § 23.

73. Restatement, Contracts (2d) § 32(1); 1 Corbin § 95; 1 Williston § 37; Parks v. Atlanta News Agency, Inc., 115 Ga.App. 842, 156 S.E.2d 137 (1967).

74. Material terms include subject matter, price, payment terms, quantity, quality, duration, and work to be done.   Given the infinite variety of contracts, it is obvious no precise definition can be formulated.   For more detailed treatment, see 1 Williston §§ 38–48; 1 Corbin §§ 95–100.

75. The requirement of definiteness cannot be pushed to extreme limits.

As Corbin says in § 95 "In considering expressions of agreement, the court must not hold the parties to some impossible, or ideal, or unusual standard.   It must take language as it is and people as they are.   All agreements have some degree of indefiniteness and some degree of uncertainty.   In spite of its defects, language renders a practical service.   In spite of ignorance as to the language they speak and write, with resulting error and misunderstanding, people must be held to the promises they make.   The court must not be overly fearful of error; it must not be pedantic or meticulous in interpretation of expressions."

76. Restatement, Contracts (2d) § 32.

number in your acceptance" and B replies "I'll take 5," there is a contract, although considered alone the offer might seem indefinite as to quantity.

If A says to B, "If you work for me for one year as the foreman of my plant I promise to pay you a fair share of the profits," it has been held that the promise is too vague and indefinite to be enforced.[77] If, however, B performs under the agreement he may obtain a quasi contractual recovery measured by the reasonable value of his services rather than by a share of the profits.[78] A promise to make a tailor-made suit for fifty dollars where the material is not specified also suffers from indefiniteness.[79] Indefiniteness of this kind can be cured by the subsequent conduct of the parties. If the tailor commences making the suit with cotton cloth and the customer acquiesces in this, the parties' own construction of the agreement will be enforced.[80] The difference between granting contractual recovery in the tailor case and quasi contractual recovery in the employment case stems from the fact that in the tailor case the indefinite promise was made definite by performance and acquiescence; in the employment case the indefinite promise was never made definite.[81]

There is an important distinction between cases in which the parties have purported to agree on a contractual provision and have done so in a vague and indefinite manner and cases in which they have remained silent as to a material term. When parties fail to mention a material term, often the reasonable conclusion is that they intended that the term be supplied by implication. Thus, if A and B agree that A will perform a service for B and no mention is made of price, it will be implied that the parties intended that a reasonable price should be paid and received.[82] The same is true if goods are involved. It will be assumed that the parties contracted in terms of a reasonable

---

77. Varney v. Ditmars, 217 N.Y. 223, 111 N.E. 822 (1916); additional cases are collected in 1 Williston § 41. A number of more liberal cases have enforced promises of this nature. See Allan v. Hargadine-McKittrick Dry Goods Co., 315 Mo. 254, 286 S.W. 16 (1926); Noble v. Joseph Burnett Co., 208 Mass. 75, 94 N.E. 289 (1911).

78. Varney v. Ditmars, supra n. 77; 1 Corbin § 102; 1 Williston § 49.

79. Factor v. Peabody Tailoring System, 177 Wis. 238, 187 N.W. 984 (1922).

80. See 1 Corbin § 101; 1 Williston § 49; City of Bremerton v. Kitsap County Sewer Dist., 71 Wash.2d 689, 430 P.2d 956 (1967). The related question of forging a good unilateral contract out of a bad bilateral contract is discussed at § 74 infra.

81. 1 Williston § 49.

82. S. F. Bowser & Co. v. F. K. Marks & Co., 96 Ark. 113, 131 S.W. 334 (1910); Konitsky v. Meyer, 49 N.Y. 571 (1872); A. M. Webb & Co. v. Robt. P. Miller Co., 157 F.2d 865 (3d Cir. 1946). The Uniform Commercial Code provides detailed rules applicable to agreements in which the price has not

price which will ordinarily be the market price.[83] Where there is no market price the reasonable price may be determined by actual cost plus a reasonable profit,[84] or other means of valuation.[85] If no time is stated for the delivery of goods,[86] or for the completion of a building contract,[87] a reasonable time is implied. However, where the subject matter of the contract such as the kind or quantity of goods [88] or the specifications of a building contract [89] have not been decided upon and no standard can be found for reasonable implication, courts have ordinarily refused to supply the missing term.[90] Unfortunately, despite the business necessity for such contracts, courts have frequently included within this category agreements to deliver one's entire output to, or to take all one's requirements of a product from, the other contracting party.[91] The Uniform Commercial Code explicitly validates such agreements.[92]

been decided upon. U.C.C. § 2–305 provides:

"(1) The parties if they so intend can conclude a contract for sale even though the price is not settled. In such a case the price is a reasonable price at the time for delivery if
  (a) nothing is said as to price; or
  (b) the price is left to be agreed by the parties and they fail to agree; or
  (c) the price is to be fixed in terms of some agreed market or other standard as set or recorded by a third person or agency and it is not so set or recorded.
"(2) A price to be fixed by the seller or by the buyer means a price for him to fix in good faith.
"(3) When a price left to be fixed otherwise than by agreement of the parties fails to be fixed through fault of one party the other may at his option treat the contract as cancelled or himself fix a reasonable price.
"(4) Where, however, the parties intend not to be bound unless the price be fixed or agreed and it is not fixed or agreed there is no contract. In such a case the buyer must return any goods already received or if unable so to do must pay their reasonable value at the time of delivery and the seller must return any portion of the price paid on account."

83. U.C.C. § 2–305.

84. Kuss Mach. Tool & Die Co. v. El-Tronics, Inc., 393 Pa. 353, 143 A.2d 38 (1958), a case decided under § 2–305 of the U.C.C. Cf. Restatement, Contracts (2d) § 32, ill. 7.

85. Economic and legal methods of valuation are considered in McCormick, Damages ch. 6 (1935).

86. U.C.C. § 2–309(1). If the place of delivery is not specified, U.C.C. § 2–308 determines the proper place.

87. American Concrete Steel Co. v. Hart, 285 F. 322 (2d Cir.1922) (reasonableness of time sometimes a question of fact, sometimes of law).

88. Guthing v. Lynn, 109 Eng.Rep. 1130 (1831); Burke v. Campbell, 258 Mass. 153, 154 N.E. 759 (1927).

89. Bissenger v. Prince, 117 Ala. 480, 23 So. 67 (1898); Peoples Drug Stores v. Fenton Realty Corp., 191 Md. 489, 62 A.2d 273 (1948); Palombi v. Volpe, 222 App.Div. 119, 226 N.Y.S. 135 (1st Dep't 1927), aff'd 249 N.Y. 194, 163 N.E. 607 (1928).

90. See 1 Williston § 42; 1 Corbin § 100.

91. See § 72 infra; 1 Corbin § 100.

92. U.C.C. § 2–306(1); see § 72 infra.

The duration of contracts for goods or services has proved a prolific source of litigation. In employment contracts, if no term is provided expressly or by factual implication, the majority of courts have held that the hiring is at will even if the parties have set the compensation at a specified sum per month, day or year.[93] Some courts have held, however, that an agreement for a specified sum per day, month, or year gives rise to a contract for such a period in the absence of evidence to the contrary.[94] Under both views it is of course possible for the parties by the use of appropriate language to bind themselves to an employment contract for a definite number of days, months, or years. If a hiring for a specified term is found, performance after the term expires usually gives rise to an implication that the parties have renewed their agreement for the same duration.[95]

Often parties agree that employment shall be "permanent." Again the majority of courts have held that a hiring at will results.[96]

93. Boatright v. Steinite Radio Corp., 46 F.2d 385 (10th Cir.1931); Watson v. Gugino, 204 N.Y. 535, 98 N.E. 18 (1912); Elliott v. Delta Air Lines, Inc., 116 Ga.App. 36, 156 S.E.2d 656 (1967).

94. Dennis v. Thermoid Co., 128 N.J.L. 303, 25 A.2d 886 (1942); accord, Restatement, Contracts (2d), § 32, ill. 6.

95. Cinefot Int'l Corp. v. Hudson Photographic Indus., 13 N.Y.2d 249, 246 N.Y.S.2d 395, 196 N.E.2d 54, 6 A.L.R. 3d 1347 (1963); Restatement, Contracts (2d) § 32, ill. 6.

There are statutes however which do not permit the inference of a continued contractual relationship even in the face of an automatic renewal provision unless notice is given by the dominant party to the subservient party. An illustration of such a statute is § 5–903 of McKinney's New York General Obligations Law which provides:

Automatic renewal provision of contract for service, maintenance or repair unenforceable by contractor unless notice thereof given to recipient of services.

1. As used in this section, "person" means an individual, firm, company, partnership or corporation.

2. No provision of a contract for service, maintenance or repair to or for

any real or personal property which states that the term of the contract shall be deemed renewed for a specified additional period unless the person receiving the service, maintenance or repair gives notice to the person furnishing such contract service, maintenance or repair of his intention to terminate the contract at the expiration of such term, shall be enforceable against the person receiving the service, maintenance or repair, unless the person furnishing the service, maintenance or repair, at least fifteen days and not more than thirty days previous to the time specified for serving such notice upon him, shall give to the person receiving the service, maintenance or repair written notice, served personally or by certified mail, calling the attention of that person to the existence of such provision in the contract.

3. Nothing herein contained shall be construed to apply to a contract in which the automatic renewal period specified is one month or less.

See also § 5–905 which makes a similar provision with respect to leases.

96. Skagerberg v. Blandin Paper Co., 197 Minn. 291, 266 N.W. 872 (1936); Arentz v. Morse Dry Dock & Repair Co., 249 N.Y. 439, 164 N.E. 342, 62 A. L.R. 231 (1928); Benson Coop. Creamery Ass'n v. First Dist. Ass'n, 276

Apparently most courts have felt that by use of this term all that is meant is that the employment is foreseen as steady rather than seasonal or for a particular project. If something like lifetime employment were meant, it is felt that the parties would be more explicit in articulating an agreement so unusual. However, if a consideration over and above the consideration supplied by the employee's service or promises of service is exchanged for the promise of permanent employment, some courts have indicated that the promise is enforceable.[97] This approach gropes toward a fair result but confuses the questions of indefiniteness and consideration. It is possible to reach just results without confusing issues so diverse. Terms such as "permanent employment" have no immutable meaning. When used in different concrete situations by different individuals different meanings may fairly be attached to the term. If the employee has paid in money or in some other way for the promise of "permanent employment" it is likely that both parties understood that employment was to endure at least as long as the employee is able to perform the work for which he is hired. The payment of an additional consideration is an evidentiary factor bearing on the proper interpretation of the parties' intention. It follows that other evidentiary factors can perform the same function. In each case all of the circumstances are to be considered. It may be shown that the parties meant or did not mean something definite. The presence or absence of an additional consideration should not be conclusive on this score. Unfortunately, however, the courts have tended to deal with the question mechanically, as if stare decisis could provide the method by which the intention of the parties could be determined.

In contrast to the employment cases, where a contracting party is franchised as a dealer in the other party's products and no definite duration or manner of termination is specified, the modern cases hold that a reasonable period of notice must be given prior to termination.[98] The Uniform Commercial Code adopts and carries these cas-

Minn. 520, 151 N.W.2d 422 (1967); Annot., 35 A.L.R. 1417; contra, 1 Williston § 39, n. 7 and cases there cited.

97. Bixby v. Wilson & Co., 196 F.Supp. 889 (D.Iowa 1961); United Security Life Ins. Co. v. Gregory, 281 Ala. 264, 201 So.2d 853 (1967); see 1 Corbin § 96; 1A Corbin § 152; 3A Corbin § 684.

98. Scanlan v. Anheuser-Busch, Inc., 388 F.2d 918 (9th Cir.1968); C. C. Hauff Hardware v. Long Mfg. Co., 257 Iowa 1127, 136 N.W.2d 276, 19 A.

L.R.3d 191 (1965); A. S. Rampell, Inc. v. Hyster Co., 3 N.Y.2d 369, 381–82, 165 N.Y.S.2d 475, 486, 144 N.E.2d 371 (1957); Colony Liquor Distributors, Inc. v. Jack Daniel Distillery, 22 A.D. 2d 247, 254 N.Y.S.2d 547 (3d Dep't 1965). For an interesting case relating to salesmen, see Entis v. Atlantic Wire & Cable Corp., 355 F.2d 759 (2d Cir.1964); cf. Weilersbacher v. Pittsburgh Brewing Co., 421 Pa. 118, 218 A.2d 806 (1966); 67 W.Va. L.Rev. 225 (1965); Muller Enterprises v. Samuel Gerber Adv. Agency, 182 Neb. 261, 153 N.W.2d 920 (1967).

es one step further, providing that "an agreement dispensing with notification is invalid if its operation would be unconscionable." [99]

It must be remembered, however, that where the parties have stated their agreement on a material term but have done so indefinitely, there is less room for implication.[1] The same has ordinarily been held true where the parties agree to agree on a material term at a later date.[2] The logic is that an agreement to agree shows a lack of present agreement. It has, however, been widely recognized of late that agreements to agree serve a valuable commercial need, especially in long term supply contracts where the parties wish to assure themselves respectively of a source of supply and an outlet for production, but are unable to foresee in a potentially fluctuating market what a reasonable price will be. In consequence the Uniform Commercial Code [3] and the new Restatement [4] adopt the modern view that an agreement to agree as to a material term does not necessarily result in fatal indefiniteness. It should also be stressed that even at common law indefiniteness as to an immaterial term is also not fatal.[5]

The Uniform Commercial Code has also resolved another problem which previously had divided the courts. The problem is illustrated by the facts in Wilhelm Lubrication Co. v. Brattrud [6] where the seller agreed to sell and the buyer agreed to buy five thousand gallons of "Worthmore Motor Oil SAE 10–70." The term "SAE 10–70" designates seven weights of oil. In this agreement the price for each weight was definite. Three weeks after the agreement was made and before any specifications were submitted the buyer repudiated the agreement. The court held that the agreement was too vague and indefinite to be enforceable because the contract was indefinite as to the quantity of each weight. There are many cases in accord which hold that unless the assortment is specified the agreement is too vague and indefinite to be enforceable and perhaps an equal number of cases which hold that the agreement is sufficiently definite.[7] The latter cases ordinari-

---

99. U.C.C. § 2–309(3).

1. See Varney v. Ditmars, supra n. 77; Factor v. Peabody Tailoring Co., supra n. 79.

2. Burgess v. Rodom, 121 Cal.App.2d 71, 262 P.2d 335 (1953); Sun Printing & Pub. Ass'n v. Remington Paper & Power Co., 235 N.Y. 338, 139 N.E. 470 (1923); Willmott v. Giarraputo, 5 N.Y.2d 250, 184 N.Y.S.2d 97, 157 N.E.2d 282 (1959); Annot., 68 A.L.R.2d 1221.

3. § 2–305(1) (b); cf. § 2–204(3).

4. Restatement, Contracts (2d) § 32, ill. 8.

5. Purvis v. United States for Use and Benefit of Associated Sand & Gravel, 344 F.2d 867 (9th Cir.1965).

6. 197 Minn. 626, 268 N.W. 634, 106 A.L.R. 1279 (1936).

7. The cases are collected in Annots., 105 A.L.R. 1101 (1936) and 106 A.L.R. 1284 (1937) and are commented upon in 11 Temp.L.Q. 250 (1936).

ly assess damages upon the alternative least onerous to the defendant.[8]

Subsection 1 of Section 2–311 of the Code resolves this problem by holding that "despite the fact that the agreement leaves particulars of performance to be specified by one of the parties," there is a contract. Under subsection 3 the contract would be breached if the buyer fails to specify the assortment or if the seller refuses to permit him to specify the assortment. Although subsection 2 says that the specifications relating to the assortment of goods are at the buyer's option, it does not mean that the buyer is free to specify or not specify as he chooses but rather he has both the right and obligation.[9] The problem of indefiniteness is solved by requiring the specification to be made in "good faith and within limits set by commercial reasonableness." [10]

In addition to the specific provisions on the question, the Uniform Commercial Code contains a general provision designed to change the emphasis of the decisions upon the necessity for definiteness. All too often in the past a contracting party, dissatisfied with his bargain, has taken refuge in the doctrine to renounce his agreement. Rarely did the uncertainty itself cause the dissatisfaction.[11] Section 2–204(3) of the Code states the guiding principle to be:

> "Even if one or more terms are left open a contract for sale does not fail for indefiniteness if the parties have intended to make a contract and there is a reasonably certain basis for giving an appropriate remedy." [12]

8. 5 Williston § 1407; Restatement, Contracts § 344. The Code sections relating to remedies and damages as they apply to this kind of case are discussed in Note, 23 U.Chi.L.Rev. 499, 505 et seq. (1956).

9. See § 2–311, Comments 1, 2.

10. § 2–311(1).

11. Where the doctrine of indefiniteness has been raised, the facts of the case usually reveal that the non-performance of the agreement was related to grounds other than the alleged lack of certainty. See, e. g., Scammell v. Ouston, [1941] 1 All E. R. 14 (1940); Foley v. Classique Coaches, Ltd., [1934] 2 K.B. 2 (C.A.); Kearns v. Andree, 107 Conn. 181, 139 A. 695; 59 A.L.R. 599 (1928); Fairmount Glass Works v. Crunden-Martin Wooden-

ware Co., 106 Ky. 659, 51 S.W. 196 (1899).

12. The intent of this section is clear. It says that not only should the courts use the "gap fillers" which they have previously used but they should go beyond this where the parties intended to make a contract and cure the indefiniteness by using any reasonably certain basis for giving an appropriate remedy. When such a basis exists must be decided on a case by case basis. In this respect Comment 3 points out: "The test is not certainty as to what the parties were to do nor as to the exact amount of damages due to the plaintiff. Nor is the fact that one or more of the terms are left to be agreed upon enough of itself to defeat an otherwise adequate agreement. Rather commercial standards on the point of "indefiniteness"

§ 24. Unilateral, Bilateral and Reverse Unilateral Contracts and Some of Their Implications

If A says to B, "If you walk across Brooklyn Bridge I will pay you $10," A has made an offer looking to a unilateral contract.[13] B cannot accept this offer by promising to walk the bridge.[14] He must accept, if at all, by performing the act. Since no promise is requested of him, at no point is he bound to perform.[15]

If A says to B, "If you promise to walk across Brooklyn Bridge, I will pay you $10," he makes an offer looking to a bilateral contract.[16] If B makes the promise, both parties are bound. If B does not make the promise, either expressly or by implication,[17] there is no contract. There is perhaps one exception to this last statement. If the offeree actually performs the act he was requested to promise to perform, there is some authority to the effect that a contract is formed if the performance is completed while the offer is still open[18] and the requisite notice of performance is given.[19] At times an offer may be phrased so as expressly to permit an acceptance either by the making of a promise or by the doing of an act.[20] Under the

are intended to be applied, this act making provision elsewhere for missing terms needed for performance, open price, remedies and the like." It is interesting to note that Professor Williston wished to limit the section to "minor" omissions. Williston, The Law of Sales In the Proposed Uniform Commercial Code, 63 Harv.L. Rev. 561 (1950). His recommendation was rejected. "This shows that those drafting the statute intended that the omission of even an important term does not prevent the finding under the statute that the parties intended to make a contract." Pennsylvania Co. v. Wilmington Trust Co., 39 Del.Ch. 453, 166 A.2d 726, 732 (1960).

13. See § 8 supra.

14. Simpson, Contracts 46 (2d ed. 1965) [hereinafter cited as Simpson].

15. This matter is discussed in greater detail in § 34 infra.

16. See § 35 infra.

17. If B walked in A's presence a promise to walk could be inferred. If not, even if B intended a promise the requisite communication would be lacking. 10 Cornell L.Q. 220 (1924).

18. Restatement, Contracts § 63; 1 Williston § 78A; see Allied Steel & Conveyors, Inc. v. Ford Motor Co., 277 F.2d 907 (6th Cir.1960). See also Goble, Is Performance Always as Desirable as a Promise to Perform?, 22 Ill. L.Rev. 789 (1928); Williston, Reply, 22 Ill.L.Rev. 791 (1928).

19. The matter of notice is discussed in § 28 infra. This exception, based on the thought that a performance is as desirable as a promise, has been eliminated in the tentative draft of the new Restatement. In so doing, the "purity of the concept of voluntary agreement" is restored. Braucher, Offer and Acceptance in the Second Restatement, 74 Yale L.J. 302, 307 (1964); cf. the Reporter's Note to Restatement, Contracts (2d) § 63, pointing out that the need for the exception has all but disappeared because of the revision of § 31. See text at notes 21, 22 infra and § 38 infra.

20. Ever-Tite Roofing Corp. v. Green, 83 So.2d 449 (La.App.1955); Lazarus v. American Motors Corp., 21 Wis.2d 76, 123 N.W.2d 548 (1963).

modern view, incorporated in the Uniform Commercial Code and the second Restatement, when the offeror has not explicitly restricted the offeree to a particular kind of acceptance the offeree may choose either manner of acceptance.[21] The original Restatement had espoused the rule that in such cases it would be presumed that the offer looked to a bilateral contract.[22]

If S places a book in B's possession saying, "If you promise to pay me $5.00 next Saturday, all of my right, title and interest in the book is now yours," it has been suggested that S has made an offer to a "reverse unilateral" contract.[23] In a unilateral contract the offeror makes the promise; in a reverse unilateral contract the offeree is the promisor.[24]

---

21. U.C.C. § 2–206; Restatement, Contracts (2d) § 31.

22. Restatement, Contracts, § 31.

23. Goble, Is An Offer A Promise? 22 Ill.Law Rev. 567 (1928); Green, Is An Offer Always A Promise? 23 Ill. Law Rev. 301 (1928); Goble, The Non-Promissory Offer, 48 Nw.U.L. Rev. 590 (1953). Williston argues at § 24A that "the present tense is here used with the meaning of the future, and the offeror's statement means, "this book shall be yours." The Restatement (2d) gives a clearer illustration of a reverse unilateral contract in illustration 1 of § 57 which reads as follows: "A applies to B, an insurance company, for a policy of life insurance, and pays the first premium on an understanding that the insurance must be approved at B's home office. B's notification that the approval has been given is an acceptance of A's offer and forms a contract of insurance." See also 1 Corbin § 71.

24. The existence of the "reverse unilateral" contract explains why every offer does not necessarily contain a promise. See § 15 supra.

D. ACCEPTANCE

Analysis

Sec.
25. Must the Offeree Know of the Offer and if so at What Point of Time?
26. Must the Offeree Intend to Accept?
27. Who May Accept the Offer?
28. Must the Offeree Give Notice of Acceptance of an Offer to a Unilateral Contract?
29. Acceptance of an Offer Looking to a Series of Contracts.
30. The Necessity for Communicating Acceptance of an Offer to a Bilateral Contract.
31. Promises Inferred from Conduct or Silence.
32. Acceptance Varying from Offer.
33. Termination of the Power of Acceptance Created by Revocable Offers.
     (a) Lapse of Time.
     (b) Death or Lack of Capacity of the Offeror.
     (c) Revocation, Direct and Indirect.
     (d) Rejection—Counter-Offer.
     (e) Death or Destruction.
     (f) Supervening Illegality.
34. Up to What Point of Time May an Offeror Revoke a Revocable Offer Looking to a Unilateral Contract?
35. Up to What Point in Time May a Revocable Offer Looking to a Bilateral Contract be Revoked?
     (a) Parties at a Distance.
     (b) Parties in the Presence of One Another.
36. Risk of Mistake in Transmission.
37. Termination of Irrevocable Offers (Option Contracts).
     (a) What Makes an Offer Irrevocable?
     (b) Termination of Irrevocable Offers.
38. Modern Trend Limiting the Importance of the Distinction Between Unilateral and Bilateral Contracts.
     (a) § 2–206 of the Uniform Code.
     (b) Proposed Restatement.

§ 25. Must the Offeree Know of the Offer and if so at What Point of Time?

As a general proposition no contract can be formed unless the offeree knew of the offer at the time of his alleged acceptance.[25] Anglo-American law generally requires that before a person can recover on a promise he must exchange his own performance or promise for the promise he seeks to enforce.[26] Under the objective theory of contracts, it is, however, possible that the offeree may be bound by an acceptance even if he does not know of the offer. The appearance of

---

25. 1 Corbin § 59; 1 Williston § 33.

26. For further development of the importance of the exchange requirement, see Ch. 4 infra.

a bargain in some circumstances is sufficient. For example, A sends an offer to B by mail. B, when he gets the letter, without opening it and without suspecting that it is an offer, decides to confuse A by sending a letter which states "I accept." Here, there is a contract even though B did not know of the offer because A as a reasonable man could rely upon B's promise.[27] The same principle operates to bind an offeree who signs a writing known to be an offer without reading it.[28] The same result may obtain even without a signature. Thus, for example, the acceptance of documents such as bills of lading, passenger tickets, insurance policies and bank books gives rise to contracts based upon the provisions contained therein which they may be reasonably expected to contain.[29] A different result has been reached as to provisions printed in small print on a parcel check because a person should not reasonably expect to find contract provisions upon a parcel check.[30]

The rule that the offeree must know of the offer certainly applies to a unilateral contract because here there is no question of the offeror relying upon a promise of the offeree. Thus, if an offer of reward has been made to the public a person who has performed the act called for has no contractual claim [31] against the offeror unless he knows of the offer.[32]

27. Restatement, Contracts (2d) § 23, Comment b; see § 12 supra.

28. Grismore § 40; 1 Williston § 35. However the result would be different if there were fraud or mistake not due to negligence. Corona v. Esposito, 4 Conn.Cir. 296, 230 A.2d 624 (1966); Bollinger v. Central Pa. Quarry Strip & Constr. Co., 425 Pa. 430, 229 A.2d 741 (1967).

29. Polonsky v. Union Federal Sav. & Loan Ass'n, 334 Mass. 697, 138 N.E.2d 115, 60 A.L.R.2d 702 (1956); see 1 Williston §§ 90A–90E. This rule may be subject to a requirement of legibility. For example, statutes sometimes provide that certain kinds of clauses be printed in specified kinds of type. E. g., McKinney's N.Y.Pers. Prop.Law, § 46–c. Apart from statute, it has been held that clauses which are virtually invisible are ineffective. Silvestri v. Italia Società per Azioni di Navigazioni, 388 F.2d 11 (2d Cir.1968).

30. Klar v. H. & M. Parcel Room, Inc., 270 App.Div. 538, 61 N.Y.S.2d 285 (1st Dep't 1946), aff'd 296 N.Y. 1044, 73 N.

E.2d 912 (1947); Berguido v. Eastern Air Lines, Inc., 378 F.2d 369 (3d Cir. 1967). There are many other policy decisions which protect a party against his failure to read a document which contains provisions which might be deemed to be unfair under the circumstances. This is particularly true of a contract of adhesion. Kessler, Contracts of Adhesion—Some Thoughts About Freedom of Contract, 43 Colum.L.Rev. 629 (1943); Henningsen v. Bloomfield Motors, Inc., 32 N.J. 358, 161 A.2d 69, 75 A.L.R.2d 1 (1960). See § 3 supra and § 56 infra.

31. In some states an offer for a reward made by a public agency is deemed to create a non-contractual liability toward a person performing the desired act. Smith v. State, 38 Nev. 477, 151 P. 512 (1915); Choice v. City of Dallas, 210 S.W. 753 (Tex.Civ. App.1919). In these jurisdictions knowledge of the offer is not a prerequisite to recovery

32. Glover v. Jewish War Veterans, 68 A.2d 233 (D.C.Mun.App.1949); Fitch v.

The principle that an offeree must know of the offer also gives rise to the rule that identical cross-offers do not create a contract.[33] For example, if A sends an offer through the mail to B offering to sell a certain item at a certain price and B in ignorance of this offer mails an offer to buy the item at the same price, it has been held that no contract results. The Restatement, Second, asserts that the two offerors could assent in advance to cross-offers and suggests that such assent may be inferred where both parties think a contract has already been made.[34] Since identical cross-offers are most likely to be made after the parties have had detailed preliminary negotiations which the parties may have believed resulted in an agreement, under the Restatement approach a contract is likely to be found in many instances where such offers are made.[35] Under § 2–204(1) and (2) of the Uniform Commercial Code, which expand upon the notion that not every mutual manifestation of assent can be pinpointed to an offer and acceptance, in sales cases it may even more easily be found that identical cross-offers have created a contract when the parties subsequently act upon the offers as if a contract had been formed.

If A offers a reward of $10.00 to anyone who finds and returns a lost watch and B finds the watch, learns of the reward and returns it to A, is B entitled to $10.00? A number of authorities have concluded that B may not recover because he did not know of the offer when he started to perform.[36] Others have concluded that it is sufficient that he completes performance with knowledge of the offer.[37]

§ 26. Must the Offeree Intend to Accept?

If the requested return promise is made in response to an offer to a bilateral contract, it is quite clear that a contract is formed even if the offeree did not intend to accept. Under the prevailing objective test,[38] he will be held to what appeared from his expression to be his intention since the offeror has a right to rely upon this appearance, unless he knows or has reason to know that the offeree did not intend to accept.[39] When the offer is to a unilateral contract, how-

Snedaker, 38 N.Y. 248, 97 Am.Dec. 791 (1868); Broadnax v. Ledbetter, 100 Tex. 375, 99 S.W. 1111 (1907).

33. Tinn v. Hoffman & Co., 29 L.T.R. (n.s.) 271 (Ex.1873).

34. Restatement, Contracts (2d) § 23, Comment d.

35. Restatement, Contracts (2d) § 23, ill. 5; cf. Morris Asinof & Sons, Inc. v. Freudenthal, 195 App.Div. 79, 186

N.Y.S. 383 (1st Dep't 1921), aff'd 233 N.Y. 564, 135 N.E. 919 (1922).

36. Restatement, Contracts § 53; Fitch v. Snedaker, supra n. 32.

37. Restatement, Contracts (2d) § 53; 1 Corbin § 60.

38. See §§ 12, 25 supra.

39. Brant v. California Dairies, Inc., 4 Cal.2d 128, 48 P.2d 13 (1935). See also

ever, the performance of the requested act is ambiguous; it is not necessarily in response to the offer. Moreover, since the offeror is the only party under a potential obligation, there is no question of reliance on his part. Consequently, the traditional view is that evidence of the offeree's subjective intention is relevant and admissible.[40] The Restatement Second takes the position that if the act is done with knowledge of the offer a contract is presumed in the absence of words or conduct indicating the contrary.[41] Apparently under the Restatement Second the offeree may not testify as to his subjective intention even though it is in issue.

An interesting question is to what extent an offeree who knows of the offer to a unilateral contract must have it in mind at the time he performs. A recent case indicates that it is sufficient that he have it at the back of his mind.[42] Other cases have indicated to the contrary.[43] A realistic reading of the cases, mostly involving offers to rewards, may indicate that they are difficult to reconcile primarily because courts seem in these cases, more than in others, to emphasize the ethical position of the particular claimant and the public policy involved in the reward situations.

§ 27. Who May Accept the Offer?

An offer may be accepted only by the person or persons to whom it is made.[44] Ordinarily, the identity of the offerees will be determined

Hotz v. Equitable Life Assur. Soc., 224 Iowa 552, 276 N.W. 413 (1937) (inadvertent acceptance).

40. Reynolds v. Eagle Pencil Co., 285 N.Y. 448, 35 N.E.2d 35 (1941), rev'g, 260 App.Div. 482, 23 N.Y.S.2d 101 (1st Dep't 1940); Simpson, Contracts 42. The conclusion is based on the traditional view, (§ 47 infra) that subjective intention is relevant when a manifestation is ambiguous.

41. Restatement Contracts (2d) § 55 Comment c. Subdivision 3 of § 55 has a strange provision which states: "Where an offer of a promise invites acceptance by performance . . . the rendering of the invited performance does not constitute an acceptance if before the offeror performs his promise the offeree manifests an intention not to accept." If this means that performing the act called for with intent to accept in a unilateral contract is not an acceptance it ap-

pears to be in conflict with sections 45 and 56. If it means that the obligation to pay does not arise if there is disclaimer before payment it would appear to violate the existing rule that consideration is ordinarily necessary to support the discharge of a contract. Under the existing rule a contract arises at least when the act is performed. See § 34 and § 339 infra.

42. Simmons v. United States, 308 F.2d 160 (4th Cir.1962).

43. Reynolds v. Eagle Pencil Co., supra n. 40; Vitty v. Eley, 51 App.Div. 44, 64 N.Y.S. 397 (4th Dep't 1900).

44. Boulton v. Jones, 157 Eng.Rep. 232 (Ex.1857); Wagner, How and by Whom May an Offer Be Accepted? 11 Villanova L.Rev. 95, 95–96 (1965); Williams, Mistake as to Party in the Law of Contract, 23 Can.B.Rev. 271, 380 (1945). An offer given for a con-

by the reasonable man test.[45] Thus, it has been determined that a reward offer ordinarily may be accepted by anyone who knows of the offer, but once the offer has been accepted no one else may accept.[46] On the other hand an offer to pay a sum of money to anyone who uses a certain medicine and contracts influenza can be accepted by anyone and by any number of persons.[47]

In a well known case Jones, a regular customer of Brocklehurst, with whom he had a running account, sent him an order for a hose. Earlier the same day Brocklehurst had sold his business to Boulton, his manager. Boulton furnished the hose without notifying Jones of the change in ownership. When Boulton sued for the contract price, he was denied a contractual recovery because the offer had been made to Brocklehurst.[48] The result might or might not have been different if Brocklehurst had been doing business under a trade name and Boulton continued to use the trade name.[49] The result would certainly have been different if Brocklehurst had accepted the offer and assigned his rights under the contract to Boulton.[50]

The offeree need not be the promisee. Thus, if A makes a promise to B, asking in exchange a return promise from C, the offeree is C, rather than the promisee, B.[51]

sideration, sometimes called an option contract, may ordinarily be assigned. See § 264 infra.

45. Restatement, Contracts (2d) § 28.

46. 1 Williston §§ 32, 33A. It has been argued that if more than one person performs the requested act the reward should be divided among them. 1 Corbin § 64; Note, 34 Mich.L.Rev. 854 (1936).

47. Carlill v. Carbolic Smoke Ball Co., [1893] 1 Q.B. 256 (C.A.1892).

48. Boulton v. Jones, n. 44 supra. Boulton might have recovered in quasi contract but only to the extent the value of the hose exceeded any set-off which Jones had against Brocklehurst. Parker v. Dantzler Foundry & Mach. Works, 118 Miss. 126, 79 So. 82 (1918). The recovery would not be calculated at Boulton's price, but at the value the hose had to Jones. Michigan Cent. R. Co. v. State, 85 Ind.App. 557, 155 N.E. 50 (1927).

49. The facts assumed are that Brocklehurst was doing business under the trade name of, for example, "Acme Supply Co." and that Boulton when he bought the business also bought the name and that the order was addressed to Acme Supply Co. Under these facts two possibilities arise: 1) that Jones intended to make the offer to "Acme Supply Co." irrespective of the ownership of the establishment or 2) that he intended to make the offer to "Acme" only so long as Brocklehurst was the proprietor. This would be a difficult decision and evidence of subjective intention would doubtless be relevant. See § 47 infra. It could well be a question of fact if different inferences could be drawn from the evidence adduced.
There are also many cases involving mistake as to the identity of a party to a contract. See, for example, Ingram v. Little, 3 All E.R. 332, 3 W.L. R. 504 (C.A.) [1960].

50. See § 260 infra.

51. Restatement, Contracts (2d) **§ 54,** Comment b and ill. 3.

§ 28.　Must the Offeree Give Notice of Acceptance of an Offer to a Unilateral Contract?

In an offer to a unilateral contract the offeror has requested not words, but deeds.　Consequently, it is well settled that the offeree need not give notice that he is going to perform.[52]　On the question of whether he must give notice of the fact that he has performed there are essentially three views.　The first is that notice is not required unless requested by the offeror.[53]　The second view, adopted by the Restatement, is that a contract arises at least upon performance, but if the offeree has reason to know that the offeror has no adequate means of learning of the performance with reasonable promptness and certitude, the duty of the offeror is discharged unless the offeree exercises reasonable diligence to notify the offeror or the offeror otherwise learns of the performance within a reasonable time or the offer expressly or by implication indicates that notification is not necessary.[54]　The third and least tenable view is the same as the second except that if notice is required, no contract is consummated unless and until the notice of performance has been communicated.[55]

It is clear everywhere, however, that the offeror as the creator of the power of acceptance may impose, as one of the terms of the offer, a requirement that notice be given and, similarly, he may dispense with the need for notice.

§ 29.　Acceptance of an Offer Looking to a Series of Contracts

The preceding discussion has largely been confined to offers looking to a single unilateral or bilateral contract.　An offer may instead look to the formation of a series of contracts, unilateral or bi-

---

52. Carlill v. Carbolic Smoke Ball Co., supra n. 47.　See generally 1 Williston § 69–69AA; Calhoun, Acceptance of Offer for Unilateral Contract—Necessity of Notice to Offeror, 4 U.Cin.L. Rev. 57 (1930); Campbell, The Notice Due to a Guarantor, 35 Mich.L.Rev. 529 (1936); Dole, Notice Requirements of Guaranty Contracts, 62 Mich.L.Rev. 57 (1963).

53. Midland Nat. Bank v. Security Elevator Co., 161 Minn. 30, 200 N.W. 851 (1924); City Nat. Bank v. Phelps, 86 N.Y. 484 (1881).

54. Restatement, Contracts (2d) § 56; Bishop v. Eaton, 161 Mass. 496, 37 N. E. 665 (1894).　The Restatement indicates that it is the exceptional case in which the offeror does not have the means of ascertaining what has transpired.

55. Kresge Dep't Stores, Inc. v. Young, 37 A.2d 448 (D.C.Mun.App.1944).　If an offer is made on November 1, the act of acceptance occurs on November 2, a revocation is effected on November 3, and notice of performance is sent on November 4, there is no contract under this view, while there could be under the Restatement view. However, under this theory it is possible to reach the same result as under the Restatement approach by application of the rule (see § 34 infra) that part performance by the offeree renders the offer irrevocable for a reasonable time.　Dole, supra note 52, at 98.

lateral. For example, A, on January 1, writes to B: "In consideration of your advancing moneys from time to time over the next twelve calendar months, up to a total of $5,000, to X, at X's request, at your option, I hereby undertake to make good any losses you may sustain in consequence." [56] In reliance upon the letter, B, lends $1,000 to X on February 1, another $1,000 on March 1, and $1,000 again on April 1. If A revoked the offer on March 15, the result is that separate unilateral contracts arose on February 1 and March 1.[57] No contract arose, however, as to the loan of April 1 because by this time the offer had been revoked.[58]

If A offers B stated quantities of certain goods as B may order from time to time during the next year at a fixed price, A has made an offer looking to a series of bilateral contracts. Each time B places an order he impliedly promises to pay. If several orders are placed, a series of bilateral contracts arise. As to the future, however, the offer remains revocable.[59]

Care must be taken to distinguish an offer looking to a series of contracts from an offer that looks to one acceptance but a number of performances.[60] Whether the offer looks to one or a series of contracts is a question of interpretation to be decided in the same manner as any question of interpretation.[61]

---

56. The illustration is based upon the facts of Offord v. Davies, 142 Eng. Rep. 1336 (C.P.1862).

57. The question of notice is not considered here. See § 28 supra. It may be observed, however, that the Restatement rule requiring notice is qualified to the extent that one notification may be sufficient for multiple acceptances of an offer to a series of unilateral contracts. Restatement, Contracts (2d) § 30, Comment b; § 56, Comment d.

58. Restatement, Contracts (2d) §§ 30, 44.

59. Great Northern Ry. v. Witham, L. R., 9 C.P. 16 (1873); Strang v. Witkowski, 138 Conn. 94, 82 A.2d 624 (1951). If the offeree in response to the original offer had replied, "I accept," no contract would be formed, since he has not committed himself to take any goods. See 1 Corbin § 65.

60. For example: A offers to sell B between 4000 and 6000 tons of certain specified type of coal; deliveries to be made in equal instalments during the months of May, June, July and August and the acceptance to specify the quantity. This offer looks to one bilateral contract which will arise when B specifies the quantity. However there will be four performances under the contract. Chicago & Great E. Ry. v. Dane, 43 N.Y. 240 (1870); Restatement, Contracts (2d) § 30, ill. 2.

Other illustrative cases are American Publishing & Engraving Co. v. Walker, 87 Mo.App. 503 (1901); Restatement, Contracts (2d) § 30, ill. 3 and § 44, ill. 3, § 56, ill. 3; United States ex rel. Wilhelm v. Chain, 300 U.S. 31, 57 S.Ct. 394, 81 L.Ed. 487 (1937).

61. See §§ 12, 22 supra; ch. 3 infra.

§ 30. The Necessity for Communicating Acceptance of an Offer to a Bilateral Contract

When an offer looks to a bilateral contract, the general rule is that the offeree's promise must be communicated to the offeror. Clearly, the offeree, as a reasonable man, should understand that the offeror expects to know that the offeree has made the requested return promise so that he may guide his conduct accordingly.[62] Whether it is necessary for the communication actually to come to the offeror's knowledge is a matter to be discussed subsequently.[63]

The offeror is the master of his offer. Just as he may specify the kind of acceptance which is required, he may dispense with the requirement of communication. Thus, where an offer for a bilateral contract—the terms of which had been set by the offeree—stated that a contract would arise when approved by an executive officer of the offeree, it was held that a contract arose upon his approval and that communication was unnecessary.[64]

§ 31. Promises Inferred from Conduct or Silence

A promise need not be expressed in words. It may be communicated by conduct and even by silence. It follows that an offer may be made by conduct and perhaps even by silence and that an acceptance may also occur in the same way. Thus, if A on passing a market picks up an apple from a box marked "10 cents each" and holds it up so that the clerk sees it and nods assent, A has made an offer by conduct and B has accepted in the same way.[65]

Most of the cases involving implied in fact promises concern the question of acceptance. Although the line is often indistinct, acceptance by silence will first be discussed, followed by the question of acceptance by conduct.

Silence ordinarily does not give rise to an acceptance of an offer or a counteroffer.[66] Thus, if A makes an unsolicited offer to B by

---

62. 1 Corbin § 67; 1 Williston § 70.

63. See § 35 infra.

64. International Filter Co. v. Conroe Gin, Ice & Light Co., 277 S.W. 631 (Tex.Com.App.1925). Although it seems true that the contract arose when approved by an executive officer of the offeree and that communication of this promise was not necessary to create the contract it would appear reasonable to imply that notice of acceptance should be required by analogy to the rules established by the Restatement for giving notice of performance in the case of a unilateral contract. Such notice would not be necessary for the formation of the contract but failure to give notice would discharge the defendant's liability. The case disagrees and states that notice of acceptance was not necessary. Cf. Restatement, Contracts (2d) § 57A, ill. 1.

65. Restatement, Contracts (2d) § 5, ill. 2.

66. Restatement, Contracts (2d) § 72, Comment a; Albrecht Chem. Co. v.

mail and states, "If I do not hear from you by next Tuesday, I shall assume you accept," everyone agrees that B need not reply. Normally, a party cannot by the wording of his offer turn the absence of a communication into an acceptance and compel the recipient of his offer to remain silent at his peril. Suppose, however, that B remained silent intending to accept. There are two views on this question. The first is that he cannot accept by remaining silent but must communicate his acceptance.[67] The other view is that since the offeree's silence is ambiguous his subjective intention in remaining silent is relevant and a contract exists if he intended to accept.[68] This view seems sounder in that B should have a right to rely on the terms of the offer and A should be held to the reasonable consequences of his words.

To be distinguished are cases where the parties have mutually agreed that silence will manifest assent. For example, A says to B "I offer to sell you my black horse for two hundred dollars." B replies, "If you do not hear from me by Tuesday you may assume I accept." A agrees. Here, B's silence will result in a contract even if he does not intend to accept.

A similar case exists when A on a number of occasions has sent goods to B who has always paid for the goods and on this occasion B takes the shipment and retains it for a period without notifying A that he does not want the goods.[69] B's silence is concededly

Anderson Trading Corp., 298 N.Y. 437, 84 N.E.2d 625 (1949); More v. N. Y. Bowery Fire Ins. Co., 130 N.Y. 537, 29 N.E. 757 (1892); Royal Ins. Co. v. Beatty, 119 Pa. 6, 12 A. 607 (1888); Beech Aircraft Corp. v. Flexible Tubing Corp., 270 F.Supp. 548 (D.Conn. 1967); Thomson v. United States, 174 Ct.Cl. 783, 357 F.2d 683 (1966).

67. Prescott v. Jones, 69 N.H. 305, 41 A. 352 (1898).

68. Restatement, Contracts § 72(1) (b). At first blush this appears to contradict § 23 of Restatement (2d) which states that in a bilateral contract a party's subjective intention is irrelevant unless the other party knows or has reason to know the other's subjective intention. See § 26 supra. In the cases discussed in that context, however, there is no question but that a promise was made and the only issue is whether the offeree may attempt to show that subjectively he did

not intend to accept. Here the issue is whether a promise is made by silence and since the silence is ambiguous evidence of subjective intent is admissible. Cavanaugh v. D. W. Ranlet Co., 229 Mass. 366, 118 N.E. 650 (1918). Since the offeror here is primarily responsible for the ambiguity it need not be determined whether he as a reasonable man interpreted the silence as a promise of acceptance.

69. These are the facts of Hobbs v. Massasoit Whip Co., 158 Mass. 194, 33 N.E. 495 (1893). The same principle is involved in Holt v. Swenson, 252 Minn. 510, 90 N.W.2d 724 (1958); Ballard v. The Tingue Mills, Inc., 128 F. Supp. 683 (D.Conn.1954). U.C.C. § 2–606 says: "Under this article 'acceptance' as applied to goods means that the buyer, pursuant to contract, takes particular goods, which have been appropriated to the contract as his own, whether or not he is obligated to do so, and whether he does so by words,

ambiguous and as a result of this ambiguity two questions arise. First, should B be permitted to give evidence of subjective intention that he did not intend to accept in remaining silent?[70] Would a reasonable man in the position of A conclude that B has made a promise of acceptance?[71] The Restatement Second answers the first question by saying that the issue of whether B made an implied promise to pay for the goods is to be decided without reference to his subjective intent.[72] This leaves the question of whether a reasonable man in the position of A would have concluded that there was an acceptance and this is undoubtedly a jury question. The original Restatement made this question turn upon the subjective understanding of the offeror.[73]

A similar problem arises when A, through a salesman, has frequently solicited orders from B, the contract to arise when approved by A at A's home office. A has always shipped the goods to B without prior notification and has billed for them after shipment. A's salesman solicits and receives another order from B and remains silent for a period of time.[74] Under the Restatement Second the question of A's acceptance is to be decided under the test of the understanding of the reasonable man in the position of the offeror, whereas under the original Restatement the subjective understanding of the offeror would control.[75]

The cases are somewhat in confusion and it is often difficult to determine whether the holding is that there is a contract or whether because the offeror has changed his position the offeree is no longer free to assert the non-existence of the contract—a theory of estoppel.[76]

---

action or silence when it is time to speak." While this section of the Code deals primarily with acceptance of goods delivered pursuant to an existing contract, it would also apply to the situation under discussion.

70. As we have seen the general rule with respect to a bilateral contract is that the offeree may not testify as to his subjective intention. There does not appear to be any reason to depart from the rule here because the ambiguity which results would appear to be more the fault of the offeree.

71. This is the type of issue discussed in § 13 supra. In other words in every contract there are two issues. First, would a reasonable man in the position of the offeree conclude there was an offer and, second, would a reasonable man in the position of the offeror think that there was an acceptance.

72. Restatement, Contracts (2d) § 72(1) (c), Comment d. The original Restatement appears to be in accord.

73. Restatement, Contracts § 72(1) (c).

74. This is a recurring fact pattern. See, for example, Anmons v. Wilson & Co., 176 Miss. 645, 170 So. 227 (1936); Hendrickson v. International Harvester Co., 100 Vt. 161, 135 A. 702 (1927). The contract arises when A approves at the home office. In this kind of case, as we have seen, notice of acceptance is not always necessary. See § 30 supra.

75. See notes 72 and 73 supra.

76. See, for example, Restatement, Contracts (2d) § 72, ill. 5. Where there

Another, and more common, instance of acceptance by silence arises where the offeree takes offered services with reasonable opportunity to reject them and with reason to believe they are offered with expectation of compensation.[77] Ordinarily, where the services are rendered within the family relationship, the presumption is that the services were rendered without expectation of compensation; moreover, the offeree ordinarily has no reason to know that compensation is expected.[78] On the other hand where the parties are strangers the presumption is that compensation is expected.[79]

has been no prior course of dealings would the facts still justify a finding that there is a contract or an estoppel? Senner & Kaplan Co. v. Gera Mills, 185 App.Div. 562, 173 N.Y.S. 265 (1st Dep't 1918) (held, no). Should an insurance company be bound if it fails to act promptly in processing a policy application? American Life Ins. Co. of Alabama v. Hutcheson, 109 F.2d 424 (6th Cir. 1940), cert. den. 310 U.S. 625, 60 S.Ct. 898, 84 L.Ed. 1397 (1940) (yes); Joseph Schultz & Co. v. Camden Fire Ins. Ass'n, 304 N.Y. 143, 106 N.E.2d 273 (1952) (no). See 12 Appleman, Insurance, Law & Practice § 7226 (1943); Annot., 32 A.L.R. 487 (1953). See also § 2–208 of the U.C.C.

77. Old Jordan Mining Co. v. Societé Anonyme des Mines, 164 U.S. 261, 17 S.Ct. 113, 41 L.Ed. 427 (1896); James v. P. B. Price Constr. Co., 240 Ark. 628, 401 S.W.2d 206 (1966); Day v. Caton, 119 Mass. 513, 20 Am.R. 347 (1876); Restatement, Contracts § 72(1) (a).

78. Taylor v. Dutton, 13 N.Y.S.2d 980 (Sup.Ct.1939); Annot., 7 A.L.R.2d 8; McDowell, Contracts in the Family, 45 B.U.L.Rev. 43 (1965). However the presumption may be rebutted, Wilhoite v. Beck, 230 N.E.2d 616 (Ind. App.1967).

79. McKeon v. Van Slyck, 223 N.Y. 392, 119 N.E. 851 (1918). In an interesting case plaintiff and defendant believed that they were husband and wife when in fact they were not. Plaintiff worked for defendant in his inn apparently without expectation of compensation. Later she found out that they were not married and sued. The court held for the defendant. In re Gorden's Estate, 8 N.Y.2d 71, 202 N.Y.S.2d 1, 168 N.E.2d 239 (1960). For another interesting case see Shapira v. United Medical Service Inc., 15 N.Y.2d 200, 257 N.Y.S.2d 150, 205 N.E.2d 293 (1965) which states quite correctly that the existence of an implied contract is ordinarily a question of fact.

At times it is difficult to decide whether a person who renders services prior to the formation of an express contract does so gratuitously in hopes of obtaining a contract or whether he expects to be paid for the preliminary services irrespective of obtaining the ultimate contract. Compare Arden v. Freydberg, 9 N.Y.2d 393, 174 N.E.2d 495, 214 N.Y.S.2d 400 (1961), 22 Maryland L.Rev. 225 (1962) and Cronin v. National Shawmut Bank, 306 Mass. 202, 27 N.E.2d 717 (1940) with Hill v. Waxberg, 16 Alaska 477, 237 F.2d 936 (9th Cir. 1956). Similar problems arise under such topics as Consideration, Promissory Estoppel and Conditions.

An interesting question arises where the services appear to be offered with the expectation of compensation but in fact the person rendering the services does not intend to charge for his services. For example, if A's car is disabled upon a highway and B, the owner of a tow truck, passes and offers to help and A assents, an implied in fact bilateral contract usually would be held to have arisen. Could B in order to avoid contractual liability for subsequent misconduct show that he intended to offer the services gratuitously? See Taylor v. Smith, 121 N.C. 76, 28 S.E. 295 (1897); Prince v. McRae, 84 N.C. 674 (1881).

Distinguishable from all of the above cases is the situation where an offeree exercises dominion over an article that is offered to him. In such cases the offeror has a number of remedies. The exercise of dominion involves the tort of conversion.[80] An ancient option allows him to "waive the tort" and obtain quasi-contractual recovery against the tort-feasor.[81] In addition, a number of cases have held that the exercise of dominion is conduct which constitutes a contractual acceptance.[82] These cases have not paid sufficient attention to the question of whether the promise implied from the offeree's exercise of dominion needs to be communicated.

80. Prosser, Torts § 94 (3rd Ed.1965).

81. Terry v. Munger, 121 N.Y. 161, 24 N.E. 272 (1890); Olwell v. Nye & Nissen Co., 26 Wash.2d 282, 173 P.2d 652, 169 A.L.R. 139 (1947); Corbin, Waiver of Tort and Suit in Assumpsit, 19 Yale L.J. 221 (1910).

82. Raible v. Puerto Rico Indus. Dev. Co., 392 F.2d 424 (1st Cir. 1968); Ferrous Products Co. v. Gulf States Trading Co., 160 Tex. 399, 332 S.W.2d 310 (1960); Louisville Tin & Stove Co. v. Lay, 251 Ky. 584, 65 S.W.2d 1002 (1933); Austin v. Burge, 156 Mo.App. 286, 137 S.W. 618 (1911); Indiana Mfg. Co. v. Hayes, 155 Pa. 160, 26 A. 6 (1893). According to the Restatement, Contracts (2d) § 72(2), the offeree is not bound by the offered terms where these are manifestly unreasonable. Wright v. Sonoma County, 156 Cal. 475, 105 P. 409 (1909). This qualification reflects the basically quasi contractual nature of such contracts. See Comment (e) to § 72. § 2–606 of the U.C.C. provides in part that acceptance of goods occurs when the buyer "does any act inconsistent with the seller's ownership; but if such act is wrongful as against the seller it is an acceptance only if ratified by him." In F. W. Lang Co. v. Fleet, 193 Pa.Super. 365, 165 A.2d 258 (1960) the defendant-buyer exercised dominion over a compressor unit contained in a freezer sent to him by the plaintiff by using it to operate an air-conditioner. This act was clearly inconsistent with the seller's ownership. Consequently, the seller by entering a judgment for the unpaid balance of the price was deemed to have ratified the sale and the buyer was charged with an acceptance of the goods. See also sections 2–327(1) (b) and 4–302(a) of the U.C.C.

In order to discourage the unsolicited sending of goods to unwary customers, several states have enacted legislation providing that it is unlawful to offer merchandise for sale by the unsolicited sending of goods and that a person who receives such goods has a complete defense to an action for the price or for the return of the goods. E. g., McKinney's N.Y.Gen.Bus.Law, § 396(2). This section reads as follows: "No person . . ., shall . . ., offer for sale goods . . ., where the offer includes the voluntary and unsolicited sending of goods . . . not actually ordered or requested by the recipient, either orally or in writing. The receipt of any such unsolicited goods, wares or merchandise shall for all purposes be deemed an unconditional gift to the recipient who may use or dispose of the same in any manner he sees fit without any obligation on his part to the sender."

Compare Neb. Rev.St. § 63–101 (1966) which provides: "No person in this State shall be compelled to pay for any newspaper, magazine, or other publication which shall be mailed or sent to him without his having subscribed for or ordered it, or which shall be mailed or sent to him after the time of his subscription or order therefor has expired, notwithstanding that he may have received it."

§ 32. Acceptance Varying from Offer

The common law rule is that if the purported acceptance varies from the terms of the offer even as to trivial detail, it operates as a counter-offer and thereby a rejection [83] of the offer.[84] The rule has been enforced with a rigor worthy of a better cause. For example, where a seller offers a delivery of five bales of cotton in September and ten bales in October, the offeree cannot accept by requiring that five bales be delivered on September 4th and ten bales on October 2nd.[85] Rigid application of the rule has proved detrimental to commerce, particularly since business today is largely done through the mails on printed forms and the buyer's and seller's forms frequently clash as to ancillary terms of the transaction. At times this common law rule has been relaxed by a process of interpretation.[86] It has been substantially changed by § 2–207 of the Uniform Commercial Code which reads as follows:

(1) A definite and seasonable expression of acceptance or a written confirmation which is sent within a reasonable time operates as an acceptance even though it states terms additional to or different from those offered or agreed upon, unless acceptance is expressly made conditional on assent to the additional or different terms.

(2) The additional terms are to be construed as proposals for addition to the contract. Between merchants such terms become part of the contract unless:

(a) the offer expressly limits acceptance to the terms of the offer;

(b) they materially alter it; or

(c) notification of objection to them has already been given or is given within a reasonable time after notice of them is received.

(3) Conduct by both parties which recognizes the existence of a contract is sufficient to establish a contract for sale although the writings of the parties do not otherwise establish a contract. In such cases the terms of the particu-

83. Restatement, Contracts § 60; Oregon-Pacific Forest Products Corp. v. Welsh Panel Co., 248 F.Supp. 903 (D. Or.1965). For further analysis of the effect of a counter-offer, see § 33 infra.

84. Poel v. Brunswick-Balke-Collender Co., 216 N.Y. 310, 110 N.E. 619 (1915), rearg. denied, 216 N.Y. 771, 111 N.E.

1098 (acceptance which insisted that its receipt be acknowledged held to constitute a counter-offer).

85. Timmons v. Bostwick, 141 Ga. 713, 82 S.E. 29 (1914).

86. Valashinas v. Koniuto, 308 N.Y. 233, 124 N.E.2d 300 (1954), 40 Cornell L.Q. 605 (1955).

lar contract consist of those terms on which the writings of the parties agree, together with any supplementary terms incorporated under any other provisions of this Act.

The section states that a "definite and seasonable expression of acceptance" operates as an acceptance even though it includes different or additional terms which at common law would have given rise to a counter-offer which operated as a rejection. Under the statute when there is a "definite and seasonable expression of acceptance" there is a rejection only when the acceptance "is expressly made conditional on assent to the additional or different terms."

Subdivision 2 states what happens to the additional terms when there is a "definite and seasonable expression of acceptance" which is not expressly "made conditional on assent to the additional or different terms." Here the section makes a distinction between merchants and non-merchants.[87] In the case of non-merchants the additional terms are treated as "proposals for addition to the contract" which is to say that they become part of the contract only if they are in turn accepted by the offeror. As between merchants the additional terms become part of the contract unless: (a) the offer expressly limits acceptance to the terms of the offer; (b) they materially alter it or (c) notification of objection to them has already been given or is given within a reasonable time after notice of them is received.[88]

Subdivision 3 of the section comes into play only when the writings of the parties do not create a contract.[89]

The operation of this section and some of the problems created by it can best be demonstrated by examining two of the leading cases which have discussed the section.

The first case is Roto-Lith, Ltd. v. F. P. Bartlett & Co.[90] In that case the plaintiff, a merchant, made an offer to buy a drum of emulsion from the defendant who was also a merchant. The offer did not refer to warranties but did state the particular purpose for which the goods were to be used. The defendant sent an acknowledgment and an invoice, both of which provided: "All goods sold without warranties, express or implied and subject to the terms on reverse side." One of those terms stated: "Seller's liability hereunder shall be

---

87. "Merchant" is defined in § 2–104(1). That the definition will present many perplexing problems has been shown in 30 Geo.L.J. 130 (1950).

88. "Different" terms, apparently those which contradict the offer, never form part of the contract unless accepted by the offeror. But cf. Comment 3 to

U.C.C. § 2–207 which equates "additional" and "different" terms.

89. Duesenberg & King, Sales & Bulk Transfers, § 3.04(1) (2d ed., 1966) [hereinafter cited as Duesenberg & King].

90. 297 F.2d 497 (1st Cir. 1962).

limited to the replacement of any goods that materially differ from the Seller's sample order on the basis of which the order for such goods was made. If these terms are not acceptable, Buyer must so notify the Seller at once." Plaintiff did not object to the terms and accepted the goods when delivered and paid for them. The action brought was one for breach of warranty.

The first question to be decided is whether there was a definite and seasonable expression of acceptance. This would appear to be the case particularly since the acknowledgment was accompanied by an invoice [91] and so the next question is whether the acceptance was expressly conditional on assent to the additional or different terms.[92] It would appear that the assent was not expressly conditional; therefore there is an "acceptance" and we go to subdivision 2 to determine the content of the contract.

The next question is whether the new term excluding warranties is an "additional" term or a "different" term. If the terms added by the defendant are different they would not become part of the contract unless accepted by the offeror.[93] However since the offer had no express provisions as to warranty it is arguable that this is an additional term which (since the parties were merchants) would have become part of the contract but for the fact that the term materially altered the contract.[94]

91. "What is necessary to constitute a 'definite and seasonable expression of acceptance' is somewhat cloudy under the Code and whether the acknowledgment form of the seller in the Roto-Lith case would otherwise have qualified cannot be learned from the report of the decision. In general, it may be ventured that if the face of the acknowledgment form repeats the terms of the written order (i. e., the names of the buyer and seller, the description of the goods, price, quantity and date of delivery) there is a 'definite and seasonable expression of acceptance'." Duesenberg & King § 3.04(1).

92. The phrase "all goods sold without warranties express or implied and subject to the terms on reverse side" would not appear to be an expressly conditional acceptance. Purely on the issue of language is it the same to say that the acceptance is subject to the terms contained therein as it is to say that the acceptance is conditional on the offeror's assent to the different

or additional terms of the purported acceptance?

There is another phrase in the acceptance which should be carefully analyzed, to wit, "If these terms are not acceptable Buyer must so notify Seller at once." Does this say I accept only on the condition that the offeror assents to the warranty terms which I have proposed. Does it say so "expressly" or only "impliedly?" Compare Construction Aggregates Corp. v. Hewitt-Robins, 404 F.2d 505 (7th Cir. 1968).

93. See n. 88 supra.

94. The case did not come within 2(a) since the offer did not expressly limit acceptance to the terms of the offer and did not come within 2(c) because notification of objection to the additional term was not given either before or after the offeror was notified of it. However, the proposal to exclude warranties "materially" altered the contract formed and so did not be-

Thus it would appear that there was a contract and that the warranty implied in law which was part of the offer became a part of the contract.

The court, however, held that the purported acceptance was not an acceptance because it inserted terms which were unilaterally burdensome to the offeror and so must be deemed to expressly condition the offeree's assent.[95] It therefore concluded that the alleged acceptance was a counter-offer which was accepted by plaintiff when it accepted and paid for the goods. This result would have been correct at common law.[96] Even if we were to assume, however, that there was a rejection because of a conditional acceptance, the decision is incorrect by virtue of the provision of subdivision (3). Under this subdivision when the contract arises through conduct as here the terms of the contract are the terms of the exchanged writings to the extent that they are consistent "together with any supplementary terms incorporated under any other provision of this Act." Thus in Roto-Lith since there was a conflict as to the warranty provisions, the warranty provisions of the Code which would favor the plaintiff should have become part of the contract.

The other leading case interpreting the section is Application of Doughboy Industries.[97] The plaintiff buyer mailed a purchase order on its own form to the defendant. The form contained the following: "None of the terms and conditions contained in this Purchase Order may be added to, modified, superseded or otherwise altered except by a written instrument signed by an authorized representative of Buyer and delivered by Buyer to Seller, and each shipment received by Buyer from Seller shall be deemed to be only upon the terms and conditions contained in the Purchase Order except as they may be added to, modified, superseded or otherwise altered, notwithstanding any terms and conditions that may be contained in any acknowledgment, invoice or other form of Seller and notwithstanding

come part of the contract unless accepted by the offeror. What is a material addition as opposed to an immaterial addition is not made clear. Comments 4 and 5 of the section give some illustrations of each.

95. That this reasoning is incorrect, see note 92 supra. The case has been criticized. See, for example, 30 U. Chi.L.Rev. 840 (1963); 42 B.U.L. 373 (1962); 76 Harv.L.Rev. 1481 (1963).

96. Indiana Mfg. Co. v. Hayes, 155 Pa. 100, 26 A. 6 (1893). Subd. (3) of U.C.

C. § 2-207 repudiates the so-called "last shot" principle under which the conflicting form of the offeree became a counter-offer which was accepted when the offeror accepted the goods. The common law rule may still apply however, if the facts indicate that the counter-offer has intentionally been accepted. Construction Aggregates Corp. v. Hewitt-Robins, Inc., 404 F.2d 505 (7th Cir. 1968).

97. 17 A.D.2d 216, 233 N.Y.S.2d 488 (1st Dep't 1962).

Buyer's act of accepting or paying for any shipment or similar act of Buyer."

On May 13 defendant sent an acknowledgment which contained a clause that read: "IMPORTANT—Buyer agrees he has full knowledge of conditions printed on the reverse side hereof; and that the same are part of the agreement between the buyer and seller and shall be binding if either the goods referred to herein are delivered to and accepted by the buyer, or if the buyer does not within ten days from the date hereof deliver to seller written objection to said conditions or any part thereof." [98] It also contained a clause providing for arbitration in New York if there was a dispute. When a dispute arose the question was whether the buyer was bound to arbitrate. The court held that, assuming the existence of a contract, under the common law of New York the buyer would not be bound to arbitrate.[99] It then gratuitously referred to § 2–207 (not yet effective) and stated the arbitration clause did not become effective whether it is viewed as a "material alteration" or contrary to the limits expressly set by the offer or as a term "different" from the terms contained in the offer. In so stating the court assumes that there was a definite and seasonable expression of acceptance and that the acceptance was not "expressly conditional, on assent to the additional or different terms." Had it been decided that there was no acceptance and had the goods been delivered (which appears to be the fact) a contract would still have arisen by conduct and the arbitration clause would not be included because the writings of the parties do not agree upon this term and because there is no provision in the Code which would imply arbitration.

Thus far we have not considered the phrase "or a written confirmation which is sent within a reasonable time" in subdivision 1. It appears strange to say that "a written confirmation" operates as an acceptance because a confirmation presumably would be a confirmation of a contract already formed. However this part of the section seems to be limited primarily to two situations: (1) "where an agreement has been reached either orally or by informal correspondence between the parties and is followed by one or both of the

98. This exercise in drawing forms designed to give advantage to the drafter has aptly been referred to as the "battle of the forms". See Apsey, The Battle of the Forms, 34 Notre Dame Law. 556 (1959); Macaulay, Non-Contractual Relations in Business: a Preliminary Study, 28 Am. Sociological Rev. 55, 59–60 (1963). See American Parts Co., Inc. v. Am. Arbitration Ass'n, 8 Mich.App. 156, 154 N.W.2d 5 (1967).

99. "As pointed out earlier, an agreement to arbitrate must be clear and direct and must not depend upon implication, inveiglement or subtlety." Application of Doughboy Industries, 17 A.D.2d 216, 220, 233 N.Y.S.2d 488, 493 (1st Dep't 1962).

parties sending formal acknowledgments or memoranda embodying the terms so far agreed upon and adding terms not discussed." [1] In this type of situation it is easy to understand that the rules previously stated with respect to "additional" terms should apply. (2) Where there are "additional" terms in the memos sent and they conflict, each party is deemed to object to the other party's term "and the conflicting terms do not become part of the contract." The contract then consists of the terms originally expressly agreed to, terms on which the confirmations agree and terms supplied by the Act including subsection 2.[2]

If a written confirmation contains terms which differ from the agreement actually reached, it would appear that the actual terms agreed upon may be proved and will govern the transaction.[3]

Courts at times have distinguished a qualified acceptance, which at common law amounts to a counter-offer, from an unqualified acceptance which by its terms is to take effect in the future. For example, in one case plaintiff-offeror was a low bidder. The defendant allegedly promised that the plaintiff would have the contract if the defendant decided to proceed with certain construction, a decision which was to be made in a day or two. Three days later the defendant accepted the offer of another bidder. The court held that there was a question of fact as to whether there was a counter-offer or an acceptance which was to take effect upon the happening of a future event.[4]

In such a case, of course, either party is entitled to withdraw until the future event actually occurs and fairness may require that the offeree give the offeror notice that the event has occurred.[5]

§ 33. Termination of the Power of Acceptance Created by Revocable Offers

The power of acceptance created by a revocable offer [6] may be terminated in a variety of ways prior to its exercise.

1. U.C.C. § 2–207, Comment 1.

2. U.C.C. § 2–207, Comment 6.

3. See U.C.C. § 2–201(2), Comment 3.

4. Reed Bros. v. Bluff City Motor Co., 139 Miss. 441, 104 So. 161 (1925), 24 Mich.L.Rev. 302 (1926); accord, Orr v. Doubleday, Page & Co., 223 N.Y. 334, 119 N.E. 552, 1 A.L.R. 338 (1918), rearg. denied 223 N.Y. 700, 119 N.E. 1064. See 1 Williston § 77A where this type of acceptance is called "an acceptance in escrow." The converse situation arises where the offeror conditions his offer to a subcontractor upon getting a construction contract and the subcontractor accepts this offer. See Frederick Raff Co. v. Murphy, 110 Conn. 234, 147 A. 709 (1929).

5. Note, 24 Mich.L.Rev. 302 (1926).

6. Restatement, Contracts § 33. For the distinction between a revocable and irrevocable offer, see § 37 infra.

(a) Lapse of time

If A sends a written offer to B and states that the offer is open for eight days, it is clear that the power of acceptance will lapse after eight days, but whether the eight days should be measured from the date it is sent or the date it is received is a matter of interpretation.[7] A leading case has held that in the absence of countervailing indications the eight days should be measured from the day the offer is received.[8]

The same problem can be complicated further by assuming that there is a delay in transmission. Should the eight days be measured from the date the offer was received or from when it should have been received? The answer appears to be that if the offeree knows, or has reason to know of the delay, the eight days should be measured from the date it should have been received.[9]

If the duration of the power of acceptance is not stated, it is deemed to be open for a reasonable time [10] and what is a reasonable time is ordinarily a question of fact depending upon the circumstances of the case including whether the transaction is speculative or not [11] and the manifest purpose of the offeror and, according to the new Restatement, whether or not the offeree is in good faith.[12]

7. 1 Williston § 53A; 1 Corbin § 35. Both writers seem to suggest that since the offeree should realize that the offer is ambiguous and the limitation is imposed for the benefit of the offeror that the eight day period should be reckoned from the date the letter is sent rather than from the date it is received. If the offer had read "You have eight days from the date hereof" the period would clearly be measured from the date of the letter. In measuring the eight days the day from which the time is reckoned should normally be excluded. West's Ann.Cal.Civ.Code, § 10; Clements v. Pasadena Finance Co., 376 F.2d 1005 (9th Cir. 1967); LSA–C.C. art. 2058; Housing Authority v. T. Miller & Sons, 239 La. 966, 120 So.2d 494 (1960); McKinney's N.Y.Gen.Constr.Law § 20; N.Y.C.P.L.R. § 780; Barnet v. Cannizzarro, 3 A.D.2d 745, 160 N.Y.S.2d 329 (2d Dep't 1957).

8. Caldwell v. Cline, 109 W.Va. 553, 156 S.E. 55, 72 A.L.R. 1211 (1930). The Restatement appears to have reached the same conclusion when it states: "Where the parties are at a distance from each other the normal understanding is that the time for acceptance is extended by at least the normal time for transmission of the offer and for the sending of the offeree's reply." Restatement, Contracts (2d) § 40, Comment e.

9. Restatement, Contracts § 51. "In most cases the offeree will have some indication of the delay from the date of the letter, the postmarks, the condition of the envelope, or statements of the messenger. All such indications must be considered." 1 Corbin § 37.

10. Restatement, Contracts § 40.

11. Minnesota Linseed Oil Co. v. Collier White Lead Co., 17 F.Cas. 447 (No. 9635) (C.C.D.Minn.1876); Brewer v. Lepman, 127 Mo.App. 693, 106 S.W. 1107 (1908); Restatement, Contracts (2d) § 40, ill. 7 and Comment f.

12. Loring v. City of Boston, 48 Mass. (7 Met.) 409 (1844); Matter of Kelly,

The offeror may stipulate in his offer that the power of acceptance shall terminate upon the happening of a certain event. If the event happens before the acceptance the power of acceptance lapses even though the offeree is not informed that the event has occurred.[13]

Where an offer is made in a face to face or telephonic conversation the offer is deemed, in the absence of a manifestation of a contrary intention, to be open only while the parties are conversing.[14]

A well known case has raised a troublesome question.[15] A made an offer to B, stating no time limitation for acceptance. Consequently, the power of acceptance was open for a reasonable time. B sent a letter of acceptance after a reasonable time had expired. The acceptance, however, crossed a letter from A indicating that the offer was still open. B sent no other acceptance. Had B accepted after receiving A's second letter it would be easy to conclude that although the offer had lapsed it had been revived by the second communication and so was effectively accepted.[16]

The court decided that there was a contract, holding that it was the original offer which had been accepted. The decision, utilizing a subjective test to determine the offeror's intent to keep the offer open, is clearly just.[17] The objective test is designed to do justice by protecting a person who puts the reasonable construction upon the words of another. Where, however, there is clear evidence that the other intended to incur greater liability than his words indicated, is not justice better done by application of a subjective test?

A similar problem is presented where A makes an offer to B, the offer to be open for one day. If B purports to accept five days later, no contract is formed but his purported acceptance operates as an offer which A may accept by a communication to B.[18] Upon

---

39 Conn. 159 (1872); cf. Carr v. Mahaska County Bankers Ass'n, 222 Iowa 411, 269 N.W. 494 (1936); Restatement, Contracts (2d) § 40.

13. Oliphant, The Duration and Termination of an Offer, 18 Mich.L.Rev. 201 (1920).

14. Akers v. J. B. Sedberry, Inc., 39 Tenn.App. 633, 286 S.W.2d 617 (1955).

15. Mactier's Adm'rs v. Frith, 6 Wend. 103, 21 Am.Dec. 262 (N.Y.1830).

16. Livingston v. Evans, [1925] 4 D.L.R. 769 (Alberta 1925).

17. The test is termed "subjective" because although the offeror had manifested his intent to extend the time of his offer this had not yet been brought to the knowledge of the offeree at the time of his acceptance. The Restatement appears to approve of the decision. Restatement, Contracts (2d) § 23, ill. 6.

18. Restatement, Contracts § 73. Contrary to what is stated in the text, a number of courts have held that the offeror may waive the tardiness of the acceptance and a contract can be formed by an uncommunicated waiver. These decisions have been severely criticized as violating "a vital principle of the law of contracts." See 1 Williston § 92.

receipt of a tardy acceptance, however, the offeror, if circumstances exist from which an acceptance may be inferred from silence, is subjected to the burden of notifying the offeree that his acceptance is late.[19]

(b) Death or Lack of Capacity of the Offeror

It is well settled in most jurisdictions that a power of acceptance is terminated when the offeror dies or is deprived of legal capacity to enter into the proposed contract prior to aceptance.[20] The rule is a frequently criticized remnant of the subjective theory.[21] The reasoning was simple: There can be no meeting of the minds if one of the parties is dead or incapable of understanding the nature and consequences of the transaction.[22] It must be carefully kept in mind that the rule has reference to death or incapacity which occurs between the making of the offer and the acceptance. To illustrate, if A makes an offer to B looking toward a bilateral contract and B accepts *after* A dies, whether or not he knows of the death,[23] there is no contract because A's death terminated the power of acceptance; but if B accepts *before* A dies there is a contract. The question then would be whether A's estate would have the defense of impossibility of performance, a matter to be discussed later.[24]

The same rules apply to unilateral contracts except that the problem of determining when there is an acceptance is more complicated than in the case of a bilateral contract. The matter is discussed in § 34 infra.

It should be carefully noted that we are not here discussing the question of capacity of the parties which would arise, for example, if A was insane when he made an offer and remained insane until B accepted.[25] This type of question as well as the question of quasi contractual recoveries in such cases are discussed in chapter 8 of this book. The point made here is that if such insanity as to-

---

19. 1 Williston §§ 92, 93; Restatement, Contracts § 73. For circumstances in which silence may give rise to acceptance, see § 31 supra.

20. New Headley Tobacco Warehouse Co. v. Gentry's Ex'r., 307 Ky. 857, 212 S.W.2d 325 (1948); Jordan v. Dobbins, 122 Mass. 168 (1877); Jones v. Union Central Life Ins. Co., 265 App.Div. 388, 40 N.Y.S.2d 74 (4th Dep't 1943), aff'd 290 N.Y. 883, 50 N.E.2d 293 (1943); Restatement, Contracts § 48.

21. See, e. g., 1 Corbin § 54.

22. This would be conclusively presumed where there had been an adjudication of insanity accompanied by the appointment of a guardian. See ch. 8 infra.

23. Knowledge of the death would more justifiably amount to a revocation.

24. See § 191 infra.

25. See 1 Williston § 62A; 1 Corbin § 54; Restatement, Contracts (2d) § 18C and authorities cited in Reporter's Note thereto.

tally deprives an offeror of his contractual capacity occurs between the time of making the offer and the acceptance, no contract results.[26]

It is also the rule that the supervening death or legal incapacity of the offeree terminates the offer.[27]

(c) Revocation, Direct and Indirect

The most obvious way of terminating the power of acceptance created by a revocable offer is by revocation [28]—a manifestation of intent not to enter into the proposed contract.[29] The question of whether particular language used is language of revocation is a question of interpretation.[30]

The general rule [31] is that revocation is effective when received [32] by the offeree, but when an offer is made to a number of persons whose identity is unknown to the offeror as, for example, in a newspaper advertisement, the power of acceptance may be terminated by giving equal publicity to the revocation.[33] Normally this is accomplished by using the same medium for the revocation as was used for the offer.[34] However, the doctrine essentially requires the best means of notice reasonably available under the circumstances of the case.[35] Should the offeror know the identity of a person who

---

26. Restatement, Contracts (2d) § 48.

27. Restatement, Contracts (2d) § 49, Comment c; Brunne-Booth Foto- chrome Corp. v. Kaufman, 18 A.D.2d 160, 238 N.Y.S.2d 26 (1st Dep't 1963), motion denied 13 N.Y.2d 753, 242 N.Y. S.2d 57, 192 N.E.2d 25, aff'd 13 N.Y.2d 1077, 246 N.Y.S.2d 403, 196 N.E.2d 60. Restatement, Contracts (2d) § 54, ill. 3, states as follows: "A makes an of- fer to B, who dies after receiving it. His executor though acting within the permitted time, cannot accept." See § 27 supra.

28. 1 Corbin § 38.

29. Restatement, Contracts § 41.

30. See, e. g., Hoover Motor Exp. Co. v. Clements Paper Co., 193 Tenn.App. 6, 241 S.W.2d 851 (1951).

31. There is an additional exception to the one listed in the text which is that "an offeror may reserve the pow- er to revoke the offer without notice, and such a reservation will be given effect whether contained in the offer or in a later communication received by the offeree." Restatement, Con- tracts (2d) § 41, Comment b.

32. A written communication is re- ceived "when the writing comes into the possession of the person ad- dressed, or of some person authorized by him to receive it for him, or when it is deposited in some place which he has authorized as the place for this or similar communications to be deposited for him." Restatement, Contracts § 69; cf. U.C.C. § 1–201(26); Howard v. Daly, 61 N.Y. 362, 19 Am. R. 285 (1875). Some states by statute have the rule that a revocation is ef- fective when dispatched. See e. g., Cal. Civil Code § 1587.

33. Shuey v. United States, 92 U.S. 73, 23 L.Ed. 697 (1875); Carr v. Mahaska County Bankers Ass'n, 222 Iowa 411, 269 N.W. 494, 107 A.L.R. 1080 (1936); Restatement, Contracts § 43.

34. Grismore § 32.

35. 1 Williston § 59A.

is taking action upon the offer the offeror must, to have an effective revocation, communicate the revocation to him.[36]

An offer may also be terminated by indirect revocation. This occurs when the offeree acquires reliable information from a third party that the offeror has engaged in conduct which would indicate to a reasonable man that the offeror no longer wished to make the offer.[37] The leading case is Dickinson v. Dodds.[38] The defendant had made an offer to sell certain land to the plaintiff. Before the plaintiff had accepted, he learned that the defendant had sold the property to another. It was held that the offer had been revoked.

The case raises three problems. Should the doctrine of indirect revocation be limited to cases involving the sale of land and chattels? The original Restatement so stated. The Restatement Second is to the contrary.[39] The second problem is, what information is reliable? The cases hold that the information must in fact be true and must come from a source which would put a reasonable man acting in good faith on inquiry.[40] The most difficult problem is what should be the result if the offeree hears reliably that the offeror is *offering* the same thing or position to another. The reasonable man might conclude that offeror would not want to make two offers and so decide that the offeror intends to revoke or he may decide that since the offeror has not bothered to communicate a revocation he is willing to run the risk of making two offers. The second view seems preferable.[41]

(d) Rejection—Counter-Offer

An offeree's power of acceptance is terminated by a rejection or a counter-offer unless the offeror or offeree manifests a contrary intention.[42] This rule has been modified, as we have seen,[43] by § 2–207 of the Commercial Code where the acceptance adds different

36. Long v. Chronicle Pub. Co., 68 Cal. App. 171, 228 P. 873 (1924); Restatement, Contracts (2d) § 43, ill. 1.

37. Restatement, Contracts § 42.

38. 2 Ch.Div. 463 (1876).

39. Restatement, Contracts § 42; Restatement, Contracts (2d) § 42, ill. 2.

40. 1 Corbin § 40.

41. Grismore § 32. Some confusion in this area may arise from the reporter's statement of facts in Dickinson v. Dodds, supra n. 38. This states that "Dodds had been offering or agreeing

to sell the property." The opinions of the judges however state that he "had in fact agreed" (James, L.J.) and the property had been "sold" (Mellish, L. J.). On the danger of relying upon the reporter's statement of facts in English law reports, see the discussion by Asquith, L.J., in Victoria Laundries (Windsor) Ltd., v. Newman Industries, Ltd., [1949] 2 K.B. 528 (C. A.).

42. Restatement, Contracts (2d) §§ 37, 38; Quinn v. Feaheny, 252 Mich. 526, 233 N.W. 403 (1930). A counter-offer

43. See note 43 on page 61.

or additional terms and the new Restatement accepts the philosophy of the Code.[44] Even as a common law proposition, however, it was necessary to distinguish a counter-offer and a rejection from a counter-inquiry, a request for a modification and a comment upon the terms.[45]

For example, if A makes an offer to B to sell an object for $5000, the offer to remain open for thirty days, and B says "I'll pay $4800," this would be a counter-offer but if B said "Will you take $4800?" this would merely be a counter-inquiry. If B had said "Send lowest cash price" this would be a request for a modification and not a rejection.[46] Even at common law an acceptance which *requests* additional or different terms is not a counter-offer.[47]

(e) Death or Destruction

The power of acceptance created by an offer is terminated by the death or destruction, prior to acceptance, of a person or thing essential for the performance of the contract.[48]

(f) Supervening Illegality

The power of acceptance is terminated by illegality supervening between the making of an offer and its acceptance.[49]

§ 34. Up to What Point of Time May an Offeror Revoke a Revocable Offer Looking to a Unilateral Contract?

May an offer to a unilateral contract be revoked after the offeree has partially performed? There are three views on the question. The classical and logical view is that the offer may be revoked at any

---

is defined in section 38 as "an offer made by an offeree to his offeror relating to the same matter as the offer and proposing a substituted bargain differing from that proposed by the original offer." Thus, if A makes an offer to B to sell him lumber which B accepts and adds "send me one saw," B has accepted and has made a separate offer and not a counter-offer.

43. See § 32 supra.

44. Restatement, Contracts (2d) § 60.

45. Restatement, Contracts (2d) § 38, Comment b.

46. Stevenson, Jaques & Co. v. McLean, 5 Q.B. 346 (1880); Home Gas Co. v.

Magnolia Petroleum Co., 143 Okl. 112, 287 P. 1033 (1930).

47. Restatement, Contracts (2d) § 62. Culton v. Gilchrist, 92 Iowa 718, 61 N.W. 384 (1894); Butler v. Foley, 211 Mich. 668, 179 N.W. 34 (1920); Valashinas v. Koniuto, 308 N.Y. 233, 124 N.E.2d 300 (1954).
An acceptance which states a condition which would have been implied in law is not a counter-offer. Thus an acceptance of an offer to sell real property conditioned on the marketability of title is an operative acceptance. Burkhead v. Farlow, 266 N.C. 595, 146 S.E.2d 802, 16 A.L.R.3d 1416 (1966).

48. Restatement, Contracts § 49.

49. Restatement, Contracts § 50.

time until the act constituting performance is completed.[50] This view follows from the fact that even after part performance the offeree is free to withdraw: a commitment has neither been requested from, nor made by, him and because it is logical to conclude that the offeror is asking for a completed act. Logic, however, is not justice. Clearly, once the offeree has relied to his detriment upon the offer he deserves some protection from an arbitrary revocation. To provide such protection it has been held that a bilateral contract arises when the offeree starts to perform.[51] This view is not only illogical but unsatisfactory in result. The offeror did not ask for a promise and the offeree by his part performance may not have intended to commit himself to pursue the act to completion.[52]

The third view is that once the offeree begins to perform[53] the offer becomes irrevocable.[54] The offeree's rights to have the offeror perform his side of the bargain do not arise, however, unless the offeree completes performance within the time allowable. If the offeror repudiates (revokes) his promise after the offeree has commenced performance, the offeree at that point has a cause of action. He must, however, mitigate damages;[55] usually, this rule requires that he cease performance.[56] If performance requires the cooperation of the offeror and cooperation is withheld, tender of part performance is the equivalent of part performance.[57]

The Uniform Commercial Code has not entirely resolved this problem although cases involving this issue are essentially placed on a different basis.[58]

50. Petterson v. Pattberg, 248 N.Y. 86, 161 N.E. 428 (1928); Wormser, The True Conception of Unilateral Contracts, 26 Yale L.J. 136 (1916); Selected Readings 307: but cf. Wormser, Book Review, 3 J. Legal Ed. 145 (1950).

51. Los Angeles Traction Co. v. Wilshire, 135 Cal. 654, 67 P. 1086 (1902).

52. See Ashley, Offers Calling for Consideration other than a Counter Promise, 23 Harv.L.Rev. 159 (1910), Selected Readings 293. If A says to B, "If you walk across Brooklyn Bridge I promise to pay you $10.00," and B replies, "I promise," B's promise is a nullity.

53. The Restatement distinguishes between beginning performance and mere preparation. See Bretz v. Union

Central Life Ins. Co., 134 Ohio St. 171, 16 N.E.2d 272 (1938).

54. Restatement, Contracts § 45; Marchiondo v. Sheck, 78 N.M. 440, 432 P. 2d 405 (1967). It should be observed that under this view the offeree does not become bound to perform.

55. Simpson § 199.

56. See § 216 infra.

57. Restatement, Contracts (2d) § 45, Comment d. It is interesting to speculate whether the word "tendered" here is used in its technical legal signficance as it apparently was by the Court of Appeals in Petterson v. Pattberg, n. 50 supra.

58. See § 2–206 (especially Comment 3), discussed at § 38 infra.

§ 35. Up to What Point in Time May a Revocable Offer Looking to a Bilateral Contract be Revoked?

(a) Parties at a Distance

A revocable offer to a bilateral contract may be revoked at any time prior to its acceptance. Thus, stated differently, the question in the caption is, when is an attempted acceptance effective? In a general way the answer is that it is operative when it is communicated.[59] As we have seen a revocation is effectively communicated when it is received,[60] and the same is true of a rejection.[61] However, as a result of historical accident some early cases held that an acceptance is effectively communicated when it is put out of the possession of the offeree.[62] This view prevails generally throughout the United States [63] with the qualification that the acceptance must be dispatched in an "authorized" manner. The Restatement states that in the absence of contrary indications, the offeror authorizes the means of communication used in transmitting the offer and any other manner customary at the time and place received.[64] The cases are in conflict [65] and may indicate that "authorization" is not

59. See § 30 supra.

60. See § 33 supra; Lynch v. Webb City School Dist. No. 92, 418 S.W.2d 608 (Mo.App.1967).

61. Restatement, Contracts § 69.

62. Adams v. Lindsell, 106 Eng.Rep. 250 (K.B.1818). The decision seems to have been rendered to protect offerees from an application of the subjective theory as previously announced in the case of Cooke v. Oxley, 100 Eng.Rep. 785 (1790). The rule that acceptance takes effect upon dispatch was reaffirmed in Dunlop v. Higgins, 9 Eng. Rep. 805 (1848). This result obtains even if the acceptance fails to arrive at its destination. Household Fire & Carriage Acc. Ins. Co., Ltd. v. Grant, 4 Ex.D. 216 (C.A.1879). For a critique of the decisions, see Macneil, Time of Acceptance: Too Many Problems for a Single Rule, 112 U.Pa.L. Rev. 947 (1964).

63. Morrison v. Thoelke, 155 So.2d 889 (Fla.App.1963); Restatement, Contracts § 64. Contra, Rhode Island Tool Co. v. United States, 130 Ct.Cl. 698, 128 F.Supp. 417 (1955) (relying on

privilege, under postal regulation, to withdraw letter from the mails). But this position has not gained any substantial recognition. Morrison v. Thoelke, supra; Note, 38 Tulane L. Rev. 566 (1964).

64. Restatement, Contracts § 66. It is also generally held that a letter which is properly addressed, stamped and mailed is presumed to have been delivered in due course of the post News Syndicate Co. v. Gatti Paper Stock Corp., 256 N.Y. 211, 176 N.E 169, rearg. denied 256 N.Y. 678, 177 N.E. 190 (1931); Charlson Realty Co. v. United States, 181 Ct.Cl. 262, 384 F.2d 434 (1967).

65. It is often held that a wire is an authorized method of accepting an offer sent by post. Stephen M. Weld & Co. v. Victory Mfg. Co., 205 F. 770 (E.D.N.C.1913); contra, Dickey v. Hurd, 33 F.2d 415 (1st Cir.1929), cert. denied 280 U.S. 601, 50 S.Ct. 82, 74 L. Ed. 646; Lucas v. Western Union Tel. Co., 131 Iowa 669, 109 N.W. 191 (1906); cf. Elkhorn-Hazard Coal Co. v. Kentucky Riv. Coal Corp., 20 F. 2d 67 (6th Cir.1927) (use of mail for acceptance not authorized where writ-

the key to the problem and that the courts have really been con-cerned with what is a reasonable medium of communication under the circumstances. The Uniform Commercial Code expressly adopts the rule that an offer may be accepted by "any medium reasonable in the circumstances." [66] If an improper medium is chosen, the weight of authority is that acceptance is effective when received rather than when sent.[67] Section 68 of the proposed new Restate-ment and Section 1–201(38) of the Uniform Commercial Code, how-ever, take the position that if an unreasonable method of acceptance is utilized, it is nevertheless effective when sent, provided it is re-ceived within the time a properly dispatched acceptance would nor-mally have arrived.

If the offer indicates that the acceptance must be made in a prescribed place, time or manner, the terms of the offer control.[68] If, for example, the offeror states, "You must accept, if at all, by telegram," a contract will be formed upon dispatch of the telegram. If the offeree uses another medium no contract is formed. When the offer mentions the manner in which the offeror wishes an ac-ceptance to be transmitted the tendency of the courts is to hold that the offeror has merely suggested, rather than required, this form of acceptance [69] and the question still is, what method of communica-tion is authorized or reasonable under the circumstances.

ten offer delivered in person). An ac-ceptance of a telegraphed offer by post has been held to be authorized, Farmers' Produce Co. v. McAlester Storage & Comm'n Co., 48 Okl. 488, 150 P. 483 (1915); contra, Richard v. Credit Suisse, 124 Misc. 3, 206 N.Y.S. 150 (Sup.Ct.1924), aff'd 214 App.Div. 705, 209 N.Y.S. 909 (1st Dep't 1925), aff'd 242 N.Y. 346, 152 N.E. 110, 45 A. L.R. 1041 (1926).

66. U.C.C. § 2–206(1) (a); accord, Re-statement, Contracts (2d) § 64.

67. Restatement, Contracts § 68. Of course the acceptance must be re-ceived before the power of acceptance has lapsed or has been revoked. 1 Williston § 87. There are some diffi-cult problems. For example, if A in Los Angeles makes an offer to B by mail in New York and a reasonable time within which to reply by mail would be two days after receipt of the letter in due course and B accepts on the third day by a telegram (assume unauthorized) and the telegram is re-ceived by the offeror "within the time within which an acceptance sent in authorized manner would probably have been received by him," (Restate-ment, Contracts § 68) there would be a contract. But would the result be the same if the offer was stated to be open for 2 days from the time it was received? The Restatement, Con-tracts (2d) § 68, Comment a, indicates that the offeree should not be allowed to use the extra time to speculate at the expense of the offeror and states in the body of the rule that the ac-ceptance must be "seasonably dis-patched."

68. Restatement, Contracts § 61; Spratt v. Paramount Pictures, Inc., 178 Misc. 682, 35 N.Y.S.2d 815 (Sup. Ct.1942).

69. Allied Steel & Conveyors, Inc. v. Ford Motor Co., 277 F.2d 907 (6th Cir.1960); Zimmerman Bros. & Co. v. First Nat. Bank, 219 Wis. 427, 263 N. W. 361 (1935); see also Restatement, Contracts (2d) § 61, ill. 5.

Even if the authorized means of communication is utilized, failure to address it properly or to take other reasonable precautions to insure safe transmission has traditionally been believed to result in the loss of the benefit of the rule that the acceptance takes effect when dispatched. If the communication actually arrives in good time, the rule has been that it is effective upon receipt;[70] in cases governed by the Uniform Commercial Code, however, section 1–201 (38) provides that it is as effective as a properly dispatched acceptance, provided that it arrives within the time a properly dispatched acceptance would normally have arrived. Section 68 of the proposed Restatement has adopted the Code position.

The offeror, it must be remembered, is master of the offer. In framing his offer he has the power to require actual receipt of an acceptance as a precondition to the formation of the contract.[71]

The rule that an acceptance is effective when sent is troublesome when the offeree sends both an acceptance and a rejection. The rejection, as we have seen, is effective when received.[72] Consider the following sequences: (a) rejection sent, acceptance sent, rejection received, acceptance received; (b) acceptance sent, rejection sent, rejection received, acceptance received. If the acceptances were dispatched in an "authorized" manner and the general rule is applied, contracts would be held to have been created in both of these sequences. Clearly these results would be unjust since the offerors should be permitted to rely on the rejections received prior to the purported acceptances. To govern the first of these sequences an exception is made to the general rule. An acceptance dispatched after a rejection has been sent is not effective until received and only if received prior to receipt of the rejection.[73] If received subsequently, it may be operative as an offer. In the second sequence hypothesized above it is generally concluded that a contract is formed upon dispatch of the acceptance. However, if the offeror changes his position in reliance upon the receipt of the rejection, the offeree is estopped from enforcing the contract.[74]

---

70. Restatement, Contracts § 67.

71. Lewis v. Browning, 130 Mass. 173 (1881). However, such a requirement must be clearly expressed. 1 Williston § 88; Vassar v. Camp, 11 N.Y. 441 (1854). It is also possible for the offeror to word his offer in such a way that the acceptance is effective when sent provided it is in fact received. Restatement, Contracts (2d) § 64, Comment b.

72. Restatement, Contracts (2d) § 69.

73. Restatement, Contracts (2d) § 39.

74. E. Frederics, Inc. v. Felton Beauty Supply Co., 58 Ga.App. 320, 198 S.E. 324 (1938); Restatement, Contracts (2d) § 64, Comment c and ill. 7. The rejection in this case may also amount to an offer to rescind the contract or to a repudiation. See also U.C.C. § 2–608.

(b) Parties in the Presence of One Another

When parties are in the presence of each other an acceptance is inoperative unless the offeror hears it or is at fault in not hearing.[75] Even if the offeror is at fault in not hearing, there still would be no contract if the offeree knew or had reason to know that the offeror had not heard.[76]

Should a conversation conducted by telephone or similar media be governed by the rules developed for face to face conversation? The textwriters all but unanimously agree that these means of communication should be governed by the *in praesentes* rules.[77] The majority of the cases appear to be to the contrary holding that the acceptance takes place when spoken by the offeree rather than when heard by the offeror, but it should be noted that they have arisen in the context of conflict of laws and concern the question of *where* the contract was formed rather than *whether* there was a contract.[78]

§ 36. Risk of Mistake in Transmission

If A intends to offer to sell his horse to B for $110, but inadvertently says, "I offer to sell you my horse for $100," it appears to be settled that if B does not know or have reason to know of A's mistake and accepts the offer a contract for the sale of the horse at $100 is formed.[79] In a well known case [80] a similar mistake was made not by A but by the telegraph company in transmitting the message. It was held that a contract was formed and this appears to be the majority view.[81] The reasons advanced are that the first

75. 1 Williston § 82A. It would be an unusual case in which the offeror is at fault in not hearing. 1 Corbin § 104.

76. 1 Corbin § 79.

77. Restatement, Contracts § 65; 1 Corbin § 79; 1 Williston § 82A.

78. Perrin v. Pearlstein, 314 F.2d 863 (2d Cir. 1963); Linn v. Employers Reins. Corp., 392 Pa. 58, 139 A.2d 638 (1958); Travelers Ins. Co. v. Workmen's Compensation Appeal Bd., 68 Cal.2d 7, 64 Cal.Rptr. 440, 434 P.2d 992 (1967).

79. Wender Presses, Inc. v. United States, 170 Ct.Cl. 483, 343 F.2d 961 (1965); Restatement, Contracts § 71(c).

80. Ayer v. Western Union Tel. Co., 79 Me. 493, 10 A. 495 (1887).

81. 1 Corbin § 105; 1 Williston § 94. The same rule prevails if the error in transmission results in a higher price, that is to say, a contract is formed upon the higher figure. 1 Corbin § 105. In other words the rule is that the message as transmitted is operative unless the other party knows or has reason to know of the mistake. If it is apparent from the face of the message that an error has been made, no contract results since the addressee is not justified in relying upon its contents. Germain Fruit Co. v. Western Union Tel. Co., 137 Cal. 598, 70 P. 658 (1902).

of the parties to utilize the telegraph should bear the risk of loss;[82] that the telegraph company is the agent of this party[83] and that this rule results in better business convenience.[84]

The minority and better view is that since the offeror is no more responsible for the mistake than the offeree there should be no contract.[85] Nor may it be argued that the majority rule is more consistent with the objective theory of contracts since even under this theory acts manifesting assent must be done either negligently or with the intent to do those acts.[86]

Attempts by telegraph companies to limit their liability have generally proved successful. This question is now governed by federal regulations.[87]

§ 37. Termination of Irrevocable Offers (Option Contracts)

(a) What makes an Offer Irrevocable?

One of the classic ways of rendering an offer irrevocable is by the acceptance of a consideration by the offeror in exchange for his promise to keep the offer open.[88] Such an offer is frequently called an option contract.[89]

---

82. This does not seem to be sound. For example, if A makes an inquiry by telegram and B sends an offer which is not properly transmitted by the telegraph company and A accepts, the risk of transmission falls on B and not upon A who was the first to adopt this medium of communication. The same would be true if the offeree delivered a message saying "no" and it came back "yes."

83. This is fallacious. The telegraph company is an independent contractor and not an agent. See 1 Corbin § 105.

84. Ultimately, the risk of loss would fall upon the telegraph company. If the offeree is held to bear the risk of transmission, he has an action in tort against the telegraph company. Webbe v. Western Union Tel. Co., 169 Ill. 610, 48 N.E. 670 (1897). However, telegraph companies enjoy limited liability. See text at n. 87 infra.

85. Western Union Tel. Co. v. Cowin & Co., 20 F.2d 103, 54 A.L.R. 1362 (8th

Cir.1927); see also Restatement, Contracts § 71; cf. Restatement, Contracts (2d) § 21A, and ch. 3 infra. This is in accord with the general rule that a person who hires an independent contractor is not liable for the negligence of the contractor. Chenoweth v. Settle Engineers, Inc., 151 W.Va. 830, 156 S.E.2d 297 (1967).

86. Whittier, The Restatement of Contracts and Mutual Assent, 17 Cal.L. Rev. 441, 447–48 (1929).

87. See Western Union Tel. Co. v. Priester, 276 U.S. 252, 48 S.Ct. 234, 72 L.Ed. 555 (1928); Annots., 20 A.L.R.2d 761, 94 A.L.R. 1056.

88. Restatement, Contracts § 46. In some jurisdictions an offer may be made irrevocable by use of a seal. See ch. 7 infra.

89. Restatement, Contracts (2d) § 24A. A down payment does not of itself render an offer irrevocable. Restatement, Contracts (2d) § 47A.

Option contracts usually take one of two forms. A may say to B, "If you pay me $100 today I promise to sell Blackacre to you for $10,000 on the condition that you tender the $10,000 within thirty days." If B pays the $100, a unilateral contract arises and there is no longer any question of the revocability of the offer. A is bound to perform if B performs the stated condition.

The second form is created when A says to B, "I offer to sell you Blackacre for $10,000, this offer to remain open for thirty days if you pay $100 for this privilege." If B pays the $100 it is commonly said that there is a collateral contract not to revoke the offer and it is clear that A is bound not to revoke. It has been suggested that in this case A has no *right* to revoke but has the *power* to revoke. Consequently, if A revoked, B would be entitled to damages for breach of the collateral contract but not to specific performance of the main promise contained in the offer.[90] This view is rejected by the modern text writers [91] and most of the decided cases.[92] Thus, when the option takes the form of a collateral contract the offeror has no power to revoke. The consequences of this form of option contract, then, are indistinguishable for this purpose from those taking the form discussed in the preceding paragraph.[93]

Certain statutes permit the creation of irrevocable offers without consideration. For example, a New York statute, set out in full in the note,[94] provides, in essence, that if the offeror in a signed writing declares that the offer is irrevocable it cannot be revoked despite the absence of consideration. There is a similar provision

90. Langdell, Summary of the Law of Contracts § 178 (1880). Since damages for breach of the collateral contract would be the same as for breach of the underlying proposed contract, the distinction between the right and the power to revoke can be raised only if specific performance is sought. McGovney, Irrevocable Offers, 27 Harv. L.Rev. 644 (1914), Selected Readings 220.

91. 1 Corbin §§ 42–44; 1 Williston §§ 61–61D.

92. Simpson & Harper v. Sanders & Jenkins, 130 Ga. 265, 60 S.E. 541 (1908); Crocker v. Page, 210 App.Div. 735, 206 N.Y.S. 481 (3rd Dep't 1924), aff'd 240 N.Y. 638, 148 N.E. 738 (1925). Time is generally considered to be of the essence in an option contract. Wesley v. United States, 384 F.2d 100 (9th Cir. 1967).

93. See 1A Corbin § 262.

94. McKinney's N.Y.Gen.Oblig.Law, § 5–1109 provides:

"Except as otherwise provided in section 2–205 of the uniform commercial code with respect to an offer by a merchant to buy or sell goods, when an offer to enter into a contract is made in a writing signed by the offeror, or by his agent, which states that the offer is irrevocable during a period set forth or until a time fixed, the offer shall not be revocable during such period or until such time because of the absence of consideration for the assurance of irrevocability. When such a writing states that the offer is irrevocable but does not state any period or time of irrevocability, it shall be construed to state that the offer is irrevocable for a reasonable time."

in the Uniform Commercial Code.[95] The two statutory formulations are compared in the notes.[96]

We have previously encountered the notion of an irrevocable offer in our discussion of the revocability of offers to unilateral contracts. According to § 45 of the Restatements—old and new—an option contract arises when the offeree begins to perform the act requested in an offer to a unilateral contract.[97]

(b) Termination of Irrevocable Offers

An irrevocable offer is terminated by lapse of time, death or destruction of a person or thing essential for the performance of the contract and supervening legal prohibition of the proposed contract. However, an irrevocable offer is not terminated by rejection,[98] revocation or supervening death or incapacity of the offeror, nor does the death or supervening incapacity of the offeree terminate the offer.[99] The weight of authority and new Restatement take the position that the acceptance of an option contract is operative when received by the offeror rather than when dispatched.[1] The rule that acceptances are effective when sent was designed to protect an offeree against a revocation. Since the offer contained in an option contract is irrevocable the protection of this rule is not required.[2]

---

95. U.C.C. § 2–205 provides:
"An offer by a merchant to buy or sell goods in a signed writing which by its terms gives assurance that it will be held open is not revocable, for lack of consideration, during the time stated or if no time is stated for a reasonable time, but in no event may such period of irrevocability exceed three months; but any such term of assurance on a form supplied by the offeree must be separately signed by the offeror."

96. At least four differences are readily perceptible. The Code section is limited to offers by merchants and is limited to offers to buy and sell goods. Under the Code, the period of irrevocability may not exceed three months. Finally, the Code provides that where the term of assurance is contained on a form supplied by the offeree, it must be separately signed by the offeror.

97. See § 34 supra. An offer may also be made irrevocable under the doctrine of promissory estoppel. See § 107 infra.

98. Restatement, Contracts (2d) § 35A. Compare § 35 supra relating to revocable offers. See Silverstein v. United Cerebral Palsy Ass'n, 17 A.D.2d 160, 232 N.Y.S.2d 968 (1st Dep't 1962); 1 Corbin § 94. Cf. Simpson, § 23, Restatement, Contracts § 47.

99. Restatement, Contracts (2d) § 48, Comment d. Although the death or supervening incapacity of the offeror or offeree does not terminate an irrevocable offer, death or incapacity create a variety of other problems. These are discussed under the heading of Prospective Inability to Perform (ch. 9 infra) and Impossibility of Performance (ch. 11 infra) and the Assignability of Option Contracts (§ 264 infra).

1. Dynamics Corp. of America v. United States, 182 Ct.Cl. 62, 389 F.2d 424 (1968); Restatement, Contracts (2d) § 64(b); 1A Corbin § 264 and cases cited therein. Contra, Becker v. Comm'r of Internal Revenue, 378 F.2d 767 (3d Cir. 1967).

2. Restatement, Contracts (2d) § 64, Comment f.

§ 38. Modern Trend Limiting the Importance of the Distinction Between Unilateral and Bilateral Contracts

We have already seen that at common law the distinction between a unilateral and bilateral contract was fundamental.[3] An offer, except in very unusual cases, looked either to an act or a promise.[4] If it looked to an act a return promise was a nullity;[5] if it looked to a promise, an act other than a promissory act was ineffective unless it was completed during the time that the offer was open.[6] If the offer was ambiguous it was presumed that the offer invited a promise.[7]

The distinction has, however, met with trenchant criticism, particularly by Karl Llewellyn, principal draftsman of the Commercial Code. The thrust of the criticism is that the distinction is artificial and the consequences of the distinction do not conform to the way businessmen think about their rights and obligations.[8] Implicit in the criticism is that the law of contracts should be brought into line with the actual expectations of contracting parties, and that commerce should not be forced to conform to academic distinctions. This philosophy, at least in part, has found its way into the Uniform Commercial Code and the Restatement Second.

(a) § 2–206 of the Uniform Commercial Code

This section reads as follows:

"(1) Unless otherwise unambiguously indicated by the language or circumstances

(a) an offer to make a contract shall be construed as inviting acceptance in any manner and by any medium reasonable in the circumstances;

(b) an order or other offer to buy goods for prompt or current shipment shall be construed as inviting acceptance either by a prompt promise to ship or by the prompt or current shipment of conforming or non-conforming goods, but such a shipment of non-conforming goods does not constitute an acceptance if the seller seasonably notifies the buyer that the shipment is offered only as an accommodation to the buyer.

---

3. See § 24 supra.

4. See § 24 supra.

5. See § 24 supra.

6. See § 24 supra.

7. See § 24 supra.

8. See Llewellyn, Our Case-Law of Contract: Offer and Acceptance, I, 48 Yale L.J. 1 (1938), II, 48 Yale L.J. 779 (1939).

"(2) Where the beginning of a requested performance is a reasonable mode of acceptance an offeror who is not notified of acceptance within a reasonable time may treat the offer as having lapsed before acceptance."

The first phrase of subdivision (1) indicates that the distinction between a unilateral and a bilateral contract will continue to be observed when the intent to have it observed is "unambiguously indicated by the language or circumstances." Where this intent is not manifested, Section 1(a) seems to say that the offer is construed as inviting acceptance in any manner; that is to say either by an act or a promise if that is reasonable under the circumstances. When a promise is used and is a reasonable manner of acceptance it will be effective when sent provided it is sent "by any medium reasonable in the circumstance." The concept of "reasonableness" is intended to be more flexible than the previously prevailing concept of an "authorized" means of transmission.[9]

Subsection 1(b) appears to be designed to accomplish two results. First, it "exemplifies the more general provision of subsection 2–206(1) (a) quoted above."[10] That is to say, it shows that an "ambiguous" offer "to buy goods for prompt or current shipment" invites an acceptance either by act or promise.[11]

Secondly, it prevents the offeree from utilizing what Hawkland calls the "unilateral contract trick." This is explained in a well written law review[12] article as follows:

"Under the common law, if an offeree-seller accepted an order by the unilateral method, i. e., by shipping the goods, a valid contract would come into existence only if the goods shipped conformed exactly to the terms of the offer. If the goods shipped were partially defective, no contract would come into existence. Under the Code, if the offeree-seller ships goods which are either partially defective or nonconforming[13] to the order, a valid contract would come into existence in the absence of notification by the seller that

9. § 2–206, Comment 1.

10. Hawkland, § 1.1303. For a contrary interpretation see n. 11 infra.

11. Duesenberg & King, § 4.02(1) contend that this subsection does not undermine the general distinction between a unilateral and a bilateral contract but does so only in connection with the fact pattern presented in Section 1(b) and is limited to that subsection. See also U.C.C. § 2–504.

12. Gilbride, The Uniform Commercial Code: Impact on the Law of Contracts, 30 Brooklyn L.Rev. 177, 185 (1964).

13. "Goods or conduct including any part of a performance are 'conforming' or conform to the contract when they are in accordance with the obligation under the contract." U.C.C. § 2–106(2).

he doesn't intend to accept the original order, and is only sending the nonconforming shipment as a substitute for the original order. For example, if B places an order for the shipment of 12 dz. Brand X men's white shirts size 15, S may accept by shipping 12 dz. Brand X white shirts size 15. Under the common law, if S inadvertently shipped 12 dz. Brand Y size 15 shirts, S would not be bound to perform the contract because the shipment of nonconforming goods would not create a binding unilateral contract. Under the Code, this nonconforming shipment would constitute an acceptance, and S would be liable if he later refused to ship the 12 dz. Brand X size 15 shirts. Thus, under this provision, the same identical act constitutes an acceptance and a breach of the contract. But if S had notified B that he didn't have Brand X, but for his convenience he was shipping Brand Y shirts, no contract would come into existence."

The reach of subdivision 2 of § 2–206 is unclear. It covers a situation where the offeree does not promise but starts to perform. If the offeree subsequently gives notice of his beginning of the requested performance within a reasonable time, the effect of the notice is to bind the offeree and to cut off the offeror's power of revocation.[14] If the offeree starts to perform but does not give notice within a reasonable time, or if beginning performance is not a reasonable mode of acceptance, the offeror may treat the offer as having lapsed.[15] Where the offeree starts to perform but does not give notice within a reasonable time the question remains whether the offeror may treat the situation as if a contract was formed. Apparently he may but only "if the beginning of performance is a reasonable mode of acceptance" and "the beginning of performance unambiguously expresses the offeree's intent to engage himself." [16] Comment 3 indicates that during the time between the beginning of performance and the reasonable time for giving notice whether the offeror is free to revoke depends upon the common law rule of the particular jurisdiction.

(b) Proposed Restatement

The new Restatement follows the lead of the Code in diminishing the importance of the distinction between a unilateral and bilateral contract. Section 31 provides: "In case of a doubt an offer is interpreted as inviting the offeree to accept either by promising to perform

14. § 2–206, Comment 3.

16. § 2–206, Comment 3.

15. § 2–206(2)

what the offer requests or by rendering the performance as the offeree chooses."

Thus the proposed Restatement sets up three types of cases:

(a) Where the offer unambiguously looks to a unilateral contract.[17] This situation is covered by the rules previously stated.[18]

(b) Where the offer unambiguously looks to a bilateral contract. This situation is covered by the rules previously stated.[19]

(c) Where the offer is ambiguous it may be accepted by promise and the rules previously stated apply. If the offeree starts to perform there is an implied promise on his part to perform [20] unless within a reasonable time the offeree exercises reasonable diligence to notify the offeror of non-acceptance.[21]

---

17. The Restatement gives as illustrations of an offer unambiguously looking to a unilateral contract, an offer of a reward, and an offer asking the offeree to refrain from drinking. Restatement, Contracts (2d) § 31 ill. 3 and 4.

18. See §§ 24, 28, 34 supra.

19. See §§ 24, 30, 35 supra.

20. Restatement, Contracts (2d) § 63(2) and § 52(2). Cf. Lazarus v. American Motors Corp., 21 Wis.2d 76, 123 N.W. 2d 548 (1963), 49 Iowa L.Rev. 960

(1964). Notice, however, may be required.

21. Accord, Restatement, Contracts (2d) § 56. It should be observed that although the new Restatement and the Uniform Commercial Code are basically in accord on questions of offer and acceptance there are often puzzling differences in phraseology. For an attempted synthesis, see Murray, Contracts: A New Design for the Agreement Process, 53 Cornell L.Rev. 785 (1968).

CHAPTER 3

PAROL EVIDENCE AND INTERPRETATION [1]

Analysis

		Sections
A.	Introduction	39
B.	The Parol Evidence Rule	40–46
C.	Interpretation	47–52

A. INTRODUCTION

Sec.
39. The Difficulty of the Subject Matter.

B. THE PAROL EVIDENCE RULE

40. The Area of Substantial Agreement.
41. The Parol Evidence Rule: The Major Area of Conflict.
42. The Parol Evidence Rule Does Not Apply Until It is Decided That There is a Contract.
43. The Parol Evidence Rule is a Rule of Substantive Law.
44. The Parol Evidence Rule Does Not Apply to Subsequent Transactions.
45. Some Miscellaneous Observations.
46. Parol Evidence and The Uniform Commercial Code.

C. INTERPRETATION

47. Standards of Interpretation.
48. Rules of Interpretation and Their Relationship to Standards of Interpretation.
49. Are Questions of Interpretation Questions of Fact or Questions of Law?
50. The Relationship Between the Parol Evidence Rule and Rules and Standards of Interpretation.
51. Some Practical Observations About Parol Evidence and Interpretation.
52. Course of Dealing, Course of Performance and Usage.

A. INTRODUCTION

Analysis

Sec.
39. The Difficulty of the Subject Matter.

1. The bulk of this chapter appeared in Calamari and Perillo, A Plea for a Uniform Parol Evidence Rule and Principles of Contract Interpretation, 42 Ind.L.J. 333 (1967).

§ 39.　The Difficulty of the Subject Matter

Professor Thayer, speaking of the parol evidence rule, aptly observed "Few things are darker than this, or fuller of subtle difficulties." [2]　Much of the fog and mystery stems from the fact that there is basic disagreement as to the meaning and effect of the parol evidence rule and as to the appropriate goals to be achieved by the process of contractual interpretation.　The cases and treatises of the contract giants tend to conceal this conflict.　While frequently masking disagreement by using the same terminology, Professors Williston and Corbin are often poles apart in the meaning they attach to the same terms.　Often starting from what superficially appear to be the same premises, they frequently advocate different results in similar fact situations.　The polarity of their views reflects conflicting value judgments as to policy issues that are as old as our legal system and that are likely to continue as long as courts of law exist.　Although many writers and courts have expressed their views on the subject and have made major contributions to it, concentration on the analyses of Professors Williston and Corbin will point up the fundamental bases upon which the conflicting cases and views rest.[3]

B.　THE PAROL EVIDENCE RULE

Analysis

Sec.
40.　The Area of Substantial Agreement.
41.　The Parol Evidence Rule: The Major Area of Conflict.
42.　The Parol Evidence Rule Does Not Apply Until It is Decided That There is a Contract.
43.　The Parol Evidence Rule is a Rule of Substantive Law.
44.　The Parol Evidence Rule Does Not Apply to Subsequent Transactions.
45.　Some Miscellaneous Observations.
46.　Parol Evidence and The Uniform Commercial Code.

§ 40.　The Area of Substantial Agreement

There is a rule of substantive law which states that whenever contractual intent is sought to be ascertained from among several ex-

---

2.　Thayer, A Preliminary Treatise on Evidence at Common Law 390 (1898).

3.　For some recent articles see, Corbin, The Interpretation of Words and the Parol Evidence Rule, 50 Cornell L.Q. 161 (1965); Farnsworth, "Meaning" in the Law of Contracts, 76 Yale L.J. 939 (1967); Murray, The Parol Evidence Rule: A Clarification, 4 Duquesne U.L.Rev. 337 (1966); Patterson, The Interpretation and Construction of Contracts, 64 Colum.L.Rev. 833 (1964); Sweet, Contract Making and Parol Evidence: Diagnosis and Treatment of a Sick Rule, 53 Cornell L.Q. 1036 (1968); Young, Equivocation in the Making of Agreements, 64 Colum. L.Rev. 619 (1964).

pressions of the parties, an earlier tentative expression will be rejected in favor of a later expression that is final.[4]   More simply stated, the contract made by the parties supersedes tentative terms set forth in earlier negotiations.   Consequently, in determining the content of the contract, the earlier tentative agreements are irrelevant.

The parol evidence rule comes into play only when the last expression is in writing.[5]   Professor Corbin states the rule as follows: "When two parties have made a contract and have expressed it in a writing to which they have both assented as the complete and accurate integration of that contract, evidence, whether parol or otherwise, of antecedent understandings and negotiations will not be admitted for the purpose of varying or contradicting the writing."[6] Professor Williston's formulation is not to the contrary: "Briefly stated," he writes, "this rule requires, in the absence of fraud, duress, mutual mistake, or something of the kind, the exclusion of extrinsic evidence, oral or written, where the parties have reduced their agreement to an integrated writing."[7]   The similarity between the parol evidence rule and the rule stated in the preceding paragraph is obvious. The main and important difference is that where the last expression is not in writing the jury determines whether the parties intended the second expression to supersede the first.[8]   This is to say that this question of intention is determined as is any other question of intention stemming from oral transactions.   Where the later expression is in writing, however, this question is usually determined by the trial judge.   At an early date it was felt (and the feeling strongly remains) that writings require the special protection that is afforded by removing this issue from the province of unsophisticated jurors.[9]

4.   3 Corbin § 573; McCormick, Evidence § 213 (1954) [hereinafter cited as McCormick].

5.   Restatement, Contracts § 228, Comment b, suggests that the words of an oral agreement may be chosen with such precision that there is an equivalent of an integration.   It adds that such a case is so unusual as not to require separate discussion.   Cf. 3 Corbin § 573 n. 11.

6.   3 Corbin § 573.

7.   4 Williston § 631.

8.   McCormick § 214.   Of course if reasonable men could reach only one reasonable conclusion the question would be one for the court.

9.   McCormick §§ 214–16;   Freeman v. Continental Gin Co., 381 F.2d 459 (5th Cir. 1967), reh. denied 384 F.2d 365. But see Murray, supra note 3, at 342, where he asks: "If the parol evidence rule is based upon distrust of juries because they lack sophistication in comparing an oral expression with a subsequent writing, why should the rule apply when both expressions are written?"

It is often assumed that the parol evidence rule protects the "haves" against the "have nots," since it is the former who ordinarily draft written contracts and the latter who receive the sympathy of the jury.   See McCormick § 210, at 427–28.   Surprisingly, however, a substantial number of the reported cases dealing with the

While it is unanimously agreed that the parol evidence rule applies to *prior* expressions, and has no application to an agreement made *subsequent* to the writing,[10] there is no unanimity as to expressions *contemporaneous* with the writing. Williston and the Restatement take the position that contemporaneous expressions should be treated the same as prior expressions except that contemporaneous writings should be deemed to be a part of the integration.[11] Corbin appears to argue that expressions are either prior or subsequent to the writing and that therefore the word "contemporaneous" merely clouds the issue.[12] Everyone agrees that the parol evidence rule does not apply to a separate agreement, that is, an agreement that has a separate consideration.[13]

A distinction is drawn between a total and a partial integration. Where the writing is intended to be *final* and *complete,* it is characterized as a total integration and may be neither contradicted nor supplemented by evidence of prior agreements or expressions. But where the writing is intended to be *final* but *incomplete,* it is said to be a partial integration; although such a writing may not be *contradicted* by evidence of prior agreements or expressions, it may be *supplemented* by evidence of consistent additional terms.[14] Thus, in approaching a writing, two questions must be asked: (1) Is it intended

rule involve sizable transactions between persons with apparently strong bargaining power. See, e. g., Hunt Foods & Indus., Inc. v. Doliner, 26 A.D. 2d 41, 270 N.Y.S.2d 937 (1st Dep't 1966) (transaction involving over $5,-000,000); Millerton Agway Co-op. v. Briarcliff Farms, 17 N.Y.2d 57, 268 N.Y.S.2d 18, 215 N.E.2d 341 (1966) ($1,000,000 guarantee); Hicks v. Bush, 10 N.Y.2d 488, 225 N.Y.S.2d 34, 180 N. E.2d 425 (1962) (involving 475,000 shares of a holding company); Crowell-Collier Pub. Co. v. Josefowitz, 5 N. Y.2d 998, 157 N.E.2d 730, 184 N.Y.S.2d 859 (1959) (sale of business for $3,-000,000).

10. Wagner v. Graziano Constr. Co., 390 Pa. 445, 136 A.2d 82 (1957); 3 Corbin § 574; 4 Williston § 632. Under certain statutes, parties may, by agreement, bar a subsequent oral modification. E. g., U.C.C. § 2–209(2); McKinney's N.Y.Gen.Obligations Law § 15–301. Even under such statutes, however, an executed oral agreement is effective. See Hohmann & Bar-

nard, Inc. v. Sciaky Bros., 333 F.2d 5 (2d Cir. 1964), 50 Cornell L.Q. 355 (1965).

11. Restatement, Contracts § 237, Comment a; 4 Williston § 628; Sonfield v. Eversole, 416 S.W.2d 458 (Tex.Civ. App.1967), ref. n. r. e. This position has been adopted by the Uniform Commercial Code. The parol evidence provision applies to "evidence of any [oral or written] prior agreement or of a contemporaneous oral agreement." U.C.C. § 2–202.

12. 3 Corbin § 577.

13. 3 Corbin § 594; 4 Williston § 637.

14. 4 Williston § 636. While Corbin is in agreement with the statement in the text, he advocates abandonment of the term "partial integration" and argues that parties rarely intend that an incomplete writing be considered final. 3 Corbin § 581; see Leyse v. Leyse, 251 Cal.App.2d 629, 59 Cal. Rptr. 680 (1967).

as a final expression? (2) Is it intended to be a complete expression?

Is the writing intended as a final expression?

Writings that evidence a contract are not necessarily "final" embodiments of the contract. Exchanges of letters or memoranda that appear to show the formation of a contract may have been intended to be read in the light of more far-ranging conversations and documents. Or, the parties may have intended their writings to be tentative and preliminary to a final draft. In these cases, the parol evidence rule does not bar enforcement of the entire agreement as proved by the writing read in the context of prior and contemporaneous expressions.[15] It is agreed that any relevant evidence is admissible to show that the writing was not intended to be final.[16] Although the question of finality is frequently characterized as one of law in order to remove it from the province of unsophisticated jurors, it is actually a question of fact—one of intention—which the trial judge determines.[17] To be considered final the writing need not be in any particular form and need not be signed. The crucial requirement is that the parties have regarded the writing as the final embodiment of their agreement.

Undoubtedly the completeness of an agreement does have some bearing on the question of finality, that is to say, the more complete and formal the instrument is the more likely it is that it is intended as an integration.[18] However, a note or memorandum is not ordinarily regarded as an integration.[19] A letter of confirmation generally acts as an integration if the other party makes no response to it at least prior to performance.[20] It does not have this effect, however, under Article 2 of the Uniform Commercial Code.[21]

---

15. Atwater v. Cardwell, 21 Ky.L.Rptr. 1297, 54 S.W. 960 (1900); Hechinger v. Ulacia, 194 App.Div. 330, 185 N.Y.S. 323 (1st Dep't. 1920).

16. Restatement, Contracts § 228, Comment a; 3 Corbin § 588; 4 Williston § 633, n. 13.

17. McCormick §§ 214–15. Corbin would allow greater participation by the jury. See 3 Corbin § 595.

18. Di Menna v. Cooper & Evans Co., 220 N.Y. 391, 397–98, 115 N.E. 993, 995 (1917); Restatement, Contracts (2d) § 21A, Comment c; 3 Corbin § 581.

19. Donald Friedman & Co. v. Newman, 255 N.Y. 340, 174 N.E. 703, 73 A.L.R.

95 (1931), motion denied 255 N.Y. 632, 175 N.E. 345.

20. Tow v. Miners Memorial Hosp. Ass'n, 305 F.2d 73 (4th Cir. 1962); Restatement, Contracts § 228, ill. 2; Newburger v. American Sur. Co., 242 N.Y. 134, 151 N.E. 155 (1926).

21. Under U.C.C. § 2–201(2) a confirmatory memorandum sent by one merchant to another merchant within a reasonable time operates to satisfy the writing requirement of the Statute of Frauds. It does not operate as an integration. The parol evidence provision, U.C.C. § 2–202, makes clear that the parol evidence rule stated therein applies in the context of writ-

Is the writing a complete or partial integration?

Once it is determined that the writing is intended to be final and therefore an integration, it becomes necessary to ascertain whether the integration is complete (so that it cannot be contradicted or supplemented) or only partial (so that it cannot be contradicted but may be supplemented by evidence of consistent additional terms). It seems to be generally agreed that this is a question of law in the sense that it is determined by the trial judge.[22]

§ 41. The Parol Evidence Rule: The Major Area of Conflict

Apparent agreement by Professors Williston and Corbin, except as noted, on the rules stated above conceals real conflict. The battleground upon which they express disagreement is a major one: the concept of total integration. This, of course, is the area in which most of the cases arise. Both assert that the existence of a total integration depends on the intention of the parties. Williston does so primarily in a section entitled, "Integration Depends Upon Intent." [23] Corbin's emphasis on intent runs throughout his entire discussion of the rule.[24] It appears, however, that in this context they use the term "intent" in ways that are remarkably dissimilar. A typical fact situation will illustrate this. A agrees to sell and B agrees to purchase Blackacre for $10,000. The contract is in writing and in all respects appears complete on its face. Prior to the signing of the contract A, in order to induce B's assent, orally promises him in the presence of a number of reputable witnesses that if B will sign the contract, A will remove an unsightly shack on A's land across the road from Blackacre. May this promise be proved and enforced? [25] This depends upon whether the writing is a total integration.

Williston argues that if the intention to have a total integration were to be determined by the ordinary process of determining intention, the parol evidence rule would be emasculated.[26] He points out that the mere existence of the collateral oral agreement would conclusively indicate that the parties intended only a partial integration and that the only question that would be presented is whether the al-

---

ten confirmations only to "terms with respect to which the confirmatory memoranda of the parties agree." This presupposes an exchange of memoranda.

22. McCormick § 215. Corbin dissents in part, arguing for the propriety of a jury verdict in many cases. 3 Corbin § 595.

23. 4 Williston § 633.

24. 3 Corbin §§ 573–96.

25. The facts given here are suggested by Mitchill v. Lath, 247 N.Y. 377, 160 N.E. 646, 68 A.L.R. 239 (1928), rearg. den. 248 N.Y. 526, 162 N.E. 511.

26. 4 Williston § 633.

leged prior or contemporaneous agreement was actually made. This would be a question of fact for the jury, thus eliminating the special protection which the trial judge should afford the writing.[27]

Williston, therefore, suggests that the issue of partial or total integration should be determined according to the following rules.

(1) If the writing expressly declares in what is sometimes referred to as a merger clause that it contains the entire agreement of the parties, the declaration conclusively establishes that the integration is total unless the document is obviously incomplete or the merger clause was included as a result of fraud or mistake or any other reason exists that is sufficient to set aside a contract.[28] As previously indicated, even a merger clause does not prevent enforcement of a separate agreement supported by a distinct consideration.[29]

(2) In the absence of a merger clause, the determination is made by looking to the writing. Consistent additional terms may be proved if the writing is obviously incomplete on its face [30] or if it is apparently complete but, as in the case of deeds, bonds, bills and notes, expresses the undertaking of only one of the parties.[31]

(3) Where the writing appears to be a complete instrument expressing the rights and obligations of both parties, it is deemed a total integration unless the alleged additional terms were such as might naturally be made as a separate agreement by parties situated as were the parties to the written contract.[32]

Thus in the hypothetical case given, Williston's view is that the collateral promise to remove the unsightly shack could not be enforced. The writing was apparently complete on its face and contracting parties would ordinarily and naturally have included such a promise in the writing. Many might agree with this result,[33] but can it be seriously argued that this result is based on the parties' intent that the agreement be integrated? How can a rule based on the

---

27. At 9 Wigmore § 2430, at 98 (1940) [hereinafter cited as Wigmore] the author states that if the judge decides that the parol evidence rule applies "he does not decide that the excluded negotiations did not take place, but merely that *if* they did take place they are nevertheless legally immaterial." If he determines that the parol evidence rule does not apply "he does not decide that the negotiations did take place, but merely that *if* they did, they are legally effective, and he then leaves to the jury the determination of fact whether they did take place." (emphasis his.)

28. 4 Williston § 633; cf. 3 Corbin § 578.

29. See text accompanying note 13 supra.

30. 4 Williston § §633, 636.

31. 4 Williston § 645; 3 Corbin § 587.

32. 4 Williston §§ 638–39.

33. As did the court in Mitchill v. Lath, 247 N.Y. 377, 160 N.E. 646, 68 A.L.R. 239 (1928), rearg. den. 248 N.Y. 526, 162 N.E. 511.

intention of the parties be emasculated by seeking to determine their actual expressed intent? It is quite clear that the expressed intent shown by overwhelming evidence is at variance with an intent to have the writing serve as their complete agreement.

Professor Corbin takes a contrary view as to the proper result in our hypothetical case: "It can never be determined by mere interpretation of the words of a writing whether it is an 'integration' of anything, whether it is 'the final and complete expression of the agreement' or is a mere partial expression of 'the agreement'." [34] Elsewhere, he states: "Since the very existence of an 'integration' . . . is dependent on what the parties thereto say and do (necessarily extrinsic to the paper instrument) at the time they draw that instrument 'in usual form,' are we to continue like a flock of sheep to beg the question at issue, even when its result is to 'make a contract for the parties,' one that is vitally different from the one they made for themselves?" [35] When Professor Corbin speaks of the intent of the parties he emphatically means their actual expressed intent.

Thus, two schools of thought are on the scene, one determined to seek out the intent of the parties, the other speaking of the intent but refusing to consider evidence of what the intent actually was. Let us examine Williston's approach further, since it is, at least linguistically, the more puzzling. A key to understanding this approach is a case such as Gianni v. R. Russel & Co.,[36] which followed the not dissimilar approaches of Williston and Wigmore.[37] The parties signed a three-year lease in which the tenant agreed not to sell tobacco in any form on the premises but was permitted to sell soft drinks. The tenant al-

---

34. 3 Corbin § 581, at 442.

35. 3 Corbin § 582.

36. 281 Pa. 320, 126 A. 791 (1924).

37. Dean Wigmore's approach is by no means similar in all respects to Professor Williston's. While Williston would ordinarily require that a writing be incomplete on its face before permitting parol evidence to be introduced (4 Williston § 633), Wigmore argues that "intent must be sought where always intent must be sought . . ., namely, in the *conduct and language* of the parties and the *surrounding circumstances*. The document alone will not suffice." 9 Wigmore § 2430, at 98 (emphasis his). They each, however, approach the

question of intent to have a total integration mechanistically. Wigmore suggests that the "chief and most satisfactory index for the judge is found in the circumstance whether or not the *particular element of the alleged extrinsic negotiation is dealt with at all* in the writing." Id. at 98–99 (emphasis his). This is somewhat different from Williston's test of "the inherent probability of parties who contract under the circumstances in question, simultaneously making both the agreement in writing which is before the court, and also the alleged parol agreement. The point is not merely whether the court is convinced that the parties before it did in fact do this, but whether parties so situated generally would or might do so." 4 Williston § 638 at 1040–41.

leged that his agreement to refrain from the sale of tobacco was in consideration of an oral promise by the defendant to give him exclusive rights to the sale of soft drinks on the premises. The court held that evidence of the oral agreement was inadmissible, citing Williston and Wigmore. The court stated:

> In cases of this kind, where the cause of action rests entirely on an alleged oral understanding concerning a subject which is dealt with in a written contract it is presumed that the writing was *intended* to set forth the entire agreement as to that particular subject.[38] (Emphasis added.)

While the court spoke of the parties' intention, it excluded evidence of that intention. Logically, since the quantum of evidence would appear to be irrelevant under the court's test, it would so rule if the transaction were entered into on a national television network and were witnessed by tens of millions of viewers. The key to the court's decision may be found elsewhere in the opinion:

> We have stated on several occasions recently that we propose to stand for the integrity of written contracts . . . .
> We reiterate our position in this regard.[39]

Fictions have been enormously important in the development of our law. In an era when the law was deemed unchangeable and eternal, they provided almost the only mechanism for avoiding the impact of rules deemed unwise. Their use today serves only to obfuscate what should be clear. Shorn of language indicating a fictitious search for intent, the courts and writers who adopt a Willistonian approach are saying this: *When parties adopt a written form that gives every appearance of being complete and final, they are required to incorporate in that form their entire agreement. If they fail to do so, unincorporated terms relating to the same subject matter are void.*

Professor Corbin has an easy task in demolishing the Willistonian approach. In treating the matter of integration as a question of intent, as Professor Williston purports to do, he shows the absurdity of excluding all relevant evidence of intent except the writing itself.

---

38. Gianni v. R. Russel & Co., 281 Pa. 320, 324, 126 A. 791, 792 (1924).

39. Id. at 325, 126 A. at 792 (citations omitted). See also Cargill Comm. Co. v. Swartwood, 159 Minn. 1, 198 N.W. 536, 538 (1924): "Without that rule there would be no assurance of the enforceability of a written contract. If such assurance were removed today from our law, general disaster would result, because of the consequent destruction of confidence, for the tremendous but closely adjusted machinery of modern business cannot function at all without confidence in the enforceability of contracts. They must not be reduced to the innocuous character of a mere 'scrap of paper.'"

But, as we have seen, Williston, and such courts as the Supreme Court of Pennsylvania in Gianni v. R. Russel & Co.,[40] are unconcerned about the true intention of the parties. Rather, shorn of rote language of fiction indicating a search for intention, they are advocating and applying a rule of form. Since (and even before) the common law had its genesis,[41] there has been a deeply-felt belief that transactions will be more secure, litigation will be reduced, and the temptation to perjury will be removed, if everyone will only use proper forms for his transactions. The Statute of Wills and the Statute of Frauds are but examples of this belief.[42] Professor Corbin, by attacking the apparent arguments of Williston's position has not expressly come to grips with the substance of his position. This is not to suggest that either he or Professor Williston have been unaware of the true nature of their disagreement. Rather, they seem for the most part to have been content not to make explicit the basis of their differing views.

The issue to be resolved is whether the public is better served by giving effect to the parties' entire agreement written and oral, even at the risk of injustice caused by the possibility of perjury and the possibility that superseded agreements will be treated as operative, or does the security of transactions require that, despite occasional injustices, persons adopting a formal writing be required, on the penalty of voidness of their side agreements, to put their entire agreement in the formal writing.[43]

The conflict is an old one. Rules excluding evidence on the ground that it is likely to be false are not strangers to the law. Formerly, parties and interested third persons were incompetent to testify on the

---

40. See text accompanying note 36, supra.

41. On the historical development of the rule see 9 Wigmore § 2426. For a classic discussion of the desirability of requiring contracts to be put in writing, see 2 Bentham, Rationale of Judicial Evidence 454–513 (1827). It is to be noted, however, that, as a prerequisite to imposition of such a rule, he advocated that the requirement be widely publicized throughout the country. Moreover, he deemed it unfair that failure to comply with the requirement should result in voidness of the agreement. Rather, an alleged agreement not made in proper form would merely be regarded with suspicion.

42. Contrast, however, the New York Retail Instalment Sales Act which adopts a radically new approach to parol evidence. Personal Property Law § 402 requires that the written contract shall contain the entire agreement of the parties with respect to the goods and services. Failure to comply with this provision is a misdemeanor and gives the instalment buyer a cause of action for recovery of all finance charges. Pers.Prop.Law § 414(1), (2). Obviously the effectuation of such a cause of action requires that the buyer be permitted to testify as to the making of a collateral oral agreement.

43. For the policy considerations involved, see 3 Corbin § 575; 4 Williston § 633; McCormick §§ 210–16.

ground that their testimony would be unworthy of belief.[44] The Statute of Frauds and the Statute of Wills embody similar considerations.[45] It is submitted, however, that the possibility of perjury is an insufficient ground for interfering with freedom of contract by refusing to effectuate the parties' entire agreement.

The whole thrust of our law for over a century has been directed to the eradication of exclusionary rules of evidence in civil cases. Thus parties may now testify, their interest in the outcome affecting only the weight and not the admissibility of the evidence. Dissatisfaction with rigid application of the parol evidence rule has resulted in the strained insertion of fact situations into the categories where the parol evidence rule is inapplicable. Thus, to circumvent the rule fraud has been found [46] and reformation has been granted [47] in situations where these concepts are not ordinarily deemed applicable. Moreover, whole categories of exceptions have been carved out; for example, a deed absolute may be shown to be a mortgage.[48] Professor Thayer's observation concerning of the parol evidence problem warrants repetition: "Few things are darker than this, or fuller of subtle difficulties." [49] When any rule of law is riddled through with exceptions and applications difficult to reconcile,[50] it is believed that litiga-

---

44. See McCormick § 65.

45. See 3 Corbin § 575.

46. E.g., Bareham & McFarland, Inc. v. Kane, 228 App.Div. 396, 240 N.Y.S.123 (4th Dep't 1930) (language sounding in warranty of performance held to be factual representations); see Sweet, Promissory Fraud and the Parol Evidence Rule, 49 Calif.L.Rev. 877, 896 (1961) ("It does not take much manipulation to classify a promise as either a warranty or a fact.").

47. E. g., Winslett v. Rice, 272 Ala. 25, 128 So.2d 94 (1960) (breach of oral collateral agreement constituted "fraud" justifying reformation).

48. 3 Corbin § 587; 9 Wigmore § 2437; 4 Williston § 635. See Fogelman, The Deed Absolute as a Mortgage in New York, 32 Fordham L.Rev. 299 (1963).

49. Thayer, op.cit. supra note 2, at 390.

50. The Supreme Court of California recently acknowledged that its decisions have not been consistent. It disapproved of the restrictive approach previously adopted in many cases. Masterson v. Sine, 68 Cal.2d 222, 65 Cal.Rptr. 545, 436 P.2d 561 (1968). Inconsistency in the Virginia decisions are discussed in Note 7 Wm. & Mary L.Rev. 189 (1966). Pennsylvania inconsistencies are discussed in Corbin § 577 n. 34 (Supp.1964).

It is interesting that an occasional jurisdiction appears to reach consistent results although on the most varied reasoning. For example, in Connecticut the leading cases appear to be State Finance Corp. v. Ballestrini, 111 Conn. 544, 150 A. 700 (1930) in which Williston's test is articulated but a result more consistent with Corbin's approach was reached; Harris v. Clinton, 142 Conn. 204, 112 A.2d 885 (1955), in which although he is not cited, the reasoning seems to be pure Corbin; Greenwich Plumbing & Heating Co. v. A. Barbaresi & Son, Inc., 147 Conn. 580, 164 A.2d 405 (1960), in which parol evidence of a collateral agreement was admitted because the writing was ambiguous. The analysis, but not the result of this last decision is criticized in 3 Corbin § 582 n. 84 (Supp.1964).

tion is stimulated rather than reduced.[51] If the policy of the parol evidence rule is to reduce the possibility of judgments predicated upon perjured testimony and superseded agreements, it may be effectuated to a large extent by continuing to leave control over determining the question of intent to integrate in the hands of the trial judge.[52] Finally, the trend of modern decisions, as Williston suggests, "is toward increasing liberality in the admission of parol agreements."[53] This tendency of the courts is in no small measure due to the influence of Professor Corbin's treatise.[54]

Lack of understanding of the rationale of the parol evidence rule results in decisions such as Townsend v. Standard Indus., Inc., 235 Ark. 951, 363 S. W.2d 535 (1962). The parties had been operating under an oral agreement for some time. They subsequently memorialized this in a writing which was held to be inoperative as a contract for lack of "mutuality of obligation." The court further held, on the pleadings, that, since the writing had been adopted as an integration, evidence of the prior oral agreement proffered to show the presence of consideration was inadmissible. The decision is scorchingly criticized in Note, 17 Ark.L.Rev. 220 (1963). An integration supersedes prior agreements because it is a final contract. A writing which is not a contract is no integration. Moreover, a glance at the writing reproduced in the opinion shows it to be a brief memorandum and, even if mutuality of obligation were shown, probably not a total integration under any test.

A degree of consistency is shown in some jurisdictions which adopt a Willistonian approach. McDonough, The Parol Evidence Rule in South Dakota and the Effect of Section 2-202 of the Uniform Commercial Code, 10 S.D.L. Rev. 60 (1965). See Comment, The Parol Evidence Rule in Missouri, 27 Mo.L.Rev. 269, 279–82 (1962). New York is one such jurisdiction. Oxford Commercial Corp. v. Landau, 12 N.Y. 2d 362, 239 N.Y.S.2d 865, 190 N.E.2d 230, 13 A.L.R.3d 309 (1963), 49 Cornell L.Q. 311 (1964); Mitchill v. Lath, 247 N.Y. 377, 160 N.E. 646, 68 A.L.R. 239 (1928), rearg. den. 248 N.Y. 526, 162

N.E. 511; Meadow Brook Nat. Bank v. Bzura, 20 A.D.2d 287, 246 N.Y.S.2d 787 (4th Dep't 1964). This apparent consistency is often achieved by strained characterization of the facts to bring the case within one of the exceptions to the parol evidence rule. See e. g., Peo v. Kennedy, 16 A.D.2d 306, 227 N.Y.S.2d 971 (4th Dep't 1962) (condition precedent to the formation of a contract); Bareham & McFarland, Inc. v. Kane, 228 App.Div. 396, 240 N.Y.S. 123 (4th Dep't 1930) (fraud).

51. See 3 Corbin § 575; see also Fisch, New York Evidence § 64, at 42 (1959): "Because the decisions are ineffective as guides to determine in advance whether or not the facts of a given transaction will come within one of the exceptions to the rule, the assumption, frequently enunciated in judicial opinions, that the rule is indispensable to business stability is specious . . . The decisions as to these matters are valueless, contrary holdings being reached on almost identical facts."

52. The most thorough text treatment of this point is in McCormick §§ 214–16; see also Murray, note 3 supra.

53. 4 Williston § 638, at 1045.

54. Ample authority for this proposition can be found in the cases relying upon Professor Corbin's analysis and cited by him in 3 Corbin § 573–95. See, more recently, United States v. Clementon Sewerage Auth., 365 F.2d 609 (3d Cir. 1966) (New Jersey law); Masterson v. Sine, 68 Cal.2d 222, 65 Cal.Rptr. 545, 436 P.2d 561 (1968).

§ 42. The Parol Evidence Rule Does Not Apply Until It is Decided That There is a Contract

It is well settled that the parol evidence rule does not prevent a party from using contemporaneous or prior negotiations or expressions to show that the writing was never intended to be operative [55] or that it was intended to be effective only upon the happening of a condition precedent, provided that the condition sought to be proved is not inconsistent with the writing,[56] nor does the parol evidence rule prevent proof that the written contract lacks consideration,[57] or that it is voidable or subject to reformation by reason of mistake,[58] or vitiated by fraud, duress or undue influence, or that it is invalidated by illegality.[59] In general it may be said that parol evidence is always admissible to show that the agreement is void or voidable.[60]

§ 43. The Parol Evidence Rule is a Rule of Substantive Law

It is generally agreed that the parol evidence rule is a rule of substantive law and not a rule of evidence.[61] Thus, it has been held that the parol evidence rule can be raised on appeal despite the absence of an objection.[62]

§ 44. The Parol Evidence Rule Does Not Apply to Subsequent Transactions

If one reviews the statement of the parol evidence rule which introduced this subject matter, it will be recalled that the parol evi-

---

55. For example, this would be the situation where the parties had made a tentative written agreement but intended that no contract would exist until a final writing was executed. 1 Williston § 28; 1 Corbin § 30. See § 40 supra.

56. Hicks v. Bush, 10 N.Y.2d 488, 225 N.Y.S.2d 34, 180 N.E.2d 425 (1962); Cosper v. Hancock, 163 Colo. 263, 430 P.2d 80 (1967).

57. Title Guar. & Trust Co. v. Pam, 232 N.Y. 441, 134 N.E.2d 525 (1922), rearg. denied 233 N.Y. 530, 135 N.E. 904. The relationship of the parol evidence rule to the question of consideration is also discussed in § 77 infra.

58. General Discount Corp. v. Sadowski, 183 F.2d 542 (6th Cir. 1950).

59. McCormick § 211. Occasionally a case is found which does not permit evidence of fraud to overcome a merg-

er clause which specifically covers the area in which the fraud is claimed. Danann Realty Corp. v. Harris, 5 N. Y.2d 317, 184 N.Y.S.2d 599, 157 N.E.2d 597 (1959); but see Millerton Agway Co-op. v. Briarcliff Farms, 17 N.Y.2d 57, 268 N.Y.S.2d 18, 215 N.E.2d 341 (1966), and Wittenberg v. Robinov, 9 N.Y.2d 261, 213 N.Y.S.2d 430, 173 N.E. 2d 868 (1961).

60. Grismore § 94, at 150.

61. 3 Corbin § 573; Fogelson v. Rackfay Constr. Co., 300 N.Y. 334, 90 N.E. 2d 881 (1950); O'Brien v. O'Brien, 362 Pa. 66, 66 A.2d 309, 10 A.L.R.2d 714 (1949). Apparently contra, Freeman v. Continental Gin Co., 381 F.2d 459 (5th Cir. 1967), reh. den. 384 F.2d 365 (Mississippi Law).

62. Dollar v. International Banking Corp., 13 Cal.App. 331, 109 P. 499 (Ct. App.1910); contra, Higgs v. De Maziroff, 263 N.Y. 473, 189 N.E. 555 (1934).

dence rule excludes evidence of prior negotiations and transactions and that there is some controversy as to its applicability to simultaneous expressions. It is, however, well settled that the parol evidence rule does not have any application to subsequent agreements; [63] therefore, evidence of subsequent modifications of an integration may be shown.

§ 45. Some Miscellaneous Observations

It is generally held that the parol evidence rule may be invoked by and against a person who is not a party to the agreement.[64] A difficult question which does not seem to have received a uniform answer is whether implied terms should be deemed to be part of the integration.[65] The queston of the admissibility of parol evidence as an aid to interpretation of a writing is discussed below.[66]

§ 46. Parol Evidence and The Uniform Commercial Code

Section 2–202 of the Uniform Commercial Code provides: "Terms with respect to which the confirmatory memoranda of the parties agree or which are otherwise set forth in a writing intended by the parties as a final expression of their agreement with respect to such terms as are included therein may not be contradicted by evidence of any prior agreement or of a contemporaneous oral agreement but may be explained or supplemented (a) by course of deal-

---

63. Wagner v. Graziano Constr. Co., 390 Pa. 445, 136 A.2d 82 (1957); Johnson v. Campagna, 200 So.2d 150 (La. App.1967). There are statutes, however, which prevent a subsequent modification or rescission if such an intent is expressed by the parties in writing. See U.C.C. § 2–209(2) which provides: "A signed agreement which excludes modification or rescission except by a signed writing cannot be otherwise modified or rescinded, but except as between merchants such a requirement on a form supplied by the merchant must be separately signed by the other party." See also McKinney's N.Y.Gen.Obligations Law § 15–301.

64. Clark v. United States, 341 F.2d 691 (9th Cir. 1965); Akamine & Sons, Ltd. v. American Sec. Bank, 50 Hawaii 304, 440 P.2d 262 (1968); Oxford Commercial Corp. v. Landau, 12 N.Y.2d 362, 239 N.Y.S.2d 865, 190 N.E.2d 230, 13 A.L.R.3d 309 (1963), 49 Cornell L. Rev. 311 (1963); Hartford Accident &

Indem. Co. v. Anderson, 155 N.W.2d 728 (N.D.1968); Contra, Great Western Cas. Co. v. Truck Ins. Exch., 358 F.2d 883 (10th Cir. 1966); see 4 Williston § 647.

65. See Hayden v. Hoadley, 94 Vt. 345, 111 A. 343 (1920); Balon v. Hotel & Restaurant Supplies, Inc., 6 Ariz.App. 481, 433 P.2d 661 (1967), vacated 103 Ariz. 474, 445 P.2d 833 (1968); Restatement, Contracts § 240, Comment c; 4 Williston § 640. Another interesting question is whether the parties by agreement may narrow or expand the content of the parol evidence rule. See Garden State Plaza Corp. v. S. S. Kresge Corp., 78 N.J.Super. 485, 189 A.2d 448 (App.Div.), certification den. 40 N.J. 226, 191 A.2d 63 (1963), 64 Colum.L.Rev. 372 (1964), which held that such an agreement would violate the public policy of the state.

66. See § 50 infra.

ing or usage of trade (Section 1–205) or by course of performance (Section 2–208); and (b) by evidence of consistent additional terms unless the court finds the writing to have been intended also as a complete and exclusive statement of the terms of the agreement."

The thrust of the Code section is to make it more difficult to have a finding that a writing is a total integration. The Code rejects Williston's rule, stated above,[67] that where the writing appears to be a complete expression of the rights and obligations of both parties, it is deemed a total integration unless the alleged additional terms were such as might *naturally* be made as a separate agreement by parties situated as were the parties to the written contract. Under the Code there is not a total integration unless the alleged additional terms "would *certainly* have been included in the document in the view of the court." [68] It is only then that "evidence of their alleged making must be kept from the trier of the fact" [69] which presumably means that in all other cases the jury is to determine whether the additional term was in fact agreed upon.[70] The only other exception would be where the evidence clearly shows the parties actually intended the writing to be a total integration. This could occur, for example, in the case of a merger clause.

Subsection (a) goes even beyond subsection (b). Here the evidence of "course of dealing or usage of trade or course of performance is,[71] unless "carefully negated," deemed to be read into the contract for purposes of ascertaining the meaning of the language even though it contradicts the apparently unambiguous language of the writing,[72] and in the case of a course of dealing, or a trade usage for the purpose of adding additional terms even though under common law rules there would be a total integration.[73] This involves a clear rejection of the plain meaning rule and even Williston's rule that extrinsic evidence may not give language a meaning at variance with the appropriate local meaning of words.[74]

---

67. See § 41 supra.

68. U.C.C. § 2–202, Comment 3 (emphasis added); Hull-Dobbs Inc. v. Mallicoat, 57 Tenn.App. 100, 415 S.W.2d 344 (1966), Ciunci v. Wella Corp., 26 A.D. 2d 109, 271 N.Y.S.2d 317 (1st Dep't, 1966).

69. § 2–202, Comment 3.

70. Hunt Foods & Indus. Inc. v. Doliner, 26 A.D.2d 41, 270 N.Y.S.2d 937 (1st Dep't, 1966).

71. These terms are discussed in § 52 infra together with the common law rules governing custom and usage.

72. This is really a part of the repudiation of the "plain meaning" doctrine which is discussed in § 50 infra.

73. U.C.C. 1–205(3). This matter is discussed in more detail in § 52 infra.

74. See § 47 and § 50 infra.

C. INTERPRETATION

Analysis

Sec.
47. Standards of Interpretation.
48. Rules of Interpretation and Their Relationship to Standards of Interpretation.
49. Are Questions of Interpretation Questions of Fact or Questions of Law?
50. The Relationship Between the Parol Evidence Rule and Rules and Standards of Interpretation.
51. Some Practical Observations About Parol Evidence and Interpretation.
52. Course of Dealing, Course of Performance and Usage.

§ 47. Standards of Interpretation

Since there is no "lawyers' Paradise" where "all words have a fixed, precisely ascertained meaning," [75] frequently [76] the problem is to interpret [77] the language and other manifestations of the parties. The Restatement says: "Interpretations of words and other manifestations of intention forming an agreement [or having reference to the formation of an agreement] [78] is the ascertainment of the meaning to be given to such words and manifestations." [79]

The question then is whose meaning is to be given to an agreement, communication, or other manifestation of intent. The Restatement lists six possible standards of interpretation, that is, six vantage points which might be used in making this interpretation.[80] These standards are:

   1.   the standard of general usage;

   2.   a standard of limited usage, which would attach the meaning given to language in a particular locality, or by a sect or those engaged in a particular occupa-

---

75. Thayer, note 2 supra, at 428–29.

76. See Shepherd, Contracts in a Prosperity Year, 6 Stan.L.Rev. 208, 223, 226 (1954).

77. On the distinction between interpretation and construction see 3 Corbin § 534; 4 Williston § 602; Patterson, note 3 supra, at 835–36. Note that these authorities are not in accord as to the proper use of these terms.

78. The words in brackets indicate that this process called interpretation is also utilized to determine whether there is a contract. Accord, 3 Corbin § 32. But § 58 of the Restatement and the Restatement Second seem to indicate that the normal process of interpretation does not apply to an acceptance. See also United States v. Braunstein, 75 F.Supp. 137 (S.D.N.Y. 1947), appeal dismissed 168 F.2d 749 (2nd Cir. 1948).

79. Restatement, Contracts § 226.

80. Id. § 227.

tion, or by an alien population or those using a local dialect (the distinction between 1 and 2 is a difference in degree, since generality of usage does not necessarily imply universality);

3. a mutual standard, which would allow only such meanings as conform to an intention common to both or all the parties, and would attach this meaning although it violates the usage of all other persons;

4. an individual standard, which would attach to words or other manifestations of intention whatever meaning the person employing them intended them to express, or that the person receiving the communication understood from it; [81]

5. a standard of reasonable expectation, which would attach to words or other manifestations of intention the meaning which the party employing them should reasonably have apprehended that they would convey to the other party;

6. a standard of reasonable understanding, which would attach to words or other manifestations of intention the meaning which the person to whom the manifestations are addressed might reasonably give to them.

Williston chooses two different standards depending upon whether there is an integration. When there is no integration the standard is the meaning that the party making the manifestation should reasonably expect the other party to give it—the standard of reasonable expectation, a test based primarily upon the objective theory of contracts.[82] However, there are two exceptions. First, where there is an ambiguity [83] the following rules are applicable:

81. Standards (3) and (4) are subjective, the others are objective.

82. 4 Williston § 605. This test is somewhat similar to, but not exactly the same as, the test of the reasonable man in the position of the party other than the one making the manifestation, a standard of reasonable understanding. See § 12 supra. The standard of reasonable understanding takes into account what the other party knows or should know, whereas the standard chosen by Williston would take this into account only where the party making the manifestation knew or should know of the

knowledge of the other party. A compromise between the two tests is employed by Corbin. See text at note 9, infra.

83. No distinction is made between latent and patent ambiguity. 4 Williston § 627. The best known illustration of a latent ambiguity is Raffles v. Wichelhaus, 159 Eng.Rep. 375 (Ex. 1864) (the "Peerless" case).

See also Young, Equivocation in the Making of Agreements, 64 Colum.L.Rev. 619 (1964); Patterson, The Interpretation and Construction of Contracts, 64 Colum.L.Rev. 833 (1964).

(a) Where neither party knows or has reason to know of the ambiguity or where both parties know or have reason to know of the ambiguity it is given the meaning that each party intended it to bear.[84] This means as a practical matter that if the parties give the ambiguous expression the same meaning there is a contract, but if they give it a different meaning there is no contract,[85] at least if the ambiguity relates to a material term. (b) Where one party knows or has reason to know of the ambiguity and the other does not, it bears the meaning given to it by the latter—an individual standard.[86] As a practical matter this means that there is a contract based upon the meaning of the party who is without fault.[87] A second exception to the standard of reasonable expectation is that "where the law gives to certain words an established meaning, this meaning is less readily controlled by the standard of interpretation . . . than is the meaning of other words."[88]

As to integrated [89] writings Williston's standard of interpretation "is the meaning that would be attached to the integration by a reasonably intelligent person acquainted with all operative usages and knowing all the circumstances prior to and contemporaneous with the making of the integration, other than oral statements by the parties of what they intended it to mean."[90] This is the standard of limited usage.[91] Local and trade usages of terms used in the contract are to be considered and, if the parties contracted with reference to them, are determinative.[92]

Basically there are two differences in Williston's approach to an integration as opposed to a non-integration.[93]

First, in the case of a non-integration the issue of ambiguity may be raised simply by the assertion that the parties mutually

84. Restatement, Contracts § 233; 4 Williston § 605.

85. Restatement, Contracts § 71; 4 Williston § 605.

86. Restatement, Contracts § 233; 4 Williston § 605.

87. Restatement, Contracts § 71; 4 Williston § 605.

88. Restatement, Contracts § 234; see also 4 Williston §§ 614, 615.

89. Williston, for the purpose of interpretation, treats a non-integrated writing which is necessary to satisfy the Statute of Frauds as if it were an integration. 4 Williston § 604.

90. Restatement, Contracts § 230.

91. 4 Williston § 607.

92. See generally Levie, Trade Usage and Custom Under the Common Law and the Uniform Commercial Code, 40 N.Y.U.L.Rev. 1101 (1965). See also U. C.C. §§ 1–205, 2–202. This is discussed in more detail in § 52 infra.

93. It should be noted that the rule relating to the situation where "the law gives to certain words an established meaning" is also applicable to integrated writings. 4 Williston §§ 614, 615.

manifested an intention to adopt a meaning different from the ordinary or local meaning; for example, that the word "horse" means "cow" or that the word "buy" means "sell." [94] However, this could not be done in the case of an integration because in determining whether there is an ambiguity "oral statements of what the parties intended it to mean," even if expressed to one another, are excluded. Stated differently, an integration contains an ambiguity only when, in the light of all of the surrounding circumstances (except the oral statements of what the parties intended), the words admit of several normal or popular meanings or there is doubt whether the normal or some local trade meaning was intended. Thus if there were evidence that in a particular locality the word "buy" meant "sell," evidence of what the parties intended would be admissible.[95]

According to Williston there is a second difference between an integrated and a non-integrated transaction. We have already seen that where both parties to a non-integrated agreement justifiably attach different meanings to a material term there is no contract.[96] But in similar circumstances if the agreement is integrated, there is, according to Williston, a contract in accordance with the meaning of "a reasonably intelligent person acquainted with all operative usages and knowing all the circumstances prior to and contemporaneous with the making of the integration." [97]   In the exceptional case in which this test produces an uncertain or ambiguous result, the rules governing the interpretation of non-integrated agreements are applicable.[98]

Williston expressly recognizes that his standards of interpretation may result in the interpretation of an agreement in such a way as to conform to the intention of neither party.[99] For him the contract acquires a life and meaning of its own, separate and apart from the meanings the parties attach to their agreement. "It is not primarily the intention of the parties which the court is seeking, but the meaning of the words at the time and place when they were used." [1] He is explicit in stating why this should be so. "A facility and certainty of interpretation is obtained, which, though not ideal, is so much greater than is obtainable" by use of a less rigid standard.[2]

---

94. 4 Williston § 605.

95. 4 Williston §§ 608–13, 617, 629, 630.

96. See text accompanying notes 82–92 supra.

97. Restatement, Contracts § 230; 4 Williston § 610A.

98. Restatement, Contracts § 231.

99. 4 Williston §§ 609–07A; Restatement, Contracts § 230, ill. 1.

1. 4 Williston § 613, at 583.

2. Id. § 612, at 577.

The certainty so obtained is "more than an adequate compensation for the slight restriction put upon the power to grant and contract." [3]

Williston's position has deep roots in our legal system. Long ago, Justice Brook thundered from the bench: "The party ought to direct his meaning according to the law, and not the law according to his meaning, for if a man should bend the law to the intent of the party rather than the intent of the party to the law, this would be the way to introduce barbarousness and ignorance and to destroy all learning and diligence." [4]

Bentham, for one, disagreed vehemently, calling such an approach "an enormity, an act of barefaced injustice . . . a practice exactly upon a par (impunity excepted) with forgery." [5] Professor Corbin, although slightly more restrained in language, agrees that in every case one must take into account "the intention and the understanding of each of the two parties." [6] If they coincide there is a contract. If they do not coincide as to material terms there is no contract unless one of the parties is more guilty than the other for the difference in meaning attached. [7] This is the position taken by the Restatement Second. [8] At first glance it might appear that, under this test, in a great many cases no contract results since rarely do the intentions of the parties completely coincide, even as to material terms. However, in determining whether the parties justifiably misunderstood one another, a standard based on a balance between the standard of reasonable expectations and the standard

---

3. Id.

4. Throckmerton v. Tracy, 75 Eng.Rep. 222, 251 (K.B.1554).

5. 5 Bentham, op. cit. supra note 41, at 590.

6. 3 Corbin § 542; Corbin, The Interpretation of Words and the Parol Evidence Rule, 50 Cornell L.Q. 161, 189 (1965).

7. 3 Corbin §§ 538, 539.

8. Restatement, Contracts (2d) § 21A reads as follows:

(1) There is no manifestation of mutual assent to an exchange if the parties attach materially different meanings to their manifestations and

  (a) neither party knows or has reason to know the meaning attached by the other; or

  (b) each party knows or each party has reason to know the meaning attached by the other.

(2) The manifestations of the parties are operative in accordance with the meaning attached to them by one of the parties if

  (a) that party does not know of any different meaning attached by the other, and the other knows the meaning attached by the first party or

  (b) that party has no reason to know of any different meaning attached by the other, and the other has reason to know the meaning attached by the first party.

It is interesting to note that although illustration 2 of § 71 of the Restatement is the same as illustration 5 of § 21A of the Restatement Second, the result reached is different.

of reasonable understanding is used.[9] A contract exists in accord with the understanding, if any, that the promisee reasonably could rely upon, provided the promisor had reason to foresee this understanding. Consequently, in the usual case, despite the presence of a misunderstanding, a contract results on the terms understood by the party who is less at fault for the misunderstanding. This properly takes into account that speech is not only and not primarily the expression of thought, but is used "in order to influence the conduct of others." [10]

§ 48. Rules of Interpretation and Their Relationship to Standards of Interpretation

In addition to the standards of interpretation just discussed there are also rules of interpretation. Here again Williston and Corbin take a different approach dictated primarily by their difference in approach to the question of standards of interpretation.

Williston distinguishes between primary and secondary rules of interpretation. The primary rules as stated in section 235 of the Restatement are set forth in footnote.[11] These primary rules apply to both integrated and non-integrated transactions and "serve merely as guides to achieving a final result, namely, the correct application of the proper standard." [12] The secondary rules set forth in footnote [13]

9. 3 Corbin § 538.

10. Gardiner, The Theory of Speech and Language 19 (1932).

11. The following rules aid the application of the standards stated in §§ 230, 233.

(a) The ordinary meaning of language throughout the country is given to words unless circumstances show that a different meaning is applicable.
(b) Technical terms and words of art are given their technical meaning unless the context or a usage which is applicable indicates a different meaning.
(c) A writing is interpreted as a whole and all writings forming part of the same transaction are interpreted together.
(d) All circumstances accompanying the transaction may be taken into consideration, subject in case of integrations to the qualifications stated in § 230.
(e) If the conduct of the parties subsequent to a manifestation of intention indicates that all the parties placed a particular interpretation upon it, that meaning is adopted if a reasonable person could attach it to the manifestation.

12. Restatement, Contracts § 235, Comment a.

13. Restatement, Contracts § 236 reads as follows:
Where the meaning to be given to an agreement or to acts relating to the formation of an agreement remains uncertain after the application of the standards of interpretation stated in §§ 230, 233, with the aid of the rules stated in § 235, the following rules are applicable:
(a) An interpretation which gives a reasonable, lawful and effective meaning to all manifestations of intention is preferred to an interpretation which leaves a part of such manifestations unreasonable, unlawful or of no effect.

are also applicable to both integrated and non-integrated transactions, but need not be invoked except where the meaning of words or other manifestations of intent remain doubtful after application of the appropriate standard of interpretation, aided by the primary rules of interpretation.[14]

Corbin, of course, does not distinguish between primary and secondary rules; the principal standard of interpretation selected by him, the intention of the parties, does not require the aid of the primary rules.[15] Further, he does not agree that the secondary rules can be applied only in the case of an ambiguity.[16] Corbin makes it clear that rules of interpretation "are to be taken as suggestive working rules only."[17]

What Williston calls the secondary rules of interpretation would appear to have little relevance once it has been determined that the applicable standard of interpretation is a mutual or an individual standard. According to Williston, a mutual or individual standard is applied when there is an ambiguity and the parties testify to their understanding;[18] according to Corbin, it is applied in every case where the parties testify to their understandings.[19] The only relevance these rules of interpretation could have is on the issue of who knows

(b) The principal apparent purpose of the parties is given great weight in determining the meaning to be given to manifestations of intention or to any part thereof.

(c) Where there is an inconsistency between general provisions and specific provisions, the specific provisions ordinarily qualify the meaning of the general provisions.

(d) Where words or other manifestations of intention bear more than one reasonable meaning an interpretation is preferred which operates more strongly against the party from whom they proceed, unless their use by him is prescribed by law.

(e) Where written provisions are inconsistent with printed provisions, an interpretation is preferred which gives effect to the written provisions.

(f) Where a public interest is affected an interpretation is preferred which favors the public.

Corbin's statement of these rules generally corresponds to Williston's. See 3 Corbin § 545–50. Corbin adds some additional rules in § 552.

14. Restatement, Contracts § 236, Comment a. In his text Williston makes it clear that in the case of an integration these secondary rules come into play "only where after the primary rules or principles have been applied, the local meaning of the writing is still uncertain or ambiguous." He adds "the same rules are applicable to informal parol agreements, but, as has been seen, the standard there sought to be applied is slightly different." 4 Williston § 617, at 703–04.

15. See note 6 supra and accompanying text.

16. 3 Corbin § 542.

17. 3 Corbin § 535.

18. 1 Williston § 95. As we have seen, in the case of an integrated writing, an ambiguity exists, according to his test, only after application of the standard of limited usage, aided by the primary rules of interpretation, fails to give the writing one definite meaning.

19. 3 Corbin § 538.

or should know of the ambiguity (Williston) or who knows or should know of the understanding of the other party (Corbin).

§ 49. Are Questions of Interpretation Questions of Fact or Questions of Law?

Williston's rules on this subject may be summarized as follows: Although the meaning of language is really a question of fact, in many instances it has been determined that this question should be treated as a question of law in the sense that the determination should be made by the trial judge. The general rule is that the interpretation of a writing is for the court.[20] Where, however, the meaning of a writing is uncertain or ambiguous [21] and extrinsic [22] evidence is introduced in aid of its interpretation, the question of its meaning should be left to the jury except where, after taking the extrinsic evidence into account, the meaning is so clear that reasonable men could reach only one conclusion, in which event the court should decide the issue as it does when the resolution of any question of fact is equally clear.[23] Where the writing is ambiguous and extrinsic evidence is not introduced, the question is one of law. Even where the contract is oral, if the exact words used by the parties are not in dispute, the court will deal with the matter in the same way as if the contract were written.[24] It would appear that Corbin is generally in accord with these views.[25]

§ 50. The Relationship Between the Parol Evidence Rule and Rules and Standards of Interpretation

Before the parol evidence rule may be invoked, the judge must determine that the parties intended the writing to be final.[26] The question of intent is determined according to the standards and rules of interpretation discussed above.[27] Conversely, the parol evidence rule should have no effect on the question of interpretation—the *meaning* of language. Stated otherwise, before the parol evidence rule can be

---

20. 4 Williston § 616; Kurland v. United Pac. Ins. Co., 251 Cal.App.2d 112, 59 Cal.Rptr. 258 (1967); Gitelson v. Du Pont, 17 N.Y.2d 46, 268 N.Y.S.2d 11, 215 N.E.2d 336 (1966).

21. It is important to recall once again that under Williston's view the word ambiguous has different connotations in the cases of integrated and noninte-grated transactions.

22. The term extrinsic evidence includes all evidence outside of the writing including parol evidence.

23. Hoover, Inc. v. McCullough Indus., Inc., 380 F.2d 798 (5th Cir.1967); Marso v. Mankato Clinic Ltd., 278 Minn. 104, 153 N.W.2d 281 (1967); Root v. Allstate Ins. Co., 272 N.C. 580, 158 S.E.2d 829 (1968).

24. See § 40 supra.

25. 3 Corbin § 554.

26. See § 40 supra.

27. See §§ 47–48 supra.

invoked to exclude evidence, the *meaning* of the writing must be ascertained since one may not determine whether a writing is being contradicted or supplemented until one knows what the writing means.

This should mean that evidence of prior and contemporaneous expressions is always admissible to aid in determining the meaning of the integration, and Corbin so states.[28] Williston is cautiously in accord. Such evidence may be introduced, he grants, but not to prove that the intention of the parties is at variance with the appropriate local meaning of the words.[29] The evidence may be considered only on the question of whether the parties contracted with reference to a local or trade usage or, if this local or trade meaning is ambiguous, on the question of what meaning the parties attached to the words. Even accepting his premise that the true intention of the parties is usually irrelevant, there are two difficulties with Williston's position on the admissibility of this evidence. First, it assumes that the court can successfully ignore the parties' real intention when it is shown by the evidence. Second, it involves a great deal of tension with the exclusionary aspects of his version of the parol evidence rule. If evidence of prior and contemporaneous expressions is not admissible to prove terms supplementary to or at variance with a total integration,[30] but is admissible to show the meaning of the integration, the astute trial lawyer will characterize his evidence on what are really supplementary or contradictory terms as evidence on the true meaning of the contract. Although the function of this evidence is to demonstrate the "meaning of the writing," once it is admitted the court may find it difficult (and unjust) to disregard what may be clear and convincing proof that the writing is not the complete agreement of the parties. Williston's grand structure meticulously separating the parol evidence rule, standards of interpretation, and primary and secondary rules of interpretation seems to collapse into this procedural pitfall.[31]

It is little wonder, then, that many courts that share Williston's concern for the "security of transactions" have retreated even further from the intention of the parties to the almost universally con-

---

28. 3 Corbin §§ 542, 542A, 543, 579; Schuman v. Gordon Inv. Corp., 247 Md. 265, 232 A.2d 256 (1967); Whitebird v. Eagle-Picher Co., 390 F.2d 831 (10th Cir.1968).

29. 4 Williston § 630.

30. See § 40 supra.

31. There are other devices to achieve the same end. "[I]t is a rare set of facts that will forestall, without any exceptional ingenuity, the inclusion in a pleading of at least one cause of action or defense, such as fraud, delivery on condition or . . . [lack] . . . of consideration, which will open the door to the introduction of extrinsic evidence." Fisch, New York Evidence § 64, at 42 (1959).

demned,[32] but generally accepted, "plain meaning rule," holding that if a writing appears clear and unambiguous on its face, its meaning must be determined from the four corners of the instrument without resort to extrinsic evidence of any nature.[33] This approach excludes evidence of trade usage and prior dealings between the parties as well as evidence of surrounding circumstances and prior and contemporaneous expressions. As previously stated the latest legislative statement on the matter, the Uniform Commercial Code, explicitly condemns the plain meaning rule [34] and explicitly allows use of evidence of a course of dealing or course of performance to explain the agreement "unless carefully negated." [35]

§ 51. Some Practical Observations About Parol Evidence and Interpretation

It is obvious from the foregoing that there is no unanimity as to the content of the parol evidence rule or the process called interpretation, and the rules are complex, technical and difficult to apply. It

---

32. 3 Corbin § 542; Grismore, § 97 (1965); McCormick § 219; Thayer, op. cit. supra § 39 n. 2 at ch. X, 9 Wigmore §§ 2461–62; 4 Williston § 629.

33. The "plain meaning" rule was previously discussed in § 46 n. 72 supra. As Corbin points out the fallacy of the rule is that it is not possible to know if a writing is clear and unambiguous without knowing the surrounding circumstances. However, the cases invoking the "plain meaning" rule are very numerous. Some recent examples include: Plymouth Mut. Life Ins. Co. v. Illinois Mid-Continent Life Ins. Co., 378 F.2d 389 (3d Cir.1967); Simpson Timber Co. v. Palmberg Constr. Co., 377 F.2d 380 (9th Cir.1967); Standard Title Ins. Co. v. United Pac. Ins. Co., 364 F.2d 287 (8th Cir.1966); San Joaquin County v. Galletti, 252 Cal. App.2d 840, 61 Cal.Rptr. 62 (1967); Donahue v. Rockford Showcase & Fixture Co., 87 Ill.App.2d 47, 230 N.E.2d 278 (1967); Perper v. Fayed, 247 Md. 639, 234 A.2d 144 (1967); Oxford Commercial Corp. v. Landau, 12 N.Y.2d 362, 239 N.Y.S.2d 865, 190 N.E.2d 230, 13 A.L.R.3d 309 (1963); Cordes v. Prudential Ins. Co., 181 Neb. 794, 150 N.W.2d 905 (1967); Nationwide Mut. Ins. Co. v. Jackson, 10 Ohio App.2d 137, 226 N.E.2d 760 (1967). Whether there is

an "ambiguity" under the "plain meaning" rule is a question of law. St. Paul Mercury Ins. Co. v. Price, 359 F.2d 74 (5th Cir. 1966). An ambiguity exists when the contract considered as a whole is fairly susceptible to different constructions. Lemke v. Larsen Co., 35 Wisc.2d 427, 151 N.W.2d 17 (1967). It does not arise merely because the parties disagree as to the meaning. Homestake-Sapin Partners v. United States, 375 F.2d 507 (1967); cf. In re Estate of Schmith, 19 N.Y.2d 398, 280 N.Y.S.2d 365, 227 N.E.2d 290 (1967). For strong judicial disapproval of the plain meaning rule, see Pacific Gas & Elec. Co. v. G. W. Thomas Drayage & Rigging Co., 69 Cal.2d 33, 69 Cal.Rptr. 561, 442 P.2d 641 (1968); Hamilton v. Wosepka, 255 Iowa 910, 124 N.W.2d 512, 154 N.W.2d 164 (1967); Atlantic N. Airlines v. Schwimmer, 12 N.J. 293, 96 A.2d 652 (1953); see also Hohenstein v. S. M. H. Trading Corp., 382 F.2d 530 (5th Cir.1967); Southern Constr. Co. v. United States, 176 Ct. Cl. 1339, 364 F.2d 439 (1966).

34. U.C.C. § 2–202, Comment 1; see also U.C.C. § 1–205.

35. U.C.C. § 2–202, Comment 2; see § 52 infra.

would, however, be a mistake to suppose that the courts follow any of these rules blindly, literally or consistently. As often as not they choose the standard or the rule that they think will give rise to a just result in the particular case.[36] We have also seen that often under a guise of interpretation a court will actually enforce a rule of "public policy" which is nothing more than an attempt to do justice.[37]

§ 52. Course of Dealing, Course of Performance and Usage

The Uniform Commercial Code has attempted to draw a careful distinction between a "course of dealing", a "course of performance" and a "trade usage" whereas the common law decisions often inartistically meshed the three together under the usual classification of a custom.[38]

A course of dealing is defined in the Code as "a sequence of previous conduct between the parties to a particular transaction which is fairly to be regarded as establishing a common basis of understanding for interpreting their expressions and other conduct." [39] A course of dealing relates to conduct prior to the agreement.[40] A course of performance relates to conduct after the agreement, according to the Code, as "where the contract for sale involves repeated occasions for performance by either party with knowledge of the nature of the performance and opportunity for objection to it by the other, any course of performance accepted or acquiesced in without objection shall be relevant to determine the meaning of the agreement." [41] The Code defines a usage of trade as "any practice or method of deal-

36. See, e. g., Crow v. Monsell, 200 So. 2d 700 (La.App.1967), writ denied 251 La. 226, 203 So.2d 558 (1967).

37. See § 3 supra and § 56 infra.

38. Duesenberg & King, Sales and Bulk Transfers § 4.08(3) [b].

39. U.C.C. § 1–205(1); accord: Sinkwich v. E. F. Drew & Co., 9 A.D.2d 42, 189 N.Y.S.2d 630 (3rd Dep't 1959).

40. U.C.C. § 1–205, Comment 2.

41. U.C.C. § 2–208(1). Under the Restatement of Contracts a course of performance is treated as a primary rule of interpretation: "If the conduct of the parties subsequent to a manifestation of intent indicates that all the parties placed a particular interpretation upon it, that meaning is adopted if a reasonable person could attach it to the manifestation." Restatement, Contracts § 235. Sometimes it has been stated that this type of evidence "is entitled to the greatest weight" or is referred to as "convincing evidence." Reconstruction Fin. Corp. v. Sherwood Distil. Co., 200 F.2d 672 (4th Cir.1952); Martinson v. Brooks Equip. Leasing Inc. 36 Wisc.2d 209, 152 N.W.2d 849 (1967), reh. denied 36 Wis.2d 209, 154 N.W.2d 353 (1968); Department of Revenue v. Jennison-Wright Corp., 393 Ill. 401, 66 N.E.2d 395 (1946). Some courts have held that the parties would be bound by a course of performance even though it did not conform to the contract. H. B. Deal Constr. Co. v. Labor Discount Center Inc., 418 S.W.2d 940 (Mo.1967).

ing having such regularity of observance in a place,[42] vocation or trade as to justify an expectation that it will be observed with respect to the transaction in question." [43]

To be enforceable at early common law a custom had to be "(1) legal, (2) notorious, (3) ancient or immemorial and continuous, (4) reasonable, (5) certain, (6) universal and obligatory." [44] These requisites, however, even as a common law proposition have been watered down so that it would be fair to say that the requirement that they be ancient or immemorial or that they be universal is no longer insisted upon.[45]

Under the Code the usage need not be ancient or immemorial or universal.[46] The requirement of certainty is also eliminated.[47] Reasonableness is also abolished and substituted in its place is the requirement against "unconscionable contracts and clauses." [48]

The other requirements appear to be maintained. The requirement that the custom be notorious is carried forth in the definition of usage in 1–205(2) which, as we have seen, requires "regularity of observance."

---

42. Although the word "place" is used here it seems clear that the Code is limited to usages in a vocation or trade in which both parties are engaged. U.C.C. § 1–205(3). The relevance of "place" is further explained by § 1–205(5) which states "an applicable usage of trade in the place where any part of performance is to occur shall be used in interpreting the agreement as to that part of performance." Cf. Restatement, Contracts § 248, Comment b.

43. U.C.C. § 1–205(2).

44. Levie, Trade Usage and Custom Under the Common Law and the Uniform Commercial Code, 40 N.Y.U.L. Rev. 1101 (1965).

45. Restatement, Contracts § 245, Comment a states: "A particular usage may be more or less widespread. It may prevail throughout a whole district, and if so the district may be a small or a large one—a city or state or a larger geographical division. A usage may prevail among all people in a geographical division or in only a

special trade or among part of the people." It need not have existed for a sufficient length of time to be generally known. See Ulmer v. Farnsworth, 80 Me. 500, 15 A. 65 (1888).

46. § 1–205(2). It is enough that it be "currently observed by the great majority of decent dealers." U.C.C. § 1–205, Comment 5.

47. § 1–205, Comment 9 states: "In cases of a well established line of usage varying from the general rules of this act where the precise amount of variation has not been worked out into a single standard, the party relying on the usage is entitled, in any event, to the minimum variation demonstrated. The whole is not to be disregarded because no particular line of detail has been established. In case a dominant pattern has been fairly evidenced, the party relying on the usage is entitled under this section to go to the trier of the fact on the question of whether such dominant pattern has been incorporated into the agreement."

48. § 1–205, Comment 6.

In one respect the Code seems to distinguish between a trade usage and other usages. If the parties are members of a trade, § 1–205(3) seems to say that they are bound by usage of the trade, unless negated, whether they know of it or should know of it. If the usage is not a trade usage, the parties are not bound by it unless "they are or should be aware" of it. However comment 7 appears to ignore this distinction.

Whether or not a custom has "regularity of observance" and whether the other party was aware or should have been aware of it so "as to justify an expectation that it will be observed with respect to the transaction in question" would appear generally to be questions of fact.[49]

A course of dealing or a custom once established at common law could be used to define the meaning of words or other manifestations of intent or to add to the agreement if "not inconsistent with the agreement or manifestations of intention."[50] Under the Code "a course of dealing between parties and any usage of the trade [may] . . . give particular meaning to, supplement or qualify terms of the agreement."[51]

As we have seen, under the Code, despite the existence of an integration a course of dealing or usage may always be introduced to show the meaning of a term unless the custom has been "carefully negated."[52] So also an additional term based upon a custom may be added since the presumption is that the parties took the custom for granted in contracting.[53] In addition this section of the Code says that a course of dealing or custom may be used to "qualify" the terms of the agreement.[54] It has been suggested that the word "qualify" means "cut down"[55] and one case has indicated that it means "contradict" despite the existence of an integration.[56]

49. § 1–205(2); cf. Restatement, Contracts §§ 247, 248.

50. Restatement, Contracts § 246.

51. U.C.C. § 1–205(3). For a similar result in a non-U.C.C. case, see Willey v. Terry & Wright Inc., 421 S.W.2d 362 (Ky.1967), where the court stated: "We think that the parties by their course of dealing [i. e. course of performance] abrogated the written approval clause. It makes no difference what name we apply to the theory on which we reach this conclusion, whether it be contemporaneous construction, waiver, estoppel, novation, or what have you. The theory simply is that by their course of dealing the parties showed that they did not intend the written approval clause to be strictly observed." Id. at 363.

52. U.C.C. § 2–202, Comment 2.

53. This is contrary to the plain meaning rule under which this evidence can be introduced only if there is an "ambiguity." United States v. Citizens and So. Nat. Bank, 367 F.2d 473 (4th Cir.1966).

54. U.C.C. § 1–205(3).

55. Levie, supra note 92, at 1112.

56. Provident Tradesmens Bank & Trust Co. v. Pemberton, 196 Pa.Super.

A "course of performance" at common law could serve two functions; first, to aid interpretation "if a reasonable man could attach it [that meaning] to the manifestation." [57]   It could also serve to modify the agreement.   Under U.C.C. section 2–208(1) "any course of performance accepted or acquiesced in without objection shall be relevant to determine the meaning of the agreement" [58] and a comment states that "a course of performance is always relevant to determine the meaning of the agreement" [59] and this would appear to be so even if it has been "carefully negated." [60]

However, the better approach is to treat the course of performance as a modification or waiver [61] and subdivision 3 provides "subject to the provisions of the next section on modification [62] and waiver, such course of performance shall be relevant to show a waiver or modification of any term inconsistent with such course of performance." [63]

The Code also sets up relative priorities.   Where all of the terms are not consistent the order of priority is (1) the express terms of the agreement, (2) course of performance, (3) course of dealing and (4) usage of the trade.[64]

It should also be noted that subdivision 6 of § 1–205 provides: "Evidence of relevant usage of trade offered by one party is not admissible unless and until he has given the other party such notice as the court finds sufficient to prevent unfair surprise to the latter." This provision seems to fall somewhere in between the decisions which provide that the usage must be alleged in a pleading [65] and those which grant an adjournment to permit rebutting evidence.[66]

180, 173 A.2d 780 (1961), affirming 24 Pa. D. & C.2d 720 (Philadelphia Mun. Ct.1960).

57. Restatement, Contracts § 235(e).

58. Cf. Restatement, Contracts § 235, Comment h which states: "Under the rule stated in this Clause the meaning of the contract cannot be stretched by the acts of the parties beyond what the language will bear. Such conduct of the parties, however, may be evidence of a subsequent modification of their contract."

59. U.C.C. § 2–208, Comment 2.

60. See § 46 supra.

61. U.C.C. § 2–208, Comment **3.**

62. The next section, U.C.C. § 2–209, is discussed in § 92 infra.

63. When the question is modification or waiver there is no question regarding the applicability of the parol evidence rule because this rule has no applicability to subsequent agreements.

64. U.C.C. §§ 1–205(4) and 2–208(2).

65. Harrison v. Birrell, 58 Or. 410, 115 P. 141 (1911).

66. Clifton Shirting Co. v. Bronne Shirt Co., 213 App.Div. 239, 209 N.Y.S. 709 (1st Dept. 1925).

CHAPTER 4

CONSIDERATION

Analysis

Sec.
53. What is Consideration?
54. Motive and Past Consideration are Not Consideration; Necessity of an Exchange.
55. Adequacy of the Detriment.
56. Unconscionable Inadequacy of Consideration and Unconscionable Contracts.
57. Conditions to Gifts Distinguished from Bargained for Detriment.
58. Of Sham and Nominal Consideration and Cases Where the Promise is Only in Part Induced by the Detriment.
59. Surrender of or Forbearance to Assert an Invalid Claim as Detriment.
60. The Pre-existing Duty Rule: Duties Imposed by Law.
61. The Pre-existing Duty Rule: The Two Party Cases.
62. The Pre-existing Duty Rule: The Three Party Cases.
63. Pre-existing Duty Rule—Agreements to Accept Part Payment as Satisfaction of a Debt: Pinnel's Case and Foakes v. Beer.
64. The Rule of Foakes v. Beer: Minority Views.
65. The Relationship of the Rule of Foakes v. Beer to the Doctrine of Accord and Satisfaction—Of Liquidated and Unliquidated Claims.
66. Consideration in Bilateral Contracts.
67. Mutuality of Obligation: Introduction.
68. The Unilateral Contract: A So-called Exception to the Mutuality Requirement.
69. Voidable and Unenforceable Promises as Consideration.
70. Illusory and Optional Promises.
71. A Conditional Promise May be Sufficient Consideration: Aleatory Promises.
72. Requirement and Output Contracts.
73. Consideration Supplied by Implied Promises.
74. A Void Contract is Not Necessarily a Nullity.
75. One Consideration Will Support Many Promises.
76. All of the Consideration Need Not be Valid.
77. Consideration and the Parol Evidence Rule.

§ 53. What is Consideration?

Apparently no legal system has ever enforced all promises. More primitive systems usually require that an enforceable promise be made pursuant to solemn forms.[1] Remnants of this notion are preserved

---

1. See Hazeltine, The Formal Contract of Early English Law, 10 Colum.L. Rev. 608 (1910), Selected Readings 1; Maine, Ancient Law Ch. IX (5th ed. 1873); 2 Corbin § 240.

in those common law jurisdictions which still give effect to the seal.[2] Many European, Latin-American, African and Asiatic countries which have derived their legal systems from Roman law require that contracts either be made in solemn form or contain the element of causa.[3]

Fundamentally, the idea is that the coercive power of the State will not be employed to impose sanctions on a defaulting promisor unless the promisor has made a commitment which the law deems socially useful[4] or has resorted to a form which indicates he has acted with deliberation.

As a condition to enforceability the common law usually requires that informal promises be made for a consideration.[5] The history of this requirement is tortuous, confused and wrapped in controversy.[6] The doctrine of consideration contains certain oddities which, in the opinion of some, interfere with the needs of modern society. The English Law Revision Committee has recommended its abolition,[7] but Parliament has not followed its counsel. The Pennsylvania legislature has made radical inroads into the doctrine but in other jurisdictions legislatures have usually been content to retain the doctrine or to modify various aspects of it.[8] The Uniform Commercial Code has significantly affected aspects of the doctrine.[9]

Since the doctrine of consideration is an historical phenomenon and therefore in some of its aspects affected by fortuitous circum-

---

2. See ch. 7 infra.

3. See Von Mehren, Civil Law Analogues to Consideration: An Exercise in Comparative Analysis, 72 Harv.L. Rev. 1009 (1959); Lorenzen, Causa and Consideration in the Law of Contracts, 28 Yale L.J. 621 (1919). On formal contracts in civil law systems derived from Roman law, see Schlesinger, The Notary and the Formal Contract in Civil Law, 1941 Report of the New York Law Revision Commission 403.

4. A modern formulation of the causa requirement is that a contract is enforceable if it is directed to the realization of interests worthy of protection in accordance with the principles of the legal system. Ital.C.Civ. art. 1322 (paraphrase).

5. On consideration, see generally, 1 & 1A Corbin §§ 110–239; 1 Williston §§ 99–137A.

6. See Ames, The History of Assumpsit, 2 Harv.L.Rev. 1, 53 (1888), Selected Readings 33; cf. Shatwell, The Doctrine of Consideration in the Modern Law, 1 Sydney L.Rev. 289 (1954).

7. Sixth Interim Report on Statute of Frauds and the Doctrine of Consideration (1937). A more recent study sponsored by the English Law Revision Committee once again recommends abolition and offers a tentative draft of a statute implementing this recommendation. Chloros, The Doctrine of Consideration and the Reform of the Law of Contract, A Comparative Analysis, 17 Int'l & Comp. L.Q. 137 (1968); see also Ashley, Doctrine of Consideration, 26 Harv.L.Rev. 429 (1913) (urging abolition).

8. See §§ 91, 96 infra.

9. See §§ 92–95 infra.

stances, an encompassing definition is perhaps impossible.[10] Nonetheless, an attempt should be made. A learned judge has identified the three elements which must concur before a promise is supported by consideration.[11]

(a) The promisee [12] must suffer legal detriment; [13] that is, do or promise to do what he is not legally obligated to do; or refrain from doing or promise to refrain from doing what he is legally privileged to do.

(b) The detriment must induce the promise. In other words the promisor must have made the promise because he wishes to exchange it at least in part for the detriment to be suffered by the promisee.

(c) The promise must induce the detriment. This means in effect, as we have already seen, that the promisee must know of the offer and intend to accept.[14]

The essence of consideration, then, is legal detriment [15] that has been bargained for and exchanged for the promise. Fundamental to the doctrine is the ideological concept that economic activity and commercial activity in particular are to be encouraged and that this is best done by encouraging trade; that is, exchanges.

It should be observed that the inquiry has been set up in terms of whether a promise is supported by consideration. Of course in a bilateral contract there are two promisors. This gives rise to some complicated problems to be discussed later.[16]

---

10. See the eloquent discussion in 1 Corbin § 109.

11. Cardozo, C.J., in Allegheny College v. Nat. Chautauqua County Bank, 246 N.Y. 369, 159 N.E. 173 (1927).

12. Although, since this is the typical fact pattern, it is common to speak of a detriment to be suffered by the promisee running to the promisor, it is well settled that the detriment may be given by a person other than the promisee and run to a person other than the promisor. Of course this assumes that the promisor so requests. Restatement, Contracts § 75(2); see also § 27 supra at n. 51.

13. The rule is generally stated in terms of legal detriment suffered by the promisee or legal benefit obtained by the promisor. Currie v. Misa, L.R. 10 Ex. 153, 162 (1875); 1 Williston § 102. The result is almost invariably the same. For a possible exception, see §§ 62–63 infra.

14. See §§ 25–26 supra. As pointed out in those sections, at times this requirement is eliminated in a bilateral contract in order to protect the expectations of the offeror.

15. The use of the term detriment in this context is criticised by 1 Corbin §§ 122–123. Its use has been avoided in the Restatement, Contracts (2d). See § 81, Comment b. The criticism of this traditional term by these authorities is based upon the thought that it is unrealistic to speak of detriment in cases involving no economic loss. This criticism has merit, but similar criticism may be directed at legal terms such as "consideration" which frequently differ in meaning from use of the same words by non-lawyers.

16. See §§ 66 et seq. infra.

§ 54. Motive and Past Consideration are Not Consideration: Necessity of an Exchange

If the promisor says to one of his sons, "In consideration of the fact that you are not as wealthy as your brothers, I promise to pay you $500.00 thirty days from today," this promise is not enforceable because the promisor has neither requested nor induced any detriment in exchange.[17] The promisor merely has stated the motive for his gratuitous promise. If the promisor had stated to his son, "In consideration of the fact that you have named your child after me I promise to pay you $500.00 thirty days from today," the promise is equally unenforceable because the detriment (naming the child after the promisor) did not induce the promise.[18] Since the detriment had already been incurred, it cannot be said to have been bargained for in exchange for the promise. Hence the statement is commonly seen that past consideration is not consideration.[19] This logically follows from the idea of consideration as a bargained for exchange. Similarly, a guaranty of payment made after the principal obligation has arisen does not bind the guarantor unless new detriment is incurred by the promisee in exchange for the guaranty.[20]

The idea of "exchange" is central to the law of contracts, as it is to any advanced economic system.[21] Should it, however, set the boundaries of the law of contract? One may question the adequacy of a legal system which refuses to enforce a promise such as this: "In consideration of your forty years of faithful service, you will be paid a pension of $200.00 per month."[22] It is not surprising that some legislatures [23] have turned their attention to promises of this kind which, if seriously made, deserve to be enforced. The requirement of an "exchange" may have seemed indispensable (with few excep-

---

17. Fink v. Cox, 18 Johns. 145 (N.Y. Sup.Ct.1820).

18. Lanfier v. Lanfier, 227 Iowa 258, 288 N.W. 104 (1939) (nor did the promise induce the detriment). If, however, the promisor bargains for the naming of the child, and thereby induces the parent to name the child after the promisor, consideration exists. Schumm v. Berg, 37 Cal.2d 174, 231 P.2d 39, 21 A.L.R.2d 1051 (1951).

19. 1 Williston § 142.

20. Hauswald v. Katz, 216 App.Div. 92, 214 N.Y.S. 705 (1st Dep't 1926); see 1 Williston § 142 n. 11 for additional cases. Cf. McMillan v. Lane Wood & Co., 361 P.2d 487 (Okla.1961) (jury can

determine if guaranty signed after principal obligation has come into being was orally agreed to simultaneously with the principal obligation and therefore supported by consideration).

21. This concept of exchange is discussed in more detail in §§ 57 and 58 infra.

22. Cf. Perreault v. Hall, 94 N.H. 191, 49 A.2d 812 (1946); and see 1 Williston § 130B; Somers and Schwartz, Pension and Welfare Plans: Gratuities or Compensation? 4 Ind. & Lab. Rel.Rev. 77 (1950); Notes, 23 Cornell L.Q. 310 (1938), 44 Geo.L.J. 145 (1955).

23. See § 96 infra.

tions) [24] to eighteenth and nineteenth century lawyers whose understanding of the proper role of contract law was conditioned by the pervasive influence of Adam Smith's theory of economics. Twentieth century lawyers seem less inclined to ideological dogmatism of any school and more inclined to ask whether the community conscience would deem a particular promise worthy of enforcement. Although the exchange requirement still remains central to the law of contracts, lawyer influenced legislation and the development of the doctrine of promissory estoppel [25] dispense with the exchange requirement in a number of instances. These instances will doubtless increase in the future.

§ 55. Adequacy of the Detriment

As a general rule it is settled that any detriment no matter how economically inadequate will support a promise. Courts have believed that it would be an unwarranted interference with freedom of contract if they were to relieve an adult party from a bad bargain.[26] This reluctance to interfere with economic freedom has been carried to its logical conclusion. In Haigh v. Brooks,[27] the defendant for a consideration had executed a document purporting to guarantee payment of £10,000 owed the plaintiffs by a third party. He subsequently promised that if the plaintiffs would return this written document to him he would pay the plaintiffs £10,000. The plaintiffs accepted his offer and surrendered the document. In an action to enforce the subsequent promise, the defendant argued that his promise was not supported by detriment because the writing surrendered to him was legally ineffective at its inception because, among other reasons, it was unstamped and therefore worthless under the existing English law. The premise of his argument was that surrender of a worthless piece of paper did not constitute detriment. In ruling for the plaintiffs the court indicated that the evidence showed that the defendant did bargain for the paper. This being so the court indicated that it was not

---

24. See ch. 5 infra.

25. See ch. 6 infra.

26. See Black Industries, Inc. v. Bush, 110 F.Supp. 801 (D.N.J.1953) ("Even if it were proved that the plaintiff was to have received a far greater profit than the defendants for a much smaller contribution, the defendant would nevertheless be bound by his agreement by the familiar rule that relative values of the consideration in a contract between business men dealing at arm's length without fraud will not

affect the validity of the contract." 110 F.Supp. at 805).

27. 113 Eng.Rep. 119 (K.B.1839); Mullen v. Hawkins, 141 Ind. 363, 40 N.E. 797 (1895) (quitclaim deed from grantor who had no interest in the premises); see also Brooks v. Ball, 18 Johns. 337 (N.Y.Sup.Ct.1820). Compare, however, the situation where a recording act requires "valuable consideration." Hood v. Webster, 271 N. Y. 57, 2 N.E.2d 43, 107 A.L.R. 497 (1936).

the court's function to concern itself with the adequacy or inadequacy of the price paid or promised for it.[28] This landmark case should be compared with another well-known case, Newman & Snell's State Bank v. Hunter,[29] in which a widow had promised plaintiff to pay the debt of her deceased husband whose estate was insolvent. In exchange the bank returned the husband's note to the widow. The court, ruling in favor of the widow, indicated that surrender of a worthless note did not constitute consideration. If the court meant that the surrender of the note was not legal detriment, the case is in radical opposition to the weight of authority.[30] However, the case might be consistent with basic concepts of contract law if it is based on the ground that economic inadequacy may constitute some circumstantial evidence of fraud, duress, over-reaching, undue influence or mistake.[31] Later in this chapter, the question of the good faith and reasonableness surrounding plaintiff's surrender of its claim against the husband's estate will be considered.[32] In the final analysis, almost without exception, the surrender of any legal right, privilege or immunity constitutes legal detriment.[33]

There is one kind of transaction in which the court will evaluate the economic adequacy of consideration. This involves an exchange, or promises to exchange a specific amount of money or fungible goods for the same or lesser amount of money or goods at the same time and place.[34] The reasoning behind this exception is that in such a

28. See 1 Corbin § 132 which also points out that since the writing in fact created no enforceable duty its surrender would not effect a change in legal relations other than a transfer of the paper itself and that if the defendant had bargained for a discharge of the duty supposed to be created by the document and the plaintiff so understood or should reasonably have so understood, the plaintiff could not recover because although there was a detriment that was not the detriment bargained for by the defendant. With the facts in this posture the result may also be explained by saying that the defendant's promise was conditioned upon the existence of an obligation and that since the parties were mistaken as to this underlying assumption their agreement is voidable for mistake. It should be noted, however, that in the same section Corbin states: "However as a matter of fact a promisor bargains for the acts he

describes rather than for a change in the legal relations they may produce."

29. 243 Mich. 331, 220 N.W. 665, 59 A. L.R. 311 (1928).

30. See criticism of the case in 1 Corbin § 127 n. 83.

31. Restatement, Contracts (2d) § 81, Comment e. Another possible explanation is that plaintiff failed to sustain its burden of proof that the desire to secure the note motivated the promisor. Cf. Restatement, Contracts (2d) § 81, ill. 6. This explanation would appear to contradict Corbin's statement that a party presumptively bargains for the act he describes. See note 28 supra.

32. See § 59 infra.

33. Hamer v. Sidway, 124 N.Y. 538, 27 N.E. 256, 12 L.R.A. 463 (1891).

34. Restatement, Contracts § 76(c). The Restatement, Contracts (2d) omits

case the court takes judicial notice of the value of the things exchanged and cannot indulge in the supposed normal presumption of equivalence between the detriment and the promise.[35]　(This exception would not apply to an exchange involving foreign currency or a rare coin since these are generally dealt with in the market place as commodities).[36]　Unthinking lawyers have sometimes run afoul of this rule by drafting such meaningless clauses as "in consideration of $1.00 by each to the other paid."[37]　To be distinguished are cases in which money is loaned and to be repaid with interest at a later date. Also to be distinguished are cases in which a sum is exchanged for the promise to return a larger sum if a contingent event occurs.　A party released from a mental institution solicited $50 from a friend for the purpose of travelling to Alaska to recover a gold mine.　He promised that if he were to be successful he would repay $10,000. It was held that since the loan was repayable only on the happening of a contingency there was sufficient consideration for this promise to pay two hundred times the amount received.[38]

Economic inadequacy, then, except in one unusual situation, does not prevent any bargained for detriment from constituting consideration.　On the other hand, economic inadequacy may constitute some circumstantial evidence of fraud, duress, over-reaching, undue influence, mistake[39] or that the detriment was not in fact bargained for.[40]　Relief from this harshly individualistic principle under the doctrine of unconscionability will be considered in the following section.

§ 56.　Unconscionable Inadequacy of Consideration and Unconscionable Contracts

In the preceding section we saw the rule that adequacy of consideration is ordinarily not important.　However there are a number of older cases which refused to enforce a contract when there was un-

---

this exception (see Reporter's Note to § 76) on the ground that an agreement of this kind is highly unlikely to be made, citing Whittier, The Restatement of Contracts and Consideration, 18 Calif.L.Rev. 611, 623 (1930).　But see Robertson v. Garvan, 270 F. 643 (S.D.N.Y.1920); text at note 37 infra.

35.　American University v. Todd, 1 A. 2d 595 (Del.Super.1938); see 1 Corbin § 129; 1 Williston § 115.

36.　1 Corbin § 129.

37.　Robertson v. Garvan, 270 F. 643 (S.D.N.Y.1920); 1 Williston § 115. Of

course, in such cases there may in addition be no bargain since the consideration is likely to be sham or nominal.　See § 58 infra.

38.　Embola v. Tuppela, 127 Wash. 285, 220 P. 789 (1923).　The case also raised problems with respect to usury and capacity which are discussed in other chapters.

39.　See n. 28 supra.

40.　See § 57 infra and 1 Williston § 112.

conscionable inadequacy of consideration.[41]   Although there are modern cases which pay lip service to the concept, it has not generally been used as the basis of decision.[42]

Section 2–302 of the Uniform Commercial Code [43] reads as follows:

> (1) If the court as a matter of law finds the contract or any clause of the contract to have been unconscionable at the time it was made the court may refuse to enforce the contract, or it may enforce the remainder of the contract without the unconscionable clause, or it may so limit the application of any unconscionable clause as to avoid any unconscionable result.

> (2) When it is claimed or appears to the court that the contract or any clause thereof may be unconscionable the parties shall be afforded a reasonable opportunity to present evidence as to its commercial setting, purpose and effect to aid the court in making the determination.

The effect of the Code upon the doctrine of unconscionable inadequacy is not yet clear.[44]   It is clear, however, that the Code section is designed to govern unconscionability of any kind and not merely unconscionable inadequacy of consideration.   The history of the law preceding the enactment of the Code is enlightening.   Courts of equity generally launched direct frontal attacks on contracts found to be unconscionable by refusing to give an equitable remedy.[45]   However, the equity court ordinarily did not take away the right to have the contract enforced at law but merely denied an equitable remedy.[46]

---

41. 1 Page, The Law of Contracts §§ 635, 636 (2d ed. 1920).   These cases can be found in both the law and equity courts.   However in the equity cases courts as a rule have not invalidated the agreement but simply have ruled that an equitable remedy is unavailable.

42. See, for example, Olson v. Rasmussen, 304 Mich. 639, 8 N.W.2d 668 (1943); Mandel v. Liebman, 303 N.Y. 88, 100 N.E.2d 149 (1951).   Courts of equity, however, have continued to use this concept to deny equitable remedies.   Restatement, Contracts § 367.

43. There are other statutes using the term unconscionable.   E. g., N.Y.Exec. Law § 63(12).

44. Compare American Home Imp., Inc. v. MacIver, 105 N.H. 435, 201 A.2d 886, 14 A.L.R.3d 324 (1964); Central Budget Corp. v. Sanchez, 53 Misc.2d 620, 279 N.Y.S.2d 391 (Civ.Ct.N.Y.1967) and cases cited therein with McNussen v. Graybeal, 146 Mont. 173, 405 P.2d 447 (1965).

45. Jackson v. Copeland, 217 Ga. 420, 122 S.E.2d 573 (1961).   This is not to say that at times equity did not resort to indirection.   See, for example, Cox v. Burgess, 139 Ky. 699, 96 S.W. 577 (1906).

46. Note, 63 Yale L.J. 560 (1954); West Ky. Coal Co. v. Nourse, 320 S.W.2d 311 (Ky.1959).

The law courts on the other hand did not directly condemn a contract as unconscionable but resorted to imaginative flanking devices to defeat the contract.[47] The law courts instead searched for and found (even though not present under ordinary rules) failure of consideration,[48] lack of consideration,[49] lack of mutual assent,[50] duress or fraud,[51] inadequacy of pleading,[52] lack of integration in a written contract,[53] or a strained interpretation after finding ambiguity where lit-

47. See Note, 45 Iowa L.Rev. 843 (1960).

48. See Laitner Plumbing & Heating Co. v. McThomas, 61 S.W.2d 270, 272 (Kansas City Mo.Ct.App.1933), in which the court said the seller of refrigeration equipment which broke down several times a month would not be permitted to recover the price of the equipment, not because a disclaimer of warranties was ineffective, but because the equipment was found to have "no value other than the material of which it was composed."

49. Faced with a contract which required that a borrower pay the lender, a bank president, $100 monthly so long as the borrower remain in business in addition to 8% interest, an Indiana court was able to discard the unconscionable provision by finding that the $5000 loan was consideration for the interest and that there was no consideration for the promise to pay the $100 monthly. Stiefler v. McCullough, 97 Ind.App. 123, 174 N.E. 823 (1931).

50. We have previously seen the rule that in the absence of fraud one who does not choose to read a contract before signing it is bound by the contract. See § 25 supra; Moreira Constr. Co., Inc. v. Moretrench Corp., 97 N.J.Super. 391, 235 A.2d 211 (1967). We have also seen that this rule has been circumvented at times by a finding that there was no mutual consent to a contract or to the terms of a contract. See §§ 25, 56 supra. This finding has been made most often in contracts of adhesion. See § 3 supra. It has also been applied extensively to exculpatory clauses. Joseph v. Sears Roebuck & Co., 224 S.C. 105, 77 S.E.2d 583, 40 A.L.R.2d 742 (1953); Lachs v.

Fidelity & Cas. Co., 306 N.Y. 357, 118 N.E.2d 555 (1954); Steven v. Fidelity & Cas. Co., 58 Cal.2d 862, 27 Cal.Rptr. 172, 377 P.2d 284 (1962). At times the same result is obtained through a process of interpretation, Hartol Products v. Prudential Ins. Co. of America, 290 N.Y. 44, 47 N.E.2d 687, 690 (1943), motion denied 290 N.Y. 744, 49 N.E.2d 1010 and in rejecting fine print. Gerhardt v. Continental Ins. Cos., 48 N.J. 291, 225 A.2d 328 (1966). At times the courts have read the exculpatory clause out of the contract expressly as a matter of public policy. Henningsen v. Bloomfield Motors, 32 N.J. 358, 161 A.2d 69, 75 A.L.R.2d 1 (1960). The same problem arises with respect to contractual exemption from tort liability. See, for example, Smith v. Kennedy, 43 Ala.App. 554, 195 So.2d 820 (1966), cert. den. 280 Ala. 718, 195 So.2d 829 (Ala.1966), 19 Ala.L.Rev. 484 (1967).
See U.C.C. § 2–719(3) which now obviates a finding of no mutual assent in some personal injury situations.

51. In McCoy v. Gas Engine & Power Co., 135 App.Div. 771, 119 N.Y.S. 864 (1909), rearg. denied 136 App.Div. 922, 120 N.Y.S. 1133, the Appellate Division had to assume that a legal fraud had been perpetrated because of a lawyer's unexplained $153,000 contingent fee, due to the lack of a doctrine of unconscionability to which to turn.

52. See Davis Motors, Dodge and Plymouth Co. v. Avett, 294 S.W.2d 882 (Tex.Civ.App.1956).

53. In V. Valente, Inc. v. Mascitti, 163 Misc. 287, 295 N.Y.S. 330, 335 (Rochester City Ct.1937), a buyer of a shortwave radio who was told by the plaintiff's salesman that it "could get Rome easily," was not compelled to

tle or no ambiguity existed.[54]

The Code seems to adopt the equity approach. Comment 1 states "This section is intended to make it possible for the courts to police explicitly against the contracts or clauses which they find to be unconscionable." The Code does not define unconscionability[55] and simply states "The basic test is whether, in the light of the general commercial background and the commercial needs of the particular trade or case, the clauses involved are so one-sided as to be unconscionable under the circumstances existing at the time of the making of the contract."[56]

Although a comment to the Code states that "The principle is one of the prevention of oppression and unfair surprise and not of disturbance of allocation of risks because of superior bargaining power,"[57] it is nevertheless clear that unequal bargaining power is an important element of unconscionability.[58] However the Code comment appears to say that superior bargaining power is of itself insufficient[59] and that there must be in addition, for example, a lack of a meaningful choice as in the case of an industry wide form contract that is offered

pay for the radio despite the lack of any warranty as to the radio's capabilities in the written contract which generally would be considered integrated.

54. See Patterson, The Delivery of a Life Insurance Policy, 33 Harv.L.Rev. 198, 222 (1919–1920), which indicates prime examples of the way language in insurance contracts is occasionally strained "out of its meaning." Such interpretations are evident in the holdings that a stipulation which requires the policy's delivery to the applicant before the policy is to be operative, is satisfied merely by a delivery to the insurer's local agent or by a mailing. The rule of interpretation to the effect that language in contracts placing one party at the mercy of the other is not favored by the courts, Tibbetts Contracting Corp. v. O & E Contracting Co., 15 N.Y.2d 324, 258 N.Y.S.2d 400, 206 N.E.2d 340 (1965), can be used to reach the same result.

55. The term "unconscionable" does not have a fixed content. It is "a general term encompassing a wide variety of factual situations." 45 Iowa L.Rev. 846 (1960). It has been suggested that

an unconscionable contract is one "such as no man in his senses and not under delusion would make on the one hand, and no honest or fair man would accept, on the other." Greer v. Tweed, 13 Abb.Pr.,N.S., 427, 429 (N.Y. 1872). Compare 1 Corbin § 128.

56. § 2–302, Comment 1.

57. § 2–302, Comment 1. But see 79 Harv.L.Rev. 1299 (1966).

58. See the cases cited in n. 61 infra and National Packing Co. v. NLRB, 377 F.2d 800 (10th Cir. 1967).

59. The Supreme Court of New Jersey, however, continuing its pioneering role in the area of unconscionability has clearly indicated that the inequality of bargaining power existing between real estate brokers and the ordinary seller of residential property is a sufficient basis for striking down any agreement requiring payment of a broker's commission when a sale is unconsummated because of the purchaser's default. Ellsworth Dobbs, Inc. v. Johnson, 50 N.J. 528, 236 A.2d 843 (1967).

on a take it or leave it basis [60] or a situation where freedom of contract is being exploited by a stronger party who has control of the negotiations due to the weaker party's ignorance, feebleness, unsophistication as to interest rates and similar business concepts or general naivete.[61]

However it would appear to be equally clear that unconscionability may exist even where the parties are on "about equal footing" and even where the oppressor is inexperienced compared to the oppressed.[62]

A question which still remains unanswered is whether a court may, in addition to not enforcing the contract or eliminating an unconscionable provision, rewrite the contract for the parties. Although the original draft did permit the court to make substitutions, this was eliminated from the final draft.[63] However, at least one case has assumed that the court could make modifications.[64]

Section 2–302 should be considered in conjunction with the obligation of good faith imposed at several places in the Code. For example § 1–203 of the Code provides that "Every contract or duty within this Act imposes an obligation of good faith in its performance or

---

60. See, for example, Campbell Soup Co. v. Wentz, 172 F.2d 80 (3d Cir. 1948).

61. In several of the few cases decided under the Code section, just such unsophisticated buyers have been protected. See Williams v. Walker-Thomas Furniture Co., 121 U.S.App. D.C. 315, 350 F.2d 445, 18 A.L.R.3d 1297 (1965), 51 Cornell L.Q. 768 (1966), in which the Court of Appeals for the District of Columbia gave protection to a consumer who had entered into an extremely harsh installment sales contract with a furniture company. The contract had a tie-in clause which the company hoped would permit it to repossess all items purchased over a number of years on default in payment of the price of any one of them.

See also American Home Imp., Inc. v. MacIver, 105 N.H. 435, 201 A.2d 886, 14 A.L.R.3d 324 (1964), in which the court was prompted, by an installment contract which required that over $2500 be paid for $1000 worth of goods, to require that consumers be told of the financing terms.

In Frostifresh Corp. v. Reynoso, 52 Misc.2d 26, 274 N.Y.S.2d 757, (Nassau County Dist. Ct.1966) rev'd in part, 54 Misc.2d 119, 281 N.Y.S.2d 964 (App. Term 2d Dep't 1967), a poor Spanish speaking person was persuaded into promising to pay $1145 for a $348 appliance.

See also State by Lefkowitz v. ITM, Inc., 52 Misc.2d 39, 275 N.Y.S.2d 303 (Sup.Ct.1966), in which the defendant-company, which received up to $658 for $80 broilers by selling them on time, was warned to tell consumers of the contract terms "in language the least educated person can understand."

Compare Lundstrom v. Radio Corp. of America, 17 Utah 2d 114, 405 P.2d 339, 14 A.L.R.3d 1058 (1965).

62. Miller v. Coffeen, 365 Mo. 204, 280 S.W.2d 100 (1955); see also Pope Mfg. Co. v. Gormully, 144 U.S. 224, 12 S.Ct. 632, 36 L.Ed. 414 (1892).

63. 63 Yale L.J. 560 (1953).

64. Frostifresh Corp. v. Reynoso, n. 61 supra.

enforcement." [65] Despite the fact that § 1–203 does not relate to the formation of a contract it has been suggested that good faith should be considered in determining unconscionability.[66]

§ 57. Conditions to Gifts Distinguished from Bargained for Detriment

If A gratuitously says to B, "If it rains tomorrow I promise to pay you $10.00," even if it rains B may not enforce the promise. A has merely made an unenforceable conditional promise to make a gift.[67]

In a well known case the defendant wrote to "Dear Sister Antillico," his sister-in-law, promising her a place to raise her family "If you will come down and see me." [68] In response to the promise she moved to the defendant's land incurring certain losses and expenses. The court held that the defendant's promise was a promise to make a gift and that her expenses arising from the move were merely necessary conditions to acceptance of the gift.[69] The defendant did not appear to be bargaining for the plaintiff's presence on his plantation; rather it appeared he wished to help her out of a difficult situation.

A similar problem may arise even in a business context. In Bard v. Kent [70] the promisor gave the promisee an "option" to renew a lease. She suggested before the "option" was given that the promisee retain an architect to check figures on the proposed improvements on the premises. This was done after the "option" was given. The court

---

65. § 1–201(19) defines good faith as "honesty in fact in the conduct or transaction concerned." In the case of a merchant it "means honesty in fact and the observance of reasonable commercial standards of fair dealing in the trade." § 2–103(1) (b).

66. Llewellyn, The Common Law Tradition 369 (1960); cf. 1955 N.Y.Law Rev.Comm'n 658; see Standard Oil Co. of Texas v. Lopeno Gas Co., 240 F.2d 504 (5th Cir. 1957) and Flash v. Powers, 99 N.Y.S.2d 765 (Sup.Ct.1950), which in attempting to define unconscionability have dwelled upon the element of lack of good faith.

67. A gift ordinarily is ineffective until there has been delivery of the subject matter. See Brown, Personal Property 83–225 (2d ed. 1955).

68. Kirksey v. Kirksey, 8 Ala. 131 (1845). Accord, In re Baer's Estate, 196 Misc. 979, 92 N.Y.S.2d 359 (Sur. Ct.1949). Compare Maughs v. Porter, 157 Va. 415, 161 S.E. 242 (1931) (prize offered to anyone who would attend auction; attendance is sufficient detriment and was bargained for, and Edwards v. Skyways, Ltd. (1964), 1 WLR 349, 80 L.Q.Rev. 316 (1964) where the term "ex gratia" in a contract was held not to mean a voluntary gift but "without admission of liability"; Bredemann v. Vaughan Mfg. Co., 40 Ill. App.2d 232, 188 N.E.2d 746 (1963), 13 De Paul L.Rev. 158 (1964).

69. For a discussion of the doctrine of promissory estoppel and its application to cases of this kind, see ch. 6 infra.

70. 19 Cal.2d 449, 122 P.2d 8 (1942).

sustained the finding of fact made in the trial court that engaging the architect did not constitute consideration for the "option" so as to make it irrevocable since it had not been bargained for in exchange for the promise.[71]

Williston suggests that an aid to making the distinction between bargained for detriment and detriment which is incurred merely as a necessary precondition to obtaining a gift is whether the happening of the contingency would be a benefit to the promisor.[72] For example, if in the case above involving "Dear Sister Antillico" the defendant had wanted his sister-in-law to come to his home as a housekeeper, the result would doubtless have been different.[73] In other words, selfish benefit to the promisor is an indication of a contractual state of mind, whereas if the benefit is merely the pleasure of altruism a gift-making state of mind is usually present. This test, however, is not conclusive. In another well known case a promise was made by an uncle to his nephew to pay $5000 if the nephew refrained from "drinking, using tobacco," etc., until he was twenty-one. The nephew fulfilled his uncle's requirements and the court held that there was sufficient evidence to sustain the lower court's finding that there was a contract.[74] Although no economic benefit had been received by the uncle, there was evidence that he was bargaining for his nephew to conduct himself in accordance with his wishes.

71. Accord, National Co. v. Navarro, 149 So.2d 648 (La.1963); Loeb v. Johnson, 142 So.2d 518 (La.1962). The two cases are noted in 23 La.L.Rev. 795 (1963); Lexington Housing Auth. v. Continental Cas. Co., 210 F.Supp. 732 (W.D.Tenn.1962). In addition to the consideration problem in Bard v. Kent the question arises whether the offeror manifested an intention to make the offer irrevocable.

72. 1 Williston § 112. In the same section it is pointed out that although the adequacy of the detriment is not important in itself, it is relevant in determining whether the promisor manifests a gift making state of mind or a bargaining state of mind since it is less likely that a promisor will bargain for a small detriment. However a small detriment is invariably sustained in option contracts and in continuing guarantees. Davis v. Wells, Fargo Express & Co., 104 U.S. 159, 26 L.Ed. 686 (1881); Chrisman v. Southern Cal. Edison Co., 83 Cal.App.2d 249, 256 P. 618 (1927); Brooks v. LeGrand, 435 P.2d 142 (Okl.1967). While most of the cases appear to treat the option and guarantee situations as involving a true exchange, the Restatement Second points out that gross disproportion between the alleged consideration and the value of the option may indicate that the alleged consideration was not in fact bargained for but was a merely nominal consideration. Restatement, Contracts (2d) § 89B, Comment b. On the question of nominal consideration see § 58 infra.

73. Davis v. Jacoby, 1 Cal.2d 370, 34 P.2d 1026 (1934); Brackenbury v. Hodgkin, 116 Me. 399, 102 A. 106 (1917).

74. Hamer v. Sidway, 124 N.Y. 538, 27 N.E. 256 (1891); see also Schumm v. Berg, 37 Cal.2d 174, 231 P.2d 39, 21 A.L.R.2d 1051 (1951) (naming of child after actor Wallace Beery).

Ultimately this question is nothing more nor less than a question of interpretation. The rules relating to subjective and objective intention and the dividing line between questions of law and fact again become relevant.[75]

§ 58. Of Sham and Nominal Consideration and Cases Where the Promise is Only in Part Induced by the Detriment

As we have seen the law generally will not concern itself with the adequacy of consideration.[76] Consequently, parties to a written agreement frequently recite that the agreement is made in consideration of $1.00 or some other small sum. A recital of this kind raises several problems.[77]

Frequently, the recited sum has not in fact been paid; the recital is a mere sham. The vast majority of cases have held that it may be shown that the consideration has not been paid and that no other consideration has been given.[78] This result does not ordinarily contravene the parol evidence rule since this rule does not prohibit the contradiction of a recital of fact.[79] There is a minority view which reaches the opposite result either upon the theory that the parties are estopped from contradicting their writing [80] or upon the theory

75. 1 Williston § 112; 1 Corbin § 151. See ch. 3 and § 22 supra.

76. See § 55 supra.

77. The word recital here is not used in its technical sense. In its technical sense a recital in a contract is usually prefixed by the word "Whereas". They are not usually drafted as promises or conditions. It appears to be generally agreed that a recital of fact is prima facie evidence of that fact, subject, however, to refutation. Eastern Plank Road Co. v. Vaughn, 14 N. Y. 546 (1856). Oregon has a statute which makes the truth of recitals in a written instrument conclusive presumptions between the parties thereto. As to the relationship of recitals to the body of the instrument the rule usually followed is the one stated by Lord Esher in Ex Parte Dawes, 17 Q. B.D. 275, 286 (1886) wherein he stated: "If the recitals are clear and the operative part is ambiguous, the recitals govern the construction. If the recitals are ambiguous, and the operative part is clear, the operative part must prevail. If both the recitals and

the operative part are clear, but they are inconsistent with each other, the operative part is to be preferred." See Note, 41 Cornell L.Q. 126 (1955) and Note, 35 Colum.L.Rev. 565 (1935).

78. Bard v. Kent, 19 Cal.2d 449, 122 P. 2d 8, 139 A.L.R. 1032 (1942); Komp v. Raymond, 175 N.Y. 102, 67 N.E. 113 (1903).

79. 1 Williston, § 115B. We have already discussed one aspect of the parol evidence rule as it relates to consideration in § 42 supra. Other aspects of this relationship are discussed in § 77 infra.

80. Real Estate Co. v. Rudolph, 301 Pa. 502, 153 A. 438 (1930). The Restatement, Contracts (2d) takes the position that promises to keep an offer firm or promises of guaranty are binding if they are in writing, and contain a "recital of purported consideration" whether or not the consideration has been paid. It should be noted that in the case of a firm offer the Restatement also requires that the offer "proposes an exchange on fair

that the recital gives rise to an implied promise to pay.[81]

Another kind of problem is presented when a small sum is promised or has actually been paid. It is important to remember in this context that the detriment to be surrendered by the promisee need not be the sole or even the predominant inducement. But it must be enough of an inducement so that it is in fact bargained for.[82] Williston gives this illustration. A is moved by friendship to sell his horse to B for $100.00. If there is an actual agreement to exchange the horse for the money a contract is formed even though A's primary motive in entering into the transaction was friendship.[83] The same would doubtless be true if A agreed, for the same motives, to sell the horse for $1.00.

A slightly different problem arises where the parties, having learned that a gratuitous promise is unenforceable, attempt to make the promise of the promisor enforceable by agreeing that a valuable promise shall be given in exchange for a small detriment. There is in fact no bargain but an attempt to make a gratuitous promise enforceable by cloaking it with the form of a bargain. It can be argued, especially in jurisdictions which have emasculated the seal, that some such mechanism should be available to achieve this result.[84] The Restatement Second and a number of other authorities take the view that the use of nominal consideration, that is, consideration in name but not in fact, as in the fact pattern supposed, will be unsuccessful.[85] There are, however, authorities to the contrary.[86]

terms within a reasonable time." §§ 89B, 89C. It should also be observed that these sections are placed in topic 2 of Chapter 4 entitled "Contracts Without Consideration". Statutes performing a similar function are discussed in § 95 infra.

81. Jones v. Smith, 206 Ga. 162, 56 S. E.2d 462 (1949).

82. 1 Corbin § 118; 1 Williston § 111; see § 58 supra.

83. 1 Williston § 111.

84. See generally Von Mehren, Civil-Law Analogues to Consideration: An Exercise in Comparative Analysis, 72 Harv.L.Rev. 1009 (1959).

85. Fischer v. Union Trust Co., 138 Mich. 612, 101 N.W. 852 (1904); Lawhead v. Booth, 115 W.Va. 490, 177 S.E. 283 (1934); Grismore § 60; Simpson § 53; Restatement, Contracts (2d) § 75, ill. 5; see Note, Restatement of Contracts (Second)—A Rejection of Nominal Consideration?, 1 Valparaiso U. L.Rev. 102 (1966). It will be recalled, however, that in a business context the second Restatement regards nominal and even sham consideration as sufficient to support an option or a continuing guarantee. See n. 80 supra.

86. The first Restatement lent support to such use (Restatement, Contracts § 84(a), ill. 1); as did the influential writings of Holmes. See Holmes, The Common Law 293–95 (1881).

§ 59. Surrender of or Forbearance to Assert an Invalid Claim as Detriment

A promise to surrender a valid claim ordinarily constitutes detriment and, if bargained for, constitutes consideration. There is no unanimity, however, with respect to the surrender of an invalid claim. Everyone has a duty not to assert an invalid claim, but if a party believes that he has a claim, should his surrender of the invalid claim still be considered non-detrimental? [87] The earliest view, still preserved in some jurisdictions, was that the surrender of an invalid claim cannot constitute detriment because a person has no right to assert an unfounded claim.[88] A more modern view, however, is that the surrender of an invalid claim may serve as consideration if the claimant has asserted it in good faith and a reasonable man could believe that the claim is well founded.[89] Still other courts have held that the only requirement is good faith.[90] The new Restatement takes the position that either good faith or objective uncertainty as to the validity of the claim is sufficient.[91] Probably, the direction of the law is toward a rule in which the surrender of a claim constitutes detriment provided the claim is neither patently ridiculous nor corruptly asserted.

The same rules apply to forbearance to assert a claim [92] although some of the earlier decisions had held that while a promise to forbear could constitute consideration, forbearance to prosecute a claim could not.[93] In short, there was an erroneous belief that there could be no unilateral contract of forbearance to prosecute a claim.

---

87. Indeed, a contract entered into and performed under threat of a claim known to be unfounded may be set aside on the ground of duress and restitution awarded to the aggrieved party. See Wise v. Midtown Motors, Inc., 231 Minn. 46, 42 N.W.2d 404, 20 A.L.R.2d 735 (1950); Chandler v. Sanger, 114 Mass. 364 (1874); Dawson, Duress Through Civil Litigation, 45 Mich.L.Rev. 571 and 679 (1947); Note, 6 Ark.L.Rev. 472 (1952); Restatement, Restitution § 71 (1937).

88. Renney v. Kimberley, 211 Ga. 396, 86 S.E.2d 217 (1955); but see Holsomback v. Caldwell, 218 Ga. 393, 128 S.E.2d 47 (1962) (good faith test).

89. Fiege v. Boehm, 210 Md. 352, 123 A.2d 316 (1956); Melotte v. Tucci, 319 Mass. 490, 66 N.E.2d 357 (1946); Re-

statement, Contracts § 76(b); 1 Williston § 125.

90. Byrne v. Padden, 248 N.Y. 243, 162 N.E. 20 (1928); see also cases cited in 1 Corbin § 140 n. 79. This requirement of good faith is often modified by insisting that the invalidity of the claim not be obvious; i.e., "unless the claim is so obviously unfounded that the assertion of good faith would affront the intelligence of the ordinary and reasonable layman." Hall v. Fuller, 352 S.W.2d 559, 562 (Ky.1961), 51 Ky.L.J. 174 (1962).

91. Restatement, Contracts (2d) § 76B.

92. In re All Star Feature Corp., 232 F. 1004 (S.D.N.Y.1916).

93. Shaw v. Philbrick, 129 Me. 259, 151 A. 423, 74 A.L.R. 290 (1930).

It is interesting to observe that the cases involving "worthless pieces of paper" and "invalid claims" are closely related.[94] Should the rules relating to invalid claims be applied where the paper is worthless because it involves an invalid claim? The Restatement, Second,[95] and Professor Corbin [96] indicate that these two kinds of cases should be kept distinct on the grounds that in one case the promisor is bargaining for the paper itself while in the other the promisor is bargaining for the discharge of a duty. If the facts so indicate, these authorities are sound in their analyses. It is doubtful, however, whether the parties ordinarily are conscious of a distinction between the paper itself and the legal obligations embodied in or evidenced by the paper.[97] Rather, it is believed that the parties are usually concerned with the substance of the claim represented by the paper. It is submitted, therefore, that these cases should be tested by the tests of good faith and reasonableness. Indeed, in the case of Haigh v. Brooks,[98] the leading "worthless paper" case, the court took pains to indicate that there was sufficient doubt at the time of contracting as to the validity of the guaranty embodied in the piece of paper subsequently found to be worthless. Consequently, the decision in Newman & Snell's State Bank v. Hunter, critically discussed above, can be supported if the unreported facts indicated that the plaintiff did not act in good faith in the transaction. In other words, it may be desirable to equate the situation in which one bargains for the discharge of a legally invalid claim represented by a writing with the situation in which the claim, although legally valid, is worthless because it is asserted against an insolvent estate.[99]

94. See § 55 supra.

95. § 81, ill. 2.

96. 1 Corbin § 127 n. 76, discussing Neikirk v. Williams, 81 W.Va. 558, 94 S. E. 947 (1918).

97. However one must clearly distinguish cases wherein the parties consciously considered the question of invalidity or worthlessness and then made an adjustment from cases where the parties did not consciously consider the question of invalidity. For example, if a disputed paternity action is settled it is quite clear that the parties have taken into account and compromised the question of paternity. However if it turned out that the girl was not pregnant, one should ascertain the intention of the parties to determine if this was a matter concluded by the compromise. Cf. St. Regis Paper Co. v. Hill, 202 So.2d 201 (Fla.1967).

98. Discussed at § 55 supra.

99. See § 55 supra.
When is a claim valid and when is it invalid? Some cases have held that a claim is invalid only if it is void but not if it is voidable. "This distinction has long been regarded as invalid." 1 Corbin, § 140. Is a claim which is unenforceable because of the Statute of Frauds or the statute of limitations to be considered valid or invalid? Compare Skinner v. Fisher, 120 Ark. 91, 178 S.W. 922 (1915) with Peterson v. Hegna, 158 Minn. 289, 197 N.W. 484 (1924). Other courts have held that even though a claim is valid "if there is no possibility of enforcement and collection, ..." it should

§ 60. The Pre-existing Duty Rule: Duties Imposed by Law

As a general proposition the courts have ruled that where a party does or promises to do what he is already legally obligated to do or promises to refrain from doing or refrains from doing what he is not legally privileged to do he has not incurred detriment. The pre-existing duty need not be contractual. Thus, for example, if a husband promised to pay his wife a thousand dollars at the end of the year if she performs her household duties, she would not be entitled to the money because she would merely have performed her legal obligation.[1] So also a sheriff may not obtain a reward for the capture of a criminal if the capture is part of his duties.[2]

§ 61. The Pre-existing Duty Rule: The Two Party Cases

If in August B hires A for a one year term to commence in November at $90.00 per week and in October the parties agree to modify the agreement so that the salary is to be $100.00 per week, B's promise to pay the additional $10.00 weekly is not enforceable because A has suffered no detriment since he is merely doing what he is legally obligated to do.[3] Some cases have disagreed on the theory that A has suffered detriment in giving up his legal right to breach his contract.[4] But this is clearly unsound. Although a contracting party

---

be treated as invalid. 1 Corbin § 140. Again if one "who would be subject to a claim or defense, if one existed, wants assurance of its non-existence" as for example where a party promises to pay for a quit claim deed his promise will be enforceable at least if the other party is not guilty of "improper pressure or deception." Restatement, Contracts (2d) § 76B(2), Comment c.

1. Lee v. Savannah Guano Co., 99 Ga. 572, 27 S.E. 159 (1896); Young v. Cockman, 182 Md. 246, 34 A.2d 428 (1943); Ritchie v. White, 225 N.C. 450, 35 S.E.2d 414 (1945); Blaechinska v. Howard Mission & Home, 130 N.Y. 497, 29 N.E. 755 (1892). Accord, Keith & Hastings v. Miles, 39 Miss. 442 (1860) (duty of ward to obey his guardian). See generally, 1A Corbin §§ 171–192; 1 Williston §§ 120–133.

2. Gray v. Martino, 91 N.J.L. 462, 103 A. 24 (1918); see Restatement, Contracts (2d) § 76A, ills. 1, 2; Maryland Cas. Co. v. Mathews, 209 F.Supp. 822

(S.D.W.Va.1962), 20 Wash. & Lee L. Rev. 395 (1963).

3. Alaska Packers Ass'n v. Domenico, 117 F. 99 (9th Cir. 1902); Continental Cas. Co. v. Wilson-Avery, Inc., 115 Ga.App. 793, 156 S.E.2d 152 (1967); Dunn v. Utica Mut. Ins. Co., 108 Ga. 368, 133 S.E.2d 60 (1963), 15 Mercer L.Rev. 506 (1964); Healy v. Brewster, 59 Cal.2d 455, 30 Cal.Rptr. 129, 380 P. 2d 817 (1963).

4. Swartz v. Liberman, 323 Mass. 109, 80 N.E.2d 5, 12 A.L.R.2d 75 (1948). In Lattimore v. Harsen, 14 Johns. 330 (N.Y.1817), the court construed a contract containing a penalty clause as giving the defendant an option to perform or pay the penalty. The decision is clearly obsolete. Wirth & Hamid Fair Booking, Inc. v. Wirth, 265 N.Y. 214, 192 N.E. 297 (1934), motion granted and rearg. denied 265 N. Y. 510, 193 N.E. 295 (1935); Bradshaw v. Millikin, 173 N.C. 432, 92 S.E. 161 (1917); Restatement, Contracts § 378; 5 Williston § 1444 (rev'd ed.

often can refuse to perform his agreement and respond in damages, his ability to breach his contract is neither a right nor a lawful exercise of a power. It is as much a wrong as the commission of a tort.[5]

In the illustration just discussed, if A assumed even a slight additional duty, detriment for the raise in salary would exist.[6] Again, if the parties had terminated their contract by mutual agreement and subsequently entered into a new employment agreement at the salary of $100.00 per week, the promise would be enforceable since A would have been under no obligation to B at the time the new agreement was entered into.[7]

The pre-existing duty rule has been the subject of debate. Two policies clash in this area. Although the pre-existing duty rule is a logical consequence of the fundamental concept that consideration requires detriment, would it not be reasonable for the law to allow adult contracting parties to modify their legal relations?[8] In conflict with the reasonableness of this last proposition is the realization that modifications are frequently agreed to under conditions that approach duress.[9] In a typical situation, the building contractor threatens to terminate operations if the price is not increased. The landowner succumbs rather than face the pitfalls of litigation and the difficulty of procuring a substitute contractor with dispatch.[10]

In dealing with this conflict of policies the courts have generally followed the pre-existing duty rule, but have, on occasion used great

1938). And see Armstrong v. Stiffler, 189 Md. 630, 56 A.2d 808 (1948) ("Forfeiture and damage clauses are means to insure performance, not optional alternatives for performance.") 56 A.2d at 810.

5. See 1A Corbin § 182.

6. Blakeslee v. Bd. of Water Comm'rs, 106 Conn. 642, 139 A. 106, 55 A.L.R. 1319 (1927).

7. Restatement, Contracts § 406, ill. 1.

8. This was the apparent policy rationale for the strained reasoning in Schwartzreich v. Bauman-Basch, Inc., 231 N.Y. 196, 131 N.E. 887 (1921), rearg. denied 231 N.Y. 602, 132 N.E. 905.

9. A threat not to perform an existing agreement is generally held, however, not to constitute duress. Secor v.

Clark, 117 N.Y. 350, 22 N.E. 754 (1889), rearg. denied 22 N.E. 1133 (1890); Colonie Constr. Corp. v. De Lollo, 25 A.D.2d 464, 266 N.Y.S.2d 283 (3d Dep't 1966), aff'd 20 N.Y.2d 917, 286 N.Y.S.2d 271, 233 N.E.2d 287 (1967). This rule appears to be modified by Comment 2 to § 2–209 U.C.C. which states that the extraction of a modification "without legitimate commercial reason is ineffective as a violation of the duty of good faith." See Farnsworth, Good Faith Purchase and Commercial Reasonableness Under the Uniform Commercial Code, 30 U.Chi. L.Rev. 666, 675–6 (1963); see also § 93 infra.

10. For another illustration, see the outrageous demands of the architect in Lingenfelder v. Wainwright Brewing Co., 103 Mo. 578, 15 S.W. 844 (1891).

ingenuity in circumventing its impact. Some courts have found, on tenuous grounds, that the pre-existing contract has been rescinded by mutual agreement even where the rescission and the new agreement are simultaneous.[11] This involves reasoning in a circle since the parties clearly intended the rescission to be contingent on the new contract, which, in turn, is contingent on the rescission.[12] This approach involves the manipulation of concepts and demonstrates the dissatisfaction of modern courts with the pre-existing duty rule.[13] In Wisconsin, the rule has been done away with by use of the fiction that the original consideration is imported into the new agreement.[14] In a number of jurisdictions the new agreement will be upheld if it was made after unforeseen difficulties have arisen in the performance of the prior agreement.[15] A few jurisdictions have ruled that no consideration is required for a modifying agreement.[16]

11. Schwartzreich v. Bauman-Basch, Inc., 231 N.Y. 196, 131 N.E. 887 (1921), rearg. denied 231 N.Y. 602, 132 N.E. 905. The rescission must be express, however, and not implied from the new agreement. Armour and Co. v. Celic, 294 F.2d 432 (2d Cir. 1961).

12. 1 Williston § 130A; 1 Corbin § 186.

13. See Rye v. Phillips, 203 Minn. 567, 282 N.W. 459, 119 A.L.R. 1120 (1938), in which the court indicated in dictum that the rule would be discarded. This dictum was followed in Winter Wolff & Co. v. Co-op Lead & Chem. Co., 261 Minn. 199, 111 N.W.2d 461 (1961).

14. Holly v. First Nat. Bank, 218 Wis. 259, 260 N.W. 429 (1935); Jacobs v. J. C. Penney Co., 170 F.2d 501 (7th Cir. 1948); accord, Mid-Century, Ltd. of America v. United Cigar-Whelan Stores Corp., 109 F.Supp. 433 (D.D.C. 1953).

15. Lange v. United States, 120 F.2d 886 (4th Cir. 1941) (Maryland Law); King v. Duluth M. & N. Ry., 61 Minn. 482, 63 N.W. 1105 (1895); Liebreich v. Tyler State Bank & Trust Co., 100 S. W.2d 152 (Tex.Civ.App.1936), error dism'd (depression as unforeseen circumstance "supplying" consideration); Restatement, Contracts § 76, ill. 8 (limited to cases where unforeseen difficulties justify termination of the contract); compare McGovern v. City of N. Y., 234 N.Y. 377, 138 N.E. 26, 25 A.L.R. 1442 (1923), rearg. denied and

remittitur amended 236 N.Y. 508, 142 N.E. 262 (1924); see 1 Corbin § 184. The Restatement, Contracts (2d) § 89D states that a modification is binding even if unsupported by consideration "if the modification is fair and equitable in view of circumstances not anticipated when the contract was made." It is interesting to note that the position of the Restatement, Contracts (2d) had been widespread in the nineteenth century. In Meech v. City of Buffalo, 29 N.Y. 198, 218 (1864), the following language appears. "The contractor, finding that the contract price must prove wholly inadequate on account of this hidden and wholly unforeseen obstacle, quitted the work and declined to proceed further without additional compensation. It was under these circumstances that the new agreement, providing for the additional compensation, was made; and the law will uphold it." One judge went further, saying "It is conceded that the parties might have cancelled the agreement, and, if they could do this, they could certainly modify it." 29 N.Y. at 213-14. Although this case has not been specifically overruled, (but see McGovern v. City of N. Y., supra), it finds no support in later decisions. For cases in other jurisdictions, see Beale, Notes on Consideration, 17 Harv.L.Rev. 71, 78 n. 6 (1903).

16. Watkins & Son, Inc. v. Carrig, 91 N.H. 459, 21 A.2d 591, 138 A.L.R. 131 (1941).

Important legislative changes have been made in this area, both in the Uniform Commercial Code and in other statutes. These are discussed in a later section.[17]

A troublesome situation is an agreement to extend an interest bearing debt. Assume that C lends $1,000.00 to D for a one year term at 6% interest. At the end of the year the parties agree to a one year extension at the same rate of interest. Under the majority view there is a binding contract supported by detriment on both sides: C surrenders his right to collect the money for an additional year and D surrenders the privilege of discharging the debt and thereby terminating the running of interest.[18] A minority of jurisdictions have incorrectly concluded that since interest accrues by operation of law on overdue debts, the debtor in promising to pay interest is merely promising to perform a pre-existing legal duty.[19] This reasoning overlooks that the debtor has surrendered his right to tender payment thereby stopping the further accumulation of interest.[20]

§ 62. The Pre-existing Duty Rule: The Three Party Cases

If A, a jockey, enters into a bilateral contract with the owner of a horse to ride in a race for $1,000 and the contract is modified by the parties to provide for compensation of $1500, the modification is not supported by consideration because A is only doing what he is legally obligated to do. But if C, an outsider, promises the jockey an additional $500 to fulfill his contract to ride, there are conflicting views. The majority of courts have taken the traditional and rigorously logical view that since the jockey is merely promising to perform his legal obligation, the agreement is a nullity.[21] A minority view, supported by both editions of the Restatement, is that a con-

---

17. See § 92 infra.

18. Adamson v. Bosick, 82 Colo. 309, 259 P. 513 (1927); Benson v. Phipps, 87 Tex. 578, 29 S.W. 1061 (1895); Restatement, Contracts (2d) § 76A, ill. 8.

19. Olmstead v. Latimer, 158 N.Y. 313, 53 N.E. 5 (1899).

20. If the debtor receives an extension of a past due obligation on his promise that he will pay "within a week", there is no consideration for the creditor's promise as the debtor has incurred no detriment. By the terms of his promise he may make payment at any time within the week. Therefore, he has not surrendered his right to

stop the accumulation of interest. Austin Real Estate & Abstract Co. v. Bahn, 87 Tex. 582, 30 S.W. 430 (1895); 1 Williston § 122.

21. McDevitt v. Stokes, 174 Ky. 515, 192 S.W. 681 (1917); Arend v. Smith, 151 N.Y. 502, 45 N.E. 872 (1897). De Cicco v. Schweizer, 221 N.Y. 431, 117 N.E. 807 (1917) is not to the contrary; it holds that there is detriment if the third party bargains for and causes the original contracting parties to refrain from rescinding their previous agreement. On the facts, the reasoning was tenuous and again reflects judicial dissatisfaction with the pre-existing duty rule.

tract is formed.[22] As a policy matter this seems sound since such agreements are less likely to be induced by coercion than in the two party situation. Analytically, acceptance of this view results in a rare case of consideration which involves no detriment to the promisee and only benefit to the promisor.[23] If the pre-existing arrangement between the jockey and owner was an offer to a unilateral contract, the jockey would not be under a duty to perform. C's promise would be enforceable.[24]

§ 63. Pre-existing Duty Rule—Agreements to Accept Part Payment as Satisfaction of a Debt: Pinnel's Case and Foakes v. Beer

The rule of Pinnel's Case [25] and Foakes v. Beer [26] is a particular application of the pre-existing duty rule. In Pinnel's Case, Lord Coke in dictum stated "that payment of a lesser sum on the [due] day in satisfaction of a greater, cannot be any satisfaction of the whole, because it appears to the Judges that by no possibility a lesser sum can be a satisfaction to the plaintiff for a greater sum." [27] This dictum does not necessarily follow from the pre-existing duty rule which is concerned with the requirement of consideration for the creation of executory duties. The question of discharge of duties, as an original proposition, could have been distinguished and exempted from the requirement of consideration.

Lord Coke's dictum was not put to the test in authoritative fashion until the case of Foakes v. Beer arose in 1884. The plaintiff had obtained a judgment of some £2000 against the defendant. The parties agreed that the plaintiff would accept in full satisfaction of the judgment, £500 in cash and the balance in installments. The defendant fully complied with the agreement and the amount of the judgment was fully paid. Plaintiff subsequently brought suit for interest on the

---

22. Abbott v. Doane, 163 Mass. 433, 40 N.E. 197 (1895); Restatement, Contracts § 84(d); Restatement, Contracts (2d) § 76A, Comment d. The Restatement, Contracts (2d), however, takes the position that if the pre-existing duty is owed to the public, a promise to perform this duty would not constitute consideration. A third view would enforce the promise of the promisor if the contract between the jockey and the third party is bilateral but not if it is unilateral. Beale, Notes on Consideration, 17 Harv.L. Rev. 71 (1903).

It should be observed that even in a jurisdiction which accepts the view that a promise to a third party to perform a pre-existing contractual duty constitutes consideration, the agreement must be scrutinized for possible illegality. The acceptance of the additional consideration may constitute bribery, a breach of an employee's duty to his employer or a similar wrong.

23. 1 Williston §§ 131, 131A.

24. Beale, supra n. 22.

25. 77 Eng.Rep. 237 (1602).

26. 9 App.Cas. 605 (1884).

27. 77 Eng.Rep. at 237.

judgment. The defendant alleged that pursuant to the agreement of the parties he was fully discharged. The House of Lords ruled that part payment, even if bargained for in satisfaction of an obligation, could not discharge the obligation.[28]

Generally, part payment by a debtor of an amount here and now indisputably due is not consideration to support a promise by a creditor to discharge the entire amount due.[29] The rule has been frequently and severely criticized because it tends to defeat fair dealing and honesty. Consequently, the courts have been eager to ferret out some kind of consideration.

Lord Coke's dictum indicated that delivery of a "horse, hawk or robe" [30] in addition to or in place of part payment of the pre-existing debt would provide the necessary detriment to support the promise to discharge the debt. Indeed, in Pinnel's Case the holding was that part payment prior to the due date would satisfy the obligation [31] and a further dictum stated that part payment at York instead of full payment at Westminster could constitute sufficient detriment.[32] It has been held that sufficient detriment exists if the debtor gives security in addition to the part payment,[33] or if the part payment is made by a third person [34] or if the debtor refrains from bankruptcy or insolvency proceedings [35] or in general does anything which he was not bound to do, for example, arranging for a voluntary composition agreement under which a number of creditors agree to take less than is due them.[36] It is generally held, however, that the debtor's execution of

---

28. See generally, Ferson, The Rule of Foakes v. Beer, 31 Yale L.J. 15 (1921); Hemingway, The Rule in Pinnel's Case, 13 Va.L.Rev. 380 (1927); Gold, The Present Status of the Rule in Pinnel's Case, 30 Ky.L.J. 72, 187 (1942).

29. See 1 Williston § 120; In re Cunningham's Estate, 311 Ill. 311, 142 N. E. 740 (1924); Bunge v. Koop, 48 N.Y. 225 (1872).

30. Pinnel's Case, 77 Eng.Rep. 237 (1602).

31. Accord, Princeton Coal Co. v. Dorth, 191 Ind. 615, 133 N.E. 386, 24 A.L.R. 1471 (1921), reh. denied 134 N. E. 275; see 1 Williston § 121 n. 7.

32. For cases in accord, see 1 Williston § 121 n. 9.

33. Jaffray v. Davis, 124 N.Y. 164, 26 N.E. 351 (1891).

34. Welsh v. Loomis, 5 Wash.2d 377, 105 P.2d 500 (1940).

35. Restatement, Contracts (2d) § 76A, ill. 6; Melroy v. Kemmerer, 218 Pa. 381, 67 A. 699 (1907).

36. Although composition agreements are invariably sustained, there has been a certain amount of difficulty in ascertaining the consideration which sustains them. As stated in Restatement, Contracts § 84, Comment d: "The consideration for which each of the assenting creditors bargains may be any or all of the following: (1). part payment of the sum due him; (2). the promise of each other creditor to forego a portion of his claim; (3). forbearance (or promise thereof) by the debtor to pay the assenting creditors more than equal proportions; (4). the action of the debtor in securing the assent of the other creditors; (5). the part payment made to other

his own promissory note or check is not sufficient consideration.[37] This holding is probably correct in most cases; the execution of the note or check is rarely bargained for as such. If the creditor in fact bargained for the note or check to secure evidence or facility of collection of his credit, sufficient consideration is present.[38]

There are decisions, even in states which adopt the rule of Foakes v. Beer which are difficult to reconcile with the rule. It is generally held that if a creditor agrees, in consideration of part payment, to discharge a retiring partner, the promise is binding.[39] There are occasional decisions holding that when a promisee is entitled to money payable in installments, as for example, under a lease or separation agreement, acceptance of a lesser sum in full payment discharges the debtor as to that installment despite the absence of detriment.[40] These cases should be carefully compared with a case such as McKenzie v. Harrison.[41] A lease called for payment of $1250.00 per quarter. The lessor subsequently agreed to accept and accepted $875.00 per quarter. Upon each payment he gave the tenant a receipt marked "payment in full." On these facts alone, under the rule of Foakes v. Beer, the lessor would have the right to demand payment of the difference between the amount called for in the lease and the amount he received. The court, however, found that the lessor had a donative intent and the receipts constituted sufficient delivery of the gift.[42]

creditors. Of these number 1 is not a sufficient consideration; but each of the other four is sufficient. Numbers 4 and 5 are seldom bargained for in fact; but numbers 2 and 3 are practically always bargained for, by reasonable implication if not in express terms. Still other considerations may be agreed upon in any case."

See White v. Kuntz, 107 N.Y. 518, 14 N. E. 423 (1887); A & H Lithoprint, Inc. v. Bernard Dunn Advertising Co. 82 Ill.App.2d 409, 226 N.E.2d 483 (1967).

37. Shanley v. Koehler, 80 App.Div. 566, 80 N.Y.S. 679 (1st Dep't 1903), aff'd 178 N.Y. 556, 70 N.E. 1109 (1904).

38. Id.

39. Ludington v. Bell, 77 N.Y. 138, 33 Am.R. 601 (1879); 1 Williston § 123 (pointing out the possibility of detriment in the event of subsequent insolvency); see also Crane, Partnership 423 (2d ed. 1952) who states that "Changing a joint obligation as partners into a separate obligation, there-

by giving the creditor a parity with other creditors of the separate estate, will operate as consideration." Query, is this the bargained for consideration?

40. Julian v. Gold, 214 Cal. 74, 3 P.2d 1009 (1931); Russo v. De Bella, 220 N.Y.S.2d 587 (Sup.Ct.1961); contra, Levine v. Blumenthal, 117 N.J.L. 23, 186 A. 457 (1936), aff'd 117 N.J.L. 426, 189 A. 54 (1937); Pape v. Rudolph Bros., Inc., 257 App.Div. 1032, 13 N.Y. S.2d 781 (4th Dep't 1939), aff'd 282 N. Y. 692, 26 N.E.2d 817 (1940). This type of case is discussed in more detail in the chapter on Discharge.

41. 120 N.Y. 260, 24 N.E. 458 (1890); see also Gray v. Barton, 55 N.Y. 68 (1873).

42. In McKenzie v. Harrison the court could properly find a completed gift since there apparently was evidence of donative intent and sufficient delivery. In the cases listed in note 40 there would not appear to be suffi-

As to future installments, the promise to accept reduced rental payments was not binding since gratuitous promises are unenforceable.

Detrimental reliance on the creditor's promise to accept part payment in full satisfaction of an obligation could result in enforceability of the promise [43] under the doctrine of promissory estoppel discussed below.[44]

Statutory changes of the rule of Foakes v. Beer, discussed below, have been made in a number of jurisdictions and by the Uniform Commercial Code.[45]

§ 64. The Rule of Foakes v. Beer: Minority Views

As indicated, despite its overwhelming acceptance, the rule of Foakes v. Beer has been persistently criticized. In Frye v. Hubbell,[46] a leading minority case, the rule was abandoned and it was determined that part payment of a debt accepted in full payment discharged liability for the balance.

Other minority cases have held that unforeseen hardships making full payment more onerous than anticipated, justifies enforcing an agreement to accept less than full payment.[47]

§ 65. The Relationship of the Rule of Foakes v. Beer to the Doctrine of Accord and Satisfaction—Of Liquidated and Unliquidated Claims

The rule of Foakes v. Beer is limited to liquidated claims; that is, claims that are undisputed as to their existence and undisputed and certain in amount.[48] As indicated above, if a claim is disputed, agreement relating to it will ordinarily be given effect, even if the claim is invalid, provided that the dispute has the degree of good faith

---

cient delivery so that the possibility of the finding of a gift is precluded. Brown, Personal Property § 62.

43. Central London Property Trust, Ltd. v. High Tree House, Ltd., [1947] 1 K.B. 130.

44. See ch. 6 infra; In re Estate of Stein, 50 Misc. 627, 271 N.Y.S.2d 449 (Sup.Ct.1966).

45. See §§ 92, 93 infra.

46. 74 N.H. 358, 68 A. 325 (1907), further explained in Watkins & Son v. Carrig, 91 N.H. 459, 21 A.2d 591, 138 A.L.R. 131 (1941). This view was

adopted in Rye v. Phillips, 203 Minn. 567, 282 N.W. 459, 119 A.L.R. 1120 (1938) (dictum); cf. Winter Wolff & Co. v. Co-op Lead and Chemical Co., 261 Minn. 199, 111 N.W.2d 461 (1961).

47. Liebreich v. Tyler State Bank & Trust Co., 100 S.W.2d 152 (Tex.Civ. App.1936), error dism. (economic depression). As we have seen some courts have adopted the same rule with respect to a modification of an executory contract. See § 61 supra.

48. Restatement, Contracts (2d) § 76B, Comment c.

and reasonableness required in the jurisdiction whose law governs the agreement.[49]

A great number of cases have arisen in what may be termed a "check cashing" context.[50] Three major categories of cases may be distinguished.

(1) If the debtor (D) owes the creditor (C) one hundred dollars here and now undisputably due so that the claim is liquidated and D sends a check for $50.00 marked "payment in full" and C cashes the check, C may nonetheless recover the balance of $50.00. D has merely paid part of what he was legally obligated to pay and therefore the attempted accord and satisfaction is without consideration.[51]

(2) On the same facts, if the debt was disputed; for example, C claiming that he was entitled to $100.00 and D claiming that C was entitled only to $50.00 and D sent a check for $75.00 marked "payment in full", which C cashed, C would not be entitled to assert the balance of his claim.[52] The claim is unliquidated and, assuming the necessary good faith and reasonableness of the dispute, there is consideration to support C's promise to accept $75.00 in full satisfaction. It avails C not at all to strike out the words "paid in full" written on the check,[53] or to notify the creditor that he is cashing the check in part payment.[54] For, in cashing the check in violation of the conditions upon which it was tendered, the creditor is held to assent to its terms much as in the cases where an offeree exercises dominion over unordered personal property sent him.[55] In the words

49. See § 59 supra.

50. See Calamari, The New York "Check Cashing" Rule, 1 N.Y.C.L.E. No. 2, p. 113 (1963). It must be emphasized that the question arises only where it has been made clear that the payment is sent as "full payment." Hudson v. Yonkers Fruit Co., Inc., 258 N.Y. 168, 179 N.E. 373, 80 A.L.R. 1052 (1932), otherwise the payment will be treated as a part payment.

51. State for Use of Warner Co. v. Massachusetts Bonding & Ins. Co., 40 Del. 274, 9 A.2d 77 (Del.Super.1939). The sending of the check is an offer of accord and the cashing of it or retention of it for an unreasonable period of time is the satisfaction. Lafferty v. Cole, 339 Mich. 223, 63 N.W.2d 223 (1954). In the case discussed in the text the point is that there is no

consideration for the accord and satisfaction.

52. Kall v. W. G. Block Co., 319 Ill. 339, 150 N.E. 254 (1926); accord, Gottlieb v. Charles Scribner's Sons, 232 Ala. 33, 166 So. 685 (1936) (dispute related to method rather than amount of payment); contra, Whittaker Chain Tread Co. v. Standard Auto Supply Co., 216 Mass. 204, 103 N.E. 695 (1913).

53. Toledo Edison Co. v. Roberts, 50 Ohio App. 74, 197 N.E. 500 (1934); O'Malley v. Yacht Kappy, 270 F.Supp. 955 (S.D.Fla.1967).

54. Olson v. Wilson & Co., 244 Iowa 895, 58 N.W.2d 381 (1953); Nassoiy v. Tomlinson, 148 N.Y. 326, 42 N.E. 715 (1896).

55. See § 31 supra.

of Chief Judge Cardozo, "Protest will be unavailing if the money is retained. What is said is overridden by what is done, and assent imputed as an inference of law." [56]

(3) If all of the facts in the preceding case are the same except that D admits that he owes $50.00 and sends his check in that amount, according to the majority of cases, the claim is still deemed unliquidated and therefore there is consideration for the accord and satisfaction.[57]

Even if the claim is unliquidated there is substantial authority to the effect that no binding accord and satisfaction would result in cases (2) and (3) if D stood in a fiduciary relation to C.[58] Nor would a binding accord and satisfaction arise in case (3) if two independent liabilities are sought to be discharged by the payment of one liability undisputably due.[59]

The Uniform Commercial Code has made inroads into the case law. Section 1–207 provides:

> "A party who with explicit reservation of rights performs or promises performance or assents to performance in a manner demanded or offered by the other party does not thereby prejudice the rights reserved. Such words as 'without prejudice', 'under protest' or the like are sufficient."

The Code thus expressly gives the creditor the privilege of cashing the check in defiance of the conditions upon which it was tendered,

---

56. Hudson v. Yonkers Fruit Co., Inc., 258 N.Y. 168, 171, 179 N.E. 373, 374, 80 A.L.R. 1052 (1932). If the check is inadvertently cashed the cases are split on the question of whether the effect of the cashing may be set aside for mistake. Relief on the grounds of mistake was granted in Dalrymple Gravel & Contracting Co. v. State, 23 A.D.2d 418, 261 N.Y.S.2d 566 (3d Dep't 1965), aff'd 19 N.Y.2d 644, 278 N.Y.S. 2d 616, 225 N.E. 210 (1967); but cf. Hotz v. Equitable Life Assur. Soc., 224 Iowa 552, 276 N.W. 413 (1937).

57. See note 52 supra. While it is true that the claim is unliquidated it does not follow there is consideration for the accord and satisfaction since it could be argued that in sending the $50.00 the debtor is only doing what he is legally obligated to do. However if he is not contractually bound by his admission then he may be doing more than he is legally obligated to

do. See Restatement, Contracts (2d) § 76B, Comment c.

58. The theory is that despite the fact that the claim is unliquidated, as a matter of public policy "[t]he law will not suffer an agent to withhold moneys collected from the principal's account by the pressure of a threat that no part of the moneys will be remitted to the owner without the approval of deductions beneficial to the agent. Such conduct is a flagrant abuse of the opportunities and powers of a fiduciary position." Hudson v. Yonkers Fruit Co., Inc., 258 N.Y. 168, 173, 179 N.E. 373, 375, 80 A.L.R. 1052 (1932); cf. Kellogg v. Iowa State Traveling Men's Ass'n, 239 Iowa 196, 29 N.W.2d 559 (1947) (insurance company held to the standard of a fiduciary in dealing with insured).

59. Manse v. Hossington, 205 N.Y. 33, 98 N.E. 203 (1912).

provided that notice is given the debtor that the acceptance is under protest.

The effect of other provisions of the Commercial Code and of other statutory provisions, dispensing with the requirement of consideration, on the "check cashing" cases is discussed below.[60]

§ 66. Consideration in Bilateral Contracts

It has sometimes been asserted that in a bilateral contract each party's promise is consideration for the promise of the other since each party in making a promise is doing something he is not legally bound to do.[61] Closer analysis of decided cases, however, shows that the uttering of the promise does not supply the consideration; rather it is the content of the promise which must be scrutinized to determine its sufficiency as consideration.[62] The cases hold that a promise in a bilateral agreement is consideration for the counter-promise only if the performance which is promised would be sufficient consideration.[63] For example, B says to A, "If you pay me the fifty dollars you owe me, I promise to give you a hat worth $10.00," B's promise is not enforceable because A, if he performs, would merely be doing what he was legally obligated to do.[64] The result would be the same if B had asked for and received A's counter-promise to pay the amount admittedly due. Therefore, it is clear that the mere utterance of words of promise does not constitute legal detriment in a bilateral contract.

§ 67. Mutuality of Obligation: Introduction

The meaning of the phrase "mutuality of obligation" as here used is best indicated by an illustration. B here and now owes A a liquidated debt of $1,000. They agree that A will not seek to collect the debt for six months and that B will pay the debt without interest at the end of this period. A's promise is not enforceable because B's promise is not detrimental to B.[65] On the other hand, B's promise

---

60. See § 94 infra.

61. See Ames, Two Theories of Consideration, 12 Harv.L.Rev. 515 (1898), 13 Harv.L.Rev. 29 (1899), Selected Readings 320 (1931).

62. See 1 Williston § 103.

63. It is possible to hypothesize a case in which one party bargains for the making of a promise rather than for its ultimate performance. For example, a nephew may, for past grievances, refuse to speak to his uncle.

The uncle makes the following offer, "I will give you $1,000 if you say 'I promise to accept.' " If the nephew speaks the requested words it may be held that he incurred sufficient detriment to support the uncle's promise. Such an hypothesis is rather remote from the generality of contract cases.

64. See § 63 supra.

65. See § 63 supra. If interest were bargained for, the result would be different in most jurisdictions. See § 61 supra.

would at first glance seem to be enforceable because it was given in exchange for a promise detrimental to A. The doctrine of mutuality is commonly expressed in the phrase that in a bilateral contract "both parties must be bound or neither is bound." From this premise it follows that since A is not bound, B is not.

While the doctrine of mutuality of obligation may have a core of validity it has clearly been over-generalized and used as a mistaken premise for decisions defeating justified expectations. It has been subjected to so many so-called exceptions and judicial circumventions that it has been suggested that the term "mutuality of obligation" should be abandoned.[66] More importantly, the misleading notion that both parties must be "bound" must be dispensed with. The following sections discuss the kinds of problems traditionally associated with the mutuality puzzle. They demonstrate that the supposed requirement of mutuality of obligation is merely one of mutuality of consideration: Each contracting party must supply consideration to the other.

§ 68. The Unilateral Contract: A So-called Exception to the Mutuality Requirement

Let us examine the typical pedagogical illustration of an offer to a unilateral contract: "If you walk across the Brooklyn Bridge, I will pay you ten dollars." At no time has the offeree been requested to bind himself to do anything. Indeed, if he should promise to walk across the bridge, his unsolicited promise would be a nullity.[67] If he should perform the requested act a contract will arise. His performance is the bargained for detriment which renders the offeror's promise enforceable. Despite the absence of "mutuality of obligation," it has long been recognized that a contract exists.[68]

The importance of the rule that unilateral contracts form an exception to the doctrine of "mutuality of obligation" cannot be over-emphasized. For example, an employer offers a bonus to employees, whose hiring is at will, if they continue their employment for a specified period. If the employees comply with the terms of the offer, they have provided consideration for, and are entitled to the promised bonus although there is no mutuality of obligation.[69] It

---

66. Modern authorities are generally in accord with the desirability of abandoning the use of this terminology. Restatement, Contracts (2d) § 81; 1A Corbin § 152; Grismore § 68.

67. See § 24 supra.

68. See 1A Corbin §§ 152–154.

69. Scott v. J. F. Duthie & Co., 125 Wash. 470, 216 P. 853 (1923); see also Chinn v. China Nat. Aviation Corp., 138 Cal.App.2d 98, 291 P.2d 91 (1955) (promise of severance pay); see generally, 1A Corbin § 153.

is inconsequential that at no time were the employees requested to or in any way obligated to continue their services.

An option contract (irrevocable offer) typically contains a promise to sell or buy in exchange for a price.[70] One party is bound to perform at the election of the other who is not bound by any obligation. The option contract is nonetheless valid.[71] Both parties have provided consideration. There is no additional requirement of mutuality of obligation. Similarly, in many agency relationships no obligation is undertaken by the agent.[72] Frequently, the agreement is merely that the agent will be paid a commission if he produces a buyer, ready, willing and able to purchase at specified terms. There is no mutuality of obligation, but if the agent produces the buyer, he has given consideration and his principal is obligated to pay the promised commission.[73]

Unilateral contract analysis can solve even more complex problems of lack of mutuality. In Pace Corporation v. Jackson,[74] a shareholder in Pace Corporation transferred his shares of stock to the Corporation partially in exchange for the Corporation's promise to supply him with cigarettes at cost for resale in his business. The shareholder made no promise to purchase any cigarettes. Nevertheless, stripped to its essentials, the transaction was held to be a unilateral contract. In consideration of the transfer of the shares, the shareholder was granted an option to purchase cigarettes at favorable prices. When both parties have provided consideration, there is no additional requirement of mutuality of obligation.

§ 69. Voidable and Unenforceable Promises as Consideration

The Restatement, Second, broadly states:[75]

The fact that a rule of law renders a promise voidable or unenforceable does not prevent it from being consideration."

At an early date it was held that an infant's power to disaffirm his contractual obligations does not prevent his promises from serving as consideration.[76] In terms of traditional thinking about a re-

---

70. See § 37 supra; Oliver v. Wyatt, 418 S.W.2d 403 (Ky.Ct.App.1967).

71. Chrisman v. S. Cal. Edison Co., 83 Cal.App. 249, 256 P. 618 (1927) ("As a unilateral contract is not founded on mutual promises, the doctrine of mutuality of obligation is inapplicable to such a contract." 256 P. at 621); Oliver v. Wyatt, supra n. 70.

72. Frequently, however the relationship is expressly or implicitly bilateral. See § 73 infra.

73. See generally, 1A Corbin § 154.

74. 155 Tex. 179, 284 S.W.2d 340 (1955).

75. Restatement, Contracts (2d) § 80; see 1 Williston § 105.

76. Holt v. Ward Clarencieux, 93 Eng. Rep. 954 (K.B.1732).

quirement of mutuality of obligation, an infant's right to enforce a bilateral contract has sometimes been considered to be an exception to the supposed requirement of mutuality of obligation.[77] Sounder reasons for the enforceability of infants' contracts can be found. An infant incurs legal detriment in making a promise which he must act affirmatively to avoid. Alternatively, it may be said that the infant's promise creates an expectation which the other party bargains for and, generally, for consideration to exist the possibility of detriment rather than the absolute certainty of detriment is sufficient.[78] This analysis is reinforced by the social and economic aspects of the situation. It would be undesirable to deny an infant the power of contracting as would be the case if a doctrine of mutuality of obligation were applied to his promise. He should be, as he is, able to enforce the promise of the adult even though he has a power of avoidance.[79]

Thus voidable and unenforceable promises are sufficient consideration for a counter-promise in a bilateral contract and no mutuality problem is presented. Other instances of voidable or unenforceable promises are promises induced by fraud or duress as well as oral promises that come within the Statute of Frauds.[80]

§ 70. Illusory and Optional Promises (alternative performances)

An illustration of a void promise is an illusory promise. An illusory promise is an expression cloaked in promissory terms, but which, upon closer examination, reveals that the promisor has committed himself not at all. Many such cases analyzed in the Offer and Acceptance chapter as cases involving indefiniteness can also be analyzed in terms of consideration. For example, in Great Northern R. Co. v. Witham,[81] an offer was made to supply "such quantities . . . as your storekeeper may order from time to time" at specified prices. The offeree purported to accept this offer. There was no manifestation of assent sufficient to constitute a contract since the offeree has made no promise to purchase any goods. For the same reason the offeree has supplied no consideration. His purported acceptance creates merely the illusion of a promise.[82]

---

77. Williston says, "[t]he rule exemplified by these cases must be regarded as an exception to the general principles of consideration." 1 Williston § 105. Restatement, Contracts (2d) § 80 does not agree.

78. See § 71 infra.

79. 1 Corbin § 146; 1 Williston § 105; Restatement, Contracts (2d) § 80.

80. 1 Corbin § 146; 1 Williston § 105; Restatement, Contracts (2d) § 80.

81. L.R. 9 C.P. 16 (1873).

82. The statement may nonetheless constitute an offer to a series of contracts. Each time a specific order is placed by the offeree a contract is formed. While the offer is bound to fill any order received prior to revoca-

Similarly, where in consideration of guaranteeing a note, the guarantor bargained for the creditor's promise to forbear from collecting it for a period of time, the creditor's promise to "hold it until such time as I want my money," commits him to nothing. He does not appear to have accepted the guarantor's offer nor has he supplied consideration for the guarantor's promise.[83]

If performance of an apparent promise is entirely optional with the promisor, the promise has been said to be illusory. In the words of the Restatement Second, "A promise or apparent promise is not consideration if by its terms the promisor or purported promisor reserves a choice of alternative performances unless (a) each of the alternative performances would have been consideration if it alone had been bargained for." [84] Since both parties' promises in a bilateral contract must be supported by consideration, the entire arrangement falls if one of the party's promises is illusory.[85] This traditionally has been explained in terms of mutuality of obligation rather than in terms of mutuality of consideration. The law reports are littered with the casualties of this tradition. Countless bargains, freely entered into and openly arrived at, have been struck down because of zealous judicial concern that one party's promise appeared illusory. It mattered not that, ordinarily, it was this party who was prepared to carry out the bargain without taking advantage of the escape route contained in his promise and the other party who reneged on the agreement. If the plaintiff has an escape route, the illusory promise doctrine has been held to require that the defendant must be allowed free access to it.

The tide has most definitely turned. It is fruitless to speak in terms of weight of authority where it is evident that new approaches are firmly taking hold. To illustrate these new approaches, agreements containing an option by one contracting party to cancel will be discussed.

If A and B enter into a bilateral agreement whereby A agrees to provide services for a year at a certain wage and B retains the power to terminate the agreement upon giving thirty days notice, there is no doubt that the agreement constitutes a contract. B has agreed to pay wages for one year or for thirty days. Both of these alternatives

tion, his power to terminate the offer *in futuro* remains intact. See § 29 supra; 1A Corbin § 157; Nat Nal Service Stations v. Wolf, 304 N.Y. 332, 107 N.E.2d 473 (1952). However, since no quantity is stated it could be argued that the statement was not even an offer.

83. Strong v. Sheffield, 144 N.Y. 392, 39 N.E. 330 (1895).

84. Restatement, Contracts (2d) § 79.

85. If the illusory promise is performed, other doctrines may come into play. See § 74 infra.

are detrimental to B.[86] Similarly, the promise is not illusory if the power to terminate is at will but conditioned upon some factor outside the promisor's unfettered discretion, such as the promisee's non-performance,[87] the happening of some event such as a strike, war, decline in business, etc.[88]

Where a party reserves the right to cancel an agreement at any time without notice the older cases have held that his promise is illusory.[89] Where a party reserves the right of cancellation simply by giving notice at any time without any specific period of notice being required the majority of the cases have said that the promise is not consideration.[90]

But Corbin and the later, better considered, decisions take the position that the requirement for notice, even though it may be given at any time, constitutes detriment.[91] Even where the language of the agreement seems to reserve the right to cancel at any time without notice the more recent cases have sustained the agreement by a process of interpretation.[92] For example in a well known case, Sylvan Crest Sand & Gravel Co. v. United States,[93] the United States promised to purchase trap rock from the plaintiff. The agreement read, "Cancellation by the Procurement Division may be effected at any time." The court took great pains to point out that the parties intended their agreement to be a contract and not a nullity. In order to effectuate their intention the court interpreted the agreement to mean that the government had promised to purchase trap rock or, alternatively, by implication, to give notice of cancellation within a reasonable time from the time of acceptance. In the court's words, "the alternative of giving notice was not difficult of performance, but it was sufficient consideration to support the contract." This frontier case goes very far toward obliterating the illusory promise problem by interpreting the cancellation clause as calling for notice of cancellation within a reasonable time. While it accords with business convenience and effectuates the agreement of the parties, is the reasoning satisfactory? It is quite correct to say that the writing and send-

86. 1A Corbin § 164; 1 Williston § 105; Long v. Foster & Associates, 242 La. 295, 136 So.2d 48 (1961), 22 La.L.Rev. 872 (1962).

87. 1A Corbin § 166; 1 Williston § 105.

88. 1A Corbin § 165; 1 Williston § 105.

89. 1A Corbin § 163; 1 Williston § 104.

90. 1 Williston § 104; Miami Coca-Cola Bottling Co. v. Orange Crush Co., 296

F. 693 (5th Cir. 1924) stating that this is the "great weight of authority".

91. 1A Corbin § 163.

92. See, for example, Russell v. Princeton Laboratories, 50 N.J. 30, 231 A.2d 800 (1967), and Franklin Co. v. United States, 180 Ct.Cl. 666, 381 F.2d 416 (1967).

93. 150 F.2d 642 (2d Cir. 1945).

ing of a letter of cancellation or even the giving of oral notice of cancellation constitutes detriment. Can it be said, however, that the plaintiff bargained for notice of cancellation in exchange for his promise to supply trap rock? In the Sylvan Crest case, and in similar cases, the presence of such a bargain is quite doubtful and the finding of consideration on such a premise seems to be a fiction designed to effectuate the parties' agreement.

Dispensing with the fiction, the Sylvan Crest case supports this proposition: A promise is not rendered insufficient as consideration by reason of a power of cancellation reserved by the promisor. The statement of the rule in these terms has the advantage of bringing the law governing a promisor's option to terminate into symmetry with the law governing contingent contracts generally and in particular with the rule governing unenforceable and voidable contracts. Moreover, it tends to carry out agreements freely entered into by which one party has willingly assumed the risk that the other party will withdraw.

Courts are likely, however, to continue with more circuitous approaches to the promisor's option to terminate.[94] The possibility that the giving of reasonable notice to terminate may be implied in the agreement is strengthened by the Uniform Commercial Code, which in § 2–309(3) provides:

> "Termination of a contract by one party except on the happening of an agreed event requires that reasonable notification be received by the other party and an agreement dispensing with notification is invalid if its operation would be unconscionable."

The purpose of this Code provision is to recognize "that the application of principles of good faith and sound commercial practice normally call for such notification of the termination of a going contract relationship as will give the other party reasonable time to seek a substitute arrangement."[95] Although the Code provision is not primarily directed to the consideration problem involved in the exercise of an option to terminate, by imposing a reasonable notice requirement, consideration, along traditional lines of thinking, is supplied. In non-Code cases the Code provisions may be applied by analogy.

Another legislative technique aimed at curtailing termination of contracts in an unfair manner is found in the Automobile Dealers

94. Indeed cases can still be found which follow the older approach. Zeyher v. S. S. & S. Mfg. Co., 319 F.2d 606 (7th Cir. 1963).

95. U.C.C. § 2–309, Comment 8.

Day in Court Act which requires an automobile manufacturer "to act in good faith . . . in terminating, cancelling or not renewing" a dealership.[96] This Congressional legislation was enacted in response to the numerous cases in which automobile manufacturers have terminated dealerships in an allegedly arbitrary fashion pursuant to one-sided adhesion agreements drafted by the manufacturers.[97] The requirement of good faith imposed as a condition to termination has the additional effect of removing any question of whether the typical dealership contract is illusory.

The same technique has been employed by courts in the absence of legislation. A well reasoned lower court case will illustrate. In Richard Bruce & Co. v. J. Simpson & Co.[98] the plaintiff, a stock brokerage firm, agreed to market a public offering of defendant's stock, reserving the right to terminate the contract, however,

> "if prior to the effective date the Underwriter, in its absolute discretion, shall determine that market conditions or the prospects of the public offering are such as to make it undesirable or inadvisable to make or continue the public offering hereunder;"

The court held that the quoted clause did not make the plaintiff's promise illusory, saying:

> "The term, 'absolute discretion' must be interpreted in context and means under these circumstances a discretion based upon fair dealing and good faith—a reasonable discretion." [99]

Although there is a strong trend toward limiting the concept of the illusory promise by adopting a judicial or legislative construction or interpretation of the agreement which will sustain it, the draftsman would do well to take note of the many cases which have failed to sustain an inartful agreement despite the parties' intention to be bound.[1] Moreover, the litigator should be aware that no proc-

---

96. 15 U.S.C.A. § 1222 (1956).

97. See generally, Kessler, Automobile Dealer Franchises: Vertical Integration by Contract, 66 Yale L.J. 1135 (1957); Brown and Conwill, Automobile Manufacturer-Dealer Legislation, 57 Colum.L.Rev. 219 (1957); Comment, 48 Cornell L.Q. 711 (1963); Southern Rambler Sales, Inc. v. American Motors Corp., 375 F.2d 932 (5th Cir. 1967), cert. denied 389 U.S. 832, 88 S. Ct. 105, 19 L.Ed.2d 92; American Motors Sales Corp. v. Semke, 384 F.2d

192 (10th Cir. 1967). For a comparative viewpoint, see Comment, Termination of a Commercial Agency in Continental Europe, 3 Texas Int'l L.F. 303 (1967).

98. 40 Misc.2d 501, 243 N.Y.S.2d 503 (Sup.Ct.1963).

99. 40 Misc.2d at 504, 243 N.Y.S.2d at 506.

1. The artful draftsman may, however, desire to create the illusion of a contract without the substance of one.

ess of interpretation or construction will sustain an agreement such as was made in Nat Nal Service Stations v. Wolf.[2] In this case, the plaintiff alleged that the defendant agreed that so long as the plaintiff ordered its requirements of gasoline from the defendant and the defendant accepted such orders, the defendant would grant the plaintiff a specified discount. It is clear that this agreement was non-contractual. The plaintiff did not agree to purchase any gasoline; the defendant did not agree to accept any orders. There was merely an arrangement by which the defendant invited offers at given terms.

§ 71. A Conditional Promise May be Sufficient Consideration: Aleatory Promises

As has been previously suggested the possibility of detriment is a sufficient basis for the existence of consideration.[3] Thus an insurance company's promise to pay a sum of money in the event of fire or other casualty supplies consideration for the insured's payment of a premium even if no casualty occurs. As indicated,[4] a valid contract exists if in consideration of $50, a promise is made to pay $10,000 "if I recover my gold mine." [5]

Suppose a man with two sons has made a will and one son makes the following proposition to the other: "You know how eccentric our father is. Let us agree now that no matter what his will contains, we will divide whatever he leaves to either of us equally." If the second son agrees, there is consideration, although it turns out that the testator bequeathed all of his assets to the second son. The first son has incurred no actual detriment, but the possibility of detriment is sufficient to support his brother's promise.[6]

Very often parties reach an agreement, the performance of which is agreed to be contingent upon some future event. There is no doubt that if the happening of the event is outside the control of the parties, the agreement does not fall for lack of consideration.[7]

See Streich v. Gen. Motors Corp., 5 Ill.App.2d 485, 126 N.E.2d 389 (1955). A more artful court, however, could have held the defendant to the illusion it tried to create. See 1A Corbin § 157.

2. 304 N.Y. 332, 107 N.E.2d 473 (1952).

3. See § 69 supra.

4. See § 55 supra.

5. Embola v. Tuppela, 127 Wash. 285, 220 P. 789 (1923). A "promise conditional on the happening of a fortuitous event, or an event supposed by the parties to be fortuitous" is known as an aleatory promise. Restatement, Contracts § 291.

6. See Beckley v. Newman, 24 Eng.Rep. 691 (Ch. 1723); Minehan v. Hill, 144 App.Div. 854, 129 N.Y.S. 873 (1911).

7. See § 70 supra; Call v. Alcan Pac. Co., 251 Cal.App.2d 442, 59 Cal.Rptr. 763 (1967).

If, however, the happening of the event is within the control of one of the parties, is his promise illusory? The modern decisions have through a process of interpretation answered in the negative.[8] Typically, the question is posed in connection with sales of real estate contingent upon the purchaser being able to obtain specified financing secured by a mortgage;[9] in sales of businesses contingent upon the purchaser being able to obtain an extended lease from the landlord; and in agreements to lease contingent upon the lessee obtaining a license for the kind of business he intends to engage in on the premises.

Agreements of this kind serve a vital purpose. They are entered into with the understanding that both parties are firmly committed to the performance of the agreement provided that cooperation is forthcoming from a financial institution, landlord or licensing authority. The purchaser or lessee has wisely protected himself, with the seller's consent, against the possibility that he will be unable to obtain the financing, lease or license.[10] In so doing, however, he has impliedly promised to use his best efforts to bring about the happening of the condition to his promise.[11] His conditional promise is thus by no means illusory.

In Di Bennedetto v. Di Rocco,[12] the Supreme Court of Pennsylvania went further than have the courts in the cases just discussed. The agreement provided that, "In the event that the buyer cannot make the settlement, he may cancel this agreement." The buyer's obligation was held not to be illusory. The Court reasoned

---

8. L. Y. Douglas v. City of Dunedin, 202 So.2d 787 (Fla.1967).

9. It is important that the terms of the contemplated mortgage financing be agreed upon. Otherwise the agreement may fail for indefiniteness. Burgess v. Rodom, 121 Cal.App.2d 71, 262 P.2d 335 (1953); Willmott v. Giarraputo, 5 N.Y.2d 250, 184 N.Y.S.2d 97, 157 N.E.2d 282 (1959); Gerruth Realty Co. v. Pire, 17 Wis.2d 89, 115 N.W. 2d 557 (1962).

10. The case of Raner v. Goldberg, 244 N.Y. 438, 155 N.E. 733 (1927) is instructive. The lessee leased certain premises for use as a dance hall. His application for a license to operate his business was denied. He sought to terminate the lease on the grounds of frustration of the venture (see § 195 infra). The court held him bound

to the lease, pointing out that he could have insisted that his duty of performance be conditioned upon obtaining the license. Having failed to protect himself by contract, the court denied him relief

11. Lach v. Cahill, 138 Conn. 418, 85 A.2d 481 (1951); Carlton v. Smith, 285 Ill.App. 380, 2 N.E.2d 116 (1936); Eggan v. Simonds, 34 Ill.App.2d 316, 181 N.E.2d 354 (1962); but see Paul v. Rosen, 3 Ill.App.2d 423, 122 N.E.2d 603 (1954). Compare Marino v. Nolan, 24 App.Div.2d 1005, 266 N.Y.S.2d 65 (2d Dep't 1965), aff'd 18 N.Y.2d 627, 272 N.Y.S.2d 776, 219 N.E.2d 291 (1966) with Glassman v. Gerstein, 10 A.D.2d 875, 200 N.Y.S.2d 690 (2d Dep't 1960).

12. 372 Pa. 302, 93 A.2d 474 (1953).

that the word "cannot" meant objective inability, rather than subjective unwillingness. Therefore, the performance of the promise was not left to the whim and caprice of the buyer. To be disapproved are numerous cases contrary in spirit to this well reasoned decision. Parties must be permitted to contract with flexibility to meet the complexities of modern life. Typical of the cases in which such flexibility serves a valuable economic need are requirement and output contracts discussed in the next section.

§ 72. Requirement and Output Contracts

A promise by which one party agrees to purchase all his requirements of a given product from the other is supported by consideration. If no other detriment can be located, it will be found in the promisor's surrender of his privilege of purchasing elsewhere. The same analysis can be applied to a promise to deliver one's entire output to the other. The promisor has surrendered his privilege of selling elsewhere. Despite the simplicity of this analysis a good deal of litigation has arisen concerning this kind of agreement. At first, they were deemed illusory because the buyer might refrain from having requirements under a requirements contract and a seller might refrain from production under an output contract.[13] This view was soon discarded.[14] Some courts, however, have sometimes refused to enforce an agreement when the promisor did not have established requirements as when he was entering a new business [15] or was a middleman.[16] In these cases, the stated thinking was that the lack of any basis for prediction of the amount of goods to be produced or purchased rendered the agreement illusory, indefinite and void, but perhaps the real reason for striking down the agreement was the onesideness of the arrangement.

13. Crane v. C. Crane & Co., 105 F. 869 (7th Cir.1901); Swindell & Co. v. First Nat. Bank, 121 Ga. 714, 49 S.E. 673 (1905) (agreement to supply required loan funds up to $30,000). See generally, Havighurst & Berman, "Requirement and Output Contracts," 27 Ill.L.Rev. 1 (1932); Note, 78 Harv.L. Rev. 1212 (1965).

14. Loudenback Fertilizer Co. v. Tenn. Phosphate Co., 121 F. 298 (6th Cir. 1903).

15. G. Loewus & Co. v. Vischia, 2 N.J. 54, 65 A.2d 604 (1949); Nassau Supply Co. v. Ice Service Co., 252 N.Y. 277, 169 N.E. 383 (1929), 43 Harv.L.Rev. 828 (1930) (a reading of the opinion may indicate that the court felt the transaction fraudulent). Cf. McMichael v. Price, 177 Okl. 186, 58 P.2d 549 (1936).

16. Oscar Schlegel Mfg. Co. v. Peter Cooper's Glue Factory, 231 N.Y. 459, 132 N.E. 148, 24 A.L.R. 1348 (1921). The case may be read less broadly, since the middleman did not expressly promise not to purchase glue elsewhere.

Output and requirements contracts are now governed by § 2–306 of the Uniform Commercial Code, which provides:

"A term which measures the quantity by the output of the seller or the requirements of the buyer means such actual output or requirements as may occur in good faith, except that no quantity unreasonably disproportionate to any stated estimate or in the absence of a stated estimate to any normal or otherwise comparable prior output or requirements may be tendered or demanded." [17]

This provision assumes the validity of requirement and output contracts even as to middlemen.[18] The problems of the middleman demanding an excessive supply in a rising market is overcome by restricting his ability to demand performance to an amount reasonably foreseeable at the time of contracting.[19] The requirement of good faith, should remove any question of the validity of a requirements contract entered into by a new business. The Code, however, is not explicit on the question of new businesses.[20]

A question which has divided the courts, is whether a purchaser who is bound by a requirements contract is privileged, without liability, to go out of business or change the manner in which he does business so that he has no further requirements of the product for which he contracted. A similar question is whether a producer under an output contract may go out of business or otherwise cease producing.

Essentially there have been three approaches to the question. These approaches are not necessarily in conflict with each other. Each case involves the interpretation or construction of the agreement in the light of the pertinent facts. Some cases have held that the buyer under a requirements contract is free to go out of business and thus have no requirements.[21] Other cases have taken the position that the buyer is liable if he goes out of business in bad faith.[22] Per-

---

17. Prior to the Code some courts held that a requirements buyer was entitled to his "normal requirements." Others held that he was entitled to his actual good faith requirements. An estimate had no effect except if made in bad faith in which event it operated as a maximum to the seller's liability. See generally the article and note cited in note 13 supra.

18. U.C.C. § 2–306, Comment 2.

19. Id.

20. Duesenberg & King § 4.05(1). But see the final sentence of § 2–708, Comment 2. The Code's attitude to new businesses expressed in this Comment may provide indirect authority under § 2–306.

21. In re United Cigar Stores of America, 8 F.Supp. 243 (S.D.N.Y.1934).

22. In re United Cigar Stores of America, 72 F.2d 673 (2d Cir.1937), cert. denied Consolidated Dairy Prod. v. Irving Trust Co., 293 U.S. 617, 55 S.Ct.

haps this test is best expressed in terms of whether the purchaser has used legitimate commercial judgment as opposed to an attempt to defeat the particular obligation in issue.[23] Still other cases indicate that the buyer has impliedly promised to maintain his business as a going concern.[24] An official comment to the Uniform Commercial Code indicates that the good faith test has been adopted,[25] stating that a plant shutdown would be permissible, without liability, for lack of orders or other good faith reason. The comment is perhaps at variance with the text of § 2–306 which states that notwithstanding good faith,

> "no quantity unreasonably disproportionate to any stated estimate or in the absence of any stated estimate to any normal or otherwise comparable prior output or requirements may be tendered or demanded."

This language could be construed to mean that the buyer may not demand disproportionately more or less than the amount reasonably foreseeable at the time of contracting. The comment is correct, however, if the text is construed to mean that the buyer may not demand disproportionately larger deliveries but may, without liability, have disproportionately smaller requirements. This second view finds support in the law reviews [26] and in other authorities.[27] No matter how the Code is interpreted, the parties are basically free to determine this question for themselves by express provision in the contract.[28]

It is important to distinguish requirement and output contracts from continuing offers. A promise by X to bottle all milk supplied by Y, is merely an offer looking to a series of contracts, revocable at will,[29] unless made irrevocable by payment of a consideration or by compliance with statutory formalities. If, however, a return

---

210, two cases, 79 L.Ed 706; Royal Paper Box Co. v. E. R. Apt Shoe Co., 290 Mass. 207, 195 N.E. 96 (1935).

23. Cf. McKeever & Co. v. Canonsburg Iron Co., 138 Pa. 184, 16 A. 97 (1888) (Defendant agreed to buy requirements of coal. Upon discovery of natural gas on its own land, defendant converted to gas. *Held*: Defendant was privileged to convert.)

24. Wells v. Alexandre, 130 N.Y. 642, 29 N.E. 142 (1891); Wigand v. Bachmann-Bechtel Brewing Co., 222 N.Y. 272, 118 N.E. 618 (1918).

25. § 2–306, Comment 2.

26. See Note, 78 Harv.L.Rev. 1212, 1220 n. 34 (citing others).

27. Neofotistos v. Harvard Brewing Co., 341 Mass. 684, 171 N.E.2d 865 (1961) is a case decided under the U. C.C., but which makes no reference to the text of the Code, relying on common law authorities. See 1A Corbin § 158 n. 49, approving the decision.

28. 1A Corbin § 158.

29. Balsam Farm, Inc. v. Evergreen Dairies, Inc., 6 A.D.2d 720, 175 N.Y.S. 2d 517 (2d Dep't 1958), rearg. and appeal denied 6 A.D.2d 829, 176 N.Y.S.2d 931.

promise by Y to supply milk is expressed or can be implied, a bilateral contract exists.[30]

§ 73. Consideration Supplied by Implied Promises

A bilateral contract may be express, implied in fact or a mixture of the two.[31] The implication of a promise for the purpose of finding sufficient consideration to support an express promise has become an important technique employed to sustain agreements which appear illusory and to avoid problems of "mutuality of obligation."

The leading case in this context is Wood v. Lucy, Lady Duff Gordon.[32] An elaborate written instrument was drafted pursuant to which Lady Duff Gordon granted the plaintiff an exclusive right to place her endorsement on fashion designs. The instrument was silent as to any obligation on the part of the plaintiff. The Court, pointed out, however, that the plaintiff had an organization adapted to the carrying out of the exclusive agency and was interested in carrying it out because of his financial self-interest. It inferred a promise on plaintiff's part to use reasonable efforts to enter into contracts pursuant to the agency. In the language of the Court:[33]

> "It is true that he does not promise in so many words that he will use reasonable efforts to place the defendant's indorsements and market her designs. We think, however, such a promise is fairly to be implied. The law has outgrown its primitive stage of formalism when the precise word was the sovereign talisman, and every slip was fatal. It takes a broader view today. A promise may be lacking, and yet the whole writing may be 'instinct with an obligation' imperfectly expressed . . .. If that is so there is a contract."

The method of the case, in finding, by inferences drawn from the facts, an implied promise so as to sustain a contract has found broad acceptance in cases involving exclusive agencies,[34] and in many other contexts.[35]

---

30. McNussen v. Graybeal, 146 Mont. 173, 405 P.2d 447 (1965); see § 73 infra.

31. See §§ 10, 24, 31 supra.

32. 222 N.Y. 88, 118 N.E. 214 (1917), rearg. denied 222 N.Y. 643, 118 N.E. 1082 (1918).

33. 222 N.Y. at 90–91, 118 N.E. at 214.

34. See 1A Corbin § 154 (pointing out that in determining whether the agent's promise is to be implied, the customs of the particular trade must be considered.)

35. E. g., Lach v. Cahill, 138 Conn. 418, 85 A.2d 481 (1951) (contract subject to obtaining a mortgage loan; implied promise to use best efforts in securing the loan); McNussen v. Graybeal,

The Uniform Commercial Code adopts and goes beyond the reasoning of Wood v. Lucy, Lady Duff Gordon. It provides in § 2–306(2):

> "A lawful agreement by either the seller or the buyer for exclusive dealing in the kind of goods concerned imposes unless otherwise agreed an obligation by the seller to use best efforts to supply the goods and by the buyer to use best efforts to promote their sale."

Of course, the Code provision has reference only to exclusive dealings in "goods" as defined by the Code.[36] It thus would not be applicable to an agreement such as was involved in the Wood case, but it adopts and extends the rationale of the Wood case by imposing the obligation of best efforts as a matter of legislative fiat rather than as a matter of interpretation. This approach had already been taken in a number of cases.[37]

§ 74.   A Void Contract is Not Necessarily a Nullity

We have seen that if there is no detriment on one side of a bilateral contract the contract is void.[38] However it does not follow that a void bilateral contract does not give rise to any legal consequences.

For example in Hay v. Fortier [39] the defendant was under an undisputed obligation to pay the plaintiff a liquidated debt. The parties entered into an agreement whereby the plaintiff agreed to forbear from suing on the obligation and the defendant promised to pay the debt at the end of the six months. Under the pre-existing duty rule, the plaintiff's promise was unsupported by consideration and thus unenforceable.[40] Consequently the agreement as a whole was void and the court so held.

However the plaintiff did forbear for six months and then brought action upon the defendant's promise to pay the liquidated debt.[41] The court found for the plaintiff despite the voidness of the bilateral contract, stating as follows: "If a contract, although not originally binding for want of mutuality, is nevertheless executed

---

146 Mont. 173, 405 P.2d 447 (1965) (output contract); Scientific Management Institute, Inc. v. Mirrer, 27 A.2d 845, 278 N.Y.S.2d 58 (2d Dep't, 1967), appeal after remand 29 A.D.2d 962, 289 N.Y.S.2d 336 (1968).

36.   U.C.C. § 2–105.

37.   See Mandel v. Liebman, 303 N.Y. 88, 100 N.E.2d 149 (1951), rearg. de-

nied 277 App.Div. 637, 102 N.Y.S.2d 563.

38.   See § 67 supra.

39.   116 Me. 455, 102 A. 294 (1917).

40.   See § 63 supra.

41.   See n. 39 supra.

by the party not originally bound, so that the party asserting the invalidity of the contract has actually received the benefit contracted for, the latter will be estopped from refusing performance on his part on the ground that the contract was not originally binding on the other, who has performed." [42]

The court in so stating appears to be invoking some species of the doctrine of promissory estoppel.[43] This process has also been referred to as forging a good unilateral contract out of a bad bilateral contract.[44] Before the forging may occur at least two requirements are essential. First, all of the requisites of the law of offer and acceptance must be fulfilled including the requirement that the promise requested must have been given by the party seeking to invoke the doctrine of forging and, secondly, the act performed by this party must be detrimental.[45]

This process of forging a good unilateral contract out of a bad bilateral contract is also relevant in cases where the agreement is void because the promises on one or both sides of a bilateral arrangement are void as being too vague and indefinite. If the promise which was originally definite is performed, obviously the promise to be enforced is still indefinite and so there is only the possibility of a quasi contractual recovery.[46] If however the side of the agreement which was too vague and indefinite becomes definite by performance, the other side of the agreement, though not originally enforceable, becomes enforceable under the doctrine of forging a good unilateral contract out of a bad bilateral contract.[47] The same type of problem arises in the case of illusory problems.[48] Another doctrine which is used to overcome the problems of indefiniteness is the doctrine that "the original indefiniteness may sometimes be cured by a subsequent definition of intended performance." [49]

Closely related to the doctrine of forging a good unilateral contract out of a bad bilateral contract is the related doctrine of forg-

---

42. 102 A. at 295. The quotation is from 6 R.C.L. 690.

43. See ch. 6 infra.

44. See Calamari, Forging a Good Unilateral Contract or a Series of Good Contracts out of a Bad Bilateral Contract, (1961) Wash.U.L.Q. 367; Finn, The Forging of Good Unilaterals out of Bad Bilaterals 3 Brooklyn L.Rev. 6 (1933).

45. See Calamari, supra n. 44.

46. 1 Williston § 49.

47. 1 Williston §§ 49 and 104.

48. See Calamari, supra n. 44.

49. 1 Williston § 49. A good illustration is the case of Perreault v. Hall, 94 N.H. 191, 49 A.2d 812 (1946), wherein the defendant promised to pay the plaintiff "well and enough." Upon retirement the defendant promised to give her a pension of $20.00 per week as long as she lived, an offer which plaintiff apparently accepted. The court specifically stated that

ing a series of good contracts out of a bad bilateral contract.[50] This process has already been illustrated in this text without reference to the label placed upon it here.[51] Another illustration here will suffice to show the nature of the process.

In Rubin v. Dairymen's League Co-op. Ass'n,[52] the defendant agreed to appoint the plaintiff as his exclusive agent within a certain territory in exchange for the plaintiff's promise to develop a market for the defendant's products. No time was stated for the duration of the contract and the court held that the contract was terminable at will.[53] The court held that although the contract was void because of indefiniteness, nevertheless the plaintiff was entitled to be paid under the agreement for the series of orders he had obtained—thus forging a series of good unilateral contracts out of a bad bilateral contract.[54]

It should also be reiterated that there are occasions where the doctrine of forging will not apply but where quasi contractual relief may be available.[55]

§ 75. One Consideration Will Support Many Promises

Typically, one or both parties to an agreement makes a number of promises to the other. Thus in consideration of an employee's promised services, the employer may promise a salary, a year-end bonus and other fringe benefits. All of the employer's promises are supported by the employee's single promise to provide services.[56] Similarly, payment of the price will support a seller's promise to deliver goods and to warrant their performance.

---

the original indefiniteness was cured by a subsequent definition of intended performance. Of course it might be concluded that the promise to give twenty dollars and the acceptance of it might be some species of accord and satisfaction. Cf. 1 Corbin § 143.

50. Calamari, supra n. 44.

51. See, for example, the case of Balsam Farms, Inc. v. Evergreen Dairies, cited in § 72 supra, n. 29 and Nat Nal Service Stations v. Wolf cited in § 70 supra, n. 2 and Great Northern R. Co. v. Witham, L.R. 9 C.P. 16 (1873); Restatement, Contracts § 33 ill. 1.

52. 284 N.Y. 32, 29 N.E.2d 458 (1940), rearg. denied 284 N.Y. 816, 31 N.E.2d 927.

53. See § 23 supra.

54. It is interesting to note that the New York Court of Appeals did not forge a series of good contracts out of a bad bilateral contract in Nassau Supply Co. v. Ice Service Co., 252 N.Y. 277, 169 N.E. 383 (1929), and in Strong v. Sheffield, 144 N.Y. 392, 39 N.E. 330 (1895) suggested that there is no such process. "The consideration is to be tested by the agreement, and not by what was done under it." (144 N.Y. at 396, 39 N.E. at 331).

55. See n. 46 supra.

56. Keane v. Aetna Life Ins. Co., 22 N. J.Super. 296, 91 A.2d 875 (1952); see 1 Corbin § 125; 1 Williston § 137A; Restatement, Contracts (2d) § 83.

The Restatement Second generalizes such cases in the following language: [57]

"There is consideration for a set of promises if what is bargained for and given in exchange would have been consideration for each promise in the set if exchanged for that promise alone."

§ 76.　All of the Consideration Need Not be Valid

If a promisor bargains for and receives several promises or performances from the other, a contract is formed if any of these promises or performances is sufficient as consideration.[58]　This idea has previously been discussed in connection with the rule of Foakes v. Beer [59] and the pre-existing duty rule.[60]　For example, if A says to B, "I promise to give you my black horse if you pay me the $50 you owe me and paint my fence," although in paying his debt, B is only doing what he is legally obligated to do, in painting the fence he is providing sufficient consideration for A's promise which is enforceable provided B paints and pays the debt.[61]　Similarly, a promise by an uncle to his nephew, "In consideration of your past good conduct and in consideration of your promise to refrain from smoking for a year, I will pay you $500," would be supported by consideration if the counter-promise were given.　The fact that part of the consdieration is past does not vitiate the sufficiency of the valid consideration.

§ 77.　Consideration and the Parol Evidence Rule

We have already seen that as a general rule a recital in a written agreement that a stated consideration has been given may be contradicted.[62]　We have also seen that an integrated writing may not

---

57.　Restatement, Contracts (2d) § 83(1). However, if a promisor reserves a choice of alternative performances unless each alternative is detrimental, the promises do not constitute consideration for a counter-promise. Restatement, Contracts (2d) § 79(a). However, subdivision (b) of this section adds that the alternative promises are consideration provided there is or appears to be to the parties a substantial possibility that events may eliminate the possibility which is not detrimental before the promisor exercises his choice.

58.　Restatement, Contracts (2d) § 83(2); 1 Corbin § 126; 1 Williston § 134.

59.　See § 63 supra.

60.　See § 61 supra.

61.　The illustration makes it clear that even though paying the debt is void as consideration it is still a condition which must be performed if B is to recover on A's promise. There is a related question in the area of illegality which is discussed in § 384 infra.

62.　See § 58 supra.

be contradicted because of the parol evidence rule.[63] These two statements appear to be contradictory. However, the great weight of authority is to the effect that the parol evidence rule does not bar evidence which would contradict, vary or supplement a recital of fact.[64] There is a minority view, however, to the effect that although a recital of consideration may be shown to be false for other purposes, such a showing may not be made for the purpose of destroying the contractual effect of a writing.[65]

The parol evidence rule will, however, bar an attempt to contradict, vary or supplement the promissory consideration stated in a total integration. Where, however, no consideration is stated on one or both sides of a written agreement, extrinsic evidence is admissible to show that consideration exists even if the consideration takes the form of a promise.[66] This is quite consistent with the parol evidence rule. A writing which does not on its face appear to be supported by consideration is not an integration.

---

63. See ch. 3 supra.

64. See, in addition to the authorities cited in § 58 supra, Kay v. Spencer, 29 Wyo. 382, 213 P. 571, 27 A.L.R. 1122 (1923); 1 Williston § 115B.

65. Schneider v. Turner, 130 Ill. 28, 22 N.E. 497, 66 L.R.A. 164 (1889); In re Emery's Estate, 362 Pa. 142, 66 A.2d 262 (1949); cf. Restatement, Contracts § 243, which would bar the introduction of parol evidence to contradict a recital of fact for the purpose of destroying the contractual effect of a writing only where the writing itself makes the fact essential to the obligation.

66. La Dam v. Squires, 127 Vt. 95, 241 A.2d 58 (1968); Restatement, Contracts § 240(2); 3 Corbin § 586.

CHAPTER 5

INFORMAL CONTRACTS WITHOUT CONSIDERATION OR DETRIMENTAL RELIANCE

Analysis

Sections

A. Past Consideration and Moral Obligation as Consideration ____ 78–89

B. Consideration Not Required in Certain Commercial and Written Contracts --- 90–96

C. Stipulations --- 97–98

A. PAST CONSIDERATION AND MORAL OBLIGATION AS CONSIDERATION

Sec.
78. Introduction.
79. The Relationship Between Past Consideration and Moral Obligation.
80. Promises to Pay Pre-existing Debts.
81. Promises to Pay for Acts Previously Performed at Request.
82. Promises to Pay for Benefits Previously Received Without Request.
83. Promises to Pay Debts Discharged by Operation of Law: Rationale.
84. Promises to Pay Debts Discharged in Bankruptcy.
85. Promises to Pay Debts—Effect on Statute of Limitations.
86. Promises to Perform Voidable Duties.
87. New Promise Based Upon a Previous Promise Within the Statute of Frauds.
88. Miscellaneous Promises Supported by Antecedent Events.
89. To Whom the Promise Must be Made.

B. CONSIDERATION NOT REQUIRED IN CERTAIN COMMERCIAL AND WRITTEN CONTRACTS

90. Scope of the Discussion.
91. The Model Written Obligation Act.
92. Modification of Contracts.
93. Modifications Under Compulsion.
94. Release and Accord and Satisfaction.
    a) Release.
    b) Accord and Satisfaction.
95. Firm Offers.
96. Past Consideration.

C. STIPULATIONS

97. Stipulations Defined.
98. Consideration and Formality in Stipulations.

A. PAST CONSIDERATION AND MORAL OBLIGATION AS CONSIDERATION

Analysis

Sec.
78. Introduction.
79. The Relationship Between Past Consideration and Moral Obligation.
80. Promises to Pay Pre-existing Debts.
81. Promises to Pay for Acts Previously Performed at Request.
82. Promises to Pay for Benefits Previously Received Without Request.
83. Promises to Pay Debts Discharged by Operation of Law: Rationale.
84. Promises to Pay Debts Discharged in Bankruptcy.
85. Promises to Pay Debts—Effect on Statute of Limitations.
86. Promises to Perform Voidable Duties.
87. New Promise Based Upon a Previous Promise Within the Statute of Frauds.
88. Miscellaneous Promises Supported by Antecedent Events.
89. To Whom the Promise Must be Made.

§ 78. Introduction

Not all contracts require consideration. The formal contract under seal survives in some jurisdictions,[1] as do recognizances and other kinds of specialities. In addition there are cases in which informal contracts are exempt from the requirement of consideration. Promises which are enforceable because they have induced unbargained for reliance are the subject for the next chapter. This chapter is concerned with informal promises which are enforceable without detrimental reliance or consideration. One group of promises of this kind, promises to perform a duty despite failure of a condition, will be discussed in chapter 9, where the context will make discussion clearer.

Lord Mansfield, perhaps the greatest judge in the history of Anglo-American law,[2] introduced revolutionary changes into the doctrine of consideration. This revolution proved abortive, but had certain residual effects on court decisions and the ideas he espoused have in part been revived by legislation. In the case of Pillans and Rose v. Van Mierop [3] he laid down two radical propositions. First, no consideration is required if a promise is expressed in a writing. Second, no consideration is required in a commercial

1. See ch. 7 infra.

2. His major achievement was the incorporation of the law merchant into the common law. In contracts, he is responsible for the doctrine of constructive conditions and substantial performance. He also introduced the Roman Law idea of quasi-contracts into the common law.

3. 97 Eng.Rep. 1035 (K.B.1765).

transaction. Both of these propositions were quickly overruled [4] but as indicated in part B of this chapter have found limited acceptance in Twentieth Century legislation.

In Lee v. Muggeridge,[5] Mansfield asserted that a promise made in fulfilment of an antecedent moral obligation was sufficiently supported by moral consideration. This assertion was reasonably well grounded in the older law.[6] It is important to observe that the promise does not create the moral obligation but that antecedent facts create the moral obligation.[7] On this point, too, he was overruled,[8] but not entirely and not in every common law jurisdiction. The first part of this chapter will discuss the moral obligation problem. This will be followed by a discussion of statutes which eliminate the necessity for consideration under certain circumstances. This chapter will close with a brief discussion of stipulations, a category unto itself.

§ 79. The Relationship Between Past Consideration and Moral Obligation

We have already seen the general rule that past consideration is not consideration.[9] We have also seen immediately above that in most common law jurisdictions it is no longer generally true that an antecedent moral obligation will support a subsequent promise. The enforcement of certain limited kinds of promises without consideration, however, has been based on the rationale that certain antecedent facts create the moral obligation which justifies the enforcement of certain subsequent promises. Thus Corbin states that "all 'past consideration' cases, or nearly all, are cases in which enforcement depends upon recognition of some pre-existing moral obligation." [10] Although it is impossible to state any general test of the existence of moral obligation the majority of the cases do tend to fall into certain definitely circumscribed categories.

§ 80. Promises to Pay Pre-existing Debts

At early common law it was well settled that a pre-existing debt was consideration for a promise to pay the debt. Under this early common law rule, if C loaned D $1,000 which was to be repaid

---

4. Rann v. Hughes, 101 Eng.Rep. 1014 n. (Ex.1778).

5. 128 Eng.Rep. 599 (C.P.1813).

6. E. g., Lampleigh v. Brathwait, 80 Eng.Rep. 255 (C.P.1615).

7. 1A Corbin §§ 230, 231, 232.

8. Eastwood v. Kenyon, 113 Eng.Rep. 482 (Q.B.1840).

10. 1A Corbin § 230.

9. See § 54 supra.

by D on January 2, 1968 and D failed to repay the loan when due, D's promise made on March 1, 1968, to repay the debt was deemed to be supported by consideration. Under modern definitions of consideration, the promise is unsupported by consideration, since the past debt was not incurred in exchange for the subsequent promise. The rule that the pre-existing debt constitutes consideration was highly important at this time. In an action on the promise to pay the pre-existing indebtedness the writ of assumpsit was available under which the plaintiff was entitled to trial by jury. If the writ of debt was employed, defendant was entitled to trial by wager of law.[11]

There is some question whether the rule continues in effect. Some authorities take the position that if the past debt is still existing and enforceable a promise to pay the debt is enforceable provided that the promise is co-extensive with the pre-existing debt.[12] Other authorities indicate that the promise is unenforceable.[13] The question is almost purely of academic interest since the creditor may sue on the original obligation.[14] The primary context in which the new promise may become important is that of the running of the statute of limitations. Promises in this context, however, have a particular set of rules, discussed below.[15]

§ 81.   Promises to Pay for Acts Previously Performed at Request

At early common law if A requested B to perform a certain act without making an express promise in return, an action for debt would not lie because the obligation was unliquidated. Assumpsit would not lie because A made no express promise.[16] For example, if A requested B to paint A's house but made no express promise to pay for the services A would not be liable to B either under the writ of debt or under the writ of assumpsit. To help overcome this unjust result it was held that a subsequent express promise to pay for the

---

11. Ames, The History of Assumpsit, 2 Harv.L.Rev. 53 (1888), Selected Reading 33.

12. 1A Corbin § 211. If the debtor promised to pay less the promise is still enforceable. 1A Corbin § 212. However, the existing debt of a third person will not support a promise.

13. 1 Williston § 143.

14. A negotiable instrument given to represent a pre-existing obligation requires no consideration. This is probably the result of the peculiar position of such instruments as mercantile specialties rather than as a consequence of the rules discussed in the text.
An account stated (§ 346 infra) is enforceable without consideration and gives the claimant certain advantages of pleading and proof. This is perhaps a result of the rule here discussed.

15. See § 85 infra.

16. Ames, The History of Assumpsit, 2 Harv.L.Rev. 1 (1888).

acts performed was enforceable.[17] In time it was held that this was true even if the services had been performed as a favor rather than in expectation of payment.[18]

Under the modern law if A requests B to perform services, A would be liable on his implied promise to pay the reasonable value of the services, unless the services were rendered gratuitously.[19] A subsequent promise defining the amount which A is willing to pay for the services, assented to by B, is, of course, supported by consideration.[20] If a promise to pay a fixed amount is made by A, and withdrawn prior to B's acceptance, no mutual assent and no consideration is present. In a number of cases it has been held that there is no reason to enforce such a promise. Under this view A's promise is at best a rebuttable evidentiary admission of the value of the services.[21]

It is, nonetheless, much more commonly held that a new promise to pay a fixed sum in payment of a pre-existing obligation arising from services rendered at request is enforceable without new consideration and without mutual assent.[22] The second Restatement,[23] Professor Corbin[24] and a number of cases[25] take the view that the promise will be enforced only to the extent that it is not disproportionate to the value of the services. Under this view the new promise is of little value except to the extent that it may be prima facie proof of the value of the prior acts. According to Professor Williston's analysis, "the weight of authority supports the validity of a subsequent promise defining the extent of the promisor's undertaking," even if the promise is disproportionate to the value of the prior acts.[26] That is, the new promise will be enforced according to its terms. Many of the cases are analytically unsatisfactory in one respect. In many, if not most, of the cases in which the court relied on the majority rule as stated by Professor Williston, the facts show that the new promise was assented to by the promisee; the promise could equally have been treated as a compromise agreement.[27]

17. Bosden v. Thinne, 80 Eng.Rep. 29 (K.B.1603).

18. Lampleigh v. Brathwait, 80 Eng. Rep. 255 (C.P.1615).

19. 1A Corbin § 233 n. 72; 1 Williston § 144–147.

20. Each party is suffering detriment in arriving at the compromise. However, the agreement may instead be an executory accord. See §§ 341–343 infra.

21. See 1 Williston §§ 144–145.

22. Restatement, Contracts (2d) § 89A.

23. Id.

24. 1A Corbin § 233.

25. In re Estate of Gerke, 271 Wis. 297, 73 N.W.2d 506 (1955).

26. 1 Williston § 146.

27. E. g., In re Bradbury, 105 App.Div. 250, 93 N.Y.S. 418, (3rd Dep't 1905); see note 20 supra.

An important problem is whether a promise to pay for services rendered at request, but as a favor, without expectation of payment, is enforceable. In a majority of jurisdictions, such a promise is unenforceable.[28] As discussed earlier,[29] past consideration is ordinarily not sufficient to support a promise. Yet, Lord Mansfield's ruling that the past consideration creates a moral obligation which supports a subsequent promise lingers on. In some jurisdictions, it continues to be held to constitute the law, although frequently the decisions are sustainable on other grounds.[30] The Restatement Second suggests that gratuitous services will support a subsequent promise to pay for them if the services were rendered in a business setting,[31] in emergencies[32] and in other marginal cases.[33] Professor Corbin is generally in accord and suggests that the moral consideration concept is part of the legal resources of all jurisdictions to be utilized "as an escape from more hardened and definitely worded rules of law."[34]

§ 82. Promises to Pay for Benefits Previously Received Without Request

Under the rules of quasi contracts, in limited circumstances, there is a right of action to recover the value of benefits conferred upon another without his request.[35] When such a right exists a promise to pay for benefits so received is governed by the same rules as is any promise to pay for acts previously performed at request.[36] In the ordinary case, however, receipt of unrequested benefits creates no legal obligation.[37] If a subsequent promise is made to pay for these benefits, the majority of cases hold that the promise is unenforceable.[38] Other

---

28. Allen v. Bryson, 67 Iowa 591, 25 N. W. 820 (1885); Moore v. Elmer, 180 Mass. 15, 61 N.E. 259 (1901); Pershall v. Elliott, 249 N.Y. 183, 163 N.E. 554 (1928).

29. See § 54 supra.

30. In re Hatten's Estate, 233 Wis. 199, 288 N.W. 278 (1940) (the decision, however, is supported by the majority view since payment for the services was promised prior to their complete rendition); Medberry v. Olcovich, 15 Cal.App.2d 263, 59 P.2d 551 (1936), appeal denied on other grounds 15 Cal. App.2d 263, 271, 60 P.2d 281, 282 (1936).

31. See Restatement, Contracts (2d) § 89A, ill. 8, 9.

32. Id. at Comment d.

33. Id. at Comment b.

34. 1A Corbin § 230.

35. Chase v. Corcoran, 106 Mass. 286 (1871) (rescue and repair of a boat); Cotnam v. Wisdom, 83 Ark. 601, 104 S.W. 164 (1937) (medical services to an unconscious person).

36. See § 81 supra.

37. Restatement, Restitution §§ 113–117.

38. In re Greene, 45 F.2d 428 (S.D.N.Y. 1930); ("the doctrine that past moral obligation is consideration is now generally exploded"); Mills v. Wyman, 20 Mass. (3 Pick.) 207 (1825) (father promised to pay for services rendered

cases, accepting the moral obligation concept, are to the contrary.[39] The Restatement Second hedges, generally taking the view that the promise be enforced if the services are rendered in an emergency or by mistake and no affirmative indication of a donative intent exists.[40]

§ 83.   Promises to Pay Debts Discharged by Operation of Law: Rationale

A promise to pay a debt discharged in bankruptcy, barred by the statute of limitations, or otherwise rendered unenforceable by operation of law [41] is enforceable without consideration.   The cases frequently articulate the rationale in terms that the debt coupled with the moral obligation to pay the debt is sufficient consideration to support the new promise to pay.[42]   Other cases speak in terms of the promise reviving a debt barred by operation of law.[43]   Others adopt the rationale that the promise operates as a waiver of the debtor's defense; the right is said to continue to exist, only the remedy being barred.[44] In truth, the rule is a particular application of the older view that an antecedent debt is sufficient consideration for a subsequent promise to pay it.   When this doctrine was abandoned by some courts, these courts generally agreed that promises to pay a debt discharged by operation of law should be enforced and apparently carved out an exception for this type of case.[45]   That the reason for the rule is historical rather than purely logical is shown by the cases holding that a promise to pay a tort claim which is barred by the statute of limitations [46] or discharged in bankruptcy [47] is unenforceable despite the

---

to ailing son; court suggests that the enforcement of such promise be left to the Tribunal of Conscience); Harrington v. Taylor, 225 N.C. 690, 36 S.E.2d 227 (1945) (plaintiff injured in saving defendant's life; promise to pay damages).

39. Webb v. McGowin, 232 Ala. 374, 168 So. 199 (1936) (plaintiff injured in saving defendant's life; promise to pay an annuity); Holland v. Martinson, 119 Kan. 43, 237 P. 902 (1925); Edson v. Poppe, 24 S.D. 466, 124 N.W. 441 (1910) (tenant orders well dug; landlord promised to pay well digger).

40. Restatement, Contracts (2d) § 89A, Comment d.

41. Other illustrations of this doctrine may be found in § 88 infra.

42. Stanek v. White, 172 Minn. 390, 215 N.W. 784 (1927); Herrington v. Davitt, 220 N.Y. 162, 115 N.E. 476, 1 A.L.

R. 1700 (1917); Kopp v. Fink, 204 Okl. 570, 232 P.2d 161 (1951).

43. See 1 Williston § 202.

44. Way v. Sperry, 60 Mass. (6 Cush.) 238 (1851).

45. See § 80 supra; 1 Williston §§ 201, 203; Stanek v. White, 172 Minn. 390, 215 N.W. 784 (1927); Carshore v. Huyck, 6 Barb. (N.Y.) 583 (1849); Restatement, Contracts (2d) §§ 86–87.

46. Marchetti v. Atchison T. & S. F. Ry., 123 Kan. 728, 255 P. 682 (1927) (negligence); Hollenbeck v. Guardian Nat. Life Ins. Co., 144 Neb. 684, 14 N. W.2d 330 (1944) (fraud); Armstrong v. Levan, 109 Pa. 177, 1 A. 204 (1885) (but promise made before the statute had run may be enforceable by estoppel).

47. Burleson v. Langdon, 174 Minn. 264, 219 N.W. 155 (1928).

fact that the elements of waiver and moral obligation are equally as strong in such cases.

§ 84.   Promises to Pay Debts Discharged in Bankruptcy

As indicated, a promise to pay a contractual debt discharged in bankruptcy is enforceable despite an absence of consideration for the promise. For example, D owes C $1,000. D goes through bankruptcy and receives a discharge of that debt. If D subsequently promises to pay the discharged debt the promise is enforceable despite the absence of consideration.

According to most authorities, an enforceable promise to pay a contractual debt discharged in bankruptcy may be made at any time after the petition in bankruptcy has been filed,[48] but, according to some, it must be made after the adjudication of bankruptcy.[49] In the absence of statute the promise may be oral,[50] but a good number of jurisdictions have statutory provisions imposing a requirement that the promise be in writing.[51]

While the action is to enforce the new promise, complaints upon the discharged obligation have been sustained by treating the new promise, alleged in the plaintiff's reply, as a waiver of the discharge.[52]

The promise to be enforceable must be clear and explicit. A promise inferrable from an acknowledgment or part payment does not revive a debt discharged in bankruptcy.[53] The promise may be

---

48. Zavelo v. Reeves, 227 U.S. 625, 33 S.Ct. 365, 57 L.Ed. 676 (1913); Restatement, Contracts (2d) § 87. Such a promise made in advance of bankruptcy is against public policy and void. Federal Nat. Bank v. Koppel, 253 Mass. 157, 148 N.E. 379, 40 A.L.R. 1443 (1925); In re Weitzen, 3 F.Supp. 698 (S.D.N.Y.1933).

49. Linzer v. Weitzen, 292 N.Y. 306, 55 N.E.2d 42 (1944); (after adjudication, but not necessary that it be made after discharge); Holt v. Akarman, 84 N.J.L. 371, 86 A. 408 (1913) (adjudication insufficient; must be made after discharge).

50. Restatement, Contracts (2d) § 87, Comment a.

51. E. g., McKinney's N.Y.Gen.Obligations Law § 5–701; see 1 Williston § 158 n. 18.

52. Lawrence v. Harrington, 122 N.Y. 408, 25 N.E. 406 (1890); accord, Little v. Blunt, 26 Mass. (9 Pick.) 488 (1830) (statute of limitations); see 1A Corbin § 219.

53. Koletsky v. Resnik, 104 Conn. 311, 132 A. 898 (1926); Lawrence v. Harrington, 122 N.Y. 408, 25 N.E. 406 (1890); Restatement, Contracts (2d) § 87, Comment a. This rule should be carefully compared with the differing rule stated in the next section with respect to the statute of limitations. The Restatement, supra, explains the difference between the rules on the ground that "In modern times discharge in bankruptcy has been thought to reflect a somewhat stronger public policy than the statute of limitations."

conditional, and in such a case the duty of payment will arise when the condition is fulfilled.[54]

A promise to pay a debt voluntarily discharged [55] is not enforceable under this exception. The rule in question applies only to a discharge by operation of law. In the words of the American Law Institute, the voluntary discharge is regarded as discharging the moral as well as the legal obligation to pay.[56] On this rationale, even in the case of a voluntary discharge, if the creditor reserves the moral obligation a subsequent promise to pay is enforceable.[57] A promise to pay a debt discharged by a composition agreement is deemed voluntary,[58] and a subsequent promise to pay unenforceable, unless the composition agreement is reached pursuant to the Bankruptcy Act.[59]

§ 85. Promises to Pay Debts—Effect on Statute of Limitations

A promise to pay a contractual debt has the effect of starting the statute of limitations running anew.[60] This is true whether the promise is made when the debt has been barred by the passage of the statutory period or whether it is not yet barred.[61] A promise not to plead the statute of limitations generally has the same effect

---

54. Herrington v. Davitt, 220 N.Y. 162, 115 N.E. 476 (1917) ("you will be paid . . . as soon as I sell the mill." 115 N.E. at 476).

55. It is to be kept in mind that under the rule of Foakes v. Beer (§ 63 supra) a voluntary discharge ordinarily requires consideration, a seal, or a statutory substitute.

56. Restatement, Contracts (2d) § 87, Comment b; see also 1A Corbin § 226.

57. Straus v. Cunningham, 159 App.Div. 718, 144 N.Y.S. 1014 (1st Dep't 1913); Restatement, Contracts (2d) § 87, ill. 3.

58. Welles-Kahn Co. v. Klein, 81 Fla. 527, 88 So. 315 (1921); Easton Furniture Mfg. Co. v. Caminez, 146 App. Div. 436, 131 N.Y.S. 157 (2nd Dep't 1911), reh. and appeal denied 147 App. Div. 904, 131 N.Y.S. 1112; 1A Corbin § 226.

59. Herrington v. Davitt, 220 N.Y. 162, 115 N.E. 476 (1917); Easton Furniture

Mfg. Co. v. Caminez, 146 App.Div. 436, 131 N.Y.S. 157 (2nd Dep't 1911), reh. and appeal denied 147 App.Div. 904, 131 N.Y.S. 1112; 1A Corbin § 222.

60. Restatement, Contracts § 86 (both editions). See generally, Kocourek, A Comment on Moral Consideration and the Statute of Limitations, 18 Ill.L. Rev. 538 (1924).

61. Harper v. Fairley, 53 N.Y. 442 (1873); 1A Corbin § 214; 1 Williston § 160. For example, assume a six year period of limitation. If A lends B $1,000 on January 2, 1965, the money to be repaid on January 2, 1966, the statute of limitations begins to run in January of 1966. If B on January 2, 1969 made a new promise to pay, the six year period would commence to run again from this date so that the debt would be barred in 1975. If instead, B in 1973 promised to pay after the statute had run, the statute would start to run again so that it will expire in 1979.

as a promise to pay the debt,[62] but, in most jurisdictions if the promise is made in the original contract or before maturity of the debt, it is void as contrary to public policy.[63]

Contrary to the rule relating to promises to pay debts discharged in bankruptcy, an acknowledgment of the existence of the debt is treated as an implied promise to pay,[64] unless there is an indication of a contrary intention. For example, a statement that "I know I owe the money . . . and I will never pay it," although an acknowledgment of the debt rebuts any implication of a promise to pay.[65]

Statutes in most of our states require the promise or the acknowledgment to be in a signed writing.[66] Part payment of principal or interest or the giving of collateral may have the same effect as an acknowledgment and be treated as equivalent of a writing.[67] To have this effect the part payment must be voluntary.[68]

The creditor's claim is based on the new promise and therefore is governed by the terms of the new promise.[69] Thus, the promise may be to pay in part or in installments [70] or on specified conditions.[71]

62. United States v. Curtiss Aeroplane Co., 147 F.2d 639 (2nd Cir. 1945); 1 Williston §§ 183–184. But if the debtor makes the promise indicating he reserves the right to raise other defenses, there is no implied promise to pay the debt. The promise may, however, be enforced if supported by consideration or if the claimant relies on the promise to his detriment. 1 Williston § 184.

63. 1 Williston § 183; Restatement, Contracts § 558; see McKinney's N.Y. C.P.L.R. 201. See also U.C.C. § 725(1) which provides:
"An action for breach of any contract for sale must be commenced within four years after the cause of action has accrued. By the original agreement the parties may reduce the period of limitation to not less than one year but may not extend it."

64. Curtiss Wright Corp. v. Intercontinent Corp., 277 App.Div. 13, 97 N.Y.S. 2d 678 (1st Dep't 1950). Some courts are reluctant to infer a promise. See Wipf v. Blake, 72 S.D. 10, 28 N.W.2d 881 (1947); Dolby v. Fisher, 1 Wash. 2d 181, 95 P.2d 369 (1939); see generally, 1A Corbin § 216; 1 Williston §§ 166–173.

65. A'Court v. Cross, 3 Bing. 329 (C.P. 1825).

66. 1 Williston 164; Restatement, Contracts (2d) § 86, Comment a; e. g., McKinney's N.Y.Gen.Obligations Law § 17–101.

67. Restatement, Contracts (2d) § 86, Comment e. The word "may" is used in the text because the question is whether the part payment is to be interpreted as an implied promise to pay the balance. This is often a question of fact. Jones v. Jones, 242 F.Supp. 979 (S.D.N.Y.1965); see also 1A Corbin § 217, 1 Williston § 174.

68. Security Bank v. Finkelstein, 160 App.Div. 315, 145 N.Y.S. 5 (1st Dep't 1913), aff'd 217 N.Y. 707, 112 N.E. 1076 (1916); Restatement, Contracts (2d) § 86, Comment e; 1 Williston § 175.

69. Tebo v. Robinson, 100 N.Y. 27, 2 N. E. 383 (1885).

70. Gillingham v. Brown, 178 Mass. 417, 60 N.E. 122 (1901); 1 Williston § 181.

71. E. g., Big Diamond Milling Co. v. Chicago, M. & St. P. R. Co., 142 Minn.

Originally, the rule enforcing new promises to pay debts barred by the statute of limitations was apparently limited to antecedent obligations enforceable pursuant to the writ known as indebitatus assumpsit or general assumpsit.[72] Generally, this writ was available to enforce claims for liquidated amounts or for the reasonable value of an executed performance.[73] New promises to pay obligations enforceable in special assumpsit or covenant were apparently not enforced; the former writ was applicable to a breach of an executory contract. Consequently, the first Restatement stated the rule that a promise to pay all or part of any antecedent contractual or quasi-contractual obligations for the payment of money, whether liquidated or not, commences the running of the statute of limitations anew.[74]

This means by way of illustration that if A, a painter, painted B's house at B's request and B subsequently promised to pay for the services B's subsequent promise would start the statute of limitations running anew even though the obligation was unliquidated.[75] However, if A and B above entered into a bilateral contract with respect to the painting and B breached the contract before A performed, a subsequent promise by B to pay the damages caused by his breach would have no effect upon the statute of limitations.[76]

With the abolition of the writ system a number of cases began to hold that the subsequent promise would have the effect of starting the obligation running anew even though the promise was to pay an obligation under seal or to pay a judgment.[77] The original Restatement took the position that the antecedent duty may be under seal but that "an antecedent duty under a judgment is not, however, included."[78] The Restatement Second takes no position with regard to sealed instruments or judgments.[79] The Restatement Second makes specific what appears to have been generally recognized that

---

181, 171 N.W. 799, 8 A.L.R. 1254 (1919); see 1 Williston §§ 179, 182.

72. Restatement, Contracts (2d) § 86, Comment b.

73. See Shipman, Common Law Pleading 254–55 (1923).

74. Restatement, Contracts § 86.

75. Restatement, Contracts § 86(1), Comment b. But some cases have held that the indebtedness must be defined by the new promise. Bell v. Morrison, 26 U.S. (1 Pet.) 351, 7 L.Ed. 174 (1828).

76. 1 Williston § 188.

77. Trustees of St. Mark's Evang. Lutheran Church v. Miller, 99 Md. 23, 57 A. 644 (1904); Spilde v. Johnson, 132 Iowa 484, 109 N.W. 1023 (1906).

78. Restatement, Contracts § 86(1), Comment b. Williston asserts that there is no logical basis for this distinction (1 Williston § 187), and Corbin takes the position that a promise to pay a specialty debt or a barred judgment should be enforceable. 1A Corbin § 220.

79. Restatement, Contracts (2d) § 86, Comment b.

a promise to pay a tort claim has no effect upon the statute of limitations unless the tort claim involves unjust enrichment.[80]

§ 86. Promises to Perform Voidable Duties

If A is induced by fraud to promise to pay B $100 in return for property worth much less, his promise is voidable. If, upon discovering the fraud, he again promises to pay $100, or some lesser sum, the new promise is enforceable without consideration,[81] provided of course, that the new promise is not itself voidable because it is induced by fraud or suffers from some other infirmity. If the second promise is made without knowledge of the fraud, it is not enforceable.[82]

The same analysis is applicable to contracts voidable on other grounds, such as duress, mistake and infancy.

The rule set forth herein has not been generally applied to void contracts [83] although there is an occasional case to the contrary.[84]

The rule of law discussed here may also be explained on grounds other than the presence or absence of consideration. A voidable promise gives the promisor the right to elect to avoid or to affirm the promise. In promising to make payment he has given notice of his election not to exercise his power of avoidance.[85]

§ 87. New Promise Based Upon a Previous Promise Within the Statute of Frauds

If A and B enter into a contract which is unenforceable under the Statute of Frauds,[86] should a subsequent oral promise based upon the previous agreement within the Statute of Frauds be enforceable? Assuming first that the arrangement within the Statute of Frauds is still executory, it might seem that the case is analogous to the voidable promises discussed above and that therefore the subsequent oral promise should be enforceable despite the absence of consideration.[87] However there is, as we have seen, an important distinction frequently made between a voidable contract and an un-

---

80. Restatement, Contracts (2d) § 86, Comment b; 1 Williston § 186.

81. Restatement, Contracts § 89 (both editions).

82. Restatement, Contracts § 93 (both editions). The promisor need only know the essential facts. It is not necessary that he know that the facts give him a legal power of avoidance or other remedy. But see § 124 infra as to infants.

83. Restatement, Contracts § 89 (both editions).

84. Sheldon v. Haxtun, 91 N.Y. 124 (1883).

85. 1 Williston § 204.

86. See ch. 16 infra.

87. See § 86 supra.

88. See § 9 supra and Restatement, Contracts (2d) § 89, Comment a.

enforceable contract, to wit, a voidable contract may be ratified but an unenforceable contract may not.[88] Since the real basis of the cases in the preceding section is the power of ratification it is clear that they are not analogous to the Statute of Frauds cases and this has been reinforced by recognition of the fact that enforcement of the subsequent oral promise would violate the policy of the Statute of Frauds which is to curtail perjured claims.[89]

A different problem would be presented if the subsequent promise were in writing. Under the Statute of Frauds it is well settled that a memorandum subsequent to the agreement which sufficiently outlines the details of the transaction satisfies the Statute of Frauds and it is immaterial that there is no consideration for the memorandum.[90] Thus, if the subsequent promise is contained in a sufficient memorandum it will be enforceable. But there is some authority for the proposition that where the writing definitely states the terms of the promise even though it does not serve as a sufficient memorandum, it should be enforceable.[91]

The situation is also different where the agreement which is unenforceable under the Statute of Frauds has been performed by one of the parties. Under these circumstances it is generally accepted that the party who has performed is entitled to a quasi-contractual recovery.[92] A subsequent promise to pay what is owing under this quasi-contractual obligation raises problems similar to the problems discussed in sections 81 and 82 above.

The cases decided in this area of the Statute of Frauds show such a broad split of authority for such a variety of reasons that complete analysis is not feasible here.[93] Suffice it to say that it is believed that the analysis set forth above would serve to reduce much of the conflict.

A major conservative force in this area has been the overgeneralized but influential note made by the reporters to the case of

---

89. Hill v. Dodge, 80 N.H. 381, 117 A. 728 (1922).

90. See § 310 infra.

91. 1 Williston § 199; Donald Friedman & Co. v. Newman, 255 N.Y. 340, 174 N.E. 703, 73 A.L.R. 95 (1931), rearg. denied 255 N.Y. 632, 175 N.E. 345, 73 A.L.R. 95.

92. See § 319 et seq. infra. But occasionally a statute is drawn in such a way as to prevent a quasi contractual recovery. In such a case the subse-

quent promise should be enforced unless the subsequent promise is included in the prohibition. 1A Corbin § 238.

93. 1 Williston § 199; 1A Corbin § 238. The Restatement, Contracts (2d) § 89A, Comment g, states that "the new promise is binding if the policy of the statute is satisfied." See, e. g., Muir v. Kane, 55 Wash. 131, 104 P. 153 (1909); Coulter v. Howard, 203 Cal. 17, 262 P. 751 (1927); Bagaeff v. Prokopik, 212 Mich. 265, 180 N.W. 427, 17 A.L.R. 1292 (1920).

Wennall v. Adney.[94] This asserted that a new promise to pay a debt that had been barred by operation of law is enforceable while a new promise to pay a debt unenforceable at its inception is not enforceable. This over-generalization frequently has been criticized in the cases [95] and the treatises,[96] and should be discarded.

§ 88. Miscellaneous Promises Supported by Antecedent Events

On moral obligation and related grounds a number of cases which have not been previously discussed have enforced promises based on antecedent events. These include promises by sureties or indorsers who have been discharged on technical grounds,[97] promises to repay sums collected by force of an erroneous but valid judgment [98] and promises to pay for benefits received under an illegal bargain when the illegality does not involve moral turpitude,[99] as well as others.[1]

§ 89. To Whom the Promise Must be Made

A new promise to pay an antecedent obligation, to be enforceable, must be made to an obligee of the antecedent duty or his representative.[2] A promise made to a stranger to the transaction has no operative effect unless it can be anticipated that this person will communicate the promise to the obligee.[3] In a few jurisdictions, where a mere admission of the indebtedness is sufficient to revive the debt, an admission or promise made to a third person is sufficient.[4]

94. 127 Eng.Rep. 137 (K.B. 1802).

95. Bagaeff v. Prokopik, 212 Mich. 265, 180 N.W. 427, 17 A.L.R. 1292 (1920); Goulding v. Davidson, 26 N.Y. 604, 25 How Pr. 483 (1863) (contract usurious in its inception); Muir v. Kane, 55 Wash. 131, 104 P. 153 (1909); but see Stout v. Humphrey, 69 N.J.L. 436, 55 A. 281 (1903).

96. 1A Corbin § 239; 1 Williston § 202.

97. 1A Corbin § 224.

98. Bentley v. Morse, 14 Johns (N.Y.) 468 (1817); 1A Corbin § 225.

99. 1A Corbin § 236.

1. 1A Corbin §§ 210–329.

2. City of Fort Scott v. Hickman, 112 U.S. 150, 5 S.Ct. 56, 28 L.Ed. 636 (1884); Restatement, Contracts (2d) § 92; 1 Williston §§ 154, 185, esp. 189. A beneficiary and a surety are included in the term obligee. Restatement, Contracts (2d) § 92, Comment b.

3. Miller v. Teeter, 53 N.J.Eq. 262, 31 A. 394 (1895).

4. In re Stratman's Estate, 231 Iowa 480, 1 N.W.2d 636 (1942).

B. CONSIDERATION NOT REQUIRED IN CERTAIN COMMERCIAL AND WRITTEN CONTRACTS

Analysis

Sec.
90. Scope of the Discussion.
91. The Model Written Obligations Act.
92. Modification of Contracts.
93. Modifications Under Compulsion.
94. Release and Accord and Satisfaction.
    (a) Release.
    (b) Accord and Satisfaction.
95. Firm Offers.
96. Past Consideration.

§ 90. Scope of the Discussion

At common law, persons wishing to enter into a contract without consideration were empowered to resort to a sealed instrument.[5] In recent decades, by legislation and judicial decision, the legal effect of the seal has been abolished or substantially curtailed in a majority of jurisdictions.[6] Partly in an attempt to fill the gap thus created legislatures have reacted with a number of statutes which provide that specified kinds of promises are enforceable without consideration. The abolition of the seal was not the only motive for these statutes. Ever since Lord Mansfield's day,[7] there has been a lingering feeling that written agreements show sufficient deliberation and that the requirement of consideration, as applied to them, tends, without sufficient justification, to defeat the expectations of the parties. Similarly, the doctrine has sometimes seemed to have defeated commercial expectations without any countervailing benefit to the state's interest in regulating private contracts.

A text of this size does not purport to attempt complete coverage of local variations. Only the most significant types of statutes will be considered.

§ 91. The Model Written Obligations Act

Pennsylvania is the only state which presently has on its books[8] the Model (formerly Uniform) Written Obligations Act.[9] This provides:

> "A written release or promise, hereafter made and signed by the person releasing or promising, shall not be in-

---

5. See ch. 7 infra.

6. Id.

7. See § 78 supra.

8. 33 P.S. § 6–8.

9. 9C U.L.A. 378 (adopted 1925).

valid or unenforceable for lack of consideration, if the writing also contains an additional express statement, in any form of language, that the signer intends to be legally bound."

Under this statute, a written promise is not sufficient; there must be "an additional express statement" indicating the promisor's intent to be bound.[10] It has been held that the following language is insufficient to meet the statutory requirements: [11]

"We, Pauline and Mike, release you from all obligations under the Lease, for the balance thereof, and will not hold you responsible whatsoever under the Lease if you sell to Mr. Brown."

If appropriate language is used, however, a gratuitous promise is enforceable.[12]

§ 92. Modification of Contracts

As previously discussed, according to the majority of cases, under the pre-existing duty rule an enforceable agreement to modify a contract requires consideration on both sides.[13] This rule has been mitigated in a number of states when unforeseen difficulties arise in the performance of the contract,[14] and eliminated by judicial decision in a distinct minority of jurisdictions.[15] There are some statutes less sweeping than the Model Written Obligations Act which relate specifically to modifications.

The Sales Article of the Uniform Commercial Code provides in § 2–209(1):

"An agreement modifying a contract within this Article needs no consideration to be binding."

The Code does not require the modifying agreement to be written except in two important instances. First, a writing is required if the contract as modified is within the Statute of Frauds provision of the Code.[16] Also, a writing is required if the original contract by its terms excludes modification or rescission [17] by mutual consent except by a

---

10. Gershman v. Metropolitan Life Ins. Co., 405 Pa. 585, 176 A.2d 435 (1962) (words, "Approved by" followed by a signature are insufficient to meet the statutory requirement).

11. Fedun v. Mike's Cafe, Inc., 204 Pa. Super. 356, 204 A.2d 776 (1964), aff'd 419 Pa. 607, 213 A.2d 638 (1965).

12. See In re Goldstein's Estate, 384 Pa. 1, 119 A.2d 278 (1956) (there was consideration, however, in this case).

13. See § 61 supra.

14. See § 61 supra.

15. See § 61 supra.

16. U.C.C. § 2–209(3). See § 316 infra.

17. Note that there is no consideration question as to rescission. A mutual rescission of contract executory on both sides is supported by the detriment incurred by each party in sur-

signed writing.[18] If the contract is between a merchant [19] and a non-merchant, a term on the merchant's form requiring that modification or rescission be in a signed writing must be separately signed by the non-merchant.[20]

Section 2–209 expressly deals with the contingency of an oral or unsigned modification or rescission even where a signed writing is required. Subdivisions (4) and (5) provide that the attempted modification or rescission can operate as a waiver. However, the waiver may be retracted by giving reasonable notification "unless the retraction would be unjust in view of a material change of position in reliance on the waiver." [21]

An illustrative case under § 2–209 is Skinner v. Tober Foreign Motors, Inc.[22] The defendant sold and delivered an airplane to the plaintiff who agreed to pay the purchase price at the rate of $200 per month. Soon after delivery, it was discovered that the engine was faulty. Apparently, the airplane was not warranted. Since the plaintiff would have to incur considerable expense in repairing the engine, defendant orally agreed that for one year plaintiff would have to pay only $100 per month toward the price.[23] Several months later, defendant demanded that the payments be increased to $200. Plaintiff refused and defendant repossessed the aircraft. It was held that the modification was binding without consideration and that defendant was liable for substantial damages.

Outside of the Uniform Commercial Code, other statutory provisions relating to modification exist. For example, there is a New York statute which relates to modifications among other things. The New York statute is substantially the same as § 2–209 of the Uniform Commercial Code, except that a writing is required in every case.[24]

rendering his rights. Schwartzreich v. Bauman-Basch, Inc., 231 N.Y. 196, 131 N.E. 887 (1921), rearg. denied 231 N.Y. 602, 132 N.E. 905.

18. U.C.C. § 2–209(2).

19. "Merchant" is defined in U.C.C. § 2–104(1). It has been pointed out that the definition will present perplexing problems. Note, 39 Geo.L.J. 130 (1950). In Cook Grains, Inc. v. Fallis, 239 Ark. 962, 395 S.W.2d 555 (1965), it was held that a farmer who sells his crops is not a merchant.

20. U.C.C. § 2–209(2).

21. U.C.C. § 2–209(5).

22. 345 Mass. 429, 187 N.E.2d 669 (1963), 65 W.Va.L.Rev. 330 (1963).

23. Since the defendant did not plead the defense of the Statute of Frauds, the court did not reach the question whether a writing was required by § 2–201 of the Code.

24. McKinney's   N.Y.Gen.Obligations Law § 5–1103, effective in 1936, as since amended, provides:
"An agreement, promise or undertaking to change or modify, or to discharge in whole or in part, any contract, obligation, or lease, or any mortgage or other security interest in personal or real property, shall not be invalid because of the absence of consideration,

§ 93. Modifications Under Compulsion

The pre-existing duty rule in addition to the conceptual ground sustaining it, has had an important policy rationale. In an early decision, a sailor who had signed for a voyage at a stipulated wage sued to recover for additional wages promised him during the voyage. Lord Kenyon, in rendering his decision, was little concerned about concepts of consideration. Rather, he urged:

> "If this action was to be supported, it would materially affect the navigation of this kingdom . . . . [I]f sailors were . . . in times of danger entitled to insist on an extra charge on such a promise as this, they would in many cases suffer a ship to sink, unless the captain would pay any extravagant demand they might think proper to make." [25]

In repeated instances, courts have defended the pre-existing duty rule as a salutary method of preventing the coerced modification of contracts.[26] Now that the Uniform Commercial Code and other legislation permit a contractual modification without consideration it seems clear that other techniques need to be developed to avoid coerced modifications.

The Code must be read as an integrated document. As the comments to § 2–209 make clear the good faith standard of § 2–103 ("the observance of reasonable commercial standards of fair dealing in the trade")[27] is applicable to a request for modification. It will, of course,

provided that the agreement, promise or undertaking changing, modifying, or discharging such contract, obligation, lease, mortgage or security interest, shall be in writing and signed by the party against whom it is sought to enforce the change, modification or discharge, or by his agent."
Compare such statutes as Mass.G.L.A. c. 4, § 9A, providing that an instrument reciting that it is a sealed instrument will be treated as a sealed instrument. Compare also such statutes as Miss. Code 1942, §§ 260–262, giving the effect of a sealed instrument to all writings. The effect of the statutes such as these depends on the effect seals have heretofore had in the particular jurisdiction. See § 120 infra.

25. Harris v. Watson, 170 Eng.Rep. at 94 (K.B. 1791); see also Stilk v. Myrick, 170 Eng.Rep. 1168 (C.P. 1809); Bartlett v. Wyman, 14 Johns (N.Y.) 260 (1817) (similar facts; cases decid-

ed on grounds of lack of consideration); see § 61 supra.

26. See, e. g., Lingenfelder v. Wainwright Brewery Co., 103 Mo. 578, 15 S.W. 844 (1891).

27. On "good faith" under the U.C.C., and some of the questions surrounding the term, see Broeker, Articles 2 and 6; Sales and Bulk Transfers, 15 U. Pitt.L.Rev. 541, 554 (1954); Farnsworth, Good Faith Performance and Commercial Reasonableness under the Uniform Commercial Code, 30 U.Chi. L.Rev. 666, 675–76 (1963) Rabel, the Sales Law in the Proposed Commercial Code, 17 U.Chi.L.Rev. 427, 431 (1950); Spies, Sales, Article II, 16 Ark.L.Rev. 6 (1961); Whitney, Contracts, 26 St. John's L.Rev. 3, 18 (1951); and particularly Note, 23 U. Pitt.L.Rev. 754 (1962) which points out that the term "good faith" is used in three different senses in the Code.

require a good deal of creative interpretation of the Code before standards are developed for distinguishing between reasonable and unreasonable demands for modification.[28]

As to modifications entered into under other statutory dispensations from the requirement of consideration, the common law doctrine of duress is relevant. The doctrine, in most jurisdictions has been rather narrow in scope. Generally, it has been held that a threat to break a contract does not constitute duress.[29] Of late, however, courts have begun to hold that various kinds of "business compulsion" constitute duress.[30] It is likely that this concept will be developed to the point where a bad faith demand for modification will be treated as duress. In this way the various statutory provisions permitting contractual modifications without consideration will be brought into harmony with the Code.

§ 94.   Release and Accord and Satisfaction

(a) Release

The pre-existing duty concept led to the rule that a release of a duty is ordinarily ineffectual without consideration.[31] Section 1–107 of the U.C.C. provides, however, that: "Any claim of right arising out of alleged breach can be discharged in whole or in part by a written waiver or renunciation signed and delivered by the aggrieved party."

---

28. Clearly, if unforeseen difficulties arise which are sufficient to excuse performance for "failure of presupposed conditions" (U.C.C. §§ 2–614, 2–615), a modification is permissible since detriment would exist in the surrender of the privilege not to perform.

If unforeseen difficulties of a less significant kind arise, such as has led a minority of states, prior to enactment of the Code, to permit a modification agreement without new detriment, [§ 61 supra; Restatement, Contracts (2d) § 89D], it seems equally clear that a modification would be enforced under the Code. Doubtless, this was the line of cases which inspired § 2–209 of the Code. Indeed, the language of the Code permits a far broader permissibility of modifications, limited only by good faith. Comment 2 to Section 2–209 indicates that "a market shift which makes performance come to in-

volve a loss" may sufficiently show good faith.

29. Hartsville Oil Mill v. United States, 271 U.S. 43, 46 S.C. 389, 70 L. Ed. 822 (1926); Doyle v. Rector, etc. of Trinity Church, 133 N.Y. 372, 31 N.E. 221 (1892); Oleet v. Pa. Exchange Bank, 285 App.Div. 411, 137 N.Y.S.2d 779 (1st Dep't 1955), see also § 61 n. 9 supra. The scope of the concept of duress is treated very narrowly in the Restatement, Contracts §§ 492–496, 499. More liberal cases include Pittsburgh Steel Co. v. Hollingshead & Blei, 202 Ill.App. 177 (1916); Hochman v. Zigler's Inc., 139 N.J.Eq. 139, 50 A.2d 97 (1946), 1 Rutgers L. Rev. 309 (1947).

30. King Constr. Co. v. W. M. Smith Elec. Co., 350 S.W.2d 940 (Tex.Civ. App.1961), 41 Texas L.Rev. 317 (1962).

31. See § 347 infra.

The section appears to relate to a discharge by way of release since the word renunciation is the word of art used to cover an oral release.[32]

The section is comparable to § 15–303 of the New York General Obligations Law which provides: "A written instrument which purports to be a total or partial release of any particular claim . . ., shall not be invalid because of the absence of consideration or of a seal." [33]

It should be noted that Code Section 1–107 applies only to a claim or right arising out of an "alleged breach" whereas the New York statute covers the release of any claim or obligations even if there has been no breach.

(b) Accord and Satisfaction

We have previously discussed a case where C claims that D owes him $100.00, D claims that he owes C $50.00 and there is a bona fide dispute. D then sends C a check marked payment in full which C cashes while protesting that the check is a partial payment. At common law C could not collect the balance due because the claim is unliquidated and so there is consideration for C's agreement to take less and an accord and satisfaction is created with the result that C's protest is unavailing.[34]

However § 1–207 of the U.C.C. provides:

"A party who with explicit reservation of rights performs or promises performance or assents to performance in a manner demanded or offered by the other party does not thereby prejudice the rights reserved. Such words as 'without prejudice', 'under protest' or the like are sufficient."

This section would certainly appear to change the result in the case discussed above in a Code-covered transaction.

The New York statute set out in note 24 supra also raises an interesting question in the area of accord and satisfaction. We have previously seen that where D owes C a liquidated debt and he sends a check for a lesser amount the debt is not discharged even if D sends a check marked "payment in full" and C cashes it. D is only doing what he is legally obligated to do and there is therefore no consideration and the alleged accord and satisfaction is therefore invalid.[35] What is the result under the New York Statute in such a

---

32. See § 349 infra.

33. Statutes similar to the New York Statute may be found in 1 Williston § 120 n. 9.

34. See § 65 supra.

35. See § 65 supra. The statute would clearly seem to apply where a creditor states in a signed writing that he will

case? It could be argued that the phrase "payment in full" is a writing and that the creditor's endorsement of the check is a signing within the meaning of the statute and that therefore there is an accord and satisfaction since, because of the statutory provision, consideration is not necessary to support it. However, this argument appears to have been rejected by the New York cases unless the evidence shows that the creditor actually consented and acted with deliberation.[36]

§ 95. Firm Offers

As previously discussed, under the U.C.C. and under a number of other state statutes, an offer may be made irrevocable without consideration, if expressed in writing.[37]

§ 96. Past Consideration

As indicated,[38] past events do not constitute consideration, in the bargain sense, for a promise. For example, a promise by C to guarantee payment of a debt owed by B to A, requires new consideration,[39] and a promise made after an employee's retirement to pay him a pension, is unenforceable.[40] A provision of the New York General Obligations Law [41] provides that:

> "A promise in writing and signed by the promisor or by his agent shall not be denied effect as a valid contractual obligation on the ground that consideration for the promise is past or executed, if the consideration is expressed in the writing and is proved to have been given or performed and would be valid consideration but for the time it was given or performed."

Similar results are obtainable under broader statutes, such as the Model Written Obligations Act.[42]

take a lesser amount in discharge of a liquidated debt and the lesser amount is paid by the debtor.

36. King Metal Products, Inc. v. Workmen's Compensation Bd., 20 A.D.2d 565, 245 N.Y.S.2d 882 (2d Dep't 1963); Glen Navigation Corp. v. Trodden, 97 N.Y.S.2d 228 (N.Y.City Ct. 1950); Horan v. John F. Trommer, Inc., 15 Misc.2d 347, 137 N.Y.S.2d 26 (Sup.Ct. 1954); Armour & Co. v. Schlacter, 159 N.Y.S.2d 135 (Westchester County Ct. 1957).

37. See § 37 supra.

38. See § 54 supra.

39. Strong v. Sheffield, 144 N.Y. 392, 39 N.E. 330 (1895).

40. Perreault v. Hall, 94 N.H. 191, 49 A.2d 812 (1946).

41. § 5–1105 (enacted in 1941, as since amended).

42. See § 91 supra.

C. STIPULATIONS

Analysis

Sec.
97. Stipulations Defined.
98. Consideration and Formality in Stipulations.

§ 97. Stipulations Defined

A stipulation is a promise or agreement with reference to a pending judicial proceeding, made by a party to the proceeding or his attorney.[43] Stipulations are favored by the courts. They tend to relieve court congestion and place the settlement of litigation or details of the litigation on the litigants where it primarily belongs.

§ 98. Consideration and Formality in Stipulations

Generally, statutes or rules of court provide that a stipulation should be in writing or made in open court.[44] Stipulations are enforced without regard to consideration [45] but as in the case of any other kind of contract, fraud or other vitiating circumstances can be shown to avoid its legal effect.[46]

An oral stipulation not made in court is not a nullity. The cannons of ethics state that it is dishonorable for an attorney to avoid performance of an oral agreement and a court will enforce an oral stipulation upon which a party relies to his detriment.[47]

43. See Restatement, Contracts (2d) § 94; 1 Williston § 204A.

44. Id.

45. Crunden-Martin Mfg. Co. v. Christy, 22 Ariz. 254, 196 P. 454 (1921); Connors v. United Metal Products Co., 209 Minn. 300, 296 N.W. 21 (1941).

46. 1 Williston § 204A. Indeed, a court has power to relieve a party from a stipulation if there is no prejudice to the other party, for reasons such as inadvertence, improvidence or excusable neglect. Hester v. New Amsterdam Cas. Co., 268 F.Supp. 623 (D.C.S. C.1967).

47. Mutual Life Ins. Co. v. O'Donnell, 146 N.Y. 275, 40 N.E. 787 (1895); Restatement, Contracts (2d) § 94(c).

CHAPTER 6

PROMISSORY ESTOPPEL: DETRIMENTAL RELIANCE AS A SUBSTITUTE FOR CONSIDERATION

Analysis

		Sections
A.	History of the Doctrine	99–105
B.	Modern Trends in Doctrine	106–111

A. HISTORY OF THE DOCTRINE

Sec.
 99. Introduction.
100. Promises in the Family.
101. Oral Gifts of Land.
102. Gratuitous Agencies and Bailments.
103. Charitable Subscriptions.
104. Other Roots of the Doctrine of Promissory Estoppel.
105. Traditional Approach to the Promissory Estoppel Doctrine.

B. MODERN TRENDS IN DOCTRINE

106. Modern Trends Generally.
107. Offers by Subcontractors.
108. Promises of Franchises: Is Promissory Estoppel a Non-contractual
        Cause of Action?
109. Pensions and Other Fringe Benefits.
110. Flexibility of Remedy.
111. The Future of Promissory Estoppel.

A. HISTORY OF THE DOCTRINE

Analysis

Sec.
 99. Introduction.
100. Promises in the Family.
101. Oral Gifts of Land.
102. Gratuitous Agencies and Bailments.
103. Charitable Subscriptions.
104. Other Roots of the Doctrine of Promissory Estoppel.
105. Traditional Approach to the Promissory Estoppel Doctrine.

§ 99. Introduction

Section 90 of the Restatement Second states the doctrine of promissory estoppel [1] in the following terms: [2]

> "A promise which the promisor should reasonably expect to induce action or forbearance on the part of the promisee or a third person and which does induce such action or forbearance is binding if injustice can be avoided only by enforcement of the promise. The remedy for breach may be limited as justice requires."

As a generalized doctrine, promissory estoppel is a twentieth century innovation. Nonetheless, it has ancient roots. It has been extracted as a general principle from a number of recurring decisions which were difficult, and sometimes impossible, to explain in terms of the doctrine of consideration. [3]

Ordinarily the key difference between a promise supported by consideration and a promise supported by promissory estoppel is that in the former case the detriment is bargained for in exchange for the promise; in the latter, there is no bargain. The detriment is a consequence of the promise but does not induce the making of the promise. Justice Holmes in arguing for strict adherence to the concept of consideration said, "It is not enough that the promise induces the detriment or that the detriment induces the promise if the other half is wanting." [4] Elsewhere, he lamented that the courts "have gone far" in losing sight of this fact. [5] The modern law has tended to hold firm to Holmes' view of consideration and to develop a separate doctrine from the cases which he had criticized as stretching the doctrine of consideration beyond its conceptual boundaries.

---

1. The distinction between promissory estoppel and equitable estoppel or estoppel *in pais* is discussed in § 166 infra; see also note 9 infra.

2. Section 90 of the first Restatement stated the doctrine in the following terms:

"A promise which the promisor should reasonably expect to induce action or forbearance of a definite and substantial character on the part of the promisee and which does induce such action or forbearance is binding if injustice can be avoided only by enforcement of the promise."

There are three significant differences between the formulations. The Second Restatement has excised the words,

"of a definite and substantial character." See 1A Corbin § 200 on the meaning of the word "definite." It added a new sentence permitting flexibility of remedy. See § 110 infra. It has also provided for the contingency of reliance by a third party.

3. See Boyer, Promissory Estoppel: Principle from Precedents (Pts. I & II), 50 Mich.L.Rev. 639, 873 (1952).

4. Wisconsin & Mich. Ry. Co. v. Powers, 191 U.S. 379, 386, 24 S.Ct. 107, 108, 48 L.Ed. 229 (1903).

5. Holmes, The Common Law 292 (1881).

This chapter will first consider some of the typical fact patterns from which the doctrine was distilled (§§ 100–103) and will conclude with illustrations of the modern application of the doctrine in new situations.

§ 100.　Promises in the Family

In the case of Devecmon v. Shaw,[6] an uncle of the plaintiff promised him that if plaintiff would take a trip to Europe, he would reimburse his expenses. The nephew made the trip but the uncle's executor [7] refused to make payment. The court concluded that the uncle's promise was supported by consideration. Surely there was detriment, but the court did not consider whether the detriment was bargained for in exchange for the promise.

The court came to grips with the conceptual problem in Ricketts v. Scothorn.[8] A grandfather had given his granddaughter a promissory note, indicating that it was for the purpose of freeing her from the necessity of working. It was clear that he was not demanding that she cease working in exchange for the note. The court recognized that there was no consideration for the note and held that the note would be enforced against the grandfather's estate on the grounds of estoppel *in pais*. Traditionally, estoppel *in pais* has been limited to cases in which one party has represented a fact to the other who relies on the representation.[9] In such cases the court bars the party who has made the representation from contradicting it. The court in Ricketts v. Scothorn extended the doctrine of estoppel to promissory expressions.

Recognition of the doctrine of promissory estoppel as an independent ground for enforcing intra-family promises can lead to a profitable reexamination of many similar cases decided on grounds of consideration.[10]

§ 101.　Oral Gifts of Land

Cases involving oral gifts of land generally arise in a family context and are related to the cases discussed in the preceding section.

6.　69 Md. 199, 14 A. 464 (1888).

7.　How often it is in these cases that the promise is not repudiated. Frequently it is the executor, conscious of the possibility of being surcharged, who refuses the payment. One cannot but conjecture the importance of this factor on the decisions.

8.　57 Neb. 51, 77 N.W. 365 (1898).

9.　Courts had traditionally held that an estoppel could not be created by reliance on a promise. See Prescott v. Jones, 69 N.H. 305, 41 A. 352 (1898) ; see also note 1 supra.

10.　E. g., Hamer v. Sidway, and Kirksey v. Kirksey, discussed at § 57 supra.

The land cases, however, involve non-compliance with the Statute of Frauds [11] as well as the absence of consideration and have an historical background somewhat different from other kinds of intra-family promises.

An oral *promise* to give land, standing alone, is unenforceable because of the lack of delivery of a conveyance to complete the gift. Not infrequently, however, acting in reliance on the oral promise or oral gift, the promisee takes possession of the land and makes improvements. Courts of equity in almost all states in such circumstances have granted the promisee specific performance [12] or other equitable remedies. [13] Traditionally, the expressed rationales of the decisions have been of two kinds. Sometimes, the court has relied on an analogy from the law of gifts, treating the entry upon the land and the making of improvements as the equivalent to physical delivery of a chattel. [14] Perhaps more frequently the courts have said that the taking of possession and the making improvements constitute "good consideration in equity." [15] Under modern ideas of the relationship between law and equity it is indeed anomalous that a different definition of consideration should prevail in the equity and law sides of the court.

It is now recognized that the decisions enforcing oral promises to give land are based on promissory estoppel. [16]

11. The Statute of Frauds generally requires that a contract to create or the creation of an interest in land be in writing. See §§ 295–296, 326–327 infra.

12. Seavey v. Drake, 62 N.H. 393 (1882); Freeman v. Freeman, 43 N.Y. 34 (1870); see also Wohlford v. Wohlford, 121 Va. 699, 93 S.E. 629 (1917). Some courts have distinguished between promises to make a gift and present gifts, stating that the former are not enforceable. Prior v. Newsom, 144 Ark. 593, 223 S.W. 21 (1920); Burris v. Landers, 114 Cal. 310, 46 P. 162 (1896); Hagerty v. Hagerty, 186 Iowa 1329, 172 N.W. 259 (1919).

13. King's Heirs v. Thompson, 34 U.S. (9 Pet.) 204, 9 L.Ed. 102 (1835) (equitable lien). In addition, an action for restitution at law or equity is available. Carter v. Carter, 182 N.C. 186, 108 S.E. 765, 17 A.L.R. 945 (1921).

14. Horsfield v. Gedicks, 94 N.J.Eq. 82, 118 A. 275 (Ch.1922), aff'd 96 N.J.Eq. 384, 124 A. 925 (1924).

15. Young v. Overbaugh, 145 N.Y. 158, 163, 39 N.E. 712, 713 (1895); Lindell v. Lindell, 135 Minn. 368, 371, 160 N. W. 1031, 1032 (1917) ("A parol promise by an owner to give land to another either by deed or will accompanied by actual delivery of possession, becomes an enforceable promise, when the promisee induced thereby has made substantial improvements upon the premises with knowledge of the promisor. The promise to give is no longer *nudum pactum*. It has become a promise upon a consideration . . .").

16. Greiner v. Greiner, 131 Kan. 760, 293 P. 759 (1930).

§ 102.　Gratuitous Agencies and Bailments

The early case of Coggs v. Bernard [17] has been highly influential in this area. A carter agreed to transport a keg of brandy for the plaintiff free of charge. By reason of the carter's negligence the freight was damaged. It was held that an action for assumpsit would lie for breach of the carter's implied promise to use due care. The court reasoned that the "bare being trusted with another man's goods, must be taken to be a sufficient consideration." [18] It is clear, however, that in such a case the gratuitous bailee does not bargain for the privilege of being trusted with the goods; consequently, the decision is not in accord with modern ideas of consideration. In cases such as Coggs v. Bernard a distinction was drawn between nonfeasance and misfeasance. If the gratuitous promisor takes possession of the goods and fails to carry out his promise with respect to the goods, liability has traditionally been found to exist.[19] If, however, he fails to take possession, traditionally there is no liability on the gratuitous promise to take the goods.[20]

A similar distinction between nonfeasance and misfeasance has been made in cases of gratuitous agencies. Here, the influential case has been Thorne v. Deas.[21] The parties were co-owners of a brig. On the day it was to sail the defendant promised to procure insurance for the voyage. Ten days later, the defendant told the plaintiff that no insurance had been procured. The plaintiff, upset at this revelation said he would procure insurance himself. The defendant, however, told the plaintiff to "make himself easy" and that he would procure coverage that very day. Defendant failed to act and the brig was wrecked. It was held that the defendant was not liable since there was no consideration for the promise and no liability for mere nonfeasance pursuant to a gratuitous promise. If, however, the defendant had negligently procured insurance that was somehow defective, he would have been guilty of misfeasance and liable in contract.[22]

The gratuitous agency and bailment cases coalesced in the case of Siegel v. Spear & Co.[23] The defendant agreed to store plaintiff's

17.　92 Eng.Rep. 107 (K.B. 1703).

18.　Id. at 114.

19.　Siegel v. Spear & Co., 234 N.Y. 479, 138 N.E. 414 (1923).

20.　Tomko v. Sharp, 87 N.J.L. 385, 94 A. 793 (Sup.Ct.1915).

21.　4 Johns. 84 (N.Y.1809), followed in Comfort v. McCorkle, 149 Misc. 826, 268 N.Y.S. 192 (Sup.Ct.1933).

22.　Barile v. Wright, 256 N.Y. 1, 175 N.E. 351 (1931); Elam v. Smithdeal Realty & Ins. Co., 182 N.C. 599, 109 S.E. 632, 18 A.L.R. 1210 (1921).

23.　234 N.Y. 479, 138 N.E. 414 (1923), 23 Colum.L.Rev. 573 (1923); accord, Schroeder v. Mauzy, 16 Cal.App. 443, 118 P. 459 (1911).

furniture free of charge and also agreed to procure insurance at the plaintiff's expense, stating that he could obtain the insurance at a cheaper rate than could the plaintiff. The defendant failed to act and the uninsured furniture was destroyed by fire. It was held that the defendant was liable on his promise. The court characterized the case as one of gratuitous bailment, indicating that once possession of the goods was taken by the bailee, failure to carry out the promise to insure was negligent misfeasance.

This was the state of the law at the time the generalized doctrine of promissory estoppel was formulated in the Restatement. This section has so changed the legal climate in this area that the New York Court of Appeals was able to overrule Thorne v. Deas without citing it and, indeed, without ever referring to the term "promissory estoppel" [24] and other courts have, in similar circumstances, applied the rule as stated in the Restatement.[25]

§ 103.   Charitable Subscriptions

With great frequency but not with complete uniformity, charitable subscriptions have been enforced in this country.[26] There are cases in which the promise to give money to a charity is supported by consideration in the strict sense of the term. The promisor may have bargained for and received a commitment from the charity that the "gift" be employed in a specified way or that a memorial be built bearing the promisor's name.[27]

---

24. Spiegel v. Metropolitan Life Ins. Co., 6 N.Y.2d 91, 188 N.Y.S.2d 486, 160 N.E.2d 40 (1959), 35 N.Y.U.L.Rev. 1486 (1960). This case is discussed in more detail in § 111 infra.

25. Lusk-Harbison-Jones, Inc. v. Universal Credit Co., 164 Miss. 693, 145 So. 623 (1933); Graddon v. Knight, 138 Cal.App.2d 577, 292 P.2d 632 (1956); Northern Commercial Co. v. United Airmotive, 13 Alaska 503, 101 F.Supp. 169 (1951).

The Restatement of Agency (2d) § 378 states a particular application of promissory estoppel in the field of agency. It provides:

One who, by a gratuitous promise or other conduct which he should realize will cause another reasonably to rely upon the performance of definite acts of service by him as the other's agent, causes the other to refrain from having such acts done by other available

means is subject to a duty to use care to perform such service or, while other means are available, to give notice that he will not perform.

26. See generally, 1 Williston §§ 116, 140; 1A Corbin § 198; Billig, The Problem of Consideration in Charitable Subscriptions, 12 Cornell L.Q. 467 (1927); Page, Consideration: Genuine and Synthetic, 1947 Wis.L.Rev. 483; Shattuck, Gratuitous Promises—A New Writ? 35 Mich.L.Rev. 908 (1937). In England, charitable subscriptions generally are not enforced. In re Hudson, 54 L.J.Ch. 811 (1885).

27. Rogers v. Galloway Female College, 64 Ark. 627, 44 S.W. 454 (1898) (in consideration of locating a college in a particular town); American Legion Christie E. Wilson Post No. 324, Rexford, Kan. v. Thompson, 121 Kan. 124, 245 P. 744 (1926) (in consideration of building a particular building).

In the usual case, however, there is no bargain in fact and the promisor manifests a gift making state of mind. Courts have, however, purported to find consideration on various tenuous theories. Some courts have found consideration on the theory that the donee impliedly promises to use the promised gifts for charitable purposes.[28] This rationale is deficient in that the charity is legally bound to use its funds for such purposes [29] and because it is unrealistic to assume that it was this for which the promisor bargained. Other cases have found consideration in the purported exchange of promises between the subscribers.[30] If such an exchange actually is bargained for and actually occurs, consideration exists.[31] But this is hardly what occurs in large fund raising campaigns. A subscriber may be motivated by the fact that others have given or will give. But motive and consideration are not equivalents.[32] Moreover, the prior subscriptions are past and therefore cannot constitute consideration.[33] Other cases have held that the subscription is an offer to a unilateral contract which is accepted by the charity's performance of the terms of the subscription [34] but this is also a rationalization because there is nothing to indicate a contract making state of mind upon the part of the promisor.

Thus wide variation in reasoning indicates the difficulty of enforcing a charitable subscription on grounds of consideration. Yet, the courts have generally striven to find grounds for enforcement, indicating the depth of feeling in this country that private philanthropy serves a highly important function in our society.

Of late, courts have tended to abandon the attempt to utilize traditional contract doctrines to sustain subscriptions and have placed their decision on grounds of promissory estoppel.[35] Surprisingly,

28. Nebraska Wesleyan Univ. v. Griswold's Estate, 113 Neb. 256, 202 N.W. 609, 38 A.L.R. 858 (1925).

29. See 1 Williston § 116.

30. First Presbyterian Church of Mt. Vernon v. Dennis, 178 Iowa 1352, 161 N.W. 183 (1917).

31. Floyd v. Christian Church Widows & Orphans Home of Kentucky, 296 Ky. 196, 176 S.W.2d 125, 151 A.L.R. 1230 (1943); 1 Williston §§ 117, 118; 1A Corbin § 198.

32. See § 54 supra.

33. See § 54 supra.

34. I. & I. Holding Corp. v. Gainsburg, 276 N.Y. 427, 12 N.E.2d 532, 115 A.L. R. 582 (1938), 39 Colum.L.Rev. 283 (1939), 7 Fordham L.Rev. 264 (1938), 12 St. John's L.Rev. 339 (1938).

35. Danby v. Osteopathic Hosp. Ass'n. of Del., 34 Del.Ch. 427, 104 A.2d 903 (1954); Allegheny College v. National Chautauqua County Bank, 246 N.Y. 369, 159 N.E. 173, 57 A.L.R. 980 (1927) (dictum); but cf. I. & I. Holding Corp. v. Gainsburg, 276 N.Y. 427, 12 N.E.2d 532, 115 A.L.R. 582 (1938) (reverting to unilateral contract analyses, applying Restatement, Contracts § 45). For an early case using an estoppel rationale, see Miller v. Western College of Toledo, 177 Ill. 280, 52 N.E. 432 (1898).

however, if promissory estoppel, in its traditional form, is widely adopted as the grounds upon which such subscriptions are to be tested, fewer subscriptions are likely to be enforced than previously. Under previous holdings, despite the conceptual inadequacy of the reasoning, promises were frequently enforced without regard to detrimental reliance on the promise. It was enough that the promisor had subscribed.[36] If enforcement of charitable subscriptions is a desirable goal, it would seem sounder to view the preponderance of the cases as supporting the proposition that a charitable subscription is enforceable without consideration and without detrimental reliance. This seems to be the position taken in the Restatement Second.[37] Recognition of such a rule would also put an end to the flood of needless litigation created by the caution of executors and administrators who, for self-protection against surcharging, will not pay out on a subscription without a court decree.

§ 104. Other Roots of the Doctrine of Promissory Estoppel

Detrimental reliance on a promise has been the basis of court relief in countless cases of the most variegated sort, although the decisions are not always articulated in those terms. Promises of marriage settlements made prior to a marriage have been enforced on this basis.[38] Similarly promises in tort cases not to plead the statute of limitations,[39] and promises otherwise unenforceable under the Statute of Frauds,[40] have been enforced where detrimental reliance has been induced by the promise.

Courts have often employed the concept of equitable estoppel in cases in which a contracting party, without consideration, has promised to waive a contractual condition and the other party has changed his position in reliance upon the promise.[41] Such waivers are promissory in nature and therefore enforcement of such promises is more akin to promissory estoppel [42] than to the older idea of equitable estoppel which, at least originally, required a misrepresentation of fact.

36. E. g., 1A Corbin § 198 ("promises of this kind are now almost universally enforced").

37. See Restatement, Contracts (2d) § 90, Comment c.

38. De Cicco v. Schweizer, 221 N.Y. 431, 117 N.E. 807 (1917), as re-explained in Allegheny College v. National Chautauqua County Bank, 246 N.Y. 369, 159 N.E. 173, 57 A.L.R. 980 (1927).

39. If the promise is made with reference to certain contract claims, no reliance is needed. See § 85 supra.

The rule here discussed is primarily applied in noncontract cases. Armstrong v. Levan, 109 Pa. 177, 1 A. 204 (1885). In New York the principle of estoppel in cases involving the statute of limitation has been codified. McKinney's N.Y.Gen. Obligations Law § 17–103.

40. Monarco v. Lo Greco, 35 Cal.2d 621, 220 P.2d 737 (1950); Loeb v. Gendel, 23 Ill.2d 502, 179 N.E.2d 7 (1961).

41. See §§ 166, 168–169 infra.

42. See 5 Williston §§ 691–692.

The Uniform Commercial Code[43] restates prior case law when it states that a waiver may not be retracted if "the retractions would be unjust in view of a material change of position in reliance on the waiver."[44]

Estoppel principles have widely been applied in promises of various kinds made by mortgagees to mortgagors to the effect that in some specified way the mortgagee will not take full advantage of his rights under the mortgage.[45]

Frequently banking officers and stockholders have given their promissory notes to the bank in a scheme to inflate the apparent assets of the bank. These notes lack consideration and in addition are sham transactions lacking mutual assent. It is usually held, nevertheless, that reliance by the public and by regulatory agencies on these apparent assets renders the notes enforceable.[46]

These categories of cases are by no means inclusive of all cases in which detrimental reliance on a promise was a strong element in the outcome.[47]

§ 105. Traditional Approach to the Promissory Estoppel Doctrine

Before looking to the doctrine of promissory estoppel the courts ordinarily look to see if conventional consideration is present. If not they determine if the elements for a promissory estoppel are present. However even if all of the elements for a promissory estoppel are present the plaintiff will lose unless a given jurisdiction accepts promissory estoppel as a substitute for consideration under the facts of a particular case. As a minimum most jurisdictions will accept the doctrine in the fact patterns discussed above. Thus, Section 90 of the Restatement has been applied to oral gifts of land,[48] gratuitous agencies,[49] charitable subscriptions,[50] and promises not to plead the statute of limitations in tort cases.[51]

---

43. U.C.C. § 2–209(5).

44. Imperator Realty Co. v. Tull, 228 N.Y. 447, 127 N.E. 263 (1920).

45. Schroeder v. Young, 161 U.S. 334, 16 S.Ct. 512, 40 L.Ed. 721 (1896); Wolfe v. Wallingford Bank & Trust Co., 124 Conn. 507, 1 A.2d 146, 117 A. L.R. 932 (1938); Cameron v. Townsend, 286 Pa. 393, 133 A. 632 (1926).

46. D'Oench, Duhme & Co. v. F. D. I. C., 315 U.S. 447, 62 S.Ct. 676, 86 L.Ed. 956 (1942), reh. denied 315 U.S. 830, 62 S.Ct. 910, 86 L.Ed. 1224 (1942); Mt. Vernon Trust Co. v. Bergoff, 272 N.Y. 192, 5 N.E.2d 196 (1936).

47. See generally, Boyer, Promissory Estoppel: Principle from Precedents (Pts. I & II), 50 Mich.L.Rev. 639, 873 (1952); 1 Williston § 140; 1A Corbin §§ 193–209.

48. Greiner v. Greiner, 131 Kan. 760, 293 P. 759 (1930).

49. Lusk-Harbison-Jones, Inc. v. Universal Credit Co., 164 Miss. 693, 145 So. 623 (1933).

50. Danby v. Osteopathic Hosp. Ass'n of Del., 34 Del.Ch. 427, 104 A.2d 903 (Sup.Ct.1954).

51. Jackson v. Kemp, 211 Tenn. 438, 365 S.W.2d 437 (1963).

B. MODERN TRENDS IN DOCTRINE

Analysis

Sec.
106. Modern Trends Generally.
107. Offers by Subcontractors.
108. Promises of Franchises: Is Promissory Estoppel a Non-contractual Cause of Action?
109. Pensions and Other Fringe Benefits.
110. Flexibility of Remedy.
111. The Future of Promissory Estoppel.

§ 106. Modern Trends Generally

The modern trend in promissory estoppel cases is not to restrict enforcement to the types of situations listed in § 105 but to enforce any promise which meets the requirements of a promissory estoppel. Since the kinds of promises which are likely to induce reliance are as varied as human ingenuity,[52] no exhaustive listing of the cases is possible in this context. A few illustrations will suffice. Each of the following statements which induced reliance have been enforced: A promise to reduce the agreed rental,[53] a release of further obligation under a lease,[54] a promise to see to it that litigation expenses would be reimbursed,[55] and a promise that a view would remain unobstructed.[56]

Three kinds of promises which have been the subject of much discussion are considered in the following three sections: bids by subcontractors, promises of dealer franchises, and promises of pensions.

§ 107. Offers by Subcontractors

An offer, unsupported by consideration, a statutorily prescribed writing, or (in a now limited number of jurisdictions) a seal, is revocable. As a general proposition, promissory estoppel will not serve to make an offer irrevocable. Ordinarily an offeree is not justified in relying on an offer. If he wishes to rely on the promise, he

---

52. This was recognized in Burgess v. California Mut. Bldg. & Loan Ass'n, 210 Cal. 180, 290 P. 1029 (1930). The promissory estoppel doctrine was applied to a requirements contract in Haveg Corp. v. Guyer, —— Del. ——, 226 A.2d 231, 19 Ala.L.Rev. 486 (1967) but was not applied to a case involving "permanent employment". Bixby v. Wilson & Co., 196 F.Supp. 889 (N.D. Iowa 1961), 47 Iowa L.Rev. 725 (1962).

53. Central London Property Trust Ltd. v. High Trees House, Ltd., [1947] 1 K.B. 130 (1946).

54. Fried v. Fisher, 328 Pa. 497, 196 A. 39, 115 A.L.R. 147 (1938).

55. Schafer v. Fraser, 206 Ore. 446, 290 P.2d 190 (1955).

56. Miller v. Lawlor, 245 Iowa 1144, 66 N.W.2d 267, 48 A.L.R.2d 1058 (1954).

need only accept it. A bid made by a subcontractor, however, to a general contractor involves somewhat different considerations.[57] It is predictable that the general contractor will only rely on the low bids received by him in calculating his bid for the overall project. May the subcontractor revoke his bid after it has been relied upon by the general contractor, but before it has been accepted?

An early case considering the application of the doctrine of promissory estoppel in this context is James Baird Co. v. Gimbel Bros., Inc.[58] Defendant made a serious miscalculation in its bid for subcontract work on a public building. Plaintiff utilized defendant's low bid as a basis for its bid for construction of the building.

After plaintiff had submitted its bid, but prior to the award to the general contractor, defendant revoked its offer. The court ruled that there was no room for the doctrine of promissory estoppel in a bargaining situation.

In subsequent cases, however, it has generally been held that the doctrine of promissory estoppel is not so narrow. The majority of courts which have considered the problem, have held that justifiable detrimental reliance on an offer renders it irrevocable.[59] Of course, there must be something upon which the contractor may justifiably rely. An estimate is not enough [60] and if the sub-contractor's bid is

---

57. See generally Schultz, The Firm Offer Puzzle: A Study of Business Practice in the Construction Industry, 19 U. Chi.L.Rev. 237 (1952) (business practice indicates to the author that subcontractor's bids should not be treated as irrevocable); Sharp, Promises, Mistake and Reciprocity, 19 U. Chi.L.Rev. 286 (1952).

58. 64 F.2d 344 (2d Cir. 1933), critically noted, 28 Ill.L.Rev. 419 (1933); see also Fridman, Promissory Estoppel, 35 Can.B.Rev. 279 (1957); 22 Minn.L.Rev. 843 (1938); 20 Va.L.Rev. 214 (1933).

59. Robert Gordon, Inc. v. Ingersoll-Rand Co., 117 F.2d 654 (7th Cir. 1941) (disapproving of James Baird Co. v. Gimbel Bros., Inc., but finding insufficient detriment for invocation of promissory estoppel); N. Litterio & Co. v. Glassman Constr. Co., 115 U.S. App.D.C. 335, 319 F.2d 736 (1963); Reynolds v. Texarkana Constr. Co., 237 Ark. 583, 374 S.W.2d 818 (1964), 18 Ark.L.Rev. 351 (1965); Drennan v. Star Paving Co., 51 Cal.2d 409, 333 P.

2d 757 (1958); E. A. Coronis Associates v. M. Gordon Constr. Co., 90 N. J.Super. 69, 216 A.2d 246 (Super.Ct. 1966); Northwestern Eng'r Co. v. Ellerman, 69 S.D. 397, 10 N.W.2d 879 (1943). Compare Harris v. Lillis, 24 So.2d 689 (La.App.1946) (bid held to be irrevocable pursuant to local custom).
To be distinguished are cases in which there is a prior contract between the sub-contractor and the prime contractor that the sub-contractor will be retained if the prime contract is awarded. In such a case the prime contractor is bound on conventional grounds of consideration. See Air Technology Corp. v. General Electric Co., 347 Mass. 613, 199 N.E.2d 538 (1964), where it was held that the prime contractor and sub-contractor had entered into a joint venture to obtain a government contract.

60. Leo F. Piazza Paving Co. v. Bebek & Brkich, 141 Cal.App.2d 226, 296 P.2d 368, 371 (1956); Robert Gordon, Inc. v. Ingersoll-Rand Co., 117 F.2d 654 (7th Cir. 1941).

so palpably low as to indicate that it is based on a mistake, reliance is not justified.[61] It may be observed that in the cases which apply the doctrine of promissory estoppel although the sub-contractor is bound by his bid, the general contractor is not bound to accept the bid.

§ 108. Promises of Franchises: Is Promissory Estoppel a Non-contractual Cause of Action?

Difficulties involved in agreements between large manufacturers and distributors and their local dealers have been previously considered. As indicated,[62] there is such a wide disparity between the bargaining power of the parties that legislation and court decisions have sought to provide a modicum of protection for the weaker party. In three significant cases the doctrine of promissory estoppel was invoked to protect applicants for local dealerships from arbitrary action.

In Goodman v. Dicker,[63] plaintiff incurred expenses in reliance upon representations that his application for a franchise had been accepted and that a franchise would be granted. The court awarded the plaintiff the amount of expenses plaintiff had incurred in reliance upon this promise to grant a franchise. Interestingly, the award was made despite the fact that the standard Emerson Radio franchise in this pre-U.C.C. era would have been terminable at will. If the franchise had been granted and immediately cancelled, plaintiff would have had less tenable claim.

Chrysler Corporation v. Quimby[64] was a more clear cut case. Defendant assured plaintiff that if he took certain steps he would be granted a dealership. At the time the assurances were made, defendant had no intention of granting the dealership. Plaintiff was awarded standard contract damages for a ninety day period since the standard Chrysler dealership of the time was cancellable on ninety days notice.

Of great interest is the more recent case of Hoffman v. Red Owl Stores.[65] Here the plaintiff was assured that if he took certain steps and raised $18,000 worth of capital he would be granted a supermarket franchise. In compliance with the recommendation of the de-

---

61. Robert Gordon, Inc. v. Ingersoll-Rand Co., 117 F.2d 654 (7th Cir. 1941).

62. See § 70 supra. Doubtless, the legislation rules and judicial decisions restricting the manufacturer's power to terminate franchises are in part predicated upon the expenditure of effort and capital by the agent in reliance upon the franchise.

63. 83 U.S.App.D.C. 353, 169 F.2d 684 (1948).

64. 51 Del. 264, 144 A.2d 123 (1958), petition for rearg. denied 51 Del. 264, 295, 144 A.2d 885 (1958).

65. 26 Wis.2d 683, 133 N.W.2d 267 (1965), 51 Cornell L.Q. 351 (1966), 65 Mich.L.Rev. 351 (1966).

fendant, he sold his bakery, purchased a grocery store to gain experience and resold it, acquired an option on land for building a franchised outlet, and moved his residence near to where the franchise was to be. He raised the necessary capital by borrowing the major portion of it from his father-in-law. This arrangement was approved by the defendant's agent. Later, however, defendant's more highly placed agents insisted that plaintiff's credit standing was impaired by this loan and demanded that plaintiff procure from his father-in-law a statement that these funds were an outright gift. Plaintiff refused and sued. The court ruled for the plaintiff on the theory of promissory estoppel, limiting his recovery to the amounts he had lost and expended in reliance on the promise.

The difficulty with the case is that at the time of the rupture of the negotiations many of the terms of the franchise had not been agreed upon. This was not a situation contemplating merely the signing of a standardized agreement. Indeed, the trial court found as a fact that the parties did not reach a final agreement. Among the details which had not been agreed upon were the "size, cost, design, and layout of the store building; and the terms of the lease with respect to rent, maintenance, renewal, and purchase options." [66]

The court specifically held that promissory estoppel can sustain a cause of action despite the absence of the elements of a contract. In the court's view promissory estoppel is more than an equivalent of or substitute for consideration. It is the basis of a cause of action that is neither contract, tort, nor quasi-contract. The court's result is close in spirit to the doctrine of *culpa in contrahendo* recognized in a number of European countries, under which, where justice demands, recovery is awarded for losses sustained as a result of unsuccessful negotiations.[67] The result in Goodman v. Dicker [68] is similar in spirit: recovery was awarded although it would not have been available under the contract contemplated by the parties.

§ 109. Pensions and Other Fringe Benefits

Many promises by employers to pay pensions and other fringe benefits are undoubtedly supported by consideration. This is particularly so if the pension plan is in effect when the employee is hired. The pension plan then becomes an express or implied in fact term of the contract. The employee's services constitute sufficient considera-

---

66. Id. at 697, 133 N.W. at 274.

67. See Kessler & Fine, Culpa in Contrahendo, Bargaining in Good Faith, and Freedom of Contract: A Comparative Study, 77 Harv.L.Rev. 401 (1964).

68. 83 U.S.App.D.C. 353, 169 F.2d 684 (1948).

tion for the payment of the pension in addition to his salary.[69] If the plan is instituted subsequent to the hiring, and if the hiring is at will, forbearance from quitting constitutes sufficient detriment.[70] This is usually bargained for, expressly or impliedly. If a bargain cannot be implied, the elements of promissory estoppel will usually be present in the facts. The promisor can foresee that continuation in employment is likely to be induced, such continuation has been induced and injustice can be avoided only by giving effect to the promise.

There are situations which are more difficult to analyze. If the promise has been made after the employee has already retired or in contemplation of his prospective retirement, consideration will be difficult to find, as the employment is past and any continued employment is not bargained for in exchange for the promise. If new consideration is found, the promise is, of course, enforceable.[71] Promissory estoppel is also difficult to apply in such circumstances, for where is the detrimental reliance to be located? In Feinberg v. Pfeiffer Co.,[72] the court found reliance in the very fact of the employee's retirement from a well paid position. Testimony showed that she would not have retired if the pension had not been proffered, moreover, after her retirement, in reliance on the pension, she sought no other employment.

With surprising frequency,[73] employers have offered pension plans, death benefits and other fringe benefits while retaining the power to withdraw or modify the offer at will. Such an offer is an illusory promise. Generally, the courts have held that reliance on the terms of the offer creates no liability.[74] By the process of interpretation of the terms of the offer so as to preclude withdrawal or modification after the employee has retired [75] or died,[76] such promises have

69. See § 75 supra.

70. See § 68 supra.

71. Specht v. Eastwood-Nealley Corp., 34 N.J.Super. 156, 111 A.2d 781 (Super.Ct.1955) (promise not to interfere with the business; as a minority shareholder he was privileged to "interfere").

72. 322 S.W.2d 163 (Mo.App.1959); accord, Bredemann v. Vaughan Mfg. Co., 40 Ill.App.2d 232, 188 N.E.2d 746 (1963); Langer v. Superior Steel Corp., 105 Pa.Super. 579, 161 A. 571 (1932) (alternative holding), rev'd on other grounds 318 Pa. 490, 178 A. 490 (1935).

73. See Note, Consideration for the Employer's Promise of a Voluntary Pension Plan, 23 U.Chi.L.Rev. 96 (1955); Note, Contractual Aspects of Pension Plan Modification, 56 Colum. L.Rev. 251 (1956).

74. Spooner v. Reserve Life Ins. Co., 47 Wash.2d 454, 287 P.2d 735 (1955) (bonus).

75. Schofield v. Zion's Co-op. Mercantile Institution, 85 Utah 281, 39 P.2d 342, 96 A.L.R. 1083 (1934) (pension); West v. Hunt Foods, Inc., 101 Cal. App.2d 597, 225 P.2d 978 (1951).

76. Mabley & Carew Co. v. Borden, 129 Ohio St. 375, 195 N.E. 697, 100 A.L.R. 511 (1935) (death benefit).

been on occasion enforced. Detrimental reliance on the promise doubtless is a primary factor in impelling the courts to so interpret the offer.

§ 110. Flexibility of Remedy

The first Restatement's formulation of the doctrine of promissory estoppel said nothing concerning the remedies available in a promissory estoppel case. The implication, was that if the elements were present, a contract was formed and therefore the ordinary remedies for breach of contract would be available. As Professor Williston explained to the American Law Institute, either a contract was formed or it was not, "you have to take one leg or the other." [77] This overly conceptual approach has very likely hindered full judicial acceptance of the doctrine. To circumvent the conceptual problem, one eminent writer has suggested that promissory estoppel be treated as the basis of a tort action.[78]

Some courts, however, have broken the conceptual barrier and have decided that the remedy need not be as broad as that which would be available for breach of a contract founded on consideration. In Goodman v. Dicker,[79] the court in enforcing a promise to grant the plaintiff dealership franchise, limited the plaintiff's recovery to the expenditures made in reliance on the promise. Such flexibility is to be encouraged. If the reliance on an extremely valuable promise is moderate, courts should not be compelled to choose between full contractual recovery or none at all.[80]

An interesting illustration of judicial flexibility is Central London Property Trust Ltd. v. High Trees House Ltd.[81] An apartment building was leased for a 99 year term. During the Second World War, the building proved unprofitable to the lessee because of a high vacancy rate. The lessor agreed in writing to reduce the rental from £2500 to £1250. In 1945, conditions had changed and the building was fully tenanted. The King's Bench held that, despite the absence of consideration, the lessor's promise to accept the reduced rental was binding

77. Williston, IV American Law Institute Proceedings, Appendix P. 103 (1926) ; 1A Corbin § 205.

78. Seavey, Reliance Upon Gratuitous Promises or Other Conduct, 64 Harv. L.Rev. 913, 926 (1951).

79. 83 U.S.App.D.C. 353, 169 F.2d 684 (1948) ; Chrysler Corp. v. Quimby, 51 Del. 264, 144 A.2d 123 (1958), adhered to 51 Del. 264, 144 A.2d 885 (full damages awarded under similar facts; additional facts, however, showed promisor never intended to perform). As we have seen the Restatement Second encourages flexibility of remedy. See § 99 note 2 supra.

80. Fuller and Perdue, The Reliance Interest in Contract Damages, 46 Yale L.J. 373, 405 (1937).

81. [1947] 1. K.B. 130 (1946).

by reason of the lessee's reliance in continuing its business. The court, however, held that the promise would be enforced only as to the period during which the high vacancy rate existed. This, the court indicated, was probably the intention of the parties; but even if it was not, there would be no reason to raise an estoppel as to the post-1945 rent.

In the case of Hoffman v. Red Owl Stores, the court not only indicated that flexibility of remedy was a permissible judicial response to promissory estoppel, but that the cause of action is non-contractual.[82]

§ 111. The Future of Promissory Estoppel

Just as the original Restatement gave great impetus to the promissory estoppel it may be expected that the Second Restatement with its liberalization of the doctrine will give added impetus to the utilization of the doctrine as a substitute for consideration [83] or, as has been suggested, as the basis of a cause of action that is neither contract, tort or quasi-contract.[84]

Added impetus may also come from the New York case of Spiegel v. Metropolitan Life Ins. Co.[85] Up until the Spiegel case it could fairly be said that New York had retained the traditional pre-Restatement approach.[86] In that case the plaintiff, as beneficiary, brought an action against the insurance company and Levy, one of the Company's agents, to recover upon a life policy written upon the life of her husband. The plaintiff did not succeed against the insurance Company because the policy had lapsed by virtue of a failure to make payment of a quarterly premium. Plaintiff testified that she told Levy that she did not have the money to pay the quarterly premium in question and that he assured her that he would "take care of the payment and look to her for reimbursement when she obtained the money from her summer rental." [87] The agent repeated the assurance before the expiration of the thirty day grace period. The insured died before the premium was paid, after the expiration of the grace period and before any other default. The trial court directed a verdict in favor of

82. Discussed at length at § 108 supra.

83. See footnote 2 and § 110 hereof. In addition to making changes in the promissory estoppel doctrine in § 90 the Restatement breaks new ground in §§ 89B(2), 89C and 89D.

84. See § 108 supra.

85. 6 N.Y.2d 91, 188 N.Y.S.2d 486, 160 N.E.2d 40 (1959).

86. See § 105 supra. Comfort v. McCorkle, 149 Misc. 826, 268 N.Y.S. 192 (Sup.Ct.1933). In fact it would appear that New York has limited the family cases to marriage settlement cases. Matter of Baer, 196 Misc. 979, 92 N.Y.S.2d 359 (Sup.Ct.1949).

87. The plaintiff rented her house for the summer.

the insurance company and Levy and the Appellate Division affirmed. The Court of Appeals reversed as to Levy stating: "However the evidence presented did require that the case against the defendant Levy be submitted to the jury. He had promised to pay the second quarterly premium in order to keep the policy in force. In short, if the jurors believed, as the plaintiff in effect testified . . . they would have been justified in holding him liable." [88]

Clearly the Court of Appeals, although it did not so state, was applying the promissory doctrine free of the restrictions inherent in the traditional approach in that under the prior approach the defendant's non-performance would have been deemed to be nonfeasance for which he would not have been liable.[89]

In view of these developments in the law of promissory estoppel it would appear that the prudent lawyer should seriously consider supplementing his consideration approach with a promissory estoppel theory.

88. Spiegel v. Metropolitan Life Ins. Co., 6 N.Y.2d 91, 95, 188 N.Y.S.2d 486, 488–9, 160 N.E.2d 40, 42 (1959).

89. The Court cited Siegel v. Spear but did not attempt to distinguish Thorne v. Deas. See § 102 supra.

CHAPTER 7

CONTRACTS UNDER SEAL

Analysis

Sec.
112. Introduction.
113. Sufficiency of the Writing.
114. What Constitutes a Seal.
115. The Adoption of a Seal Already On the Instrument.
116. Delivery of a Sealed Instrument.
117. Is Acceptance by the Obligee Necessary to Complete a Delivery?
118. Delivery in Escrow—Conditional Delivery.
119. Some Effects of the Seal.
120. Statutory Changes Affecting the Seal.

§ 112. Introduction

For centuries before the doctrine of consideration was developed and long before informal contracts were enforced, contracts under seal were enforced.[1] As we have seen, a contract under seal is one type of formal contract;[2] indeed, the outstanding kind of formal contract from the late middle ages down to recent times, at least in non-mercantile transactions.[3] The sealed instrument required no consideration, although, at times, courts, losing sight of its historical origins, have said that the seal "imports a consideration."[4] The promise under seal is enforced because of the form of the instrument. The required formalities are three: a sufficient writing, a seal, and delivery.[5]

1. 1A Corbin § 252; 1 Williston § 205.

2. See § 7 supra. The efficacy of the seal has not been limited to contracts. Traditionally, many executed transactions such as conveyances and releases have been under seal.

3. This is not to say that sealed instruments have not been used in mercantile transactions, but other forms of formal instruments are more important in commercial law; e. g., negotiable instruments and corporate securities.

4. See discussion of this terminology in Hartford-Connecticut Trust Co. v. Divine, 97 Conn. 193, 116 A. 239, 21 A.

L.R. 34 (1922); Thomason v. Bescher, 176 N.C. 622, 97 S.E. 654, 2 A.L.R. 626 (1918)

5. Restatement, Contracts (2d) § 95. In addition the promisor and promisee must have legal capacity and the contract must not be void as, for example, because of illegality. In addition, if the promisee is to render some performance under the contract, such performance may be required as a condition precedent to enforcement of the promise under the same rules as are applicable to an informal contract. See ch. 9 infra; In re Conrad's Estate, 333 Pa. 561, 3 A.2d 697 (1939).

§ 113. Sufficiency of the Writing

The sealed instrument "must be written on paper or parchment, but an instrument written or printed on any substance capable of receiving and retaining legible characters, would probably have equal validity." [6] Although today sealed instruments are invariably signed, a signature is not a requirement to the efficacy of the instrument.[7] The instrument must contain a promise which is sufficiently definite as to be capable of performance.[8] In addition the promisor and the promisee must be named or sufficiently described in the instrument so as to be capable of identification.[9] Thus, for example, the rule of agency law that a principal may sue or be sued on a contract, although the contract by its terms appears to be made with an agent, is inapplicable to sealed instruments.[10] Some courts, however, have circumvented this rule in part by holding that if the contract was such that no seal was required, it will be treated as an informal contract.[11]

Although there was an initial reluctance to permit a suit by a third party beneficiary upon a sealed contract, the prevailing view today is that there is no greater obstacle to such an action than in the case of informal contracts.[12]

§ 114. What Constitutes a Seal

For some period in history seals were required to consist of wax affixed to the parchment or paper on which the terms of the instrument were written. The wax was required to have an identifiable impression made upon it.[13] Usually this was made by a signet ring.

In time when ordinary people learned to read and write and such people did not have signet rings, it was to be expected that substitutes for the traditional seal would be accepted by the law. Thus, today it would be generally accurate to say that a seal may consist of wax, a gummed wafer, an impression on the paper, the word "seal," the letters "L.S." (locus sigilli) or even a pen scratch.[14]

---

6. 1 Williston § 206.

7. Restatement, Contracts (2d) § 95, Comment c.

8. On definiteness, see § 23 supra.

9. Restatement, Contracts (2d) § 108.

10. Crowley v. Lewis, 239 N.Y. 264, 146 N.E. 374 (1925); 1 Williston § 215.

11. Harris v. McKay, 138 Va. 448, 122 S.E. 137, 32 A.L.R. 156 (1924); contra, New England Dredging Co. v. Rock-

port Granite Co., 149 Mass. 381, 21 N.E. 947 (1889).

12. Wilmington Housing Authority for use of Simeone v. Fidelity & Deposit Co., 43 Del. 381, 47 A.2d 524, 170 A.L.R. 1288 (1946); Coster v. Mayor of Albany, 43 N.Y. 399 (1871); 1A Corbin § 255; Restatement, Contracts § 134.

13. Coke, 3 Institutes 169 (1812). See 1A Corbin § 241; 1 Williston § 207.

14. Loraw v. Nissley, 156 Pa. 329, 27 A. 242 (1893); Restatement, Contracts

To have a sealed instrument in addition to the formalities mentioned above, it must appear that the party executing it intended it to be a sealed instrument.[15] The most common way in which this intent is shown is by a witnessing clause; that is, a clause which states "In Witness Whereof I have hereunto set my hand and seal" or words to that effect. Some states have held that a recital is necessary at least where the seal is other than a wax impression.[16] Others, contrary to the formerly prevailing view that one must determine from the face of the instrument whether it is sealed, have admitted extrinsic evidence to show the necessary intention.[17] The Restatement of Contracts Second adopts the approach that a recital of sealing is neither required nor conclusive.[18] Generally, however, an objective test of sealing is incorporated in its definition of a seal as "a manifestation in tangible and conventional form of an intention that a document be sealed." [19] The Restatement recognizes, however, that extrinsic evidence should be freely admitted to determine whether or not there was a manifestation of intention to seal.[20]

§ 115. The Adoption of a Seal Already on the Instrument

In the discussion in the section above it was assumed as a fact that the seal which appeared upon the writing was placed there by the promisor before delivery. It is to be noted, however, that under modern practice very often the parties adopt a printed form purchased from a legal stationer upon which the word "seal," the letters "L.S." or some other form of seal has been printed or otherwise affixed, or they adopt a form prepared by the attorney for one of the parties. It is well settled that the promisor need not himself attach

(2d) § 96; 1A Corbin § 241; 1 Williston § 207. This listing is not necessarily completely accurate in each jurisdiction. For example, a pen scrawl was held to be insufficient in Woodbury v. U. S. Cas. Co., 284 Ill. 227, 120 N.E. 8 (1918).

15. Empire Trust Co. v. Heinze, 242 N. Y. 475, 152 N.E. 266 (1926). However, there are cases indicating that the intent to seal is sufficient, as for example, where there is a clause which says "In Witness Whereof, I have hereunto set my hand and seal," not accompanied by a seal. Beach v. Beach, 141 Conn. 583, 107 A.2d 629 (1954).

16. Dawsey v. Kirven, 203 Ala. 446, 83 So. 338, 7 A.L.R. 1658 (1919).

17. Matter of Pirie, 198 N.Y. 209, 91 N.E. 587 (1910), modified, 199 N.Y. 524, 91 N.E. 1144 (1910).

18. Restatement, Contracts (2d) § 100.

19. Restatement, Contracts (2d) § 96(1).

20. Restatement, Contracts (2d) § 100, Comment b: "A recital may give meaning to a manifestation of intention, indicating that a dash or scrawl after a signature is intended as a seal or that the promisor intends to adopt a seal affixed by another party . . . . [R]ecitals are often false and their falsity may be shown by any relevant evidence."

the seal [21] and that one seal may serve for several persons.[22]　In other words a seal which is on the instrument may be adopted.　Since the question of adoption is one of intent and the writing is seldom unambiguous, extrinsic evidence is ordinarily admissible to determine this issue of adoption.[23]　It also seems to be generally agreed that if the instrument contains a recital of sealing and some form of seal, all who signed will be presumed to have adopted the seal.[24]

§ 116.　Delivery of a Sealed Instrument

It is unanimously agreed that delivery of a sealed instrument is required for its validity.[25]　The question which has given the courts difficulty is what constitutes delivery.　The earlier cases seemed to have assumed that when the obligor placed the instrument in the possession of the offeree or of some third person as agent of the promisee delivery was effectuated.[26]　But it soon became recognized that possession of the paper could be relinquished without an intent that the obligation should exist as, for example, when it was merely given for inspection.　Consequently, it was held that in addition to the surrendering of possession an intent to deliver was required.[27]　Under the more modern cases, the only requirement is an intent to deliver, that is to say, a manifestation of intent by the obligor that the document be immediately operative, even where the instrument has never left the possession of the obligor.[28]　This view is not sufficiently widespread, however, to cause the Second Restatement to depart from the traditional rule that the promisor must part with possession.[29]

§ 117.　Is Acceptance by the Obligee Necessary to Complete a Delivery?

There are cases which have held that an expression of assent by the other party is necessary to complete a delivery.[30]　However, this

---

21.　Commonwealth v. Gutelius, 287 Pa. 441, 135 A. 214 (1926).

22.　Restatement, Contracts (2d) § 99.

23.　Restatement, Contracts (2d) § 98; 1 Williston § 208.

24.　Cammack v. J. B. Slattery & Bro., Inc., 241 N.Y. 39, 148 N.E. 781 (1925); Branton v. Martin, 243 S.C. 90, 132 S. E.2d 285 (1963).

25.　Restatement, Contracts (2d) § 95(1) (b).

26.　If the instrument is transferred to an agent or custodian of the obligor, there is no delivery by virtue of the transfer of possession.　1A Corbin § 244.

27.　Moore v. Trott, 162 Cal. 268, 122 P. 462 (1912).

28.　Maciaszek v. Maciaszek, 21 Ill.2d 542, 173 N.E.2d 476 (1961).

29.　Restatement, Contracts (2d) § 102, Comment b.

30.　Bowen v. Prudential Ins. Co., 178 Mich. 63, 144 N.W. 543 (1913); 1 Williston § 213.

is obviously not true where the instrument expresses an obligation only on the part of the obligor because in such a case an effective delivery can be made without an expression of assent.[31] It has sometimes been said that the promisee's assent is presumed absent a disclaimer from him. A more direct statement is that the instrument is effective upon delivery without assent, but that it may be disclaimed within a reasonable time after learning of the existence of the instrument.[32]

The situation is different if the instrument delivered by the obligor calls for a return promise. In such a case in order for the promisee to be bound by a sealed promise he must seal and deliver the instrument (or another instrument). If the promisee does not seal and deliver, but makes the required return promise, the parties are bound by a bilateral contract. The original promisor is bound by a promise under seal and the second promisor is bound by his informal promise.[33] It is sometimes held, however, that acceptance of the sealed instrument containing a return promise justifies a holding that the acceptor is liable on the instrument by adoption or estoppel.[34] Since such a transaction involves consideration, the effects of the distinction between action on a sealed promise and an informal promise are primarily two: (1) where common law pleading survives, the action on the sealed promise is in covenant rather than assumpsit; and (2) in many jurisdictions the statutory period of limitations is appreciably longer in the case of an action on a sealed instrument.

Under any view of the matter, if the sealed instrument calls for a return promise, the delivery is deemed conditional until the return promise is made as the promisor has no intent to deliver until there is an expression of assent by the other party.[35]

§ 118. Delivery in Escrow—Conditional Delivery

We have already seen that delivery can be effectuated by the transfer of possession to a third party other than an agent of the

---

31. Restatement, Contracts (2d) § 104.

32. Branton v. Martin, 243 S.C. 90, 132 S.E.2d 285 (1963); Restatement, Contracts (2d) § 104(2); 1 Williston § 213; 1A Corbin § 245.

33. Restatement, Contracts (2d) § 107; 1A Corbin § 256; 1 Williston § 214.

34. Atlantic Dock Co. v. Leavitt, 54 N. Y. 35 (1873); 1 Williston § 214. In Blass v. Terry, 156 N.Y. 122, 50 N.E. 953 (1898), the court held that suffi-

cient delivery of a deed so as to vest title in the grantee did not necessarily result in a sufficient manifestation of assent to a mortgage assumption clause in the deed. Under the facts the grantee was not given the opportunity to read the deed. Under ordinary circumstances the grantee who accepts a deed is chargeable with its contents whether he reads it or not. See § 25 supra.

35. Diebold Safe & Lock Co. v. Morse, 226 Mass. 342, 115 N.E. 431 (1917).

promisor. The question here is the effect of such a delivery when instructions are given to the third party to deliver the instrument to the grantee or promisee only upon the occurrence of a condition not specified in the instrument itself. The function of the conditional delivery is to make the promisor bound upon the instrument in the sense that, unless the power of revocation is reserved, the instrument is irrevocable;[36] however the obligor is not bound to perform until the condition takes place.[37] When the condition occurs he is bound even though the third party does not deliver the instrument.[38] The main legal problem presented by this fact pattern is with the parol evidence rule. However, the weight of authority is to the effect that the parol evidence rule is no bar to proof that the delivery was conditional.[39]

A similar problem arises where the instrument is delivered not to a third person but to the promisee and is delivered subject to the occurrence of a condition not stated in the instrument. Many of the older cases, particularly those involving conveyances, held that the condition not stated in the writing should be disregarded because of the parol evidence rule.[40] The weight of authority under the modern cases is contrary.[41]

Of course it is possible in the cases discussed above that the condition is one which prevents any delivery from taking place at all so that the instrument is not effective in any way. For example, if A hands B a sealed instrument which contains a promise in favor of B and says "hold this for me until tomorrow," there is no delivery and therefore the instrument is not effective.[42] At times it is difficult to determine whether the condition imposed prevents a delivery or whether it is merely a condition to performance. "Without doubt, interpretations have been variable and inconsistent."[43]

§ 119. Some Effects of the Seal

As we have seen a sealed instrument is binding without consideration.[44] At early common law it was held that the discharge or

---

36. Moore v. Downing, 289 Ill. 612, 124 N.E. 557 (1919); Restatement, Contracts (2d) § 103.

37. Sunset Beach Amusement Corp. v. Belk, 31 N.J. 445, 158 A.2d 35 (1960).

38. Gardiner v. Gardiner, 36 Idaho 664, 214 P. 219 (1923).

39. Restatement, Contracts (2d) § 103; Corbin, Conditional Delivery of Written Contracts, 36 Yale L.J. 443, 455 (1927). 1A Corbin § 249; 1 Williston § 212.

40. Hume v. Kirkwood, 216 Ala. 534, 113 So. 613 (1927).

41. 1A Corbin § 250; 1 Williston § 212.

42. See § 116 supra.

43. 1A Corbin § 251; see also Puckett v. Hoover, 146 Tex. 1, 202 S.W.2d 209 (1947); 1 Williston § 212.

44. See § 112 supra. However the absence of consideration will be taken into account by a court of equity in

modification of a sealed contract could be accomplished only by another sealed instrument.[45] Later it was held that a sealed instrument could be discharged or modified by an accord and satisfaction but not by an unperformed executory bilateral contract.[46] The more modern view is that a sealed instrument may be modified or rescinded in the same manner as any other instrument.[47]

Under common law pleading an action on a sealed instrument was required to be brought under the writ of covenant rather than assumpsit. While the distinction between the writs is now largely a matter of history, it still remains the law in a good number of jurisdictions that a longer statutory period of limitations is applicable to an action on an instrument under seal.[48]

§ 120. Statutory Changes Affecting the Seal

In its original conception, the sealing of an instrument was surrounded by impressive solemnity. Such individuals who owned signet rings or similar devices guarded them as they would guard treasure. The community was aware of the consequences of the ceremony of sealing and delivery. As times changed and the ceremony was abandoned and supplanted by the mere presence on a printed form of the word "seal" or the initials "L.S." [49] on or near the signature line, the community lost its awareness of the distinction between sealed and unsealed instruments.

Taking cognizance of the change in community expectations, legislatures have enacted statutes affecting the seal.[50] Some statutes

---

determining whether specific performance should be granted. See Restatement, Contracts § 366.

45. See 1A Corbin § 253.

46. Tussing v. Smith, 125 Fla. 578, 171 So. 238 (1936).

47. Koth v. County Bd. of Educ. of Jasper County, 141 S.C. 448, 140 S.E. 99, 55 A.L.R. 682 (1927); Restatement, Contracts § 407.

48. See the statutory note preceding Restatement, Contracts (2d) § 95 which compiles the relevant statutes.

49. The abandonment of the ceremony apparently occurred early in American history. "He was a bold fellow, who first in these colonies, and particularly in Pennsylvania, in 'time whereof the memory of man runneth not to

the contrary', substituted the appearance of a seal, by the circumflex of a pen, which has been sanctioned by usage and the adjudication of the courts, as equipollent with a stamp containing some effigies, or inscription on stone or metal. . . . In fact the circumflex *is usually made by the scrivener drawing the instrument*, and the word seal inscribed in it." Brackenridge, J., in Alexander v. Jameson, 5 Binn. 238, 244 (Pa.1812), quoted in the learned decision, Loraw v. Nissley, 156 Pa. 329, 27 A. 242 (1893).

50. The courts had previously taken cognizance of the deterioration of the ceremony of sealing. Their piecemeal attempts to deal with the problem, however, tended to place the law in confusion. On the chaotic state of

make private seals wholly inoperative.[51]　The Uniform Commercial Code is in this class.　It "makes it clear that every effect of the seal which relates to 'sealed instruments' is wiped out insofar as contracts for sale are concerned." [52]　In some states where the effectiveness of the seal has been abolished, and under the Uniform Commercial Code, as we have seen, it has been deemed necessary to enact statutory substitutes to perform one or more of its functions, particularly the function of sustaining a transaction without consideration.[53]

Another group of statutes has abolished the distinction between sealed and unsealed instruments but provide that any written promise is rebuttably presumed to be supported by consideration.[54]　A third group of statutes provide that a seal is only presumptive evidence of consideration on executory instruments, generally leaving unchanged the effect of the seal on executed instruments such as releases.[55] There are, of course, variations within these groups and no lack of additional statutes of miscellaneous types.

Not all statutes of the same type have received similar interpretations.　For example, the New Jersey legislature enacted legislation

the New York law prior to abolition of the private seal, see Crane, The Magic of the Private Seal, 15 Colum. L.Rev. 24 (1915), Selected Readings 598.

51.　Arkansas, Illinois, Indiana, Minnesota, Nebraska, New York, Ohio, Utah, Wyoming.　The presence or absence of a seal has always been irrelevant in Louisiana.　See the statutory note preceding Restatement, Contracts (2d) § 95.　Another statutory classification appears in 1 Williston § 219A.

52.　§ 203, Comment 1.　Comment 2 states: "This section leaves untouched any aspects of a seal which relate merely to signatures or to authentication of execution and the like.　Thus, a statute providing that a purported signature gives prima facie evidence of its own authenticity or that a signature gives prima facie evidence of consideration is still applicable to sales transactions even though a seal may be held to be a signature within the meaning of such a statute.　Similarly, the authorized affixing of a corporate seal bearing the corporate name to a contractual writing purporting to be made by the corporation may have effect as a signature with-

out any reference to the law of sealed instruments."

53.　See §§ 90–96 supra.

54.　Arizona, California, Idaho, Iowa, Kansas, Kentucky, Missouri, Montana, Nevada, North Dakota, Oklahoma, Tennessee, Texas.　Two states, Mississippi and New Mexico, have statutes which appear to have elevated all written contracts to the level of sealed instruments in that all written promises are binding without consideration.　In each state, however, the court decisions must be consulted to determine the interpretation given to the local statute.

Citations to the statutes are compiled in the statutory note preceding Restatement, Contracts (2d) § 95.

The rebuttable presumption of consideration conferred on all written promises can have a significant impact upon the decision of a concrete case. See Patterson v. Chapman, 179 Cal. 203, 176 P. 37, 2 A.L.R. 1467 (1918).

55.　Alabama, Connecticut, Florida, Michigan, New Jersey, Oregon, Washington, Wisconsin.　See the Restatement's statutory note.

to the effect that the seal is merely presumptive evidence of consideration. This was held not to deprive a sealed gratuitous promise of its efficacy if no bargained for exchange was intended.[56] A subsequent statutory change was enacted to the effect that in an action on a sealed promise the defendant may prove the absence of consideration with the same effect as if the instrument were not sealed. In the face of this statute the court still adhered to its view that no consideration is necessary on a sealed instrument.[57]

It is apparent that the different kinds of statutes may give rise to different results. Thus, for example, if a jurisdiction has not over-ruled the common law principle that a sealed instrument may only be modified or rescinded by an instrument under seal,[58] a statute abolishing the effect of a seal would obliterate this rule, but a statute which modifies the effect of a seal by providing that it is presumptive evidence of consideration would have no effect on this rule as it relates only to consideration.

The same analysis would apply in the case of the common law rule that an undisclosed principal may not sue or be sued upon a sealed instrument.[59] Under a statute providing that the seal gives rise to a presumption of consideration, this common law rule would not be changed.

---

56. Aller v. Aller, 40 N.J.L. 446 (1878); see 1A Corbin § 254; 1 Williston § 219. Cf. Cochran v. Taylor, 273 N.Y. 172, 7 N.E.2d 89 (1937), decided under the former New York statute that a seal created a presumption of consideration. It was held that the parties were estopped from contradicting a recital of $1.00 as consideration. An estoppel is not created in New York by such a recital on an unsealed instrument. See § 58 supra.

57. Zirk v. Nohr, 127 N.J.L. 217, 21 A. 2d 766 (1941).

58. See § 119 supra.

59. Of course, the courts could change the common law rule as has been done by courts in other jurisdictions. Indeed, the legislative policy to reduce the sanctity of a sealed instrument should be given effect even as to rules such as this. A similar analysis is applicable to the rule retained by some jurisdictions that a third party beneficiary may not sue on a sealed instrument.

CHAPTER 8

CAPACITY OF PARTIES

Analysis

		Sections
A.	Infants	122–129
B.	The Mentally Infirm	130–135

Sec.
121. Introduction.

A. INFANTS

122. Introduction.
123. Transactions Which the Infant Cannot Avoid.
124. Avoidance and Ratification.
    (a) Failure to Make a Timely Disaffirmance.
    (b) Express Ratification.
    (c) Ratification by Conduct.
125. Effect Upon Ratification of Ignorance of Law or Fact.
126. Obligations of Restitution upon Disaffirmance.
    (a) Infant as Defendant.
    (b) Infant as Plaintiff.
127. Torts Connected with Contracts.
    (a) Infant's Torts Stemming from His Contracts.
    (b) False Representations by the Infant.
    (c) Torts and Agency Relationships.
128. Liability of an Infant for Necessaries.
129. Infant's Liability for Benefits Received: The New Hampshire View.

B. THE MENTALLY INFIRM

130. Introduction.
131. Requirement of Restitution.
132. Avoidance and Ratification.
133. Liability for Necessaries.
134. Intoxicated Persons.
135. Exploitation of Alcoholics and Weak Minded Persons.

§ 121. Introduction

There are certain classes of persons whose contractual capacity is limited. Their agreements are either void, or more often, voidable.

197

These classes include infants and persons suffering from mental infirmity.[1]

A. INFANTS

Analysis

Sec.
122. Introduction.
123. Transactions Which the Infant Cannot Avoid.
124. Avoidance and Ratification.
    (a) Failure to Make a Timely Disaffirmance.
    (b) Express Ratification.
    (c) Ratification by Conduct.
125. Effect upon Ratification of Ignorance of Law or Fact.
126. Obligations of Restitution Upon Disaffirmance.
    (a) Infant as Defendant.
    (b) Infant as Plaintiff.

1. Other classes exist. Formerly, the agreements of married women were void. This disability has largely been eliminated by statutory enactments. The statutes are compiled in 2 Williston §§ 269–269A. Some disabilities of married women continue to exist in various jurisdictions. See United States v. Yazell, 382 U.S. 341, 86 S.Ct. 500, 15 L.Ed.2d 404 (1966) (Texas law). In a number of jurisdictions a spendthrift may be placed under guardianship and his contracts are voidable. See Lilienthal v. Kaufman, 239 Or. 1, 395 P.2d 543 (1964) (Oregon spendthrift may avoid promissory notes although creditor was unaware of his disability and loan was made in California).

Convicts are under disabilities which vary from state to state. See 2 Williston § 272; Note, 14 Colum.L.Rev. 592 (1914); Note, 5 Cornell L.Q. 320 (1920).

The problem of capacity to contract arises as to corporations in connection with the doctrine of ultra vires; that is, in relation to agreements entered into outside the scope of the powers of the corporation. This doctrine is extensively discussed in works on corporation law. For summary treatment, see 2 Williston § 271.

A related problem exists in relation to the contracts of municipal corporations and other public agencies. Public contracts not awarded pursuant to the procedures provided by law are void or voidable. There is much confusion in the cases as to whether and under what circumstances the private party who has performed under such a contract may recover in quasi contract. Extensive discussion and citations will be found in America-LaFrance, Inc. v. City of Philadelphia, 183 Miss. 207, 184 So. 620 (1938); Hudson City Contracting Co. v. Jersey City Incinerator Authority, 17 N.J. 297, 111 A.2d 385 (1955); Federal Paving Corp. v. City of Wauwatosa, 231 Wis. 655, 286 N.W. 546 (1939). Some jurisdictions will in almost no case grant such relief. See Seif v. City of Long Beach, 286 N.Y. 382, 387–88, 36 N.E.2d 630, 632 (1941), motion denied 287 N.Y. 836, 41 N.E.2d 164 (1942) ("this court has given emphatic warning that equitable powers of the courts may not be invoked to sanction disregard of statutory safeguards and restrictions."); but see Gerzof v. Sweeney, 22 N.Y.2d 297, 292 N.Y.S.2d 640, 239 N.E.2d 521 (1968). See also Haight, The Problem of the Defective Public Contract in New York State, 14 Syracuse L.Rev. 426 (1963).

Sec.
127. Torts Connected with Contracts.
      (a) Infant's Torts Stemming from His Contracts.
      (b) False Representations by the Infant.
      (c) Torts and Agency Relationships.
128. Liability of an Infant for Necessaries.
129. Infant's Liability for Benefits Received: The New Hampshire View.

§ 122. Introduction

At common law a person remained an infant until he reached the age of twenty-one. Generally under present day legislation and decisions this common law rule continues in effect, although by statute in some states infancy terminates for some or all purposes at a younger age.[2] In accordance with the maxim that the law often disregards fractions of a day, it is commonly held that infancy ends at the very first moment of the day preceding the twenty-first birthday.[3] Emancipation of the infant by his parents does not enlarge his capacity to contract.[4]

Formerly it was the rule that the contracts of infants were void.[5] Later it was held that they were voidable but that certain kinds of transactions entered into by an infant such as his appointment of an

2. According to a recent report, one state fixes the age of majority for most purposes at 18 (Kentucky), one at 19 (Alaska), one at 20 (Hawaii) and nine states regard females as having attained majority at age 18 (Arkansas, Idaho, Illinois, Montana, Nevada, North Dakota, Oklahoma, South Dakota, Utah). Study and Recommendations to Improve and Simplify the Practice Relating to the Settlement of Infants' Claims, Thirteenth Annual Report of the New York Judicial Conference 300, 301 (1968). Various ages are fixed by the states for testamentary capacity and capacity to marry. See Note, 15 Syr.L.Rev. 705 (1964).

3. Nelson v. Sandkamp, 227 Minn. 177, 34 N.W.2d 640, 5 A.L.R.2d 1136 (1948). In several jurisdictions, an infant attains his majority at the first moment of his twenty-first birthday. See 2 Williston § 224.

4. Commonwealth v. Graham, 157 Mass. 73, 31 N.E. 706 (1892); Schoenung v. Gallet, 206 Wis. 52, 238 N.W. 852, 78 A.L.R. 387 (1931). Emancipa-tion occurs upon the express or implied renunciation by his parents of their common law right of control over the infant and particularly of the infant's obligation to provide his parent with his services and to turn over to them his earnings. In most jurisdictions emancipation also occurs by operation of law upon the infant's marriage. See 2 Williston § 225. In some jurisdictions it is also held that contractual capacity is attained upon marriage, but this is a distinctly minority view. See Succession of Hecker, 191 La. 302, 185 So. 32 (1938). Several jurisdictions permit judicial emancipation upon the petition of the minor and the decree may also remove in whole or in part the infant's lack of capacity. See 1938 Report of the New York Law Revision Commission 139, for discussion of such statutes in Alabama, Florida, Kansas, Louisiana, Oklahoma, Tennessee and Texas.

5. For the historical development of this rule, see the learned opinion in Henry v. Root, 33 N.Y. 526 (1865); see also 2 Williston § 226.

agent, his execution of a promissory note and his agreement to be surety were void. It is now almost everywhere agreed that even such transactions are voidable rather than void.[6] Not only a contract, but also an executed transaction, such as a sale, conveyance or release may be avoided. The power of avoidance resides only in the infant [7] or in the event of his death, in his heirs, administrators or executors.[8] Occasional decisions permitting a parent or other guardian to disaffirm the infant's contract can, however, be found and would seem to be sound if the infant is not emancipated.[9] It is quite clear that an adult party to the transaction cannot avoid the contract on the ground of the other's infancy.[10]

Because of the one-sided power of avoidance held by the infant it might seem anomalous to speak in terms of the limited capacity of infants. To some observers it has seemed that the infant has capacity to contract coupled with an additional power of disaffirmance. It has been said that "the law confers a privilege rather than a disability." [11] This, however, represents but one side of the coin. Adult parties frequently will refuse to contract with or sell to infants because an infant is incapable of giving legal assurance that he will not disaffirm.[12]

6. See Casey v. Kastel, 237 N.Y. 305, 142 N.E. 671, 31 A.L.R. 995 (1924); 2 Williston § 226.

7. Quality Motors, Inc. v. Hays, 216 Ark. 264, 225 S.W.2d 326 (1949) (father cannot disaffirm for son); Oliver v. Houdlet, 13 Mass. 237 (1816) (guardian may not disaffirm for ward); Dostal v. Magee, 272 Wis. 509, 76 N.W.2d 349 (1956) (father cannot ratify for son).

8. Gendreau v. North American Life & Cas. Co., 158 Minn. 259, 197 N.W. 257 (1924); Eagan v. Scully, 29 App.Div. 617, 51 N.Y.S. 680 (3d Dep't 1898), aff'd, 173 N.Y. 581, 65 N.E. 1116 (1902); cf. Kline v. L'Amoureaux, 2 Paige's Ch. 419 (N.Y.1831) (upon obtaining majority, infant was declared mentally incompetent; committee for the incompetent could disaffirm).

9. Crockett Motor Co. v. Thompson, 177 Ark. 495, 6 S.W.2d 834 (1928); Hughes v. Murphy, 5 Ga.App. 328, 63 S.E. 231 (1908) (action brought by guardian to disaffirm sale permissible although infant objected); Champa v. New York Central Mut. Relief Ass'n, 57 Ohio App. 522, 15 N.E.2d 172 (1936).

10. Holt v. Ward Clarencieux, 93 Eng. Rep. 954 (K.B. 1732); Shaw v. Philbrick, 129 Me. 259, 151 A. 423, 74 A.L. R. 290 (1930). For the relationship between this rule and the doctrine of "mutuality of obligation," see § 69 supra.

A contract between two infants is voidable at the option of either. Hurwitz v. Barr, 193 A.2d 360 (D.C.App.1963) (sale of motor scooter).

11. Simpson, Contracts 216.

12. As a practical matter the adult party may refuse to contract with the infant unless the infant's parent or other responsible adult agrees to become jointly liable with the infant. In such a case, disaffirmance by the infant does not discharge his co-obligor. Campbell v. Fender, 218 Ark. 290, 235 S.W.2d 957 (1951); 2 Williston § 327.

From this point of view the infant is under both a legal and practical disability.[13]

After the infant has exercised his power to avoid the contract the transaction is treated for many purposes as if it were void from the beginning. Thus, by disaffirming his conveyance the infant may reclaim the real property from a subsequent purchaser who purchased in good faith and without notice of the fact that an infant had preceded his vendor in the chain of title.[14] So also an infant may disaffirm his liability on a negotiable instrument even as to a holder in due course.[15] As to sales of goods, however, the Uniform Sales Act provided that a subsequent bona fide purchaser for value obtained goods free from an infant's power of disaffirmance [16] and this rule has been continued by the Uniform Commercial Code.[17]

§ 123. Transactions Which the Infant Cannot Avoid

There are certain situations where the infant cannot avoid the contract. No clear-cut test can be formulated except to state that the infant cannot disaffirm certain contracts because public policy so requires or because a statute so provides or because he has done or promised to do something which the law would compel him to do even in the absence of the contract.[18] Thus, if an infant contracts to support his illegitimate child his promise cannot be disaffirmed as infants are under an obligation to support their illegitimate children.[19] An infant employee's promise not to utilize secret customer lists will be enforced by injunction as his promise merely defines the scope of a legal duty existing apart from the express contractual provision.[20] An infant is generally held liable on his bail bonds on the ground that public policy would otherwise be offended.[21]

---

13. See Warner Bros. Pictures, Inc. v. Brodel, 31 Cal.2d 766, 192 P.2d 949, 3 A.L.R.2d 691 (1948), cert. denied 335 U.S. 844, 69 S.Ct. 67, 93 L.Ed. 394 (1948), reh. denied 335 U.S. 873, 69 S. Ct. 165, 93 L.Ed. 417, for a discussion of how the infant's power of avoidance often works against his best interests.

14. Ware v. Mobley, 190 Ga. 249, 9 S. E.2d 67 (1940) (collecting cases).

15. U.C.C. § 3–305(2) (a). But he may not assert any claim against a holder in due course predicated upon his infancy. U.C.C. § 3–207.

16. Uniform Sales Act § 24. For judicial application of this provision, see Jones v. Caldwell, 216 Ark. 260, 225 S.W.2d 323, 16 A.L.R.2d 1416 (1949), 28 Chi.-Kent L.Rev. 253 (1950).

17. U.C.C. § 2–403.

18. 2 Williston § 228.

19. Gavin v. Burton, 8 Ind. 69 (1856); Township of Bordentown v. Wallace, 50 N.J.L. 13, 11 A. 267 (1887).

20. Mutual Milk & Cream Co. v. Prigge, 112 App.Div. 652, 98 N.Y.S. 458 (1st Dep't 1906) (decided on other grounds).

21. Commonwealth v. Harris, 11 Pa.D. & C. 1, 2, 77 U.Pa.L.Rev. 279 (1928).

Exceptions to the general rule of the voidable nature of infant's contract can be found in the statutes of most jurisdictions. Insurance legislation, banking laws, educational loan statutes,[22] federal and state legislation regarding military enlistments,[23] and the like, must be consulted. Some statutes provide that a contract made by an infant may not be disaffirmed when it has been approved by a court.[24] It is nonetheless probably true everywhere that the great bulk of infants' transactions continue to be voidable.

To be distinguished from legislation permitting infants to contract are statutes in almost all jurisdictions permitting a guardian to sell the property of an infant under specified conditions. Usually a court order is required to effectuate such a sale, and when made pursuant to the statutory procedure, the sale is not disaffirmable.[25] To facilitate gifts of securities to minors almost all jurisdictions have enacted the Uniform Gifts to Minors Act which permits a custodian of the securities given to the minor pursuant to the terms of the Act to sell the infant's securities and to reinvest the proceeds with great freedom and without the possibility of disaffirmance.[26]

§ 124. Avoidance and Ratification

As we have seen, the general rule is that an infant's contract is voidable by him. The exercise of this power of avoidance is often called disaffirmance. The effective surrender of this power is known as ratification. An effective ratification obviously cannot take place prior

22. Statutes on the subject in one jurisdiction include: McKinney's N.Y. Gen. Obligations Law § 3–101 (contracts of infants over eighteen years of age who are engaged in business and which were reasonable and provident when made); McKinney's N.Y. Gen. Obligations Law § 3–103 (contracts pursuant to Servicemen's Readjustment Act); McKinney's N.Y.Educ. Law § 654 (certain educational loans); McKinney's N.Y.Banking Law § 134 (certain banking transactions); McKinney's N.Y.Ins.Law § 145 (certain insurance transactions). See also note 24 infra.

23. See United States v. Williams, 302 U.S. 46, 58 S.Ct. 81, 82 L.Ed. 39 (1937), 12 St.John's L.Rev. 346 (1938).

24. West's Ann.Cal.Civ.Code, § 36(2) (contracts of employment as a performing artist or athlete); West's

Ann.Cal.Labor Code, § 1700.37 (contracts with theatrical employment agencies and artists' managers); McKinney's N.Y.Gen.Obligations Law § 3–105 (certain contracts with infant professional athletes or performing artists); McKinney's N.Y.C.P.L.R. 1207 (compromise of infant's claims). It will be recalled that in several states, a court may in whole or in part remove the disabilities of infants. See note 4, supra.

25. See 4 Tiffany, Real Property § 1244 (3d ed. 1939).

26. See generally, Newman, The Uniform Gifts to Minors Act in New York and Other Jurisdictions—Tax Consequences, Possible Abuses, and Recommendations, 49 Cornell L.Q. 12 (1963); Newman, Tax and Substantive Aspects of Gifts to Minors, 50 Cornell L.Q. 446 (1965).

to the attainment of majority; any purported ratification prior to that time suffers from the same infirmity as the contract itself.[27]

An infant may disaffirm his contract at any time prior to ratification. Except as to his conveyance of real property, it is clear that a disaffirmance may effectively be made during infancy and once made is irrevocable.[28] It seems to be the weight of authority, however, that a conveyance of real property executed by an infant may be disaffirmed only after his majority,[29] but sound modern authority permits disaffirmance during minority.[30] The older rule based on a desire to protect the infant's interests has a tendency to keep land unmarketable for an excessive period.

No particular form of language or conduct is required to effectuate a disaffirmance. It may be oral. Any manifestation of unwillingness to be bound by the transaction is sufficient.[31] Often disaffirmance is manifested for the first time by a plea of infancy as a defense,[32] or by the commencement of an action to set aside the transaction.[33]

Ratification may take place in three ways: failure to make a timely disaffirmance, express ratification, and conduct manifesting an intent to ratify.

(a) Failure to Make a Timely Disaffirmance

Leaving aside for the moment special rules in connection with conveyances, an infant may disaffirm his contracts until a reasonable time after reaching majority.[34] What is a reasonable time is

27. Elkhorn Coal Corp. v. Tackett, 261 Ky. 795, 88 S.W.2d 943 (1935); Morris v. Glaser, 106 N.J.Eq. 585, 151 A. 766 (1930), aff'd 110 N.J.Eq. 661, 160 A. 578 (1932).

28. Smith v. Wade, 169 Neb. 710, 100 N.W.2d 770 (1960); McNaughton v. Granite City Auto Sales, Inc., 108 Vt. 130, 183 A. 340 (1936). Michigan appears to stand alone in holding that no effective disaffirmance may occur until majority. Poli v. National Bank of Detroit, 355 Mich. 17, 93 N.W.2d 925 (1959).

29. 2 Williston § 235.

30. New Domain Oil & Gas Co. v. McKinney, 188 Ky. 183, 221 S.W. 245 (1920) (infant's action to set aside conveyance). Even in jurisdictions in which it is held that the infant may not disaffirm during his minority it

has been held that the infant may enter onto the land to take profits or recover the income of the premises conveyed. Sims v. Bardoner, 86 Ind. 87 (1882); Bool v. Mix, 17 Wend. 119 (N.Y. 1836).

31. Tracey v. Brown, 265 Mass. 163, 163 N.E. 885 (1928); McNaughton v. Granite City Auto Sales, Inc., 108 Vt. 130, 183 A. 340 (1936).

32. Lesnick v. Pratt, 116 Vt. 477, 80 A. 2d 663 (1951).

33. Del Santo v. Bristol County Stadium, Inc., 273 F.2d 605 (1st Cir. 1960) (disaffirmance of release accomplished by bringing suit on underlying negligence claim).

34. In some jurisdictions this is the rule by statute and is applicable to executory and executed transactions.

often a question of fact dependent upon such circumstances as whether or not there has been any performance by either or both parties, the nature of the transaction and the extent to which the other party has been prejudiced by any extensive delay in disaffirming.[35]

A good many cases speak in terms of a firm rule that executed contracts are binding if not disaffirmed within a reasonable time after majority, but executory contracts are not binding unless ratified by words or conduct after majority.[36] The rule is a carryover from the older view that an infant's executory contract is void rather than voidable.[37] It is apparent, however, that this "rule" as to executory contracts is not applied when the infant's failure to disaffirm within a reasonable time after attaining his majority works injustice.[38] Ordinarily, however, if the infant has obtained no benefits under the contract[39] as will usually be the case if the contract is wholly executory or executed only by the infant, there is no reason to bar the infant from disaffirming at any time up until the time the statute of limitations has run. Where it has been executed by the adult or by both parties, it will ordinarily be inequitable to permit the infant to retain the benefits of the contract for a long time and then disaffirm. However, for example, it has been pointed out that where pursuant to contract the infant received and paid for services during his minority, there is no reason not to permit the infant to disaffirm long after reaching his majority as the infant's inaction constituted neither benefit to him nor prejudice to the other.[40] In summary, the true rule, re-

See Pottawatomie Airport & Flying Service, Inc. v. Winger, 176 Kan. 445, 271 P.2d 754 (1954). Similar statutory provisions exist in California, Idaho, Iowa, Montana, Utah and Washington. Statutes in North Dakota, Oklahoma and South Dakota limit the infant's power of disaffirmance to one year after attaining majority. 1938 Report of the New York Law Revision Commission 132–137.

35. Harrod v. Kelly Adjustment Co., 179 A.2d 431 (D.C.Mun.App.1962); Adamowski v. Curtiss-Wright Flying Service, Inc., 300 Mass. 281, 15 N.E.2d 467 (1938); Johnson v. Storie, 32 Neb. 610, 49 N.W. 371 (1891); International Text Book Co. v. Connelly, 206 N.Y. 188, 99 N.E. 722 (1912); Merchants' Credit Bureau v. Kaoru Akiyama, 64 Utah 364, 230 P. 1017 (1924); and see Wooldridge v. Lavoie, 79 N.H. 21, 104 A. 346 (1918), where disaffirmance at trial was deemed reasonable.

36. Nichols & Shepard Co. v. Snyder, 78 Minn. 502, 81 N.W. 516 (1900).

37. See Henry v. Root, 33 N.Y. 526 (1865), where the court traces the historical changes in the law of infant's contracts.

38. E. g., Jones v. Godwin, 187 S.C. 510, 198 S.E. 36 (1938) (in reliance upon a mortgage executed by infant, creditor advanced money to infant's father after infant attained majority).

39. Whether or not the infant had received any benefit was said to be the test in Cassella v. Tiberio, 150 Ohio St. 27, 80 N.E.2d 426, 5 A.L.R.2d 1 (1948).

40. Adamowski v. Curtiss-Wright Flying Service, Inc., 300 Mass. 281, 15 N.E.2d 467 (1938).

flecting what the courts have done in fact, has been expressed in a Texas case in terms of "the effect which mere nonaction by the minor has upon the respective rights of interests of the parties, rather than upon arbitrary test of whether the contract be regarded as executed or executory in whole or in part." [41]

In a good number of cases often cited as announcing a rule on the question, close reading of the opinion indicates that the court merely held that there were sufficient facts to sustain the verdict of the jury or findings of fact of the trial court,[42] and ordinarily the question is the factual one of whether because of the passage of time after attaining full legal capacity it is unreasonable to disaffirm.

As to conveyances of real property, it is the general rule that these also are ratified if not disaffirmed within a reasonable time after reaching majority,[43] but many cases hold that in the absence of estoppel, the former infant has the right to avoid his conveyance until the statute of limitations has run.[44]

(b) Express Ratification

In the absence of statute an express ratification may be oral.[45] It has been said frequently that "ratification depends upon intent"[46]

41. Walker v. Stokes Bros. & Co., 262 S.W. 158 (Tex.Civ.App.1924).

42. Adamowski   v.   Curtiss-Wright Flying Service, Inc., 300 Mass. 281, 15 N.E.2d 467 (1938); Johnson v. Storie, 32 Neb. 610, 49 N.W. 371 (1891); International Text Book Co. v. Connelly, 206 N.Y. 188, 99 N.E. 722 (1912).

43. Sims v. Everhardt, 102 U.S. 300, 26 L.Ed. 87 (1880); Martin v. Elkhorn Coal Corp., 227 Ky. 623, 13 S.W.2d 780 (1929); Sprecher v. Sprecher, 206 Md. 108, 110 A.2d 509 (1955); Muncey v. Norfolk & Western Ry. Co., 106 W.Va. 348, 145 S.E. 581 (1928); cf. 2 Williston § 239.

44. Gibson v. Hall, 260 Ala. 539, 71 So. 2d 532 (1954); Walker v. Ellis, 212 Ark. 498, 207 S.W.2d 39 (1947); Mott v. Iossa, 119 N.J.Eq. 185, 181 A. 689 (1935). Of course, many of the same factors which go into a finding of whether there is an estoppel are the same as those which go into a determination under the majority rule of whether a reasonable time has elapsed. The equitable doctrine of laches may also be applicable and much the same factors as create an estoppel give rise to the application of that doctrine. Curtis v. Curtis, 398 Ill. 442, 75 N.E.2d 881 (1947). Thus, the concrete result reached in a given case under either the reasonable time rule or the estoppel rule should often be the same. Very often it is unclear which rule the court is applying. E. g., Green v. Green, 69 N.Y. 553 (1877).

45. Statutes requiring that a ratification be in writing exist in Arkansas, Kentucky, Maine, Mississippi, Missouri, New Jersey, South Carolina, Virginia and West Virginia. See 1938 Report of the New York Law Revision Commission 139.

46. International Text Book Co. v. Connelly, 206 N.Y. 188, 99 N.E. 722 (1912). If ratification occurs because of failure to make a timely disaffirmance, it is obvious that subjective intention is immaterial.

and, as to contracts not yet performed by the former infant, many cases hold that a mere acknowledgment of the contract is not enough [47] and that nothing less than a promise will suffice.[48] Still, a jury may be entitled to find that a promise can reasonably be implied from the language and circumstances.[49] It has been pointed out in an able opinion that the requisite that there be a new promise is an erroneous carryover from the obsolete view that the contracts of infants are void,[50] and that therefore a ratification must, by analogy, meet the requisites of a new promise to pay a debt discharged in bankruptcy.[51]

The authorities agree that if the contract is fully executed, an acknowledgment or other words consistent with an intention to stand on the transaction is sufficient to constitute ratification.[52]

(c) Ratification by Conduct

Ratification by failure to make a timely disaffirmance, previously discussed, may be considered a kind of ratification by conduct; at least if inaction be deemed conduct. Retention and enjoyment of property received pursuant to contract for more than a reasonable time after attaining majority involves both kinds of conduct; that is, active use of the property coupled with a failure to disaffirm. Under such circumstances a ratification will often be found to have occurred.[53] Receipt of performance from the other party after attaining majority will also be normally considered to be a ratification.[54] On the other hand part payment or other performance by the infant, without more, will not ordinarily be deemed a ratification.[55] Frequently the question is for the jury to determine.

47. E. g., Lee v. Thompson, 124 Fla. 494, 168 So. 848 (1936). See 2 Page, Contracts § 1372 (2d ed. 1920). "By the weight of authority the rule in ratification of an infant's contract . . . is that mere acknowledgment that the obligation has been incurred, or even a part payment thereon is not a ratification. Even payment of interest, part payment of principal, and a mere acknowledgment of the debt, or a statement, 'I owe a debt and you will get your pay' was held not to be a ratification."

48. Thus, it is generally held that part payment made by an infant after attaining his majority is not, without more, a ratification. International Accountants Soc'y v. Santana, 166 La. 671, 117 So. 768, 59 A.L.R. 276 (1928).

49. Camp v. Bank of Bentonville, 230 Ark. 414, 323 S.W.2d 556 (1959); Hook v. Harmon Nat'l Real Estate Corp., 250 App.Div. 689, 251 App.Div. 722, 295 N.Y.S. 249 (2d Dep't 1937).

50. Henry v. Root, 33 N.Y. 526 (1865). Inconsistent language in subsequent New York opinions should be disapproved.

51. On these requisites, see § 84 supra.

52. E. g., Lee v. Thompson, 124 Fla. 494, 168 So. 848 (1936).

53. See notes 38–41 supra.

54. Turner v. Little, 70 Ga.App. 567, 28 S.E.2d 871 (1944); Clark v. Kidd, 148 Ky. 479, 146 S.W. 1097 (1912).

55. See notes 47, 48 supra.

§ 125. Effect Upon Ratification of Ignorance of Law or Fact

The former infant's ratification is ineffective unless he knows the facts upon which his liability depends,[56] but the cases are in conflict as to whether he must know that the law gives him the power to avoid the original contract. Perhaps the majority of cases have applied the maxim that everyone is presumed to know the law and have held that lack of knowledge of the law is immaterial.[57] A significant number of cases, however, have held that there can be no ratification without full knowledge of the legal consequences.[58]

§ 126. Obligations of Restitution upon Disaffirmance

A variety of questions and a number of conflicting views exist as to the adjustment of the economic relations of the parties after an infant has disaffirmed. If either or both parties have rendered some performance questions of restitution may arise.

(a) Infant as Defendant

If an infant has purchased an automobile on credit [59] and effectively disaffirms, in an action against him for the balance of the price his avoidance is an affirmative defense.[60] It would be an obvious injustice, however, if he were to be allowed to retain the automobile while escaping from his obligation to pay. Thus it is everywhere recognized that the infant is under an obligation to return any consideration which he has received and still possesses.[61] If he no longer

56. Thus in a case in which an infant partner upon reaching majority was alleged to have ratified his partnership obligations by accepting benefits under the partnership, it was held that he did not ratify certain outstanding bad checks of which he was unaware. Tobey v. Wood, 123 Mass. 88 (1877).

57. Shepherd v. Shepherd, 408 Ill. 364, 97 N.E.2d 273 (1951); Campbell v. Sears, Roebuck & Co., 307 Pa. 365, 161 A. 310 (1932); see Annot., Ignorance of Legal Right to Avoid Contract or Conveyance Made During Infancy as Affecting Ratification Thereof upon Attaining Majority, 5 A.L.R. 137 (1920).

58. Trader v. Lowe, 45 Md. 1 (1876); International Text Book Co. v. Connelly, 206 N.Y. 188, 99 N.E. 722 (1912). An intermediate position was taken in Ogborn v. Hoffman, 52 Ind. 439 (1876), where it was held that the presumption that everyone knows the law is applicable as a rebuttable presumption only.

59. It is assumed here that the automobile is not a necessary. If it is a necessary other rules come into play. See § 128, infra.

60. Clark, Code Pleading 611, 621 (2d ed. 1947).

61. It is generally agreed that the infant need not tender restitution of the consideration as a condition precedent to a defensive plea of infancy. 2 Williston § 238.

"When property is bought by an infant on credit, and being sued for the price, he pleads infancy, the seller may recover at law the property, the title being revested in him by the re-

has the consideration he need not return it. This is true even if he has squandered, wasted or negligently destroyed what he has received.[62] Thus the infant purchaser of the automobile on credit is not accountable for the automobile if he no longer has it.[63] This rule is subject to one exception. If the infant has exchanged or sold the property and still possesses the property received in the exchange or the investment, the infant will be liable as if he still had the original consideration or such portion of it as is represented by the exchange or investment.[64]

(b) Infant as Plaintiff

Suppose that instead of purchasing an automobile on credit, the infant purchases the automobile for $5,000, pays cash and proceeds to wreck it. If the infant then disaffirms and brings an action for restitution, application of the rule that an infant need account only for that part of the consideration which he retains would seem to dictate that the infant may have full recovery of the $5,000 upon restoration of the wreck. This is the traditional view.[65] Many courts have, however, ruled that the infant's recovery will be offset by the value of the use to him of the automobile and the amount of depreciation in value of the vehicle.[66] Although the texts have not usually em-

sult of the suit for the price . . .. A fortiori is the principle applicable in a court of equity." Evans v. Morgan, 69 Miss. 328, 329, 12 So. 270–71 (1891) (citations omitted).

62. Drude v. Curtis, 183 Mass. 317, 67 N.E. 317, 62 L.R.A. 755 (1903) (rule applied where both parties were infants).

63. 2 Williston § 238.

64. MacGreal v. Taylor, 167 U.S. 688, 17 S.Ct. 961, 42 L.Ed. 326 (1897) (subrogation theory); Whitman v. Allen, 123 Me. 1, 121 A. 160, 36 A.L.R. 776 (1923) (infant had proceeds of sale); Evans v. Morgan, 69 Miss. 328, 12 So. 270 (1891) (infant businessmen purchased goods from plaintiffs on credit and goods were intermingled with other stock; plaintiffs could execute on entire stock).

65. Quality Motors, Inc. v. Hays, 216 Ark. 264, 225 S.W.2d 326 (1949) (wrecked automobile); Carpenter v. Grow, 247 Mass. 133, 141 N.E. 859

(1923); Rotondo v. Kay Jewelry Co., 84 R.I. 292, 123 A.2d 404 (1956) (burden of proof on adult party that infant still has the consideration); Hines v. Cheshire, 36 Wash.2d 467, 219 P.2d 100 (1950) (return of damaged automobile); Annot., Return of Property Purchased by Infant as Condition of Recovery of Purchase Money Paid, 16 A.L.R. 1475 (1922); Return of Property Purchased by Infant as Condition of Recovery of Purchase Price Paid, 36 A.L.R. 782 (1925).

66. Myers v. Hurley Motor Co., Inc., 273 U.S. 18, 47 S.Ct. 277, 71 L.Ed. 515, 50 A.L.R. 1181 (1927) (depreciation caused by negligent use of automobile); Worman Motor Co. v. Hill, 54 Ariz. 227, 94 P.2d 865, 124 A.L.R. 1363 (1939); Creer v. Active Automobile Exchange, Inc., 99 Conn. 266, 121 A. 888 (1923) (value of depreciation deducted from infant's recovery but not value of use); Marceiliac v. Stevens, 206 Ky. 383, 267 S.W. 229 (1924) (rental value of house; alternate ground as house was also a necessary); La-

phasized the distinction in result based upon whether the infant is the plaintiff or defendant in the action, it explains a good many cases which otherwise appear contradictory. The distinction has been recognized explicitly in some of the decisions.[67] A distinction in result based upon the procedural position of the parties may seem arbitrary, but to some extent it reflects the risks foreseeable to the parties. A seller on credit recognizes that he is assuming legal and practical risks of nonpayment. A seller for cash would usually be astounded if he were made to restore the price paid without receiving in return the goods delivered. There is rough justice in holding that an infant who takes a flight from New York to Los Angeles and pays cash may not demand his money back after taking the flight;[68] but that if he flies on the "pay later plan," the risk of nonpayment is taken by the extender of credit. What is involved is an attempt to protect an infant from improvident commitments; but not from improvident cash expenditures, at least where protection of the infant would work a harsh forfeiture against the other party. This approach, pioneered in New Hampshire,[69] has led to a complete breakthrough in the ordinary rules relating to infancy in that jurisdiction, discussed in § 129 infra.

§ 127. Torts Connected with Contracts

Very often tort liability is intimately connected with a contractual relation. Although an infant is not generally liable on his con-

trobe v. Dietrich, 114 Md. 8, 78 A. 983 (1910); Johnson v. Northwestern Mut. Life Ins. Co., 56 Minn. 365, 57 N.W. 934, aff'd, 56 Minn. 365, 59 N.W. 992, 26 L.R.A. 187 (1894) (infant must account for benefits received); Wooldridge v. Lavoie, 79 N.H. 21, 104 A. 346 (1918) (infant must account for benefit received from use but not depreciation caused by negligence); Rice v. Butler, 160 N.Y. 578, 55 N.E. 275, 45 L.R.A. 303 (1899); Pettit v. Liston, 97 Ore. 464, 191 P. 660, 11 A.L.R. 487 (1920) (value of use of motorcycle); Barber v. Gross, 74 S.D. 254, 51 N.W. 2d 696 (1952) (statutory result). See also Annot., Infant's Liability for Use or Depreciation of Subject Matter, In Action to Recover Purchase Price upon His Disaffirmance of Contract to Purchase Goods, 12 A.L.R.3d 1174 (1967).

67. The distinction is suggested in 2 Kent's Commentaries * 240. Many of the cases making the distinction rely upon and cite these influential commentaries. E. g., Rice v. Butler, 160 N.Y. 578, 55 N.E. 275, 45 L.R.A. 303 (1899), and Pettit v. Liston, 97 Ore. 464, 191 P. 660, 11 A.L.R. 487 (1920).

68. Vichnes v. Transcontinental & Western Air, Inc., 173 Misc. 631, 18 N.Y.S.2d 603 (App.T.1940), 15 St. John's L.Rev. 98 (1940); contra, Adamowski v. Curtiss-Wright Flying Service, Inc., 300 Mass. 281, 15 N.E.2d 467 (1938) (on the theory that the duty of the infant to account for depreciation and use is limited to cases involving tangibles and inapplicable to cases involving services), criticized 27 Georgetown L.J. 233 (1938), 7 Fordham L.Rev. 445 (1938).

69. Hall v. Butterfield, 59 N.H. 354 (1879); Bartlett v. Bailey, 59 N.H. 408 (1879); Wooldridge v. Lavoie, 79 N.H. 21, 104 A. 346 (1918).

tracts he is liable for his torts.[70] At least three kinds of problems arise from the interplay of tort and contract liability in cases involving infants.

(a) Infant's Torts Stemming from His Contracts

The other party to a contractual relation may not sue the infant for tort if the tort is in essence a breach of contractual duty. While it is possible in some jurisdictions to frame an action for negligence in respect to a bailment in terms of tort or in terms of breach of contract,[71] the almost universal holding is that the action cannot be brought against the infant no matter how it is couched.[72] It is believed that to allow such an action would in effect be enforcing the contract. The infant, however, would be liable if he converted the chattel since this kind of wrong is deemed to be independent of the contract, rather than a breach of an implied promise not to convert.[73] The same analysis is made as to breach of warranty, although such a breach may often give rise to an action in tort, since it stems from a contract, it is not maintainable against an infant.[74]

(b) False Representations by the Infant

If the infant wilfully misrepresents his age, the majority view is that he nevertheless may exercise his power of avoidance.[75] How-

70. See Prosser, Torts § 128 (3d ed. 1964).

71. Although a bailment is not a contract, it is often formed by a contract, (see § 2 supra) and as a common law proposition, "assumpsit" could be brought for negligence in relation to a bailment.

72. Jones v. Milner, 53 Ga.App. 304, 185 S.E. 586 (1936); Eaton v. Hill, 50 N.H. 235 (1870); Brunhoelzl v. Brandes, 90 N.J.L. 31, 100 A. 163 (1917); contra, Daggy v. Miller, 180 Iowa 1146, 162 N.W. 854 (1917). Similarly, it has been held that an infant is not liable for breach of contract of safe carriage when for a fee he drove other minors to school. Brown v. Wood, 293 Mich. 148, 291 N.W. 255, 127 A.L.R. 1436 (1940). As a result of disaffirmance of the contract the passengers had the status of guests and were barred from recovery by a "guest statute."

73. Williams v. Buckler, 264 S.W.2d 279 (Ky.1959); Young v. Muhling, 48 App.Div. 617, 63 N.Y.S. 181 (2d Dep't 1900); Vermont Acceptance Corp. v. Wiltshire, 103 Vt. 219, 153 A. 199, 73 A.L.R. 792 (1931).

74. Collins v. Gifford, 203 N.Y. 465, 96 N.E. 721, 38 L.R.A.,N.S., 202 (1911).

75. Myers v. Hurley Motor Co., Inc., 273 U.S. 18, 47 S.Ct. 277, 71 L.Ed. 515, 50 A.L.R. 1181 (1927); Del Santo v. Bristol County Stadium, 273 F.2d 605 (1st Cir. 1960); Creer v. Active Automobile Exchange, Inc., 99 Conn. 266, 121 A. 888 (1923); Tracey v. Brown, 265 Mass. 163, 163 N.E. 885 (1928); Sternlieb v. Normandie Nat'l Sec. Corp., 263 N.Y. 245, 188 N.E. 726, 90 A.L.R. 1437 (1934). The result may be different as a result of a statute, Thosath v. Transport Motor Co., 136 Wash. 565, 240 P. 921 (1925); or decision, La Rosa v. Nichols, 92 N.J.L. 375, 105 A. 201, 6 A.L.R. 412 (1918).

ever, it often has been held that in equity the rule is different to the extent that if the infant wishes to disaffirm under these circumstances he must place the adult party in the status quo ante.[76]

Despite the general recognition of the rule that a misrepresentation of age does not inhibit the infant's power of avoidance, there is a marked split of authority on the question of whether an infant is liable in tort for a wilful misrepresentation of his age. The division stems from the rule that a tort action will not lie against an infant if in essence it involves the enforcement of a contract. Some courts assert that ultimately the fraud action is based on the contract.[77] Others take the position that the tort is sufficiently independent of the contract and that the granting of tort relief does not involve indirect enforcement of the contract.[78] A case can be made for either point of view. The basic dispute is as to what extent the law's policy of protecting infants should apply to a fraudulent infant. The same kind of split of authority exists as to other kinds of fraudulent statements made by infants in connection with their contracts.[79]

It is recognized that the infant's fraudulent misrepresentation as to his age or other material facts will permit the other party to avoid the contract on grounds of fraud.[80]

See generally, Miller, Fraudulent Misrepresentations of Age as Affecting the Infant's Contract—A Comparative Study, 15 U.Pitts.L.Rev. 73 (1953).

76. Lewis v. Van Cleve, 302 Ill. 413, 134 N.E. 804 (1922); Stallard v. Sutherland, 131 Va. 316, 108 S.E. 568, 18 A.L.R. 516 (1921); contra, Sims v. Everhardt, 102 U.S. 300, 26 L.Ed. 87 (1880); Watson v. Billings, 38 Ark. 278 (1881). In line with the usual flexibility of equitable doctrine, however, the decisions have varied with questions such as whether the infant is the plaintiff or defendant and whether the contract is executed or executory. See Note, Liability of the Infant in Contract, 20 Iowa L.Rev. 785, 790–91 (1935).

77. Drennen Motor Car Co. v. Smith, 230 Ala. 275, 160 So. 761 (1935); Slayton v. Barry, 175 Mass. 513, 56 N.E. 574 (1900); Sternlieb v. Normandie Nat'l Sec. Corp., 263 N.Y. 245, 188 N. E. 726, 90 A.L.R. 1437 (1934); Greensboro Morris Plan Co. v. Palmer, 185 N.C. 109, 116 S.E. 261 (1923).

78. Keser v. Chagnon, 159 Colo. 209, 410 P.2d 637 (1966) (adult may counterclaim for fraud in infant's action for restitution); Byers v. Lemay Bank & Trust Co., 365 Mo. 341, 282 S. W.2d 512 (1955); Wisconsin Loan & Finance Corp. v. Goodnough, 201 Wis. 101, 228 N.W. 484, 67 A.L.R. 1259 (1930). See generally, Miller, supra note 75. This article contains an exhaustive appendix showing the state of the law in each jurisdiction.

79. Not liable: Collins v. Gifford, 203 N.Y. 465, 96 N.E. 721, 38 L.R.A.,N.S., 202 (1911); Lesnick v. Pratt, 78 A.2d 487 (1951), rearg. denied 116 Vt. 477, 80 A.2d 663 (1951). Liable: Wisconsin Loan & Finance Co. v. Goodnough, 201 Wis. 101, 228 N.W. 484, 67 A.L.R. 1259 (1930).

80. Beardsley v. Clark, 229 Iowa 601, 294 N.W. 887 (1940), 39 Mich.L.Rev. 1417 (1941); Neff v. Landis, 110 Pa. 204, 1 A. 177 (1885) (seller permitted to avoid the contract and replevy the goods); Fredeking v. Grimmett, 140 W.Va. 745, 86 S.E.2d 554, 50 A.L.R.2d

(c) Torts and Agency Relationships

Under the doctrine of respondeat superior a principal is liable for the torts of his agent committed within the scope of the agent's employment. An infant may appoint an agent but such an appointment is subject to disaffirmance. Accordingly the majority view is that infants may avoid their liability for the torts of their agents,[81] at least insofar as the tort liability stems from respondeat superior.[82]

§ 128. Liability of an Infant for Necessaries

It is well settled that an infant is liable for necessaries furnished him, and it is generally recognized that this liability is quasi contractual rather than contractual. As a consequence of the quasi contractual nature of the action, the infant may disaffirm an executory contract for necessaries.[83] Moreover, the infant is not liable for the contract price, but for the reasonable value of the necessaries furnished.[84]

The concept of "necessaries" is relative to the infant's status in life.[85] It would seem clear that the range of what is necessary is considerably larger if the infant is emancipated, and larger yet if he is married,[86] as compared with what is necessary for an unemancipated infant. Thus it is a somewhat fruitless quest to analyze the cases to determine, for example, whether an automobile is a necessary.[87] When reasonable men would differ, the question is for the

1346 (1955). See generally Miller, supra note 75, and appendix thereto.

81. Palmer v. Miller, 380 Ill. 256, 43 N. E.2d 973 (1942); Payette v. Fleischman, 329 Mich. 160, 45 N.W.2d 16 (1950); Hodge v. Feiner, 338 Mo. 268, 90 S.W.2d 90, 103 A.L.R. 483 (1936); Covault v. Nevitt, 157 Wis. 1113, 146 N.W. 1115, 51 L.R.A.,N.S., 1092 (1914) (infant businessman not liable for negligence of his janitor); contra, Scott v. Schisler, 107 N.J.L. 397, 153 A. 395, 44 Harv.L.Rev. 1292 (1931). See generally Gregory, Infant's Responsibility for His Agent's Torts, 5 Wis.L.Rev. 453 (1930).

82. Cf. Sikes v. Johnson, 16 Mass. 389 (1820) (infant procured another to commit a battery).

83. Gregory v. Lee, 64 Conn. 407, 30 A. 53, 25 L.R.A. 618 (1894); Wallin v.

Highland Park Co., 127 Iowa 131, 102 N.W. 839 (1905).

84. Sceva v. True, 53 N.H. 627 (1873); see 2 Williston §§ 240–244; Woodward, Quasi Contracts § 202 (1913).

85. "The word 'necessaries' as used in the law is a relative term, except when applied to such things as are obviously requisite for the maintenance of existence, and depends on the social position and situation in life of the infant as well as upon his own fortune and that of his parents." International Text Book Co. v. Connelly, 206 N.Y. 188, 195, 99 N.E. 722, 725 (1912).

86. Ragan v. Williams, 220 Ala. 590, 127 So. 190, 68 A.L.R. 1182 (1930); Spaulding v. New England Furniture Co., 154 Me. 330, 147 A.2d 916 (1959).

87. Generally the cases have held that the automobile was not a necessary

jury. It is obvious, however, that food,[88] shelter,[89] and clothing [90] are necessaries. But the kind of food,[91] shelter,[92] and clothing [93] is another question. Medical services can generally be considered as necessaries.[94] Legal services are necessaries in many instances, particularly for the enforcement or defense of tort claims and criminal prosecutions,[95] but are often not considered such if the attorney is retained to protect property rights. This result is reached on the ground that a guardian should be appointed to protect such rights and the attorney should contract with the guardian.[96]

Education is of course a necessary, but the kind of education which is necessary is dependent upon the circumstances of the infant. While a basic public school education is recognized as a necessary, it appears that generally a college education has not been deemed to be,[97] but education in a trade has been said to qualify as a necessary.[98] The language of the decisions shows sufficient flexi-

under the facts of the particular case. See Harris v. Raughton, 37 Ala.App. 648, 73 So.2d 921 (1954), 6 Hastings L.J. 112 (1954) (an excellent note pointing out the changing place of the automobile in society). Contra, Ehrsam v. Borgen, 185 Kan. 776, 347 P.2d 260 (1959); Bancredit, Inc. v. Bethea, 65 N.J.Super. 538, 168 A.2d 250 (1961) (remanded for jury determination).

88. O'Donniley v. Kinley, 220 Mo.App. 284, 286 S.W. 140 (1926) (loan to purchase groceries).

89. Ragan v. Williams, 220 Ala. 590, 127 So. 190, 68 A.L.R. 1182 (1930) (house rental for married infant); Gregory v. Lee, 64 Conn. 407, 30 A. 53, 25 L.R.A. 618 (1894) (lodging for Yale student); but see Moskow v. Marshall, 271 Mass. 302, 171 N.E. 477 (1930) (lodging for Harvard student).

90. Lynch v. Johnson, 109 Mich. 640, 67 N.W. 908 (1896).

91. Kline v. L'Amoureux, 2 Paige's Ch. 419 (N.Y.1831); L'Amoureux v. Crosby, 2 Paige's Ch. 422 (N.Y.1831) (liquor not a necessary).

92. The purchase of a house was held to be a necessary in Johnson v. Newberry, 267 S.W. 476 (Tex.Com.App. 1924), 13 Georgetown L.J. 416 (1925), although this would not ordinarily be the case.

93. Lefils & Christian v. Sugg, 15 Ark. 137 (1854) (cologne, cravats, kid gloves, and walking canes not necessaries).

94. Cole v. Wagner, 197 N.C. 692, 150 S.E. 339, 71 A.L.R. 220 (1929).

95. Crafts v. Carr, 24 R.I. 397, 53 A. 275 (1902); Plummer v. Northern Pac. Ry. Co., 98 Wash. 67, 167 P. 73, 7 A. L.R. 104 (1917). See Annot., 13 A.L. R.3d 1251 (1967).

96. Grissom v. Beidleman, 35 Okl. 343, 129 P. 853 (1913); 2 Williston § 242.

97. Moskow v. Marshall, 271 Mass. 302, 171 N.E. 477 (1930); La Salle Extension University v. Campbell, 131 N.J. L. 343, 36 A.2d 397 (1944); Middlebury College v. Chandler, 16 Vt. 683 (1844).

98. Mauldin v. Southern Shorthand & Bus. Univ., 126 Ga. 681, 55 S.E. 922 (1906) (stenography may qualify, but not under the facts); Curtiss v. Roosevelt Aviation School, 5 Air.L.Rev. 382 (Mun.Ct.N.Y.1934) (mechanical training course). In Siegel & Hodges v. Hodges, 20 Misc.2d 243, 191 N.Y.S.2d 984 (Sup.Ct.1959), aff'd 10 App.Div.2d 646, 197 N.Y.S.2d 246 (2d Dep't 1960), aff'd 9 N.Y.2d 747, 174 N.E.2d 533, 214 N.Y.S.2d 452 (1961), it was held that voice training could constitute a nec-

bility, however, to allow for changing community standards in this regard.[99]

If the infant borrows money for the purpose of purchasing necessaries and so uses it, the infant is liable to the lender as if the lender had supplied the necessaries.[1] The same result should follow if a loan is in fact used for necessaries although there was no agreement with the lender as to the use to which the money is to be put.[2] If the funds are advanced for the purpose of purchasing necessaries but are squandered for other purposes, the cases are divided as to the infant's liability.[3]

The liability of an infant for necessaries is relative not only to his status in life but also is dependent upon whether or not he has an existing supply of necessaries, or parents or guardians who are able and willing to supply him with the necessities of life.[4] The mere fact that the goods or services are in general considered necessaries does not make them necessary to the particular infant if he is already supplied with them.[5] Also an infant who has not been emancipated can-

essary for a ten year old prodigy who made many television appearances, but that a parent could not recover from the child, as the primary duty of furnishing the necessaries is upon the parent. See also Siegel v. Hodges, 15 App.Div.2d 571, 222 N.Y.S.2d 989 (2d Dep't 1961).

It was subsequently held that whether a third person could recover for managerial and coaching services as necessaries was a question of fact for the jury. Siegel v. Hodges, 24 App.Div.2d 456, 260 N.Y.S.2d 405 (2d Dep't 1965).

99. "A proper education is a necessary, but what is a proper education depends upon circumstances. A common school education is doubtless necessary in this country, because it is essential to the transaction of business and the adequate discharge of civil and political duties. A classical or professional education, however, has been held not to come within the term . . . . . Still, circumstances not found in the cases cited may exist where even such an education might properly be found a necessary as matter of fact." International Text Book Co. v. Connelly, 206 N.Y. 188, 195, 99 N.E. 722, 725 (1912) (citations omitted).

Cases in other contexts, e. g., family court support orders, petitions for invasion of trust funds, welfare program administration, etc., have indicated that a college education can be a necessary. 1961 Report of the New York Law Revision Commission 283–84.

1. Norwood Nat. Bank v. Allston, 152 S.C. 199, 149 S.E. 593, 65 A.L.R. 1334 (1929), 43 Harv.L.Rev. 498 (1930). Sometimes this result is attained by the equitable doctrine of subrogation by which the lender is placed in the position of the party who supplied the necessaries. Price v. Sanders, 60 Ind. 310 (1878).

2. 2 Williston § 243 argues strongly for this position.

3. The infant was held to be liable in Norwood Nat. Bank v. Allston, 152 S. C. 199, 149 S.E. 593, 65 A.L.R. 1334 (1929), 43 Harv.L.Rev. 498 (1930). A strong contrary dictum appears in Randall v. Sweet, 1 Denio 460 (N.Y. 1845).

4. 2 Williston § 244.

5. Conboy v. Howe, 59 Conn. 112, 22 A. 35 (1890); Trainer v. Trumbull, 141 Mass. 527, 6 N.E. 761 (1886).

not be liable for necessaries unless his parent or guardian refuses to supply him with his needs and broad discretionary latitude is granted the parent or guardian in determining the manner in which he will meet the needs of his child or ward.[6] Moreover, even if all other tests of what is necessary are met it must appear that the goods or services were supplied on the credit of the infant and not of his parent, guardian or third person.[7] Therefore, the mere fact that the creditor has supplied necessaries to the family unit of which the infant is a part does not render the infant liable unless he contracted for the necessaries.[8] Thus, the liability, although quasi contractual, requires that there be a contract with the infant. The basis of this liability is thus considerably different from the liability of a parent for necessaries furnished his children.[9]

§ 129. Infant's Liability for Benefits Received: The New Hampshire View

It has been pointed out that many jurisdictions now require that an infant who seeks to disaffirm a contract and obtain restitution must return or account for the benefits he has received under the contract.[10] If, however, the infant is a defendant and sets up a defense of infancy the infant is liable only for necessaries[11] or for the value of tangible consideration he still retains.[12]

In New Hampshire, however, the courts have taken the position that it is immaterial whether the infant is plaintiff or defendant. If the infant has received benefits, whether necessaries or not, he is liable in an action for restitution for the value of the benefits. Thus,

---

6. Mauldin v. Southern Shorthand & Bus. Univ., 126 Ga. 681, 55 S.E. 922 (1906); International Text Book Co. v. Connelly, 206 N.Y. 188, 99 N.E. 722 (1912).
"It would be subversive of parental authority and dominion if interested third persons could assume to judge for the parent, and subject him to liability for their unauthorized interference in supplying the supposed wants of the child." Lefils & Christian v. Sugg, 15 Ark. 137, 140 (1854).
"A third party has no right to usurp the rights and duties of the guardian. Even if the money paid was, in some sense, for the infant's benefit . . . if the guardian in good faith, and in the exercise of a wise discretion, and with reference to the best interests of his ward, supplied her wants and contributed means suitable to her age

and station in life, and in view of his estate, then the infant would not be liable for the money, as necessaries." McKanna v. Merry, 61 Ill. 177, 180 (1871).

7. McManus v. Arnold Taxi Corp., 82 Cal.App. 215, 255 P. 755 (1927); Mackey v. Shreckengaust, 27 S.W.2d 752 (Kan.City, Mo.Ct.App.1930); Foster v. Adcock, 161 Tenn. 217, 30 S.W.2d 239, 70 A.L.R. 569 (1930).

8. Foster v. Adcock, 161 Tenn. 217, 30 S.W.2d 239, 70 A.L.R. 569 (1930).

9. See § 10 supra.

10. See § 126 supra.

11. Id.

12. Id.

it has been held that an infant dealer in milk is liable for the value
of milk supplied to him in the course of his business,[13] and that an infant orphan is liable for the reasonable value of legal services received
to contest the appointment of a particular guardian, the court deem-
ing it irrelevant to determine whether or not the services were necessary.[14] The approach adopted by New Hampshire commends itself
to good sense as it protects the infant from executory contracts, and
transactions which are not beneficial to him. At the same time it
recognizes the legitimate interest of those who have dealt with the
infant.

B.   THE MENTALLY INFIRM

Analysis

Sec.
130.   Introduction.
131.   Requirement of Restitution.
132.   Avoidance and Ratification.
133.   Liability for Necessaries.
134.   Intoxicated Persons.
135.   Exploitation of Alcoholics and Weak Minded Persons.

§ 130.   Introduction

Although there is older authority to the effect that the contracts
and executed transactions of the mentally infirm are void,[15] the overwhelming weight of modern authority is to the effect that they are
merely voidable,[16] except that if the person so afflicted has been adjudicated an incompetent and a guardian has been appointed prior to
entering into the transaction, in many jurisdictions it is deemed
void.[17]

---

13. Bartlett v. Bailey, 59 N.H. 408 (1879).

14. Porter v. Wilson, 106 N.H. 270, 209 A.2d 730, 13 A.L.R.2d 1247 (1965); accord, under a statute, Spencer v. Col-
lins, 156 Cal. 298, 104 P. 320 (1909).
Similar reasoning is found in Pankas
v. Bell, 413 Pa. 494, 198 A.2d 312
(1964), in enjoining a former infant
employee from violation of a covenant
not to compete.

15. Hovey v. Hobson, 53 Me. 541 (1866).
A most thorough treatment of the
subject is Comment, Mental Illness
and the Law of Contracts, 57 Mich.L.
Rev. 1020 (1959).

16. See 2 Williston §§ 249–252. As one
consequence of this rule, as in the
case of infancy, a bona fide purchaser
of personal property takes free of the
incompetent's interest in the property.
See 2 Williston § 252.

As to real property, unlike in the case
of infants, the majority rule protects
the bona fide purchaser on the basis
of the rule requiring restoration of
the status quo, discussed in the next
section. See Note, 47 Colum.L.Rev.
675 (1947).

17. Church v. Rosenstein, 85 Conn. 279,
82 A. 568 (1912); Hughes v. Jones,
116 N.Y. 67, 22 N.E. 446, 5 L.R.A. 637

Although the problems we are now considering are ordinarily grouped under the heading of "Contracts of Insane Persons,"[18] a significant number of the cases do not deal with insanity, but with other forms of mental infirmity, such as senility, mental retardation,[19] temporary delirium deriving from physical injuries sustained in accidents [20] and intoxication.[21]

It is generally said that insanity exists where a party does not understand the nature and consequences of his act at the time of the transaction.[22]   This test, as well as subsidiary tests of whether the transaction was entered into during a "lucid interval" or whether the person was rational except for "insane delusions" as to the particular transaction in question, has been attacked as unscientific.[23] Some observers have pointed out, however, that the very fact that psychiatric tests are not employed has enabled the courts to work out just results.[24]   In other words, if the contract is fair and beneficial

(1889); John P. Bleeg Co. v. Peterson, 51 S.D. 502, 215 N.W. 529 (1927), 41 Harv.L.Rev. 536 (1928). An adjudication without appointment of a guardian is merely evidence of incompetency. McCormick v. Littler, 85 Ill. 62 (1877). An appointment of a guardian is prima facie evidence that the person was incapable of contracting just prior to the adjudication but is not conclusive. Hughes v. Jones, 116 N.Y. 67, 22 N.E. 446, 5 L.R.A. 637 (1889); cf. L'Amoureux v. Crosby, 2 Paige's Ch. 422 (N.Y.1831) (judgment entered by confession void where judgment creditor knew incompetency proceedings were pending against judgment debtor).

It is often held that if the guardianship falls into disuse because the ward has regained sanity, the ward's contracts are enforceable. Fugate v. Walker, 204 Ky. 767, 265 S.W. 331 (1924); Schultz v. Oldenburg, 202 Minn. 237, 277 N.W. 918 (1938).

18. E. g., 2 Williston ch. 10.

19. E. g., Edmunds v. Chandler, 203 Va. 772, 127 S.E.2d 73 (1962).

20. E. g., Kilgore v. Cross, 1 F. 578 (E. D.Ark.1880).

21. See § 134 infra.

22. Poole v. Hudson, 46 Del. 339, 83 A. 2d 703 (1951); Schneider v. Johnson, 357 Mo. 245, 207 S.W.2d 461 (1948). See Guttmacher and Weihofen, Mental Incompetency, 36 Minn.L.Rev. 179 (1952); Note 32 Colum.L.Rev. 504 (1932).

23. See Comment, "Civil Insanity": The New York Treatment of the Issue of Mental Incapacity in Non-Criminal Cases, 44 Cornell L.Q. 76, 88–93 (1958) (collecting various psychiatric criticisms)

24. A series of articles by Green demonstrates that the legal fact of insanity or sanity tends to be determined by the finding which will better serve the interests of the alleged incompetent. The courts are primarily concerned, he demonstrates, with the question of whether the transaction was abnormal, tending to determine the question of sanity by that criterion. Green, Fraud, Undue Influence, and Mental Incompetency, 43 Colum. L.Rev. 176 (1943); Green, Public Policies Underlying the Law of Mental Incompetency, 38 Mich.L.Rev. 1189 (1940); Green, Judicial Tests of Mental Incompetency, 6 Mo.L.Rev. 141 (1941); Green, The Operative Effect of Mental Incompetency on Agree-

to the alleged incompetent there will be a great tendency to find that he was sane; otherwise the tendency is to find him incompetent.[25] Of course, a tendency must not be confused with doctrine, and there must be some arguable basis for a determination of incompetency and this tendency merely reflects judicial treatment of borderline cases.

§ 131. Requirement of Restitution

To some extent the rationale of the rules concerning the transactions of infants and incompetents coincide. The law desires to protect these classes of persons from their own presumed improvidence. As to incompetents an additional factor is present. Contracts are based on mutual assent. A person incapable of rational volition cannot give his intelligent assent. Under a purely subjective test his contracts would be void. But under a purely objective test the inquiry would be whether he appeared to a reasonable man in the position of the other to be capable of rational assent. This purely objective approach, however, conflicts with the policy of protecting the incompetent from his own improvidence.

Under the majority view a kind of compromise has evolved. Contracts which are executory,[26] or based upon grossly inadequate consideration [27] are voidable, but if the transaction is executed and the other party took no advantage of the incompetent and had no reason to know of his infirmity, it is not voidable unless the incompetent can place the other party in the status quo ante.[28] If the incompetency

ments and Wills, 21 Tex.L.Rev. 554 (1943); Green, Proof of Mental Incompetency and the Unexpressed Major Premise, 53 Yale L.J. 271 (1944). See also Virtue, Restitution from the Mentally Infirm, 26 N.Y.U.L.Rev. 132 and 291 (1951).

25. E. g., in discussing the contests surrounding life support contracts frequently entered into by aged persons, one observer concludes "if it was a reasonable contract and the recipient was a worthy object of trust and faith, then that shows sufficient capacity to uphold the contract; but if support was not given, or if there was fraud, then the grantor was incapacitated because no one in his right mind would have made such a contract." Virtue, supra note 24, at 151. It is to be noted that in many of such cases, it is the heirs of the alleged incompetent who are attempting to set aside

the contract or conveyance, thereby seeking to frustrate a bargain which was beneficial to the deceased.

26. Cundell v. Haswell, 23 R.I. 508, 51 A. 426 (1902). The English rule is contrary. Where the other party did not take advantage of the incompetent and had no reason to know of his mental infirmity the executory contract is enforceable. York Glass Co., Ltd. v. Jubb, 134 L.T.R. (N.S.) 36 (C. A.1925). See Note, Insanity as a Defense to Executory Contracts, 25 Colum.L.Rev. 230 (1925).

27. Alexander v. Haskins, 68 Iowa 73, 25 N.W. 935 (1885) (land conveyed for about one third of its value).

28. Sparrowhawk v. Erwin, 30 Ariz. 238, 246 P. 541, 46 A.L.R. 413 (1926); Coburn v. Raymond, 76 Conn. 484, 57 A. 116 (1904); Perper v. Edell, 160

would be obvious to a reasonable man there is no obligation upon the incompetent to make restitution if the consideration has been consumed or dissipated.[29]   Under a minority view the appearance of sanity is immaterial and the incompetent need restore the consideration only if he still has it.[30]

§ 132.   Avoidance and Ratification

As in the case of infants' contracts there is no power of avoidance in the competent party.[31]   The power of avoidance and ratification is reserved to the incompetent and his heirs or personal representative after death.[32]   If a guardian is appointed the power is vested in the guardian.[33]   Once the incompetent recovers his capacity he may ratify the contract.[34]   As in the case of infants' contracts ratification can

---

Fla. 477, 35 So.2d 387, 47 Mich.L.Rev. 269 (1948) (incompetent must pay real estate broker's commission); Atlanta Banking & Savings Co. v. Johnson, 179 Ga. 313, 175 S.E. 904, 95 A.L.R. 1436 (1934); cf. Georgia Power Co. v. Roper, 201 Ga. 760, 41 S.E.2d 226 (1947), prior judgment vacated 74 Ga. App. 750, 41 S.E.2d 342; Verstandig v. Schlaffer, 296 N.Y. 62, 70 N.E.2d 15 (1946), motion granted 296 N.Y. 997, 73 N.E.2d 573, 47 Colum.L.Rev. 675 (1947); Edmunds v. Chandler, 203 Va. 772, 127 S.E.2d 73 (1962). Restoration of the status quo ante often requires a complex evaluation of the equities and a complex accounting as, for example, when a conveyance is avoided the price received by the incompetent is offset against the rental value during the period it was held by the grantee. For exhaustive treatment, see Virtue, supra note 24, esp. at 291–320.

It is to be observed that the modern tendency is to bring the rules regarding infants contracts into harmony with those governing the contracts of mental incompetents. See § 126 supra as to infants' obligations to make restitution.

29.   Spence v. Spence, 239 Ala. 480, 195 So. 717 (1940); Hardy v. Dyas, 203 Ill. 211, 67 N.E. 852 (1903).

30.   The leading case is Seaver v. Phelps, 28 Mass. (11 Pick.) 304 (1821).

31.   Atwell v. Jenkins, 163 Mass. 362, 40 N.E. 178 (1895).   But logically the competent party could obtain a declaration of nullity of a transaction entered into with an incompetent under guardianship as such a transaction is void rather than merely voidable.

32.   Orr v. Equitable Mortgage Co., 107 Ga. 499, 33 S.E. 708 (1899); 2 Williston § 253.   See also Reed v. Brown, 215 Ind. 417, 19 N.E.2d 1015 (1939) (administrator prevailed over adversary grantee-heir); Bullard v. Moor, 158 Mass. 418, 33 N.E. 928 (1893) (administrator's ratification binding on heirs).

Some jurisdictions permit creditors of the incompetent to attack transfers of his property.   Chandler v. Welborn, 156 Tex. 312, 294 S.W.2d 801 (1956).

33.   Finch v. Goldstein, 245 N.Y. 300, 157 N.E. 146 (1927) (ratification); Kline v. L'Amoureaux, 2 Paige's Ch. 419 (N.Y.1831) (avoidance); 2 Williston § 253; contra, Gingrich v. Rogers, 69 Neb. 527, 96 N.W. 156 (1903).

Strangers cannot generally avail themselves of the incompetency of a party to the transaction.   Safe Deposit & Trust Co. of Baltimore v. Tait, 54 F. 2d 383 (D.C.Md.1931) (Commissioner of Internal Revenue).

34.   Strodder v. Southern Granite Co., 99 Ga. 595, 27 S.E. 174 (1896).

be effected by conduct or words, and once ratified the contract may not be avoided.[35]

§ 133. Liability for Necessaries

As in the case of an infant, a mental incompetent is liable in a quasi contractual action for necessaries furnished him [36] or his family.[37] Roughly the same classes of goods and services considered necessaries for infants are necessaries for incompetents, including money advanced to procure necessaries.[38] Obviously, the incompetent's need for nursing and medical attention is salient among his necessaries.[39] Also legal services availed of to procure release from custody and guardianship, whether or not successful, are ordinarily compensable.[40]

§ 134. Intoxicated Persons

When a person is so far intoxicated or under the influence of narcotics that he does not understand the nature and consequences of the transaction in issue, the legal effect is much the same as in the case of any other kind of mental infirmity having the same effect.[41] Since the incompetency is self-induced, however, there is a different emphasis in the cases and particularly in the older cases, a good deal of moral indignation is often voiced at the intoxicated person [42] or the person plying him with liquor.[43]

---

35. Bunn v. Postell, 107 Ga. 490, 33 S. E. 707 (1899).

36. Coffee v. Owen's Adm'r, 216 Ky. 142, 287 S.W. 540 (1926), 15 Ky.L.J. 361 (1927).

37. Dalton v. Dalton, 172 Ky. 585, 189 S.W. 902 (1916); Linch v. Sanders, 114 W.Va. 726, 173 S.E. 788 (1934).

38. Bank of Rector v. Parrish, 131 Ark. 216, 198 S.W. 689 (1917); Henry v. Knight, 74 Ind.App. 562, 122 N.E. 675 (1919).

39. In re Weber's Estate, 256 Mich. 61, 239 N.W. 260 (1931), 17 Cornell L.Q. 502 (1932).

40. Kay v. Kay, 53 Ariz. 336, 89 P.2d 496, 121 A.L.R. 1496 (1939); Carr v. Anderson, 154 Minn. 162, 191 N.W. 407, 26 A.L.R. 557 (1923); Carter v. Beckwith, 128 N.Y. 312, 28 N.E. 582 (1891); In re Weightman's Estate, 126 Pa.Super. 221, 190 A. 552 (1937), 85 U.Pa.L.Rev. 852 (1937).

41. See Poole v. Hudson, 46 Del. 339, 83 A.2d 703 (1951); Seminara v. Grisman, 137 N.J.Eq. 307, 44 A.2d 492 (1945); Lucy v. Zehmer, 196 Va. 493, 84 S.E.2d 516 (1954).
See generally, McCoid, Intoxication and its Effect upon Civil Responsibility, 42 Iowa L.Rev. 38 (1956); Annot., Intoxication as Ground For Avoiding Contract, 36 A.L.R. 619 (1925); 2 Williston §§ 258–263.
Chronic alcoholism is ground in many jurisdictions for an adjudication of incompetency and for the appointment of a guardian.

42. See Cook v. Bagnell Timber Co., 78 Ark. 47, 94 S.W. 695 (1906), expressing a minority view that intoxication per se is never a defense. If coupled with fraud by the other, the transaction is voidable on grounds of fraud. Accord, Burroughs v. Richman, 13 N.J.L. 233 (1832). See also Somers v. Ferris, 182 Mich. 392, 148 N.W. 782 (1914).

43. See L'Amoureux v. Crosby, 2 Paige 422 (N.Y.1831), where the Chancellor

The contract of an intoxicated person is voidable by him but only under circumstances similar to those available to other classes of the mentally infirm. Cases permitting avoidance on intoxication alone are rare. This may be explainable on grounds that it would be unusual for the admittedly competent party to contract unknowingly with a person who is so intoxicated as not to understand the nature and consequences of his acts.[44] Where the other party is aware of the intoxication the rules alluded to in the next section come into play.

§ 135. Exploitation of Alcoholics and Weak Minded Persons

Mental infirmity, feebleness of intellect or intoxication may exist to a lesser degree than required by law for the avoidance of a contract. In such a case the person so afflicted is of course bound by his contract if no other grounds for avoidance exist. The cases, however, frequently reveal exploitation of such persons. The law offers a number of other doctrines for their protection. It is obvious that where a feeble minded illiterate woman is made to execute a conveyance at pistol point the transaction is voidable.[45] The woman's mental powers are barely relevant in such circumstances. The factual patterns, however, usually involve more subtle forms of duress, fraud, undue influence or overreaching. To ply an alcoholic with liquor and then induce him to enter into a contract for a grossly inadequate consideration has been deemed a species of fraud.[46] Such cases are not decided on grounds of lack of capacity, but the person's limited mental ability coupled with unconscionable exploitation by the other. This is further illustrated by cases holding that a hard bargain aggressively pressed upon a sober alcoholic by a party who knows of his consuming desire for cash to obtain liquor is voidable for overreaching.[47]

The situation in which persons who suffer from some infirmity but who are not legally insane have been exploited are as varied as the expressions of human avarice. Typical situations which recur in-

---

expressed regret that he did not possess the power of English Chancellor to commit plaintiff innkeeper to Fleet Prison.

44. See 2 Williston § 259.

45. This illustration is suggested by Phillips v. Bowie, 127 S.W.2d 522 (Tex.Civ.App.1939).

46. Thackrah v. Haas, 119 U.S. 499, 7 S.Ct. 311, 30 L.Ed. 486 (1886); Tubbs

v. Hilliard, 104 Colo. 164, 89 P.2d 535 (1939); Matthis v. O'Brien, 137 Ky. 651, 126 S.W. 156 (1910).

47. Kendall v. Ewert, 259 U.S. 139, 42 S.Ct. 444, 66 L.Ed. 862 (1922), leave to present petition for reh. granted 42 S. Ct. 587; 3 Tenn.L.Rev. 84 (1925); Harlow v. Kingston, 169 Wis. 521, 173 N.W. 308, 6 A.L.R. 327 (1919).

volve deeds extracted from the aged bedridden,[48] and releases extracted from injured persons suffering great shock or pain.[49] In each case the court has the difficult task of sifting through the facts. Some degree of infirmity coupled with the unfairness of the bargain will often result in a finding of fraud, undue influence, overreaching or even mental incapacity. The recent enlargement of the doctrine of unconscionability offers another and perhaps more forthright approach to cases of this kind.[50]

48. An analysis of 123 cases involving contracts and conveyances with aged persons attacked for want of capacity leads one observer to conclude that in addition to evidence of the extent of the infirmity and the fairness of the bargain the courts place emphasis on whether there is a fiduciary relationship, secrecy or unkindness. Of the 62 transactions which were set aside, undue influence and fraud rather than want of capacity seems to have been the basis of most of the decisions. The observer concludes: "These are perhaps the most difficult cases of all for the courts, which are virtually without doctrinal guidance, and must base their decisions solely on the individual equities, as disclosed by witnesses who are usually deeply involved emotionally in some variant of the King Lear situation." Virtue, supra note 24, at 298–99.

49. Union Pacific Ry. Co. v. Harris, 158 U.S. 326, 15 S.Ct. 843, 39 L.Ed. 1003 (1895) (release signed while injured person was under the influence of morphine); Carr v. Sacramento Clay Products Co., 35 Cal.App. 439, 170 P. 446 (1918) (plaintiff was still physically injured, in the "depths of dispair," unable to work, had less than $1.00, owed considerable medical bills, adjuster falsely represented that statute limited liability to $217, doctor testified that plaintiff had "traumatic neurosis"; court found fraud, undue influence and incompetency). For additional cases, see Virtue, supra note 24, at 296–97; see also Keefe, Validity of Releases Executed Under Mistake of Fact, 14 Fordham L.Rev. 135 (1945).

50. See § 56 supra.

CHAPTER 9

CONDITIONS

Analysis

		Sections
A.	General Principles	136–149
B.	Express Conditions	150–154
C.	Constructive Conditions	155–163
D.	Excuse of Condition	164–173

A. GENERAL PRINCIPLES

Sec.
136. Meaning of Condition in a Contract.
137. Classification of Conditions.
138. Conditions Precedent.
139. Concurrent Conditions.
140. Conditions Subsequent.
141. Express (True) and Constructive Conditions.
142. Illustrations and Effect of Express Conditions.
143. Distinction Between an Express Condition and a Promise.
144. Express Language of Condition May be Implied Language of Promise.
145. Express Language of Promise Giving Rise to Implied or Constructive Conditions.
146. The History of Constructive Conditions.
147. Constructive Conditions Distinguished from Implied in Fact Conditions.
148. Conditions as Related to Unilateral and Bilateral Contracts.
149. Importance of Distinguishing Between Express and Constructive Conditions: Substantial Performance and Material Breach.

B. EXPRESS CONDITIONS

150. Strict Compliance.
151. Conditions of Satisfaction.
152. Conditions of Satisfaction: Satisfaction of a Third Person.
153. Conditions of Satisfaction: Satisfaction of a Party to the Contract.
154. Demand as a Condition.

C. CONSTRUCTIVE CONDITIONS

155. Introduction.
156. Required Order of Performance in a Bilateral Contract.

Sec.
157. Material Breach and Substantial Performance.
    (a) Material Breach.
    (b) Substantial Performance.
158. A Note on Terminology: "Failure of Consideration."
159. Recovery for Less than Substantial Performance: Quasi Contractual and Statutory Relief.
160. Recovery by a Party in Default: Divisibility.
161. Divisibility: Other Uses of the Concept.
162. Independent Promises.
163. Present or Prospective Inability and Unwillingness to Perform as Constructive Conditions.

D. EXCUSE OF CONDITION

164. Introduction.
165. Hindrance or Failure to Cooperate as an Excuse of Condition: Duty to Cooperate.
166. Estoppel and Waiver Compared.
167. Waiver Contemporaneous with the Formation of the Contract.
168. Waiver and Estoppel: Waiver before Failure of Condition but after Formation of the Contract.
169. Waiver after Failure of Condition: Election.
170. Giving Unjustifiable Reasons for Refusing to Perform as an Excuse of a Condition.
171. Waiver of Condition is Not Waiver of Right to Damages for Breach.
172. Excuse of Conditions Involving Forfeitures.
173. Excuse of Condition by Impossibility.

A. GENERAL PRINCIPLES

Analysis

Sec.
136. Meaning of Condition in a Contract.
137. Classification of Conditions.
138. Conditions Precedent.
139. Concurrent Conditions.
140. Conditions Subsequent.
141. Express (True) and Constructive Conditions.
142. Illustrations and Effect of Express Conditions.
143. Distinction Between an Express Condition and a Promise.
144. Express Language of Condition May be Implied Language of Promise.
145. Express Language of Promise Giving Rise to Implied or Constructive Conditions.
146. The History of Constructive Conditions.
147. Constructive Conditions Distinguished from Implied in Fact Conditions.
148. Conditions as Related to Unilateral and Bilateral Contracts.
149. Importance of Distinguishing Between Express and Constructive Conditions: Substantial Performance and Material Breach.

§ 136.　Meaning of Condition in a Contract

The formation of a contract is usually conditioned upon the existence of an offer, an acceptance and a consideration. This chapter, however, is not concerned with conditions to the formation of contracts. Rather, it deals primarily with conditions to the performance of contractual duties after a contract has been formed. At times there is an overlap between performance and creation of duties. This is particularly true in the case of a unilateral contract.

Traditionally, a condition is defined as an act, or event, other than a lapse of time, which affects a duty to render a promised performance.[1] A duty (promise) is said to be absolute (independent or unconditional) if nothing but a lapse of time is necessary to make its performance due immediately. To illustrate, when a party promises to pay $100 to another if a specified ship comes into port, the performance of his promise is conditioned upon the arrival of the ship. If the promise is to pay if the ship arrives before July 15th, performance of the duty of payment is conditioned upon arrival of the ship by that date. If, however, the promise is merely to pay $100 on July 15th, the promise is said to be unconditional.[2] It is said that in the last illustration the "nonoccurrence is not conceivable by the human mind and . . . is therefore disregarded in describing the promise and the duty." [3]

1. See Restatement, Contracts § 250. The term "condition" is also used to describe the provision in a contract by which it is agreed that a given act or event will affect a duty to render a promised performance. This use of the term is disapproved in 3A Corbin § 627.

2. The example is purely for illustrative purposes. Under the facts presented the question of conditions is academic because there is no consideration for the promise.

3. Corbin, Conditions in the Law of Contract, 28 Yale L.Rev. 739, 742 (1919), Selected Readings 871, 874. This rationale is not entirely convincing. The writers are seemingly unanimous in this view that a mere lapse of time cannot be a condition. It is said that a condition must be "future and uncertain." Ashley, Conditions in Contract, 14 Yale L.J. 424, 425 (1905),

Selected Readings 866, 867. See Grismore § 109; 5 Williston § 663. Why this should be so does not seem to be explained adequately by Professor Corbin's reasoning. If a duty is not to be performed until a certain day in the future, the duty is for most purposes treated as conditional. (In the law of negotiable instruments, however, the characterization of such a promise as unconditional is meaningful.) For example, in the absence of a repudiation an action brought prior to the due date to enforce the promise will be dismissed. One suspects that the requirement of "future and uncertain" was borrowed from rules governing conditional estates in land, where major substantive distinctions exist between estates conditioned on uncertain events and estates limited by definite time periods. See Blackstone's Commentaries, Book II, ch. 10.

§ 137. Classification of Conditions

Conditions may be classified in at least two different ways. A classification is frequently made based upon the time when the conditioning event is to happen in relation to the promisor's duty to perform. Under this division, conditions are labelled as conditions precedent, conditions concurrent and conditions subsequent. A second classification is based upon the manner in which the condition arises; that is, whether it is imposed by the parties or whether it is created by law. Under this division conditions are divided into express conditions and constructive conditions.

§ 138. Conditions Precedent

A condition precedent is an act or event, other than a lapse of time, which must exist or occur before a duty of immediate performance of a promise arises.[4] For example, if A has promised for a consideration to pay B $100 if a specified ship arrives in port, A's duty of payment does not arise unless and until the ship arrives. Similarly, if A offers to pay $10 to B if B walks across the Brooklyn Bridge, A's duty to pay does not become absolute until B performs the requested act. In this instance of an offer to a unilateral contract B's performance is a condition precedent to A's duty of payment. It is also, under the classical view,[5] a condition precedent to the formation of the contract—that is to say, performance of the act is the acceptance of the offer.[6] It should be stressed again, however, that the term "condition" is ordinarily reserved to describe acts or events which must occur before a duty of performance under an existing contract becomes absolute.

§ 139. Concurrent Conditions

A concurrent condition is a particular kind of condition precedent.[7] It exists where the parties are to exchange performances at the same time. For example, if A agrees to sell and B agrees to buy a certain book, in the absence of agreement to the contrary, payment and delivery are ordinarily concurrent conditions. This means that in order for A to put B in default he must make conditional tender of the book or show that tender is excused, and in order for B to put A in default he must make conditional tender of the price or show that tender is excused.[8] Concurrent conditions principally occur in contracts for the sale of goods and contracts for the conveyance of land.

---

4. Restatement, Contracts § 250(a).

5. See § 34 supra.

6. See § 34 supra.

7. See Restatement, Contracts § 251.

8. See 3A Corbin § 629; McFadden v. Wilder, 6 Ariz.App. 60, 429 P.2d 694 (1967); see § 156 infra.

§ 140. Conditions Subsequent

A condition subsequent is any fact the existence or occurrence of which, by agreement of the parties, operates to discharge a duty of performance after it has become absolute.[9] For example, insurance policies frequently contain conditions for the protection of the insurer. Often the policy will provide that no claims will be paid unless proof of loss is filed with the insurer within sixty days of the loss. Such a provision is usually interpreted as a condition precedent. The insurer's duty of payment does not become absolute unless this condition is complied with.[10] In addition, the policy will often contain a provision that no action may be brought to recover under the policy after the expiration of twelve months from the occurrence of the loss. The passage of twelve months without the commencement of an action extinguishes the duty of payment which became absolute upon filing of the proof of loss.[11] It is, therefore, characterized as a condition subsequent.[12]

In the law of contracts, conditions precedent are quite common while true conditions subsequent are rare.[13] From a substantive point of view the characterization of a condition as precedent or subsequent is relatively unimportant. Procedurally, however, the distinction is often crucial. The party to whom the duty is owed usually has the burden of proving the occurrence of the conditions precedent to

---

9. Restatement, Contracts § 250(b).

10. Lawson v. American Motorists Ins. Corp., 217 F.2d 724 (5th Cir. 1954); Harris v. North British & Mercantile Ins. Co., 30 F.2d 94 (5th Cir. 1929), cert. denied, 279 U.S. 852, 49 S.Ct. 348, 73 L.Ed. 995 (1929). For such a provision in an employment contract, see Inman v. Clyde Hall Drilling Co., 369 P.2d 498, 4 A.L.R.3d 430 (Alaska 1962), 14 Syracuse L.Rev. 109 (1963).

11. Berman v. The Palatine Ins. Co., 379 F.2d 371 (7th Cir. 1967); Barza v. Metropolitan Life Ins. Co., 281 Mich. 532, 275 N.W. 238, 112 A.L.R. 1283 (1937). In some jurisdictions contractual clauses curtailing the statute of limitations are invalid, (See Annot. 112 A.L.R. 1288), or regulated by Statute. E. g., McKinney's N.Y. Ins.Law §§ 164(3) (A) (11), 168(6). But such clauses frequently are utilized even outside the insurance field and

are generally upheld. Soviero Bros. Contracting Corp. v. City of New York, 286 App.Div. 435, 142 N.Y.S.2d 508 (1st Dep't 1955), aff'd 2 N.Y.2d 924, 161 N.Y.S.2d 888, 141 N.E.2d 918 (1957); Restatement, Contracts § 218; Williston § 183. The U.C.C. specifically validates such clauses in § 2-725(1).

12. Although this characterization is made by the writers of law books and restatements, the courts have not generally labelled such a condition as a condition subsequent. E. g., Graham v. Niagara Fire Ins. Co., 106 Ga. 840, 32 S.E. 579 (1899) (characterization as condition precedent). See Harnett and Thornton, The Insurance Condition Subsequent: A Needle in a Semantic Haystack, 17 Ford.L.Rev. 220 (1948).

13. Kindler v. Anderson, 433 P.2d 268 (Wyo.1967).

the performance of the duty.[14]   The party burdened by the duty, however, usually has the burden of proving the discharge of his duty by the occurrence of a condition subsequent.[15]

Thus in the illustrations previously given the assured would have the burden of proof on the issue of whether notice has been duly given, but the insurance company would have the burden on the question of whether the action has been duly commenced within one year.

Contract draftsmen frequently use language which in form appears to make provision for a condition subsequent but which actually operates to provide for a condition precedent. For example, in the well known case of Gray v. Gardner,[16] the defendants executed two notes in consideration of a quantity of whale oil sold to them by the plaintiff. One of the notes was unconditional in terms. The second note was conditioned to be void if a greater quantity of whale oil entered New Bedford and Nantucket between April 1st and October 1st than had arrived during the same period as the previous year. It is fairly obvious that the parties intended the second note to be payable only if less oil arrived in these whaling ports than had arrived in the previous year and that it would not be payable until October 2d when the existence of this condition could be ascertained. As such, by definition, payment would be subject to a condition precedent, despite the use of language of condition subsequent. The court decided, however, that the parties would be held to the form of language used, indicating that since defendant had freely adopted this language, it saw no reason to upset the effect of the language chosen. The use of language of condition subsequent proved to be crucial to the outcome of the case since, in the light of the conflicting evidence, the party bearing the burden of proof was bound to have judgment entered against him.

Conditions subsequent in form but precedent by definition are particularly common in insurance policies and surety bonds. Perhaps more often than not, courts will, for purposes of pleading and burden

---

14. Formerly, the party to whom the duty is owed (usually the plaintiff) also had the burden of alleging the occurrence of all conditions precedent. Shipman, Common Law Pleading 246–49 (3d ed. 1923). Under Code pleading, a general allegation of due compliance with all conditions precedent is generally sufficient. Clark, Code Pleading 280–82 (2d ed. 1947); 5 Williston § 674. Under recent procedural enactments even this requirement is dispensed with. The simplification of pleading requirements does not, however, change the burden of proof. Although the burden is placed on the defendant to deny the occurrence of a condition precedent, once he has made the denial, the burden is placed on the plaintiff to prove its occurrence. McKinney's N.Y.C.P.L.R. § 3015.

15. Gray v. Gardner, 17 Mass. 188 (1821).

16. Id.

of proof, treat the condition as if it were a condition subsequent. There is no universal consistency and a good deal of subtlety has gone into the refinements of the problem,[17] without, however, resulting in any satisfactory resolution of the basic problem.[18]

§ 141.   Express (True) and Constructive Conditions

An express condition is provided for by the parties.[19] It may be spelled out clearly in so many words or it may be implied in fact; that is, "gathered from the terms of the contract as a matter of interpretation."[20]

Constructive conditions, sometimes called conditions implied in law, are neither expressed nor implied in the words chosen by the parties. These are imposed by law to meet the ends of justice.[21]

In a given agreement it may be difficult to determine whether a condition has been expressed in words or whether it is implied in fact in the words and conduct of the parties. It is not important that this determination be made since the same general rule applies to both, that is, a true condition must be literally complied with.[22] Since there is no difference in consequences, implied in fact conditions and conditions set forth in so many words are both denominated as express conditions.[23]

The dividing line between a true condition and a constructive condition is often equally indistinct.[24] Whether in a given case the court has found a condition as a matter of interpretation or has imposed it as a matter of construction is often difficult to discern. Yet,

---

17. 5 Williston §§ 667, 667A, 674; Clark, Code Pleading 282-83 (2d ed. 1947).

18. Compare 3A Corbin §§ 749-51 with the authorities in the preceding note. Corbin appears to argue that, unless social policy dictates another conclusion, the burden of proof should be allocated in accordance with whether or not the condition is a true condition subsequent and that the form in which the condition is couched should be disregarded. Compare with this argument Anson, Contract 434 (Corbin's ed. 1924), wherein it is stated:

"Thus it is evident, in spite of very general assumptions to the contrary, that the burden of allegation and the burden of proof cannot be determined by the test of such descriptive adjectives as precedent and subsequent. It is no doubt true that the law on this subject needs entire reconstruction and restatement, that there is no existing test capable of logical definition, and that the rules are largely arbitrary as well as conflicting. Such rules as now exist will frequently be found to be based on false logic and on more or less ill-defined notions of public policy."

19. Restatement, Contracts § 252.

20. Costigan, The Performance of Contracts 50 (2d ed. 1927).

21. Restatement, Contracts § 253.

22. See § 150 infra.

23. See Restatement, Contracts § 258.

24. See Williston § 668.

the distinction is often of crucial importance. In contrast to the general rule governing express conditions, the general rule as to constructive conditions is that substantial compliance is sufficient.[25] This distinction is pursued at greater length in the sections which follow. It is important to observe that at the heart of this distinction is the distinction between a condition and a promise.[26]

§ 142. Illustrations and Effect of Express Conditions

In an admiralty case,[27] a ship was chartered with an option granted to the charterers to cancel "if the steamer does not arrive at port of loading, and be ready to load on or before midnight of 10th of October." The ship arrived at 11 P.M. on the day specified but could not be loaded until she was inspected by a health officer on the morning of October 11th. It was held that the charterers properly exercised their option to cancel, although for all practical purposes they were not prejudiced by the failure of the condition. Literal compliance with an express condition is usually necessary before a duty of performance will become absolute.[28]

The easiest way for a contract draftsman to create an express condition is, of course, to state that a given fact or act will operate as a condition. Thus, a provision of a contract stating that filing of a notice of claim with the other contracting party within thirty days after any claim arises "shall be a condition precedent to any recovery"[29] creates a condition precedent in the most explicit fashion and strict compliance with the condition will ordinarily be required.

As a rule of thumb, provisions which commence with words such as "if,"[30] "on condition that,"[31] and "provided,"[32] create conditions to performance. Each case, however, involves the process of interpretation. Particularly difficult problems of interpretation arise in cases in which a duty is agreed to be performed "when" (rather than "if") a given event occurs. A simple illustration will show the nature of the problem. If a television repairman extends credit to a

25. See § 149 infra.

26. See § 143 infra.

27. The Austin Friars, 71 L.T.R. (n.s.) 27 (Adm.1894).

28. Arizona Land Title & Trust Co. v. Safeway Stores, Inc., 6 Ariz.App. 52, 429 P.2d 686 (1967); 5 Williston § 675.

29. Inman v. Clyde Hall Drilling Co., 369 P.2d 498, 4 A.L.R.3d 430 (Alaska 1962).

30. Guerrette v. Cheetham, 289 Mass. 240, 193 N.E. 836 (1935).

31. Simpson 305.

32. Goodwin v. Jacksonville Gas Corp., 302 F.2d 355 (5th Cir. 1962); Hamilton Constr. Co. v. Board of Public Instruction of Dade County, 65 So.2d 729 (Fla.1953).

customer upon the customer's promise to pay "when I receive my Christmas bonus," most probably neither party understood that payment for the repairs would be contingent upon whether or not the customer's employer sees fit to grant him a bonus. If the customer receives no bonus, it will almost certainly be held that the parties had reference to the time when payment would be due rather than to a condition to payment. That is, the contract will be interpreted to mean that "I will pay around Christmas time." Most cases involving this sort of language are more difficult to resolve. In a recurring situation, a prime contractor agrees to make payment to a subcontractor "as received from the owner" or language to this effect. The question, put in practical terms is, who assumed the risk of the owner's non-payment? In the usual case no dogmatic answer can be given and its resolution may be dependent upon extrinsic evidence introduced at trial.[33] Certainly, custom and usage in the particular field will be of great weight in the determination of the probable intention of the parties.[34] When personal services are rendered it will not lightly be assumed that payment was contingent upon the happening of an event outside the control of the party rendering the services.[35] If, however, the services are of the kind that are frequently rendered on a contingent fee basis, the result will be otherwise. Thus, a promise to pay a brokerage commission "on the closing of title" will be held to be conditioned upon the closing of title.[36] A large number of cases are concerned with the interpretation of a promise to pay

33. Mascioni v. I. B. Miller, Inc., 261 N.Y. 1, 184 N.E. 473 (1933) (trial court's finding that a condition was intended not erroneous as a matter of law); see DeWolfe v. French, 51 Me. 420 (1864) making it clear that the issue is one of the intention of the parties when it states: "If the parties intend that a debt shall be contingent . . . then it will be so held by the Court. If, on the contrary, they intend that the debt shall be absolute, and fix upon the future event as a convenient time for payment merely . . . and, if the future event does not happen as contemplated, the law will require payment to be made within a reasonable time." Accord: North American Graphite Corp. v. Allan, 87 U.S.App.D.C. 154, 184 F.2d 387 (1950); but see Mignot v. Parkhill, 237 Or. 450, 391 P.2d 755 (1964) where, as a matter of law, the following language was held not to create a condition: "It is fully understood by

and between the parties hereto that Contractor shall not be obligated to pay Subcontractor for any of the work until such time as Contractor has himself received the money from Bates Lumber Co."

34. Thus, in Thos. J. Dyer Co. v. Bishop Int'l Eng'r Co., 303 F.2d 655 (6th Cir. 1962), the court took judicial notice that the general contractor rather than the subcontractor normally takes the risk of the owner's non-payment.

35. North American Graphite Corp. v. Allan, 184 F.2d 387, 87 U.S.App.D.C. 154 (1950) (engineer's services).

36. Amies v. Wesnofske, 255 N.Y. 156, 174 N.E. 436, 73 A.L.R. 918 (1931) (collecting cases); see also Matthews v. Staritt, 252 Cal.App.2d 884, 60 Cal. Rptr. 857 (1967) (broker's commission was "subject to" right of tenant to exercise option to purchase).

"when able." Although there is said to be a "majority rule" interpreting this language as language of condition and a "minority rule" interpreting such a promise to mean that payment will be made in a reasonable time,[37] it is likely that many of the seemingly conflicting cases can be reconciled if it is realized that in each case the language must be interpreted in its verbal and factual context. If, as is often the case, the promise to pay "when able" is a new promise to pay a debt that otherwise would be barred by bankruptcy or the statute of limitations, it is gratuitous and interpretation of the promise as conditional would seem to be justified.[38] Similarly, if a major stockholder renders services to the corporation on the understanding that he will be paid "as the financial condition of the corporation permits out of profits" it can readily be inferred from the relationship of the parties that the corporation's promise was intended to be conditional.[39] Where, however, the promise is to pay for services rendered, goods delivered, or property conveyed, in the absence of special circumstances, it would be unreasonable to assume that the promisee intended more than to allow the promisor a reasonable time in which to effectuate payment.[40]

§ 143. Distinction Between an Express Condition and a Promise

A says to B, "If you walk across the Brooklyn Bridge I will pay you $10.00," A's duty of payment is subject to the express condition precedent that B walk across the bridge, but if B does not cause this condition to occur, he is under no liability to A. He has made no promise. If, however, A had said to B, "I will pay you $10.00 if you walk across the Brooklyn Bridge, provided in addition that you promise to perform," and B so promises two consequences follow if B does not walk across the bridge. First, A's duty to pay does not become absolute, and, in fact, is discharged. Second, B is liable for breach of contract for failure to perform his express promise.

Very often it is difficult to determine whether particular language in a contract is language of promise or language of condition.

An illustration of this difficulty is supplied by the "standard mortgagee" clause found in many insurance contracts. This pro-

---

37. See 5 Williston § 804; Annot. 94 A.L.R. 721 (1935). Some cases take an intermediate position, holding that the promisor is obligated at least to use reasonable efforts to become able to pay. See 3A Corbin § 641.

38. Tebo v. Robinson, 100 N.Y. 27, 2 N. E. 383 (1885).

39. Booth v. Booth & Bayliss Commercial School, Inc., 120 Conn. 221, 180 A. 278, 99 A.L.R. 1517 (1935).

40. Sanford v. Luce, 245 Iowa 74, 60 N.W.2d 885 (1953) (construction work); Mock v. Trustees of First Baptist Church of Newport, 252 Ky. 243, 67 S.W.2d 9, 94 A.L.R. 716 (1934) (architectural services).

vides in effect that the loss is payable to the mortgagee "provided, however, that in case the mortgagor shall neglect to pay any premium the mortgagee shall, on demand, pay the same." The question is whether the mortgagee has promised to pay on demand or whether his payment on demand is a condition precedent to the liability of the insurer. The cases are not in harmony.[41] The Restatement's approach in cases of this kind where the proper interpretation is doubtful is that one should inquire whose words these purport to be. If they purport to be the words of the party who is to do the act they should be interpreted as promissory in nature. If they purport to be the words of the party who is not to do the act they should be deemed to create a condition.[42] As to the standard mortgagee clause, the Restatement reasons that since the language of an insurance policy— typically a unilateral contract—is the language of the insurer and since the insurance company is not to do the act in question (payment of the premium) the language of the mortgagee clause is language of condition. From this conclusion it follows that the mortgagee is not liable for payment of the premium because he has made no promise to pay. It also follows, however, that he may not recover on the policy if the condition is not satisfied.

No exclusive test exists to determine whether a particular provision creates a promise or a condition. Of course, if the language is clearly promissory or clearly creates a condition, interpretation is not difficult.[43] Where, however, the language is not clear the Restatement test is often used.[44] If the Restatement test does not prove helpful, a promissory interpretation is favored since this ordinarily tends to protect both parties.[45]

§ 144. Express Language of Condition May be Implied Language of Promise

Not only is it difficult to determine whether particular language is language of condition or language of promise but the problem is further complicated by the fact that express language of condition may be implied language of promise (discussed in this section) and

---

41. Most of the cases interpret this clause as creating a condition. General Credit Corp. v. Imperial Cas. & Indem. Co., 167 Neb. 833, 95 N.W.2d 145 (1959); 14 Appleman, Insurance Law and Practices § 7842. See also Goble, The Liability of a Mortgagee for Premiums and Assessments under a Standard Mortgage Clause, J. Am.Ins. 13 (Feb. 1935).

42. Restatement, Contracts § 260.

43. See ch. 3 supra.

44. Graham v. American Eagle Fire Ins. Co., 182 F.2d 500 (4th Cir. 1950).

45. O'Neal v. George E. Breece Lumber Co., 38 N.M. 492, 35 P.2d 314 (1934); Restatement, Contracts § 261.

express language of promise may be implied language of condition (to be discussed in the next section).

To illustrate, A and B enter into a contract for the sale and purchase of real property. The contract contains a clause that performance is "contingent upon B obtaining" a described mortgage loan. The phrase in the quotation is obviously language of condition and B is not obligated to perform unless he obtains the mortgage loan.[46] In addition, however, B has impliedly promised to use reasonable efforts to obtain mortgage financing.[47] Stated in other terms, he has impliedly promised to use reasonable efforts to cause the condition to occur.[48]

In the same transaction, however, if B conditioned his promise upon the Dow Jones average reaching 1000 at some point between the time of the signing of contract and the time for performance, it is obvious that although B would not be bound to perform if the condition did not arise, he is not impliedly promising to use reasonable efforts to cause the condition to occur.[49]

No simple rule can be set forth which explains when express language of condition will or will not give rise to implied language of promise. One of the important factors to be considered is whether the conditioning event is within the control of the party who it is alleged made an implied promise. Thus in the mortgage illustration it was within B's control to use reasonable efforts to obtain a mortgage; but in the case relating to the Dow Jones average it was not within B's power to cause the Dow Jones average to reach 1000. A related question is discussed in section 165.

46. Sheldon Builders, Inc. v. Trogan Towers, 255 Cal.App.2d 781, 63 Cal. Rptr. 425 (1967).

47. Lach v. Cahill, 138 Conn. 418, 85 A.2d 481 (1951); Carlton v. Smith, 285 Ill.App. 380, 2 N.E.2d 116 (1936); Eggan v. Simonds, 34 Ill.App.2d 316, 181 N.E.2d 354 (1962); but see Paul v. Rosen, 3 Ill.App.2d 423, 122 N.E.2d 603 (1954). Compare Marino v. Nolan, 24 A.D.2d 1005, 266 N.Y.S.2d 65 (2d Dep't 1965), aff. 18 N.Y.2d 627, 272 N.Y.S.2d 776, 219 N.E.2d 291 (1966), with Glassman v. Gerstein, 10 A.D.2d 875, 200 N.Y.S.2d 690 (2d Dep't 1960). In the Marino case the contract vendee was held to be under a duty to accept a purchase money mortgage loan offered by the vendor, while in the Glassman case it was held that such a duty did not exist where the duty of performance was contingent upon obtaining a mortgage loan from a "lending institution." These cases illustrate the difficulty of determining the *extent* of the admitted duty of cooperation. It might also be observed that if this promise were not implied there would be no contract because otherwise B's obligation would be illusory.

48. See generally Patterson, Constructive Conditions in Contracts, 42 Colum.L.Rev. 903, 928–42 (1942).

49. Simpson 306.

§ 145. Express Language of Promise Giving Rise to Implied or Constructive Conditions

In the preceding section we examined the problem of express language of condition giving rise to an implied promise. The converse question is presented here. However, here we must distinguish whether the condition which arises from language of promise is constructive or implied in fact.[50] This can best be explained through an historical approach.

§ 146. The History of Constructive Conditions

At early common law if S agreed to sell and B agreed to buy 100 cases of oranges, S without tendering performance could sue B and conversely B without tendering performance could sue S.[51] But subsequently the courts held that such express mutual promises gave rise to constructive concurrent conditions. This means that although neither party expressly conditioned his promise on performance by the other, the law, to do justice, constructs a condition that tender of performance by one party is a condition precedent to the liability of the other party.[52] Constructive conditions are discussed in more detail in sections 155 to 163.

§ 147. Constructive Conditions Distinguished from Implied in Fact Conditions

In section 141 supra we saw that implied in fact conditions are true conditions and therefore are to be treated as express conditions and that constructive conditions are governed by a different rule. However, because both constructive conditions and implied in fact conditions arise from promises, they are difficult to distinguish. The theoretical difference is that in the case of an implied in fact condition the parties have impliedly agreed to the condition, whereas in the case of a constructive condition the court constructs a condition in the interests of justice. The courts prefer to find constructive conditions rather than implied in fact conditions because constructive conditions are flexible instruments for justice. The principal area in which implied in fact conditions are found is in the area of promises of cooperation. For example, if A promised to paint B's house and B promised to supply the paint, since A cannot perform without B keeping his promise to supply the paint, B's supplying the paint is an implied in fact condition to A's duty to paint even though this is not expressly stated in the contract.

50. See § 141 supra.

51. Nichols v. Raynbred, Hob. 88b (K. B.1615).

52. Kingston v. Preston, Lofft 194, 2 Doug. 684 (K.B.1773). See § 139 supra.

§ 148. Conditions as Related to Unilateral and Bilateral Contracts

Unilateral contracts invariably involve express conditions and even under the rule of section 45 of the Restatement, the offeror is entitled to literal performance. Section 45 specifically states that offeree must "completely perform within the time stated." It is in bilateral contracts that constructive conditions ordinarily will be found.

§ 149. Importance of Distinguishing Between Express and Constructive Conditions: Substantial Performance and Material Breach

The importance of distinguishing between language of promise and language of condition and consequently between express and constructive conditions can be illustrated by the following fact pattern. A was the owner in possession of a vessel in England who agreed in a bilateral contract to charter the vessel to B who was in the United States. By the terms of the agreement A was to supply the vessel and B was to pay for the use of it when it arrived.[53] The critical clause in the agreement stated: "The vessel to sail from England on or before the 4th day of February." The vessel in fact did not sail by the 4th.

The clause in question could be interpreted in three possible ways 1) as an express condition to B's obligation to perform, 2) as a promise by A to cause the vessel to sail on or before the 4th, and 3) both as an express condition to B's obligation to perform and as a promise by A to cause the vessel to sail.

If the clause is interpreted as an express condition to B's obligation to perform, then B is free not to proceed if he so desires because, as we have seen, as a general proposition a true condition must be literally performed—A is not liable for any breach, however, because by hypothesis he has not made a promise to cause the vessel to sail by February 4th.

If the clause is interpreted to be a promise to sail on the date specified, failure to perform this promise raises the question of the relationship of the doctrine of constructive conditions and substantial performance on the one hand and material breach on the other. If B sued A, the case would be approached from the point of view of material breach.[54] If the breach is material, B would be free not to proceed and could sue for a total breach; but if the breach is immaterial, B would still be required to perform and could only sue for a partial breach.[55]

53. The fact pattern is suggested by Glaholm v. Hays, 2 Mann & Granger 257 (C.P.1841).

54. See § 157 infra.

55. See § 157 infra.

But if A sued B for the price the case would be approached under the doctrine of constructive conditions. Under the agreement, by hypothesis, there is no express condition but it is clear that A is to perform before B is to perform and, therefore, A's performance is a constructive condition precedent to B's duty.[56] The question then is whether A has substantially performed the constructive condition. If he has, the constructive condition has been satisfied and the breach can only be immaterial.[57] All of these matters are treated in more detail elsewhere herein.

If the language quoted were language of express condition and implied language of promise B would be free not to proceed and A would be guilty of a breach which, although it may be immaterial, would be treated as if it were a material breach justifying an action for a total breach.[58]

The Court ruled that the sailing by February 4th was an express condition; therefore B was justified in cancelling the contract. A similar holding was made in Shadforth v. Higgin [59] where the ship was to be laden with cargo "provided she arrives out and ready by the 25th of June." On the other hand, in Bornmann v. Tooke,[60] where the agreement was, "the captain must sail with the first favourable wind direct to the port of Portsmouth," this provision was held to constitute a promise rather than a condition. Thus, in this case, since the breach was immaterial, the defendant is required to pay for the freight, but is entitled to damages caused by the captain's breach.

B. EXPRESS CONDITIONS

Analysis

Sec.
150. Strict Compliance.
151. Conditions of Satisfaction.
152. Conditions of Satisfaction: Satisfaction of a Third Person.
153. Conditions of Satisfaction: Satisfaction of a Party to the Contract.
154. Demand as a Condition.

§ 150. Strict Compliance

We have already seen the general rule that express conditions must literally be complied with. As is the case with most general rules there are situations in which the rule is not always rigidly adhered to. These are discussed in sections 151–153. In addition part D of this

---

56. See § 157 infra.

57. See § 157 infra.

58. Simpson 305.

59. 3 Camp. 385 (N.P.1813).

60. 1 Camp. 376 (K.B.1807).

chapter discusses the circumstances under which compliance with a condition is excused.

§ 151. Conditions of Satisfaction

Very often contracting parties agree that one party's duty of performance is conditioned upon his satisfaction with the performance of the other contracting party or upon the satisfaction of a third person. When a contract provides that a party is to perform only upon the condition that he or some third person is satisfied with the performance of the other contracting party, the language could mean that personal satisfaction is contemplated or it could mean that a reasonably satisfactory performance will satisfy the condition.[61]

§ 152. Conditions of Satisfaction: Satisfaction of a Third Person

Contracts in which one party's duty of performance is expressly conditioned upon a third person's satisfaction are particularly prevalent in the construction industry where the satisfaction or approval of a named architect or engineer, evidenced by his certificate, is often made a condition precedent to the duty of payment, or at least, of final payment. Although the third person whose approval is made a condition precedent is usually retained by the party for whom the structure is to be built, the parties have agreed to rely on his professional integrity. Generally, courts have applied the same standard to this kind of a condition precedent that has been applied to other conditions precedent. Strict compliance with the condition is the rule.[62] The court will not substitute the approval or satisfaction of judge or jury for that of the chosen expert. Nevertheless, if it can be proved that the expert acted dishonestly or in bad faith, the condition that he express his approval in a certificate or otherwise will be dispensed with.[63] The expert's dishonesty is a question of fact and the burden of proof on the question is on the party who alleges it. Although unreasonableness may be circumstantial evidence of dis-

---

61. In this kind of case a preliminary question is whether or not the language used creates a condition of satisfaction. If a party merely promises to satisfy the other, no express condition of satisfaction is created; performance of the promise may, however, be a constructive condition. See 3A Corbin § 645. A condition of satisfaction may or may not create in addition an implied promise to give satisfaction. This problem is presented in Fursmidt v. Hotel Abbey Holding Corp., 10 A.D.2d 447, 200 N.Y.S.2d 256 (1st Dep't 1960), rearg. denied 11 A.D. 2d 649, 203 N.Y.S.2d 1012.

62. Pope v. King, 108 Md. 37, 69 A. 417 (1908); cf. Restatement, Contracts § 303; see generally 3A Corbin §§ 647–652; 5 Williston §§ 675–675B. Quasi contractual relief, however, is available to the builder in a number of jurisdictions. See Restatement, Contracts § 357; 5A Corbin § 1125–85. See also § 159 infra.

honesty [64] in most jurisdictions, the mere fact that the refusal is unreasonable is insufficient grounds for dispensing with compliance with the condition.[65]

There are a number of cases, however, especially in New York, which go far in remaking the contract for the parties. In Nolan v. Whitney,[66] plaintiff builder sued for the last installment of a building contract in the amount of $2,700. An express condition precedent to the payment of the final installment was the issuance of an architect's certificate of satisfaction. No certificate was issued. The trier of fact found that although plaintiff had substantially complied with the contract, performance was defective in the amount of $200. The court held that the refusal of the architect to issue the certificate was unreasonable and that plaintiff could recover the final installment less damages. Looked at from the architect's point of view it is difficult to ascertain why it is unreasonable to refuse to certify as performed satisfactorily that which is unsatisfactory. From the defendant's point of view, he is held to a bargain not of his making. The case was subsequently explained by the Court of Appeals as resting "upon the basis that enforcement of the contract according to its strict terms would cause forfeiture of compensation for work done or materials furnished." [67] The Court consequently refused to extend the holding to a contract involving the sale of goods, the quality of which was to be approved by a third person. Absent fraud, the third person's judgment was held to be final. No forfeiture or extreme hardship resulted since the goods which were unsatisfactory to the expert were retained by the seller and presumably the goods were readily salable upon the open market.

The interference with contractual freedom represented by Nolan v. Whitney was further restricted by a subsequent appellate division holding that:

"Substantial performance might make compliance with an express condition unnecessary, but only when the depar-

63. Rizzolo v. Poysher, 89 N.J.L. 618, 99 A. 390 (1916); Zimmerman v. Marymor, 290 Pa. 299, 138 A. 824, 54 A.L. R. 1252 (1927) (collusion); Restatement, Contracts § 303.

64. 3A Corbin § 645.

65. Hebert v. Dewey, 191 Mass. 403, 77 N.E. 822 (1906).

66. 88 N.Y. 648 (1882); accord, Coplew v. Durand, 153 Cal. 278, 95 P. 38 (1908); Richmond College v. Scott Nuckols Co., 124 Va. 333, 98 S.E. 1 (1919). For an extended criticism of this view see Mehler, Substantial Performance Versus Freedom of Contract, 33 Brooklyn L.Rev. 196 (1967).

67. Van Iderstine Co. v. Barnet Leather Co., 242 N.Y. 425, 434, 152 N.E. 250, 252, 46 A.L.R. 858 (1926); but see Vought v. Williams, 120 N.Y. 253, 24 N.E. 195 (1890) (title was to be satisfactory to purchaser's attorney; reasonableness of attorney's opinion may be reviewed by court).

ture from full performance is an inconsiderable trifle having no pecuniary importance." [68]

§ 153. Conditions of Satisfaction: Satisfaction of a Party to the Contract

When a contract provides that performance is to be satisfactory, it could contemplate the personal satisfaction of the party to whom performance is tendered or it could be interpreted as contemplating the satisfaction of a reasonable man. In case of doubt the preferred interpretation is that the contract calls for a performance which is objectively satisfactory.[69]

In a well-known case [70] the defendant had promised to pay for an enlargement of a photograph only if he were to be personally satisfied with the enlarged picture. The defendant indicated to the plaintiff that he was not satisfied and testified at trial to his dissatisfaction. The court sustained the judgment of the trial court entered upon a verdict in favor of the defendant, thus holding that an express condition precedent to the defendant's duty had not been fulfilled.[71]

A number of interesting problems are concealed in this case. The agreement clearly called for the defendant's personal satisfaction. Does this mean, however, that his statement with respect to his satisfaction must be accepted? If such were the agreement, it would be illusory.[72] Thus, where personal satisfaction is called for it is almost invariably held that the dissatisfaction must in fact exist in good faith and must not merely be simulated.[73] Such an interpretation removes the contract from the class of illusory agreements.

In a large class of cases a further requirement is imposed, as a matter of law, that the dissatisfaction be not only honest but reasonable.[74] Generally, where the suitability of the performance is a mat-

---

68. Witherell v. Lasky, 286 App.Div. 533, 145 N.Y.S.2d 624 (4th Dep't 1955).

69. Hawkins v. Graham, 149 Mass. 284, 21 N.E. 312 (1889); Restatement, Contracts § 265.

70. Gibson v. Cranage, 39 Mich. 49 (1878).

71. At one point the court expressed doubt whether the parties' agreement constituted a contract. Although it did not pursue the question the court could have regarded the parties' conversations as creating an offer to a unilateral contract; that is, that the defendant offered to pay if a satisfac-

tory enlargement were delivered. Or it could have regarded the conversations as creating a bilateral agreement in which the defendant's promise was illusory since it might appear that the performance of his promise to pay was entirely within the defendant's control. See § 70 supra.

72. See § 70 supra.

73. Mattei v. Hopper, 51 Cal.2d 119, 330 P.2d 625 (1958); Tow v. Miners Mem'l Hosp. Ass'n, 305 F.2d 73 (4th Cir. 1962), 35 Colo.L.Rev. 272 (1963).

74. American Oil Co. v. Carey, 246 F. Supp. 773 (E.D.Mich.1965) (in whichev-

ter of "mechanical fitness, utility, or marketability" the contract is construed as imposing only a requirement that the performance be objectively satisfactory.[75] It must be recognized that this construction often involves the remaking of the contract for the parties. Perhaps lurking in the background of these cases is the thought that literal compliance with the contract would be unconscionable.

Where, however, the object of the contract is to gratify taste, serve personal convenience, or satisfy individual preference the courts refuse to intervene and test only the good faith of the party expressing dissatisfaction. Illustrations of cases in this class include contracts to provide art work,[76] valet services [77] and household draperies.[78] Also subject to the good faith test are contracts of employment in which a condition of satisfaction has been agreed to,[79] and contracts conditioned upon one party's satisfaction with the financial status or credit rating of the other.[80]

The court's tendency to remake the contract for the parties in cases involving mechanical fitness, utilities or marketability can be criticized on the ground that under the guise of interpretation the

---

er class the case falls, the agreement is not illusory).

75. American Oil Co. v. Carey, 246 F. Supp. 773 (E.D.Mich.1965) ("obtain . . . permits satisfactory to Purchaser," id at 774); Alper Blouse Co. v. E. E. Connor & Co., 309 N.Y. 67, 127 N.E.2d 813 (1955) (sale of goods); Doll v. Noble, 116 N.Y. 230, 22 N.E. 406 (1889) (rubbing and staining woodwork); Duplex Safety Boiler Co. v. Garden, 101 N.Y. 387, 4 N.E. 749 (1886) (remodernization of a boiler); contra, Thompson-Starett Co. v. La Belle Iron Works, 17 F.2d 536 (2d Cir. 1927), cert. denied 274 U.S. 748, 47 S.Ct. 763, 71 L.Ed. 1330 (contract to build houses—reasonableness of honest dissatisfaction immaterial); Gerisch v. Herold, 82 N.J.L. 605, 83 A. 892 (1912) (taste or fancy of owner may be an important element in a dwelling house).

76. Davis v. General Goods Corp., 21 F.Supp. 445 (S.D.N.Y.1937); Gibson v. Cranage, 39 Mich. 49 (1878).

77. Fursmidt v. Hotel Abbey Holding Corp., 10 App.Div.2d 447, 200 N.Y.S.2d 256 (1st Dep't 1960) rearg. denied 11 App.Div.2d 649, 203 N.Y.S.2d 1012.

Note that satisfaction, although a condition in this case, was not necessarily also a promise. Thus, defendant's counter-claims for damages, alleging that defendant did not receive satisfactory services will not be allowed unless the plaintiff also promised to satisfy. The court avoids the point, reserving it for later consideration, but, even if the plaintiff promised to satisfy, would it not be possible to use a reasonableness test as to the breach of promise, and the good faith test as to the failure of condition?

78. Scott v. Erdman, 9 Misc.2d 961, 173 N.Y.S.2d 843 (App.T.1957), appeal denied 5 App.Div.2d 849, 172 N.Y.S.2d 542.

79. Kendall v. West, 196 Ill. 221, 63 N. E. 683 (1902), aff'g 98 Ill.App. 116 (1901); Ferris v. Polansky, 191 Md. 79, 59 A.2d 749 (1948); contra, Johnson v. School Dist. No. 12, Wallowa County, 210 Or. 585, 312 P.2d 591 (1957).

80. Stribling v. Ailion, 223 Ga. 662, 157 S.E.2d 427 (1967); Holton v. Monarch Motor Car Co., 202 Mich. 271, 168 N. W. 539 (1918).

courts ignore the manifest intention of the parties.[81] In many of the cases such interference with freedom of contract may be justified on the ground that literal compliance with the contract would unjustly enrich the person who received the performance and would be unduly harsh on the person who rendered the performance.[82] If this is the basis of the decisions, it is submitted that forthright recognition should be given to this underlying rationale and a distinction drawn between cases involving unjust enrichment and forfeiture on the one hand, and cases in which these elements are not present on the other.

Under the good faith test, it is of course difficult for the plaintiff to make out a *prima facie* case. He must show that the defendant is in fact satisfied with the performance rendered or tendered and has other motives for testifying to his dissatisfaction. He may show the defendant's true state of mind by evidence showing that the defendant made statements giving other reasons for his rejection of the performance,[83] that he has refused to examine the performance,[84] or that he has a motive to simulate dissatisfaction. According to some authorities evidence of the unreasonableness of the defendant's expressed dissatisfaction is admissible to justify an inference of bad faith.[85]

§ 154. Demand as a Condition

When a promise is made to render a performance on demand, a demand must be made as a condition precedent to enforcement of the promise.[86] One of the consequences of this rule is that the statute

---

81. See Grismore § 131.

82. Compare the minority holdings discussed in the preceding section involving the satisfaction of third persons where a distinction is drawn along the lines here suggested.

83. Restatement, Contracts § 265, ill. 1.

84. Restatement, Contracts § 265, ill. 2; Frankfort Distilleries, Inc. v. Burns Bottling Mach. Works, 174 Md. 12, 197 A. 599 (1938).

85. Grobarchik v. Nasa Mort. & Inv. Co., 117 N.J.L. 33, 186 A. 433 (1936); Fursmidt v. Hotel Abbey Holding Corp., 10 App.Div.2d 447, 200 N.Y.S.2d 256 (1st Dep't 1960); Restatement, Contracts § 265, ill. 3; 3A Corbin § 645.

86. A provision in a contract requiring notice to be given does not necessarily give rise to an express condition. In Standard Oil Co. of Cal. v. Perkins, 347 F.2d 379 (9th Cir. 1965), the contract provided that: "In the event of any breach by Standard . . . consignee shall give Standard written notice of any such breach," id. at 383. The court said: "Nowhere in this agreement is notice made an express condition precedent to suit. And a court will not imply that a covenant is a condition unless it clearly appears the parties so intended it . . . . It bears emphasis that we here deal with a so-called 'adhesion' contract." Id. If the court had ruled that the notice requirement was a condition the action would have been dismissed and could not have been reinstituted because of the passage of a limitation period stipulated in the contract.

of limitations commences to run from the date of demand.[87]   There is a well recognized exception to this rule.   It is generally held that a debtor's promise to pay his own liquidated debt upon demand is enforceable without demand.[88]   There is no good reason for this exception which is rooted in history.   The exception may be practical in that the complaint itself constitutes a demand and it would be perhaps foolish to dismiss a complaint which can be filed again the same day. The exception, however, has the additional consequence that the statute of limitations commences to run from the date of the promise;[89] a result perhaps not contemplated by parties not advised by counsel. It should be noted that despite the exception interest imposed by law runs only from the time of demand.[90]

C. CONSTRUCTIVE CONDITIONS

Analysis

Sec.
155.   Introduction.
156.   Required Order of Performance in a Bilateral Contract.
157.   Material Breach and Substantial Performance.
          (a) Material Breach.
          (b) Substantial Performance.
158.   A Note on Terminology: "Failure of Consideration."
159.   Recovery for Less than Substantial Performance: Quasi Contractual and Statutory Relief.
160.   Recovery by a Party in Default: Divisibility.
161.   Divisibility: Other Uses of the Concept.
162.   Independent Promises.
163.   Present or Prospective Inability and Unwillingness to Perform as Constructive Conditions.

§ 155. Introduction

We have already seen that constructive conditions are created by the courts in order to do justice.[91]   We shall now consider this

---

87.   Town of Warren v. Ball, 341 Mass. 350, 170 N.E.2d 341 (1960).   It is sometimes held, however, that if demand is not made within a reasonable time, the statutory period will commence from the expiration of a reasonable time.   Campbell v. Whoriskey, 170 Mass. 63, 48 N.E. 1070 (1898); see 3A Corbin § 643; Restatement, Contracts § 264.

88.   3A Corbin § 643; Restatement, Contracts § 264.   If the promisor is a surety for the debt of another payable on demand, a demand is a precondition to enforcement of the surety's

duty.   First Nat. Bank v. Story, 200 N.Y. 346, 93 N.E. 940 (1911); McDonald v. Filice, 252 Cal.App.2d 613, 60 Cal.Rptr. 832 (1967).

89.   Miguel v. Miguel, 184 Cal. 311, 193 P. 935 (1920).   The statute of limitations of a number of jurisdictions contain legislative qualifications of the general rules.   E. g., McKinney's N.Y. C.P.L.R. § 206(a).

90.   White v. Schrafft, 94 N.H. 467, 56 A.2d 62, 175 A.L.R. 242 (1947).

91.   See § 141 supra.

concept in more detail particularly as it relates to topics such as the order of performance in a bilateral contract, the effect of prospective inability or unwillingness to perform, whether one party's performance of some but not all of the promises undertaken by him entitles him to any performance by the other.

§ 156.　Required Order of Performance in a Bilateral Contract

In a bilateral contract the parties quite often neglect to state the order in which their promises are to be performed. Volumes could be written about the rules of law which have been forged to fill gaps of this kind in the parties' agreement. Fortunately, the rules are in general firmly rooted in common sense, or at least the average person is familiar with them by reason of his business experience.

The first and simplest rule is that a party who is to perform work must perform before he is entitled to payment.[92]　In other words, performance of work is a constructive condition precedent to payment.　Periodic payments are not implied.[93]　If, however, periodic payments have been agreed upon a different situation is present.　In such cases a series of alternating constructive conditions precedent exist.　Performance is a constructive condition precedent to the first periodic payment (unless the parties have agreed to some payment in advance) and the first payment is a condition precedent to the next stage of the work, and so on.[94]

Where the promised acts are capable of simultaneous performance, each duty of performance is constructively conditioned upon conditional tender of the other.　The primary application of this rule is in contracts for the sale of personal or real property.[95]　In such

---

92.　Bright v. Ganas, 171 Md. 493, 189 A. 427, 109 A.L.R. 467 (1937) (for years of faithful performance plaintiff was to receive $20,000 out of employer's estate, but with employer on his death bed plaintiff wrote a love letter to employer's wife, i.e., was unfaithful); Coletti v. Knox Hat Co., 252 N.Y. 468, 472, 169 N.E. 648, 649 (1930) ("when the performance of a contract consists in doing (faciendo) on one side, and in giving (dando) on the other side, the doing must take place before the giving."); Restatement, Contracts § 270.

93.　Smoll v. Webb, 55 Cal.App.2d 456, 130 P.2d 773 (1942); LeBel v. McCoy, 314 Mass. 206, 49 N.E.2d 888 (1943);

Stewart v. Newbury, 220 N.Y. 379, 115 N.E. 984, 2 A.L.R. 519 (1917).

94.　Guerini Stone Co. v. P. J. Carlin Constr. Co., 248 U.S. 334, 39 S.Ct. 102, 63 L.Ed. 275 (1919); K & G Constr. Co. v. Harris, 223 Md. 305, 164 A.2d 451 (1960); but see Palmer v. Watson Constr. Co., 265 Minn. 195, 121 N.W.2d 62 (1963).

95.　The Uniform Commercial Code is explicit on the point. U.C.C. § 2–507(1) provides: "Tender of delivery is a condition to the buyer's duty to accept the goods and, unless otherwise agreed, to his duty to pay for them. Tender entitles the seller to acceptance of the goods and to payment ac-

cases constructive concurrent conditions will normally be imposed in the following circumstances:

"(a) the same time is fixed for the performance of each promise; or

(b) a fixed time is stated for the performance of one of the promises and no time is fixed for the other; or

(c) no time is fixed for the performance of either promise; or

(d) the same period of time is fixed within which each promise shall be performed." [96]

Where each party is to perform an act which takes time, the performances are concurrent at least in the sense that one need not proceed with his performance unless the other performance is proceeding apace.[97]

§ 157. Material Breach and Substantial Performance

(a) Material Breach

As we have seen, where a party fails to perform a promise according to its terms, ordinarily it is important to determine whether the breach is material. Two consequences stem from this determination. If the breach is material the aggrieved party may sue for "total breach." If the breaching party's performance is a constructive condition to the aggrieved party's duty of performance the latter may also treat the material breach as a failure of condition. In other words, he has the power to cancel the contract. If the breach is not material, the aggrieved party may sue for "partial breach," [98] but may not cancel the contract.[99] There is no simple test to ascertain whether a breach is material.[1] Among the factors to be considered are: 1) to what extent, if any, the contract has been performed at the

cording to the contract." U.C.C. § 2–511(1) provides: "Unless otherwise agreed tender of payment is a condition to the seller's duty to tender and complete any delivery." As to Real Property, see McFadden v. Wilder, 6 Ariz.App. 60, 429 P.2d 694 (1967).

96. Restatement, Contracts § 267.

97. Grismore, Contracts § 143.

98. The terms "total breach" and "partial breach" are defined in Restatement, Contracts § 313 as follows:

"(1) A total breach of contract is a breach where remedial rights provided by law are substituted for all the existing contractual rights, or can be so substituted by the injured party.

(2) A partial breach of contract is a breach where remedial rights provided by law can be substituted by the injured party for only a part of the existing contractual rights."

99. See § 149 supra.

1. See 4 Corbin §§ 945–46; 3A Corbin §§ 700–12; 6 Williston §§ 812–86.

time of the breach. The earlier the breach the more likely it will be regarded as material.[2] 2) A wilful breach is more likely to be regarded as material than as a breach caused by negligence or by extraneous circumstances.[3] 3) A quantitatively serious breach is more likely to be considered material.[4] In addition, the consequences of the determination must be taken into account. The degree of hardship on the breaching party is an important consideration particularly when considered in conjunction with the extent to which the aggrieved party has or will receive the substantial benefit of the promised performance and the adequacy with which he may be compensated by damages.[5]

2. A breach which occurs at the very beginning is more likely to be deemed material even if it is relatively small. See Note, 21 Colum.L.Rev. 358 (1921). The reason for this is that it is fair, in determining the materiality of the breach, to consider what has been done and the benefits which the nonbreaching party has received. At times the same problem arises in another form where there is in fact a breach which is excused. Thus, if a school teacher is absent for five weeks at the beginning of school due to illness although her performance is excused under the doctrine of impossibility of performance, nevertheless the employer is free to discharge her if the employer is deprived of an important part of what he bargained for. Hong v. Independent School Dist. No. 245 of Polk County, 181 Minn. 309, 232 N.W. 329, 72 A.L.R. 280 (1930).

3. Since the basic question in determining materiality of the breach is one of fairness, it is obvious that whether the breaching party was guilty of wilful negligence or behavior is relevant. Thus where an employee absents himself from his employer's business for three days to care for his own business where permission has been denied by the employer the breach was deemed wilful and material. Jerome v. Queen City Cycle Co., 163 N.Y. 351, 57 N.E. 485 (1900). The result would have been different if the employee had been sick and, undoubtedly, even if he had been sick as a result of intoxication. The question of wilfulness as it relates to substantial performance is discussed below.

4. It is apparent that the ratio of the part performed to the part to be performed is an important question in determining substantial performance and so also an important question in determining material breach. However it is equally true that a breach which might ordinarily be insignificant could be deemed material if it prevents the other party from obtaining what he bargained for. However in the case of a sale of goods under a non-installment contract the buyer need not take any number less than called for in the contract. U.C.C. § 2–601, set out in note 8 infra.

5. In Boone v. Eyre, 126 Eng.Rep. 160 (K.B. 1777), the plaintiff agreed to sell an estate and certain slaves (number unknown) to the defendant. The defendant agreed to pay £ 500 and an annuity of £ 160 for a number of years. Plaintiff sued on the annuity and defendant answered that plaintiff did not have good title to one or more of the slaves. The court held that in the way the answer was framed the defendant admitted that the plaintiff had substantially performed. Therefore there was no material breach. The court was undoubtedly influenced by the fact that in view of the extensive performance by both parties under the contract it was fairer to allow the plaintiff a recovery under the contract with an off-set to the defendant for the small number of slaves to which the plaintiff did not have title. See generally, Restatement, Contracts § 275; 4 Corbin §§ 945–46, 3A Corbin §§ 700–12; 6 Williston §§ 812–816.

Perhaps the most frequent question raised in this area is whether delay in performance constitutes a material breach. In the case of a mercantile contract the common law rule was that any delay in the delivery of goods was material.[6] The modern authorities appear to have relaxed this rule somewhat.[7] The Uniform Commercial Code, however, appears to have reinstituted the stricter common law approach at least as to non-installment contracts.[8] Delay by a buyer in making payment has been regarded as less serious than delay in delivery [9] because money can usually be borrowed on a short term loan or, at least, the delay may be compensated for by the payment of interest. However, if literally interpreted, the Uniform Commercial Code would seem to regard late payment of a non-installment contract as a material breach.[10]

In other cases, however, the general rule is that time is not of the essence unless the contract expressly so provides.[11] Thus with respect to real estate transactions the modern view at law as well as in equity is that time is not of the essence unless the parties have manifested such an intent.[12] The same is generally true in construction contracts [13] and in contracts relating to the manufacture of goods.[14]

TIME NOT OF ESSENCE UNLESS REQUEST.

6. Norrington v. Wright, 115 U.S. 188, 6 S.Ct. 12, 29 L.Ed. 366 (1885); Oshinsky v. Lorraine Mfg. Co., 187 F. 120 (1911) (delivery day was set at Nov. 15; tender on Nov. 16 properly refused); 6 Williston § 847.

7. Continental Grain Co. v. Simpson Feed Co., 102 F.Supp. 354 (E.D.Ark. 1951), modified 199 F.2d 284 (8th Cir. 1952); DeStefano v. Associated Fruit Co., 318 Ill. 345, 149 N.E. 284 (1925); see 3A Corbin § 718; 6 Williston § 847; Williston on Sales § 453d.

8. Section 2–601 of the Uniform Commercial Code provides that the buyer under a non-installment contract, unless otherwise agreed, "if the goods or the tender of delivery fails in any respect to conform to the contract, the buyer may

  (a) reject the whole; or
  (b) accept the whole; or
  (c) accept any commercial unit or units and reject the rest."

The inflexibility of this provision is criticized in Note, 16 Wyo.L.J. 178, 182–84 (1962).

9. Vulcan Trading Corp. v. Kokomo Steel & Wire Co., 268 F. 913 (7th Cir. 1920).

10. U.C.C. § 2–703 lists the remedies available to a seller when the buyer "fails to make a payment due on or before delivery." Among other options, the seller may elect to cancel the contract. § 2–703(f).

11. Burwick v. Saetz, 154 N.W.2d 679 (N.D.1967).

12. Cohen v. Kranz, 12 N.Y.2d 242, 238 N.Y.S.2d 928, 189 N.E.2d 473 (1963); Restatement, Contracts § 276.

It is generally recognized, however, that time is of the essence in an option contract. Page v. Shainwald, 169 N.Y. 246, 62 N.E. 356 (1901); 6 Williston § 853.

13. Glen Cove Marina, Inc. v. Vessel Little Jennie, 269 F.Supp. 877 (E.D.N.Y.1967); Walton v. Denhart, 226 Or. 254, 359 P.2d 890 (1961); see 3A Corbin § 720; 6 Williston § 849.

14. 3A Corbin § 719.

(b) Substantial Performance

The doctrine of substantial performance is a natural outgrowth of the doctrine of constructive conditions. If a constructive condition had to be literally performed, as does a true condition, the doctrine of constructive conditions which was developed as an instrument for justice could have been a vehicle for injustice. However it was soon held that a constructive condition requires only substantial performance.[15]

Substantial performance is the antithesis of material breach. Thus if it is determined that a breach is material it follows that substantial performance has not been rendered. Just as the question of materiality of breach depends upon many factors (discussed above) so also the question of substantial performance depends to a large extent upon the same factors.[16]

For the doctrine of substantial performance to apply the part unperformed must not destroy the value or the purpose of the contract; [17] this, of course, is another way of saying that the breach must not have been material. The doctrine is applicable to all bilateral contracts for an agreed exchange [18] with the exception of contracts for the sale of goods where any delay or variation in specifications by the seller seems to be deemed material.[19] Its primary application in the cases has been with respect to building contracts where a considerable default is sometimes treated as immaterial.[20] The reasons for the radically different approaches in sales contracts

15. Boone v. Eyre, 126 Eng.Rep. 160 (K.B. 1777).

16. 3A Corbin § 700.

17. Plante v. Jacobs, 10 Wis.2d 567, 103 N.W.2d 296 (1960).

18. Simpson, Contracts 323.

19. As we have seen in the case of a non-installment contract under the Code, a delay in delivery and payment is deemed to be material and the buyer need not take goods in number or kind which do not conform to the contract. See notes 6–10, supra. It should also be recalled that if the goods are defective, but curable, the purchaser must allow the seller to make good the deficiency or repair the defect unless the time for performance has elapsed. Wilson v. Scampoli, 228 A.2d 848 (D.C.App. 1967); U.C.C. § 2–508(1). Under the Code the seller may cure the defective tender even after the time for performance has passed if he had reasonable grounds to believe that the nonconforming tender would be acceptable. U.C.C. § 2–508(2).

20. Chinigo v. Ehrenberg, 112 Conn. 381, 152 A. 305 (1930) (default involved about one-third of the value of the promised performance); Jardine Estates, Inc. v. Donna Brook Corp., 42 N.J.Super. 332, 126 A.2d 372 (1956); but see Schieven v. Emerick, 220 App. Div. 468, 221 N.Y.S. 780 (1927) (five per cent deviation; no substantial performance). Nor is there substantial performance where there is a structural defect. Spence v. Ham, 163 N.Y. 220, 57 N.E. 412 (1900).

and building contracts stems from the differing practical consequences in these cases. A dissatisfied buyer of goods has the burden of returning the goods or of refusing delivery if the goods are defective. A dissatisfied landowner retains the defective structure built on his land. The possibilities of unjust enrichment are thus inherent in the building contract situation.

The doctrine of substantial performance does not apply where the breach is willful. "The willful transgressor must accept the penalty of his transgression."[21] Trivial defects, however, even if willful are to be ignored under the doctrine of *de minimis non curat lex*.[22]

It must be remembered that substantial performance is not full performance and that the party who relies on this doctrine has breached his contract. Consequently, he is liable in damages to the aggrieved party. If, as is usually the case, the defaulting party is the plaintiff in the action the aggrieved party's damages must be subtracted from the contract price and the burden of proof of the amount of the subtraction is on the party who claims to have rendered substantial performance.[23]

21. Cardozo, C.J., in Jacob & Youngs, Inc. v. Kent, 230 N.Y. 239, 244, 129 N. E. 889, 891 (1921), rearg. denied 230 N.Y. 656, 130 N.E. 933; accord, Bowen v. Kimball, 203 Mass. 364, 89 N.E. 542 (1909). The word wilful in this context is not easily defined. See Corbin § 707, Williston § 842. An intentional variation from the contract, even if made with good motives, is deemed by some courts to be wilful. See Shell v. Schmidt, 164 Cal.App.2d 350, 330 P.2d 817, 76 A.L.R.2d 792 (1958), cert. denied 359 U.S. 959, 79 S. Ct. 799, 3 L.Ed.2d 766 (1959); contra, Handy v. Bliss, 204 Mass. 513, 90 N.E. 864 (1910).

22. Van Clief v. Van Vechten, 130 N.Y. 571, 29 N.E. 1017 (1892); 3A Corbin § 707.

23. Lowy v. United Pac. Ins. Co., 67 Cal.2d 87, 60 Cal.Rptr. 225, 429 P.2d 577 (1967); Treiber v. Schaefer, 416 S.W.2d 576 (Tex.Civ.App.1967); Silos v. Prindle, 127 Vt. 91, 237 A.2d 694 (1967). Assuming substantial performance, some courts say that the measure of damages is the difference between the value of the house as

built and the value it would have had had it been constructed according to the contract. White v. Mitchell, 123 Wash. 630, 213 P. 10 (1923); Venzke v. Magdanz, 243 Wis. 155, 9 N.W.2d 604 (1943). On the other hand there are jurisdictions which hold that ordinarily the defaulting party will be allowed to recover the contract price less the cost of correction of the defects of the unfinished work. Bellizzi v. Huntley Estates, Inc., 3 N.Y.2d 112, 164 N.Y.S.2d 395, 143 N.E.2d 802 (1957). But where this measurement would be unfair, as where correction of a usable structure containing no structural defect would require substantial tearing down of the structure and its rebuilding, the deduction will be for the difference between the value of the structure had it been built according to specifications and its value as constructed. Jacob & Youngs, Inc. v. Kent, 230 N.Y. 239, 129 N.E. 889 (1921), rearg. denied 230 N.Y. 656, 130 N.E. 933; see Annot. 76 A.L.R.2d 805 (1961). It should also be noted that these formulae are also used in determining whether there is substantial performance. See note 20 supra.

Although ordinarily the existence of an immaterial breach indicates that substantial performance has been rendered, this is not always so.[24] For example, in a contract in which time is not of the essence slight delay does not create a material breach, but at the same time (for example, in a construction contract) substantial performance may not have been rendered. Under these circumstances a party may by proper notice to the other set a reasonable date for performance and specify that time is of the essence. If a reasonable period of time is provided in the notice, it will be effective to make failure to perform by the specified date a material breach of the contract.[25]

§ 158. A Note on Terminology: "Failure of Consideration"

This volume nowhere utilizes the concept of "failure of consideration" as an operative concept. Use of this phrase, although gradually falling into disfavor, is sufficiently widespread that some discussion of it is in order. If S promises to sell and deliver a chattel to B on February 1st in exchange for B's promise to pay $100 on the preceding January 30th, a bilateral contract is formed. The promises of the parties are consideration for each other. If B fails to make payment on January 30th, S need not deliver the chattel since payment by B is a constructive condition precedent to S's performance of his duty of delivery. Sometimes this result is articulated in this fashion: S need not perform because B's breach of contract constitutes a failure of consideration.

The use of the term "failure of consideration" involves a major difficulty. The consideration for each of the promises in the contract was the content of the return promise. Thus when the term "failure of consideration" is used, "consideration" has a different meaning than it has in the phrase "lack of consideration." As stated by an English judge:[26]

> "[I]n the law relating to the formation of contract, the promise to do a thing may often be the consideration; but, when one is considering the law of failure of consideration . . . it is, generally speaking, not the promise which is referred to as the consideration, but the performance of the promise."[27]

---

24. See for example § 149 supra.

25. 3A Corbin § 723.

26. Lord Simon in Fibrosa Spolka Akcyjna v. Fairbairn Lawson Combe

Barbour, Ltd., [1943] A.C. 32, [1942] 2 All E.R. 122 (H.L.).

27. [1942] 2 All E.R. at 129.

The use of the term consideration in these two different senses appears to be an unnecessary invitation to confusion.[28]

§ 159. Recovery for Less than Substantial Performance: Quasi Contractual and Statutory Relief

As a starting point for this discussion it should be reiterated that a defaulting plaintiff may not recover on the contract unless his performance falls within the doctrine of substantial performance,[29] or one of the other exceptions to the general rule not previously mentioned: divisibility of the contract,[30] or independency of the promise.[31]

In Stark v. Parker,[32] an early Massachusetts case, the plaintiff was hired to work for one year for the sum of $120. Before the end of this agreed upon period the plaintiff, without cause, left the defendant's employment. He framed his complaint for services rendered in the quasi contractual form of action known as indebitatus assumpsit. The Supreme Judicial Court found the plaintiff's complaint "strange," and "repugnant," saying

"The law indeed is most reasonable in itself. It denies only to a party an advantage from his own wrong. It requires him to act justly by a faithful performance of his own engagements, before he exacts the fulfilment of dependent obligations on the part of others. It will not admit of the monstrous absurdity, that a man may voluntarily and without cause violate his agreement, and make the very breach of that agreement the foundation of an action which he could not maintain under it."[33]

Although this case probably still constitutes the weight of authority, the contrary reasoning of another old and still widely cited case continues to make converts and to influence legislation. In a nearly identical fact situation, the Supreme Court of Judicature of New Hampshire in Britton v. Turner[34] ruled that the defaulting plaintiff,

28. Accord, Harriman, Contracts § 524 (2d ed. 1901); Grismore § 145. The use of this terminology is supported in 6 Williston § 814.

29. See § 157 supra.

30. See §§ 160, 161 infra.

31. See § 162 infra.

32. 19 Mass. (2 Pick.) 267 (1824).

33. Id. at 275.

34. 6 N.H. 481 (1834); see Ashley, Britton v. Turner, 24 Yale L.J. 544 (1915); Corman, The Partial Performance Interest of the Defaulting Employee, 38 Marq.L.Rev. 61, 139 (1954–55); Laube, The Defaulting Employee—Britton v. Turner Re-viewed, 83 U.Pa.L.Rev. 825 (1935); Williston, The Defaulting Employee—A Correction, 84 U.Pa.L.Rev. 69 (1935), Laube, The Defaulting Employee—No Retraction, 84 U.Pa.L.Rev. 69 (1935); Laube, The Right of An Employee Discharged for Cause, 20 Minn.L.Rev. 597 (1936).

although unable to recover on the contract could recover under a quasi contractual theory for the reasonable value of his services less any damages suffered by the defendant. The Court laid stress on the injustice of the defendant's retention, without payment, of benefits received under the contract. It also took note that the general understanding of the community is that payment should be made for services actually received.

, The conflict of authority extends beyond employment contracts to all kinds of contracts not governed by statute. Thus, the majority rule is that a defaulting purchaser of land may not recover his down payment,[35] while a minority allows restitution of the down payment to the extent it exceeds the seller's damages.[36] Some jurisdictions permit quasi contractual relief under a building or other service contract even where the performance is less than substantial.[37]

The modern trend is toward recognition that a party in substantial default should not be treated as an outlaw.[38] To a large extent this trend is expressed in legislation. Labor legislation in most states requires the payment of wages to workingmen at periodic intervals, and the payment of accrued wages at the termination of employment regardless of any contractual condition to the contrary.[39] The Uniform Commercial Code permits a defaulting buyer to obtain restitution of payments made by him to the extent that these exceed $500 or 20% of the value of the buyer's obligation, whichever is

---

35. Lawrence v. Miller, 86 N.Y. 131 (1881), reaffirmed in 32 Beechwood Corp. v. Fisher, 19 N.Y.2d 1008, 281 N.Y.S.2d 843, 228 N.E.2d 823 (1967).

36. Freedman v. Rector, Wardens & Vestrymen of St. Mathias Parish, 37 Cal.2d 16, 230 P.2d 629, 31 A.L.R. 2d 1 (1951) (even where breach is wilful). The minority view is supported by Corbin, The Right of a Defaulting Vendee to the Restitution of Instalments Paid, 40 Yale L.J. 1013 (1931).

37. Kirkland v. Archbold, 113 N.E.2d 496 (Ohio 1953); Burke v. McKee, 304 P.2d 307 (Okl.1956) (contract to clear land of timber); Lynn v. Seby, 29 N. D. 420, 151 N.W. 31 (1915) (contract to thresh grain). See Norstrom & Woodland, Recovery by Building Contractor in Default, 20 Ohio St.L.J. 193 (1959). Although generally where substantial performance is rendered, recovery is allowed on the contract, in some juris-

dictions only quasi contractual relief is permitted. Allen v. Burns, 201 Mass. 74, 87 N.E. 194 (1909).

38. 5A Corbin § 1123; see Judge Clark's able discussion in Amtorg Trading Corp. v. Miehle Printing Press & Mfg. Co., 206 F.2d 103 (2d Cir. 1953) prophesying a change in New York law. The prophesy has not been fulfilled. See also Kitchin v. Mori, —— Nev. ——, 437 P.2d 865 (1968) which asserts that the weight of authority now permits a party in default to recover the value of his performance less the aggrieved party's damages.

39. E. g., McKinney's N.Y.Labor Law § 196 (wages of mechanics, workingmen and laborers payable weekly); see Corman, The Partial Performance Interest of the Defaulting Employee, II, 38 Marq.L.Rev. 139, 162–68 (1955).

smaller.[40] The buyer's claim for restitution is subject to an offset in the amount of the seller's actual damages and the value of benefits received by the buyer as a result of the contract: [41] the buyer's rights may be curtailed or expanded by a valid liquidated damages clause in the contract.[42]

Elsewhere the Code generally allows a defaulting debtor under a secured transaction any surplus on a sale of the security by the creditor.[43]

A seller may recover although the goods do not conform to the contract provided the goods are accepted: [44] of course, the buyer may set off any damages the non-conformity has caused him.[45] Other remedies for defaulting parties also exist. For centuries defaulting mortgagors have been protected by a variety of rules fashioned by courts of equity.[46]

Despite the inroads of statutes and fairly wide acceptance of the doctrine of Britton v. Turner, the majority of jurisdictions continue to adhere to the general principle that a defaulting party has no remedy notwithstanding the degree of hardship and forfeiture he may suffer. The general principle is punitive, but is not rational in meting out punishment. The penalty is not fashioned to meet the specific wrong. Rather, the amount of penalty depends upon the fortuitous circumstances of the transaction. Paradoxically, the more the defaulting party has performed, the greater his forfeiture and the greater the unearned enrichment of the other party.[47]

§ 160. Recovery by a Party in Default: Divisibility

Some contracts are said to be "entire" while others are said to be "divisible." If it is divisible, the contract, for certain purposes, is treated as if it were a number of contracts. A contract is said to be divisible if "performance by each party is divided into two or more parts" and "performance of each part by one party is the agreed ex-

---

40. U.C.C. § 2–718(2) (b).

41. U.C.C. § 2–718(3).

42. U.C.C. § 2–718(2) (a). On the validity of liquidated damages clauses, see § 232 et seq. infra.

43. U.C.C. § 9–504(2).

44. U.C.C. § 2–607(1).

45. U.C.C. §§ 2–607(2), 2–714.

46. Osborne, Mortgages 16–29 (1951).

47. In Freedman v. Rector, Wardens & Vestrymen of St. Mathias Parish, 37 Cal.2d 16, 230 P.2d 629, 31 A.L.R.2d 1 (1951), the court, in granting restitution to a defaulting purchaser of land stated that the majority rule, in effect, grants punitive damages to the non-breaching party. But this award has no "rational relationship to its purpose. . . . It not only fails to take into consideration the degree of culpability but its severity increases as the seriousness of the breach decreases." 37 Cal.2d at 22, 230 P.2d at 632.

change for a corresponding part by the other party." [48] Although it is often said that whether a contract is divisible is a question of interpretation, the process of interpretation in such cases is frequently result-oriented. It is easier to understand the distinction between divisible and entire contracts if one understands the consequences of the determination.

If A and B agree that A will act as B's secretary for one year at a salary of $100 per week, the contract is said to be divisible.[49] On the other hand where defendant agreed to make extensive alterations to the plaintiff's property for $3,075 to be payable in instalments, $150 upon signing of the contract, $1,000 on delivery of material and start of the work, $1500 upon completion of the rough carpentry and $425 upon completion of the job, the contract was held to be entire.[50]

Once the secretary has worked one week she becomes entitled to $100 irrespective of any subsequent events. Thus even if she breaches the contract by wrongfully leaving B's employment, she is nonetheless entitled to $100.[51] B is entitled, of course, to sue her or to counterclaim for damages. Expressed in terms of conditions, the

48. Restatement, Contracts § 266 Comment e; 6 Williston § 860.

49. White v. Atkins, 62 Mass. (8 Cush.) 367 (1851); Wrightsman v. Brown, 181 Okl. 142, 73 P.2d 121 (1937); Yeargin v. Bramblett, 115 Ga.App. 862, 156 S.E.2d 97 (1967) (physicians' services over a period of years to patient afflicted with chronic diseases held to be severable for purposes of statute of limitations).

50. New Era Homes Corp. v. Forster, 299 N.Y. 303, 86 N.E.2d 757, 22 A.L.R. 2d 1338 (1949). Note that in this case the building contractor performed and the defendant defaulted in payment of the third instalment. The court held that the contractor could not recover the instalment as such; he had to prove his damages.

If all that was in issue was the right to payment of the instalment, the contractor should have been awarded judgment on his action for this partial breach of contract. Rich v. Arancio, 277 Mass. 310, 178 N.E. 743, 82 A.L.R. 313 (1931) (analyzed in 3A Corbin § 695 n. 54). But the decision would

be justified if the plaintiff had elected to treat the breach as total and ceased to perform. Under such circumstances he is required to sue for total rather than partial breach. 3A Corbin § 697 n. 68. Cf. Shapiro Eng'r. Corp. v. Francis O. Day Co., 215 Md. 373, 137 A.2d 695 (1958).

For a case involving an entire contract in which a manufacturer undertook a four stage project for research and development of production facilities for military supplies in which the last stage was to be implemented only in the event of a national emergency, see Pennsylvania Exchange Bank v. United States, 145 Ct.Cl. 216, 170 F.Supp. 629 (1959).

51. However there are cases holding that even though she is entitled to be paid for the severable performance rendered, nevertheless if she breaches the employer would not be guilty of a breach in failing to pay this sum at least as long as he does not retain an amount in excess of his damages. Grismore § 164. Accord U.C.C. § 2-717.

situation is this. Each week's performance on her part is a constructive condition precedent to her right to a week's salary. Her right to the salary is not conditioned on performance of her obligation to work for one year. In effect, for this purpose,[52] the contract is deemed to be divided into 52 exchanges of performances. In the construction case, however, if the rough carpentry were completed, but by reason of the contractor's default the balance of the work was not completed, the contractor could not recover $1500; at most (and only in a minority of jurisdictions) he could bring a quasi contractual action.[53]

The test of divisibility is whether, had the parties thought of it, they would be willing to exchange the part performances irrespective of what transpired subsequently or whether the divisions made are merely for the purpose of requiring periodic payments as the work progresses. It is rare that the parties express an intention on this question. The results reached in this area depend largely upon the kind of contract involved. Building contracts are generally deemed to be entire [54] while employment contracts tend to be held to be divisible.[55]

The Uniform Commercial Code has extensive rules governing instalment contracts. Unless otherwise expressly or implicitly agreed, contracts for the sale of goods are entire, in the sense that all goods called for under the contract must be delivered in one lot.[56] If the contract permits instalment deliveries and if the price can be apportioned, a proportionate share of the price is payable, unless otherwise agreed, upon tender of delivery of each instalment.[57]

---

52. The point is that although a divisible contract is divisible for some purposes it is not divisible for all purposes. Thus, in the case of the secretary, if she did not work for four days out of a week ordinarily she would not be guilty of a material breach because the question of materiality is decided on the ratio of four days to a year rather than four days to a week. See note 60 infra.

53. See § 159 supra.

54. New Era Homes Corp. v. Forster, 299 N.Y. 303, 86 N.E.2d 757, 22 A.L.R. 2d 1338 (1949). But cf. Lowy v. United Pac. Ins. Co., 67 Cal.2d 87, 60 Cal. Rptr. 225, 429 P.2d 577 (1967) which combined the doctrines of divisibility and substantial performance. The contract provided that contractor was

to do excavation work and street improvement work and a unit price was allocated to each phase. The contract was held to be divisible and the contractor was permitted to recover for substantial performance of the first phase, although he defaulted entirely on the second phase and in part as to the first phase.

55. White v. Atkins, 62 Mass. (8 Cush.) 367 (1851); Wrightsman v. Brown, 181 Okl. 142, 73 P.2d 121 (1937).

56. U.C.C. § 2–307. For prior case law in accord see Baker v. Higgins, 21 N. Y. 397 (1860) (contract for delivery of 75,000 bricks; no duty to pay for an instalment delivery of 21,000.

57. U.C.C. § 2–307.

There is another group of rules concerning the tender of nonconforming instalments where instalment deliveries are permitted under the contract.[58] The buyer may reject a non-conforming instalment only if the non-conformity substantially impairs the value of that instalment.[59] The buyer may treat non-conformity or default with respect to any instalment as a total breach if the value of the contract as a whole is substantially impaired.[60] These rules contrast strangely with the general rule of the Sales Article of the Code. As to non-instalment sales, strict compliance is required. The doctrine of substantial performance is not recognized.[61]

§ 161. Divisibility: Other Uses of the Concept

Although the concept of divisibility is, perhaps, employed primarily in connection with the problem of whether a party in default may recover, it is used in other contexts. It is often used to determine whether a contract tainted with illegality can be severed into a legal and enforceable portion and an illegal and unenforceable portion.[62] The concept is also utilized to determine the allocation of risks where performance of contractual duties in part becomes impossible.[63] The question of divisibility may be raised in connection with the running of the statute of limitations [64] and the applicability of the Statute of Frauds,[65] as well as with the question of whether the aggrieved party has one cause of action or several.[66]

---

58. These rules have no application to a situation where the buyer has made several distinct deliveries of goods of the same kind under separate contracts. Performance of a separate contract is not a condition precedent to the performance of any other contract. Rock v. Gaede, 111 Kan. 214, 207 P. 323, 27 A.L.R. 1152 (1922). Nonperformance of one contract may, however, give rise to reasonable grounds for insecurity and to the right to demand assurance. See § 163 infra.

59. U.C.C. § 2–612(2).

60. U.C.C. § 2–612(3); accord under prior law, Helgar Corp. v. Warner's Features, Inc., 222 N.Y. 449, 119 N.E. 113 (1918). The question of substantial impairment will frequently be a question of fact for the jury. Monroe v. Diamond, 279 Pa. 310, 123 A. 817 (1924).

61. See § 159 supra. The Code rules on instalment sales are the subject of critical comment in Peters, Remedies for Breach of Contracts Relating to the Sale of Goods Under the Uniform Commercial Code: A Road Map For Article Two, 73 Yale L.J. 199, 223–27 (1963).

62. See § 384 infra. However, as we shall see, the word is not necessarily used in the same sense in which it is used here.

63. See Restatement, Contracts § 463.

64. See Rich v. Arancio, 277 Mass. 310, 178 N.E. 743, 82 A.L.R. 313 (1931).

65. See United States Rubber Co. v. Bercher's Royal Tire Service, Inc., 205 F.Supp. 368 (D.C.Ark.1962).

66. See Armstrong v. Illinois Bankers Life Ass'n, 217 Ind. 601, 29 N.E.2d 415, 131 A.L.R. 769 (1940), reh. denied 217 Ind. 601, 29 N.E.2d 953, 131 A.L.R. 769.

Given the wide variety of contexts in which the question of divisibility is raised, it is fairly obvious that the contours of the concept will be reshaped to provide a just result in the particular context in which the concept is raised.

§ 162. Independent Promises

As we have seen a promise is, by definition, independent (unconditional) if nothing but a lapse of time is necessary to make the promise enforceable.[67] Thus if A promises to build a house for B and B promises to pay X dollars, A's promise is by definition unconditional since he must perform before B does anything, but B's promise is constructively conditional upon A's substantial performance.[68]

A more complicated situation arises where there is more than one promise on one or both sides of a bilateral contract. For example, Williston [69] suggests a situation where A promises to deliver to B an automobile and to change a flat tire for B in exchange for B's promise to pay $3,500.00. B's promise is clearly constructively conditional on A's performance. However, delivery of the automobile would undoubtedly amount to substantial performance of the constructive condition. If this is so then, in a sense, B's promise is independent of (not conditioned upon) A's promise to deliver the tire.[70]

---

67. See § 136 supra.

68. See § 141 supra.

69. 6 Williston § 822.

70. Strictly speaking, however, B's promise is conditional because it is conditioned on the delivery of the automobile. It is not, however, conditional upon repair of the flat tire. A similar situation with an opposite result is presented in the case of Palmer v. Fox, 274 Mich. 252, 264 N.W. 361, 104 A.L.R. 1057 (1936), in which the vendor agreed to deliver title to a certain lot and to cinderize the streets in the subdivision in which the lot was located. The vendor tendered his deed and sued for the last installment. The vendee set up as a defense that the vendor had not cinderized the street. The court held that the final payment was not only conditioned upon tendering the deed but also upon cinderizing the streets. This was another way of saying that under the circumstances the vendor had not sub-

stantially performed. Accord, on similar facts, DeBisschop v. Crump, 24 F.2d 807 (5th Cir. 1928); Horowitz v. Bergan Associates, Inc., 162 Misc. 430, 295 N.Y.S. 33 (Sup.Ct.1937) (purchasers were permitted to rescind and obtain restitution); but cf. Zambetti v. Commodores Land Co., 102 Fla. 586, 136 So. 644 (1931).

Contrary to the modern approach expressed in Palmer v. Fox, supra, it was formerly the view that breach of a covenant which "goes only to part of the consideration on both sides" would not be deemed a failure of constructive condition. This was Rule 3 of the famous "Sergeant Williams' Rules" first published in an annotation to Pordage v. Cole, 1 Wm.Saund. 319 (1798). These rules are reprinted in 6 Williston § 820. Also illustrative of the modern approach is Tichnor Bros. v. Evans, 92 Vt. 278, 102 A. 1031 (1918) (sale of postcards to defendant with collateral promise not to sell similar cards to defendant's competitors; held, breach of collateral

In a similar sense a promise is regarded as independent in cases to which the doctrine of constructive conditions does not apply. This occurs where the performance on one side or both sides of a contract is made to depend upon a fortuitous event—the so-called aleatory contract.

The commonest illustration is an insurance policy in which the assured promises to pay the premium. If the doctrine of constructive conditions applied one would expect that the insurance company's obligation would be constructively conditioned on the payment of the premium so that the assured could not recover if he did not pay the premium. However under the cases, the assured may recover even though he has not paid the premium because the promise of the insurance company is deemed to be independent of the payment of premiums.[71] The theory is that the payment of a premium is so small with respect to the promise of the insurance company that the promise of the insurance company is independent and not conditional on the promise to pay premiums. It should be noted here that this is not a question of substantial performance, but rather that the courts simply refuse to apply the doctrine of constructive conditions, and so, as at early common law, each party may sue the other upon the promise of the other party. To avoid this result the insurance company may expressly condition its promise upon the payment of the premium.

At times promises which were originally independent may become conditional with the passage of time. For example, in a transaction for the sale and purchase of real property B agrees to pay the purchase price in three installments and S agrees to convey at the time of the payment of the final installment. It is clear that the buyer's promises to pay the first two installments are unconditional but that his promise to pay the last installment is concurrently conditional with the tender of the deed.[72] However, if B has not paid the first two installments when the third installment becomes due, S may not, under the majority view, sue for the first two installments without tendering the deed. Thus promises which were orig-

---

promise did not "go to the essence" of the contract); cf. Brown v. Fraley, 222 Md. 480, 161 A.2d 128 (1960). Compare Specialties Development Corp. v. C–O–Two Fire Equip. Co., 207 F.2d 753 (3d Cir. 1953), cert. denied 347 U.S. 919, 74 S.Ct. 519, 98 L.Ed. 1074 (licensor of patent breached covenant to prosecute infringers; breach held to be material).

71. Dwelling House Ins. Co. v. Hardie, 37 Kan. 674, 16 P. 92 (1887); Restatement, Contracts § 293. However by definition the promise of the insurance company is not independent because it is conditioned on the occurrence of the fortuitous event. It is, however, independent of the policy holder's performance.

72. Kane v. Hood, 30 Mass. (13 Pick.) 281 (1832).

inally unconditional became conditional, presumably in an attempt to do justice.[73]

A lease is a peculiar instrument. It acts as a conveyance of a leasehold interest in real property. Usually it also is a bilateral contract in which the tenant agrees to pay rent and the landlord may agree to make repairs. Courts have generally focused on the property rather than the contract aspects of the lease. As a result of this orientation it is generally held that a tenant's duty to pay rent is independent of his landlord's promise to repair or to provide services,[74] a result which has contributed to the decay of urban housing and to the phenomenon of the "rent strike."[75] The rule is mitigated by the holding that if the landlord's non-performance is extreme it may amount to a "constructive eviction" justifying termination of the lease by the tenant.[76]

§ 163.   Present or Prospective Inability and Unwillingness to Perform as Constructive Conditions

Actual failure of performance will, as we have seen, result either in a material or immaterial breach.[77] So, too, when the non-performance is prospective there are also questions of degree.[78] Under some circumstances where there is prospective non-performance the other party may be justified only in suspending his performance; at other times he may be justified in regarding the contract as cancelled or in changing his position.[79] Where there is a repudiation of prospective performance he may be able to sue immediately under a theory of anticipatory breach.[80]

Prospective inability or unwillingness to perform is ordinarily manifested by a statement of unwillingness or inability to perform,[81]

73. Jozovich v. Central Cal. Berry Grower's Ass'n, 183 Cal.App.2d 616, 6 Cal.Rptr. 617 (1960); Beecher v. Conradt, 13 N.Y. 108 (1885); but cf. Gray v. Meek, 199 Ill. 136, 64 N.E. 1020 (1902) (all but last installment may be recovered without tender).

74. Restatement, Contracts § 290; Means v. Dierks, 180 F.2d 306 (10th Cir. 1950); Hosang v. Minor, 205 Cal. App.2d 269, 22 Cal.Rptr. 794 (1962); Thomson-Houston Elec. Co. v. Durant Land Imp. Co., 144 N.Y. 34, 39 N.E. 7 (1894).

75. See Simmons, Passion and Prudence: Rent Withholding under New York's Spiegel Law, 15 Buffalo L.Rev. 572 (1966).

76. Charles E. Burt, Inc. v. Seven Grand Corp., 340 Mass. 124, 163 N.E. 2d 4 (1959).

77. See § 157 supra.

78. Restatement, Contracts § 280, Comment a.

79. See generally, 6 Corbin §§ 1259–61; 5 Williston § 699; 6 Williston §§ 875–79; Restatement, Contracts §§ 280–87.

80. This phase of the problem is discussed in chapter 10 infra as well as the question of retraction of a statement of prospective unwillingness to perform.

81. Restatement, Contracts § 280.

destruction of the subject matter,[82] death or illness of a person whose performance is essential under the contract,[83] encumbrance or lack of title in a contract vendor,[84] existing or supervening illegality of a promised performance,[85] insolvency of a party [86] and defective performances rendered in other contracts or other instalments of the present contract.[87]

To illustrate, S agrees to sell and B agrees to buy a specific second hand car, delivery to be made and title to pass on June 1, and B agrees to pay the purchase price on May 1. If the car is destroyed by fire on April 25th, B could not successfully enforce the contract against S, for as we shall see, S would have the defense of impossibility of performance.[88] Although B's promise to pay prior to delivery was independent of any performance on the part of S, it is constructively conditioned upon S's apparent ability to perform his part of the agreed exchange.[89] It is thus clear that whenever a party to a contract has the defense of impossibility of performance, the other party has a defense of prospective inability.[90] Where prospective inability is caused by destruction of the subject matter, the contract is discharged without any requirement of a change of position.[91]

But suppose that in the same case there is no fire but rather S on April 25th unconditionally sells the car to X, and B on April 26th buys a different car. The authorities agree that B, by virtue of S's prospective non-performance, was justified in changing his position by buying a different car and therefore was not obliged to perform on May 1st and in addition was discharged from his obligations under the contract.[92]

If it be assumed, however, that B did not buy another car on April 26th but merely told S that he would not proceed with the

82. Restatement, Contracts § 281.

83. Restatement, Contracts § 282.

84. Restatement, Contracts §§ 283–84.

85. Restatement, Contracts §§ 285–86.

86. Restatement, Contracts § 287.

87. U.C.C. § 2–609, Comment 3.

88. Dexter v. Norton, 47 N.Y. 62 (1871); see § 187 infra.

89. Thus illustration 4 of § 282 reads as follows:
"A contracts with B, a tutor, to instruct A's son during the year beginning Jan. 1 at a salary of $300 a month.

A's son dies in February. A is not bound to pay the salary for the remainder of the year." The point is that B has the defense of impossibility of performance and A has the defense of prospective inability to perform.

90. See § 187 infra.

91. Restatement, Contracts § 281. The same rule applies to real property. Restatement, Contracts § 284.

92. Brimmer v. Salisbury, 167 Cal. 522, 140 P. 30 (1914); Fort Payne Coal & Iron Co. v. Webster, 163 Mass. 134, 39 N.E. 786 (1895); James v. Burchell, 82 N.Y. 108 (1880).

transaction and S on April 27 re-obtained the auto in question, a more difficult question is presented.[93] Some authorities indicate that B was justified in stating that he would not proceed and that he is no longer bound despite the fact that S re-obtained the auto.[94] The Restatement rules say that there must be a change of position but do not indicate whether B's notification could be considered a change of position.[95]

In the same illustration, if S instead of selling the car on April 25 tells B that he positively will not perform and B buys a different automobile, B would not be bound to pay S on May 1 because of S's prospective unwillingness to perform and, because he has changed his position, he would be discharged from the contract.[96]

Some of the cases in this area involve contracts for the sale of realty where the vendor does not have title to the property at the time the contract of sale is entered into. Unless the vendee has knowledge of the lack of title [97] he may invoke the doctrine of prospective inability to perform in such a situation [98] unless the vendor has a right to become owner or a justifiable expectation of becoming owner in time to perform.[99]

The Restatement announces the same rule where the vendor has title but the title is not marketable.[1] However the better view is that where time is not of the essence and the vendor has the power to remedy the defect within a reasonable time, the vendee does not have the right to change his position and cancel his duties under the con-

---

93. If S did not reacquire the automobile there can be no doubt that his probable non-performance would justify B in not paying the purchase price on May 1 even if he had not stated that he would not proceed with the transaction.

94. Simpson 340.

95. Restatement, Contracts § 284.

96. Windmuller v. Pope, 107 N.Y. 674, 14 N.E. 436 (1887). On the question of change of position see note 91 supra. In addition to B having a defense because of the prospective unwillingness to perform (repudiation) B would have a cause of action against S based upon a theory of anticipatory breach. See § 177 infra.

97. Tague Holding Corp. v. Harris, 250 N.Y. 422, 165 N.E. 834 (1929), mo-

tion to dismiss appeal denied 250 N.Y. 557, 166 N.E. 323. If the vendee has such knowledge he must make payments as they fall due since he has consciously accepted the risk of not getting an agreed exchange; if, of course, marketable title is not delivered, the vendee has his action for damages or restitution.

98. This means that if the contract calls for installment payments prior to delivery of the deed the vendee may suspend his payments and in any event may change his position or, according to another view, merely notify the seller that he (the buyer) is no longer bound and thereby his duties under the contract are discharged.

99. Restatement, Contracts § 283.

1. Restatement, Contracts § 283.

tract.[2] As has been stated "The question must resolve itself into one of degree and of probability;"[3] that is, the degree of the encumbrance and the probability of its being cleared.[4]

The insolvency or bankruptcy of one of the parties to a contract also presents questions of prospective unwillingness and inability to perform.[5] For example, if S agrees to sell and deliver certain goods to B on May 1 for which B is to pay on August 1, and on April 30th B is insolvent,[6] must S deliver the goods according to the terms of the contract?

The rule is that, if B is insolvent, or adjudicated a bankrupt, or his property taken under a receivership, or a petition in bankruptcy or for a receiver is pending against him, S's duty to deliver the goods is suspended until B either tenders payment in cash for the goods or until B furnishes adequate security for payment in August.[7] According to the weight of authority the failure of the insolvent party to tender cash or security within a reasonable time discharges the duty of the solvent party altogether.[8]

2. Cohen v. Kranz, 12 N.Y.2d 242, 238 N.Y.S.2d 928, 189 N.E.2d 473 (1963) (vendor could have cured title by moving a fence; vendee not justified in terminating contract).

3. 6 Williston § 879.

4. Depositor's Trust Co. v. Bruneau, 144 Me. 142, 66 A.2d 86 (1949); De Felice v. Peace, 13 N.J.Super. 236, 80 A.2d 321 (1951); Kadow v. Cronin, 97 N.J.L. 301, 116 A. 427 (1922).

5. The rules stated herein relate only to the insolvency of a party who is receiving credit or who is delivering property which is subject to being levied upon by his creditors. Restatement, Contracts § 287, ill. 3; Grismore § 156. Bankruptcy is discussed in § 181 infra.

6. "Insolvent" in this context means that the debtor is unable to pay the debts as they mature. Restatement, Contracts § 287(2).

7. Restatement, Contracts § 287. This section also indicates that the solvent party may "reasonably and materially change his position" and thus also discharge his obligation. The Uniform Commercial Code adopts the philosophy of this rule in § 2–702 which provides:

(1) Where the seller discovers the buyer to be insolvent he may refuse delivery except for cash including payment for all goods theretofore delivered under the contract, and stop delivery under this article (Section 2–705).

(2) Where the seller discovers that the buyer has received goods on credit while insolvent he may reclaim the goods upon demand made within ten days after receipt, but if misrepresentation of solvency has been made to a particular seller in writing within three months before delivery the ten day limitation does not apply. Except as provided in this subsection the seller may not base a right to reclaim goods on the buyer's fraudulent or innocent misrepresentation of solvency or of intent to pay.

(3) The seller's right to reclaim under subsection (2) is subject to the rights of a buyer in ordinary course or other good faith purchaser or lien creditor under this article. (Section 2–403). Successful reclamation of goods excludes all other remedies with respect to them.

8. Leopold v. Rock-ola Mfg. Corp., 109 F.2d 611 (5th Cir. 1940); Hanna v.

Also relevant in this area is § 2–609 of the Uniform Commercial Code which reads as follows:

Right to Adequate Assurance of Performance

(1) A contract for sale imposes an obligation on each party that the other's expectation of receiving due performance will not be impaired. When reasonable grounds for insecurity arise with respect to the performance of either party the other may in writing demand adequate assurance of due performance and until he receives such assurance may if commercially reasonable suspend any performance for which he has not already received the agreed return.

(2) Between merchants the reasonableness of grounds for insecurity and the adequacy of any assurance offered shall be determined according to commercial standards.

(3) Acceptance of any improper delivery or payment does not prejudice the aggrieved party's right to demand adequate assurance of future performance.

(4) After receipt of a justified demand failure to provide within a reasonable time not exceeding thirty days such assurance of due performance as is adequate under the circumstances of the particular case is a repudiation of the contract.

The Code innovation in this section is to impose an obligation upon each party to the contract to provide assurance to the other when there is reasonable ground for insecurity. Failure to give adequate assurance not only acts as a failure of a constructive condition of demonstrating continued willingness and ability to perform, but acts as a breach of contract,[9] unless the inability to perform is excused as, for example, by impossibility. Although the term "adequate assurance" is left intentionally vague, the Code Comment indicates that standards of commercial reasonableness are involved, and, depending upon the nature of the insecurity and the reputation of the parties, these standards may at one extreme be satisfied by a simple letter stating an intention to perform, and at the other extreme, may require posting of a guaranty.[10]

Florence Iron Co. of Wisconsin, 222 N.Y. 290, 118 N.E. 629 (1918); but cf. Keppelon v. W. M. Ritter Flooring Corp., 97 N.J.L. 200, 116 A. 491 (1922) which holds that the solvent party must tender or at least inquire whether the insolvent can furnish the required security or cash.

9. See U.C.C. § 2–609(4). This matter is discussed in more detail in ch. 10 infra.

10. A difficult problem of interpretation of the Code arises where the grounds for insecurity stem from a defective performance or default un-

D. EXCUSE OF CONDITION

Analysis

Sec.
164. Introduction.
165. Hindrance or Failure to Cooperate as an Excuse of Condition: Duty to Cooperate.
166. Estoppel and Waiver Compared.
167. Waiver Contemporaneous with the Formation of the Contract.
168. Waiver and Estoppel: Waiver before Failure of Condition but after Formation of the Contract.
169. Waiver after Failure of Condition: Election.
170. Giving Unjustifiable Reasons for Refusing to Perform as an Excuse of a Condition.
171. Waiver of Condition is Not Waiver of Right to Damages for Breach.
172. Excuse of Conditions Involving Forfeitures.
173. Excuse of Condition by Impossibility.

§ 164. Introduction

As a general proposition a conditional duty remains conditional until the condition occurs. There are situations, however, in which it would be patently unjust to insist upon fulfillment of the condition. The most obvious example of such a situation is where the party in whose favor the condition exists prevented the occurrence of the express or constructive condition to his duty.

§ 165. Hindrance or Failure to Cooperate as an Excuse of Condition: Duty to Cooperate

The question of wrongful prevention or substantial hindrance or failure to cooperate as an excuse of condition, expressed in functional terms is, may a plaintiff who has failed to perform recover from the defendant when the failure to perform is somehow caused by the defendant's wrongful prevention or active hindrance or passive non-cooperation? [11] In a well known case [12] plaintiff agreed to

der an instalment contract. Certainly, the purchaser would have a right to demand assurance under U.C.C. § 2–609. The difficulty is in determining where the purchaser may, instead, reject the instalment or cancel the contract pursuant to U.C.C. § 2–612. A discussion of this problem requires deeper analysis of the Code than is possible here. See Duesenberg & King, Sales & Bulk Transfers under the Uniform Commercial Code § 14.02 [3] (1966); Peters, Remedies for Breach of Contracts Relating to the

Sale of Goods under the Uniform Commercial Code: A Roadmap for Article Two, 73 Yale L.J. 199, 223–27 (1963).

11. A related question is whether a plaintiff may recover although he prevented the defendant from performing. Of course he may not. This kind of fact pattern does not involve an excuse of condition; it involves the implication or construction of a condi-

12. See note 12 on page 265.

care for his granduncle until the uncle died. He was prevented from doing so when he was without cause ordered to leave. The court held that the complaint stated a cause of action for recovery on the contract even though plaintiff had not fulfilled the condition precedent to the defendant's promise. The condition was excused.[13] Decisions in cases of this kind involving active prevention are clear cut and pose no particular difficulty.

A difficult problem is to determine when, if ever, a condition is excused by mere passive non-cooperation. In Amies v. Wesnofske,[14] plaintiff's right to a brokerage commission from a vendor was, by agreement, conditioned upon closing of title. The vendee defaulted under the contract but the vendor took no legal action against the defaulting vendee and agreed with the vendee that the vendee was discharged from his duties under the contract in consideration of the vendor being permitted to retain the down payment. The broker insisted that he was entitled to the commission, arguing that the occurrence of the condition was excused because of the vendor's failure to bring an action for specific performance against the vendee. Such an action was incumbent upon the vendor, he argued, by virtue of the vendor's implied duty of cooperation. The court held, however, that while the promisor must refrain from active conduct preventing

tion. There is probably an implied in fact and at least a constructive condition in every contract that each party will not unjustifiably hinder the other from performing.

12. Barron v. Cain, 216 N.C. 282, 4 S. E.2d 618 (1939).

13. When one says that the condition is excused one means that even though the condition did not take place, the plaintiff may recover on the contract provided he can show that he would have been ready, willing and able to perform but for the prevention. Restatement, Contracts § 315. When the condition is excused it does not follow that the promisee will receive the amount called for by the contract. Thus in the case under discussion the promisee would obtain a recovery diminished by what he could reasonably have earned by being excused from performing the remainder of his contract. However if the condition which is excused is only an incident of performance as for example where a contractor is excused from producing an architect's certificate

(see § 194 infra) then if the contractor has otherwise performed he is entitled to recover the amount called for in the contract.

But, if defendant had merely been disagreeable and difficult to live with, the condition would not be excused. This is the kind of risk that one assumes in a contract of this type. Godburn v. Meserve, 130 Conn. 723, 37 A.2d 235 (1944).

14. 255 N.Y. 156, 174 N.E. 436, 73 A.L. R. 918 (1931); accord, Beattie-Firth, Inc. v. Colebank, 143 W.Va. 740, 105 S.E.2d 5, 74 A.L.R.2d 431 (1958). For illustrations of a principal's liability to a broker where there is active hindrance or intentional conduct causing the other party's non-performance, as for example where the seller refuses to convey without cause, see Westhill Exports, Ltd. v. Pope, 12 N.Y.2d 491, 240 N.Y.S.2d 961, 191 N.E.2d 447 (1963); Langfan v. Walzer, 13 N.Y.2d 171, 244 N.Y.S.2d 305, 194 N.E.2d 124 (1963) (agreement that vendor not liable to broker even if he is at fault for non-consummation).

or hindering the fulfilment of the condition,[15] in remaining passive and neutral he was not guilty of wrongful prevention.

There are many cases, however, in which a duty of affirmative cooperation will be implied or imposed. In Patterson v. Meyerhofer,[16] plaintiff agreed to sell certain real property to the defendant. Plaintiff informed defendant that he did not have title to the property and expected to acquire it at a foreclosure sale. The defendant outbid the plaintiff at the foreclosure sale. Two results followed: first, the plaintiff was excused from non-performance of his promise, performance of which was a condition precedent to defendant's duty to pay; second, defendant was guilty of a breach of an implied promise of cooperation for which defendant was made to respond in damages.

The term implied promise of cooperation is used to cover situations which are not necessarily factually similar. If a building contract requires the landowner to select the site upon which the structure is to be erected, it is apparent that the builder needs the cooperation of the owner in order to render his own performance. In this type of case it is usually held that if the party who must cooperate to insure the performance of the other party fails to do so he not only excuses the performance of the other party by his prevention but also breaches an implied promise of cooperation.[17]

The term promise of cooperation might also be employed in another sense in a case such as Amies v. Wesnofske previously discussed. There, it was clear that the broker could perform without the cooperation of the seller. The question there is whether the vendor must cooperate by bringing an action to insure that the condition to the broker's obtaining his fee shall occur.[18] A case of the

15. Accord: Ellsworth Dobbs, Inc. v. Johnson, 50 N.J. 528, 236 A.2d 843 (1967); contra, Tarbell v. Bomes, 48 R.I. 86, 135 A. 604, 51 A.L.R. 1386 (1927).

16. 204 N.Y. 96, 97 N.E. 472 (1912).

17. Suburban Land Co. v. Brown, 237 Mass. 166, 129 N.E. 291 (1921); Bruson Heights Corp. v. State, 281 App. Div. 371, 120 N.Y.S.2d 73 (3d Dept. 1953) (owner was to select fixtures for the building); Levicoff v. Richard I. Rubin & Co., 413 Pa. 134, 196 A.2d 359 (1964) (lessee neglected to provide plans for store which lessor was to build); Kehm Corp. v. United States, 119 Ct.Cl. 454, 93 F.Supp. 620 (1950) (the government failed to supply the

proper tail assemblies for bombs to be made by the plaintiff). So also it is generally held that a general contractor must take reasonable measures to insure that his subcontractor is not delayed. McGrath v. Electrical Constr. Co., 230 Or. 295, 364 P.2d 604 (1961), reh. denied 370 P.2d 231 (1962).

18. See E. I. Dupont de Nemours Powder Co. v. Schlottman, 218 F. 353 (2d Cir. 1914), cert. denied 235 U.S. 705, 35 S.Ct. 282, 59 L.Ed. 434 (defendant agreed to pay an additional $25,000 for the purchase of a factory if certain production goals could be met after one year and if in the defendant's judgment the factory was worth it; defendant's sale of the factory ex-

Amies type could equally well have been discussed under the heading of express language of condition being implied language of promise.[19] As we saw there, whether or not such a promise will be implied does not depend upon any mechanical rule.[20] Rather the court's instinct for the commercial setting, the ethical position of the parties, the probable understanding that they would have reached had they considered the matter and many other considerations enter into the determination.[21]

Of course, a party may assume the risk of hindrance of his own performance either expressly or impliedly in which event the hindrance would not be wrongful. If a seller promises to sell and deliver 1000 bales of hemp six months from the date of the contract, he assumes the risk of market conditions. This risk includes the possibility that his purchaser will buy large quantities of hemp from other suppliers thus inflating the market price to a point where it is burdensome for the seller to obtain hemp to perform the contract.[22] Courts have felt that this is a foreseeable commercial risk. Where, however, the buyer interferes with what he knows to be the seller's only source of supply, the seller's duty is discharged.[23] A discharge would also result if the purchaser cornered the market [24] or, according to some authorities, if he caused the market price to be inflated in an attempt to corner the market.[25] There is no rule which explains the

cused the condition); Mackay v. Dick, 6 App.Cas. 251 (H.L.1881) (buyer promised to pay for a machine provided it tested satisfactorily; his refusal to test the machine excuses the condition, making his duty to pay absolute); Swartz v. War Memorial Commission of Rochester, 25 A.D.2d 90, 267 N.Y.S.2d 253 (4th Dep't 1966) (landlord was to be paid rent based on a percentage of sales; held licensee impliedly promised to obtain a beer license to increase landlord's rent).

19. See § 144 supra.

20. See § 144 supra.

21. Patterson, Constructive Conditions in Contracts, 42 Colum.L.Rev. 903, 928–42 (1942).

22. United States v. Fidelity & Deposit Co. of Maryland, 152 F. 596 (2d Cir. 1907); Iron Trade Products v. Wilkoff Co., 272 Pa. 172, 116 A. 150 (1922); see 6 Corbin § 1264; 6 Williston §§ 677–77A.

23. Patterson v. Meyerhofer n. 16 supra; and see El Ranco, Inc. v. First National Bank of Nevada, 406 F.2d 1205 (9th Cir. 1968), where defendant enticed away some of plaintiff's employees and entered into a conspiracy with plaintiff's agent to prevent performance of the contract. The defendant was liable in tort as well as breach of contract.

24. United States v. Peck, 102 U.S. 64, 26 L.Ed. 46 (Ct.Cl.1880). When one uses the phrase "cornered the market," one must determine what is the relevant market. In this case the court stated that the parties contemplated as the relevant market "the Big Meadows near the mouth of the Tongue River—which was, indeed, the only hay which the claimant could have procured within hundreds of miles, and which it was known he relied upon."

25. Restatement, Contracts § 315, ill. 3.

result in all of these cases except the court's instinct for justice in allocating the risks it thinks the parties would have assumed had they thought of the contingency which gave rise to the litigation.

§ 166. Estoppel and Waiver Compared

The doctrine of estoppel in pais (equitable estoppel) in its traditional form states that a party who is guilty of a misrepresentation of existing *fact* upon which the other party justifiably relies to his detriment is estopped from denying his utterances or acts to the detriment of the other party.[26] For example, if M is the owner of real property and S, her son, forges her name to a mortgage which S gives to X for a consideration and M having learned of the existence of the mortgage, makes payments on the mortgage upon which the mortgagee relies to his detriment, M by her payments impliedly represented that the mortgage was valid and would be estopped from asserting the invalidity of the mortgage.[27]

Similar cases may arise where, although there is no misrepresentation of existing fact, a party makes a promise upon which the other relies to his detriment. For example, if a party promised before breach to accept a late payment and as a result the other party did not pay on time the party who promised to accept the late payment would be estopped from asserting the lateness of the payment [28] unless the condition was reinstated before the promisee relied thereon to his detriment.[29] It should be observed that here a promise is being enforced even though there is no consideration for it.[30] This is a species of promissory estoppel, except that ordinarily the term promissory estoppel is used in reference to the *formation* of a contract and not to the modification of a contract.[31] At any rate it is now

---

26. 1 Williston § 139. Carruthers v. Whitney, 56 Wash. 327, 105 P. 831 (1909).

27. Rothschild v. Title Guarantee & Trust Co., 204 N.Y. 458, 97 N.E. 879 (1912). This case does not strictly speaking involve any question of excuse of condition and is used solely to illustrate the doctrine of estoppel in pais.

28. Dreier v. Sherwood, 77 Colo. 539, 238 P. 38 (1925).

29. Meyer Milling Co. v. Baker, 328 Mo. 1246, 43 S.W.2d 794 (1931); Imperator Realty Co. v. Tull, 228 N.Y. 447, 127 N.E. 263 (1920). This point is expanded upon in § 168 infra. It

should be observed that this illustration, contrary to the Rothschild case, involves the excuse of conditions.

30. See ch. 4 supra. U.C.C. § 2–209(5) reads:

"A party who has made a waiver affecting an executory portion of the contract may retract the waiver by reasonable notification received by the other party that strict performance will be required of any term waived, unless the retraction would be unjust in view of a material change of position in reliance on the waiver."

31. See ch. 6 supra; B. F. Goodrich Co. v. Parker, 282 Ala. 151, 209 So.2d 647 (1968).

clear that under the modern doctrine of estoppel a misrepresentation of *fact* is not necessary—a promise or an innocent representation of fact being sufficient to form the basis of an estoppel, whether it be denominated "equitable" or "promissory." [32]

A waiver may be defined as an intentional relinquishment of a known right [33] but it must be emphasized that a voluntarily relinquishment of a known right is not necessarily effective. [34] At times such a voluntary relinquishment may be effective without consideration and without detrimental reliance. Often, however, a waiver is ineffective unless supported by consideration, detrimental reliance or some equivalent ground. The following sections proceed to examine waiver contemporaneous with the formation of the contract, waiver after formation of the contract but before failure of condition, and waiver (election) after failure of condition.

§ 167.　Waiver Contemporaneous with the Formation of the Contract

It is obvious that a "waiver" contemporaneous with the formation of the contract is not, strictly speaking, a waiver. It is part of the parties' agreement supported by the same consideration which supports other aspects of the agreement. It is common to speak in terms of waiver, however, where an agent for a party (usually an insurance company) allegedly "waives" certain conditions of the printed text of the form upon which the agreement of the parties is manifested.

As an illustration of the problem, an insurance policy may provide that it is void if the same property is covered by other insurance. May it be shown that the insurance company "waived" this provision at the time of delivery of the policy? Aside from any question of the insurance agent's authority, the so called waiver is a valid term of the parties' agreement if it is not barred by the parol evidence rule. Under most formulations of the parol evidence rule it would appear that evidence of the term would be barred as it would

---

32. Moline I.F.C. Fin. Inc. v. Soucinek, 91 Ill.App.2d 257, 234 N.E.2d 57 (1968); Arrow Lathing & Plastering Inc. v. Schaulat Plumbing Sup. Co., 83 Ill.App.2d 394, 228 N.E.2d 209 (1967); Dart v. Thompson, —— Iowa ——, 154 N.W.2d 82 (Iowa 1967); American Bank & Trust Co. v. Trinity Universal Ins. Co., 251 La. 445, 205 So.2d 35 (1967); Triple Cities Constr. Co. v. Maryland Cas. Co., 4 N.Y.2d 443, 176 N.Y.S.2d 292, 151 N.E.2d 856 (1958).

33. Hoxie v. Home Ins. Co., 32 Conn. 21, 40 (1864); DeCruz v. Reid, 258 Cal.App. 367, 65 Cal.Rptr. 698 (1968), vacated 70 Cal.Rptr. 550, 444 P.2d 342.

34. Rennie & Laughlin, Inc. v. Chrysler Corp., 242 F.2d 208 (9th Cir. 1957); Restatement, Contracts § 297. Corbin points out that the word "waiver" has been given various definitions and that no one definition is "correct." 3A Corbin § 752.

contradict what appears to be an integrated writing.[35] A minority of courts have followed this logic.[36] A majority, however, on a variety of theories, especially on grounds of equitable estoppel, have held that the parol evidence rule does not bar proof of the "waiver." [37] Other cases have proceeded on the theory that reformation of the instrument is available even in an action at law.[38] Whatever the analytic grounds which may be advanced to support these cases, it is clear that the courts have been influenced by the relative bargaining positions of the parties and have attempted to mitigate the "take it or leave it" nature of printed form policies.[39] Statutory enactments in a number of states have put this problem on a new basis. The power of the insurer is reduced by requiring the policy to conform to statutory standards; at the same time, the insured's right to rely on oral waivers is removed or severely restricted.[40]

§ 168. Waiver and Estoppel: Waiver before Failure of Condition but after Formation of the Contract

It is well settled that a waiver of a condition which forms a material part of the agreed exchange after the contract is made, but before its performance is due, is ineffective unless the waiver is supported by consideration or induces detrimental reliance so as to give rise to an estoppel.[41] A waiver which is under seal or which satis-

---

35. See ch. 3 supra.

36. Lumber Underwriters of New York v. Rife, 237 U.S. 605, 35 S.Ct. 717, 59 L.Ed. 1140 (1915); see 5 Williston §§ 748–49.

37. See 5 Williston § 750 (collecting cases). Note that the estoppel here is promissory in nature. This illustrates once again that promissory estoppel is not merely a substitute for consideration, since the "waiver" is supported by consideration.

In New York it has been held that while a condition may be "waived" a warranty that the insured had not been denied insurance by any other company is not waivable. Satz v. Massachusetts Bonding & Ins. Co., 243 N.Y. 385, 153 N.E. 844, 59 A.L.R. 606 (1926), 75 U.Pa.L.Rev. 477 (1926).

38. Wilhide v. Keystone Ins. Co., 195 F.Supp. 659 (M.D.Pa.1961); Grand View Bldg. Ass'n v. Northern Assur. Co. of London, 73 Neb. 149, 102 N.W.

246 (1905), aff'd 203 U.S. 106, 27 S.Ct. 27, 51 L.Ed. 109 (1906). For the availability of reformation at law, see Restatement, Contracts § 507.

39. See 5 Williston § 747.

40. Metropolitan Life Ins. Co. v. Alterovitz, 214 Ind. 186, 14 N.E.2d 570, 117 A.L.R. 770 (1938); Johnson v. Mutual Benefit Health & Accident Ass'n of Omaha, Neb., 5 A.D.2d 103, 168 N.Y.S. 2d 879 (1957), resettled 6 A.D.2d 947, 176 N.Y.S.2d 250 (3d Dep't 1958), modified 5 N.Y.2d 1031, 185 N.Y.S.2d 552, 158 N.E.2d 251; see 5 Williston § 750A.

41. Rennie & Laughlin, Inc. v. Chrysler Corp., 242 F.2d 208 (9th Cir. 1957); see Restatement, Contracts § 297. The party asserting the existence and effectiveness of the waiver has the burden of proof on these issues. Scaduto v. Orlando, 381 F.2d 587 (2d Cir. 1967).

fies a statutory writing requirement may also, in certain jurisdictions, be effective without consideration. As has been noted, traditionally only a misstatement of fact was believed to be sufficient grounds for creation of an estoppel.[42] Frequently, however, the waiver is a promise to forgo the benefit of a condition. If such a promise induces detrimental reliance it will be given effect even in jurisdictions which have not formally adopted the doctrine of promissory estoppel.[43] Very often the alleged waiver arises from the conduct of the party for whose benefit the condition exists.

Various aspects of the doctrine of waiver can be illuminated by variations on a building contract situation. Assume that, pursuant to a building contract, the owner is required to make progress payments upon completion of specified portions of the work. The completion of each portion is a condition precedent to a payment; each payment is a condition precedent to continuance of the work. If the owner makes a progress payment although the stipulated amount of work has not been completed he has effectively waived the condition to that payment. Once the payment is executed the waiver of condition cannot be retracted.[44] If, however, the owner had promised to dispense with the condition, this promise, unless supported by consideration or its equivalent, could be retracted unless the builder in reliance upon the promise has materially changed his position, as, for example, by forgoing other opportunities for financing his payroll.[45]

Repeated waivers will not in themselves create waivers of later conditions.[46] Thus, in the illustration under consideration, repeated progress payments made by the owner prior to performance of the conditions requiring the payments will not prevent the owner from insisting upon the fulfilment of the condition precedent to the next progress payment.[47] At times, however, the repeated waivers may

42. See § 166 supra.

43. Imperator Realty Co. v. Tull, 228 N.Y. 447, 127 N.E. 263 (1920).

44. 3A Corbin § 752.

45. Accord, U.C.C. § 2-209(5) which provides: "A party who had made a waiver affecting an executory portion of the contract may retract the waiver by reasonable notification received by the other party that strict performance will be required of any term waived, unless the retraction would be unjust in view of a material change of position in reliance on the waiver."

46. United Shoe Mach. Co. v. Abbott, 158 F. 762 (8th Cir. 1908); Daniels v. Boston & M. R. Co., 184 Mass. 337, 68 N.E. 337 (1903) (repeated waivers of an employee's breaches of duties does not estop employer from discharging employee for subsequent breach).

47. Cases are collected in 3A Corbin § 754 n. 13. Waiver by a road commission of a condition in one contract with the plaintiff does not estop the commission from insisting upon compliance with a similar condition in another contract. W. P. Harlin Constr. Co. v. Utah State Road Comm'n, 19 Utah 2d 364, 431 P.2d 792 (1967). Making payments on the purchase of

be such as to cause the builder justifiably to change his position so that a demand for compliance with future conditions would be manifestly unjust. In such a case an estoppel will be raised against the owner and he will be held to have effectively waived his right to insist upon compliance with future conditions of the same kind, unless, a reasonable period of notice is granted that strict compliance will be demanded.[48]

Different rules are believed to govern the waiver of a condition if the condition is not a material part of the agreed exchange. A waiver of a condition of this kind is effective without consideration, but if it takes the form of a promise it too is subject to retraction if sufficient time for compliance is granted and there has been no detrimental reliance upon the waiver. In a well known case [49] a writer of law books promised to write a series of books to be compensated at the rate of $2 a page but if he totally abstained from alcoholic beverages he was to be paid an additional $4 a page. He did not comply with the conditions of total abstinence but produced 3,469 pages which were satisfactory to the publisher. The writer alleged that at various times the publisher had assured him that strict compliance with this condition would not be insisted upon. The court held that the waiver was effective and that the writer was entitled to $6 a page: the plaintiff's sobriety was not a material part of the consideration, but a detail of performance which was effectively waivable. Reasoning of this kind is frequent where the condition waived relates to the time for performance. If a builder agrees to build a structure before January 1st and time is made of the essence, the condition that it be completed by that date may be effectively waived without consideration,[50] but waiver of the condition that the structure be built requires consideration. The time limitation, once waived, may be reimposed, if there has been no change of position in reliance upon the waiver, or a new time limitation may be set by the promisor provided a reasonable time is allotted.[51]

an interest in real property prior to delivery of a deed does not waive the condition of delivery as to future payments. Gail v. Gail, 127 App.Div. 892, 112 N.Y.S. 96 (4th Dep't 1908).

48. Kummli v. Myers, 130 U.S.App.D.C. 303, 400 F.2d 774 (1968) (mortgagee who has consistently waived lateness of payments may not without prior reasonable notice refuse a late payment and institute foreclosure proceedings); Fox v. Grange, 261 Ill. 116,

103 N.E. 576 (1913). Additional cases are collected in 3A Corbin § 754 n. 15.

49. Clark v. West, 193 N.Y. 349, 86 N. E. 1 (1908).

50. Restatement, Contracts (2d) § 88. See also Restatement, Contracts § 297; 3A Corbin § 754.

51. Restatement, Contracts (2d) § 88, Comment f.

§ 169.   Waiver after Failure of Condition: Election

After a failure of an express condition or a material failure of a constructive condition, the party for whose benefit the condition exists normally has the power to elect to cancel his performance or to proceed with performance.[52] Thus, for example, in a case where there was an express condition that a certain vessel was to sail on or before February 4th and it sailed on the 5th, the party for whose benefit the condition was inserted could elect to continue with the contract despite the non-performance of the condition. If the failure of condition is also a material breach the same rule can be expressed in other terms; that is, he ordinarily has the right to sue for a total breach or to elect to continue performance and sue for partial breach. If the breaching party has also repudiated his obligations, however, the aggrieved party cannot elect to continue performance.[53] An effective election affects both parties; not only is the party who has waived the condition obligated to perform, but the party in default is held to the performance of the rest of his contractual obligations.[54]

An election may be, and often is, manifested by conduct. Thus an election to waive a condition exists if the promisor continues his own performance [55] (if the performance was dependent upon the condition) or by acceptance and retention of a defective performance.[56] Thus the acceptance and retention of an instalment delivery of goods of inferior quality constitutes a waiver by the buyer of his right to reject a subsequent instalment of conforming goods.[57] An exception

52. Sitlington v. Fulton, 281 F.2d 552 (10th Cir. 1960); Lichter v. Goss, 232 F.2d 715 (7th Cir. 1956); Graham v. San Antonio Mach. & Sup. Corp., 418 S.W.2d 303 (Tex.Civ.App.1967) (waiver of condition of notice of claim); Restatement, Contracts § 309; 4 Corbin § 954.

53. See § 183 infra.

54. Brunswick Corp. v. Vineberg, 370 F.2d 605 (5th Cir. 1967); K. & G. Constr. Co. v. Harris, 223 Md. 305, 164 A.2d 451 (1960); S. S. Steiner, Inc. v. Hill, 191 Or. 391, 230 P.2d 537 (1951).

55. Foster v. L.M.S. Development Co., 346 S.W.2d 387 (Tex.Civ.App.1961) (continuing to pay rent); see 3A Corbin § 755; Restatement, Contracts § 309.

56. Specialities Development Corp. v. C-O-Two Fire Equip. Co., 207 F.2d 753 (3rd Cir. 1953), cert. denied 347 U.S. 919, 74 S.Ct. 519, 98 L.Ed. 1074; Longenecker v. Brommer, 59 Wash.2d 552, 368 P.2d 900 (1962); see 3A Corbin § 755; Restatement, Contracts § 309.

57. John Service, Inc. v. Goodnow-Pearson Co., 242 Mass. 594, 136 N.E. 623, 29 A.L.R. 1513 (1922); Cahen v. Platt, 69 N.Y. 348 (1877); see Annot. 29 A.L.R. 1513 (1924). Repeated elections to continue performance do not ordinarily bind the party electing to the same course in the event that he has a right to make another election. United Shoe Mach. Co. v. Abbott, 158 F. 762 (8th Cir. 1908); Daniels v. Boston & M. R. Co., 184 Mass. 337, 68 N. E. 337 (1903); W. P. Harlin Constr. Co. v. Utah State Road Comm'n, 19 Utah 2d 364, 431 P.2d 792 (1967); Fox v. Grange, 261 Ill. 116, 103 N.E. 576 (1913). Additional cases are collected in 3A Corbin § 754 n. 15.

is made where the promisor merely retains possession of his own property, as where he utilizes a structure which fails to meet the test of substantial performance. Such use does not in itself create an election.[58] As we have seen, an election to continue performance is often manifested by conduct; that is, by accepting performance despite the breach. An election by conduct requires no consideration.[59] An election made in the form of a promise, however, according to the Restatement, requires consideration or detrimental reliance unless the condition was not a material part of the agreed exchange.[60] A good number of cases, however, hold that even in the case of an election expressed in words neither consideration nor detrimental reliance is required.[61]

§ 170.   Giving Unjustifiable Reasons for Refusing to Perform as an Excuse of a Condition

In stating his reasons for rejecting performance or his objections to a performance which he has accepted a promisee runs the risk of excusing other grounds upon which he might have rejected a defective performance at least under some of the decided cases.[62] But the better view is that this result should obtain only where there is in the fact pattern a basis for an estoppel.[63] The Uniform Commercial Code outlines in some detail the burden thrust on the buyer to particularize his objections. First, in the case of accepted goods he is barred from any remedy if he does not notify the seller of his breach within a reasonable time after discovery.[64] Second, in the case of rejected goods he has the burden of notifying the seller of defects which are ascertainable by reasonable inspection. He is barred from relying upon any such unstated defect if the seller could have cured the defect if it had been stated seasonably.[65] Moreover, between merchants, if the seller requests in writing a full statement of all defects upon which the buyer proposes to rely, the buyer is deemed to have waived all defects which he could have ascertained by reason-

---

58. Cawley v. Weiner, 236 N.Y. 357, 140 N.E. 724 (1923).

59. Brede v. Rosedale Terrace Co., 216 N.Y. 246, 110 N.E. 430 (1915); Restatement, Contracts § 309.

60. Restatement, Contracts § 310.

61. Champion Spark Plug Co. v. Automobile Sundries Co., 273 F. 74 (2d Cir. 1921); Bowman v. Surety Fund Life Ins. Co., 149 Minn. 118, 182 N.W. 991 (1921); Thompson v. Postal Life Ins. Co., 226 N.Y. 363, 123 N.E. 750 (1919).

62. Cummings v. Connecticut Gen. Life Ins. Co., 102 Vt. 351, 148 A. 484 (1930).

63. New England Structures, Inc. v. Loranger, 354 Mass. 62, 234 N.E.2d 888 (1968); Cawley v. Weiner, 236 N.Y. 357, 140 N.E. 724 (1923); Restatement, Contracts §§ 304, 305.

64. U.C.C. § 2–607(3).

65. U.C.C. § 2–605(1) (a); cf. U.C.C. § 2–508.

able inspection which are not particularized in his reply to the seller's request.[66] The Code provisions, although placing a considerable burden upon the buyer are somewhat less burdensome than the rule announced in a number of pre-Code cases which had held that when an objection was made, all other objections not stated were waived.[67] It is to be noted that under these Code provisions the waiver operates not only as a waiver of condition but also as a renunciation of the right to damages.[68]

§ 171. Waiver of Condition is Not Waiver of Right to Damages for Breach

The facts which constitute a failure of condition often also constitute a breach of contract. For example, if a building contract contains a promise that the structure will be completed before January 1st and that time is of the essence, completion of the building on January 30th involves both a breach of contract and a failure of condition. If the person for whose benefit the condition was agreed upon effectively elects to continue performance he has merely lost the right to terminate his performance and to reject the performance of the other party; he does not thereby lose his right to damages for the breach,[69] although he may be required to indicate within a reasonable time after breach that he intends to assert these rights.[70] It should be pointed out, however, that the language or conduct of the aggrieved party may indicate not only a waiver of condition but also a renunciation of rights to damages.[71]

---

66. U.C.C. § 2–605(1) (b).

67. E. g., Littlejohn v. Shaw, 159 N.Y. 188, 53 N.E. 810 (1899).

68. See §§ 171, 339 infra.

69. Phillips & Colby Constr. Co. v. Seymour, 91 U.S. 646, 23 L.Ed. 341 (1875); Federal Welding Serv., Inc. v. Dioguardi, 295 F.2d 882 (2d Cir. 1961); Glen Cove Marina, Inc. v. Vessel Little Jennie, 269 F.Supp. 877 (E.D.N.Y. 1967); Barton v. Morin, 281 Mass. 98, 183 N.E. 170 (1932); Dunn v. Steubing, 120 N.Y. 232, 24 N.E. 315 (1890). The distinction between waiver of condition and discharge of a right to damages is sometimes lost sight of. See Western Transmission Corp. v. Colorado Mainline, Inc., 376 F.2d 470 (10th Cir. 1967), where the court, although reaching a correct result, assumed that plaintiff's continued acceptance of defendant's performance after breach ordinarily results in a waiver of a right to damages. The court found a supposed exception to this supposed rule. Compare Sitlington v. Fulton, 281 F.2d 552 (10th Cir. 1960); Robberson Steel Co. v. Harrell, 177 F.2d 12 (10th Cir. 1949) for sounder analyses.

70. See, e. g., U.C.C. § 2–607(3) (a): "the buyer must within a reasonable time after he discovers or should have discovered any breach notify the seller of breach or be barred from any remedy; . . ." This provision applies to accepted goods. For rejected goods see U.C.C. § 2–605.

71. See § 339 infra.

The terminology utilized in the Uniform Commercial Code is apt to cause confusion on this point. Although the Code in Section 2–209 utilizes the term "waiver" in the same sense as it is used in the Restatement and in this book, that is, in the sense of waiver of condition, in Section 1–107 the word seems to be used in a different sense. This provision reads:

> "Any claim or right arising out of an alleged breach can be discharged in whole or in part by a written waiver or renunciation signed and delivered by the aggrieved party."

After a material breach the aggrieved party has at least two "rights." One of these is the power to declare his obligations at an end; the other is the right to sue for damages. If the aggrieved party "waives" his rights to damages, under this section, it is a valid release without consideration. If he waives his power to declare the contract at an end (that is, elects to continue performance), under pre-Code law neither a writing nor a consideration is required. It is doubtful whether the draftsmen of the Code intended to impose a writing requirement in this second situation. It is likely that the term "waiver" is used in this section solely in the sense of "release." This conclusion is reinforced by the use in this section of the term "discharged," which, as a term of art, is used in connection with "release."

§ 172. Excuse of Conditions Involving Forfeitures

In Ledford v. Atkins,[72] the plaintiff was the assignee of a lease of mineral rights. Pursuant to the lease he had expended about $250,000 in exploring for oil on the premises. Plaintiff failed to make a required rental payment to his assignor on May 1st: On that day, and for two months prior to that day he was bedridden with a serious illness. On May 13th the rental payment plus interest was tendered to, and refused by, the defendant. Ordinarily, in oil leases, time is considered to be of the essence.[73] Failure to make payment on the due date results in a forfeiture of the lessee's interests. The Court, recognizing this general rule, nevertheless held that the failure of condition should be excused in the light of the lack of wilfulness of the breach and the harsh forfeiture which would otherwise result.[74] The dissenting judge took a more traditional view.

---

72. 413 S.W.2d 68 (Ky.1967).

73. See Annot. 5 A.L.R.2d 993 (1949).

74. Mere illness of the obligor does not give rise to an excuse by virtue of impossibility of performance; the duty to pay could have been delegated to another. See § 197 infra. Cf. Berry v. Crawford, 237 Ark. 380, 373 S.W.2d 129 (1963); Note, 18 Ark.L.Rev. 175 (1964).

"When grown men have seen fit to place such a requirement in the contract, without condition, qualification or provision against unforeseen circumstances, I do not feel a court should modify it."

The Restatement generalizes cases of this kind in section 302.

"A condition may be excused without other reason if its requirement

     (a) will involve extreme forfeiture or penalty, and

     (b) its existence or occurrence forms no essential part of the exchange for the promisor's performance."

Courts seldom rely on the Restatement rule quoted above, and generally continue to articulate the rule that strict compliance with an express condition precedent is required. Nevertheless, it is also true that the doctrines of substantial performance and divisibility are based primarily on the idea of relieving a forfeiture. So too are the increasing statutory enactments and expanding quasi contractual remedies designed to grant relief to a defaulting plaintiff. Moreover, a waiver or other excuse of condition will more readily be found when a forfeiture would otherwise result than when it would not. Where these mitigating doctrines are inapplicable, in a proper case, the rule of Restatement § 302 provides a sound outlet for the court's instinct for justice.

§ 173. Excuse of Condition by Impossibility

At times, a condition may be excused by impossibility. Discussion of this kind of excuse is best reserved for later consideration when the question of impossibility is considered in all its aspects.[75]

75.   See § 194 infra.

CHAPTER 10

BREACH OF CONTRACT—REPUDIATION

Analysis

Sec.
174. Introduction.
175. Repudiation.
176. What Constitutes a Repudiation.
177. Positive Statement of Unwillingness or Inability to Perform as a Repudiation.
178. Transferring or Contracting to Transfer Specific Property to a Third Person or Performing Any Voluntary Affirmative Act Which Renders Performance Substantially Impossible.
179. Repudiation and Good Faith.
180. What Constitutes Repudiation Under the Uniform Commercial Code.
181. Insolvency and Bankruptcy as Equivalents of Repudiation.
182. Retraction of a Repudiation.
183. Courses Open to the Promisee.
184. Does a Repudiation Always Justify an Immediate Action for Total Breach?
185. Successive Actions for Breach—Splitting an Indivisible Cause of Action.

§ 174. Introduction

Any failure to perform a contractual duty which has become absolute constitutes a breach.[1] This is so even if the party who was to have received the performance has benefited by its non-performance.[2] Many aspects of the subject matter of breach have previously been discussed, such as the distinction between a material (total) breach and an immaterial (partial) breach and the consequences of the distinction.[3] Thus the subject matter of this chapter is rather limited. Two questions not discussed elsewhere in this volume are discussed here; first, the question of breach by repudiation and second, the question of whether more than one action may be brought on a contract, a problem generally discussed under the rubric of "splitting a cause of action."

§ 175. Repudiation

We have previously considered the effect of prospective inability or unwillingness to perform from the point of view of whether the party whose right to receive the performance is endangered may sus-

1. Restatement, Contracts § 312.

2. Beattie v. New York, N. H. & H. R. R., 84 Conn. 555, 80 A. 709 (1911).

3. See § 157 supra.

278

pend or cancel his duty of performance.[4] In the context of this chapter the question discussed is whether a party to whom a repudiation has been communicated may institute an action for breach of contract. If the repudiation takes place at the time performance is due, clearly a breach has been committed. However, if the repudiation takes place before the time for performance the problem is more complicated. Since no performance is yet due, there is no failure of performance of an absolute duty. The effect of such a repudiation has received a good deal of attention by the courts and writers.[5]

All discussion of the problem revolves around the case of Hochster v. De La Tour.[6] In April 1852 the plaintiff and defendant entered into a contract by the terms of which the plaintiff was to work for a fixed period commencing on June 1, 1852. On May 11, 1852, the defendant stated he would not perform. The plaintiff brought an action for breach of contract on May 22, 1852 and issue was joined on the defendant's contention that as of that point no breach had occurred.

The court in upholding a jury verdict for the plaintiff ruled that the action was not premature. It reasoned erroneously that unless the plaintiff were free to sue immediately he would have to wait for an actual breach (which under the court's analysis could not possibly occur before June 1)[7] before he could change his position by, for example, getting another job. As the court saw the problem the plaintiff would otherwise be caught in a dilemma: to remain idle and hope

4. See § 163 supra.

5. Leading articles are Ballantine, Anticipatory Breach and the Enforcement of Contractual Duties, 22 Mich. L.Rev. 329 (1924), Selected Readings 1072; Limburg, Anticipatory Repudiation of Contracts, 10 Cornell L.Q. 135 (1925), Selected Readings 1090; Vold, The Tort Aspect of Anticipatory Repudiation of Contracts, 41 Harv.L. Rev. 340 (1928), Selected Readings 1127; Vold, Withdrawal of Repudiation after Anticipatory Breach of Contract, 5 Texas L.Rev. 9 (1926), Selected Readings 1154; Wardrop, Prospective Inability in the Law of Contracts, 20 Minn.L.Rev. 380 (1936); Williston, Repudiation of Contracts (pts. 1 & 2), 14 Harv.L.Rev. 317, 421 (1901), Selected Readings 1044, 1055.

6. 118 Eng.Rep. 922 (Q.B.1853).

7. Under the facts it might be argued that the defendant would not commit a present breach until he was required by the contract to make the first payment. However, it is clear that a breach would have occurred on June 1, if the defendant on that date refused to permit the plaintiff to perform the services for which he was engaged as this would have been a breach of the defendant's duty of cooperation. Indeed, it could be argued that a repudiation may constitute a breach of a duty of cooperation even before any performance is due. See 11 Williston § 1316. For a suggestion that a repudiation always has this effect, see Equitable Trust Co. of New York v. Western Pac. Ry. Co., 244 F. 485, 501–02 (S.D.N.Y.1917), aff'd 250 F. 327 (2d Cir. 1918), cert. denied 246 U.S. 672, 38 S.Ct. 423, 62 L.Ed. 932 (1918). This question is discussed in more detail below in this section.

in the future for a favorable court judgment or to obtain other employment thereby forfeiting his rights against the defendant as he could not then prove that he was ready, willing and able to perform at the agreed time.[8] The court, misled by defendant's counsel,[9] overlooked the rule that where a party manifests prospective unwillingness to perform the other party may suspend his performance and change his position without surrendering his right to sue after the breach occurs. In other words, the court might have looked at the repudiation as (1) a defense to any action brought by the defendant against the employee and (2) in an action brought by the plaintiff after June 1 as an excuse of the constructive condition that the plaintiff be ready, willing and able to perform.[10]

Although based on erroneous premises, the doctrine of anticipatory breach, or more properly, breach by virtue of anticipatory repudiation, has been generally followed both in England and in the United States.[11] Massachusetts maintains its striking position in American contract law as the guardian of rearguard positions by its non-acceptance of the doctrine.[12]

Since the case which introduced the doctrine was based on erroneous premises, it has been hostilely received by many influential writers. Partially as a result of this academic hostility a number of limitations which are not inherent in the nature of the doctrine have been accepted by the courts. To illustrate the depth of this hostility,

8. This in essence was the argument of defendant's counsel, although he also argued that the repudiation should be regarded as an offer to a mutual rescission which the plaintiff was free to accept or reject.

9. The case illustrates very pointedly one aspect of the art of advocacy. Defendant's counsel understated radically the plaintiff's equities and rights. The understatement was counter-productive. It led the court to invent new doctrine to protect the plaintiff.

10. See § 183 infra.

11. See 4 Corbin § 959; 11 Williston § 1312.

12. Daniels v. Newton, 114 Mass. 530, 19 Am.Rep. 384 (1874) is the leading case. For a qualification, see Tucker v. Connors, 342 Mass. 376, 173 N.E.2d 619, 623 (1961) (equitable action for specific performance).

Nebraska has been cited as being in opposition to the doctrine, but see the analysis of the Nebraska cases in Vold, Repudiation of Contracts, 5 Neb.L.Bull. 269 (1927).

Even under the Massachusetts view of the matter, the promisee may cancel the contract, J. K. Welding Co. v. W. J. Halloran Steel Erection Co., 178 F. Supp. 584 (D.R.I.1959) (applying Massachusetts law), and recover the value of any performance he has rendered in a quasi-contractual action. Johnson v. Starr, 321 Mass. 566, 74 N.E.2d 137 (1947); 11 Williston § 1314.

Massachusetts also permits an action for total breach where there is a present breach coupled with a repudiation of further obligations stemming from the contract. Parker v. Russell, 133 Mass. 74 (1882) (promise to support plaintiff for life).

the following quotation from Professor Terry of Columbia will suffice. In a book review complimenting Professor Williston's treatment of the doctrine, he states that the "fearlessness with which the author stamps in no uncertain terms and with clearness of logic and irrefutable argument those vicious errors which have crept in, in one way or another, but which should be extirpated for the everlasting good of the science, can be illustrated in no better way than by his attack upon the false doctrine of 'anticipatory breach.' That doctrine, as the author well demonstrates, is not and never has been defensible. . . . There can be no fine-spun reasoning which will successfully make that a breach of promise which, in fact, is not a breach of promise. . . . To say that it may be broken by anticipation is to say that which, in the nature of things, cannot be so." [13]

Is it indeed possible that a doctrine which in a few generations swept practically the entire common law world is so illogical as to violate the "nature of things?" On the contrary, it is submitted that the doctrine does not offend logic and is supported by practical wisdom. As far as logic goes, a contract is usually formed by promises, but the obligation of a contract is the sum of duties thrust by law on the promisor or promisors by virtue of the promises. There is no lack of logic in the law's imposition of a duty not to repudiate, as, for example, it has imposed constructive conditions and duties of cooperation on the contracting parties. This duty not to repudiate imposed by law may be breached although the express promise is not.[14] Whether this duty is articulated in terms of an implied promise that neither party "will do anything to the prejudice of the other inconsistent with that [contractual] relation" [15] or in terms that "the promisee has an inchoate right to the performance of the bargain . . . he has a right to have the contract kept open as a subsisting and effective contract," [16] is unimportant. There is no lack of power in a common law court to develop the law by imposing duties. The exercise of this power is no offense to logic, much less to "the nature of things." As far as the wisdom of imposing a duty not to repudiate, there is much to say for it. Very often a repudiation is made because the repudiator believes he is justified in so doing. The sooner this issue is resolved, the better. Let it be resolved when memories are fresh and witnesses available. From a more substantive point of view, a right to a future performance is of present economic value. Usually, it may be dealt with in the market as an asset, either

13. Book Review, 34 Harv.L.Rev. 891, 894 (1921), Selected Readings 1259, 1263.

14. See Ballantine, supra note 5.

15. Hochster v. De La Tour, 118 Eng. Rep. 922, 926 (Q.B. 1853).

16. Frost v. Knight [1872] L.R. 7 Ex. 111.

by outright assignment or by assignment as security for a loan. Apart from this possibility, its presence or absence on a balance sheet affects credit standings. A repudiated right, however, is of little value on the market or on an honest financial statement since the statement usually must indicate that the right in question is contested. Moreover, a promisee has a valuable interest, trite as it may seem, in peace of mind. Will his expectation of a future benefit materialize? The sooner the community enables him to obtain an answer, the sooner it will have performed one of the most valuable functions the law can serve.

With the advent and acceptance of the doctrine of anticipatory breach it was predictable that generally speaking the same rules would apply whether a repudiation is anticipatory or present. Therefore, in the remainder of the discussion no distinction will be drawn between anticipatory and present repudiations except where a distinction exists in the cases.

§ 176. What Constitutes a Repudiation

The Restatement of Contracts lists three actions which constitute repudiation. These are: "(a) a positive statement to the promisee or other person having a right under the contract, indicating that the promisor will not or cannot substantially perform his contractual duties; (b) transferring or contracting to transfer to a third person an interest in specific land, goods, or in any other thing essential for the substantial performance of his contractual duties; (c) any voluntary affirmative act which renders substantial performance of his contractual duties impossible, or apparently impossible." [17] In addition, the Uniform Commercial Code adds to this list a kind of constructive repudiation and, for some purposes, an adjudication of bankruptcy is treated as the equivalent of a repudiation.

§ 177. Positive Statement of Unwillingness or Inability to Perform as a Repudiation

We have previously seen that if S agrees to sell a car to B on June 1 and B agrees to pay on May 1 and S wrongfully repudiates his obligation under the contract in April, B may suspend his performance and change his position under the doctrine of prospective unwillingness to perform.[18] Under the doctrine of anticipatory repudiation B may sue immediately after the repudiation because the statement by S that he will not perform constitutes an anticipatory breach.[19]

17. Restatement, Contracts § 318.

18. See § 163 supra.

19. Hochster v. De La Tour, 118 Eng. Rep. 922 (Q.B.1853); Wells v. Hart-

However, a statement by the seller to the effect that "I doubt that I will perform" does not amount to a repudiation and therefore would not permit an immediate action under the doctrine of anticipatory breach but of course would justify the application of the doctrine of prospective unwillingness to perform.[20] In other words, the buyer would not be permitted to sue for breach of contract but could suspend his performance and demand assurances and take such other measures as are permitted under the doctrine of prospective unwillingness or inability to perform. So, also, if the promisor states that he will not perform unless a specified event occurs, this is deemed not to be a positive statement even though the event is not likely to happen.[21]

It should be observed that a repudiation occurs when a promisor positively states that he cannot perform. If he cannot perform but does not so state, subject to the rules stated in the next section, there is not a repudiation,[22] although once again the doctrine of prospective inability to perform may come into play.

§ 178. Transferring or Contracting to Transfer Specific Property to a Third Person or Performing Any Voluntary Affirmative Act Which Renders Performance Substantially Impossible

We have discussed in detail the effect of a transfer to a third person of anything essential for the substantial performance of the promisor's promise from the point of view of prospective inability or unwillingness to perform. The question here is whether such a transfer amounts to a repudiation. The all but unanimous view is that such conduct if it amounts to prospective unwillingness or inability to perform also amounts to a repudiation.[23]

So also if A contracts to work and B contracts to employ A for a year beginning in ten days and A embarks for a voyage around the world there is not only a prospective inability and unwillingness to perform but also a repudiation.[24]

ford Manilla Co., 76 Conn. 27, 35, 55 A. 599, 602 (1903) ("the renunciation must be so distinct that its purpose is manifest, and so absolute that the intention to no longer abide by the terms of the contract is beyond question."); Marek v. McHardy, 234 La. 841, 101 So.2d 689 (1958); 4 Corbin § 973; 11 Williston § 1322.

20. Restatement, Contracts § 280; 11 Williston § 1331.

21. Dingley v. Oler, 117 U.S. 490, 6 S. Ct. 850, 29 L.Ed. 984 (1886); McCloskey & Co. v. Minweld Steel Co., 220 F.2d 101 (3d Cir. 1955).

22. Restatement, Contracts § 318, Comment h.

23. Miller v. Baum, 400 F.2d 176 (5th Cir. 1968); Pappas v. Crist, 223 N.C. 265, 25 S.E.2d 850 (1943); Allen v. Wolf River Lumber Co., 169 Wis. 253, 172 N.W. 158, 9 A.L.R. 271 (1919).

24. Restatement, Contracts § 318, ill. 6.

§ 179. Repudiation and Good Faith

Frequently a party states that he will not perform or takes some action which objectively constitutes a repudiation and does so with the most honorable of motives. In good faith he believes that the contract entitles him to act as he did or that he has a lawful excuse for his action. There is respectable authority to the effect that a good faith disclaimer is not a repudiation.[25] By far the prevailing view, however, is that the test should be objective and that good faith is immaterial.[26]

§ 180. What Constitutes Repudiation Under the Uniform Commercial Code

The Uniform Commercial Code contains several provisions which bear upon the problem of anticipatory repudiation. It does not define what constitutes a repudiation and therefore prior law remains viable as authority on the point.[27] A comment to § 2–610, however, states that "Repudiation can result from action which reasonably indicates a rejection of the continuing obligation."[28] This statement indicates a less rigid test than had existed under prior law. It is unfortunate that if this was the intent of the codifiers, they failed to enunciate this test in the text of the Code.[29]

The Code, however, has clearly added an additional form of repudiation to those known under prior law. As we have seen, the Code provides that when reasonable grounds for insecurity arise a party may demand adequate assurance of due performance and suspend his performance until he receives such assurance.[30] The same section of the Code provides: "After receipt of a justified demand failure to provide within a reasonable time not exceeding thirty days such assurance of due performance as is adequate under the circumstances of the particular case is a repudiation of the contract."

§ 181. Insolvency and Bankruptcy as Equivalents of Repudiation

It has been previously noted that insolvency gives rise to application of the doctrine of prospective inability to perform. It is generally held, however, that under ordinary circumstances the insolven-

---

25. New York Life Ins. Co. v. Viglas, 297 U.S. 672, 56 S.Ct. 615, 80 L.Ed. 971 (1936); Grismore § 184.

26. 4 Corbin § 973; 11 Williston § 1323; Restatement, Contracts § 318 set forth in § 176 supra.

27. § 1–103 of the Code provides: "Unless displaced by the particular provi-

sions of this Act, the principles of law and equity . . . shall supplement its provisions."

28. U.C.C. § 2–610, Comment 2.

29. U.C.C. § 2–609(1); see § 163 supra.

30. U.C.C. § 2–609.

cy of a promisor does not have the effect of a repudiation because it is not voluntarily caused.[31] The Uniform Commercial Code puts this rule on a new basis. Actual or apparent insolvency creates reasonable grounds for insecurity and, as discussed in § 180 above, permits the insecure party to demand assurance and to sue for breach if he does not receive it. In addition, the Code provides for other means whereby a party may protect himself in the event of the other's insolvency.[32] These provisions do not, however, involve the concept of anticipatory breach.

It is well established that bankruptcy of a party is the equivalent of a repudiation [33] provided that the trustee in bankruptcy does not adopt the contract within a reasonable time.[34] It is quite clear that this rule was adopted, not as a logical consequence of the doctrine of anticipatory breach, but as a policy decision to facilitate allowance of unmatured claims in bankruptcy proceedings.[35] If a petition in bankruptcy is filed but does not result in an adjudication of bankruptcy,

---

31. Restatement, Contracts § 324; 4 Corbin § 985.

32. U.C.C. § 2–502:

(1) Subject to subsection (2) and even though the goods have not been shipped a buyer who has paid a part or all of the price of goods in which he has a special property under the provisions of the immediately preceding section may on making and keeping good a tender of any unpaid portion of their price recover them from the seller if the seller becomes insolvent within ten days after receipt of the first installment on their price.

(2) If the identification creating his special property has been made by the buyer he acquires the right to recover the goods only if they conform to the contract for sale.

U.C.C. § 2–702:

(1) Where the seller discovers the buyer to be insolvent he may refuse delivery except for cash including payment for all goods theretofore delivered under the contract, and stop delivery under this Article (Section 2–705).

(2) Where the seller discovers that the buyer has received goods on credit while insolvent he may reclaim the goods upon demand made within ten

days after the receipt, but if misrepresentation of solvency has been made to the particular seller in writing within three months before delivery the ten day limitation does not apply. Except as provided in this subsection the seller may not base a right to reclaim goods on the buyer's fraudulent or innocent misrepresentation of solvency or of intent to pay.

(3) The seller's right to reclaim under subsection (2) is subject to the rights of a buyer in ordinary course or other good faith purchaser under this Article (Section 2–403). Successful reclamation of goods excludes all other remedies with respect to them.

33. Here, as in the case of prospective inability to perform, there is no repudiation if the promised performance does not require financial ability on the part of the promisor. See § 163 supra; Restatement, Contracts § 324, ill. 2; 4 Corbin § 985.

34. Central Trust Co. of Illinois v. Chicago Auditorium Ass'n, 240 U.S. 581, 36 S.Ct. 412, 60 L.Ed. 811 (1916); Restatement, Contracts § 324, Comment a.

35. 4 Corbin § 985; 11 Williston § 1325.

the legal effect is similar to that of a withdrawal of a repudiation.[36] It follows that if the claim is provable in bankruptcy under the doctrine here discussed, failure of the promisee to prove his claim in the bankruptcy proceedings will terminate his rights against the bankrupt.[37]

§ 182. Retraction of a Repudiation

Section 2–611(1) of the U.C.C. states: "Until the repudiating party's next performance is due he can retract his repudiation unless the aggrieved party has since the repudiation cancelled or materially changed his position or otherwise indicated that he considers the repudiation final." This is in general accord with the common law rule that a repudiation may be retracted until the other party has commenced an action thereon or has otherwise changed his position.[38] The Code makes it clear, however, that it is sufficient if the aggrieved party states that he relies upon the repudiation.[39] No other act in reliance is necessary.

Retraction of a repudiation is ordinarily written or verbal; but where the repudiation consists of acts inconsistent with the contract the retraction may consist in the repudiator's regaining his ability to perform.[40] However, to be effective this fact must be communicated.[41]

In the case of anticipatory repudiation, if the repudiation is withdrawn in time it is generally held, somewhat anomalously, that there is no breach.[42] The Uniform Commercial Code does not completely

36. Restatement, Contracts § 324, Comment a. On the effect of a withdrawal of a repudiation, see § 182 infra.

37. Restatement, Contracts § 324, ill. 3; but cf. ill. 2 as to certain obligations which are not discharged in bankruptcy.

38. Roehm v. Horst, 178 U.S. 1, 20 S. Ct. 780, 44 L.Ed. 953 (1900); Guerrieri v. Severini, 51 Cal.2d 12, 330 P.2d 635 (1958). The change of position need not be communicated. Bu-Vi-Bar Petroleum Corp. v. Krow, 40 F.2d 488, 69 A.L.R. 1295 (10th Cir. 1930).

39. Accord, United States v. Seacoast Gas Co., 204 F.2d 709 (5th Cir. 1953), cert. denied 346 U.S. 866, 74 S.Ct. 106, 98 L.Ed. 377 (1953); Louisville Packing Co. v. Crain, 141 Ky. 379, 132 S. W. 575 (1910); Simpson, § 128.

40. 11 Williston § 1335.

41. Restatement, Contracts § 319. § 2–611(2) of the Code provides: "Retraction may be by any method which clearly indicates to the aggrieved party that the repudiating party intended to perform, but must include any assurance justifiably demanded under the provisions of this Article (Section 2–609)."

42. Restatement, Contracts § 319, Comment a. Another peculiarity of the anticipatory breach doctrine is that the courts hold that the statute of limitations does not begin to run until there is a failure to perform. Brewer v. Simpson, 53 Cal.2d 567, 2 Cal.Rptr. 609, 349 P.2d 289 (1960); Ga Nun v. Palmer, 202 N.Y. 483, 96 N.E. 99, 36 L.R.A.,N.S., 922 (1911); Restatement, Contracts § 322; 4 Corbin § 989.

adopt this concept when it provides: "Retraction reinstates the repudiating party's rights under the contract with due excuse and allowance to the aggrieved party for any delay occasioned by the repudiation." [43]

§ 183.   Courses Open to the Promisee

After the enunciation of the doctrine of anticipatory breach in Hochster v. De La Tour,[44] the courts had a great deal of difficulty in coherently working out all of its ramifications—a difficulty commonly occurring in the wake of any new doctrine.   An early English case interpreted the doctrine as granting the promisee the power to elect to treat the repudiation as a breach or not as he saw fit.[45] This rule, seemingly fair, had some unfortunate logical consequences [46] which have resulted in some unjust decisions. The more recent cases, however, have placed the law on a sounder footing.

Under the concept of election the courts, as indicated in the previous section, satisfactorily worked out the rule that no retraction of a repudiation is possible after a change of position by the promisee; the change of position being regarded as a sufficient election.

Suppose, however, the promisee elects to ignore the repudiation and proceeds with his performance. Suppose, for example, the promisor contracts to pay for the building of a bridge and in advance of any performance repudiates.[47] May the promisee elect to proceed with his performance? Under the election theory a number of American cases reached the conclusion that the promisee may elect to perform.[48] The modern cases representing the great weight of authority hold that the duty to mitigate damages overrides the concept of election and the promisee must not perform if the effect of performance would be

43.   U.C.C. § 2–611(3).

44.   118 Eng.Rep. 922 (Q.B.1853).

45.   Johnstone v. Milling, [1886] 16 Q.B. 460, 472.

46.   Although the American cases often utilize the same terminology as the English cases, they have largely avoided the consequences which the English courts have drawn from the concept of election. 11 Williston § 1320.

47.   This illustration is derived from Rockingham County v. Luten Bridge Co., 35 F.2d 301, 66 A.L.R. 735 (4th Cir. 1929). This case, however, did not involve an anticipatory breach, but a present breach coupled with a

repudiation. Well before the doctrine of anticipatory breach originated, it was well established that a duty to mitigate damages existed in cases of this kind. Clark v. Marsiglia, 1 Denio 317, 43 Am.Dec. 670 (N.Y.1845).

48.   Reliance Cooperage Corp. v. Treat, 195 F.2d 977 (8th Cir. 1952); John A. Roebling's Sons Co. v. Lock-Stitch Fence Co., 130 Ill. 660, 22 N.E. 518 (1889). Many of the cases relying on this reasoning are sustainable on other grounds. E. g. Barber Milling Co. v. Leichthammer Baking Co., 273 Pa. 90, 116 A. 677, 27 A.L.R. 1227 (1922) (dealer in goods need not sell at time of buyer's repudiation to minimize damages; this rule explained in the chapter on Damages at § 216).

to enhance damages.[49] Conversely, suppose it is the party who is to build the bridge who repudiates: must the other party mitigate damages by securing another contractor? Again the modern view incorporated in the Uniform Commercial Code is, yes.[50] The Code (although of course not applicable to a construction contract) provides that the aggrieved party may "for a commercially reasonable time await performance by the repudiating party."[51] Comment 1 to this section adds: "But if he awaits performance beyond a commercially reasonable time he cannot recover resulting damages which he should have avoided." The Code is thus quite consistent with the general theory of mitigation; a doctrine which requires reasonable and not absolutely successful efforts to minimize damages.[52]

Similar problems arise when there is a repudiation which is not anticipatory but present. Here, under any theory, the rule of mitigation of damages is applicable and the non-breaching party has no right to recover for a subsequent performance which will enhance damages.[53] Since such a repudiation almost always will be a material breach, this rule acts as an exception to the general rule that in the face of a material breach the aggrieved party has the power to elect to continue his performance and sue for partial breach or to cancel the contract and sue for a total breach.[54]

An additional question is what is the legal consequence if the promisee urges or insists that the other party perform. An illustrative case is Bernstein v. Meech.[55] The plaintiff had contracted to perform in December at the defendants' theater. In August plaintiff wrote that he would not honor the engagement unless the promised remuneration were increased. Defendants replied insisting that the plaintiff comply with the contract. Defendants heard nothing further from plaintiff and booked other entertainers for the period in question. In December the plaintiff appeared at the theater and tendered his services which, for obvious reasons, were refused. The court, applying the election theory, held that the defendants by insist-

49. Bu-Vi-Bar Petroleum Corp. v. Krow, 40 F.2d 488, 69 A.L.R. 1295 (10th Cir. 1930); Cameron v. White, 74 Wis. 425, 43 N.W. 155, 5 L.R.A. 493 (1889). Other cases are collected in 4 Corbin § 983; 11 Williston §§ 1301–1303. Problems concerning mitigation and anticipatory breach are also considered in the chapter on Damages at § 216 et seq.

50. See the authorities cited in the previous note.

51. U.C.C. § 2–610(a).

52. See § 216 infra.

53. 11 Williston § 1336.

54. See § 163 supra.

55. 130 N.Y. 354, 29 N.E. 255 (1891); subsequent New York cases have overruled this case by implication. See, e. g., De Forest Radio Tel. & Tel. Co. v. Triangle Radio Supply Co., Inc., 243 N.Y. 283, 153 N.E. 75 (1926), rearg. denied 243 N.Y. 618, 154 N.E. 629.

ing on performance had elected to keep the contract alive and therefore were liable for breach of contract. Fortunately, the weight of authority,[56] the Restatement[57] and the Uniform Commercial Code take a position contrary to this decision. It is generally recognized that the presence or absence of a breach is dependent upon the repudiating party's actions alone. The aggrieved party's demand that his primary rights to performance of the contract be honored should not operate, without more, to divest him of his secondary rights to damages. The Code states that the non-repudiating party may "resort to any remedy for breach . . ., even though he has notified the repudiating party that he would await the latter's performance and has urged retraction."[58]

Another course open to the non-repudiating party is to do nothing and to institute an action for breach after the time for performance. Under the majority view he may bring such an action without tendering his own performance or even alleging or proving that he was ready, willing and able to perform.[59] He must show, however, that he would have been ready, willing and able to perform but for the repudiation.[60]

§ 184. Does a Repudiation Always Justify an Immediate Action for Total Breach?

We have seen that as a general rule a repudiation justifies an immediate action for a total breach. However there are exceptions.

For example, if B says to A, "If you walk across Brooklyn Bridge I'll pay you $10.00 one year after you finish walking" and A walks and B repudiates his obligation, A could not bring an immediate action for the $10.00. The anticipatory repudiation does not justify an

---

56. Renner Co. v. McNeff Bros., 102 F. 2d 664 (6th Cir. 1939), cert. denied 308 U.S. 576, 60 S.Ct. 92, 84 L.Ed. 483; Tri-Bullion Smelting & Dev. Co. v. Jacobsen, 233 F. 646 (2d Cir. 1916); Canada v. Wick, 100 N.Y. 127, 2 N.E. 381 (1885); 11 Williston §§ 1333, 1334.

57. Restatement, Contracts § 320.

58. U.C.C. § 2–610(b). This rule can on occasion be rather harsh on the repudiating party. See Duesenberg and King, Sales & Bulk Transfers § 14.-06[2] [a]. It may be pointed out, however, that the repudiator is responsible for his own plight.

59. Plunkett v. Comstock, Cheney Co., 211 App.Div. 737, 208 N.Y.S. 93 (1st Dep't 1925); Midwest Eng. Co. v. Electric Regulator Corp., 435 P.2d 89 (Okl.1957); Hurwitz v. David K. Richards & Co., 20 Utah 2d 232, 436 P.2d 794 (1968); 11 Williston § 1337.

60. Spartans Industries, Inc. v. John Pilling Shoe Co., 385 F.2d 495 (1st Cir. 1967); Model Vending Co. v. Stanisci, 74 N.J.Super. 12, 180 A.2d 393 (1962); Ufitec, S.A. v. Trade Bank & Trust Co., 21 A.D.2d 187, 249 N.Y.S.2d 557 (1st Dep't 1964), aff'd 16 N.Y.2d 698, 261 N.Y.S.2d 893, 209 N.E.2d 551.

immediate action. The same would be true if the arrangement were bilateral and A had performed.[61]

So also if A loaned B $12,000.00 and B promised to repay $1,000.00 per month over the period of the next twelve months and B not only failed to pay his first instalment but unjustifiably repudiated his obligation, A could only recover $1,000.00 and could not recover for the other instalments until they severally matured.[62]

A similar problem arises in the case of a disability insurance policy where the insurance company claiming that the insured is not disabled refuses to make a monthly or a weekly payment called for by the policy and states that it will not make any further payments. Here again the majority of the cases have held that the insured even though disabled may sue only for instalments that are presently due.[63]

All of these cases have two factors in common. First, the plaintiff has completely performed and, second, the plaintiff is entitled to a fixed payment of money either at one time or in instalments. In other words, the defendant is under a unilateral obligation to pay a fixed amount of money at a fixed time or times. Apparently where these two conditions concur a repudiation does not permit an action for a payment which has not matured.[64] This is undoubtedly the ma-

---

61. Restatement, Contracts § 318, as amended in 1946; 4 Corbin §§ 962–969; 11 Williston §§ 1326–1330. Texas is in a distinct minority to the contrary. See Placid Oil Co. v. Humphrey, 244 F.2d 184 (5th Cir. 1957); Pollack v. Pollack, 23 S.W.2d 890 (Tex.Civ.App.1929), 39 S.W.2d 853 (Tex.Com.App.1931), reh. denied, 46 S.W.2d 292, 45 Harv.L.Rev. 585 (1932), 10 Tex.L.Rev. 236 (1932); 11 Williston § 1330.

62. Phelps v. Herro, 215 Md. 223, 137 A.2d 159 (1957).

63. N.Y. Life Ins. Co. v. Viglas, 297 U. S. 672, 56 S.Ct. 615, 80 L.Ed. 971 (1936); contra, Federal Life Ins. Co. v. Rascoe, 12 F.2d 693 (6th Cir. 1926), cert. denied 273 U.S. 722, 47 S.Ct. 112, 71 L.Ed. 859. For additional cases, see 4 Corbin § 969; 11 Williston § 1329. In a number of cases the court although limiting the plaintiff's recovery to instalments due at the time of commencement of the action, (or in some jurisdictions, at the date of judgment), also issued a decree for specific performance as to payment of

future instalments. John Hancock Mut. Life Ins. Co. v. Cohen, 254 F.2d 417 (9th Cir. 1958); Equitable Life Assur. Soc. v. Goble, 254 Ky. 614, 72 S.W.2d 35 (1935).

64. This problem is not limited to cases involving repudiation. For example, in the Viglas case cited in the previous note Mr. Justice Cardozo held that there was no repudiation because of the good faith of the insurance company. See § 179 supra. However even if there was no repudiation it is certainly arguable that there was a material breach, which under the general rule would allow an action for a total breach. 4 Corbin §§ 963, 966 and 967 and § 157 supra. However, despite the materiality of the breach there is no total breach because the two factors referred to in the text coexist. It should also be noted that the result reached is built into the Restatement definition of total breach which is defined in § 313 as "a breach where remedial rights provided by law are substituted for all the existing contractual rights, or can be so substi-

jority view although there are a number of cases to the contrary and this result has been much criticized.[65]

However where either one of these elements is missing the result is different. For example, "A transfers a farm to B in consideration of B's promise to support C for life. After supporting C for a week, B ceases to support C and repudiates the contract." The Restatement says that an action may be brought for a total breach so that damages for breach of the entire contract may be obtained in one action.[66] Here although A has completely performed there is no fixed amount or time for payment or payments and so one of the factors set forth above is missing.

Another interesting situation which recurs with some regularity arises when a life insurance company unjustifiably refuses to accept a premium. The majority view is that an action for total breach lies either for the recovery of premiums paid or for damages.[67] There is a minority view which refuses to permit an action for damages because the insured's rights can be protected in an action in equity for a declaratory judgment.[68] It would appear that the majority rule is correct even in terms of the rule previously stated because the plaintiff must still pay premiums under the contract to keep it in force.

It is the function of a book of this kind to state basic rules of contract law and to give some explanation of the rationale of the rules. In this section the task is rather difficult since no sound logical or practical ground has been advanced for the rule that no action lies for

tuted by the injured party." In the type of case under discussion since the plaintiff may recover only for instalments as they severally mature, it is clear that the remedial rights provided by law are not substituted for his contractual rights.

65. See, for example, 4 Corbin §§ 962–969. In a number of cases involving leases under which the only executory obligation is to pay rent, the court has allowed damages for breach when the lessee repudiated the obligation. E g., Novak v. Fontaine Furniture Co., 84 N.H. 93, 146 A. 525 (1929); cf. Sliman v. Fish, 177 La. 38, 147 So. 493 (1933) (action allowed for future rent and not merely damages). For an excellent decision in accord see Sagamore Corp. v. Willcutt, 120 Conn. 315, 180 A. 464 (1935), where the court placed the decision on the broad ground that an action for total breach

will lie where there has been a present breach coupled with a repudiation. Contra, Hermitage Co. v. Levine, 248 N.Y. 333, 162 N.E. 97, 59 A.L.R. 1015 (1928) (action for damages must await end of the term).

66. Restatement, Contracts § 317, ill. 6; see 4 Corbin § 970; 11 Williston § 1326.

67. Van Werden v. Equitable Life Assur. Soc., 99 Iowa 621, 68 N.W. 892 (1896); but cf. Barlow v. Grand Lodge A.O.U.W., 179 Iowa 1149, 162 N.W. 757 (1917); O'Neil v. Supreme Council Am. Legion of Honor, 70 N.J. L. 410, 57 A. 463 (Sup.Ct.1904); American Ins. Union v. Woodward, 118 Okl. 248, 247 P. 398, 48 A.L.R. 102 (1926).

68. Kelly v. Security Mut. Life Ins. Co., 186 N.Y. 16, 78 N.E. 584 (1906).

a repudiation of a unilateral obligation to pay money at a fixed time or times. Professor Williston, expressing hostility to the entire doctrine of anticipatory breach states that the rule as to unilateral obligations is justified because "it seems undesirable to enlarge the boundaries of the doctrine." [69] Such reasoning seems as sound as stating that the doctrine should exclude contracts made on Thursdays. He continues his argument by asserting that to permit such an action "is truly nothing but a direct bonus to the promisee beyond what he was promised and a direct penalty to the promisor." [70] By this is meant that to grant enforcement of the promise prior to maturity would be to remake the contract to the benefit of the promisee and to the injury of the promisor. If this argument were sound, it would be sound in any case in which damages are granted for breach of a contract involving performances to be rendered in the future. In an action for damages, however, the promise is not enforced as such, but a remedy is granted for breach of the obligations contained in the contract. There is no reason why the granting of the remedy of damages is any more of a bonus and penalty in this context as in any other.

In the cases involving disability insurance and other contracts for the payment of instalments for life, it has been argued that it would be much too speculative to award damages as the duration of the disability and of the plaintiff's life cannot be proved with absolute certainty.[71] While this is a plausible argument, such obstacles are routinely surmounted in tort cases and cases involving breach, anticipatory or otherwise, of executory bilateral contracts.

Another reason for the rule has been advanced: "The reason why a contract to pay money at a definite time in the future is an exception to the rule is that money is not a commodity which is sold and bought in the market and the market value of which fluctuates, as is the case with grain, stocks, and other similar articles." [72] This argument also misses its mark. Although, inflation aside, money does not fluctuate in value, the creditor's right to payment does fluctuate in value and, when repudiated by the debtor becomes nearly valueless as an asset.[73]

69. 11 Williston § 1326 at p. 150.

70. Id. at 150.

71. 11 Williston § 1329; and see Mabery v. Western Cas. & Sur. Co., 173 Kan. 586, 250 P.2d 824 (1952).

72. Alger-Fowler Co. v. Tracy, 98 Minn. 432, 437, 107 N.W. 1124, 1126 (1906).

73. See § 175 supra.

§ 185.   Successive Actions for Breach—Splitting an Indivisible Cause of Action

In earlier times, it was held that only one action could be maintained on one contract.[74] This rule has been replaced by the rule that an indivisible cause of action may not be split. The rationale for the present rule is that multiple actions would be unjust and vexatious to the defendant.[75] Consequently, if an action is brought, all damages which could have been, but were not, claimed in the action are lost.

Despite numerous attempts to arrive at a workable definition,[76] it is probably true that the term "cause of action" "has no such consistent and commonly accepted definition that it can be used to advantage." [77]   It is perhaps better to concentrate upon the question of the possible kinds of breaches of a contract.

When the contract is divisible, it seems generally to be agreed that a breach of each severable portion gives rise to a separate cause of action,[78] and there is a sound tendency to treat each breach of an obligation performable in instalments as a separate cause of action even if the contract is entire.[79] This proper resolution of the question whether successive actions may be brought for breach of an instalment of an entire contract is logically dependent upon the broader question of the relationship between the doctrines of material and partial breach on the one hand and of the aggrieved party's power to waive the failure of condition caused by a material breach.

It has previously been stated that where there has been a partial breach the aggrieved party does not have the power to cancel his obligation to perform but may institute an action for the damages caused him by the partial breach.[80] An illustration will show the problem. A agrees to build a number of cottages at staggered intervals for B who agrees to pay $35,000 upon completion of the entire contract. Periodic payments are not provided for in the contract. The first cottage is completed several months after the date provided for in the contract. B sues and recovers for partial breach as he has a right to. A subsequently abandons the work. What was a partial

---

74.   4 Corbin § 949.

75.   4 Corbin § 950; Clark, Code Pleading § 73 (2d ed. 1947); Clark, Joinder and Splitting of Causes of Action, 25 Mich.L.Rev. 393 (1926).

76.   See Clark, Code Pleading § 19 (2d ed. 1947).

77.   4 Corbin § 955; cf. Restatement, Judgments, Introductory Note to Ch.

3, Topic 2, Title D (1942), which indicates that the meaning of the term varies with the context.

78.   Restatement, Judgments § 62, Comment i; Kennedy v. City of N.Y., 196 N.Y. 19, 89 N.E. 360 (1909).

79.   4 Corbin § 949.

80.   See §§ 149, 157 supra.

breach has become a total breach. Logically, B should be permitted to institute another action for his additional damages. He should not be barred from recovery of those damages which he could not have recovered in the prior action.[81] There is another view of the matter which in effect takes the position that the aggrieved party should defer bringing the action until the consequences of the breach are clear and that if it should turn out that the breaching party will not perform his contract the plaintiff should take the risk of his haste in having brought the action.[82] Under this view the exercise of a legal right becomes a snare for the innocent.

A similar problem arises where there has been a material breach and the non-breaching party elects to continue the contract and sue for partial breach. He may make this election unless the breach is coupled with a repudiation.[83] Again, the better view is to the effect that recovery for partial breach does not bar an action for a subsequent breach which occurs after the first suit was instituted.[84] There is another view to the effect that in recovering in the first action the plaintiff has split a single cause of action.[85] Under this view the plaintiff by exercising his legal right to bring an action is forced to assume the risk that no future breaches of the contract will occur.

The same problem exists in instalment contracts which are entire rather than divisible. For example, if S fails to deliver the first instalment of goods under an entire contract and B sues for this breach and later S fails to deliver another instalment, may B sue for failure to deliver this instalment? It has sometimes been held that B cannot sue for the second breach because he could have sued for a total breach in the first action.[86] However, these decisions ignore

81. Restatement, Contracts § 449, Comment e; Restatement, Judgments § 62, Comment h; cf. Clark, Code Pleading § 74 (2d ed. 1947).

82. 11 Williston § 1293. None of the cases cited by this authority supports this broad a proposition. With the exception of Pakas v. Hollingshead, discussed at n. 86, infra, all of the cited cases involve either dictum or a clear repudiation by the breaching party.

83. It is almost universally accepted that if there is a breach coupled with a repudiation of a kind that permits an action for total breach, the plaintiff must bring his action for damages in one action. Arnold v. Masonic Country Club, 268 Mich. 430, 256 N.W.

472 (1934); Jameson v. Board of Ed., 78 W.Va. 612, 89 S.E. 255 (1916); 4 Corbin § 946; Clark, Code Pleading § 74 (2d ed. 1947); Restatement, Contracts § 449, Comment e; Restatement, Judgments § 62, Comment h; contra, Barron G. Collier, Inc. v. Rawson, 202 Iowa 1159, 211 N.W. 704 (1927) (employing the unfortunate concept of election in the face of a repudiation; see § 183 supra).

84. Restatement, Contracts § 449, Comment e; Restatement, Judgments § 62, Comment h.

85. 11 Williston § 1294.

86. Pakas v. Hollingshead, 184 N.Y. 211, 77 N.E. 40 (1906). There is, however, language in the opinion which

the power of the aggrieved party to waive the failure of condition and to continue the contract in force. A majority of cases appear to have permitted B to recover on the second breach.[87] The Uniform Commercial Code seems to have adopted this majority view as to instalment contracts. In Section 2–612(3) it provides: "the aggrieved party reinstates the contract . . . if he brings an action with respect only to past installments . . . ." By implication this means if there is a subsequent breach of the reinstated contract there is a new cause of action. The Code makes it clear, however, that there is no right of reinstatement by the aggrieved party if the defaulter repudiates his obligations.[88]

Closely related in policy to the rule against splitting a cause of action is the rule that even though there are successive breaches the plaintiff must sue for all of the breaches that have occurred prior to the commencement of his action or lose his right to any cause of action not included.[89] This rule is not generally deemed to apply to separate and distinct contracts.[90] However, if separate and distinct contracts constitute a running account [91] then the general rule stated above applies so that a suit on less than all of the breaches which have occurred will result in the loss of those claims not joined in the action.[92]

indicates that the first breach was accompanied by a repudiation. If this was indeed the case, the opinion is sound. This case should be compared with Perry v. Dickerson, 85 N.Y. 345 (1881) where the court appears to have reached an opposite result in the case of an employment contract, holding that upon discharge an employee may bring an action for damages and a second action for past due wages. This decision violates the rule stated at n. 89, infra.

87. Goodwin v. Cabot Amusement Co., 129 Me. 36, 149 A. 574 (1930). Although some cases have suggested that a different rule should apply to a "continuing" contract than applies to instalment contracts, this distinction is rejected by Corbin as rendering "no service" and operating "to dim or to conceal the true reasons on which a decision is or ought to be based." 4 Corbin § 956.

88. U.C.C. § 2–612, Comment 6. It is important to recall, however, that not every repudiation gives a right of ac-

tion for total breach. See § 184 supra. If there is no right of action for total breach it is clear that the plaintiff does not split his cause of action by suing for matured instalments only.

89. Thomas v. Carpenter, 123 Me. 241, 122 A. 576 (1899); See v. See, 294 Mo. 495, 242 S.W. 949, 24 A.L.R. 880 (1922); 4 Corbin § 952; 11 Williston § 1294.

90. Lozier Auto. Exchange v. Interstate Cas. Co., 197 Iowa 935, 195 N.W. 885 (1923). Negotiable bills and notes have long been regarded as separate contracts. 4 Corbin § 952.

91. Whether or not there is a running account appears to be a question of intent, often manifested by submission and acceptance of a consolidated bill for multiple purchases or services rendered. Corey v. Jaroch, 229 Mich. 313, 200 N.W. 957 (1924).

92. Kruce v. Lakeside Biscuit Co., 198 Mich. 736, 165 N.W. 609 (1917)

CHAPTER 11

IMPOSSIBILITY OF PERFORMANCE AND FRUSTRATION OF THE VENTURE

Analysis

Sec.
186. Impossibility of Performance: Introduction.
187. Destruction, Deterioration or Unavailability of the Subject Matter or Tangible Means of Performance.
188. Failure of the Contemplated Mode of Delivery or Payment.
189. Supervening Prohibition or Prevention by Law.
190. Failure of the Intangible Means of Performance.
191. Death or Illness.
192. Reasonable Apprehension of Impossibility or Danger.
193. Impracticability.
194. Impossibility as an Excuse of Condition.
195. Frustration of the Venture.
196. Temporary Impossibility or Frustration.
197. Personal versus Objective Impossibility or Frustration.
198. Contributory Fault, Foreseeability, Assumption of the Risk.
199. Assumption of the Risk—Technological Impossibility.
200. Effect of Impossibility Upon a Prior Repudiation.
201. Impossibility and Frustration Under the Uniform Commercial Code.

§ 186. Impossibility of Performance: Introduction

When an unforeseen event which makes impossible the performance of a contractual duty occurs subsequent to the formation of the contract and prior to the time when the duty to perform becomes absolute, it is often held that the promisor is excused from performing.[1] Such holdings are exceptions to the general rule that when a contractual promise is made, the promisor must perform or pay damages for his failure to perform no matter how burdensome performance has become as a result of unforeseen circumstances.[2]

The doctrine of supervening impossibility is a late development in the law, and therefore, its contours are less developed than many of the other doctrines of the law of contracts. Indeed, until 1863 it was generally assumed that impossibility of performance was no defense

---

1. If facts exist at the time an agreement is made which make performance impossible, the agreement does not create a contract, except if the promisor has reason to know of these facts or agrees to assume the risk of impossibility. Restatement, Contracts § 456; compare Restatement, Contracts § 35(1) (c), (d), (f).

2. Taylor v. Caldwell, 122 Eng.Rep. 309 (K.B.1863).

to an action for damages.[3] Since that year there has been a steady growth of exceptions to that assumption. These have generally been articulated in the terms of implied or constructive conditions. The parties are said to have contemplated the continued existence of a state of facts, and if these facts change so as to render impossible a party's performance, it is often said that there is a condition precedent to the promisor's duty that the facts contemplated continue to exist.

In determining whether such a condition will be imposed or implied, the key question is which party assumed the risk of the unforeseen circumstances; or, if no clear assumption is shown, to which party should the risk be allocated.[4] Another question is to what extent the rules which have been developed as to impossibility should be extended to situations in which performance, although possible, would be impracticable.

A modern statement of the impossibility doctrine appears in a recent case:[5]

> The doctrine of impossibility of performance has gradually been freed from the earlier fictional and unrealistic strictures of such tests as the 'implied term' and the parties' 'contemplation'. [citations omitted.] It is now recognized that 'A thing is impossible in legal contemplation when it is not practicable; and a thing is impracticable when it can only be done at an excessive and unreasonable cost,' [citations omitted]. The doctrine ultimately represents the ever-shifting line, drawn by courts hopefully responsive to commercial practices and mores, at which the community's interest in having contracts enforced according to their terms is outweighed by the commercial senselessness of requiring performance. When the issue is raised, the court is asked to construct a condition of performance based on changed circumstances, a process which involves at least three reasonably definable steps. First, a contingency—something unexpected—must have occurred. Second, the risk of the unexpected occurrence must not have been allocated either by agreement or by custom. Finally, occurrence of the contingency must have rendered performance commercially impracticable.

3. Id.

4. See 6 Corbin §§ 1320–72; Patterson, The Apportionment of Business Risks Through Legal Devices, 24 Colum.L. Rev. 335 (1924).

5. Transatlantic Financing Corp. v. United States, 124 U.S.App.D.C. 183, 363 F.2d 312, 315 (1966).

Although impossibility of performance may arise in many different ways, the tendency has been to classify the cases into several categories. These are: 1) Destruction, deterioration or unavailability of the subject matter or the tangible means of performance; 2) Failure of the contemplated mode of delivery or payment; 3) Supervening prohibition or prevention by law; 4) Failure of the intangible means of performance and 5) Death or illness. Closely related to the doctrine of impossibility is the doctrine of excuse of performance by reasonable apprehension of impossibility and also the doctrine of frustration of the venture. With the understanding that these categories are convenient groupings rather than conceptually distinct classifications, they will be discussed seriatim.

§ 187. Destruction, Deterioration or Unavailability of the Subject Matter or Tangible Means of Performance

The modern doctrine of impossibility can be traced to Taylor v. Caldwell.[6] In this case the defendant promised, for a consideration, to permit the plaintiff to use his music hall for the giving of concerts. Prior to the time for performance a fire destroyed the music hall. The court held that the defendant was excused from performance; that is, his failure to perform did not constitute a breach of contract.[7] Of course, the plaintiff in such a situation is also excused from performance under the doctrine of prospective or present inability to perform.[8] Since this case was decided, it has rather consistently been held that impossibility is an excuse for performance when there has been a fortuitous destruction, material deterioration, or unavailability of the subject matter[9] or tangible means of performance of the contract.

6. 122 Eng.Rep. 309 (K.B.1863). For a discussion of the law prior to this decision and its development thereafter, see Page, The Development of the Doctrine of Impossibility of Performance, 18 Mich.L.Rev. 589 (1920), Selected Readings 979.

7. An excuse from performance should be distinguished from an excuse of condition. The former discharges a duty so that a party under a duty is not liable for his failure of performance. An excuse of condition operates to transform a conditional duty into an absolute duty notwithstanding the non-occurrence of the condition to the duty.

8. See § 163 supra.

9. It is important to note that in the music hall case the plaintiff had a license rather than a lease to use the music hall. There are certain rules of property law which may lead to a different result where the subject matter of the contract is destroyed. For example, if on April 1, S agrees to sell and B agrees to buy a specific second hand car, title to pass and payment to be made on May 1, and the car was destroyed by fire on April 25 without the fault of either party, the result would be exactly the same as in the music hall case. But if title passed to B on April 24, under the common law rule that risk of loss follows title, S would be deemed to have performed and B would be required to

Thus, if A promised to deliver 2000 tons of Regent potatoes to be grown upon his farm in Elmira, New York, he would be excused from performance if, without any fault on his part, a pestilence destroyed his crop.[10]   If, however, the contract did not specify that the potatoes were to be raised upon designated land but the parties, as a matter of course, assumed that the crop was to be grown on specific land, the cases are not easily reconcilable.   Some cases have construed the contract to mean that the subject matter of the contract need not come from any particular source and therefore performance of the contract is not impossible.[11]   Other courts have concluded that since the parties contemplated a particular source of supply, destruction of the source results in an excuse for performance.[12]   The same dicho-

pay. 2 Williston, Sales § 301 (rev. ed. 1948); Uniform Sales Act § 22. The Uniform Commercial Code modifies this approach somewhat because it abandons the "title" concept. However, U.C.C. § 2–613 specifically recognizes that the risk of loss may pass to the buyer. It provides as follows:

Casualty to Identified Goods

Where the contract requires for its performance goods identified when the contract is made, and the goods suffer casualty without fault of either party before the risk of loss passes to the buyer, or in a proper case under a "no arrival, no sale" term (Section 2–324) then

(a) if the loss is total the contract is avoided; and

(b) if the loss is partial or the goods have so deteriorated as no longer to conform to the contract the buyer may nevertheless demand inspection and at his option either treat the contract as avoided or accept the goods with due allowance from the contract price for the deterioration or the deficiency in quantity but without further right against the seller.

The rules relating to risk of loss are set forth in U.C.C. § 2–509; see also U.C. C. § 2–501.

A similar problem arises where real property is destroyed between the time a contract is signed and the time for closing of title.   The majority view places the risk of loss on the buyer while a minority view places the risk upon the seller.   The Uniform Purchaser and Vendor Risk Act places the risk of loss upon the party who is in possession.   A similar problem also arises under the common law rule with respect to leases which regards the lessor as having completely performed when the lease is given so that risk of loss is placed upon the lessee.   This rule has been changed in many jurisdictions by statute or judicial decision.

10. Howell v. Coupland, 1 Q.B.D. 258 (1876), 46 L.J.Q.B. 147 (1876); Ontario Deciduous Fruit-Growers' Ass'n v. Cutting Fruit-Packing Co., 134 Cal. 21, 66 P. 28 (1901); accord, Bruce v. Indianapolis Gas Co., 46 Ind.App. 193, 92 N.E. 189 (1910) (oil or gas from named well); Ward v. Vance, 93 Pa. 499 (1880) (water from named well).

11. Anderson v. May, 50 Minn. 280, 52 N.W. 530 (1892) (failure of bean crop); accord, Whitman v. Anglum, 92 Conn. 392, 103 A. 114 (1918) (failure of milk supply caused by death of cows); Oakland Elec. Co. v. Union Gas & Elec. Co., 107 Me. 279, 78 A. 288 (1910) (failure of electricity supply caused by injury to dam).

12. International Paper Co. v. Rockefeller, 161 App.Div. 180, 146 N.Y.S. 371 (3d Dep't 1914) (parol evidence admitted to show parties intended wood to be supplied from a specific tract of land); Snipes Mountain Co. v. Benz

tomy exists in cases stemming from the destruction of factories. If it is not specifically agreed, but only assumed, that the subject matter will be produced at a given factory, does fortuitous destruction of the plant excuse performance? [13] While the differing results in cases of this kind may be to some extent attributable to differing factual circumstances surrounding the contracts involved in the cases, it is probable that there is a difference among judges on the question of which of two innocent parties must bear the risk of non-performance. Leading cases [14] and the Uniform Commercial Code make the allocation of the risk turn on the question of whether the particular source of supply was a "basic assumption on which the contract was made." [15] Judicial disagreement over which innocent party will bear the risk of non-performance will doubtless continue and find expression in disagreement of how basic to the particular contract was a given assumption and, in view of the blamelessness of the parties, decisions often are, under the Commercial Code as in the past, likely to be based upon subtle equities. How diligent was the party who seeks to be excused? [16] How foreseeable was the risk that performance would be impossible? [17] In addition, other criteria will be employed.

Bros., 162 Wash. 334, 298 P. 714, 74 A.L.R. 1287 (1931) (suit in equity for reformation); cf. Unke v. Thorpe, 75 S.D. 65, 59 N.W.2d 419 (1953) (decided on ground of mutual mistake as to the amount of seed in the farmer's crop).

In two interesting cases, crop failures in a given part of the country were held to excuse delivery, although the parties did not contemplate that the crop was to be produced on the promisor's land. Rather, it was contemplated that he would acquire the crop from farmers in the vicinity. Mitchell Canneries, Inc. v. United States, 111 Ct.Cl. 228, 77 F.Supp. 498 (1948) (promisor's performance excused); Dillon v. United States, 140 Ct.Cl. 508, 156 F.Supp. 719 (1957) (extra compensation granted to promisor who went out of state to procure hay).

13. In Booth v. Spuyten Duyvil Rolling Mill Co., 60 N.Y. 487 (1875), destruction of the factory was held not to be an excuse although the factory was named in the contract. The court argued that the contract did not prohibit the manufacturer from producing the goods at another plant. More-

over, in the view of the court, the goods could have been produced prior to the date on which the factory was destroyed. Compare Stewart v. Stone, 127 N.Y. 500, 28 N.E. 595 (1891).

14. "The inquiry is merely this, whether the continuance of a special group of circumstances appears from the terms of the contract, interpreted in the setting of the occasion, to have been a tacit or implied presupposition in the minds of the contracting parties, conditioning their belief in a continued obligation." Cardozo, C. J., in Canadian Indus. Alcohol Co. v. Dunbar Molasses Co., 258 N.Y. 194, 198–99, 179 N.E. 383 (1932) (citations omitted).

15. U.C.C. § 2–615(a).

16. Cf. Canadian Indus. Alcohol Co. v. Dunbar Molasses Co., 258 N.Y. 194, 198, 179 N.E. 383, 384 (1932); see § 198 infra.

17. Cf. Transatlantic Financing Corp. v. United States, 124 U.S.App.D.C. 183, 363 F.2d 312 (1966); see § 198 infra.

Principally, the question is, if the parties had thought about the matter, which of them would have assumed the risk of the unexpected event.

This method of allocation of risks is illustrated in the building contract field. In a common factual pattern a contractor agrees to construct a building on land owned by the other party to be completed and delivered by a certain date, say, May 5. On April 30, the nearly completed building is destroyed by fire without fault on the part of the contractor.[18] It would appear that as a practical matter performance is impossible. Yet, although the Restatement of Contracts accepts "extreme impracticability" as the equivalent of "impossibility,"[19] it deals with this situation under the heading of "unanticipated difficulty" which does not provide an excuse for non-performance.[20] In this analysis it is in accord with the great weight of authority.[21] How can this situation be distinguished from Taylor v. Caldwell?[22] One could say that in Taylor v. Caldwell[23] the contract related to the existing music hall, while in the building case the contract related to a completed building constructed on the site, not necessarily the first. It is much more realistic to say, however, that the risk should be allocated to the builder because this is what the parties would probably have agreed upon if they had paused to consider the matter.[24]

The foregoing situation is further complicated if the building is destroyed or rendered less valuable because of defective plans and specifications supplied by the owner. Earlier cases took the position that the builder by accepting the owner's plans promises to produce the result called for by the plans and accepts the risks attendant upon using the owner's specifications.[25] It was believed that the owner relied upon the builder's technical knowledge. The modern cases, how-

18. The fact pattern is suggested by School District No. 1 v. Dauchy, 25 Conn. 530 (1857).

19. Restatement, Contracts § 454.

20. Restatement, Contracts § 467, ill. 1. Under the concept of "temporary impossibility" it may be that the contractor is excused from performing by the agreed completion date. Restatement, Contracts § 462; see § 196 infra.

21. School District No. 1 v. Dauchy, 25 Conn. 530 (1857); Tompkins v. Dudley, 25 N.Y. 272 (1862); see Note, 54 Harv.L.Rev. 106 (1940). The concept of "an act of God" is irrelevant in any discussion of "impossibility of performance." See 6 Williston § 1936 (rev'd ed. 1938).

22. 122 Eng.Rep. 309 (K.B.1863).

23. Id.

24. Cf. Parker & Adams, The A.I.A. Standard Contract Forms and the Law 45–48, 131–34 (1954) (owner's obligation under standard forms to procure insurance).

25. Superintendent & Trustees v. Bennett, 27 N.J. 513 (1859); Stees v. Leonard, 20 Minn. 494 (1874).

ever, generally hold that where plans and specifications are prepared by professionals hired by the owner, unless the language of the contract or the circumstances otherwise indicate,[26] the owner warrants that the plans are adequate to produce the desired result [27] unless the builder has reason to know of the inadequacy.[28] As indicated in this statement of the rule the parties are free to allocate the risks by their agreement. Thus, if the builder expressly warrants that the owner's plans are adequate, he may not claim the excuse that they are inadequate.[29] If the parties agree upon contingency plans or payments in the event of unexpected soil conditions, the agreement will be given effect despite any alleged inadequacy of the specifications, or of any agreed upon additional payment or whether or not the unexpected conditions were grossly outside the reasonable contemplation of the parties.[30]

Contracts to repair or alter an existing building are distinguished from contracts to construct a building. A different allocation of risk is made. If a structure is destroyed, the contractor is excused from performance of his duty to repair or alter.[31] The continued existence of the building is deemed to be a basic assumption upon which the

26. Compare Faber v. City of New York, 222 N.Y. 255, 118 N.E. 609 (1918), with Application of Semper, 227 N.Y. 151, 124 N.E. 743 (1919).

27. United States v. Spearin, 248 U.S. 132, 39 S.Ct. 59, 63 L.Ed. 166 (1918); Simpson Timber Co. v. Palmberg Constr. Co., 377 F.2d 380 (9th Cir. 1967); North American Philips Co. v. United States, 175 Ct.Cl. 71, 358 F.2d 980 (1966); State v. Commercial Cas. Ins. Co., 125 Neb. 43, 248 N.W. 807, 88 A.L.R. 790 (1933); MacKnight Flintic Stone Co. v. Mayor of New York, 160 N.Y. 72, 54 N.E. 661 (1899); see 35 N. Y.L.J. 232 (1947); 5 Okla.L.Rev. 480 (1930); 6 A.L.R.3d 1394. Some courts appear to proceed on a negligence rather than a warranty theory. In either case it would be relevant to ascertain whether the plans were the proximate cause of the failure to complete. Kinser Constr. Co. v. State, 204 N.Y. 381, 97 N.E. 871 (1912).

The defective specifications not only provide an excuse for non-performance, but also a basis for an action for recovery of increased expenses involved in producing the desired result. Montrose Contracting Co. v. County of

Westchester, 80 F.2d 841 (2d Cir. 1936), cert. denied, 298 U.S. 662, 56 S. Ct. 746, 80 L.Ed. 1387 (1936), second appeal 94 F.2d 580 (2d Cir. 1938); Simpson Timber Co. v. Palmberg Constr. Co., 377 F.2d 380 (9th Cir. 1967).

28. Banducci v. Hickey, 93 Cal.App.2d 658, 209 P.2d 398, 399 (Dist.Ct.App. 1949); Montrose Contracting Co. v. Westchester County, 94 F.2d 580 (2d Cir. 1938).

29. Philadelphia Housing Authority v. Turner Constr. Co., 343 Pa. 512, 23 A. 2d 426 (1942).

30. Simpson Timber Co. v. Palmberg Constr. Co., 377 F.2d 380 (9th Cir. 1967); Depot Constr. Co. v. State, 19 N.Y.2d 109, 278 N.Y.S.2d 363, 224 N.E. 2d 866 (1967).

31. See Note, Building Contracts—Contract to Furnish Part of Labor and Materials for Another's Building—Contract to Repair—Accidental Destruction—Intervening Impossibility, 14 Minn.L.Rev. 51 (1929), Selected Readings 1038.

parties contracted. The contractor is entitled to quasi contractual recovery to the extent he has performed.[32] The same concepts have been applied to excuse sub-contractors from their duty of performance when a building under construction is destroyed. Here, too, quasi contractual relief will be awarded to the sub-contractors.[33] By extension of the reasoning in the repair and sub-contractor cases, builders have in several cases been excused from performance of a contract to construct a building and have received a quasi contractual recovery where the owner was cooperating in the project by supplying some labor.[34]

§ 188. Failure of the Contemplated Mode of Delivery or Payment

The Uniform Commercial Code now governs cases involving failure of the contemplated mode of delivery or payment at least as to transactions involving goods. The section is basically a codification of the better reasoned common law cases.[35] Section 2–614 provides:

(1) Where without fault of either party the agreed berthing, loading, or unloading facilities fail or an agreed type of carrier becomes unavailable or the agreed manner of delivery otherwise becomes commercially impracticable but a commercially reasonable substitute is available, such substitute performance must be tendered and accepted.

---

32. F. M. Gabler, Inc. v. Evans Laboratories, 129 Misc. 911, 233 N.Y.S. 408 (App.T. 1st Dep't 1927) (collecting cases). Some cases proceed on the theory that repairs or alterations have been wrought into the building, thus becoming fixtures. Under this theory contractor's recovery is limited to the value of the fixtures incorporated into the building. Hipskind Heating & Plumbing Co. v. General Industries, Inc., 136 Ind.App. 647, 194 N.E.2d 733 (1964), petition denied, 246 Ind. 215, 204 N.E.2d 339 (1965) (value of preliminary work of $7400 not recoverable). But cf. Haynes, Spencer & Co. v. Second Baptist Church, 88 Mo. 285 (1885) (value of materials destroyed at job site recoverable); F. M. Gabler, Inc. v. Evans Laboratories, 129 Misc. 911, 233 N.Y.S. 408 (App.T. 1st Dep't 1927) (same). For a third view see Albre Marble and Tile Co. v. John Bowen Co., 338 Mass. 394, 155 N.E.2d 437 (1959), where recovery for expenses in preparation for performance (drawings, tests, samples) was awarded.

The court pointed out that although the defendant was discharged by impossibility, the defendant was not entirely blameless. It was held that in such a case expenditures made in reliance on the contract should be reimbursed.

33. Hayes v. Gross, 9 App.Div. 12, 40 N.Y.S. 1098 (3d Dep't 1896), aff'd 162 N.Y. 610, 57 N.E. 1112 (1900).

34. Butterfield v. Byron, 153 Mass. 517, 27 N.E. 667 (1891). It has been held that if the owner merely supplies materials the case is not within the repair doctrine and impossibility is not an excuse for performance. Vogt v. Hecker, 118 Wis. 306, 95 N.W. 90 (1903).

35. E. g. Meyer v. Sullivan, 40 Cal.App. 723, 181 P. 847 (1919); Iasigi v. Rosenstein, 141 N.Y. 414, 36 N.E. 509 (1894); see § 201 infra for a general discussion of impossibility under the Code.

(2) If the agreed means or manner of payment fails because of domestic or foreign governmental regulation, the seller may withhold or stop delivery unless the buyer provides a means or manner of payment which is commercially a substantial equivalent. If delivery has already been taken, payment by the means or in the manner provided by the regulation discharges the buyer's obligation unless the regulation is discriminatory, oppressive or predatory.

Impossibility of performance is treated differently in this situation than in situations where the impossibility goes to the essence of the contract. Mode of delivery and manner of payment, although important, are incidental to the principal obligations which are that the goods be delivered and paid for. Thus, impossibility as to these incidental matters does not excuse performance if a commercially reasonable substitute is available. If payment in accordance with the terms of the agreement becomes illegal under applicable foreign or domestic regulations it is obvious that the payor's duty should not be discharged; instead, payment in some other manner is required.[36] Similarly, if one vessel is destroyed, a substitute vessel, if available, should be used.

§ 189. Supervening Prohibition or Prevention by Law

When parties enter into a lawful agreement they usually assume that the law will continue to permit performance. It is well settled that supervening prohibition of performance by law or administrative regulation of the United States, a state, or municipality provides an excuse for nonperformance.[37] Thus, lawful performance is impossible.

There has been some dispute concerning whether prevention by court or administrative order, such as an injunction, excuses performance. Obviously it is not argued that the promisor can perform by violating the order. Rather, the argument is that the impossibility

---

36. Exceedingly complex problems have arisen in regard to currency regulations of foreign countries. Treaty obligations, such as the Bretton Woods Agreement, are often applicable. In the absence of treaty, traditionally, domestic courts have refused to recognize foreign restrictive regulations on the movement of currency. See Banco Do Brasil v. A. C. Israel Commodity Co., Inc., 12 N.Y.2d 371, 190 N.E.2d 235, 239 N.Y.S.2d 872 (1963), cert. denied 376 U.S. 906, 84 S.Ct. 657, 11 L.

Ed.2d 605 (1964); Ehrenzweig, Conflict of Laws § 191 (1962). The Code's recognition of these regulations is potentially a radical innovation. The provision is open to various interpretations, however, on the question of when the restrictive currency regulation is applicable to the case. This is a question of Conflict of Laws, not clearly answered by the Code, cf. U. C.C. § 1–105.

37. Restatement, Contracts § 458.

is personal to the promisor and the impossibility is subjective rather than objective,[38] and also that the court or administrative order was issued because of some fault of the promisor.[39] Where, however, the order is not caused by the promisor's fault, there is no reason why it should not provide as much an excuse for performance as any other kind of legal prohibition.[40] Indeed, non-judicial action by a governmental agency which affects a particular party rather than the public generally has been held to excuse performance; for example, the requisition of a factory for war production has been held to excuse performance of civilian contracts for production at the factory.[41] There is no reason why judicial action affecting a party to a contract, without fault on his part, should not equally be an excuse. The Uniform Commercial Code speaks in terms of "any applicable . . . governmental regulation or order." [42] This wording is broad enough to encompass an administrative or judicial order in an individual case as well as regulations and orders of a general nature.

The early cases generally took the position that prevention or prohibition by foreign law was not an excuse for non-performance.[43] Although this rule has been discarded in most modern cases,[44] some courts have continued arbitrarily to distinguish between domestic and foreign law.[45] The Uniform Commercial Code explicitly equates foreign law with domestic law as an excuse for non-performance.[46]

---

38. Klauber v. San Diego Street Car Co., 95 Cal. 353, 30 P. 555 (1892) (the promisor was also at fault).

39. Peckham v. Industrial Sec. Co., 31 Del. 200, 113 A. 799 (1921); see § 198 infra.

40. Boston Plate & Window Glass Co. v. John Bowen Co., 335 Mass. 697, 141 N.E.2d 715 (1957); Kuhl v. School Dist. No. 76, 155 Neb. 357, 51 N.W.2d 746 (1952); People v. Globe Mut. Life Ins. Co., 91 N.Y. 174 (1883).

41. Israel v. Luckenbach S.S. Co., 6 F. 2d 996 (2d Cir. 1925), cert. denied 268 U.S. 691, 45 S.Ct. 510, 69 L.Ed. 1159 (1924) (vessel commandeered); Mawhinney v. Millbrook Woolen Mills, Inc., 231 N.Y. 290, 132 N.E. 93, 15 A. L.R. 1506 (1921) (output of factory requisitioned); see Note, 28 Yale L.J. 399 (1919).

42. U.C.C. § 2–615(a).

43. Jacobs, Marcus & Co. v. Credit Lyonnais, 12 Q.B.D. 589 (1884).

44. Texas Co. v. Hogarth Shipping Co., Ltd., 256 U.S. 619, 41 S.Ct. 612, 65 L. Ed. 1123 (1921) (ship requisitioned by British Government); Rothkopf v. Lowry & Co., 148 F.2d 517 (2d Cir. 1945); Held v. Goldsmith, 153 La. 598, 96 So. 272 (1923) (contract by German to ship goods to U.S. on British vessel discharged by outbreak of war between Germany and Britain). The Restatement, Contracts § 458, Comment b, points out that prevention by foreign law should be regarded "as cases of impossibility due to change of fact rather than of law" and makes a cross reference to § 461 which involves failure of the intangible means of performance discussed in the next section.

45. Vanetta Velvet Corp. v. Kakunaka & Co., 256 App.Div. 341, 10 N.Y.S.2d 270 (1st Dep't 1939).

46. U.C.C. § 2–615(a).

§ 190. Failure of the Intangible Means of Performance

Decisions concerning the failure of intangible means of performance have not been uniform. Logically, there should be no distinction between the failure of tangible and intangible means of performance and this is the position taken by the Restatement.[47] A difference in result is often justifiable, however, on the grounds that the failure of intangible means of performance is usually more foreseeable than in the case of destruction of the tangible means of performance. Often it is also the kind of risk which the business community more normally considers to have been assumed by the promisor.

The chief illustration of the failure of the intangible means of performance are prevention under foreign law, which has already been discussed, and strikes. In strikes a wide variety of factors must be considered so that no general rule can be stated.

The first distinction which must be made is whether it is the promisor's own employees who are on strike or the employees of a third party. Where the promisor's own employees are on strike there is a great deal of authority to the effect that the promisor must yield to the demands of his employees [48] and that if he does not he is guilty of fault which bars the use of the defense of impossibility.[49] However, there is authority to the effect that the employer need not yield to unreasonable demands.[50] Another factor which has been deemed important in this situation is whether the strike has been accompanied by violence. Where it is accompanied by violence the cases are inclined to hold that the employer is excused.[51] It should be noted, however, that most of the cases are of doubtful authority in that they are based on assumptions about labor relations existing prior to the advent of modern labor law and practices. The Uniform Commercial Code does not appear to specifically cover the subject of strikes.[52]

---

47. Restatement, Contracts § 461, which deals with the problem under the heading of "Non-Existence of Essential Facts Other than Specific Things or Persons."

48. 6 Corbin § 1340; Richland S.S. Co. v. Buffalo Dry Dock Co., 254 F. 668 (2nd Cir.) cert. denied 248 U.S. 582, 39 S.Ct. 133, 63 L.Ed. 432 (1918).

49. See § 198 infra.

50. Empire Transp. Co. v. Philadelphia & R. Coal & Iron Co. 77 F. 919 (8th Cir. 1896); 6 Williston § 1951A (rev'd ed. 1938) appears to agree.

51. Geismer v. Lake Shore and Michigan So. Ry., 102 N.Y. 563, 7 N.E. 828 (1886); The No. C–4, 300 F. 757 (S.D. N.Y.1923), aff'd Galt v. Willingham, 11 F.2d 757 (1926). It has been held that where all the employees belong to the same union a peaceable strike would have the ultimate effect of a violent strike, since the promisor was prevented from proceeding just as effectively as if there was violence. Barnum v. Williams, 115 App.Div. 694, 102 N.Y.S. 844 (2nd Dep't 1906), aff'd 190 N.Y. 539, 83 N.E. 1122 (1907).

52. But see U.C.C. § 2–615, particularly Comment 4.

As a result of the uncertainties in the cases it has been customary for the parties to include strike clauses in their contracts with the result that there has been a substantial amount of litigation relating to the interpretation of these clauses.[53]

§ 191. Death or Illness

We have already seen that ordinarily the death of the offeror terminates the power of acceptance created by his offer.[54] But death does not necessarily terminate a contract. However, if a contract calls for personal performance by the promisor [55] or a third person,[56] and the person who is to render performance dies or becomes so ill as to make performance by him impossible or seriously injurious to his health, the promisor's duty is excused. If the act to be performed is delegable, however, the death or illness of the promisor or of a third person who is expected to perform the act does not excuse performance.[57]

The personal representative of the deceased employee is entitled to quasi-contractual recovery for the reasonable value of the services rendered. The contract rate is evidence of this value but is not conclusive, except that it sets the upward limit of recovery.[58] Although the death of the employee who is to render personal services is in no sense a breach, a number of jurisdictions have permitted the employer

53. See, for example, Davis v. Columbia Min. Co., 170 Mass. 391, 49 N.E. 629 (1898); Normandie Shirt Co. v. J. H. & C. K. Eagle Inc., 238 N.Y. 218, 144 N.E. 507, 35 A.L.R. 714 (1924).

54. See note 33 supra.

55. Herren v. Harris, Cortner & Co., 201 Ala. 577, 78 So. 921 (1918); Buccini v. Paterno Constr. Co., 253 N.Y. 256, 170 N.E. 910 (1930). Conversely, the promisee need not accept a performance tendered by the deceased promisor's personal representative. Smith v. Preston, 170 Ill. 179, 48 N.E. 688 (1897); cf. 6 Corbin § 1335.

56. Spalding v. Rosa, 71 N.Y. 40 (1877); Phillips v. Alhambra Palace Co., [1901] 1 Q.B. 59.

57. Chamberlain v. Dunlop, 126 N.Y. 45, 26 N.E. 966 (1891). Restatement, Contracts § 459, Comment c makes this clear when it states: "Whether performance can be rendered only by a particular person is the same question, put in another form, as whether

performance can be delegated to another. A question of this sort is involved not only in cases where a contractor dies or becomes ill, but in those where he voluntarily delegates the performance to another person and his power to do this is disputed. If a contractor without violation of duty can go abroad and perform by means of another, his death or illness will not make subsequent performance of his contract impossible." See §§ 277–278 infra.

58. Buccini v. Paterno Constr. Co., 253 N.Y. 256, 170 N.E. 910 (1930). Difficult problems arise where the deceased was to be paid a contingent fee. See Rowland v. Hudson County, 7 N.J. 63, 80 A.2d 433 (1951), 65 Harv. L.Rev. 702 (1952) (architect to receive percentage of construction costs; plans were incomplete; building never built); Morton v. Forsee, 249 Mo. 409. 155 S.W. 765 (1913) (death of attorney); City of Barnsdall v. Curnutt, 198 Okl. 3, 174 P.2d 596 (1945) (death of attorney).

to set off his damages for non-performance of the contract against the estate's claim for quasi contractual recovery for part performance.[59]

The same principles should govern the death or serious illness of an employer. If the employee was to work under the personal direction and supervision of the employer, the employer's incapacity makes the performance in accordance with the contract impossible. The employee is discharged because of impossibility and the employer or his estate is discharged because of the employer's inability to perform.[60] Thus, the question is whether the employer's duty and right of supervision is delegable and assignable.[61] Although perhaps most of the cases are reconcilable with this test, too often courts have indulged in sweeping generalizations and have indicated that a rule of mutuality is applied to the effect that if the employee's duties are personal, death of the employer discharges the employee.[62]

§ 192.   Reasonable Apprehension of Impossibility or Danger

Closely related to the doctrine of impossibility is the doctrine that reasonable apprehension of impossibility or reasonable apprehension of danger to life or health gives rise to an excuse for non-performance.[63] Thus, an actor is excused from performing if he has symptoms of what may be a serious disease and enters a hospital for an examination. It matters not that the examination reveals that his illness is not serious.[64] A ship is excused from sailing into submarine infested waters and the shipowner is excused from his failure to deliver its cargo, although it subsequently is shown that the ship could have arrived at its destination several hours prior to the outbreak of hostilities.[65] An employee is discharged from his duty to work in an area where an epidemic of a serious contagious disease appears to be in progress.[66]

59. Clark v. Gilbert, 26 N.Y. 279 (1863); Patrick v. Putnam, 27 Vt. 759 (1855); 46 Mich.L.Rev. 401, 421 (1948); see 69 Yale L.J. 1054 (1960).

60. See 6 Corbin § 1335.

61. See §§ 261, 277, 278 infra.

62. See 6 Williston § 1941 (rev'd ed. 1938). A mixture of sound analysis and sweeping over-generalizations is often found. See, e. g., Minevitch v. Puleo, 9 A.D.2d 285, 193 N.Y.S.2d 833 (1st Dep't 1959).

63. See Restatement, Contracts § 465. The rules stated herein are subject to the qualifications stated in § 198 infra.

64. Wasserman Theatrical Enterprise v. Harris, 137 Conn. 371, 77 A.2d 329 (1950) (the producer who has contracted to put on a show featuring the actor is also excused).

65. The Kronprinzessin Cecilie, 244 U. S. 12, 37 S.Ct. 490, 61 L.Ed. 960 (1917).

66. Lakeman v. Pollard, 43 Me. 463 (1857); see also Hanford v. Connecticut Fair Ass'n, 92 Conn. 621, 103 A. 838 (1918).

§ 193. Impracticability

The Restatement equates extreme impracticability with impossibility; [67] the Uniform Commercial Code utilizes the term "impracticable" to encompass "impossible." [68] Courts, however, have been extremely reluctant to accept anything short of impossibility as an excuse for performance. When the promisor is faced with unforeseen difficulties and increased costs of performance, many jurisdictions have been willing to enforce an agreement made without consideration for increased compensation.[69] In the absence of agreement, however, the promisor has generally been held to have assumed the risk of unforeseen difficulties and increased costs. Typical of holdings in most jurisdictions is Columbus Railway, Power & Light Co. v. City of Columbus,[70] which held that a street car company was not excused from its long-term obligation to sell rides at eight for a quarter despite greatly increased costs resulting in annual deficits. California has led the way toward relaxation of this rigorous rule. In the leading case, Mineral Park Land Co. v. Howard,[71] the defendant agreed to take his requirements of gravel needed on a bridge building project by removing it from plaintiff's land and to pay for it at the rate of five cents per yard. The defendant removed all of the gravel above water level but refused to take gravel below water level on the grounds that the cost of removal would be ten to twelve times the usual cost of removing gravel. The court held that the defendant was excused from performing. It reasoned that although it was not impossible to remove additional gravel, for practical purposes no additional gravel was available and, therefore, performance was excused because of the non-existence, for practical purposes, of the subject matter of the contract. A good number of cases [72] in accord concerning mineral leases had previously been decided on a variety of grounds, mostly as a matter of interpretation of the lease but also on grounds of mutual mistake of fact.[73] The case, however, is noteworthy as equating impracticability with impossibility.

67. Restatement, Contracts § 454.

68. U.C.C. § 2–615.

69. See § 61 supra.

70. 249 U.S. 399, 39 S.Ct. 349, 63 L.Ed. 669, 6 A.L.R. 1648 (1919). For a large number of cases in accord, holding that unforeseen financial hardship does not excuse performance, see 6 Corbin § 1333; 6 Williston § 1963 (rev'd ed. 1938).

71. 172 Cal. 289, 156 P. 458 (1916), critically noted in 4 Calif.L.Rev. 407 (1916).

72. E. g., Swiss Oil Corp. v. Riggsby, 252 Ky. 374, 67 S.W.2d 30 (1934); Carozza v. Williams, 190 Md. 143, 57 A. 2d 782 (1948); Brick Co. v. Pond, 38 Ohio St. 65 (1882).

73. Petrey v. John F. Buckner & Sons, 280 S.W.2d 641 (Tex.Civ.App.1955), ref. n. r. e.; Paddock v. Mason, 187 Va. 809, 48 S.E.2d 199 (1948).

Very few cases have squarely relied on impracticability as a basis for decision. It has been held that a blizzard excused performance of a contract to deliver fuel oil.[74] Cases applying California law have held that where the cost of performance is considerably more than was originally contemplated, performance is excused. In these cases, however, the increased cost was a result of the necessity of performing in a manner radically different than originally contemplated. In one case a construction contractor was required to excavate well over twice the yardage originally estimated.[75] In another case, the City of Los Angeles had entered into a long term contract for the disposal of sewage of a neighboring community. When the State required Los Angeles to treat sewage in a modern plant, the increased cost of performance was caused by the necessity of performing its contract in a manner not originally contemplated.[76] Stricter courts would have held, however, that the contractor and the City had promised to produce given results and the means utilized to secure these results were of no concern to the promisees. An official comment to the Commercial Code [77] states that "increased cost alone does not excuse performance unless the rise in cost is due to some unforeseen contingency which alters the essential nature of the performance. Neither is a rise or collapse in the market in itself a justification, for that is exactly the type of business risk which business contracts made at fixed prices are intended to cover. But a severe shortage of raw materials or of supplies due to a contingency such as war, embargo, local crop failure, unforeseen shutdown of major sources of supply or the like, which either causes a marked increase in cost or altogether prevents the seller from securing supplies necessary to his performance, is within the contemplation of this section."

§ 194. Impossibility as an Excuse of Condition

The preceding discussion has considered impossibility of performance from the point of view of an excuse for non-performance. A separate question is whether a condition is excused when its occurrence is impossible.[78] In other words, may a conditional promise

---

74. Whelan v. Griffith Consumers Co., 170 A.2d 229 (D.C.Mun.App.1961); but see Stevens & Elkins v. Lewis-Wilson-Hicks Co., 168 Ky. 645, 182 S.W. 840, modified, 170 Ky. 238, 185 S.W. 873 (1916).

75. Transbay Constr. Co. v. City of San Francisco, 35 F.Supp. 433 (N.D.Cal. 1940), rev'd 134 F.2d 468 (9th Cir.), cert. denied 320 U.S. 749, 64 S.Ct. 52, 88 L.Ed. 445.

76. City of Vernon v. City of Los Angeles, 45 Cal.2d 710, 290 P.2d 841 (1955).

77. U.C.C. § 2–615, Comment 4; accord, Mitchell Canneries, Inc. v. United States, 111 Ct.Cl. 228, 77 F.Supp. 498 (1948); Dillon v. United States, 140 Ct.Cl. 508, 156 F.Supp. 719 (1957) (increased hardships caused by local crop failures).

78. See § 173 supra.

be enforced when it is impossible for the condition to occur? The answer to this question varies with the nature of the condition and with what has been done under the contract. Generally, if the condition is a material part of the agreed exchange such as a constructive or express condition of performance, impossibility will not excuse the condition.[79] Otherwise, the promisor would be obligated to perform despite the fact that he has not gotten what he has bargained for in exchange for his promised performance.

If the condition is incidental to the agreed exchange, impossibility will very likely excuse the condition especially if a forfeiture would otherwise occur.[80] Thus, for example, if a building contractor cannot produce the certificate of a named architect because of the architect's death or incapacity, failure to produce the certificate will be excused.[81] Any other result would cause an extreme forfeiture and do violence to what the parties doubtless would have agreed upon had they thought about the matter. Since the element of forfeiture is the principal consideration, if the architect had died prior to the contractor's performance, it may well be that the ruling would be otherwise; that is, it could be held that since the contract is impossible to perform pursuant to its terms, performance on both sides is discharged. Cases concerning the sale of goods support this distinction. Prior to the enactment of the Uniform Commercial Code, if goods were to be sold at a price to be fixed by an appraiser, the buyer was excused from performance if the price was not so fixed.[82] If the goods were delivered and accepted, however, the buyer's duty of performance was not discharged; rather the condition to his duty of performance was excused. He was required to pay reasonable value.[83] The Code puts cases of this kind

79. Restatement, Contracts § 301(b); Lazzara v. Wisconsin Boxing Club, 29 F.2d 483 (7th Cir. 1928), cert. denied, 279 U.S. 851, 49 S.Ct. 347, 73 L.Ed. 994 (1928).

80. Restatement, Contracts § 301(b). There is a marked split of authority as to whether a condition of notice imposed by an insurance policy is excused when the insured is mentally disabled. See Mutual Life Ins. Co. v. Johnson, 293 U.S. 335, 55 S.Ct. 154, 79 L.Ed. 398 (1934) (collecting cases).

81. Restatement, Contracts § 303(a).

82. Louisville Soap Co. v. Taylor, 279 F. 470 (6th Cir. 1922), cert. denied 259

U.S. 583, 42 S.Ct. 586, 66 L.Ed. 1075 (1921) (price to be that prevailing on Savannah market; market was inactive); Stern v. Farah Bros., 17 N. Mex. 516, 133 P. 400 (1913); Turman Oil Co. v. Sapulpa Ref. Co., 124 Okl. 150, 254 P. 84 (1926); see U.C.C. § 2–305, Comment 4.

83. Hood v. Hartshorn, 100 Mass. 117 (1868). But see U.C.C. § 2–305, which requires a contrary result if it is shown that the parties do not intend to be bound unless the particular expert fixes the price. If such an intent exists the buyer must return the goods to avoid liability for their value.

on a somewhat different basis.[84] If the price is not fixed in the manner agreed, the contract will be construed to mean that a reasonable price must be paid. If, however, the parties intend not to be bound unless the price is fixed in the manner agreed upon, as when they rely on the expertise of an appraiser in a situation where no clear market standards exist, the contract is discharged if the appraiser cannot set the price. The buyer must return goods already received. If this is not possible, he must pay reasonable value.

§ 195. Frustration of the Venture

The doctrine of frustration of the venture had its origin in what are generally known as the coronation cases. In Krell v. Henry [85] the plaintiff had granted the defendant a license to use his apartment for two days to view the coronation of King Edward VII and the defendant agreed to pay £75 for this privilege. The coronation was cancelled because the King was stricken by perityphlitis. It was held that the defendant was excused from his duty of payment. It is apparent that performance was impossible on neither side. The premises were available for viewing the site where the coronation was to have taken place and there was no impossibility involved in making payment. It is also clear that there was no failure of constructive condition of performance as the plaintiff made no promise that the coronation would occur. Rather, there is the imposition of a constructive condition of another type. Where the object of one of the parties is the basis upon which both parties contract, the duties of performance are constructively conditioned upon the attainment of that object.[86] Although the application of this rule is rather clear in the coronation cases, most other cases in which the applicability of the doctrine has been urged by counsel have been more difficult to resolve.

The courts agree that the doctrine of frustration of the venture does not apply unless the frustration is "total or nearly total." [87] However there is difficulty in determining what is "total or nearly total" frustration. The lease cases are good illustrations of the problem.[88]

84. U.C.C. § 2–305; see § 23 supra.

85. [1903] 2 K.B. 740.

86. See Restatement, Contracts § 288;
      6 Corbin §§ 1353–61.

87. Lloyd v. Murphy, 25 Cal.2d 48, 153
      P.2d 47 (1944).

88. It should be observed that some cases have doubted whether a lease can ever be discharged by frustration. Viewed as a matter of property law, a lease is a conveyance of an estate in land, performance being complete on the execution of the lease. In Paradine v. Jane, 82 Eng.Rep. 897 (1647) it was held that a lessee was required to

In Doherty v. Monroe Eckstein Brewing Co.,[89] the defendant was in possession under a lease which provided: "It being expressly agreed that the only business to be carried on in said premises is the saloon business."[90]   During the term of the lease Congress passed a national prohibition law which made the sale of alcoholic beverages illegal.   It is obvious that this is not a case of supervening illegality of the lease; it is not illegal for the tenant to pay rent on unused premises.   Rather the courts have held that there was frustration even though the defendant could still have used the premises to sell cigars, cigarettes, near beer and the like.   Thus the holding is to the effect that the frustration was nearly total.[91]   Although it is difficult to generalize it would appear that where the principal use is completely frustrated the frustration will ordinarily be deemed to be nearly total but where the principal use is not completely frustrated then the frustration will be called partial and the holding will be to the effect that the defense of frustration is not available.[92]   A contract to buy machines for the purpose of exporting them to Russia is not discharged by supervening licensing restrictions which prohibit their export.[93]   The purchaser may be able to find a market for the goods in this or some other country.   If, however, the contract had called for shipment to Russia the contract would have been discharged by reason of impossibility caused by supervening illegality.

Once it has been decided that a contract has been discharged by reason of frustration, a difficult question is to what extent is the court empowered to adjust the relations of the parties.   The coronation cases were most unsatisfactory in this respect.   While in Krell v. Henry[94] it was held that the defendant was excused from paying for use of the premises, in the related case of Chandler v. Webster[95]

pay rent although the premises were occupied by alien enemies.

89.   198 App.Div. 708, 191 N.Y.S. 59 (1st Dep't 1921).

90.   Id. at 708, 191 N.Y.S. 59.   Such a restrictive covenant is often deemed essential to present a question of frustration of a lease.

91.   Accord, The Stratford v. Seattle Brewing and Malting Co., 94 Wash. 125, 162 P. 31 (1916).   Contra, Proprietors' Realty Co. v. Wohltmann, 95 N.J. L. 303, 112 A. 410 (1921).   Some courts, despite what is said above, speak in terms of supervening illegality.

92.   Lloyd v. Murphy, 25 Cal.2d 48, 153 P.2d 47 (1944) (auto dealership);

Wood v. Bartolino, 48 N.Mex. 175, 146 P.2d 883 (1944) (gasoline station); Colonial Operating Corp. v. Hannan Sales & Service, Inc., 265 App.Div. 411, 39 N.Y.S.2d 217 (2d Dep't 1943), appeal granted 266 App.Div. 742, 41 N.Y.S.2d 953 (auto dealership).

93.   Bardons & Oliver, Inc. v. Amtorg Trading Corp., 123 N.Y.S.2d 633 (Sup. Ct. 1948), aff'd 275 App.Div. 748, 88 N.Y.S.2d 272 (1st Dep't 1949), aff'd 301 N.Y. 622, 93 N.E.2d 915 (1950); accord, Swift Canadian Co. v. Banet, 224 F.2d 36 (3d Cir. 1955).

94.   [1903] 2 K.B. 740.

95.   [1904] 1 K.B. 493.

it was held that a defendant who had made a substantial down payment and had agreed to pay the balance in advance of the coronation was not entitled to restitution and furthermore was liable to pay the balance. The rule was simply that the parties should be placed in the position they should have been in at the occurrence of the frustrating event. Chandler v. Webster was subsequently overruled by the Fibrosa case [96] which, however, produced an equally arbitrary rule. Restitution of a down payment was granted, placing the parties in the position they enjoyed prior to contracting. This ruling was not flexible enough to take into account the relative extent to which the parties might be out of pocket by reason of action in reliance on the contract. As suggested by the Law Lords in the Fibrosa case, the English Parliament enacted legislation [97] permitting recovery under a contract discharged by reason of impossibility or frustration for the value of benefits received, "if it considers it just to do so, having regard for all the circumstances." Pursuant to this enactment, the court may deduct for expenses incurred in reliance on the contract, taking into consideration the circumstances giving rise to the frustration or impossibility. In the United States, courts have generally taken the view that when a contract is discharged by impossibility or frustration the parties must make restitution for the benefits conferred upon them. Sometimes, the concept of "benefit" is stretched to include expenses incurred in preparation for performance.[98] An occasional case apportions the losses sustained without regard to conceptual niceties.[99]

§ 196. Temporary Impossibility or Frustration

Temporary impossibility or frustration merely suspends the duty of performance until the impossibility ceases. If, however, after the cessation of the impossibility or frustration, the burden of the promised performance would be substantially different from what

---

96. Fibrosa Spolka Akeyjna v. Fairbarn Lawson Combe Barbour, Ltd., H.L., (1943) A.C. 32, [1942] 2 All Eng. Rep. 122, Annot. 144 A.L.R. 1298, 91 U.Pa.L.Rev. 262 (1942).

97. Law Reform (Frustrated Contracts) Act, 1943, 6 & 7 Geo. 6, c. 40. For a suggested American statute, see Comment, 69 Yale L.J. 1054 (1960).

98. The American cases are ably analyzed in Comment, 69 Yale L.J. 1054 (1960). A landmark case has recognized explicitly that "reliance" expenses incurred by the promisee may

be recoverable when the equities are on his side. Albre Marble & Tile Co. v. John Bowen Co., 338 Mass. 394, 155 N.E.2d 437 (1959), modified 343 Mass. 777, 179 N.E.2d 321 (1962).

99. See, e. g., Kinser Constr. Co. v. State, 125 N.Y.S. 46 (Ct.Cl.1910), aff'd 145 App.Div. 41, 129 N.Y.S. 567 (3d Dep't 1911), aff'd 204 N.Y. 381, 97 N. E. 871 (1912); but see The Isle of Mull, 278 F. 131 (4th Cir. 1921) disapproving the District Court's attempt equitably to adjust the rights of the parties.

it would have been had there been no supervening impossibility, the promisor's duty is discharged.[1] The rule thus stated permits great flexibility. It allows consideration of such questions as how essential is the time of performance under the contract, the duration of the period in which performance was impossible or futile,[2] and the reasonableness of any change of position made by either of the parties as a result of the impossibility. In connection with this last factor, it is highly relevant to consider whether at the time performance became impossible, the date at which performance would be possible was reasonably foreseeable.

§ 197. Personal versus Objective Impossibility or Frustration

For impossibility or frustration to operate as an excuse, it must be objective rather than subjective. "It is the difference between 'the thing cannot be done' and 'I cannot do it.'"[3] The excuse for non-performance granted because of death or illness does not violate this distinction. Such an excuse is available only where the performance is non-delegable. Since no substitute may perform, the performance is objectively as well as subjectively impossible.[4]

The primary application of this distinction is in cases where performance is impossible because of inability to pay money or render any other performance as a result of insolvency or other financial problems. Such inability is personal to the obligor and does not excuse performance.[5] It is perhaps more realistic to state, however, that when entering into a contract each party assumes the risk that he will have the financial ability to perform. In Taylor v. Caldwell[6] it was held that the destruction of a music hall discharged its proprietor's duty to make it available for theatrical performances. In a subsequent English case[7] it was properly held that foreclosure of a music hall did not discharge the proprietor's obligation. This, the court said, was not the kind of "unforeseen calamity" which merits remaking the contract for the parties.

---

1. See 6 Corbin § 1348; 6 Williston §§ 1957–58 (rev'd ed. 1938); Restatement, Contracts § 462; Patterson, Temporary Impossibility of Performance of Contract, 47 Va.L.Rev. 798 (1961).

2. See Patch v. Solar Corp., 149 F.2d 558 (7th Cir. 1945), cert. denied 326 U.S. 741, 66 S.Ct. 53, 90 L.Ed. 442 (1945) (patent license could not be utilized during wartime; frustration not total because usable after end of war; duty to pay royalty suspended).

3. Restatement, Contracts § 455, Comment a.

4. See Restatement, Contracts § 455, ill. 4.

5. Christy v. Pilkinton, 244 Ark. 407, 273 S.W.2d 533 (1954); Title & Trust Co. v. Durkheimer Inv. Co., 155 Or. 427, 451, 63 P.2d 909, 919 (1936).

6. 122 Eng.Rep. 309 (K.B.1863).

7. Phillips v. Alhambra Palace Co., [1901] 1 Q.B. 79.

§ 198. Contributory Fault, Foreseeability, Assumption of the Risk

As we have seen the doctrines of impossibility and frustration involve the allocation of risks of unexpected occurrences which make the performance of contractual duties more burdensome than originally contemplated. Various more or less standardized rules have been formulated to allocate risks of this kind. All of these rules involve consideration of whom, if the parties did not allocate the risk themselves, would the community normally expect to assume the risk of the unexpected occurrence. If the occurrence is reasonably foreseeable, courts normally take the position that the promisor has assumed the risk of impossibility or frustration. Thus, it has been held that promises to transport goods through the Suez Canal were not excused by the closing of the canal in 1956, as the possibility of military action in that area was widely discussed at the time the contracts were entered into.[8] So, too, the possibility of American entry into World War II was foreseeable when a dealer entered into a lease for an automobile showroom in August 1941.[9] It is to be noted, however, that foreseeability was not the sole ground of these decisions. It was still possible to sail around Africa and it was still possible to sell some new automobiles as well as used automobiles.[10] Rarely is only one criterion determinative.

It has almost universally been held that when a lessee enters into a lease for the purpose of engaging in a business which requires a license, his duty is not discharged if the license is denied.[11] It is foreseeable that a license may not be issued and ordinarily parties provide for such a contingency in their agreement.[12] Failure to make provision for denial of the license therefore indicates an assumption of the risk.

The excuse of performance on the grounds of impossibility of performance involves the construction of a condition in the interests of justice. Consequently, if the promisor is in some respects responsible for the event which makes performance of his promise impossible, justice does not dictate that he be excused. Thus destruction of the subject matter is no defense if the destruction was

---

8. Glidden Co. v. Hellenic Lines, Ltd., 275 F.2d 253 (2d Cir. 1960); Transatlantic Financing Corp. v. United States, 124 U.S.App.D.C. 183, 363 F.2d 312 (1966), 41 Tul.L.Rev. 709 (1967), 8 Wm. & Mary L.Rev. 679 (1967).

9. Lloyd v. Murphy, 25 Cal.2d 48, 153 P.2d 47 (1944). Pregnancy does not excuse performance of an employment contract where the pregnancy is known by the employee to exist at the time of contracting. Jennings v. Lyons, 39 Wis. 553 (1876).

10. See § 195 supra.

11. Raner v. Goldberg, 244 N.Y. 438, 155 N.E. 733 (1927).

12. See § 195 supra.

caused by the promisor's wilful or negligent act and [13] impossibility caused by governmental act is no defense if the promisor induced the government to act in the manner it did.[14]

The interplay of the problems presented by the doctrines of contributory fault and assumption of the risk can be well illustrated in the concrete by considering the facts in the case of Canadian Industrial Alcohol Co. v. Dunbar Molasses Co. and some variations thereon.[15]

The plaintiff agreed to buy and the defendant, a middleman, agreed to sell approximately 1,500,000 gallons of molasses of the usual run from the National Sugar Refinery, Yonkers, N.Y., to test around 60% sugars.[16] The output of the factory fell below its capacity and so the defendant was able to deliver only 344,083 gallons. When sued the defendant employed the defense of impossibility. The court held, inter alia, that the defendant could not avail itself of that defense because it was guilty of contributory fault in failing to enter into a contract with the refinery.

If the refinery had burned down and there was still no contract between the defendant and the refinery the court indicates that the defendant would have the defense of impossibility of performance. Here it could be said that the fault of the defendant did not contribute to defendant's failure to perform but rather the proximate cause was the destruction of the refinery, a risk which was not assumed by the defendant.[17] This seems fair, because on this assumption the defendant would not have a cause of action against the refinery even if he had entered into a contract with the refinery.

If it were assumed further that the defendant did make a contract with the refinery and the refinery nevertheless curtailed its output, should the defendant have the defense of impossibility? The answer should be that the defendant does not have a defense of impossibility because although the defendant would be liable to the plaintiff, he in turn would have an action against the refinery. The result would be different if the parties had agreed that the contract and its performance was contingent upon the defendant obtaining a contract with the refinery and performance by the refinery.

13. Restatement, Contracts §§ 457, 460.

14. Restatement, Contracts § 458.

15. 258 N.Y. 194, 179 N.E. 383, 80 A.L. R. 1173 (1932).

16. It is clear that the court assumes that this is not merely language of de-scription but that the molasses must come from this particular refinery.

17. Cf. Sunseri v. Garcia & Maggini Co., 298 Pa. 249, 148 A. 81, 67 A.L.R. 1428 (1929).

A parallel situation arises if "A contracts with B to sell him ½ the grapes contracted to be purchased by A from C under a specified contract between A and C." Under these circumstances it has been held that, if C defaults on his contract to deliver, A's duty to B is discharged by virtue of the provisions of the contract.[18] This result is justifiable, if as a matter of interpretation the contract between A and B is conditioned upon performance of the contract between A and C.

§ 199. Assumption of the Risk—Technological Impossibility

In a number of cases, mostly involving government contracts for the manufacture of new products, or the use of new processes, the manufacturer has contended that compliance with the contract has proved impossible, at least under existing technology. Generally, the cases have held that the contractor has assumed the risk that production was possible.[19]

On the other hand, where detailed specifications of manufacturing processes, as opposed to specifications which the end product must meet, are provided by the government, it has been held that the government warrants that the specifications will produce the desired result.[20]

In a recent interesting and unprecedented case [21] a contractor agreed to produce artillery shells for the government using a new process. In the course of negotiations the contractor argued that the process would not produce the result desired unless certain machinery were used to remove excess steel. The government, however, insisted that such equipment was not needed. The plaintiff succumbed to the government's insistence and agreed to produce the shells pursuant to the process at a fixed price. After costly experimentation the government agreed that the process would not work without

---

18. Restatement, Contracts § 460, ill. 12; Scialli v. Correale, 97 N.J.L. 165, 117 A. 255 (1922); Mosby v. Smith, 194 Mo.App. 20, 186 S.W. 49 (1916).

19. United States v. Wegematic Corp., 360 F.2d 674 (2d Cir. 1966) (applying the U.C.C. as "federal common law"); Austin Co. v. United States, 161 Ct.Cl. 76, 314 F.2d 518, cert. denied 375 U.S. 830, 84 S.Ct. 75, 11 L.Ed.2d 62 (1963); Rolin v. United States, 142 Ct.Cl. 73, 160 F.Supp. 264 (1958).

20. Helene Curtis Indus., Inc. v. United States, 160 Ct.Cl. 437, 312 F.2d 774

(1963). Where the government merely suggests rather than requires a given production process, the government does not warrant that the process will produce the desired result. Clark Grave Vault Co. v. United States, 178 Ct.Cl. 52, 371 F.2d 459 (1967). Compare these cases with the cases discussed in § 187 supra ns. 25–30.

21. National Presto Indus., Inc. v. United States, 167 Ct.Cl. 749, 338 F.2d 99 (1964).

equipment such as plaintiff had originally urged and permitted the plaintiff to make use of such equipment.   The plaintiff sued for extra compensation based upon the losses sustained as a result of the added expenses incurred in attempting to make the original specifications work.   The court rightly held that the plaintiff could not recover under breach of implied warranty.   The specific negotiations concerning the adequacy of the specifications negatived any justifiable reliance on them.   The court, however, held that the plaintiff was entitled to reformation of the contract on grounds of mutual mistake.   The plaintiff and the defendant were required by the court to share the losses as if they had been engaged in a joint venture rather than in a fixed price contract.   The decision has received less than favorable comment in the law reviews [22] and the court clearly and admittedly departed from principles ordinarily governing mutual mistake and reformation.   Although impossibility of performance was not discussed, it is clear that performance in the manner agreed was in fact impossible.   Under traditional analysis, however, impossibility would not have excused performance because the plaintiff foresaw and even complained about the risk.   Either the decision will be deemed "wrong" and ignored in the future or it will help point the way to a more flexible allocation of the parties' risks without reference to their agreement [23]—a further move from contract to status.

§ 200.   Effect of Impossibility Upon a Prior Repudiation

If A and B enter into an agreement under which A is to serve B for a year and B repudiates before the time for performance arrives, and A dies within that time, as we have seen, although A had a cause of action for the repudiation, his estate could not recover, because it would be necessary to show that A would have been ready, willing and able to perform but for the repudiation.[24]

The converse of this situation exists where, after a party repudiates, events occur which make his own performance impossible. Should the subsequent impossibility be taken into account in adjusting the rights of the parties? Some have taken the position that it should not because the rights of the parties became fixed by the repudiation.[25]

22. 65 Colum.L.Rev. 542 (1965); 33 Fordham L.Rev. 507 (1965).

23. See Cuneo & Cromwell, Impossibility of Performance—Assumption of the Risk or Act of Submission?, 29 Law & Contemp. Prob. 531, 533 (1964), where the authors state: "Neither the common law nor the *Restatement* furnish the necessary tools for an adequate analysis of space age impossibility under fixed-price contracts." Id. at 533.

24. See § 183 supra.

25. See Simpson, Contracts § 175.

The better rule appears to be that subsequent impossibility will discharge an anticipatory breach and will ordinarily limit damages in the case of a non-anticipatory breach.[26]

Thus under the majority rule in the illustration previously given if A repudiated before the time for performance and died before the time for performance, B would not be entitled to any recovery.[27] If A repudiated before the time for his performance and died one month after performance was to begin, B would be entitled to damages for only one month.[28] So also if A performed for two weeks and then repudiated and A died two weeks later, B would be entitled to damages for only two weeks.[29]

§ 201. Impossibility and Frustration Under the Uniform Commercial Code

The Commercial Code has a number of sections bearing upon impossibility of performance and frustration of the venture. Reference has been made to section 2–614 which governs failure of the contemplated means of delivery or payment[30] and to section 2–613 entitled "Casualty to Identified Goods."

The basic section of the Code dealing with "Impossibility of Performance" is section 2–615 which reads as follows:

Excuse by Failure of Presupposed Conditions

Except so far as a seller may have assumed a greater obligation and subject to the preceding section on substituted performance:

(a) Delay in delivery or non-delivery in whole or in part by a seller who complies with paragraphs (b) and (c) is not a breach of his duty under a contract for sale if performance as agreed has been made impracticable by the occurrence of a contingency the non-occurrence of which was a basic assumption on which the contract was made or by compliance in good faith with any applicable foreign or domestic governmental regulation or order whether or not it later proves to be invalid.

(b) Where the causes mentioned in paragraph (a) affect only a part of the seller's capacity to perform, he must allocate production and deliveries among his customers but may at his option include regular customers not then

---

26. See generally 6 Corbin § 1341; 6 Williston § 1967A (rev'd ed. 1938).

27. Restatement, Contracts § 457, Comment d.

28. Id., ill. 4.

29. Id., Comment d.

30. See § 188 supra.

under contract as well as his own requirements for further manufacture. He may so allocate in any manner which is fair and reasonable.

(c) The seller must notify the buyer seasonably that there will be delay or non-delivery and, when allocation is required under paragraph (b), of the estimated quota thus made available for the buyer.

Paragraph (a) states the doctrines of impossibility and frustration in broad general terms of the basic assumptions of the parties, which, as we have seen, is the theory underlying the doctrine. Comment 2 indicates that generalized rather than particularized language was adopted deliberately so that the courts may apply the reason and purpose of the section to any given set of facts.

The section continues the rule that "where a particular source of supply is exclusive under the agreement and falls through casualty," the doctrine of impossibility applies.[31] The Code also adopts the same rule where a source of supply, contemplated by both parties but not mentioned in the agreement, is fortuitously destroyed.[32] The Code, following the lead of California and of the Restatement embraces a test of impracticability,[33] and also recognizes the well established rule that the doctrine of impossibility should not be available to one who has been guilty of negligence.[34] The Code equates impossibility caused by domestic and foreign law and recognizes both as a defense.[35]

The Code has no provision explicitly relieving the buyer, who, by reason of a development not mentioned in the buyer-seller contract, has found it impracticable to perform: the impracticability section of the Code provides for the excuse of seller only. It seems, therefore, that the pre-Code law would be consulted to supplement the Code in the case of the buyer's claim of excuse.[36]

Subsection (b), which requires fair and reasonable allocation in the event partial delivery is practicable, appears to be in substantial accord with the present law.[37] Section 2–616 ties into subdivision (c) of section 2–615, which provides that in case of impossibility, "the

---

31. U.C.C. § 2–615, Comment 5.

32. Id.

33. See § 193 supra.

34. U.C.C. § 2–615, Comment 5.

35. Id., Comment 10.

36. Note, 105 U.Pa.L.Rev. 880, 904 (1957); U.C.C. § 2–605, Comment 9.

37. Mawhinney v. Millbrook Woolen Mills, Inc., 234 N.Y. 244, 137 N.E. 318 (1922) (government requisitioned much, but not all, of manufacturer's output); County of Yuba v. Mattoon, 160 Cal.App.2d 456, 325 P.2d 162 (1958); 6 Corbin § 1342; 6 Williston § 1974 (rev'd ed. 1938); Restatement, Contracts § 464.

seller must notify the buyer seasonably that there will be a delay or non-delivery" and, in a proper case, estimate the quota which will be available to the buyer.

Section 2–616 states the rights of the buyer when he receives such a notice. The section is self-explanatory and it reads as follows:

(1) Where the buyer receives notification of a material or indefinite delay or an allocation justified under the preceding section he may by written notification to the seller as to any delivery concerned, and where the prospective deficiency substantially impairs the value of the whole contract under the provisions of this Article relating to breach of installment contracts (Section 2–612), then also as to the whole,

(a) terminate and thereby discharge any unexecuted portion of the contract; or

(b) modify the contract by agreeing to take his available quota in substitution.

(2) If after receipt of such notification from the seller the buyer fails so to modify the contract within a reasonable time not exceeding thirty days the contract lapses with respect to any deliveries affected.

(3) The provisions of this section may not be negated by agreement except insofar as the seller has assumed a greater obligation under the preceding section.

These provisions relating to notice are new; there were no comparable provisions in the Sales Act.

CHAPTER 12

DAMAGES

Analysis

		Sections
A.	Introduction	202
B.	Non-compensatory Damages	203–204
C.	Compensatory Damages	205
D.	Foreseeability	206–208
E.	Certainty	209–212
F.	The Concept of Value	213–215
G.	Avoidable Consequences	216–218
H.	Damages in Particular Actions	219–231
I.	Agreed Damages	232–236

A. INTRODUCTION

Sec.
202. Damages Defined.

B. NON–COMPENSATORY DAMAGES

203. Nominal Damages.
204. Punitive Damages.

C. COMPENSATORY DAMAGES

205. The General Standard.

D. FORESEEABILITY

206. The Rule of Hadley v. Baxendale.
207. Application of the Rule in Carrier and Telegraph Cases.
208. Application of the Rule in Other Cases.

E. CERTAINTY

209. Certainty as a Limitation Upon Recovery of Damages.
210. Alternative Recovery: Reliance Interest Protected Where Expectation Interest is Uncertain or Nonexistent.
211. Alternative Recovery: Value of a Chance or Opportunity.
212. Alternative Recovery: Rental Value of Property that Might have Produced Profits.

F. THE CONCEPT OF VALUE

213. Market Value as the Usual Standard.
214. Proof of Value.
215. Value a Variable Concept.

G. AVOIDABLE CONSEQUENCES

Sec.
216. The "Duty" to Mitigate Damages.
217. Non-exclusive Contracts—An Apparent Exception to the Doctrine of Avoidable Consequences.
218. Recovery of Expenses Sustained in Avoiding Consequence of a Breach.

H. DAMAGES IN PARTICULAR ACTIONS

219. Wrongful Discharge of Employee.
220. Wrongful Termination by Employee.
221. Total Breach of Sales Contracts—Buyer's General Damages.
222. Buyer's General Damages for Seller's Breach of Warranty or Fraud.
223. Consequential and Incidental Damages for Seller's Breach.
224. Seller's General Damages for Non-acceptance or Repudiation.
225. Seller's General Damages Following Resale.
226. Seller's Consequential and Incidental Damages.
227. Seller's Action for the Price.
228. Seller's Damages for Contracts to Manufacture Special Goods Under the Code.
229. Construction Contracts: Measure of Recovery by Contractor.
230. Construction Contracts: Measure of Recovery by Owner.
231. Contracts to Sell Realty: Measure of Damages for Total Breach.

I. AGREED DAMAGES

232. Liquidated Damages Distinguished from Penalties.
233. Two Pitfalls of Draftsmanship: The Shotgun Clause and the Have Cake and Eat It Clause.
234. Availability of Specific Performance When Damages are Liquidated.
235. Liquidated Damages and Penalties Distinguished from Alternative Promises.
236. Liquidated Damages Under the Uniform Commercial Code.

A. INTRODUCTION

Analysis

Sec.
202. Damages Defined.

§ 202. Damages Defined

In the later stages of the system of common law pleading in an action to enforce a contract, two basic writs were available.[1] If the plaintiff had fully performed all or a severable part of his contractual obligation and if the agreed exchange for his performance was the

---

[1.] A common law pleader would find this statement and ensuing discussion greatly over-simplified. For a discussion of the writs formerly available in contract cases, see Shipman, Common Law Pleading 132–169 (3d ed. Ballantine 1923).

payment of money, the writ of general assumpsit was available to him. The plaintiff's recovery was the agreed price, or, if no price had been agreed upon, the reasonable value of the labor or services he had rendered or the property which he had transferred to the defendant. Although such recovery was sometimes referred to as "damages," [2] it is conceptually and practically different from an award of damages as that term is generally understood.

When the defendant breached his contract prior to a completed performance by the plaintiff, the appropriate writ was special assumpsit. In this case the plaintiff was not entitled to recover the agreed price, but only the amount of the pecuniary injury, if any, he had suffered. It is sometimes said that the plaintiff's contract rights are primary rights and upon breach by the defendant, these primary rights are discharged and in substitution the law grants the plaintiff secondary rights.[3] The law of remedies defines the scope of these secondary rights.

Modern law has kept the distinction made in these common law writs. This is not necessarily because the common law writs continue to rule us from the grave; rather the distinction makes good economic sense. When the plaintiff has fully performed, it would be anomalous not to award him the agreed price. The Uniform Commercial Code labels a lawsuit seeking this kind of recovery an "action for the price." [4] When the plaintiff has not fully performed it would often be unduly generous to him and unduly harsh on the defendant to award him the price. Rather, the inquiry should be and is: what was the extent of his economic injury? Usually, this will be less than the agreed exchange; but sometimes it will be more. Compensation allowed by law for this injury is known as damages. In addition, two categories of recoveries—nominal damages and punitive damages—have other non-compensatory functions. These play a rather small role in contract actions and will be discussed briefly at the outset of this chapter.

---

2. Indeed, the plaintiff would allege as follows:

"But the said [defendant] to pay the same, or any part thereof, hath hitherto wholly refused, and still refuses, to the damage of the said [plaintiff] of —— pounds; and therefore he brings this suit, etc."

Stephen, Principles of Pleading in Civil Actions 361 (2d ed. Andrews 1901).

3. 5 Corbin § 995. The Restatement, looking at the right-duty relationship from the perspective of the obligor's duty, states that the obligor's contractual duty is discharged and in substitution a duty to make compensation is placed upon him. Restatement, Contracts § 399(1).

4. U.C.C. § 2–709. Unlike the rule under the common law writs, in an action for the price, incidental damages may sometimes be recovered in addition to the price. See § 223 infra; 5 Corbin § 995; U.C.C. § 2–709.

B. NON–COMPENSATORY DAMAGES

Analysis

Sec.
203. Nominal Damages.
204. Punitive Damages.

§ 203. Nominal Damages

For every legal wrong there is a legal remedy.[5] Thus, for every breach of contract a cause of action exists. If the aggrieved party has suffered no damage he is entitled to a judgment for nominal damages,[6] usually in the amount of six cents or one dollar,[7] to symbolize vindication of the wrong done to him.

As a practical matter an award of nominal damages in a contract action may serve either of two functions. First, the plaintiff may bring an action knowing that he will at best obtain nominal damages in order to establish a precedent in a test case or in a dispute that is likely to recur in a continuing relationship.[8] Today, under modern statutes, he is more likely to bring an action for a declaratory judgment. Second, and more frequently, the plaintiff is likely to institute his action in the belief that he is entitled to substantial damages. At trial he establishes that the contract was breached, but fails to establish that he has suffered actual damages. He thus is entitled to a judgment for nominal damages.[9] Traditionally, since he has established his cause of action he is also entitled to the costs of the action. It is sometimes said that nominal damages is a "peg to hang costs on." [10] In recent years this function of nominal damages has been somewhat curtailed. Statutory provisions frequently provide that if the action could have been brought in a court of inferior jurisdiction costs will not be recovered unless a specified minimum judgment is entered.[11] These statutes are designed to relieve congestion in the major trial courts.

5. Ashby v. White, 92 Eng.Rep. 126 (Q. B. 1703).

6. Manhattan Sav. Institution v. Gottfried Baking Co., 286 N.Y. 398, 36 N. E.2d 637 (1941); Restatement, Contracts §§ 327–328.

7. Hasselbusch v. Mohmking, 76 N.J.L. 691, 73 A. 961 (1909); Manhattan Sav. Institution v. Gottfried Baking Co., 286 N.Y. 398, 36 N.E.2d 637 (1941).

8. McCormick, Damages 95–96 (1935) [hereinafter cited as McCormick, Damages].

9. Beattie v. New York, N.H. & Hartford Ry., 84 Conn. 555, 80 A. 709 (1911). On the additional question involved in this case of whether a judgment for the defendant will be reversed and remanded when it appears that the plaintiff is entitled merely to nominal damages, see Note, 25 Colum. L.Rev. 963 (1925).

10. Stanton v. New York & E. Ry., 59 Conn. 272, 282, 22 A. 300, 303 (1890).

11. E. g., McKinney's N.Y.C.P.L.R. 8102; see McCormick, Damages 94–95.

§ 204. Punitive Damages

Punitive damages are granted to punish malicious or wilful and wanton conduct.[12] The purpose of such an award is to deter the wrongdoer from similar conduct in the future as well as to deter others from engaging in such conduct. Punitive damages awards are of growing importance in tort litigation. Traditionally, however, punitive damages are not awarded in contract actions, no matter how malicious the breach.[13]

Where, however, the breach constitutes or is accompanied by an independent malicious or wanton tort, punitive damages are available.[14] They are also awarded where the breach also involves the malicious or wanton violation of a fiduciary duty.[15]

C. COMPENSATORY DAMAGES

Analysis

Sec.
205. The General Standard.

§ 205. The General Standard

For breach of contract the law of damages seeks to place the aggrieved party in the same economic position he would have had if the contract had been performed.[16] This involves an award of both the "losses caused and gains prevented by the defendant's breach, in

---

12. See McCormick, Damages 275–299. Punitive damages are also known as exemplary damages.

13. J.J. White, Inc. v. Metropolitan Merchandise Mart, 48 Del. 526, 107 A. 2d 892 (1954); American Ry. Exp. Co. v. Bailey, 142 Miss. 622, 107 So. 761 (1926); Restatement, Contracts § 342; see Simpson, Punitive Damages for Breach of Contract, 20 Ohio St.L.J. 284 (1959); annot., 84 A.L.R. 1345 (1933).

14. I.H.P. Corp. v. 210 Central Park South Corp., 12 N.Y.2d 329, 239 N.Y. S.2d 547, 189 N.E.2d 812 (1963) (breach of lease constituted tort of forcible entry and detainer). For additional cases see Simpson, note 13 supra at 287.

In South Carolina, a breach of contract accompanied by a fraudulent act, in a broad sense of the term "fraudulent," is a basis for an award of punitive damages. See Howser, The Awarding of Punitive Damages for Breach of Insurance Contracts in South Carolina, 1 S.C.L.Q. 150 (1948); Note, Punitive Damages for Breach of Contract, 10 S.C.L.Q. 444 (1958).

15. Brown v. Coates, 102 U.S.App.D.C. 300, 253 F.2d 36 (1958), 33 N.Y.U.L. Rev. 878 (1958) (real estate broker); cf. International Bhd. of Boilermakers v. Braswell, 388 F.2d 193 (5th Cir. 1968), cert. denied 391 U.S. 935, 88 S. Ct. 1848, 20 L.Ed.2d 854 (union wrongfully expelled member); Hoche Productions, S.A. v. Jayark Films Corp., 256 F.Supp. 291 (S.D.N.Y.1966) (film distributor fraudulently accounted for gross receipts).

16. 5 Corbin § 992; McCormick, Damages 561; 11 Williston § 1338.

excess of savings made possible." [17]   An illustrative case is Lieberman v. Templar Motors Co.[18]   The plaintiff contracted to manufacture a number of specially designed automobile bodies.   The contract was repudiated by the defendant after production had commenced and about one-quarter of the bodies had been delivered.   Since there was no market for auto bodies of this special design, the plaintiff could not mitigate his damages by completing the manufacture of the remaining bodies and selling them on the market.   It was held that the plaintiff could recover his gains prevented calculated by the difference of what would have been the cost of performance and the contract price;   in other words, the profit the defendant would have made if the contract had been fully performed.   In addition, the plaintiff was permitted to recover the amount of his losses sustained.   These consisted of payments for labor and material, reasonably made in part performance of the contract, to the extent that these were wasted; that is, to the extent that the labor product and materials could not be salvaged.[19]

There are many rules of damages for particular kinds of contracts;   for example, contracts for the sale of goods,[20] construction contracts,[21] employment contracts,[22] etc.   With only a few exceptions, mainly in the real property area,[23] these specialized rules implement the general standard of gains prevented and losses sustained. It sometimes happens that because of the particular facts of a case the specialized rule usually applicable does not fulfill its purpose of providing an accurate formula for determining the gains prevented and losses sustained.   In such a case the courts will turn to the general standard.[24]

Recently, a new analysis of the elements of contract damages has been made.[25]   It has been pointed out that a contracting party has

---

17.   Restatement, Contracts § 329.

18.   236 N.Y. 139, 140 N.E. 222, 29 A.L. R. 1089 (1923).

19.   Also included are "overhead expenses" such as an allocated share of the cost of management, plant, electric power, etc.   See Conditioned Air Corp. v. Rock Island Motor Transit Co., 253 Iowa 961, 114 N.W.2d 304, 3 A.L.R.2d 679 (1962), cert. denied 371 U.S. 825, 83 S.Ct. 46, 9 L.Ed.2d 64 (1962).

20.   See §§ 221–28 infra.

21.   See §§ 229–30 infra.

22.   See §§ 219–20 infra.

23.   See § 231 infra.

24.   See, e. g., Great Atlantic & Pacific Tea Co. v. Atchison, T. & S. F. Ry., 333 F.2d 705 (7th Cir. 1964), cert. denied 379 U.S. 967, 85 S.Ct. 661, 13 L. Ed.2d 560 (1965); Liberty Navig. & Trading Co. v. Kinoshita & Co., 285 F.2d 343 (2d Cir. 1960), cert. denied 366 U.S. 949, 81 S.Ct. 1904, 6 L.Ed.2d 1242 (1961); Abrams v. Reynolds Metals Co., 340 Mass. 704, 166 N.E.2d 204 (1960).

25.   Fuller & Perdue, The Reliance Interest in Contract Damages, 46 Yale L.J. 52, 373 (1936–37).

three legally protected interests: a restitution interest, a reliance interest, and an expectation interest. The first of these represents his interest in the benefits he has conferred upon the other. The reliance interest represents the detriment he may have incurred by changing his position. The expectation interest represents the prospect of gain from the contract. This analysis does not conflict with the gains prevented and losses sustained analysis; it merely represents a different breakdown of the same economic harm suffered. The use of this newer analysis is gaining acceptance as it often permits a clearer way of determining the actual economic harm.

D.　FORESEEABILITY

Analysis

Sec.
206.　The Rule of Hadley v. Baxendale.
207.　Application of the Rule in Carrier and Telegraph Cases.
208.　Application of the Rule in Other Cases.

§ 206.　The Rule of Hadley v. Baxendale

Prior to 1854 there were almost no rules of contract damages. The assessment of damages was pretty much left to the unfettered discretion of the jury.[26] Such broad discretion, however, was unsuited to the now mature commercial economy of England. In that year the case of Hadley v. Baxendale [27] was decided. It has won universal acceptance in the common law world and remains the leading case in the field.

The plaintiffs operated a grist mill which was forced to suspend operations because of a broken shaft. An employee of the plaintiff brought the broken shaft to the defendants for shipment to an engineering company which was to manufacture a new shaft, using the broken one as a model. The defendants unexcusably delayed the shipment for several days. As a result the mill was shut down for a greater period of time than it would have been had the shipment been seasonably dispatched.[28] A judgment entered upon jury verdict for

26.　McCormick, Damages 562–563; Washington, Damages in Contract at Common Law, 47 Law Q.Rev. 345 (1931), 48 Law Q.Rev. 90 (1932).

27.　156 Eng.Rep. 145 (1845).

28.　Many discussions of the case have demonstrated that there has been confusion as to the facts of the case. According to the reporter's statement of the facts the plaintiff's servant told the clerk that the mill was stopped and the shaft was to be sent immediately. But the opinion of the court states: "We find that the only circumstances here communicated by the plaintiffs to the defendants at the time the contract was made were that the article to be carried was the broken shaft of a mill, and the plaintiffs

the plaintiff which included an award of damages for the lost profits of the mill was reversed.

The court laid down two rules. First, the aggrieved party may recover those damages "as may fairly and reasonably be considered . . . arising naturally, i.e., according to the usual course of things, from such breach of contract itself." Second, he may recover damages "such as may reasonably be supposed to have been in the contemplation of both parties, at the time they made the contract, as the probable result of the breach of it." [29] A several days delay in the shipment of a shaft does not "in the usual course of things" result in catastrophic consequences. Usually, delay in shipment of a chattel results in a loss of the value of its use for the period of delay; that is, its rental value.[30] Liability for damages in excess of that value, according to the second rule of Hadley v. Baxendale, will only be awarded if such additional damages were in the contemplation of both parties as a probable consequence of a breach. As applied in this case and subsequent cases, this means that such consequences must be foreseeable.[31] Thus, if the shipper had known that the mill was shut down

were millers of that mill." Even as careful a scholar as McCormick uncritically accepted the reporter's statement of the facts. McCormick, Damages 564; McCormick, The Contemplation Rule as a Limitation upon Damages for Breach of Contract, 19 Minn.L.Rev. 497, 509 (1935). A subsequent English case has pointed out the error of reliance on the reporter's statement insofar as it conflicts with the court's analysis of the facts. Victoria Laundry (Windsor) Ltd. v. Newman Industries, Ltd., [1949] 2 K.B. 528, 537. In this case the court indicated that if the reporter's headnote were correct, the decision would have gone the other way. Unfortunately some cases have relied on the headnote, thereby reaching erroneous results. E. g., Moss Jellico Coal Co. v. American Ry. Exp. Co., 198 Ky. 202, 248 S.W. 508 (1923).

29. 156 Eng.Rep. at 151.

30. New Orleans & N. E. R. R. v. J. H. Miner Saw Mfg. Co., 117 Miss. 646, 78 So. 577 (1918); Chapman v. Fargo, 223 N.Y. 32, 119 N.E. 76 (1918). If, however, the goods are shipped for the purpose of sale, the aggrieved party may recover any depreciation in the market value of the goods which may have occurred between the time the goods should have arrived and the time of their arrival. Ward v. New York Cent. R.R., 47 N.Y. 29 (1871); but cf. Great Atlantic & Pacific Tea Co., Inc. v. Atchison, T. & S. F. Ry., 333 F.2d 705 (7th Cir. 1964), cert. denied 379 U.S. 967, 85 S.Ct. 661, 13 L. Ed.2d 560 (1965) (no damages awarded where wholesale price declined but goods were resold at price originally contemplated).

31. Cf. Restatement, Contracts § 330, which provides:

"In awarding damages, compensation is given for only those injuries that the defendant had reason to foresee as a probable result of his breach when the contract was made. If the injury is one that follows the breach in the usual course of events, there is sufficient reason for the defendants to foresee it; otherwise, it must be shown specifically that the defendant had reason to know the facts and to foresee the injury."

For the intimate relationship between the doctrine of foreseeability and the doctrine of avoidable consequences, see § 216 infra.

because of the want of the shaft and that no substitute shaft was available, the shipper would have been liable for consequential damages consisting of the lost profits of the mill.

When parties enter into a contract their minds are usually fixed on performance rather than on breach. To the extent that this is true, it is fictional to speak in terms of the damages which are in the subjective contemplation of the parties.[32] When courts speak in terms of the "contemplation of the parties," they use this terminology within the framework of the objective theory of contracts. Under the first rule of Hadley v. Baxendale, certain damages will so naturally and obviously flow from the breach that every one is deemed to contemplate them. Frequently such damages are known as "general" damages. Under the second rule, less obvious kinds of damages are deemed to be contemplated if the promisor knows or has reason to know the special circumstances which will give rise to such damages. Such damages are frequently known as "special" or "consequential" damages.

A number of English cases subsequently applied a stricter rule than that announced in Hadley v. Baxendale. According to these cases, mere notice of special circumstances is an insufficient basis for imposing liability for consequential damages. These decisions required that the knowledge of special circumstances "must be brought home to the party to be charged under such circumstances that he must know that the person he contracts with reasonably believes that he accepts the contract with the special condition attached to it." [33] In other words there must be an express or implied manifestation of intent to assume the risk of foreseeable consequential damages. This "tacit agreement" test was adopted by Mr. Justice Holmes for the United States Supreme Court as Federal common law,[34] but has attracted few followers among the state courts.[35] This additional quali-

32. "I think a more precise statement of this rule is, that a party is liable for all the direct damages which both parties to the contract would have contemplated as flowing from the breach, if at the time they entered into it they had bestowed proper attention upon the subject, and had been fully informed of the facts. In this case then, in what may be called the fiction of law . . .." Leonard v. New York, Albany and Buffalo Electro-Magnetic Tel. Co., 41 N.Y. 544, 567 (1870).

33. British Columbia Saw-Mill Co. v. Nettleship, L.R. 3 C.P. 499, 500 (1868);

accord, Horne v. Midland R.R., L.R. 7 C.P. 583 (1872), L.R. 8 C.P. 131 (1873).

34. Globe Ref. Co. v. Landa Cotton Oil Co., 190 U.S. 540, 23 S.Ct. 754, 47 L. Ed. 1171 (1903). With the general abandonment of Federal common law, in diversity cases the Federal courts must now apply state law in such cases. Krauss v. Greenbarg, 137 F.2d 569 (3d Cir. 1943), cert. denied 320 U. S. 791, 64 S.Ct. 207, 88 L.Ed. 477, reh. denied 320 U.S. 815, 64 S.Ct. 368, 88 L.Ed. 492 (1944).

35. See McCormick, Damages 579–80. It has also been attacked by writers

fication of the Rule of Hadley v. Baxendale appears to have been abandoned in England [36] and has been repudiated by the Uniform Commercial Code.[37]   The "tacit agreement" test was based on the dubious assumption that damages for breach of contract are based upon the contracting parties implied or express promise to pay damages in the event of breach, rather than based upon a secondary duty imposed by law as a consequence of the breach.[38]

§ 207. Application of the Rule in Carrier and Telegraph Cases

Hadley v. Baxendale itself was a carrier case. It indicated that a carrier will be liable for consequential damages if it is on notice of the particular purpose the cargo will serve and the fact that there is no available substitute for the cargo which is delayed, lost or injured in transit. If there were an available substitute the aggrieved party by virtue of the doctrine of avoidable consequences would not be able to recover those damages which could have been avoided by employment of the substitute.[39]

Applying this test, a carrier is not liable for consequential damages consisting of lost profits when it delays shipment of motion picture film to a theater if it has no notice that the theater could not procure a substitute film.[40]   Similarly a carrier was held not liable for a lost engagement suffered by a vaudeville artist caused by delay in shipment of his baggage where, although the carrier knew the contents of baggage, it did not know that the artist was engaged for a performance at the point of destination.[41]

On the other hand, if the shipment is of such a character that its purpose is obvious and the consequences of non-delivery equally obvious, the carrier will be held liable for consequential damages. Thus, when a carrier undertakes to transport scenery for a road show and

on contracts. 11 Williston § 1357; 5 Corbin § 1010. It is supported by Bauer, Consequential Damages in Contract, 80 U.Pa.L.Rev. 687 (1931).

36. Victoria Laundry (Windsor) Ltd. v. Newman Industries Ltd., [1949] 2 K.B. 528, seems to have slightly liberalized the Hadley v. Baxendale test. Consequential damages were allowed where the defendant had "reason to know" the special circumstances although these were not communicated by the plaintiff.

37. U.C.C. § 2–715, Comment 2. It seems no longer to be followed by Federal courts in the application of federal statutes, such as the Carmack Amendment, 49 U.S.C.A. § 20(11), concerning the liability of land carriers in interstate commerce. See, e. g., L. E. Whitlock Truck Serv. v. Regal Drilling Co., 333 F.2d 488 (10th Cir. 1964).

38. See 5 Corbin § 1010; 11 Williston § 1357.

39. See § 216 infra.

40. Chapman v. Fargo, 223 N.Y. 32, 119 N.E. 76, 1918F L.R.A. 1040 (1918).

41. Rives v. American Ry. Exp. Co., 227 App.Div. 375, 237 N.Y.S. 429 (1st Dep't 1929).

knows the date of the scheduled theatrical performance it will be liable for consequential damages suffered by the road company as the carrier should be aware that no substitute scenery will be available.[42] In a decision perhaps more liberal than most a carrier was held liable for loss of a herd of hogs caused by its delay in the shipment of hog cholera serum.[43] The Court indicated that the carrier should be aware of the probable use and probable consequences of the delay although it did not know, for example, that the consignee was a farmer. A stronger case is made out when the carrier is actually told the special circumstances. Thus, if the carrier is told that an oil well drilling rig is the only one the consignor has and the consequent importance of timely delivery, it is liable for the loss of profit attributable to the lack of prompt delivery.[44] If, however, other rigs were available on a short term basis on the rental market, the decision would go the other way.

Decisions involving the liability of telegraph companies are closely aligned to those involving carriers. Telegraph companies share with common carriers a duty to serve everyone on an equal basis. In addition they both receive a relatively small compensation for services which, if not duly performed, could result in catastrophic financial losses to their clients. The courts have been highly reluctant to shift these losses to the carrier in view of the disproportion between the compensation received and the potentially large burden of damages. Thus, the courts have tended towards particular strictness in these classes of cases in applying the test of foreseeability. If a telegraph message clearly indicates the nature of the transaction, the telegraph company is liable for consequential damages flowing from negligence in failing to transmit a message or in transmitting it erroneously.[45] If the message conveys nothing to the company as to the nature of the transaction, clearly there is no liability for consequential damages.[46] Where, as is often the case, the message is obviously a business message, but the nature of the transaction is not clear, there is not a sufficient basis for recovery of consequential damages. "Notice of the

42. Weston v. Boston & M. R. R., 190 Mass. 298, 76 N.E. 1050, 4 L.R.A.,N.S., 569 (1906).

43. Adams Exp. Co. v. Allen, 125 Va. 530, 100 S.E. 473 (1919).

44. L. E. Whitlock Truck Serv., Inc. v. Regal Drilling Co., 333 F.2d 488 (10th Cir. 1964).

45. Leonard v. New York, Albany and Buffalo Electro-Magnetic Tel. Co., 41 N.Y. 544 (1870) (message as transmitted read, "Send 5,000 casks of salt immediately," instead of "send 5,000 sacks of salt immediately."); Allen v. Western Union Tel. Co., 209 S.C. 157, 39 S.E.2d 257, 167 A.L.R. 1392 (1946); contra, Daugherty v. American Union Tel. Co., 75 Ala. 168 (1883) (rejecting rule of Hadley v. Baxendale).

46. Primrose v. Western Union Tel. Co., 154 U.S. 1, 14 S.Ct. 1098, 38 L.Ed. 883 (1893) (message in private code).

business, if it is to lay the basis for special damages, must be sufficiently informing to be notice of the risk." [47]

In any modern case involving a common carrier or telegraph company, an additional factor to be considered is limitation of the carrier's liability under applicable state and federal regulatory legislation.[48] While these statutes do not overrule the contemplation of the parties test, they frequently curtail the amount of recovery by setting a maximum limit, or permit the parties to set such a limit by agreement.

§ 208. Application of the Rule in Other Cases

The doctrine of foreseeability is applicable not only in carrier cases but in all contract cases. The discussion in this chapter dealing with damages in particular kinds of contract actions will consider both general and consequential damages in such actions.

E.   CERTAINTY

Analysis

Sec.
209.   Certainty as a Limitation Upon Recovery of Damages.
210.   Alternative Recovery: Reliance Interest Protected Where Expectation Interest is Uncertain or Nonexistence.
211.   Alternative Recovery: Value of a Chance or Opportunity.
212.   Alternative Recovery: Rental Value of Property that Might have Produced Profits.

§ 209. Certainty as a Limitation Upon Recovery of Damages

Ordinarily, prior to rendering its verdict a jury is charged by the judge to render a decision based on the "preponderance of the evidence." [49] The jury's verdict may be set aside only if the court concludes "that no reasonable man would solve the litigation in the way the jury has chosen to do." [50] Frequently, however, a different standard is applied in cases involving contract damages. The jury's verdict will be set aside if the standard of "certainty" is not met. It has

---

47. Kerr S.S. Co. v. Radio Corp. of America, 245 N.Y. 284, 288, 157 N.E. 140, 55 A.L.R. 1139 (1927); accord, Einbinder v. Western Union Tel. Co., 205 S.C. 15, 30 S.E.2d 765, 154 A.L.R. 704 (1944).

48. Cf. U.C.C. § 7–309 as to carriers' limitations of liability, with citations in the official comments to other legislation. On the question of preemp-

tion of state law by federal legislation, see Western Union Tel. Co. v. Priester, 276 U.S. 252, 48 S.Ct. 234, 72 L.Ed. 555 (1928); Western Union Tel. Co. v. Abbott Supply Co., 45 Del. 345, 74 A.2d 77, 20 A.L.R.2d 754 (1950).

49. McCormick, Evidence § 319 (1954).

50. Rapant v. Ogsbury, 279 App.Div. 298, 109 N.Y.S.2d 737 (3rd Dep't 1952).

been said that the damages "must be certain, both in their nature and in respect to the causes from which they proceed." [51] It seems to be generally recognized that absolute certainty is not required; "reasonable certainty" will suffice.[52]

Courts do not as a rule impose the requirement of certainty except where the damages in issue involve lost profits on transactions other than the transaction on which the breach occurred.[53] To illustrate, if there is a contract for the delivery of sugar at six cents a pound and at the time the buyer learns of the breach the market price is seven cents, the purchaser has suffered gains prevented in the amount of one cent per pound. The courts do not insist upon a standard of certainty in establishing this loss.[54] If, however, the seller has reason to know that the sugar will be used by the buyer for the baking of cakes for resale and no other supply of sugar will seasonably be available to the buyer, the seller may be liable for the profits which would have been made upon resale of the cakes.[55] It is to profits such as these that the standard of certainty is applied. The baker must show with certainty that he would have made profits on the sale of the cakes as not all bakery operations necessarily result in profits. He must also establish with certainty the amount of such profits.

There is no satisfactory way of defining what is meant by "certainty" or "reasonable certainty." It means, however, that the quality of the evidence must be of a higher caliber than is needed to establish most other factual issues in a lawsuit. Although the courts have been using more or less the same language for well over a century, the stringency of its application has tended to vary in different decades dependent upon the makeup and philosophy of the bench in a particular jurisdiction at a particular time.[56]

It has usually been held that lost profits caused by a breach of contract to produce a sporting event,[57] theatrical performance or

---

51. Griffin v. Colver, 16 N.Y. 489 (1858).

52. Restatement, Contracts § 331(1); McCormick, Damages 401.

53. Corbin §§ 1020–1028; McCormick, Damages 104–106.

54. Market price may in fact be uncertain or fictitious. See § 213 infra.

55. See § 221 infra.

56. Compare the liberal attitude and the relaxed standard of certainty in Wakeman v. Wheeler & W. Mfg. Co.,

101 N.Y. 205, 4 N.E.2d 264 (1886), with the stringent standard of Judge Cardozo in Broadway Photoplay Co. v. World Film Corp., 225 N.Y. 104, 121 N.E. 756 (1919), and the return to a relaxed standard in Duane Jones Co. v. Burke, 306 N.Y. 172, 117 N.E.2d 237 (1952); Spitz v. Lesser, 302 N.Y. 490, 99 N.E.2d 540 (1951), 9 Wash. & Lee L.Rev. 75 (1952).

57. Chicago Coliseum Club v. Dempsey, 265 Ill.App. 542 (1932); Carnera v. Schmeling, 236 App.Div. 460, 260 N.Y. S. 82 (1st Dep't 1932).

other form of entertainment,[58] are too uncertain for recovery. Evidence of profits made by other performances of a similar kind or by the same performance in a different city has been deemed insufficiently probative of whether profits would have been made and, in any event, of the amount which would have been made. Similarly, new businesses have not been successful in establishing with certainty what their profits, if any, would have been in cases where the defendant's breach prevented or delayed their opening for business. This has been the result, despite evidence of earnings subsequent to their opening or earnings of similar businesses elsewhere.[59] It is interesting to note, however, that in actions based upon antitrust law violations, new businesses have been awarded damages based upon lost profits.[60] The difference in treatment accorded to contract actions reveals rather clearly that the standard of certainty, like the rule of foreseeability, is based at least partly upon a policy of limiting contractual risks.[61]

As a rule, established businesses can prove lost profits on transactions of a kind in which the particular business has traditionally engaged with sufficient certainty.[62] Even here, however, a verdict

58. Narragansett Amusement Co. v. Riverside Park Amusement Co., 260 Mass. 265, 157 N.E. 532 (1927); Bernstein v. Meech, 130 N.Y. 354, 29 N.E. 255 (1892); Willis v. Branch, 94 N.C. 142 (1886). But compare Orbach v. Paramount Pictures Corp., 233 Mass. 281, 123 N.E. 669 (1919), where the theater was able to recover on the basis of proof of net profits prior and subsequent to the period of breach and of the profits of another theater in the same city, with Broadway Photoplay Co. v. World Film Corp., 225 N.Y. 104, 121 N.E. 756 (1919), where similar proof of damages was held to be too uncertain.

59. Central Coal & Coke Co. v. Hartman, 111 F. 96 (8th Cir. 1901); Thrift Wholesale, Inc. v. Malkin-Illion Corp., 50 F.Supp. 998 (E.D.Pa.1943); Marvell Light & Ice Co. v. General Elec. Co., 162 Ark. 467, 259 S.W. 741 (1924); California Press Mfg. Co. v. Stafford Packing Co., 192 Cal. 479, 221 P. 345, 32 A.L.R. 114 (1923); Paola Gas Co. v. Paola Glass Co., 56 Kan. 614, 44 P. 621 (1896); Evergreen Amusement Corp. v. Milstead, 206 Md. 610, 112 A. 2d 901 (1955); Cramer v. Grand Rap-

ids Showcase, 223 N.Y. 63, 119 N.E. 227, 1 A.L.R. 154 (1918); Barbier v. Barry, 345 S.W.2d 557 (Tex.Civ.App. 1961).

60. William Goldman Theatres v. Loew's, 69 F.Supp. 103 (E.D.N.Y.1946), review denied 163 F.2d 241, (2d Cir.), aff'd 164 F.2d 1021, cert. denied 334 U.S. 811, 68 S.Ct. 1016, 92 L.Ed. 1742 (1948).

61. Botta v. Brunner, 42 N.J.Super. 95, 126 A.2d 32 (1956), modified 26 N.J. 82, 138 A.2d 713, 60 A.L.R.2d 1331 (1958); cf. McCormick, Damages 105; Fuller & Perdue, supra note 25, at 373–77. Indeed, courts have on occasion intermingled the foreseeability and certainty tests into a single doctrine. See Archer-Daniels Midland Co. v. Paull, 293 F.2d 389 (8th Cir. 1961), 48 Iowa L.Rev. 147 (1962); Witherbee v. Meyer, 155 N.Y. 446, 50 N.E. 58 (1898).

62. Natural Soda Prod. Co. v. City of Los Angeles, 23 Cal.2d 193, 143 P.2d 12 (1943), cert. denied 321 U.S. 793, 64 S.Ct. 790, 88 L.Ed. 1082, reh. denied 322 U.S. 768, 64 S.Ct. 942, 88 L.Ed. 1594 (1944). The cases which are per-

for the plaintiff will be set aside if the court is not convinced that the record contains the best available evidence upon which an informed verdict can be based.[63]

There are said to be several modifying doctrines of the rule of certainty. Leading among these is the statement that "where the defendant's wrong has caused the difficulty of proof of damage, he cannot complain of the resulting uncertainty." [64] If this statement were literally true, no verdict could be set aside on the ground of uncertainty except in the case where plaintiff's counsel has failed to produce the best available evidence of the fact and amount of lost profits. Yet courts frequently rely on this supposed modifying doctrine.[65] It is also clear that they frequently do not.[66] It has been suggested that there is a tendency to relax the rule of certainty and to apply this modifying doctrine where the breach is wilful.[67] What is clear is that there is no universal application of the rule of certainty, and that, within a given jurisdiction, case authority which applies a stringent test often exists along with other cases which, in express terms [68] or, in effect, hold that certainty is not a requirement.

haps most cited on the point today are cases involving private actions to recover treble damages under the anti-trust laws. Bigelow v. RKO Radio Pictures, Inc., 327 U.S. 251, 66 S.Ct. 574, 90 L.Ed. 652 (1946), reh. denied 327 U.S. 817, 66 S.Ct. 815, 90 L.Ed. 1040; Eastman Kodak Co. v. Southern Photo Materials Co., 273 U.S. 359, 47 S.Ct. 400, 71 L.Ed. 684 (1927). Reliance on the relatively relaxed standard applied in these cases, particularly in the Bigelow case, has had a notably liberalizing effect upon contract decisions.

A small number of decisions take the position that lost profits on resale are inherently too speculative for proof and refuse to allow any evidence on the point. See Paris v. Buckner Feed Mill, 279 Ala. 148, 182 So.2d 880 (1966).

63. Center Chem. Co. v. Avril, Inc., 392 F.2d 289 (5th Cir. 1968); Alexander's Dep't Stores, Inc. v. Ohrbach's, Inc., 269 App.Div. 321, 56 N.Y.S.2d 173 (1st Dep't 1945); Allen, Heaton & McDonald, Inc. v. Castle Farm Amusement Co., 151 Ohio St. 522, 86 N.E.2d 782, 17 A.L.R.2d 963 (1949); McCormick, Damages 107–10. For an excellent summary of the kind of evidence deemed acceptable, see Note, 14 Minn.L.Rev. 820 (1930); see also Commonwealth Trust Co. of Pittsburgh v. Hachmeister-Lind Co., 320 Pa. 233, 181 A. 787 (1935).

64. McCormick, Damages 101.

65. Bigelow v. RKO Radio Pictures, Inc., 327 U.S. 251, 66 S.Ct. 574, 90 L. Ed. 652 (1946), reh. denied 327 U.S. 817, 66 S.Ct. 815, 90 L.Ed. 1040; (anti-trust case); Milton v. Hudson Sales Corp., 152 Cal.App.2d 418, 313 P.2d 936 (1957); Wakeman v. Wheeler & W. Mfg. Co., 101 N.Y. 205, 4 N.E. 264 (1886).

66. Broadway Photoplay Co. v. World Film Corp., 225 N.Y. 104, 121 N.E. 756 (1919); and see the cases cited at notes 57, 58, 59 supra.

67. Bauer, The Degree of Moral Fault as Affecting Defendant's Liability, 81 U.Pa.L.Rev. 586, 592 (1931).

68. Cases which have expressly stated that certainty is not a requirement include Hacker Pipe & Supply Co. v. Chapman Valve Mfg. Co., 17 Cal.App. 2d 265, 61 P.2d 944 (1936) (standard of

More commonly than is the case in other fields of contract law, the decision as to a particular set of facts cannot be predicted by the application of abstract legal rules. The Uniform Commercial Code in a comment indicates that in Code governed cases the standard of proof must be flexibly applied and certainty will not be insisted upon where the facts of the case do not permit more than an approximate estimate.[69]

If the aggrieved party is unable to prove his damages with sufficient certainty it does not follow that he may not have any recovery. The next three sections will consider alternative measures of recovery where lost profits cannot be established.

§ 210. Alternative Recovery: Reliance Interest Protected Where Expectation Interest is Uncertain or Nonexistent

When the aggrieved party cannot establish his loss of profits with sufficient certainty, he is permitted to recover his expenses of preparation and of part performance, as well as other foreseeable expenses incurred in reliance upon the contract. This relief is awarded on "the assumption that the value of the contract would at least have covered the outlay." [70]

Thus, for example, where the defendant's breach of contract prevents the staging of a theatrical event, it is very unlikely that the plaintiff can establish with sufficient certainty the amount of profits he would have made had the performance taken place, but he will be permitted to recover his expenses in preparation for performance.[71] A farmer who purchases and plants defective seed, may or may not be able to prove what the value of his crop would have been if the seed had been of merchantable quality.[72] If not, he is permitted to recover the amount paid for the seed, the rental value of the land on which it was sown and the cost of preparing the land and sowing

---

reasonable probability); Tobin v. Union News Co., 18 A.D.2d 343, 239 N.Y. S.2d 22 (4th Dep't 1963), aff'd mem. 13 N.Y.2d 1155, 247 N.Y.S.2d 385, 196 N. E.2d 735 (1964) ("A reasonable basis for the computation of approximate result is the only requisite"). Such cases in the present state of the law should be viewed skeptically.

69. U.C.C. § 1–106, Comment 1.

70. McCormick, Damages 586. This rationale is also expressed in Holt v. United Security Life Ins. Co., 76 N.J.

L. 585, 72 A. 301, 21 L.R.A.,N.S., 691 (1909).

71. Chicago Coliseum Club v. Dempsey, 265 Ill.App. 542 (1932) (promotor's expenses in preparing for boxing match); Bernstein v. Meech, 130 N.Y. 354, 29 N.E. 255 (1892).

72. In many cases the farmer has been successful in proving the value the crop would have had. E. g., Henderson v. Berce, 142 Me. 242, 50 A.2d 45, 168 A.L.R. 572 (1946); White v. Miller, 71 N.Y. 118 (1877).

the seed.[73] A distributor whose franchise is wrongfully terminated may or may not be able to prove his lost profits; if not, he may elect to claim his reliance expenditures. It is to be noted that such expenditures include not only expenses incurred in part performance and in preparation for performance, but also such foreseeable collateral expenses as amounts expended in advertising the manufacturer's product.[74] The owner of a plant who incurs expenses by building a foundation on which to install machinery may recover these expenses if the machines are not delivered.[75] Of course, to the extent that the reliance expenditures are salvageable no recovery will be allowed.[76]

Since the allowance of recovery for reliance expenditures is based on the assumption that the aggrieved party would at least have broken even if the contract had been performed, if it can be shown that the contract would have been a losing proposition for him, an appropriate deduction should be made for the loss which was not incurred. It has been held that the burden of proof that a loss would have occurred is upon the wrongdoer.[77]

Not all contracting parties contemplate a direct and identifiable profit from the contract. A manufacturer may contract to have a product shipped to a convention for display in the hopes of attracting interest in its products, rather than immediate sales. If the shipper is aware of the manufacturer's purpose, it can foresee that in reliance upon the contract the manufacturer will rent exhibition space and incur other expenses. In the event of breach such reliance expenditures are recoverable.[78]

§ 211. Alternative Recovery: Value of a Chance or Opportunity

In Chaplin v. Hicks [79] the plaintiff was one of fifty semi-finalists in a beauty contest in which twelve finalists would receive prizes. The de-

73. Crutcher & Co. v. Elliott, 13 Ky. Law Rep. 592 (1892); 5 Corbin, Contracts § 1026.

74. Hardin v. Eska Co., 256 Iowa 371, 127 N.W.2d 595 (1964); accord, Sperry & Hutchinson Co. v. O'Neill-Adams Co., 185 F. 231 (2d Cir. 1911) (advertising and other expenses in connection with promotion of trading stamps).

75. L. Albert & Son v. Armstrong Rubber Co., 178 F.2d 182, 17 A.L.R.2d 1289 (2d Cir. 1949).

76. Royce Chemical Co. v. Sharples Corp., 285 F.2d 183 (2d Cir. 1961); Gruber v. S-M News Co., 126 F.Supp. 442 (S.D.N.Y.1954).

77. United States v. Behan, 110 U.S. 338, 4 S.Ct. 81, 28 L.Ed. 168 (1884); L. Albert & Son v. Armstrong Rubber Co., 178 F.2d 182, 17 A.L.R.2d 1289 (2d Cir. 1949); Matter of Yeager Co., 227 F.Supp. 92 (N.D.Ohio 1963); Restatement, Contracts § 333(d); see 5 Corbin § 1033.

78. Security Stove & Mfg. Co. v. American Ry. Exp. Co., 227 Mo.App. 175, 51 S.W.2d 572 (1932).

79. [1911] 2 K.B. 786.

fendant, promotor of the contest, breached the contract by failing properly to notify the plaintiff of the time and place of the competition. The jury assessed the damages at £100, about one quarter of the value of the lowest prize. The judgment entered upon the jury's verdict was affirmed on appeal. It is obvious that not only was the amount of damages uncertain, but also the fact of damage. The court, nonetheless, indicated that the chance of winning had value which could be assessed by the law of averages. The Restatement of Contracts has accepted the rationale of this decision but only under circumscribed conditions. In general the Restatement allows recovery for the value of a chance only if the promised performance is aleatory; that is, conditioned upon an event that is not within the control of the parties.[80] As such, its primary fields of applicability are in the cases of contests [81] and in cases of wrongful cancellation of insurance contracts by the insurer.[82] It has also been applied in some cases to contracts to drill exploratory oil or gas wells.[83]

One may well question the wisdom of the limitation imposed upon the doctrine by the Restatement. If damages based upon a theory of probability is a sound approach to aleatory contracts, why is it unsound as to other contracts? [84] For example, if a manufacturer wrongfully terminates a distributorship, it will frequently be impossible to prove that the distributorship would have made a profit and the amount, if any, of such profits. Aside from the possibility of electing to claim mere reliance damages, the distributor in such a case faces an all or nothing prospect. Full recovery for the profits he would have made or merely nominal damages. If, as an alternative he were permitted to recover the value of the lost opportunity to strive for the profit, the hazards and possible injustice of the all or nothing approach would be reduced. Recovery would be allowed on the basis

---

80. Restatement, Contracts § 332.

81. Recovery for the value of a chance in contest cases has been granted in Mange v. Unicorn Press, Inc., 129 F. Supp. 727 (S.D.N.Y.1955); Wachtel v. National Alfalfa Journal Co., 190 Iowa 1293, 176 N.W. 801 (1920); Kansas City, M. & O. Ry. v. Bell, 197 S.W. 322 (Tex.Civ.App.1917); contra, Phillips v. Pantages Theatre Corp., 163 Wash. 303, 300 P. 1048 (1931); Collatz v. Fox Wis. Amusement Corp., 239 Wis. 156, 300 N.W. 162 (1941).

82. Caminetti v. Manierre, 23 Cal.2d 94, 142 P.2d 741 (1943); Commissioner of Ins. v. Massachusetts Acc. Co., 314 Mass. 558, 50 N.E.2d 801 (1943); Peo-

ple v. Empire Mut. Life Ins. Co., 92 N.Y. 105 (1883).

83. Because of the speculative nature of exploratory drilling, a wide variety of approaches have been taken toward the assessment of damages. See Scott, Measure of Damages for Breach of a Covenant to Drill a Test Well for Oil and Gas, 9 U.Kan.L.Rev. 281 (1961); 5 Corbin § 1093; Annot., 4 A.L.R.2d 284 (1949).

84. For an excellent student comment relating legal theory to mathematical probability theory, see Comment, Damages Contingent Upon Chance, 18 Rutgers L.Rev. 875 (1964).

of the price that a reasonable businessman would pay for the opportunity.[85] Despite authority for such an approach in an excellently reasoned old American case,[86] counsel in this country seem seldom to have made this argument,[87] although this approach is now well accepted in England.[88]

§ 212. Alternative Recovery: Rental Value of Property that Might have Produced Profits

If the evidence in Hadley v. Baxendale had established that the defendants had sufficient notice to be able to foresee the prolonged shut-down of the mill as a consequence of their breach, it nevertheless might have been impossible for the plaintiff to establish the fact and amount of his loss with sufficient certainty. The plaintiff would, however, be able to obtain recovery under an alternative theory, formulated in the Restatement in the following language: "[if] the breach is one that prevents the use and operation of property from which profits would have been made, damages may be measured by the rental value of the property or by interest on the value of the property." [89] The Restatement rule is based upon ample authority.[90]

---

85. See Kessler, Automobile Dealer Franchises: Vertical Integration by Contract, 66 Yale L.J. 1135, 1188–89 (1957); Comment, The Elusive Measure of Damages for Wrongful Termination of Automobile Dealership Franchises, 74 Yale L.J. 354 (1964).

86. Taylor v. Bradley, 39 N.Y. 129 (1868), where the court said: "he is deprived of his adventure; what was this opportunity which the contract had apparently secured to him worth?" 39 N.Y. at 144.

87. The argument is, however, persuasively put forth in McCormick, Damages 117–23. Interestingly, it has been applied in a negligence case in which the plaintiff suffered slight permanent damage of her voice which deprived her of the opportunity of commencing a career as an opera singer, a field of endeavor in which the chances of of success are speculative and remote. Grayson v. Irvmar Realty, 7 A.D.2d 436, 184 N.Y.S.2d 33 (1st Dep't 1959).

88. Hall v. Meyrick, [1957] 2 Q.B. 455, rev'd on other grounds 2 Q.B. 473;

Domine v. Grimsdall, [1937] 2 All E.R. 119 (K.B.).

89. Restatement, Contracts § 331(2). Hadley v. Baxendale is discussed in § 206 supra.

90. New York & Colorado Mining Syndicate & Co. v. Fraser, 130 U.S. 611, 9 S.Ct. 665, 32 L.Ed. 1031 (1889) (defective machinery rendered silver mill inoperative; rental value of mill calculated at the rate of legal interest on the cost of the mill in absence of other competent testimony of rental value); Witherbee v. Meyer, 155 N.Y. 446, 50 N.E. 58 (1898) (failure to provide sufficient waterpower to a mill; damages awarded for diminution in rental value); Dixon-Woods Co. v. Phillips Glass Co., 169 Pa. 167, 32 A. 432 (1895) (defective furnace installed; damages awarded for rental value of glass factory); Livermore Foundry & Mach. Co. v. Union Compress & Storage Co., 105 Tenn. 187, 58 S.W. 270 (1900) (rental value of compressing plant for entire season); see 5 Corbin § 1029; but cf. Natural Soda Prod. Co. v. City of Los Angeles, 23 Cal.2d 193, 143 P.2d 12 (1943), cert. denied

F. THE CONCEPT OF VALUE

Analysis

Sec.
213. Market Value as the Usual Standard.
214. Proof of Value.
215. Value a Variable Concept.

§ 213. Market Value as the Usual Standard

One of the most pervasive concepts of our law is that of "value." In practically every tort and contract case in which damages are to be assessed there is some reference to value. The concept also is widely used in cases of condemnation, taxation, quasi-contract, administrative rate making, and even in criminal law.

By and large in contract cases the standard of valuation considered is market value in contradistinction to any peculiar value the object in question may have had to the owner.[91] This standard offers no particular problems as to goods and securities which are actively traded upon stock and commodity exchanges. As to these there is in the literal sense a market place and a market price.[92] When the standard is applied to other objects, such as commodities and shares of stock which are not actively traded, land, unique chattels, and professional services, the determination of a market value involves something of a fiction. What is sought is the sum of money which a willing seller

321 U.S. 793, 64 S.Ct. 790, 88 L.Ed. 1082, reh. denied 322 U.S. 768, 64 S.Ct. 942, 88 L.Ed. 1594, a tort case in which the court states: "Expert opinion as to the market value of such a plant is likely to be based on nothing more substantial than the probable returns from the operations of the plant. A more accurate assessment of damage can be obtained by estimating loss of profit directly."

91. See McCormick, Damages § 44. Occasionally value to the owner is used as a standard where market value does not compensate fully for the peculiar use of the property by the owner. See Alfred Atmore Pope Found., Inc. v. New York, N. H. & Hartford Ry., 106 Conn. 423, 138 A. 444 (1927) (negligence action; forest attached to forestry school was destroyed by fire). The use of such a standard would be

highly unusual, however, in a contract action.

Occasionally courts reject any single standard of value. See McAnarney v. Newark Fire Ins. Co., 247 N.Y. 176, 159 N.E. 902, 56 A.L.R. 1149 (1928) (action on a fire insurance policy; structure destroyed was a brewery rendered obsolete by national prohibition).

92. But even as to shares of stock listed on stock exchanges the current price is not necessarily the value if special circumstances exist. Seas Shipping Co. v. Commissioner, 371 F. 2d 528 (2d Cir. 1967), cert. denied 387 U.S. 943, 87 S.Ct. 2076, 18 L.Ed.2d 1330 (1967) (large block of shares in a corporation whose shares were traded rather inactively); Kahle v. Mt. Vernon Trust Co., 22 N.Y.S.2d 454 (Sup.Ct.1940).

would pay to a willing buyer.[93] The main issues which arise in making this factual determination involve the kind of evidence which may be admitted.

§ 214. Proof of Value

Publications reporting the price of goods regularly bought and sold in any established commodity market are admissible.[94] If goods of the kind in issue have not been traded at the relevant time or place, evidence is admissible of prices prevailing at any reasonable times prior or subsequent to the relevant time and at any place which could reasonably serve as a substitute, with due allowance for transportation costs to that place.[95]

Other relevant evidence includes the opinions of qualified experts as to value,[96] original cost less depreciation,[97] reproduction cost less an allowance for depreciation,[98] and sales of comparable personalty or realty.[99] Also admissible is the sale price of the property if it was resold to another soon after the breach.[1] Offers to purchase the prop-

93. Standard Oil Co. of N. J. v. Southern Pac. Co., 268 U.S. 146, 45 S.Ct. 465, 69 L.Ed. 890 (1925); Heiman v. Bishop, 272 N.Y. 83, 4 N.E.2d 944 (1936) rearg. denied 273 N.Y. 497, 6 N. E.2d 422 (1937), Allen v. Chicago & N. W. R. R., 145 Wis. 263, 129 N.W. 1094 (1911).

94. U.C.C. § 2–724.

95. U.C.C. § 2–723.

96. Standard Oil Co. of N.J. v. Southern Pac. Co., 268 U.S. 146, 45 S.Ct. 465, 69 L.Ed. 890 (1925). This is said to be the commonest sort of evidence of value. McCormick, Damages 175.

97. Standard Oil Co. of N. J. v. Southern Pac. Co., 268 U.S. 146, 45 S.Ct. 465, 69 L.Ed. 890 (1925) (ship); Thornton v. City of Birmingham, 250 Ala. 651, 35 So.2d 545, 7 A.L.R.2d 773 (1948) (price paid for land two years previously). Original cost of goods some years prior to the wrong, standing alone, is not sufficient evidence of value. Some evidence as to depreciation must also be introduced. Rauch v. Wander, 122 Misc. 650, 203 N.Y.S. 553 (App.T.1924), as well as evidence of changes in market values, Watson v. Loughran, 112 Ga. 837, 38 S.E. 82 (1901).

98. Standard Oil Co. of N. J. v. Southern Pac. Co., 268 U.S. 146, 45 S.Ct. 465, 69 L.Ed. 890 (1925); Alabama G. S. R. R. v. Johnston, 128 Ala. 283, 29 So. 771 (1901); Missouri Pac. R. R. v. Fowler, 183 Ark. 86, 34 S.W.2d 1071 (1931).

99. Village of Lawrence v. Greenwood, 300 N.Y. 231, 90 N.E.2d 53 (1949). It must first be shown, however, that the other property was substantially of the same kind as the property in issue. Redfield v. Iowa State Comm., 251 Iowa 332, 99 N.W.2d 413, 85 A.L. R.2d 96 (1960); Amory v. Massachusetts, 321 Mass. 240, 72 N.E.2d 549, 174 A.L.R. 370 (1947). In a substantial minority of jurisdictions, however, such evidence is not admissible as to real property and unique chattels. Walnut Street Fed. Sav. & Loan Ass'n v. Bernstein, 394 Pa. 353, 147 A.2d 359 (1959).

1. Louis Steinbaum Real Estate Co. v. Maltz, 247 S.W.2d 652, 31 A.L.R.2d 1052 (Mo.App.1952) (fraud case); Wolff v. Meyer, 75 N.J.L. 181, 66 A. 959 (1907), aff'd 76 N.J.L. 574, 70 A. 1103 (1908); Triangle Waist Co., Inc. v. Todd, 223 N.Y. 27, 119 N.E. 85 (1918) (breach by employee; salary

erty are inadmissible on the grounds that the fabrication of such evidence would be too easy.[2] Offers to sell the property however, may be introduced in evidence but only as evidence against the offeror.[3]

§ 215. Value a Variable Concept

It is obvious that property may have more than one market value. There is a wholesale and a retail market for many products. The appropriate market is the one in which the aggrieved party may obtain replacement of the property. Thus, for the consumer the retail market is normally the appropriate standard, while for the dealer it is the wholesale market.[4] Less obvious is the fact that a given object can have different market values dependent upon various uses which it may have.[5] A cow may be used for beef production, milk production or primarily for breeding. The aggrieved party is entitled to an evaluation based upon the most profitable use to which he reasonably could have put the object.[6]

paid by new employer evidence of value of employee's services).

2. Sharp v. United States, 191 U.S. 341, 24 S.Ct. 114, 48 L.Ed. 211 (1903); Thornton v. City of Birmingham, 250 Ala. 651, 35 So.2d 545, 7 A.L.R.2d 773 (1948). On the realistic ground that tax assessments of real property are notoriously unreliable as indicia of value, the overwhelming weight of authority is to the effect that such evidence is inadmissible. Commonwealth of Kentucky v. Gilbert, 253 S.W.2d 264, 39 A.L.R.2d 205 (Ky.App.1952). The owner's statements to the tax assessing authorities are admissible against him, however, as admissions. San Diego Land & Town Co. v. Jasper, 189 U.S. 439, 23 S.Ct. 571, 47 L. Ed. 892 (1903).

3. Cotton v. Boston Elevated R.R., 191 Mass. 103, 77 N.E. 698 (owner's listing price); McAnarney v. Newark Fire Ins. Co., 247 N.Y. 176, 159 N.E. 902, 56 A.L.R. 1149 (1928).

4. Illinois Cent. R. R. v. Crail, 281 U.S. 57, 50 S.Ct. 180, 74 L.Ed. 699, 67 A.L. R. 1423 (1930); Wehle v. Haviland, 69 N.Y. 448 (1877).

5. "A loblolly pine tree at sixty years that would produce a fifty-foot piling would be worth fifty dollars peeled and loaded on a truck, for saw timber it would be worth $4.80." Shirley and Graves, Forest Ownership for Pleasure and Profit 32 (1967); cf. Spink v. New York, N. H. & H. R. R., 26 R.I. 115, 58 A. 499 (1904) (standing timber destroyed in fire may be valued on the basis of prices for poles and piles rather than cordwood).

6. Campbell v. Iowa Central Ry., 124 Iowa 248, 99 N.W. 1061 (1904) (brood mare); Southwestern Tel. & Tel. Co. v. Krause, 92 S.W. 431 (Tex.Civ.App. 1906) (milk cows not valued on basis of value of beef cattle).

G.   AVOIDABLE CONSEQUENCES

Analysis

Sec.

216.   The "Duty" to Mitigate Damages.

217.   Non-exclusive Contracts—An Apparent Exception to the Doctrine of Avoidable Consequences.

218.   Recovery of Expenses Sustained in Avoiding Consequence of a Breach.

§ 216.   The "Duty" to Mitigate Damages

As an almost inflexible proposition a party who has been wronged by a breach of contract may not unreasonably sit idly by and allow damages to accumulate.[7] The law does not permit him to recover from the wrongdoer those damages which he "should have foreseen and could have avoided by reasonable effort without undue risk, expense, or humiliation."[8] This absence of a right of recovery for enhanced damages, often improperly called a "duty to mitigate,"[9]

7. An exception to the doctrine of avoidable consequences exists as to leases of real property. Upon the tenant's abandonment of the premises the landlord may elect to terminate the tenancy and sue for damages, or to continue the tenancy. If he elects to continue the tenancy he may sue for the agreed rent although he makes no effort to secure a substitute tenant. This is based on the property concept that the landlord has conveyed a leasehold to the tenant, therefore performing the agreed exchange. Enoch C. Richards Co. v. Libby, 136 Me. 376, 10 A.2d 609, 126 A.L.R. 1215 (1940); Sancourt Realty Co. v. Dowling, 220 App.Div. 660, 222 N.Y.S. 288 (1st Dep't 1927).

8. Restatement, Contracts § 336(1).

9. "The statement is made not infrequently in treatise and decision that a servant wrongfully discharged is 'under a duty' to the master to reduce the damages, if he can. The phrase is accurate enough for most purposes, yet susceptible of misunderstanding, if emphasised too sharply . . . The servant is free to accept employ- ment or reject it according to his uncensored pleasure. What is meant by the supposed duty is merely this: That if he unreasonably reject, he will not be heard to say that the loss of wages from then on shall be deemed the jural consequence of the earlier discharge. He has broken the chain of causation, and loss resulting to him thereafter is suffered through his own act. It is not damage that has been caused by the wrongful act of the employer." McClelland v. Climax Hosiery Mills, 252 N.Y. 347, 358–59, 169 N.E. 605, 614 (1930), remittitur amended 253 N.Y. 533, 171 N.E. 770, rearg. denied 253 N.Y. 558, 171 N.E. 781 (Cardozo, C. J., concurring opinion).

In an attempt to employ the legal classifications developed by Hohfeld, others have referred to a "disability" to recover damages which could have been avoided, rather than the more accurate "no right" to recover. Rock v. Vandine, 106 Kan. 588, 189 P. 157 (1920); Notes 28 Yale L.J. 827 (1920), 32 Yale L.J. 380 (1923); cf. 5 Corbin § 1039.

is at the root of many of the rules of the law of damages. Thus, for example, the rule of Hadley v. Baxendale becomes clearer when viewed in terms of the doctrine of avoidable consequences. Under that decision the defendant would have been liable for the lost profits of the mill if it had had reason to know that no substitute shaft was available. In other words liability for consequential damages stems from reason to know that the plaintiff will be unable to mitigate his damages. The doctrine of avoidable consequences is also an unspoken premise in most rules of general damages. Thus, the rule in sales contracts that damages for breach by the seller are measured by the difference between the market price and the contract price is based on the thought that in the event of breach the plaintiff can minimize his damages by purchasing similar goods on the open market.

In addition to its role as an implied premise in many other rules and doctrines, the doctrine of avoidable consequences is frequently used as an independent basis for a decision. For example, where a municipality breaches a contract to fill in waterfront land, the aggrieved party may not sit idle for many years and then recover the rental value the filled land would have had during the period the land was unfilled. Rather, he may have such recovery measured by a reasonable period of time, as it was incumbent upon the plaintiff, if feasible, to have the land filled by other means.[10] Likewise where an experienced farmer is supplied patently defective seed he will not be permitted to enhance his damages by planting the seed and losing a crop.[11] Similarly, the doctrine is employed in every manner of contract including contracts of employment,[12] sale,[13] construction,[14] and in the United States, even in cases of breach by anticipatory repudiation.[15]

The doctrine merely requires reasonable efforts to mitigate damages. Thus, if reasonable, the efforts need not be successful.[16] Under the rule of reasonableness, the wronged party need not act if the cost of avoidance would involve unreasonable expense.[17] He need

10. Losel Realty Corp. v. City of New York, 254 N.Y. 41, 171 N.E. 899 (1930).

11. Wavra v. Karr, 142 Minn. 248, 172 N.W. 118 (1919).

12. See §§ 219–20 infra.

13. See generally §§ 221–28 infra.

14. See §§ 229–30 infra.

15. See § 224 infra; § 183 supra.

16. Ninth Avenue & Forty-Second St., Corp. v. Zimmerman, 217 App.Div. 498, 217 N.Y.S. 123 (1st Dep't 1926) (unsuccessful suit against third party to clear title).

17. Taylor v. Steadman, 143 Ark. 486, 220 S.W. 821 (1920); Chambers v. Belmore Land Co., 33 Cal.App. 78, 164 P. 404 (1917); 5 Corbin § 1041.

not commit a wrong, as by breaching other contracts, in order to minimize damages,[18] nor need he jeopardize his credit rating.[19]

One troublesome issue has vexed and divided the courts. Must the aggrieved party accede to a wrongful demand by the wrongdoer if his accession would minimize damages? The problem is illustrated in its extreme form in a case where a water company unjustifiably asked for the yearly payment of $58.00 in instalments in advance instead of at the end of contract period as provided in the contract. The plaintiff, an owner of an irrigated vineyard refused to accede to this change of company policy. As a consequence the water supply was shut off and the plaintiff lost his crop. The court ruled that the trivial extra cost (interest on the advance payments) amounting to less than $2.00, viewed in relation to the large amount of injury foreseeably ensuing, was such that the plaintiff should have acceded to the unjustified demand.[20] On similar facts other courts have disagreed,[21] while still others have let the jury decide whether the plaintiff's refusal was reasonable.[22] On the other hand, where the demand is not trivial in relation to the ensuing damages, most courts have ruled that the plaintiff need not bend his will to that of the wrongdoer even if it would have the effect of minimizing damages.[23]

Frequently, the aggrieved party does accede to the demands of the other, often because any other course of action would result in a major disruption of his business or personal affairs. When this is done, it may be held that the aggrieved party is without remedy be-

---

18. Leonard v. New York, Albany and Buffalo Electro-Magnetic Tel. Co., 41 N.Y. 544 (1870); McCormick, Damages 141 (1935); contra, Western Union Tel. Co. v. Southwick, 214 S.W. 987 (Tex.Civ.App.1919), rev'd on other grounds 255 U.S. 565, 41 S.Ct. 446, 65 L.Ed. 788 (1921), 33 Harv.L.Rev. 728 (1920).

19. Audiger, Inc. v. Town of Hamilton, 381 F.2d 24 (5th Cir. 1967).

20. Severini v. Sutter-Butte Canal Co., 59 Cal.App. 154, 210 P. 49 (1922). The decision was distinguished in a subsequent case involving similar facts except that the water company's unjustified demand was in the amount of about $100. The court deemed this to be a substantial rather than trivial demand. Schultz v. Town of Lakeport, 5 Cal.2d 377, 54 P.2d 1110, 108 A.L.R. 1168 (1936), modified 55 P.2d 485, 108 A.L.R. 1168.

21. Southwestern Gas & Elec. Co. v. Stanley, 45 S.W.2d 671 (Tex.Civ.App. 1931), aff'd, 123 Tex. 157, 70 S.W.2d 413 (1934).

22. Key v. Kingwood Oil Co., 110 Okl. 178, 236 P. 598 (1924).

23. Coppola v. Marden, Orth & Hastings, 282 Ill. 281, 118 N.E. 499 (1918); Seeley v. Peabody, 139 Wash. 382, 247 P. 471 (1926), aff'd 141 Wash. 696, 250 P. 469 (1926); see 5 Corbin § 1043; McCormick, Damages § 39 (1935). This point is further illustrated by the rule that an employee whose employment is pursuant to an employment contract need not mitigate damages by accepting an offer from his employer for employment in a different position or on other different terms. Billetter v. Posell, 94 Cal. App.2d 858, 211 P.2d 621 (1949); and see § 219 infra.

cause he has entered into a substituted agreement discharging the prior contract.[24] This result may be avoided under the Uniform Commercial Code by surrendering to the demand while indicating that accession is under protest.[25]

§ 217. Non-exclusive Contracts—An Apparent Exception to the Doctrine of Avoidable Consequences

A full time employee owes a duty to his employer not to work for others on his employer's time. If the employee is wrongfully discharged, his damages are reduced by any earning from employment he secures or could with reasonable diligence secure during the contract period.[26] If it were not for the breach such employment could not lawfully be obtained.

If the relation between the parties is such that the wronged party was legally free to enter into similar contracts with others, the fact that subsequent to the breach the wronged party could have or actually has made similar contracts in no way reduces the damages to which he is entitled. Thus, for example, if the lessee of automobiles from a car rental company breaches the lease, damages will not be reduced by the fact that the lessor leases, or could have leased, the automobiles to another.[27] The lessor was free to obtain as many customers as it was willing and able to secure, provided that as a practical matter it could secure additional automobiles for such customers. On the other hand, if the lease is of a unique chattel such as an ocean going freighter, the lessor's damages will be reduced by any amount earned or earnable by chartering the ship to another, each ship being regarded as unique.[28] Similar considerations exist where a purchaser breaches a contract for sale.[29] Construction contracts are non-exclusive and a construction contractor's damages are not normally reduced by any earnings attributable to contracts made subsequent to the breach.[30] Similarly a publisher's damages re-

---

24. See Comment, Effect of Second Contract With Defaulter upon Rights for Breach of First, 19 N.C.L.Rev. 59 (1940).

25. U.C.C. § 1–207.

26. See § 219 infra.

27. Mount Pleasant Stable Co. v. Steinberg, 238 Mass. 567, 131 N.E. 295, 15 A.L.R. 749 (1921) (teams of horses and wagons); Locks v. Wade, 36 N.J.Super. 128, 114 A.2d 875 (1955) (juke box).

28. Liberty Nav. & Trading Co. v. Kinoshita & Co., 285 F.2d 343 (2d Cir. 1960), cert. denied 366 U.S. 949, 81 S. Ct. 1904, 6 L.Ed.2d 1242 (1961).

29. See generally §§ 225–28 infra.

30. Koplin v. Faulkner, 293 S.W.2d 467 (Ky.App.1956); M. & R. Contractors & Builders, Inc. v. Michael, 215 Md. 340, 138 A.2d 350 (1958); Olds v. Mapes-Reeve Constr. Co., 177 Mass. 41, 58 N.E. 478 (1900). In a celebrated case the court seems inappropriately to have applied the general rule. The

sulting from breach of an advertising contract are not to be reduced under the doctrine of avoidable consequences [31] unless the publication has limited space for advertising, in which case it would be incumbent upon the publisher to attempt to secure additional advertisers to fill the space vacated as a result of the breach.[32]

§ 218.　Recovery of Expenses Sustained in Avoiding Consequences of a Breach

The doctrine of avoidable consequences is a two edged sword. That it may reduce the aggrieved party's damages has been considered in the preceding discussion. It may, also, act to provide recovery for certain kinds of expenses not otherwise recoverable. This aspect of the doctrine is best illustrated by the leading tort case.[33] The plaintiff, a steamship company flying the neutral flag of Norway during World War I was accused by the defendant newspaper publisher of carrying on illegal activities for the benefit of the German war effort. In order to protect its reputation it placed paid advertisements in other newspapers refuting the defendant's libel. It was held that the plaintiff could recover these expenses as a reasonable effort, whether or not successful, to mitigate damages.

The same principle finds wide application in cases involving breach of contract,[34] and is implicitly recognized by the Uniform Commercial Code in its provisions regarding "cover" [35] and "inci-

---

plaintiff contracted with X corporation to install certain apparatus in X's plant. X, because of insolvency, repudiated the contract. X's receivers sold the plant to Y corporation. Y contracted with the plaintiff to make the same installation. This contract was performed. Nevertheless, on the ground that it was not a contract for personal services, plaintiff was permitted to recover damages against X's receivers for breach of the first contract without a deduction for the profit made on the second contract despite the fact that but for the breach of the first contract plaintiff could not have entered into the second. Grinnell Co. v. Voorhees, 1 F.2d 693 (3d Cir. 1924), cert. denied 266 U.S. 629, 45 S.Ct. 195, 69 L.Ed. 477 (1925), 34 Yale L.J. 553 (1925); accord, Olds v. Mapes-Reeve Constr. Co., 177 Mass. 41, 58 N.E. 478 (1900); contra, Canton-Hughes Pump Co. v. Llera, 205 F. 209 (6th Cir. 1913); cf. Kunkle v. Jaffe, 71 N.E.2d 298 (Ohio App.1946).

31. Western Grain Co. v. Barron G. Collier, Inc., 163 Ark. 369, 258 S.W. 979, 35 A.L.R. 1534 (1924); Western Adv. Co. v. Mid-West Laundries, 61 S. W.2d 251 (Mo.App.1933); J. K. Rishel Furniture Co. v. Stuyvesant Co., 123 Misc. 208, 204 N.Y.S. 659 (Mun.Ct. 1924).

32. Barron G. Collier, Inc. v. Women's Garment Store, 152 Minn. 475, 189 N. W. 403 (1922).

33. Den Norske Ameriekalinje Actiesselskabet v. Sun Printing & Pub. Ass'n, 226 N.Y. 1, 122 N.E. 463 (1919); accord, Restatement Contracts § 336(2); see 5 Corbin § 1044; McCormick, Damages § 42.

34. See, e. g., Audiger, Inc. v. Town of Hamilton, 381 F.2d 24 (5th Cir. 1967).

35. See § 221 infra.

dental" damages.[36] It has been held that the cost of procuring a substitute outlet for water is recoverable where the defendant breached his contract to allow the use of his ditch.[37] In another case,[38] the plaintiff was the general contractor in Detroit for the building of a ship and the defendant was the subcontractor for the manufacture of the boilers. In the event delivery of the ship were to be delayed the plaintiff was known by the defendant to be under an obligation to pay liquidated damages in the sum of $200 per day. When the defendant was late in completing the manufacture of the boilers at Duluth, it was held not to be unreasonable for the plaintiff to pay $1500 to a steamer captain to induce him to await departure until the defendant boiler company completed manufacture so that he could deliver the boilers to Detroit as no other ship would be leaving until the next season. Such reasonable expenditures are recoverable even if hindsight shows that the expenditure made is in excess of the amount by which damages are diminished.[39]

H. DAMAGES IN PARTICULAR ACTIONS

Analysis

Sec.
219. Wrongful Discharge of Employee.
220. Wrongful Termination by Employee.
221. Total Breach of Sales Contracts—Buyer's General Damages.
222. Buyer's General Damages for Seller's Breach of Warranty or Fraud.
223. Consequential and Incidental Damages to Seller's Breach.
224. Seller's General Damages for Non-acceptance or Repudiation.
225. Seller's General Damages Following Resale.
226. Seller's Consequential and Incidental Damages.
227. Seller's Action for the Price.
228. Seller's Damages for Contracts to Manufacture Special Goods Under the Code.
229. Construction Contracts: Measure of Recovery by Contractor.
230. Construction Contracts: Measure of Recovery by Owner.
231. Contracts to Sell Realty: Measure of Damages for Total Breach.

36. See §§ 223, 226 infra.

37. Hoehne Ditch Co. v. John Flood Ditch Co., 76 Colo. 500, 233 P. 167 (1925).

38. Northwestern Steam Boiler Mfg. Co. v. Great Lakes Eng'r Works, 181 F. 38 (8th Cir. 1910); accord, Apex Mining Co. v. Chicago Copper & Chemical Co., 306 F.2d 725 (8th Cir. 1962) (defendant failed to deliver ore; plaintiff purchased jaw crusher to process substitute ore of a different type).

39. Apex Mining Co. v. Chicago Copper & Chem. Co., 306 F.2d 725 (8th Cir. 1962); Hogland v. Klein, 49 Wash.2d 216, 298 P.2d 1099 (1956).

§ 219.   Wrongful Discharge of Employee

When an employee is wrongfully discharged he is entitled to the salary [40] that would have been payable during the remainder of the term reduced by the income which he has earned, will earn, or could with reasonable diligence earn during the unexpired term.[41] This rule takes into consideration the employee's burden of mitigation. In carrying out this burden, however, the employee need not seek or accept a position of lesser rank,[42] or at a reduced salary,[43] or at a location unreasonably distant from his former place of employment.[44] The authorities agree that an employee has properly mitigated his damages by going into business for himself with the knowledge that the prospects for earnings from the business are minimal in its initial stages.[45]   It was wisely held in one such case, however, that his re-

---

40. The problem of the valuation of fringe benefits as an element of salary has yet to be explored thoroughly by the courts. For one discussion, see McAleer v. McNally Pittsburgh Mfg. Co., 329 F.2d 273 (3rd Cir. 1964) (no recovery for loss of group life insurance protection).

41. Sutherland v. Wyer, 67 Me. 64 (1877); Hollwedel v. Duffy-Mott Co., 263 N.Y. 95, 188 N.E. 266, 90 A.L.R. 1312 (1933); Godson v. McFadden, 162 Tenn. 528, 39 S.W.2d 287 (1931); Galveston H. & S. A. R. R. v. Eubanks, 42 S.W.2d 475 (Tex.Civ.App.1931), aff'd 59 S.W.2d 825 (Com.App.1933). If the unexpired term is of lengthy duration, the recovery is to be discounted at a reasonable rate of interest inasmuch as the plaintiff will recover well in advance of the dates on which future salary payments would have been payable. Hollwedel v. Duffy-Mott Co., supra; Dixie Glass Co. v. Pollak, 341 S.W.2d 530, 91 A.L.R.2d 662 (Tex.Civ. App.1960), aff'd 162 Tex. 440, 347 S. W.2d 596 (1961).

The old English doctrine of "constructive service" pursuant to which a wrongfully discharged employee who held himself ready, willing and able to resume his employment was entitled to his salary in full has almost everywhere been abandoned. 5 Corbin § 1095; McCormick, Damages § 158.

A small minority of jurisdictions permit the discharged employee to recover damages suffered only up to the time of trial. The authorities on this question are collected in Dixie Glass Co. v. Pollak, supra, where the minority view is repudiated.

42. Cooper v. Stronge & Warner Co., 111 Minn. 177, 126 N.W. 541, 27 L.R. A.,N.S. 1011, 20 Ann.Cas. 663 (1910) (department manager need not accept position as sales clerk at same salary); State ex rel. Freeman v. Sierra County Bd. of Ed., 49 N.Mex. 54, 157 P.2d 234 (1945) (principal need not accept post as teacher at reduced salary); Mitchell v. Lewensohn, 251 Wis. 424, 29 N.E.2d 748 (1947).

43. Crabtree v. Elizabeth Arden Sales Corp., 105 N.Y.S.2d 40 (Sup.Ct.1951), aff'd 279 App.Div. 992, 112 N.Y.S.2d 494 (1st Dep't 1952), aff'd 305 N.Y. 48, 110 N.E.2d 551 (1953).

44. American Trading Co. v. Steele, 274 F. 774 (9th Cir. 1921) (resident of China need not seek employment in U. S.); San Antonio & A. P. R. R. v. Collins, 61 S.W.2d 84 (Tex.Com.App.1933) (resident of Houston need not accept employment in San Antonio).

45. Ransome Concrete Mach. Co. v. Moody, 282 F. 29 (2d Cir. 1922); Cornell v. T. V. Development Corp., 17 N.Y.2d 69, 268 N.Y.S.2d 29, 215 N.E.2d 349 (1966).

covery should be reduced by the value of his services in building up the business.[46]

Generally speaking a public officer's right to compensation is not dependent upon contract, but on public law. If he is wrongfully denied his office the doctrine of avoidable consequences is inapplicable. Therefore, his recovery is not diminished by the amount he has earned or could have earned during his term of office.[47] Most persons on the public payroll, however, are employees rather than officers [48] and are subject to the doctrine of avoidable consequences.[49]

Rarely are special damages awarded for wrongful discharge. Damages for injury to the employee's reputation are ordinarily said to be too remote and not in the contemplation of the parties.[50] There is considerable authority in England [51] and some in the United States for an award of consequential damages where the contract contemplates that performance will enhance the employee's reputation, as where a script writer is promised screen credit [52] and where a disc jockey is promised exposure to a large audience.[53]

§ 220. Wrongful Termination by Employee

When an employee wrongfully terminates his employment, the employer's recovery is measured by the additional market cost of obtaining substitute help for the unexpired contract term; that is, the difference between the market value of such services and the con-

46. Kramer v. Wolf Cigar Stores Co., 99 Tex. 597, 91 S.W. 775 (1906).

47. Gentry v. Harrison, 194 Ark. 916, 110 S.W.2d 497 (1937); Corfman v. McDevitt, 111 Colo. 437, 142 P.2d 383, 150 A.L.R. 97 (1943).

48. For the distinction between public office and public employment see C.J. S. Officers § 5; Annot., 140 A.L.R. 1076; see also Punke, Breach of Teacher Contracts, and Damages, 26 Ala.Law. 243, 265–74 (1965).

49. Stockton v. Department of Employment, 25 Cal.2d 264, 153 P.2d 741 (1944); People ex rel. Bourne v. Johnson, 32 Ill.2d 324, 205 N.E.2d 470 (1965); Spurck v. Civil Service Bd., 231 Minn. 183, 42 N.W.2d 720 (1950).

50. Mastoras v. Chicago, M. & St. P. Ry., 217 F. 153 (D.C.Cir. 1914); Gary v. Central of Georgia Ry., 37 Ga. 744, 141 S.E. 819 (1928); Tousley v. Atlan-

tic City Ambassador Hotel Corp., 25 N.J.Misc. 88, 50 A.2d 472 (1947).

51. Tolnay v. Criterion Film Productions, [1936] 2 All. E.R. 1225; Marbe v. George Edwards, Ltd., [1928] 1 K.B. 269, 56 A.L.R. 888 (1928).

52. Paramount Productions v. Smith, 91 F.2d 863 (9th Cir. 1937), cert. denied 302 U.S. 749, 58 S.Ct. 266, 82 L. Ed. 579.

53. Colvig v. RKO General, Inc., 232 Cal.App.2d 56, 42 Cal.Rptr. 473 (1965). Such holdings are consistent with the related rule that if the services to be rendered will be of benefit to the employee as by enhancing his skill or reputation, the employer is obliged not only to pay his salary but also to provide work of the kind contemplated. Sigmon v. Goldstone, 116 App.Div. 490, 101 N.Y.S. 984 (1st Dep't 1906); Restatement, Second, Agency § 433.

tract rate of compensation.[54] Although courts do not generally deny the possibility of an award of consequential damages against the employee, the rules of foreseeability, mitigation and certainty have been so strictly applied as to indicate a strong policy against such awards against employees.[55]

§ 221. Total Breach of Sales Contracts—Buyer's General Damages

The traditional measure of general damages for a total breach of contract by the seller is the difference between the market price and the contract price. This rule has been retained by the Uniform Commercial Code [56] but the Code has added an alternative measure. The buyer may cover; that is, he may make a good faith purchase or contract to purchase substitute goods without unreasonable delay.[57] He may then recover the difference between the cost of cover and the contract price.[58] While this measure of damages will often produce the same result as the traditional market price minus contract price rule, this will not always be so. When notified of a breach the purchaser may be forced to go outside his normal sources of supply and to pay more than the normal price which constitutes the "market." [59] Or he may pay a higher than market price unaware that the goods were available at the market price from some suppliers. He may find that goods of the same quality and specifications are not readily available and procure as a reasonable substitute goods of a somewhat higher quality and cost. In all of these circumstances the cover price minus contract price result produces a more reasonable result.[60] In addition the often difficult, expensive and time con-

---

54. Roth v. Speck, 126 A.2d 153, 61 A. L.R.2d 1004 (D.C.Mun.App.1956); Triangle Waist Co. v. Todd, 223 N.Y. 27, 119 N.E. 85 (1918); 5 Corbin § 1096; 5 Williston § 1362A (rev. ed. 1937).

55. See Riech v. Bolch, 68 Iowa 526, 27 N.W. 507 (1886); Peters v. Whitney, 23 Barb. 24 (N.Y.1856); Winkenwerder v. Knox, 51 Wash.2d 582, 320 P.2d 304 (1958). For a rare case awarding such damages, see Stadium Pictures, Inc. v. Walker, 224 App.Div. 22, 229 N.Y.S. 313 (1928).

56. U.C.C. § 713(1).

57. U.C.C. § 712(1).

58. U.C.C. § 712(2).

59. For example, an article in the Financial Section of the New York Times, dated January 1, 1967, discussing the tight supply of sulphur points out that while two large producers charged $28.50 per ton, "Demand is so strong that some consumers have been paying more than $50 a ton for spot supplies . . . . Authorities said overseas markets had been chaotic and prices had been hard to catalogue. They were reported to have ranged recently from $40 to $65 a ton."

60. Cf. 3 Williston, Sales § 599 (rev. ed. 1948) where the older view is expressed: "[I]f the buyer pays more than the market price, it is not the seller's wrong but his own error of judgment which was the cause of the excessive payment."

suming task of proving market price at trial can be obviated. This provision, although one of the simplest, is yet one of the most useful innovations to appear in the Commercial Code.

In the event that the buyer chooses to utilize the market price minus contract price rule, the market price is that which is in effect at the time the buyer learned of the breach.[61] The majority view under prior law was to the contrary, holding that the applicable market price was that of the date on which delivery should have been made.[62] The Commercial Code rule has the doctrine of avoidable consequences built into it. The appropriate time is the time when the buyer learns of the breach for this is the time when he reasonably should cover on the market.

§ 222. Buyer's General Damages for Seller's Breach of Warranty or Fraud

The Commercial Code adopts the measure of general damages which previously prevailed for breach of warranty. The measure is the difference between the value of the goods accepted and the value they would have had if they had been as warranted.[63] Value is determined, however, at the time and place of acceptance, rather than, as under the Sales Act, the time and place of delivery.[64]

The Uniform Commercial Code provides that remedies for fraud shall be the same as for breach of contract.[65] In an action for damages, therefore, it would seem that the measure of damages would be the same as for breach of warranty. This has the almost unnoticed effect of repealing, at least in the context of sales of goods, the "out of pocket" rule previously applicable to actions for fraud in a number of jurisdictions.[66] Pursuant to this rule the defrauded purchaser was

---

61. U.C.C. § 2-713(1). It is important to note that in the event of a breach by the buyer the rule is different and the applicable market price is that in effect at the date of delivery. See § 224 infra.

62. Reliance Cooperage v. Treat, 195 F.2d 977 (8th Cir. 1952); Segall v. Finlay, 245 N.Y. 61, 156 N.E. 97 (1927); McCormick, Damages § 175; Restatement, Contracts § 338.

63. U.C.C. § 2-714(2).

64. Uniform Sales Act § 69(7).

65. U.C.C. § 2-721.

66. The leading cases establishing this rule are Peek v. Derry, L.R. 37 Ch. Div. 541 (1887); and Reno v. Bull, 226 N.Y. 546, 124 N.E. 144, rearg. denied 227 N.Y. 591, 125 N.E. 924 (1920), 5 Cornell L.Q. 167 (1919). See McCormick, Damages § 448. The contrary "benefit of the bargain" rule adopted by the Uniform Commercial Code has support in prior law in a good number of jurisdictions. Hartwell Corp. v. Bumb, 345 F.2d 453, 13 A.L.R.3d 868 (9th Cir. 1965), cert. denied 382 U.S. 891, 86 S.Ct. 182, 15 L.Ed.2d 148 (1965).

permitted to recover only the difference between the amount paid and the value of the goods received rather than the difference between the value the goods would have had if they were as represented and actual value which may now be recovered.

§ 223.   Consequential and Incidental Damages for Seller's Breach

In the ordinary case the buyer is made whole by application of the rules of general damages. Thus if the buyer contracted to purchase sugar at four cents per pound and the seller breaches when the market price is seven cents the purchaser is entitled to damages of three cents per pound. This ordinarily provides full compensation because the purchaser may go out on the market and purchase the sugar at no cost except the original unpaid contract price plus the damages to which he is entitled. Suppose, however, there is no sugar on the market or no sugar available for delivery in time for the purchaser to keep his commitments for resale to retail outlets or for keeping his bakery in operation. The lost profits and other proximate damages, as, for example, damages he must pay to aggrieved retailers, are recoverable by him only if these were foreseeable to the seller. Prior to the Uniform Commercial Code many cases held that such consequential damages were awardable only if the seller knew two things at the time of contracting: first, the buyer's purpose in making the purchase and, second, that no substitute would be available to the purchaser in the event of a breach by the seller.[67] The Code seems to have relaxed the requirement of foreseeability considerably. Section 2–715(2) provides that consequential damages include:

> "any loss resulting from general or particular requirements and needs of which the seller at the time of contracting had reason to know and which could not reasonably be prevented by cover or otherwise. . . ."

Under the Code it is not necessary that the seller have reason to know at the time of contracting that no substitute will be available to the buyer.[68] It is sufficient that at the time of the breach no sub-

---

67.   Czarnikow-Rionda Co. v. Federal Sugar Ref. Co., 255 N.Y. 33, 173 N.E. 913, 88 A.L.R. 1426 (1930); Thomas Raby, Inc. v. Ward-Meehan Co., 261 Pa. 468, 104 A. 750 (1918).

68.   Accord under prior law, Lukens Iron & Steel Co. v. Hartmann-Greiling Co., 169 Wis. 350, 172 N.W. 894 (1919)

(steel shortage occurred after the contract was formed). The intimation in § 2–715, Comment 2, that the common law has been "modified by refusing to permit recovery unless the buyer could not reasonably have prevented the loss by cover or otherwise," is erroneous. Prior law was at least as insistent as the Code on this point.

stitute is reasonably available [69] and that the seller had reason to know the buyer's needs.

As under prior law, consequential damages for breach of warranty also include injury to person or property proximately resulting from the breach.[70]

The Code expressly permits the parties to limit or exclude consequential damages by agreement, unless the limitation or exclusion is unconscionable. An attempt to limit damages for injury to the person in connection with a sale of consumer goods is, however, "prima facie unconscionable but limitation of damages where the loss is commercial is not." [71]

The Code has adopted a category of damages known as incidental damages. Included in this category are "expenses reasonably incurred in inspection receipt, transportation and care and custody of goods rightfully rejected. . . ." [72] Under prior law such damages would have been recoverable but often would have been characterized as direct or consequential damages.[73]

Also included in the Code category of incidental damages are "any commercially reasonable charges, expenses or commissions in connection with effecting cover . . .." [74] Such damages were also available under prior law as damages incurred in a proper attempt to mitigate damages.[75]

In addition "any other reasonable expense incidental to the delay or other breach" are recoverable as incidental damages.[76]

§ 224. Seller's General Damages for Non-acceptance or Repudiation

The seller's general damages for nonacceptance or repudiation by the buyer is the difference between the market price and the un-

---

69. As to "reasonable availability," see Oliver-Electrical Mfg. Co. v. I. O. Teigen Constr. Co., 177 F.Supp. 572 (D. Minn.1959), motion denied 183 F.Supp. 768 where defendant proved that a substitute supplier was available but failed to prove that plaintiff should have known this.

70. U.C.C. § 2–715(2) (b); see Prosser, Torts § 97 (3d ed. 1964).

71. U.C.C. § 2–719(3).

72. U.C.C. § 2–715(1).

73. Messmore v. New York Shot & Lead Co., 40 N.Y. 422 (1869) (direct). Often such damages were permitted to

be recovered without any characterization. Taylor v. Saxe, 134 N.Y. 67, 31 N.E. 258 (1892).

74. U.C.C. § 2–715(1).

75. § 218 supra.

76. U.C.C. § 2–715(1).

77. U.C.C. § 2–708(1). In an unorthodox and highly sophisticated series of articles, Professor Harris has formulated a rule for the measurement of seller's damages in terms differing from that of the Code and conventional analyses. "The rule is: Plaintiff should recover (minuend minus subtrahend) plus incidental damages. The 'minuend' is always the value to

paid contract price.[77] The appropriate market price is the price at the "time and place for tender." [78] There is a marked difference between this rule and the rule applicable to buyer's damages where the appropriate market price is the price in effect "at the time when the buyer learned of the breach." [79] The reason for the rule as to buyers, as previously discussed,[80] is that the buyer upon learning of the breach should reasonably go into the market to replace the goods. A seller, however, is in a different position, and upon learning of the breach, if he resells the goods his damages are not measured by the difference between market price and unpaid contract price. Instead, separate provisions of the Code govern the eventuality of resale.[81] On the other hand, at the time of learning of the breach he does not necessarily have the goods which he has promised to deliver and, if he has them, he has not necessarily appropriated any particular goods from his inventory for the contract. Consequently, this rule of damages gives the seller the benefit of his bargain as of the time when delivery would have been made.[82]

plaintiff of the difference between what defendant promised to do and what he in fact actually did in the way of performance. The 'subtrahend' is always the value to plaintiff of being relieved by defendant's breach from all or part of plaintiff's scheduled performance." Harris, A Radical Restatement of the Law of Damages: New York Results Compared, 34 Fordham L.Rev. 23, 28 (1965); see also Harris, A General Theory for Measuring Seller's Damages for Total Breach of Contract, 60 Mich.L.Rev. 577 (1962); Harris, A Radical Restatement of the Law of Seller's Damages: Michigan Results Compared, 61 Mich.L.Rev. 849 (1963); Harris & Graham, A Radical Restatement of the Law of Seller's Damages: California Results Compared, 18 Stan.L.Rev. 553 (1965); Harris, A Radical Restatement of the Law of Seller's Damages: Sales Act and Commercial Code Results Compared, 18 Stan.L.Rev. 66 (1965).

78. U.C.C. § 2–708(1). If the case comes to trial prior to the date for performance, damages will be determined as of the time the seller learned of the breach. U.C.C. § 2–723(1).

79. U.C.C. § 2–713(1).

80. See § 221 supra.

81. See § 225 infra.

82. Under prior case law, it was held in a number of jurisdictions that the seller's damages should be measured by reference to the market price at the time of learning of the breach. Such holdings were ostensibly based on the doctrine of avoidable consequences. It was thought that the seller should mitigate damages in a falling market by selling the goods on the market as soon as possible after learning of the breach. See, e. g., Crane Iron Works v. Cox & Sons Co., 28 F.2d 328 (3rd Cir. 1928). This argument overlooks the fact that it is dubious that anyone should be forced to prognosticate that the market will continue to fall. It also overlooks that if the seller could procure additional supplies of the goods, any additional sale of such goods are for the benefit of the seller and are not attributable to the plaintiff's breach. See Williston, Sales §§ 587, 588 (rev. ed. 1948).

It is quite clear, however, that very often the seller will not be placed in as good a position by this measure of damages as performance would have. For example, if a dealer contracts to sell an automobile at the market price of $3,000, upon a breach by the buyer recovery on the basis of the difference between market price and contract price would result in a recovery of only nominal damages.[83] But in fact the dealer has lost the profit on the sale measured by the difference between the cost to him of the automobile and the contract price. In order to give full compensation in such cases the Uniform Commercial Code provides that if the difference between market price and contract price provides inadequate recovery, "the measure of damages is the profit (including reasonable overhead) which the seller would have made from full performance by the buyer." [84] Recovery of the lost profit would be appropriate in any case in which the seller has, for practical purposes, an unlimited supply of goods of the kind involved in the transaction.

§ 225. Seller's General Damages Following Resale

In the event of any breach by the buyer, whether by wrongful nonacceptance of the goods, repudiation, or failure to make a payment when due,[85] the seller may identify the goods to the contract[86] and resell them at a private or public sale. He may then recover from the buyer the difference between the resale price and contract price.[87] This, of course, is the counterpart of the buyer's remedy of cover.[88] The seller need not account to the buyer for any profit made on the resale.[89] It is unclear, however, how any part payment made by the buyer is to be allocated.[90]

§ 226. Seller's Consequential and Incidental Damages

According to Section 1–106 of the Uniform Commercial Code consequential damages are not available unless specifically provided

---

83. This was the result in a number of jurisdictions under the Sales Act. Charles Street Garage Co. v. Kaplan, 312 Mass. 624, 45 N.E.2d 928 (1942); A. Lenobel, Inc. v. Senif, 252 App.Div. 533, 300 N.Y.S. 226 (2d Dep't 1937), order resettled 253 App.Div. 813, 1 N.Y. S.2d 1022, 22 Cornell L.Q. 581 (1937); contra, Stewart v. Hansen, 62 Utah 281, 218 P. 959, 44 A.L.R. 340 (1923), 24 Colum.L.Rev. 210 (1924).

84. U.C.C. § 2–708(2).

85. U.C.C. § 2–703.

86. U.C.C. § 2–704.

87. U.C.C. § 2–706(1).

88. See § 221 supra.

89. U.C.C. § 2–706(6).

90. Discussions of this problem is inappropriate in a basic contract text. See Nordstrom, Seller's Damages Following Resale Under Article Two of the Uniform Commercial Code, 65 Mich.L.Rev. 1299 (1967).

for by the Code or other rule of law and none of the provisions of the Code dealing with seller's damages allow for the recovery of consequential damages. In the last analysis almost every breach by the buyer involves a failure or refusal to pay the contract price.[91] Even under prior case law the buyer's failure to pay the price or indeed his failure to pay any liquidated indebtedness was never a sufficient basis for the award of consequential damages no matter how foreseeable the injury to the creditor. The only recovery allowable was the sum of money owed with interest.[92] Thus, a seller's claim for consequential damages faces difficult obstacles indeed.

The Code expressly, however, permits recovery for incidental damages suffered by the seller. These "include any commercially reasonable charges, expenses or commissions incurred in stopping delivery, in the transportation, care and custody of goods after the buyer's breach, in connection with return or resale of the goods or otherwise resulting from the breach."[93] Incidental damages are recoverable whether he sues for damages following resale,[94] for damages without reference to resale,[95] or if he sues for the price.[96]

§ 227. Seller's Action for the Price

Although an action by the seller for the price is not an action for damages,[97] brief consideration of the circumstances under which such an action is available seems appropriate to round out the discussion of the various kinds of money judgments available to an aggrieved seller. Such an action is available if the goods have been accepted by

---

91. Occasionally, the breach by the buyer may take other forms, as where the buyer breaches his duty of cooperation in providing specifications, resulting in delayed production and additional cost to the seller. Kehm v. United States, 119 Ct.Cl. 454, 93 F. Supp. 620 (1950). While the Code permits the seller to cancel (U.C.C. § 2–711), or to perform in any reasonable manner as by providing his own specifications (U.C.C. § 2–311), it apparently leaves him remediless if he exercises patience, awaits the buyer's specifications and thereby suffers a loss, unless such damages may be characterized as incidental damages.

92. Loudon v. Taxing Dist., 104 U.S. 771, 26 L.Ed. 923 (1881); 11 Williston § 1410. There is an exception to this rule where the payment is to be made to a third person. In such cases the creditor is permitted to recover special damages suffered by him, often consisting of injury to his credit and reputation. Cf. U.C.C. § 4–402 (liability of bank to depositor for wrongful dishonor); see also Dillon v. Lineker, 266 F. 688 (9th Cir. 1920) (damages of $28,000 sustained by failure of defendant to pay off creditor's mortgage of $3,000); Miholevich v. Mid-West Mut. Auto Ins. Co., 261 Mich. 495, 246 N.W. 202, 86 A.L.R. 633 (1933) (liability insurer failed to pay judgment recovered against insured, held liable for damages as a result of a body execution levied on insured).

93. U.C.C. § 2–710.

94. U.C.C. § 2–706(1).

95. U.C.C. § 2–708(1), (2).

96. U.C.C. § 2–709(1).

97. See § 224 supra.

the buyer.[98] It is also available if the seller identifies the goods to the contract and the seller is unable after reasonable effort to resell them at a reasonable price, or if the circumstances reasonably indicate that such effort will be unavailing.[99] In this event the seller must hold the goods for the buyer, but if resale subsequently becomes practicable the seller may resell them at any time prior to collection of a judgment for the price.[1]

The seller also has an action for the price if the goods are lost or damaged within a commercially reasonable time after risk of their loss has passed to the buyer.[2] Analysis of this provision would require discussion of the complexities of when risk of loss passes [3] and the relation of these complexities to the question of insurance coverage.[4] This is best left to works on Sales.[5]

§ 228. Seller's Damages for Contracts to Manufacture Special Goods Under the Code

There is no explicit provision in the Code measuring damages for repudiation by the buyer of a contract to manufacture special goods. It is clear that if the manufacture is completed the seller may maintain an action for the price if the goods are not reasonably resaleable [6] and if resaleable, he may utilize the resale remedy [7] or maintain an action for damages.[8]

The problem arises where the repudiation occurs prior to completion of manufacture. The Code has an express provision as to mitigation in this eventuality. The seller "in the exercise of reasonable commercial judgment for the purposes of avoiding loss and of effective realization" has two options.[9] He may complete the manufacture, appropriate the goods to the contract and then exercise his remedy of resale or of an action for the price. His second option is to "cease

---

98. U.C.C. § 2–709(1) (6). It is unclear whether this includes the situation where the buyer accepts the goods and subsequently wrongfully purports to revoke his acceptance because of alleged defects. See Duesenberg & King § 13.06 [2] [a] (such situations are included); Peters, Remedies for Breach of Contracts Relating to the Sale of Goods Under the Uniform Commercial Code: A Roadmap for Article Two, 73 Yale L.J. 199, 241–43 (1963) (such situations are not included; revocation is equivalent of rejection by buyer).

99. U.C.C. § 2–709(1) (b).

1. U.C.C. § 2–709(2).

2. U.C.C. § 2–709(1) (a).

3. U.C.C. § 2–509; see § 187 supra.

4. U.C.C. § 2–510.

5. See Duesenberg & King § 13.06 [3].

6. See § 227 supra.

7. See § 225 supra.

8. See § 224 supra.

9. U.C.C. § 2–704(2).

manufacture and resell for scrap or salvage value or proceed in any other reasonable manner." If he exercises this option, the Code does not indicate his remedy. It seems clear, however, that he may, under the Code, sue for damages measured by the difference between the market price and contract price plus incidental damages or for the profit which he would have made.[10] Recovery of profit alone, however, would not compensate him for his losses sustained. Under prior law in addition to his gains prevented he would have been entitled to his losses sustained measured by the expenditures made pursuant to the contract to the extent that the product of such expenditures are not salvagable.[11] The Code appears to continue to permit such recovery in addition to lost profits by requiring "due allowance for costs reasonably incurred."[12]

§ 229.   Construction Contracts: Measure of Recovery by Contractor

The construction contractor is in many respects in the position of a seller of goods. The major difference is that his performance is affixed to land of another. Thus, such remedies as resale or replevin are unavailable. If he has completely performed he is unquestionably entitled to the agreed price.[13] If, however, the contract is repudiated by the owner or if the contractor justifiably cancels the contract because of a breach by the owner, the contractor's remedy is in damages.[14] If no work has been done the builder is entitled to the profit he would have made measured by the difference between the contract price and the prospective cost of performance.[15] If the work has commenced the contractor is entitled to the unpaid contract price less the amount it would have cost him to complete his performance.[16] The measure of recovery is sometimes expressed in a somewhat different formula. Under this second formula the contractor is en-

10. Anchorage Centennial Dev. Co. v. Van Wormer & Rodrigues, Inc., 443 P.2d 596 (Alaska 1968); see § 224 supra.

11. Lieberman v. Templar Motor Co., 236 N.Y. 139, 140 N.E. 222, 29 A.L.R. 1089 (1923); see § 226 supra.

12. U.C.C. § 2–708(2). For discussions of damages for breach of manufacturing contracts, see Duesenberg & King § 13.07 [4]; Peters, Remedies for Breach of Contract Relating to the Sale of Goods Under the Uniform Commercial Code: A Roadmap for Article Two, 73 Yale L.J. 199, 273–75 (1963).

13. McCormick, Damages 640.

14. He also has a remedy in restitution, discussed in § 239 infra.

15. McCormick, Damages § 164; 11 Williston § 1363. For a thorough discussion of the rules discussed in this section, see Patterson, Builder's Measure of Recovery for Breach of Contract, 31 Cal.L.Rev. 1286 (1934).

16. Guerini Stone Co. v. P. J. Carlin Constr. Co., 240 U.S. 264, 280, 36 S.Ct. 300, 307, 60 L.Ed. 636 (1915); Millen v. Gulesian, 229 Mass. 27, 118 N.E. 267 (1917); Restatement, Contracts § 346(2) (a).

titled to the profit he would have made plus the cost of work actually performed, less any progress payments he may have received.[17]   A third formula has also found judicial approval. This permits the builder to recover "such proportion of the contract price as the cost of the work done bears to the total cost of doing the job, plus, for the work remaining, the profit that would have been made on it."[18] In most cases each of these formulas yields the same result. Where the contract would have been performed at a loss to the contractor, however, each of the formulas may produce a different result.[19] It should be noted, however, that on a losing contract, the contractor would frequently find that his recovery would be greater in an action for restitution than in an action for damages.[20]

§ 230. Construction Contracts: Measure of Recovery by Owner

When a building contract is defectively performed, as a general rule the owner is entitled to damages measured by the cost of remedying the defect.[21] Frequently, however, it has been held that this measure of recovery would be inappropriate. For example, if the builder installs plumbing lines which are substantially in compliance with the contract but consisting of a different brand of pipe than specified by the contract, it will be held that the owner is entitled merely to the difference between the value of the structure if built to specifications and the value it has as constructed.[22] It is usually said that this second measure of recovery is appropriate "[i]f it is made to appear that

17. United States v. Behan, 110 U.S. 338, 344, 4 S.Ct. 81, 28 L.Ed. 168 (1884); Warner v. McLay, 92 Conn. 427, 103 A. 113 (1918). For a discussion of the similarity of result usually achieved by the application of this and the previous formula, see Petropoulos v. Lubienski, 220 Md. 293, 152 A.2d 801 (1959).

18. McCormick, Damages 641. Cases utilizing this formula include McGrew v. Ide Estate Inv. Co., 106 Kan. 348, 187 P. 887 (1920); Kehoe v. Borough of Rutherford, 56 N.J.L. 23, 27 A. 912 (1893).

19. The following illustration is given in McCormick, Damages 642. "Assume an extreme case: The contract price is $10,000, the work already done has cost $5,000, and the unfinished part would cost $10,000 to complete. Here under the three formulas

the builder would recover (1) zero, (2) $5,000, and (3) $3,333.33."

20. See § 240 infra.

21. Shell v. Schmidt, 164 Cal.App.2d 350, 330 P.2d 817, 76 A.L.R.2d 792 (1958) cert. denied 359 U.S. 959, 79 S.Ct. 799, 3 L.Ed.2d 766 (1959); Groves v. John Wunder Co., 205 Minn. 163, 286 N.W. 235, 123 A.L.R. 502 (1939); Bellizzi v. Huntley Estates, 3 N.Y.2d 112, 164 N.Y.S.2d 395, 143 N.E.2d 802 (1957); 5 Corbin § 1089; McCormick, Damages § 168; 11 Williston § 1363. Caveat: if the owner has not fully paid the price and performance by the builder is not substantial, in many jurisdictions the owner need pay nothing, or nothing further, on the contract. See § 159 supra.

22. Jacob & Youngs v. Kent, 230 N.Y. 239, 125 N.E. 889, 23 A.L.R. 1429 (1921).

physical reconstruction and completion in accordance with the contract will involve unreasonable economic waste by destruction of usable property or otherwise." [23]   It seems apparent, however, that the true rationale is that recovery for the cost of remedying the defect would involve unjust enrichment.   In all likelihood if the owner were to recover this amount in such circumstances he would pocket the recovery.   Most likely he would not undertake to remedy the defect by tearing the structure apart and changing the brand of pipe.   The end result would be that the owner would have a structure substantially in compliance with the contract and a sum of money far in excess of the pecuniary harm done to him.   Economic waste, then, is merely a criterion by which one can determine whether or not the owner reasonably would remedy the defect or would utilize the building in its defective state.   Another criterion is whether the owner's purpose is to gratify personal taste and fancy.   If so, he may be entitled to damages measured by the cost of completion even if this involves economic waste.[24]

It cannot usually be said that there is unreasonable economic waste if the structure is unusable or unsafe in its present condition. Thus, the owner's measure of damages in such a case is the cost of remedying the defect.[25]

In the event the builder abandons the construction prior to completion, normally the measure of damages is the reasonable cost of completion,[26] plus any damages suffered by the consequent delay in

23.   5 Corbin § 1090 at p. 493; accord, Eastern S.S. Lines, Inc. v. United States, 125 Ct.Cl. 422, 112 F.Supp. 167 (1953) (performance of contract to restore ship to pre-war condition would cost $4,000,000; after restoration ship would be worth $2,000,000); Peevyhouse v. Garland Coal & Min. Co., 382 P.2d 109 (Okl.1962), cert. denied 375 U.S. 906, 84 S.Ct. 196, 11 L.Ed.2d 145 (1963) (performance of promise to restore strip mined land would cost $29,000; restored land would be worth $5,000); Restatement, Contracts § 346(1) (a) (ii); McCormick, Damages § 168; contra, Groves v. John Wunder Co., 205 Minn. 163, 286 N.W. 235, 123 A.L.R. 502 (1939) (performance of promise to grade gravel and sand pit would cost $60,000; land as restored would be worth $12,-000).

Some cases have qualified the difference in value rule by holding that it is applicable only if the breach is not intentional.   Shell v. Schmidt, 164 Cal. App.2d 350, 330 P.2d 817, 76 A.L.R.2d 792 (1958).

24.   Groves v. John Wunder Co., 205 Minn. 163, 286 N.W. 235, 123 A.L.R. 502 (1958) (dissenting opinion); Chamberlain v. Parker, 45 N.Y. 569 (1871) (A man may choose "to erect a monument to his caprice or folly on his premises . . . ."); cf. Restatement, Contracts § 346, ill. 4.

25.   Bellizzi v. Huntley Estates, Inc., 3 N.Y.2d 112, 164 N.Y.S.2d 395, 143 N.E. 2d 802 (1957).

26.   State for Use of County Court of Randolph Cty. v. R. M. Hudson Paving & Constr. Co., 91 W.Va. 387, 113 S.E. 251 (1922); McCormick, Damages. § 169.

completion.[27] Damages for delay normally consist of the rental or use value the premises would have had during the period of delay.[28] If the requisite foreseeability and certainty exist, special damages are also recoverable.[29]

§ 231. Contracts to Sell Realty: Measure of Damages for Total Breach

Among the earliest rules of damages laid down in England were those relating to real property.[30] In 1776 it was held in Floreau v. Thornhill [31] that upon a vendor's breach of a contract because of an inability to convey good title the vendee may not recover for his loss of bargain. About half of the American states have accepted this English rule.[32] In such jurisdictions the vendee generally may recover only his down payment plus the reasonable expenses in examining title.[33] In its inception the limitation on the vendee's recovery was based upon the difficulty besetting a vendor in ascertaining whether his title was marketable in view of the lack of adequate land registries.[34] In those jurisdictions in which the limitation is accepted, despite the presence of adequate land registries, the rule is so well established and known to the legal profession and to land-owners that any judicial overturning of the rule would be unwarranted. Nevertheless, the original rationale must be strictly borne in mind in applying the rule. If the vendor has good title but refuses to convey he will be liable for ordinary contract damages, measured by the difference between the value of the land and the contract price, together with con-

---

27. Noonan v. Independence Indem. Co., 328 Mo. 706, 41 S.W.2d 162, 76 A.L.R. 931 (1931).

28. Wing & Bostwick Co. v. U. S. Fidelity & Guaranty Co., 150 F. 672 (W.D. N.Y.1906); Standard Oil Co. of N. Y. v. Central Dredging Co., 225 App.Div. 407, 233 N.Y.S. 279 (3rd Dep't), aff'd 252 N.Y. 545, 170 N.E. 137 (1929); McCormick, Damages § 170. The owner, however, under the doctrine of avoidable consequences may not enhance damages by prolonging the period of delay. See Losei Realty Corp. v. City of New York, 254 N.Y. 41, 171 N.E. 899 (1930), a case which pushes the doctrine to extreme limits, holding that although the defendant did not expressly abandon the contract and manifested an intention of eventually performing, the plaintiff as a reasonable man should have miti-

gated damages by putting an end to the contract.

29. Reilly v. Connors, 65 App.Div. 470, 72 N.Y.S. 834 (2d Dep't 1901); J. T. Stark Grain Co. v. Harry Bros. Co., 57 Tex.App. 529, 122 S.W. 947 (1909), error ref.

30. Other early rules limiting damages, not here considered, relate to breaches of covenants in conveyances. See McCormick, Damages § 185.

31. 96 Eng.Rep. 635 (1776).

32. McCormick, Damages §§ 177, 179 (lining up the jurisdictions).

33. McCormick, Damages § 182.

34. This is the explanation given in subsequent English cases. Day v. Singleton, [1899] 2 Ch. 320, 333.

sequential damages.[35]   Similarly, he will be so liable if he was aware of the defect in title at the time of contracting [36] or if a previously unknown curable defect is discovered and the vendor fails to utilize his best efforts to remove the defect.[37]   All of these cases are frequently said to come within a "bad faith" exception to the English rule, although in many such cases the question of whether or not the vendor was in bad faith is not so much in issue as is the question of whether the vendor knowingly assumed the risk that he would acquire marketable title.[38]   In cases where the vendee is permitted to recover for his loss of bargain, he may not also recover his expenses in examining title.[39]

In jurisdictions following the "American rule," the vendee is entitled to recover in all cases his loss of bargain together with consequential damages pursuant to the general principles of contract damages.[40]

In the event of breach by the vendee, it seems to be the rule everywhere that the vendor may recover standard contract damages: the difference between the contract price and the market value of the land.[41]   In an appropriate case the vendor may recover consequential damages measured by the profit which the vendor would have made on the transaction.[42]

---

35.   Pearce v. Hubbard, 223 Ala. 231, 135 So. 179 (1931). Of course, as a prerequisite to the recovery of consequential damages the vendee must meet the tests of foreseeability and certainty. Gilmore v. Cohen, 95 Ariz. 34, 386 P.2d 81, 11 A.L.R.3d 714 (1963).

36.   Stone v. Kaufman, 88 W.Va. 588, 107 S.E. 295 (1921); Arentsen v. Moreland, 122 Wis. 167, 99 N.W. 790 (1904); see also Potts v. Moran's Ex'rs, 236 Ky. 28, 32 S.W.2d 534 (1932), which collects many of the cases and adopts a somewhat different view to the effect that the vendor will be liable in such a case for loss of bargain only if he fails to utilize good faith in an attempt to remove the defect. See Carnahan, The Kentucky Rule of Damages for Breach of a Contract to Convey, 20 Ky.L.J. 304 (1932), an excellent article not limited to Kentucky law.

If the vendee is aware of the vendor's lack of marketable title at the time of contracting, as where the vendor merely has a contract to purchase the realty, some cases take the position that since there is a lack of bad faith, the vendor will not be liable for loss of bargain where he cannot perfect his title. Northridge v. Moore, 118 N. Y. 419, 23 N.E. 570 (1890); contra, Edgington v. Howland, 111 Neb. 171, 195 N.W. 934 (1923).

37.   Braybrooks v. Whaley, [1919] 1 K. B. 435.

38.   See Hammond v. Hannin, 21 Mich. 374, 386–87 (1870); Arentsen v. Moreland, 122 Wis. 167, 99 N.W. 790 (1904); McCormick, Damages 689–91.

39.   Schultz & Son v. Nelson, 256 N.Y. 473, 177 N.E. 9 (1931).

40.   Doherty v. Dolan, 65 Me. 87 (1876); McCormick, Damages § 177; Annot., 48 A.L.R. 12, 68 A.L.R. 137.

41.   McCormick, Damages § 186.

42.   Tague Holding Corp. v. Harris, 250 N.Y. 422, 165 N.E. 834 (1929), motion to dismiss appeal denied 250 N.Y. 557, 166 N.E. 323 (vendor had a contract to purchase from the owner).

I. AGREED DAMAGES

Analysis

Sec.
232. Liquidated Damages Distinguished from Penalties.
233. Two Pitfalls of Draftsmanship: The Shotgun Clause and the Have Cake and Eat It Clause.
234. Availability of Specific Performance When Damages are Liquidated.
235. Liquidated Damages and Penalties Distinguished from Alternative Promises.
236. Liquidated Damages Under the Uniform Commercial Code.

§ 232. Liquidated Damages Distinguished from Penalties

Historically, a rule developed in Equity that penalties agreed upon by the parties would not be enforced. This equitable rule, designed to prevent over-reaching and to give relief from hard bargains, was later adopted by courts of law.[43] Given the deeply rooted principle of freedom of contract and the reluctance of courts to inquire into the wisdom of a bargain except when fraud or something like it is proved, it has seemed somewhat anomalous that common law courts have continued assiduously to refuse enforcement of penalty clauses. The answer seems to be that in general parties are free to enter into a contract containing whatever terms they wish regarding the establishment of primary rights, but except within narrow limits they are not free to determine what remedial rights will be provided.[44] Remedies are provided by the state and are defined by public rather than private law. Therefore, for example, a contractual clause providing that in the event of breach specific performance will be granted will not be given effect.[45]

While parties are not empowered to provide for penalties in the event of a breach, they are permitted under certain conditions to determine in advance what damages will be assessed in the event of a breach.

---

43. Liquidated damages are discussed in McCormick, Damages §§ 146–157, and the historical development of the doctrine in § 147. See generally, Crowley, New York Law of Liquidated Damages Revisited, 4 N.Y.Cont. Leg.Ed.No. 1, 59 (1966); MacNeil, Power of Contract and Agreed Remedies, 47 Cornell L.Q. 495 (1962).

44. For a somewhat similar analysis, predicated, however, on the premise that the rule against penalties is not an abridgment of freedom of contract, see MacNeil, supra note 43.

45. But the clause may be influential in determining how the court will exercise its discretion. The cases are collected in MacNeil, supra note 43, at 521–22.

A penalty is designed to deter a party from breaching his contract and to punish him in the event the deterrent is ineffective.[46] Courts ritualistically list three criteria by which a valid liquidated damages clause may be distinguished from a penalty: first, the injury caused by the breach must be difficult or impossible of accurate estimation; second, the parties must intend to provide for damages rather than for a penalty, and; third, the sum stipulated must be a reasonable pre-estimate of the probable loss. Yet, analysis of what the courts have decided in fact demonstrates that the first two of these criteria are of limited importance and that in most cases the third criterion is determinative.[47] That the first criteria is of limited importance is shown by decisions where liquidated damage clauses are upheld although actual damages are readily calculable.[48] It is nonetheless true, however, that a liquidated damages clause is most useful to the parties and most likely to be upheld in cases where actual damages are most difficult to prove, as in the case of breach of a covenant not to compete ancillary to the sale of a business.[49] That intention is of little moment is indicated by decisions upholding clauses which the parties have labelled as penalty clauses [50] and striking down clauses which parties have labelled as providing for liquidated damages.[51] Moreover, even if it be shown that the parties conscientiously intended to provide for liquidated damages, the clause will be struck down if the amount stipulated is out of proportion to the probable damage.[52]

46. Berger v. Shanahan, 142 Conn. 726, 118 A.2d 311 (1955); Shields v. Early, 132 Miss. 282, 95 So. 839 (1923). Compare the function of punitive damages and the general lack of availability of such damages in contract actions. See § 204 supra. Note also that an attempt by a trade association to "fine" its member pursuant to a contract permitting the board of directors to levy such fines in the event of violation of the rules of the association, may also be invalid as a penalty. Continental Turpentine & Rosin Co. v. Gulf Naval Stores Co., 244 Miss. 465, 142 So.2d 200 (1962).

47. This is convincingly demonstrated in McCormick, Damages §§ 148–149; Crowley, supra note 43, at 60–66.

48. Callanan Road Imp. Co. v. Colonial S. & S. Co., 190 Misc. 418, 72 N.Y.S.2d 194 (Sup.Ct.1947) (excellent discussion). For additional cases see McCormick, Damages 605–06.

49. Jaquith v. Hudson, 5 Mich. 123 (1858), which contains one of the better discussions of the relative significance of intention, uncertainty and disproportion, is such a case.

50. United States v. Bethlehem Steel Co., 205 U.S. 105, 27 S.Ct. 450, 51 L. Ed. 731 (1907); Pierce v. Fuller, 8 Mass. 223 (1811); Tode v. Gross, 127 N.Y. 480, 28 N.E. 469, 13 L.R.A. 652 (1891).

51. Caesar v. Rubinson, 174 N.Y. 492, 67 N.E. 58 (1903); and see Seeman v. Biemann, 108 Wis. 365, 84 N.W. 490 (1900) ("While courts adhere to the doctrine that the intention of the parties must govern . . . the judicial power thus exercised cannot properly be justified under any ordinary rules of judicial construction.").

52. J. Weinstein & Sons v. New York, 264 App.Div. 398, 35 N.Y.S.2d 530 (1st Dep't), aff'd 289 N.Y. 741, 46 N.E.2d 351 (1942); 5 Corbin § 1058. Signifi-

It is generally agreed that reasonableness must be judged as of the time of contracting rather than as of the time of the breach and ensuing damage. Nevertheless, this general agreement breaks down when the extreme case is reached; that is, where no actual loss results although at the time of contracting a loss was foreseeable and reasonably estimated. A number of cases have ruled that in such circumstances the clause is unenforceable.[53] Before such a ruling is reached, however, the facts should be scrutinized to determine if the breaching party would be unjustly enriched by the breach,[54] as where a seller has been paid a premium price for prompt delivery, but delivers tardily with no actual damage to the buyer.[55]

§ 233.   Two Pitfalls of Draftsmanship: The Shotgun Clause and The Have Cake and Eat It Clause

Many contracts contain a number of covenants of varying importance. Damages for breach of each of these covenants may vary greatly. Thus a lessee may promise to pay rent, maintain fire insurance, keep the corridors lighted, etc. A clause which stipulates that in the event the lessee breaches the lease a given sum will be paid as liquidated damages (or that a given security deposit will be forfeited), cannot be a reasonable pre-estimate of the loss for breach of each of

cantly, neither the Restatement of Contracts § 339, nor the U.C.C. § 2–718 consider the question of intention to be relevant to the issue.

The overwhelming majority of cases involve the contention that the damages were set at a disproportionately high sum. Yet, where the damages are set at an unconscionably low figure, the clause will also be stricken. Bonhard v. Gindin, 104 N.J.L. 599, 142 A. 52 (1928); cf. U.C.C. § 2–718, Comment 1; see generally, Fritz, "Underliquidated" Damages as Limitation of Liability, 33 Tex.L.Rev. 196 (1954).

53.   Massman Constr. Co. v. City of Greenville, 147 F.2d 925 (5th Cir. 1945) (one factor in decision); Rispin v. Midnight Oil Co., 291 F. 481, 34 A.L. R. 1331 (9th Cir. 1923); Norwalk Door Closer Co. v. The Eagle Lock & Screw Co., 153 Conn. 681, 220 A.2d 263 (1966); McCann v. City of Albany, 158 N.Y. 634, 53 N.E. 673 (1899). Such cases are criticized in Crowley, supra note 43, at 64; and discussed

with approval in MacNeil, supra note 43, at 504–509. Cases to the contrary include Frick Co. v. Rubel Corp., 62 F.2d 765 (2d Cir. 1933) (evidence of lack of any actual damages was excluded, an erroneous decision because under any view such evidence should be admissible as bearing on what losses were foreseeable); Blackwood v. Liebke, 87 Ark. 545, 113 S.W. 210 (1908); McCarthy v. Tally, 46 Cal.2d 577, 297 P.2d 981 (1956), 9 Stan.L.Rev. 381 (1957).

54.   Berger v. Shanahan, 142 Conn. 726, 118 A.2d 311 (1955).

55.   United States v. Bethlehem Steel Co., 205 U.S. 105, 27 S.Ct. 450, 51 L. Ed. 731 (1907). It should be noted that although it is common to speak of penalty clauses in government contracts, such clauses are valid only if they conform to the requirements of liquidated damage clauses generally. See Laurent, Legal Aspects of Defense Procurement 159–62 (1962).

the lessee's covenants and thus will be deemed a penalty.[56]   On occasion, however, it will be possible to interpret such a clause so as to confine it to breach of the major covenant in which event if the stipulated sum is a reasonable pre-estimate of the loss for the breach of that covenant the clause will be upheld.[57]

Another pitfall into which contract draftsmen have plunged involves an attempt to fix damages in the event of a breach with an option on the part of the aggrieved party to sue for such additional actual damages as he may establish.   These have been struck down as they do not involve a reasonable attempt definitively to pre-estimate the loss.[58]

§ 234. Availability of Specific Performance When Damages are Liquidated

Despite the presence in a contract of a valid liquidated damages clause, if the criteria for equitable relief are met, the court will issue a decree for specific performance.   The fact that damages have been liquidated does not give the party who has promised to pay liquidated damages an option to perform the basic agreement or to pay damages at his discretion.[59]   In issuing its decree for specific performance a court of equity may also award damages for injury sustained between the period of the breach and the issuance of the decree.[60]

§ 235. Liquidated Damages and Penalties Distinguished from Alternative Promises

If a builder promises to build two houses by a specified day or pay the other party $4,000, several interpretations of the agreement are possible.   The parties may have regarded their agreement as calling for a firm commitment to build the houses, and on default, the builder

56.   Lenco, Inc. v. Hirschfeld, 247 N.Y. 44, 159 N.E. 718 (1928); Jolley v. Georgeff, 92 Ohio App. 271, 110 N.E. 2d 23 (1952); Management, Inc. v. Schassberger, 39 Wash.2d 321, 235 P. 2d 293 (1951).   See MacNeil, supra note 43, at 509–13, who points out that if such holdings are pressed to their logical conclusions, no liquidated damage clause would be valid because even as to the major covenant a breach may take varying forms.

57.   Ward v. Haren, 183 Mo.App. 569, 167 S.W. 1064 (1914); Hackenheimer v. Kurtzmann, 235 N.Y. 57, 138 N.E. 735 (1923); Hathaway v. Lynn, 75 Wis. 186, 43 N.W. 956 (1889); cf. Ann Arbor Asphalt Constr. Co. v. City of

Howell, 226 Mich. 647, 198 N.W. 195 (1924).

58.   Jarro Bldg. Indus. Corp. v. Schwartz, 54 Misc.2d 13, 281 N.Y.S.2d 420 (App.T.1967).

59.   Rubenstein v. Rubenstein, 23 N.Y.2d 293, 244 N.E.2d 49, 296 N.Y.S.2d 354 (1968); Bradshaw v. Millikin, 173 N. C. 432, 92 S.E. 161, L.R.A.1917E, 880 (1917); Restatement, Contracts § 378; 11 Williston § 1444.

60.   Wirth & Hamid Fair Booking Co. v. Wirth, 265 N.Y. 214, 192 N.E. 297, rearg. denied 265 N.Y. 510, 193 N.E. 295 (1934).

is to pay $4,000 as damages or as a penalty. Another interpretation is also possible. The parties may have meant that the builder was to have the privilege of not building; the price of this privilege was fixed at $4,000. Thus interpreted the agreement would be an option contract, with a price fixed for the exercise of an option to terminate.[61] Such agreements are sustained,[62] but the form of the agreement is not controlling. The court must determine whether the parties actually bargained for an option.

§ 236. Liquidated Damages Under the Uniform Commercial Code

The Uniform Commercial Code provides that liquidated damages may be agreed upon, "but only at an amount which is reasonable in the light of the anticipated or actual harm caused by the breach, the difficulties of proof of loss, and the inconvenience or non-feasibility of otherwise obtaining an adequate remedy. A term fixing unreasonably large liquidated damages is void as a penalty." [63]

The Code appears to have made one significant change in the law. Under the Code there are two moments at which the liquidated damages clause may be judged rather than one. Thus, contrary to the rule at common law, if the stipulated sum is not a reasonable forecast of the probable damages, but is reasonable in the light of the actual harm [64] it will be upheld.[65] It is difficult to assess the significance of the rather vague requirement that the clause must be viewed in the light of the difficulty of proof and of the availability of other remedies. Prior to enactment of the Code these factors were at best makeweights.[66] It is hoped that this will continue to be the case.[67]

61. This was the holding in the fact pattern discussed in the text. Pearson v. Williams' Adm'rs, 24 Wend. 244 (N.Y.1840), which, however, was later affirmed on the theory that the promise to pay was a valid liquidated damages clause. 26 Wend. 630 (N.Y.1841).

62. Pennsylvania Retreading Tire Co. v. Goldberg, 305 Ill. 54, 137 N.E. 81 (1922), 32 Yale L.J. 618 (1924) (promise to deliver shares of stock or pay $50,000); Edward G. Acker, Inc. v. Rittenberg, 255 Mass. 599, 152 N.E. 87 (1926) (defendant to give leasehold or pay $4,000).

63. U.C.C. § 2–718(1).

64. It is unclear whether actual harm refers to all harm suffered or merely actual damages. It will be recalled that unforeseeable harm actually

caused are not damages. See Crowley, supra note 43, at 74.

65. 1 Hawkland, A Transactional Guide to the Uniform Commercial Code 171; cf. Crowley, supra note 43, at 58–59, where a contrary interpretation is discussed and rejected. This interpretation is that the amount fixed may be disproportionate neither to a reasonable forecast of probable harm nor to the actual damages realized at the breach.

66. See § 232 supra.

67. Cf. Crowley, supra note 43, at 78 ("The statutory provisions relating to liquidated damages in the Uniform Commercial Code have not reduced the sense of confusion . . .. Rather . . . the statutory provisions appear to have increased the confusion.").

CHAPTER 13

RESTITUTION AS A REMEDY FOR BREACH

Analysis

Sec.
237. Introduction.
238. What is Meant by Restitution? The Concept of Unjust Enrichment.
239. Restitution as an Alternative Remedy for Breach.
240. Measure of Recovery in an Action for Restitution Based on Breach.
241. Restitution Not Available if a Debt Has Been Created.
242. May the Plaintiff Recover Both Damages and Restitution?

§ 237. Introduction

While the aim of the law of contract damages is generally to place the aggrieved party in the same economic position he would have had if the contract had been performed, the aim of restitution is to place both of the parties in the position they had prior to entering into the transaction. Throughout this volume reference has been made to the availability in particular circumstances of a quasi contractual or other restitutionary recovery. The availability of such remedies has been discussed or alluded to in the context of performance pursuant to agreements which are too indefinite to constitute contracts,[1] agreements made by persons lacking full contractual capacity,[2] contracts which are unenforceable because of the Statute of Frauds,[3] contracts which are discharged because of impossibility of performance or frustration of the venture,[4] agreements which are illegal,[5] and situations in which a defaulting plaintiff seeks to recover for part performance.[6]

This chapter has a twofold objective: first, to discuss briefly the common principles which underlie the law of restitution; and second, to discuss restitution as an alternative remedy for breach of contract.

§ 238. What is Meant by Restitution? The Concept of Unjust Enrichment

As the term is generally used today, "restitution" has a very flexible meaning. It encompasses recovery in quasi contract in which form of action the plaintiff recovers a money judgment. It is also

1. See § 23 supra.

2. See §§ 128, 133 supra.

3. See §§ 320 et seq. infra.

4. See §§ 187, 191, 195 supra.

5. See §§ 383–386 infra.

6. See § 159 supra.

used to encompass equitable remedies for specific relief such as decrees which cancel deeds or impose constructive trusts or equitable liens as well as some recoveries in Equity for sums of money.

The common thread which draws these actions together is that "one person is accountable to another on the ground that otherwise he would unjustly benefit or the other would unjustly suffer loss."[7] At the core of the law of restitution is the principle that "A person who has been unjustly enriched at the expense of another is required to make restitution to the other. . . ."[8] It should be emphasized, however, that this is a principle which underlies many particular rules rather than an operative rule.[9] Taken as a rule it would at the same time be too broad and too narrow. Too broad, because there are situations in which one's sense of justice would urge that unjust enrichment has occurred, yet no relief is available. Too narrow, because very often restitution is available where there has been no enrichment of the defendant but the plaintiff has suffered a loss. For example, where the plaintiff seeks restitution for the value of his performance pursuant to a contract unenforceable under the Statute of Frauds, the measure of recovery is ordinarily the losses sustained by the plaintiff (but not the gains prevented) as a result of the breach.[10] Not infrequently, however, this result is articulated in manipulative terms by artificially labelling the losses sustained by the plaintiff as benefits conferred upon the defendant.[11] In other contexts, however, such as in those limited areas where the plaintiff may recover for benefits conferred upon another without request, courts are rather strict in seeking to limit recovery to the amount by which the defendant has actually been enriched.[12]

§ 239. Restitution as an Alternative Remedy for Breach

In the event of a total breach of contract,[13] the aggrieved party may cancel the contract and pursue his remedies, one of which is restitution. In former times, if he sued for damages he was deemed to

7. Restatement, Restitution 1 (1937).

8. Restatement, Restitution 1 (1937).

9. Restatement, Restitution 11 (1937).

10. See § 323 infra.

11. Id.

12. Discussion of recovery for benefits conferred without request is outside the scope of this volume. An illustration of such a recovery is restitution awarded against a parent to one who unofficiously supplies necessaries to an infant. Greenspan v. Slate, 12 N. J. 426, 97 A.2d 390 (1953); Note, 39 Cornell L.Q. 337 (1954). See generally, Wade, Restitution for Benefits Conferred Without Request, 19 Vanderbilt L.Rev. 1183 (1966).

13. Restitution is not available as a remedy for a partial breach. Rudd Paint & Varnish Co. v. White, 403 F. 2d 289 (10th Cir. 1968); 5 Corbin § 1104.

be seeking to enforce the contract. If he decided to obtain restitution it was deemed that he elected to rescind the contract and pursue a quasi contractual remedy not based on the contract. Although for a considerable number of decades it has been recognized that the right to damages or restitution are both remedial rights based on the contract,[14] the older view that an action for restitution is not based on the contract has left its imprint on the rules governing the availability of, and measure of, recovery under this remedy. Thus, for restitution to be available, it was the rule that the plaintiff must give prompt notice that he cancels (under older terminology, "rescinds" or "disaffirms") the contract.[15] He may cancel only if the breach may be characterized as a total breach.[16] Such notice is now required, however, only if the plaintiff retains some tangible benefit from the contract,[17] or failure to give notice operates as a waiver of condition.[18] Indeed, some courts have gone further. Judge Cardozo put the rule in this fashion: "notice may be given at any time within the period of the Statute of Limitations unless delay would be inequitable." [19]

As a prerequisite to an action for restitution, at common law the plaintiff was required to tender [20] back all tangible benefits he had re-

14. See 5 Corbin § 1106; Woodward, Quasi Contracts § 260 (1913). The argument whether an action for restitution based on breach is a contract remedy or a quasi contractual action is not devoid of practical significance. For example, the United States has not waived its immunity under the Tucker Act as to quasi contractual actions. Knight Newspapers, Inc. v. United States, 395 F.2d 353 (6th Cir. 1968). An action for restitution based on breach may, however, be brought under the Act, Acme Process Equip. Co. v. United States, 171 Ct.Cl. 324, 347 F.2d 509 (1965), on the theory that the action is on the contract. Rev'd on other grounds 385 U.S. 138, 87 S.Ct. 350, 17 L.Ed.2d 249, reh. denied 385 U.S. 1032, 87 S.Ct. 738, 17 L.Ed.2d 680 (1967).

15. Woodward, supra note 14, at 429; accord, U.C.C. § 2–602(1) (notice of rejection by buyer).

16. Buffalo Builder's Supply Co. v. Reeb, 247 N.Y. 170, 159 N.E. 899 (1928); Sidney Stevens Imp. Co. v. Hintze, 92 Utah 260, 67 P.2d 632, 111

A.L.R. 331 (1937); cf. Rosenwasser v. Blyn Shoes, Inc., 246 N.Y. 340, 159 N.E. 84 (1927); 5 Corbin § 1104; Woodward, supra note 14, at § 263. The use of the term "rescission" in this context is to be avoided, as the legal relations resulting from a mutual rescission and from a decision by an aggrieved party to cancel the contract are quite distinct, but have often been confused because of the semantic trap caused by utilization of the same term to describe distinct concepts. The Uniform Commericial Code avoids this difficulty by adopting the term "cancel." See U.C.C. §§ 2–106(4); 2–703(f); 2–711(1); see also § 339 infra.

17. Ripley v. Hazelton, 3 Daly (N.Y.) 329 (1870).

18. Crofoot Lumber, Inc. v. Thompson, 163 Cal.App.2d 324, 329 P.2d 302 (1958); 5 Corbin § 1104.

19. Richard v. Credit Suisse, 242 N.Y. 346, 351, 152 N.E. 110, 111, 45 A.L.R. 1041, 1044 (1926).

20. The Restatement, Contracts § 349, avoids the technical term "tender"

ceived pursuant to the contract as a precondition to commencement of the action.[21] In Equity, however, actual tender was not always required, as a court of Equity could condition its decree upon restitution by the plaintiff to offset the value of the benefits retained.[22] Today, in a good number of jurisdictions the Equity rule has not been adopted at law.[23] Although the Restatement of Contracts continues to require an offer (but not a tender) by the plaintiff to make restoration, it provides for a number of exceptions.[24]

§ 240. Measure of Recovery in an Action for Restitution Based on Breach

The basic aim of restitution is to place the plaintiff in the same economic position as he enjoyed prior to contracting. Thus, unless specific restitution is obtained in Equity, the plaintiff's recovery is for the reasonable value of services rendered, goods delivered, or property conveyed less the reasonable value of any counter-performance received by him.[25]

and requires merely an offer to return. The Uniform Commercial Code requires neither a tender nor an offer to return. The buyer must merely hold the goods at the seller's disposition. U.C.C. § 2–602(2)(b).

21. Woodward, supra note 14, at § 265. As a corollary to this rule a plaintiff who had received intangible benefits, such as services, could not bring an action at law for restitution. This is no longer the prevailing view. Timmerman v. Stanley, 123 Ga. 850, 51 S. E. 760, 1 L.R.A.,N.S., 379 (1905); Brown v. Woodbury, 183 Mass. 279, 67 N.E. 327 (1903).

22. See 5 Corbin §§ 1102–1103, 1115–1116; 5 Williston §§ 1460, 1460A, 1463 (rev. ed. 1937).

23. See 5 Corbin §§ 1102–1103, 1115–1116; 5 Williston § 1460 (rev. ed. 1937).

24. Section 349(2) provides:

"A failure to offer to return the performance received does not make restitution unavailable as a remedy if

(a) it was wholly worthless; or

(b) it has been destroyed or harmed by the defendant or has per-

ished or deteriorated because of defects constituting a breach of the defendant's contract; or

(c) it is merely money paid by the defendant, the amount of which is credited to him; or

(d) it is the one for which a price is apportioned by the contract and that price is not included in the demand for restitution; or

(e) it constitutes a comparatively small part of the whole consideration and either is of such nature that its return has been from the time of its receipt impossible, or it has been disposed of by the plaintiff without reason to know of the defendant's breach, and its value can be determined and credited to the defendant."

25. Woodward, supra note 14, at § 268. The plaintiff recovers the reasonable value of his performance whether or not the defendant in any economic sense benefited from the performance. Schwasnik v. Blandin, 65 F.2d 354 (2d Cir. 1933); Rogers v. Becker-Brainard Milling Mach. Co., 211 Mass. 559, 98 N.E. 592 (1912); Mooney v. York Iron Co., 82 Mich. 263, 46 N.W. 376 (1890).

By the weight of authority the plaintiff is not restricted to the contract rate of payment although the contract price is admissible as evidence of the value of his performance.[26] Thus, in Boomer v. Muir,[27] the plaintiff on a construction project justifiably cancelled because of the defendant's breach. Had he completed the work he would have been entitled to an additional payment of $20,000. Rather than sue for damages, however, the plaintiff elected at trial to sue for restitution. Judgment entered upon a verdict in the amount of $257,965.06 was affirmed on appeal.

§ 241. Restitution Not Available if a Debt Has Been Created

It is an anomaly of the law of restitution that if the plaintiff in Boomer v. Muir, discussed in the preceding section, had completed the performance and was aggrieved by the defendant's failure to pay, his maximum recovery would have been $20,000. It is firmly established that if the plaintiff's performance has created a contract debt in money because of the plaintiff's full performance of his obligations,[28] he may not have restitution.[29] He is restricted to an action for recovery of the debt. No justification for this rule appears to exist other than such a result appears to have been established early in the history of the writ of indebitatus assumpsit.[30]

An interesting case pointing up the anomaly is Oliver v. Campbell,[31] in which plaintiff, an attorney, was retained as counsel in a divorce action for the agreed fee of $750. At the conclusion of divorce trial, but before judgment, plaintiff was discharged. The court found that the reasonable value of his services was $5,000. The majority of the court, however, took the position that plaintiff

---

26. The cases and arguments are ably discussed in Palmer, The Contract Price as a Limit on Restitution for Defendant's Breach, 20 Ohio St.L.J. 264 (1959).

27. 24 P.2d 570 (Cal.App.1933), hearing dism'd.

28. Lynch v. Stebbins, 127 Me. 203, 142 A. 735 (1928); Farron v. Sherwood, 17 N.Y. 227 (1858); 5 Corbin § 1110; Comment, Restitution—Availability as an Alternative Remedy Where Plaintiff Has Fully Performed a Contract to Provide Goods or Services, 57 Mich.L.Rev. 268 (1958).

29. There is authority for the proposition that restitution is available, however, if any part of the defendant's

obligation involves something other than the payment of money. Restatement, Contracts § 350; Bailey v. Interstate Airmotive, Inc., 358 Mo. 1121, 219 S.W.2d 333, 8 A.L.R.2d 710 (1949). This appears, however, to be a minority view. See Comment, Restitution— Availability as an Alternative Remedy Where Plaintiff Has Fully Performed a Contract to Provide Goods or Services, 57 Mich.L.Rev. 268 (1958).

30. Keener, Quasi Contracts 301–02 (1893); Woodward, supra note 14, at 415; cf. 5 Corbin § 1110.

31. 43 Cal.2d 298, 273 P.2d 15 (1954); cf. Matter of Montgomery, 272 N.Y. 323, 6 N.E.2d 40, 109 A.L.R. 669 (1936) (plaintiff attorney was promised $5,-

had fully performed and thus could recover only $750, while the dissenting judges were of the opinion that he had not fully performed and was therefore entitled to $5,000.

It also has been stated to be the rule that if any severable portion of the contract has been performed the plaintiff may not obtain restitution as to that portion, but only the apportioned price.[32] Conversely, if the contract is severable, the plaintiff may obtain restitution of the breached portions without cancelling those portions which are performed.[33]

It should be noted, however, that the criteria for severability developed in other contexts have not been mechanically applied in this connection. The mere fact that unit price has been established by contract per ton of coal delivered or per unit of earth excavated should not result in a finding of severability if it appears that the contract price is based on an average of the estimated future market price which fluctuates seasonally or an average value per unit of excavation of ground of varying difficulty, and the plaintiff's deliveries were made during the period when the market price was highest[34] or the ground excavated was of more than average difficulty.[35]

§ 242. May the Plaintiff Recover Both Damages and Restitution?

As a general rule a plaintiff may not have both restitution and damages for breach of contract.[36] At some stage he must elect his remedies; the time at which such an election must be made varies with local practice, but the modern tendency is to dispense with the earlier requirement that an election be made in the pleadings.[37]

000 for agreed services; after completing five-sixths of the agreed services he was discharged; recovery of $13,000 was sustained).

32. Dibol v. Minott, 9 Iowa 403 (1859); Restatement, Contracts § 351.

33. Czarnikow-Rionda Co. v. West Market Grocery Co., 21 F.2d 309 (2d Cir. 1927), cert. denied 275 U.S. 558, 48 S. Ct. 118, 72 L.Ed. 425; Portfolio v. Rubin, 233 N.Y. 439, 135 N.E. 843 (1922); cf. U.C.C. §§ 2–703, 2–711.

34. Wellston Coal Co. v. Franklin Paper Co., 57 Ohio St. 182, 48 N.E. 888 (1897) (coal has a higher market value in winter); accord, Clark v. Manchester, 51 N.H. 594 (1872) (contract of employment for one year at $25 per month; plaintiff discharged after working during season when wages were generally highest); see also Davidson v. Laughlin, 138 Cal. 320, 71 P. 345, 5 L.R.A.,N.S., 579 (1903); Williams v. Bemis, 108 Mass. 91 (1871).

35. Clark v. Mayor of N.Y., 4 N.Y. 338 (1850); cf. Palmer, supra note 26, at 276 (1959).

36. Downs v. Jersey Central Power & Light Co., 117 N.J.Eq. 138, 174 A. 887 (1934).

37. See, e. g., Barron and Holtzoff, Federal Practice and Procedure § 282 (1960); Clark, Code Pleading § 77 (2d ed. 1937); Moore, Federal Practice § 2.06 [3] (1967); Weinstein, Korn and Miller, New York Civil Practice §

It should carefully be noted, however, that in an award for damages, the plaintiff's restitutionary interest is usually protected.[38] He is entitled to losses sustained (benefits conferred on the other as well as reliance expenditures) as well as gains prevented. Until the advent of the Uniform Commercial Code, however, in an action for restitution the plaintiff's expectation interest usually received no protection. If defective machinery were delivered to the buyer and if he elected to return the machinery, he was entitled to restitution of payments made and often certain reliance expenditures,[39] but he received no compensation for any additional cost of replacing the machinery. Under the Uniform Commercial Code, however, the buyer may exercise the remedy of restitution and recover damages as well.[40] It would also appear, although not explicitly, that a seller may recover in restitution for the value of goods delivered (if a severable price is not apportioned) and also damages for breach as well.[41]

3002.04 (1968); cf. Restatement, Contracts § 381.

38. See generally, Fuller and Perdue, The Reliance Interest in Contract Damages, 46 Yale L.J. 52, 373 (1936–37).

39. Freight charges were recovered in International Harvester Co. v. Olson, 62 N.D. 256, 243 N.W. 258 (1932); Houser & Harnis Mfg. Co. v. McKay, 53 Wash. 337, 101 P. 894, 27 L.R.A.,N. S., 925 (1909). Expenses incurred in attempting to utilize defective purchases were recovered in Granette Products Co. v. Arthur H. Newmann & Co., 200 Iowa 572, 203 N.W. 935, modified 205 N.W. 205 (1925), af-

firmed 208 Iowa 24, 221 N.W. 197 (1928); National Sand & Gravel Co. v. R. H. Beaumont Co., 9 N.J.Misc. 1026, 156 A. 441 (1931). Consequential damages resulting from personal injuries were recovered in Russo v. Hochschild Kohn & Co., 184 Md. 462, 41 A.2d 600, 157 A.L.R. 1070 (1945). See 5 Williston § 1464; Anderson, Quasi Contractual Recovery in the Law of Sales, 21 Minn.L.Rev. 529 (1937); Rooge, Damages upon Rescission for Breach of Warranty, 28 Mich.L.Rev. 26 (1929); Notes, 21 Minn.L.Rev. 111 (1936); 45 Yale L.J. 1313 (1936).

40. U.C.C. § 2–711(1).

41. U.C.C. § 2–703, Comment 1.

CHAPTER 14

THIRD PARTY BENEFICIARIES

Analysis

Sec.
243. Introduction.
244. Categories of Beneficiaries.
    (a) Creditor and Donee Beneficiaries.
    (b) Intended and Incidental Beneficiaries.
245. Relationship of Third Party Beneficiary Doctrine to the Statute of Wills.
246. The Mortgage Assumption Cases and Vrooman v. Turner.
247. Public Contracts.
248. Intent to Benefit in the Creditor Beneficiary Context—Promises of Indemnity.
249. The Surety Bond Cases.
250. Promisor's Defenses.
251. Vesting—Voluntary Discharge or Modification.
252. Rights of the Beneficiary Against the Promisee.
253. Rights of the Promisee Against the Promisor.

§ 243. Introduction

It was firmly established in nineteenth century England that a person not in "privity" could not sue on a contract.[1] Although "privity" is used in several senses, in this context it refers to those who exchange the promissory words or those to whom the promissory words are directed.[2] Some earlier cases had been to the contrary. In Dutton v. Poole,[3] the defendant had promised his father to pay defendant's sister £1,000 if the father would forbear from selling certain property. The father performed and the sister was permitted to enforce the promise even though she was not in privity. The court reasoned that the close family relationship between the plaintiff and the promisee was a substitute for privity. Although the English courts subsequently repudiated the third party beneficiary doctrine, to do justice they are "very ready to torture such a contract into a trust."[4]

1. Price v. Easton, 110 Eng.Rep. 518 (K.B.1833); Tweddle v. Atkinson, 121 Eng.Rep. 762 (Q.B.1861); Dunlop Pneumatic Type Co. v. Selfridge & Co., [1915] A.C. 847; Green v. Russell, [1959] 1 Q.B. 28, 44.

2. 4 Corbin § 778.

3. Dutton v. Poole, 83 Eng.Rep. 523 (K.B.1677), aff'd 83 Eng.Rep. 156 (Ex. Ch.1679).

4. 1 Scott on Trusts § 14.4, at 152. The English decisions are analyzed in 4 Corbin §§ 836–55.

While there appear to have been earlier cases in the United States permitting a third party beneficiary to enforce a contract,[5] the case of Lawrence v. Fox [6] is generally credited with creation of new doctrine. In this case Holly, the promisee, owed $300.00 to Lawrence. Holly loaned $300.00 to Fox in exchange for Fox's promise to pay $300.00 to Lawrence. Since he took no part in this agreement, Lawrence was not in privity with the agreement. Although there was some discussion of trusts and agency in the decision,[7] ultimately the case held that Lawrence could recover as a third party beneficiary because it was manifestly just that he should.

§ 244. Categories of Beneficiaries

(a) Creditor and Donee Beneficiaries

The authorities generally distinguish between donee and creditor beneficiaries.[8] In essence the distinction is based on the purpose of the promisee in extracting the promisor's commitment to render a performance to the third party. If the promisee enters into the contract to confer a gift in the form of a promise upon the third party, as in Dutton v. Poole,[9] the third party is said to be a donee beneficiary; [10] but if the purpose of the promisee is to discharge an obligation which the promisee owes, or according to the Restatement, believes he owes, to the beneficiary, the third party is said to be a creditor beneficiary.[11] Under the original Restatement if the promisee has neither of these purposes, the third party was said to be an incidental beneficiary and as such has no rights under the contract.[12]

---

5. See 4 Corbin § 827 (N.Y. Cases); § 826 (Massachusetts cases).

6. 20 N.Y. 268 (1859).

7. The concurring judges preferred to rest the decision on an agency theory, that is to say that Holly was acting as agent for Lawrence. On the facts this theory was of doubtful applicability. This is a popular approach in Massachusetts where the third party beneficiary doctrine has not been fully accepted. See, e. g., Green v. Green, 298 Mass. 19, 9 N.E.2d 413 (1937) (recognizing that the agency rests "in some degree upon legal fiction"). See Restatement, Contracts (2d) § 133, Comment f. All references in this chapter to the Second Restatement are to Tentative Draft No. 3, except that references to § 133 are to the revision of that section appearing in Tentative Draft No. 4.

8. Restatement, Contracts § 133; 4 Corbin § 774; 2 Williston § 356.

9. See note 3 supra and accompanying text.

10. Restatement, Contracts § 133(1) (a). Contrary to the ordinary rule governing gifts, delivery is not necessary because the gift is the result of a contract. In re Estate of Sheimo, —— Iowa ——, 156 N.W.2d 681 (1968).

11. Restatement, Contracts § 133(1) (b).

12. Willard v. Claborn, 220 Tenn. 501, 419 S.W.2d 168 (1967); Stephens v. Great So. Sav. & Loan Ass'n, 421 S. W.2d 332 (Mo.App.1967); Restatement, Contracts § 133(c).

The Restatement Second avoids the use of the terms "donee" and "creditor" beneficiary because they "carry overtones of obsolete doctrinal difficulties" and instead uses the concept of "intended" beneficiary which is explained in the following section.[13]

(b) Intended and Incidental Beneficiaries

It is obvious that not everyone who would be benefited by performance of a contract, however remotely or indirectly, should be permitted to enforce it. The test by which the line is ordinarily said to be drawn between protected and incidental beneficiaries is the test of "intent to benefit" the beneficiary.[14]

Of whose intent do the courts speak and how is the intent to be ascertained? One view, distinctly in the minority, is that both parties must intend to benefit the third party and that such intention must be found in the contract.[15] In general, however, the courts are agreed that it is the promisee's intention which is more important.[16] The original Restatement determines "intent to benefit" by looking at the purpose of the promisee in the light of the terms of the promise and the accompanying circumstances.[17]

The Restatement Second takes the position that, "unless otherwise agreed,"[18] if "recognition of a right to performance in the beneficiary is appropriate to effectuate the intention of the parties," the beneficiary will be protected in two situations. First, if "performance of a promise will satisfy an obligation of the promisee to pay money

---

13. Restatement, Contracts (2d) Introductory Note to Ch. 6 and Reporter's Note to § 133. This would appear to bring the Restatement into conformity with the large number of court decisions which have made intent to benefit the primary test of enforceability. See, for example, Visintine & Co. v. New York, Chicago & St. Louis R.R., 169 Ohio St. 505, 160 N.E.2d 311 (1959). Another difficulty with the "creditor" "donee" terminology is that it is difficult to classify all cases of protected beneficiaries into these categories. 2 Williston §§ 356, 356A. For an example of this difficulty see the discussion of the surety bond cases at § 249 infra.

14. Robins Dry Dock & Repair Co. v. Flint, 275 U.S. 303, 48 S.Ct. 134, 72 L. Ed. 290 (1927).

15. Austin v. Seligman, 18 F. 519 (2d Cir. 1883); Spires v. Hanover Fire

Ins. Co., 364 Pa. 52, 70 A.2d 828 (1950); O'Boyle v. Du Bose-Killeen Properties Inc., 430 S.W.2d 273 ref. n. r. e. (Tex.Civ.App.1968) (On the peculiarities of the Pennsylvania decisions, see 4 Corbin § 828.) For an opposite extreme, see Beardsley v. Stephens, 134 Okl. 243, 273 P. 240 (1928) which seems to indicate that the writing itself is always insufficient to establish an intention to benefit.

16. Hamill v. Maryland Cas. Co., 209 F.2d 338 (10th Cir. 1954); McCulloch v. Canadian Pac. Ry., 53 F.Supp. 534 (D.Minn.1943) (New York law applied); 4 Corbin § 776; 2 Williston § 356A, at 839.

17. Restatement, Contracts § 133(1) (a) & (b).

18. See note 23 infra.

to a beneficiary." [19]   Second, if "the promisee manifests an intention to give the beneficiary the benefit of the promised performance." [20] Ultimately, according to the Second Restatement, intent to benefit is ascertained by whether "the beneficiary would be reasonable in relying upon the promise as manifesting an intention to confer a right on him.   Where there is doubt whether such reliance would be reasonable, considerations of procedural convenience and other factors not strictly dependent on the manifested intention of the parties may affect the question whether . . . recognition of a right in the beneficiary is appropriate." [21]   As in other cases in which intention is to be ascertained, there are differences in opinion as to the kind of evidence which may be introduced and how it may be evaluated. [22]

Under any approach to contractual interpretation, however, the agreement itself is the primary evidence which must be examined. Thus, if the parties explicitly agree that the third party shall or shall not have an enforceable right, their express agreement on this point will be given effect. [23]   A key which unlocks many of the cases is the determination of to whom the performance is to be rendered.   If the performance is to run directly to the promisee, the third party is ordinarily an unprotected incidental beneficiary, [24] but if it is to run to the third party, he is ordinarily an intended beneficiary with enforceable rights. [25]   Thus, for example, if a bank promised A a loan to pay his creditors, the creditors would most probably be deemed incidental beneficiaries; but if the bank promised to pay the money directly to the creditors they generally would be classified as intended beneficiaries. [26]   This test, however, is not conclusive.   For example, in Lucas

19.   Restatement, Contracts (2d) § 133(1) (a).

20.   Id., § 133(1) (b).

21.   Id., § 133, Comment d.   Matters of policy of course play an important part in the determination.   Westerhold v. Carroll, 419 S.W.2d 73 (Mo. 1967); Forman v. Forman, 17 N.Y.2d 274, 270 N.Y.S.2d 586, 217 N.E.2d 645 (1966).

22.   See ch. 3 supra.

23.   Borough of Brooklawn v. Brooklawn Housing Corp., 124 N.J.L. 73, 11 A.2d 83 (1940) (contract reserved enforcement to the promisee).

24.   McConnico v. Marrs, 320 F.2d 22 (10th Cir. 1963); Tomaso, Feitner and Lane, Inc. v. Brown, 4 N.Y.2d 391, 175 N.Y.S.2d 73, 151 N.E.2d 221 (1958).

25.   Fidelity & Deposit Co. of Baltimore v. Rainer, 220 Ala. 262, 125 So. 55, 77 A.L.R. 13 (1929); Carson, Pirie Scott & Co. v. Parett, 346 Ill. 252, 178 N.E. 498, 81 A.L.R. 1262 (1931); Lenz v. Chicago & N. W. Ry., 111 Wis. 198, 86 N.W. 607 (1901) ("Payment direct to the third person is, of course, a benefit to him, and, if that is required by a contract, the intent to so benefit is beyond question." 86 N.W. at 609).

26.   This distinction would reconcile, for example, the well known cases of H. R. Moch Co. v. Rensselaer Water Co., 247 N.Y. 160, 159 N.E. 896, 62 A. L.R. 1199 (1928) (contract to supply a given amount of water pressure to a city is not for the benefit of property owners) and La Mourea v. Rhude, 209 Minn. 53, 295 N.W. 304 (1940) (promisor agreed to be "liable for any dam-

v. Hamm [27] a lawyer promised to draft a will for the promisee. Under the will, the plaintiffs were to be beneficiaries. Because the will was improperly drawn, the plaintiffs received $75,000 less from the testator's estate than the testator had intended. It was held that the plaintiffs were intended beneficiaries of the testator's contract with the lawyer. Conversely, if an uncle promises his nephew that if he forbears from smoking cigarettes for one year, he will purchase for his nephew a new Aston-Martin automobile from the nearest distributor, the vendor of Aston-Martin cars will have no enforceable right, despite the fact that the uncle's promise cannot be performed without paying money to the vendor.[28] It is fairly obvious on these bare facts that there is no intent to benefit the vendor who is then characterized as an incidental beneficiary.

There have been a number of difficulties with the intent to benefit test. First of all, while many cases have been based on this test as an original proposition, certain hardened categories have emerged which are decided as a matter of law, without reference to any particular intention revealed in the facts of the particular case.[29] Second, in the donee cases at least two lines of cases may be traced. In the cases where there is a close tie of family or friendship between the promisee and beneficiary, the courts seem primarily concerned with the subjective intention of the promisee.[30] In a quest for subjective intention, more clearly than in a search for objective intention, extrin-

---

ages done to the work or other structure or public or private property and injuries sustained by persons"). The implications of the La Mourea case are discussed in Massengale v. Transitron Electric Corp., 385 F.2d 83 (1st Cir. 1967) wherein a buyer was held to be obligated to pay a broker who had been hired by the seller.

27. 56 Cal.2d 583, 15 Cal.Rptr. 821, 364 P.2d 685 (1961), cert. denied 368 U.S. 987, 82 S.Ct. 603, 7 L.Ed. 525 (1962); see also United States v. Carpenter, 113 F.Supp. 327 (E.D.N.Y.1949) (agreement between exporters and U.S. importer to restrict use of potatoes imported into U.S. to seed purposes, the U.S. Government held to be an intended beneficiary); TSS Sportswear Ltd. v. The Swank Shop (Guam) Inc., 380 F.2d 512 (9th Cir. 1967) (agreement between seller and buyer of stock that corporate debtor would no longer owe any money to seller or firms controlled by him.)

28. Restatement, Contracts § 133, ill. 12.

29. E. g., the cases relating to contractors' sureties, § 249 infra. The Restatement, Security (1941) in the introductory note to chapter 7 states that certain rules are so well established "that they can no longer be considered merely rules of interpretation." See also Note, Third Party Beneficiaries and the Intention Standard, 54 Va.L.Rev. 1166 (1968).

30. See Ridder v. Blethen, 24 Wash.2d 552, 166 P.2d 834 (1946) where the court said, in a donee situation, "resort, of necessity, must be had to extrinsic evidence to ascertain whether it was the purpose and intent of the parties to the contract to bestow a benefit or gift upon a third party." 166 P.2d at 836. Accord, Restatement, Contracts § 133(1) (a), which speaks of the promisee's "purpose" rather than of his intention.

sic evidence of all surrounding circumstances, including the promisee's own statements about his intention, must be admitted and weighed. However, in cases arising in a commercial [31] or governmental context,[32] the courts are not generally concerned with the subjective intention of the promisee. More objective tests of intention are sought, although evidence showing the circumstances surrounding the execution of the contract may be relevant to establish objective intention.

As suggested elsewhere in the book the best approach to any question of intention is a balance between the standard of reasonable understanding and the standard of reasonable expectations.[33] If these standards are adapted to the third-party beneficiary situation the test would be as follows: Would a reasonable man in the position of the promisor conclude that the promisee manifested an intention that the promisor's promised performance was sought at least in part for the benefit of the alleged beneficiary, and, assuming that the answer to the first question is in the affirmative, would a reasonable man in the position of the promisee conclude that the promisor acquiesced in the intention of the promisee? Although the test is phrased in terms of manifest intent here again evidence of subjective intent and other evidence extrinsic to the writing should be permitted in accordance with the parol evidence rule and the principles of interpretation previously discussed. Under this test the question of intent would often be a question of fact.[34]

A good number of states have enacted statutes governing the question of third party beneficiaries. By and large, the questions

---

31. E. g., note the manner in which the court found "intent to benefit" in McCulloch v. Canadian Pac. Ry., 53 F.Supp. 534 (D.Minn.1943), by relying on evidence of the circumstances which brought about the contract and without reference to anyone's statement of what his intention was. See also the surety bond cases, discussed at § 249 infra, where any attempt to ascertain subjective intention would clearly be inappropriate. See also Oxford Commercial Corp. v. Landau, 12 N.Y.2d 362, 239 N.Y.S.2d 865, 190 N.E. 2d 230, 13 A.L.R.3d 309 (1963), where the court excluded parol evidence proferred to contradict an unambiguous contract which showed an intent to benefit. But see Cutler v. Hartford Life Ins. Co., 22 N.Y.2d 245, 292 N.Y. S.2d 430, 239 N.E.2d 361 (1968).

32. See the municipality cases, § 247 infra. Even in such cases, the instru-

ment may not show whether the third parties were intended donee beneficiaries. Full development of the surrounding circumstances should be permitted.

33. See § 47 supra.

34. See, e. g., United States v. Carpenter, 113 F.Supp. 327 (E.D.N.Y.1949) where it was suggested that the question of intent to benefit is often a factual question. Compare Cutler v. Hartford Life Ins. Co., 22 N.Y.2d 245, 292 N.Y.S.2d 430, 239 N.E.2d 361 (1968) where the court explored the surrounding circumstances and determined that someone other than the named beneficiary of a life insurance policy was the ultimate intended beneficiary, but so ruled as a matter of law. Compare further, Hylte Bruks Aktiebolag v. Babcock & Wilcox Co., 399 F.2d 289 (2d Cir. 1968).

which arise and solutions which have been reached are the same as those in non-statutory states.[35]

§ 245. Relationship of Third Party Beneficiary Doctrine to the Statute of Wills

Under the Statute of Wills and its modern descendants a testamentary disposition must usually be in writing, signed and witnessed in a rather rigidly specified manner. If a contract for the benefit of a third party makes the beneficiary's rights conditional upon his surviving the promisee, some courts have held that he acquires no rights because of non-compliance with the Statute of Wills.[36] This is clearly incorrect. The promisee is not disposing of an existing right but is creating a present conditional right by contract.[37] If compliance with the Statute of Wills were required, no life insurance policy would be enforceable.

§ 246. The Mortgage Assumption Cases and Vrooman v. Turner

A mortgage is a security interest in real property typically given in exchange for a loan. The loan is usually evidenced by a bond or note. Suppose that A in exchange for a loan gives a bond and mortgage to B and A subsequently sells the mortgaged property to C. The transaction can be negotiated in two ways. C may "assume" the mortgage, which in common usage means that he promises A that he will pay the mortgage indebtedness to B. In such a case the situation is in essence the same as Lawrence v. Fox.[38] A's purpose in requiring C's covenant of assumption, it may be assumed, is to have the debt discharged. It is generally agreed that B is a third party beneficiary of C's promise made to A.[39] Continuing with this illustration, if C conveyed the property to D, who validly assumed the mortgage, B would be a third party beneficiary of D's promise to C.[40]

If, in the conveyance, C had merely taken subject to the mortgage; that is, recognized that there was a security interest in the

35. A table of statutes appears in 2 Williston § 367. For a discussion see id. at § 365; Note, The Third Party Beneficiary Concept: A Proposal, 57 Colum.L.Rev. 406, 414–15 (1957).

36. Coley v. English, 235 Ark. 215, 357 S.W.2d 529 (1962); McCarthy v. Pieret, 281 N.Y. 407, 24 N.E.2d 102 (1939), rearg. denied 282 N.Y. 800, 27 N.E.2d 207 (1940); but see Freer v. J. G. Putnam Funeral Home, Inc., 195 Ark. 307, 111 S.W.2d 463 (1937); In re Estate of Hillowitz, 22 N.Y.2d 107, 291 N.Y.S.2d 325, 238 N.E.2d 723 (1968).

37. Grismore § 237, at 387. If, however, the promisor undertakes by contract to provide for the beneficiary by will, in some jurisdictions the Statute of Frauds provides that his promise must be in writing. See McKinney's N.Y. E.P.T.L. 13–2.1(2).

38. 20 N.Y. 268 (1859).

39. Burr v. Beers, 24 N.Y. 178 (1861); 4 Corbin § 796; 2 Williston § 383.

40. The Home v. Selling, 91 Or. 428, 179 P. 261, 21 A.L.R. 403 (1919).

land but assumed no personal obligation in regard to the indebtedness, B clearly would not be a third party beneficiary since C has not made any promise with respect to payment of the indebtedness. Suppose, however, C, despite the absence of any personal obligation on his part, in a subsquent conveyance to D causes D to assume the mortgage. This was the situation in the well known case of Vrooman v. Turner.[41]

The court ruled that D's promise to pay the indebtedness was not enforceable by B.[42] It stated that before a party may qualify as a third party beneficiary two requirements must be met. First, there must be an intent to benefit, which the court apparently found to exist, and, second, there must be an obligation owing from the promisee to the beneficiary. This second requisite was lacking because C had not assumed the mortgage and thus was not indebted to B.

An interesting question with respect to cases such as Vrooman v. Turner, is why did C, the promisee, who was under no liability, extract an assumption from D. It is generally agreed that there is no basis for a finding that C's purpose was to confer a gift upon B.[43] Nor will it usually be found that the assumption clause was placed there inadvertently or by mistake.[44] Rather, generally it will be found that C's purpose was to guard against a supposed liability upon his part.[45] The court, however, ruled that the existence of a supposed liability was insufficient as a predicate for third party beneficiary status. About one half of the jurisdictions are in accord with Vrooman v. Turner.[46]

It is difficult to reconcile Vrooman v. Turner with decisions such as Rouse v. United States,[47] which are generally recognized to be the

---

41. 69 N.Y. 280 (1877).

42. The promisee in such a case would have a right of action against the promisor, but in the usual case he would be unable to prove any damage. On the possibility of an action for specific performance in such circumstances, see § 253 infra.

43. In some cases a motive can be found. See Federal Bond & Mortgage Co. v. Shapiro, 219 Mich. 13, 188 N.W. 465 (1922) (promisee wished to protect his second mortgage on the premises) and Schneider v. Ferrigno, 110 Conn. 86, 147 A. 303 (1929).

44. Parol evidence is admissible to strike out an assumption clause on grounds of mistake, to reform the instrument, or to show that the clause was inserted in the deed without the assent of the promisor. Kilmer v. Smith, 77 N.Y. 226 (1879) (clause stricken out); Blass v. Terry, 156 N. Y. 122, 50 N.E. 953 (1898) (no assent); cf. Ross v. Warren, 196 Iowa 659, 195 N.W. 228 (1923) (insufficient evidence to justify reformation).

45. 2 Williston § 386A.

46. 4 Corbin § 796, at 151.

47. 94 U.S.App.D.C. 386, 215 F.2d 872 (1954); accord Restatement, Contracts § 144.

law even in states which follow Vrooman v. Turner.[48] In the Rouse
case the plaintiff's assignor sold an oil burner to B on credit pursuant
to a conditional sales contract. When B sold the house, the defendant purchaser agreed to assume the payments still due on the oil
burner contract. The defendant failed to make payment and sought
to interpose as a defense that plaintiff's assignor had breached a
warranty made to B. One would expect that in states following
Vrooman v. Turner the defendant would be permitted to raise this
defense; he is attemping to show that there is no obligation owing
from the promisee to the beneficiary. The court, however, ruled that
the defendant, by his assumption, promised to pay irrespective of any
defense the promisee might have. This is the usual holding in a case
where there is an assumption of a specific alleged debt.[49]

The rationale employed by the court in Vrooman v. Turner is no
longer accepted in New York where the case was decided. It is obvious that if there must be an obligation owing from the promisee to
the beneficiary, a donee beneficiary could not qualify as a protected
beneficiary. However, a few years after the decision in Vrooman v.
Turner it was held in New York that a donee beneficiary may recover if there is a close family relationship between the beneficiary and
the promisee.[50] Subsequent cases have erased the necessity for such
a relationship.[51] This is the prevailing view in the country,[52] although
occasional decisions to the contrary may be found.[53]

The result in Vrooman v. Turner, still accepted by a large number of jurisdictions,[54] is best looked at as a living fossil, limited to

48. E. g., Bennett v. Bates, 94 N.Y. 354
     (1884) (invalidity of mortgage). See 4
     Corbin §§ 821–822; 2 Williston § 399.

49. The Restatement, Contracts (2d)
     takes the same position in § 144, Com-
     ment b, when it states: "Nonexistence
     of the supposed duty does not estab-
     lish a mistake where the terms of the
     promise provide for the case. Thus if
     the promisor promises to perform
     whatever duty is owed and none is
     owed, the beneficiary has no right
     against the promisor. Likewise, a
     promise to render a performance
     whether or not there is a pre-existing
     duty is effective according to its
     terms. Prima facie an unqualified
     promise to render the performance
     has the same effect, but mistake as to
     the existence of the duty may make
     the contract voidable."

50. Seaver v. Ransom, 224 N.Y. 233,
     120 N.E. 639, 2 A.L.R. 1187 (1918).

51. Oxford Commercial Corp. v. Lan-
     dau, 12 N.Y.2d 362, 239 N.Y.S.2d 865,
     190 N.E.2d 230 (1963); Lait v. Leon,
     40 Misc.2d 60, 242 N.Y.S.2d 776 (Sup.
     Ct.1963).

52. See Restatement, Contracts § 133.

53. Cases indicating that there must be
     some kind of obligation or relation-
     ship between the promisee and benefi-
     ciary even in a donee situation in-
     clude West v. Norcross, 190 Ark. 667,
     80 S.W.2d 67 (1935); Scheidl v. Uni-
     versal Aviation Equip., Inc., 159 N.Y.
     S.2d 278 (Sup.Ct.1957).

54. It seems to have been reaffirmed in
     New York. Nicholson v. 300 Broad-
     way Realty Corp., 7 N.Y.2d 240, 196

mortgage assumption cases and surviving from the era when there was great uncertainty as to the limits of the then radical third party beneficiary doctrine. An attempt at an analytic reconciliation of the case with prevailing principles, however, can possibly be made. Unlike the situation in Rouse v. United States, there was no antecedent promise running from the promisee to the beneficiary. Restated, Vrooman v. Turner may be said to require that for an intended creditor beneficiary to recover there must be at least an ability by the supposed creditor to show the color of a claim against the promisee.[55]

§ 247. Public Contracts

Every contract made by a governmental unit is made for the benefit of its inhabitants. If a city contracts to have a police station, fire house, tax office, or park built, it does so to enhance the general welfare and, thus, to benefit the public. Yet, in such a case, no individual inhabitant has a right to enforce the contract on his own behalf.[56]

There are, however, at least three classes of cases in which members of the public will be classified as protected beneficiaries. The

N.Y.S.2d 945, 164 N.E.2d 832 (1959). According to 2 Williston § 386A the majority of cases are in accord; but see 4 Corbin § 796, at 151, stating that the majority of cases have held for the beneficiary. There is a fairly even split and certain distinctions are sometimes made within a given jurisdiction. A leading case to the contrary is Schneider v. Ferrigno, 110 Conn. 86, 147 A. 303 (1929) where the court said "The cases which deny liability . . . do not seem fully to recognize the extent and force of the rule which permits a third party beneficiary to sue upon a contract as it has now been developed."

55. Although the Restatement Second does not undertake to reconcile the two cases it is clear that it provides a basis for reconciling them along the grounds suggested because it attaches great significance to the question of whether the promisee is a surety. It reasons that where the duty of the promisee is voidable (as in Rouse) or

unenforceable the promisee is still a surety and so although the promise of the promisee will satisfy only a voidable duty of the promisee nevertheless "the beneficiary is automatically treated as an intended beneficiary." § 144, Comment a. See the text at note 19. However in the Vrooman case since the promisee is under no duty (not even a voidable one), he is not a surety and so if the beneficiary is to qualify as an intended beneficiary he must do so under the test of intent to benefit as outlined in § 244 supra. Illustration 3 under § 144 indicates that ordinarily under the facts of Vrooman v. Turner an intent to benefit should be found.

56. Restatement (2d) § 145, Comment a. In some jurisdictions, individual residents may bring a "taxpayer's action" to enforce a government contract. In such cases, however, the action is on behalf of the governmental unit and any recovery goes into the public treasury.

original Restatement makes specific reference to but two of these classes; both on the borderland of tort liability.[57]

First, if the contractor agrees to perform services which the municipality is under a legal duty to perform to individual members of the public,[58] the contractor's failure properly to perform his contract which results in injury to an individual will create liability to the individual.[59] The primary illustration of this rule has been in cases where contractors have assumed the city's duty to repair or otherwise maintain a public street or highway.

The second situation contemplated by the Restatement involves the exaction of a promise by the governmental body from the contractor to compensate members of the public for injury done them in situations where the city owes no duty to the public. If there is an intent that injured persons recover from the contractor "manifested in the contract, as interpreted in the light of the circumstances surrounding its formation," [60] these individuals are donee beneficiaries.[61] In a great number of jurisdictions cases have arisen in which, in violation of their contracts with municipalities, water companies have failed to maintain the promised degree of water pressure, resulting in fire losses. Far the greater number of cases have found on these facts that there was no intent to benefit the individual property owner.[62] In all likelihood, courts have been impelled to this conclusion at

---

57. Restatement, Contracts § 145. The Restatement Second recognizes that in some respects the original Restatement was too restrictive. In addition to making provision for the two situations provided for in the old Restatement, it adds that "The rules stated in this Chapter apply to contracts with a government or governmental agency except to the extent that the application would contravene the policy of the law authorizing the contract or prescribing remedies for its breach." § 145(1). While the old Restatement stated the rule in terms of the United States, a State or a municipality, the Restatement Second speaks in terms of a "government or governmental agency."

58. When or whether such a duty exists involves questions of tort law, the doctrine of sovereign immunity and, at times, questions of interpretation of statutes.

59. This matter is discussed in some detail in § 248 infra and will not be repeated here.

60. Restatement, Contracts § 145(a). Contrast the language of § 133(1) (a) of the original Restatement which places great stress on the purpose of the promisee. The Restatement Second seems to exclude even surrounding circumstances when it allows an action by the third party only when "the terms of the promise provide for such liability." § 145(2) (a). But see id., Comment c.

61. Restatement, Contracts § 145(a). In these cases it is unnecessary to prove tort liability, the contractor having agreed to pay "any damages" or words to that effect. See La Mourea v. Rhude, 209 Minn. 53, 295 N.W. 304 (1940); Anderson v. Rexroad, 175 Kan. 676, 266 P.2d 320 (1954).

62. The leading case is perhaps H. R. Moch Co. v. Rensselaer Water Co., 247

least in part by a fear that too crushing a burden would be placed on the water company.[63]

A third kind of case, which the Restatement does not consider in a separate category, involves contracts which a governmental unit enters into in order to secure advantages for the public and not merely to protect the public from harm. Thus, contracts with water,[64] gas [65] and other utility companies,[66] as well as common carriers,[67] specifying maximum rates to be charged, have generally been held to create enforceable rights in individual consumers. So also, contracts specifying minimum wages to be paid to employees have been held to be enforceable by the employees.[68] The Restatement Second appears to have provided for these cases in subdivision 1 of § 145 previously quoted.[69]

Interestingly, it has generally been held that if the contract can be characterized as a contract for the benefit of third persons, it is immaterial that the individual seeking to enforce the contract is not an inhabitant of the political unit which has entered into the contract.[70]

N.Y. 160, 159 N.E. 896, 62 A.L.R. 1199 (1928). For citations to other jurisdictions, see 4 Corbin § 806 n. 75; 2 Williston § 373 n. 11. But see Doyle v. South Pittsburgh Water Co., 414 Pa. 199, 199 A.2d 875 (1964) (negligence claim allowed). A leading case allowing contractual recovery is Gorrell v. Greensboro Water Supply Co., 124 N.C. 328, 32 S.E. 720 (1899).

63. In the Moch case, note 62, supra, Chief Judge Cardozo wrote: "An intention to assume an obligation of indefinite extension to every member of the public is seen to be the more improbable when we recall the crushing burden that the obligation would impose . . . .. If the plaintiff is to prevail, one who negligently omits to supply sufficient pressure to extinguish a fire started by another, assumes an obligation to pay the ensuing damage, though the whole city is laid low. A promisor will not be deemed to have had in mind the assumption of a risk so overwhelming for any trivial reward." 247 N.Y. at 165–66, 159 N.E. at 897–98. The Restatement Second recognizes the policy aspect of the problem in Comment d to § 133. See note 21 supra. In addition it should be noted that perform-

ance ran to the promisee. See § 244 supra, particularly note 25 supra.

64. Pond v. New Rochelle Water Co., 183 N.Y. 330, 76 N.E. 211 (1906).

65. Farnsworth v. Boro Oil & Gas Co., 216 N.Y. 40, 109 N.E. 860 (1915).

66. Rochester Tel. Co. v. Ross, 195 N.Y. 429, 88 N.E. 793 (1909).

67. International Ry. v. Rann, 224 N.Y. 83, 120 N.E. 153 (1918).

68. H. B. Deal & Co. v. Head, 221 Ark. 47, 251 S.W.2d 1017 (1952) (time and a half for overtime); Novosk v. Reznick, 323 Ill.App. 544, 56 N.E.2d 318 (1944) (minimum wage); Stover v. Winston Bros. Co., 185 Wash. 416, 55 P.2d 821 (1936), 46 Yale L.J. 706 (1937).

69. See note 57 supra.

70. Wilson v. Oliver Costich Co., 231 App.Div. 346, 247 N.Y.S. 131, aff'd mem. 256 N.Y. 629, 177 N.E. 169 (1931). This case supports the conclusion that in donee beneficiary cases there is no need for any special relationship between the promisee and the beneficiary.

§ 248.   Intent to Benefit in the Creditor Beneficiary Context—Promises of Indemnity

It has been argued in creditor beneficiary cases that, since the purpose of the promisee is to discharge an obligation that he owes to the creditor, the promisee does not intend to benefit the creditor.[71] This argument as a universal misses the mark because, although the promisee's purpose is to benefit himself, nevertheless, in many cases he intends that this purpose be accomplished by having the promisor perform directly to the creditor and such an intention is distinctly beneficial to the creditor.[72]

However, even in the context of a creditor beneficiary it would appear possible to have difficult questions as to the existence of an intent to benefit. We have seen that if A is obligated to B and C agrees to assume A's obligation, there is "an intent to benefit" B who is characterized as a third party creditor beneficiary.[73] But what if C promises A that he will discharge A's legal liability in the event that A becomes liable to B? C's status is that of an indemnitor against liability. This is the situation presented under a liability insurance policy. Quite often it is held in such a case, apparently contrary to the rules previously stated, that B is not a third party beneficiary of C's promise to a A.[74] This holding is often a result of specific language in the insurance contract providing that no action shall be brought against the insurer,[75] but also often a result of a policy against having the jury be aware that an insurer will ultimately pay the damages the jury assesses.[76]

71.   See, e. g., National Bank v. Grand Lodge, 98 U.S. 123, 25 L.Ed. 75 (1878).

72.   The distinction is convincingly presented in Grismore § 238.

73.   §§ 244, 246 supra.

74.   Jefferson v. Sinclair Ref. Co., 10 N.Y.2d 422, 223 N.Y.S.2d 863, 179 N.E. 2d 706 (1961); Restatement, Contracts, (2d) § 145, ill. 6; cf. United States v. Lutz, 295 F.2d 736 (5th Cir. 1961).

75.   Litigation concerning the validity and effect of such language has been especially prolific in conflict of laws cases. A number of jurisdictions by statute permit direct action against the insurer despite language in the policy attempting to exclude such an action. Such statutes may be constitutionally applied to insurance policies negotiated and issued outside the state provided that the state has a legitimate interest, under the facts, in applying its own law. Watson v. Employers Liability Assur. Corp., 348 U. S. 66, 75 S.Ct. 166, 99 L.Ed. 74 (1954), reh. denied 348 U.S. 921, 75 S.Ct. 289, 99 L.Ed. 722 (1955). For discussions of the problems of contract law and conflict of laws, see MacDonald, Direct Action Against Liability Insurance Companies, 1957 Wis.L.Rev. 612; Note, 57 Colum.L.Rev. 256 (1957); Note, 74 Harv.L.Rev. 357 (1960).

76.   Morton v. Maryland Cas. Co., 1 A. D.2d 116, 148 N.Y.S.2d 524 (2d Dep't 1955), aff'd 4 N.Y.2d 488, 176 N.Y.S.2d 329, 151 N.E.2d 881 (1958). This policy has been somewhat relaxed in New York, but only as to cases in which the law of another jurisdiction is applicable. Oltarsh v. Aetna Ins. Co., 15

A different problem arises when C promises A that he will reimburse A in the event that A is compelled to pay B. Here C is called an indemnitor against loss. Under the test of "to whom is the performance to run" it would seem clear that B should be held to be an incidental beneficiary and the majority of the authorities have so held.[77]

However, particularly in the area of the municipality cases, there has been a tendency to treat a promise of indemnity against loss as a third party beneficiary situation.[78] This is in part perhaps due to the influence of H. R. Moch Co. v. Rensselaer Water Co.[79] and the original Restatement[80] which seem to imply that in a municipality case the contractor is liable to the inhabitant if the city owed a duty to the inhabitants to render the services which the contractor has agreed to perform irrespective of any "intent to benefit" the inhabitant, even though performance under the contract is to run to the municipality.

The Restatement Second handles this problem by stating "Where there is government liability, and the question of interpretation is in doubt, there is liability if a direct action is appropriate in view of the factors referred in Comment a."[81]

A problem related to the cases discussed above occurs when a promisor agrees to procure liability insurance for the promisee and fails to do so. A number of cases have held that an injured party could successfully sue the promisor although a contrary result might have been reached on the ground that the performance was to run to the promisee.[82]

N.Y.2d 111, 256 N.Y.S.2d 577, 204 N.E. 2d 622 (1965).

77. Restatement, Contracts § 133, ill. 9; Restatement, Contracts (2d) § 133, ill. 3.

78. Stewart v. Sullivan County, 196 Tenn. 49, 264 S.W.2d 217 (1953), 7 Vand.L.Rev. 793 (1954); O'Connell v. Merchants' & Police Dist. Tel. Co., 167 Ky. 468, 180 S.W. 845 (1915); Rigney v. New York Cent. & H. R. R. Co., 217 N.Y. 31, 111 N.E. 226 (1916); cf. Coley v. Cohen, 169 Misc. 933, 9 N.Y.S.2d 503 (Sup.Ct.), aff'd 258 App.Div. 292, 117 N.Y.S.2d 101 (4th Dep't 1939), aff'd 289 N.Y. 365, 45 N.E.2d 913, (1942).

79. 247 N.Y. 160, 159 N.E. 896 (1928).

80. Restatement, Contracts § 145(b).

81. Restatement, Contracts (2d) § 145, Comment c. Illustration 4 would appear to illustrate this comment. Compare illustration 6.

82. Johnson v. Holmes Tuttle Lincoln-Mercury, Inc., 160 Cal.App.2d 290, 325 P.2d 193 (1958); James Stewart & Co. v. Law, 149 Tex. 392, 233 S.W.2d 558 (1950). Contra, Anderson v. Howard Hall Co., 278 Ala. 491, 179 So.2d 71 (1965), 19 Ala.L.Rev. 491 (1967). Similar results have been obtained where the promisor has agreed to take out a policy of life insurance upon the life of the promisee and to name his wife as beneficiary and fails to do so; after the death of the promisee the wife has been permitted to sue the promisor, Weiner v. Physicians News Serv., Inc., 13 A.D.2d 737, 214 N.Y.S.2d 474 (1st Dep't 1961), rev'g 27 Misc.2d 470,

§ 249. The Surety Bond Cases

When a contractor undertakes to construct a building for an owner or a public works project for the United States or other political body, it is common to require that the contractor, as principal, obtain a surety bond. At times the bond is "conditioned to be void" upon the contractor's faithful performance of the contract. Such bonds are commonly known as performance bonds. At times the bond is a payment bond, that is, "conditioned to be void" upon payment by the contractor to subcontractors, materialmen and laborers. At times both conditions are combined in a single performance—payment bond.

Since the laborers, materialmen and subcontractors are not parties to the bond[83] the question is whether they are third party beneficiaries of the instrument.[84] Obviously they are not third party beneficiaries of a performance bond. This kind of bond is merely designed to assure payment of damages to the owner in the event of the contractor's nonperformance. But where the bond is a performance-payment bond or a payment bond the decisions have not been harmonious.[85] It is generally conceded that the primary question is one of intent to benefit.[86]

A leading case has indicated that, where there is a performance-payment bond, at least presumptively the bond is intended to inure solely to the benefit of the promisee-owner; otherwise the bond might be dissipated in paying third party beneficiaries without paying the promisee.[87] Even in the case of a payment bond it has often been doubted whether subcontractors, laborers and materialmen are third party beneficiaries. This has been particularly true where the promisee-owner is a private owner. It is often concluded that his intent is to

211 N.Y.S.2d 429 (Sup.Ct.1960), 37 N. D.Lawyer 254 (1961); and where a promisor promised the promisee to pay life insurance premiums upon a policy of which the plaintiff was named as a beneficiary and failed to do so. Walker Bank & Trust Co. v. First Security Corp., 9 Utah 2d 215, 341 P.2d 944 (1959).

83. The parties to the contract are the contractor and the surety, both of whom are promisors, and the owner as promisee.

84. No attempt will be made in this brief exposition to take into account variations between statutes and be-

tween language in bonds which may account for some of the differences in results.

85. See 4 Corbin §§ 799–803; 2 Williston § 372.

86. Ibid.

87. Fosmire v. National Sur. Co., 229 N.Y. 44, 127 N.E. 472 (1920). This and subsequent New York cases are discussed in Notes, 41 Cornell L.Q. 482 (1956); 27 Ford.L.Rev. 262 (1958). Contra, Byram Lumber & Supply Co. v. Page, 109 Conn. 256, 146 A. 293 (1929).

protect himself against mechanics' liens and so the third parties are incidental beneficiaries.[88] When the owner is the United States or a political subdivision, however, it has generally been held that the third parties are intended donee beneficiaries because a mechanics' lien may not be obtained against such a governmental unit.[89] This result is often dictated by statute.[90] The trend today seems to be to abolish this distinction between public and private promisees and to hold that these third parties are protected beneficiaries of a payment bond. The courts have recognized that although the *motive* of the promisee may be to protect himself the *intent* is in part to benefit the third parties.[91]

A question of interest is whether a beneficiary of a payment bond is a donee or a creditor beneficiary.[92] Since the promisee is under no personal liability to the beneficiaries, a traditional creditor beneficiary case is not made out. On the other hand, the promisee has no real donative intent. In a private construction project, since the beneficiaries ordinarily have the privilege of asserting mechanics' liens against the real property, the situation is closely analogous to a creditor beneficiary situation.[93] No mechanics' lien is ordinarily available, however, on real property owned by a public instrumentality. The rights of the beneficiary in such a case must be viewed as *sui generis*. In other words, the donee and creditor beneficiary categories must not be viewed as encompassing all categories of protected beneficiaries.

§ 250. Promisor's Defenses

If A promises not to cut down certain timber in exchange for B's promise to pay C $1,000, would C be entitled to enforce B's promise even if A cut down the timber? Although C is an intended donee beneficiary he may not recover because of A's total breach of con-

88. See Fidelity & Deposit Co. v. Rainer, 220 Ala. 262, 125 So. 55, 77 A.L.R. 13 (1929). The court, however, reversed its position on rehearing, reported with the cited opinion.

89. See 2 Williston § 372, at 919–20.

90. See, e. g., Miller Act, 40 U.S.C.A. §§ 270a–270e; Graybar Elec. Co. v. John A. Volpe Constr. Co., 387 F.2d 55 (5th Cir. 1967).

91. Socony-Vacuum Oil Co. v. Continental Cas. Co., 219 F.2d 645 (2d Cir. 1955); Daniel Morris Co. v. Glens Falls Indem. Co. 308 N.Y. 464, 126 N.E.2d 750 (1955); 2 Williston § 372; Restatement, Contracts (2d) § 133, ill. 11.

92. Compare Restatement, Security § 165, Comment b, with 4 Corbin § 802. It has been suggested that no point is served in pursuing this distinction, particularly in the surety bond context. Simpson, Annual Survey of American Law (Contracts), 31 N.Y.U. L.Rev. 471, 474 (1956).

93. It is closely analagous to Vrooman v. Turner.

tract.[94] It is fundamental that the beneficiary's rights stem from the contract. The promisor may, therefore, usually assert against the beneficiary any defense which he could assert against the promisee if the promisee were suing on the contract.[95] This would include such defenses as fraud,[96] mistake,[97] lack of consideration, failure of condition,[98] etc.[99] The major exception is ordinarily discussed under the confusing label of "vesting," the subject of the next section.[1]

It is possible for the parties to agree that the beneficiary will have an enforceable right despite any defenses which the promisor might have against the promisee. This is most frequently done in fire insurance contracts containing the "standard mortgagee clause," which provides that a mortgagee may recover on a policy despite any "act or neglect" of the mortgagor-promisee. Under this clause it is possible for the mortgagee to recover a casualty loss from the insurer despite fraud or non-payment of premium by the promisee.[2]

94. Sedgwick v. Blanchard, 170 Wis. 121, 174 N.W. 459 (1919). Accord, Kyner v. Clark, 29 F.2d 545 (8th Cir. 1928) (creditor beneficiary).

95. This applies as well to creditor beneficiaries. Restatement, Contracts (2d) § 140. It should be recalled that in a creditor beneficiary context the promisor usually cannot assert defenses which the promisee might have raised against the creditor in an action on the creditor's antecedent claim. See § 246 supra. This is distinguishable from the question of the promisor's use of defenses he has on the third party beneficiary contract itself. See Rouse v. United States, 94 U.S.App.D.C. 386, 215 F.2d 872 (1954), where the distinction is well drawn.

96. While the beneficiary's rights are subject to the defense of fraud, the promisor may not retain the benefits of the transaction if he wishes to rely on the defense. Arnold v. Nichols, 64 N.Y. 117 (1876).

97. Page v. Hinchee, 174 Okl. 537, 51 P.2d 487 (1935).

98. Williams v. Paxson Coal Co., 346 Pa. 468, 31 A.2d 69 (1943) ("failure of consideration," i. e., failure of constructive condition in a donee situation); Alexander H. Revell & Co. v.

C. H. Morgan Grocery Co., 214 Ill. App. 526 (1919); Gennett v. Smith, 244 App.Div. 3, 278 N.Y.S. 478 (3rd Dep't 1935) (same in creditor situations).

99. 2 Williston § 394.

1. The other exceptions are few. They include collective bargaining agreements, Lewis v. Benedict Coal Corp., 361 U.S. 459, 80 S.Ct. 489, 4 L.Ed.2d 442 (1960); and cases involving surety bonds where the surety would have a defense against the promisee but may not assert it against the beneficiary, Doll v. Crume, 41 Neb. 655, 59 N.W. 806 (1894). At times the promisor will be estopped from asserting defenses that he has against the promisee. See Levy v. Empire Ins. Co., 379 F.2d 860 (5th Cir. 1967) (beneficiary who purchased debentures in reliance on terms of written contract permitted to recover although the written contract was subject to conditions precedent not stated in the writing).

2. General Credit Corp. v. Imperial Cas. & Indem. Co., 167 Neb. 833, 95 N.W.2d 145 (1959); Goldstein v. National Liberty Ins. Co., 256 N.Y. 26, 175 N.E. 359 (1931); Prudential Ins. Co. v. Franklin Fire Ins. Co., 180 S.C. 250, 185 S.E. 537 (1936).

There are very few cases dealing with the question of whether the promisor may assert counterclaims against the beneficiary which he might assert against the promisee.[3] The situation is analogous to the problem of whether the obligor may assert counterclaims against an assignee which he might have asserted against the assignor.[4]

§ 251. Vesting—Voluntary Discharge or Modification

A beneficiary's rights stem from a contract to which he is not a party. May the contracting parties who have created these rights destroy or modify them?[5] The resolution of this question is usually said to turn on when the beneficiary's rights become vested.

According to the original Restatement, the rights of a creditor beneficiary vest when he brings action to enforce the contract or otherwise materially changes position before he knows of the discharge or modification.[6] Another view is that his rights vest upon learning of the contract and assenting to it.[7] This second view seems prefer-

3. The promisor may assert against the beneficiary "Partial defenses by way of recoupment for breach by the promisee . . . unless precluded by the terms of the agreement or considerations of fairness or public policy." Restatement, Contracts (2d) § 140, Comment c. But the promisor may not assert against the beneficiary a claim he has against the promisee arising out of a separate transaction. "The conduct of the beneficiary, however, like that of any obligee, may give rise to defenses and claims which may be asserted against him by the obligor." Id.

4. See § 270 infra.

5. Another interesting question not previously discussed is whether and up to what point the beneficiary may disclaim the rights created for him by the contract between the promisor and the promisee. The answer appears to be that although the beneficiary is presumed to accept the benefits bestowed upon him he may prior to actual acceptance within "a reasonable time after learning of its existence and terms render any duty to him inoperative from the beginning by disclaimer." Restatement, Contracts (2d) § 137. "But once the beneficiary has manifested assent, disclaimer is opera-

tive only if the requirements are met for discharge of a contractual duty," Id., Comment b. The effect of disclaimer upon the rights of the promisee and third persons is beyond the scope of this treatise.

6. Restatement, Contracts § 143; Restatement, Contracts (2d) § 142; accord, Crowell v. Currier, 27 N.J.Eq. 152 (1876), aff'd Crowell v. Hospital of St. Barnabas, 27 N.J.Eq. 650 (1876) (rescission permitted; no change of position); cf. Hartman v. Pistorius, 248 Ill. 568, 94 N.E. 131 (1911) (rescission permitted; court indicates that creditor beneficiary's rights do not vest while the performances running between promisee and promisor are still executory, unless the beneficiary changes his position in reliance upon the contract).

7. Copeland v. Beard, 217 Ala. 216, 115 So. 389 (1928) (on theory that creditor's assent makes him a party to the contract); Gifford v. Corrigan, 117 N.Y. 257, 22 N.E. 756 (1889). Sometimes assent is presumed. Lawrence v. Fox, 20 N.Y. 268 (1859) (dictum; presumption of assent); see Annot., 44 A.L.R.2d 1266 (1955). This is especially true if the beneficiary is an infant. Rhodes v. Rhodes, 266 S.W.2d 790, 44 A.L.R.2d 1266 (Ky.1953);

able in that once he has assented to the contract the creditor is likely to rely in subtle ways, not readily provable, upon the security of the contract.[8]

When the beneficiary is a donee, according to the original Restatement, the rights of the beneficiary vest immediately upon the making of the contract and a subsequent voluntary discharge or modification would be ineffective to curtail the rights of the beneficiary unless the power to discharge or modify the contract is reserved.[9] This view is supported by a good number of life insurance cases,[10] and a few other decisions.[11] A strong trend, however, has questioned the soundness of the original Restatement's position.[12] A number of courts have, it is believed, justly rebelled at the concept that a donee should have greater rights than a creditor. The only justification for the view of the original Restatement appears to be an analogy with the law of trusts and gifts.[13] It is believed, however, that a much closer analogy is the law governing the creditor beneficiary.[14]

The Restatement Second appears to have noted these criticisms and has set forth a rule which applies equally well to all intended beneficiaries. Under this rule the promisor and the promisee may by agreement create a right in the beneficiary which cannot be varied by

Plunkett v. Atkins, 371 P.2d 727 (Okl. 1962); Restatement, Contracts (2d) § 142, Comment d.

8. This line of thought seems to underly the decision in Gifford v. Corrigan, 117 N.Y. 257, 22 N.E. 756 (1889), where the court said that from the moment the creditor beneficiary assents to the contract "he must be assumed to act or omit to act in reliance upon it." Id. at 263, 22 N.E. at 758.

9. Restatement, Contracts § 142. Frequently, courts do not distinguish between creditor and donee beneficiaries in this context. See Comment, The Third Party Beneficiary Concept: A Proposal, 57 Colum.L.Rev. 406, 418–20 (1957).

10. See, e. g., Ford v. Mutual Life Ins. Co., 283 Ill.App. 325 (1936); Whitehead v. New York Life Ins. Co., 102 N.Y. 143, 6 N.E. 267 (1886). See Vance, the Beneficiary's Interest in a Life Insurance Policy, 31 Yale L.J. 343 (1922).

11. Logan v. Glass, 136 Pa.Super. 221, 7 A.2d 116 (1939) (following Restatement), aff'd 338 Pa. 489, 14 A.2d 306 (1940).

12. McCulloch v. Canadian Pac. Ry., 53 F.Supp. 534 (D.Minn.1943) (reliance required); Lehman v. Stout, 261 Minn. 384, 112 N.W.2d 640 (1961); Salesky v. Hat Corp., 20 A.D.2d 114, 244 N.Y. S.2d 965 (1st Dep't 1963). See Page, The Power of the Contracting Parties to Alter a Contract for Rendering Performance to a Third Person, 12 Wis.L.Rev. 141 (1937).

13. 2 Williston § 396 supports the Restatement view by use of this analogy, but in § 396B he indicates that in most jurisdictions for this purpose donee beneficiaries are not distinguished from creditor beneficiaries.

14. As indicated in note 9 supra, many courts do not distinguish between donee and creditor beneficiary cases for this purpose and apply the creditor rule to donee cases. E. g., Blackard v. Monarch's Mfrs. and Distribs., 131 Ind.App. 514, 169 N.E.2d 735, 97 A.L. R.2d 1255 (1960).

agreement without the beneficiary's consent.[15] When no provision of this kind is made in the agreement the parties retain the power to modify or discharge the rights of the beneficiary [16] unless the beneficiary "materially changes his position in justifiable reliance on the promise or brings suit on it or manifests assent to it in a manner invited or required by the promisor or promisee," provided this occurs "before he receives notification of the discharge or modification." [17]

If the promisee wrongfully attempts to discharge or modify the promisor's duty and receives a consideration in exchange, according to the original Restatement the beneficiary was required to elect whether he would assert a right against the consideration so received or whether he would pursue his original right.[18] Under the Restatement Second the requirement for an election is eliminated [19] and substituted therefor is a rule of what is equitable under the circumstances.[20]

A third party beneficiary contract may exist even if the beneficiary is not named, identifiable, or even in being at the time of contracting. It is sufficient that he be identifiable when the time arrives for the performance of the promise for the benefit of the third person.[21] If the beneficiary is not in being or not identifiable at the time the contract is rescinded or modified, ordinarily he cannot contend that his rights were vested.[22]

The troublesome question of vesting may as we have seen be avoided to some extent by a provision in the contract reserving to the contracting parties the power to amend or discharge their contract. This is nearly always done in modern life insurance policies,[23] employee death benefit plans [24] and the like.

---

15. Restatement, Contracts (2d) § 142(1), Comments a and b. Conversely the promisor and the promisee may retain a power to discharge or to modify the promisor's duty. In such a case the Comment j provides: "Whether the exercise of such a power is rightful or wrongful may depend upon facts other than the promise."

16. Id., § 142(3).

17. Id., § 142(2); see Comments f, g, and h; cf. Comment d relating to the assent of the infant.

18. Restatement, Contracts § 142. By its terms the section was limited to donee beneficiaries.

19. Restatement, Contracts (2d) § 142(4).

20. Id., Comment j.

21. Restatement, Contracts § 139. The Restatement Second adds that this is one of the factors to be considered in determining whether the beneficiary is an intended or incidental beneficiary.

22. Freer v. J. G. Putnam Funeral Home, Inc., 195 Ark. 307, 111 S.W.2d 463 (1937); Stanfield v. W. C. McBride, 149 Kan. 567, 88 P.2d 1002 (1939).

23. See, e.g., New York Life Ins. Co. v. Cook, 237 Mich. 303, 211 N.W. 648 (1927). See also Restatement, Contracts (2d) § 142, Comments c and e.

24. Salesky v. Hat Corp., 20 A.D.2d 114, 244 N.Y.S.2d 965 (1st Dep't 1963).

If the promisee has merely extracted from the promisor an offer to a unilateral contract for the benefit of a third person, the offer may be revoked pursuant to the rules governing such offers.[25] Until the power created by the offer has ripened into a right, there can be no question of any right vesting in the beneficiary.

The doctrine of vesting forms an exception to the general rule that the promisor may assert against the beneficiary any defense he could assert against the promisee. After the rights of the beneficiary vest he is not subject to any defense which the promisor has against the promisee based upon a subsequent agreement between the promisor and promisee which purports to vary or discharge the beneficiary's rights.

§ 252. Rights of the Beneficiary Against the Promisee

If A is indebted to T and causes B, for a consideration, to assume this indebtedness, T acquires enforceable rights against the promisor, B, in T's new status as third party beneficiary. T does not, however, thereby lose his rights against A. The original obligation continues unimpaired.[26]

If T agrees to release A in exchange for B's assumption of the obligation, there is said to be a novation.[27] Some courts have erroneously held that when B assumes the obligation, A and B have made an implied offer to a novation, which T accepts if he elects to enforce B's promise.[28] Under this view, if T elects to proceed against A, he is precluded from later proceeding against B because he has elected to reject the offer.[29] Far the greater number of states have taken the sounder positions that T may obtain a judgment against both A and B, but is entitled to only one satisfaction.[30]

25. See § 34 supra.

26. See § 277 infra.

27. On the nature of a novation, see § 345 infra.

28. Henry v. Murphy, 54 Ala. 246 (1875). This rationale was disapproved in Copeland v. Beard, 217 Ala. 216, 115 So. 389 (1928) ("We now adopt the doctrine that by acceptance of the promise made for his benefit, and action thereon, the creditor does not release the original debtor, unless so stipulated in the contract and made known to the creditor"). Id. at 318, 115 So. 391.

29. Bohanan v. Pope, 42 Me. 93 (1856); Wood v. Moriarty, 15 R.I. 518, 9 A. 427 (1887).

30. Copeland v. Beard, 217 Ala. 216, 115 So. 389 (1928); Vulcan Iron Works v. Pittsburgh-Eastern Co., 144 App.Div. 827, 129 N.Y.S. 676 (3d Dep't 1911); Erickson v. Grande Ronde Lumber Co., 162 Or. 556, 94 P.2d 139 (1939); see also Restatement, Contracts (2d) § 141(1). It will generally be possible for the beneficiary to join the original debtor and the assuming promisor as defendants in the same action.

As between A and B, the relationship is that of surety and principal. B who has promised to pay A's debt is the principal debtor.[31] The main consequence of this relationship is that if A is compelled to pay the indebtedness, he may proceed against B for reimbursement and damages.[32]

A donee beneficiary, of course, has no rights against the promisee except where, as we have seen in the previous section, the promisee has received a consideration to discharge the promisor. There is no antecedent duty owed by him to the beneficiary and he has undertaken none by the contract. It is possible, however, to conceive of a bilateral contract in which both parties have made promises for the benefit of a third person. In which case, the beneficiary could assert rights against both promisors.

§ 253. Rights of the Promisee Against the Promisor

Although there have been some cases holding that the promisee may not sue the promisor for breach of a contract [33] for the benefit of a third person, the majority view is that the promisee has a cause of action.[34] The difficulty, however, is that the promisee very frequently suffers no actual damages. In a donee situation it is clear that ordinarily he is entitled merely to nominal damages.[35] It has, therefore, been held that the promisee may bring an action for specific performance.[36] An action for restitution may also be available.[37]

In an action by the promisee on a creditor beneficiary contract, according to the majority view, he may recover the amount of the debt.[38] Since the beneficiary is also entitled to the full value of the promise, a possibility of double recovery exists.[39] To avoid this pos-

31. Restatement, Contracts (2d) § 146 and § 141, Comments a and b.

32. 4 Corbin § 825. Generally speaking a surety is also entitled to exoneration and subrogation.

33. North Ala. Dev. Co. v. Short, 101 Ala. 333, 13 So. 385 (1893).

34. Heins v. Byers, 174 Minn. 350, 219 N.W. 287 (1928); Restatement, Contracts §§ 135(b) and 136(1) (b). The same rule is continued in the Restatement Second.

35. Restatement, Contracts § 345; Restatement, Contracts (2d) § 136, Comment a. For an exceptional case in which the promisee sustained actual damages, see Vineyard v. Martin, 29

N.Y.S.2d 935 (Sup.Ct.1941) (promises exchanged between shareholders to advance money to corporation; promisee may recover his damages).

36. Drewen v. Bank of Manhattan, 31 N.J. 110, 155 A.2d 529, 76 A.L.R.2d 221 (1959); Croker v. New York Trust Co., 245 N.Y. 17, 156 N.E. 81 (1927).

37. Restatement, Contracts § 136, Comment c, § 356.

38. See 5 Williston § 1408 (rev'd ed. 1938); Restatement, Contracts (2d) § 136.

39. When a double recovery is allowed this would appear to violate the rule that the promisor may assert against the beneficiary any defense which he

sibility, some courts have ruled that the promisee may recover the debt only if he has paid it.[40] Of course, the promisor may protect himself against double recovery by paying the creditor beneficiary prior to judgment. In addition, he may ordinarily insure that both the promisee and the creditor participate in the same action by utilizing interpleader procedure or other procedural techniques. In the event this is not done, the remote possibility of double recovery can be avoided by the flexibility possessed by a modern court in which law and equity are merged; for example, the court may order that the judgment be payable to the creditor even if the action is brought by the promisee.[41]

has against the promisee. However the answer would appear to be that the promisor is responsible for his own plight.

40. White v. Upton, 255 Ky. 562, 74 S. W.2d 924 (1934) (promisee, however,

may sue the promisor to compel him to pay the debt).

41. See Heins v. Byers, 174 Minn. 350, 219 N.W. 287 (1928).

CHAPTER 15

ASSIGNMENT AND DELEGATION

Analysis

Sec.
254. Terminology.
255. History.
256. Nature of an Assignment.
257. Coverage of the Uniform Commercial Code and of this Chapter.
258. Formalities.
259. Gratuitous Assignments.
260. Are There Rights Which Are Not Assignable? Problem in General.
261. Where the Assignment Would Materially Change the Duty of the Other Party.
262. Where the Assignment Would Vary Materially the Burden or Risk of the Obligor.
263. Where the Assignment Would Impair Materially the Other Party's Chance of Obtaining Return Performance: Executory Bilateral Contracts.
264. The Assignability of Option Contracts.
265. Necessity of Precise Distinctions: Partnership as an Illustration.
266. Assignments Contrary to Public Policy.
267. Effect of Contractual Prohibition or Authorization of an Assignment.
268. Voidable Assignments, Assignments of Conditional Rights and Conditional Assignment of Rights.
269. Defenses of the Obligor Against the Assignee.
270. Other Limitations Upon the Rights of the Assignee: Counterclaims, Set-off, and Recoupment.
271. Other Limitations Upon the Rights of the Assignee: Latent Equities.
272. Priorities Between Successive Assignees of the Same Claim.
273. Rights of the Assignee Against an Attaching Creditor.
274. Assignment of Future Rights: Equitable Assignments.
275. Partial Assignments.
276. Implied Warranties of the Assignor and Sub-Assignor.
277. Delegation of Duties: Generally.
278. Non-delegable Duties.
279. Liability of the Delegate.
280. Effect of Repudiation by Delegating Party.
281. Effect of Delegation of a Non-delegable Duty.

§ 254. Terminology

The words "assignment," "delegation" and "assumption" are words of art. Perhaps more frequently than is the case with other terms of art, lawyers seem prone to use the word "assignment" inartfully, frequently intending to encompass within the term the distinct concepts of delegation and assumption.[1] An assignment involves the transfer of rights. A delegation involves the appointment of another to perform one's duties. An assumption of duties occurs if the person who has been delegated to perform makes a promise to perform which is intended to benefit the person to whom the duty is owed.

§ 255. History

At early common law an attempted assignment of a contract right was ordinarily ineffective.[2] It was believed that the contractual relation was too personal to permit the interjection of a third person into the relationship without the consent of the obligor. This idea was reinforced by the law's policy against maintenance and champerty. It was believed that assignments would be employed to stir up and finance litigation.[3] The rule against assignments was, however, circumvented by use of a power of attorney appointing an agent to enforce the right and permitting him to retain the proceeds.[4] Purported assignments were treated as if they were powers of attorney of this kind. Under this concept the assignee's rights were not secure; assignments were terminable by the assignor's death, bankruptcy or revocation. In time, however, equity held that such an assignment

1. A classic article which has helped to unsnarl the terminological confusion in the area is Corbin, Assignment of Contract Rights, 74 U.Pa.L.Rev. 207 (1926), Selected Readings 718. See also Restatement, Contracts (2d) § 160, Comment a, § 148, Comment c.

2. The historical background of the law of assignments is traced in Holdsworth, History of the Treatment of Choses in Action by the Common Law, 33 Harv.L.Rev. 997 (1920), Selected Readings 706; Bailey, Assignments of Debts in England from the Twelfth to the Twentieth Century, 47 L.Q. 516 (1931), 48 L.Q.Rev. 248, 547 (1932). There were some exceptions to the rule of nonassignability, such as assignments by the government. These are but of historical interest. Under the Law Merchant bills and notes were transferable. These mercantile instruments continue to be governed by a separate body of law, until recently governed by the Uniform Negotiable Instruments Law and

presently largely by Article 3 of the Uniform Commercial Code.

3. Lord Coke utilized this rationale to explain the rule against assignments. Lamper's Case, 77 Eng.Rep. 994, 997 (K.B.1613). For a discussion of champerty and maintenance, see § 368 infra.

4. Mallory v. Lane, 79 Eng.Rep. 292, (Ex.Ch.1615). An interesting historical parallel is found in Roman law. The Roman rule against assignments was circumvented in the same manner. Radin, Roman Law 53, 290–92 (1927).

The concept of champerty is sometimes used to strike down an arrangement by which plaintiff is authorized to bring an action on the obligee's claim and to retain a portion of the proceeds. See Kenrich Corp. v. Miller, 377 F.2d 312 (3d Cir. 1967) (Pennsylvania law), where the transaction was in form of power of attorney rather than an assignment.

was not terminable and the law courts followed suit,[5] although it was generally necessary for the assignee to sue in the assignor's name and to make the assignor a party to the action. Almost everywhere, statutes have been enacted permitting the assignee to sue in his own name.[6]

The history of the law of assignments is an interesting illustration of the struggle between commercial needs and the tenacity of legal conceptualism. The common law developed when wealth was primarily land and secondarily chattels. Intangibles hardly mattered. In a developed economy, however, wealth is primarily represented by intangibles: bank accounts, securities, accounts receivable, etc. The free alienability of these assets is essential to commerce.[7] This is fully recognized by the Uniform Commercial Code.[8]

§ 256. Nature of an Assignment

Ordinarily parties to an assignment have one of two purposes in mind. They may intend an outright transfer of the right or they may intend that the right be transferred as collateral security for an indebtedness. In either case an assignment is a manifestation of intent by the owner of the right to effectuate a present transfer of an interest in the right to the assignee.[9] Ordinarily an outright assignment extinguishes the right in the assignor and transfers it to the assignee.[10] An assignment made as collateral security transfers a security interest to the assignee.[11] In either case an assignment is

5. See Cook, The Alienability of Choses in Action 29 Harv.L.Rev. 816 (1916), Selected Readings 738 (1931); Williston, Is the Right of an Assignee of a Chose in Action Legal or Equitable? 30 Harv.L.Rev. 97 (1916), Selected Readings 754, and 31 Harv.L.Rev. 822 (1918), Selected Readings 790.

6. See Clark & Hutchins, The Real Party in Interest, 34 Yale L.J. 259 (1924). The introductory note to Chapter 7 of the Restatement, Contracts Second contains a list and analysis of state real party in interest statutes.

7. In this country the value of receivables which have been assigned to obtain financing amounts to tens of billions of dollars at any given moment. See Coogan & Gordon, The Effect of the Uniform Commercial Code upon Receivables Financing—Some Answers and Some Unsolved Problems, 76 Harv.L.Rev. 1529, 1530 (1963).

8. U.C.C. § 9–318(4), § 2–210(2), discussed at § 267 infra.

9. Restatement, Contracts § 149 (both editions).

10. Restatement, Contracts § 149. When this result is accomplished the assignment is sometimes said to be "effective." Restatement, Contracts § 150; Restatement, Contracts (2d) § 149, Comment a. The reason why the word "ordinarily" is used here is explained in §§ 259, 268 infra.

11. For certain purposes the Uniform Commercial Code views outright assignments as creating security interests. U.C.C. §§ 1–201(37) and 9–102(1) (b). This approach is explained in § 257 infra.

not a contract because it involves an executed transaction either in the nature of a sale or a security device.[12]   Thus, a promise to pay money when the promisor receives it from a specified source is not an assignment.   There is no present transfer.[13]   So also a promise to assign or to pay out of a specified existing fund does not result in an assignment.[14]   The same is true when a creditor authorizes his debtor to pay a third person and to charge his account.[15]

§ 257.   Coverage of the Uniform Commercial Code and of this Chapter

It is with some hesitancy that an introduction to the provisions of the Uniform Commercial Code governing assignments is here presented.   The provisions of Article 9 are so inter-related with the general field of commercial financing that separation of rules relating to assignments is somewhat strained and artificial.   Even more strained and artificial is the attempt to separate the Code rules relating to outright assignments and security assignments.   This discussion proceeds with this caveat in mind.

12.   At times courts have caused decisions to turn upon whether title to the security is in the secured party or whether he merely has a lien.   See, for example, Ralston Purina Co. v. Como Feed & Milling Co., 325 F.2d 844 (5th Cir. 1963).   The Uniform Commercial Code rejects this approach.   See the official comment to § 9–101.

13.   Bass v. Olson, 378 F.2d 818 (9th Cir. 1967); Donovan v. Middlebrook, 95 App.Div. 365, 88 N.Y.S. 607 (1st Dep't 1904); 4 Corbin § 877.

14.   State Central Sav. Bank v. Hemmy, 77 F.2d 458 (8th Cir. 1935); Myers v. Forest Hill Gardens Co., 103 N.J.Eq. 1, 141 A. 808 (1928), aff'd, 105 N.J.Eq. 584, 147 A. 911 (1929).   However since a promise to assign or transfer proceeds may be specifically enforceable the promisee may have rights which resemble those of the assignee of a future right.   See § 274 infra.   Restatement, Contracts (2d) § 162, Comment c.   Sometimes it is said that the promisee has an equitable lien.   Morrison Flying Service v. Deming Nat. Bank, 404 F.2d 856 (10th Cir. 1968), cert. denied 393 U.S. 1020, 89 S.Ct. 628, 21 L.Ed.2d 565 (1969.)

15.   However the result is different if the instrument refers to the duty which the obligor owes to the creditor and expressly or impliedly conditions the obligor's duty to pay the third person upon the existence of such duty.   Restatement, Contracts § 163; Restatement, Contracts (2d) § 157.   Compare Structural Gypsum Corp. v. National Comm. Title & Mortg. Guar. Co., 105 N.J.Eq. 424, 148 A. 199 (1929), rev'd on other grounds 107 N.J.Eq. 32, 151 A. 839 (1930), with Andrews Elec. Co. v. St. Alphonse Catholic Total Abstinence Soc., 233 Mass. 20, 123 N.E. 103 (1919); see 4 Corbin §§ 879–880.   Since a check or draft is an unconditional order, the Uniform Commercial Code provides: "A check or other draft does not of itself operate as an assignment   . . ."   U.C.C. § 3–409(1).   The Code here restates pre-existing law.   Griffin v. Louisville Trust Co., 312 Ky. 145, 226 S.W.2d 786 (1950); Burrows v. Burrows, 240 Mass. 485, 137 N.E. 923, 20 A.L.R. 174 (1922).   Pursuant to special agreement, however, a check may be an assignment.   See Banco Longoria, S. A. v. El Paso Nat. Bank, 415 S.W.2d 1 (Tex.Civ. App.1967), ref. n. r. e.

Section 9–102(1) (a) of the Uniform Commercial Code states that Article 9 of the Code regulates security interests in personal property and fixtures, "including goods, documents, instruments, general intangibles, chattel paper, accounts or contract rights." [16] Since this subdivision deals with security devices it is outside our primary concern—outright assignments. However § 9–102(1) (b) states that Article 9 of the Code also regulates any outright "sale [assignment] of accounts, contract rights or chattel paper." [17]

Again we are not primarily concerned with "chattel paper" for "chattel paper" primarily relates to security. Thus, insofar as the Code is concerned we are primarily interested in its coverage of "accounts" and "contract rights." " 'Account' means any right to payment for goods sold or leased or for services rendered which is not evidenced by an instrument [18] or chattel paper." [19] " 'Contract right' means any right to payment under a contract not yet earned by performance and not evidenced by an instrument or chattel paper." [20]

Thus, insofar as the Code is involved we are concerned primarily with the sale (assignment) of an "account" or a "contract right."

In addition to discussing the aspects of the Code which relate to outright assignments, we shall also consider the common law rules relating to outright assignments. When one speaks of an assignment in this sense one refers to a transfer of a "chose in action" as opposed to the sale of a tangible chattel, sometimes called a "chose in possession." [21] However, the term "chose in action" in its broadest sense includes "debts of all kinds, tort claims, and rights to recover ownership or possession of real or personal property; it has been extended to instruments and documents embodying intangible property rights, to such intangible property as patents and copyrights, and even to equitable rights in tangible property." [22]

In general the Restatement Second limits its coverage to contractual choses in action.[23] We shall also limit our discussion in this

---

16. These terms are defined in U.C.C. § 9–105 except for "account," "contract right" and "general intangible" which are defined in U.C.C. § 9–106.

17. " 'Chattel paper' means a writing or writings which evidence both a monetary obligation and a security interest in or a lease of specific goods." § 9–105(1) (b).

18. Instrument means negotiable instruments and certain specialties. § 9–105(1) (g).

19. § 9–106.

20. § 9–106.

21. 4 Corbin § 859.

22. Restatement, Contracts (2d) § 148, Comment a.

23. Restatement, Contracts (2d) § 148, Comment a. The comment adds: "The rules stated here may have same application to non-contractual choses in action, but the transfer of non-contractual rights is beyond the scope of the Restatement of this subject."

chapter to the common law rules relating to the assignment of contractual choses in action and how these rules have been affected by the Uniform Commercial Code in the case of "accounts" and "contract rights."

Under the Code if the assignment arises from a sales transaction it is also governed by the assignment provisions of Article 2 of the Code.[24]

It should also be observed that § 9–104 completely excludes a variety of matters from the coverage of Article 9. Among the exclusions are wage assignments;[25] any outright assignment in connection with the sale of a business from which the rights assigned arose; assignments for purposes of collection only; and a transfer of rights to an assignee who is also to do performance under a contract.[26] As a result these transactions are still to a large extent governed by common law rules although other statutory enactments and Article 2 of the Code must also be consulted in appropriate cases.

§ 258. Formalities

In the absence of an applicable statute the manifestation of intention required for an assignment need not be in writing.[27] Under present statutory law the requirement of a writing is heavily emphasized. A "security interest" governed by Article 9 of the Uniform Commercial Code is not enforceable against the debtor or third persons unless the debtor has signed a "security agreement," or unless the assignee has possession of collateral.[28] Since the term "security agreement" includes any outright assignment which is governed by Article 9 of the Code,[29] it follows that an outright assignment of an "account" or "contract right" is unenforceable unless in a signed security agreement. If the assignee has possession of a note or other writing which is customarily deemed to incorporate the debt, no written security agreement is needed.[30]

---

24. U.C.C. § 2–210; see also U.C.C. § 9–113.

25. U.C.C. § 9–104(d).

26. U.C.C. § 9–104(f).

27. Anaconda Alumium Co. v. Sharp, 243 Miss. 9, 136 So.2d 585, 99 A.L.R.2d 1307 (1962); Jemison v. Tindall, 89 N.J.L. 429, 99 A. 408 (1916); Brown v. Fore, 12 S.W.2d 114, 63 A.L.R. 435 (Tex.Comm.App.1929); Restatement, Contracts § 157; Restatement, Contracts (2d) § 156, Comment a; 4 Corbin § 879.

28. U.C.C. § 9–203.

29. "Security agreement" is defined by U.C.C. § 9–105(h) to mean "an agreement which creates or provides for a security interest." "Security interest" is defined in U.C.C. § 1–201(37) to include "any interest of a buyer of accounts, chattel paper, or contract rights which is subject to Article 9."

30. U.C.C. § 9–203(1) (a) dispenses with the need for a signed security agree-

Section 1–206 of the Code requires a writing signed by the assignor of any chose-in-action if the amount sought to be enforced in court exceeds $5,000. This section applies to all assignments not within the coverage of Articles 8 or 9 of the Code.[31]

§ 259. Gratuitous Assignments

It is well settled that the obligor may not assert as a defense the fact that the assignee did not provide consideration for the assignment.[32] An assignment is an executed transaction and requires no consideration.[33] However, unless something is done to complete the gift, a gratuitous assignment [34] is terminable by the death of the assignor, by a subsequent assignment of the same right, or by a notice of revocation communicated to the assignee or to the obligor.[35]

The law of gifts requires that a gift be completed by delivery.[36] Since a right cannot be physically delivered the law has validated certain substitutes for delivery. Thus, if the assignee obtains payment from or judgment against the obligor, or enters into a substituted contract with the obligor, the assignment will be deemed completed.[37] If the right assigned is evidenced by a writing which the creditor is required to surrender upon payment (what the Second Restatement refers to as a "symbolic writing") and the writing is

ment when the creditor has possession of collateral. Collateral is defined in U.C.C. § 9–105(c) and Comment 3 thereto to include writings which customarily are deemed to incorporate a debt. See also U.C.C. § 9–105(g).

31. This section is discussed in more detail in § 297 infra. Article 8 relates to investment securities such as shares of stock and corporate bonds. It has a writing requirement in § 8–319.

32. Restatement, Contracts § 150. Generally speaking an obligor may not assert a defense which the assignor has against the assignee. In re Holden, 271 N.Y. 212, 2 N.E.2d 631 (1936).

33.   4 Corbin § 909.

34. An assignment is not deemed gratuitous if it is given as security or in total or partial satisfaction of a pre-existing debt. Abramson v. Boedeker, 379 F.2d 741 (5th Cir. 1967), cert. denied 389 U.S. 1006, 88 S.Ct. 563, 19 L.

Ed.2d 602 (1967). Such an assignment is deemed an "assignment for value." Restatement, Contracts § 149; Restatement, Contracts (2d) § 164(5). The Code definition of "value" is contained in § 1–201(44).

35. Restatement, Contracts § 158; Restatement, Contracts (2d) § 164. The Uniform Commercial Code does not govern donative assignments as its coverage is limited to "sales" of rights or their assignment as security.

36. Adams v. Merced Stone Co., 176 Cal. 415, 178 P. 498, 3 A.L.R. 928 (1917); Biehl v. Biehl's Adm'x, 263 Ky. 710, 93 S.W.2d 836 (1936); Cook v. Lum, 55 N.J.L. 373, 26 A. 803 (1893); see Williston, Gifts of Rights under Contracts in Writing by Delivery of the Writing, 40 Yale L.J. 1 (1930); Bruton, The Requirement of Delivery as Applied to Gifts of Choses in Action, 39 Yale L.J. 837 (1930).

37. Restatement, Contracts § 158(2); Restatement, Contracts (2d) § 164(3).

delivered to the assignee, the gift is also deemed completed.[38] Writings in this class include bonds and mortgages, savings account books, life insurance policies and stock certificates.[39] A number of cases have gone beyond this, holding that delivery of the obligor's informal written contract constitutes sufficient delivery of the rights evidenced by it even though it is not a symbolic writing.[40]

A gift assignment may also be made irrevocable by estoppel. If the assignor should reasonably foresee that the assignee will change his position in reliance on the assignment and such detrimental reliance does occur the assignment is irrevocable.[41] In many jurisdictions a gratuitous assignment may be completed by a deed of gift or a written instrument under seal.[42] In some jurisdictions a gift assignment may even be completed by an informal signed writing.[43] This result is obtained in New York by a statute which provides: "An assignment shall not be denied the effect of irrevocably transferring the assignor's rights because of the absence of consideration, if such an assignment is in writing and signed by the assignor, or by his agent." [44]

Even in jurisdictions which permit gift assignment by informal signed writings, there still seems to be a good deal of conflict as to the resolution of two interesting questions.[45] First, is an unsealed but signed written gratuitous assignment effective without delivery? For the most part, the cases hold that delivery is needed.[46] A second, and more controversial, question is whether delivery of a writ-

---

38. Restatement, Contracts § 158(1) (b); Restatement, Contracts (2d) § 164(1) (b).

39. Brooks v. Mitchell, 163 Md. 1, 161 A. 261, 84 A.L.R. 547 (1932) (delivery of suitcase containing savings bank book sufficient delivery to create assignment of bank account); 4 Corbin §§ 915–920; 3 Williston §§ 438A–440.

40. In re Huggin's Estate, 204 Pa. 167, 53 A. 746 (1902) (gift of rights under a contract for the sale of real property effected by delivery of the written contract); Restatement, Contracts (2d) § 164, Comment d.

41. Restatement, Contracts § 158(1) (c); Restatement, Contracts (2d) § 164(4).

42. Restatement, Contracts § 158(1) (a); Restatement, Contracts § 164(1) (a); Sweeney v. Veneziano, 70 N.J.Super. 185, 175 A.2d 241 (1961).

43. Berl v. Rosenberg, 169 Cal.App.2d 125, 336 P.2d 975 (1959); Smith v. Smith, 313 S.W.2d 753 (Mo.App.1958); Thatcher v. Merriam, 121 Utah 191, 240 P.2d 266 (1952); 4 Corbin § 921; 3 Williston § 438A.

44. McKinney's   N.Y.Gen.Obligations Law § 5–1107; see Speelman v. Pascal, 10 N.Y.2d 313, 222 N.Y.S.2d 324, 178 N.E.2d 723 (1961).

45. See generally, Williston, Gifts of Rights under Contracts in Writing by Delivery of the Writing, 40 Yale L.J. 1 (1930).

46. Biehl v. Biehl's Adm'x, 263 Ky. 710, 93 S.W.2d 836 (1936); Cooney v. Equitable Life Assur. Soc., 235 Minn. 377, 51 N.W.2d 285 (1952); Restatement, Contracts (2d) 164, Comment b.

ten, gratuitous assignment is sufficient to transfer a right which is embodied in a symbolic writing or whether, if under the circumstances it is not unduly burdensome, the document incorporating the right must itself be delivered.[47]   The controversy revolves around the purpose of the requirement of delivery.   Is delivery a talismanic act which changes the legal ownership of the thing delivered or is the delivery requirement imposed merely to assure a secure evidentiary base for a finding of a completed gift?   It is submitted that in modern law the requirement that the subject matter of the gift be delivered serves primarily an evidentiary purpose.   Consequently, delivery of a writing which purports to complete a gift of intangibles should be held to effect a transfer of property rights in those intangibles.

§ 260. Are There Rights Which Are Not Assignable? Problem in General

In contrast with the earlier law the modern view is emphatically to the effect that ordinarily rights are assignable.[48]   Both Restatements [49] and Article 2 of the Uniform Commercial Code,[50] however, provide that a right is not assignable in the following circumstances: (1) if the assignment would materially change the duty of the other party, (2) increase materially the burden or risk imposed on him by his contract, or (3) impair materially his chance of obtaining return performance.[51]   In addition, on various policy grounds, the law restricts the assignability of certain kinds of rights on other grounds.

§ 261. Where the Assignment Would Materially Change the Duty of the Other Party

Almost any assignment changes, to a degree, the duty of the obligor.   Nevertheless, it is generally recognized that in practically

47. To the effect that delivery of the document evidencing the chose in action is not required, see Thatcher v. Merriam, 121 Utah 191, 240 P.2d 266 (1952). In the case of an assignment for value, as defined in note 34 supra, delivery of the instrument evidencing the chose in action is not necessary to complete the assignment. Sweers v. Malloy, 28 A.D.2d 955, 281 N.Y.S.2d 693 (3d Dep't 1967). However, as we shall see in § 272 infra, the failure of the assignee to take possession of such instrument may affect his rights against third parties.

48. See U.C.C. § 9–318(4), § 2–210(2); McKinney's N.Y.Gen.Obligations Law

§ 13–101; S & L Vending Corp. v. 52 Thompkins Ave. Rest., Inc., 26 A.D. 2d 935, 274 N.Y.S.2d 697 (2d Dep't 1966).

49. Restatement, Contracts § 151(a); Restatement, Contracts (2d) § 149(2) (a).

50. U.C.C. § 2–210(2).

51. The new Restatement adds "or materially reduce its value to him," that is, the value of the return performance.

every case a right to the payment of money is assignable.[52] So too is a right to the delivery of goods.[53] The obligor's duty is changed to the extent that he must make payment or delivery to a different party. Such a variation in the obligor's duty is not deemed material enough to defeat the validity of an assignment. But if A agreed to paint B's portrait for a fee, B could not assign to C his right to have his portrait painted (but could assign his right to have the completed portrait delivered). A's duty would be changed materially.[54] So also an employer may not, in the absence of an agreement to the contrary,[55] assign his rights to the services of an employee where the employee was hired to work under the supervision and direction of the particular employer.[56] It was frequently held that contract rights to receive one's requirements or to tender one's output were not assignable.[57] This result appears to have been changed by the Uniform Commercial Code [58] which has adopted a broad policy of permissiveness toward assignments while supplying objective criteria for construing requirement and output contracts,[59] removing the arbitrary power of the parties to gauge their requirements or output. The Code continues, however, to prohibit the assignment of rights whose contours are definable only by the material personal discretion of the owner of the rights.[60]

§ 262. Where the Assignment Would Vary Materially the Burden or Risk of the Obligor

A typical illustration under this heading is a purported assignment of a fire insurance policy. If A owns a building which is insured by X insurance company against loss due to fire and sells the

---

52. American Lithographic Co. v. Ziegler, 216 Mass. 287, 103 N.E. 909 (1914); U.C.C. § 2–210(2), last sentence; U.C.C. § 9–318(4).

53. Rochester Lantern Co. v. Stiles & Parker Press Co., 135 N.Y. 209, 31 N.E. 1018 (1892).

54. The attempted assignment would not amount to a material breach until B persisted in his refusal to have his own portrait painted. See 3 Williston § 420.

55. For example, the so-called "Reserve Clause" in the contracts of professional athletes.

56. Wooster v. Crane & Co., 73 N.J.Eq. 22, 66 A. 1093 (1907); Globe & Rutgers Fire Ins. Co. v. Jones, 129 Mich. 664, 89 N.W. 580 (1902); Restatement, Contracts § 152; Restatement, Contracts § 166, particularly Comment e. The same type of problem arises whenever the obligor's duty is conditioned on the personal cooperation of the original obligee.

57. Crane Ice Cream Co. v. Terminal Freezing & Heating Co., 147 Md. 588, 128 A. 280, 39 A.L.R. 1184 (1925).

58. See U.C.C. § 2–210, Comment 4.

59. See § 72 supra.

60. See U.C.C. § 2–210, Comment 4.

property to B, A may not, without the assent of the insurer, assign his rights under the policy to B.[61] The insurer in theory at least had in part made its determination to issue the policy upon its assessment of the character of the insured. Although transfer of the policy to another owner of the property would involve no material change in the insurer's duties, it involves a material change in the insurer's risk. Although the Restatement [62] and the Uniform Commercial Code [63] speak in terms of a material *increase* in the burden or risk of the obligor, the courts will not ordinarily inquire into whether the burden or risk is greater or lesser than it was prior to the attempted assignment; rather, the inquiry is whether the burden or risk would be *changed* in a material way. If so, the assignment is ineffective.[64]

§ 263. Where the Assignment Would Impair Materially the Other Party's Chance of Obtaining Return Performance: Executory Bilateral Contracts

Probably no other area of the law of assignments is as confusing as the cases under this heading. The cases must be carefully read to separate what the courts have actually held from the expressed rationale of the cases. The primary source of confusion is the penchant of lawyers and judges to use the term "assignment" to encompass not only the assignment of rights but also the delegation of duties.

Certainly if S agrees to sell and deliver 1,000 bushels of potatoes to B in exchange for B's promise to pay $1,000 on delivery, and S, prior to delivery assigns his rights to payment to T, the assignment would to a degree impair B's chance of obtaining a return performance because S may lack incentive to perform. Yet in this kind of case the courts have overwhelmingly held that the assignment is effective.[65] This result is appropriate because B's duty of payment does not mature until the potatoes are delivered.[66] If B were obligated under the contract to pay in advance of delivery, however, a number of cases have indicated that the assignment would be ineffective.[67]

---

61. Central Union Bank v. New York Underwriters Inc., 52 F.2d 823, 78 A. L.R. 494 (4th Cir. 1931) (but insured may assign his rights to payment as security).

62. Restatement, Contracts § 151(a).

63. U.C.C. § 2–210(2).

64. The Restatement Second adds, as we have seen (note 51 supra), "or materially reduces its value to him."

65. Rockmore v. Lehman, 129 F.2d 892 (2d Cir. 1942), cert. denied 317 U.S. 700, 63 S.Ct. 525, 87 L.Ed. 559 (1943). On the question of whether such an assignment of an unmatured right is to be considered a "legal" or "equitable" assignment, see § 274 infra.

66. See 4 Corbin § 869.

67. See Restatement, Contracts § 151, ill. 1. If the assignment is for security, however, there is no question that

It is believed that this kind of problem should have been placed on a new footing by the Uniform Commercial Code. Article 2 of the Code provides generally that if there is reasonable ground to believe that the expectation of due performance has been impaired, the insecure party, in accordance with Section 2–609(1), may "demand adequate assurance of due performance and until he receives such assurance may if commercially reasonable suspend any performance for which he has not already received the agreed return." Thus if an assignment creates reasonable grounds for belief that the other party will not receive the return performance it would seem that the codifiers could have achieved consistency by providing that the assignment would not thereby be ineffective. Rather, the insecure party could suspend performance until adequate assurance was obtained. If the assurance is not forthcoming the insecure party could then treat the assignment as ineffective. The Code, however, instead of relying on the procedure for insecurity, appears to provide that an attempted assignment which impairs materially the chance of obtaining return performance need not be honored.[68] This provision continues the vagaries of prior case law.

Subdivision 5 of Section 2–210 of the Uniform Commercial Code does, however, authorize a demand for assurance in one kind of fact pattern. The provision reads:

> "The other party may treat any assignment which delegates performance as creating reasonable grounds for insecurity and may without prejudice to his rights against the assignor demand assurances from the assignee."

What this subdivision is designed to cover and not to cover can be made clear by using the well-known case of Paige v. Faure [69] as an illustration. The defendant gave Paige and Linder an exclusive agency in return for their promise to use their best efforts to promote the defendant's product. Subsequently Linder assigned his rights and delegated his duties under the contract to Paige. The Court held the assignment ineffective, stating broadly: "Rights arising out of a contract cannot be transferred if they are coupled with liabilities." The court's analysis was defective [70] because if the du-

---

it should be upheld. American Lithographic Co. v. Ziegler, 216 Mass. 287, 103 N.E. 909 (1914).

68. U.C.C. § 2–210(2).

69. 229 N.Y. 114, 127 N.E. 898, 10 A.L. R. 649 (1920).

70. Similar language occurs in Delaware County Comm'rs v. Diebold Safe

& Lock Co., 133 U.S. 473, 10 S.Ct. 399, 33 L.Ed. 674 (1890); Paper Product Mach. Co. v. Safepack Mills, 239 Mass. 114, 131 N.E. 288 (1921); cf. Fisher v. Berg, 158 Wash. 176, 290 P. 984 (1930). For an analysis of cases of this kind, see 4 Corbin § 867; 3 Williston § 418.

ties had been delegable duties the assignment of rights which consisted primarily of rights to the delivery of tires would have been enforced as a matter of course.[71] Thus the real ground for the holding in this and similar cases is that the assignment of rights is coupled with the delegation of non-delegable duties,[72] and since the obligor would not receive the performance owed him under his contract, he was justified in refusing to continue the arrangement.

Under the Code when a contracting party assigns assignable rights together with a delegation of performance, two situations must be distinguished. If the duties are delegable, the assignment and delegation are effective. The other contracting party may, however, suspend his performance until adequate assurance is received from the assignee-delegate that the counter-performance will be forthcoming.[73] If the duties are non-delegable as too personal in nature or made non-delegable by provisions in the contract, the attempted assignment coupled with the purported delegation will be ineffective.

§ 264.   The Assignability of Option Contracts

The rule of law that an offer may be accepted only by the person or persons for whom it is intended has previously been discussed.[74] It follows that an offer is not assignable. The prohibition is based on the idea that everyone has the privilege of choosing with whom he may contract.[75] This is true whether the offer looks to a bilateral or a unilateral contract and even though the offeree is only to pay money. Thus, if A offers to sell his car to B for $100.00 the offer cannot be accepted by C. But once an offer has ripened into a contract, the rights thus created are usually assignable. This seeming anomaly is at least partially explainable. An assignor by his assignment divests himself of rights; he cannot divest himself of his duties. While he may sometimes delegate his duties he remains liable for their due performance.[76] The other contracting party is thus not frustrated from having the right to enforce his contract against the person on whose credit and reputation he relied in entering into the contract.[77]

---

71. Restatement, Contracts (2d) § 149, Comment d.

72. Since both Paige & Linder were to use their best efforts to develop sales the defendant would not get what he bargained for if only one did. See U. C.C. § 2–210, Comment 4. The question of delegation is discussed in more detail in § 278 infra.

73. U.C.C. § 210(5) must be read with § 2–609 which grants the insecure party the privilege of suspending performance.

74. See § 27 supra.

75. This privilege is not absolute. In some cases antitrust and civil rights legislation forbid discriminatory refusals to deal.

76. See § 277 infra.

77. This rule also explains the liability of an agent who does not disclose his

In determining the assignability of an option contract it must be recalled that an option contract is both an offer and a contract. In addition it should be recalled that option contracts are of two types.[78]

For example, if A offers to sell property to B in exchange for B's promise to pay $10,000.00 and asks B for $100.00 to keep the offer open for ten days, which B pays, there is an option contract. The offer underlying the option contract can be accepted only by B's promise and the validity of any attempted assignment depends upon the promise being made.[79]

However, the option contract may also be of such a nature as to require no promise on the part of B. In such a case the option contract is as assignable as is any other contract. Thus, if A for a consideration gives B a binding option to purchase real property for a sum of money in cash, B can assign the option to C, who upon proper tender of cash can compel conveyance by A.[80] This is so because no promise on B's part is required and it is immaterial who pays the money. On the other hand, if the option given to B is a right to purchase the property on credit or for personal services to be rendered by B, although the rights under the option are assignable the duty is nondelegable. In other words A is not required to accept C's note or services in substitution. C may, however, enforce the underlying contract if B performs his part of the contract.[81]

§ 265. Necessity of Precise Distinctions: Partnership as an Illustration

From the discussion in this chapter it should be obvious that each assignment must be scrutinized with some care and precision to determine its effectiveness and consequences. The Uniform Partnership Act has approached the problem of the assignability of partnership rights with a good deal of precision and can provide a model for analysis. If the question is asked whether the rights of a partner in a partnership are assignable, the Uniform Partnership Act makes it clear that a question of such broad scope is not helpful. One must ask more specific questions once it becomes apparent that a partner has a considerable number of rights, the exercise of which have dif-

principal. See Seavey, Agency § 123 (1964). However, it does not explain why an offer is not assignable if all that is required of the offeree is payment in cash.

78. See § 37 supra.

79. 1 Corbin § 57.

80. Cochran v. Taylor, 273 N.Y. 172, 7 N.E.2d 89 (1937).

81. Cochran v. Taylor, 273 N.Y. 172, 183, 7 N.E.2d 89, 93 (1937); 1 Corbin § 57; 4 Corbin § 883. In other words the problem here is not one of assignability of rights but of delegation of duties.

fering effects on his co-partners. Among other rights,[82] a partner is entitled to share in the profits and surplus of the firm, to share in the management of the enterprise, to full disclosure of all information affecting the partnership, to inspect and copy the books, and to be indemnified for payments and liabilities incurred by him in the ordinary and proper conduct of partnership business.

According to Section 27(1) of the Uniform Partnership Act a partner may assign his interest in the partnership, but such assignment "does not . . . entitle the assignee, during the continuance of the partnership to interfere in the management or administration of the partnership business or affairs, or to require any information or account of partnership transactions, or to inspect the partnership books; but it merely entitles the assignee to receive in accordance with his contract the profits to which the assigning partner would otherwise be entitled." In addition, Section 27(2) grants the assignee a right to receive his assignor's share of the surplus on dissolution of the partnership.

In other terms, the Partnership Act permits the partner to assign his rights to profits and capital, but not his right to participate in partnership affairs. A transfer of such rights by a partner to an assignee would materially change the burden assumed by his co-partners. They have a right to select the person with whom they wish to share management prerogatives.

§ 266. Assignments Contrary to Public Policy

Many states have statutes or common law rules restricting the power of assignment.[83] For example, a good number of state statutes regulate wage assignments by outright prohibition or by limiting their duration or effect.[84] These are designed to prevent a wage earner from, in effect, mortgaging his entire wage earning capacity. Federal statutes limit the assignability of claims against the United States.[85]

Certain assignments are condemned by public policy. The most common illustrations are the nonassignability in most jurisdictions

---

82. The rights of partners, except as varied by agreement, are outlined primarily in Parts IV and V of the Uniform Partnership Act.

83. See Restatement, Contracts § 547.

84. E. g., McKinney's N.Y.Pers.Prop. Law Art. 3–A. See generally Fortas, Wage Assignments in Chicago, 42 Yale L.Rev. 526 (1933); Strasburger, The Wage Assignment Problem, 19 Minn.L.Rev. 536 (1935); Comment, 31 Mich.L.Rev. 236 (1932). On grounds that a contrary result would infringe personal liberties and create pauperism, wage assignments do not survive the wage earner's bankruptcy. Local Loan Co. v. Hunt, 292 U.S. 234, 54 S. Ct. 695, 78 L.Ed. 1230, 93 A.L.R. 195 (1933).

85. E. g., 31 U.S.C.A. § 203; 41 U.S.C. A. § 15.

of the salary or other remuneration of a public officer which has not yet been earned,[86] and the nonassignability of government pensions,[87] and unmatured alimony claims.[88]　The securing of assignments for the purpose of stirring up litigation is also against public policy.[89]　This is especially the case if the assignee is a lawyer.[90]

§ 267.　Effect of Contractual Prohibition or Authorization of an Assignment

Some cases have held that a contractual provision prohibiting the assignment of rights created by the contract is an unlawful restraint on alienation.[91]　The majority of cases, however, have refused to interfere with the parties' freedom of contract in so explicit a manner.　Rather, they have indicated that a provision of this kind is effective.[92]　At the same time, however, they have tended to find that the particular provision before the court was not drafted with sufficient clarity to accomplish its purpose of prohibiting assignment. They have often emasculated the provision by holding it to be merely a promise not to assign.[93]　Under such a construction the assignment

---

86. See 3 Williston § 417. There is no unanimity on the question of who is a "public officer," but generally even subordinate clerical employees are deemed public officers for this purpose. See Bliss v. Lawrence, 58 N.Y. 442 (1874), where the rationale of the prohibition was expressed in these terms: "The public service is protected by protecting those engaged in performing public duties; and this not upon the ground of their private interest, but upon that of the necessity of securing the efficiency of the public service, by seeing to it that the funds provided for its maintenance should be received by those who are to perform the work . . . .."

87. See 5 U.S.C.A. § 8346(a).

88. Welles v. Brown, 226 Mich. 657, 198 N.W. 180 (1924).

89. See Kenrich Corp. v. Miller, 377 F. 2d 312 (3d Cir. 1967), which, in form, involved a power of attorney rather than an assignment. The obligor's defense of champerty was sustained.

90. See § 368 infra. Cf. Ellis v. Frawley, 165 Wis. 381, 161 N.W. 364 (1917).

91. Portuguese-American Bank v. Welles, 242 U.S. 7, 37 S.Ct. 3, 61 L.Ed. 116 (1916); Jankowski v. Jankowski, 311 Mich. 340, 18 N.W.2d 848 (1945) (valid while assignor's performance is still executory, but not thereafter); cf. State St. Furniture Co. v. Armour & Co., 345 Ill. 160, 177 N.E. 702, 76 A. L.R. 1298 (1931) (contractual provision purporting to void assignments held not binding on assignee).

92. Masterson v. Sine, 68 Cal.2d 222, 65 Cal.Rptr. 545, 436 P.2d 561 (1968) (oral agreement not to assign written option upheld); see generally, Grismore, Effect of a Restriction on Assignment in a Contract, 31 Mich.L.Rev. 299 (1933).

93. E. g., in Manchester v. Kendall, 51 Super. (19 Jones & Spencer) 460 (N.Y. 1885), aff'd 103 N.Y. 638 (1886), the following contractual provision was held not to bar an assignment: "This contract not to be assigned, or any part thereof, or any installments to grow due under the same." It has also been held that there is no violation of an anti-assignment clause when the assignment is made because of a change in the form of the assignor's business, as where an individual

is effective but the obligor has a cause of action against the assignor for breach of contract.[94] Since damages for such a breach ordinarily will be merely nominal, the anti-assignment provision is of no practical value. If, however, the provision explicitly states that any assignment shall be void, or uses other equivalent language, the courts have generally held that a purported assignment is ineffective [95] unless the obligor consents to the assignment.[96]

The Uniform Commercial Code has adopted the rule that an anti-assignment clause is ineffective to prohibit the assignment of an "account" or "contract right" [97] or, in a sales situation, the assignment of a right to damages for total breach or a right arising out of the assignor's due performance of his entire obligation.[98] The basic purpose of these provisions of the Code is to prohibit restraints on the assignability of most rights to receive money and goods which have been paid for.[99] The Code adopted a general policy of free assignability to bring the law in conformity with business convenience and on the grounds that the courts had already "construed the heart out of" anti-assignment provisions in contracts.[1]

The Code also contains a provision relating to interpretation which bears on the problem. The Code provides that in a sales situation a clause prohibiting assignment of "the contract" should be, unless the circumstances indicate the contrary, construed as barring only the delegation of duties.[2] Thus, a generally phrased anti-assignment clause is to be read as permitting assignment but forbidding delegation. The codifiers, it is believed, took proper notice of what the parties, despite an improper use of terminology, ordinarily intend by such a clause.

proprietor forms a corporation and assigns his contractual rights to the corporation. Ruberoid Co. v. Glassman Constr. Co., 248 Md. 97, 234 A.2d 875 (1967).

94. Hull v. Hostettler, 224 Mich. 365, 194 N.W. 996 (1923).

95. Allhusen v. Caristo Constr. Corp., 303 N.Y. 446, 103 N.E.2d 891 (1952); Restatement, Contracts § 151(c); Restatement, Contracts (2d) § 149(c), particularly Comment c.

96. Sillman v. 20th Century Fox Film Corp., 3 N.Y.2d 395, 165 N.Y.S.2d 498, 144 N.E.2d 387 (1957); Metropolitan Life Ins. Co. v. Dunne, 2 F.Supp. 165 (S.D.N.Y.1931); Restatement, Con-

tracts § 176; Restatement, Contracts (2d) § 154(d).

97. U.C.C. § 9–318(4); see also U.C.C. § 5–116 as to letters of credit.

98. U.C.C. § 2–210(2); accord, Restatement, Contracts (2d) § 154(b) (as a rule of construction).

99. For a discussion of the coverage of Article 9, see § 257 supra.

1. U.C.C. § 9–318, Comment 4; see Gilmore, The Commercial Doctrine of Good Faith Purchase, 63 Yale L.J. 1057, 1118–20 (1954).

2. U.C.C. § 2–210(3); accord, Restatement, Contracts (2d) § 154(a).

If the contract contains a provision permitting assignment it will be honored even if the rights under the contract would not otherwise be assignable.[3] However, a merely routine clause to the effect that the contract shall inure to the benefit of the heirs and assigns of the parties will not by itself have the effect of rendering the rights assignable or the duties delegable.[4]

§ 268. Voidable Assignments, Assignments of Conditional Rights and Conditional Assignment of Rights

We have previously seen that a gratuitous assignment is in some instances terminable by the assignor.[5] An assignment may also be voidable by the assignor because of infancy, insanity, duress, fraud, etc.[6] In each of these situations, although there is a present transfer of the right, nevertheless the right of the assignor is not completely extinguished as is the case in the ordinary assignment.

So also if the assignment is conditional the right of the assignor is not extinguished until the condition occurs.[7] The Restatement gives this illustration. A has a right to $400 against B and assigns the right to C in payment for an automobile delivered by C on condition that the car run 1000 miles without needing repairs. Although there is an assignment, the right to $400 belongs to A and not C until the condition occurs or is excused.[8]

This situation is to be carefully distinguished from the assignment of a conditional right. In the previous case the assignment was conditional; the condition arose as a result of the agreement between the assignor and the assignee. Here, the assigned right is conditional; the condition arises as a result of the agreement between the obligor and the assignor. The existence of the condition does not prevent the assignment,[9] but if the condition is not performed the case

---

3. Restatement, Contracts § 162(1); Restatement, Contracts (2d) § 155(1); 3 Williston § 423.

4. Standard Chautauqua Sys. v. Gift, 120 Kan. 101, 242 P. 145 (1926); Paige v. Faure, 229 N.Y. 114, 127 N.E. 898, 10 A.L.R. 649 (1920); Restatement, Contracts (2d) § 155, Comment b.

5. See § 259 supra.

6. Restatement, Contracts (2d) § 170, Comment g. However such an assignment bars action by the assignor until he revokes or avoids it. As we have seen a gratuitous assignment is no longer revocable after the gift is completed. See § 259 supra. In the case

of a voidable assignment the obligor's duty to the assignor is discharged if the obligor pays the assignee in good faith without notice. Restatement, Contracts (2d) § 170, Comment g. If the obligor pays the assignee with reason to know that the assignment is voidable, however, he does so at his peril.

7. Restatement, Contracts (2d) § 163, Comment b.

8. Restatement, Contracts (2d) § 163, ill. 1.

9. Restatement, Contracts (2d) § 152, § 153, Comment a.

will come within the rule of the next section; that is, that the obligor may assert against the assignee any defense which the obligor may assert against the assignor.[10]

§ 269. Defenses of the Obligor Against the Assignee

We saw in the previous Chapter that a promisor may ordinarily assert against a third party beneficiary any defense which he may assert against the promisee.[11] A similar rule prevails here; that is, the obligor may generally assert against the assignee the defenses he could have asserted against the assignor.[12] However, just as in the third party beneficiary context there is an exception discussed under the doctrine of "vesting," [13] a related exception exists in the context of assignments. The assignee is not bound by any defense resulting from an agreement reached between the obligor and assignor or payment made to the assignor after the obligor has notice of the assignment.[14] In other words, notice received by the obligor of the assignment vests the rights of the assignee in the sense that after notice his rights are not defeasible by agreement of the original contracting parties or payment made by the obligor to the assignor.[15]

The Uniform Commercial Code continues these rules, with some modifications. Article 9 of the Code provides that the obligor may continue to pay the assignor until he receives notice of the assignment and of his duty to pay the assignee.[16] The Code has clarified the question of the kind of notice required. First, the notice must "rea-

10. The same rule applies in a case such as Paige v. Faure, discussed in § 263, supra, where the obligor attempts to delegate a nondelegable duty. Since the condition to the other party's duty is not being performed he may decline to perform even though the right in question is assignable.

11. See § 250 supra.

12. Sponge Divers' Ass'n, Inc. v. Smith, Kline & French Co., 263 F. 70 (1st Cir. 1920); Jones v. Martin, 41 Cal.2d 23, 256 P.2d 905 (1953).

13. See § 251 supra.

14. Welch v. Mandeville, 14 U.S. (1 Wheat.) 233, 4 L.Ed. 79 (1816) (obligor may not release assignor after notice of the assignment); Continental Purchasing Co. v. Van Raalte, 251 A.D. 151, 295 N.Y.S. 867 (4th Dep't 1937).

(obligor may not pay assignor after notice of assignment); Terino v. Le Clair, 26 A.D.2d 28, 270 N.Y.S.2d 51 (4th Dep't (1966). Until the obligor has received notice, he is, of course, free to deal with the assignor. Van Keuren v. Corkins, 66 N.Y. 77 (1876) (payment after assignment of bond and mortgage; recording is not notice to obligor).

15. Even prior to notice, the rights of the assignee cannot be varied by an agreement between the obligor and assignor unless the obligor gives value. Restatement, Contracts (2d) § 170(1). Value is defined in Comments c and d. In other words a gratuitous release of the obligor is ineffective except in the case of a revocable or voidable assignment.

16. U.C.C. § 9–318(3).

sonably identify the rights assigned." [17]   Moreover, if requested by the obligor the assignee must furnish proof that the assignment had been made.[18]   The Code also provides that despite notification [19] of the assignment to the obligor, if the assigned contract right has not become an account, the original contracting parties may agree to modify or substitute the contract in good faith and in accordance with reasonable commercial standards.[20]   Under this provision the assignee is bound by the modification but acquires rights under the modified or substituted contract.[21]

Since it is a general rule that the obligor may assert against the assignee any defense which he can assert against the assignor, it is often stated that the assignee stands in the shoes of the assignor; that is, the assignee does not have any better rights than his assignor.[22]

17.   U.C.C. § 9–318(3).

18.   U.C.C. § 9–318(3). At common law no specific kind of notice or proof was required. A rule of reasonableness prevailed. 3 Williston § 437. The Code has adopted a more stringent notice and proof requirement, such as had been adopted by judicial decision for the protection of banks in cases involving assignment of bank accounts. Gibraltar Realty Corp. v. Mt. Vernon Trust Co., 276 N.Y. 353, 12 N.E.2d 438, 115 A.L.R. 322 (1938). On the question of bank deposits and commercial instruments, see also Restatement, Contracts (2d) § 171, Comment c.

19.   A person receives notification under the Code (§ 1–201(26)) when it comes to his attention or is duly delivered at a place held out by him as the place for receipt of such communication.

20.   New York in passing this section also required that the modificiation be "without material adverse effect upon the assignee's right under or the assignor's ability to perform the contract." The Permanent Editorial Board of the Code rejected the change upon the ground that it was implicit in the Code. Report No. 2, Variations to Code in Adopting States, p. 225 (1965).

21.   U.C.C. § 9–318(2). This, of course, changes the common law rule and also overrules cases such as Homer v. Shaw, 212 Mass. 113, 98 N.E. 697 (1912), which held that the assignee acquires no rights under the substituted contract. The Restatement, Contracts (2d) § 170(2), adopts the Code rule. For a detailed discussion of this provision, see Gilmore, The Assignee of Contract Rights and His Precarious Security, 74 Yale L.J. 217 (1964).

22.   It is interesting to compare the law of sales with the law of assignments on this point. If B, by fraud, obtains title to and possession of a horse from A and sells the horse to T for value and without notice of A's rights, T acquires good title to the horse. U.C.C. § 2–403. (But the result is different if T purchases from a thief. Linwood Harvestore, Inc. v. Cannon, 427 Pa. 434, 235 A.2d 377 (1967)). If B, as a result of his fraud acquires a non-negotiable note from A and assigns it to C for value and without notice of A's rights, C acquires no better rights than B and is subject to A's defense of fraud. It is believed that the difference between the results reached in sales cases and in the law of assignments is justified. In obtaining an assignment, the assignee understands that he is entering into a relationship with the obligor, and, if he wishes to protect himself may ask the obligor if he claims any defenses. In obtaining the horse, however, there is usually no reliable way of determining from whom and the conditions under which

There are, however, exceptions. First as we have seen, under the doctrine of vesting, this is not wholly true. In addition, the ubiquitous doctrine of estoppel may come into play. Thus, if A gives his non-negotiable note to B, who assigns and delivers the note to C, notwithstanding lack of notice, A's payment to B will not necessarily be available as a defense in an action by C to enforce the note against A. On making payment A had the right and the burden of demanding the surrender of the note. His failure to insist upon its surrender may estop him from asserting the defense of payment.[23]

Special rules govern the question of the obligor's right to assert set-off or recoupment against the assignee which he might have asserted against the assignor. Although these are in a sense matters of defense, they are better discussed in connection with the question of the permissibility of counter-claims.[24]

A pressing current question is whether, by agreement, the obligor and assignor may effectively provide that the assignee shall not be bound by a defense which the obligor has against the assignor. If such a clause is valid, it is obvious that sellers of goods will automatically have such a clause printed in their form contracts for credit sales. While some jurisdictions have held such clauses to be void as against public policy,[25] others have upheld them.[26] The Uniform Commercial Code validates such clauses where the assignee takes in good faith for value without notice of the defense, but not with respect to defenses which would be denominated as real defenses to a negotiable instrument.[27] These are set out set out in Section 3–305 of the Code and include such defenses as infancy, incapacity, duress, misrepresentation of a serious kind, and bankruptcy. However, the Code subordinates this provision "to any statute or decision which establishes a different rule for buyers or lessees of consumer goods." [28]

---

the seller acquired title. Nor is the purchaser of tangibles entering into any particular relationship with the prior owner. In traditional terms, his rights are *in rem* rather than *in personam*.

23. Assets Realization Co. v. Clark, 205 N.Y. 105, 98 N.E. 457 (1912); Restatement, Contracts § 170(4); Restatement, Contracts (2d) § 170(4).

24. See § 270 infra.

25. American Nat. Bank v. A. G. Sommerville, Inc., 191 Cal. 364, 216 P. 376 (1923); Quality Fin. Co. v. Hurley, 337 Mass. 150, 148 N.E.2d 385 (1958); Motor Contract Co. v. Van der Volgen,

162 Wash. 449, 298 P. 705, 79 A.L.R. 29 (1931).

26. United States ex rel. Adm'r of F. H. A. v. Troy Parisian, Inc., 115 F.2d 224 (9th Cir. 1940), cert. denied sub. nom. Troy Parisian, Inc. v. United States, 312 U.S. 699, 61 S.Ct. 739, 85 L.Ed. 1133 (1941).

27. U.C.C. § 9–206(1); see General Elec. Credit Corp. v. Tidenberg, 78 N.M. 59, 428 P.2d 33 (1967).

28. U.C.C. § 9–206(1). Restatement, Contracts § 168, Comment f; see also Comment g, relating to the possibility of estoppel against an obligor even though the agreement not to assert a

§ 270. Other Limitations Upon the Rights of the Assignee: Counterclaims, Set-off, and Recoupment

To what extent may the obligor assert against the assignee claims which he has against the assignor? The resolution of this question has tended to differ in various jurisdictions.[29] This is one instance in which the existence of substantive rights has often turned upon the wording of procedural statutes. Article 9 of the Uniform Commercial Code has adopted the solution which had perhaps received the widest acceptance.

Under the Code, if the obligor's claim arises out of the same contract from which the assignee's rights stem, the obligor may assert this claim against the assignee, whether the claim arose prior or subsequent to notice of assignment.[30] The obligor's plea in this instance is, under traditional terminology, known as recoupment. The obligor may assert this claim as a subtraction from the assignee's judgment. The obligor may not under such a pleading obtain a judgment against the assignee for any excess over the assignee's claim.[31]

If the obligor's claim is in the nature of a set-off, that is, arises from a collateral transaction between the assignor and the obligor, it may be asserted against the assignee only if it matured before the obligor received notice of the assignment.[32] Again, the obligor may utilize a set-off by way of subtraction from the assignee's claim and

---

defense is invalid. Cf. President and Directors of Manhattan Co. v. Monogram Associates Inc., 276 App.Div. 766, 92 N.Y.S.2d 579 (2d Dep't 1949). It should also be noted that the U.C. C. §§ 9–201, 9–203 subordinate the provisions of Article 9 to statutes regulating retail installment sales. See generally, Hogan, a Survey of Retail Installment Sales Legislation, 44 Cornell L.Q. 38 (1958); McAlister, Retail Instalment Credit: Growth and Legislation (1964). For an example of a local statute see McKinney's N.Y.Pers. Prop.Law Arts. 9, 10, and particularly § 403(3) (a).

29. See 4 Corbin §§ 896–897.

30. U.C.C. § 9–318(1) (a); American Bridge Co. v. City of Boston, 202 Mass. 374, 88 N.E. 1089 (1909); Seibert v. Dunn, 216 N.Y. 237, 110 N.E. 447 (1915); Cronkleton v. Hastings Theatre & Realty Corp., 134 Neb. 168, 278 N.W. 144 (1938).

31. Restatement, Contracts (2d) § 168, Comment d. However there is an exception where the obligor and assignor have agreed to the contrary.

32. U.C.C. § 9–318(1) (b); Restatement, Contracts (2d), particularly Comment d. The Uniform Commercial Code appears to have rejected the case of Stafford Security Co. v. Kremer, 258 N.Y. 1, 179 N.E. 32, 78 A.L.R. 822 (1931) which is to the effect that the obligor is limited on his set-off to the amount that has been earned by the assignor prior to the assignment. This is made clear by the fact that the rule announced by the Code relates to "account debtors" which by definition (§ 9–105(1) (a)) includes a person obligated under a "contract right" which relates to a right of payment not yet earned and so it appears that the Code does not limit the set-off to the amount that has been earned by the assignor prior to the assignment. Cf. McKinney's N.Y.Gen. Obligations Law § 13–105.

may not obtain a judgment against the assignee for any excess over the assignee's claim. The obligor may counterclaim against the assignee for an affirmative judgment only if he has a claim against the assignee himself.[33]

The rules discussed in this section also apply to sub-assignees; that is subsequent assignees of the original assignee.[34]

§ 271. Other Limitations Upon the Rights of the Assignee: Latent Equities

It is a truism that a subsequent legal title will cut off prior equities if the legal title is acquired in good faith for value, without notice of the existence of the equities.[35] As between two competing equities, however, prior in time is prior in right.[36] Thus, if the question is posed as to whether an assignee takes free from latent equities, (that is, an equity which exists in a party other than the obligor) the answer is made to depend on whether an assignment vests legal or equitable title in the assignee. Under the older view an assignment is equitable and is thus subject to latent equities.[37] The modern approach is to consider an assignment as vesting a legal interest in the assignee. Therefore, if the assignee takes his assignment in good faith for value and without notice of the prior equities, these are cut off.[38] Even under the modern approach, however, assignments of so-called "future rights" are often deemed equitable,[39] and if a conceptual approach is adopted, latent equities will survive the assignment.

---

33. His right to counterclaim on an unrelated transaction may be limited for trial convenience by procedural rules. See Restatement, Contracts (2d) § 168, Comment c.

34. Restatement, Contracts (2d) § 168, Comment e. The contrary rule stated in the original Restatement in § 167(3) was eliminated to bring the Restatement into harmony with the Uniform Commercial Code. See Reporter's note following § 168.

35. Holt v. American Woolen Co., 129 Me. 108, 150 A. 382 (1930); McClintock, Equity 69–71 (1948).

36. Id. at 52.

37. Owen v. Evans, 134 N.Y. 514, 31 N. E. 999 (1892). This view is strongly supported by 3 Williston § 447, where he states that it is supported by the weight of authority. See also 3 Williston § 438. His policy rationale, ("it is to be observed that intangible choses in action are not primarily intended for merchandising, as chattels are") stated in § 447 is no longer an accurate statement of commercial practice.

38. Glass v. Springfield L. I. Cemetery Soc., 252 App.Div. 319, 299 N.Y.S. 244 (1st Dep't 1937), lv. to app. denied 276 N.Y. 687, 13 N.E.2d 479; Restatement, Contracts § 174; Restatement, Contracts (2d) § 175. Corbin describes this as the prevailing view. 4 Corbin § 900. This rule is not applied where the protection of the purchaser would impair the rights of the obligor. Restatement, Contracts (2d) § 175, Comment b.

39. See § 274 infra.

§ 272.　Priorities Between Successive Assignees of the Same Claim

If A assigns to B a right to the payment of $1,000 which is owed to A by X and A subsequently assigns this same right to C who pays value and takes without notice of the assignment to B, who prevails? A has obviously acted unlawfully in making the second assignment, and if solvent and brought to justice can be made to pay for his wrongful act.[40] As between the two innocent assignees there are essentially three views on the question of priority. The English view is that as between successive assignees the second will prevail if he is the first to give notice and acts in good faith without notice of the first assignment and pays value.[41] This rule is unsatisfactory in view of the widespread business usage of non-notification financing of accounts receivable in this country. The New York rule is that first in time is first in right.[42] The Restatement adopted as an intermediate approach the so called "four horsemen" rule that first in time is first in right unless a second assignee who pays value in good faith without notice (a) obtains payment from the obligor, (b) recovers judgment, (c) enters into a new contract with the obligor, or (d) receives delivery of a tangible token or writing, the surrender of which is required by the obligor's contract (a symbolic writing).[43]

Even in states which adopt the New York rule it is clear that the second assignee will prevail if the first assignment is gratuitous and not yet a completed gift or is voidable.[44] So also, if the necessary elements are present, the first assignee may be estopped from asserting priority as, for example, where he has failed to take possession of a symbolic writing.[45]

---

40. See § 276 infra, relating to the warranties of the assignor.

41. This is the rule of Dearle v. Hall, 38 Eng.Rep. 475 (ch. 1827). It adopts the theory that failure to give notice to the debtor is a species of negligence. Accord, Graham Paper Co. v. Pembroke, 124 Cal. 117, 56 P. 627 (1899); Anaconda Aluminum Co. v. Sharp, 243 Miss. 9, 136 So.2d 585, 99 A.L.R.2d 1307 (1962).

42. Superior Brassiere v. Zimetbaum, 214 App.Div. 525, 212 N.Y.S. 473 (1st Dep't 1925). Thus, if the second assignee receives payment from the obligor, in New York, the first assignee may proceed against him to recover this sum. Superior Brassiere Co. v. Zimetbaum, supra; contra, Rabinowitz v. People's Nat'l Bank, 235 Mass. 102, 126 N.E. 289 (1920) (applying Re-

statement rule). It should be noted, however, that it is undisputed that the obligor is discharged by payment to the second assignee, if he has no notice of the first assignment. This follows from the discussion in § 269 supra.

43. Restatement, Contracts § 173(b); Restatement, Contracts (2d) § 174; Restatement, Contracts (2d) § 164, Comment c.

44. Cf. Perkins v. City Nat. Bank, 253 Iowa 922, 114 N.W.2d 45 (1962); Restatement, Contracts (2d) § 174, Comment d. The same is true in the case of an assignment of a future right if the second assignee pays value and takes without notice. See § 274 infra.

45. Restatement, Contracts (2d) § 174, Comment f. Thus even under the

The problem of successive assignments is not extremely important in itself, since such conduct is rare. Yet there has been a highly dramatic side effect of the rule governing successive assignments. In Corn Exchange National Bank & Trust Co. v. Klauder,[46] the United States Supreme Court ruled that assignments of accounts receivable in Pennsylvania, where the English rule prevailed, were not "perfected" liens within the protection of the Bankruptcy Act. This was because of the remote possibility that the assignor could have assigned to a second assignee, who would, under Pennsylvania Law, acquire priority over the first assignee. In effect, the decision deprived creditors who had advanced money on the security of accounts receivable of their lien, placing them in the category of unsecured creditors. The legislative response was prompt and a majority of states enacted legislation to give the first assignee greater security.[47] In some, the New York rule was enacted, in some, a system of marking the debtor's books was adopted, and, in others, a filing system was instituted.

Against this background[48] the Commercial Code provided in Article 9 for a filing system. However, as we have seen, certain assignments are excluded from the coverage of Article 9.[49] In addition the filing provisions of Article 9 are inapplicable to "an assignment of accounts or contract rights which does not alone or in conjunction with other assignments to the assignee transfer a significant part of the outstanding accounts or contract rights of the assignor."[50] If

New York rule if the first assignee fails to take possession of what the Restatement Second calls a symbolic writing his rights may be inferior to those of the second assignee by virtue of the doctrine of estoppel. Cf. Salem Trust Co. v. Mfrs' Finance Co., 264 U.S. 182, 44 S.Ct. 266, 68 L.Ed. 628, 31 A.L.R. 867 (1924) (adopting the New York view but leaving open the question of equitable estoppel against the first assignee); 4 Corbin § 902.

46. 318 U.S. 434, 63 S.Ct. 679, 87 L.Ed. 884, 144 A.L.R. 1189 (1943). The "four horsemen" rule, however, was held to give the assignee sufficient security so that his lien could be deemed perfected. In re Rosen, 157 F.2d 997 (3d Cir. 1946), cert. den. 330 U.S. 835, 67 S.Ct. 972, 91 L.Ed. 1282 (1947).

47. The Statutes are analyzed in Comment, 67 Yale L.J. 402 (1958).

48. However amendments to the Bankruptcy Act in 1950 reduced the significance of the problem. Craig, Accounts Receivable Financing: A Reappraisal of Validation Statutes in the Light of Amended 60(a), 65 Harv.L. Rev. 627 (1952).

49. See § 9–104 of the Code. We have previously indicated that among the exclusions are: wage assignments (subd. d), and "a sale of accounts, contract rights or chattel paper as part of a sale of the business out of which they arose, or an assignment of accounts, contract rights or chattel paper which is for the purpose of collection only, or a transfer of a contract right to an assignee who is also to do the performance under the contract;" (subd. f). See § 257 supra.

50. U.C.C. § 9–302(1) (e). There are other exemptions from filing set forth in § 9–302 and in §§ 9–304 and 9–305.

the filing provision is applicable to the transaction a second assignee who files first will generally prevail over an unfiled first assignee to the extent that the second assignee gives value.[51]

§ 273.　Rights of the Assignee Against an Attaching Creditor

An assignee clearly has rights superior to the general creditors of the assignor. The assignee, unlike general creditors, has a specific property interest in the right assigned. An attaching creditor also obtains an interest in the specific right attached. Thus, if the creditor secures an attachment of a specific right prior to assignment, the creditor has priority over the claims of the assignee. The converse is usually true. An assignment which preceded an attachment will have priority over the attachment.[52] This rule, however, if absolute, could work to the prejudice of the obligor. It is therefore held that under certain circumstances the assignee is estopped from asserting his priority.[53] There are at least two formulations of this rule of estoppel. One version bars the assignee if the obligor has not received notice of the assignment in sufficient time to call the assignment to the attention of the court in the attachment proceeding.[54] Other cases hold that notice after the entry of judgment in the attachment proceeding, but prior to payment of the judgment claim, is sufficient to protect the assignee's priority.[55]

The Uniform Commercial Code, to a large extent, resolves the priority problem by its filing system. Under the Code a "perfected" assignment is superior to a lien obtained by a subsequent lien cred-

---

These are beyond the scope of this work.

51. U.C.C. § 9–312(5). Literally interpreted, the first assignee to file has priority even if he has knowledge of an unfiled prior assignment. However, since there is a general obligation of good faith (U.C.C. § 1–201(19); 1–203), it might be argued that obtaining an assignment with knowledge of a prior assignment constitutes a violation of this obligation.

52. Stathos v. Murphy, 26 A.D.2d 500, 276 N.Y.S.2d 727 (1st Dep't 1966), aff'd, 19 N.Y.2d 883, 281 N.Y.S.2d 81, 227 N.E.2d 880 (1967); 4 Corbin § 903; 3 Williston § 434.

53. Since a creditor does not qualify as a purchaser for value by virtue of his attachment, he can obtain priority over an assignee only by virtue of the doctrine of estoppel or by the terms of a particular statute. Restatement, Contracts (2d) § 173, Comment a. However an attaching creditor who is subsequent to an assignee will have superior rights if the assignment is terminable or voidable. Restatement, Contracts (2d) § 173, Comment b; cf. Restatement, Contracts § 172(1).

54. Restatement, Contracts § 172(2).

55. McDowell, Pyle & Co. v. Hopfield, 148 Md. 84, 128 A. 742, 52 A.L.R. 105 (1925); Greentree v. Rosenstock, 61 N.Y. 583 (1875); Goldfarb v. C. & K. Purchasing Corp., 170 Misc. 90, 9 N. Y.S.2d 952 (App.Term 1939). See Annot., 52 A.L.R. 109; Restatement, Contracts (2d) § 173(2).

itor.[56] An attaching creditor is a lien creditor.[57] Thus, if the assignment is of the kind which comes under the filing provision of the Code, a filed assignment is perfected and takes priority over the lien of a subsequent attachment if a financing statement is filed. An assignment which is subject to the filing requirements, but which has not been filed, is subordinate to a subsequent attachment if the attaching creditor is without knowledge of the security interest.[58] If the assignment is governed by the Code, but is not within its filing requirements the assignment takes priority if it attaches prior to the lien of the creditor.[59]

§ 274. Assignment of Future Rights: Equitable Assignments

The cases are in confusion as to the distinction between future and present rights. Suppose a builder under an existing contract is to be paid progress payments of $1,000 per month, conditioned upon his performance of a specified amount of work each month. If at the end of the first month of due performance he assigned his right to payment of the first installment, this is unquestionably an assignment of a present existing right. If, however, at the end of the first month he assigned his right to the second installment some would say that this is the assignment of a present conditional right,[60] but others would say that this is the assignment of a future right.[61] Everyone agrees that if A assigns his rights under a contract which he expects to enter into this is the assignment of a future right.[62]

56. U.C.C. § 9–301(1)(b) provides that an unperfected security interest is subordinate to the rights of a person who becomes a lien creditor without knowledge of the security interest and before it was perfected. Restatement, Contracts (2d) § 173, Comment d.

57. U.C.C. § 9–301(3).

58. U.C.C. § 9–301(1) (b).

59. That is to say the assignment in this case is perfected upon attachment. U.C.C. § 9–301; U.C.C. § 9–305, Comment 1. Under the facts assumed the assignment attaches immediately. U.C.C. § 9–204.

60. See § 268 supra; Restatement, Contracts § 154(1); Restatement, Contracts (2d) § 153(1); Simpson § 128; Rockmore v. Lehman, 129 F.2d 892 (2d Cir. 1942), cert. denied, 317 U.S. 700, 65 S.Ct. 525, 87 L.Ed. 559 (1943); Stathos v. Murphy, 26 A.D.2d 500, 276 N.Y.S.2d 727 (1st Dep't 1966), aff'd 19 N.Y.2d 883, 281 N.Y.S.2d 81, 227 N.E. 2d 880 (1967); In Re Holt, 28 A.D.2d 201, 284 N.Y.S.2d 208 (3d Dep't 1967). Under this view the fact that the "contract" is terminable at will would be immaterial. In Re Wright, 157 F. 544 (2d Cir. 1907). A strange peculiarity in this area is to treat the assignment of non-contractual conditional rights, such as rights to refunds of liquor license deposits, as future rights. Matter of City of N. Y. v. Bedford Bar & Grill, 2 N.Y.2d 429, 161 N.Y.S.2d 67, 141 N.E.2d 575 (1957). Under the Uniform Commercial Code such deposits would be considered "general intangibles." See § 257 supra.

61. Grismore § 252; Comment, 27 Ford.L.Rev. 579 (1959).

62. Restatement, Contracts § 154(2); cf. Restatement, Contracts (2d) § 153(2).

An assignment of a present right, is, according to the prevailing view,[63] a legal assignment. An assignment for value [64] of a future right has generally been held to be an equitable assignment upon the theory that although one may not effect a present transfer of what he does not have, equity will treat the purported assignment as a promise to assign and will ordinarily order specific performance of the promise after the right comes into existence.[65]

As between the assignor and assignee it usually matters little whether the assignment is to be labeled as legal or equitable.[66] The most important consequence of the distinction is that the rights of an equitable assignee are inferior to the rights of a subsequent legal assignee for value without notice and also inferior to the rights of a subsequent attaching creditor without notice.[67] Consequently, an equitable assignee's security is not recognized in the event of the assignor's bankruptcy.[68]

The Uniform Commercial Code has made radical changes in this area.[69] The Code authorizes a creditor to extract a security agreement from his debtor which will cause all after-acquired property

63. See Simpson §§ 127–128.

64. Simpson § 126. The theory is that equity will not ordinarily grant specific performance of a promise unless the promisee gives value.

65. Holt v. American Woolen Co., 129 Me. 108, 150 A. 382 (1930); Robert Wise Plumbing & Heating Inc. v. Alpine Develop. Co., 72 Wash.2d 172, 432 P.2d 547 (1967). The original Restatement in § 154(2) indicates the obligor is not bound by the assignment. However the Restatement Second does not so provide. See Restatement, Contracts (2d) § 153, Comment d. As previously indicated (see § 256 supra), under a promise to assign or to transfer proceeds, the promisee may have rights which resemble those of an assignee of a future right.

66. An equitable assignment of wages; that is, a purported assignment of wages from employment not yet obtained may be against public policy. See Orkow v. Orkow, 133 Cal.App. 50, 23 P.2d 781 (1933). This question is now generally regulated by statute. See § 266 supra.

67. Restatement, Contracts § 154(2); Restatement, Contracts (2d) § 153(2); State Factors Corp. v. Sales Factors

Corp., 257 A.D. 101, 12 N.Y.S.2d 12 (1st Dep't 1939).

68. Taylor v. Barton-Child Co., 228 Mass. 126, 117 N.E. 43 (1917); see Rockmore v. Lehman, 128 F.2d 564 (2d Cir. 1942), revs'd on rehearing 129 F. 2d 892, cert. denied 317 U.S. 700, 63 S.Ct. 525, 87 L.Ed. 559 (1943), in which the U. S. Court of Appeals at first held that an assignment of rights to payment under an existing contract was equitable because payment was conditioned on the assignor's due performance of its side of a bilateral contract. It was held therefore that the assignment did not constitute a lien valid against the trustee in bankruptcy. The court subsequently vacated its decision, holding that the transfer of a present conditional right was a legal assignment, effective against the trustee in bankruptcy. For extensive comment on this and similar cases, see 4 Corbin § 903 (Pocket Parts 1964).

69. See generally, Coogan & Gordon, The Effect of the Uniform Commercial Code upon Receivables Financing —Some Answers and Some Unresolved Problems, 76 Harv.L.Rev. 1529 (1963).

to secure all obligations covered by the security agreement.[70]   When the financing statement is filed it gives constructive notice of the possibility that the security agreement may contain an after-acquired property clause.[71]   Thus the Code permits creation of a security interest in after-acquired contract rights as well as after-acquired tangible property.   In the past, courts had often deemed such agreements as against public policy on the grounds that other creditors could be unduly prejudiced.[72]

Under the Code if a security agreement contains an after-acquired property clause and the creditor files a financing statement he will have priority over all subsequent parties with certain exceptions.[73] If the financing statement has not been filed his security interest is not perfected and will be subordinate to the rights of lien creditors of the debtor without notice and purchasers of accounts, contract rights and general intangibles to the extent that these assignees give value without notice before the filing of the financing statement.[74]

§ 275.   Partial Assignments

At common law a partial assignment was unenforceable over the objection of the obligor because of the rule against splitting a cause of action; moreover, because procedure at law limited any suit to two parties, the obligor would be subjected to multiplicity of suits.[75]   In time, however, partial assignments were recognized in equity where the interests of all parties could be adjudicated in one lawsuit.[76]   Today, the majority view, often as a result of Code procedure, is that the equity rule is applicable at law.   Therefore, the partial assignee may sue at law provided that all of the interested

---

70.   Certain exceptions are made as to crops and consumer goods. U.C.C. § 9–204(4).

71.   U.C.C. § 9–204(4), Comment 3, speaks in terms of "everything he has or will have." See Industrial Packaging Prods. Co. v. Fort Pitt Packaging Int'l, Inc., 399 Pa. 643, 161 A.2d 19 (1960).

72.   Taylor v. Barton-Child Co., 228 Mass. 126, 117 N.E. 43, 44 (1917) ("A door would be opened for the accomplishment of fraud in business . . . . The principles and spirit of our jurisprudence have been that owners of personal property ought not to acquire any false credit by creating encumbrances more or less secret and unknown to the world.").

73.   U.C.C. § 9–204(3). A possible exception exists in the case of a purchase money security interest. U.C.C. §§ 9–301(2), 9–312(3) and (4). A purchase money security interest was also recognized at common law. Fricker v. Uddo & Taormina Co., 48 Cal.2d 696, 312 P.2d 1085 (1957); cf. Cosmopolitan Mut. Cas. Co. v. Monarch Concrete Corp., 6 N.Y.2d 383, 189 N.Y.S.2d 893, 160 N.E.2d 643 (1959).

74.   U.C.C. § 9–301(1) (d), § 9–301(2).

75.   Andrews Electric Co., Inc. v. St. Alphonse Catholic Total Abstinence Soc., 233 Mass. 20, 123 N.E. 103 (1919).

76.   Id.; see also Annot. 80 A.L.R. 413 (1932).

parties have been joined, or procedural rules dispensing with the necessity of joinder have been complied with.[77]

§ 276. Implied Warranties of the Assignor and Sub-Assignor

As in the case of other consensual transactions, the parties to an assignment are, within broad limits, free to negotiate the terms. Thus, the assignor will be held to any express warranty or representations he may make.[78] Conversely, it may be agreed that the transfer is without warranty, express or implied.[79]

Where the parties are silent on the subject, the law implies certain warranties. Generally an assignor is held to warrant: (1) that he will do nothing to defeat or impair the value of the assignment; (2) that the right exists and is subject to no defenses or limitations except as stated or apparent, and (3) that any document delivered as part of transaction is genuine and what it purports to be. The assignor does not warrant that the obligor is solvent or that he will perform.[80]

In the absence of a contrary manifestation of intent the warranties of an assignor to an assignee do not run to a sub-assignee.[81]

§ 277. Delegation of Duties: Generally

We have already adverted to the importance of the distinction between assignment and delegation. Rights are assigned; duties are delegated.[82] When a right is assigned, the assignor ordinarily no longer has any interest in the claim.[83] When a duty is delegated,

---

77. Schwartz v. Horowitz, 131 F.2d 506 (2d Cir. 1942); Zurcher v. Modern Plastic Mach. Corp., 24 N.J.Super. 158, 93 A.2d 778 (1952), aff'd 12 N.J. 465, 97 A.2d 437 (1953); Prudential Fed. Sav. & Loan Ass'n v. Hartford Acc. & Indem. Co., 7 Utah 2d 366, 325 P.2d 899 (1958); see 4 Corbin § 889; cf. 3 Williston §§ 442–443. See also Terino v. Le Clair, 26 A.D.2d 28, 270 N.Y.S.2d 51 (4th Dep't 1966) (obligor who continued to pay assignor after notice of the partial assignment held liable to the assignee); Geo. V. Clark Co., Inc. v. N. Y., N. H. & H. R. Co., 279 App. Div. 39, 107 N.Y.S.2d 721 (1st Dep't 1951) (specific performance of partial assignment of right to purchase land).

78. Warner v. Seaboard Fin. Co., 75 Nev. 470, 345 P.2d 759 (1959); Restatement, Contracts (2d) § 165(3).

79. Brod v. Cincinnati Time Recorder Co., 82 Ohio App. 26, 77 N.E.2d 293 (1947); Restatement, Contracts (2d) § 165, Comment b.

80. Restatement, Contracts § 175; Restatement Contracts (2d) § 165(1); 4 Corbin § 904; 3 Williston § 445.

81. Restatement, Contracts (2d) § 165(4); cf. § 270 supra.

82. See § 254 supra.

83. See § 256 supra. As we have seen, if the assignment is revocable, voidable, unenforceable or conditional, the assignor often retains some interest in the assigned right. See §§ 259, 268 supra. Also, if the assignment is for security, the assignor merely transfers a security interest.

however, the delegating party continues to remain liable. If this were not so, every solvent person could obtain freedom from his debts by delegating them to an insolvent. Delegation involves the appointment by the obligor of another to render performance on his behalf. It does not free the obligor from his duty to see to it that the performance is rendered.[84] In this context the party making the delegation may be discharged, prior to performance, by a novation; that is, a three party agreement whereby the delegate assumes the duty of the original obligor and this assumption is accepted by the obligee in substitution for the original obligor's liability.[85] It should be carefully noted, however, that not every delegation involves an assumption of duties by the delegate and that an assumption by a delegate is not ordinarily accepted by the obligee in substitution for the obligor's duties.

§ 278. Non-delegable Duties

Just as there are rights which are not assignable, there are duties which are not delegable. Here again the modern law has come a long way from the era when contractual relations were deemed strictly personal. *Delectus Personae* was the Law Latin catch phrase to indicate that a party had a right to choose with whom he would deal. Today, however, the general proposition is that, subject to exceptions, duties are delegable.

A duty is non-delegable where performance by the delegate would vary materially from performance by the obligor.[86] In other words the test is whether performance by the original obligor or under his personal supervision is of the essence of the contract.[87] If the contract was premised on the artistic skill or unique abilities of a party, the duties are not delegable. There is no objective standard by which the performance of the delegate can be determined to be the equivalent of the obligor's if the performance is to paint a portrait,[88] or to

---

84. U.C.C. § 2–210(1) restates the law thus: "No delegation of performance relieves the party delegating of any duty to perform or any liability for breach." See also 3 Williston § 419; Restatement, Contracts § 160(4).

85. Restatement, Contracts (2d) § 150(3), and Comment d thereto.

86. Restatement, Contracts § 160. The rule is stated in U.C.C. § 2–210(1) in the following language: "A party may perform his duty through a delegate . . . unless the other party has a substantial interest in having his orig-

inal promisor perform or control the acts required by the contract." The same formulation is found in the Restatement, Contracts (2d) § 150(2) and § 151(2).

87. Devlin v. Mayor, 63 N.Y. 8 (1875).

88. See Taylor v. Palmer, 31 Cal. 240 (1866) ("All painters do not paint portraits like Sir Joshua Reynolds, nor landscapes by Claude Lorraine, nor do all writers write dramas like Shakespeare or fiction like Dickens. Rare genius and extraordinary skill are not transferable, and contracts for their

produce an entertainment.[89]   Also non-delegable are duties which involve a close personal relationship, such as the duties owed by an attorney to his client [90] or a physician to his patient.[91] An employer may not delegate his duty of supervision where the contract contemplated personal supervision and direction of the employer.[92] "Service," said Mr. Justice Holmes, "is like marriage, which in the old law, was a species of it. It may be repeated, but substitution was unknown." [93]

It is generally held that duties under construction contracts are delegable because it is contemplated that the work will be performed by a person other than the obligor.[94] So too, duties under other contracts calling for mechanical skills which can be tested by objective standards are generally delegable,[95] at least where it is not contemplated that a given individual perform or supervise the work. A seller's duty to deliver goods is also generally delegable.[96]

It is immaterial that the credit of the delegate is less sound than the credit of the delegating party whose liability continues despite the delegation. If, however, one of the duties sought to be delegated is the execution of a promissory note or other instrument of credit, the delegation is ineffective [97] unless the delegate is willing and able to tender cash or the instrument of the delegating party.[98]

employment are therefore personal, and cannot be assigned [correction, delegated].   But rare genius and extraordinary skill are not indispensable to the workmanlike digging down of a sand hill or the filling up of a depression to a given level, or the construction of brick sewers with manholes and covers, and contracts for such work are not personal, and may be assigned [delegated]."

89. Standard Chautauqua System v. Gift, 120 Kan. 101, 242 P. 145 (1926).

90. Corson v. Lewis, 77 Neb. 446, 109 N.W. 735 (1906).

91. Deaton v. Lawson, 40 Wash. 486, 82 P. 879 (1905).

92. Leet v. Jones, 19 La.App. 452, 139 So. 711 (1932); Board of Education v. State Board, 81 N.J.L. 211, 81 A. 163 (1911), aff'd 85 N.J.L. 384, 91 A. 1068 (1913). See § 261 supra where the same situation is discussed with respect to assignment of rights.

93. American Colortype Co. v. Continental Colortype Co., 188 U.S. 104, 107, 23 S.Ct. 265, 47 L.Ed. 404 (1903).

94. New England Iron Co. v. Gilbert El. R. Co., 91 N.Y. 153 (1883). The well known custom of builders to "sub-contract" parts of a building project involves partial delegation of performance. Duties under building contracts were, however, held non-delegable in Swarts v. Narragansett Elec. Lighting Co., 26 R.I. 338, 59 A. 77 (1904), reh. denied 26 R.I. 436, 59 A. 111; Johnson v. Vickers, 139 Wis. 145, 120 N.W. 837 (1909).

95. British Waggon Co. v. Lea & Co., 5 Q.B.D. 149 (1880) (duty to keep railway cars in repair); Devlin v. Mayor, 63 N.Y. 8 (1875) (duty to clean streets).

96. U.C.C. § 2–210(1).

97. E. M. Loew's, Inc. v. Deutschmann, 344 Mass. 765, 184 N.E.2d 55 (1962).

98. Cochran v. Taylor, 273 N.Y. 172, 7 N.E.2d 89 (1937); see § 264 supra.

It has been intimated that the duty of a corporation is always delegable because a corporation necessarily performs by delegation of duties to individuals.[99] This is perhaps too broad a statement. It is easy to conceive of a contract under which the basis of the bargain is the personal performance of particular individuals within the corporate structure and delegation to another corporation or person would be ineffective.[1]

In contrast with rules favoring free alienation of rights which limit the validity of clauses purporting to prohibit assignments, there seems to be no restriction on the parties' ability to provide in their contract that duties shall be non-delegable.[2] Once more it should be recalled that it is common for contract draftsmen to utilize the word "assignment" where "delegation" is meant. Taking notice of this proclivity, the Commercial Code provides: "Unless the circumstances indicate the contrary a prohibition of assignment of 'the contract' is to be construed as barring only the delegation to the assignee of the assignor's performance."[3] Of course delegation of particular duties may also be prohibited by statute or by a rule of public policy.[4]

---

99. New England Iron Co. v. Gilbert El. R. R., 91 N.Y. 153, 167 (1883). To be distinguished are cases where delegation was held improper when coupled with liquidation of the corporation delegating performance. Wetherell Bros. v. United States Steel Co., 200 F.2d 761 (1st Cir. 1952); New York Bank Note Co. v. Hamilton Bank Note Engraving & Printing Co., 180 N.Y. 280, 293, 73 N.E. 48, 52 (1905). In these cases the expectations which the other party to the contract has of obtaining return performance are impaired by the liquidation and the case is quite similar to the situation discussed in § 280 infra where the delegating party repudiates.

1. E. g., a corporation producing motion pictures for a distribution company could not delegate its duties to another corporation if the effect of the delegation is to deprive the other party to the contract of the contemplated performance of given "stars," directors or other key figures within the delegating corporation's structure. An interesting question is posed if X, knowing that A will not deal with him, causes Y to enter into a contract with A and immediately accepts from Y an assignment of Y's rights and a

delegation of his duties. Similar cases have arisen in the law of agency where Y acts as an agent for X without disclosing to A the fact that he is not acting on his own behalf. A split of authority exists in the agency cases. The majority of the decisions deny enforcement, generally regarding the non-disclosure as a kind of misrepresentation. See Mechem, Outlines of the Law of Agency §§ 165–172 (4th ed. 1952); Seavey, Agency § 112 (1964).

2. U.C.C. § 2–210(1); Restatement, Contracts § 160(3) (c); Restatement, Contracts (2d) § 150(1), § 151(1).

3. U.C.C. § 2–210(3); accord, Restatement, Contracts (2d) § 154(a). A similar interpretation was adopted in Arnold Productions, Inc. v. Favorite Films Corp., 298 F.2d 540 (2d Cir. 1962), where however, the clause was even more narrowly construed. It was construed to permit delegation of duties to "franchise holders," provided the delegating party did not "abdicate responsibility" for performance.

4. Restatement, Contracts § 160(3) (b); Restatement, Contracts (2d) § 150(1), § 151(1).

§ 279. Liability of the Delegate

Sometimes the delegate merely has an option to perform and is under no liability for his failure to perform.[5] Often, however, the delegate assumes the duty which has been delegated to him. That is, he has made a promise to the obligor for the benefit of the obligee that he will perform. In such a case the delegate is liable both to his promisee and to the third person who is a third party creditor beneficiary of the delegate's promise.[6] Frequently, however, he may promise to perform in terms which indicate that the promise is for the benefit of the promisee alone. This is the usual interpretation in cases where the delegate is an employee [7] or subcontractor of the obligor; the delegate's liability runs solely to the obligor.[8]

A common question of interpretation arises when a party to a bilateral contract uses general language such as, "I assign this contract to T." Although the question should be treated as a question of interpretation of the transaction in the light of the particular circumstances of the case,[9] it has frequently been treated as if it were governed by the mechanics of stare decisis. Some courts have adhered to the rule that such general phraseology creates merely an assignment of rights,[10] while a more modern view is that the probable intention is to create not only an assignment of rights but also a delegation and assumption of duties.[11] The sales article of the Commercial Code adopts the latter presumption.[12]

5. Restatement, Contracts § 160(2); Restatement, Contracts (2d) § 150, Comment b.

6. Imperial Refining Co. v. Kanotek Refining Co., 29 F.2d 193 (8th Cir. 1928); see § 246 supra.

7. 4 Corbin § 779E.

8. 4 Corbin § 779D.

9. This was admirably done in Chatham Pharmaceuticals, Inc. v. Angier Chemical Co., 347 Mass. 208, 196 N.E. 2d 852 (1964).

10. Loegler v. C. V. Hill & Co., 238 Ala. 606, 193 So. 120 (1940); Meyer v. Droegemueller, 165 Minn. 245, 206 N. W. 391 (1925); State ex rel. Hoyt v. Shain, 338 Mo. 1208, 93 S.W.2d 992 (1936), conformed to 231 Mo.App. 143, 99 S.W.2d 145 (1937); Langel v. Betz, 250 N.Y. 159, 164 N.E. 890 (1928); see generally, Grismore, Is the Assignee of a Contract Liable for the Non-Performance of Delegated Duties?, 18 Mich.L.Rev. 284 (1920), Selected Readings 802; 4 Corbin § 906; 3 Williston § 418A.

11. Art Metal Constr. Co. v. Lehigh Structural Steel Co., 116 F.2d 57 (3d Cir. 1940); [but compare the decision after trial where it was found as a fact that no assumption was intended. 126 F.2d 134 (1941), cert. den. 316 U.S. 694, 62 S.Ct. 1296, 86 L.Ed. 1764]; Restatement, Contracts § 164. The Restatement, Contracts (2d) § 160, which is generally in accord, points out, however, that the overwhelming weight of authority in land contract cases is in accord with Langel v. Betz (see note 10 supra) and therefore it takes no position with respect to land contracts. For a rationalization of an exception for land contracts see Restatement, Contracts (2d) § 160, Comment c.

12. U.C.C. § 2–210(4).

At times the question arises as to whether there has been an implied assumption of a duty by conduct. For example, in Epstein v. Gluckin,[13] the New York Court of Appeals held that the assignee of a right to purchase property who had not assumed the duty at the time of the assignment, assumed it subsequently by bringing an action for specific performance. In a later case the same court held that the purchaser of a building who had taken subject to a lease of air conditioners assumed the obligation by refusing to allow the lessor of the air conditioners to remove them.[14]

§ 280. Effect of Repudiation by Delegating Party

As we have seen, when the delegating party delegates his duty his liability ordinarily continues. But what if he delegates his duty and asserts that he refuses to remain liable? For example, A and B enter into a bilateral contract, B delegates his duty to C who agrees to assume. If B tells A that he regards his liability to be at an end, it is clear that A need not deal with C and may sue B for a total breach at least if B persists in this position.[15] But what if A deals with C? There is substantial authority to the effect that B is making an offer of novation to A which A accepts by dealing with C.[16] Such holdings are unfortunate; they permit the repudiating party to profit from his wrongful act. Unless the obligee in such circumstances actually agrees to release his obligor, no novation should be held to exist. His acceptance of the delegate's proffered performance should merely be construed as a reasonable effort to mitigate damages.[17] The Sales Article of the Commercial Code seems to have adopted a position of this kind. It provides that the obligee may "without prejudice to his rights against the assignor" demand assurances of performance from the assignee.[18]

---

13. 233 N.Y. 490, 135 N.E. 861 (1922).

14. Conditioner Leasing Corp. v. Sternmor Realty Corp., 17 N.Y.2d 1, 266 N. Y.S.2d 801, 213 N.E.2d 884 (1966).

15. Western Oil Sales Corp. v. Bliss & Wetherbee, 299 S.W. 637 (Tex.Com. App.1927). A similar problem arises where the delegating party is a corporation and is dissolved. See § 278 note 99 supra; 4 Corbin § 865. As to the effect of the insolvency of the assignor, see 3 Williston § 420; 6 Williston § 880; U.C.C. § 2-609.

16. 3 Williston § 420; cf. 4 Corbin § 870. The Restatement indicates that the obligee may defeat the occurrence of a novation by notifying either the assignee or assignor that he intends to retain unimpaired his contract rights. Restatement, Contracts § 165; accord, Restatement, Contracts (2d) § 161(2), particularly Comment c; cf. U.C.C. § 1-207.

17. See § 216 supra.

18. U.C.C. § 2-210(5).

§ 281.   Effect of Delegation of a Non-delegable Duty

If an obligor purports to delegate a non-delegable duty it is clear that the obligee need not accept the delegate's performance and if the obligor persists in the attempted delegation he is liable for breach of contract.[19]

If the obligee deals with the delegate he may no longer complain of the delegation and at times it has been concluded that he has entered into a novation,[20] but the better view is that, absent evidence of an intent to enter into a substituted agreement with the delegate, no novation occurs.   There is merely a waiver of the non-delegability of the obligor's duty.[21]

19.   4 Corbin § 865; 3 Williston § 411.

20.   American Colortype Co. v. Continental Colortype Co., 188 U.S. 104, 23 S.Ct. 265, 47 L.Ed. 404 (1903).

21.   Seale v. Bates, 145 Colo. 430, 359 P.2d 356 (1961).

CHAPTER 16

STATUTE OF FRAUDS

Analysis

		Sections
I.	When a Writing is Necessary	282–306
	A. Suretyship Agreements	283–293
	B. Agreements in Consideration of Marriage	294
	C. Agreements for the Sale of Land or of Interests in Land	295–296
	D. Agreements for the Sale of Goods: The Uniform Commercial Code	297
	E. Contracts Not to be Performed Within one Year	298–306
II.	What is a Sufficient Writing or Memorandum and the Effect Thereof	307–318
III.	Restitutionary Remedies	319–325
IV.	Estoppel	326–327

I. WHEN A WRITING IS NECESSARY

Sec.
282. Introduction.

A. SURETYSHIP AGREEMENTS

283. Promise by Executor or Administrator.
284. Promise to Answer for the Debt, Default or Miscarriage of Another.
285. Cases Where There is No Prior Obligation Owing from TP to C to Which D's Promise Relates.
    (a) TP Must Come Under at Least a Voidable Obligation to C.
    (b) There Must be a Principal-Surety Relationship Between TP and D.
    (c) C Must Know or Have Reason to Know of the Principal-Surety Relationship.
    (d) The Promise Must Not be Joint.
    (e) Summary.
286. Cases Where There is a Prior Obligation Owing from TP to C to Which D's Promise Relates.
    (a) Novation.
    (b) Where the Promise to Pay is Made to TP.
    (c) Where the Promise is Made to C but is Co-extensive with D's Obligation to C.
287. The Main Purpose (or Leading Object) Rule.
288. Some Illustrations.
289. The Peculiar New York Rule.
290. Promises of Indemnity.
291. The Promise of the Del Credere Agent.
292. The Promise of the Assignor to His Assignee Guaranteeing Performance by the Obligor.
293. A Promise to Buy a Claim.

B.   AGREEMENTS IN CONSIDERATION OF MARRIAGE

Sec.
294.   When the Statute of Frauds Applies.

C.   AGREEMENTS FOR THE SALE OF LAND OR
INTERESTS IN LAND

295.   Contracts for the Sale of Land.
       (a) Introduction.
       (b) Is a Promise to Pay for an Interest in Real Property Within
           the Statute?
       (c) Interests in Land.
           1.   In General.
           2.   Liens.
           3.   Fructus Industriales.
           4.   Standing Timber, Buildings Attached to the Land and
                Other Things Attached to the Earth Not Included in
                the Concept Fructus Industriales.
           5.   Miscellaneous Items Deemed Not to be Within this Section
                of the Statute of Frauds Relating to Interests in Land.
296.   Performance as Causing a Contract Within the Statute to be En-
       forceable.

D.   AGREEMENTS FOR THE SALE OF GOODS: THE
UNIFORM COMMERCIAL CODE

297.   Contracts for the Sale of Goods.
       (a) Introduction.
       (b) Price or Value.
       (c) Goods.
       (d) Choses in Action.
       (e) Part Performance.
           1.   Accept and Receive.
           2.   Payment or Earnest.
       (f) Admission in Court.

E.   CONTRACTS NOT TO BE PERFORMED WITHIN ONE YEAR

298.   Computation of the One Year Period.
299.   Possibility of Performance Within One Year.
300.   Promises Performable Within One Year but Conditional Upon an
       Uncertain Event.
301.   A Promise of Extended Performance that Comes to an End Upon
       the Happening of a Condition that May Occur Within a Year.
302.   Contracts for Alternative Performances and Contracts with Option
       to Terminate, Renew or Extend.
303.   Is a Promise or a Contract Within the One Year Section of the
       Statute of Frauds?
304.   Effect of Performance Under the One Year Section.
305.   Unilateral Contracts.
306.   Relationship of the One Year Provision with Other Subdivisions of
       the Statute.

II. WHAT IS A SUFFICIENT WRITING OR MEMORANDUM AND THE EFFECT THEREOF

Sec.
307. Introduction.
308. Parol Evidence and the Memorandum.
309. The Contents of the Memorandum.
310. The Form of the Contract and When It is to be Prepared—Necessity for Delivery.
311. Signed by the Party to be Charged.
312. Problems Presented When the Memorandum is Contained in More Than One Writing.
313. The Memorandum Under U.C.C. § 2–201—The Sale of Goods Section.
314. Is the Oral Contract Which Does Not Comply with the Statute "Unenforceable" or "Void"?
315. Effect of Part of a Contract being Unenforceable Because of the Statute.
316. Oral Rescission or Variation of a Contract Within the Statute.
317. To What Extent May an Oral Contract Which is Not Enforceable Because of the Statute of Frauds be Used as a Defense?
318. Some Miscellaneous Rules.

III. RESTITUTIONARY REMEDIES

319. Introduction.
320. The Plaintiff Must Not be in Default.
321. Effect of Defendant's Restoration of the Status Quo.
322. Restitution Denied Where Policy of the Statute Would be Thwarted.
323. Measure of Recovery.
324. The Contract Price as Evidence of Value: Contrast Between Damages and Restitution.
325. Specific Restitution in Equity.

IV. ESTOPPEL

326. Equitable Estoppel and the Statute of Frauds.
327. Promissory Estoppel.

I. WHEN A WRITING IS NECESSARY

Analysis

Sec.
282. Introduction.

A. SURETYSHIP AGREEMENTS

283. Promise by Executor or Administrator.
284. Promise to Answer for the Debt, Default or Miscarriage of Another.

Sec.

285. Cases Where There is No Prior Obligation Owing from TP to C to Which D's Promise Relates.
    (a) TP Must Come Under at Least a Voidable Obligation to C.
    (b) There Must be a Principal-Surety Relationship Between TP and D.
    (c) C Must Know or Have Reason to Know of the Principal-Surety Relationship.
    (d) The Promise Must Not be Joint.
    (e) Summary.

286. Cases Where There is a Prior Obligation Owing from TP to C to Which D's Promise Relates.
    (a) Novation.
    (b) Where the Promise to Pay is Made to TP.
    (c) Where the Promise is Made to C but is Co-extensive With D's Obligation to C.

287. The Main Purpose (or Leading Object) Rule.

288. Some Illustrations.

289. The Peculiar New York Rule.

290. Promises of Indemnity.

291. The Promise of the Del Credere Agent.

292. The Promise of the Assignor to His Assignee Guaranteeing Performance by the Obligor.

293. A Promise to Buy a Claim.

B. AGREEMENTS IN CONSIDERATION OF MARRIAGE

294. When the Statute of Frauds Applies.

C. AGREEMENTS FOR THE SALE OF LAND OR OF INTERESTS IN LAND

295. Contracts for the Sale of Land.
    (a) Introduction.
    (b) Is a Promise to Pay for an Interest in Real Property Within the Statute?
    (c) Interests in Land.
        1. In General.
        2. Liens.
        3. Fructus Industriales.
        4. Standing Timber, Buildings Attached to the Land and Other Things Attached to the Earth Not Included in the Concept Fructus Industriales.
        5. Miscellaneous Items Deemed Not to be Within this Section of the Statute of Frauds Relating to Interests in Land.

296. Performance as Causing a Contract Within the Statute to be Enforceable.

D. AGREEMENTS FOR THE SALE OF GOODS: THE
UNIFORM COMMERCIAL CODE

Sec.

297. Contracts for the Sale of Goods.
    (a) Introduction.
    (b) Price or Value.
    (c) Goods.
    (d) Choses in Action.
    (e) Part Performance.
        1. Accept and Receive.
        2. Payment or Earnest.
    (f) Admission in Court.

E. CONTRACTS NOT TO BE PERFORMED WITHIN ONE YEAR

298. Computation of the One Year Period.
299. Possibility of Performance Within One Year.
300. Promises Performable Within One Year but Conditional Upon an Uncertain Event.
301. A Promise of Extended Performance that Comes to an End Upon the Happening of a Condition that May Occur Within a Year.
302. Contracts for Alternative Performances and Contracts with Option to Terminate, Renew or Extend.
303. Is a Promise or a Contract Within the One Year Section of the Statute of Frauds?
304. Effect of Performance Under the One Year Section.
305. Unilateral Contracts.
306. Relationship of the One Year Provision to Other Subdivisions of the Statute.

§ 282. Introduction

At early common law, oral promises were generally not enforced by the king's courts, but this changed with the advent and gradual expansion of the writ of assumpsit.[1] When oral promises became enforceable perjury and subornation of perjury appear to have become commonplace.[2] In 1677 Parliament enacted an Act for the Prevention of Fraud and Perjuries.[3] This Statute contained twenty-five sections which dealt with conveyances, wills, trusts, judgment and execution in addition to contracts.

Only two sections, the fourth and the seventeenth are important for contract purposes. These sections read as follows:

"Sec. 4. And be it further enacted by the authority aforesaid, That from and after the said four and twentieth

---

1. 2 Corbin § 275.

2. See 6 Holdsworth, A History of English Law 379–97 (1927).

3. 29 Car. II, c. 3, 8 St. at Large 405.

day of June no action shall be brought [(1)] whereby to charge any executor or administrator upon any special promise, to answer damages out of his own estate; (2) or whereby to charge the defendant upon any special promise to answer for the debt, default, or miscarriage of another person; (3) or to charge any person upon any agreement made upon consideration of marriage; (4) or upon any contract or sale of lands, tenements or hereditaments, or any interest in or concerning them; (5) or upon any agreement that is not to be performed within the space of one year from the making thereof; (6) unless the agreement upon which such action shall be brought, or some memorandum or note thereof, shall be in writing, and signed by the party to be charged therewith, or some other person thereunto by him lawfully authorized.

"Sec. 17. And be it further enacted by the authority aforesaid, That from and after the said four and twentieth day of June no contract for the sale of any goods, wares and merchandizes, for the price of ten pounds sterling or upwards, shall be allowed to be good, except the buyer shall accept part of the goods so sold, and actually receive the same, or give something in earnest to bind the bargain, or in part of payment, or that some note or memorandum in writing of the said bargain be made and signed by the parties to be charged by such contract, or their agents thereunto lawfully authorized."

While the writing requirements are imposed in large part to obviate perjury, it is clear that other policy bases for the requirement exist. An agreement reduced to writing promotes certainty; false testimony stems from faulty recollection as well as from faulty morals. In addition, the required formality of a writing "promotes deliberation, seriousness, . . . and shows that the act was a genuine act of volition." [4] While all will agree that to a lesser or greater extent these are desirable goals, it is obvious that the carrying out of these goals may well frustrate honesty and fair dealing. As with the case of a strict application of the parol evidence rule, the quest for certainty and deliberation involves the exclusion of evidence of what the parties may have actually agreed upon. Oral agreements are made and are performed. If the oral agreement is within the Statute of Frauds and the Statute is enforced with vigor, the

---

4. Rabel, The Statute of Frauds and Comparative Legal History, 63 L.Q. Rev. 174, 178 (1947).

expectations of the person who had performed would be frustrated and the person who had breached the oral agreement would be unjustly enriched. If such were the result, the Statute would encourage fraud and sanction unethical conduct.

The ability of the Statute to cause injustice has had a strong impact on judicial decisions. Often the courts have viewed the Statute with disfavor and have tended to give it a narrow construction as to the kinds of contracts covered. In addition, they have developed devices for "taking the contract outside" the Statute. Finally, a variety of legal and equitable remedies have been forged to grant relief to a party who has performed an oral agreement within the statutory terms. Other courts have tended to view the basic policy of the Statute as sound and have given it a broad construction. It is not surprising that the decisions rendered throughout its almost 300 year history are not entirely harmonious. In 1954 the British Parliament repealed all but two provisions of the Statute; [5] similar repeal in the United States is, however, not considered likely within the foreseeable future.

Indeed, in the United States the policy of requiring a writing has been extended by legislation to other areas. For example, as we have seen, in most states a promise to pay a debt discharged in bankruptcy must be in writing, and in some states this is also true of a promise which has the effect of extending the statute of limitations.[6] However, the discussion here will be limited to the provisions contained in the original Statute because these provisions have been substantially re-enacted by most of the states. There are variations in wording and interpretation, some of which will be noted as we proceed.

A. SURETYSHIP AGREEMENTS

§ 283. Promise by Executor or Administrator

A promise by an administrator or executor "to answer damages out of his own estate" is within the Statute of Frauds.[7] The clause

---

5. 2 & 3 Eliz. II, c. 34. The two provisions retained relate to contracts for the sale of land and promises to answer for the debt, default or miscarriage of another.

6. This goes back to Lord Tenterden's Act, 9 Geo. IV, c. 14, enacted in England in 1829. See §§ 84–85 supra. Other areas to which the policy of the Statute has often been extended by legislation include contracts to leave property by will; contracts to pay a real estate broker his commission; and a promise to pay a debt contracted during infancy. See also Restatement, Contracts (2d), statutory note to ch. 8.

7. The term "contract within the Statute of Frauds" means that it is covered by the Statute and therefore is

is somewhat unclear because it does not state what or whose damages the executor or administrator is promising to pay. The cases have made it clear, however, that the Statute applies only where the executor or administrator promises to pay out of his own property a debt of the deceased.[8] It does not apply to promises to pay debts of the deceased out of the assets of the estate.[9]

Since this is the accepted view of the meaning of this section it is clear that this provision is merely a particular application of the second subdivision relating to promises to answer for the debt, default or miscarriage of another and that what is said with reference to that subdivision will also be applicable here.[10]

§ 284. Promises to Answer for the Debt, Default or Miscarriage of Another [11]

The task here is to determine which oral promises contravene this section of the Statute, and which promises are not condemned by the Statute even though they are oral. When a promise contravenes this section because it is not in writing, it is said to be collateral; when it does not, it is called original. These words are generally used to express a result and do not help in ascertaining which promises are enforceable.[12]

It is apparent from the wording of the section that almost all of the factual situations governed by it will be tripartite. One party has made the promise and now pleads the Statute as a defense. We will refer to him as the promisor, and since he is invariably the defendant in these cases, by the letter D. The person to whom the promise is made we will refer to as the creditor (C). Invariably he will be the plaintiff in the action. The person for whom the promisor promises we shall refer to as the third party (TP).[13]

---

not enforceable unless it is in a satisfactory writing or unless it is enforceable for some other reason despite the absence of such writing.

8. Bellows v. Sowles, 57 Vt. 164 (1884).

9. Piper v. Goodwin, 23 Me. 251 (1843); Norton v. Edwards, 66 N.C. 367 (1872).

10. Bellows v. Sowles, 57 Vt. 164 (1884); 2 Corbin § 346, Restatement, Contracts (2d) § 179.

11. Much of this discussion is based upon Calamari, The Suretyship Stat-

ute of Frauds, 27 Ford.L.Rev. 332 (1958).

12. 3 Williston § 463. "If the terms are of any service, they can be so only as terms descriptive of a result arrived at on grounds quite independent of the terms themselves." 2 Corbin § 348.

13. This terminology is used rather than P (principal) and S (surety) to minimize the possibility of begging the question by assuming that one of the parties is the principal and another the surety. Compare 2 Corbin § 353.

At the outset a distinction must be drawn between cases where there is no prior obligation owed by the third party (TP) to the creditor (C) to which D's promise relates, and cases where there is such a prior obligation.[14] This distinction is of extreme importance, since, as we shall see, there are different rules governing the two situations. We shall discuss first the cases where there is no prior obligation.

§ 285. Cases Where There is No Prior Obligation Owing from TP to C to Which D's Promise Relates

An illustration will serve to bring this category of cases into focus. D says to C, "Deliver these goods to TP and I will see that you are paid." C delivers the goods. Is D's promise enforceable? This depends upon the answers to a number of questions, some contract, some suretyship. Some of these questions will now be explored.

(a) TP Must Come Under at Least a Voidable Obligation to C

It is frequently said and apparently is the law,[15] that D's promise can be collateral only where TP eventually [16] comes under an obligation to C. If TP does not come under an obligation to C, it is reasoned that the promise must be original because in that case D is not promising to pay the debt of another, there being no other debt. It would appear, then, that the first inquiry which must be made is whether TP eventually came under at least a voidable obligation to C.[17]

In the illustration given, did TP come under any such obligation to C? The first requisite for any contract is that the offeror manifest a contractual state of mind,[18] and this is true in determining whether TP came under obligation to C in the illustration given.[19] This explains why the courts place so much emphasis on the question

---

14. 3 Williston § 462; 2 Corbin § 350. The word obligation is here used to include all duties recognized by law, whether contractual or not. Restatement, Contracts (2d) § 180, Comment b.

15. See 3 Williston § 454; Simpson, Suretyship 122–27 (1950).

16. Of course it is arguable that D's promise has to be original since at the time he makes his promise there is no obligation owing from TP to C. This contention was rejected in the early case of Jones v. Cooper, 1 Cowp. 228, 98 Eng.Rep. 1058 (K.B. 1774). See 2

Williston § 461 (rev. ed. 1936); 2 Corbin § 350.

17. This means that for the purposes of this rule a voidable obligation is an obligation, but that a void obligation is not. 3 Williston § 454; Simpson, Suretyship 126–27 (1950); 2 Corbin § 356.

18. 1 Williston §§ 22–27.

19. In the illustration given, although D is the offeror in relation to C, C may be and usually is an offeror in relation to TP.

of whether C extended credit to TP,[20] for this is merely another way of inquiring whether C manifested an intention to contract with TP. Charging TP as a debtor upon C's books is strong evidence that credit was extended to TP [21] but is not conclusive.[22] The question is ordinarily one of fact.[23]

If C has extended credit to TP, obviously the only remaining question to determine whether TP came under an obligation to C is to ascertain whether TP accepted C's offer.[24] In many of the reported cases [25] there is no discussion of what transpired after D made his promise to C. In such a case, however, whether TP accepted C's offer must be determined under the rules relating to acceptance by silence or exercise of dominion, as well as other forms of manifestation of assent by conduct.[26]

An instructive case on the question of acceptance is Mease v. Wagner.[27] The defendant (D), a friend of the deceased, Mrs. Bradley, told the plaintiff (C), an undertaker, to bury Mrs. Bradley in a certain manner and to charge the estate of Dr. Bradley (TP) (the husband of Mrs. Bradley who had predeceased her) or a certain nephew (also TP) of Mrs. Bradley and "if they don't pay I will." It may be assumed that the plaintiff extended credit to the estate of Dr. Bradley and to the nephew. However the estate of Dr. Bradley never became liable because it did nothing to manifest an acceptance and would not otherwise be liable.[28] Although the nephew promised to pay after the services were rendered, he never became liable be-

---

20. For example, this is true of all of the cases in Simpson, Cases on Suretyship (1942) which deal with this phase of the problem.

21. Wood v. Dodge, 23 S.D. 95, 120 N. W. 774 (1909); Simpson, Suretyship 124 (1950).

22. Hammond Coal Co. v. Lewis, 248 Mass. 499, 143 N.E. 309 (1924); Annot., 99 A.L.R. 79, 83 (1935).

23. Lawrence v. Anderson, 108 Vt. 176, 184 A. 689 (1936); Burdick, Suretyship and the Statute of Frauds, 20 Colum.L.Rev. 153, 155 (1920). "The existence or non-existence of a duty in the third person to pay for the goods or service is a mixed question of law and fact; but in most cases the facts that determine that duty are sufficiently in doubt to make this mixed issue a question for the jury." 2 Corbin § 352.

24. Of course TP might have some defense which would make the agreement void or voidable but this has already been considered. See note 17 supra.

25. For example, this is true of all of the cases in Simpson, Cases on Suretyship 1–10 (1942) which deal with this problem.

26. See Restatement, Contracts §§ 72–73 (1932). See § 15 supra.

27. 1 McCord (S.C.) 395 (1821).

28. The estate of a deceased husband is not ordinarily liable even for the necessaries of a wife. His death, generally speaking, terminates his duty to support. Wilson v. Hinman, 182 N.Y. 408, 75 N.E. 236 (1905).

cause of the familiar doctrine that past consideration is not consideration.[29]

The court concluded that since neither the estate of Dr. Bradley nor the nephew came under an obligation to the plaintiff the promise of the defendant had to be original and therefore was enforceable notwithstanding the absence of a writing. The court did not consider whether the estate of Mrs. Bradley became liable.[30] The theory was that it is "settled doctrine that when no action will lie against the party undertaken for, it is an orignal (sic) promise."[31] Here the third parties were the estate of Dr. Bradley and the nephew. Since they did not come under an obligation the promise is original,[32] irrespective of whether the estate of Mrs. Bradley became liable. In a word, for the purpose of the Statute of Frauds,[33] TP is the person for whom the defendant undertakes.

To summarize: In the category of cases under discussion, the courts reason that if TP does not come under an obligation (at least voidable) to C, the promise is original. If TP does come under obligation, *so far as we know now,*[34] the promise is collateral.[35]

There is another contract question which must be considered. It can perhaps best be introduced by a simple illustration. D says to C, "Deliver these goods to TP and, provided you extend credit to TP, I will pay if he does not." Assume that the goods are delivered to TP but that C extends no credit to TP. Is D liable to C?

It is clear under the rules previously considered that D's promise is original because TP never came under an obligation to C. Yet this question can only be of academic interest. D should not be liable to C since, in failing to extend credit to TP, C has not accepted D's

---

29. See 1 Williston § 142 (rev. ed. 1936).

30. Under long established principles of quasi contract the estate of a decedent is liable for burial expenses. Cape Girardeau Bell Tel. Co. v. Hamil, 160 Mo.App. 521, 140 S.W. 951 (1911); Annot., 35 A.L.R.2d 1399 (1954), 82 A.L.R.2d 873 (1962). This liability would exist even if the undertaker did not specifically intend to charge her estate but only whomever proved ultimately responsible. Restatement, Restitution § 113, Comment e.

31. Mease v. Wagner, 1 McCord (S.C.) 395, 396 (1821).

32. Simpson, Suretyship 125 (1950).

33. On the assumptions made, the defendant would be a non-consensual surety in relation to the estate of Mrs. Bradley. Matthews v. Aikin, 1 N.Y. 595 (1848); Campbell, Non-Consensual Suretyship, 45 Yale L.J. 69 (1935).

34. The emphasized words are meant to indicate that although TP comes under an obligation to C, the promise, due to factors discussed below, may still be original.

35. Drummond v. Pillsbury, 130 Me. 406, 156 A. 806 (1931); Wood v. Dodge, 23 S.D. 95, 120 N.W. 774 (1909).

offer. In the logical order, of course, this question should be considered before adverting to whether the promise is original or collateral, for if there is no contract between C and D the question of whether the promise is original or collateral under the Statute of Frauds can only be of academic interest.

This simple illustration makes it clear that in every case it is important to determine whether C has accepted D's offer and performed.[36] Some authorities do not emphasize this in the least and seem to imply that C in every case is free to extend or not extend credit as he sees fit.[37] The better view, however, is that in the ordinary case whether D has insisted as a condition precedent to his liability that credit be extended to TP or that TP come under an obligation to C is a question of interpretation and very often a jury question.[38]

In summary, the first inquiry to be made in this type of case [39] is whether TP eventually comes under an obligation to C. If he does not, the promise is original. If he does, the promise is collateral unless it is rendered original for one of the reasons now to be discussed.

(b) There Must be a Principal-Surety Relationship Between TP and D

Even though TP comes under an obligation to C, D's promise will still be original if there is not a principal-surety relationship [40] be-

---

36. 3 Williston § 454.

37. Simpson, Suretyship 125 (1950) seems to imply this:
"Nevertheless, the form of the promise has its bearing on presumptions which obtain where there is lack of evidence to refute them. If C sues S [D in this discussion] on an oral promise, 'Deliver the goods to P [TP] and I will pay for them,' proof of the promise and the delivery of the goods will entitle C to a judgment in absence of evidence that P [TP] also was obligated to C. On the other hand, if C sues S [D] on a promise alleged to be in form 'Deliver goods to P [TP] and if he does not pay for them, I will,' S's [D's] promise is in form collateral to an apparent obligation on the part of P [TP]. The burden will then be upon the plaintiff [C], where faced with the defense of the statute of frauds, to rebut the presumption of a collateral promise by showing affirmatively that S's [D's] promise was in substance original because no obliga-

tion was ever assumed by P [TP] nor was any credit extended to him." Cf. 2 Corbin § 353.

38. Duca v. Lord, 331 Mass. 51, 117 N. E.2d 145 (1954); Simpson Suretyship 273–77 (1950); 3 Williston § 454.

39. One where TP is not under a prior obligation to C to which D's promise relates at the time D makes his promise to C.

40. Restatement, Contracts (2d) § 180; Restatement, Security § 82 (1941) defines suretyship as follows: "Suretyship is the relation which exists where one person has undertaken an obligation and another person is also under an obligation or other duty to the obligee, who is entitled to but one performance, and as between the two who are bound, one rather than the other should perform." This is a good working definition since it points out that the essence of suretyship is that, even though the plaintiff (C)

tween TP and D.[41] To illustrate, assume that TP makes a purchase
from C and at the same time [42] D guarantees payment and credit is
extended to TP who becomes obligated. Under the rules thus far
considered D's promise would be collateral. But if it were established
thta TP was acting as D's agent in this transaction, would D's promise be collateral? The answer is in the negative.[43] As pointed out
above, for D's promise to be collateral there must not only be an obligation on the part of TP [44] but there must also be a principal-surety
relationship between TP and C. Here that relationship does not exist.[45]

(c) C Must Know or Have Reason to Know of the Principal-Surety Relationship

Even if TP comes under an obligation to C and there is in fact
a principal-surety relationship between TP and D, D's promise will
still be original if C does not know or have reason to know of the relationship.[46] One illustration will suffice.[47] When goods are being

may recover from D, D may in turn
recover from TP. Whether this definition includes an indemnitor shall be
discussed infra at § 290.

41. "The promisor and the third person
must both be under obligation to the
promisee, either for the very same
performance or for different performances either one of which will discharge both duties, in order to be a
case within the statute. If the performances promised by the two persons are different and full performance by either of them would not discharge the other, neither one is a
surety and the statute does not apply."
2 Corbin § 349. "But a promise
the performance of which will not operate as a discharge of the debt either
in whole or in part is not within the
statute." Id. § 364; Restatement,
Contracts (2d) § 180, Comment d.

42. This case is still within the first
category, for if TP and D became
bound at the same time, there was no
prior obligation on the part of TP to
C at the time that D made his promise.

43. Lesser-Goldman Cotton Co. v. Merchants' & Planters' Bank, 182 Ark.
150, 30 S.W.2d 215 (1930); cf. Bartolatta v. Calvo, 112 Conn. 385, 152 A.
306 (1930).

44. Here, under the assumption made,
TP would be liable to C as an agent
who has not disclosed his principal.
Ferson, Principles of Agency § 170
(1954).

45. TP is the agent and D is the principal. Though it is probably true that
as between the two, D should ultimately pay [Thomas J. Nolan, Inc. v.
Martin & William Smith, Inc., 193
Misc. 877, 85 N.Y.S.2d 380 (New York
City Mun.Ct.), aff'd 195 Misc. 50, 85
N.Y.S.2d 387 (App.T.1949)], so that
there may be additionally a principal
and surety relationship under the Restatement definition, still the relationship between TP and D is not principal and surety but surety and principal. When the rule states that there
must be a principal-surety relation between TP and D it means that TP
must be the principal and D the surety and not vice versa.

46. Restatement, Contracts (2d) § 180;
3 Williston § 475; 2 Corbin § 362.

47. Restatement, Contracts § 180, ill. 11
(1932); compare with the cases discussed in 2 Corbin § 355 (1950), particularly Colbath v. Everett D. Clark
Seed Co., 112 Me. 277, 91 A. 1007
(1914).

purchased from C, D promises to pay and TP states he will guarantee D's payment. C is informed that the goods are to be delivered to D. As a matter of fact the arrangement between TP and D is that D shall turn the goods over to TP and this is done. Credit is extended to both. Though TP came under an obligation to C [48] and there is a principal-surety relationship between TP and D,[49] D's promise is still original because C did not know or have reason to know of the principal-surety relationship between TP and D.[50] In the illustration, TP would also be liable to C.[51]

(d) The Promise Must Not be Joint

By the great weight of authority,[52] even though TP comes under an obligation to C and there is a principal-surety relationship between TP and D and C knows of this relationship, D's promise is still original if his promise and TP's promise are joint.[53] The theory of these cases is that since the promise is joint there is only one obligation (a joint one) and that, therefore, the obligation *in toto* must be original.[54] The rule does not apply where the obligation is joint and several because in such a case more than one obligation results.[55]

---

48. TP is the principal debtor and so does not have the defense of Statute of Frauds. See note 50 infra.

49. TP is the principal debtor because the goods came to him and as between him and D he should ultimately pay.

50. C knows that there is a principal-surety relationship but he thinks TP is the surety and that the defendant (D) is the principal. The rule means that before the promise of the defendant (D) can be collateral, the creditor must know, or have reason to know, that the defendant (D) is the surety. This is only fair, otherwise the creditor, even if he knew of the Statute of Frauds, might not require a writing. This result is at times explained by saying that the sale to D makes him the principal, "[a]nd ordinarily it makes no difference what he did with the goods after conveyance to him; he may have destroyed, sold, or given them away, yet he remains a debtor notwithstanding." 2 Corbin § 355. This is undoubtedly what the author of the Restatement of Contracts means when, after giving the illustration he states that D's promise is not subject to the Statute of Frauds, "since the duty to pay is in truth his." Restatement, Contracts § 180, ill. 11 (1932); see also id., ill. 10.

51. He is in fact the principal debtor and so is promising only to pay his own debt.

52. Boyce v. Murphy, 91 Ind. 1 (1883); 2 Corbin § 361; 2 Williston § 466 (rev. ed. 1936); Restatement, Contracts § 181 (1932).

53. The rules which establish when a promise is joint, joint and several, or several, are discussed in 4 Corbin §§ 923–42; 2 Williston §§ 316–46; § 329 infra.

54. "If they say 'we promise' or 'we jointly promise,' they are said to be joint promisors and the technical rules of joint contracts are applicable. In such a case there is a fiction that there is only one promise made, even though there are several persons who at different times go through the factual process of promising. This one promise is supposed to create an indivisible 'obligation' . . . ." 2 Corbin § 361. The joint nature of the promise does not prevent a surety relationship from arising. Simpson, Contracts §§ 98–105 (1954). On the question of joint and joint several obligations, see § 329 infra.

55. Simpson, Suretyship 132 (1950).

(e) Summary

From what has been said it is concluded that where there is no prior obligation on the part of TP to C at the time that D's promise is made, the promise will be original unless all of the following conditions concur:

1.   TP comes under an obligation at least voidable to C.

2.   There is a principal-surety relationship between TP and D.

3.   C knows or has reason to know of the principal-surety relationship between TP and D.

4.   The promise is not joint (in jurisdictions which posit this requirement).

5.   The main purpose rule is not satisfied.

If all of these conditions concur the promise is collateral; otherwise it is original. The main purpose rule will not be discussed here but will be discussed in § 287 infra.

§ 286.   Cases Where There is a Prior Obligation Owing from TP to C to Which D's Promise Relates

In the previous section consideration was directed to the cases where there is no obligation owing from TP to C at the time that D makes his promise. Here the rules covering the situation where TP is obligated to C at that time shall be discussed.

It is readily apparent that the words of the Statute clearly apply to such a situation. It is not surprising, therefore, to find that where TP is obligated to C at the time of D's promise, the promise will be held to be collateral [56] and therefore subject to the requirement of a writing, unless it falls within one of a number of recognized exceptions to the Statute which will now be discussed.

(a) Novation

The first exception which is universally recognized arises where there is a novation.[57] This is so whether the novation be denominated legal or equitable.[58] A practical reason for the exception is that if the

---

56. Colpitts v. L. C. Fisher Co., 289 Mass. 232, 193 N.E. 833 (1935); 2 Corbin § 350; 3 Williston § 469.

57. Hill v. Grat, 247 Mass. 25, 141 N.E. 593 (1923); Annot., 74 A.L.R. 1025 (1931); 2 Corbin § 365.

58. 2 Williston § 477.

promise of D causes TP's obligation to be discharged and if D's promise were held to be collateral, C would be in the unfortunate position of being unable to collect the obligation from either TP or D. The legal reason usually given is that advanced by Lord Mansfield in Anstey v. Marden,[59] wherein he states, "I did not see how one person could undertake for the debt of another, when the debt, for which he was supposed to undertake, was discharged by the very bargain."[60]

(b) Where the Promise to Pay is Made to TP

The second exception arises where D makes his promise to TP rather than to C.[61] A typical illustration is the situation where the assuming grantee (D) promises the grantor (TP) that he will pay a mortgage debt according to its terms to the mortgagee (C). In that case, C may ordinarily enforce D's promise made to TP under the theory of third party beneficiary [62] or, in some jurisdictions, under the theory of equitable subrogation.[63] The Statute of Frauds provision under discussion is not a defense to D.[64] The best reason given as to why this should be is that as a result of the promise D becomes the principal debtor and is, therefore, merely promising to pay his own debt.[65]

(c) Where the Promise is Made to C but is Co-Extensive with D's Obligation to C

The question then arises as to what extent a promise made by D to C, after D's promise to TP, is enforceable. Assume a situation in which C is an employee of TP under a hiring at will. TP owes C wages of $1000. TP enters into an agreement with D whereby TP agrees to turn the business over to D in consideration *inter alia* of D's promise to pay TP's obligation to C. As we have seen, D's promise made to TP to pay C is enforceable by C.

But suppose that one week later D personally promises C to pay him. Is this promise enforceable? So far as the Statute of Frauds is concerned the promise is original. Since D is already the principal debtor [66] he is merely promising to pay his own debt. The courts

---

59. 1 Bos. & Pul. (N.R.) 124, 127 Eng. Rep. 406 (C.P.1804).

60. Id. at 131, 127 Eng.Rep. at 409.

61. People's State Sav. Bank v. Cross, 197 Iowa 750, 198 N.W. 70 (1924); 3 Williston § 460; 2 Corbin § 357.

62. Osborne, Mortgages § 261 (1951); see § 246 supra.

63. Id. § 262.

64. In some states a promise to assume a mortgage must be in writing because of a different statute. See, e. g., N.Y.Gen.Obligations Law § 5–705.

65. Aldrich v. Ames, 75 Mass. (9 Gray) 76 (1857); Restatement, Security § 100, Comment a (1941).

66. This is a result of his promise made to TP. See text at note 60 supra. For the same reason, where one

do not usually consider whether there is consideration for D's promise, but this is a situation where his promise is enforceable without consideration.[67]

Suppose in the illustration given that D's promise to TP was that he would pay TP's debt to C out of profits and that D makes the same promise to C later. Both of these promises are enforceable despite the absence of a writing.[68]

Suppose further in the illustration given that when D makes his promise to TP, he promises to pay C out of proceeds. Subsequently, D says to C, "If you agree to continue the work that you were doing for TP for six months, I promise to pay you $100 per week and to pay TP's debt to you after one month." [69] There is consideration for D's promises.[70] Is the promise to pay TP's debt after one month original? If not, is the other promise to pay $100 per week enforceable, or must both promises stand or fall together? The answers to these questions depend to a great extent upon the so-called main purpose rule which is discussed in the next section.

§ 287.   The Main Purpose (or Leading Object) Rule

The main purpose rule may be stated in substance as follows: "Where the party promising has for his object a benefit which he did not enjoy before his promise, which benefit accrues immediately to himself, his promise is original, whether made before, after or at the time of the promise of the third party, notwithstanding that the effect is to promise to pay or discharge the debt of another." [71]

It should be noted that the main purpose rule applies whether there was or was not a prior obligation owing from TP to C to which the promise relates.[72]

of several co-partners promises personally to pay the whole debt of the partnership, the promise is not within the Statute of Frauds. For this and other cases where this principle applies, see 2 Corbin § 391.

67. 1 Williston §§ 143–44. "[A]nd since it is based upon, and coextensive with, an already existing, legally enforceable duty, it would be held to have a sufficient consideration and to be enforceable as a contract." 2 Corbin § 363; see § 80 supra.

68. As pointed out above, when D makes his promise to TP he becomes the principal, and so when he makes the same promise to C he is merely promising to pay his own debt. Con-

tra, Ackley v. Parmenter, 98 N.Y. 425 (1885). Cases where TP has not consented to D's promise to pay from property of TP under D's control have not been uniform. See 2 Corbin § 363.

69. These facts are suggested by the facts in the case of Belknap v. Bender, 75 N.Y. 446 (1878).

70. Though there may be other reasons why there is consideration, it is clear that C, in promising to work six months when the original hiring by TP was at will, is suffering detriment.

71. Nelson v. Boynton, 44 Mass. (3 Met) 396 (1841).

72. See § 286 supra.

It is also clear that two elements are necessary to cause the main purpose rule to apply (a) there must be consideration for D's promise and (b) the consideration must be beneficial to him. The benefit to be obtained has been described by adjectives such as personal, immediate, pecuniary and direct.[73]

It is obvious that this rule involves difficult distinctions as to the degree of benefit and as to purpose and motive so that no extended discussion of these matters is possible here.[74] However a few typical situations will be discussed in the next section.

§ 288. Some Illustrations

If TP is indebted to C and C has a lien upon TP's property and D promises to pay the debt in order to discharge the lien of the property does the main purpose rule apply? The answer is that it depends upon whether D has some interest to protect as would be the case where he had taken subject to a mortgage.[75] It is otherwise however if the lien surrendered is upon property in which D has no interest to protect as, for example, where he is a first mortgagee and has no other reason to pay the second mortgage.[76]

Another common situation involving the main purpose rule occurs when a stockholder of a corporation makes a promise to a creditor of the corporation which induces action which is at least indirectly beneficial to the stockholder. For example, in one case [77] defendant was a substantial stockholder in a particular corporation and the plaintiff, a creditor, had been furnishing merchandise to the corporation which had not paid its bills. Defendant thereupon promised to be responsible for these bills and for future deliveries if the plaintiff would continue to supply the corporation which plaintiff did. The court held that the main purpose rule did not apply because stock ownership is too indirect and remote to satisfy the main purpose rule. This is the generally accepted view.[78] Where the defendant was the sole stockholder, the cases are not in harmony but it

---

73. Hurst Hardware Co. v. Goodman, 68 W.Va. 462, 69 S.E. 898 (1910). Restatement, Contracts (2d) § 184 states the rule in terms of whether the promisor desires his own "economic advantage."

74. See 2 Corbin §§ 366–372.

75. Kahn v. Waldman, 283 Mass. 391, 186 N.E. 587, 88 A.L.R. 699 (1933).

76. Griffin v. Hoag, 105 Iowa 499, 75 N.W. 372 (1898).

77. Hurst Hardware Co. v. Goodman, 68 W.Va. 462, 69 S.E. 898 (1910).

78. Richardson Press v. Albright, 224 N.Y. 497, 121 N.E. 362, 8 A.L.R. 1195 (1918); Mid-Atlantic Appliances, Inc. v. Morgan, 194 Va. 324, 73 S.E.2d 385, 35 A.L.R.2d 899 (1952).

would appear that the better view is that the main purpose rule should apply.[79]

A number of cases have arisen where D, the owner of unimproved realty, employs TP, a general contractor, to build a house for D on the latter's land. TP orders material from C who makes deliveries for which TP fails to pay. C tells TP that he will not fill further orders but subsequently agrees to fill further orders of TP when D agrees to pay the overdue debt of TP and to pay for subsequent deliveries. C fills the orders, TP does not pay. C sues D who sets up the defense of Statute of Frauds. Is the Statute in whole or in part a defense?

There are three views. One view is that the promise to pay for past deliveries is unenforceable but the promise to pay for future deliveries is enforceable.[80] Under this view the promises are said to be severable. The Restatement of Security rejects the doctrine of severability and carries the main purpose rule to its logical conclusion when it holds both promises enforceable because of the benefit conferred.[81] New York, for reasons to be discussed in the next section holds both promises to be unenforceable.[82]

§ 289.   The Peculiar New York Rule

It is generally agreed that the New York main purpose rule is different from the main purpose rule as it exists elsewhere.[83] A discussion of this difference and its extent may begin with a brief review of the landmark cases [84] which culminated in the decision of White v. Rintoul.[85]

Leonard v. Vredenburgh [86] held that so long as the promisor (D) received new consideration for his promise the promise was original. The fallacy of this position was demonstrated in Mallory v. Gillett.[87]

79. To the effect that the main purpose rule does not apply see Bulkley v. Shaw, 289 N.Y. 133, 44 N.E.2d 398 (1942) ; Goldie-Klenert Distrib. Co. v. Bothwell, 67 Wash. 264, 121 P. 60 (1912). Contra, Davis v. Patrick, 141 U.S. 479, 12 S.Ct. 58, 35 L.Ed. 826 (1891) ; Eastern Wood Products Co. v. Metz, 370 Pa. 636, 89 A.2d 327 (1952). See 2 Corbin § 372; Simpson, Suretyship § 38 (1950).

80. Peterson v. Paxton-Pavey Lumber Co., 102 Fla. 89, 135 So. 501 (1931).

81. Restatement, Security § 93, ill. 1 (1941) ; Restatement, Contracts (2d) § 184, ill. 3 ; cf. Abraham v. H. V. Mid-

dleton, Inc., 279 F.2d 107 (10th Cir. 1960).

82. Witschard v. A. Brody & Sons, Inc., 257 N.Y. 97, 177 N.E. 385 (1931).

83. Conway, Subsequent Oral Promise to Perform Another's Duty and the New York Statute of Frauds, 22 Fordham L.Rev. 119 (1953).

84. Id. at 124–30 has an extended discussion of these cases.

85. 108 N.Y. 222, 15 N.E. 318 (1888).

86. 8 Johns. 29 (N.Y.1811).

87. 21 N.Y. 412 (1860).

In that case, the plaintiff (C) had made repairs upon the boat of TP and therefore had a lien.[88] D went to C and promised that if C would surrender possession of the boat, he (D) would pay for the repairs. C surrendered possession and when he was not paid brought his action against D. It is clear that under the test of Leonard v. Vredenburgh the promise would be original because D's promise to pay is supported by consideration.[89] The court pointed out that to say that new consideration makes the promise original effectively eliminates the Statute of Frauds since consideration is necessary to support the new promise in any event. The court added that for the main purpose rule to apply not only is consideration for D's promise necessary but in addition the consideration must be directly beneficial to the promisor. At this point New York had adopted the main purpose rule in its generally accepted form.[90]

In Brown v. Weber [91] the Court of Appeals introduced a third element to the content of the New York law when it stated as dictum:

> The language shows that the test to be applied to every case is, whether the party sought to be charged is the principal debtor, primarily liable, or whether he is only liable in case of the default of a third person; in other words, whether he is the debtor, or whether his relation to the creditor is that of surety to him for the performance, by some other person, of the obligation of the latter to the creditor.[92]

The Court of Appeals explained, or attempted to explain, the meaning of this language in the leading case of White v. Rintoul. In that case, Wheatcroft and Rintoul (TP) made two notes in favor of the plaintiff (C). Before the maturity date of the notes, D, who was the father of one of the members of the firm, requested that C forebear collection and stated that if C would do so he would see that C was paid. D was a secured creditor of the firm. C complied with D's request and sought to recover from D on his promise. It is apparent that the court might simply have stated that the promise was collateral because the consideration for the promise of D was not sufficiently beneficial to him.[93] However, the court reviewed the earlier cases and concluded as follows:

> These four cases, advancing by three distinct stages in a common direction, have ended in establishing a doctrine in

88. McKinney's N.Y.Lien Law § 80.

89. The surrender of the boat and the lien is consideration.

90. Conway, supra note 83, at 125.

91. 38 N.Y. 187 (1868).

92. Id. at 189. Before talking about the Statute of Frauds the court had held that C had not performed his contract with D.

93. The benefit, in the sense in which the word is being used, was to TP and not D.

the courts of this state which may be stated with approximate accuracy thus, that where the primary debt subsists and was antecedently contracted, the promise to pay it is original when it is founded on a new consideration moving to the promisor and beneficial to him, and such that the promisor thereby comes under an independent duty of payment irrespective of the liability of the principal debtor.[94]

A reading of this language compels the conclusion that three elements must be satisfied before the main purpose rule will apply:

(a) there must be consideration.

(b) it must be beneficial to the promisor, and

(c) the situation must be such that "the promisor thereby comes under an independent duty of payment irrespective of the liability of the principal debtor."

The same thought is expressed in different language in Richardson Press v. Albright,[95] when the Court of Appeals said that D's promise "is regarded as original only where the party sought to be charged clearly becomes, within the intention of the parties [TP and D] a principal debtor primarily liable."

We have seen in the preceding section that in New York the promise of an owner to pay a subcontractor for goods delivered by the general contractor has the defense of Statute of Frauds since the main purpose rule does not apply.[96] The reason is that the court feels that the third element of White v. Rintoul is not satisfied. It is difficult to determine what this requirement means because of the paucity of cases which appear to have decided that this requirement is satisfied.[97]

§ 290. Promises of Indemnity

Although the word indemnity is used in many senses, as used here, indemnitor means one who agrees to save a promisee harmless from some loss or liability irrespective of the liability of a third

---

94. 108 N.Y. 222, 227, 15 N.E. 318, 320 (1888).

95. 224 N.Y. 497, 502, 121 N.E. 362, 364, 8 A.L.R. 1195 (1917).

96. See note 82 supra.

97. This requirement was held to be satisfied in Raabe v. Squier, 148 N.Y. 81, 42 N.E. 516 (1895) and Rosenkranz v. Schreiber Brewing Co., 287 N.Y. 322, 39 N.E.2d 257 (1942). These cases are analyzed extensively in Calamari, The Suretyship Statute of Frauds, 27 Fordham L.Rev. 332 (1958). See also Biener Contr. Corp. v. Elberon Restaurant Corp., 7 A.D.2d 391, 183 N.Y. S.2d 756 (1st Dep't 1959), rearg. and appeal denied 8 A.D.2d 698, 185 N.Y. S.2d 746, 28 Fordham L.Rev. 384 (1959).

person.[98] The overwhelming weight of authority is to the effect that a promise of indemnity is not within the Statute of Frauds.[99]

For example, a contract of collision insurance is a contract of indemnity. The insurance company promises to pay the insured for the property damage suffered, regardless of whether the accident is the result of the negligence of another party.

A common problem which has divided the courts is presented when the defendant requests the plaintiff to become a surety on the obligation of TP to C and orally promises the plaintiff that if he is forced to pay, the defendant will reimburse him. If the plaintiff complies and is compelled to pay, may he sue the defendant upon his oral promise or is the promise collateral? Some courts have concluded that the promise is original, as one of indemnity, because the promise was made to a debtor, the surety.[1] However as some courts have pointed out the surety is also a creditor for he has a right to reimbursement from the principal and so these courts conclude that the promise is collateral.[2]

We have seen that when a promise is made to a debtor it can be safely concluded that it is not within the Statute of Frauds. However when a promise is made to a creditor it is very difficult to determine whether the promise is one of indemnity or one of suretyship (a promise to answer for the debt, default or miscarriage of another). Part of the difficulty stems from the fact that the authorities are not in total accord on the test to be used in making this determination. Williston states that there is suretyship and not indemnity where the parties, the plaintiff (C) and defendant (D), expect that a third party (TP) will come under an obligation to C.[3] Professor Corbin states that there is a promise of indemnity where the contract is made solely for the benefit of the promisee (C) and not for the accommodation or benefit of some third person.[4] Professor Corbin, in answering the question of whether a third party was being accommodated, places

---

98. See Restatement, Security § 82, Comment e (1941). This statement takes into account the distinction between an indemnitor against loss who promises to pay only after a loss and an indemnitor against liability who promises to pay after the promisee becomes liable and before loss. See Sorenson v. Overland Corp., 142 F.Supp. 354 (D.Del.1956), aff'd 242 F.2d 70 (3d Cir. 1957).

99. Corbin, Contracts of Indemnity and the Statute of Frauds, 41 Harv.L.Rev. 689 (1928).

1. Restatement, Contracts (2d) § 186; Tighe v. Morrison, 116 N.Y. 263, 22 N.E. 164 (1889); Newbern v. Fisher, 198 N.C. 385, 151 S.E. 875, 68 A.L.R. 345 (1930). See § 286 supra.

2. Restatement, Contracts (2d) § 186; Green v. Cresswell, 10 Ad. & El. 453, 113 Eng.Rep. 172 (1839); Restatement, Security § 96.

3. 3 Williston § 482; Restatement, Security § 82, Comment e (1941).

4. 2 Corbin §§ 384, 388.

great weight on whether the third party is an indeterminate third person or a specific third person.[5]

A good illustration of the difference in approach is a case of credit insurance. According to Williston credit insurance involves suretyship and not indemnity because the parties expect that a third party will come under an obligation.[6] Under Corbin's view a contract of credit insurance would be a contract of indemnity because the contract is for the benefit of the promisee and not for the accommodation of a third person.[7] Both agree that a contract of collision insurance involves indemnity[8] and that a contract of fidelity insurance involves suretyship.[9] It might also be noted that if the contract is one of suretyship the premium received by the insurance company does not bring the case within the main purpose rule.[10]

§ 291. The Promise of the Del Credere Agent

A del credere agent is one who receives possession of the goods for sale upon commission and who guarantees to his own principal that those to whom he sells will perform. The Statute of Frauds problem arises when the principal seeks to enforce the oral promise of the del credere agent. In the terminology that has been employed herein, the agent is D, his principal is the creditor and the third persons are the unknown persons to whom the agent sells.

It is uniformly held that the oral promise of the del credere agent is not within the Statute of Frauds.[11] A variety of reasons are assigned for the holding. Thus, for example, Corbin explains the result on the ground that this is a promise of indemnity because it is not for the accommodation or benefit of the third parties.[12] Williston explains the case by saying that the guarantee is incidental to a larger contract.[13] That is to say, that the guaranty is merely incidental to the agency in that it is part and parcel of the arrangement for compensation.

§ 292. The Promise of The Assignor to His Assignee Guaranteeing Performance by the Obligor

It is well settled that the promise of an assignor to his assignee guaranteeing performance by the obligor is not within the Statute of

5. Id.

6. See note 3 supra.

7. See notes 4 and 5 supra.

8. See notes 3, 4 and 5 supra.

9. 2 Corbin § 371 and note 3 supra.

10. 3 Williston § 472; Restatement, Contracts (2d) § 184, Comment c.

11. 2 Corbin § 389; Restatement, Contracts (2d) § 189(2).

12. Id.

13. 3 Williston § 484.

Frauds.[14] Here the obligor is TP, the assignee is C and the assignor is D. Here again Corbin explains the result upon the theory that this is a promise of indemnity,[15] and Williston again explains it by saying that the guarantee is incidental to a larger contract.[16]

§ 293. A Promise to Buy a Claim

If A owes B one hundred dollars and B promises to assign his right to payment to C and C promises to pay a stated sum for the assignment, it is clear that C's promise to pay said sum is not a promise to answer for the debt, default or miscarriage of another. C is not promising to pay the debt, but rather it is contemplated that the claim will continue with C as the holder of the claim.[17]

B. AGREEMENTS IN CONSIDERATION OF MARRIAGE

§ 294. When the Statute of Frauds Applies

The Statute of Frauds covers "any agreement made upon consideration of marriage." It has consistently been held however that the Statute does not apply to mutual promises to marry.[18] This is not inherent in the language of the Statute but rather appears to be a policy decision,[19] although there is some indication that the draftsmen of the act did not intend to encompass mutual promises to marry within this terminology.[20] However it does apply to promises to give money or property or anything else in exchange for marriage or a promise of marriage.[21] It would even apply to a negative covenant given in exchange for the consideration of marriage.[22]

But the courts have held that the Statute does not apply if the promise is made merely in contemplation of marriage, that is to say, if marriage is not truly a consideration for the promise but is merely an occasion for the promise, or a condition of it.[23]

---

14. 2 Corbin § 390; Restatement, Contracts (2d) § 189(1).

15. Id.

16. See note 13 supra.

17. 3 Williston § 480; Restatement, Contracts (2d) § 190.

18. Clark v. Pendleton, 20 Conn. 495 (1850); Blackburn v. Mann, 85 Ill. 222 (1877); Brock v. Button, 187 Wash. 27, 59 P.2d 761 (1936).

19. Short v. Stotts, 58 Ind. 29 (1877); Kellner v. Kellner, 196 Misc. 774, 90 N.Y.S.2d 743 (Sup.Ct.1949).

20. See Costigan, Has There Been Judicial Legislation in the Interpretation and Application of the "Upon Consideration of Marriage" and Other Contract Clauses of the Statute of Frauds?, 14 Ill.L.Rev. 1 (1919).

21. Chase v. Fitz, 132 Mass. 359 (1882).

22. Williams v. Hankins, 75 Colo. 136, 225 P. 243 (1924).

23. Riley v. Riley, 25 Conn. 154 (1856); Restatement, Contracts § 192, ill. 5.

A promise made by a third party in consideration of the marriage of two oth-

The fact that the marriage ceremony has taken place is not sufficient performance to make the promise enforceable.[24] If there has been part performance other than the marriage itself the unperformed part of the contract may become enforceable.[25] As usual, full performance on both sides eliminates any question of the Statute of Frauds.[26]

C. AGREEMENTS FOR THE SALE OF LAND OR OF INTERESTS IN LAND

§ 295. Contracts for The Sale of Land

(a) Introduction

The original Statute by its terms applied to "any contract or sale of lands, tenements or hereditaments, or any interest in or concerning them." The language used would appear to encompass both the conveyance of an interest in land and an executory contract to transfer an interest in land. However, other sections of the original Statute covered conveyances, and it is common even today to find conveyances governed by a separate statute. The clause under discussion has been interpreted as if it had said "contract for the sale of land or interests in land" and this is the wording which is commonly adopted today. The phrase "tenements or hereditaments" is not of great significance today and many of the modern Statutes do not use this phraseology.[27]

(b) Is a Promise to Pay for an Interest in Real Property Within the Statute?

Setting aside questions of part performance which are discussed later,[28] one of the most troublesome questions has been whether the Statute, which obviously applies to a promise to transfer an interest in land, also applies to a promise to pay for the interest. There is substantial authority for the proposition that a contract for the pur-

---

er persons is within this subdivision of the Statute of Frauds. In re Peterson's Estate, 55 S.D. 457, 226 N.W. 641 (1929); Restatement, Contracts § 192.

24. Busque v. Marcou, 147 Me. 289, 86 A.2d 873, 30 A.L.R.2d 1411 (1952).

25. Restatement, Contracts (2d), § 192, Comment d; Ferrell v. Stanley, 83 Kan. 491, 112 P. 155 (1910); Thomp-

son v. St. Louis Union Trust Co., 363 Mo. 667, 253 S.W.2d 116 (1952).

26. McDonald v. McDonald, 215 Ala. 179, 110 So. 291 (1926); Bernstein v. Prudential Ins. Co. of America, 204 Misc. 775, 124 N.Y.S.2d 624 (Sup.Ct. 1953).

27. 2 Corbin § 396.

28. See § 296 infra.

chase and sale of an interest in realty is unenforceable against either party absent a sufficient memorandum.[29] However, under the wording of some Statutes, the memorandum to be enforceable must be signed by the "vendor" rather than the "party to be charged." Under such Statutes it would seem clear that the purchaser's promise could be enforced without a memorandum signed by him.[30]

(c) Interests in Land

A difficult question which is presented by the Statute is whether the subject matter of a particular contract constitutes an interest in land.[31] Some of the problems in this area are discussed below.

1. In General

Not only is a promise to transfer a legal estate in lands covered but also a promise to create, or transfer or assign a lease,[32] or easement,[33] or rent,[34] or according to the majority view, a restriction on land.[35] Also included are promises relating to equitable interests in land including the assignment of a contract to sell.[36]

2. Liens

A promise to give a mortgage or other lien as security for money loaned has ordinarily been held to be within this section of the Stat-

---

29. Restatement, Contracts (2d) § 193, Comment d; 2 Corbin § 397. This is because, as we shall see, contracts, rather than promises are within the Statute of Frauds. §§ 303, 315 infra.

30. Krohn v. Dustin, 142 Minn. 304, 172 N.W. 213 (1919). Some courts have held that in such a case the vendor must introduce a memorandum signed by him and delivered to the purchaser or otherwise accepted by him as a correct memorandum. 300 West End Ave. Corp. v. Warner, 250 N.Y. 221, 165 N.E. 271 (1929); cf. Thomas v. Dickenson, 12 N.Y. 364 (1855).

31. For a listing of things that have been held to constitute an interest in land see 3 Williston § 491.

32. Most Statutes exclude a lease of short duration—usually from one to three years—from the operation of this subdivision of the Statute. 2 Corbin § 402; Restatement, Contracts (2d) § 193, Comment b.

33. Canell v. Arcola Housing Corp., 65 So.2d 849 (Fla.1953); Estabrook v. Wilcox, 226 Mass. 156, 115 N.E. 233 (1917). Unlike an easement, a license is not within the Statute. 2 Corbin § 404; Restatement, Contracts, (2d) § 198, Comment b.

34. "The common law regarded rent as 'issuing from the land.' Although the conception is artificial, an agreement to transfer the right to rent must, in many jurisdictions, be in writing; but a promise by an assignee of a lease to assume payment of rent need not be." 3 Williston § 491.

35. Sargent v. Leonardi, 223 Mass. 556, 112 N.E. 633 (1916) represents the majority view; Thornton v. Schobe, 79 Colo. 25, 243 P. 617 (1926) the minority. The Restatement of Contracts Second is in accord with the majority view. § 195, Comment b.

36. Traiman v. Rappaport, 41 F.2d 336, 71 A.L.R. 475 (3d Cir. 1930).

ute of Frauds even though the Statute refers to the "sale" of land.[37] But the Statute does not apply to an interest in land that arises by operation of law, for example, a grantor's lien or a constructive trust.[38] However, once a mortgage is created a promise to assign it is not considered by most courts as the sale of an interest in land, but rather as the assignment of a chose in action since the assignment is ordinarily in connection with the transfer of the debt which the mortgage secures.[39]

3. *Fructus Industriales*

Products of the soil, such as annual crops, obtained by the labor and cultivation of man, are not considered an interest in land even though at the time of the making of the contract the crops are attached to the soil.[40] "It has also been held to be true of crops that are gathered annually even though borne on perennial trunks or stems, such as apples, small fruits, and hardy shrubs and bulbs."[41] The Sales Article of the Uniform Commercial Code adopts this approach when it states, "[t]he concept of 'industrial' growing crops has been abandoned, for under modern practices fruit, perennial hay, nursery stock and the like must be brought within the scope of this Article."[42]

4. *Standing Timber, Buildings Attached to the Land and Other Things Attached to the Earth Not Included in the Concept Fructus Industriales*

Whether a contract to sell any of the above is a contract for the sale of an interest in land is one upon which the decided cases are not in agreement. It has generally been accepted that, if the contract contemplates that title will pass before severance, an interest in land is involved. On the other hand, if the purchaser did not become the owner until after its severance, then he was deemed to have a license to take goods and, as we have seen, a license is not within the Statute.[43] Other courts have made the solution depend upon whether the parties have dealt with the subject matter of the contract as land or as chattels.[44] Still others have made it depend upon how soon it is contemplated that the thing is to be removed.[45]

37. Sleeth v. Sampson, 237 N.Y. 69, 142 N.E. 355, 30 A.L.R. 1400 (1923); Nixon v. Nixon, 100 N.J.Eq. 437, 135 A. 516 (1927).

38. 2 Corbin § 401.

39. Osborne, Mortgages § 65 (1951).

40. Restatement, Contracts § 200; Uniform Sales Act § 76.

41. 2 Corbin § 410.

42. U.C.C. § 2–105, Comment 1.

43. Baird v. Elliott, 63 N.D. 738, 249 N.W. 894, 91 A.L.R. 1274 (1933); Hurley v. Hurley, 110 Va. 31, 65 S.E. 472 (1909). That a license is not within the Statute see note 33 supra.

44. Home Owners' Loan Corp. v. Gotwals, 67 S.D. 579, 297 N.W. 36 (1941).

45. Slingluff v. Franklin Davis Nurseries, Inc., 136 Md. 302, 110 A. 523 (1920).

The Uniform Commercial Code provides: "A contract for the sale of timber, minerals or the like or a structure or its materials to be removed from realty is a contract for the sale of goods within this Article if they are to be severed by the seller .   . .." [46] "If the buyer is to sever, such transactions are considered contracts affecting land   .   . .." [47]

The Code further provides: " a contract for the sale apart from land of growing crops or other things attached to realty and capable of severance without material harm thereto but not described in subsection (1) [48] is a contract for the sale of goods within this Article whether the subject matter is to be severed by the buyer or by the seller even though it forms part of the realty at the time of contracting, and the parties can by identification effect a present sale before severance." [49]

The Code in the above section uses the phrase "things attached" to the realty and avoids the use of the word fixture. [50]

5.   *Miscellaneous Items Deemed Not to be Within this Section of the Statute of Frauds Relating to Interests in Land*

If the subject matter of the contract is not the transfer of an interest in realty it does not come within the Statute although the end result would be an interest in land. For example, a contract to build a building or to do work on land is not within the Statute,[51] and the same would be true of a promise to lend money with which to buy land,[52] and of a contract between partners to buy and sell real estate and to divide the profits.[53]

---

46. U.C.C. § 2–107(1).

47. U.C.C. § 2–107, Comment 1.

48. Set forth in the preceding paragraph in the text.

49. U.C.C. § 2–107(2).

50. U.C.C. § 2–107, Comment 2. "Tenant's fixtures are regarded as part of the real property as long as they are unsevered; but the tenant has an irrevocable privilege of severance during the tenancy; and a sale of such fixture by him is held to be a sale of his privilege and power and not a sale of goods or of an interest in land. . . . Fixtures attached by the general owner of the party are part of the land; and they remain such as against a grantee by deed, in spite of previous

oral contract to sell them." 2 Corbin § 409.

51. Plunkett v. Meredith, 72 Ark. 3, 77 S.W. 600 (1903); Scales v. Wiley, 68 Vt. 39, 33 A. 771 (1895).

52. Horner v. Frazier, 65 Md. 1, 4 A. 133 (1886).

53. Evanovich v. Hutto, 204 So.2d 477 (Miss.1967); see 2 Corbin § 411. The same is true of the promise to pay a real estate broker his commission for finding a purchaser. Atlantic Coast Realty Co. v. Robertson, 240 F. 372 (4th Cir. 1917). In several states the broker's contract must be in writing because of a separate statute to this effect. Boundary line and partition agreements are generally held to be within this section of the Statute of Frauds, subject to the rules of part

§ 296. Performance as Causing a Contract Within the Statute to be Enforceable

It appears to be well settled that if the vendor of the property conveys to the vendee, the oral promise of the vendee is enforceable.[54]

This rule is different from the so called "part performance" rule which ordinarily operates in favor of the purchaser.[55] Under the "part performance" rule, payment by the buyer in whole or in part is not deemed to be sufficient to permit the court to specifically enforce the oral promise to convey,[56] since he has the quasi-contractual remedy of recovering back what he has paid.[57]

In addition, payment by the buyer is not sufficient because for the part performance doctrine to apply "there must be performance 'unequivocally referable' to the agreement—performance which alone and without the aid of words of promise is unintelligible or at least extraordinary unless as an incident of ownership, assumed if not existing . . .. [W]hat is done must itself supply the key to what is promised. It is not enough that what is promised may give significance to what is done." [58]

This occurs in some jurisdictions where there is payment and possession by the vendee or the making by the vendee of valuable improvements upon the land with the consent of the vendor.[59] But in other jurisdictions all of these elements need not concur although it is clear that these are always important factors to be considered.[60] A very small number of states do not recognize the doctrine of part performance.[61]

---

performance discussed in the next section. Restatement, Contracts (2d) § 196.

54. Restatement, Contracts (2d) § 193(3); Dangelo v. Farina, 310 Mass. 758, 39 N.E.2d 754 (1942).

55. 3 Williston § 494, Restatement, Contracts § 197, ill. 4.

56. "The 'part performance' rule was exclusively an equity rule, the available remedy being a decree for specific performance and not money damages." 2 Corbin § 419; Restatement, Contracts (2d) § 197, Comment c.

57. Restatement, Contracts § 197, ill. 3.

58. Burns v. McCormick, 233 N.Y. 230, 135 N.E. 273 (1922).

59. Baker v. Rice, 37 So.2d 837 (Fla. 1948).

60. 2 Corbin § 434.

61. Mississippi, North Carolina, Tennessee. See 2 Corbin § 443.

The Restatement, Contracts (2d) § 197, indicates that enforcement has been justified on the theory that part performance in reliance upon the promise may result in a virtual fraud if the promise is not specifically enforced. Although the Restatement adds that the power to enforce should "be exercised with caution," it indicates that acts in reliance upon the contract, even if not unequivocally referable to the contract, may justify specific performance. Restatement, Contracts (2d) § 197, Comment d.

D. AGREEMENTS FOR THE SALE OF GOODS: THE UNIFORM COMMERCIAL CODE

§ 297. Contracts for the Sale of Goods

(a) Introduction

Prior to enactment of the Uniform Commercial Code, the Uniform Sales Act was the law of sales prevailing generally throughout the United States. Section 4 of the Sales Act,[62] based on Section 17 of the original Statute of Frauds, continues to deserve examination, since Section 2–201 of the Uniform Commercial Code is to a large extent a restatement of the Sales Act provision with modifications and clarifications.[63] To a large extent, therefore, cases decided under the

---

62. Section 4 of the Uniform Sales Act provided:

(1) A contract to sell or a sale of any goods or choses in action of the value of five hundred dollars or upwards shall not be enforceable by action unless the buyer shall accept part of the goods or choses in action so contracted to be sold or sold, and actually receive the same, or give something in earnest to bind the contract, or in part payment, or unless some note or memorandum in writing of the contract or sale be signed by the party to be charged or his agent in that behalf.

(2) The provisions of this section apply to every such contract or sale, notwithstanding that the goods may be intended to be delivered at some future time or may not at the time of such contract or sale be actually made, procured, or provided, or fit or ready for delivery, or some act may be requisite for the making or completing thereof, or rendering the same fit for delivery; but if the goods are to be manufactured by the seller especially for the buyer and are not suitable for sale to others in the ordinary course of the seller's business, the provisions of this section shall not apply.

(3) There is an acceptance of goods within the meaning of this section when the buyer, either before or after delivery of the goods, expresses by words or conduct his assent to becoming the owner of those specific goods.

Variations on the uniform provision were enacted in a number of states. Many of the jurisdictions adopted a value of fifty rather than five hundred dollars. A number of states did not enact any Statute of Frauds provision regarding the sale of goods.

63. Section 2–201 of the U.C.C. provides:

Formal   Requirements;   Statute   of Frauds

(1) Except as otherwise provided in this section a contract for the sale of goods for the price of $500 or more is not enforceable by way of action or defense unless there is some writing sufficient to indicate that a contract for sale has been made between the parties and signed by the party against whom enforcement is sought or by his authorized agent or broker. A writing is not insufficient because it omits or incorrectly states a term agreed upon but the contract is not enforceable under this paragraph beyond the quantity of goods shown in such writing.

(2) Between merchants if within a reasonable time a writing in confirmation of the contract and sufficient against the sender is received and the party receiving it has reason to know

Sales Act continue to be authoritative. The Sales Act provision was applicable to "A contract to sell or sale of goods;" the Commercial Code provision refers to "a contract for the sale of goods." Since the Code in Section 2–106(1) defines "Contract for sale" as encompassing "both a present sale of goods and a contract to sell goods at a future time," there is no substantive difference between the Sales Act and the Code in this respect. The Statute of Frauds thus applies equally well if the contract for sale is executed or executory.[64]

(b) Price or Value

The Sales Act applied to goods "of the *value* of five hundred dollars or upwards," while the Code refers to "the *price* of $500 or more." To what extent the Codifiers intended a substantive change is unclear. In ordinary speech "price" is far less vague a term than "value" and thus it may be that the Codifiers intended to eliminate problems of (1) whether the Statute of Frauds applies when goods are sold for a price less than their value [65] and (2) when, in addition to a monetary consideration, other benefits are conferred on the seller.[66] The resolution of the second of these problems, however, is complicated by § 2–304(1) which provides that: "the price can be made payable in money or otherwise." This definition makes clear that the Statute of Frauds continues to apply if goods are exchanged not for money but for other property or services of a value of five hundred dollars or more.[67] The gray area in which the Code is unclear, then, is case of a

its contents, it satisfies the requirements of subsection (1) against such party unless written notice of objection to its contents is given within ten days after it is received.

(3) A contract which does not satisfy the requirements of subsection (1) but which is valid in other respects is enforceable

(a) if the goods are to be specially manufactured for the buyer and are not suitable for sale to others in the ordinary course of the seller's business and the seller, before notice of repudiation is received and under circumstances which reasonably indicate that the goods are for the buyer, has made either a substantial beginning of their manufacture or commitments for their procurement; or

(b) if the party against whom enforcement is sought admits in his pleading, testimony or otherwise in court that a contract for sale was made, but the contract is not enforceable under this provision beyond the quantity of goods admitted; or

(c) with respect to goods for which payment has been made and accepted or which have been received and accepted (Section 2–606).

64. See 2 Corbin § 468.

65. See Duesenberg and King, Sales and Bulk Transfers § 2.02 [2] (1966).

66. See Hawkland, Sales and Bulk Sales 33 (1958).

67. This was the weight of authority under the Sales Act. Misner v. Strong, 181 N.Y. 163, 73 N.E. 965 (1905).

sale of goods for basically a monetary consideration coupled with incidental benefits conferred on the seller.

The Code offers no solution to a frequently recurring problem under pre-existing law. Often parties contract for the exchange of a number of chattels having an aggregate value in excess of five hundred dollars but which individually have a value below this statutory amount. The test, often difficult to apply, is whether there is one contract or several.[68]

(c) Goods

The Sales Act, like Article 2 of the Uniform Commercial Code is basically concerned with contracts for the sale of goods. A contract for labor or other services is not within the Statute. It is well established that a contract to furnish labor and materials in erecting a structure or repairing a chattel is not within the Statute unless there is a transfer of title to goods prior to annexation.[69]

Prior to enactment of the Sales Act there were wide divergencies among the authorities on the applicability of the Statute of Frauds to contracts for the manufacture of goods. The Commercial Code provision is largely based on the compromise solution enacted in the Sales Act. A contract for sale of goods to be manufactured is within the Statute, unless "the goods are to be specially manufactured for the buyer and are not suitable for sale to others in the ordinary course of the seller's business and the seller, before notice of the repudiation is received and under circumstances which reasonably indicate that the goods are for the buyer, has made either a substantial beginning of their manufacture or commitments for their procurement." This exception to the writing requirement contains two significant innovations. Under the Sales Act, the writing requirement was dispensed with for contracts for sale of specially manufactured goods only if the seller was also the manufacturer. Under the Code it is clear that the seller need not also be the manufacturer, but may be a third party. The Sales Act exempted all contracts for sale of specially manufactured goods from coverage of the Statute of Frauds. The Code exemption applies, however, only if the seller has acted in reliance upon the contract by making a substantial beginning toward manufacturing or has made commitments for the procurement of the goods.

It is of course obvious that items which are considered realty or interests in realty are not included in the term "goods." This matter has been discussed sufficiently in § 295 supra.

---

68. See Williston, Sales § 70 (rev. ed. 1948); Duesenberg and King, supra note 65, at § 2.02 [2].

69. 2 Corbin § 476.

(d) Choses in Action

The Statute of Frauds provision of the Uniform Sales Act specifically encompassed choses in action as well as goods. Section 2–201 of the Uniform Commercial Code is restricted solely to contracts for the sale of goods. Three sections of the Code govern writing requirements in connection with the transfer of choses in action. Section 8–319 relates to investment securities and Section 9–203 relates to the creation of security interests.[70]

Section 1–206 governs all contracts for the sale of personal property not specifically governed by the other three Statute of Frauds provisions of the Code.[71] Principally this section is intended to govern the assignment of rights which are not governed by Article 9 of the Code.

(e) Part Performance

The original sales Statute of Frauds provided that no writing was required if the buyer accepted or received the goods or gave something in earnest to bind the bargain or made a part payment. The Sales Act reenacted these exceptions.[72] The Code, however, has made significant departures from preexisting law.[73]

1. Accept and Receive

Prior to the Code the entire oral contract was enforceable if the buyer had accepted and received part of the goods.[74] Acceptance re-

---

70. A security interest which is not evidenced by a signed writing is subordinate to the claims of a subsequent attaching creditor although the secured creditor has filed a financing statement. Mid-Eastern Electronics, Inc. v. First Nat'l Bank, 380 F.2d 355 (4th Cir. 1967).

71. Many problems in the interpretation of this Section are discussed in Comment, The Uniform Commercial Code, Section 1–206—A New Departure in the Statute of Frauds?, 70 Yale L.J. 603 (1961). The Section reads as follows:

(1) Except in the cases described in subsection (2) of this section a contract for the sale of personal property is not enforceable by way of action or defense beyond five thousand dollars in amount or value of remedy unless there is some writing which indicates that a contract for sale has been made between the parties at a defined or stated price, reasonably identifies the subject matter, and is signed by the party against whom enforcement is sought or by his authorized agent.

(2) Subsection (1) of this section does not apply to contracts for the sale of goods (Section 2–201) nor of securities (Section 8–319) nor to security agreements (Section 9–203).

72. See note 62 supra.

73. See note 63 supra. The Code provision referring to specially manufactured goods, discussed above, may be considered as another category in which part performance creates an exception to the writing requirement.

74. Uniform Sales Act § 4(1). This was true although the buyer denied con-

lated to title [75] and receipt had to do with possession.[76] The Code continues preexisting law only in part. The writing requirement is dispensed with only as to those items which have been received and accepted.[77] Receipt continues to mean the taking of physical possession of the goods.[78] Acceptance, however, has a somewhat different meaning under the Code. It is not a question of whether the buyer accepted title to the goods but whether he has indicated an intention to keep the goods.[79] This represents a shift in emphasis from a legal conclusion to a factual one.

2. Payment or Earnest

"Something in earnest," a phrase used in the original Statute of Frauds and in the Sales Act sounds rather remote from modern commercial practice. The phrase apparently has reference to an old custom of giving a sum of money or some tangible object to cement a bargain. "Earnest" is not part payment as it is not applied to the price.[80] Because of the disappearance or, at least, rarity of this practice, the Code has abolished this exception to the writing requirement.

tracting for any quantity beyond what he had accepted and received. John Thallon & Co. v. Edsil Trading Corp., 302 N.Y. 390, 98 N.E.2d 572 (1951).

75. See Restatement, Contracts § 201.

76. See Restatement, Contracts § 202.

77. U.C.C. § 2–201(3) (c).

78. U.C.C. § 2–103(1) (c) provides: "'Receipt' of goods means taking physical possession of them."

79. U.C.C. § 2–606 provides:
(1) Acceptance of goods occurs when the buyer

  (a) after a reasonable opportunity to inspect the goods signifies to the seller that the goods are conforming or that he will take or retain them in spite of their nonconformity; or

  (b) fails to make an effective rejection (subsection (1) of Section 2–602), but such acceptance does not occur until the buyer has had a reasonable opportunity to inspect them; or

  (c) does any act inconsistent with the seller's ownership; but if such act is wrongful as against the seller it is an acceptance only if ratified by him.

(2) Acceptance of a part of any commercial unit is acceptance of that entire unit.

One authority argues that the Code definition of "acceptance" does not apply to the Statute of Frauds provision and that more flexible pre-Code decisions should continue to be applied in this context. Duesenberg and King, supra note 65, at § 2.04 [4] [a]. This argument is difficult to accept in view of the express cross-reference to U.C. C. § 2–606 found in U.C.C. § 2–201(3) (c).

The question of whether a revocation of acceptance on grounds of non-conformity of the goods (U.C.C. § 2–608) revives the writing requirement is discussed in Duesenberg and King, supra note 65. The Code is silent on the point.

80. See 2 Corbin § 494; 3 Williston § 564. Some cases have held that "earnest" and part payment are the same thing. Scott v. Mundy & Scott, 193 Iowa 1360, 188 N.W. 972, 23 A.L.R. 460 (1922).

Under prior law if payment in whole or in part was made by the buyer and accepted by the seller, the entire contract was enforceable.[81] The Code seems to have significantly changed this rule by providing that the contract is enforceable only as to "goods for which payment has been made and accepted." [82]   Part payment, therefore, would seem to give rise only to partial enforcement.[83]

(f) Admission in Court

The Uniform Commercial Code expressly provides that a contract is enforceable "if the party against whom enforcement is sought admits in his pleading, testimony or otherwise in court that a contract for sale was made, but the contract is not enforceable under this provision beyond the quantity of goods admitted." [84]

This provision is new, although to some extent the problems it concerns itself with were raised in prior case law.[85]   The principal question the Code provision raises is whether and to what extent the party against whom enforcement is sought can be compelled to admit the existence of the oral contract either during the trial or in pretrial proceedings.   That is, may he object to the question on the grounds that he is asserting the Statute of Frauds as an affirmative defense or must he answer the question under oath as to whether the oral contract was made? [86]

E.   CONTRACTS NOT TO BE PERFORMED WITHIN ONE YEAR

§ 298.   Computation of the One Year Period

Subdivision 5 of Section 4 of the original Statute of Frauds provided that a writing is required for "an agreement that is not to be

---

81.   2 Corbin § 495; 3 Williston § 565; Restatement, Contracts § 205. These authorities also consider the question of what constitutes payment in situations where payment is alleged to have been made by means other than cash.   On this point, see also Duesenberg and King, supra note 65, at § 2.-04 [5] [a].

82.   U.C.C. § 2–201(3) (c).

83.   Williamson v. Martz, 11 Pa.D. & C. 2d 33 (1958).   Thus, a $100 deposit on an item costing $1,000 would not permit enforcement of the contract, although the purchaser could recover his part payment in a quasi-contractual action.   This literal interpreta-

tion of the Code provision is criticised in Hawkland, A Transactional Guide to the Uniform Commercial Code § 1.-1202 (1964); and see Starr v. Freeport Dodge, Inc., 54 Misc.2d 271, 282 N.Y. S.2d 58 (Dist.Ct.1967), in which a $25.-00 down payment made on an automobile was held to render the contract enforceable.

84.   U.C.C. § 2–201(3) (b).

85.   See 2 Corbin §§ 317–320; Note, 38 Cornell L.Q. 604 (1953).

86.   For a prediction that the courts will divide on the resolution of this question, see Duesenberg and King, supra note 65, at § 2.04 [3].

performed within the space of one year from the making thereof."
The test is not how long the performance will take, but when will it
be complete. Thus, if on January 10, 1969, A in a bilateral contract
promises to make a one hour television appearance on February 1,
1970, the contract is within the Statute.

It is generally accepted that if A contracts to work for B for one
year, his work to begin more than one day after making the agreement, the contract is within the one year section; but if the work is
to begin the very next day the contract is not within the Statute on
the theory that the law disregards fractions of a day.[87]

§ 299. Possibility of Performance Within One Year

The one year section of the Statute of Frauds has never been a
favorite of the courts and so it has been interpreted in such a way as
to narrow its scope as much as possible. Thus it has been interpreted
to mean that it only applies to a promise or agreement [88] which by its
terms does not admit of performance within one year from time of its
making. If by its terms performance is possible within one year, however unlikely or improbable that may be, the agreement or promise is
not within this subdivision of the Statute of Frauds. Thus a promise
made in October 1920 to cut down and deliver certain timber on or before April 1, 1922 is not within the Statute.[89] It is immaterial whether or not the actual period of performance exceeded one year. The
same is true of a promise to build a house within fifteen months.[90] A
promise to perform upon completion of a dam is not within the Statute
although it is contemplated that the dam will be completed in three
years and in fact completion takes three years.[91] However, a promise

---

87. Restatement, Contracts § 198, Comment d; 2 Corbin § 448; 3 Williston §
502. If the contract is restated at the
beginning of work and the restatement can be regarded as the making
or remaking of the contract, the year
starts to run from that time. "Courts
have been very liberal in holding that
the restatement was itself a contract."
2 Corbin § 448; 3 Williston § 503; Restatement, Contracts (2d) § 198, Comment c.

88. The question of whether "promises"
or "agreements" are within this subdivision of the Statute of Frauds is discussed in § 303 infra.

89. Gallagher v. Finch, Pruyn & Co.,
211 App.Div. 635, amended 212 App.
Div. 847, 207 N.Y.S. 403 (3d Dept.

1925). Numerous cases in accord are
collected in 2 Corbin § 444.

90. Plimpton v. Curtiss, 15 Wend. 336
(N.Y.1836).

91. Restatement, Contracts (2d) § 198,
Comment a; Gronvold v. Whaley, 39
Wash.2d 710, 237 P.2d 1026 (1951);
accord, Walker v. Johnson, 96 U.S.
424, 24 L.Ed. 834 (1877); Swain v.
Harmount & Woolf Tie Co., 226 Ky.
823, 11 S.W.2d 940 (1928). A distinct
minority of cases have taken into account how the parties intended and
expected that the contract would be
performed. That is, even if by its
terms it conceivably may be performed within one year without violating the terms of the contract, if it
cannot be performed within a year in

by A to work for B for a period in excess of one year [92] or a promise not to compete for two years is within the Statute,[93] as is a promise by B to pay in monthly instalments extending over a period of two years.[94]

§ 300. Promises Performable Within One Year but Conditional Upon an Uncertain Event

If A promises to pay B $10,000 upon the sale of certain property, A's promise is not within the Statute because the act of payment obviously can be performed within a year and it is possible that the condition will occur within a year.[95] Insurance contracts for more than one year are not within the one year section because the contingency upon which payment is promised may occur within the year.[96] A warranty that a pressure cooker will not explode is not within the one year provision even if the explosion upon which suit is brought occurs two years after the making of the warranty.[97]

So too, the one year provision does not bar enforcement of a contract to leave a bequest by will [98] or to pay a sum at the death of a

the manner in which the parties intended and expected, it is within the Statute of Frauds. 2 Corbin § 446; 3 Williston § 500. On the peculiar line of New York cases in agency situations, see § 305 infra.

92.   Carroll v. Palmer Mfg. Co., 181 Mich. 280, 148 N.W. 390 (1914); Chase v. Hinkley, 126 Wis. 75, 105 N.W. 230 (1905). It has been held that a contract whereby an employee is to be paid a bonus or commission on an annual basis but which cannot be calculated and paid until after the books have been closed is not within the Statute although the bonus cannot be calculated until after the end of the year. White Lighting Co. v. Wolfson, 68 Cal.2d 347, 66 Cal.Rptr. 697, 438 P. 2d 345 (1968); Dennis v. Thermoid Co., 128 N.J.L. 303, 25 A.2d 886 (1942).

93.   Higgins v. Gager, 65 Ark. 604, 47 S.W. 848 (1898); McGirr v. Campbell, 71 App.Div. 83, 75 N.Y.S. 571 (1st Dept. 1902); Restatement, Contracts § 198, ill. 4; contra, Restatement, Contracts (2d) § 198, ill. 9; Doyle v. Dixon, 97 Mass. 208 (1867); see 2 Corbin § 453; 3 Williston § 497. The theory of the authorities cited as contra is

that although the contract cannot be performed within a year nevertheless its purpose is attained within a year if the promisor dies. See § 301 infra.

94.   Sophie v. Ford, 230 App.Div. 568, 245 N.Y.S. 470 (4th Dept. 1930); Thompson v. Ford, 145 Tenn. 335, 236 S.W. 2 (1921); but see Restatement, Contracts (2d) § 198, Comment d.

95.   Sullivan v. Winters, 91 Ark. 149, 120 S.W. 843 (1909); Bartlett v. Mystic River Corp., 151 Mass. 433, 24 N.E. 780 (1890).

96.   Sanford v. Orient Ins. Co., 174 Mass. 416, 54 N.E. 883 (1899); Struzewski v. Farmers' Fire Ins. Co., 179 App.Div. 318, 166 N.Y.S. 362 (4th Dept. 1917), rev'd on other grounds 226 N.Y. 338, 123 N.E. 661 (1919).

97.   Joseph v. Sears Roebuck & Co., 224 S.C. 105, 77 S.E.2d 583, 40 A.L.R.2d 742 (1953).

98.   Dixon v. Lamson, 242 Mass. 129, 136 N.E. 346 (1922); Carlin v. Bacon, 322 Mo. 435, 16 S.W.2d 46, 69 A.L.R. 1 (1929). Such an agreement may, however, be within the real property provision.

named person.[99] The contingency of death could occur within the year and therefore it is immaterial whether it occurred within the year or many years later. It should be noted, however, that legislation in some jurisdictions has extended the Statute of Frauds to contracts which are not performable before the end of a lifetime [1] and to contracts to make a testamentary disposition.[2]

§ 301. A Promise of Extended Performance that Comes to an End Upon the Happening of a Condition that May Occur Within a Year

If A promises to supply B with goods for the duration of the war A's promise is not within the Statute because the war may end within a year.[3] So too if A promises to support X for life or to employ X for life or to employ X permanently, the promise is not within the Statute because the contract by its terms is conditioned upon the continued life of X and the condition may cease to exist within a year because X may die within a year.[4]

In Duncan v. Clarke [5] a promise was made to pay for the support of an illegitimate child by paying sixty dollars per month until the child became twenty-one. At the time of the promise the child was four years of age. The majority of opinion held that if the child were to die the agreement would be fully performed and since the child could die within a year the promise by its terms could be performed within a year.[6]

99. Riddle v. Backus, 38 Iowa 81 (1874).

1. See, e. g., McKinney's N.Y.Gen. Obligations Law § 5–701(1).

2. See, e. g., McKinney's N.Y.E.P.T.L. § 13–2.1(2).

3. Canister Co. v. National Can Corp., 63 F.Supp. 361 (D.Del.1945), motion denied 64 F.Supp. 808, appeal dism'd 163 F.2d 683 (3d Cir. 1947).

4. Quirk v. Bank of Commerce & Trust Co., 244 F. 682 (6th Cir. 1917); Hobbs v. Brush Elec. Light Co., 75 Mich. 550, 42 N.W. 965 (1889); Fidelity Union Trust Co. v. Reeves, 96 N.J.Eq. 499, 125 A. 582 (1924), aff'd 98 N.J.Eq. 412, 129 A. 922 (1925). These cases should be compared with the cases cited at note 94 supra. There it was said that if A promised to work for B for two years A's promise is within the Statute of Frauds. But isn't it equally possible there that A could die within

one year? Obviously it is, but if A dies there is not *performance* merely *termination*. That is to say the contract is not phrased in terms of the life of A.

5. 308 N.Y. 282, 125 N.E.2d 569, 49 A. L.R.2d 1287 (1955).

6. The minority opinion says that the death of the child would result in *termination* and not performance. The weight of authority is in accord with the majority opinion. As Corbin states: "Even though the promise is to render a performance throughout a specified period of years, it is generally held not to be within the Statute if the continued life of some person is necessary to enable performance to be made and if upon that person's death the essential purpose of the parties is completely attained." 2 Corbin § 446; Restatement, Contracts (2d) § 198, Comment b.

§ 302. Contracts for Alternative Performances and Contracts with Option to Terminate, Renew or Extend

Where a contractor promises one of two or more performances in the alternative, the promise is not within the one year section if any of the alternatives can be performed within one year from the time of the making thereof.[7]

If A and B enter into an oral contract by the terms of which A promises to perform services for B for five years and B promises to pay for the services at a fixed rate over that period and one or both have the right by the terms of the contract to terminate the contract by giving 30 days notice within the year, is the one-year section a defense? One view is that the Statute is a defense because although *termination* is possible within a year *performance* is not.[8]

The other view is that the contract is not within the Statute of Frauds.[9] It is reasoned that alternative promises are provided: (1) either to perform for the full period or (2) to perform up to the time of election and then exercise the option to cancel.[10] As we have seen if one of the alternative promises may be performed within a year the one year section does not apply.[11]

The same type of problem exists in the case where there is a contract that may be performed by its terms within one year or less but

---

7. 2 Corbin § 454. It does not matter which party has the right to name the alternative. For example, if A can perform by working for B for two years or by delivering twenty bales of cotton within six months, since one of the alternative performances may, by its terms, be performed within a year, the promise is not within the one year section of the Statute of Frauds.

8. Coan v. Orsinger, 105 U.S.App.D.C. 201, 265 F.2d 575 (1959); Barth v. Women's City Club, 254 Mich. 270, 236 N.W. 778 (1931); Deevy v. Porter, 11 N.J. 594, 95 A.2d 596 (1953); see 3 Williston §§ 498A–498B.

9. Restatement, Contracts (2d) § 198, Comment b, ill. 6; Fothergill v. McKay Press, 361 Mich. 666, 106 N.W.2d 215 (1960); see 2 Corbin § 449.

10. Hopper v. Lennen & Mitchell, Inc., 146 F.2d 364, 161 A.L.R. 282 (9th Cir. 1944); Johnston v. Bowersock, 62 Kan. 148, 61 P. 740 (1900); Blake v. Voigt, 134 N.Y. 69, 31 N.E. 256 (1892).

The subsequent history of the case of Blake v. Voigt in New York is interesting. The earlier New York cases interpreted Blake as holding that the Statute does not apply if either party has an option of termination within a year. However, later cases have held the Statute does not apply if the option of termination is bilateral or if the option is in the defendant but that the Statute would be a defense if the option of termination is only in the plaintiff. "For in such cases defendant's liability endures indefinitely subject only to the uncontrolled voluntary act of the party who seeks to hold the defendant. Under such circumstances it is illusory, from the point of view of the defendant, to consider the contract terminable or performable within one year." Harris v. Home Indemnity Co., 6 A.D.2d 861, 175 N.Y.S.2d 603 (1st Dept. 1958).

11. See note 7 supra. However, is a provision for *termination*, an alternative performance in the same sense as that term was used in note 7 supra?

by the terms of the contract one party has a right to extend or renew the contract so that performance beyond a year would be required. The same split of authority evidenced in the option to terminate cases above also appears here.[12]

§ 303. Is a Promise or a Contract Within the One Year Section of the Statute of Frauds? [13]

It appears to be settled that where any of the promises on either side of a bilateral contract cannot be fully performed within one year from the time of the formation of the contract, all of the promises in the contract are within the one year section of the Statute of Frauds.[14] This means that the contract is unenforceable by either party in the absence of a sufficient memorandum or in the absence of performance, the effect of which is discussed in the next section.

§ 304. Effect of Performance Under the One Year Section

Courts have had to deal with the question of part and full performance on one side under each subdivision of the Statute of Frauds. Different doctrines have been forged for many of these subdivisions. Under the majority view, full performance on one side renders a contract within the one year section enforceable.[15] Some of the jurisdictions adopting this view, however, qualify this position by requiring that the performance must have actually taken place within one year from the making of the contract.[16] A minority of jurisdictions, however, hold that performance is ineffective to render the contract enforceable, restricting the performing party to his quasi contractual remedy.

It seems everywhere to be agreed that part performance on one side does not entitle either party to sue at law to enforce the con-

---

12. Hand v. Osgood, 107 Mich. 55, 64 N.W. 867 (1895) holding that the Statute is a defense. Contra, Ward v. Hasbrouck, 169 N.Y. 407, 62 N.E. 434 (1902). Just as the holding in the Blake case, note 8 supra has been modified by subsequent New York decisions so also has the holding in Ward v. Hasbrouck. See Belfert v. Peoples Planning Corp. of America, 22 Misc.2d 753, 199 N.Y.S.2d 839 (Sup.Ct. 1959), aff'd 11 A.D.2d 760, 202 N.Y.S. 2d 101 (1st Dept. 1960), appeal dismissed 8 N.Y.2d 1054, 207 N.Y.S.2d 267, 170 N.E.2d 403, motion denied 9 N.Y.2d 678, 212 N.Y.S.2d 413, 173 N.E. 2d 235 (1961) (if option is in the plain-

tiff alone, the contract is within the Statute; if bilateral or in the defendant contract is performable within one year); see generally 2 Corbin § 450.

13. See note 88 supra.

14. Restatement, Contracts § 198; 2 Corbin § 456; Restatement, Contracts (2d) § 198(1).

15. Restatement, Contracts § 198, Comment a; 2 Corbin § 456; Restatement, Contracts (2d) § 198(2).

16. See 2 Corbin § 457.

tract,[17] unless according to some authorities, the contract is divisible.[18] There are, however, a number of cases in which enforcement has been granted on the basis of estoppel.[19]

§ 305. Unilateral Contracts

There is a great deal of authority to the effect that unilateral contracts are enforceable without reference to the one year Statute of Frauds.[20] This stems in part from the majority rule that where the plaintiff has fully performed his side of the bargain the one year provision of the Statute is not a defense.[21]

Even in jurisdictions adopting the minority view, however, it is still arguable that a unilateral contract would not ordinarily be within the Statute of Frauds. If A said to B, "if you walk across Brooklyn Bridge three years from today, I promise to pay you $10.00 immediately after you walk," the promise logically would not be within the one year provision of the Statute because by its terms its performance is to take place immediately after the contract is formed.[22] The result would logically be different if A's promise was to pay more than one year after B performed the act which created the contract.[23]

A series of decisions in New York, a minority jurisdiction, are of interest in this context. Among the more interesting of these cases is Martocci v. Greater N. Y. Brewery, Inc.[24] The defendant had promised to pay the plaintiff a 5% commission on all sales made by the defendant to P. Lorillard & Co., if the plaintiff introduced P. Lorillard & Co. to the defendant. The plaintiff performed and the defendant set up the defense of the one year provision of the Statute of Frauds.

There are a number of preliminary observations to be made. First, the plaintiff had completely performed, and, therefore, under the majority view the Statute of Frauds would have been satisfied.

17. Chevalier v. Lane's, Inc., 147 Tex. 106, 213 S.W.2d 530, 6 A.L.R.2d 1045 (1948); Restatement, Contracts (2d) § 198, Comment e.

18. Blue Valley Creamery Co. v. Consolidated Products Co., 81 F.2d 182 (8th Cir. 1936) (instalment sales of dairy products); but see § 315 infra.

19. See §§ 326–327 infra.

20. Restatement, Contracts § 198, Comment a; the cases are collected in 2 Corbin § 457.

21. See § 304 supra.

22. This is logical where the Statute speaks in terms of an "agreement," but not necessarily so when it speaks in terms of a "promise."

23. See Simpson, Contracts 172 (2d ed. 1965); Restatement, Contracts (2d) § 198, Comment c.

24. 301 N.Y. 57, 92 N.E.2d 887, motion denied, 301 N.Y. 662, 92 N.E.2d 926 (1950). This and subsequent N.Y. cases are discussed in 25 Fordham L.Rev. 720 (1957).

Secondly, the contract was unilateral as it did not arise until the plaintiff had performed.

The Court of Appeals held, however, that the defendant's promise was within the Statute, stating "If the terms of the contract here had included an event which might end the contractual relationship of the parties within a year, defendant's possible liability beyond that time would not bring the contract within the Statute. Since, however, the terms of the contract are such that the relationship will continue beyond a year, it is within the Statute, even though the continuing liability to which defendant is subject is merely a contingent one. The endurance of the defendant's liability is the deciding factor. The mere cessation of orders from Lorillard to defendant would not alter the contractual relationship between the parties; it would not constitute performance; plaintiff would still be in possession of his contractual right, though it may have no monetary value, immediately or ever."[25]

The court here distinguished the kind of case typified by a promise to deliver goods for the duration of the war. In such a case the contingency is expressed in the contract and the contingency terminates the contractual relationship; thus the promise by its terms may be performed within a year. In a case such as Martocci, the promise endures continuously into the future. The court does not take into account the possibility that P. Lorillard may cease to exist within a year. We have previously seen that if a promise is limited by the life of a person, or even if the essential purpose of the contract for a period of years is attained upon the death of a person, it is not within the one year section. In the Martocci case, however, it is quite clear that by its terms the performance of the defendant was not limited by the life of the customer, P. Lorillard & Co., and it would also appear that the essential purpose of the parties would not be achieved if the corporation ceased to exist.

To be distinguished from the Martocci case are cases such as Nat Nal Service Stations, Inc. v. Wolf,[26] where there is no contract but only an offer looking to a series of contracts. Since in such a situation, as we have seen,[27] the offeror may revoke his offer at any time, the one year section of the Statute of Frauds does not apply.

25. The court apparently assumes that the arrangement was to last in perpetuity. 301 N.Y. at 62–63, 92 N.E.2d at 889; accord, Zupan v. Blumberg, 2 N.Y.2d 547, 161 N.Y.S.2d 428, 141 N.E.2d 819 (1957) (commission payable to salesman on any account he brought in so long as account remained active); Nurnberg v. Dwork, 12 A.D.2d 612, 208 N.Y.S.2d 799 (1st Dep't 1960), aff'd mem. 12 N.Y.2d 776, 234 N.Y.S.2d 721, 186 N.E.2d 568 (1962) (commission on percentage of sales if at any future times plaintiff obtains concessions for defendant at designated stores).

26. 304 N.Y. 332, 107 N.E.2d 473 (1952).

27. See § 29 supra.

In a recent Court of Appeals case,[28] the plaintiff, pursuant to an oral agreement entered into in October of 1960, was promised the exclusive distributorship of the defendant's beer in a specified area for as long as defendant sold beer in the area. The defendant designated a new distributor in 1962. Plaintiff sued for breach and defendant set up as a defense the one year section of the Statute of Frauds. The Court of Appeals held that the Statute was not a defense. The Court indicates first that since by the terms of the contract the defendant could at any time discontinue its beer sales in the area, the defendant under the New York view could perform in less than a year by withdrawing its product from the market in the area.

The Court distinguishes the Martocci case by saying that there the plaintiff had completely performed and therefore there is greater opportunity for fraud in that type of case, and, secondly, that in the Martocci case the agreement could not by its terms be terminated by either party to the contract,[29] whereas here at least as pointed out above the defendant had a right to terminate the arrangement.[30]

§ 306. Relationship of the One Year Provision to Other Subdivisions of the Statute

The one year section applies to all contracts no matter what their subject matter. Thus, for example, a contract for the sale of goods must comply with both the one year and the sale of goods provisions of the Statute.[31] According to the weight of authority, mutual promises to marry not performable within one year are within the one year provision,[32] although not within the consideration of marriage subdivision.[33]

---

28. North Shore Bottling Co. v. C. Schmidt and Sons, Inc., 22 N.Y.2d 171, 292 N.Y.S.2d 86, 239 N.E.2d 189 (1968).

29. However it might have been terminated by the dissolution of the third party corporation—but not by its terms.

30. The Court of Appeals expressly overrules certain decisions of the Second Circuit as, for example, Perrin v. Pearlstein, 314 F.2d 863 (2d Cir. 1963) where the court held a contract to be within the New York Statute of Frauds where it was to endure "as

long as I am in the dog food business and you are in the food brokerage business." A later case which followed Perrin and which was also overruled is Ginsberg Mach. Co. v. J. & H. Label Processing Corp., 341 F.2d 825 (2d Cir., 1965).

31. Bryant v. Credit Service, Inc., 36 Del. 360, 175 A. 923 (1934). However, an exception is generally made in the case of a short term lease and in the case of mutual promises to marry.

32. 2 Corbin §§ 455, 461.

33. See § 294 supra.

II. WHAT IS A SUFFICIENT WRITING OR MEMORANDUM AND THE EFFECT THEREOF

Analysis

Sec.
307. Introduction.
308. Parol Evidence and the Memorandum.
309. The Contents of the Memorandum.
310. The Form of the Contract and When It is to be Prepared—Necessity for Delivery.
311. Signed by the Party to be Charged.
312. Problems Presented When the Memorandum is Contained in More Than One Writing.
313. The Memorandum Under U.C.C. § 2–201—The Sale of Goods Section.
314. Is the Oral Contract Which Does Not Comply with the Statute "Unenforceable" or "Void"?
315. Effect of Part of a Contract being Unenforceable Because of the Statute.
316. Oral Rescission or Variation of a Contract Within the Statute.
317. To What Extent May an Oral Contract Which is Not Enforceable Because of the Statute of Frauds be Used as a Defense?
318. Some Miscellaneous Rules.

§ 307. Introduction

Assuming that a contract is within the Statute of Frauds, it is clear that it is enforceable if there is a sufficient writing or memorandum. This was spelled out in Section 4 of the English Statute which made the contract enforceable if "the agreement . . ., or some memorandum or note thereof, shall be in writing, and signed by the party to be charged therewith, or some other person thereunto by him lawfully authorized." This language in substance has been adopted by most of the states. However, there are variations from state to state. All that can be said is the variations are not so great as to prevent general discussion but that in every case the words of the particular statute should be considered.

§ 308. Parol Evidence and the Memorandum

The relationship between the parol evidence rule and the Statute of Frauds is wrapped in much the same controversy and confusion as the parol evidence rule itself.[34] It is clear that a memorandum sufficient to satisfy the Statute of Frauds need not be an integrated writing.[35] Yet the distinction between an integrated writing and a nonintegrated writing is important in at least one respect.

---

34. See ch. 3 supra.

35. "A written memorandum of a contract is not identical with a written

Where the writing is not integrated it may be shown that the oral agreement made contained terms different from or additional to those stated in the memorandum. When the memorandum is thus exposed as inaccurate, the party sought to be charged may obtain a dismissal of the case against him because the memorandum does not contain the terms of the agreement [36]—one of the more bizarre results of the often criticized Statute of Frauds.[37] However, if there is a total integration, the writing may not be varied, contradicted or supplemented in order to show that it is inaccurate.[38]

But the situation is quite different when a party seeks to introduce oral evidence in order to establish terms not found in the memorandum because the memorandum does not contain all of the essential terms. Here whether the memorandum is integrated or not makes no difference, because for this purpose the Statute of Frauds has its own built in exclusionary rule which excludes oral evidence offered to vary or supplement the writing.[39] However, oral evidence should be admissible in aid of interpretation unless the plain meaning rule prevents the introduction of the extrinsic evidence.[40]

contract. A written contract will indeed serve as a memorandum, but a memorandum includes also any writing which states the terms agreed upon, though not intended or adopted by the parties as a final complete statement of their agreement."

36. 2 Corbin § 498; 4 Williston § 575. The statement does not take into account the possibility of a court of equity granting reformation, a question which is beyond the purview of this work. See Donald Friedman & Co. v. Newman, 255 N.Y. 340, 174 N.E. 703, 73 A.L.R. 95 (1931), rearg. denied 255 N.Y. 632, 175 N.E. 345, 73 A.L.R. 95; Restatement, Contracts (2d) § 207 Comment g.

37. See 2 Corbin § 275; see also 4 Williston § 599 at p. 275, n. 12, urging a uniform liberalized statute.

38. Lyon v. Big Bend Developing Co., 7 Ariz.App. 1, 435 P.2d 732 (1968); N. E. D. Holding Co. v. McKinley, 246 N.Y. 40, 157 N.E. 923 (1927); Restatement, Contracts § 207, ill. 11. If the writing is a partial integration it may not be contradicted for this purpose but it may be supplemented. Again the possibility of reformation is not considered.

39. "Unless the writing, considered alone, expresses the essential terms with sufficient certainty to constitute an enforceable contract, it fails to meet the demands of the statute. Accordingly, where the Statute of Frauds, rather than the parol evidence rule is invoked, it follows that recovery may not be predicated upon parol proof of material terms omitted from the written memorandum, even though the oral understanding is entirely consistent with, and in no way tends to vary or contradict, the written instrument." 4 Williston § 575, quoting from Ellis v. Klaff, 96 Cal. App.2d 471, 216 P.2d 15 (1950). Cf. 2 Corbin § 527.

40. See § 50 supra and Stanley v. A. Levy & J. Zentner Co., 60 Nev. 432, 112 P.2d 1047 (1941); Marsico v. Kessler, 149 Conn. 236, 178 A.2d 154 (1962).

§ 309. The Contents of the Memorandum

The memorandum must state with *reasonable* certainty: (a) the identity of both contracting parties; however, the party need not be named if he is sufficiently described since extrinsic evidence to clarify the description is admissible; [41] (b) the subject matter of the contract so that it can be identified either from the writing or if the writing is not clear by the aid of extrinsic evidence; [42] (c) the essential terms and "conditions of all the promises constituting the contract and by whom and to whom the promises are made." [43]

It should be repeated that the "essential terms"—a term of considerable flexibility itself—must be stated with only "reasonable" certainty.[44] A leading case which ilustrates this rule is Marks v. Cowdin.[45] In 1911 the plaintiff was employed under a written contract for two years as "sales manager". When this period expired the parties made an oral agreement for further employment. The memorandum, signed some time later, read: "It is understood . . . that the arrangements made for employment of L. Marks in our business on January 1, 1913 for a period of three years from that date at a salary of $15,000 per year plus 5 per cent of the gross profits earned in our business which we agree shall not be less than $5,000 per year—continues in force until Jan. 1, 1916."

It is apparent that the memorandum does not state the nature of the employment to be performed by Marks, the plaintiff. The court held that the memorandum was sufficient to permit the plaintiff to show that he had been employed as a "sales manager" and that the employment had been continued.

---

41. Restatement, Contracts § 207(a); Restatement, Contracts (2d) § 207(2) adds that the memorandum should indicate that a contract has been made.

42. Restatement, Contracts § 207(b); 2 Corbin § 505; Malin v. Ward, 21 A.D. 2d 926, 250 N.Y.S.2d 1009 (3d Dep't, 1964).

43. Restatement, Contracts § 207(c); Restatement, Contracts (2d) § 207(c). Whether the consideration for each promise must be stated in the memorandum is a question which is still in dispute. 2 Corbin § 501. However, there is a great deal of authority, if the suit is upon a unilateral contract or upon a bilateral contract which has become unilateral by full performance on the part of the plaintiff, that plaintiff's consideration need not be stated in the memorandum. Standard Oil Co. v. Koch, 260 N.Y. 150, 183 N.E. 278 (1932), rearg. denied 261 N.Y. 535, 185 N.E. 727 (1933); cf. Restatement, Contracts (2d) § 207(c) and Comment h.

44. Restatement, Contracts § 207; Restatement, Contracts (2d) § 207, Comment g.

45. 226 N.Y. 138, 123 N.E. 139 (1919).

§ 310.   The Form of the Contract and When It is to be Prepared— Necessity for Delivery

The memorandum that satisfies the Statute may be in almost any form. It may be a receipt [46] or a telegram [47] or an exchange of correspondence [48] or the record books of a business [49] or a letter which acknowledges the contract and repudiates it.[50]

The memorandum need not be prepared with the purpose of satisfying the Statute,[51] nor at the same time that the contract is made; but it must according to the first Restatement be made before the suit is instituted.[52] It is also generally agreed that the memorandum need not be delivered.[53] It is also clear that the memorandum need not be in existence at the time of suit; it is sufficient that it existed at one time.[54]

§ 311.   Signed by the Party to be Charged

The term "signature" includes any memorandum, mark or sign, written, printed, stamped, photographed, engraved, or otherwise placed upon any instrument or writing with intent to execute or *authenticate* such instrument or writing.[55] The important thing is that the instrument be *authenticated* by the party to be charged. If the name is inscribed at the end, that constitutes prima facie evidence of au-

---

46. Goetz v. Hubbell, 66 N.D. 491, 266 N.W. 836 (1936).

47. Brewer v. Horst & Lachmund Co., 127 Cal. 643, 60 P. 418 (1900).

48. United States v. City of New York, 131 F.2d 909 (2d Cir. 1942), cert. denied 318 U.S. 781, 63 S.Ct. 858, 87 L. Ed. 1149 (1943).

49. Al-Sco Realty Co. v. Suburban Apt. Corp., 138 N.J.Eq. 497, 48 A.2d 838 (1946), aff'd 141 N.J.Eq. 40, 55 A.2d 296 (1947).

50. See Restatement, Contracts § 209; Schmoll Fils & Co. v. Wheeler, 242 Mass. 464, 136 N.E. 164 (1922); Webb v. Woods, 176 Okl. 306, 55 P.2d 959 (1936). For the memorandum to be sufficient it must "amount to acknowledgment by the party to be charged that he has assented to the contract that is asserted by the other party." 2 Corbin § 517.

51. Annot. 85 A.L.R. 1184, 1215 (1933); Restatement, Contracts (2d) § 209

which makes an exception in the case of a contract in consideration of marriage.

52. Restatement, Contracts §§ 214 and 215. Restatement, Contracts (2d) takes a different position and omits § 215 of the original Restatement "as procedural and as contrary to the spirit of modern procedural reforms."

53. Restatement, Contracts (2d) § 207, Comment d; Kludt v. Connett, 350 Mo. 793, 168 S.W.2d 1068, 145 A.L.R. 1014 (1943); contra, Main v. Pratt, 276 Ill. 218, 114 N.E. 576 (1916). Of course a deed must be delivered to be effective as a deed but there is no such requirement for it to be effective as a memorandum.

54. Hiss v. Hiss, 228 Ill. 414, 81 N.E. 1056 (1907).

55. See McKinney's N.Y.Gen. Construction Law § 46, which restates the common law; 2 Corbin § 522; Restatement, Contracts (2d) § 210; U.C. C. § 1–201 (39).

thentication. "If the name is inscribed elsewhere . . . the contrary presumption may arise, making other evidence requisite to convince the court that the inscribed name was intended to be a signature." [56]

The memorandum need not be signed by both parties, it need only be signed by the party to be charged.[57] The party to be charged is ordinarily the defendant, but in case of a counterclaim it is the plaintiff. Since the memorandum need be signed only by the party to be charged it is apparent that there will be situations where the contract is enforceable against one party and not the other as, for example, where one party sends a signed written offer and the other party orally accepts.[58] Some Statutes do not use the phrase signed "by the party to be charged" but rather use the phrase "signed by the vendor or lessor." Under such Statutes it would appear that the vendee's promise could be enforced without a memorandum; [59] but some courts have held that the vendor must introduce a memorandum signed by him and delivered to the purchaser or otherwise accepted by the purchaser as a correct memorandum.[60]

The original Statute of Frauds expressly provided that a memorandum is sufficient if signed by an authorized agent of the party to be charged. Generally the American statutes have expressly or implicitly continued this rule. By the great weight of authority, the agent's power to sign a written instrument need not be vested in him by a written instrument.[61] Thus an oral grant of authority is suf-

56. 2 Corbin § 521. Some states have, as to some or all provisions of the Statute of Frauds, imposed the requirement that the writing be "subscribed" rather than "signed." Some courts have held that because of this language the writing must be signed at the end. 300 West End Ave. Corp. v. Warner, 250 N.Y. 221, 165 N.E. 271 (1929). Others, however, have held that "subscribed" and "signed" are basically synonymous. California Canneries Co. v. Scatena, 117 Cal. 447, 49 P. 462 (1897). See 2 Corbin § 521.

57. Ullsperger v. Meyer, 217 Ill. 262, 75 N.E. 482 (1905).

58. Tymon v. Linoki, 16 N.Y.2d 293, 266 N.Y.S.2d 357, 213 N.E.2d 661 (1965). No mutuality problem is created because under the majority view the defense of the Statute of Frauds makes the contract unenforceable rather than void. This matter is discussed in more detail in § 314 infra.

59. Krohn v. Dustin, 142 Minn. 304, 172 N.W. 213 (1919).

60. 300 West End Ave. Corp. v. Warner, 250 N.Y. 221, 165 N.E. 271 (1929); Restatement, Contracts (2d) § 209 Comment b.

61. See 2 Corbin § 526; Seavey, Agency § 19F (1964).

The problem of the relationship between rules governing agents for undisclosed principals, the Statute of Frauds and the parol evidence rule are not considered in this book. See, on the subject, Dodge v. Blood, 299 Mich. 364, 300 N.W. 121, 138 A.L.R. 322 (1941), 42 Col.L.Rev. 475 (1942), 40 Mich.L.Rev. 900 (1942), and compare Jaynes v. Petoskey, 309 Mich. 32, 14 N.W.2d 566 (1944).

ficient.   A number of states, however, have by statute provided that if the contract is within the Statute of Frauds, the agent's authority must be evidenced by a writing.[62]   Often, however, this requirement is limited to the real property Statute of Frauds.[63]

§ 312.   Problems Presented When the Memorandum is Contained in More Than One Writing

If there is more than one writing and all of the writings are signed by the party to be charged and it is clear by their contents that they relate to the same transaction, no particular problem is presented.[64]

But if the party to be charged has signed only one of the documents comprising the memorandum, the problem becomes a little more complicated because it is more difficult to say that the complete memorandum has been authenticated by the party to be charged. When the unsigned document is physically attached to the signed document at the time it is signed, the Statute is satisfied.[65]   This is also true when the signed document by its terms expressly refers to the unsigned document.[66]

However the cases are in conflict where the signed document is not attached to or does not refer to the unsigned papers.   One view is that in such a situation the memorandum is not sufficiently authenticated.[67]   The other and better view is that even if the signed document does not expressly refer to the unsigned document it is still sufficient if the documents by internal evidence refer to the same subject matter or transaction and in that event extrinsic evidence is admissible to help show the connection between the documents.[68]

§ 313.   The Memorandum Under U.C.C. § 2–201—The Sale of Goods Section

Section 2–201 of the Uniform Commercial Code introduces several innovations with respect to the contents of the memorandum and

---

62.   See 2 Corbin § 526.

63.   E. g., McKinney's N.Y.Gen. Obligations Law § 5–703.

64.   Forman v. Gadouas, 247 Mass. 207, 142 N.E. 87 (1924).

65.   Tallman v. Franklin, 14 N.Y. 584 (1856).

66.   Leach v. Crucible Center Co., 388 F.2d 176 (1st Cir. 1968); Tampa Shipbldg. & Eng'r Co. v. General Constr. Co., 43 F.2d 309, 85 A.L.R. 1178 (5th Cir. 1930).

67.   Ezzell v. S. G. Holland Stave Co., 210 Ala. 694, 99 So. 78 (1924).

68.   Crabtree v. Elizabeth Arden Sales Corp., 305 N.Y. 48, 110 N.E.2d 551 (1952); Restatement, Contracts (2d) § 208, Comment a; but see Intercontinental Planning, Ltd. v. Daystrom, Inc., 24 N.Y.2d 372, 300 N.Y.S.2d 817, 248 N.E.2d 576 (1969).

the necessity of a writing signed by the party to be charged. Only three definite and invariable requirements as to the memorandum are made by this subsection. First, it must evidence a contract for the sale of goods;[69] second, it must be "signed" a word which includes any authentication which identifies the party to be charged; and third, it must specify a quantity.[70]

We have already seen that as a general rule, it may be shown that the oral agreement contained terms not set forth in the memorandum, with the result that the memorandum is insufficient under the Statute of Frauds unless a court of equity would grant reformation based upon mistake.[71] Under the Code if the memorandum is in error as to any term, other than the quantity term, extrinsic evidence is admissible to correct the error.[72] If the quantity term is not accurately stated, recovery is limited to the amount stated, presumably unless the other party is able to get reformation.[73]

When merchants have concluded an oral contract it is quite common for one to send to the other a letter of confirmation, or perhaps a printed form of contract. Naturally, this confirmation will serve as a memorandum and will be signed only by the party who sent it, thus leaving one party at the mercy of the other. The Code remedies this situation by providing: "Between merchants if within a reasonable time a writing in confirmation of the contract and sufficient against the sender is received and the party receiving it has reason to know

---

69. This represents a significant relaxation of the writing requirement. All that is required is that "there is some writing sufficient to indicate that a contract for sale has been made." Thus, it is not necessary that all essential terms be included. See U.C.C. § 2–201, Comment 1; Harry Rubin & Sons, Inc. v. Consolidated Pipe Co. of America, Inc., 396 Pa. 506, 153 A.2d 472 (1959); Julian C. Cohen Salvage Corp. v. Eastern Elec. Sales Co., 205 Pa.Super. 26, 206 A.2d 331 (1965). However, a notation on a check stating: "tentative deposit on tentative purchase," is not a sufficient writing as it shows a lack of commitment to the purchase. Arcuri v. Weiss, 198 Pa.Super. 506, 184 A.2d 24 (1962). See Restatement, Contracts (2d) § 207, Comment b.

70. U.C.C. § 2–201, Comment 1. The same comment states with respect to the memorandum "It need not indicate which party is the buyer and

which the seller. . . . The price, time and place of payment or delivery, the general quality of the goods, or all particular warranties may be omitted. . . . Of course if the 'price' consists of goods rather than money the quantity of goods must be stated."

71. See note 36 supra; 2 Corbin § 288. Reformation is beyond the purview of this text. For discussions on the availability of reformation of a contract within the Statute of Frauds, see 2 Corbin §§ 335, 336, 338, 342; 5 Williston §§ 1552, 1555 (rev. ed. 1937).

72. 2 Corbin § 531.

73. U.C.C. § 2–201, Comment 1. In addition the statute states: "A writing is not insufficient because it omits or incorrectly states a term agreed upon but the contract is not enforceable under this paragraph beyond the quantity of goods shown in such writing."

its contents, it satisfies the requirements of subsection (1) against such party unless written notice of objection to its contents is given within ten days after it is received." [74]

Finally this section of the Code provides that the agreement is enforceable despite the absence of a memorandum "if the party against whom enforcement is sought admits in his pleading, testimony or otherwise in court that a contract for sale was made, but the contract is not enforceable under this provision beyond the quantity of goods admitted." [75]

§ 314.   Is the Oral Contract Which Does Not Comply with the Statute "Unenforceable" or "Void"?

The many Statutes of Frauds which have been adopted have not been uniform in describing the effect of non-compliance with the Statute. The fourth section of the English Statute says "no action shall be brought," the seventeenth section says "no action shall be allowed to be good." The Uniform Commercial Code states that the oral contract "is not enforceable by way of action or defense." [76] Some states say that the oral contract is "void" [77] and at least one state talks in terms of admissibility of evidence.[78]

Partly as a result of the difference in wording above and partly as a result of judicial interpretation the effect of non-compliance has not always been deemed to be the same.

The vast majority of the cases have held that the Statute merely makes the contract unenforceable but that the oral contract is operative for a wide variety of purposes.[79] However, the courts which say that the oral contract is void or that the oral contract is not admissible have held that the oral contract is inoperative at least for some of these purposes.[80]

---

74. U.C.C. § 2–201(2). This means that under the circumstances provided for in the Code, the receiver of the memorandum is in the equivalent position of having signed the writing so that it may be enforced against him.

75. U.C.C. § 2–201(3) (b). Cf. Martocci v. Greater N. Y. Brewery, 301 N.Y. 57, 92 N.E.2d 887 (1950), motion denied 301 N.Y. 662, 93 N.E.2d 926 (1950). Comment 7 adds: "Under this section it is no longer possible to admit the contract in court and still treat the statute as a defense. However, the contract is not thus conclusively established. The admission so made by a party is itself evidential against

him of the truth of the facts so admitted and of nothing more; as against the other party, it is not evidential at all." See also § 297 supra.

76. U.C.C. § 2–201(1).

77. E. g., McKinney's New York Gen. Obligations Law § 5–701.

78. Iowa Code Ann. § 622.32.

79. 2 Corbin § 279 lists ten purposes for which the oral contract is effective under this view.

80. 2 Corbin §§ 284, 288. Because a statute says that the oral contract is void it does not follow that such lan-

This difference probably can be best understood in the light of a few illustrations. We have already seen that under the majority view if the memorandum is signed by only one party it is enforceable against him.[81] However under the minority view, since the return promise of the unsigned party is not sufficient consideration, being void, the entire contract is unenforceable under the doctrine of mutuality.[82]

Again under the majority view the Statute of Frauds must be pleaded as an affirmative defense.[83] However under the minority view, since the oral agreement is no contract at all, this may be shown under a general denial,[84] or, if no writing is pleaded, a motion to dismiss for failure to state a cause of action.[85] But even here it cannot be raised for the first time upon appeal.[86]

Again where the contract has been fully performed on both sides it is unanimously agreed that the Statute has no effect, thus indicating that the oral agreement is not void.[87] So also the general rule is that the Statute of Frauds is personal to the party to the contract and those in privity with him, and so a third party may not assert its invalidity, thus indicating that the oral agreement is not void.[88] However, the opposite result has been reached where the Statute was deemed to make the contract void.[89]

Finally, the oral contract is shown to be unenforceable by the rule, previously referred to, that the memorandum may be made at a time other than the time of contracting.[90] However, if the oral contract was "void" the writing would have to come into existence at the same time as the agreement or at least while both parties were still in agreement.[91]

guage is literally interpreted. For example, the New York Statute (see note 77 supra) says void but has often been interpreted as meaning "voidable" or unenforceable. Crane v. Powell, 139 N.Y. 379, 34 N.E. 911 (1893).

81. See § 311, note 58 supra.

82. Wilkinson v. Heavenrich, 58 Mich. 574, 26 N.W. 139 (1886).

83. Gentile Bros. Corp. v. Rowena Homes, Inc., 352 Mass. 584, 227 N.E.2d 338 (1967); Crane v. Powell, 139 N.Y. 379, 34 N.E. 911 (1893).

84. Jones v. Pettigrew, 25 S.D. 432, 127 N.W. 538 (1910).

85. Leonard v. Martling, 378 Pa. 339, 106 A.2d 585 (1954).

86. Iverson v. Cirkel, 56 Minn. 299, 57 N.W. 800 (1894).

87. Restatement, Contracts § 219; Blackwell v. Blackwell, 196 Mass. 186, 81 N.E. 910 (1907).

88. Restatement, Contracts § 218; Pasquay v. Pasquay, 235 Ill. 48, 85 N.E. 316 (1908); Amsinck v. American Ins. Co., 129 Mass. 185 (1880).

89. Gerndt v. Conradt, 117 Wis. 15, 93 N.W. 804 (1903).

90. See § 310, note 52 supra.

91. Wilkinson v. Heavenrich, 58 Mich. 574, 26 N.W. 139 (1886).

§ 315.   Effect of Part of a Contract being Unenforceable Because of the Statute

Where some of the promises in a contract are within the Statute and others are not, the general rule is that no part of the contract is enforceable.[92]   Any other approach would appear to be unfair.   A large number of cases have applied the same rule even though the contract might be considered divisible.[93]   But there are cases to the contrary which hold that if the contract is divisible and the part which is not within the Statute is performed, the corresponding promise may be enforced.[94]

There are exceptions to the general rule stated above.   The first is where all of the promises which are within the Statute have been performed, then all of the other promises become enforceable.   The second exception occurs where the party who is to receive the performance under the only promise or promises within the Statute agrees to abandon that part of the performance.[95]

It should also be recalled that under some of the sections of the Statute of Frauds full performance or even part performance may make the contract enforceable.

However, where a promisor makes a promise of alternative performances, one of which is within the Statute and the other without, it is generally held that the promisee may enforce the promise which is without the Statute.[96]

§ 316.   Oral Rescission or Variation of a Contract Within the Statute

We have seen that as a general rule a written contract may be rescinded or modified orally and that the only question which is usually presented is one of consideration.[97]   Does the same rule apply when a contract is within the Statute of Frauds and is evidenced by a sufficient memorandum?

There are some cases which hold that when a contract is within the Statute of Frauds and is in writing, it may not be modified or re-

---

92.   Restatement, Contracts § 221; contra, White Lighting Co. v. Wolfson, 68 Cal. 347, 66 Cal.Rptr. 697, 438 P.2d 345 (1968).

93.   Hurley v. Donovan, 182 Mass. 64, 64 N.E. 685 (1902).

94.   Blue Valley Creamery Co. v. Consolidated Products Co., 81 F.2d 182 (8th Cir. 1936); Belleville Lumber & Supply Co. v. Chamberlain, 120 Ind. App. 12, 84 N.E.2d 60 (1949).

95.   Restatement, Contracts § 221; Restatement, Contracts (2d) § 221(3) states that the exception does not apply to a contract to transfer property on the promisor's death.

96.   The cases are collected in 13 A.L.R. 267 (1921).   But see § 302 supra which relates only to the one year section.

97.   See § 61 supra.

scinded by an oral agreement.[98] The better rule, however, is that if the new agreement is not within the Statute of Frauds it is not only enforceable without a writing but also serves to discharge the previous written agreement.[99] If the new agreement is within the Statute of Frauds and is unenforceable because it is oral, the former written contract remains enforceable [1] so long as the conduct of the party attempting to enforce is not operative as a waiver.[2] But the waiver may be retracted by reasonable notice that strict performance will be required of any term waived, "unless the retraction would be unjust in view of a material change of position in reliance on the waiver." [3]

§ 317. To What Extent May an Oral Contract Which is Not Enforceable Because of the Statute of Frauds be Used as a Defense?

It is certainly the general rule that a contract which is not enforceable because of the Statute of Frauds may not be used "by way of action or defense." [4] This obviously means that the oral contract may not be used by way of counterclaim, set-off, or recoupment.[5]

There are a number of exceptions to the rule, some of which are discussed in the sections which follow. One occurs when the plaintiff is suing in quasi-contracts but is in default and the defendant is not in default and has never refused to sign a sufficient memorandum when requested by the plaintiff.[6] This matter is discussed in more detail in section 320 infra.

So also an agreement which is unenforceable because of the Statute of Frauds may operate to prevent a tort from occurring.[7] For

98. Bradley v. Harter, 156 Ind. 499, 60 N.E. 139 (1901).

99. ABC Outdoor Advertising, Inc. v. Dolhun's Marine, Inc., 38 Wis.2d 457, 157 N.W.2d 680 (1968); Restatement, Contracts § 222; 2 Corbin § 302; 4 Williston § 592. As to land contracts, see Restatement, Contracts (2d) § 222, Comment c and § 223(1).

1. Lieberman v. Templar Motor Co., 236 N.Y. 139, 140 N.E. 222 (1923); accord, U.C.C. § 2–209(3).

2. Van Iderstine Co. v. Barnet Leather Co., 242 N.Y. 425, 152 N.E. 250, 46 A. L.R. 858 (1926); accord, U.C.C. § 2–209(4).

3. U.C.C. § 2–209(5); Imperator Realty Co. v. Tull, 228 N.Y. 447, 127 N.E. 263 (1920).

4. U.C.C. § 2–201(1); Restatement, Contracts § 217.

5. It is also obvious that if the plaintiff is suing upon an oral contract and has a sufficient memorandum signed by the defendant alone, the defendant may still use any defense arising out of the terms and conditions of the contract. Oxborough v. St. Martin, 169 Minn. 72, 210 N.W. 854, 49 A.L.R. 1115 (1926); Restatement, Contracts (2d) § 217B.

6. Restatement, Contracts § 217(1) (b). On the question of refusing to sign a memorandum, see Restatement, Contracts (2d) 217C(2), Comment b.

7. Restatement, Contracts § 217(c); Restatement, Contracts (2d) § 217D.

example, if A has entered into possession under the provisions of an unenforceable contract or lease, he is not a trespasser until he receives notice of repudiation from the vendor or lessor.[8]

§ 318. Some Miscellaneous Rules

The Statute of Frauds does not apply to formal contracts. Included in the concept "formal contracts" are contracts under seal, recognizances and negotiable instruments.[9] In the case of a contract that is within the Statute of Frauds an oral promise to execute a sufficient memorandum is not enforceable for the simple reason that, if it were, the very purpose of the Statute could be circumvented.[10]

It must also be noted that a contract may be within one or more sections of the Statute of Frauds and that ordinarily the various clauses of the Statute of Frauds apply separately. However, where a land contract is specifically enforceable under the doctrine of part performance the other clauses of the Statute do not prevent enforcement.

III. RESTITUTIONARY REMEDIES

Analysis

Sec.
319. Introduction.
320. The Plaintiff Must Not be in Default.
321. Effect of Defendant's Restoration of the Status Quo.
322. Restitution Denied Where Policy of the Statute Would be Thwarted.
323. Measure of Recovery.
324. The Contract Price as Evidence of Value: Contrast Between Damages and Restitution.
325. Specific Restitution in Equity.

§ 319. Introduction

It is neither illegal nor against public policy to enter into an oral agreement of the kind governed by the Statute of Frauds. A party who in whole or part performs under such an agreement is not an outlaw.[11] Thus, as we have seen, the courts have developed doctrines under which the oral agreement will be enforced if sufficient perform-

---

8. Rosenstein v. Gottfried, 145 Minn. 243, 176 N.W. 844 (1920).

9. 2 Corbin § 280.

10. 2 Corbin § 283. On the question of refusing to sign a memorandum, see also Restatement, Contracts (2d) § 217C. Comment b.

11. On the contrary, it has been suggested that a defendant's attorney who automatically raises the defense of the Statute in any case in which it is applicable may be guilty of unethical conduct. Stevens, Ethics and the Statute of Frauds, 37 Cornell L.Q. 355 (1952).

ance has been rendered on one side.[12]   As indicated in the prior discussion, the circumstances under which performance will be a sufficient predicate for enforcement of the contract varies with respect to the particular subdivision of the Statute in question and from jurisdiction to jurisdiction.

It seems everywhere to be agreed that a plaintiff who has rendered some performance and has not defaulted may recover in quasi contract for the value of the benefits he [13] has conferred on the defendant [14] and in some instances he may have specific restitution.[15]   The majority of such cases involves a performance which is not sufficient to bring into operation the rules which would permit enforcement of the contract.   There is substantial authority to the effect that even in a case in which the plaintiff could secure enforcement of the contract on grounds of performance, he may elect a restitutionary remedy.[16] Restitutionary remedies include quasi contractual relief in which the recovery is always and solely for a sum of money.   Also included are equitable remedies in which specific restitution is granted, such as by cancellation of a conveyance or imposition of a constructive trust, and the legal remedy of replevin.

§ 320.   The Plaintiff Must Not be in Default

According to the great weight of authority, a plaintiff who is entitled to restitution for his performance under an unenforceable contract must not be in default under the agreement,[17] which of course means that the defendant must have repudiated or otherwise materially breached the agreement.[18]   It is obvious that proof of the oral

---

12. See § 296 supra, as to real estate transactions; § 304 supra, as to the one year section; § 295 supra as to contracts for the sale of goods.

13. Apparently very few cases have considered the question of whether a third party beneficiary may recover in quasi contract for the value of the performance rendered by the promisee under an unenforceable contract. Recovery has been denied on the ground that the plaintiff had conferred no benefit on the defendant. Pickelsimer v. Pickelsimer, 257 N.C. 696, 127 S.E. 2d 557 (1962), 41 N.C.Rev. 890 (1963). The same theory led a court to grant restitution to the promisee under an oral contract for the conveyance of land to a third person. Graham v. Graham, 134 App.Div. 777, 119 N.Y.S.

1013 (3d Dept. 1909).   Cf. Restatement, Contracts § 356.

14. Ricks v. Sumler, 179 Va. 571, 19 S. E.2d 889 (1942); 2 Corbin § 321; 3 Williston § 534.

15. 2 Corbin § 323; 3 Williston § 535.

16. 2 Corbin § 323; 3 Williston § 535.

17. Watkins v. Wells, 303 Ky. 728, 198 S.W.2d 662, 169 A.L.R. 185 (1946); Bendix v. Ross, 205 Wis. 581, 238 N. W. 381 (1931); 2 Corbin §§ 332–34; 3 Williston § 538; see also Keener, Quasi Contracts 234–39 (1893); Woodward, Quasi Contracts § 98 (1913).

18. "There is no right of restitution against a defendant who is not in default and who is willing to perform the contract or to execute a memoran-

agreement is admissible to establish the obligations of the parties, otherwise a breach could not be proved.

In a minority of jurisdictions, under the doctrine of Britton v. Turner,[19] a defaulting party may have quasi contractual relief under an enforceable contract. It logically follows that in such jurisdictions a defaulting party may have quasi contractual relief under a contract unenforceable under the Statute of Frauds.[20] The same result has been reached in a number of other jurisdictions on the theory that if the decision were made to turn on which party was in default, the court would be indirectly enforcing the contract.[21]

§ 321.   Effect of Defendant's Restoration of the Status Quo

According to the Restatement,[22] if the defendant tenders restoration of specific property delivered to him pursuant to an unenforceable contract, the plaintiff's right to quasi contractual relief is divested. This is on the theory that the defendant's obligation is primarily that of making specific restitution.[23] There is a paucity of case authority on the point and the leading case is to the contrary.[24]

§ 322.   Restitution Denied Where Policy of the Statute Would be Thwarted

According to the Restatement, "[t]he remedy of restitution is not available if the Statute that makes the contract unenforceable so provides, or if the purpose of the Statute would be nullified by granting such a remedy." [25] This exception to the general rule does not apply to the original Statute of Frauds nor to the reenactment of its basic provisions.[26] The exception seems to have been confined largely to statutes enacted in a number of jurisdictions requiring a promise to pay a commission for services as a real estate broker to be in writing. The courts in these jurisdictions have generally refused quasi con-

dum sufficient to make it enforceable." Restatement, Contracts § 355(4); accord, Restatement, Contracts (2d) § 217(c).

19.   6 N.H. 481 (1834); see § 159 supra.

20.   3 Williston § 538.

21.   Freeman v. Foss, 145 Mass. 361, 14 N.E. 141 (1887); accord, Reedy v. Ebsen, 60 S.D. 1, 242 N.W. 592 (1932), adhered to 61 S.D. 54, 245 N.W. 908 (1933), on the additional ground that in South Dakota an oral contract within the Statute of Frauds is void rather than unenforceable.

22.   Restatement, Contracts § 355(2).

23.   Keener, Quasi Contracts 285–89 (1893); 3 Williston § 535.

24.   Hawley v. Moody, 24 Vt. 603 (1852); supported by 2 Corbin § 324.

25.   Restatement, Contracts § 355(3).

26.   2 Corbin § 324.

tractual recovery to the broker who alleges performance under an oral agreement.[27]

§ 323.   Measure of Recovery

In quasi contract cases it is usually stated that the plaintiff's recovery is the value of "benefits conferred" upon the defendant.[28]   As discussed elsewhere in this book,[29] the concept of "benefit" is so flexible as to be misleading.   Indeed, the weight of decided cases supports a rule to the effect that the measure of recovery is the detriment incurred by the plaintiff in rendering the bargained for performance.[30]   There is, however, only limited authority allowing recovery with respect to detriment incurred in preparation for performance.

Typical of the cases which wrestle with the concept of benefit is Fabian v. Wasatch Orchard Co.[31]   The plaintiff was employed as a

27. Baugh v. Darley, 112 Utah 1, 184 P.2d 335 (1947); Hale v. Kreisel, 194 Wis. 271, 215 N.W. 227, 56 A.L.R. 780 (1927); accord, under a statute limited to certain business brokerage contracts, N.Y.Gen.Obligations Law § 5–701(10); contra, Clinkinbeard v. Poole, 266 S.W.2d 796, 41 A.L.R.2d 901 (Ky. 1954).

Although no right to restitution exists, a subsequent promise to pay may be enforced under the moral obligation doctrine (§ 87 supra).   Coulter v. Howard, 203 Cal. 17, 262 P. 751 (1927); Ekelman v. Freeman, 350 Mich. 665, 87 N.W.2d 157 (1957); Muir v. Kane, 55 Wash. 131, 104 P. 153 (1909); Elbinger v. Capital & Teutonia Co., 208 Wis. 163, 242 N.W. 568 (1932).

28. See generally, Jeanblanc, Restitution Under the Statute of Frauds: Measurement of the Legal Benefit Unjustly Retained, 15 Mo.L.Rev. 1 (1950); Jeanblanc, Restitution Under the Statute of Frauds: What Constitutes an Unjust Retention, 48 Mich.L. Rev. 923 (1950); Jeanblanc, Restitution Under the Statute of Frauds: What Constitutes a Legal Benefit, 26 Ind.L.J. 1 (1950).

29. See § 240 supra.

30. 3 Williston § 536, collecting cases at p. 830, n. 6.   It must be recognized,

however, that although the courts permit recovery based on the detriment incurred by the defendant, they tend to couch their decisions in terms of benefit or constructive benefit.   See Fuller and Perdue, The Reliance Interest in Contract Damages, 46 Yale L.J. 373, 394 (1937), where the authors state:

"When the benefit received by the defendant has become as attenuated as it is in some of the cases cited, and when this benefit is 'measured' by the plaintiff's detriment, can it be supposed that a desire to make the defendant disgorge is really a significant part of judicial motivation? When it becomes impossible to believe this, then the courts are actually protecting the reliance interest."

A leading case to the contrary, Boone v. Coe, 153 Ky. 233, 154 S.W. 900, 51 L.R.A.,N.S. 907 (1913), held that expenses incurred in moving from Texas to Kentucky in order to commence performance of an oral tenancy agreement within the Statute of Frauds were not recoverable as no benefit had been received.

31. 41 Utah 404, 125 P. 860, L.R.A. 1916D, 892 (1912); but see Baugh v. Darley, 112 Utah 1, 184 P.2d 335 (1947).

salesman on a commission basis under an oral contract not performable within one year. Acting under the contract the plaintiff procured a number of orders which were filled by the defendant. In an action by the plaintiff for quasi contractual relief, the defendant argued that the products were sold at a loss and therefore it had not received a benefit. The court, however, ruled that any performance rendered pursuant to agreement and accepted by the defendant constituted a benefit whether or not it resulted in economic enrichment.[32]

A different kind of situation was presented in Riley v. Capital Airlines, Inc.[33] in which the plaintiff entered into an oral contract to supply defendant's requirements of methanol for a five year period. Upon the defendant's repudiation of the agreement the plaintiff was permitted to recover his losses based on expenditures made as a necessary prerequisite to performance. The plaintiff had purchased special tanks and pumps to produce and store the methanol and was forced by the breach to resell these at a loss. In no sense were these losses a benefit to the defendant. Both of the leading contract treatises assert, without qualification, that in the absence of receipt by the defendant of the plaintiff's property or services, no quasi contractual relief is possible.[34] Yet, sporadic decisions like the Riley case do occur [35] and demonstrate attempts by the courts to prevent the Statute of Frauds from operating as an instrument of injustice. The groping of the courts for a solution of this problem has also led other courts in similar circumstances to enforce the contract on a theory of estoppel.[36]

§ 324. The Contract Price as Evidence of Value: Contrast Between Damages and Restitution

If A orally agrees to perform services for a two year period in return for B's promise to pay $2,000 at the end of the period, the contract is within the Statute of Frauds. If B discharges A at the end of six months, may A introduce the contract price as evidence of the value of his services? The great weight of authority is to the effect that

32. Accord, Matousek v. Quirici, 195 Ill.App. 391 (1915) (plaintiff required to pay reasonable rental value of premises orally leased although he never occupied the premises); Randolph v. Castle, 190 Ky. 776, 228 S.W. 418 (1921) (employees may recover for value of their time while on the job site although they performed no services).

33. 185 F.Supp. 165 (S.D.Ala.1960).

34. 2 Corbin § 327; 3 Williston § 536 at p. 832.

35. Randolph v. Castle, 190 Ky. 776, 228 S.W. 418 (1921), 5 Minn.L.Rev. 567 (1921); Rineer v. Collins, 156 Pa. 342, 27 A. 28 (1893) (tort theory); McCrowell v. Burson, 79 Va. 290 (1884) (implied in fact contract theory).

36. See § 326 infra.

the price is admissible into evidence [37] despite the fact that in many cases the jury's verdict will often be the equivalent of what it would have been in an action on the contract.

If the preceding sections have not made it clear, however, it should be explicitly stated that in many instances the plaintiff's judgment in an action for quasi contract may differ markedly from the result which would be obtainable if he could have enforced the contract in an action for damages. One illustration may suffice. Suppose an uncle orally promised his nephew to devise to him all of his real property in exchange for the nephew's promise to take care of him for life.[38] Suppose further that several weeks later the uncle repudiated and soon thereafter died. In a quasi contractual action for the value of his services, the nephew may realistically hope to recover several hundred or perhaps even several thousand dollars. In an action for damages to enforce the contract he would be entitled to the benefit of his bargain; that is, the value of the real property, conceivably millions of dollars, with a deduction for the expenses saved as a result of the repudiation.

On the other hand, in an action for restitution, the plaintiff's recovery may sometimes be greater than would have been available in an action on the contract for damages. Thus, an employee who alleged that he was hired for a three year period under an oral agreement and had been compensated at the rate of $18 to $25 per week before his wrongful discharge was permitted to plead and prove that the value of the services he had rendered was $50 per week.[39]

37. Grantham v. Grantham, 205 N.C. 363, 171 S.E. 331 (1933); Bennett Leasing Co. v. Ellison, 15 Utah 2d 72, 387 P.2d 246, 21 A.L.R.3d 1 (1963); Cochran v. Bise, 197 Va. 483, 90 S.E. 2d 178 (1955); 2 Corbin § 328; 3 Williston § 536 at p. 838; Restatement, Contracts § 217(2); Restatement, Contracts (2d) § 217E. The reader is warned to beware of statements couched in terms of "weight of authority." Consider that in one jurisdiction the following cases deem the contract price admissible: In re Schweizer's Estate, 231 N.Y.S.2d 534 (Surr.Ct.1962); Leahy v. Campbell, 70 App.Div. 127, 75 N.Y.S. 72 (1st Dept. 1902); Gall v. Gall, 27 App.Div. 173, 50 N.Y.S. 563 (1st Dept. 1898), motion granted and appeal dism'd 160 N.Y. 696, 55 N.E. 1095 (1900); and the following cases deem it inadmissible: Erben v. Lorillard, 19 N.Y. 299 (1859);

Schlanger v. Cowan, 13 A.D.2d 739, 214 N.Y.S.2d 784 (1st Dep't 1961); Parver v. Matthews-Kadetsky Co., 242 App.Div. 1, 273 N.Y.S. 44 (1st Dept. 1934); Black v. Fisher, 145 N.Y.S.2d 142 (Sup.Ct.1955); and see Galvin v. Prentice, 45 N.Y. 162 (1871).

38. It is generally held that a promise to leave real property by will is within the real property Statute of Frauds. See 2 Corbin § 398. In addition some jurisdictions have a specific provision of the Statute of Frauds applicable to contracts to make a testamentary disposition. E. g., McKinney's N.Y.E.P.T.L. § 13–2.1(2).

39. McGilchrist v. F. W. Woolworth Co., 138 Or. 679, 7 P.2d 982 (1932); accord, Schanzenbach v. Brough, 58 Ill.App. 526 (1895) (contract price does not set a maximum).

§ 325. Specific Restitution in Equity

Equity has forged an armory of remedies to aid a deserving petitioner. It is not feasible in a book on basic contract law to attempt even superficial coverage of these remedies. Rather, one recurring fact pattern will be considered to suggest the kind of analysis utilized in equity in cases involving specific restitution.

Very frequently a grantor conveys land to the defendant upon the defendant's oral promise to reconvey it to the grantor upon demand or to hold it in trust for the grantor or some third person.[40] The oral promise may be within the Statute of Frauds provision regarding the transfer of interests in land. In addition, in most jurisdictions there is a specific provision of the Statute of Frauds requiring a writing for the creation of express trusts.[41] It is obvious that the oral promise cannot be enforced as such without conflicting with the Statute. It is also obvious that the grantee who violates the oral agreement has been unjustly enriched.

Equity in such a case may impose a constructive trust on the land or the proceeds if the grantee has sold the land. The trust is said to be "constructive" because it is not based on the agreement but is imposed by law to avoid unjust enrichment and inequitable conduct.

The conditions under which the constructive trust will be imposed, however, is a matter of dispute among the jurisdictions. The weight of authority supports the imposition of a constructive trust (1) where the conveyance was procured by fraud, misrepresentation, duress, undue influence or mistake, (2) where the transferee is a fiduciary, or (3) where the transfer was made as security only.[42] A minority of jurisdictions will construct a trust in any case where there is a violation of an oral agreement to convey.[43] Massachusetts appears to stand alone in refusing to construct a trust for violation of an oral promise, relegating the grantor to a quasi contractual action for the value of the land.[44]

---

40. Sometimes this is done to defraud creditors in which case the grantor is faced with the additional difficulty of recovering under an illegal bargain. See Wantulok v. Wantulok, 67 Wyo. 22, 214 P.2d 477, 21 A.L.R.2d 572, reh. denied, 67 Wyo. 45, 223 P.2d 1030, 21 A.L.R.2d 572 (1950), 37 Va.L.Rev. 453 (1951), 5 Wyo.L.J. 152 (1951).

41. See 2 Corbin § 401.

42. Moses v. Moses, 140 N.J.Eq. 575, 53 A.2d 805, 173 A.L.R. 273 (1947); Re-statement, Restitution § 182; Restatement, Trusts § 44. On conveyances made for purposes of security, see Fogelman, The Deed Absolute as a Mortgage in New York, 32 Fordham L.Rev. 299 (1963).

43. Orella v. Johnson, 38 Cal.2d 693, 242 P.2d 5 (1952), 40 Calif.L.Rev. 621 (1952).

44. Kemp v. Kemp, 248 Mass. 354, 142 N.E. 779 (1924).

While the Restatement of Restitution states that one of the grounds for the imposition of a constructive trust where there has been a violation of an oral agreement to reconvey is the existence of a "fiduciary" relation,[45] many of the cases go well beyond this and hold that any pre-existing confidential relationship is sufficient. This would include such a relationship as husband and wife, father and son, brother and sister, lawyer and client, doctor and patient, priest and parishioner.[46]

It is generally recognized that in order to obtain relief of the kind described here the plaintiff must establish his case by more than the preponderance of the evidence. The cases speak in terms of clear and convincing evidence or of establishing the oral promise beyond a reasonable doubt.[47]

IV. ESTOPPEL

Analysis

Sec.
326. Equitable Estoppel and the Statute of Frauds.
327. Promissory Estoppel.

§ 326. Equitable Estoppel and the Statute of Frauds

Probably all jurisdictions recognize that if the elements of equitable estoppel are present, the party to be charged will not be permitted to avail himself of the defense of the Statute of Frauds. It will be recalled that equitable estoppel requires justifiable detrimental reliance upon a factual representation or conduct of the other. Thus, if the Statute of Frauds of a given jurisdiction requires that an agent's authority be granted in writing, the principal will be estopped from asserting this Statute as a defense if he has indicated to the other contracting party that the agent is duly authorized to act on his behalf.[48]

---

45. Restatement, Restitution § 182.

46. These relationships are specifically enumerated in Fraw Realty Co. v. Natonson, 261 N.Y. 396, 402, 185 N.E. 679 (1933). These are not, however, exclusive. See generally, Newman, Some Reflections on the Function of the Confidential Relationship Doctrine in the Law of Trusts, in Perspectives in Law: Essays for Austin Wakeman Scott 286 (Pound ed. 1964); Talbott, Restitution Remedies in Contract Cases: Finding a Fiduciary or Confidential Relationship to Gain Remedies, 20 Ohio St.L.J. 320 (1959).

47. E. g., for an especially strong statement, Strype v. Lewis, 352 Mo. 1004, 180 S.W.2d 688, 155 A.L.R. 99 (1944), where it was said that the evidence must be so clear, cogent and convincing as to exclude every reasonable doubt from the Chancellor's mind.

48. Fleming v. Dolfin, 214 Cal. 269, 4 P.2d 776, 78 A.L.R. 585 (1931), 20 Cal. L.Rev. 663 (1932); Levy v. Rothfeld, 271 App.Div. 973, 67 N.Y.S.2d 497 (2d Dep't 1947).

So also if the party to be charged by words or conduct represents that he has signed a written memorandum of the contract he will be estopped from pleading the Statute.[49]

§ 327. Promissory Estoppel

It is obvious that the cases which hold that part performance takes a case out of the Statute of Frauds can be explained on grounds of promissory estoppel in the sense that relief is granted because of a party's detrimental reliance on a promise. It must be pointed out, however, that the doctrine of part performance antedated the generalized concept of promissory estoppel and has it own particularized set of rules.

There has been a tendency, however, in a good number of jurisdictions to depart on occasion from the narrower doctrines of part performance and to base a decision on grounds of estoppel whenever the plaintiff's equities are so great as to make a contrary decision unconscionable.[50] In a few jurisdictions, such as California, the tendency to rely upon estoppel has been so great as to result in obliteration of the doctrine of part performance and its incorporation into the more generalized doctrine of estoppel.[51]

Since the appearance of the first Restatement a number of courts have relied upon the doctrine of promissory estoppel stated in Section 90 of the Restatement as a basis of taking a case out of the Statute. Alaska Airlines, Inc. v. Stephenson,[52] is indicative of this tendency which foreshadows a major new approach to cases under the Statute in which there has been substantial reliance upon an oral contract. The plaintiff had been employed as a pilot with Western Airlines, a position which apparently afforded a good deal of employment security. He accepted a position as general manager of the defendant airline. The oral agreement was to the effect that the plaintiff would take a six month leave of absence from his employment with Western to work for the defendant and, if the defendant received a franchise to fly from Seattle to Alaska, the plaintiff would receive a written contract for two years employment. The plaintiff moved his family from

49. McKay Products Corp. v. Jonathan Logan, Inc., 54 Misc.2d 385, 283 N.Y.S.2d 82 (Sup.Ct.1967); Restatement, Contracts § 178, Comment f.

50. See 2 Corbin § 422A (Supp.1964), § 440; 4 Williston § 533A; and see Boesiger v. Freer, 85 Idaho 551, 381 P.2d 802 (1963) (part performance insufficient, but other actions in reliance raised an estoppel); Somerset

Acres West Homes Ass'n v. Daniels, 191 Kan. 583, 383 P.2d 952 (1963); Vogel v. Shaw, 42 Wyo. 333, 294 P. 687, 75 A.L.R. 639 (1930), 29 Mich.L.Rev. 1075 (1931).

51. Monarco v. Lo Greco, 35 Cal.2d 621, 220 P.2d 737 (1950); Seymour v. Oelrichs, 156 Cal. 782, 106 P. 88 (1910).

52. 15 Alaska 272, 217 F.2d 295 (1954).

California to Alaska, abandoned his tenure rights with his former employer and occupied the position of general manager. When the franchise was obtained, no written contract was forthcoming. The plaintiff was discharged. The court in ruling for the plaintiff explicitly based its decision on promissory estoppel, suggesting that this approach "will generally be followed throughout the country." [53] It has been suggested that "such a holding is clearly impossible of justification on any theory, in view of the language of the statute." [54] This suggestion appears to be based upon a misunderstanding of the relationship between common law doctrines and legislation. The doctrine of estoppel, promissory or otherwise, is as much a part of our law as the Statute of Frauds. It is for the courts to harmonize the Statute and common law doctrine into a coherent and just pattern within our legal system—certainly a difficult task. Until the Statute of Frauds is reformed so as to take into account the many problems which almost three hundred years of history have shown were unforeseen by its draftsmen, the courts should be encouraged in their creative work of doing justice by utilizing all doctrines available to them.

---

53. Id. at 298. The decision is specifically approved in Restatement, Contracts (2d) § 217A, ill. 2. For another case explicitly utilizing the term promissory estoppel in connection with enforcement of an oral agreement within the Statute of Frauds, see Miller v. Lawlor, 245 Iowa 1144, 66 N.W.2d 267, 48 A.L.R.2d 1058 (1954). Note that in this context promissory estoppel is not applied as a substitute for consideration as the oral contracts are supported by consideration.

54. Grismore § 284.

CHAPTER 17

JOINT AND SEVERAL CONTRACTS

Analysis

Sec.
328. Multiple Promisors.
329. When Promisors are Bound Jointly, Severally, or Jointly and Severally.
330. Consequences of Joint Liability.
    (a) Compulsory Joinder of Joint Promisors.
    (b) The Discharge of Other Joint Promisors by a Judgment Against One.
    (c) Only a Joint Judgment Can be Entered Against Joint Promisors.
    (d) The Rule of Survivorship.
    (e) A Discharge of One Joint Obligor Releases the Others.
331. Consequences of Joint and Several Liability.
332. Consequences of Several Liability.
333. Relation of Co-Obligors to Each Other—Contribution.
334. Multiple Promisees.
335. Compulsory Joinder of Joint Obligees.
336. Discharge by One Joint Obligee.
337. Survivorship of Joint Rights.

§ 328. Multiple Promisors

In this chapter we are concerned with rights and duties created by multiple promises of the *same* performance. We are not concerned with multiple promises of *different* performances. Whether or not multiple promises refer to the same performance or to different performances is a question of interpretation and beyond the purview of a treatise of this size.[1] For example, if A and B each promise to pay C $500.00 they are promising different performances. However, if A and B each promise to pay C a total of $1000.00 so that each is liable for $1000.00, but C is entitled to collect it only once, then they are promising the same performance.

---

[1]. Restatement, Contracts (2d), Chapter 5, Introductory Note; 4 Corbin §§ 926, 927. § 111 of the Restatement (2d) states:

(1) Where two or more parties to a contract make a promise or promises to the same promisee, the manifested intention of the parties determines whether they promise that the same performance or separate performances shall be given.

(2) Unless a contrary intention is manifested, a promise by two or more promisors is a promise that the same performance shall be given.

What we are concerned with here is the old common law doctrine of joint, joint and several, and several obligations.[2] This problem does not arise unless the promises relate to the same performance. The question here is whether multiple promisors of the same performance have promised as a unit (jointly), or have promised the same performance separately (severally), or both as a unit and separately (jointly and severally). Having made this determination, the question then is the effect at common law of joint, joint and several, or several obligations, and finally what changes have been made (ordinarily by statute) in the arbitrary and unfortunate common law rules.

§ 329. When Promisors are Bound Jointly, Severally, or Jointly and Severally

The old common law rule was to the effect that promises of the same performance were joint [3] "unless the promises took a linguistic form appropriate to several duties." [4] Thus if A & B as promisors stated, "we jointly promise to pay the same obligation," there would be nothing to overcome the presumption of a joint obligation. However, if A & B stated "each of us independently promises to pay the obligation," the presumption of a joint obligation would be overcome by the words of severance.[5] If A & B promised by saying, "we and each of us promise to pay," the obligation is joint and several [6] and the same is true where two or more persons promise in the first person singular.[7] In the case of a joint and several obligation involving two promisors there are three obligations, the joint obligation and the two several obligations.

The old common law tended to view the problem "as a deduction from legal concepts." [8] The more modern approach is that the question is one of the intention of the parties and, although the presumption in favor of joint liability continues to exist, it is more easily overcome.[9]

---

2. There is a similar problem where a promise is made to multiple promisees. This problem is discussed at the end of this chapter.

3. Restatement, Contracts (2d) § 112(2); 4 Corbin § 425.

4. Restatement, Contracts (2d) § 112, Comment b.

5. Restatement, Contracts (2d) § 112, ill. 7. Subscription contracts, that is promises in one instrument to make individual payments are held to be several even though reading, "We, the undersigned, subscribe and promise to pay the amounts set opposite our names." 4 Corbin § 927.

6. Lorimer v. Goff, 216 Mich. 587, 185 N.W. 791 (1922).

7. Restatement, Contracts § 115; Continental Ill. Bank & Trust Co. v. Clement, 259 Mich. 167, 242 N.W. 877 (1932).

8. Restatement, Contracts (2d) § 112, Comment b.

9. Restatement, Contracts (2d) § 112, Comments b and c; 4 Corbin § 925;

The fact that one of the parties is a principal and the other a surety does not change these rules,[10] and the same is true even where the parties have agreed inter se, unknown to the promisee that, each shall be liable to the promisee for an aliquot share of the undertaking.[11]

In many states there are statutes which state that promises which are joint under the common law rules should be treated as if they were joint and several.[12]

§ 330. Consequences of Joint Liability

There are at least five common law doctrines relating to joint obligations which have proved unsatisfactory. They are as follows: 1) compulsory joinder of joint promisors; 2) the discharge of other joint promisors by a judgment against one; 3) only a joint judgment can be entered against joint promisors; 4) the rule of survivorship which barred an action against the estate of a deceased joint obligor; and 5) the rule that a discharge of one joint promisor released the others. These doctrines shall now be considered seriatim.

(a) Compulsory Joinder of Joint Promisors

If A & B are joint obligors and C, the obligee, brought a suit against A, at early common law it was held that A could demur to the declaration and the demurrer would be sustained. This was true even though B was insolvent or beyond the jurisdiction. The theory was that A and B had promised as a unit and therefore had to be sued as a unit.[13] In time the rule was modified so that the fact of non-joinder could be raised only by a plea in abatement, unless the non-joinder appeared on the face of the declaration,[14] and in the United States at least the plea could be defeated if the joint obligor not joined was not

Douglas v. Bergere, 94 Cal.App.2d 267, 210 P.2d 727 (1949). But, the vitality of the common law presumption of joint liability should not be underestimated. See United States Printing & Lithograph Co. v. Powers, 233 N.Y. 143, 134 N.E. 225 (1922); 2 Williston § 320.

10. Restatement, Contracts (2d) § 112, Comment c; City of Philadelphia v. Reeves, 48 Pa.St. 472 (1865).

11. Knowlton v. Parsons, 198 Mass. 439, 84 N.E. 798 (1908).

12. The statutes are collected in the Restatement, Contracts (2d) in the In-

troductory Note to Chapter 5 pp. 245–246, as well as in 2 Williston §§ 336–336A; but see Uniform Partnership Act § 15 as to a partner's liability for partnership obligations, which in most instances is joint, but is some instances joint and several.

13. 4 Corbin § 929; 2 Williston § 327; see generally, Reed, Compulsory Joinder of Parties in Civil Actions, 55 Mich.L.Rev. 327 (1927).

14. Rice v. Shute, 96 Eng.Rep. 409 (1770); see Shipman, Common Law Pleading § 277 (1923).

alive or not subject to process.[15] The rule of compulsory joinder continues to be the general rule in the United States today in the absence of a statute.[16] But exceptions have also been made "for dormant partners, bankrupt co-promisors, and promisors against whom a claim is barred by the Statute of Limitations." [17]

The statutes referred to above have changed the common law rule in a variety of ways. One type of statute allows less than all of the joint obligors to be sued (provided all are named) in the discretion of the court. These statutes further provide that the judgment binds the joint property of all of the joint obligors but the separate property only of those served.[18] A second type of statute is similar to the first except that it eliminates the requirement that all of the joint obligors be named.[19] Another type of statute permits an action against those served without any necessity for naming the other obligors or without any element of discretion in the judge.[20] Many states also have statutes which permit partners to be sued in the firm name irrespective of whether the obligation is joint.[21]

(b) The Discharge of Other Joint Promisors by a Judgment Against One

In subsection (a) above we discussed the common law rule whereby a joint obligor could object to the non-joinder of other joint obligors and cause the action to be dismissed. If he did not object, obviously the action would proceed to judgment. We discuss here the result where the judgment is in favor of the plaintiff and against the

---

15. Camp v. Gress, 250 U.S. 308, 39 S. Ct. 478, 63 L.Ed. 997 (1917); see Shipman, Common Law Pleading § 277 (1923).

16. Restatement, Contracts (2d) § 117.

17. Restatement, Contracts (2d) § 117, Comment b.

18. This type of statute is now effective in Alaska, Indiana, Nevada, New York, North Carolina, North Dakota, Oklahoma, Oregon, South Carolina, Washington and Wisconsin. See, e. g., McKinney's N.Y. C.P.L.R. 1501 which reads as follows: "Where less than all of the named defendants in an action based upon a joint obligation, contract or liability are served with the summons, the plaintiff may proceed against the defendants served, unless the court otherwise directs, and if the judgment is for the plaintiff it

may be taken against all the defendants."

19. Statutes in Iowa, Kentucky, Mississippi and West Virginia appear to be of this type.

20. California, Georgia, Idaho, Nebraska, New Jersey, Ohio, Utah, Virginia and Wyoming have this type of statute. See West's Ann.Cal. Code Civ. Proc. § 414 which reads as follows:

"Where the action is against two or more defendants jointly or severally liable on a contract, and the summons is served on one or more, but not on all of them, the plaintiff may proceed against the defendants served in the same manner as if they were the only defendants."

21. See Crane and Bromberg, Partnership § 60 (1968); 2 Rowley, Partnerships § 49.3 (2d ed. 1960).

joint obligor or obligors served. The result reached was that the judgment against the joint obligor or obligors sued merged the entire claim so that no further action could be maintained against the other joint obligors, even though the parties sued proved to be insolvent.[22] In time exceptions came to be made in the case of promisors who were out of the jurisdiction, for foreign judgments, for cases of estoppel, and for judgments on promises given as conditional payment or collateral security.[23]

Today there are many statutes which provide that a judgment against a joint promisor or promisors does not bar an action against other joint promisors, and some have permitted the joint property of those not served to be bound subject to later proceeding wherein they may be required to show cause why they should not be bound.[24]

(c) Only a Joint Judgment Can be Entered Against Joint Promisors

In the preceding subsection we discussed the problem presented where the plaintiff obtained a judgment against the joint promisor or promisors served. Here the question is the effects of a judgment in favor of one of the joint obligors served. The common law took the position that as against joint obligors only a joint judgment could be entered. This meant that it was impossible to have a verdict against the plaintiff in favor of one promisor and in favor of the plaintiff against another promisor. In other words if the plaintiff lost to one joint obligor he must lose as to all.[25]

Eventually an exception was made where a defendant won the case because of a defense personal to him as, for example, lack of capacity, discharge in bankruptcy and statute of limitations.[26]

The Restatement Second in § 118 sets forth the modern rule when it states: "In an action against promisors of the same performance, whether their duties are joint, several, or joint and several, judgment can properly be entered for or against one even though no judgment or a different judgment is entered with respect to another, except that

---

22. Ward v. Johnson, 13 Mass. 148 (1816); Mitchell v. Brewster, 28 Ill. 163 (1862).

23. Restatement, Contracts (2d) § 119, Comment b; 2 Williston § 327.

24. The statutes are collected in the Introductory Note to § 111 of the Restatement (2d). See, e. g., McKinney's N.Y.Gen.Obligations Law § 15–102 (based on the Model Joint Obligations Act) which reads: "A judgment against one or more of several obligors, or against one or more of joint, or of joint and several obligors shall not discharge a co-obligor who was not a party to the proceeding wherein the judgment was rendered."

25. Simpson, Contracts § 137 (2d ed. 1965). Although the judgment is joint, a successful plaintiff could levy against the individual assets of any joint obligor who was served.

26. Restatement, Contracts (2d) § 118, Comment a.

a judgment for one and against another is improper where there has been a determination on the merits and the liability of one cannot exist without the liability of the other." [27]

(d) The Rule of Survivorship

At early common law if a joint obligor died his estate could not be sued and so the creditor could proceed only against the surviving co-obligors.[28] If all of the joint obligors died only the estate of the last one to die was liable to the creditor.[29] Obviously this rule worked unfairly particularly where the remaining obligor or obligors were insolvent. The Courts of Chancery did not rigidly apply this doctrine and invented various procedures in order to do justice.[30]

Today whether by statute or by case decisions this rule has been abolished in most states.[31] However, there are still some decisions to the effect that a surety who is a joint obligor is discharged upon his death.[32]

(e) A Discharge of One Joint Obligor Releases the Others

The joint nature of a joint obligation also led the common law courts to hold that a discharge of one or more joint obligors discharged the other joint obligors.[33] This was true whether the discharge occurred by virtue of release, rescission or accord and satisfaction and irrespective of the intention of the parties.[34] Since the rule was without any rational basis and operated very unfairly, some of the courts held that the rule operated only in the case of a formal release under seal.[35]

---

27. Accord, 4 Corbin § 929. The exception at the end of the statement is based upon principles of res judicata or collateral estoppel by judgment.

28. Davis v. Van Buren, 72 N.Y. 587 (1878); McLaughlin v. Head, 86 Or. 361, 168 P. 614 (1917); 2 Williston § 344. The fact the deceased joint obligor or his estate was no longer liable to the creditor did not effect the estate's obligation of contribution to a joint obligor who had been compelled to pay.

29. Restatement, Contracts § 126.

30. 4 Corbin § 930; 2 Williston § 344.

31. Restatement, Contracts (2d) § 125, Comment b. A statutory table appears in 2 Williston § 344A.

32. 4 Corbin § 930.

33. 4 Corbin § 931; 2 Williston § 333; see generally Havighurst, The Effect of a Settlement with One Co-Obligor upon the Obligations of the Others, 45 Cornell L.Q. 1 (1951).

34. Restatement, Contracts § 121; Brooks v. Neal, 223 Mass. 467, 112 N. E. 78 (1916); Pacific Southwest Trust & Sav. Bank v. Mayer, 138 Wash. 85, 244 P. 248 (1926); 2 Williston § 333A.

35. Deering v. Moore, 86 Me. 181, 29 A. 988 (1893); Line v. Nelson, 38 N.J.L. 358 (1876); 2 Williston § 333A.

The harsh common law was soon circumvented by using a covenant not to sue.[36] While a release is an executed transaction, a covenant not to sue is executory and even when it is breached it is not specifically enforced in favor of the covenantee, and so it is held that a covenant not to sue is not a defense either to the covenantee or the other joint obligors. The covenantee may be sued but he is protected by requiring the creditor to refrain from levying against the property of the covenantee.[37]

Another device to circumvent the rule was a release containing a reservation of rights against the other obligors.[38] Such a reservation of rights caused the release to be interpreted as a covenant not to sue provided that it was concurrent with the purported release and in the same instrument.[39]

The Restatement Second adopts the common law rule but adds: "Modern decisions have converted it from a rule defeating intention to a rule of presumptive intention," and adds that where a contrary intention is manifested the release or discharge should be treated as a covenant not to sue.[40]

There are also many states which have changed the common law rule by statute. For example, the Model Joint Obligations Act provides that a release or discharge of one or more of joint, joint and several or several obligors does not discharge co-obligors against whom rights are reserved in writing and as part of the same transaction.[41] If there is no reservation of rights, then if the obligee knows or has reason to know "that the obligor released or discharged did not pay so much of the claim as he was bound by his contract or relation with that co-obligor to pay, the obligee's claim against that co-obligor shall be satisfied to the amount which the obligee knew or had reason to know that the released or discharged obligor was bound to such co-obligor to pay." [42]

For example, X, Y and Z are jointly obligated to C in the sum of $18,000 (that is to say each is liable to C for $18,000). Assume that

36. 4 Corbin § 932; 2 Williston §§ 338, 338C.

37. Restatement, Contracts § 124; Restatement, Contracts (2d) § 122.

38. 4 Corbin § 933; 2 Williston § 338.

39. The requirement that the reservation of rights must be in writing and concurrent stems from the parol evidence rule. See Oxford Commercial Corp. v. Landau, 12 N.Y.2d 362, 239 N.Y.S.2d 865, 190 N.E.2d 230, 13 A.L. R.3d 309 (1963). Corbin criticizes the application of the rule to this set of facts upon the grounds that there is no integration and that the oral covenant does not contradict or vary the writing. 4 Corbin § 934.

40. Restatement, Contracts (2d) § 121, Comment a.

41. See, e. g., McKinney's N.Y.Gen.Obligations Law § 15–104.

42. See, e. g., McKinney's N.Y.Gen.Obligations Law § 15–105(1).

they have agreed inter se that X will be liable for ½ and Y for ¼ and Z for ¼. If C, knowing this, releases X, then Y and Z will be liable for only $9,000.

The statute goes on to say that, in the illustration given, if C did not know or have reason to know of the agreement of the parties inter se then Y and Z will be discharged to the extent of the lesser of two amounts:[43] (1) "The amount of the fractional share of the obligor released or discharged," which on the facts in the illustration is $6,000 that is ⅓ (since there are three co-obligors involved) of $18,000. (2) "The amount that such obligor was bound by his contract or relation with his co-obligor to pay" which on the facts is $9,000.

Since the lesser sum is $6,000, it is obvious that C could still proceed against Y and Z for $12,000 ($18,000 − $6,000). It is equally apparent that if Y and Z pay the $12,000 they should still be entitled to collect $3,000 from X.

What has been said does not apply to a suretyship situation. As we have seen it is perfectly possible for a principal and a surety to promise as joint promisors and normally the same rules will apply despite the principal suretyship relation.[44] However it is a definite rule of suretyship law, which has not been changed by statute or by case law, that a creditor who releases a principal with knowledge of the suretyship relation releases the surety in the absence of a reservation of rights.[45] Conversely a discharge of a surety does not discharge a principal debt.[46]

§ 331. Consequences of Joint and Several Liability

As we have seen, if A and B promise jointly and severally there are actually three liabilities, the several liability of A, the several liability of B, and the joint liability of A and B.[47] Therefore, many of the problems which exist with respect to joint liability also exist with respect to joint and several liability.

On the question of joinder, the rule was that the plaintiff could elect to sue one or he could elect to sue all, but he could not elect to

---

43. See, e. g., McKinney's N.Y.Gen.Obligations Law § 15–105(2).

44. See § 329 supra.

45. Restatement, Security § 122.

46. Restatement, Contracts (2d) § 121(1) (a). The principal is ordinarily credited with any consideration which the surety pays. The surety is entitled to reimbursement for the part payment and upon full payment is in addition entitled to be subrogated. Restatement, Security §§ 104, 141. If there is an agreement that the payment by the surety is not to be credited upon the obligation, the surety loses his right of reimbursement. Restatement, Contracts (2d) § 121(3), Comment g.

47. See § 329 supra.

sue more than one unless he sued all.[48] Thus, if the creditor sued one of the obligors on his several promise and recovered, there was no merger and separate actions and separate judgments could be obtained against the others.[49] But, if the creditor brought suit against more than one and less than all of the obligors, the rule of merger with respect to joint obligors would apply.[50]

If the creditor sues one of the several obligors without joining the other obligors and loses, the doctrine of merger would not apply and his only problem would be under the doctrine of collateral estoppel by judgment.[51] The result would be otherwise if more than one was sued or if all were sued, in which event the rule with respect to joint obligors would obtain.[52]

The common law doctrine of survivorship which applied to joint obligations did not apply to joint and several obligations in the sense that the creditor could sue the representative of the deceased obligor on his several obligation.[53] But, where the creditor sought to sue the representative of the deceased obligor along with other co-obligors, the action could be resisted by the representative.[54]

As we have seen the general common law rule is that a voluntary release of one joint obligor releases the others.[55] Strangely enough the same rule was applied to a joint and several obligation.[56]

Just as the rules with respect to joint obligations have been changed by statute and court decisions,[57] so the rules as to joint and several obligations which followed the joint obligations rules have also been changed.

§ 332.   Consequence of Several Liability

There is very little to be said concerning the consequences of several liability because none of the consequences that arose with respect to joint and joint and several liability arise here except where suretyship principles may be involved.[58] Indeed, since the obligations were

---

48. Koenig v. Curran's Restaurant & Baking Co., 306 Pa. 345, 159 A. 553 (1932). This common law rule has been largely eliminated by modern rules of procedure. 4 Corbin § 937.

49. Gruber v. Friedman, 104 Conn. 107, 132 A. 395 (1926).

50. Restatement, Contracts (2d) § 118, Comment a.

51. 4 Corbin § 937.

52. Restatement, Contracts (2d) § 119, Comment a.

53. Eggleston v. Buck, 31 Ill. 254 (1863).

54. Fisher v. Chadwick, 4 Wyo. 379, 34 P. 899 (1893).

55. See § 330 supra.

56. Dwy v. Connecticut Co., 89 Conn. 74, 92 A. 883 (1915).

57. See the preceding section.

58. Simpson, Contracts § 139 (2d ed. 1965).

considered separate, at common law it was not possible to join the several obligors in one action. If the plaintiff did in fact join several obligors in one action and at trial demonstrated that the defendants were severally liable, judgment would be entered against the plaintiff because only joint or joint and several obligors could be joined as defendants.[59] Under modern procedural statutes several obligors can generally be joined as defendants.[60]

§ 333. Relation of Co-Obligors to Each Other—Contribution

We have discussed the consequences of joint, joint and several, and several liability of co-obligors liable for the same performance from the point of view of their liability to the obligee. The question here is the rights and liabilities of the co-obligors inter se. This does not depend upon whether the liability of the co-obligors is joint, joint and several, or several but depends upon suretyship principles.[61]

It is obvious that any payment, whether full or partial, by any co-obligor will inure to the benefit of the other co-obligor in the sense that there is a partial discharge of the obligation.[62] An agreement to the contrary is not effective.[63]

If C builds a house for X and Y at an agreed price of $18,000 and X pays the full $18,000, it is obvious that X should recover $9,000 from Y in the absence of any particular agreement between X and Y. This result is generally stated by saying that a co-obligor who has paid more than his proportionate share is entitled to contribution.[64] What is the proportionate share of a co-obligor depends upon the agreement between or among the co-obligors and, if there is no agreement between or among the parties, upon equitable principles. Thus, in the illustration given, in the absence of an agreement, X and Y as between themselves would be liable for $9,000 each.[65] But if X and Y agreed between themselves that X was responsible for ⅔ and Y for ⅓, X would be entitled to only $6,000 from Y.[66]

59. Jones and Carlin, Non-Joinder and Misjoinder of Parties—Common Law Actions, 28 W.Va.L.Q. 266, 266–76 (1922).

60. See Clark, Code Pleading §§ 60–61 (2d ed. 1947).

61. Aspinwall v. Sacchi, 57 N.Y. 331 (1874); 2 Williston § 345.

62. 4 Corbin § 936.

63. Restatement, Contracts (2d) § 121 (3) and 122(3). The only exception, as we have seen, is where the payment comes from a surety and it is express-

ly agreed that the amount paid should not be credited against the obligation. In such an event, the surety loses his right to reimbursement to the extent that he agrees that the amount paid shall not be credited to the obligation. See § 330 supra.

64. Simpson, Contracts § 143.

65. As to C, of course, we are assuming that both X and Y are liable for the full $18,000.

66. 2 Williston § 345; Restatement, Restitution § 81 (1937).

The situation would be different if C made a loan of $18,000 to X which X and Y agreed to repay.   Here although X and Y are still co-obligors X is the principal and Y the surety,[67] and so when X pays the $18,000 he is not entitled to contribution.[68]   The situation would also be different if the loan was to Y, in which event X would be the surety.   Here if X paid he would not be entitled to contribution ($9,000), but to reimbursement ($18,000).[69]   In addition, he would be entitled to all other rights which a surety has including the right of exoneration.[70]

In a sense there is also suretyship involved in the original illustration (where C built a house for X and Y).   Here, as between X and Y, X is primarily liable for $9,000 and Y is his surety for that $9,000. Conversely Y is primarily liable for $9,000 and X is his surety for that $9,000.[71]   Thus, in the illustration given, X is only entitled to be reimbursed for the $9,000 on which he is a surety;   he is not entitled to recover the $9,000 on which he is the principal.[72]

§ 334.   Multiple Promisees

Previously we dealt with the question of multiple promisors.   In this section we are concerned with multiple promisees.   Here again we are not concerned with promises which promise different performances to multiple promisees but rather are concerned with promises which promise the *same* performance to multiple promisees.[73]   Today, it is well established that "rights may be either 'joint' or 'several' or some combination." [74]

Under the modern view, at least, the question is one of intention, and where the intention is not clearly shown the rights of obligees of the same performance are deemed to be joint except where "the interests of the obligee in the performance or in the remedies for breach are distinct." [75]   This means that the surrounding circumstanc-

---

67.   The reason why Y is the surety is that as between X and Y, X is the one who should ultimately pay because all of the consideration came to him.   Restatement, Security § 82.

68.   Obviously the principal debtor does not have rights against the surety.

69.   Restatement, Security § 104.

70.   Restatement, Security § 112.   The right to exoneration is enforced by an equitable decree compelling the principal to fulfill his obligation to the creditor.   Glades County v. Detroit Fidelity & Sur. Co., 57 F.2d 449 (5th Cir. 1932).

71.   Lorimer v. Knack Coal Co., 246 Mich. 214, 224 N.W. 362, 64 A.L.R. 210 (1929);   Wold v. Grozalsky, 277 N.Y. 364, 14 N.E.2d 437, 122 A.L.R. 518 (1938).

72.   See notes 69 and 70 supra.

73.   This distinction is drawn in the Restatement, Contracts (2d) § 128, Comment a.

74.   Restatement, Contracts (2d) § 128, Comment a.

75.   Restatement, Contracts (2d) § 128; see 4 Corbin §§ 939–940; 2 Williston § 321.

es will be considered to determine whether or not promisees have distinct interests or a unitary interest in the promised performance.[76] Thus, for example, if A promised to pay B and C $1,000 for work to be done by B and C in the construction of a road, the question of whether B and C are joint promisees is resolved by interpreting the wording of the contract in the light of the nature of the relationship between B and C. If they are partners, they have a community of interest in the profits and losses of the transaction and as a matter of law their rights are joint.[77] If they were not in a formal sense partners, but joined together for this particular project with an intention to share profits and losses, the same result would likely follow.[78] Here too they would be operating as a business organization even if on an ad hoc basis. If, however, B and C were merely employees of A there would be no community of interest between B and C and their rights would be several. In a leading case,[79] A, B, and C promised to care for D's herd of cattle for two years and D promised to pay them one-half of the selling price in excess of $36,000. Although the promise in form might appear to have been made to the promisees jointly, the court took note of the fact that the promisees were but employees and had no community of interest in any capital investment and would not share any losses and held that B could sue separately for his one-sixth interest in the excess over $36,000. Similarly, where a coal merchant in a single document promised to take all of his requirements from three coal companies in equal shares, it was held that each of the coal companies was a several obligee, there being no connection between them other than the contract itself.[80] It should be pointed out, however, that if each of the coal companies desired to join in one action against the merchant, there is little question that the action should be permitted even in the face of a statute which permits

76. "It is the law of New York, and the general rule of the Common Law, that when two or more persons undertake a contractual obligation there arises a presumption of law that they undertake jointly and that words of severance are necessary to overcome this primary presumption . . .. But no similar presumption arises when a promise is made to several persons . . .." St. Regis Paper Co. v. Stuart, 214 F.2d 762 (1st Cir. 1954), cert. denied 348 U.S. 915, 75 S.Ct. 296, 99 L.Ed. 717 (1955).

77. Crane and Bromberg, Partnership § 57 (1968).

78. Id. at § 35.

79. Beckwith v. Talbot, 95 U.S. 289, 24 L.Ed. 496 (1877); accord, St. Regis Paper Co. v Stuart, 214 F.2d 762 (1st Cir. 1954), cert. denied 348 U.S. 915, 75 S.Ct. 296, 99 L.Ed. 717 (1955) (two salesmen worked as a team and were promised a team commission; despite absence of words of severability, held that one of the salesmen could bring an action for his share of the commission).

80. Shipman v. Straitsville Central Mining Co., 158 U.S. 356, 15 S.Ct. 886, 39 L.Ed. 1015 (1895); compare Donzella v. New York State Thruway Authority, 7 A.D.2d 771, 180 N.Y.S.2d 108 (3d Dep't 1958).

joinder of plaintiffs only when they have a "joint" right.[81] If necessary, the rights of the obligees should be classified as "joint" for permitting joint action by them and "several" for the purpose of permitting separate actions by them.

§ 335. Compulsory Joinder of Joint Obligees

Where there are multiple promisees and they have a joint right, the promisor has a right to expect that he will not be harassed by a multiplicity of actions.[82] Thus, where less than all of the joint promisees bring an action the defendant as a common law proposition may raise this issue and prevent a judgment.[83] Statutes which have relaxed the rule of compulsory joinder of joint obligors generally also relax the rule as to joint obligees.[84] Even though a joint obligee refuses to join in the action he may be joined as a plaintiff or an additional party defendant.[85] The fact that one of the joint obligees is out of the jurisdiction does not vary the situation because any joint obligee should be able to sue in the name of all of the joint obligees.[86]

§ 336. Discharge by One Joint Obligee

Does a joint obligee have the power to discharge the joint obligation? For example, if A and B are joint obligees and the obligor pays A, does B lose all of his rights against the obligor? The law is that one joint obligee has the right to act for the other and he may discharge the rights of his co-obligees; for example, by accepting payment, by an accord and satisfaction or by release.[87] There is an exception to this rule in the case of negotiable instruments.[88] Another exception occurs where the discharge is in violation of a duty to a co-obligee who may then avoid the discharge to the extent necessary to protect himself "except to the extent that the promisor has given

---

81. See 4 Corbin § 940. It should also be observed that almost everywhere several obligees of the same performance are now permitted to join as plaintiffs.

82. 4 Corbin § 939; see generally, Reed, supra note 13.

83. Lee v. Ricca, 29 Ariz. 309, 241 P. 508 (1925).

84. See, e. g., Fed. R. Civ.P. 19; N.Y. C.P.L.R. § 1001; § 330 supra.

85. Hand v. Heslet, 81 Mont. 68, 261 P. 609 (1927).

86. There are exceptions to this rule in the case of negotiable instruments, where the joint obligees have made a contrary agreement, or where bringing the action would amount to the violation of a duty to a co-obligee. Restatement, Contracts (2d) § 129(2).

87. Restatement, Contracts (2d) § 130.

88. U.C.C. § 3–116.

value or otherwise changed his position in good faith and without knowledge or reason to know of the violation." [89]

§ 337. Survivorship of Joint Rights

The rule of survivorship with respect to joint obligors also applied to joint obligees.[90] That is to say that if a joint promisee died his executor no longer had any right to sue the obligor for a money judgment.[91] If all of the joint obligees died the personal representative of the last survivor could alone sue the obligor.[92] Ordinarily, at least, the death of a joint obligee would not deprive him of his right to an accounting from the co-obligee who received performance or settled the claim.[93] The rule set forth above has not been changed and is justified as a matter of convenience because "it is unnecessary to join the personal representative of a deceased co-obligee in an action for a money judgment." [94]

89. Restatement, Contracts (2d) § 131(2). Thus if the obligor knows that the obligee he has released is violating his duty to his co-obligees, the release is effective only to the extent of the released obligee's share of the performance. An exhaustive review of the authorities appears in Freedman v. Montague Associates, Inc., 18 Misc. 2d 1, 187 N.Y.S.2d 636 (Sup.Ct.1959) (which, however, reached a contrary conclusion), rev'd mem., 9 A.D.2d 936, 195 N.Y.S.2d 392 (2d Dep't 1959), lv. to appeal denied, 10 A.D.2d 637, 197 N.Y. S.2d 441 (2d Dep't 1960).

90. See § 330 supra.

91. Israel v. Jones, 97 W.Va. 173, 124 S.E. 665 (1924).

92. Restatement, Contracts (2d) § 132.

93. Hill v. Breeden, 53 Wyo. 125, 79 P. 2d 482 (1938). Thus, for example, in a partnership, only the surviving partners may enforce partnership claims, but the estate of the deceased partner has a beneficial interest in the proceeds of the litigation. Contrariwise, upon the death of a joint tenant, the estate of the deceased tenant has no such beneficial interest. The result turns on the substantive law of partnership and real property, rather than on merely procedural rules.

94. Restatement, Contracts (2d) § 132, Comment b. This comment adds: "Where equitable relief is sought, joinder of such a representative is permitted and when necessary to complete adjudication is required."

CHAPTER 18

DISCHARGE OF CONTRACTS

Analysis

		Sections
A.	Rescission	339
B.	Destruction or Surrender	340
C.	Executory Bilateral Contract of Accord—Accord and Satisfaction—Substitute Agreement—Unilateral Accord	341–344
D.	Three Party Situations	345
E.	Account Stated	346
F.	Release and Covenant Not to Sue	347–348
G.	Gifts and Rejection of Tender	349
H.	Merger	350
I.	Union of Right and Duty in the Same Person	351
J.	Alteration	352
K.	Bankruptcy	353
L.	Performance	354

———

Analysis

Sec.
338. Introduction.

A. RESCISSION

339. Mutual Rescission.

B. DESTRUCTION OR SURRENDER

340. Cancellation or Surrender, if the Contract is Formal.

C. EXECUTORY BILATERAL CONTRACT OF ACCORD— ACCORD AND SATISFACTION—SUBSTITUTE AGREEMENT—UNILATERAL ACCORD

341. Background of the Problem.
342. Consequences of Enforceability of an Executory Bilateral Contract of Accord.
343. Distinguishing an Executory Bilateral Contract of Accord from a Substituted Agreement.
344. An Offer of Accord Looking to a Unilateral Contract.

515

D. THREE PARTY SITUATIONS

Sec.
345. Assignment, Novation or Contract for the Benefit of a Third Person.

E. ACCOUNT STATED

346. Account Stated.

F. RELEASE AND COVENANT NOT TO SUE

347. Release.
348. Covenant Not to Sue.

G. GIFTS AND REJECTION OF TENDER

349. Renunciation, Rejection of Tender, or Executed Gift.

H. MERGER

350. Merger.

I. UNION OF RIGHT AND DUTY IN THE SAME PERSON

351. Acquisition by the Debtor of the Correlative Right.

J. ALTERATION

352. Discharge by Alteration.

K. BANKRUPTCY

353. Bankruptcy.

L. PERFORMANCE

354. Performance of the Duty—To Which Debt Should Payment be Applied.

§ 338. Introduction

The Restatement of Contracts lists twenty-two ways in which a contract may be discharged.[1] Some of these have been discussed previously so that these need not be considered here. Included in this category are "occurrence of a condition subsequent;" [2] "breach by the other party or failure of consideration, or frustration;" [3] "exercise of the power of avoidance if the duty is avoidable;" [4] "impossibili-

---

1. Restatement, Contracts § 385. The Restatement distinguishes between the discharge of a contractual duty and the discharge of a duty to make compensation for a breach. Although the discussion in this chapter focuses upon the discharge of contractual duties, for the most part the rules governing the discharge of duties to make compensation are the same. It should be noted that a contractual duty is not invariably discharged by the facts enumerated. See Restatement, Contracts § 385, Comment b.

2. See § 140 supra.

3. See § 149 and § 195 supra.

4. See e. g. § 124 supra and Restatement, Contracts § 431.

ty;"[5] "illegality of a contract or of its enforcement;"[6] "the failure of a condition precedent to exist or to occur;"[7] "incapacity of the parties to retain the right duty relationship;"[8] and "the rules governing joint debtors."[9] Two of the methods of discharge listed, "res judicata," and "the rules governing sureties" are beyond the scope of this treatise. The remaining twelve, some of which have been mentioned elsewhere will be discussed briefly here.

A. RESCISSION

§ 339. Mutual Rescission

If A and B enter into an executory bilateral contract they are free to terminate the agreement by a mutual agreement and the surrender of rights under the original agreement by each party is the consideration for the mutual agreement of rescission.[10]

If the original agreement has been performed in part by one of the parties before the agreement of mutual rescission the question frequently presented is whether the performance which has been rendered should be paid for. The question is one of the intention of the parties.[11] Very often, however, the parties have expressed no intention on the matter, expressing themselves in broad terms such as "Let's call the whole deal off." Some courts have ruled that in such a case a promise to pay for the performances rendered should be implied.[12] Others have indulged in the presumption that unless an

---

5. See ch. 11 supra.

6. See ch. 19 infra.

7. See § 142 supra.

8. See e. g. ch. 8 supra.

9. See ch. 17 supra.

10. Kirk v. Brentwood Manor Homes, Inc., 191 Pa.Super. 488, 159 A.2d 48 (1960); Restatement, Contracts § 406, Comment a. Formerly, a sealed instrument could be discharged by a subsequent agreement only if the subsequent agreement was under seal. Today, however, the prevailing view in jurisdictions which have retained the seal is that an agreement under seal may be modified, rescinded, or substituted by an oral agreement or an unsealed written agreement. Kirk v. Brentwood Manor Homes, Inc., supra; Restatement, Contracts § 407,

Comment c; 5A Corbin § 1236; 6 Corbin § 1316; 6 Williston §§ 1834–1836 (rev. ed. 1938); and see § 119 supra.

A similar problem arises under modern statutes such as U.C.C. § 2–209(2) which provides in part that "a signed agreement which excludes modification or rescission except by a signed writing cannot be otherwise modified or rescinded." For a fuller discussion, see § 44 supra. The requirement of a writing for a rescission as it affects a contract which comes under the Statute of Frauds has been discussed in § 316 supra.

11. Restatement, Contracts § 409; 5A Corbin § 1236; 6 Williston § 1827 (rev. ed. 1938).

12. Anderson v. Copeland, 378 P.2d 1006 (Okl.1963); Johnston v. Gilbert, 234 Or. 350, 382 P.2d 87 (1963).

affirmative agreement to the contrary appears the parties intended that payment need not be made for services rendered prior to rescission.[13] As in any case involving intention, stare decisis should play but a suggestive role and each case should be decided on its facts.[14]

A similar problem arises where a party cancels the contract because of a material breach. Section 2–720 of the Uniform Commercial Code provides that "Unless the contrary intention clearly appears, expressions of 'cancellation' or 'rescission' of the contract or the like shall not be construed as a renunciation or discharge of any claim in damages for an antecedent breach." The Code language and comment make it clear that this provision applies after a breach and it is designed to avoid an involuntary loss of a remedy for breach by the use of language by the aggrieved party to the effect that the contract is called off. The Code primarily addresses itself to a number of unsound decisions that have held that when a contract is cancelled for breach it is logically impossible to permit an action on the contract since the contract is nonexistent; therefore only quasi-contractual relief is available.[15] The Code takes cognizance of the fact that the term "rescission" is often used by lawyers, courts and businessmen in many different senses; for example, termination of a contract by virtue of an option to terminate in the agreement, cancellation for breach and avoidance on the grounds of infancy or fraud.[16] In the interests of clarity of thought—as the consequences of each of these forms of discharge may vary—the Commercial Code carefully distinguishes three circumstances. "Rescission" is utilized as a term of art to refer to a mutual agreement to discharge contractual duties.[17] "Termination" refers to the discharge of duties by the exercise of a power granted by the agreement.[18] "Cancellation" refers to the putting an end to the contract by reason of a breach by the other party.[19] Section 2–720, however, takes into account, however, that the parties do not necessarily use these terms in this way.

13. Coletti v. Knox Hat Co., 252 N.Y. 468, 169 N.E. 648 (1930).

14. Restatement, Contracts § 409; 5A Corbin § 1236; 6 Williston § 1827 (rev. ed. 1938); and see Montgomery v. Stuyvesant Ins. Co., 393 F.2d 754 (4th Cir. 1968).

15. Walter-Wallingford Coal Co. v. A. Himes Coal Co., 223 Mich. 576, 194 N. W. 493 (1923); Thackeray v. Knight, 57 Utah 21, 192 P. 263 (1920); see Woodward, Quasi Contracts ch. 19 (1913); 5A Corbin § 1237; see also Annot. 1 A.L.R.2d 1084 (1948).

16. See, e. g., Annot., 1 A.L.R.2d 1084 (1948) ("Notice of Rescission as Irrevocable Election When Other Party Refuses to Assent Thereto"), where the annotator brings together cases involving significantly different issues merely because the court utilized the term "rescission."

17. U.C.C. § 2–209. Comment 3.

18. U.C.C. § 2–106(3).

19. U.C.C. § 2–106(4).

To return to the topic of mutual rescission, if one of the parties has fully performed under a bilateral contract or as offeree of a unilateral contract, a mutual agreement to put the contract to an end is ineffective as the party whose duties remain executory has incurred no detriment and therefore the promise of the party who has performed is not supported by consideration. Under some circumstances this purported rescission may be effective as a "release," a concept discussed below.[20]

Rescission also occurs where the parties enter into a new contract which is substituted for the original contract. The old agreement is discharged but the parties are still bound contractually. At times new terms are added to an existing contract. It is obvious that the lines between three situations are indistinct:

(1) Unconditional rescission of an existing contract followed by a subsequent entering into of a new agreement.

(2) Rescission of an existing contract contemporaneous with and conditioned on the entering into of a new agreement.

(3) Retention of an existing contract with an agreement as to new terms.

The manner of distinguishing among these situations has not been authoritatively answered and it may be that the variation in factual settings is so extensive that no test can be formulated.[21] The necessity for distinguishing these categories is not merely academic. For example, the presence or absence of consideration [22] and the necessity of complying with the Statute of Frauds [23] may vary, dependent upon the category into which the transaction falls.

B.　DESTRUCTION OR SURRENDER

§ 340.　Cancellation or Surrender, if the Contract is Formal

At early common law the normal method of discharging a formal obligation was the cancellation of the instrument by its physical destruction or mutilation.[24] The theory was that the instrument itself

---

20. See § 94 supra and § 347 infra.

21. A test appears in Travelers Ins. Co. v. Workmen's Compensation Appeals Bd., 434 P.2d 992, 998, 64 Cal.Rptr. 440, 446, 68 Cal.2d 7 (1967). "An alteration of details of the contract which leaves undisturbed its general purpose constitutes a modification rather than a rescission of the contract."

22. See the discussion in § 61 supra especially as it refers to Schwartzreich v. Bauman-Basch, Inc., 231 N.Y. 196, 131 N.E. 887 (1921), rearg. denied 231 N.Y. 602, 132 N.E. 905 (1921).

23. See § 316 supra.

24. Ames, Specialty Contracts and Equitable Defences, 9 Harv.L.Rev. **49** (1895).

was the obligation and not merely evidence of the obligation; therefore cancellation of the instrument discharged the obligation irrespective of the intention of the parties. So also surrender (delivery) of the formal instrument did not amount to a discharge irrespective of the intention of the parties.[25] However under present law a formal instrument, such as a negotiable instrument,[26] insurance policy or instrument under seal, may be discharged by either cancellation or surrender provided that the party having the right intends to discharge the duty.[27] Surrender or cancellation of an informal contract may be evidence of an intent to discharge but, in addition, consideration,[28] or one of its substitutes, or the elements of a gift, would be required.[29]

C. EXECUTORY BILATERAL CONTRACT OF ACCORD— ACCORD AND SATISFACTION—SUBSTITUTED AGREEMENT—UNILATERAL ACCORD

§ 341. Background of the Problem

An executory bilateral contract of accord is "an agreement embodying a promise express or implied to accept at some future time a stipulated performance in satisfaction or discharge in whole or in part of any present claim, cause of action, contract, obligation, . . and a promise express or implied to render such performance in satisfaction or in discharge of such claim, cause of action, contract, obligation . . .." [30] For example, C (creditor) writes to D (debtor) "I promise to discharge the debt you owe me upon delivery of your black horse if you promise to deliver the horse to me within a

---

25. 6 Williston § 1877 (rev.ed.1938).

26. U.C.C. § 3–605(1) (negotiable instruments). But if a negotiable instrument is discharged by surrender, a subsequent holder in due course will be permitted to enforce the instrument. U.C.C. § 3–602.

27. Restatement, Contracts § 432; 6 Williston § 1878 (rev.ed.1938); 5A Corbin § 1250. If the formal instrument is bilateral both parties must join in or consent to the surrender or cancellation. Restatement, Contracts § 432(2).

28. If the contract is bilateral and executory on both sides, surrender or cancellation joined in by both parties would constitute a mutual rescission. See Schwartzreich v. Bauman-Basch, Inc., 231 N.Y. 196, 131 N.E. 887 (1921), rearg. denied 231 N.Y. 602, 132 N.E. 905 (1921).

29. See chs. 4, 5, 6 supra; 5A Corbin § 1250; 6 Williston §§ 1876, 1879 (rev. ed.1938).

30. McKinney's N.Y.Gen. Obligations Law § 15–501(1); see also 6 Corbin § 1268; Restatement, Contracts § 417. Non-textual treatments of this kind of agreement include Gold, Executory Accords, 21 Boston U.L.Rev. 465 (1941); Havighurst, Reflections on the Executory Accord, in Perspectives of Law; Essays for Austin Wakeman Scott 190 (1964).

reasonable time." D promises. This agreement is an executory bilateral contract of accord.

If D delivers the horse and C accepts it there is an accord and satisfaction, the accord being the agreement and the satisfaction being the performance of the agreement.[31] That an accord and satisfaction operate to discharge a contract if supported by consideration we have already seen.[32]

Formerly an executory bilateral contract of accord was without any effect even if as in the illustration given it was supported by consideration. An executory accord could not be used as a defense nor did its breach give rise to a cause of action.[33] The reason for the rule is purely historical. Informal contracts supported by consideration were not recognized under the early common law and so it was very often held that an executory bilateral contract of accord was not enforceable. When informal bilateral contracts came to be enforced, apparently the courts failed to recognize that an executory bilateral contract of accord was nothing more or less than a bilateral contract and continued to apply the old rule of unenforceability to them.[34]

This common law rule is well illustrated by the case of Reilly v. Barrett. In that case the plaintiff had sustained personal injuries allegedly as a result of the negligence of the defendant. The plaintiff brought an action in tort and defendant interposed an affirmative defense which stated as follows: "That on or about the 10th day of December, 1913, an agreement was made between the plaintiff and the defendant, through their respective attorneys, by which the defendant agreed to pay to the plaintiff in full settlement of the cause of action . . . two hundred dollars, and the plaintiff, in consideration thereof, agreed to accept the said sum in full settlement of the action, and upon payment thereof to discontinue the action without costs." [35] The court held that since the plaintiff promised to discharge his claim only when the $200.00 was received, the defendant's plea merely stated an executory bilateral accord and was an insufficient defense.

An executory bilateral contract of accord must be distinguished from a substituted agreement because even now significantly different results stem from the two kinds of transactions. If we change slightly the illustration previously given we can also illustrate a substituted

---

31. 6 Corbin § 1269.

32. See § 65 supra.

33. Reilly v. Barrett, 220 N.Y. 170, 115 N.E. 453 (1917); see also Larscy v. T. Hogan & Sons, Inc., 239 N.Y. 298, 146

N.E. 430 (1925), rearg. denied 240 N.Y. 580, 148 N.E. 713 (1926).

34. 6 Corbin § 1271; 6 Williston §§ 1839–40 (rev.ed.1938).

35. 220 N.Y. 170, 172, 115 N.E. 453, 454 (1917).

agreement. C (creditor) writes to D (debtor), "If you will promise to deliver your black mare within 30 days I will immediately treat the debt you owe me as satisfied and discharged." D accepts the offer. Here we have a substituted agreement.

What is the factual difference in the two illustrations which permits one to be labeled an executory bilateral contract and the other a substituted agreement? First, it should be observed that both agreements are similar in that they are bilateral and are supported by consideration.[36] The difference lies in the fact that in the second case involving a substituted agreement C asks for and accepts D's new promise in satisfaction of the original claim so that the original claim is discharged upon the making of the new promise by D. In the case of an executory bilateral contract of accord as shown by the first illustration, C has made it clear that the original claim will not be discharged until the debtor performs the new agreement.[37] Thus it was logically held at common law that in the case of a substituted agreement the original claim was merged in the new agreement so that the original claim could no longer be enforced, in the absence of an express agreement to the contrary, but rather suit must be brought upon the substituted agreement.[38]

The common law rule with respect to executory bilateral contracts of accord has been overturned by judicial decisions in many states so that today they are generally deemed to be enforceable.[39] In New York the common law rule with respect to executory bilateral contracts of accord has been changed by statute but only where such

---

36. In this context as in others, promissory estoppel may substitute for consideration. Boshart v. Gardner, 190 Ark. 104, 77 S.W.2d 642, 96 A.L.R. 1130 (1935) (an executory accord mistakenly labelled a "novation," but treated as an executory accord; expenses incurred in reliance on the accord a substitute for consideration).

37. 1937 N.Y.Law Rev.Comm.Rep. 214.

38. Moers v. Moers, 229 N.Y. 294, 128 N.E. 202, 14 A.L.R. 225 (1920); see Restatement, Contracts § 418; 6 Williston § 1846 (rev.ed.1938). Thus what is here called a substituted agreement operates as, and is sometimes called, an "accord and satisfaction." This terminology is not used here as it may prove confusing; this situation is factually distinct from an accord and satisfaction created by the performance of an executory accord.

39. Very v. Levy, 54 U.S. 345, 14 L.Ed. 173 (1851); Union Central Life Ins. Co. v. Imsland, 91 F.2d 365 (8th Cir. 1937); Trenton St. Ry. v. Lawlor, 74 N.J.Eq. 828, 71 A. 234 (Ct.Err. & App. 1908); Dobias v. White, 239 N.C. 409, 80 S.E.2d 23 (1954), 240 N.C. 680, 83 S.E.2d 785 (1954); Ladd v. General Ins. Co., 236 Or. 260, 387 P.2d 572 (1963); Restatement, Contracts § 417; 6 Corbin §§ 1271–1273; 6 Williston § 1845 (rev.ed.1938). The common law view retains some adherents. Karvalsky v. Becker, 217 Ind. 524, 29 N.E.2d 560, 131 A.L.R. 1074 (1940); Bartlett v. Newton, 148 Me. 279, 92 A.2d 611 (1952).

an agreement is in writing and signed by the party "against whom it is sought to enforce the accord" "or by his agent." [40]

§ 342. Consequences of Enforceability of an Executory Bilateral Contract of Accord

In the preceding section we saw that a substituted agreement is enforceable and that by the terms of the agreement the original claim is merged into the substituted agreement and is no longer enforceable. We also saw that under the modern view, contrary to the earlier view, an executory bilateral contract of accord is now enforceable. It is quite important to observe, however, that a bilateral executory accord has considerably different effects from a substituted agreement. The original obligations of the parties are, by definition, not satisfied until the bilateral executory accord is performed. Under the view which seems to have gained general acceptance, the executory accord has a suspensive effect on the prior obligations. In the event the debtor breaches the agreement, however, the prior obligation revives and the creditor has the option of enforcing the original claim or the executory bilateral contract of accord.[41] There is authority to the effect that the same option exists if the debtor manifests prospective inability or unwillingness to perform his side of the accord and the creditor changes his position in reliance upon this manifestation.[42]

If the creditor breaches, as by refusing the debtor's tender of his part of the executory accord, a similar rule exists. The Restatement states:

> "The debtor's original duty is not discharged. The debtor acquires a right of action for damages for the breach, and if specific enforcement of that contract is practicable, he acquires an alternative right to specific enforcement thereof. If the contract is enforced specifically, his original duty is discharged." [43]

This means that the debtor's obligation is not discharged by the tender. However, the debtor may in a proper case enforce the accord

---

40.   McKinney's N.Y.Gen. Obligations Law § 15–501.

41.   Ladd v. General Ins. Co., 236 Or. 260, 387 P.2d 572 (1963); Restatement, Contracts § 417. It has been held that the creditor need not elect between the original obligation and the executory accord until after all the evidence has been adduced by both parties. Plant Steel Corp. v. National Mach. Exch., Inc., 23 N.Y.2d 472, 297 N.Y.S.2d 559, 245 N.E.2d 213 (1969).

42.   Restatement, Contracts § 417.
    Part performance by the debtor followed by unjustified failure to complete does not prevent an action by the creditor. Stratton v. West States Construction, 21 Utah 2d 60, 440 P.2d 117 (1968).

43.   Restatement, Contracts § 417(d).

by exercising his right to specific performance in which event the original duty is discharged.[44] If specific performance is not available, or the debtor does not desire it, the debtor may recover damages for breach of the accord.[45]

§ 343. Distinguishing an Executory Bilateral Contract of Accord from a Substituted Agreement

The distinction between an executory bilateral contract of accord and a substituted compromise agreement has been discussed in the preceding sections. It must be observed, however, that it is often difficult to apply the distinction in the concrete. Thus, it is generally stated that the question is one of the intention of the parties and very often a question of fact.[46] If the claim is disputed or unliquidated the presumption should be that there is a substituted agreement rather than an executory bilateral contract of accord. This is reasonable since it is presumed that the creditor in entering into the new agreement desires the certainty of the debtor's subsequent promise and is therefore willing to forgo his rights under his former claim.[47] Even in such a case, however, the determination is likely to turn on the degree of deliberation and formality which has gone into the agreement. The more deliberate and formalized the agreement, the more likely the parties intended to substitute the present agreement for prior claims.[48] In cases involving liquidated undisputed obligations, however, it will generally be presumed that the creditor did not intend to surrender his prior rights unless and until the new agreement is actually performed.[49]

§ 344. An Offer of Accord Looking to a Unilateral Contract

Although most accords are bilateral it is possible to have an offer of accord looking to a unilateral contract. For example, to vary the illustration previously used in section 341 supra, C writes to D "If you deliver your black horse within a reasonable time I promise to discharge your debt." If D tendered the horse and C accepted it there would be an accord and satisfaction. If D tendered the horse and C

---

44. Union Central Life Ins. Co. v. Imsland, 91 F.2d 365 (8th Cir.1937).

45. Restatement, Contracts § 417, Comment d.

46. Moers v. Moers, 229 N.Y. 294, 128 N.E. 202, 14 A.L.R. 225 (1920); Langlois v. Langlois, 5 A.D.2d 75, 169 N. Y.S.2d 170 (3rd Dep't 1957).

47. Restatement, Contracts § 419; but see McFaden v. Nordblom, 307 Mass. 574, 30 N.E.2d 852 (1941).

48. Goldbard v. Empire State Mut. Life Ins. Co., 5 A.D.2d 230, 171 N.Y.S.2d 194 (1st Dep't 1958).

49. Restatement, Contracts § 419; 6 Williston § 1847 (rev.ed.1938); 6 Corbin §§ 1268, 1271, 1293.

refused it there would be a unilateral contract at least under the provisions of § 45 of the Restatement.[50] Until quite recently, however, the rule was that C was free to reject the tender without being guilty of any legal wrong.[51] This result has also been changed by the modern authorities [52] and in New York by statute if the offer is in writing and signed by the offeror or by his agent.[53] Under the modern view the debtor could sue for damages for breach of the accord or in a proper case could sue for specific performance of the accord by keeping his tender good. Specific enforcement of the accord would obviously defeat an action upon the original claim, as would allowance of the accord to be pleaded and proved as an affirmative defense provided the debtor continues ready to perform his part of the bargain.[54]

D. THREE PARTY SITUATIONS

§ 345. Assignment, Novation or Contract for the Benefit of a Third Person

The common characteristic of the kinds of transactions grouped under this heading is that three parties are involved.

Assignments were discussed in chapter 15. Subject to the qualifications stated in that chapter an effective assignment transfers the assignor's interests to the assignee and thereby discharges the obligor's duty to the assignor.

Contracts for the benefit of a third person were discussed in chapter 14. The making of such a contract creates new duties and often discharges prior duties. If D owes C $100 and they enter into a contract whereby D promises to pay this sum to T, a duty to pay T is substituted for the duty to pay C. C, as promisee has an interest in the performance of this contract, but this interest now stems not from the original contract but from the substituted contract.[55]

50. See § 34 supra.

51. Harbor v. Morgan, 4 Ind. 158 (1853); Kromer v. Heim, 75 N.Y. 574, 31 Am.Rep. 491 (1879); see generally 1937 N.Y.Law Rev.Comm.Rep. 212, 233–35.

52. Restatement, Contracts § 417, Comment a; 6 Corbin § 1272.

53. McKinney's N.Y.Gen.Obligations Law § 15–503.

54. Cf. Restatement, Contracts § 417(d).

55. Cf. Restatement, Contracts § 426. In an interesting case a mortgagor was in arrears in payments. The creditor approved an arrangement whereby a contract purchaser agreed with the mortgagor to make instalment payments to the creditor. It was held that no novation had been formed. The creditor was a third party beneficiary of the agreement between the mortgagor and the contract purchaser and did not accept the contract purchaser's obligation as a substitute for the mortgagor's obligation and for its security interest in the land. Nevertheless, the creditor was held to be estopped from proceeding with foreclosure of the land so long

Although the word "novation" has been used in a variety of senses, it is commonly restricted today to describe a substituted contract involving at least one new party who replaces in whole or in part one of the parties to the prior contract. It thus differs from other substituted contracts in that it involves at least three parties—the original contracting parties and at least one additional party, who may be a new obligor or obligee or, indeed may be both an obligor and obligee.

A contract is a novation if it does three things: "(a) discharges immediately a previous contractual duty or a duty to make compensation, and (b) creates a new contractual duty, and (c) includes as a party one who neither owed the previous duty nor was entitled to its performance." [56] An assignment is not a novation because it is not a contract, but an executed transaction.[57] A contract to assign may be a novation within this definition,[58] but is not commonly denominated such. Many third party beneficiary contracts are novations [59] but are not usually so labelled. Indeed, the utility of the classification of novation is doubtful. Its legal effect is that of any substituted contract.[60] The development of a separate category under the rubric "novation" is doubtless traceable to problems of consideration formerly thought to be present in such contracts because of the former common law rule that consideration must be supplied by the promisee.[61] This rule has long been laid to rest almost everywhere.

Since a novation involves the discharge of a duty by virtue of an agreement it is obvious that the person to whom the duty is owed must assent to the discharge and since it may involve the creation of a new contractual duty it is equally obvious that the new obligor must

as the contract purchaser was not in default. The court might just as well have held that there was a tripartite accord in which the contract purchaser had become an additional obligor and the creditor's power of foreclosure had been suspended until the accord was breached. Bank of Fairbanks v. Kaye, 16 Alaska 23, 227 F.2d 566 (1955).

56.   Restatement, Contracts § 424.

57.   See § 256 supra.

58.   Compare Restatement, Contracts § 424, Comment c, with 6 Williston § 1867A (rev.ed.1938). Is the right of the assignor "discharged" or "transferred" or both?

59.   Restatement, Contracts § 426.

60.   See Mello v. Coy Real Estate Co., —— R.I. ——, 234 A.2d 667 (1967), at n. 1 of the opinion, where court indicates that "novation" and "substituted contract" may be used interchangeably.

Extensive discussions of novations in Restatement, Contracts §§ 424–430; 6 Corbin §§ 1297–1302; 6 Williston §§ 1865–1875 are valuable for their analyses of the variety of factual situations in which a novation has been or is alleged to have been created. For a discussion of one common situation involving the assignment of rights and assumption of duties by a stranger to the contract coupled with a repudiation by the assignor, see § 279 supra.

61.   See 6 Williston § 1866 (rev.ed.1938).

assent.[62] Although some of the cases have held that the consent of the original obligor must be obtained, the later authorities make it clear that this is not necessary. As a third party beneficiary of the agreement between the obligee and the new obligor, the prior obligor need not express assent to his discharge, although he is empowered to disclaim this discharge if he so desires.[63]

It is necessary to distinguish an executory accord from a novation. A novation is a substituted contract which operates immediately to discharge an obligation. If the discharge is to take place upon performance, the tripartite agreement is merely an executory accord.[64]

E. ACCOUNT STATED

§ 346. Account Stated

An account stated arises where there have been transactions between debtor and creditor resulting in the creation of matured debts and the parties by agreement compute a balance which the debtor promises to pay and the creditor promises to accept in full payment for the items of account.[65] It is relatively infrequent that an account stated results from an express agreement. Usually the cases involve an implied agreement arising when one party sends an itemized account to the other who retains it without objection for more than a reasonable time.[66]

62. It should be reiterated that the mere assumption of a duty by a new obligor with the consent of the obligee is not a novation since no duty is discharged by such an assumption unless the obligee also agrees to discharge the original obligor. See Mansfield v. Lang, 293 Mass. 386, 200 N.E. 110 (1936); Credit Bureaus Adjustment Dep't, Inc. v. Cox Bros., 207 Or. 253, 295 P.2d 1107, 61 A.L.R.2d 750 (1956); and § 279 supra.

63. F. I. Somers & Sons, Inc. v. Le Clerc, 110 Vt. 408, 8 A.2d 663, 124 A. L.R. 1494 (1939); Restatement, Contracts § 427; 6 Corbin § 1299; 6 Williston §§ 1870–1871 (rev.ed.1938). Note that an obligor may be discharged by an actual performance by a third person, accepted by an obligee in full or partial satisfaction of his claim. Jackson v. Pennsylvania R. R., 66 N.J.L. 319, 49 A. 730, 55 L.R.A. 87 (Ct. Err. & App.1901); Restatement,

Contracts § 421. This is not a substituted contract or a novation but an executed accord and satisfaction.

64. See Trudeau v. Poutre, 165 Mass. 81, 42 N.E. 508 (1895) (question of fact whether agreement was to discharge original obligor immediately or only on condition that new obligor perform his promise to execute mortgages); see generally 6 Corbin § 1300.

65. Restatement, Contracts § 422; 6 Corbin § 1303; West v. Holstrom, 261 Cal.App.2d 89, 67 Cal.Rptr. 831 (1968).

66. Griffith v. Hicks, 150 Ark. 197, 233 S.W. 1086, 18 A.L.R. 882 (1921); R. E. Tharp, Inc. v. Miller Hay Co., 261 Cal.App.2d 81, 67 Cal.Rptr. 854 (1968); Meagher v. Kavli, 251 Minn. 477, 88 N.W.2d 871 (1958); Gerstner v. Lithocraft Studios, Inc., 258 S.W.2d 250 (Mo.App.1953); Rodkinson v. Haecker, 248 N.Y. 480, 162 N.E. 493 (1928).

The chief advantage of an account stated from the plaintiff's point of view is the facility of the requirements of pleading and proof.[67] In an action on the account the creditor need not plead and prove the making and performance of each contract (goods sold and delivered, money loaned, services rendered, etc.) which went into the account.

In its narrowest sense an account stated involves mere computation of liquidated debits and credits. It is not a compromise agreement.[68] No consideration is present in striking such a balance. The account is supported by the survival in this area of the common law rule that a pre-existing debt is consideration for a promise to pay the debt.[69] However such a promise is enforceable only to the extent of the previous obligation.[70] Thus if the computation is incorrect the primary effect of the account stated is merely to shift the burden of going forward with the evidence to the party who claims the account is incorrect.[71] If, however, a party has changed his position in reliance upon the account, the other party is estopped from proving that the account was in error.[72] Another effect of an account stated is that it is often held that the account is enforceable even as to items it contains which would otherwise be unenforceable because of the statute of limitations or Statute of Frauds.[73]

The debtor's silence is equivocal, however, and raises but an inference of assent which may be rebutted by other inferences from the facts, as by a prior disagreement between the parties as to the amount of the indebtedness. Sunshine Dairy v. Jolly Joan, 234 Or. 84, 380 P.2d 637 (1963). Whether or not the debtor's silence constitutes assent may be a jury question. Polichio v. Oliver Well Works, Inc., 147 Colo. 158, 362 P.2d 1056 (1961).

67. Under common law pleading an action on an account stated could be brought upon one of the common counts of assumpsit known as insimul computassent.

68. 6 Corbin § 1312.

69. See § 80 supra. When an account stated is agreed upon are the previous obligations discharged or may the creditor instead sue on the original obligations? Corbin indicates that he may. 6 Corbin § 1314. The Restatement is to the contrary. Restate-ment, Contracts § 422; see also 6 Williston § 1862 (rev.ed.1938).

70. Trafton v. Youngblood, 69 Cal.2d 17, 69 Cal.Rptr. 568, 442 P.2d 648 (1968). Thus, it may be shown that the account contradicts the contractually agreed upon method of computation. Hopwood Plays, Inc. v. Kemper, 263 N.Y. 380, 189 N.E. 461 (1934); Norfolk Hosiery & Underwear Mills Co. v. Westheimer, 121 Va. 130, 92 S.E. 922 (1917).

71. Dodson v. Watson, 110 Tex. 355, 220 S.W. 771, 11 A.L.R. 583 (1920); 6 Corbin §§ 1307, 1308, 1310, 1311.

72. First Nat. Bank of Missouri Valley v. Williamson, 205 Iowa 925, 219 N.W. 32 (1928).

73. 6 Corbin § 1309; 6 Williston § 1863 (rev.ed.1938). The result in any given jurisdiction is often dependent in part on statutory interpretation. See Boatner v. Gates Bros. Lumber Co., 224 Ark. 494, 275 S.W.2d 627, 51 A.L.R.2d 326 (1955).

Very often, however, the term "account stated" is used in a broader sense to encompass transactions involving more than arithmetical computation. Indeed the Restatement, under the heading of Account Stated gives an illustration that is in no way distinguishable from a substituted contract:

> "A orders goods from B his grocer, no price being fixed. B employs A, an attorney-at-law, to render certain services for which no price is fixed. A and B agree that the value of the groceries is $125 and the value of the legal services is $100, and the balance due B is $25. There is an account stated." [74]

It should be noted that more than arithmetical computations is involved in their agreement. They have liquidated prior unliquidated obligations. Their agreement is supported by consideration and under the general rule that the adequacy of consideration is for the parties to decide, it is irrelevant whether the legal services or groceries were worth far more than the account provided for.[75] Much more is involved than the facilitation of pleading and proof.

F.   RELEASE AND COVENANT NOT TO SUE

§ 347. Release

A release is often defined as a writing manifesting an intention to discharge another from an existing or an asserted duty.[76] Yet it is not infrequently held that a release supported by consideration may be oral.[77] The traditional vehicle for a release has been the delivery of an instrument under seal.[78] Today with the abolition of the seal in many jurisdictions it would appear that in these jurisdictions a release must be supported by consideration or one of the substitutes for con-

---

74. Restatement, Contracts § 422, ill. 2.

75. See 6 Corbin §§ 1305, 1312; compare § 55 supra.

A case which is different than any of those discussed arises if A has performed services for B at B's request and sends a bill for $2000.00. It seems to be agreed that if B remains silent there is ordinarily no accord or substituted agreement. There is authority however that if B remains silent this is an admission which justifies a suit upon a theory of account stated. Richardson On Evidence § 302. However Corbin disagrees and states that there is no admission on B's part in remaining silent and therefore no possibility of an account stated. 6 Corbin § 1313.

76. 5A Corbin § 1238; Restatement, Contracts § 402(1).

77. Reserve Ins. Co. v. Gayle, 393 F.2d 585 (4th Cir. 1968); Bank of United States v. Manheim, 264 N.Y. 45, 189 N.E. 776 (1934), rearg. denied 264 N.Y. 511, 191 N.E. 540.

78. Pitman v. J. C. Pitman & Sons, Inc., 324 Mass. 371, 86 N.E.2d 649 (1949).

sideration [79] as, for example, a statute which does away with the necessity of consideration.[80] If the release is supported by consideration it is not clear whether delivery is required.[81] There seems to be no reason, however, in principle why delivery should be necessary.

A release may be conditional. If the condition is contained in the release and is precedent, the discharge is effective upon the happening of the condition.[82] If the condition is subsequent the release operates as a covenant not to sue unless and until the condition occurs.[83] A condition which is not contained in the release is also effective because the parol evidence rule does not prevent the showing of the condition.[84]

As we have seen a conditional release may also be used to circumvent the common law rule that the release of one joint obligor releases another.[85] If the obligee in the release reserves his right against the other joint obligor or obligors the reservation is effective and the instrument is treated in effect as a covenant not to sue the obligor to whom the "release" is given.[86] Covenants not to sue are discussed in the next section.

79. Restatement, Contracts § 402. Corbin is not in accord for he states in § 1238: "It seems not improbable, however, that, in states that have abolished the common law effect of a seal by legislative action, a formal written release would be effective, even though there was no consideration."

A gratuitous release may be sustained on a theory of promissory estoppel. Fried v. Fisher, 328 Pa. 497, 196 A. 39, 115 A.L.R. 147 (1938).

It should also be observed that a release, like any other voluntary act, may be void or voidable for mistake, incapacity, duress, etc. See Wells v. Rau, 129 U.S.App.D.C. 253, 393 F.2d 362 (1968); Keefe, Validity of Releases Executed under Mistake of Fact, 14 Fordham L.Rev. 135 (1945).

80. See, for example, McKinney's N.Y. Gen.Obligations Law § 15–303 which provides:

"A written instrument which purports to be a total or partial release of all claims, debts, demands or obligations, or a total or partial release of any particular claim, debt, demand or obligation, or a release or discharge in whole or in part of a mortgage, lien, security interest or charge upon personal or real property, shall not be invalid because of the absence of consideration or of a seal." And § 1–107 of the Uniform Commercial Code which provides: "Any claim or right arising out of an alleged breach can be discharged in whole or in part without consideration by a written waiver or renunciation signed and delivered by the aggrieved party." See also U.C.C. § 3–605 relating to negotiable instruments. See § 94 supra.

81. 5A Corbin § 1238 (no delivery required); Restatement, Contracts § 402(1) and Comment d (delivery required). U.C.C. § 1–107 imposes a requirement of delivery as to a release without consideration, but the Code is silent as to a release supported by consideration. See also U.C.C. § 3–605 which requires delivery of a writing discharging a negotiable instrument.

82. Restatement, Contracts § 404(1).

83. Restatement, Contracts § 404(2).

84. See § 42 supra.

85. See § 330 supra.

86. 5A Corbin § 1239. When the creditor releases the principal debtor the

§ 348. Covenant Not to Sue

A release is an executed transaction. A covenant not to sue is a promise by the creditor not to sue either permanently or for a limited period.

If the promise is one never to sue it operates as a discharge just as does a release.[87] The theory is that should the creditor sue despite his promise not to, the debtor has a counterclaim for damages for breach of the creditor's covenant not to sue which is equal to and wipes out the original claim. To avoid circuity of action, despite the promissory form, the promise is given the effect of a discharge of the claim.[88]

As we saw in the preceding section the release of one of a number of joint obligors containing a reservation of rights against the others is treated as a covenant not to sue. However, in this situation, and in the case of an express covenant not to sue one joint obligor, the creditor is permitted to sue the "released" obligor despite his covenant not to sue [89] but is precluded from levying execution.[90] The reason for this rule as we have seen is to be found in the historical and present intricacy of the rules concerning joint obligors, especially the rule that all joint obligors are necessary parties to an action on the obligation.[91]

If the covenant is not to sue for a limited time the modern view is that the covenant may be raised as an affirmative defense to any action brought in violation of the covenant. The only exception is, as explained above, in the case of joint obligors.[92]

G.   GIFTS AND REJECTION OF TENDER

§ 349. Renunciation, Rejection of Tender, or Executed Gift

A renunciation is nothing more than an oral gratuitous release and under the majority view is not enforceable because of the absence of consideration.[93] This topic is directly related to the general neces-

surety is discharged unless the obligee reserves his rights against the surety. If the rights are reserved, the release is treated as a covenant not to sue. See § 330 supra.

87. Seligman v. Pinet, 78 Mich. 50, 43 N.W. 1091 (1889).

88. Restatement, Contracts § 405, Comment a; 5A Corbin § 1251.

89. 53 A.L.R. 1461 (1928).

90. Restatement, Contracts § 405(2); 5A Corbin § 1239. See § 330 supra.

91. See § 330 supra.

92. Restatement, Contracts § 405.

93. Burns v. Beeny, 427 S.W.2d 772 (Mo.Rpp.1968); 5A Corbin §§ 1240, 1241. It must be recalled, however, that where a contract has not been fully performed on both sides, a breach whether material or immateri-

sity for delivery in making a gift, as discussed in connection with the doctrine of consideration and the question of gratuitous assignments.[94]

Tender has legal effects in a number of contexts.[95] In this context the effect of tender as a discharge of a debt is considered. The question is what is the effect of a refusal of a valid tender upon or after the maturity of the debt.[96] The tender does not discharge the debt but if the tender is kept good it will stop the running of interest and costs.[97] The tender may also have the effect of discharging a mortgage or other lien which secures the debt.[98]

H. MERGER

§ 350. Merger

The term "merger" may be used in a broad or narrow sense. In a broad sense anytime a contract supersedes and incorporates all or part of an earlier agreement it may be said that the earlier agreement is merged into the later. In this sense a substituted contract results in a discharge by merger.[99] Also an earlier tentative agreement is merged into an integration.[1]

In a narrower sense, a common law rule emerged in the 1600's to the effect that a merger occurred if a "lower form" of obligation was superseded by a "higher form."[2] Thus, for example, where an obli-

al may be discharged in the sense that a promise not to sue upon the breach is enforceable. See § 339 supra; and Restatement, Contracts §§ 410, 411. There may also be a discharge by a voluntary acceptance of a defective performance. See § 169 supra and Restatement, Contracts §§ 412, 413.

The Uniform Commercial Code now provides in § 2–511(2) that:

"Tender of payment is sufficient when made by any means or in any manner current in the ordinary course of business unless the seller demands payment in legal tender and gives any extension of time reasonably necessary to procure it."

94. That delivery is not always necessary see Restatement, Contracts, § 414. See § 63 and § 259 supra. The subject matter of gifts is generally beyond the scope of this volume.

95. 6 Williston §§ 1808 and 1809.

96. For the requisites of valid tender see 6 Williston §§ 1810 to 1815 (rev. ed.1938). The rule has been that unless the contract otherwise provides, tender of payment may be refused if it is not "legal tender;" that is, cash.

97. 6 Williston §§ 1816–1817. In each jurisdiction local procedural statutes should be consulted for modifications of and substitutions for the common law rule. See, e. g., McKinney's N.Y. C.P.L.R. 3219.

98. Kortright v. Cady, 21 N.Y. 343, 78 Am.Dec. 145 (1860).

99. See § 343 supra.

1. See ch. 3 supra.

2. The historical development and effect of this rule is exhaustively treat-

gation arising under a contract is reduced to judgment the only obligation which remains is the obligation under the judgment,[3] so also where the obligation arising under an informal contract is superseded by a sealed instrument or other specialty.[4]   The primary effect of such a discharge of the earlier obligation was an almost total exclusion of parol evidence of the prior contract in an attempt to vary or contradict the higher obligation, or indeed even to explain it.[5]   The judgment or specialty was itself the obligation and not merely evidence of it.   This early rule of integration preceded the parol evidence rule as applied to informal integrations.   Today, the merger of an informal contract into a specialty raises basically the same problems as the merger of an informal contract into an integrated informal contract; that is, the extent to which the prior expressions of agreement are admissible into evidence.   Thus, the existence of a separate heading of "discharge by merger" in Restatements, treatises, and texts is largely an anachronism.   What is involved is merely a substituted obligation.

Although a negotiable instrument is regarded as a specialty and is a "higher" form of obligation, it has generally been held that the acceptance of a negotiable instrument from the obligor does not discharge the underlying obligation unless it is given and accepted in satisfaction of the underlying obligation.   This rule created a good deal of litigation as to the factual question of whether or not the instrument was accepted in satisfaction.   The Uniform Commercial Code Article on commercial paper makes it clear that in the usual case the instrument acts as an executory accord, suspending the underlying obligation.   In the event the instrument is dishonored, the obligee may sue on the instrument or the prior obligation.[6]

Merger by judgment is today largely considered as one aspect of the doctrine of res judicata and treated in depth in works on judgments.

I.   UNION OF RIGHT AND DUTY IN THE SAME PERSON

§ 351.   Acquisition By the Debtor of the Correlative Right

Closely analogous to merger is a discharge by virtue of a union of right and duty in the same person.   The Restatement states the

ed in 9 Wigmore, Evidence § 2426 (3d ed.1940); see also 6 Williston § 1875E (rev.ed.1938).

3.   Restatement, Contracts § 444.   The same is true of an arbitration award. Restatement, Contracts § 445.

4.   Restatement, Contracts § 446.

5.   See 9 Wigmore, Evidence § 2426 (3d ed.1940).

6.   U.C.C. § 3–802; see also § 2–511(3).

general rule as follows: "Where a person subject to a contractual duty, or to a duty to make compensation, acquires the correlative right in the same capacity in which he owes the duty, the duty is discharged." [7] The simplest illustration is where a creditor assigns his claim against a debtor to the same debtor.[8] The Restatement rule, however, is to be disapproved as an overly sweeping generalization. Especially in the field of mortgages, difficult questions arise as to merger of the right-duty relation in the same person and often enough that person's intention to keep the two aspects of the relation separate will be given effect.[9]

J. ALTERATION

§ 352. Discharge by Alteration

The modern rule [10] is that a material alteration of a written contract by one who asserts a right under it extinguishes his right and discharges the obligation of the obligor if the alteration was made with fraudulent intent.[11] An alteration [12] is material if the rights of the obligee under the altered contract would be varied as to the party making the alteration or as to a third party.[13] A discharge caused by an alteration is nullified by a subsequent assent to or forgiveness of the alteration even though the promise to forgive is not supported by consideration.[14] So also if the contract is bilateral and the innocent party knowing of the alteration asserts his rights under the contract the duties of both parties are revived.[15] If the arrangement is unilateral, alteration discharges the rights of the party who is guilty of the alteration but does not discharge the rights of the other party who

---

7. Restatement, Contracts § 451.

8. Wright v. Anderson, 62 S.D. 444, 253 N.W. 484, 95 A.L.R. 81 (1934).

9. See, for example, Osborne, Mortgages §§ 272 to 276 (1951).

10. At early common law the doctrine of discharge by alteration appears to have applied only to formal contracts and any material alteration whether fraudulent or not or whether caused by the obligee or not or resulted in discharge. 6 Williston § 1881 (rev. ed. 1938). For more detailed treatment, see Williston, Discharge of Contracts by Alteration (Pts. I & II), 18 Harv. L.Rev. 105, 165 (1904–1905), Selected Readings 1221, 1232.

11. Knapp v. Knapp, 251 Iowa 44, 99 N.W.2d 396 (1959); Restatement, Contracts § 434. Corbin suggests that the rules should apply to only sealed instruments, integrations and a memoranda which satisfy the Statute of Frauds. 6 Corbin § 1317.

12. An alteration may be made by an erasure, an interlineation, addition, etc.

13. Restatement, Contracts § 435. Cf. § 124 of the Uniform Negotiable Instruments Law which has been changed by U.C.C. § 3–407.

14. Restatement, Contracts § 437.

15. Restatement, Contracts § 436.

must, however, if he wishes to assert his rights, perform any acts which he is required to perform under the agreement.[16]

K. BANKRUPTCY

§ 353. Bankruptcy

A bankrupt is discharged by operation of law with respect to his provable debts. The cases sometimes indicate that merely the remedy is barred or suspended by the decree in bankruptcy,[17] but others speak in terms of an actual discharge.[18] The differences in theory affect the analysis of cases involving new promises to pay debts unenforceable because of bankruptcy.[19]

L. PERFORMANCE

§ 354. Performance of the Duty—To Which Debt Should Payment be Applied

A contractual duty is obviously discharged by performance.[20] When the debtor owes the creditor more than one debt and a payment is made by the debtor or upon his behalf the question arises as to which debt the payment should be applied. Except as later indicated: (a) If the debtor manifests an intention in this respect at or before the time of payment, the creditor must apply the payment in accordance with the directions manifested by the debtor.[21] (b) If the debtor makes no manifestation, the creditor may within a reasonable time make the application.[22] (c) If neither the creditor nor the debtor makes a seasonable manifestation, the law will apply the payment in the manner which is most equitable.[23]

There is an exception to the rule stated in (a) above where the payor is under a duty to a third person, for example, a surety, to apply

16. 6 Corbin § 1317.

17. Zavelo v. Reeves, 227 U.S. 625, 33 S.Ct. 365, 57 L.Ed. 676 (1913).

18. Henry v. Root, 33 N.Y. 526 (1865).

19. See § 84 supra.

20. Restatement, Contracts § 386.

21. Schreiber v. Armstrong, 70 N.M. 419, 374 P.2d 297 (1962). A manifestation once made cannot be changed without the consent of the other party.

22. J. & G. Constr. Co. v. Freeport Coal Co., 147 W.Va. 563, 129 S.E.2d 834 (1963); Debelak Bros. Inc. v. Mille, 38 Wis.2d 373, 157 N.W.2d 644 (1968).

23. Carozza v. Brannan, 186 Md. 123, 46 A.2d 198 (1946). This and other equitable rules are listed in § 394 of the Restatement of Contracts. For example, it is applied to an unsecured debt rather than a secured debt. Contra, Jones v. Benedict, 83 N.Y. 79 (1880).

the money to a particular debt and the creditor knows or has reason to know of the facts which create the duty. Under these circumstances the creditor must apply the payment in discharge of the debt in which the third party is interested.[24]

There are also exceptions to the rule stated in (b). The creditor may not apply the payment to an unmatured claim, or a disputed claim or an illegal claim and must apply it to a debt which if not paid by the debtor will result in a forfeiture or violate a duty owed by the debtor to a third party, provided the creditor knows or has reason to know of this duty.[25]

---

24. Bounds v. Nuttle, 181 Md. 400, 30 A.2d 263 (1943); Restatement, Contracts § 388.

25. Restatement, Contracts § 389. However, under the majority view "the creditor can apply the payment in discharge of a debt that is unsecured rather than one that is secured or even in discharge of a debt that is barred by a statute of limitations or is not enforceable because of the statute of frauds." 5A Corbin § 1231.

CHAPTER 19

ILLEGAL BARGAINS

Analysis

		Sections
I.	Illegal Bargains	356–374
	A. Bargains in Restraint of Trade	356–359
	B. Bargains Harmful to Public or to Fiduciary Duties	360–364
	C. Bargains to Commit a Tort or to Exonerate or Indemnify from Tortious Liability	365–367
	D. Bargains Tending to Obstruct the Administration of Justice	368–369
	E. Bargains Harmful to Marriage	370
	F. Other Illegal Bargains	371–374
II.	The Effect of Illegality	375–387
	A. Illegal Executory Contracts	376–377
	B. Illegal Contract Which is Performed in Whole or Part	378–387

Sec.
355. Introduction.

I. ILLEGAL BARGAINS

A. BARGAINS IN RESTRAINT OF TRADE

356. Agreement by a Seller of a Business Not to Compete with the Buyer.
357. Agreement by an Employee Not to Compete after the Termination of His Employment.
358. Divisibility of a Contract in Restraint of Trade.
359. Monopolies and Restraint.

B. BARGAINS HARMFUL TO PUBLIC OR TO FIDUCIARY DUTIES

360. Lobbying Agreements to Influence Legislative Action.
361. Bargain to Procure Government Contracts.
362. Some Other Bargains Harmful to Public Service.
363. Bargain in Breach of a Fiduciary Obligation.
364. Agreement by a Citizen to Violate a Civic Duty.

C. BARGAINS TO COMMIT A TORT OR TO EXONERATE OR INDEMNIFY FROM TORTIOUS LIABILITY

Sec.
365. Bargain to Commit a Tort or Injure Third Persons.
366. Bargains to Indemnify Against the Consequences of Illegal and Tortious Acts.
367. Agreement to Exempt a Person from Willful or Negligent Misconduct.

D. BARGAINS TENDING TO OBSTRUCT THE ADMINISTRATION OF JUSTICE

368. Maintenance and Champerty.
369. Agreements Tending to Interfere with the Proper Functioning of the Judicial Machinery.

E. BARGAINS HARMFUL TO MARRIAGE

370. Contracts Tending to Prevent or Disrupt the Marriage Relationship.

F. OTHER ILLEGAL BARGAINS

371. Sunday Contracts: What Activities Included.
372. Effect of Violation of a Sunday Law Statute.
373. Wagering Contracts and Lotteries.
374. Usurious Bargains.
     (a) Was there a Loan of Money?
     (b) Does the Loan Exceed the Legal Rate of Interest?

II. THE EFFECT OF ILLEGALITY

375. Introduction.

A. ILLEGAL EXECUTORY CONTRACTS

376. General Rule.
377. Cases Where a Party May Successfully Sue Upon an Illegal Executory Bilateral Contract.
     (a) Ignorance of Facts and Law.
     (b) Bargain Illegal by Virtue of Wrongful Purpose.
     (c) Where a Particular Statute is Directed Against One of the Parties.

B. ILLEGAL CONTRACT WHICH IS PERFORMED IN WHOLE OR PART

378. Introduction.
379. Will the Courts Always Deny a Remedy in the Case of an Illegal Bargain Which Violates a Criminal Statute?
380. Effect of Licensing Statutes.
381. Remoteness of the Illegality.
382. A Mere Depositary May Not Assert the Defense of Illegality.
383. Quasi Contractual Recoveries Based Upon Performance.
384. Divisibility of Illegal Bargains.

Sec.
385. The Doctrine of Pari Delicto.
386. Locus Poenitentiae.
387. Change of Law or Facts after the Bargain is Made.

§ 355. Introduction

This chapter conveniently divides itself into two parts: first, what makes a bargain illegal and, second, the effect of the illegality. The Restatement states that "a bargain is illegal . . . if either its formation or its performance is criminal, tortious or otherwise opposed to public policy." [1] The subject matter of torts is obviously beyond the scope of this volume. Nor is it possible to consider the wide variety of situations which might make a bargain criminal or contrary to public policy. Rather it is sufficient for the purpose of a book of this size to discuss only the most common types of bargains which are illegal, tortious or contrary to public policy. The question of the effect of illegality will be discussed in more detail.

I. ILLEGAL BARGAINS

Analysis

A. BARGAINS IN RESTRAINT OF TRADE

Sec.
356. Agreement by a Seller of a Business Not to Compete with the Buyer.
357. Agreement by an Employee not to Compete after the Termination of His Employment.
358. Divisibility of a Contract in Restraint of Trade.
359. Monopolies and Restraint.

B. BARGAINS HARMFUL TO PUBLIC OR TO FIDUCIARY DUTIES

360. Lobbying Agreements to Influence Legislative Action.
361. Bargain to Procure Government Contracts.
362. Some Other Bargains Harmful to Public Service.
363. Bargain in Breach of a Fiduciary Obligation.
364. Agreement by a Citizen to Violate a Civic Duty.

C. BARGAINS TO COMMIT A TORT OR TO EXONERATE OR INDEMNIFY FROM TORTIOUS LIABILITY

365. Bargain to Commit a Tort or Injure Third Persons.
366. Bargains to Indemnify Against the Consequences of Illegal and Tortious Acts.
367. Agreement to Exempt a Person from Willful or Negligent Misconduct.

1. Restatement, Contracts § 512.

D. BARGAINS TENDING TO OBSTRUCT THE ADMINISTRATION OF JUSTICE

Sec.
368. Maintenance and Champerty.
369. Agreements Tending to Interfere with the Proper Functioning of the Judicial Machinery.

E. BARGAINS HARMFUL TO MARRIAGE

370. Contracts Tending to Prevent or Disrupt the Marriage Relationship.

F. OTHER ILLEGAL BARGAINS

371. Sunday Contracts: What Activities Included.
372. Effect of Violation of a Sunday Law Statute.
373. Wagering Contracts and Lotteries.
374. Usurious Bargains.
    (a) Was there a Loan of Money?
    (b) Does the Loan Exceed the Legal Rate of Interest?

A. BARGAINS IN RESTRAINT OF TRADE

§ 356. Agreement by a Seller of a Business Not to Compete with the Buyer

An agreement by a person to refrain from exercising his trade or calling standing alone is viewed as being illegal and contrary to public policy because it is inimical to the interests of society in a free competitive market and to the interests of the person restrained in earning a livelihood.[2] But if the covenant not to compete forms part of a legitimate transaction a different problem is presented. Such a covenant is often described as an "ancillary restraint" to indicate its connection with a legitimate transaction.[3]

Thus for many years it is and has been common in the purchase of a business as a going concern to purchase along with the other assets of the business the "good will" in the hope that the customers of the concern will patronize the new owners. To protect this expecta-

---

2. United States v. Addyston Pipe & Steel Co., 85 F. 271 (6th Cir. 1898), modified and aff'd, 175 U.S. 211, 20 S. Ct. 96, 44 L.Ed. 136 (1898); 6A Corbin §§ 1379–1384.

3. This chapter discusses covenants not to compete ancillary to sales of going businesses and ancillary to employment contracts. Rules similar to those applicable to these transactions have been forged for other ancillary restraints, such as restraints ancillary to the sale of corporate shares (6A Corbin § 1388), ancillary to the sale or lease of real property [6A Corbin § 1389; 5 Williston § 1642 (rev'd ed. 1937)], ancillary to partnership agreements [5 Williston § 1644 (rev'd ed. 1937)], and ancillary to stock option agreements. Fox v. Avis Rent-A-Car Systems, Inc., 223 Ga. 571, 156 S.E.2d 910 (1967).

tion it is common to provide that the seller shall not reopen his business in competition with the business sold.

The earlier English cases in this situation made the question of legality depend upon whether the restraint imposed was "general" or "limited." [4] Thus in some of the early cases in the United States a restraint that covered an entire state was deemed to be per se illegal [5] and in others a restraint that did not cover the entire country was deemed to be limited and therefore legal.[6] This test has now generally been abandoned and the test is whether the restraint of trade is unreasonable.[7]

"A promise by a seller not to compete with the buyer is illegal and unenforceable insofar as the restraint is in excess of the extent of the good will purchased." [8] Thus, if the restraint covers territory in which the seller had no good will, it is an unreasonable restraint of trade and the same is true if the restraint covers lines of trade in which the seller was not engaged.[9]

Although there are a number of cases to the effect that the duration of the restrictive covenant is immaterial,[10] the better view appears to be that a restraint is invalid if it is to continue "for a longer time than the good will built up by the seller and sold to the buyer can reasonably be expected to continue."[11]

§ 357. Agreement by an Employee Not to Compete after the Termination of His Employment

There are very many cases in which an employee promises his employer that upon the completion of the employment he will not

4. Mitchel v. Reynolds, 24 Eng.Rep. 347 (Ch. 1711).

5. Parish v. Schwartz, 344 Ill. 563, 176 N.E. 757, 78 A.L.R. 1032 (1931).

6. Diamond Match Co. v. Roeber, 106 N.Y. 473, 13 N.E. 419 (1887).

7. Jewel Box Stores Corp. v. Morrow, 272 N.C. 659, 158 S.E.2d 840 (1968); Restatement, Contracts § 514. Thus, if the business is national in extent, a covenant not to compete anywhere in the nation may be upheld if otherwise reasonable. See Diamond Match Co. v. Roeber, 106 N.Y. 473, 13 N.E. 419 (1887), where, however, Nevada and Montana were excluded from the restraint.

8. 6A Corbin § 1387. "When a business is sold with its good will, but without any express promise not to compete, the seller is privileged to open up a new business in competition with the buyer; but he is under obligation not to solicit his former customers or to conduct his business under such a name and in such a manner as to deprive the buyer of the 'good will' that he paid for." 6A Corbin § 1386.

9. Schultz v. Johnson, 110 N.J.Eq. 566, 160 A. 379 (Ct.Err. & App.1932); Purchasing Associates Inc. v. Weitz, 13 N.Y.2d 267, 246 N.Y.S.2d 600, 196 N.E. 2d 245 (1963).

10. Beatty v. Coble, 142 Ind. 329, 41 N. E. 590 (1895).

11. 6A Corbin § 1391.

compete with his employer either in his own business or by working for another. If the employee learns no secrets and does not have any contact with the customers of the employer there is no reason for enforcing such a restrictive covenant and the covenant should be struck down as imposing an undue hardship upon the person restricted.[12] It is generally agreed that if an employee learns a trade secret, a promise not to disclose it or use it will be enforced.[13] Indeed, even in the absence of an express covenant, employees may not, even after termination of employment disclose or make use of trade secrets, including secret customer lists.[14]

The most difficult cases appear to be the ones where an employee has contact with his employer's customers so that he obtains the good will of the customers—a good will that is likely to follow him. Here, as in the cases involving a sale of the business discussed in section 356 supra, if the restraint in space and time is greater than is necessary to protect the employer it will be deemed to be invalid.[15] However, even if the covenant is not excessive as to time or space it may still not be enforced, particularly by way of injunction, if enforcement will result in a disproportionate hardship to the employee[16] or if failure to issue an injunction will cause no irreparable harm to the employer.[17] As Corbin states, "Before granting an injunction preventing an employee from earning his living in his customary trade or employment, the court should make sure, not only that he contracted to forbear and is guilty of a breach, but also that the former employer is suffering substantial harm, that the employee is soliciting former customers or otherwise depriving his employer of business good will that he has paid wages for helping to create, and that the employee will not be deprived of opportunity to support himself and his family in reasonable comfort."[18] As usual all of the facts and circumstanc-

---

12. Crowell v. Woodruff, 245 S.W.2d 447 (Ky.1952); Restatement, Contracts § 515(b).

13. McCall Co. v. Wright, 198 N.Y. 143, 91 N.E. 516 (1910). The same is true of the sale of a secret process. Tode v. Gross, 127 N.Y. 480, 28 N.E. 469 (1891). An agreement by an employee to assign to his employer inventions made in the course of his employment is valid. 6A Corbin § 1394A.

14. Town & Country House & Home Serv. v. Newberry, 3 N.Y.2d 554, 170 N.Y.S.2d 328, 147 N.E.2d 724 (1958).

15. Purchasing Associates Inc. v. Weitz, 13 N.Y.2d 267, 246 N.Y.S.2d 600, 196 N.E.2d 245 (1963); see Note, 30 Tenn.L.Rev. 454 (1963).

16. Cogley Clinic v. Martini, 253 Iowa 541, 112 N.W.2d 678 (1962), 48 Iowa L.Rev. 159 (1962); Standard Oil Co. v. Bertelsen, 186 Minn. 483, 243 N.W. 701 (1932).

17. Menter Co. v. Brock, 147 Minn. 407, 180 N.W. 553, 20 A.L.R. 857 (1920).

18. 6A Corbin § 1394; Taylor Freezer Sales Co. v. Sweden Freezer Eastern Corp., 224 Ga. 160, 160 S.E.2d 356 (1968).

es should be considered in making this determination of unreasonable hardship.[19]

Because there is likely to be greater hardship on an employee than on the seller of a business, courts have stated on a number of occasions that they are more reluctant to uphold and to enforce covenants not to compete entered into by employees than those agreed to by sellers of businesses.[20]

§ 358.　Divisibility of a Contract in Restraint of Trade

The doctrine of divisibility is discussed in more detail below.[21] However, a word here with respect to the divisibility of a contract in restraint of trade would not be inappropriate.

As we have seen an agreement in restraint of trade may be reasonable as to some of the territory included but unreasonable as to other territory included. May the party who seeks to enforce this excessive promise enforce the lawful part of it? There are three views. One view is that the valid portion of the promise is enforceable only if the promise is so worded that the valid portion is divisible from the invalid portion.[22] In other words the promise is enforceable, if by striking out some of the words in the promise the words that are left constitute a valid restraint.[23] The second and better view is that irrespective of the language used, if the violation of the covenant takes place within the area in which the restraining covenant would be reasonable, the covenant should be enforced by the issuance of an injunction limited to the area in which the restraint is reasonable.[24] In many cases, however, the courts have refused to invoke the doctrine of divisibility and have stricken the entire covenant.[25]

It is often stated that a party to an illegal bargain may not recover for its breach.[26] From this proposition it has been thought to

19. Blake, Employee Covenants Not To Compete, 73 Harv.L.Rev. 625 (1960); Note, 17 Drake L.Rev. 69 (1967).

20. The Day Companies, Inc. v. Patat, 403 F.2d 792 (5th Cir. 1968), cert. denied 393 U.S. 1117, 89 S.Ct. 993, 22 L. Ed.2d 122 (1969); Morgan's Home Equip. Corp. v. Martucci, 390 Pa. 618, 136 A.2d 838 (1957).

21. See § 384 infra.

22. General Bronze Corp. v. Schmeling, 208 Wis. 565, 243 N.W. 469 (1932).

23. Welcome Wagon Int'l, Inc. v. Pender, 255 N.C. 244, 120 S.E.2d 739 (1961), 41 N.Car.L.Rev. 253 (1963).

24. Tobin v. Cody, 343 Mass. 716, 180 N.E.2d 652 (1962); Eldridge v. Johnston, 195 Or. 379, 245 P.2d 239 (1952); Jacobson & Co. v. Int'l Environment Corp., 427 Pa. 439, 235 A.2d 612 (1967).

25. Welcome Wagon, Inc. v. Morris, 224 F.2d 693 (4th Cir. 1955); McLeod v. Meyer, 237 Ark. 173, 372 S.W.2d 220 (1963), 18 Ark.L.Rev. 168 (1964); Weatherford Oil Tool Co. v. Campbell, 161 Tex. 310, 340 S.W.2d 950 (1960), 40 Tex.L.Rev. 152 (1961).

26. See 376 infra.

follow that a party from whom a promise in unreasonable restraint of trade has been extracted cannot enforce the return promise made to him. Thus, a local grocer who sells his business for $5,000, payable in instalments, would be barred from recovering if he has unreasonably promised not to engage in the grocery business in the United States. This harsh result has been reached in a number of cases.[27] Most courts, however, seem to have reached more equitable results, permitting the seller to recover the sale price less the proportionate value of the illegal part of the covenant[28] or full recovery.[29]

§ 359. Monopolies and Restraint

At common law an attempt to monopolize was illegal.[30] Today this matter is covered by such statutes as the Sherman Antitrust Act,[31] the Clayton Act[32] and also by State antitrust laws.

B. BARGAINS HARMFUL TO PUBLIC OR TO FIDUCIARY DUTIES

§ 360. Lobbying Agreements to Influence Legislative Action

Any public official who sells his vote or surrenders his discretion for a consideration is obviously guilty of a criminal act.[33] However, we are concerned here with the contract between a lobbyist and the person who hires him to cause the enactment or defeat of legislation. Many of the early cases held that such a contract was illegal per se if the compensation promised to the lobbyist was contingent upon success even though no unlawful acts were contemplated or performed.[34]

---

27. More v. Bonnet, 40 Cal. 251 (1871); Bishop v. Palmer, 146 Mass. 469, 16 N.E. 299 (1888); cf. 5 Williston § 1650 (rev. ed. 1937).

28. Wesley v. Chandler, 152 Okl. 22, 3 P.2d 720 (1931), 45 Harv.L.Rev. 750 (1932), 30 Mich.L.Rev. 1111 (1932); Hartman v. Everett, 158 Okl. 29, 12 P.2d 543 (1932); cf. Saratoga County Bank v. King, 44 N.Y. 87 (1870) where the court denied the seller recovery of the final instalment. The rule of partial recovery is supported in 6A Corbin § 1390.

29. Nicholson v. Ellis, 110 Md. 322, 73 A. 17 (1909); Rosenbaum v. United States Credit-System Co., 65 N.J.L. 255, 48 A. 237 (Ct.Err. & App.1901).

30. Standard Oil Co. v. United States, 221 U.S. 1, 31 S.Ct. 502, 55 L.Ed. 619 (1911).

31. 15 U.S.C.A. §§ 1–7.

32. 15 U.S.C.A. §§ 12–27.

33. United States v. Manton, 107 F.2d 834 (2d Cir. 1938), cert. denied, 309 U. S. 664, 60 S.Ct. 590, 84 L.Ed. 1012 (1940).

34. Trist v. Child, 88 U.S. (21 Wall.) 441, 22 L.Ed. 623 (1874). However this rule was not applied to a contingent fee for professional services such as collecting facts, preparing arguments, etc. Chesebrough v. Conover, 140 N.Y. 382, 35 N.E. 633 (1893).

The more modern view is that a contingent fee is merely a factor to be considered in determining the question of legality.[35]

The difficult question is what conduct by the lobbyist is illegal and what conduct is legal. It seems clear that the lobbyist is permitted to influence the legislative body or its members so long as he does it by presenting facts and arguments and provided he does this in a proper forum.[36] It is equally clear that he is not permitted to promise to use or to use personal or political influence to procure legislation.[37]

§ 361. Bargain to Procure Government Contracts

The validity of a bargain to procure a government contract is regulated by very much the same rules as the lobbying agreement. The factual difference is that in one case legislative action is influenced whereas in the other administrative action is influenced. Here again if the agent uses personal or political influence in an attempt to get the contract, or it is contemplated that he will, the contract is illegal.[38] But if all that is contemplated and occurs is that the public official is to be persuaded by the merits of the goods or of the contractor or any other desirable public ground, then the agreement is perfectly valid.[39]

In this area also there are a large number of cases which have held that the contract is illegal per se if there is a contingent fee arrangement.[40] However, there are also cases which hold that this is only one of the factors to be considered.[41]

35. Restatement, Contracts § 563.

36. Restatement, Contracts § 559. Comment a to this section states in part: "The proper way, so far as it is available for bringing such facts and arguments before legislative bodies, is by public argument before their committees. In some cases this is not possible. In the Congress of the United States public hearings are held and can be held, with reference to only a small fraction of the bills that are introduced. It is the practice for individual congressmen to receive in their offices persons interested in promoting legislation, and to hear their arguments. On these arguments the question may depend whether a committee will give a hearing on a bill."

37. Ewing v. National Airport Corp., 115 F.2d 859 (4th Cir. 1940), cert. denied, 312 U.S. 705, 61 S.Ct. 828, 85 L. Ed. 1138 (1941).

38. Mahoney v. Lincoln Brick Co., 304 Mich. 694, 8 N.W.2d 883 (1943).

39. Coyne v. Superior Incinerator Co., 80 F.2d 844 (2d Cir. 1936); Restatement, Contracts § 562.

40. Providence Tool Co. v. Norris, 69 U.S. (2 Wall.) 45, 17 L.Ed. 868 (1865).

41. Valdes v. Larrinaga, 233 U.S. 705, 34 S.Ct. 750, 58 L.Ed. 1163 (1914); Ferrell v. Elkins, 159 Ark. 31, 251 S. W. 380 (1923); Lyon v. Mitchell, 36 N.Y. 235 (1867); Glass v. Swimaster Corp., 74 N.D. 282, 21 N.W.2d 468 (1946); cf. Restatement, Contracts § 561, which provides: "A bargain to procure a pardon or to solicit by personal influence the granting of a par-

The problem has been further complicated by executive order and legislation which require that in specified federal government contracts the contractor must warrant that no one, excepting bona fide employees or commercial selling agents maintained by the contractor, has been employed or retained on a contingent fee basis to secure the contract and that in the event of a breach of the warranty the government has the right to cancel the contract or to deduct the amount of the fee from the contract price.[42] Two principal problems arise in the interpretation and effect of this warranty. First, there is a division of authority as to what constitutes the "maintaining" of a bona fide agent.[43] Second, there is a division of authority as to the effect of the executive order on the agent's rights against the contractor. Some courts take the position that an agent who is not a maintained agent may not recover a contingent fee no matter how upright his conduct.[44] Others have taken the position that in the absence of actual or contemplated improper conduct the agent may recover his fee from the contractor.[45] Still another view would allow quasi-contractual relief for legitimate services.[46] There is also disagreement as to whether the rights of the agent as against the contractor are governed by federal common law or state common law.[47]

don, is illegal; but a bargain to prepare a petition for a pardon and to make an argument in support of it before the pardoning power, is not illegal."

42. See generally McClelland, The Covenant against Contingent Fees as a Method of Eliminating the "5-Percenter," 41 Cornell L.Q. 399 (1956).

43. United States v. Paddock, 178 F.2d 394 (5th Cir. 1949), cert. den. 340 U.S. 813, 71 S.Ct. 41, 95 L.Ed. 597 (1950); Le John Mfg. Co. v. Webb, 95 U.S. App.D.C. 358, 222 F.2d 48 (1955) (agent must not be an independent contractor); Companhia Atlantica v. United States, 180 F.Supp. 342 (Ct.Cl. 1950), cert. denied 364 U.S. 862, 81 S. Ct. 103, 5 L.Ed.2d 85 (1960), 81 S.Ct. 106 (agent may be an independent contractor).

44. Le John Mfg. Co. v. Webb, 95 U.S. App.D.C. 358, 222 F.2d 48 (1955); Mitchell v. Flintkote Co., 185 F.2d 1008 (2d Cir. 1950), cert. denied 341 U.S. 931, 71 S.Ct. 804, 95 L.Ed. 1361 (1951).

45. Buckley v. Coyne Elec. School, 343 Ill.App. 420, 99 N.E.2d 370 (1951), cert. denied 342 U.S. 927, 72 S.Ct. 366, 96 L.Ed. 691 (1952); Gendron v. Jacoby, 337 Mich. 150, 59 N.W.2d 128 (1953); Ebeling v. Fred J. Swaine Mfg. Co., 357 Mo. 549, 209 S.W.2d 892 (1948); Bradford v. Durkee Marine Prods. Corp., 180 Misc. 1049, 40 N.Y.S.2d 448 (Sup.Ct.1943).

46. Browne v. R & R Engineering Co., 264 F.2d 219 (3d Cir. 1959); contra, Weitzel v. Brown-Neil Corp., 152 F. Supp. 540 (N.D.W.Va.1957), aff'd 251 F.2d 661 (4th Cir. 1958).

47. Although Erie R. R. Co. v. Tompkins, 304 U.S. 64, 58 S.Ct. 817, 82 L. Ed. 1188, 114 A.L.R. 1487 (1938), is generally cited for the proposition that there is no federal common law, the proposition is an overgeneralization. Federal judge-made law supplements federal legislation and is generally applicable if the case involves a federal question. See, e. g., D'Oench, Duhme & Co. v. F. D. I. C., 315 U.S. 447, 62 S.Ct. 676, 86 L.Ed. 956 (1942), reh. denied 315 U.S. 830, 62

A federal statute makes it a criminal offense for sub-contractors to pay kickbacks to prime contractors or their agents with respect to negotiated government contracts.[48] The statute provides for criminal penalties and for recovery by the government of the illegal kickback. Although the statute is silent in this respect, it has been held that when an illegal kickback is made by the sub-contractor to the contractor the prime contract is illegal.[49]

§ 362. Some Other Bargains Harmful to Public Service

What has been said above applies in general to bargains to influence other forms of governmental action. Thus it is clear that a bargain for the sale of public office is illegal as is a promise that a certain person will be appointed to public office.[50] So also "a bargain for either increasing or diminishing compensation fixed by law for a public official is illegal." [51] It is obvious that excessive payment would deplete the public funds. As to reduced payments these have often been accompanied by an improper purpose and so have been condemned.[52] However, there are many cases where a policeman or a workman has accepted a lesser wage without protest. Here, absent some corrupt purpose, considerations of illegality should not be presumed to be present.[53] Rather, the case should be decided in terms of

S.Ct. 910, 86 L.Ed. 1224; Friendly, In Praise of Erie—and of the New Federal Common Law, 39 N.Y.U.L.Rev. 383 (1964). For example, federal government contracts have generally been held to be governed by federal common law and the United States Court of Appeals for the Second Circuit has held that it will look to the Uniform Commercial Code as a source of federal common law. United States v. Wegematic Corp., 360 F.2d 674 (2d Cir. 1966).

In actions brought by agents to recover contingent fees for procuring government contracts it has been held by some federal courts that the federal common law is applicable. Mitchell v. Flintkote Co., 185 F.2d 1008 (2d Cir. 1950), cert. denied 341 U.S. 931, 71 S. Ct. 804, 95 L.Ed. 1361 (1951); Weitzel v. Brown-Neil Corp., 152 F.Supp. 540 (N.D.W.Va.1957), aff'd 251 F.2d 661 (4th Cir. 1958). The state courts, however, have generally proceeded on the assumption that the matter is governed by state law. See cases cited in n. 45, supra. The question is as

yet unresolved. See Stone v. Roberts Numbering Mach. Co., 146 N.Y.S.2d 199 (Sup.Ct.1955), aff'd 1 A.D.2d 770, 148 N.Y.S.2d 124 (1st Dep't 1956) in which the court avoided resolving the question.

48. 41 U.S.C. §§ 51–54, generally known as the Anti-Kickback Act.

49. United States v. Acme Process Equip. Co., 385 U.S. 138, 87 S.Ct. 350, 17 L.Ed.2d 249 (1966), reh. denied 385 U.S. 1032, 87 S.Ct. 738, 17 L.Ed.2d 680 (1967).

50. Robertson v. Robinson, 65 Ala. 610, 39 Am.Rep. 17 (1880); Goodrich v. Northwestern Tel. Exch. Co., 161 Minn. 106, 201 N.W. 290 (1924); Restatement, Contracts § 560.

51. Restatement, Contracts § 565.

52. 6A Corbin § 1453.

53. However many cases have decided the issue on this basis. E. g., City of Louisville v. Thomas, 257 Ky. 540, 78 S.W.2d 767 (1935).

lack of consideration or in terms of executed gift.[54]   As Corbin states: "Bargains for reduced salary or fees, made before services rendered, should be closely examined for illegal elements; but a discharge after salary earned should often be found to have no illegal element." [55]

Somewhat related is the rule that a public officer or an employee may not assign salary or pay not yet due.[56]   It is felt that a public employee might not have sufficient interest in performance if he has already assigned what is due to him.[57]   The same rule applies to a pension "granted in consideration at least in part of continuing future services." [58]

Conflict of interest legislation prohibits governmental agents from serving two masters. They may not do business on behalf of the government with themselves or with businesses in which they have an interest. A contract entered into in contravention of such legislation is illegal even if it is fair and conscionable.[59]

§ 363.   Bargain in Breach of a Fiduciary Obligation

An agreement by a fiduciary to act contrary to the best interests of the person for whom he acts is generally regarded as illegal and contrary to law.[60]   Thus, the director of a corporation is deemed to be a fiduciary and must act so as to advance the interests of the corporation rather than his own personal interests.[61]

Public service corporations, such as carriers, are deemed to be quasi-public corporations and therefore are in a fiduciary relationship to the public. Thus it has often been held that an agreement by a railroad to locate its stations in a manner opposed to the public interest is illegal.[62]

---

54. See § 63 supra.

55. 6A Corbin § 1453.

56. Restatement, Contracts § 547(1) (a).

57. Roesch v. W. B. Worthen Co., 95 Ark. 482, 130 S.W. 551 (1910).

58. Restatement, Contracts § 547(1) (b). Wage assignments, and particularly assignments by public officials of wages or salaries are frequently regulated or prohibited by statute. Many statutes also curtail the assignability of pension payments. See § 266 supra.

59. United States v. Mississippi Val. Generating Co., 364 U.S. 520, 81 S.Ct. 294, 5 L.Ed.2d 268 (1960), reh. denied 365 U.S. 855, 81 S.Ct. 798, 5 L.Ed.2d 820; Spadanuta v. Village of Rockville Centre, 15 N.Y.2d 755, 257 N.Y.S. 2d 329, 205 N.E.2d 525 (1965); but see Stroud v. Pulaski County Special School Dist., 244 Ark. 161, 424 S.W.2d 141 (1968) (not illegal where contract is let by competitive bidding).

60. This matter is considered in depth in other courses such as trusts, agency and corporations. See 6A Corbin §§ 1456, 1457.

61. Restatement, Contracts § 569.

62. Williamson v. Chicago, R. I. & P. R., 53 Iowa 126, 4 N.W. 870 (1880).

§ 364. Agreement by a Citizen to Violate a Civic Duty

A citizen has a duty to perform certain civic duties. Thus he has a legal right and civic duty to vote and any agreement made by him to sell his vote or even to refrain from exercising it would be illegal.[63] The same would be true of any civic duty which the citizen has.[64]

C. BARGAINS TO COMMIT A TORT OR TO EXONERATE OR INDEMNIFY FROM TORTIOUS LIABILITY

§ 365. Bargain to Commit a Tort or Injure Third Persons

As we have seen an agreement to commit a tort against a third party makes the bargain illegal within the Restatement definition of illegality.[65] Thus a bargain is illegal if it is made with the purpose of or would have the effect of defrauding a third person.[66] It is important to observe that when one party induces another to enter into a contract by fraud the contract is not only generally deemed to be voidable, but the defrauding party is guilty of a tort. Where two or more parties enter into an agreement to defraud a third person this agreement is illegal.[67] Other illustrations of illegal agreements under the heading being discussed would be an agreement to place false and deceptive labels on goods to be used to deceive purchasers [68] and also a bargain "the making or performance of which involves breach of a contract with a third person." [69] The same is true of a bargain by a creditor for a preference over other creditors.[70]

§ 366. Bargains to Indemnify Against the Consequences of Illegal and Tortious Acts

A promise to indemnify one against the consequences of illegal action is not enforceable unless the party who performs the illegal action acts in good faith and without knowledge of the illegality.[71] This

63. 6A Corbin § 1454.

64. Restatement, Contracts § 567.

65. See § 355 supra.

66. Restatement, Contracts § 577.

67. 6A Corbin § 1455.

68. Materne v. Horwitz, 101 N.Y. 469, 5 N.E. 331 (1886).

69. Restatement, Contracts § 576; Reiner v. North American Newspaper Alliance, 259 N.Y. 250, 181 N.E. 561, 83 A.L.R. 23 (1932).

70. Crandall v. Durham, 348 Mo. 240, 152 S.W.2d 1044 (1941). The subject of fraudulent conveyances is beyond the scope of this work. For a brief discussion see 6A Corbin §§ 1458 to 1466.

71. Continental Corp. v. Gowdy, 283 Mass. 204, 186 N.E. 244, 87 A.L.R. 1039 (1933). The Restatement formulation of this rule is as follows: "A bargain to indemnify another against the consequences of committing a tortious act is illegal unless the performance of the tortious act is only an undesired possibility in the performance

rule applies to a promise to indemnify against the consequences of a fraud [72] or other intentional tort.[73] It is generally agreed that a promise to indemnify a person against the consequences of his own negligence is not illegal.[74]

§ 367. Agreement to Exempt a Person from Willful or Negligent Misconduct

The question in this section is whether A and B may enter into an agreement by the terms of which A agrees not to hold B liable for B's future tortious conduct. In the preceding section the question was whether if A was liable to B, C could validly agree to indemnify A. The rule here is that an agreement by A not to hold B liable for B's willful misconduct is illegal.[75]

Despite a good number of exceptions, it is a general rule that it is not unlawful for one contracting party to agree not to hold the other liable for his negligence.[76] Historically the major exception to this general rule of contractual freedom has been in the area of contracts entered into by public servants in the performance of their public duties for compensation. Common carriers are the most common example of such public servants.[77] However, a common carrier or other person charged with a public duty [78] may limit "to a reasonable agreed valuation the amount of damages recoverable for injury to property by a non-willful breach of duty" [79] provided that Federal and State

of the bargain, and the bargain does not tend to induce the act." Restatement, Contracts § 572. Thus, for example, a publisher may in good faith lawfully procure indemnity insurance against liability for libel, but may not lawfully enter into a contract of indemnity to protect himself from such liability where he knows that material to be published is libelous.

72. Small v. Sullivan, 245 N.Y. 343, 157 N.E. 261 (1927), reorg. denied 245 N.Y. 621, 157 N.E. 883.

73. Restatement, Contracts § 572.

74. Messersmith v. American Fidelity Co., 232 N.Y. 161, 133 N.E. 432, 19 A. L.R. 876 (1921).

75. Restatement, Contracts § 575; see Thomas v. Atlantic Coast Line R. R., 201 F.2d 167 (5th Cir. 1953) (willful and wanton negligence).

76. Ciofalo v. Vic Tanny Gyms, Inc., 10 N.Y.2d 294, 220 N.Y.S.2d 962, 177 N.E. 2d 925 (1961); 6A Corbin § 1472; 6 Williston § 1751 (rev. ed. 1938); Von Hippel, The Control of Exemption Clauses, A Comparative Study, 16 Int'l & Comp.L.Q. 591 (1967); Johnston, The Control of Exemption Clauses: A Comment, 17 Int'l & Comp.L.Q. 232 (1968); Note, 42 Chi.-Kent.L.Rev. 82 (1965).

77. Boston & M. R. R. v. Piper, 246 U. S. 439, 38 S.Ct. 354, 62 L.Ed. 820 (1918).

78. "It must be remembered, that differences exist in views as to whether a particular service bargained for falls within the field of 'public service,' differences that may be based on statutory provisions. This is particularly true of warehousemen and other kinds of bailees." 6A Corbin § 1472.

79. Restatement, Contracts § 575(2).

statutes and regulations are complied with.[80]　Generally, the person charged with the performance of the public duty must offer a choice of rates pursuant to which a greater amount of liability will be assumed if a higher rate is paid.[81]

Public carriers and other public servants, however, are not the only category of contracting parties who have been barred from benefiting from a clause exculpating them from their own negligence.　In a scholarly opinion, the Supreme Court of California has summarized these cases as follows:[82]

> "The attempted but invalid exemption involves a transaction which exhibits some or all of the following characteristics.　It concerns a business of a type generally thought suitable for public regulation.　The party seeking exculpation is engaged in performing a service of great importance to the public, which is often a matter of practical necessity for some members of the public.　The party holds himself out as willing to perform this service for any member of the public who seeks it, or at least for any member coming within certain established standards.　As a result of the essential nature of the service, in the economic setting of the transaction, the party invoking exculpation possesses a decisive advantage of bargaining strength against any member of the public who seeks his services.　In exercising a superior bargaining power the party confronts the public with a standardized adhesion contract of exculpation, and makes no provision whereby a purchaser may pay additional reasonable fees and obtain protection against negligence.　Finally, as a result of the transaction, the person or property of the purchaser is placed under the control of the seller, subject to the risk of carelessness by the seller or his agents.

80.　In the event of non-compliance, the carrier will be held to pay full damages for its negligence. W. R. Grace & Co. v. Railway Exp. Agency, Inc., 8 N.Y.2d 103, 168 N.E.2d 362, 202 N.Y.S. 2d 281 (1960), cert. denied 364 U.S. 830, 81 S.Ct. 69, 5 L.Ed.2d 57 (1960), 25 Albany L.Rev. 160 (1961), 109 U. Pa.L.Rev. 606 (1961), 36 Notre Dame Law. 202 (1961).

81.　In the case cited in the previous note a shipment of platinum was declared by the shipper to be general merchandise valued at $50.　The shipper made this declaration in order to save shipping charges as the carrier had only one high rate for the shipment of precious metals.　Since the shipper was not offered a choice of rates for shipment of the goods as platinum, it was held that the carrier was liable for the actual value of $56,000.

82.　Tunkl v. Regents of the Univ. of Calif., 60 Cal.2d 92, 32 Cal.Rptr. 33, 37–39, 383 P.2d 441, 445–447 (1963) (clause exculpating charity hospital with no duty to serve the public held invalid).　See § 56 supra.

"While obviously no public policy opposes private, voluntary transactions in which one party, for a consideration, agrees to shoulder a risk which the law would otherwise have placed upon the other party, the above circumstances pose a different situation. In this situation the releasing party does not really acquiesce voluntarily in the contractual shifting of the risk, nor can we be reasonably certain that he receives an adequate consideration for the transfer. Since the service is one which each member of the public, presently or potentially, may find essential to him, he faces, despite his economic inability to do so, the prospect of a compulsory assumption of the risk of another's negligence."

Basically on considerations such as indicated in the above quotation, it is now well settled that an employer may not bargain for exemption from liability to an employee for harm caused by negligence in the course of employment.[83] Landlords, however, generally are permitted to exculpate themselves from negligence by provisions in the lease.[84] Legislatures have tended to enter this field of exculpation with sporadic piecemeal legislation covering limited circumstances.[85]

Many courts have adhered to the view of the general validity of exculpation clauses while striking them down by indirection. Thus it may be found that there was no mutual assent with respect to the exculpation.[86] The most popular covert approach, however, is to construe the clause so artificially as to make it inapplicable to the facts at hand.[87]

83. Johnston v. Fargo, 184 N.Y. 379, 77 N.E. 388 (1906). Today this is statutory. Employees are generally covered by Workmen's Compensation Acts under which negligence is immaterial. But even under the Federal Employers' Liability Act, under which a railroad employee may sue his employer for negligence, the same rule applies. Brant v. Chicago & A. R. R., 294 Ill. 606, 128 N.E. 732 (1920).

For another example of invalidity of an exculpation clause where there is no duty to serve the public, see Bisso v. Inland Waterways Corp., 349 U.S. 85, 75 S.Ct. 629, 99 L.Ed. 911 (1955).

84. O'Callaghan v. Waller & Beckwith Realty Co., 15 Ill.2d 436, 155 N.E.2d 545 (1958); but see Mayfair Fabrics v. Henley, 48 N.J. 483, 226 A.2d 602 (1967) where the court distinguishes, on grounds of relative bargaining power, between commercial and residential leases.

85. E. g., Ill.Rev.Stat. ch. 80, § 15a (1965) (leases; statute overturns case cited in previous note); McKinney's N.Y.Gen.Obl.Law § 5–321 (leases); § 5–322 (caterers); § 5–323 (building service and maintenance contractors); § 5–324 (architects, engineers, surveyors); § 5–325 (garages and parking lots).

86. General Grain, Inc. v. International Harvester Co., —— Ind.App. ——, 232 N.E.2d 616 (1968) (garage work order); Klar v. H. & M. Parcel Room, Inc., 270 App.Div. 538, 61 N.Y.S.2d 285 (1st Dep't 1946), aff'd 296 N.Y. 1044, 73 N.E.2d 912 (1947) (parcel check).

87. E. g., Willard Van Dyke Prods. v. Eastman Kodak Co., 12 N.Y.2d 301, 239 N.Y.S.2d 337, 189 N.E.2d 693 (1963). See § 56 supra.

D. BARGAINS TENDING TO OBSTRUCT THE ADMINISTRATION OF JUSTICE

§ 368. Maintenance and Champerty

Maintenance occurs when one person who has no legitimate interest in the matter pays the costs and expenses of another in bringing an action.[88] Champerty is the same as maintenance with the added element that the party who maintains the action is to receive a share of the proceeds of the litigation.[89] The early common law took a severe view with respect to such conduct and treated maintenance and champerty as crimes.[90]

However the more modern view is that such bargains are not illegal "if entered into from charitable motives and without an intention to make a profit, or in order to determine a question on which a right or duty of the maintaining party depends."[91] There is, however no uniform law of maintenance and champerty in the United States.[92]

A contingent fee arrangement with an attorney is usually permissible so long as the attorney does not undertake to pay the expenses of the suit.[93] However, it is illegal for a contingent fee arrangement to provide that the owner shall not settle without the consent of the attorney.[94] It is also illegal for an attorney to undertake a criminal case or a divorce or annulment action on a contingent fee basis.[95]

The fact that an agreement between the client and attorney is champertous is not a defense in favor of the party against whom the client has a cause of action.[96] It is sometimes held that an attorney

---

88. Restatement, Contracts § 540(1).

89. Kenrich Corp. v. Miller, 377 F.2d 312 (3d Cir. 1967); Fordson Coal Co. v. Garrard, 277 Ky. 218, 125 S.W.2d 977, 121 A.L.R. 841 (1939).

90. Winfield, The History of Maintenance and Champerty, 35 Law Q.Rev. 50 (1919).

91. Restatement, Contracts § 541. It is enough that the maintaining party reasonably believes that he has an interest in the claim. Restatement, Contracts § 543.

92. 6A Corbin § 1424.

93. In Re Gilman's Adm'x, 251 N.Y. 265, 167 N.E. 437 (1929). However, it is generally illegal to hire an investigator on a contingent fee basis. Porter v. Jones, 176 F.2d 87 (10th Cir. 1949), cert. denied 338 U.S. 885, 70 S. Ct. 188, 94 L.Ed. 543 (1949); Whelchel v. Stennett. 192 Miss. 241, 5 So.2d 418 (1942).

94. Butler v. Young, 121 W.Va. 176, 2 S.E.2d 250, 121 A.L.R. 1119 (1939); but cf. Rice v. Farrell, 129 Conn. 362, 28 A.2d 7 (1942).

95. McCarthy v. Santangelo, 137 Conn. 410, 78 A.2d 240 (1951); Restatement, Contracts § 542(2).

96. Powell v. Bowen, 279 Mo. 280, 214 S.W. 142 (1919).

employed under a champertous arrangement is not only deprived of a recovery upon the contract but also in quasi-contract for the fair and reasonable value of his services,[97] but there are many decisions to the contrary.[98]

§ 369. Agreements Tending to Interfere with the Proper Functioning of the Judicial Machinery

A bargain the purpose of which is to prevent the prosecution of a crime or an alleged crime is illegal whether or not prosecution has been started at the time the agreement is made.[99] This rule applies whether the crime in question is a misdemeanor or a felony.[1] It is also generally agreed that a party who settles a civil claim arising out of an act which is also criminal is not preventing the prosecution of a crime so long as the consideration given to him is not in part for forbearance to prosecute the crime or a promise of such forbearance.[2]

The law is strenuously opposed to stirring up litigation and so it is held that an agreement whereby a lawyer agrees to pay a layman for procuring clients is illegal.[3]

Any agreement which tends to induce parties to give false testimony is illegal.[4] Thus a bargain to pay a witness who is in the jurisdiction and subject to subpoena an amount more than the fees to which he is entitled by law is illegal.[5] This rule does not apply to expert witnesses or to a witness out of the jurisdiction provided that compensation is not made contingent on success or on his testifying in a prescribed manner.[6] A bargain for the suppression of evidence is also obviously illegal,[7] as is, except in limited circumstances, a bargain to pay for evidence.[8]

97. Hinckley v. Giberson, 129 Me. 308, 151 A. 542 (1930).

98. Kamerman v. United States, 278 F. 2d 411 (2d Cir. 1960); Ownby v. Prisock, 243 Miss. 203, 138 So.2d 279, 100 A.L.R.2d 1375 (1962). For an analysis of the division of authority on another question, see Comment, Loans to Clients for Living Expenses, 55 Calif. L.Rev. 1419 (1967).

99. Winter v. Lewis, 132 Ark. 399, 200 S.W. 981 (1918).

1. 6A Corbin § 1421.

2. Id.

3. Waychoff v. Waychoff, 309 Pa. 300, 163 A. 670, 86 A.L.R. 190 (1932).

4. Lawrence v. Hicks, 132 S.C. 370, 128 S.E. 720 (1925).

5. Dodge v. Stiles, 26 Conn. 463 (1857).

6. 6A Corbin § 1430.

7. Restatement, Contracts § 554.

8. Restatement, Contracts § 553 provides that a bargain to pay for evidence is not illegal if the evidence is in writing and the party in possession has no duty to disclose it. Also it is legal to pay one's adversary to make a written admission. It is also legal to promise a reward for the revelation of information.

Until recently, arbitration agreements were not generally looked upon with much favor particularly where the arbitrators were to determine matters other than disputed issues of fact.[9] Today most states have statutes making arbitration agreements specifically enforceable.[10]

E.   BARGAINS HARMFUL TO MARRIAGE

§ 370.   Contracts Tending to Prevent or Disrupt the Marriage Relationship

Our law has always looked upon the institution of marriage as of importance to the state. Therefore agreements "in derogation of marriage" are held to be illegal.[11] The older view was that any restraint upon marriage, however limited, was contrary to public policy.[12]

The more modern view is that it is only a general restraint of marriage which is condemned and that other restraints should be judged in the light of the reasonableness of the restraint under the circumstances of the case.[13] However, there is authority to the effect that even a general restraint will be sustained in the case of a person who has previously been married.[14]

Again, even a general restraint has been sustained if it is reasonable and is incidental to another lawful purpose of the bargain.[15] The most common type of case is where a plaintiff promises to care for the defendant for life and to remain single.[16] A result favorable to plaintiff in these cases may be explained not only on the basis

---

9.   6A Corbin § 1437.

10.   6A Corbin § 1441.

11.   Chapin v. Cooke, 73 Conn. 72, 46 A. 282 (1900).

12.   Marriage, Contracts, and Public Policy, 54 Harv.L.Rev. 473 (1941).

13.   "We are inclined to think, in the light of all the authorities, and having in mind the basis of the rule, to wit, the interest the public has in the matter, that the term 'general restraint' as used in the rule should be construed to mean restraint which binds a competent person not to marry anyone at any time, and that the validity of a contract, where the restraint it imposes is only against marrying a particular person, or a person of a particular class, or within a specified limited time, should be determined with reference to the reasonableness of such restraint under the circumstances of the particular case." Barnes v. Hobson, 250 S.W. 238, 242, 243 (Tex.Civ.App.1923), error ref'd; see also Gleason v. Mann, 312 Mass. 420, 45 N.E.2d 280 (1942).

14.   Nunn v. Justice, 278 Ky. 1, 129 S. W.2d 564 (1939).

15.   Matheson v. Gullickson, 222 Minn. 369, 24 N.W.2d 704 (1946), 31 Minn.L. Rev. 496 (1947); contra, Lowe v. Doremus, 84 N.J.L. 658, 87 A. 459 (Ct. Err. & App.1913).

16.   See cases in preceding note.

of the rule stated above but also upon the ground that the promise to remain single is not illegal consideration but only void consideration and that therefore the services rendered are sufficient consideration to support the promise of the defendant.[17]

A bargain prior to marriage by which one party or both parties agree to separate under given conditions is illegal;[18] so too is a bargain of this kind made subsequent to marriage unless it is made after the parties have separated in fact or are contemplating immediate separation.[19] Agreements to procure or consent to a divorce are void and, traditionally, a separation agreement conditioned upon procurement of, or consent to, a divorce have also been held illegal.[20] A recent tendency has developed, however, to uphold separation agreements conditioned upon procuring a divorce where the marriage is no longer viable and no fraud on the court is contemplated.[21] A bargain to change the essential incidents of marriage is also illegal,[22] as for example, an agreement that relieves a husband of his duty to support[23] or one that relieves a wife of a duty to have sexual relations.[24] A marriage brokerage contract which is a contract to pay a fee to a third party for bringing the marriage partners together is also illegal apparently upon the theory such a contract will tend to bring about unhappy marriages.[25]

17. King v. King, 63 Ohio St. 363, 59 N.E. 111 (1900).

18. In re Duncan's Estate, 87 Colo. 149, 285 P. 757, 70 A.L.R. 824 (1930).

19. Smith v. Smith, 190 Ark. 418, 79 S. W.2d 265 (1935); Restatement, Contracts § 584; see Clark, Separation Agreements, 28 Rocky Mt.L.Rev. 149 (1956).

20. Viles v. Viles, 14 N.Y.2d 365, 251 N.Y.S.2d 672, 200 N.E.2d 567 (1964), 33 Fordham L.Rev. 519 (1965).

21. Hill v. Hill, 23 Cal.2d 82, 142 P.2d 417 (1943); Schulz v. Fox, 136 Mont. 152, 345 P.2d 1045 (1959). A 1966 amendment to § 5–311 of the New York General Obligations Law contains this language: "An agreement, heretofore or hereafter made between a husband and wife, shall not be considered a contract to alter or dissolve the marriage unless it contains an express provision requiring the dissolution of the marriage or provides for the procurement of grounds for divorce." The many ambiguities lurking in this amendment are analyzed in 33 Brooklyn L.Rev. 308 (1967).

22. Restatement, Contracts § 587.

23. French v. McAnarney, 290 Mass. 544, 195 N.E. 714, 98 A.L.R. 530 (1935).

24. Mirizio v. Mirizio, 242 N.Y. 74, 150 N.E. 605, 44 A.L.R. 714 (1926).

25. Duval v. Wellman, 124 N.Y. 156, 26 N.E. 343 (1891).

F. OTHER ILLEGAL BARGAINS

§ 371. Sunday Contracts: What Activities Included

There is no common law rule relating to the illegality of Sunday contracts. The entire matter is statutory. Some statutes only provide against work being done on Sundays but the majority of statutes also provide against a contract being made on Sunday. The most common type of statute prohibits the doing of secular business on Sunday excluding works of necessity and charity. Such a statute usually proscribes contracts made or to be performed on Sunday. Other statutes prohibit the transaction of business within one's ordinary calling. There are many cases, sometimes contradictory of what constitutes "ordinary calling" or "work of necessity or charity." [26]

Under a statute which condemns the making of a contract on Sunday preliminary negotiations which occur on Sunday do not violate the statute.[27] This is well illustrated by a case in which a department store advertised goods in the Sunday paper and received calls (offers) from its customers but filled the order (completed the unilateral contract) on Monday.[28]

§ 372. Effect of Violation of a Sunday Law Statute

It may be stated as a general rule that the violation of a Sunday statute makes the contract illegal and the court will leave the parties where it finds them.[29] However, there are exceptions. First, the statute does not operate against a party who acts innocently, that is, without knowledge of the facts, for example, where a party does not know that the other party executed the contract on Sunday.[30]

It seems to be generally agreed that if a contract is made on Sunday, contrary to statute, but is performed on a secular day that the contract is enforceable,[31] or, if not, that at least a quasi-contractual

---

26. 6A Corbin § 1477. A contract made on a legal holiday is not necessarily subject to the same rules as contracts made on a Sunday. The statute establishing the holiday must be examined to determine the activities prohibited on that day. Meyer v. World Concrete, Inc., 431 P.2d 403 (Okl.1967) (auction on New Year's day lawful).

27. Maher v. Haycock, 301 Mass. 594, 18 N.E.2d 348 (1938).

28. People v. Gimbel Bros., Inc., 202 Misc. 229, 115 N.Y.S.2d 857 (Ct.Spec. Sess.1952).

29. Restatement, Contracts § 538. The entire matter of the effect of illegality is discussed in more detail in §§ 376–388 infra.

30. Simmons v. Simmons, 215 Iowa 654, 246 N.W. 597 (1933).

31. 6A Corbin § 1478; Restatement, Contracts § 539, ill. 2; contra, Win-

recovery is available, the theory being that there is some sort of ratification or adoption.

A more difficult question is presented when a bargain which is made on a secular day is to be performed on Sunday. Here the very performance is illegal and so there is no room to argue ratification or adoption.[32] Thus there are many decisions that a party who has performed on Sunday is not entitled to a contractual recovery.[33] If part of the work is done on Sunday and part is done on a secular day the possibility of divisibility arises but the courts in this type of case generally apply the doctrine of divisibility only where the contract provides a separate amount to be paid for the two performances.[34]

We may expect that in the present climate in which we live that Sunday Laws will either be repealed or that their effects on contracts will be drastically limited.[35]

§ 373. Wagering Contracts and Lotteries

As we have seen an aleatory contract is one in which at least one of the promises is made performable upon the happening of a fortuitous event.[36] A wagering contract is an aleatory contract with one important additional element: neither of the parties has an interest in the contingency prior to the formation of the contract.[37] Thus, if A bets upon a number in a roulette game neither he nor the owner of the roulette wheel has any interest in which number wins except for the wager which they have made. But if A owns a house and obtains a fire insurance policy upon it this is not a wagering contract because the house owner has an interest in the fortuitous event (the burning down of the house) prior to making the contract. In

field v. Dodge, 45 Mich. 355, 7 N.W. 906 (1881).

32. Vinz v. Beatty, 61 Wis. 645, 21 N. W. 787 (1884).

33. Carson v. Calhoun, 101 Me. 456, 64 A. 838 (1906).

34. 6A Corbin § 1480. For a more detailed discussion of the question of divisibility as it relates to illegality see § 384 infra.

35. See Comment, Sunday Statutes in a Modern Community, 61 Yale L.J. 427 (1952).

36. See § 162 supra; Restatement, Contracts § 291.

37. 6A Corbin § 1481. There is a conflict of authority as to the enforceability of a gambling obligation which is legally incurred in one jurisdiction and which is sought to be enforced in a jurisdiction where it could not lawfully have been incurred. See Ciampittiello v. Campitello, 134 Conn. 51, 54 A.2d 669, 173 A.L.R. 691 (1947) (lawful gambling obligation incurred in Rhode Island held unforceable in Connecticut); contra, Intercontinental Hotels Corp. (P.R.) v. Golden, 15 N.Y. 2d 9, 254 N.Y.S.2d 527, 203 N.E.2d 210 (1964), 33 Fordham L.Rev. 493 (1965) (Puerto Rican gambling obligation enforceable in New York).

the terminology of insurance law the house owner is said to have an "insurable interest." But if A took out a policy on the house of another in which he had no interest, then the contract would be a wagering contract and in insurance parlance A would have no insurable interest in this house.[38] Wagering contracts, as here defined, are generally held to be illegal.[39]

The common law rule was that a bargain for the actual purchase and sale of a commodity whether or not the commodity is traded upon an exchange is not a wager even though the buyer purchases on credit (margin) or the seller sells when he does not have the item which he is to deliver (sells short) so long as the parties actually intend to exchange the goods for the money. But, according to the common law, if the parties agreed that upon the day fixed for delivery and payment one of them will pay the other the difference between the contract price and the market price, then there is a wagering contract because neither party has any interest in the goods irrespective of his contract with the other.[40] Naturally, the language of the agreement was not controlling in determining whether the parties have made an illegal bargain "for the payment of the difference" and extrinsic evidence was admissible to show that the contract was not what it purported to be.[41] The law has been placed upon a different footing by Federal legislation and by an appreciation of the stabilizing force upon the market of trading in commodity futures.[42] In the fiscal year 1956–1957, on federally regulated exchanges alone almost nine million futures transactions took place involving over thirty-five billion dollars [43] and many commodities which are the subject of futures trading are not federally regulated.[44] About 99% of these transactions are settled in cash.[45] The volume of transactions

38. 6A Corbin § 1482.

39. Bernhard v. Taylor, 23 Or. 416, 31 P. 968 (1893).

40. Riordon v. McCabe, 341 Ill. 506, 173 N.E. 660, 83 A.L.R. 512 (1930). A hedging contract by a manufacturer, in the absence of a specific statutory prohibition, is not ordinarily deemed to be a wagering contract. Browne v. Thorn, 260 U.S. 137, 43 S.Ct. 36, 67 L. Ed. 171 (1922). Many state statutes have been directed against "dealings in futures," prohibiting such hedging and other speculative transactions although they would not be considered "wagers" within the ordinary meaning of that word. These statutes are reviewed in 45 Harv.L.Rev. 912 (1932).

See also Patterson, Hedging and Wagering on Produce Exchanges, 40 Yale L.J. 843 (1931).

41. 6A Corbin § 1493.

42. See Campbell, Trading in Futures Under the Commodity Exchange Act, 26 Geo.Wash.L.Rev. 215 (1957); Note, 64 Yale L.J. 906 (1955); Note, Federal Regulation of Commodity Futures Trading, 60 Yale L.J. 822 (1951).

43. Campbell, supra n. 42, at 220.

44. See, e. g., Sinva, Inc. v. Merrill Lynch, Pierce, Fenner & Smith, Inc., 253 F.Supp. 359 (S.D.N.Y.1966).

45. Campbell, supra n. 42, at 217.

has doubtless increased in the subsequent decade. It is unclear to what extent state statutes and common law rules prohibiting such transactions as wagering have been superseded by federal law; that they have to a significant degree been superseded is, however, clear.[46]

Lotteries are also generally held to be illegal.[47] A lottery has been defined as a "gambling scheme in which (a) the players pay or agree to pay something of value for chances . . . and (b) the winning chances are to be determined by a drawing or by some other method based upon the element of chance; and (c) the holders of the winning chances are to receive something of value." [48] However, no lottery exists where a party pays an entrance fee in order to compete for a prize with others on the basis of particular skills such as in a golf or bridge tournament, even though part or all of the entrance fees are added to the prize of the winner so long as the prize money is not solely made up of fees paid by the competitors.[49] If the offeror of the prize may compete then the transaction is likely to be a wager,[50] although specific statutes must be consulted in every case.

§ 374. Usurious Bargains

There is no common law of usury. However every state has adopted a usury statute and as may be expected there are variations among the states.[51] Usury has been defined as follows: "A bargain under which a greater profit than is permitted by law is paid, or is agreed to be paid to a creditor by or on behalf of the debtor for a loan of money, or for extending the maturity of a pecuniary debt, is usurious and illegal." [52]

---

46. Id. at 250–53.

47. Some states have statutes permitting lotteries under certain circumstances; for example, New Hampshire has authorized a lottery.

48. N.Y.Penal Law § 225.00(10).

49. Harris v. White, 81 N.Y. 532 (1880); Porter v. Day, 71 Wis. 296, 37 N.W. 259 (1888).

50. Cooney v. Hauck, 112 Kan. 562, 211 P. 617, 29 A.L.R. 427 (1923).

51. For example, the effect of usury is different in various states. In some states the entire interest is forfeited, in others only the interest in excess of the maximum rate is forfeited. In some states such as New York in some circumstances both principal and interest are forfeited. For a brief survey of state sanctions, see Comment, Usury in the Conflict of Laws, 55 Calif.L.Rev. 123, 232–43 (1967).

52. Restatement, Contracts § 526. It should be observed that in most states a much higher rate of interest is allowed on so-called small loans and that corporate borrowers are usually exempted from the operation of the usury laws. 6A Corbin § 1499. Naturally, such an exemption has opened the door to the imposition by the lender of a requirement that the borrower form a dummy corporation for the purpose of receiving the loan at a higher rate of interest than would be permissible on a loan to the borrower himself. Generally, the courts will

(a) Was there a Loan of Money?

The first requisite for the existence of usury is that there must be a loan of money or an agreement to extend the maturity of a pecuniary debt. Thus if all that is involved is the sale of real property, a chattel, a chose in action, or a note no question of usury can arise.[53] The weight of case authority holds that it is not usurious to have a time-price differential in excess of the permissible rate of interest. For example, if an auto dealer offers a car for sale at $2,000 cash or $4,000 payable in instalments for one year, the sale of the auto on the latter terms is not usurious because no loan has been made.[54] As far as the purchaser is concerned, however, the economic effect is the same as if he had borrowed $2,000 at 100% interest. Most states have in recent years adopted retail instalment sales acts, many of which regulate the maximum time-price differential which may be charged.[55] The effect of over-charging varies with the particular statute.

Usury is not involved in the assignment of a chose in action or note even though the assignee buys it at a discount greater than the legal rate of interest because no loan is involved in the transaction.[56]

Although a bona fide sale cannot be usurious there are many cases involving the question of whether a particular transaction was really a sale or a cover for a usurious loan.[57] Thus, for example, there are many cases where A, the owner of property, desires a loan of, say, $10,000. B is willing to make the loan but instead of taking a mortgage to secure the loan insists upon a deed to the property and to further camouflage the transaction gives to A right to repurchase in one year at a price of $12,500. Here the form of the trans-

uphold such loans as lawful. Hoffman v. Lee Nashem Motors, Inc., 20 N.Y.2d 513, 285 N.Y.S.2d 68, 231 N.E. 2d 765 (1967).

53. Murphy v. Leiber, 76 Ariz. 79, 259 P.2d 249 (1953); Spence v. Erwin, 197 Ga. 635, 30 S.E.2d 50, 154 A.L.R. 1057 (1944). The same is true if the loan is not of money but, for example, of a chattel.

54. Harper v. Futrell, 204 Ark. 822, 164 S.W.2d 995, 143 A.L.R. 235 (1942); Petersen v. Philco Finance Corp., 91 Idaho 644, 428 P.2d 961 (1967) (holding, however, that an *extension* of such an agreement for a price is within the usury laws); Lundstrom v. Radio

Corp. of America, 17 Utah 2d 114, 405 P.2d 339, 14 A.L.R.3d 1058 (1965); 6A Corbin § 1500.

55. See generally, Hogan, A Survey of State Retail Instalment Sales Legislation, 44 Cornell L.Q. 38 (1958).

56. Commercial Credit Co. v. Tarwater, 215 Ala. 123, 110 So. 39, 48 A.L.R. 1437 (1926).

57. That usurious loans may be disguised in many forms, see 6A Corbin § 1501; and see American Acceptance Corp. v. Schoenthaler, 391 F.2d 64 (5th Cir. 1968), cert. denied 392 U.S. 928, 88 S.Ct. 2287, 20 L.Ed.2d 1387 (1968).

action is a sale by A with a right to repurchase. But the actual substance of the transaction may well be a loan of $10,000 with the result that if A wants to pay off the loan pursuant to the terms of the contract he is obliged to pay $12,500 in one year—a clearly usurious transaction.[58]

Another common situation which is not always what it appears to be on its face is as follows: A is the owner of land and B wishes to purchase it. They agree upon a sale price of $10,000 but B has only $3,000 in cash and so A sells to B for $14,000 taking back a $11,000 purchase money mortgage to be paid off over a period of say five years. The mortgage is immediately assigned by A to C who pays $7,000 for the assignment. If the transaction was what it appeared to be there would be no usury under the rules previously stated. However, if B offers evidence showing that actually C was making a loan to him and that it was usurious, there is a question of fact as whether the mortgage transaction was a bargain as to price with A who sold to C or whether it was a loan made by C.[59] Obviously, in these cases parol and extrinsic evidence must be admitted to show the true nature of the transaction.[60]

(b) Does the Loan Exceed the Legal Rate of Interest?

Assuming that a loan has actually been made the next question is does it exceed the legal rate of interest. If A makes a loan and agrees to pay the maximum rate and the loan is discounted by subtracting all or part of interest due in advance is the transaction usurious? As a general rule the answer appears to be that the loan is not made usurious in the case of short term loans but is deemed usurious in the case of long term loans.[61]

A similar problem arises where the borrower agrees to pay the maximum rate of interest plus the expenses of making the loan such as a title search. So long as the expenses are reasonable and neces-

---

58. In re 716 Third Ave. Holding Corp., 340 F.2d 42 (2d Cir. 1964), cert. denied A. G. V. Associates, Inc. v. Cross, 381 U.S. 913, 85 S.Ct. 1535, 14 L.Ed.2d 434 (1965); Carter v. Zachary, 243 Ark. 104, 418 S.W.2d 787 (1967); Kline v. Robinson, 83 Nev. 244, 428 P.2d 190 (1967); Horn v. Keteltas, 46 N.Y. 605 (1871); see Fogelman, The Deed Absolute as a Mortgage in New York, 32 Fordham L.Rev. 299 (1963).

59. Evers v. Guaranty Inv. Co., 244 Ark. 925, 428 S.W.2d 68 (1968); Del

Rubio v. Duchesne, 284 App.Div. 89, 130 N.Y.S.2d 572 (1st Dep't 1954).

60. Kent v. Agard, 24 Wis. 378 (1869); Despard v. Walbridge, 15 N.Y. 374 (1857).

61. 6A Corbin § 1504. However the Small Loan Act, adopted in New York and some other states, prohibits the deduction of interest in advance. Madison Personal Loan, Inc. v. Parker, 124 F.2d 143 (2d Cir. 1941).

sary there is no usury [62] but if the charges are designed not merely for reimbursement of the lender's costs but to serve as a cover for usurious intent then there is usury.[63]

Other problems which commonly arise are with respect to acceleration and pre-payment clauses. Under an acceleration clause the entire principal and interest is made to become due upon a default in the payment of an instalment. Such a provision creates no problem with respect to usury.[64] Even if the acceleration clause calls for interest to the date of maturity it is deemed that there is no usury because the excessive interest is regarded as a penalty and as such is not enforceable.[65] A pre-payment clause gives the lender the right to pay prior to the maturity date of the loan. It is not usurious to provide that he must pay interest to the date of maturiy for the privilege of pre-payment.[66] If the borrower promises in addition to, or instead of, the payment of interest, to repay the principal amount plus a share of profits, the transaction is generally usurious if the legal rate of interest is exceeded.[67] Such a transaction must be care-

62. Harris v. Guaranty Financial Corp., 244 Ark. 218, 424 S.W.2d 355 (1968) (title insurance and credit report charges); Equitable Life Assur. Soc. of the U. S. v. Scali, 38 Ill.2d 544, 232 N.E.2d 712 (1968) (requirement that borrower purchase life insurance from lender); Oliver v. United Mortgage Co., 230 A.2d 722 (D.C.Ct.App.1967) (fee paid to loan broker).

63. First Nat. Bank of Ada v. Phares, 70 Okl. 255, 174 P. 519, 21 A.L.R. 793 (1918); Savings Loan & T. Co. v. Yokley, 174 N.C. 573, 94 S.E. 102 (1917). An unlawful intent is a necessary element of usury. Whether the intent of one party or both parties is necessary appears to be in conflict. See Restatement, Contracts § 537. A borrower's knowledge of the usurious nature of the transaction, particularly when coupled with other equities in favor of the creditor may result in an estoppel against him to take advantage of the usury law. White v. Seitzman, 230 Cal.App.2d 756, 41 Cal.Rptr. 359, 16 A.L.R.3d 500 (1965).

64. Braniff Inv. Co. v. Robertson, 124 Tex. 524, 81 S.W.2d 45, 100 A.L.R. 1421 (1935).

65. Cissna Loan Co. v. Gowley, 87 Wash. 438, 151 P. 792 (1915); contra,

Shropshire v. Commerce Farm Credit Co., 120 Tex. 400, 30 S.W.2d 282, 84 A.L.R. 1269 (1930), cert. denied 284 U. S. 675, 52 S.Ct. 130, 76 L.Ed. 571 (1931). If a loan agreement provides for a legal rate of interest but calls for interest in excess of the legal rate if the loan is not paid at maturity, it is not generally deemed to be usurious because the borrower may avoid the excessive interest by payment at maturity. However, the additional interest agreed to be paid may constitute an unenforceable penalty. Oil Investment Co. v. Dallea Petroleum Corp., 152 N.W.2d 415 (N.D.1967). Of course if the parties contemplate that the loan shall not be paid at maturity, it will be deemed to be usurious. Restatement, Contracts § 536.

66. Southland Life Ins. Co. v. Egan, 126 Tex. 160, 86 S.W.2d 722 (1935); Marley v. Consolidated Mortgage Co., — R.I. —, 229 A.2d 608 (1967); Lyons v. National Sav. Bank, 280 App.Div. 339, 113 N.Y.S.2d 695 (3rd Dep't 1952).

67. American Insurers Life Ins. Co. v. Regenold, 243 Ark. 906, 423 S.W.2d 551 (1968); Maze v. Sycamore Homes, Inc., 230 Cal.App.2d 746, 41 Cal.Rptr. 338, 16 A.L.R.3d 464 (1964); Moore v.

fully analyzed, however, to ascertain whether or not the parties contemplated a joint venture or a capital investment rather than a loan.[68]

It should also be observed that where the debtor is obliged to pay only upon the happening of a contingency which is not certain to occur there is no usury: any charge in excess of the legal rate is regarded as an exchange for the possible non-occurrence of the condition.[69]

II. THE EFFECT OF ILLEGALITY

Analysis

Sec.
375. Introduction.

A. ILLEGAL EXECUTORY CONTRACTS

376. General Rule.
377. Cases Where a Party May Successfully Sue Upon an Illegal Executory Bilateral Contract.
   (a) Ignorance of Facts and Law.
   (b) Bargain Illegal by Virtue of Wrongful Purpose.
   (c) Where a Particular Statute is Directed Against One of the Parties.

B. ILLEGAL CONTRACT WHICH IS PERFORMED IN WHOLE OR PART

378. Introduction.
379. Will the Courts Always Deny a Remedy in the Case of an Illegal Bargain Which Violates a Criminal Statute?
380. Effect of Licensing Statutes.
381. Remoteness of the Illegality.
382. A Mere Depositary May Not Assert the Defense of Illegality.
383. Quasi Contractual Recoveries Based Upon Performance.
384. Divisibility of Illegal Bargains.
385. The Doctrine of Pari Delicto.
386. Locus Poenitentiae.
387. Change of Law or Facts after the Bargain is Made.

Plaza Commercial Corp., 9 A.D.2d 223, 192 N.Y.S.2d 770 (1st Dep't 1959), aff'd 8 N.Y.2d 813, 202 N.Y.S.2d 321, 168 N.E.2d 390 (1960).

68. Orvis v. Curtiss, 157 N.Y. 657, 52 N.E. 690 (1899), rearg. denied 159 N.Y. 527, 53 N.E. 1129.

69. Embola v. Tuppela, 127 Wash. 285, 220 P. 789 (1923) (promise to pay $10,000 in exchange for $50 if the promisor recovered his gold mine); Restatement, Contracts § 527. If the lender is not really taking a risk and the bargain is cast in this form to evade the usury laws, then usury will exist. 6A Corbin § 1503.

§ 375. Introduction

The question of the effect of illegality may be divided into two parts. First, the effect of illegality upon an executory bilateral contract and, second, its effect where there has been some performance under the contract.

A. ILLEGAL EXECUTORY CONTRACTS

§ 376. General Rule

It can safely be stated that a bargain, which is illegal, is as a general rule void.[70] It must be recalled that to form a valid bilateral contract there must be consideration on both sides.[71] If A makes a promise to do something lawful and B makes a promise to do something unlawful there can be no action for breach of contract on either side. B may not sue because his illegal promise does not constitute consideration for A's promise and A may not sue, even though he promises to do something lawful, because of the doctrine of "mutuality of obligation." [72]

§ 377. Cases Where a Party May Successfully Sue Upon an Illegal Executory Bilateral Contract

Despite the general rule stated in the preceding section, there are cases where a party may successfully sue upon an illegal executory bilateral contract.

(a) Ignorance of Facts and Law

If a party enters into an illegal bargain and is justifiably ignorant of the facts creating the illegality and the other is not, the innocent party may recover on the contract if he can show that he would have been ready, willing and able to perform but for the illegality.[73] A simple illustration is the case of a man who is already married who promises to marry another woman. She, assuming her ignorance of his marital status, in a state that still recognizes such an action, could bring an action for breach of contract to marry.[74] We have already seen another illustration in the case where a party was unaware that the other party entered into the contract on Sunday.[75] It has been held that a trucking company could sue an unli-

---

70. Restatement, Contracts §§ 598, 607.

71. See § 67 supra.

72. Restatement, Contracts § 607, Comment a; cf. 6A Corbin § 1523.

73. Symcox v. Zuk, 221 Cal.App.2d 383, 34 Cal.Rptr. 462 (1963).

74. Restatement, Contracts § 549, ill. 1.

75. See § 372 n. 30 supra.

censed sub-contractor for breach of contract of carriage where the plaintiff had no knowledge that the defendant was unlicensed.[76]   A seller of land was permitted to recover damages for breach of a contract which was illegal because the purchaser was an enemy alien when the seller was ignorant of the purchaser's nationality.[77]

Cases such as this do not violate the general rule that ignorance of the law is no excuse.[78]   There is even an exception to the general rule that ignorance of the law is no excuse which arises where the illegality is minor and the party who is ignorant of the illegality justifiably relies upon an assumed special knowledge of the other of the requirements of law. This usually occurs where the other is in the business to which the contract relates.[79]

(b) Bargain Illegal by Virtue of Wrongful Purpose

Since a bargain may be illegal by reason of the wrongful purpose of one or both of the parties, in a case where only one party has an illegal purpose and the other does not, the innocent party may recover for breach of contract.[80]   Even if the innocent party knows of the purpose of the other party he may still recover on the contract unless the intended purpose involves serious moral turpitude [81] or unless he does something in connection with the contract that facilitates the illegal purpose of the other party.[82]

76.   Archbolds (Freightage) Ltd. v. Spanglett Ltd., [1961] 2 W.L.R. 170 (C.A.).

77.   Branigan v. Saba, [1924] N.Z.L.R. 481 (1923); see also Eastern Expanded Metal Co. v. Webb Granite & Const. Co., 195 Mass. 356, 81 N.E. 251 (1907); Hoekzema v. Van Haften, 313 Mich. 417, 21 N.W.2d 183 (1946); Barna v. Clifford Country Estates, Inc., 143 Misc. 813, 258 N.Y.S. 671 (N.Y.City Ct.1932).

78.   6A Corbin § 1539.

79.   Restatement, Contracts § 599; Municipal Metallic Bed Mfg. Corp. v. Dobbs, 253 N.Y. 313, 171 N.E. 75, 68 A.L.R. 1376 (1930) (action on landlord's warranty that lease did not violate zoning requirements).

80.   Restatement, Contracts § 602.

81.   Howell v. Stewart, 54 Mo. 400 (1873).

82.   Watkins v. Curry, 103 Ark. 414, 147 S.W. 43 (1912). Thus if A agrees to sell or sells goods knowing that B intends to smuggle the goods into the country A may recover, there being no serious moral turpitude, Holman v. Johnson, 98 Eng.Rep. 1120 (K.B.1775), but if he packs the goods in a manner convenient for that purpose with knowledge of the purpose he could not recover. Biggs v. Lawrence, 100 Eng. Rep. 673 (K.B.1789). In Graves v. Johnson, 179 Mass. 53, 60 N.E. 383 (1901), the court enforced a contract for the sale of liquor in Massachusetts although the seller knew that the purchaser intended to resell it unlawfully in Maine. On the other hand, in Hull v. Ruggles, 56 N.Y. 424 (1874), the court refused to enforce a contract for the sale of silverware and candy where the seller packaged lottery tickets in each box of candy to aid in the use of these products in a lottery. For variations on this problem, see Williams Mfg. Co. v. Prock, 184 F.2d 307 (5th Cir. 1950) (amuse-

(c) Where a Particular Statute is Directed Against One of the Parties

There are statutes under which only one party is a wrongdoer since the statute was passed to protect the other party.[83] Blue Sky laws are a typical illustration of such statutes.[84] In such a case the innocent party may enforce the contract.[85]

B. ILLEGAL CONTRACT WHICH IS PERFORMED IN WHOLE OR PART

§ 378. Introduction

Where performance has been entered upon under an illegal bargain the general rule is that the court will leave the parties to the illegal bargain where it finds them.[86] As the New York Court of Appeals has said "It is the settled law of this State (and probably of every other State) that a party to an illegal contract cannot ask a court of law to help him carry out his illegal object, nor can such a person plead or prove in any court a case in which he, as a basis for his claim, must show forth his illegal purpose." [87] This position is taken not out of solicitude for the defendant but the question is one "of public policy in the administration of the law." [88] However, there

---

ment machines offering free plays to winner); Hart Publications, Inc. v. Kaplan, 228 Minn. 512, 37 N.W.2d 814 (1949) (contract to print lottery tickets); Carroll v. Beardon, 142 Mont. 40, 381 P.2d 295 (1963) (contract to sell house to be used for prostitution); Fineman v. Faulkner, 174 N.C. 13, 93 S.E. 384 (1917) (contract to sell phonograph to prostitute).

83. 6A Corbin § 1540.

84. Kneeland v. Emerton, 280 Mass. 371, 183 N.E. 155, 87 A.L.R. 1 (1932).

85. State ex rel. American Surety Co. of N. Y. v. Haid, 325 Mo. 949, 30 S. W.2d 100 (1930). In Bolivar v. Monnat, 232 App.Div. 33, 248 N.Y.S. 722 (4th Dep't 1931), during prohibition the plaintiff purchased alcohol from the defendant. The alcohol was denatured and plaintiff lost his eyesight as a result of consuming it. He was permitted to recover for breach of warranty on the theory that while it was illegal to sell alcohol it was not illegal to purchase it.

86. Womack v. Maner, 227 Ark. 786, 301 S.W.2d 438, 60 A.L.R.2d 1271 (1957) (bribery of judge); Mascari v. Raines, 220 Tenn. 234, 415 S.W.2d 874 (1967) (sale of liquor on credit).

87. Stone v. Freeman, 298 N.Y. 268, 271, 82 N.E.2d 571, 572, 8 A.L.R.2d 304, 306 (1948). "No right of action can spring from an illegal contract and . . . courts do not sit to give protection to cheaters or to act 'as paymaster(s) of the wages of crime'." Seagirt Realty Corp. v. Chazanof, 13 N.Y.2d 282, 287, 246 N.Y.S.2d 613, 196 N.E.2d 254, 257 (1963) (dissent).

88. Fleigenheimer v. Brogan, 284 N.Y. 268, 272, 30 N.E.2d 591, 592, 132 A.L. R. 613, 615 (1940). "No court of justice can in its nature be made the handmaid of iniquity. . . ." or "become auxiliary to the consummation

are a number of exceptions to this rule and a wide variety of conflicting decisions so that here more than usual it is apparent that the courts pick and choose among the legal rules, to arrive at what individual judges believe to be a just result. Indeed, the courts have on occasion clearly articulated this. As indicated by the New York Court of Appeals, "We are not working here with narrow questions of technical law. We are applying fundamental concepts of morality and fair dealing." [89] These problems are considered in the sections which follow. [90]

§ 379. Will the Courts Always Deny a Remedy in the Case of an Illegal Bargain Which Violates a Criminal Statute?

There are countless statutes in the United States which prohibit certain conduct by attaching a certain criminal sanction to the conduct. For example, a New York statute provided in part that any person who gives or offers an agent, employee or servant a commission or bonus to influence his action in relation to his principal's or employer's business without the knowledge or consent of the principal or employer "shall be guilty of a misdemeanor and shall be punished by a fine of not less than ten dollars nor more than five hundred dollars, or by such fine and by imprisonment for not more than one year." [91]

In Sirkin v. Fourteenth St. Store [92] the plaintiff sold and delivered certain hosiery to the defendant pursuant to a contract which plaintiff had obtained by paying the defendant's purchasing agent $75 as an inducement to place the order. The plaintiff's conduct in bribing the agent clearly violated the statute. [93] However, although plaintiff for

---

of violations of law." Bank of the United States v. Owens, 27 U.S. (2 Pet.) 527, 538, 7 L.Ed. 508, 512 (1829).

Professor Havighurst's assessment of the effectiveness of this policy is thought provoking. "The policy against enforcing contracts calling for an illegal performance is a simple one and does not require extensive comment. It accomplishes very little in discouraging the performance of illegal acts, but it keeps the courts respectable." Havighurst, The Nature of Private Contract 53 (1961).

89. McConnell v. Commonwealth Pictures Corp., 7 N.Y.2d 465, 470, 497, 199 N.Y.S.2d 483, 486, 166 N.E.2d 494 (1960).

90. The number of exceptions and the variety of conflicting or ad hoc decisions is undoubtedly due to the fact that, as Burrough, J., said: "[Public policy] is a very unruly horse, and once you get astride it you never know where it will carry you. It may lead you from the sound law. It is never argued at all but when other points fail." Richardson v. Mellish, 130 Eng.Rep. 294, 303 (1824). See also 6A Corbin § 1375 wherein he discusses "Public Policy as a Basis of Illegality."

91. This provision was § 384–r of the Penal Code of 1881, added in 1905. At present the subject matter appears in § 180.00 of the Penal Law.

92. 124 App.Div. 384, 108 N.Y.S. 830 (1st Dep't 1908).

93. It seems clear that the purchasing agent could not have recovered from

the sake of argument conceded that his conduct violated the statute, he argued inter alia [94] that the statute did not provide for any civil sanction upon a contract made in contravention of the statute and that it would be unfair for him to suffer not only a penal sanction but also the loss of the price of the goods which had already been delivered to the defendant. Although the minority opinion agreed with the plaintiff, the majority held that a contract induced by a violation of this criminal statute was invalid even though the statute does not specifically so provide.[95]

The conflict in the opinions shows that ultimately what is involved is a question of ascertaining legislative intent.[96] If the legislature states the effect of a violation of a criminal statute upon a contract that expression of intention should of course be followed. Legislatures, however, do not usually provide for the civil consequences of the violation of the criminal law. In such a case the matter is one for judicial determination. No general rule can be set down which will cover every situation. However where there is no explicit provision in the statute it seems generally to be agreed that a plaintiff who has performed under the illegal bargain may recover if the statute is merely malum prohibitum "and the denial of relief is wholly out of proportion to the requirements of public policy or appropriate individual punishment, ..." [97] An English judge has made sound

his own principal because of his double dealing and could not have recovered from the plaintiff because of his breach of his fiduciary duty.

94. Another argument which the plaintiff made was that the illegality was "too remote," a matter to be discussed in § 381 infra.

95. Similar cases are collected in Annot., 55 A.L.R.2d 481.

96. Ets-Hokin & Galvan, Inc. v. Maas Transport, Inc., 380 F.2d 258 (8th Cir. 1967), cert. den. 389 U.S. 977, 88 S.Ct. 481, 19 L.Ed.2d 471 (1968). Among the factors taken into consideration are the language of the statute, its nature, object and purpose, its subject matter and reach, the wrong or evil which the statute seeks to remedy or prevent, the nature of the prohibited act as malum in se or malum prohibitum and the legislative history. Mascari v. Raines, 220 Tenn. 234, 415 S. W.2d 874 (1967). Ultimately the question of legislative intent may resolve

itself into a question of ascertaining the policy of the statute and the best method of carrying it out. In construing the Anti-Kickback Act (§ 361 supra) the United States Supreme Court reasoned that since Congress had expressed a policy decidedly hostile to kickbacks, this policy should be implemented by denying enforceability to contracts even indirectly tainted by kickbacks paid to managerial personnel of the prime contractor. United States v. Acme Process Equip. Co., 385 U.S. 138, 87 S.Ct. 350, 17 L.Ed.2d 249 (1966), reh. denied 385 U.S. 1032, 87 S.Ct. 738, 17 L.Ed.2d 680 (1967). See generally Annot., 55 A.L.R.2d 481 (1957).

97. John E. Rosasco Creameries, Inc. v. Cohen, 276 N.Y. 274, 278, 11 N.E.2d 908, 909, 118 A.L.R. 641, 644 (1937); Restatement, Contracts § 600; Spadanuta v. Village of Rockville Centre, 15 N.Y.2d 755, 205 N.E.2d 525, 257 N. Y.S.2d 329 (1965). Thus the basis of the holding in the Sirkin case is that

observations in this regard. Judge Devlin in St. John Shipping Corp. v. Joseph Rank Ltd.,[98] stated: "Caution in this respect is, I think, especially necessary in these times when so much of commercial life is governed by regulations of one sort or another, which may easily be broken without wicked intent . . . . Commercial men who have unwittingly offended against one of a multiplicity of regulations may nevertheless feel that they have not thereby forfeited all right to justice."

§ 380. Effect of Licensing Statutes

Much of the same principles govern licensing statutes; that is, statutes which require that certain persons obtain a license or certificate or diploma as a condition precedent to the right to engage in a particular profession or enterprise. The violation of such a statute is ordinarily a criminal offense,[99] but the question remains whether a person who performs services without the license is entitled to recover for the services performed. The question is ordinarily made to turn upon whether the licensing statute is merely a revenue raising statute or whether the statute is enacted under the police power "for the protection of the public welfare, health and morality against fraud and incompetence . . . ."[1] If it is a revenue raising statute recovery is permitted.[2] But a person who practices law without a license is ordinarily denied a recovery.[3] However, the test of revenue raising as opposed to exercise of police power is not the ultimate test but merely an aid in arriving at legislative intent. Ultimately the question is, as explained above, one of legislative intent.[4]

---

public policy requires that commercial bribery be dealt with severely.

98. [1957] 1 Q.B. 267, 288, 289.

99. Restatement, Contracts § 580(d).

1. Cope v. Rowlands, 150 Eng.Rep. 707 (Exch.P.1836); 6A Corbin § 1512.

2. Howard v. Lebby, 197 Ky. 324, 246 S.W. 828, 30 A.L.R. 830 (1923) (licensing fees assessed on building contractors constituted an occupation tax). A contractor's failure to obtain a permit did not prevent his recovery in Measday v. Sweazea, 78 N.M. 781, 438 P.2d 525 (1968).

3. Spivak v. Sachs, 16 N.Y.2d 163, 211 N.E.2d 329, 263 N.Y.S.2d 953 (1965) (California attorney may not recover for services rendered in New York), rev'g 21 A.D.2d 348, 250 N.Y.S.2d 666 (1st Dep't 1964), 33 Fordham L.Rev. 483 (1965); cf. Spanos v. Skouras Theatres Corp., 235 F.Supp. 1 (S.D.N.Y.1964), aff'd 364 F.2d 161 (2d Cir.), cert. denied 385 U.S. 987, 87 S.Ct. 597, 17 L.Ed.2d 448 (1966).

4. John E. Rosasco Creameries, Inc. v. Cohen, 276 N.Y. 274, 11 N.E.2d 908, 118 A.L.R. 641 (1937) (unlicensed milk dealer permitted recovery); cf. Carmine v. Murphy, 285 N.Y. 413, 35 N.E.2d 19 (1941) (unlicensed liquor dealer not permitted to recover). As to real estate brokers, see Galbreath-Ruffin Corp. v. 40th and 3rd Corp., 19 N.Y.2d 354, 280 N.Y.S.2d 126, 227 N.E.2d 30 (1967).

§ 381. Remoteness of the Illegality

In Sirkin v. Fourteenth Street Store discussed in section 379 supra where the plaintiff bribed the purchasing agent of the defendant contrary to statute, the plaintiff in addition to the point previously discussed raised the issue that the illegality was "too remote." The argument was that although the contract between the plaintiff and the purchasing agent was illegal, there was nothing illegal about a contract for the sale of hosiery upon which the plaintiff was suing and that therefore the illegality was "too remote." The majority of the Appellate Division did not agree with this contention.

A similar problem arose in a later case in the Court of Appeals.[5] In that case the defendant promised that if the plaintiff should succeed in negotiating a contract with a certain motion picture producer whereby the defendant would get the right to distribute certain motion pictures, the defendant would pay to the plaintiff $10,000 and in addition a certain percentage of defendant's gross receipts from distribution of the pictures. Plaintiff obtained the contract with the motion picture producer by bribing its agent and sued upon defendant's promise for a percentage of the gross receipts. Plaintiff argued that the illegality here was even more remote than in Sirkin for in Sirkin the bribe caused the formation of the very contract sued upon whereas here the agent of a third party was bribed which resulted in *performance* of the plaintiff's contract with the defendant.[6] The majority of the court held that although the illegality was more remote than in Sirkin it was not "too remote" to remove the taint from the plaintiff's cause of action.

How remote is "too remote" is obviously a question of degree. "The line of proximity varies somewhat according to the gravity of the evil apprehended." [7]

§ 382. A Mere Depositary May Not Assert the Defense of Illegality

It is well settled that a mere depositary who is not himself a party to the illegal transaction may not assert the defense of illegality if he is sued by the party for whose benefit the deposit of illegally

---

5. McConnell v. Commonwealth Pictures Corp., 7 N.Y.2d 465, 166 N.E.2d 494, 199 N.Y.S.2d 483 (1960).

6. This case also shows that a bargain which is legal in its formation may become illegal by its performance. See the definition of illegality in § 355 supra. For another illustration of a contract lawful in its inception but illegally performed, see Tocci v. Lembo,

325 Mass. 707, 92 N.E.2d 254 (1950), where a builder constructed a house without obtaining approval from the Civilian Production Administration, as then required by penal statutes and implementing regulations. He was denied recovery although the contract itself was legal.

7. Restatement, Contracts § 597, Comment b; 6A Corbin §§ 1529 and 1530.

gotten gains is made. Thus, if A makes a deposit of money or goods with B for the benefit of C pursuant to an illegal arrangement between A and C, C may obtain the deposit from B because B may not assert the defense of illegality against C or A. The theory is that the illegal transaction is regarded as completed and the undertaking by the agent is regarded as separate from the illegal transaction.[8]

It must be carefully observed that the rule does not apply where the depositary is a party to the illegal transaction. Thus, where the plaintiff, a clothing jobber, advanced money to the defendant broker to be used to bribe purchasing agents and the plaintiff sought the return of part of the money which had not been used, the court held that the defendant was not a mere depositary and therefore could use the defense of illegality.[9]

However, at times, this factor in the rule as well as the theory enunciated above upon which the rule is based have not been too carefully observed.[10] Thus, for example, in Southwestern Shipping Corp. v. National City Bank,[11] the plaintiff was a purchasing agent in New York for Garmoja, an Italian importer, who placed an order for goods with the plaintiff and promised to pay in American dollars. Such payment was prohibited under Italian law unless a license was obtained. Corti had such a license and in a scheme to evade the licensing requirement Garmoja deposited lire to cover the purchase price ($37,-222) with Corti's bank in Italy and that bank transferred dollars to the defendant bank in New York to be credited to the account of one Anlyan, who had already executed an irrevocable assignment of this credit to the plaintiff. The defendant negligently paid the money to Anlyan who absconded. When sued by the plaintiff the defendant set up the defense of illegality. The court held that the defendant was a mere depositary and so could not use the defense of illegality although it would appear that the defendant participated in the wrong and that the payment by him to the plaintiff was to be the consummation of the illegal transaction.[12]

---

8. In re Lowe's Estate, 104 Neb. 147, 175 N.W. 1015 (1920).

9. Stone v. Freeman, 298 N.Y. 268, 82 N.E.2d 571, 8 A.L.R.2d 304 (1948). This case also involves the doctrine of locus poenitentiae. See § 386 infra.

10. 6A Corbin § 1531.

11. 6 N.Y.2d 454, 160 N.E.2d 836, 190 N.Y.S.2d 352 (1959), cert. den. 361 U.S. 895, 80 S.Ct. 198, 4 L.Ed.2d 151 (1959).

12. The public policy aspect is apparent. An evasion of a foreign currency law is not as repugnant as the bribery of purchasing agents. On the attitude of American courts towards foreign currency regulations, see § 188 supra.

The case therefore could perhaps have been decided upon the theory that the illegality was only malum prohibitum and denial of relief is wholly out of proportion to the requirements of public policy or appropriate individual punishment.

§ 383.   Quasi Contractual Recoveries Based Upon Performance

Although, as we have seen, there are relatively few cases where one may sue to enforce an illegal executory contract, nevertheless where there has been some performance the courts will at times make additional exceptions to the general rule that it will leave the parties to an illegal agreement where it finds them and allow a contractual or quasi-contractual recovery.   This result is also accomplished by three doctrines not previously discussed: (1) divisibility,[13] (2) pari delicto and (3) locus poenitentiae.

§ 384.   Divisibility of Illegal Bargains

An agreement may consist of a single promise based upon a single consideration.   In such a case if either the promise or the consideration for this promise is illegal there is no room to apply the doctrine of divisibility.[14]   The same would be true if several lawful promises were given in exchange for one illegal consideration or if several lawful considerations were given in exchange for one illegal promise.[15]

However what is the result where one lawful consideration is given for two promises, one of which is lawful and the other unlawful?   The general rule is that if the lawful consideration is performed the lawful promise is enforceable.[16]   For example, if A painted B's house in exchange for B's promise to pay $1000 and to smuggle cer-

---

13.   The recovery under the doctrine of divisibility may be on the contract or may be quasi-contractual in character.

14.   The theory is that if there is only one promise or one consideration the contract is entire and not divisible. See § 161 supra.   However at times by a process of interpretation what would ordinarily be deemed one consideration may be treated as two considerations.   For example, in Lund v. Bruflat, 159 Wash. 89, 292 P. 112 (1930), the plaintiff entered into a contract with the defendant whereby the plaintiff was to do a certain plumbing and heating work for a fixed sum.   The plaintiff did not have a license and so under the rules stated in § 380 supra the defendant had a defense to an action for the price. The court, however, allowed the plaintiff to recover for the materials furnished but not for the labor performed.   Thus the court severed the materials from the illegal services and allowed a recovery for the materials as if the rendering of services was a separate consideration from the furnishing of materials, although there was in reality only one promise and one consideration.   But see American Store Equip. & Constr. Corp. v. Jack Dempsey's Punch Bowl, Inc., 174 Misc. 436, 21 N.Y.S.2d 117 (Sup.Ct. 1939), aff'd 283 N.Y. 601, 28 N.E.2d 23 (1940).   Once the contract is interpreted to be divisible as in Lund v. Bruflat then the case is one where the promise of payment is lawful and part of the consideration for it is lawful and part unlawful.   This situation is discussed in the text corresponding with n. 19.   This type of decision tends to show, as Corbin argues, that divisibility is not determined according to fixed rules, but by the judicial instinct for justice.   6A Corbin § 1520.

15.   Restatement, Contracts § 606.

16.   Osgood v. Central Vt. R. R., 77 Vt. 334, 60 A. 137 (1905).

tain goods into the country, B's promise to pay $1000 would be enforceable. However there is an exception to this rule where the illegal promise is criminal or immoral to a high degree. In such a case the legal promise will not be enforced.[17] For example, if A paints B's house in exchange for B's promise to pay $1000 and to shoot Jones, even if A has painted he may not enforce the promise to pay $1000. It is obvious that the different result in the two illustrations is based upon public policy considerations. It is equally obvious that the phrase "criminal or immoral in high degree" involves a moral judgment as to the viciousness of the illegality.[18]

The converse situation to the one discussed in the preceding paragraph is presented where the promise is lawful but part of the consideration for it is lawful and part unlawful. Here the general rule is that if any part of the consideration which is given is unlawful, the promise, though lawful, is unenforceable.[19] For example, A promises to pay $1000 if B cuts wood for a month and smuggles certain goods into the country. A's promise would not be enforceable even though B cut the wood. However, this rule is also not without exception. If the illegal consideration is very slight in degree then the promise will be enforced or at least a quasi-contractual recovery allowed.[20]

Although we have been talking about the divisibility of contracts, it is quite apparent that the term divisible is not being used in the same sense as that word was used to explain the concept of a divisible as opposed to an entire contract in § 161. However, where the contract is divisible in that sense the rule with respect to illegality is that a promise which is illegal and which has its own separately apportioned consideration is enforceable except where the other part of the bargain is criminal or immoral in a high degree.[21]

§ 385. Doctrine of Pari Delicto

A party who has performed under an illegal bargain is entitled to a quasi-contractual recovery if he was not guilty of serious moral turpitude and, although blameworthy, is not equally as guilty as the other party to the illegal bargain.[22]

---

17. Kukla v. Perry, 361 Mich. 311, 105 N.W.2d 176 (1960).

18. 6A Corbin § 1522.

19. Hanley v. Savannah Bank & Trust Co., 208 Ga. 585, 68 S.E.2d 581 (1952). Compare this statement with the rule stated in § 76 where one of the considerations for a promise is void and one is valid.

20. 6A Corbin § 1525.

21. Hill v. Schultz, 71 Idaho 145, 227 P.2d 586 (1951) (mortgage and lease on gambling premises severed; mortgage enforced as it was in consideration of a loan; lease not enforced as it was in consideration of a percentage of gambling revenues); In re Craig's Estate, 298 Pa. 235, 148 A. 83 (1929).

22. Restatement, Contracts § 604; see generally, Grodecki, In Pari Delicto Potior est Conditio Defendentis, 71 L.

What constitutes serious moral turpitude is obviously a question of degree. A person who bribes or attempts to bribe a public official or agent is usually believed to be guilty of serious moral turpitude.[23] Yet, in a case in which the plaintiff, a Jewish refugee, gave jewels to the defendant to be used in bribing the Portuguese Consul to issue a visa so that plaintiff could escape Hitler's army, it was held that the plaintiff might recover back the jewels from the defendant as he was not in pari delicto.[24] The court refused to attach the stigma of moral turpitude to an agreement made by a person in dire necessity and motivated by the instinct of self-preservation.[25]

The second question which must be asked in determining whether the parties are in pari delicto is whether the parties are equally at fault. The cases which allow recovery on the ground that the performing plaintiff is not equally at fault tend to come within several flexible categories. Foremost among these categories are cases in which the transaction is outlawed in order to protect a class of persons of which the plaintiff is a member.[26] Thus, as we have seen a borrower may recover excess interest paid, and often a penalty as well, from a usurer. Anti-trust laws are aimed, in large part, at enterprises enjoying considerable market power in order to protect enterprises having a significantly lesser amount of market power. Thus, it will usually be held that a dealership is not in pari delicto with the manufacturer although the contracts between the manufacturer and its dealers contain illegal provisions in restraint of trade.[27] In some juris-

---

Q.Rev. 254 (1955); Higgins, The Transfer of Property Under Illegal Transactions, 25 Modern L.Rev. 149 (1962); Wade, Restitution of Benefits Acquired through Illegal Transactions, 95 U.Pa.L.Rev. 261 (1947).

23. See §§ 360–362 supra.

24. Liebman v. Rosenthal, 185 Misc. 837, 57 N.Y.S.2d 875 (Sup.Ct.), aff'd, 269 App.Div. 1062, 59 N.Y.S.2d 148 (2nd Dep't 1945). See 6A Corbin § 1536. Sometimes the doctrine is worded in terms that the plaintiff "is not in particips criminis."

25. Subsequent developments in American criminal law reflect the same kind of thinking which went into the decision of this case. Emergency measures to avoid imminent injury may be taken, under modern criminal codes, despite the fact that such measures under ordinary circumstances would constitute a criminal act. See Model Penal Code § 3.02; McKinney's N.Y.Penal Law § 35.05. It should also be noted that in the Liebman case neither party appears to have raised the conflict of laws question of the effect of their agreement under French law.

For another illustration where urgency of motive was the basis of finding a party not in pari delicto, see Karpinski v. Collins, 252 Cal.App.2d 711, 60 Cal.Rptr. 846 (1967) (dairyman permitted to recover kickbacks paid to president of supplier where no other supply of milk was available).

26. Singh v. Kulubya, [1963] 3 All E.R. 499, 27 Modern L.Rev. 225 (1964); see 6 Corbin § 1540; Wade, supra n. 22, at 270–72. See § 377 supra.

27. Perma Life Mufflers, Inc. v. Int'l Parts Corp., 392 U.S. 134, 88 S.Ct. 1981, 20 L.Ed.2d 982 (1968); Simpson

dictions it has been held that a bettor is not in pari delicto with a professional bookmaker as the gambling laws are aimed primarily against organized gambling.[28]

Another class of cases in which a party is not in pari delicto exists when "he was induced to participate in the illegality by fraud or duress or by the use of influence derived from superior knowledge, mental power, or economic position."[29] A famous series of cases involving the Buckfoot gang illustrates this proposition. The gang had various operatives whose business it was to lure wealthy westerners to their headquarters at an athletic club in Missouri. One of their techniques was to induce their guests into betting on races allegedly "fixed" in their favor, when actually they were "fixed" for their man to lose. The courts allowed recovery against the gang on the grounds that the parties were not on an equal footing. These highly organized frauds, arranged with consummate skill, were no match for the relatively naive bettors.[30] It has been held that a plaintiff who has paid a marriage brokerage fee may recover it because the transaction inherently involves undue influence.[31] Perhaps a more satisfactory reason is that the rules against marriage brokerage are designed for the protection of the unmarried. Similar considerations provide the foundation for the rule that when an illegal agreement is made between parties in a fiduciary relation such as attorney-client, it will be held that the client is not in pari delicto with the fiduciary,[32] at least where the client is acting on the advice of the fiduciary.[33] Intertwined in

v. Union Oil Co., 377 U.S. 13, 84 S.Ct. 1051, 12 L.Ed.2d 98 (1964), reh. denied 377 U.S. 949, 84 S.Ct. 1349, 12 L.Ed.2d 313, on remand 270 F.Supp. 754 (1967); Crawford v. Colby Broadcasting Corp., 387 F.2d 796 (7th Cir. 1967); Beloit Culligan Soft Water Serv., Inc. v. Culligan, Inc., 274 F.2d 29 (7th Cir. 1959); cf. Eastman Kodak Co. v. Southern Photo Materials Co., 273 U.S. 359, 47 S.Ct. 400, 71 L. Ed. 684 (1927) (question of pari delicto left to jury). For another example of legislation designed to protect a class, see McAllister v. Drapeau, 14 Cal.2d 102, 92 P.2d 911, 125 A.L.R. 800 (1939) (mortgage in violation H.O.L.C. Act).

28. Watts v. Malatesta, 262 N.Y. 80, 186 N.E. 210, 88 A.L.R. 1072 (1933); contra, Elias v. Gill, 92 Ky. 569, 18 S. W. 454 (1892) (professional permitted to set off his losses).

29. 6A Corbin § 1537.

30. Stewart v. Wright, 147 F. 321 (8th Cir.), cert. denied 203 U.S. 590, 27 S. Ct. 777, 51 L.Ed. 330 (1906); Lockman v. Cobb, 77 Ark. 279, 91 S.W. 546 (1905); Hobbs v. Boatright, 195 Mo. 693, 93 S.W. 934 (1906); Falkenberg v. Allen, 18 Okl. 210, 90 P. 415 (1907); see also Catts v. Phalen, 43 U.S. (2 How.) 376, 11 L.Ed. 306 (1844); Grim v. Cheatwood, 208 Okl. 570, 257 P.2d 1049, 39 A.L.R.2d 1209 (1953).

31. Duval v. Wellman, 124 N.Y. 156, 26 N.E. 343 (1891).

32. Berman v. Coakley, 243 Mass. 348, 137 N.E. 667, 26 A.L.R. 92 (1923), 32 Yale L.J. 745 (1923); Place v. Hayward, 117 N.Y. 487, 23 N.E. 25 (1889); Peyton v. Margiotti, 398 Pa. 86, 156 A.2d 865 (1959).

33. The parties are in pari delicto where the client is the "dominant

these cases are considerations of the superior influence which an attorney may exercise on his clients as well as the consideration that an attorney must not be permitted to abuse his quasi public office.

A person entering into an illegal transaction under duress may not be in pari delicto with the party exercising the coercion.[34] Foremost among the cases in which this question arises are those in which a plaintiff seeks restitution for his performance the consideration for which was the defendant's agreement not to press criminal charges against the plaintiff or against a close relative of the plaintiff. The majority of these cases have indicated, that absent special circumstances, the parties are in pari delicto and the plaintiff may have no recovery whether or not the defendant has kept his illegal promise.[35] A number of cases have indicated, however, that if the party was innocent of the crime for which prosecution was threatened, he may have restitution.[36] Restitution has generally been allowed in cases in which a debtor has been coerced secretly to pay a creditor more than his agreed proportion under a composition agreement with creditors.[37] The degree of duress in such cases is doubtless no stronger than in the cases involving threatened criminal prosecutions. The different degrees of moral turpitude are, it is believed, the basis for the differing results.

§ 386. Locus Poenitentiae

Another exception to the general rule that the courts leave the parties to an illegal bargain where it finds them is the doctrine of locus poenitentiae. Even if the plaintiff is in pari delicto and therefore as blameworthy or more blameworthy than the defendant he is entitled to rescind the bargain and obtain restitution if he acts in time to prevent the attainment of the illegal purpose for which the bargain

mind" in the transaction. Schermerhorn v. De Chambrun, 64 F. 195 (2d Cir. 1894).

34. 6A Corbin § 1537; Wade, supra n. 22, at 272–76.

35. Baker v. Citizens Bank of Guntersville, 282 Ala. 33, 208 So.2d 601 (1968); Union Exch. Nat. Bank v. Joseph, 231 N.Y. 250, 131 N.E. 905, 17 A.L.R. 323 (1921); Ellis v. Peoples Nat. Bank, 166 Va. 389, 186 S.E. 9 (1936); contra, Gorringe v. Read, 23 Utah 120, 63 P. 902 (1901). The mere fact that an agreement is made to make restitution for a criminal act does not make the agreement illegal.

The question is whether there has been a promise to stifle prosecution. Blair Milling Co. v. Fruitager, 113 Kan. 432, 215 P. 286, 32 A.L.R. 416 (1923).

36. Sykes v. Thompson, 160 N.C. 348, 76 S.E. 252 (1912). Restitution may be granted if the person exercising the duress did not believe in the charge. Union Exch. Nat. Bank v. Joseph, 231 N.Y. 250, 131 N.E. 905, 17 A.L.R. 323 (1921) (dictum).

37. Batchelder & Lincoln Co. v. Whitmore, 122 F. 355 (1st Cir. 1903); Brown v. Everett-Ridley-Ragan Co., 111 Ga. 404, 36 S.E. 813 (1900).

was made unless the mere making of the bargain involves serious moral turpitude.[38]

The doctrine has been justified on the grounds that it frustrates the carrying out of illegal schemes [39] and that in fairness and morality the plaintiff should have an opportunity to repent. Repentance in a moral sense is not, however, usually required and the courts will not generally inquire into what motivated the plaintiff in repudiating the bargain.[40] Indeed, in cases for restitution of money deposited with a stakeholder for wagering purposes it is often held that recovery may be had even after the event wagered upon has occurred.[41] In such cases it is usually apparent that the plaintiff does not repent having violated the law but repents only having lost the wager.

The plaintiff is generally not permitted to withdraw if any part of the illegal performance is consummated.[42] Some cases, however, permit withdrawal any time before the illegal aspects are substantially performed.[43]

Although restitution is generally not granted when the bargain involves moral turpitude, at least one jurisdiction has made a strong case to the contrary,[44] arguing that the basis of the doctrine is

"to protect society from the influence of contracts made in disregard of the public weal by reducing the number of

---

38. Restatement, Contracts § 605; 6A Corbin § 1541; 6 Williston § 1788 (rev. ed. 1938).

39. Cleveland, C., C. & St. L. Ry. v. Hirsch, 204 F. 849 (6th Cir. 1913); Harrington v. Bochenski, 140 Md. 24, 116 A. 836 (1922).

40. See Aikman v. City of Wheeling, 120 W.Va. 46, 195 S.E. 667, 669 (1938), where the court says:

"The law is a reasonable institution, built on the experience of mankind through the ages. Among other things, it takes into account human frailties and emotions. To him who moves in deliberation and premeditation it is unyielding, but to him who acts under passionate impulse it is merciful. . . . If there was a turning back, that becomes paramount and the reasons for the change of action are inconsequential. The spirit of the law is magnanimity, not vindictiveness. Penalties are imposed for

wrongful conduct not for improper intentions uncrystallized."

41. Lewy v. Crawford, 5 Tex.Civ.App. 293, 23 S.W. 1041, 1043 (1893) ("not a question of sorrow and repentance, but one of disaffirming and destroying a contract made in violation of law and morals."); Restatement, Contracts § 524; 6A Corbin §§ 1484, 1541.

42. See Stone v. Freeman, 298 N.Y. 268, 82 N.E.2d 571, 8 A.L.R.2d 304 (1948) (part of the bribe money reached its destination); but cf. Gehres v. Ater, 148 Ohio St. 89, 73 N.E.2d 513, 172 A.L.R. 693 (1947) (recovery permitted for value of bond deposited as security for payment of a gambling debt).

43. Kearley v. Thomson, [1870] 24 Q.B. D. 742, 747 (C.A.); Ware v. Spinney, 76 Kan. 289, 91 P. 787 (1907).

44. Town of Meredith v. Fullerton, 83 N.H. 124, 139 A. 359, 365 (1927); accord, Greenberg v. Evening Post Ass'n, 91 Conn. 371, 99 A. 1037 (1917).

such transactions to a minimum, and by interrupting the progress of illegal undertakings before the evil purpose has been fully consummated. To hold that the hand of the court is stayed merely because of the pernicious character of the illegal promise, or solely because its performance was not sooner arrested seems like a perversion of the real purpose of the doctrine. . . . The real question at issue in any particular case is whether the ends of the law will be further-ed or defeated by granting relief."

Although it is generally said that repentance comes too late if it comes only after the other party to the bargain has indicated he will not perform or after attainment of the unlawful purpose is seen to be impossible,[45] this rule also finds its exceptions.[46]

§ 387. Change of Law or Facts after the Bargain is Made

If A and B enter into a contract which is legal at the time the contract is formed and subsequently the contract becomes illegal, the problems presented are covered under the topic of impossibility of performance.[47]

A different problem is presented if the contract is illegal when formed but subsequently contracts of that type become legal as a re-sult of a change in fact or a change in law. The general rule is that a change of law does not validate a contract which was originally illegal and unenforceable.[48] However there are exceptions when the repeal-ing statute expressly so states or where this is implied as for example "when the policy underlying the original statute or the extent of its prohibition is doubtful." [49]

Where the bargain is illegal and a change of facts removes the cause of the illegality the contract does not thereby become enforce-

---

45. Bigos v. Bousted, [1951] 1 All E.R. 92 (K.B.); 6A Corbin § 1541.

46. Liebman v. Rosenthal, 185 Misc. 837, 57 N.Y.S.2d 875 (Sup.Ct.), aff'd 269 App.Div. 1062, 59 N.Y.S.2d 148 (2nd Dep't 1945) (alternative ground).

47. See § 189 supra; Restatement, Contracts § 608.

48. Fitzsimons v. Eagle Brewing Co., 107 F.2d 712, 126 A.L.R. 681 (3d Cir. 1939); but see Bloch v. Frankfort Distillery, Inc., 273 N.Y. 469, 6 N.E.2d 408 (1936).

49. 6A Corbin § 1532 (e. g., Sunday law statutes and usury statutes). The problem here discussed is but one as-pect of the general problem of the ret-roactive applicability of civil legisla-tion. For a thorough survey of the general area, although centered on corporation laws, see McNulty, Corpo-rations and the Intertemporal Conflict of Laws, 55 Calif.L.Rev. 12 (1967).

able except where either party did not know or have reason to know of the illegality.[50] Where a change in fact occurs which removes the cause of the illegality the parties may subsequently ratify the agreement.[51]

50. Restatement, Contracts § 609. This is of course a rare situation. Usually one party will know or have reason to know of the illegality.

51. 6A Corbin § 1532.

TABLE OF CASES

References are to Pages

Abbott v. Doane, 124

ABC Outdoor Advertising, Inc. v. Dolhun's Marine, Inc., 490

Abraham v. H. V. Middleton, Inc., 455

Abrams v. Reynolds Metals Co., 328

Abramson v. Boedeker, 407

Ackley v. Parmenter, 453

Acme Process Equip. Co. v. United States, 373

A'Court v. Cross, 158

Adamowski v. Curtiss-Wright Flying Service, Inc., 204, 205, 209

Adams v. Bosick, 123

Adams v. Lindsell, 63

Adams v. Merced Stone Co., 407

Adams Exp. Co. v. Allen, 333

A. G. V. Associates, Inc. v. Cross, 562

Aikman v. City of Wheeling, 578

Air Technology Corp. v. General Electric Co., 181

Akamine & Sons, Ltd. v. American Sec. Bank, 87

Akers v. J. B. Sedberry, Inc., 57

Alabama G. S. R. R. v. Johnston, 343

Alaska Airlines, Inc. v. Stephenson, 499

Alaska Packers Ass'n v. Domenico, 120

Albrecht Chem. Co. v. Anderson Trading Corp., 45

Albre Marble & Tile Co. v. John Bowen Co., 303, 314

Aldrich v. Ames, 452

A. Leonobel, Inc. v. Senif, 358

Alexander v. Haskins, 218

Alexander v. Jameson, 194

Alexander H. Revell & Co. v. C. H. Morgan Grocery Co., 394

Alexander's Dep't Stores, Inc. v. Ohrbach's, Inc., 337

Alfred Atmore Pope Found., Inc., v. New York, N. H. & Hartford Ry., 342

Alger-Fowler Co. v. Tracy, 292

Allan v. Hargadine-McKittrick Dry Goods Co., 30

Allegheny College v. National Chautauqua County Bank, 105, 177, 178

Allen v. Bryson, 154

Allen v. Burns, 252

Allen v. Chicago & N. W. R. R., 343

Allen v. Western Union Tel. Co., 333

Allen v. Wolf River Lumber Co., 283

Allen, Heaton & McDonald, Inc. v. Castle Farm Amusement Co., 337

Aller v. Aller, 196

Allhusen v. Caristo Constr. Corp., 417

Allied Steel & Conveyors, Inc. v. Ford Motor Co., 36, 64

All Star Feature Corp., In re, 118

Alper Blouse Co. v. E. E. Connor & Co., 241

Al-Sco Realty Co. v. Suburban Apt. Corp., 483

America-La-France, Inc. v. City of Philadelphia, 198

American Acceptance Corp. v. Schoenthaler, 561

American Bank & Trust Co. v. Trinity Universal Ins. Co., 269

American Bridge Co. v. City of Boston, 422

American Colortype Co. v. Continental Colortype Co., 432, 436

American Concrete Steel Co. v. Hart, 31

American Home Imp., Inc. v. MacIver, 110, 113

American Ins. Union v. Woodward, 291

American Insurers Life Ins. Co. v. Regenold, 563

American Legion Christie E. Wilson Post No. 324, Rexford, Kan. v. Thompson, 176

American Life Ins. Co. of Alabama v. Hutcheson, 48

American Lithographic Co. v. Ziegler, 410, 412

American Motors Sales Corp. v. Semke, 137

American Nat. Bank v. A. G. Sommerville, Inc., 421

American Oil Co. v. Carey, 240, 241

American Parts Co. v. Am. Arbitration Ass'n, 54

American Publishing & Engraving Co. v. Walker, 44

American Ry. Exp. Co. v. Bailey, 327

American Store Equip. & Constr. Corp. v. Jack Dempsey's Punch Bowl, Inc., 573

American Trading Co. v. Steele, 351

American University v. Todd, 109

Amies v. Wesnofske, 231, 265

Amory v. Massachusetts, 343

Amsinck v. American Ins. Co., 488

Amtorg Trading Corp. v. Miehle Printing Press & Mfg. Co., 252

A. M. Webb & Co. v. Robt. P. Miller Co., 30

Anaconda Aluminum Co. v. Sharp, 406, 424

Anchorage Centennial Dev. Co. v. Van Wormer & Rodrigues, Inc., 361

Anderson v. Backlund, 18

Anderson v. Copeland, 517

Anderson v. Howard Hall Co., 391

Anderson v. May, 299

Anderson v. Rexroad, 388

Anderson v. Wisconsin Cent. Ry. Co., 23

Andrews Electric Co. v. St. Alphonse Catholic Total Abstinence Soc., 404, 429

Anmons v. Wilson & Co., 47

Ann Arbor Asphalt Constr. Co. v. City of Howell, 369

Anstey v. Marden, 452

Apex Mining Co. v. Chicago Copper & Chemical Co., 350

Archbolds (Freightage) Ltd. v. Spanglett, Ltd., 566

Archer-Daniels Midland Co. v. Paull, 336

Arcuri v. Weiss, 486

Arden v. Freydberg, 48

Arend v. Smith, 123

Arentsen v. Moreland, 365

Arentz v. Morse Dry Dock & Repair Co., 32

Arizona Land Title & Trust Co. v. Safeway Stores, Inc., 230

Armour & Co. v. Celic, 122

Armour & Co. v. Schlacter, 169

Armstrong v. Illinois Bankers Life Ass'n, 256

Armstrong v. Levan, 155, 178

Armstrong v. Stiffler, 121

Arnold v. Masonic Country Club, 294

Arnold v. Nichols, 394

Arnold Productions, Inc. v. Favorite Films Corp., 433

Arrow Lathing & Plastering, Inc. v. Schaulat Plumbing Supply Co., 269

Art Metal Constr. Co. v. Lehigh Structural Steel Co., 434

Ashby v. White, 326

Aspinwall v. Sacchi, 510

A. S. Rampell, Inc. v. Hyster Co., 33

Assets Realization Co. v. Clark, 421

Atlanta Banking & Savings Co. v. Johnson, 219

Atlantic Coast Realty Co. v. Robertson, 464

Atlantic Dock Co. v. Leavitt, 192

Atlantic N. Airlines v. Schwimmer, 98

Atwater v. Cardwell, 78

Atwell v. Jenkins, 219

Audiger, Inc. v. Town of Hamilton, 347, 349

Austin v. Burge, 49

Austin v. Seligman, 380

Austin Co. v. United States, 318

Austin Friars, The, 230

Austin Real Estate & Abstract Co. v. Bahn, 123

Ayer v. Western Union Tel. Co., 66

A & H Lithoprint, Inc. v. Bernard Dunn Advertising Co., 126

Baer, Matter of, 186

Baer's Estate, In re, 114

Bagaeff v. Prokopik, 161, 162

Bailey v. Interstate Airmotive, Inc., 375

Baird v. Elliott, 463

Baker v. Citizens Bank of Guntersville, 577

Baker v. Higgins, 255

Baker v. Rice, 465

Balfour v. Balfour, 16

Ballard v. The Tingue Mills Inc., 46

Balon v. Hotel & Restaurant Supplies, Inc., 87

Balsam Farm, Inc. v. Evergreen Dairies, Inc., 142, 146

Banco Do Brasil v. A. C. Israel Commodity Co., 304

Banco Longoria, S. A. v. El Paso Nat. Bank, 404

Bancredit, Inc. v. Bethea, 213

Banducci v. Hickey, 302

Bank of Fairbanks v. Kaye, 526

Bank of Rector v. Parrish, 220

Bank of United States v. Manheim, 529

Bank of the United States v. Owens, 568

Barber v. Gross, 209

Barber Milling Co. v. Leichthammer Baking Co., 287

Barbier v. Barry, 336

Bard v. Kent, 114, 116

Bardons & Oliver, Inc. v. Amtorg Trading Corp., 313

Bareham & McFarland, Inc. v. Kane, 84, 85

Barile v. Wright, 175

Barlow v. Grand Lodge A.O.U.W., 291

Barna v. Clifford Country Estates, Inc., 566

Barnes v. Hobson, 555

Barnet v. Cannizzarro, 56

Barnsdall, City of v. Curnutt, 307

Barnum v. Williams, 306

Barron v. Cain, 265

Barron G. Collier, Inc. v. Rawson, 294

Barron G. Collier, Inc. v. Women's Garment Store, 349

Barth v. Women's City Club, 475

Bartlett v. Bailey, 209, 216

Bartlett v. Mystic River Corp., 473

Bartlett v. Newton, 522

Bartlett v. Wyman, 166

Bartolatta v. Calvo, 449

Barton v. Morin, 275

Barza v. Metropolitan Life Ins. Co., 227

Bass v. Olson, 404

Batchelder & Lincoln Co. v. Whitmore, 577

Baugh v. Darley, 494

Beach v. Beach, 190

Beardsley v. Clark, 211

Beardsley v. Stephens, 380

Beattie v. New York, N. H. & H. R. R., 278, 326

Beattie-Firth, Inc. v. Colebank, 265

Beatty v. Coble, 541

Beecher v. Conradt, 259

Beechwood Corp. v. Fisher, 252

Becker v. Comm'r of Internal Revenue, 69

Beckley v. Newman, 138

Beckwith v. Talbot, 512

Beech Aircraft Corp. v. Flexible Tubing Corp., 46

Belfert v. Peoples Planning Corp. of America, 476

Belknap v. Bender, 453

Bell v. Morrison, 159

Belleville Lumber & Supply Co. v. Chamberlain, 489

Bellizzi v. Huntley Estates, Inc., 249, 362, 363

Bellows v. Sowles, 444

Beloit Culligan Soft Water Serv., Inc. v. Culligan, Inc., 576

Bendix v. Ross, 492

Benjamin v. First Citizens Bank & Trust Co., 19

Bennett v. Bates, 386

Bennett Leasing Co. v. Ellison, 496

Benson v. Phipps, 123

Benson Coop. Creamery Ass'n v. First Dist. Ass'n, 32

Bentley v. Morse, 162

Berger v. Shanahan, 367, 368

Berguido v. Eastern Air Lines, Inc., 39

Berl v. Rosenberg, 408

Berman v. Coakley, 576

Berman v. The Palatine Ins. Co., 227

Berman v. Rosenberg, 27

Bernard v. Taylor, 559

Bernstein v. Meech, 288, 336, 338

Bernstein v. Prudential Ins. Co. of America, 461

Berry v. Crawford, 276

B. F. Goodrich Co. v. Parker, 268

Biehl v. Biehl's Adm'x, 407, 408

Biener Contracting Corp. v. Elberon Restaurant Corp., 457

Big Diamond Milling Co. v. Chicago, M. & St. P. R. Co., 158

Bigelow v. RKO Radio Pictures, Inc., 337

Biggs v. Lawrence, 566

Bigos v. Bousted, 579

Billetter v. Posell, 347

Biothermal Process Corp. v. Cohu & Co., 28

Bishop v. Eaton, 43

Bishop v. Palmer, 544

Bissenger v. Prince, 31

Bisso v. Inland Waterways Corp., 552

Bixby v. Wilson & Co., 33, 180

Black v. Fisher, 496

Black Industries, Inc. v. Bush, 107

Blackard v. Monarch's Mfrs. and Distribs., 396

Blackburn v. Mann, 460

Blackwell v. Blackwell, 488

Blackwood v. Liebke, 368

Blaechinska v. Howard Mission & Home, 120

Blair Milling Co. v. Fruitager, 577

Blake v. Voight, 475

Blakeslee v. Bd. of Water Comm'rs, 121

Blakeslee v. Nelson, 19

Blass v. Terry, 192, 385

Bliss v. Lawrence, 416

Bloch v. Frankfort Distillery, Inc., 579

Blue Valley Creamery Co. v. Consolidated Products Co., 477, 489

Board of Education v. State Board, 432

Boatner v. Gates Bros. Lumber Co., 528

Boatright v. Steinite Radio Corp., 32

Boesiger v. Freer, 499

Bohanan v. Pope, 398

Bolivar v. Monnat, 567

Boll v. Sharp & Dohme, Inc., 6

Bollinger v. Central Pa. Quarry Strip & Constr. Co., 39

Bonhard v. Gindin, 368

Bool v. Mix, 203

Boomer v. Muir, 375

Boone v. Coe, 494

Boone v. Eyre, 246, 248

Booth v. Booth & Bayliss Commercial School, Inc., 232

Booth v. Spuyten Duyvil Rolling Mill Co., 300

Bordentown, Township of v. Wallace, 201

Borough of. See under name of borough

Bosden v. Thinne, 153

Boshart v. Gardner, 522

Boston Plate & Window Glass Co. v. John Bowen Co., 305

Boston & M. R. R. v. Piper, 550

Botta v. Brunner, 336

Boulton v. Jones, 41, 42

Bounds v. Nuttle, 536

Bowen v. Kimball, 249

Bowen v. Prudential Ins. Co., 191

Bowman v. Surety Fund Life Ins. Co., 274

Boyce v. Murphy, 450

Brackenbury v. Hodgkin, 115

Bradbury, In re, 153

Bradford v. Durkee Marine Prods. Corp., 546

Bradley v. Harter, 490

Bradshaw v. Millikin, 120, 369

Braniff Inv. Co. v. Robertson, 563

Branigan v. Saba, 566

Brant v. California Dairies, Inc., 40

Brant v. Chicago & A. R. R., 552

Branton v. Martin, 191, 192

Braybrooks v. Whaley, 365

Brede v. Rosedale Terrace Co., 274

Bredemann v. Vaughan Mfg. Co., 114, 184

Bremerton, City of v. Kitsap County Sewer Dist., 30

Bretz v. Union Central Life Ins. Co., 62

Brewer v. Horst & Lachmund Co., 483

Brewer v. Lepman, 56

Brewer v. Simpson, 286

Brick Co. v. Pond, 309

Bright v. Ganas, 244

Brimmer v. Salisbury, 260

British Columbia Saw-Mill Co. v. Nettleship, 331

British Waggon Co. v. Lea & Co., 432

Britton v. Turner, 251, 493

Broadnax v. Ledbetter, 40

Broadway Photoplay Co. v. World Film Corp., 335, 336, 337

Brock v. Button, 460

Brod v. Cincinnati Time Recorder Co., 430
Brooklawn, Borough of v. Brooklawn Housing Corp., 381
Brooks v. Ball, 107
Brooks v. LeGrand, 115
Brooks v. Mitchell, 408
Brooks v. Neal, 506
Brown v. Coates, 327
Brown v. Everett-Ridley-Ragan Co., 577
Brown v. Fore, 406
Brown v. Fraley, 258
Brown v. Weber, 456
Brown v. Wood, 210
Brown v. Woodbury, 374
Browne v. R & R Engineering Co., 546
Browne v. Thorn, 559
Bruce v. Indianapolis Gas Co., 299
Brunhoelzl v. Brandes, 210
Brunne-Booth Fotochrome Corp. v. Kaufman, 59
Brunswick Corp. v. Vineberg, 273
Bruson Heights Corp. v. State, 266
Bryant v. Credit Service, Inc., 479
Buccini v. Paterno Constr. Co., 307
Buckley v. Coyne Electrical School, 546
Buffalo Builder's Supply Co. v. Reeb, 373
Bulkley v. Shaw, 455
Bullard v. Moor, 219
Bunge v. Koop, 125
Bunn v. Postell, 220
Burgess v. California Mut. Bldg. & Loan Ass'n, 180
Burgess v. Rodom, 34, 139
Burke v. Campbell, 31
Burke v. McKee, 252
Burkhead v. Farlow, 61
Burleson v. Langdon, 155
Burns v. Beeny, 531
Burns v. McCormick, 465
Burr v. Beers, 384
Burris v. Landers, 174
Burroughs v. Richman, 220
Burrows v. Burrows, 404
Burwick v. Saetz, 247
Busque v. Marcou, 461
Butler v. Foley, 61
Butler v. Young, 553
Butterfield v. Byron, 303
Bu-Vi-Bar Petroleum Corp. v. Krow, 286, 288
Byers v. Lemay Bank & Trust Co., 211
Byram Lumber & Supply Co. v. Page, 392
Byrne v. Padden, 118

Caesar v. Rubinson, 367
Cahen v. Platt, 273
Caldwell v. Cline, 56
California Canneries Co. v. Scatena, 484
California Press Mfg. Co. v. Stafford Packing Co., 336

Call v. Alcan Pac. Co., 138
Callanan Road Imp. Co. v. Colonial S. & S. Co., 367
Cameron v. Townsend, 179
Cameron v. White, 288
Caminetti v. Manierre, 340
Cammack v. J. B. Slattery & Bro., Inc., 191
Camp v. Bank of Bentonville, 206
Camp v. Gress, 504
Campbell v. Fender, 200
Campbell v. Iowa Central Ry., 344
Campbell v. Sears, Roebuck & Co., 207
Campbell v. Whoriskey, 243
Campbell Soup Co. v. Wentz, 113
Canada v. Wick, 288
Canadian Industrial Alcohol Co. v. Dunbar Molasses Co., 300, 317
Canell v. Arcola Housing Corp., 462
Canister Co. v. National Can Corp., 474
Canton-Hughes Pump Co. v. Llera, 349
Cape Girardeau Bell Tel. Co. v. Hamil, 447
Cargill Commission Co. v. Swartwood, 82
Carlill v. Carbolic Smoke Ball Co., 22, 42, 43
Carlin v. Bacon, 473
Carlton v. Smith, 139, 234
Carmine v. Murphy, 570
Carnera v. Schmeling, 335
Carozza v. Brannan, 535
Carozza v. Williams, 309
Carpenter v. Grow, 208
Carr v. Anderson, 220
Carr v. Mahaska County Bankers Ass'n, 57, 59
Carr v. Sacramento Clay Products Co., 222
Carroll v. Beardon, 567
Carroll v. Palmer Mfg. Co., 473
Carruthers v. Whitney, 268
Carshore v. Huyck, 155
Carson v. Calhoun, 558
Carson, Pirie Scott & Co. v. Parett, 381
Carter v. Beckwith, 220
Carter v. Carter, 174
Carter v. Zachary, 562
Case v. Fitz, 460
Casella v. Tiberio, 204
Casey v. Kastel, 200
Catts v. Phalen, 576
Cavanaugh v. D. W. Ranlet Co., 46
Cawley v. Weiner, 274
C. C. Hauff Hardware v. Long Mfg. Co., 33
Center Chem. Co. v. Avril, Inc., 337
Central Budget Corp. v. Sanchez, 110
Central Coal & Coke Co. v. Hartman, 336
Central London Property Trust, Ltd. v. High Tree House, Ltd., 127, 180, 185
Central Trust Co. of Illinois v. Chicago Auditorium Ass'n, 285

Central Union Bank v. New York Underwriters, Inc., 411

Chamberlain v. Dunlop, 307

Chamberlain v. Parker, 363

Chambers v. Belmore Land Co., 346

Champa v. New York Central Mut. Relief Ass'n, 200

Champion Spark Plug Co. v. Automobile Sundries Co., 274

Chandler v. Sanger, 118

Chandler v. Webster, 313

Chandler v. Welborn, 219

Chapin v. Cooke, 555

Chaplin v. Hicks, 339

Chapman v. Fargo, 330, 332

Charles E. Burt, Inc. v. Seven Grand Corp., 259

Charles Street Garage Co. v. Kaplan, 358

Charlson Realty Co. v. United States, 63

Chase v. Corcoran, 154

Chase v. Hinkley, 473

Chatham Pharmaceuticals, Inc. v. Angier Chem. Co., 434

Chenoweth v. Settle Engineers, Inc., 67

Chesbrough v. Conover, 544

Chevalier v. Lane's Inc., 477

Chicago Coliseum Club v. Dempsey, 335, 338

Chicago & Great E. Ry. v. Dane, 44

Chiles v. Good, 15

Chinigo v. Ehrenberg, 248

Chinn v. China Nat. Aviation Corp., 131

Choice v. City of Dallas, 39

Chrisman v. Southern Cal. Edison Co., 115, 132

Christy v. Pilkinton, 315

Chrysler Corp. v. Quimby, 182, 185

Church v. Rosenstein, 216

Ciampittiello v. Campitello, 558

Cinefot Int'l Corp. v. Hudson Photographic Industry, 32

Ciofalo v. Vic Tanny Gyms, Inc., 550

Cissna Loan Co. v. Gowley, 563

City Nat. Bank v. Phelps, 43

City of. See under name of city

Ciunci v. Wella Corp., 88

Clark v. Gilbert, 308

Clark v. Kidd, 206

Clark v. Manchester, 376

Clark v. Marsiglia, 287

Clark v. Mayor of N. Y., 376

Clark v. Pendleton, 460

Clark v. United States, 87

Clark v. West, 272

Clark Grave Vault Co. v. United States, 318

Clements v. Pasadena Finance Co., 56

Cleveland, C., C. & St. L. Ry. v. Hirsch, 578

Clifton Shirting Co. v. Bronne Shirt Co., 102

Clinkinbeard v. Poole, 494

Coan v. Orsinger, 475

Coburn v. Raymond, 218

Cochran v. Bise, 496

Cochran v. Taylor, 196, 414, 432

Coffee v. Owen's Adm'r, 220

Coggs v. Bernard, 175

Cogley Clinic v. Martini, 542

Cohen v. Kranz, 247, 262

Colbath v. Everett D. Clark Seed Co., 449

Cole v. Wagner, 213

Coletti v. Knox Hat Co., 244, 518

Coley v. Cohen, 391

Coley v. English, 384

Collatz v. Fox Wis. Amusement Corp., 340

Collins v. Gifford, 210, 211

Colonial Operating Corp. v. Hannan Sales & Service, Inc., 313

Colonie Constr. Corp. v. De Lollo, 121

Colony Liquor Distributors, Inc. v. Jack Daniel Distillery, 33

Colpitts v. L. C. Fisher Co., 451

Columbus Railway, Power & Light Co. v. City of Columbus, 309

Colvig v. RKO General, Inc., 352

Comfort v. McCorkle, 175, 186

Commercial Credit Co. v. Tarwater, 561

Commissioner of Ins. v. Massachusetts Acc. Co., 340

Commonwealth v. Graham, 199

Commonwealth v. Gutelius, 191

Commonwealth v. Harris, 201

Commonwealth of Kentucky v. Gilbert, 344

Commonwealth Trust Co. of Pittsburgh v. Hachmeister-Lind Co., 337

Companhia Atlantica v. United States, 546

Conboy v. Howe, 214

Conditioned Air Corp. v. Rock Island Motor Transit Co., 328

Conditioner Leasing Corp. v. Sternmor Realty Corp., 435

Connors v. United Metal Products Co., 170

Conrad's Estate, In re, 188

Consolidated Dairy Prod. v. Irving Trust Co., 141

Construction Aggregates Corp. v. Hewitt-Robins, Inc., 52, 53

Continental Cas. Co. v. Wilson-Avery, Inc., 120

Continental Corp. v. Gowdy, 549

Continental Grain Co. v. Simpson Feed Co., 247

Continental Ill. Bank & Trust Co. v. Clement, 502

Continental Purchasing Co. v. Van Raalte, 419

Continental Turpentine & Rosin Co. v. Gulf Naval Stores Co., 367

Cook v. Bagnell Timber Co., 220

Cook v. Lum, 407

Cook Grains, Inc. v. Fallis, 165

Cooke v. Oxley, 63

Cooney v. Equitable Life Assur. Soc., 408

Cooney v. Hauck, 560

Cooper v. Stronge & Warner Co., 351
Cope v. Rowlands, 570
Copeland v. Beard, 395, 398
Coplew v. Durand, 239
Coppola v. Marden, Orth & Hastings, 347
Cordes v. Prudential Ins. Co., 98
Corey v. Jaroch, 295
Corfman v. McDevitt, 352
Corn Exchange Nat. Bank & Trust Co. v. Kluader, 425
Cornell v. T. V. Development Corp., 351
Corona v. Esposito, 39
Corson v. Lewis, 432
Cosmopolitan Mut. Cas. Co. v. Monarch Concrete Corp., 429
Cosper v. Hancock, 86
Coster v. Mayor of Albany, 189
Cotnam v. Wisdom, 154
Cotton v. Boston Elevated R. R., 344
Coulter v. Howard, 161, 494
County of. See under name of county
Courteen Seed Co. v. Abraham, 20, 21
Covault v. Nevitt, 212
Cox v. Burgess, 110
Coyne v. Superior Incinerator Co., 545
Crabtree v. Elizabeth Arden Sales Corp., 351, 485
Craft v. Elder & Johnston Co., 21
Crafts v. Carr, 213
Craig's Estate, In re, 574
Cramer v. Grand Rapids Showcase, 336
Crandall v. Durham, 549
Crane v. C. Crane & Co., 140
Crane v. Powell, 488
Crane Ice Cream Co. v. Terminal Freezing & Heating Co., 410
Crane Iron Works v. Cox & Sons Co., 357
Crawford v. Colby Broadcasting Corp., 576
Credit Bureaus Adjustment Dep't, Inc. v. Cox Bros., 527
Creer v. Active Automobile Exchange, Inc., 208, 210
Crocker v. Page, 68
Crockett Motor Co. v. Thompson, 200
Crofoot Lumber, Inc. v. Thompson, 373
Croker v. New York Trust Co., 399
Cronin v. National Shawmut Bank, 48
Cronkleton v. Hastings Theatre & Realty Corp., 422
Crow v. Monsell, 99
Crowe v. Hertz Corp., 22
Crowell v. Currier, 395
Crowell v. Hospital of St. Barnabas, 395
Crowell v. Woodruff, 542
Crowell-Collier Pub. Co. v. Josefowitz, 77
Crowley v. Lewis, 189
Crummer & Co. v. Nuveen, 22
Crunden-Martin Mfg. Co. v. Christy, 170
Crutcher & Co. v. Elliott, 339
Culton v. Gilchrist, 61

Cummings v. Connecticut Gen. Life Ins. Co., 274
Cundell v. Haswell, 218
Cunningham's Estate, In re, 125
Currie v. Misa, 105
Curtis v. Curtis, 205
Curtiss v. Roosevelt Aviation School, 213
Curtiss Wright Corp. v. Intercontinent Corp., 158
Cutler v. Hartford Life Ins. Co., 383
Czarnikow-Rionda Co. v. Federal Sugar Ref. Co., 355
Czarnikow-Rionda Co. v. West Market Grocery Co., 376

Daggy v. Miller, 210
Dalrymple Gravel & Contracting Co. v. State, 129
Dalton v. Dalton, 220
Danann Realty Corp. v. Harris, 86
Danby v. Osteopathic Hosp. Ass'n of Del., 177, 179
Dangelo v. Farina, 465
Daniel Morris Co. v. Glens Falls Indem. Co., 393
Daniels v. Boston & M. R. Co., 271, 273
Daniels v. Newton, 280
Dart v. Thompson, 269
Daugherty v. American Union Tel. Co., 333
Davidson v. Laughlin, 376
Davis v. Columbia Min. Co., 307
Davis v. Davis, 15
Davis v. General Goods Corp., 241
Davis v. Jacoby, 115
Davis v. Patrick, 455
Davis v. Van Buren, 506
Davis v. Wells, Fargo Express & Co., 115
Davis Motors, Dodge & Plymouth Co. v. Avett, 111
Dawes, Ex parte, 116
Dawsey v. Kirven, 190
Day v. Caton, 11, 48
Day v. Singleton, 364
Day Companies, Inc., The v. Patat, 543
Dearle v. Hall, 424
Deaton v. Lawson, 432
Debelak Bros., Inc. v. Mille, 535
DeBisschop v. Crum, 257
De Cicco v. Schweizer, 123, 178
DeCruz v. Reid, 269
Deering v. Moore, 506
Deevy v. Porter, 475
De Felice v. Peace, 262
De Forest Radio Tel. & Tel. Co. v. Triangle Radio Supply Co., 288
Delaware County Comm'rs v. Diebold Safe & Lock Co., 412
Del Rubio v. Duchesne, 562
Del Santo v. Bristol County Stadium, Inc., 203, 210
Dennis v. Thermoid Co., 32, 473
Den Norske Ameriekalinje Actiesselskabet v. Sun Printing & Publishing Ass'n, 349
Department of Revenue v. Jennison-Wright Corp., 99

Depositors Trust Co. v. Bruneau, 262
Depot Constr. Co. v. State, 302
Despard v. Walbridge, 562
DeStefano v. Associated Fruit Co., 247
Devecmon v. Shaw, 173
Devlin v. Mayor, 431, 432
DeWolfe v. French, 231
Dexter v. Norton, 260
Diamond Match Co. v. Roeber, 541
Di Bennedetto v. Di Rocco, 139
Dibol v. Minott, 376
Dickey v. Hurd, 63
Dickinson v. Dodds, 60
Diebold Safe & Lock Co. v. Morse, 192
Dillon v. Lineker, 359
Dillon v. United States, 300, 310
Di Menna v. Cooper & Evans Co., 78
Dingley v. Oler, 283
Disken v. Herter, 28
Dixie Glass Co. v. Pollak, 351
Dixon v. Lamson, 473
Dixon-Woods Co. v. Phillips Glass Co., 341
Dobias v. White, 522
Dodge v. Blood, 484
Dodge v. Stiles, 554
Dodson v. Watson, 528
D'Oench, Duhme & Co. v. Federal Deposit Ins. Corp.,
    179, 546
Doherty v. Dolan, 365
Doherty v. Monroe Eckstein Brewing Co., 313
Dohrman v. Sullivan, 27
Dolby v. Fisher, 158
Doll v. Crume, 394
Doll v. Noble, 241
Dollar v. International Banking Corp., 86
Domine v. Grimsdall, 341
Donahue v. Rockford Showcase & Fixture Co., 98
Donald Friedman & Co. v. Newman, 78, 161, 481
Donovan v. Middlebrook, 404
Donzella v. New York State Thruway Authority, 512
Dostal v. Magee, 200
Doughboy Industries, Application of, 53, 54
Douglas v. Bergere, 503
Downs v. Jersey Central Power & Light Co., 376
Doyle v. Dixon, 473
Doyle v. Rector, etc. of Trinity Church, 167
Doyle v. South Pittsburgh Water Co., 389
Dreier v. Sherwood, 268
Drennan v. Star Paving Co., 181
Drennen Motor Car Co. v. Smith, 211
Drew v. John Deere Co. of Syracuse, Inc., 23, 24
Drewen v. Bank of Manhattan, 399
Drude v. Curtis, 208
Drummond v. Pillsbury, 447
Duane Jones Co. v. Burke, 335
Duca v. Lord, 448

Duncan v. Clarke, 474
Duncan's Estate, In re, 556
Dunlop v. Higgins, 63
Dunlop Pneumatic Type Co. v. Selfridge & Co., 378
Dunn v. Steubing, 275
Dunn v. Utica Mut. Ins. Co., 120
Duplex Safety Boiler Co. v. Garden, 241
Dutton v. Poole, 378
Duval v. Wellman, 556, 576
Dwelling House Ins. Co. v. Hardie, 258
Dwy v. Connecticut Co., 509
Dynamics Corp. of America v. United States, 69

E. A. Coronis Associates v. M. Gordon Constr. Co., 181
Eastern Expanded Metal Co. v. Webb Granite & Const.
    Co., 566
Eastern Plank Road Co. v. Vaughn, 116
Eastern S. S. Lines, Inc. v. United States, 363
Eastern Wood Products Co. v. Metz, 455
Eastman Kodak Co. v. Southern Photo Materials Co.,
    337, 576
Easton Furniture Mfg. Co. v. Caminez, 157
Eastwood v. Kenyon, 151
Eaton v. Hill, 210
Ebeling v. Fred J. Swaine Mfg. Co., 546
Edgington v. Howland, 365
Edmunds v. Chandler, 217, 219
Edson v. Poppe, 155
Edward G. Acker, Inc. v. Rittenberg, 370
Edwards v. Skyways, Ltd., 114
E. Frederics, Inc. v. Felton Beauty Supply Co., 65
Egan v. Scully, 200
Eggan v. Simonds, 139, 234
Eggleston v. Buck, 509
Ehrsam v. Borgen, 213
E. I. Dupont de Nemours Powder Co. v. Schlott-
    man, 266
Einbinder v. Western Union Tel. Co., 334
Ekelman v. Freeman, 494
Elam v. Smithdeal Realty & Ins. Co., 175
Elbinger v. Capital & Teutonia Co., 494
Eldrige v. Johnston, 543
Elias v. Gill, 576
Elkhorn Coal Corp. v. Tackett, 203
Elkhorn-Hazard Coal Co. v. Kentucky Riv. Coal Corp.,
    63
Elliott v. Delta Air Lines, Inc., 32
Ellis v. Frawley, 416
Ellis v. Klaff, 481
Ellis v. Peoples Nat. Bank, 577
Ellsworth Dobbs, Inc. v. Johnson, 112, 266
El Ranco, Inc. v. First Nat. Bank of Nevada, 267
Embola v. Tuppela, 109, 138, 564
Emery's Estate, In re, 148
E. M. Loew's, Inc. v. Deutschmann, 432

Empire Transp. Co. v. Philadelphia & R. Coal & Iron Co., 306

Empire Trust Co. v. Heinze, 190

Enoch C. Richards Co. v. Libby, 345

Entis v. Atlantic Wire & Cable Corp., 33

Epstein v. Gluckin, 435

Equitable Life Assur. Soc. v. Goble, 290

Equitable Life Assur. Soc. of the U. S. v. Scali, 563

Equitable Trust Co. of New York v. Western Pac. Ry. Co., 279

Erben v. Lorillard, 496

Erickson v. Grande Ronde Lumber Co., 398

Erie R. R. Co. v. Tompkins, 546

Estabrook v. Wilcox, 462

Ets-Hokin & Galvan, Inc. v. Maas Transport, Inc., 569

Evanovich v. Hutto, 464

Evans v. Morgan, 208

Evergreen Amusement Corp. v. Milstead, 336

Evers v. Guaranty Inv. Co., 562

Ever-Tite Roofing Corp. v. Green, 36

Ewing v. National Airport Corp., 545

Ezzell v. S. G. Holland Stave Co., 485

Faber v. City of New York, 302

Fabian v. Wasatch Orchard Co., 494

Factor v. Peabody Tailoring System, 30, 34

Fairmount Glass Works v. Crunden-Martin Woodenware Co., 21, 25, 35

Falkenberg v. Allen, 576

Farmers' Produce Co. v. McAlester Storage & Commission Co., 64

Farnsworth v. Boro Oil & Gas Co., 389

Farron v. Sherwood, 375

Federal Bond & Mortgage Co. v. Shapiro, 385

Federal Life Ins. Co. v. Rascoe, 290

Federal Nat. Bank v. Koppel, 156

Federal Paving Corp. v. City of Wauwatosa, 198

Federal Welding Serv., Inc. v. Dioguardi, 275

Fedun v. Mike's Cafe, Inc., 164

Feinberg v. Pfeiffer Co., 184

Ferrell v. Elkins, 545

Ferrell v. Stanley, 461

Ferris v. Polansky, 241

Ferrous Products Co. v. Gulf States Trading Co., 49

Fibrosa Spolka Akcyjna v. Fairbairn Lawson Combe Barbour, Ltd., 250, 314

Fidelity Union Trust Co. v. Reeves, 474

Fidelity & Deposit Co. of Baltimore v. Rainer, 381, 393

Fiege v. Boehm, 118

Finch v. Goldstein, 219

Fineman v. Faulkner, 567

Fink v. Cox, 106

First Nat. Bank v. Story, 243

First Nat. Bank of Ada v. Phares, 563

First Nat. Bank of Missouri Valley v. Williamson, 528

First Presbyterian Church of Mt. Vernon v. Dennis, 177

Fischer v. Union Trust Co., 117

Fisher v. Berg, 412

Fisher v. Chadwick, 509

F. I. Somers & Sons, Inc. v. Le Clerc, 527

Fitch v. Snedaker, 39, 40

Fitzsimons v. Eagle Brewing Co., 579

Flash v. Powers, 114

Fleigenheimer v. Brogan, 567

Fleming v. Dolfin, 498

Floureau v. Thornhill, 364

Floyd v. Christian Church Widows & Orphans Home of Kentucky, 177

F. M. Gabler, Inc. v. Evans Laboratories, 303

Foakes v. Beer, 124, 126, 147, 157

Fogelson v. Rackfay Constr. Co., 86

Foley v. Classique Coaches, Ltd., 35

Ford v. Mutual Life Ins. Co., 396

Fordson Coal Co. v. Garrard, 553

Forman v. Forman, 381

Forman v. Gadouas, 485

Fort Payne Coal & Iron Co. v. Webster, 260

Fort Scott, City of v. Hickman, 162

Fosmire v. National Sur. Co., 392

Foster v. Adcock, 215

Foster v. L.M.S. Development Co., 273

Fothergill v. McKay Press, 475

Fox v. Avis Rent-A-Car Systems, Inc., 540

Fox v. Grange, 272, 273

Frankfort Distilleries, Inc. v. Burns Bottling Mach. Works, 242

Franklin Co. v. United States, 135

Fraw Realty Co. v. Natonson, 498

Fredeking v. Grimmett, 211

Frederick Raff Co. v. Murphy, 55

Freedman v. Montague Associates, Inc., 514

Freedman v. Rector, Wardens & Vestrymen of St. Mathias Parish, 252, 253

Freeman v. Continental Gin Co., 76, 86

Freeman v. Foss, 493

Freeman v. Freeman, 174

Freeman v. Poole, 24

Freer v. J. G. Putnam Funeral Home, Inc., 384, 397

French v. McAnarney, 556

Frick Co. v. Rubel Corp., 368

Fricker v. Uddo & Taormina Co., 429

Fried v. Fisher, 180, 530

Frost v. Knight, 281

Frostifresh Corp. v. Reynoso, 113

Frye v. Hubbell, 127

Fugate v. Walker, 217

Fursmidt v. Hotel Abbey Holding Corp., 238, 241, 242

F. W. Lang Co. v. Fleet, 49

Gail v. Gail, 272

Galbreath-Ruffin Corp. v. 40th and 3rd Corp., 570

Gall v. Gall, 496
Gallagher v. Finch, Pruyn & Co., 472
Galt v. Willingham, 306
Galveston, H. & S. A. R. R. v. Eubanks, 351
Galvin v. Prentice, 496
Ga Nun v. Palmer, 286
Garden State Plaza Corp. v. S. S. Kresge Corp., 87
Gardiner v. Gardiner, 193
Garnette Products Co. v. Arthur H. Newmann & Co., 377
Gary v. Central of Georgia Ry., 352
Gavin v. Burton, 201
Gehres v. Ater, 578
Geismer v. Lake Shore & Michigan So. Ry., 306
Gendreau v. North American Life & Cas. Co., 200
Gendron v. Jacoby, 546
General Bronze Corp. v. Schmeling, 543
General Credit Corp. v. Imperial Cas. & Indem. Co., 233, 394
General Discount Corp. v. Sadowski, 86
General Electric Credit Corp. v. Tidenberg, 421
General Grain, Inc. v. International Harvester Co., 552
Gennett v. Smith, 394
Gentile Bros. Corp. v. Rowena Homes, Inc., 488
Gentry v. Harrison, 352
Geo. V. Clark Co. v. New York, N. H. & H. R. Co., 430
Georgia Power Co. v. Roper, 219
Georgian Co. v. Bloom, 21
Gerhardt v. Continental Ins. Cos., 111
Gerisch v. Herold, 241
Gerke, In re Estate of, 153
German Fruit Co. v. Western Union Tel. Co., 66
Gerndt v. Conradt, 488
Gerruth Realty Co. v. Pire, 139
Gershman v. Metropolitan Life Ins. Co., 164
Gerstner v. Lithocraft Studios, Inc., 527
Gerzof v. Sweeney, 198
Gianni v. R. Russel & Co., 81, 82, 83
Gibraltar Realty Corp. v. Mt. Vernon Trust Co., 420
Gibson v. Cranage, 240, 241
Gibson v. Hall, 205
Gifford v. Corrigan, 395, 396
Gillingham v. Brown, 158
Gilman's Adm'x, In re, 553
Gilmore v. Cohen, 365
Gingrich v. Rogers, 219
Ginsberg Mach. Co. v. J. & H. Label Processing Corp., 479
Gitelson v. Du Pont, 96
Glades County v. Detroit Fidelity & Sur. Co., 511
Glaholm v. Hays, 236
Glass v. Springfield L. I. Cemetery Soc., 423
Glass v. Swimaster Corp., 545
Glassman v. Gerstein, 139, 234
Gleason v. Mann, 555

Glen Cove Marina, Inc. v. Vessel Little Jennie, 247, 275
Glen Navigation Corp. v. Trodden, 169
Glidden Co. v. Hellenic Lines, Ltd., 316
Globe Ref. Co. v. Landa Cotton Oil Co., 331
Globe & Rutgers Fire Ins. Co. v. Jones, 410
G. Loewus & Co. v. Vischia, 140
Glover v. Jewish War Veterans, 39
Godburn v. Meserve, 265
Godson v. McFadden, 351
Goetz v. Hubbell, 483
Goldbard v. Empire State Mut. Life Ins. Co., 524
Goldfarb v. C. & K. Purchasing Corp., 426
Goldie-Klenert Distrib. Co. v. Bothwell, 455
Goldstein v. National Liberty Ins. Co., 394
Goldstein's Estate, In re, 164
Goodman v. Dicker, 182, 183, 185
Goodrich v. Northwestern Tel. Exch. Co., 547
Goodwin v. Cabot Amusement Co., 295
Goodwin v. Jacksonville Gas Corp., 230
Gorden's Estate, In re, 48
Gorrell v. Greensboro Water Supply Co., 389
Gorringe v. Read, 577
Gottlieb v. Charles Schribner's Sons, 128
Goulding v. Davidson, 162
Graddon v. Knight, 176
Graham v. American Eagle Fire Ins. Co., 233
Graham v. Graham, 492
Graham v. Niagara Fire Ins. Co., 227
Graham v. San Antonio Mach. & Supply Corp., 273
Graham Paper Co. v. Pembroke, 424
Grand View Bldg. Ass'n v. Northern Assur. Co. of London, 270
Grantham v. Grantham, 496
Graves v. Johnson, 566
Graves v. Northern N. Y. Pub. Co., 15
Gray v. Barton, 126
Gray v. Gardner, 228
Gray v. Martino, 120
Gray v. Meek, 259
Graybar Electric Co. v. John A. Volpe Constr. Co., 393
Grayson v. Irvmar Realty, 341
Great Atlantic & Pacific Tea Co. v. Atchison, T. & S. F. Ry., 328, 330
Great Northern R. Co. v. Witham, 44, 133, 146
Great Western Cas. Co. v. Truck Ins. Exch., 87
Green v. Cresswell, 458
Green v. Green, 205, 379
Green v. Russell, 378
Greenberg v. Evening Post Ass'n, 578
Greene, In re, 154
Greensboro Morris Plan Co. v. Palmer, 211
Greenspan v. Slate, 11, 372
Greentree v. Rosenstock, 426
Greenwich Plumbing & Heating Co. v. A. Barbaresi & Son, Inc., 84
Greer v. Tweed, 112

Gregory v. Lee, 212, 213
Greiner v. Greiner, 174, 179
Griffin v. Colver, 335
Griffin v. Hoag, 454
Griffin v. Louisville Trust Co., 404
Griffith v. Hicks, 527
Grim v. Cheatwood, 576
Grinnell Co. v. Voorhees, 349
Grissom v. Beidleman, 213
Grobarchik v. Nasa Mort. & Inv. Co., 242
Gronvold v. Whaley, 472
Groves v. John Wunder Co., 362, 363
Gruber v. Friedman, 509
Gruber v. S–M News Co., 339
Guerini Stone Co. v. P. J. Carlin Constr. Co., 244, 361
Guerrette v. Cheetham, 230
Guerrieri v. Severini, 286
Guthing v. Lynn, 31

Hackenheimer v. Kurtzmann, 369
Hacker Pipe & Supply Co. v. Chapman Valve Mfg. Co., 337
Hadley v. Baxendale, 329–332, 341, 346
Hagerty v. Hagerty, 174
Haigh v. Brooks, 107, 119
Haldey v. Baxendale, 333
Hale v. Kreisel, 494
Hall v. Butterfield, 209
Hall v. Fuller, 118
Hall v. Meyrick, 341
Hamer v. Sidway, 108, 115, 173
Hamill v. Maryland Cas. Co., 380
Hamilton v. Wosepka, 98
Hamilton Constr. Co. v. Board of Public Instruction of Dade County, 230
Hammond v. Hannin, 365
Hammond Coal Co. v. Lewis, 446
Hand v. Heslet, 513
Hand v. Osgood, 476
Handy v. Bliss, 249
Hanford v. Connecticut Fair Ass'n, 308
Hanley v. Savannah Bank & Trust Co., 574
Hanna v. Florence Iron Co. of Wisconsin, 262
Harbor v. Morgan, 525
Hardin v. Eska Co., 339
Hardy v. Dyas, 219
Harlow v. Kingston, 221
Harper v. Fairley, 157
Harper v. Futrell, 561
Harrington v. Bochenski, 578
Harrington v. Taylor, 155
Harris v. Clinton, 84
Harris v. Guaranty Financial Corp., 563
Harris v. Home Indemnity Co., 475
Harris v. Lillis, 181
Harris v. McKay, 189
Harris v. North British & Mercantile Ins. Co., 227

Harris v. Raughton, 213
Harris v. Watson, 166
Harris v. White, 560
Harrison v. Birrell, 102
Harrod v. Kelly Adjustment Co., 204
Harry Rubin & Sons, Inc. v. Consolidated Pipe Co. of America, Inc., 486
Hart Publications, Inc. v. Kaplan, 567
Hartford Accident & Indem. Co. v. Anderson, 87
Hartford-Connecticut Trust Co. v. Divine, 188
Hartman v. Everett, 544
Hartman v. Pistorius, 395
Hartol Products v. Prudential Ins. Co. of America, 111
Hartsville Oil Mill v. United States, 167
Hartwell Corp. v. Bumb, 354
Harvey v. Facey, 20
Hasselbusch v. Mohmking, 326
Hathaway v. Lynn, 369
Hatten's Estate, In re, 154
Hauswald v. Katz, 106
Haveg Corp. v. Guyer, 180
Hawkins v. Graham, 240
Hawkins v. McGee, 18
Hawley v. Moody, 493
Hay v. Fortier, 144
Hayden v. Hoadley, 87
Hayes v. Gross, 303
Haynes, Spencer & Co. v. Second Baptist Church, 303
H. B. Deal Constr. Co. v. Labor Discount Center, Inc., 99
H. B. Deal & Co. v. Head, 389
H. B. Zachry Co. v. O'Brien, 27
Healy v. Brewster, 120
Hebert v. Dewey, 239
Hechinger v. Ulacia, 78
Hecker, Succession of, 199
Heiman v. Bishop, 343
Heins v. Byers, 399, 400
Held v. Goldsmith, 305
Helene Curtis Indus., Inc. v. United States, 318
Helgar Corp. v. Warner's Features, Inc., 256
Henderson v. Berce, 338
Hendrickson v. International Harvester Co., 47
Henningsen v. Bloomfield Motors, Inc., 6, 39, 111
Henry v. Knight, 220
Henry v. Murphy, 398
Henry v. Root, 199, 204, 206, 535
Hermitage Co. v. Levine, 291
Herren v. Harris, Cortner & Co., 307
Herrington v. Davitt, 155, 157
Hester v. New Amsterdam Cas. Co., 170
Hicks v. Bush, 77, 86
Higgins v. Gager, 473
Higgins v. Lessig, 15
Higgs v. De Maziroff, 86
Hill v. Breeden, 514
Hill v. Dodge, 161

Hill v. Grat, 451
Hill v. Hill, 556
Hill v. Schultz, 574
Hill v. Waxberg, 48
Hillowitz, In re Estate of, 384
Hinckley v. Giberson, 554
Hines v. Cheshire, 208
Hipskind Heating & Plumbing Co. v. General Industries, Inc., 303
Hiss v. Hiss, 483
Hobbs v. Boatright, 576
Hobbs v. Brush Electric Light Co., 474
Hobbs v. Massasoit Whip Co., 46
Hoche Productions, S. A. v. Jayark Films Corp., 327
Hochman v. Zigler's, Inc., 167
Hochster v. De La Tour, 279–282, 287
Hodge v. Feiner, 212
Hoehne Ditch Co. v. John Flood Ditch Co., 350
Hoekzema v. Van Haften, 566
Hoffman v. Lee Nashem Motors, Inc., 561
Hoffman v. Red Owl Stores, 182, 183, 186
Hogland v. Klein, 350
Hohenstein v. S. M. H. Trading Corp., 98
Hohmann & Barnard, Inc. v. Sciaky Bros., 77
Holden, In re, 407
Holland v. Martinson, 155
Hollenbeck v. Guardian Nat. Life Ins. Co., 155
Hollwedel v. Duffy-Mott Co., 351
Holly v. First Nat. Bank, 122
Holman v. Johnson, 566
Holsomback v. Caldwell, 118
Holt, In re, 427
Holt v. Akarman, 156
Holt v. American Woolen Co., 423, 428
Holt v. Swenson, 46
Holt v. United Security Life Ins. Co., 338
Holt v. Ward Clarencieux, 132, 200
Holton v. Monarch Motor Car Co., 241
Home, The v. Selling, 384
Home Gas Co. v. Magnolia Petroleum Co., 61
Home Owners' Loan Corp. v. Gotwals, 463
Homer v. Shaw, 420
Homestake-Sapin Partners v. United States, 98
Hong v. Independent School Dist. No. 245 of Polk County, 246
Hood v. Hartshorn, 311
Hood v. Webster, 107
Hook v. Harmon Nat. Real Estate Corp., 206
Hoover, Inc. v. McCullough Indus., Inc., 96
Hoover Motor Exp. Co. v. Clements Paper Co., 59
Hopper v. Lennen & Mitchell, Inc., 475
Hopwood Plays, Inc. v. Kemper, 528
Horan v. John F. Trommer, Inc., 169
Horn v. Ketelas, 562
Horne v. Midland R. R., 331
Horner v. Frazier, 464
Horowitz v. Bergan Associates, Inc., 257

Horsfield v. Gedicks, 174
Hosang v. Minor, 259
Hotchkiss v. National City Bank of N. Y., 14
Hotz v. Equitable Life Assur. Soc., 41, 129
Household Fire & Carriage Acc. Ins. Co. v. Grant, 63
Houser & Harnis Mfg. Co. v. McKay, 377
Housing Authority v. T. Miller & Sons, 56
Hovey v. Hobson, 216
Howard v. Daly, 59
Howard v. Lebby, 570
Howell v. Coupland, 299
Howell v. Stewart, 566
Hoxie v. Home Ins. Co., 269
H. R. Moch Co. v. Rensselaer Water Co., 381, 388, 389, 391
Hudson, In re, 176
Hudson v. Yonkers Fruit Co., 128, 129
Hudson City Contracting Co. v. Jersey City Incinerator Authority, 198
Huggin's Estate, In re, 408
Hughes v. Jones, 216, 217
Hughes v. Murphy, 200
Hull v. Hostettler, 417
Hull v. Ruggles, 566
Hull-Dobbs, Inc. v. Mallicoat, 88
Hume v. Kirkwood, 193
Hunt Foods & Indus., Inc. v. Doliner, 77, 88
Hurley v. Donovan, 489
Hurley v. Hurley, 463
Hurst Hardware Co. v. Goodman, 454
Hurwitz v. Barr, 200
Hurwitz v. David K. Richards & Co., 289
Hylte Bruks Aktiebolag v. Babcock & Wilcox Co., 383

Iasigi v. Rosenstein, 303
I. H. P. Corp. v. 210 Central Park South Corp., 327
Illinois Cent. R. R. v. Crail, 344
Imperator Realty Co v. Tull, 179, 268, 271, 490
Imperial Refining Co. v. Kanotek Refining Co., 434
Indiana Mfg. Co. v. Hayes, 49, 53
Industrial Packaging Prods. Co. v. Fort Pitt Packaging Int'l, Inc., 429
Ingram v. Little, 42
Inman v. Clyde Hall Drilling Co., 227, 230
Intercontinental Hotels Corp. (P.R.) v. Golden, 558
Intercontinental Planning, Ltd. v. Daystrom, Inc., 485
International Accountants Soc'y v. Santana, 206
International Broth. of Boilermakers v. Braswell, 327
International Filter Co. v. Conroe Gin, Ice & Light Co., 45
International Harvester Co. v. Olson, 377
International Paper Co. v. Rockefeller, 299
International Ry. v. Rann, 389
International Text Book Co. v. Connelly, 204, 205, 208, 212, 214, 215
Iron Trade Products v. Wilkoff Co., 267
Isle of Mull, The, 314

Israle v. Jones, 514
Israle v. Luckenbach S. S. Co., 305
Iverson v. Cirkel, 488
I. & I. Holding Corp. v. Gainsburg, 177

Jackson v. Copeland, 110
Jackson v. Kemp, 179
Jackson v. Pennsylvania R. R., 527
Jacob & Youngs, Inc. v. Kent, 249, 362
Jacobs v. J. C. Penney Co., 122
Jacobs, Marcus & Co. v. Credit Lyonnais, 305
Jacobson & Co. v. International Environment Corp., 543
Jaffray v. Davis, 125
James v. Burchell, 260
James v. P. B. Price Constr. Co., 48
James Baird Co. v. Gimbel Bros., Inc., 181
James Stewart & Co v. Law, 391
Jameson v. Board of Ed., 294
Jankowski v. Jankowski, 416
Jaquith v. Hudson, 367
Jardine Estates, Inc. v. Donna Brook Corp., 248
Jarro Bldg. Indus. Corp. v. Schwartz, 360
Jaynes v. Petoskey, 484
Jefferson v. Sinclair Ref. Co., 390
Jemison v. Tindall, 406
Jennings v. Lyons, 316
Jerome v. Queen City Cycle Co., 246
Jewel Box Stores Corp. v. Morrow, 541
J. J. White, Inc. v. Metropolitan Merchandise Mart, 327
J. K. Rishel Furniture Co. v. Stuyvesant Co., 349
J. K. Welding Co. v. W. J. Halloran Steel Erection Co., 280
John A. Roebling's Sons Co. v. Lock-Stitch Fence Co., 287
John E. Rosasco Creameries, Inc. v. Cohen, 569, 570
John Hancock Mut. Life Ins. Co. v. Cohen, 290
John P. Bleeg Co. v. Peterson, 217
John Service, Inc. v. Goodnow-Pearson Co., 273
John Thallon & Co. v. Edsil Trading Corp., 470
Johnson v. Campagna, 87
Johnson v. Capital City Ford Co., 22
Johnson v. Holmes Tuttle Lincoln-Mercury, Inc., 391
Johnson v. Mutual Benefit Health & Accident Ass'n of Omaha, Neb., 270
Johnson v. Newberry, 213
Johnson v. Northwestern Mut. Life Ins. Co., 209
Johnson v. School Dist. No. 12, Wallowa County, 241
Johnson v. Starr, 280
Johnson v. Storie, 204, 205
Johnson v. Vickers, 432
Johnston v. Bowersock, 475
Johnston v. Fargo, 552
Johnston v. Gilbert, 517
Johnston v. Rodis, 18
Johnston Bros. v. Rogers Bros., 26

Johnstone v. Milling, 287
Jolley v. Georgeff, 369
Jones v. Benedict, 535
Jones v. Caldwell, 201
Jones v. Cooper, 445
Jones v. Godwin, 204
Jones v. Jones, 158
Jones v. Martin, 419
Jones v. Milner, 210
Jones v. Pettigrew, 488
Jones v. Smith, 117
Jones v. Union Central Life Ins. Co., 58
Jordan v. Dobbins, 58
Joseph v. Sears Roebuck & Co., 111, 473
Joseph Schultz & Co. v. Camden Fire Ins. Ass'n, 48
Jozovich v. Central Cal. Berry Grower's Ass'n, 259
J. T. Stark Grain Co. v. Harry Bros. Co., 364
Julian v. Gold, 126
Julian C. Cohen Salvage Corp. v. Eastern Electric Sales Co., 486
J. Weinstein & Sons v. New York, 367
J. & G. Constr. Co. v. Freeport Coal Co., 535

Kadow v. Cronin, 262
Kahle v. Mt. Vernon Trust Co., 342
Kahn v. Waldman, 454
Kall v. W. B. Block Co., 128
Kamerman v. United States, 554
Kane v. Hood, 258
Kansas City, M. & O. Ry. v. Bell, 340
Karpinski v. Collins, 575
Karvalsky v. Becker, 522
Kay v. Kay, 220
Kay v. Spencer, 148
Keane v. Aetna Life Ins. Co., 146
Kearley v. Thomson, 578
Kearns v. Andree, 35
Kehm Corp. v. United States, 266, 359
Kehoe v. Borough of Rutherford, 362
Keith & Hastings v. Miles, 120
Keller v. Holderman, 15
Kellner v. Kellner, 460
Kellogg v. Iowa State Traveling Men's Ass'n, 129
Kelly, Matter of, 56
Kelly v. Security Mut. Life Ins. Co., 291
Kemp v. Kemp, 497
Kendall v. Ewert, 221
Kendall v. West, 241
Kennedy v. City of N. Y., 293
Kenrich Corp. v. Miller, 402, 416, 553
Kent v. Agard, 562
Keppelon v. W. M. Ritter Flooring Corp., 263
Kerr S. S. Co. v. Radio Corp. of America, 334
Keser v. Chagnon, 211
Key v. Kingwood Oil Co., 347
Kilgore v. Cross, 217
Kilmer v. Smith, 385

Kindler v. Anderson, 227
King v. Duluth, M. & N. Ry., 122
King v. King, 556
King Constr. Co. v. W. M. Smith Elec. Co., 167
King Metal Products, Inc. v. Workmen's Compensation Bd., 169
King's Heirs v. Thompson, 174
Kinser Constr. Co. v. State, 302, 314
Kinston v. Preston, 235
Kirk v. Brentwood Manor Homes, Inc., 517
Kirkland v. Archbold, 252
Kirksey v. Kirksey, 114, 173
Kitchin v. Mori, 252
Klar v. H. & M. Parcel Room, Inc., 39, 552
Klauber v. San Diego Street Car Co., 305
Kline v. L'Amoureaux, 200, 213, 219
Kline v. Robinson, 562
Kludt v. Connett, 483
Knapp v. Knapp, 534
Kneeland v. Emerton, 567
Knight Newspapers, Inc. v. United States, 373
Knowlton v. Parsons, 503
Koenig v. Curran's Restaurant & Baking Co., 509
Koletsky v. Resnik, 156
Komp v. Raymond, 116
Konitsky v. Meyer, 30
Koplin v. Faulkner, 348
Kopp v. Fink, 155
Kortright v. Cady, 532
Koth v. County Bd. of Educ. of Jasper County, 194
Kramer v. Wolf Cigar Stores Co., 352
Krauss v. Greenbarg, 331
Krell v. Henry, 312, 313
Kresge Dep't Stores, Inc. v. Young, 43
Krohn v. Dustin, 462, 484
Kromer v. Heim, 525
Kronprinzessin Cecilie, The, 308
Kruce v. Lakeside Biscuit Co., 295
Kuhl v. School Dist. No. 76, p. 305
Kukla v. Perry, 574
Kummli v. Myers, 272
Kunkle v. Jaffe, 349
Kurland v. United Pac. Ins. Co., 96
Kuss Mach. Tool & Die Co. v. El-Tronics, Inc., 31
Kyner v. Clark, 394
K & G Constr. Co. v. Harris, 244, 273

Lach v. Cahill, 139, 143, 234
Lachs v. Fidelity & Cas. Co., 111
La Dam v. Squires, 148
Ladd v. General Ins. Co., 522, 523
Lafferty v. Cole, 128
Lait v. Leon, 386
Laitner Plumbing & Heating Co. v. McThomas, 111
Lakeman v. Pollard, 308
L. Albert & Son v. Armstrong Rubber Co., 339
La Mourea v. Rhude, 381 382, 388

L'Amoureux v. Crosby, 213, 217, 220
Lamper's Case, 402
Lampleigh v. Brathwait, 151, 153
Lanfier v. Lanfier, 106
Lange v. United States, 122
Langel v. Betz, 434
Langer v. Superior Steel Corp., 184
Langfan v. Walzer, 265
Langlois v. Langlois, 524
La Rosa v. Nichols, 210
Larscy v. T. Hogan & Sons, Inc., 521
La Salle Extension University v. Campbell, 213
Latrobe v. Dietrich, 208
Lattimore v. Harsen, 120
Lawhead v. Booth, 117
Lawrence v. Anderson, 446
Lawrence v. Fox, 379, 384, 395
Lawrence v. Harrington, 156
Lawrence v. Hicks, 554
Lawrence v. Miller, 252
Lawrence, Village of v. Greenwood, 343
Lawson v. American Motorists Ins. Corp., 227
Lazarus v. American Motors Corp., 36, 73
Lazzara v. Wisconsin Boxing Club, 311
Leach v. Crucible Center Co., 485
Leahy v. Campbell, 496
LeBel v. McCoy, 244
Ledford v. Atkins, 276
Lee v. Muggeridge, 151
Lee v. Ricca, 513
Lee v. Savannah Guano Co., 120
Lee v. Thompson, 206
Leet v. Jones, 432
Lefils & Christian v. Sugg, 213, 215
Lefkowitz v. Great Minneapolis Surplus Store, 22
Lehman v. Stout, 396
Le John Mfg. Co. v. Webb, 546
Lemke v. Larsen Co., 98
Lenco, Inc. v. Hirschfeld, 369
Lenz v. Chicago & N. W. Ry., 381
Leo F. Piazza Paving Co. v. Bebek & Brkich, 181
Leonard v. Martling, 488
Leonard v. New York, Albany & Buffalo Electro-Magnetic Tel. Co., 331, 333, 347
Leonard v. Vredenburgh, 456
Leopold v. Rock-ola Mfg. Corp., 262
Lesnick v. Pratt, 203, 211
Lesser-Goldman Cotton Co. v. Merchants' & Planters' Bank, 449
Levicoff v. Richard I. Rubin & Co., 266
Levine v. Blumenthal, 126
Levy v. Empire Ins. Co., 394
Levy v. Rothfeld, 498
L. E. Whitlock Truck Serv., Inc. v. Regal Drilling Co., 332, 333
Lewis v. Benedict Coal Corp., 394

Lewis v. Browning, 65
Lewis v. Van Cleve, 211
Lewy v. Crawford, 578
Lexington Housing Authority v. Continental Cas. Co., 115
Leyse v. Leyse, 77
Liberty Navigation & Trading Co. v. Kinoshita & Co., 328, 348
Lichter v. Goss, 273
Lieberman v. Templar Motor Co., 328, 361, 490
Liebman v. Rosenthal, 575, 579
Liebreich v. Tyler State Bank & Trust Co., 122, 127
Lilienthal v. Kaufman, 198
Linch v. Sanders, 220
Lindell v. Lindell, 174
Line v. Nelson, 506
Lingenfelder v. Wainwright Brewing Co., 121, 166
Linn v. Employers Reins. Corp., 66
Linwood Harvestore, Inc. v. Cannon, 420
Linzer v. Weitzen, 156
Little v. Blunt, 156
Littlejohn v. Shaw, 275
Livermore Foundry & Mach. Co. v. Union Compress & Storage Co., 341
Livingston v. Evans, 57
Lizza & Sons, Inc. v. D'Onfro, 28
Lloyd v. Murphy, 312, 313, 316
Local Loan Co. v. Hunt, 415
Lockman v. Cobb, 576
Locks v. Wade, 348
Loeb v. Gendel, 178
Loeb v. Johnson, 115
Loegler v. C. V. Hill & Co., 434
Loew v. Doremus, 555
Logan v. Glass, 396
Long v. Chronicle Publishing Co., 60
Long v. Foster & Associates, 135
Longenecker v. Brommer, 273
Loraw v. Nissley, 189, 194
Lorimer v. Goff, 502
Lorimer v. Knack Coal Co., 511
Loring v. City of Boston, 56
Los Angeles Traction Co. v. Wilshire, 62
Losei Realty Corp. v. City of New York, 346, 364
Loudenback Fertilizer Co. v. Tenn. Phosphate Co., 140
Loudon v. Taxing Dist., 359
Louis Steinbaum Real Estate Co. v. Maltz, 343
Louisville, City of v. Thomas, 547
Louisville Packing Co. v. Crain, 286
Louisville Soap Co. v. Taylor, 311
Louisville Tin & Stove Co. v. Lay, 49
Lovett v. Frederick Loeser & Co., 21
Lowe's Estate, In re, 572
Lowy v. United Pac. Ins. Co., 249, 255
Lozier Auto. Exchange v. Interstate Cas. Co., 295

Lucas v. Hamm, 381
Lucas v. Western Union Tel. Co., 63
Lucy v. Zehmer, 15, 220
Ludington v. Bell, 126
Lukens Iron & Steel Co. v. Hartmann-Greiling Co., 355
Lumber Underwriters of New York v. Rife, 270
Lund v. Bruflat, 573
Lundstrom v. Radio Corp. of America, 113, 561
Lusk-Harbison-Jones, Inc. v. Universal Credit Co., 176, 179
L. Y. Douglas v. City of Dunedin, 139
Lynch v. Johnson, 213
Lynch v. Stebbins, 375
Lynch v. Webb City School Dist. No. 92, p. 63
Lynn v. Seby, 252
Lyon v. Big Bend Developing Co., 481.
Lyon v. Mitchell, 545
Lyons v. National Savings Bank, 563

Maberry v. Western Cas. & Sur. Co., 292
Mabley & Carew Co. v. Borden, 184
McAleer v. McNally Pittsburgh Mfg. Co., 351
McAllister v. Drapeau, 576
McAnarney v. Newark Fire Ins. Co., 342, 344
McCall Co. v. Wright, 542
McCann v. City of Albany, 368
McCarthy v. Pieret, 384
McCarthy v. Santangelo, 553
McCarthy v. Tally, 368
McClelland v. Climax Hosiery Mills, 345
McCloskey & Co. v. Minweld Steel Co., 283
McClurg v. Terry, 15
McConnell v. Commonwealth Pictures Corp., 568, 571
McConnico v. Marrs, 381
McCormick v. Littler, 217
McCoy v. Gas Engine & Power Co., 111
McCrowell v. Burson, 495
McCulloch v. Canadian Pac. Ry., 380, 383, 396
McDevitt v. Stokes, 123
McDonald v. Filice, 243
McDonald v. McDonald, 461
McDowell, Pyle & Co. v. Hopfield, 426
McFadden v. Wilder, 226, 245
McFaden v. Nordblom, 524
McGilchrist v. F. W. Woolworth Co., 496
McGirr v. Campbell, 473
McGovern v. City of N. Y., 122
McGrath v. Electrical Constr. Co., 266
MacGreal v. Taylor, 208
McGrew v. Ide Estate Inv. Co., 362
Maciaszek v. Maciaszek, 191
McKanna v. Merry, 215
Mackay v. Dick, 267
McKay Products Corp. v. Jonathan Logan, Inc., 499
McKeever & Co. v. Canonsburg Iron Co., 142
McKenzie v. Harrison, 126

McKeon v. Van Slyck, 48
Mackey v. Shreckengaust, 215
MacKnight Flintic Stone Co. v. Mayor of New York, 302
McLaughlin v. Head, 506
McLeod v. Meyer, 543
McManus v. Arnold Taxi Corp., 215
McMichael v. Price, 140
McMillan v. Lane Wood & Co., 106
McNaughton v. Granite City Auto Sales, Inc., 203
McNussen v. Graybeal, 143
Mactier's Adm'rs v. Frith, 57
Madison Personal Loan, Inc. v. Parker, 562
Maher v. Haycock, 557
Mahoney v. Lincoln Brick Co., 545
Main v. Pratt, 483
Malin v. Ward, 482
Mallory v. Gillett, 455
Mallory v. Lane, 402
Management, Inc. v. Schassberger, 369
Manchester v. Kendall, 416
Mandel v. Liebman, 110, 144
Mange v. Unicorn Press, Inc., 340
Manhattan Savings Institution v. Gottfried Baking Co., 326
Manse v. Hossington, 129
Mansfield v. Lang, 527
Marbe v. George Edwards, Ltd., 352
Marceiliac v. Stevens, 208
Marchetti v. Atchison T. & S. F. Ry., 155
Marchiondo v. Sheck, 62
Marek v. McHardy, 283
Marino v. Nolan, 139, 234
Marks v. Cowdin, 482
Marley v. Consolidated Mortgage Co., 563
Marsico v. Kessler, 481
Marso v. Mankato Clinic, Ltd., 96
Martin v. Elkhorn Coal Corp., 205
Martinson v. Brooks Equip. Leasing, Inc., 99
Martocci v. Greater N. Y. Brewery, Inc., 477, 478, 479, 487
Marvell Light & Ice Co. v. General Electric Co., 336
Maryland Cas Co. v. Mathews, 120
Mascari v. Raines, 567, 569
Mascioni v. I. B. Miller, Inc., 231
Massengale v. Transitron Electric Corp., 382
Massman Constr. Co. v. City of Greenville, 368
Masterson v. Sine, 84, 85, 416
Mastoras v. Chicago, M. & St. P. Ry., 352
Materne v. Horwitz, 549
Matheson v. Gullickson, 555
Matousek v. Quirici, 495
Mattei v. Hopper, 240
Matthews v. Aikin, 447
Matthews v. Staritt, 231
Matthis v. O'Brien, 221

Maughs v. Porter, 114
Mauldin v. Southern Shorthand & Bus. Univ., 213, 215
Mawhinney v. Millbrook Woolen Mills, Inc., 305, 321
Mayfair Fabrics v. Henley, 552
Maze v. Sycamore Homes, Inc., 563
Meadow Brook Nat. Bank v. Bzura, 85
Meagher v. Kavli, 527
Means v. Dierks, 259
Measday v. Sweazea, 570
Mease v. Wagner, 446, 447
Medberry v. Olcovich, 154
Meech v. City of Buffalo, 122
Mellen v. Johnson, 19
Mello v. Coy Real Estate Co., 526
Melotte v. Tucci, 118
Melroy v. Kemmerer, 125
Menter Co. v. Brock, 542
Merchants' Credit Bureau v. Kaoru Akiyama, 204
Meredith, Town of v. Fullerton, 578
Merritt-Chapman & Scott Corp. v. Public Utility Dist. # 2, p. 28
Messersmith v. American Fidelity Co., 550
Messmore v. New York Shot & Lead Co., 356
Metropolitan Life Ins. Co. v. Alterovitz, 270
Metropolitan Life Ins. Co. v. Dunne, 417
Meyer v. Droegemueller, 434
Meyer v. Sullivan, 303
Meyer v. World Concrete, Inc., 557
Meyer Milling Co. v. Baker, 268
Miami Coca-Cola Bottling Co. v. Orange Crush Co., 135
Michigan Cent. R. Co. v. State, 42
Mid-Atlantic Appliances, Inc. v. Morgan, 454
Mid-Century, Ltd. of America v. United Cigar-Whelan Stores Corp., 122
Middlebury College v. Chandler, 213
Mid-Eastern Electronics, Inc. v. First Nat. Bank, 469
Midland Nat. Bank v. Security Elevator Co., 43
Midwest Eng. Co. v. Electric Regulator Corp., 289
Mignot v. Parkhill, 231
Miguel v. Miguel, 243
Miholevich v. Mid-West Mut. Auto Ins. Co., 359
Miles v. City of Wichita, 27
Millen v. Gulesian, 361
Miller v. Baum, 283
Miller v. Coffeen, 113
Miller v. Lawlor, 180, 500
Miller v. Teeter, 162
Miller v. Western College of Toledo, 177
Millerton Agway Co-op. v. Briarcliff Farms, 77, 86
Mills v. Wyman, 154
Milton v. Hudson Sales Corp., 337
Minehan v. Hill, 138
Mineral Park Land Co. v. Howard, 309

Minevitch v. Puleo, 308

Minnesota Linseed Oil Co. v. Collier White Lead Co., 56

Minton v. F. G. Smith Piano Co., 22

Mirizio v. Mirizio, 556

Misner v. Strong, 467

Missouri Pac. R. R. v. Fowler, 343

Mitchel v. Reynolds, 541

Mitchell v. Brewster, 505

Mitchell v. Flintkote Co., 546, 547

Mitchell v. Lewensohn, 351

Mitchell Canneries, Inc. v. United States, 300, 310

Mitchill v. Lath, 79, 80, 85

Mock v. Trustees of First Baptist Church of Newport, 232

Model Vending Co. v. Stanisci, 289

Moers v. Moers, 522, 524

Moline I.F.C. Finance, Inc. v. Soucinek, 269

Monarco v. Lo Greco, 178, 499

Monroe v. Diamond, 256

Montgomery, Matter of, 375

Montgomery v. Stuyvesant Ins. Co., 518

Montgomery Ward & Co. v. Johnson, 23

Montrose Contracting Co. v. County of Westchester, 302

Mooney v. York Iron Co., 374

Moore v. Downing, 193

Moore v. Elmer, 154

Moore v. Plaza Commercial Corp., 563

Moore v. Trott, 191

More v. Bonnet, 544

More v. New York Bowery Fire Ins. Co., 46

Moreira Constr. Co. v. Moretrench Corp., 111

Morgan's Home Equip. Corp. v. Martucci, 543

Morris v. Glaser, 203

Morris Asinof & Sons, Inc. v. Fruenthal, 40

Morrison v. Thoelke, 63

Morrison Flying Service v. Deming Nat. Bank, 404

Morton v. Forsee, 307

Morton v. Maryland Cas. Co., 390

Mosby v. Smith, 318

Moses v. Moses, 497

Moskow v. Marshall, 213

Moss Jellico Coal Co. v. American Ry. Exp. Co., 330

Motor Contract Co. v. Van der Volgen, 421

Mott v. Iossa, 205

Moulton v. Kershaw, 23, 26

Mount Pleasant Stable Co. v. Steinberg, 348

Mt. Vernon Trust Co. v. Bergoff, 16, 179

Muir v. Kane, 161, 162, 494

Mullen v. Hawkins, 107

Muller Enterprises v. Samuel Gerber Adv. Agency, 33

Muncey v. Norfolk & Western Ry. Co., 205

Municipal Metallic Bed Mfg. Corp. v. Dobbs, 566

Murphy v. Leiber, 561

Mutual Life Ins. Co. v. Johnson, 311

Mutual Life Ins. Co. v. O'Donnell, 170

Mutual Milk & Cream Co. v. Prigge, 201

Myers v. Forest Hill Gardens Co., 404

Myers v. Hurley Motor Co., 208, 210

M. & R. Contractors & Builders, Inc. v. Michael, 348

Narragansett Amusement Co. v. Riverside Park Amusement Co., 336

Nassau Supply Co. v. Ice Service Co., 140, 146

Nassoiy v. Tomlinson, 128

National Bank v. Grand Lodge, 390

National Co. v. Navarro, 115

National Packing Co. v. NLRB, 112

National Presto Indus., Inc. v. United States, 318

National Sand & Gravel Co. v. R. H. Beaumont Co., 377

Nationwide Mut. Ins. Co. v. Jackson, 98

Nat Nal Service Stations v. Wolf, 134, 138, 146, 478

Natural Soda Prod. Co. v. City of Los Angeles, 336, 341

Nebraska Wesleyan Univ. v. Griswold's Estate, 177

N. E. D. Holding Co. v. McKinley, 481

Neff v. Landis, 211

Neikirk v. Williams, 119

Nelson v. Boynton, 453

Nelson v. Sandkamp, 199

Neofotistos v. Harvard Brewing Co., 142

Newburger v. American Sur. Co., 78

Newbern v. Fisher, 458

New Domain Oil & Gas Co. v. McKinney, 203

New England Dredging Co. v. Rockport Granite Co., 189

New England Iron Co. v. Gilbert El. R. Co., 432, 433

New England Structures, Inc. v. Loranger, 274

New Era Homes Corp. v. Forster, 254, 255

New Headley Tobacco Warehouse Co. v. Gentry's Ex'r, 58

Newman & Snell's State Bank v. Hunter, 108, 119

New Orleans & N. E. R. R. v. J. H. Miner Saw Mfg. Co., 330

News Syndicate Co. v. Gatti Paper Stock Corp., 63

New York Bank Note Co. v. Hamilton Bank Note Engraving & Printing Co., 433

New York Life Ins. Co. v. Cook, 397

New York Life Ins. Co. v. Viglas, 284, 290

New York, City of, Matter of v. Bedford Bar & Grill, 427

New York Trust Co. v. Island Oil & Transport Corp., 16

New York & Colorado Mining Syndicate & Co. v. Fraser, 341

Nice Ball Bearing Co. v. Bearing Jobbers, 16

Nichols v. Raynbred, 235

Nichols & Shepard Co. v. Snyder, 204

Nicholson v. Ellis, 544

Nicholson v. 300 Broadway Realty Corp., 386
Ninth Avenue & Forty-Second St. Corp. v. Zimmerman, 346
Nixon v. Nixon, 463
N. Litterio & Co. v. Glassman Constr. Co., 181
Noble v. Joseph Burnett Co., 30
Nolan v. Whitney, 239
Noonan v. Indepedence Indem. Co., 364
Norfolk Hosiery & Underwear Mills Co. v. Westheimer, 528
Normandie Shirt Co. v. J. H. & C. K. Eagle, Inc., 307
Norrington v. Wright, 247
North Ala. Dev. Co. v. Short, 399
North American Graphite Corp. v. Allan, 231
North American Philips Co. v. United States, 302
Northern Commercial Co. v. United Airmotive, 176
Northridge v. Moore, 365
North Shore Bottling Co. v. C. Schmidt & Sons, Inc., 479
Northwestern Engineering Co. v. Ellerman, 181
Northwestern Steam Boiler Mfg. Co. v. Great Lakes Engineering Works, 350
Norton v. Edwards, 444
Norwalk Door Closer Co. v. The Eagle Lock & Screw Co., 368
Norwood Nat. Bank v. Allston, 214
Novack v. Bilnor Corp., 17
Novak v. Fontaine Furniture Co., 291
Novosk v. Reznick, 389
No. C–4, The, 306
Nunn v. Justice, 555
Nurnberg v. Dwork, 478
Nussen v. Graybeal, 110

Oakland Electric Co. v. Union Gas & Electric Co., 299
O'Boyle v. Du Bose-Killeen Properties, Inc., 380
O'Brien v. O'Brien, 86
O'Callaghan v. Walter & Beckwith Realty Co., 552
O'Connell v. Merchants' & Police Dist. Tel. Co., 391
O'Donniley v. Kinley, 213
Offord v. Davies, 44
Ogborn v. Hoffman, 207
Oil Investment Co. v. Dallea Petroleum Corp., 563
Old Jordan Mining Co. v. Societé Anonyme des Mines, 48
Olds v. Mapes-Reeve Constr. Co., 348, 349
Oleet v. Pennsylvania Exchange Bank, 167
Oliver v. Campbell, 375
Oliver v. Houdlet, 200
Oliver v. United Mortgage Co., 563
Oliver v. Wyatt, 132
Oliver-Electrical Mfg. Co. v. I. O. Teigen Constr. Co., 356
Olmstead v. Latimer, 123
Olson v. Rasmussen, 110

Olson v. Wilson & Co., 128
Oltarsh v. Aetna Ins. Co., 390
Olwell v. Nye & Nissen Co., 49
O'Malley v. Yacht Kappy, 128
O'Neal v. George E. Breece Lumber Co., 233
O'Neil v. Supreme Council Am. Legion of Honor, 291
Ontario Deciduous Fruit-Growers' Ass'n v. Cutting Fruit-Packing Co., 299
Orbach v. Paramount Pictures Corp., 336
Oregon-Pacific Forest Products Corp. v. Welsh Panel Co., 50
O'Reilly v. Mitchel, 16
Orella v. Johnson, 497
Orkow v. Orkow, 428
Orr v. Doubleday, Page & Co., 55
Orr v. Equitable Mortgage Co., 219
Orvis v. Curtiss, 564
Oscar Schlegal Mfg. Co. v. Peter Cooper's Glue Factory, 140
Osgood v. Central Vt. R. R., 573
Oshinsky v. Lorraine Mfg. Co., 247
Owen v. Tunison, 19
Owens v. Evans, 423
Ownby v. Prisock, 554
Oxborough v. St. Martin, 490
Oxford Commercial Corp. v. Landau, 85, 87, 98, 383, 386, 507

Pace Corp. v. Jackson, 132
Pacific Gas & Electric Co. v. G. W. Thomas Drayage & Rigging Co., 98
Pacific Southwest Trust & Savings Bank v. Mayer, 506
Paddock v. Mason, 309
Page v. Hinchee, 394
Page v. Shainwald, 247
Paige v. Faure, 412, 418, 419
Pakas v. Hollingshead, 294
Palmer v. Fox, 257
Palmer v. Miller, 212
Palmer v. Watson Constr. Co., 244
Palombi v. Volpe, 31
Pankas v. Bell, 216
Paola Gas Co. v. Paola Glass Co., 336
Pape v. Rudolph Bros., Inc., 126
Paper Product Mach. Co. v. Safepack Mills, 412
Paradine v. Jane, 312
Paramount Productions v. Smith, 352
Paris v. Buckner Feed Mill, 337
Parish v. Schwartz, 541
Parker v. Dantzler Foundry & Mach. Works, 42
Parker v. Russell, 280
Parks v. Atlanta News Agency, Inc., 29
Parver v. Matthews-Kadetsky Co., 496
Pasquay v. Pasquay, 488

Patch v. Solar Corp., 315
Patrick v. Putnam, 308
Patterson v. Chapman, 195
Patterson v. Meyerhofer, 266, 267
Paul v. Rosen, 139, 234
Payette v. Fleischman, 212
Payne v. Cave, 23
Pearce v. Hubbard, 365
Pearl v. Lesnick, 18
Pearson v. Williams' Adm'rs, 370
Peckham v. Industrial Sec. Co., 305
Peek v. Derry, 354
Peevyhouse v. Garland Coal & Min. Co., 363
Pennsylvania Co. v. Wilmington Trust Co., 36
Pennsylvania Exchange Bank v. United States, 254
Pennsylvania Retreading Tire Co. v. Goldberg, 370
Peo v. Kennedy, 85
People v. Empire Mut. Life Ins. Co., 340
People v. Gimbel Bros., Inc., 557
People v. Globe Mut. Life Ins. Co., 305
People ex rel. Bourne v. Johnson, 352
Peoples Drug Stores, Inc. v. Fenton Realty Corp.,
     27, 31
People's State Savings Bank v. Cross, 452
Perkins v. City Nat. Bank, 424
Perma Life Mufflers, Inc. v. International Parts
     Corp., 575
Perper v. Edell, 218
Perper v. Fayed, 98
Perreault v. Hall, 106, 145, 169
Perrin v. Pearlstein, 66, 479
Perry v. Dickerson, 295
Pershhall v. Elliott, 154
Peters v. Bower, 19
Peters v. Whitney, 353
Petersen v. Philco Finance Corp., 561
Peterson v. Hegna, 119
Peterson v. Paxton-Pavey Lumber Co., 455
Peterson's Estate, In re, 461
Petrey v. John F. Buckner & Sons, 309
Petropoulos v. Lubienski, 362
Petterson v. Pattberg, 62
Pettit v. Liston, 209
Peyton v. Margiotti, 576
Phelps v. Herro, 290
Philadelphia, City of v. Reeves, 503
Philadelphia Housing Authority v. Turner Constr.
     Co., 302
Phillips v. Alhambra Palace Co., 307, 315
Phillips v. Bowie, 221
Phillips v. Pantages Theatre Corp., 340
Phillips & Colby Constr. Co. v. Seymour, 275
Pickelsimer v. Pickelsimer, 492
Pierce v. Fuller, 367
Pinnel's Case, 124, 125

Piper v. Goodwin, 444
Pirie, Matter of, 190
Pitman v. J. C. Pitman & Sons, Inc., 529
Pittsburgh Steel Co. v. Hollingshead & Blei, 167
Place v. Hayward, 576
Placid Oil Co. v. Humphrey, 290
Plante v. Jacobs, 248
Plant Steel Corp v. National Mach. Exch., Inc., 523
Plimpton v. Curtiss, 472
Plummer v. Northern Pac. Ry. Co., 213
Plunkett v. Atkins, 396
Plunkett v. Comstock, Cheney Co., 289
Plunkett v. Meredith, 464
Plymouth Mut. Life Ins. Co. v. Illinois Mid-Continent
     Life Ins. Co., 98
Poel v. Brunswick-Balke-Collender Co., 50
Poli v. National Bank of Detroit, 203
Polichio v. Oliver Well Works, Inc., 528
Pollack v. Pollack, 290
Polonsky v. Union Federal Savings & Loan Ass'n, 39
Pond v. New Rochelle Water Co., 389
Poole v. Hudson, 217, 220
Pope v. King, 238
Pope Mfg. Co. v. Gormully, 113
Pordage v. Cole, 257
Porter v. Day, 560
Porter v. Jones, 553
Porter v. Wilson, 216
Portfolio v. Rubin, 376
Portuguese-American Bank v. Welles, 416
Pottawatomie Airport & Flying Service, Inc. v. Wing-
     er, 204
Potts v. Moran's Ex'rs, 365
Powell v. Bowen, 553
Prescott v. Jones, 46, 173
President and Directors of Manhattan Co. v. Mono-
     gram Associates, Inc., 422
Press v. Albright, 457
Price v. Easton, 378
Price v. Sanders, 214
Primrose v. Western Union Tel. Co., 333
Prince v. McRae, 48
Princeton Coal Co. v. Dorth, 125
Prior v. Newsom, 174
Proprietors' Realty Co. v. Wohltmann, 313
Providence Tool Co. v. Norris, 545
Provident Tradesmens Bank & Trust Co. v. Pemberton,
     101
Prudential Fed. Savings & Loan Ass'n v. Hartford
     Acc. & Indem. Co., 430
Prudential Ins. Co. v. Franklin Fire Ins. Co., 394
Puckett v. Hoover, 193
Purchasing Associates, Inc. v. Weitz, 541, 542
Purvis v. United States for Use and Benefit of As-
     sociated Sand & Gravel Co., 34

Quality Fin. Co. v. Hurley, 421
Quality Motors, Inc. v. Hays, 200, 208
Quinn v. Feaheny, 60
Quirk v. Bank of Commerce & Trust Co., 474

Raabe v. Squier, 457
Rabinowitz v. People's Nat. Bank, 424
Raffles v. Wichelhaus, 90
Ragan v. Williams, 212, 213
Raible v. Puerto Rico Indus. Dev. Co., 49
Ralston Purina Co. v. Como Feed & Milling Co., 404
Randall v. Morgan, 19
Randall v. Sweet, 214
Randolph v. Castle, 495
Raner v. Goldberg, 139, 316
Rann v. Hughes, 151
Ransome Concrete Mach. Co. v. Moody, 351
Rapant v. Ogsbury, 334
Rauch v. Wander, 343
Real Estate Co. v. Rudolph, 116
Reconstruction Fin. Corp. v. Sherwood Distil. Co., 99
Redfield v. Iowa State Commission, 343
Reed v. Brown, 219
Reed Bros. v. Bluff City Motor Co., 55
Reedy v. Ebsen, 493
Reilly v. Barrett, 521
Reilly v. Connors, 364
Reiner v. North American Newspaper Alliance, 549
Reliance Cooperage Corp. v. Treat, 287, 354
Rennedy v. Kimberley, 118
Renner Co. v. McNeff Bros., 288
Rennie & Laughlin, Inc. v. Chrysler Corp., 269, 270
Reno v. Bull, 354
Reserve Ins. Co. v. Gayle, 529
R. E. Tharp, Inc. v. Miller Hay Co., 527
Reynolds v. Eagle Pencil Co., 41
Reynolds v. Texarkana Constr. Co., 181
Rhode Island Tool Co. v. United States, 63
Rhodes v. Rhodes, 395
Rice v. Butler, 209
Rice v. Farrell, 553
Rice v. Shute, 503
Rich v. Arancio, 254, 256
Richard v. Credit Suisse, 64, 373
Richard Bruce & Co., v. J. Simpson & Co., 137
Richardson v. Mellish, 568
Richardson Press v. Albright, 454
Richland S. S. Co. v. Buffalo Dry Dock Co., 306
Richmond College v. Scott Nuckols Co., 239
Ricketts v. Scothorn, 173
Ricks v. Sumler, 492
Ridder v. Blethen, 382
Riddle v. Backus, 474
Riech v. Bolch, 353
Rigney v. New York Cent. & H. R. R. Co., 391
Riley v. Capital Airlines, Inc., 495

Riley v. Riley, 460
Rineer v. Collins, 495
Riordon v. McCabe, 559
Ripley v. Hazelton, 373
Rispin v. Midnight Oil Co., 368
Ritchie v. White, 120
Rives v. American Ry. Exp. Co., 332
Rizzolo v. Poysher, 239
Robberson Steel Co. v. Harrell, 275
Robert Gordon, Inc. v. Ingersoll-Rand Co., 181, 182
Robertson v. Garvan, 109
Robertson v. Robinson, 547
Robert Wise Plumbing & Heating, Inc. v. Alpine Dev. Co., 428
Robins v. Finestone, 18
Robins Dry Dock & Repair Co. v. Flint, 380
Rochester Lantern Co. v. Stiles & Parker Press Co., 410
Rochester Tel. Co. v. Ross, 389
Rock v. Gaede, 256
Rock v. Vandine, 345
Rockingham County v. Luten Bridge Co., 287
Rockmore v. Lehman, 411, 427, 428
Rodkinson v. Haecker, 527
Roehm v. Horst, 286
Roesch v. W. B. Worthen Co., 548
Rogers v. Becker-Brainard Milling Mach. Co., 374
Rogers v. Galloway Female College, 176
Rolin v. United States, 318
Root v. Allstate Ins. Co., 96
Rose v. Van Mierop, 150
Rose & Frank Co. v. J. R. Crompton, 17
Rosen, In re, 425
Rosenbaum v. United States Credit-System Co., 544
Rosenkranz v. Schreiber Brewing Co., 457
Rosenstein v. Gottfried, 491
Rosenwasser v. Blyn Shoes, Inc., 373
Ross v. Warren, 385
Roth v. Speck, 353
Rothkopf v. Lowry & Co., 305
Rothschild v. Title Guarantee & Trust Co., 268
Roto-Lith, Ltd. v. F. P. Bartlett & Co., 51
Rotondo v. Kay Jewelry Co., 208
Rouse v. United States, 385, 387, 394
Rowland v. Hudson County, 307
Royal Ins. Co. v. Beatty, 46
Royal Paper Box Co. v. E. R. Apt Shoe Co., 142
Royce Chemical Co. v. Sharples Corp., 339
Rubenstein v. Rubenstein, 369
Ruberoid Co. v. Glassman Constr. Co., 417
Rubin v. Dairymen's League Co-op. Ass'n, 146
Russell v. Princeton Laboratories, 135
Russo v. De Bella, 126
Russo v. Hochschild Kohn & Co., 377
Ruud Paint & Varnish Co. v. White, 372
Rye v. Phillips, 122, 127

Safe Deposit & Trust Co. of Baltimore v. Tait, 219

Sagamore Corp. v. Willcutt, 291

St. Paul Mercury Ins. Co. v. Price, 98

St. Regis Paper Co. v. Hill, 119

St. Regis Paper Co. v. Stuart, 512

Salem Trust Co. v. Mfrs. Finance Co., 425

Salesky v. Hat Corp., 396, 397

San Antonio & A. P. R. R. v. Collins, 351

Sancourt Realty Co. v. Dowling, 345

Sanders v. Pottlitzer Bros. Fruit Co., 27

San Diego Land & Town Co. v. Jasper, 344

Sanford v. Luce, 232

Sanford v. Orient Ins. Co., 473

San Joaquin County v. Galletti, 98

Saratoga County Bank v. King, 544

Sargent v. Leonardi, 462

Satz v. Massachusetts Bonding & Ins. Co., 270

Savings Loan & Trust Co. v. Yokley, 563

Scaduto v. Orlando, 270

Scales v. Wiley, 464

Scammell v. Ouston, 35

Scanlan v. Anheuser-Busch, Inc., 33

Sceva v. True, 212

Schafer v. Fraser, 180

Schanzenbach v. Brough, 496

Scheidl v. Universal Aviation Equip., Inc., 386

Schenectady Stove Co. v. Holbrook, 23

Schermerhorn v. De Chambrun, 577

Schieven v. Emerick, 248

Schlanger v. Cowan, 496

Schmith, In re Estate of, 98

Schmoll Fils & Co. v. Wheeler, 483

Schneider v. Ferrigno, 385, 387

Schneider v. Johnson, 217

Schneider v. Turner, 148

Schoenung v. Gallet, 199

Schofield v. Zion's Co-op. Mercantile Institution, 184

School Dist. No. 1 v. Dauchy, 301

Schreiber v. Armstrong, 535

Schroeder v. Mauzy, 175

Schroeder v. Young, 179

Schultz v. Johnson, 541

Schultz v. Oldenburg, 217

Schultz v. Town of Lakeport, 347

Schultz & Son v. Nelson, 365

Schulz v. Fox, 556

Schuman v. Gordon Inv. Corp., 97

Schumm v. Berg, 106, 115

Schwartz v. Greenburg, 14

Schwartz v. Horowitz, 430

Schwartzreich v. Bauman-Basch, Inc., 121, 122, 165, 519, 520.

Schwasnik v. Blandin, 374

Schweizer's Estate, In re, 496

Scialli v. Correale, 318

Scientific Management Institute, Inc. v. Mirrer, 144

Scott v. Erdman, 241

Scott v. J. F. Duthie & Co., 131

Scott v. Mundy & Scott, 470

Scott v. Schisler, 212

Seagirt Realty Corp. v. Chazanof, 567

Seale v. Bates, 436

Seas Shipping Co. v. Commissioner, 342

Seaver v. Phelps, 219

Seaver v. Ransom, 386

Seavey v. Drake, 174

Secor v. Clark, 121

Security Bank v. Finkelstein, 158

Security Stove & Mfg. Co. v. American Ry. Exp. Co., 339

Sedgwick v. Blanchard, 394

See v. See, 295

Seeley v. Peabody, 347

Seeman v. Biemann, 367

Segall v. Finlay, 354

Seibert v. Dunn, 422

Seif v. City of Long Beach, 198

Seligman v. Pinet, 531

Seminara v. Grisman, 220

Semper, Application of, 302

Senner & Kaplan Co. v. Gera Mills, 48

716 Third Ave. Holding Corp., In re, 562

Severini v. Sutter-Butte Canal Co., 347

Seymour v. Armstrong, 22

Seymour v. Oelrichs, 499

S. F. Bowser & Co. v. F. K. Marks & Co., 30

Shanley v. Koehler, 126

Shapira v. United Medical Service, Inc., 48

Shapiro Engineering Corp. v. Francis O. Day Co., 254

Sharp v. United States, 344

Shaw v. Philbrick, 118, 200

Sheimo, In re Estate of, 379

Sheldon v. Haxtun, 160

Sheldon Builder's, Inc. v. Trogan Towers, 234

Shell v. Schmidt, 249, 362, 363

Shepherd v. Shepherd, 207

Shields v. Early, 367

Shipman v. Straitsville Central Mining Co., 512

Short v. Stotts, 460

Shropshire v. Commerce Farm Credit Co., 563

Shuey v. United States, 59

Sidney Stevens Imp. Co. v. Hintze, 373

Siegel v. Hodges, 214

Siegel v. Spear & Co., 175, 187

Siegel & Hodges v. Hodges, 213

Sigmon v. Goldstone, 352

Sikes v. Johnson, 212

Sillman v. 20th Century Fox Film Corp., 417

Silos v. Prindle, 249

Silverstein v. United Cerebral Palsy Ass'n, 69

Silvestri v. Italia Societa per Azioni di Navigazioni, 39

Simmons v. Simmons, 557

Simmons v. United States, 41

Simpson v. Union Oil Co., 575

Simpson Timber Co. v. Palmberg Constr. Co., 98, 302

Simpson & Harper v. Sanders & Jenkins, 68

Sims v. Bardoner, 203

Sims v. Everhardt, 205, 211

Singh v. Kulubya, 575

Sinkwich v. E. F. Drew & Co., 99

Sinva, Inc. v. Merrill, Lynch, Pierce, Fenner & Smith, Inc., 559

Sirkin v. Fourteenth St. Store, 568, 571

Sitlington v. Fulton, 273, 275

Skagerberg v. Blandin Paper Co., 32

Skinner v. Fisher, 119

Skinner v. Tober Foreign Motors, Inc., 165

Slayton v. Barry, 211

Sleeth v. Sampson, 463

Sliman v. Fish, 291

Slingluff v. Franklin Davis Nurseries, Inc., 463

Small v. Sullivan, 550

Smissaert v. Chiodo, 27

Smith v. Kennedy, 111

Smith v. MacDonald, 17

Smith v. Preston, 307

Smith v. Smith, 408, 556

Smith v. State, 39

Smith v. Wade, 203

Smoll v. Webb, 244

Snipes Mountain Co. v. Benz Bros., 299

Socony-Vacuum Oil Co. v. Continental Cas. Co., 393

Somers v. Ferris, 220

Somerset Acres West Homes Ass'n v. Daniels, 499

Sonfield v. Eversole, 77

Sophie v. Ford, 473

Sorenson v. Overland Corp., 456

Southern Constr. Co. v. United States, 98

Southern Rambler Sales, Inc. v. American Motors Corp., 137

Southland Life Ins. Co. v. Egan, 563

Southwestern Gas & Electric Co. v. Stanley, 347

Southwestern Shipping Corp. v. National City Bank, 572

Southwestern Tel. & Tel. Co. v. Krause, 344

Soviero Bros. Contracting Corp. v. City of New York, 227

Spadanuta v. Village of Rockville Centre, 548, 569

Spalding v. Rosa, 307

Spanos v. Skouras Theatres Corp., 570

Sparrowhawk v. Erwin, 218

Spartans Industries, Inc. v. John Pilling Shoe Co., 289

Spaulding v. New England Furniture Co., 212

Specht v. Eastwood-Nealley Corp., 184

Specialties Development Corp. v. C–O–Two Fire Equip. Co., 258, 273

Speelman v. Pascal, 408

Spence v. Erwin, 561

Spence v. Ham, 248

Spence v. Spence, 219

Spencer v. Collins, 216

Spencer v. Harding, 23

Sperry & Hutchinson Co. v. O'Neill-Adams Co., 339

Spiegel v. Metropolitan Life Ins. Co., 176, 186, 187

Spink v. New York, N. H. & H. R. R., 344

Spires v. Hanover Fire Ins. Co., 380

Spitz v. Lesser, 335

Spivak v. Sachs, 570

Sponge Divers' Ass'n, Inc. v. Smith, Kline & French Co., 419

Sponner v. Reserve Life Ins. Co., 184

Spratt v. Paramount Pictures, Inc., 64

Sprecher v. Sprecher, 205

Spurck v. Civil Service Bd., 352

S. S. Steiner, Inc. v. Hill, 273

Stadium Pictures, Inc. v. Walker, 353

Stafford Security Co. v. Kremer, 422

Stallard v. Sutherland, 211

Standard Chautauqua System v. Gift, 418, 432

Standard Oil Co. v. Bertelsen, 542

Standard Oil Co. v. Koch, 482

Standard Oil Co. v. United States, 544

Standard Oil Co. of Cal. v. Perkins, 242

Standard Oil Co. of N. J. v. Southern Pac. Co., 343

Standard Oil Co. of N. Y. v. Central Dredging Co., 364

Standard Oil Co. of Texas v. Lopeno Gas Co., 114

Standard Title Ins. Co. v. United Pac. Ins. Co., 98

Stanek v. White, 155

Stanfield v. W. C. McBride, 397

Stanley v. A. Levy & J. Zentner Co., 481

Stanton v. New York & E. Ry., 326

Stark v. Parker, 251

Starr v. Freeport Dodge, Inc., 471

State v. Commercial Cas. Ins. Co., 302

State by Lefkowitz v. ITM, Inc., 113

State Central Savings Bank v. Hemmy, 404

State ex rel. American Surety Co. of N. Y. v. Haid, 567

State ex rel. Freeman v. Sierra County Bd. of Ed., 351

State ex rel. Hoyt v. Shain, 434

State Factors Corp. v. Sales Factors Corp., 428

State Finance Corp. v. Ballestrini, 84

State for Use of County Court of Randolph Cty. v. R. M. Hudson Paving & Constr. Co., 363

State for Use of Warner Co. v. Massachusetts Bonding & Ins. Co., 128

State St. Furniture Co v. Armour & Co., 416

Stathos v. Murphy, 426, 427

Stees v. Leonard, 301

Stein, In re Estate of, 127

Stephen M. Weld & Co. v. Victory Mfg. Co., 63

Stephens v. Great So. Savings & Loan Ass'n, 379

Stern v. Farah Bros., 311

Sternlieb v. Normandie Nat. Sec. Corp., 210, 211

Steven v. Fidelity & Cas. Co., 111

Stevens & Elkins v. Lewis-Wilson-Hicks Co., 310

Stevenson, Jaques & Co. v. McLean, 61

Stewart v. Hansen, 358

Stewart v. Newbury, 244

Stewart v. Stone, 300

Stewart v. Sullivan County, 391

Stewart v. Wright, 576

Stiefler v. McCullough, 111

Stilk v. Myrick, 166

Stockton v. Department of Employment, 352

Stone v. Freeman, 567, 572, 578

Stone v. Kaufman, 365

Stone v. Roberts Numbering Mach. Co., 547

Stout v. Humphrey, 162

Stover v. Winston Bros. Co., 389

Strang v. Witkowski, 44

Stratford, The v. Seattle Brewing & Malting Co., 313

Stratman's Estate, In re, 162

Stratton v. West States Construction, 523

Straus v. Cunningham, 157

Streich v. General Motors Corp., 138

Stribling v. Ailion, 241

Strodder v. Southern Granite Co., 219

Strong v. Sheffield, 134, 146, 169

Stroud v. Pulaski County Special School Dist., 548

Structural Gypsum Corp. v. National Comm. Title & Mortg. Guar. Co., 404

Struzewski v. Farmers' Fire Ins. Co., 473

Strype v. Lewis, 498

Suburban Land Co. v. Brown, 266

Sullivan v. Winters, 473

Sun Printing & Publishing Ass'n v. Remington Paper & Power Co., 34

Sunseri v. Garcia & Maggini Co., 317

Sunset Beach Amusement Corp. v. Belk, 193

Sunshine Dairy v. Jolly Joan, 528

Superintendent & Trustees v. Bennett, 301

Superior Brassiere v. Zimetbaum, 424

Sutherland v. Wyer, 351

Swain v. Harmount & Woolf Tie Co., 472

Swarts v. Narragansett Electric Lighting Co., 432

Swartz v. Liberman, 120

Swartz v. War Memorial Commission of Rochester, 267

Sweeney v. Veneziano, 408

Sweers v. Malloy, 409

Swift Canadian Co. v. Banet, 313

Swindell & Co. v. First Nat. Bank, 140

Swiss Oil Corp. v. Riggsby, 309

Sykes v. Thompson, 577

Sylvan Crest Sand & Gravel Co. v. United States, 135

Symcox v. Zuk, 565

S & L Vending Corp. v. 52 Thompkins Ave. Rest., Inc., 409

Tague Holding Corp. v. Harris, 261, 365

Tallman v. Franklin, 485

Tampa Shipbldg. & Engineering Co. v. General Constr. Co., 485

Tarbell v. Bomes, 266

Taylor v. Barton-Child Co., 428, 429

Taylor v. Bradley, 341

Taylor v. Caldwell, 296–298, 301, 315

Taylor v. Dutton, 48

Taylor v. Palmer, 431

Taylor v. Saxe, 356

Taylor v. Smith, 48

Taylor v. Steadman, 346

Taylor Freezer Sales Co. v. Sweden Freezer Eastern Corp., 542

Tebo v. Robinson, 158, 232

Terino v. Le Clair, 419, 430

Terry v. Munger, 49

Texas Co. v. Hogarth Shipping Co., 305

Thackeray v. Knight, 518

Thackrah v. Haas, 221

Thatcher v. Merriam, 408, 409

Theiss v. Weiss, 15

Thomas v. Atlantic Coast Line R. R., 550

Thomas v. Carpenter, 295

Thomas v. Dickenson, 462

Thos. J. Dyer Co. v. Bishop Int'l Eng'r Co., 231

Thomas J. Nolan, Inc. v. Martin & William Smith, Inc., 449

Thomas Raby, Inc. v. Ward-Meehan Co., 355

Thomason v. Bescher, 188

Thompson v. Ford, 473

Thompson v. Postal Life Ins. Co., 274

Thompson v. St. Louis Union Trust Co., 461

Thompson-Starett Co. v. La Belle Iron Works, 241

Thomson v. United States, 46

Thomson-Houston Electric Co. v. Durant Land Imp. Co., 259

Thorne v. Deas, 175, 187

Thornton v. City of Birmingham, 343, 344

Thornton v. Schobe, 462

Thosath v. Transport Motor Co., 210

300 West End Ave. Corp. v. Warner, 462, 484

Thrift Wholesale, Inc. v. Malkin-Illion Corp., 336

Throckmerton v. Tracy, 93

Tibbetts Contracting Corp. v. O & E Contracting Co., 112

Tichnor Bros. v. Evans, 257

Tighe v. Morrison, 458
Timmerman v. Stanley, 374
Timmons v. Bostwick, 50
Tinn v. Hoffman & Co., 40
Title Guaranty & Trust Co. v. Pam, 86
Title & Trust Co. v. Durkheimer Inv. Co., 315
Tobey v. Wood, 207
Tobin v. Cody, 543
Tobin v. Union News Co., 338
Tocci v. Lembo, 571
Tode v. Gross, 367, 542
Toledo Edison Co. v. Roberts, 128
Tolnay v. Criterion Film Productions, 352
Tomaso, Feitner & Lane, Inc. v. Brown, 381
Tomko v. Sharp, 175
Tompkins v. Dudley, 301
Tousley v. Atlantic City Ambassador Hotel Corp., 352
Tow v. Miners Memorial Hosp. Ass'n, 78, 240
Town of. See under name of town
Town & Country House & Home Serv. v. Newberry, 542
Townsend v. Standard Indus., Inc., 85
Township of. See under name of township
Tracey v. Brown, 203, 210
Trader v. Lowe, 207
Trafton v. Youngblood, 528
Traiman v. Rappaport, 462
Trainer v. Trumbull, 214
Transatlantic Financing Corp. v. United States, 297, 300, 316
Transbay Constr. Co. v. City of San Francisco, 310
Travelers Ins. Co. v. Workmen's Compensation Appeal Bd., 66, 519
Treiber v. Schaefer, 249
Trenton St. Ry. v. Lawlor, 522
Triangle Waist Co. v. Todd, 343, 353
Tri-Bullion Smelting & Dev. Co. v. Jacobsen, 288
Triple Cities Constr. Co. v. Maryland Cas. Co., 269
Trist v. Child, 544
Troy Parisian, Inc. v. United States, 421
Trudeau v. Poutre, 527
Trustees of Dartmouth College v. Woodward, 3
Trustees of St. Mark's Evang. Lutheran Church v. Miller, 159
TSS Sportswear, Ltd. v. The Swank Shop (Guam) Inc., 382
Tubbs v. Hilliard, 221
Tucker v. Connors, 280
Tunkl v. Regents of Univ. of Cal., 6, 551
Turman Oil Co. v. Sapulpa Ref. Co., 311
Turner v. Central Hardware Co., 22
Turner v. Little, 206
Tussing v. Smith, 194
Tweddle v. Atkinson, 378
Tymon v. Linoki, 484

Ufitec, S. A. v. Trade Bank & Trust Co., 289
Ullsperger v. Meyer, 484
Ulmer v. Farnsworth, 100
Union Central Life Ins. Co. v. Imsland, 522, 524
Union Exch. Nat. Bank v. Joseph, 577
Union Pac. Ry. Co. v. Harris, 222
United Cigar Stores of America, In re, 141
United Security Life Ins. Co. v. Gregory, 33
United Shoe Mach. Co. v. Abbott, 271, 273
United States v. Acme Process Equip. Co., 547, 569
United States v. Addyston Pipe & Steel Co., 540
United States v. Behan, 339, 362
United States v. Bethlehem Steel Co., 367, 368
United States v. Braunstein, 20, 89
United States v. Carpenter, 382, 383
United States v. Citizens & So. Nat. Bank, 101
United States v. City of New York, 483
United States v. Clementon Sewerage Authority, 85
United States v. Curtiss Aeroplane Co., 158
United States v. Fidelity & Deposit Co. of Maryland, 267
United States v. Lutz, 390
United States v. Manton, 544
United States v. Mississippi Val. Generating Co., 548
United States v. Paddock, 546
United States v. Peck, 267
United States v. Seacoast Gas Co., 286
United States v. Spearin, 302
United States v. Wegematic Corp., 318, 547
United States v. Williams, 202
United States v. Yazell, 198
United States ex rel. Adm'r of F. H. A. v. Troy Parisian, Inc., 421
United States ex rel. Wilhelm v. Chain, 44
United States Printing & Lithograph Co. v. Powers, 503
United States Rubber Co. v. Bercher's Royal Tire Service, Inc., 256
Unke v. Thorpe, 300

Valashinas v. Koniuto, 50, 61
Valdes v. Larrinaga, 545
Van Clief v. Van Vechten, 249
Vanetta Velvet Corp. v. Kakunaka & Co., 305
Van Iderstine Co. v. Barnet Leather Co., 239, 490
Van Keuren v. Corkins, 419
Van Werden v. Equitable Life Assur. Soc., 291
Varney v. Ditmars, 30, 34
Vassar v. Camp, 65
Venzke v. Magdanz, 249
Vermont Acceptance Corp. v. Wiltshire, 210
Vernon, City of v. City of Los Angeles, 310
Verstandig v. Schlaffer, 219
Very v. Levy, 522
Vichnes v. Transcontinental & Western Air, Inc., 209

Victoria Laundries (Windsor) Ltd. v. Newman Industries, Ltd., 60, 330, 332
Viles v. Viles, 556
Village of. See under name of village
Vineyard v. Martin, 399
Vinz v. Beatty, 558
Visintine & Co. v. New York, Chicago & St. Louis R. R., 380
Vitty v. Eley, 41
Vogel v. Shaw, 499
Vogt v. Hecker, 303
Vought v. Williams, 239
Vrooman v. Turner, 385, 386, 393
Vulcan Iron Works v. Pittsburgh-Eastern Co., 398
Vulcan Trading Corp. v. Kokomo Steel & Wire Co., 247
V. Valente, Inc. v. Mascitti, 111

Wachtel v. National Alfalfa Journal Co., 340
Wagner v. Graziano Constr. Co., 77, 87
Wakeman v. Wheeler & W. Mfg. Co., 335, 337
Walker v. Ellis, 205
Walker v. Johnson, 472
Walker v. Stokes Bros. & Co., 205
Walker Bank & Trust Co. v. First Security Corp., 392
Wallin v. Highland Park Co., 212
Walnut Street Fed. Savings & Loan Ass'n v. Bernstein, 343
Walter-Wallingford Coal Co. v. A. Himes Coal Co., 518
Walton v. Denhart, 247
Wantulok v. Wantulok, 497
Ward v. Haren, 369
Ward v. Hasbrouck, 476
Ward v. Johnson, 505
Ward v. New York Cent. R. R., 330
Ward v. Vance, 299
Ware v. Mobley, 201
Ware v. Spinney, 578
Warner v. McLay, 362
Warner v. Seaboard Fin. Co., 430
Warner Bros. Pictures, Inc. v. Brodel, 201
Warren, Town of v. Ball, 243
Warrior Constructors, Inc. v. International Union, 27
Wasserman Theatrical Enterprise v. Harris, 308
Watkins v. Curry, 566
Watkins v. Wells, 492
Watkins & Son, Inc. v. Carrig, 122, 127
Watson v. Billings, 211
Watson v. Employers Liability Assur. Corp., 390
Watson v. Gugino, 32
Watson v. Loughran, 343
Watts v. Malatesta, 576
Wavra v. Karr, 345

Way v. Sperry, 155
Waychoff v. Waychoff, 554
Weatherford Oil Tool Co. v. Campbell, 543
Webb v. McGowin, 155
Webb v. Woods, 483
Webbe v. Western Union Tel. Co., 67
Weber's Estate, In re, 220
Wehle v. Haviland, 344
Weightman's Estate, In re, 220
Weilersbacher v. Pittsburgh Brewing Co., 33
Weiner v. Physicians News Serv., Inc., 391
Weitzel v. Brown-Neil Corp., 546, 547
Weitzen, In re, 156
Welch v. Mandeville, 419
Welcome Wagon, Inc. v. Morris, 543
Welcome Wagon Int'l, Inc. v. Pender, 543
Welles v. Brown, 416
Welles-Kahn Co. v. Klein, 157
Wells v. Alexandre, 142
Wells v. Hartford Manilla Co., 282
Wells v. Rau, 530
Wellston Coal Co. v. Franklin Paper Co., 376
Welsh v. Loomis, 125
Wender Presses, Inc. v. United States, 66
Wennall v. Adney, 162
Wesley v. Chandler, 544
Wesley v. United States, 68
West v. Holstrom, 527
West v. Hunt Foods, Inc., 184
West v. Norcross, 386
West Ky. Coal Co. v. Nourse, 110
Westerhold v. Carroll, 381
Western Adv. Co. v. Mid-West Laundries, 349
Western Grain Co. v. Barron G. Collier, Inc., 349
Western Oil Sales Corp. v. Bliss & Wetherbee, 435
Western Transmission Corp. v. Colorado Mainline, Inc., 275
Western Union Tel. Co. v. Abbott Supply Co., 334
Western Union Tel. Co. v. Cowin & Co., 67
Western Union Tel. Co. v. Priester, 67, 334
Western Union Tel. Co. v. Southwick, 347
Westhill Exports, Ltd. v. Pope, 265
Weston v. Boston & M. R. R., 333
Wetherell Bros. v. United States Steel Co., 433
Wharton v. Stoutenburgh, 27
Whelan v. Griffith Consumers Co., 310
Whelchel v. Stennett, 553
White v. Atkins, 254, 255
White v. Kuntz, 126
White v. Miller, 338
White v. Mitchell, 249
White v. Rintoul, 455–457
White v. Schrafft, 243
White v. Seitzman, 563
White v. Upton, 400
White Lighting Co. v. Wolfson, 473, 489

Whitebird v. Eagle-Picher Co., 97

Whitehead v. Burgess, 22

Whitehead v. New York Life Ins. Co., 396

Whitman v. Allen, 208

Whitman v. Anglum, 299

Whittaker Chain Tread Co. v. Standard Auto Supply Co., 128

Wigand v. Bachmann-Bechtel Brewing Co., 142

Wilhelm Lubrication Co. v. Brattrud, 34

Wilhide v. Keystone Ins. Co., 270

Wilhoite v. Beck, 48

Wilkinson v. Heavenrich, 488

Willard v. Claborn, 379

Willard Van Dyke Prods. v. Eastman Kodak Co., 552

Willey v. Terry & Wright, Inc., 101

William Goldman Theatres v. Loew's, 336

Williams v. Bemis, 376

Williams v. Buckler, 210

Williams v. Hankins, 460

Williams v. Paxson Coal Co., 394

Williams v. Walker-Thomas Furniture Co., 113

Williams Mfg. Co. v. Prock, 566

Williamson v. Chicago, R. I. & P. R. Co., 548

Williamson v. Martz, 471

Willis v. Branch, 336

Willmott v. Giarraputo, 34, 139

Wilmington Housing Authority for Use of Simeone v. Fidelity & Deposit Co., 189

Wilson v. Hinman, 446

Wilson v. Oliver Costich Co., 389

Wilson v. Scampoli, 248

Windmuller v. Pope, 261

Winfield v. Dodge, 557

Wing & Bostwick Co. v. U. S. Fidelity & Guaranty Co., 364

Winkenwerder v. Knox, 353

Winslett v. Rice, 84

Winter v. Lewis, 554

Winter Wolff & Co. v. Co-op Lead & Chem. Co., 122, 127

Wipf v. Blake, 158

Wirth & Hamid Fair Booking, Inc. v. Wirth, 120, 369.

Wisconsin Loan & Finance Corp. v. Goodnough, 211

Wisconsin & Mich. Ry. Co. v. Powers, 172

Wise v. Midtown Motors, Inc., 118

Witherbee v. Meyer, 336, 341

Witherell v. Lasky, 240

Witschard v. A. Brody & Sons, Inc., 455

Wittenberg v. Robinov, 86

Wohlford v. Wohlford, 174

Wold v. Grozalsky, 511

Wolfe v. Wallingford Bank & Trust Co., 179

Wolff v. Meyer, 343

Womack v. Maner, 567

Wood v. Bartolino, 313

Wood v. Dodge, 446, 447

Wood v. Lucy, Lady Duff Gordon, 143

Wood v. Moriarty, 398

Woodbury v. United States Cas. Co., 190

Wooldridge v. Lavoie, 204, 209

Wooster v. Crane & Co., 410

Worman Motor Co. v. Hill, 208

W. P. Harlin Constr. Co. v. Utah State Road Commission, 271, 273

W. R. Grace & Co. v. Railway Exp. Agency, Inc., 551

Wright, In re, 427

Wright v. Anderson, 534

Wright v. Sonoma County, 49

Wrightsman v. Brown, 254, 255

Yeager Co., Matter of, 339

Yeargin v. Bramblett, 254

York Glass Co. v. Jubb, 218

Young v. Cockman, 120

Young v. Muhling, 210

Young v. Overbaugh, 174

Yuba, County of v. Mattoon, 321

Zambetti v. Commodores Land Co., 257

Zavelo v. Reeves, 156, 535

Zeyher v. S. S. & S. Mfg. Co., 136

Zimmerman v. Marymor, 239

Zimmerman Bros. & Co. v. First Nat. Bank, 64

Zirk v. Nohr, 196

Zuhak v. Rose, 24

Zupan v. Blumberg, 478

Zurcher v. Modern Plastic Mach. Corp., 430

INDEX

References are to Pages

ABILITY TO PERFORM
Condition precedent, recovery for anticipatory breach, 289.
Impairment of credit, insolvency, 262–263.
Land sale, vendor without title, 261–262.
Proof, necessity after repudiation, 289.

ACCEPTANCE
See also Counter Offer.
Benefits, results of accepting or retaining, 47–49, 128.
Communication,
Bilateral contracts, 45.
Loss in mails, 63.
Mistake in transmission, 66–67.
Offer, dispensing with communication when return promise requested, 45.
Unilateral contracts, 43.
Conditional acceptance,
Acceptance on condition, new terms, 50–55.
Future acceptance distinguished from, 55.
Rejection, condition implied in offer, 61.
Requests or suggestions as, 61.
Conversion by acceptance, 49, 128.
Error, 66–67.
Future, acceptance to take effect in future, 55.
How made,
Bilateral contract, 36, 45, 63–68, 70–73.
Unilateral contract, 36, 43, 61–62, 70–73.
Implied from conduct, 10–11, 36, 45–49.
Acceptance of document, 39.
Accepting or retaining benefits, 47.
Exercise of dominion, 49.
Performance of act requested, 61–62.
Silence, 45–49.
Starting performance, 62, 70–73.
Identical cross offers as, 40.
Intent to accept, necessity, 40–41.
Knowledge of offer, necessity, 38–40.
Late acceptance, 57–58.
Notice, necessity,
Bilateral contracts, 45.
Unilateral contracts, 43.
Offeree, necessity of being promisee, 42.
Offeree signing contract without reading, 39.
Series of contracts, offer, 43–44.
Signature as, 39.
Uniform Commercial Code, 37, 40, 70–73.
Variation from offer, 50–55.
When must knowledge of offer arise, 40.
Who may accept, 41–42.

ACCORD AND SATISFACTION
See also Discharge of Contracts.
Cashing check as assent to offer of accord, 127–130.
Composition with creditors, 125.
Discharge of contract or tort liability, 127–130, 168–169, 521.
Executory bilateral accord at common law, 520–524.
Legislation, 168–169.
Part payment,
Debt before maturity, 124–127.
Liquidated debt, 125.
Substituted agreement compared with executory accord, 524.
Unilateral contract of accord, 524–525.

ACCOUNT STATED
See Discharge of Contracts.

ADEQUACY
See Consideration.

ADVERTISEMENT
Offers, 21–23.
Revocation of offer by, 59.
Reward offered by, 22, 40, 42.

AGREEMENT
Implied, 10, 11.
Leaving an option to one party, effect, 67–68, 133–140.
Mutual assent manifested, 13.
Parties, 9, 13.
Requires communication, 45.

ALEATORY CONTRACTS
Consideration, 138–140.
Definition, aleatory promise, 258.
Duties of performance, independence in, 258.
Kinds, 257–259.
Wagering contract and lottery as, 558–560.

ALTERATION
See also Discharge of Contracts.
Discharge of contract, 534–535.
Nullification by assent or assertion of rights, 534.

AMBIGUITY
Admissibility of extrinsic evidence, 88–94.
Effect, 88, 90–91, 95–96.
Known to offeror, unknown to offeree, 90–93.

ANTICIPATORY REPUDIATION
Alternative remedies after, 287–289.
Applicability, types of contracts, 289–292.

ANTICIPATORY REPUDIATION—Continued
Duty to mitigate damages, 287–288, 346, 357.
Effect of subsequent impossibility, 319–320.
Election, 287–288.
Good faith denial of liability, 284.
Insurance policies, 290–291.
Leases, 291.
Manifested by conduct, 282–283.
Necessity for election, 287–288.
Origin and reasons for doctrine, 278–282.
Present breach of contract, 278–282.
Prospective inability to perform compared, 278–279.
Repudiation, positive, 281–282.
Retraction, 286–287.
Uniform Commercial Code, 284–287.
Unilateral contract, 289–292.

ARBITRATION AND AWARD
See Illegal Contracts.

ARCHITECTS
Certificate, express condition, 238–240.
Condition excused by impossibility, 239, 310–312.
Fraudulent or unreasonable refusal, 238–239.

ASSIGNMENT
Account defined, 405.
Assignor's liability after delegation, 430–431, 435.
Chose in action, meaning, 405.
Conditional assignment, 418.
Conditional rights, 418–419.
Consideration, necessity, 407.
Contract right defined, 405.
Counter-claims against assignee, 422–423.
Defenses available against assignee,
    Anti-assignment provision, 416–417.
    Assignee not to use available defense, parties providing, 421.
    Estoppel, 421.
    Modification of contract, 420.
    Payment, 419.
Defined, 401.
Delegate, liability, 434.
Delegation, meaning, 402, 430–431.
Double assignment, 424–425.
Duties, delegation, 402, 430–431.
Effect,
    Assignment, 403.
    Authorization of assignment, 418.
    Delegating non-delegable duty, 436.
    Prohibition of assignment, 416–417.
    Repudiation by delegating party, 435.
Equitable assignments, 423, 427–429.
Filing by assignee, 425.
Formality required, 406–407.
Future rights, 423, 427–429.
Gratuitous assignments, 407–409.
History, 402–403.
Implied warranties in connection with, 430.
Insolvency of assignor, 435.
Interpretation, 417–418, 434.
Latent equities, 423.
Nature, 403–404.
Non-delegable duties, 431–433.

ASSIGNMENT—Continued
Notice to debtor, 419–420.
Offer, assignment of, 413.
Option contract, assignment of, 413–414.
Order on debtor as, 404.
Partial assignments, 429–430.
Partnership rights, 414–415.
Perfection of assignee's interest, 425.
Priorities,
    Between assignee and attaching creditor, 426–427.
    Between successive assignees, 424–425.
Public policy, assignment contrary to, 415–416.
Revocable assignments, 407.
Rights assignable, 409.
Rights not assignable, 409–413.
    Burden, risk of obligor, materially varying, 410–411.
    Impairment of obtaining return performance, 411–413.
    Materially changing duty of other party, 409–410.
Security agreement, 406.
Security assignment, 405.
Set-offs against assignee, 422–423.
Statute of Frauds, 469.
Sub-assignees, 423.
Uniform Commercial Code, 404–406, 410, 412–413, 417, 425–426, 426–427.
Vesting, 419–420.
Voidable assignments, 418.
Wages, 406, 415–416, 425.

ASSUMPTION OF RISK
Non-cooperation, 264–268.
Reason, denying defense of impossibility and frustration, event foreseeable, 316–317.

AUCTION
By-bidder, 25.
Reserve with and without reserve, 23–24.
Uniform Commercial Code, 23–25.
Who makes offer, 23–24.

AVOIDABLE DAMAGES
See Damages.

BANKRUPTCY
Discharge of the contract, 284–286, 535.
New promise to pay debt discharged by, 155–157.
Prospective inability to perform, 262–263.
Repudiation, 284–286.

BENEFICIARIES
See Third Party Beneficiaries.

BENEFIT
See Consideration.

BID
Offer, 23.
Use of Sub-contractor's bid by prime contractor, 180–182.

BILATERAL CONTRACT
Acceptance by post or telegraph, 63–65.
Communication of acceptance, 45.
Defined, 9–10.

BILATERAL CONTRACT—Continued
Distinguished from unilateral contract, 9–10, 70–73.
Implication, 10–11, 36–37, 45–49.
Intent to accept, necessity, 40–41.
Knowledge of offer, necessity, 38–39.
Mutual promises as, 9–10, 36–37.
Nature, 36.
Offer, series of bilateral contracts, 43–44.
Presumption in favor, 37.

BREACH OF CONTRACT
Accord executory, breach, 520–524.
Anticipatory repudiation, 278–282.
Character, 236–237, 245–247.
Discharge, material breach, election of other party to
    discharge, 236–237, 245–247.
Effect of partial and total breach, 236–237, 245–247.
Materiality, determining factors, 245–247.
Prevention as, 264–268.
    Present breach, 266–268.
Repudiation, 278–282.
    Total breach, 289–292.
Remedies, 287–289.
    Party who commits, 253–257.
Successive actions for breach, 293–295.
Time is of the essence, 247.
Uniform Commercial Code, 284–287.

CANCELLATION
See Discharge of Contracts.

CAPACITY
    See also Corporations; Drunken Persons; Infants;
        Insane Persons.
Convicts, 198.
Married woman, 198.
Municipal corporations, 198.
Spendthrifts, 198.

CERTAINTY
Agreement to agree, 34.
Automatic renewal agreements, 32.
Damages, 334–341.
Effect,
    Indefiniteness, 32, 143–146.
    Part performance of indefinite agreement, 30, 143–
        146.
    Promise, either promise indefinite, 143–146.
Forging, good unilateral contract out of bad bilateral
    contract, 30, 144–146.
Franchise agreement, 33–34.
Hiring at will, 32.
Indefiniteness,
    Duration, 32–34.
    Immaterial terms, 34.
    Material terms, 29.
    Price term, 30–31.
    Quantity term, 21–22, 25–26, 31, 34.
    Subject matter, 31.
    Subsequent definition, cure by, 30, 143–146.
    Time term, 32–34.
Offer, definiteness, necessity, 29.
Permanent employment, 32–33.
Quasi contractual recovery, 30.

CERTAINTY—Continued
Requirements contracts, 31, 140–143.
Terms implied, 30–35.
Terms not implied, 30–35.
Uniform Commercial Code, 31, 33–35.
Where one party may specify assortment, 34–35.

CHAMPERTY
See Illegal Contracts.

CHANGE OF CIRCUMSTANCES, EFFECT
See Conditions.

COMPOSITION WITH CREDITORS
Lesser sum, valid discharge of debt, 124–127.

CONDITION WITHIN PROMISOR'S CONTROL
Collateral duty to bring it about, 139–140, 233–234.

CONDITIONAL ACCEPTANCE
Acceptance, 50–55.
Counter offer, 50–55.
Rejection, 50, 60.

CONDITIONAL DELIVERY
Extrinsic condition, parol evidence, 86, 192–193.
Escrow sealed contracts, 192–193.

CONDITIONS
    See also Constructive Conditions; Express Condi-
        tions.
Absolute promise distinguished from conditional
    promise, 225.
Bilateral and unilateral contracts, conditions related
    to, 236.
Classification, 226.
Condition concurrent, 225.
Condition precedent, 226.
Condition subsequent, 227–229.
Constructive and express conditions distinguished,
    226, 229–230.
Definition, 225.
Demand as, 242–243.
Distinction between condition and promise, 229, 232–
    233.
Duty, performance on occurrence of certain event,
    230–232.
Election, 273–274.
Estoppel and promissory estoppel compared, 268–269.
Estoppel and waiver compared, 268–269.
Excuse of condition by impossibility, 277.
Excuse of condition involving forfeitures, 238–240,
    276–277.
Giving unjustifiable reasons for refusing to perform,
    274–275.
Hindrance or prevention, 264–268.
Importance of distinction between express and con-
    structive conditions, 236–237.
Meaning, 225.
Relationship,
    Express condition to promise, 232–233.
    Formation of contract, 225–226.
    Substantial performance and material breach, 236–
        237, 245–250.

CONDITIONS—Continued
Waiver,
After failure of condition, 273–274.
Before failure of condition, 270–272.
Contemporaneous with the formation of the contract, 269–270.
Words of condition distinguished from words of promise, 232–233.

CONSEQUENTIAL DAMAGES
See Damages.

CONSIDERATION
Act as, 130.
Adequacy, 107–109.
All need not be valid, 147.
Bargain theory, 105–107, 117.
Benefit and detriment meaning, 105–107.
Bilateral contracts, 105, 130.
Condition of gratuitous promise distinguished, 114–116.
Contingent and conditional promises, 138–140.
Definition, 103–105.
Detriment,
Test of value, 105–107, 114–115.
To induce promise, 105–107, 114–115.
Economic inadequacy, 107–109.
Elements, 105.
Exchange element, 105–107, 114–115.
Exchange of fixed values, 108–109.
Failure of, material breach, 250–251.
Forbearance to enforce claim, 118–119.
Forging a good unilateral contract out of bad bilateral contract, 30, 144–146.
History, 103–104.
Motive, element, 106, 117.
Mutual promises,
Alternative performances, 134–135.
Illegality, 565.
Illusory promises, 133–140.
Indefinite promise, consideration, 133–134, 145–146.
Non-detrimental promises, sufficiency, 130.
Requested promise, implication, 143–144.
Requirements and Output Contracts, 140–144.
Reserved option, cancel, 134–138.
Void contract, nullity, 144–146.
Voidable and unenforceable promises, sufficiency, 132–133.
Mutuality of obligation, 130–131.
Nature, 103–105.
Necessity, 103–105.
Nominal consideration, 117.
One consideration, support of many promises, 146–147.
Parol evidence rule, 86, 116–117, 141–148.
Past consideration, 106, 169.
Pre-existing duty rule,
Imposed by law, 120.
Minority view, 126–127.
Payment by debtor of part of debt as,
Composition agreements, 124–127.
Rent cases, 126–127.
Unliquidated and liquidated claims, 127–130.

CONSIDERATION—Continued
Pre-existing duty rule—Continued
Performances of legal duty as consideration,
Promise of,
Party to contract, 120–123.
Third party, 123–124.
Unexpected difficulties, effect, 122.
Possibility of detriment, sufficiency, 138–140.
Recitals, 116, 147–148.
Relationship to duress, 121.
Sham consideration, 116–117.
Sufficiency,
Surrender of claim, 118–119.
Unconscionable contracts, 109–114.
Unconscionable inadequacy, 107–114.
Unilateral contract, mutuality of obligation, 131–132.
Who must furnish, 105.
Wisconsin fiction, 122.

CONSTRUCTIVE CONDITIONS
Absolute promises, conditional, 235.
Aleatory contracts, 258.
Arise from promises, 235.
Concurrent, 226, 244–245.
Defined, 229–230.
Distinguished,
Express conditions, 236–237.
Implied in fact conditions, 229–230, 236–237.
Divisible contracts, 253–256.
Relationship to illegality, 256–257.
Relationship to impossibility, 256–257.
Relationship to Statute of Frauds, 256–257.
Relationship to Statute of Limitations, 256–257.
Entire contracts, 253.
Failure of,
Consideration, 250–251.
Quantity term, 246.
Time term, 247.
Wilful breach, 246.
History of doctrine, 235.
Independent promises, 225, 257–259.
Insolvency, 262–263.
Instalment contracts, 255–256.
Language of promise giving rise to, 235.
Nature and purposes, 229–230, 237, 243–244.
Order of performance, bilateral contract, 244–245.
Precedent, 226, 244–245.
Progress payments, 244.
Prospective failure of performance, 259–263.
Relationship, material breach and substantial performance, 236–237, 245–250.
Required order of performance, bilateral contract, 244–245.
Substantial performance, fulfillment of, 229–230, 248–250.
Time, performances due at different times, 244–245.

CONTRACTS
Adhesion, 5–6.
Aleatory, 258.
Bilateral, definition, 9, 36–37.
Charter, 3.

CONTRACTS—Continued
Classification, 9.
Definition, 1–3.
Distinguished from executed agreements, 3–4.
Divisible, 253–256.
Entire, 253.
Express and implied, 10–11.
Formal, 9.
Freedom, 4–6.
Illusory, 133–138.
Informal, 9.
Objective and subjective theory, 14–15.
Quasi contracts, see Quasi Contract.
Recognizance, 9.
Restatement of, 7.
Reverse unilateral, 17, 36–37.
Scope of law, 6.
Sources of law, 6–8.
Unconscionable, 6, 109–114.
Unenforceable, 10.
Uniform Commercial Code, 3.
Unilateral, definition, 9–10, 36.
Void and voidable, 10.

CONTRACTS UNDER SEAL
Acceptance, necessity, 191–192.
Adoption, seal already on instrument, 190–191.
Consideration, necessity, 188.
Delivery, 191.
    Escrow, 191–192.
Effects of seal, 120–121.
Recital of sealing, 190–191.
Seal, 189–190.
Signature, necessity, 189.
Statutory changes, 194–195.
Sufficiency of Writing, 189.
Third party beneficiaries, 189.

CORPORATIONS
Ultra vires contract, effect, 198.

COUNTER OFFER
Defined, 50.
Distinguished from future acceptance, 55.
Effect, 50, 60.
Nature, 50, 60.
Uniform Commercial Code, 50–55.

COURSE OF DEALING, 88, 97–98, 99.

COURSE OF PERFORMANCE, 88, 102.

DAMAGES
Accrual after anticipatory breach, 287–288.
Avoidable consequences, 345–350.
Certainty,
    Alternative recovery where lacking, 338–341.
    Necessity, 334–338.
Compensatory, 334–338.
Computation, 33.
Consequential damages, 325, 327–365.
Construction contract,
    Recovery by contractor, 361–362.
    Recovery by owner, 362–364.

DAMAGES—Continued
Contemplation of parties, 329–332.
Cost of correction rule compared to diminished value rule, 362–364.
Cover by buyer of goods, 353–354.
Defined, 324–325.
Duty to mitigate, 62, 287–288, 345–350.
Exemplary damages, 324, 327.
Employment contracts, 351–353.
Foreseeability,
    Carrier and telegraph cases, 332–334.
    Other cases, 334.
    Rule of Hadley v. Baxendale, 329–331.
General principles, 327–329.
Liquidated damage clauses,
    Availability of specific performance, 369.
    Distinguished from alternative promises, 369–370.
    Distinguished from penalties, 366–368.
    Pitfalls of draftsmanship, 368–369.
    Uniform Commercial Code, 370.
Nominal damages, 325–326.
Partial and total breach, 245–247.
Profits, recovery, 329–332.
Public official, 352.
Punitive, 324, 327, 334–338.
Purpose, 327–329.
Realty, 364–365.
Recovery, expenses to mitigate loss, 349–350.
Reliance interest, 328–329.
Sale of goods,
    Action for price, 359–360.
    Breach by seller, 353–354.
    Breach of warranty or fraud, 354–355.
    Consequential and incidental damages, 355–356, 358–359.
    Contract to manufacture special goods, 360–361.
    Sellers' damages, 356–358.
Uniform Commercial Code, 353–361, 370.
Value in measuring damages,
    Market value, standard, 342–343.
    Proof of value, 343–344.
    Variable concept, 344.

DAY
    Fraction,
        Infancy cases, 199.
        One year Statute of Frauds, 472.

DEATH
Joint promisee, effect, 514.
Joint promisor, effect, 506.
Offeror, as terminating offer, 58–59.
Revocation of gratuitous assignment, 407.

DEBT OF ANOTHER
See Statute of Frauds.

DEFINITENESS
See, generally, Certainty.

DELEGATION
See Assignment.

DELIVERY
See also Contracts under Seal; Statute of Frauds.
Requisite to gift, 114.

DEMAND
Express condition, 242–243.

DETRIMENT
See Consideration.

DISCHARGE OF CONTRACTS
Acceptance of defective performance, 273–274.
Accord and satisfaction, 124–130, 168–169, 521.
Account stated, 152, 527–529.
Acquisition of correlative right, 533–534.
Alteration, 534–535.
Bankruptcy, 535.
Cancellation, 519–520.
Contract under seal, 193–194.
Covenant not to sue, 506–507, 531.
Executory bilateral contract of accord,
    Background of problem, 520–523.
    Consequences of enforceability, 523–524.
    Distinguished from substituted agreement, 524.
Gift, 114–115, 126, 531–532.
Merger, 532, 533.
Methods, 516–517.
Modification by agreement, 119–123, 164–167.
Mutual rescission, 122, 517–519.
Novation, 525–527.
Offer of accord looking to unilateral contract, 524–525.
Payment, 535–536.
Rejection of tender, 531–532.
Release, 167–168, 529–530.
Renunciation, 167–168.
Substituted contract, 524.
Tender, rejection, 531–532.
Uniform Commercial Code, 164–168.

DISPUTED CLAIM
Consideration for release, 118–119, 127–130, 167–168.
Forbearance to sue, consideration, 118–119, 127–130.

DIVISIBLE CONTRACTS
Constructive conditions, 254–255.
Definition, 253–254.
Employment contracts, 254–255.
Illegal bargain, 573–574.
Sales contracts, 255–256.
Statute of Frauds, 489.
Uniform Commercial Code, 255–256.

DOMINION
Acceptance of offered goods, 46–48.

DRUNKEN PERSONS
Avoidance by, 220–221.
Exploitation of alcoholic persons, 221–222.
Ratification and avoidance, 220–221.
Required extent of incapacity, 220–221.

DURESS
Relation to pre-existing duty rule, 121–122, 166–167.
Threat not to perform contract, 121.
Threat to sue on invalid claim, 118.

ENTIRE CONTRACTS
Definition, 253.
Uniform Commercial Code, 255.

ESCROW
Condition, 192–193.

ESTOPPEL
See also Conditions; Promissory Estoppel.
Compared with election, 273–274.
Compared with waiver, 268–269.
Elements, 178–179, 268–269.
Modern view, 268.
Statute of Frauds, 498–499.

EXCHANGE
Bilateral bargains usually involve, 105–107, 117.
Gift on condition compared, 114–116.
Idea of consideration, 105–107, 117.
Pension promise, 183–185.

EXCUSE FOR NON-PERFORMANCE
See also Conditions; Frustration of Purpose.
Lack of demand, 242–243.
Material breach by other party, 236, 245–247.
Prevention of performance, 264–268.
Repudiation, 278–282.

EXCUSE OF CONDITION
Acceptance of benefits after breach of condition, 273–274.
Hindrance, 264–268.
Impossibility, 277.
Improper reason for refusal to perform, 274–275.
Inability or unwillingness of promisor to perform promise subject to condition, 259–268.
Prevention, 264–268.
Re-establishing time limit for performance after excuse of delay, 250, 272.
Repudiation, 278–282.
Waiver,
    After breach, 273–274.
    Before breach, 270–272.
    Compared with estoppel, 268–269.
    Compared with promissory estoppel, 178–179, 268.
    Contemporaneous with written instrument, 269–270.

EXECUTORS AND ADMINISTRATORS
See Statute of Frauds.

EXPRESS CONDITIONS
Approval, 238–242.
Architects, 238–239.
Compliance with, 229–230.
Definition, 229.
Demand, 242–243.
Distinction between an express condition and promise, 232–233.
Distinguished from constructive condition, 236–237.
Effect of non-occurrence, 230–232.
Express language of condition, implied language of promise, 233–234.
Illustrations, 230–232.
Implied in fact conditions distinguished from constructive conditions, 235.

EXPRESS CONDITIONS—Continued
Includes implied in fact conditions, 229.
Language of promise may give rise to implied in fact condition, 235.
Literal performance necessity for, 235.
Precedent, 226.
Procedural effect, 228.
Sale of goods, 226.
Satisfaction,
  Condition, 238.
    Party to the contract, 240–242.
    Third person, 238–240.
Subsequent, 227–229.
Time, condition impliedly promised, 233–234.
Words of condition, 230–232.

EXPRESS CONTRACT
Generally, 10–11.

FAILURE OF CONSIDERATION
Effect, 250–251.
Meaning, 250–251.
Prevention, 264–268.
Prospective, 259–263.
Repudiation, 278–282.

FIRM OFFER
Effect, 67–69.
What makes offer irrevocable, 67–69.
  Common law, 67–68.
  Statutes, 68–69, 169.

FORBEARANCE
Generally, 118–119.

FORFEITURE
Impossibility excuses express condition to avoid, 277.
Interpreting express condition to avoid, 239, 242, 276–277.

FORMAL CONTRACTS
Contracts under seal, 9, 188.
Definition, 9.
Kinds, 9.

FRAUDS, STATUTE OF
See Statute of Frauds.

FRUSTRATION OF PURPOSE
Coronation cases, 312.
Death and illness, 307–308.
Export licenses, 313.
Leases, 313.
Restitution, 314.
Sale of goods, 320–322.
Temporary, 314–315.
Uniform Commercial Code, 320–322.
War, 308, 316.

GRATUITOUS PROMISES
  See also Consideration; Promissory Estoppel; Substitutes for Consideration.

IGNORANCE OF OFFER
Effect on acceptance, 38–39.

ILLEGAL CONTRACTS
Agreements,
  Aid of illegal purpose of contracting parties, 566.
  Arbitrate, 555.
  Buy and sell futures, 559–560.
  Citizen to violate civic duty, 549.
  Commit a tort, 549.
  Defraud creditors, 549.
  Divorce, facilitating, 556.
  Exempt another from liability for negligence, 550–552.
  Indemnify against liability for wrongful acts, 549–550.
  Obstruct justice, 554–555.
  Private fiduciary obligation, violation, 548.
  Restraint of marriage, 555–556.
  Restraint of trade, 540–544.
  Tending to interfere with functioning of judicial machinery, 554–555.
  Use personal influence, 544–547.
Assignment, salary by public officer, 548.
Bargains harmful to public service, 547–548.
Basis of illegality, 539.
Blue laws, 567.
Champerty and maintenance, 553–554.
Change of fact, effect, 579–580.
Change of law, effect, 579–580.
Commission or contingent fee, 544–547.
Corruption of agents, 568–571.
Depository, assertion of defense, 571–572.
Effect,
  Ignorance of fact, 565–566.
  Illegality, 565, 567–568.
  Licensing statutes, 570.
  Statutes on the legality of a contract, 568–569.
Lobbying agreements, 544–546.
Marriage brokerage contracts, 556.
Meaning, 539.
Monopolies, 544.
Pari delicto, 574–577.
Partial illegality, effect, 543–544, 573–577.
Procurement of government contracts, 545–547.
Promise,
  Payment to public officer, 547.
  Refrain from carrying on business, 540–541.
  Traffic in public office, 547.
Public policy, 539, 561–570.
Remoteness, 571.
Restitution, 573–579.
Severability, 543–544, 573–577.
Statute directed against one party, 567.
Sunday contracts, 557–560.
Unconscionable bargains, 6, 109–114.
Usury, 560–564.
Wagering contracts and lotteries, 558–560.
Wrongful purpose, 566.

ILLUSORY PROMISE
Generally, 133–140.

IMPLIED CONDITION
See Conditions.

IMPLIED CONTRACTS
See Contracts.

IMPLIED PROMISE
Bilateral contract, 143–144.
Conduct, 10–11, 36, 49.
Consideration, 143–144.
Definition of, 10–11.
Relation to conditions, 232–235.
Silence, 45–48.

IMPOSSIBILITY OF PERFORMING CONDITION
Condition excused, 277, 310–312.
Condition not excused, 277, 310–312.

IMPOSSIBILITY OF PERFORMING PROMISE
Absolute undertakings, 296.
Act of God, 301.
Apprehension, 308.
Assumption of the risk, 316–319.
Building contracts, 301.
Condition, excuse, 310–312.
Contract of repair, 302–303.
Crop shortage, 299.
Death or illness, 307–308.
Destruction,
    Specific subject matter, 298–303.
    Tangible means of performance, 298–303.
Economic impracticability, 309–310, 315.
Effect upon prior repudiation, 319–320.
Failure,
    Contemplated mode of delivery or payment, 303–304.
    Intangible means of performance, 306–307.
Fault, 316–318.
Foreign law, 305.
Foreseeability, 316–318.
History, 296–297.
Illegality, supervening, 304–305.
Increase in cost, 309–310, 315.
Music hall case, 298.
Objective impossibility, 315.
Plans, insufficiency, 301–302.
Rationale, 296–298.
Reasonable apprehension of impossibility or danger, 308.
Restitution, 303, 307.
Sale of goods, 298.
Strikes, 306–307.
Subjective, 315.
Temporary, 314–315.
Transportation difficulties, 303–304.
Uniform Commercial Code, 298–300, 304–306, 320–322.

INDEFINITENESS
See Certainty.

INDEMNITY
See also Third Party Beneficiaries.
Promise,
    Illegal, 549.
    Within statute of frauds, 457–459.

INDEPENDENT PROMISES
Aleatory contracts, 258.
Definition, 225.

INFANTS
Avoidance of contract by, 202.
Effect,
    Ratification in ignorance of law or fact, 207.
    Where contract authorized by law, 201–202.
False representations by infant, 211.
Implied ratification by, 206.
Liability for necessaries, 212–215.
Obligations of restitution upon disaffirmance, 207.
Ratification, 205–206.
Time of avoidance, 201–202.
Torts connected with contracts, 209–211.
Transactions which cannot be avoided, 201–202.
What amounts to disaffirmance, 203.
What are necessaries, 212–215.
When disaffirmance necessary, 203–205.

INFORMAL CONTRACTS
See Formal Contracts.

INSANE PERSONS
Effect of insanity on contract, 216.
Liability for necessaries, 220.
Ratification and avoidance, 219–220.
Requirements for restitution, 218–219.
Test, 217–218.

INSOLVENCY
Meaning, 262.
Prospective inability to perform, 262–263.
Repudiation, 284–286.

INSTALLMENT CONTRACTS
See also Divisible Contracts.
Building contracts, 254.
Sale of goods, 255–256.

INTEGRATION
See Interpretation; Parol Evidence Rule.

INTENT TO CONTRACT
Necessity, 16–17.

INTENTION TO MEMORIALIZE AN AGREEMENT
Compared with intending legal consequences, 27–28.
Effect upon existence of contract, 27–28.

INTERPRETATION
Course of dealing, 88, 97–98, 99.
Course of performance, 88, 102.
Effect of ambiguity, 88, 90, 95–96.
Formation of contract, 20, 89.
Latent and patent ambiguity, 90.
Plain meaning rule, 97–98.
Question of law or fact, 96.
Relationship between Parol Evidence Rule and rules and standards of interpretation, 96–98.
Rules of interpretation, 94–96.
    Corbin's approach, 95.
    Distinction between primary and secondary rules, 94–95.

INTERPRETATION—Continued
Rules of interpretation—Continued
Primary rules,
Interpret as whole, 94.
Surrounding circumstances, 94.
Technical terms, 94.
Words to be given ordinary meaning, 94.
Relationship between standards and rules of interpretation, 94.
Secondary rules,
Apparent purpose of parties, 95.
Inconsistency between general and specific provisions, 95.
Intention to be carried out, 95.
Meaning given to all manifestations, 94.
When rules come into play, 94–95.
Where manifestations bear more than one reasonable meaning, 95.
Where provisions are inconsistent, 95.
Where public interest is affected, 95.
Standards of Interpretation,
Applied to an integration, 15, 91–92.
Applied to a non-integration, 14–15, 90–92.
Corbin's approach, 93–94.
Effect of ambiguity, 90–91.
Individual standard, 90–91.
Mutual standard, 90.
Standard of general usage, 89.
Standard of limited usage, 89.
Standard of reasonable expectation, 90.
Standard of reasonable understanding, 90.
When ambiguity exists, 90–93.
Williston's approach, 90–94.
Uniform Commercial Code, 97.
Usage, 88, 97, 100–101.

INTOXICATION
Effect, 220–221.
Exploitation of intoxicated person, 221–222.
What constitutes, 220.

INVITATION TO DEAL
Distinguished from offers, 19–20.

IRREVOCABLE OFFERS
At common law, 67–68.
By beginning to perform a unilateral contract, 61–62, 69.
By statute, 68–69, 169.
Mutuality of obligation, 132.
Termination of, 69.

JEST
Offers made in jest, 15.

JOINDER
Joint promisees, 513.
Joint promisors, 503–504.

JOINT AND SEVERAL LIABILITY
Consequences, 508–509.
Joint liability, 503–506.
Joint rights, 511–514.
Several liability, 509–510.
Several rights, 513–514.

JOINT AND SEVERAL LIABILITY—Continued
Covenant not to sue, 507.
Death,
Joint and several promisor, 509.
Joint promisee, 514.
Joint promisor, 506.
Discharge by one joint obligee, 513–514.
Discharge of joint obligor, 506–508.
Effect of principal-surety relationship, 503, 507, 510–511.
General nature, 501–502.
Judgment,
Against one promisor, 504–505.
Favor of one promisor, 505–506.
Multiple promises,
Different performances, 501.
Same performance, 501–502.
Relation of joint promisors to each other, 510–511.
Release of joint and several promisor, 509.
Release of joint promisor, 506–508.
Release with reservation of right, 507.
Statutory changes, 502, 504, 505, 506, 507, 509, 510.
When are obligations joint, joint and several or several, 502–503.
When are rights joint, 511–513.

JUDGMENT
Against joint obligor, 505–506.
Favor of joint obligor, 504–505.

LAND
See Statute of Frauds.

LAPSE OF OFFERS
Reasonable time, 56.
Time specified, 56–57.

LEGAL CONSEQUENCES
Compared with intending legal consequences, 27–28.
Intent, must parties intend, 16–17.

LICENSE
See Statute of Frauds.

LIMITATION OF ACTION
See Substitutes for Consideration.

LIQUIDATED DAMAGES
See Damages.

LOBBYING CONTRACTS
See Illegal Contracts.

LOCUS POENITENTIAE
See Illegal Contracts.

MAINTENANCE
See Illegal Contracts.

MATERIAL BREACH
As an excuse for non-performance, 149, 236, 245–247.
Breach in limine, 246.
Distinguished from substantial performance, 237, 245–250.
Measured quantitively, 246.
Time of performance, 247.

MEASURE OF DAMAGES
See Damages.

MEMORANDUM
Relation to parol evidence rule, 480–481.
Sufficiency to satisfy Statute of Frauds, 480–487.

MERGER
See Discharge of Contracts.

MINORS
See Infants.

MISTAKE
Identity of party, 41–42.
Negligence in failing to read, 39.
Reformation, 76, 86, 481, 486.
Telegraph company in transmittal, 66–67.
Transmission of offer, 66–67.

MITIGATION OF DAMAGES
See Damages.

MODIFICATION
Binding without consideration,
    Estoppel or waiver, 268–269.
    Statute, 164–167.
Consideration, 119–123, 164–165.
Effect of agreement requiring writing, 165.
Necessity for consideration, 119–123.

MORAL OBLIGATION
See Substitutes for Consideration.

MORTGAGE ASSUMPTION AGREEMENT
See Third Party Beneficiary.

MUNICIPALITY
See Third Party Beneficiary.

MUTUAL ASSENT
Effect, one party's assent conditional, 50–55, 60.
Identical cross offers, 40.
Intent to formalize writing, 27–28.
Jest, etc., 15–16.
Manifestations, reference to each other, 13, 38–40.
Nature of, 13–15.
Necessity, 13.
Need, subjectiveness, 14–15.
Objective manifestation, 14–15.
When subjective assent material, 14–15, 47, 89–90.

MUTUALITY OF OBLIGATION
Both parties bound or neither, 130–131.
Cancellation clauses, 133–138.
Forging a good unilateral contract out of bad bilateral
    contract, 30, 144–146.
Meaning of doctrine, 130–131.
Necessity in unilateral contracts, 131–132.
Void promises as consideration, 133–138.
Voidable promises as consideration, 132–133.
Where alternative performances promised, 133–138.

NOMINAL CONSIDERATION
Effect, 117.
Meaning, 117.

NEGOTIABLE INSTRUMENTS
Formal contract, 9.

NOVATION
See Discharge of Contracts.

OBJECTIVE IMPOSSIBILITY
See Impossibility of Performance.

OBJECTIVE THEORY
Contract formation, 14–15.
Contract interpretation, 14–15, 89–95.

OBSTRUCTING JUSTICE
See Illegal Contracts.

OFFER
Act or promise requested, 9–10.
Advertisement, 22.
Assignment, 413.
Auctions, who makes offer, 23–24.
Catalogue, 23.
Characteristics in general, 17.
Circular letter, 23.
Conduct which creates inference, 10–11, 45–49.
Contract to hold open, 67–69.
Counter-offer, effect, 50–55, 60–61.
Death of offeror, effect, 58–59.
Definiteness, 29.
Definition, 17.
Distinguished from expression of opinion, 17–19.
Duration, 56–57.
    Uncommunicated intent, 57.
    When no time limit set, 56–58.
    When time limit specified, 56.
Effect, 17.
Error in transmission, 66–67.
Expenses in preparation, 48.
Firm offer, 169.
Implication, additional terms, 30–35.
Implied in fact, 45–49.
Indefiniteness, 29.
Intention to formalize agreement, effect, 27–28.
Irrevocability, 67–69.
Jest, 15–16.
Knowledge, necessity, 38–40.
Must be communicated, 38–40.
Option contracts, 67–69.
Preliminary negotiations, 19–20.
Price lists, 23.
Price quotation distinguished, 25–26.
Public generally, offer to, 21–23, 39, **42.**
Request for bids, 25.
Statement of intention, 19–20.
Termination of revocable offer by,
    Conditional acceptance, 50–55.
    Counter offer, 50–55, 60–61.
    Death or destruction of an essential person **or**
        thing, 61.
    Death or insanity, 58–59.
    Lapse of time, 56–58.
    Rejection, 60–61.

OFFER—Continued

Termination of revocable offer by—Continued
Revocation, 59–60.
    After part performance, 61–62.
    Communication of revocation, 59–63.
    Contract to keep offer open, 67–69.
    Offer to general public, 59–60.
    When made irrevocable by statute, 67–69.
  Supervening illegality, 61.
To whom made, 41–42.
Uniform Commercial Code, 50–55, 68–69.
What is, 17.
Who may accept, 41–42.
Without intent to contract, 14–17.

OPTION CONTRACTS

See Irrevocable Offers and Statute of Frauds.

PAROL EVIDENCE RULE

Agreements,
    Subsequent to written integration, 77, 86–87.
    With separate consideration, 77.
Conditions, 86.
Consideration, 86, 116–117, 147–148.
Corbin's view and Williston's view, 75–85.
Contemporaneous writings, 77, 86–87.
Course of dealing, 88, 97–98, 99.
Course of performance, 88, 102.
Definition, 75–76.
Difficulty of subject matter, 75.
Exceptions,
    Application to subsequent agreements, 77, 85–86.
    Conditional delivery, 192–193.
    Fraud, duress, 77, 86.
    Illegality, 86.
    Lack of consideration, 86.
    Reformation for mistake, 76, 86.
    Writing, not intended to be operative, 86.
Implied terms, 30–35, 87.
Integration,
    Partial, 79–85.
    Total, 79–85.
Invoked for or against a third party, 87.
Justification, 76.
Merger clause, 80.
Persons who may invoke rule, 87.
Plain meaning rule, 98.
Proof of custom or usage, 88.
Question of fact or law, 76.
Recitals, 116, 147.
Rule of substantive law, 85.
Relationship to rules of interpretation, 96–98.
Relationship to Statute of Frauds, 480–481.
Some practical observations 98–99.
Uniform Commercial Code, 78, 87–88, 98, 99–102.
Usage, 88, 98, 100–101.

PARTIAL ASSIGNMENTS

See Assignments.

PARTIAL BREACH

Meaning, breach not material, 236–237, 245.
Restitution not available, 372.
Successive actions for, 293–295.
Total breach distinguished, 236–237, 245.

PART PERFORMANCE

Compliance with Statute of Frauds, 465, 469, 489.
Defaulting plaintiff, 251–253.
Effect on revocability of offer, 61–62.
Frustration of venture, 312–314.
Taking oral contract out of land section of Statute of
    Frauds, 465.

PAST CONSIDERATION

See Consideration; Substitutes for Consideration.

PAYMENT

Delay, material breach, 247.
Discharge of contract, 535–536.
Lesser sum, consideration, 124–127.
One joint obligee, 513–514.

PENALTY

See Damages.

PERFORMANCE

Agreed exchange bilateral contracts, 244–245, 255–259.
Constructive condition to duty, 243, 244–245.
Encumbrance of property as prospective failure, 261–
    262.
Failure,
    Aleatory contracts, 258.
    Leases, 259.
    Performance not agreed, exchange for each other,
        258–259.
    Prospective, 259–263.
Required order of,
    Acts capable of simultaneous performance, 244–
        245.
    Continuing concurrent performances, 244–245.
    Performance due at different times, 244–245.
    Performances which take time, 244–245.
    Uniform Commercial Code, 244.

PRE-EXISTING DUTY

See Consideration and Substitute for Consideration.

PRELIMINARY NEGOTIATIONS

Advertisements, 21–22.
Auctions, 23–25.
Catalogs and circular letters, 23.
Distinguished from offers, 19–20.
Effect on formation, 19–20.
Exclusion by parol evidence rule, 76–77.
Inquiry, 19–20.
Intent, agreement be formalized, 27–28.
Invitation to make offer, 19–20.
Price lists, 23.
Price quotations, 25–26.
Requests for bids, 25.
Statements of intention, 19–20.
Use in interpretation, 89.

PREVENTION

See also Condition.
As a breach of contract, 266–268.
As excuse for nonperformance of a duty, 264–266.
As excuse of a condition to a promisor's duty, 264–266.
By a third party, 238–239.
Constitutes a total breach, 266–268.

PREVIOUS DEALINGS
Affecting acceptance by silence, 44–49.
Uses in interpretation, 99.

PRICE QUOTATIONS
Distinguished from offers, 25–26.

PRIORITIES
See Assignments.

PRIVITY OF CONTRACT
See Third Party Beneficiaries.

PROGRESS PAYMENTS
See Constructive Conditions.

PROMISE
Defined, 17–18.
Gift promise, 114–116.
Illusory, 133.
Implied, 10–11, 36–37, 45–49, 143–144.
Language of condition as, 233–234.

PROMISSORY ESTOPPEL
Charitable subscriptions, 176–178.
Compared with waiver, 178–179.
Consideration, substitute for, 179.
Dealer franchises, 182–183.
Distinguished from,
   Consideration, 172.
   Estoppel, 173, 178–179.
Flexibility of remedy, 185–186.
Future of doctrine, 186–187.
Gratuitous agency, 175–176.
Gratuitous bailee, 175–176.
Insurance cases, 175–176, 186–187.
Introduction, 172–173.
Marriage settlements, 178.
Oral gifts of land, 173–174.
Pensions and other fringe benefits, 183–185.
Promises in family, 173.
Reliance upon promise of subcontractor, 180–182.
Statute of Frauds, 499–500.
Traditional approach to doctrine, 179.

PROSPECTIVE FAILURE OF PERFORMANCE
Destruction of subject matter, 260.
Insolvency or bankruptcy, 262–263.
Lack of title, 261–262.
Supervening illegality, 260.
Unwillingness to perform, 260–261.

PUBLIC OFFICERS
See Illegal Contracts and Damages.

QUANTUM MERUIT
See Quasi Contracts.

QUASI CONTRACT
   See also Restitution.
Amount of recovery, 374–375, 494–495.
Benefit conferred without request, 10–11, 154, 155.
Defaulting party as claimant, 251–253, 492–493.
Defined, 10–11.
Distinguished from express and implied in fact contract, 10–11.

QUASI CONTRACT—Continued
Emergency, 153–155.
Gratuitousness, 48, 153–155, 407–409.
Indefiniteness, 30.
Mistake, 155.
Necessaries, 212–215, 220.
Part performance,
   Defaulting plaintiff, 251–259.
   Frustration of venture, 313–314.
   Impossibility of performance, 303, 307–308.
   Statute of Frauds, 491–495.
Performance of duty of another, 10–11.
Physician's right to recover for services, 10–11.
Relation to substantial performance, 251–253.

QUESTIONS OF LAW AND FACT
   Generally, 28–29.
Offer or preliminary negotiation, 19–20.
Offer or opinion, 17–18.

QUOTATION
Distinguished from offer, 25–26.

REALTY
See Statute of Frauds.

RECEIPT OR RETENTION OF DEFECTIVE PERFORMANCE
Effect on right to damages for breach, 275–276.
Waiver of condition, 273–274.

RECITALS
See Consideration; Parol Evidence Rule

RECOGNIZANCE
Formal contract, 9.

REFORMATION
Parol evidence, 76, 86.
Statute of Frauds, 481, 486.

REJECTION OF OFFER
Counter-offer, 50–55, 60–61.
Effect, 60–61.

RELEASE
See Discharge of Contracts; Joint and Several Contracts.

REMEDIES FOR BREACH OF CONTRACT
See Damages; Restitution; Specific Performance.

REPUDIATION
Anticipatory, as present breach, 278–282.
Excuse of conditions, 278–279.
Excuse of promisor's duty, 278–279.
Good faith, 284.
Material breach, 289–292.
Remedies after, 287–289.
Retraction, 286–287.
Time retraction possible, 286–287.
What constitutes, 282–283.

RESCISSION
Consideration, 122–123.
Discharge of contract, 122–123, 517–519.
Meaning, 518.

RESCISSION—Continued
Requirement for restitution, 373.
Statute of Frauds, 489–490.

RESTITUTION
See also Quasi Contracts.
Alternative remedy to damages, 372–374, 496.
Breach is partial, 372.
Concept of unjust enrichment, 371–372.
Damages and restitution as inconsistent remedies, 376–377.
Defaulting plaintiffs, 251–253, 492–493.
Limitation by contract price, 374–375, 495–496.
Measure of recovery, 374–375, 494, 495.
Remedy conditioned on return of consideration, 373.
Severable contract, 376.
Specific restitution, 373, 497–498.
When not available remedy, 375–376.
When plaintiff discharged by impossibility, 303, 307.

RETRACTION OF WAIVER
See Waiver.

REVOCATION OF OFFER
See also Irrevocable Offers.
After part performance, 61–62.
Continuing offers, 43–44.
Direct, 59–60.
Effective when received, 59, 63.
Ends offeree's power of acceptance, 59–60.
General offers, 59–60.
Indirect, 60.

REWARD OFFER
Revocation, 59–60.
Right to adequate assurance of performance, 263.
Who may accept, 41–42.

SATISFACTION
Condition, excused, 238–242.
Express condition, 238.
Subjective and objective test as to compliance, 238–242.

SEAL
See Contracts under Seal.

SEVERABILITY
See Divisible Contracts.

SEVERAL CONTRACTS
See Joint and Several Contracts.

SICKNESS
See Impossibility of Performance.

SILENCE
Acceptance of offer, 45–48.
Waiver, after condition failed, 273–274.

SPECIFIC PERFORMANCE
Liquidated damage clause prevention, 369.
Specific restitution, 374–375, 497–498.

STATUTE OF FRAUDS
Admission of oral contracts, 471.
Choses in action, 469.

STATUTE OF FRAUDS—Continued
Contracts for sale of goods,
Acceptance and receipt of goods, 469–470.
Choses in action, 469.
Payment or earnest, 470–471.
Price or value, 467–468.
Sufficient part performance, 469.
Uniform Commercial Code, 466–471.
What are goods, 468.
Contracts for sale of land,
Effect of part performance, 465.
Interests in land, 461–464.
Contracts in consideration of marriage, 460–461.
Contracts not to be performed before end of lifetime, 474.
Contracts not to be performed within one year,
Alternative and option contracts, 475–476.
Calculating term of year, 471–472.
Effect of performance, 476–477.
Possibility of performance within a year, 472–473.
Promise conditioned upon an uncertain event, 473–474.
Promise of extended performance, 474.
Relationship of one year section with other subdivisions, 479.
Restitutionary remedy, 476–477.
Unilateral contracts, 477–479.
Contracts of executors and administrators, 443–444.
Contracts to answer for debts of another,
Cases where no prior obligation exists, 445–451.
Cases where prior obligation exists, 451–453.
Joint promises, 450.
Main purpose rule, 453–457.
Necessity for principal-surety relationship and knowledge thereof, 448–449.
No debt of another, 445–448.
Novation, 451–452.
Promise by del credere agent, 459.
Promise by executor or administrator, 443–444.
Promise co-extensive with obligation to creditor, 452–453.
Promise made to debtor, 452.
Promise of assignor, 459–460.
Promise of indemnity, 457–459.
Promise to buy claim, 460.
Promisor already under identical duty, 452–453.
Terminology, 444.
Earnest, 470–471.
Effect,
Alternative performances, 475–476.
Non-compliance, 487–488.
Oral contract to make a written contract, 491.
Performance, 465, 476–477.
Enforceability of part outside statute, 489.
Estoppel under, 498–500.
Formal contract, 491.
History and Text, 441–443.
Justification, 442–443.
Memorandum,
Consideration, necessity of stating, 148.
Contents, 482.
Delivery, 483.

STATUTE OF FRAUDS—Continued

Memorandum—Continued

Destruction, 483.

Form, 483.

Formal contracts, 491.

Identification,

Parties, 482.

Subject matter, 482.

Negotiable instruments, 491.

Parol evidence rule, 480–481.

Reformation, 481, 486.

Rescission or variation of contract, 489–490.

Several papers composing, 485.

Signature, 483.

Signed by agent, 484–485.

Time of making, 483.

Uniform Commercial Code, 485–487.

Oral contract as defense, 490–491.

Restitutionary Remedies,

Contract price, evidence of value, 495–496.

Damages compared, 496.

Effect of defendant's restoration of status quo, 493.

Estoppel, 497–500.

Measure of recovery, 494–495.

Plaintiff, default, 492–493.

Specific restitution, 497–498.

Where denied, 493–494.

STATUTE OF LIMITATIONS

Acknowledgment of debt, after running of statute, 157–160.

Barred claims, revived by new promise, 157–160.

SUBJECTIVE IMPOSSIBILITY

See Impossibility of Performance.

SUBJECTIVE THEORY

See Objective Theory.

SUBSTANTIAL PERFORMANCE

Building contracts, 248.

Compliance with a constructive condition, 237, 248, 250.

Delay in performance, 250.

Determination, 248–250.

Intentional deviation, 249.

Relationship to material breach, 248.

Sale of goods, 248–249.

Uniform Commercial Code, 248.

SUBSTITUTE CONTRACT

Consideration necessary, 120–123.

Discharge, 524.

SUBSTITUTES FOR CONSIDERATION

Moral obligation,

Effect of writing, 150.

Past act, result of request, 152–154.

Persons to whom promise must be made, 162.

Promise based upon previous promise within Statute of Frauds, 160–162.

Promise of discharged surety or indorser, 162.

SUBSTITUTES FOR CONSIDERATION—Continued

Moral obligation—Continued

Promise to correct an error in judgment, 162.

Promise to pay,

Acts previously performed at request, 152–154.

Benefits previously received without request, 154–155.

Pre-existing debt, 151–152.

Promise to pay a debt,

Barred by statute of limitations, 157–159.

Discharged by operation of law, 155–156.

Discharged in bankruptcy, 156–157.

Voluntarily discharged, 157.

Promise to pay for benefits received, 154–155.

An illegal bargain, 162.

Promise to perform a void or a voidable undertaking, 160.

Relationship between past consideration and moral obligation, 151.

Promissory estoppel. See Promissory Estoppel.

Relationship between past consideration and moral obligation, 151.

Seal as substitute for consideration, 188.

See also Contracts under Seal.

Statutes as substitute for consideration,

Firm offers, 169.

Past consideration, 169.

Model Written Obligations Act, 163–164.

Modification of contracts, 164–167.

Release and accord and satisfaction, 167–169.

Stipulations,

Defined, 170.

Consideration and formality in, 170.

SURETY

Assumption of another's debt, 430–431.

Effect on joint and joint and several obligations, 503, 510–511.

Promise within Statute of Frauds, 443–460.

SURRENDER AND CANCELLATION

See Discharge of Contract.

SURVIVORSHIP

See Joint and Several Contracts.

TELEGRAPH

Acceptance by, 64–65.

Error in transmitting, 66–67.

Limitation of liability for error in transmitting, 67, 333–334.

TENDER

Concurrent conditions, 226.

Discharge, 531–532.

Land sale, 226.

Requirements of valid tender, 531–532.

Sale of goods, 226.

TERMINATION OF OFFER

Counter-offer, 50–55, 60–61.

Death or mental incapacity, 58–59.

Lapse,

Reasonable time, 56–57.

Specified time, 56.

TERMINATION OF OFFER—Continued
Rejection by offeree, 60–61.
Revocation, 59–60.
Supervening illegality, 61.

THIRD PARTY BENEFICIARIES
Agency, 378.
American rule, 379–384.
Beneficiary, protection, 378, 379–384.
Benefit of minor, 395.
Counterclaims, 395.
Creditor beneficiary, 379, 390.
Defenses available against beneficiary, 386, 394.
Disclaimer by beneficiary, 395.
Donee beneficiary, 379.
Enforcement by promisee, 399–400.
English law, 378.
History, 378–379.
Incidental beneficiaries, 380.
Indemnity contract compared, 390–391.
Insurance agreements, 390–391.
Intended beneficiaries, 380–384.
Intent to benefit, tests, 380–384, 390.
Mortgage assumption agreements, 384.
Mortgagee beneficiaries, 384–387.
Municipal contracts, 387–389.
Nature of beneficiary's rights, 393.
Promises of indemnity, 390–391.
Public contracts, 387–389.
Relationship to Statute of Wills, 384.
Remedies of promisee against promisor, 399–400.
Requirement of privity, 378.
Restatement categories, 379–384.
Rights against promisee, 398–399.
Sealed contract, parties, 189.
Suretyship bonds, 392–393.
Testamentary dispositions, 384.
Third party, identification, 397.
Trusts, 378, 379.
Vesting of rights, 395–398.

TIME
See also Day.
Computation of, 56.
Express condition, 236–237, 247.
Time of essence, 236–237, 247.

TIME OF PERFORMANCE
Building and manufacturing contracts, 247–248.
Delay in delivery of goods, 247–248.
Delay in payment, 247–248.
Land contracts, 247.
Time of essence, 247.

TRUSTS
See Third Party Beneficiary.

UNCONSCIONABLE CONTRACTS
Adequacy of consideration, 107–114.
Conditions of notice, 136.
Contracts of adhesion, 6.
Termination clause, 136.
Traditional approach, 109–110.
Uniform Commercial Code, 6, 109–114, 136.

UNENFORCEABLE CONTRACTS
See Contracts.

UNILATERAL CONTRACTS
Anticipatory breach doctrine, application, 289–292.
Defined, 9–10.
Distinguished from bilateral, 36–37, 70–73.
Intent to accept, necessity, 40–41.
Knowledge of offer, necessity, 38–40.
Mutuality of obligation doctrine, application, 131–132.
Nature, 36–37.
Notice of acceptance, 43.
Offer looking to series of unilateral contracts, 43–44.
Part performance, effect, 61–62.

UNJUST ENRICHMENT
See Quasi Contract and Restitution.

UNLIQUIDATED DEBT
Defined, 127.
Payment of lesser sum in discharge of, 127–130.

USAGE AND CUSTOM, 88, 98, 100–101.

USURY
See Illegal Contracts.

VOID AND VOIDABLE CONTRACTS
See Contracts.

WAIVER AND BREACH
Continuing to receive other's performance, 273–274.
Effect on promisor, 273–274.
Election to continue, 273–274.
Omission to state a ground for defense, 274–275.
Promisor continuing to perform, 273–274.
Retention of defective performance, 273–274.

WAIVER BEFORE BREACH
Contemporaneous with written contract, 269.
Inferred from conduct, 271–272.
Reliance, not binding without reliance, 270.
Requirements to reinstate condition, 272.

WILLFUL BREACH
Affecting materiality of breach, 246.
Defined, 249.
Precludes recovery on substantial performance, 249.

WRITING
See Parol Evidence Rule; Statute of Frauds and Substitutes for Consideration.